ISAIAH

THE NIV
APPLICATION
COMMENTARY

From biblical text . . . to contemporary life

THE NIV APPLICATION COMMENTARY SERIES

THE NIV APPLICATION COMMENTARY

From biblical text . . . to contemporary life

JOHN N. OSWALT

ZONDERVAN™

GRAND RAPIDS, MICHIGAN 49530 USA

The NIV Application Commentary: Isaiah
Copyright © 2003 by John N. Oswalt

Requests for information should be addressed to:
Zondervan, *Grand Rapids, Michigan 49530*

Library of Congress Cataloging-in-Publication Data
Oswalt, John N.
   Isaiah / John Oswalt.
     p. cm.— (The NIV application commentary)
  Includes bibliographical references and index.
     ISBN 0-310-20613-8
     1. Bible. O.T. Isaiah—Commentaries. I. Title: Isaiah. II. Series.
  BS1515.53.O88 2003
  224'.1077—dc21   2003002527
                                                      CIP

This edition printed on acid-free paper.

Printed in the United States of America

03 04 05 06 07 08 09 /❖ DC/ 10 9 8 7 6 5 4 3 2

Contents

The NIV Application Commentary Series

When complete, the NIV Application Commentary
will include the following volumes:

Old Testament Volumes

Genesis, John H. Walton

Exodus, Peter Enns

Leviticus/Numbers, Roy Gane

Deuteronomy, Daniel I. Block

Joshua, Robert Hubbard

Judges/Ruth, K. Lawson Younger

1-2 Samuel, Bill T. Arnold

1-2 Kings, Gus Konkel

1-2 Chronicles, Andrew E. Hill

Ezra/Nehemiah, Douglas J. Green

Esther, Karen H. Jobes

Job, Dennis R. Magary

Psalms Volume 1, Gerald H. Wilson

Psalms Volume 2, Gerald H. Wilson

Proverbs, Paul Koptak

Ecclesiastes/Song of Songs, Iain Provan

Isaiah, John N. Oswalt

Jeremiah/Lamentations, J. Andrew Dearman

Ezekiel, Iain M. Duguid

Daniel, Tremper Longman III

Hosea/Amos/Micah, Gary V. Smith

Jonah/Nahum/Habakkuk/Zephaniah,
    James Bruckner

Joel/Obadiah/Malachi, David W. Baker

Haggai/Zechariah, Mark J. Boda

New Testament Volumes

Matthew, Michael J. Wilkins

Mark, David E. Garland

Luke, Darrell L. Bock

John, Gary M. Burge

Acts, Ajith Fernando

Romans, Douglas J. Moo

1 Corinthians, Craig Blomberg

2 Corinthians, Scott Hafemann

Galatians, Scot McKnight

Ephesians, Klyne Snodgrass

Philippians, Frank Thielman

Colossians/Philemon, David E. Garland

1-2 Thessalonians, Michael W. Holmes

1-2 Timothy/Titus, Walter L. Liefeld

Hebrews, George H. Guthrie

James, David P. Nystrom

1 Peter, Scot McKnight

2 Peter/Jude, Douglas J. Moo

Letters of John, Gary M. Burge

Revelation, Craig S. Keener

To see which titles are available,
visit our web site at www.zondervan.com

11/00

NIV Application Commentary
Series Introduction

THE NIV APPLICATION COMMENTARY SERIES is unique. Most commentaries help us make the journey from our world back to the world of the Bible. They enable us to cross the barriers of time, culture, language, and geography that separate us from the biblical world. Yet they only offer a one-way ticket to the past and assume that we can somehow make the return journey on our own. Once they have explained the *original meaning* of a book or passage, these commentaries give us little or no help in exploring its *contemporary significance*. The information they offer is valuable, but the job is only half done.

Recently, a few commentaries have included some contemporary application as *one* of their goals. Yet that application is often sketchy or moralistic, and some volumes sound more like printed sermons than commentaries.

The primary goal of the NIV Application Commentary Series is to help you with the difficult but vital task of bringing an ancient message into a modern context. The series not only focuses on application as a finished product but also helps you think through the *process* of moving from the original meaning of a passage to its contemporary significance. These are commentaries, not popular expositions. They are works of reference, not devotional literature.

The format of the series is designed to achieve the goals of the series. Each passage is treated in three sections: *Original Meaning, Bridging Contexts,* and *Contemporary Significance.*

THIS SECTION HELPS you understand the meaning of the biblical text in its original context. All of the elements of traditional exegesis—in concise form—are discussed here. These include the historical, literary, and cultural context of the passage. The authors discuss matters related to grammar and syntax and the meaning of biblical words.[1] They also seek to explore the main ideas of the passage and how the biblical author develops those ideas.

---

1. Please note that in general, when the authors discuss words in the original biblical languages, the series uses a general rather than a scholarly method of transliteration.

After reading this section, you will understand the problems, questions, and concerns of the *original audience* and how the biblical author addressed those issues. This understanding is foundational to any legitimate application of the text today.

THIS SECTION BUILDS a bridge between the world of the Bible and the world of today, between the original context and the contemporary context, by focusing on both the timely and timeless aspects of the text.

God's Word is *timely*. The authors of Scripture spoke to specific situations, problems, and questions. The author of Joshua encouraged the faith of his original readers by narrating the destruction of Jericho, a seemingly impregnable city, at the hands of an angry warrior God (Josh. 6). Paul warned the Galatians about the consequences of circumcision and the dangers of trying to be justified by law (Gal. 5:2–5). The author of Hebrews tried to convince his readers that Christ is superior to Moses, the Aaronic priests, and the Old Testament sacrifices. John urged his readers to "test the spirits" of those who taught a form of incipient Gnosticism (1 John 4:1–6). In each of these cases, the timely nature of Scripture enables us to hear God's Word in situations that were *concrete* rather than abstract.

Yet the timely nature of Scripture also creates problems. Our situations, difficulties, and questions are not always directly related to those faced by the people in the Bible. Therefore, God's word to them does not always seem relevant to us. For example, when was the last time someone urged you to be circumcised, claiming that it was a necessary part of justification? How many people today care whether Christ is superior to the Aaronic priests? And how can a "test" designed to expose incipient Gnosticism be of any value in a modern culture?

Fortunately, Scripture is not only timely but *timeless*. Just as God spoke to the original audience, so he still speaks to us through the pages of Scripture. Because we share a common humanity with the people of the Bible, we discover a *universal dimension* in the problems they faced and the solutions God gave them. The timeless nature of Scripture enables it to speak with power in every time and in every culture.

Those who fail to recognize that Scripture is both timely and timeless run into a host of problems. For example, those who are intimidated by timely books such as Hebrews, Galatians, or Deuteronomy might avoid reading them because they seem meaningless today. At the other extreme, those who are convinced of the timeless nature of Scripture, but who fail to discern its timely element, may "wax eloquent" about the Melchizedekian priesthood to a sleeping congregation, or worse still, try to apply the holy wars of the Old Testament in a physical way to God's enemies today.

The purpose of this section, therefore, is to help you discern what is timeless in the timely pages of the Bible—and what is not. For example, how do the holy wars of the Old Testament relate to the spiritual warfare of the New? If Paul's primary concern is not circumcision (as he tells us in Gal. 5:6), what *is* he concerned about? If discussions about the Aaronic priesthood or Melchizedek seem irrelevant today, what is of abiding value in these passages? If people try to "test the spirits" today with a test designed for a specific first-century heresy, what other biblical test might be more appropriate?

Yet this section does not merely uncover that which is timeless in a passage but also helps you to see *how* it is uncovered. The authors of the commentaries seek to take what is implicit in the text and make it explicit, to take a process that normally is intuitive and explain it in a logical, orderly fashion. How do we know that circumcision is not Paul's primary concern? What clues in the text or its context help us realize that Paul's real concern is at a deeper level?

Of course, those passages in which the historical distance between us and the original readers is greatest require a longer treatment. Conversely, those passages in which the historical distance is smaller or seemingly nonexistent require less attention.

One final clarification. Because this section prepares the way for discussing the contemporary significance of the passage, there is not always a sharp distinction or a clear break between this section and the one that follows. Yet when both sections are read together, you should have a strong sense of moving from the world of the Bible to the world of today.

THIS SECTION ALLOWS the biblical message to speak with as much power today as it did when it was first written. How can you apply what you learned about Jerusalem, Ephesus, or Corinth to our present-day needs in Chicago, Los Angeles, or London? How can you take a message originally spoken in Greek, Hebrew, and Aramaic and communicate it clearly in our own language? How can you take the eternal truths originally spoken in a different time and culture and apply them to the similar-yet-different needs of our culture?

In order to achieve these goals, this section gives you help in several key areas.

(1) It helps you identify contemporary situations, problems, or questions that are truly comparable to those faced by the original audience. Because

contemporary situations are seldom identical to those faced by the original audience, you must seek situations that are analogous if your applications are to be relevant.

(2) This section explores a variety of contexts in which the passage might be applied today. You will look at personal applications, but you will also be encouraged to think beyond private concerns to the society and culture at large.

(3) This section will alert you to any problems or difficulties you might encounter in seeking to apply the passage. And if there are several legitimate ways to apply a passage (areas in which Christians disagree), the author will bring these to your attention and help you think through the issues involved.

In seeking to achieve these goals, the contributors to this series attempt to avoid two extremes. They avoid making such specific applications that the commentary might quickly become dated. They also avoid discussing the significance of the passage in such a general way that it fails to engage contemporary life and culture.

Above all, contributors to this series have made a diligent effort not to sound moralistic or preachy. The NIV Application Commentary Series does not seek to provide ready-made sermon materials but rather tools, ideas, and insights that will help you communicate God's Word with power. If we help you to achieve that goal, then we have fulfilled the purpose for this series.

The Editors

General Editor's Preface

ONE OF THE DIFFICULTIES of applying the wisdom of Isaiah to the perplexities of twenty-first-century life is audience. It always seems as if Isaiah is talking to someone else. Let me explain.

Isaiah, son of Amoz, spends much of his writing time relating visions of destruction and visions of blessings about the divided nation of Israel and her surrounding neighbors. Listen to some of the subject headings the NIV editors scatter throughout the book: "A Rebellious Nation" (ch. 1); "Judgment on Jerusalem and Judah" (ch. 3); "Woes and Judgments" (ch. 5); "Assyria, the Lord's Instrument" (ch. 8). The list goes on and on through the sixty-six chapters of the book.

Admittedly this can make for exciting reading, particularly if you enjoy hearing about other people's problems. But it is difficult to see what the Lord-defying words and deeds of Israel have to do with us. One of the great strengths of this commentary on Isaiah, written by John Oswalt, is that he shows how to read this book—that is, how to avoid reading it solely as a chronicle of others people's problems and to see instead how it relates directly to us. Put another way, even though Isaiah seems to be warning a country that has an immoral domestic and foreign policy, at a deeper level the warnings and judgments are for you and me.

So how are we to read this book in a way that best communicates God's message to us?

(1) Expect to hear God's voice to us in Isaiah's words. This means bringing one's faith to a reading of the text. When Isaiah tells Israel to "go into the rocks, hide in the ground from dread of the LORD and the splendor of his majesty" (Isa. 2:10), it may not be necessary to load up your backpack and head for the Colorado Rockies. But it is necessary to expect that in that admonition there is a message for me.

(2) Recognize that the message is not in narrative prose but is embedded in visions, oracles, metaphors, and allusions. Isaiah was not a straight-talking prophet; he was a poetic prophet. Look at the way the type is laid out on the pages of your Bible. It looks like poetry. Only rarely in the pages of Isaiah do you see the blocks of type we associate with the narrative portions of the Bible or with other books we read.

In order to understand this kind of writing we need to think about why someone chooses to write in poetic form. The most important reason is that poetry is best at communicating the sort of wisdom that our culture makes it difficult to hear.

(3) Notice that a subtle shift takes place in Isaiah that moves us away from seeing these visions as oracles aimed directly, solely, at the nation of Israel. To see this shift, a little history reminder is in order. Most of the people of Isaiah's day (including the Israelites) were henotheists by upbringing. That is, they were used to thinking of gods as tribal gods. Each tribe, each people group, had their own god. The question was not primarily whether those gods were real (the assumption was that they were). The real question was whose god was the most powerful.

Contrast that with the way we look at God today. Most of us today assume that God is strong; our focus is on God's relating to individuals, not to groups of people. As a result, many modern exegetes of Isaiah think that the subtle shift apparent in Isaiah is from viewing the gods as tribal gods to viewing God as the God of individuals. Perhaps. There is no question that the image we end up with in taking the Old Testament texts as a whole is not henotheistic but monotheistic, a righteous God concerned about individual persons.

But the *real shift* in Isaiah is toward a view of God as the Lord not of just tribes, not of just individuals, but as the Lord of all:

> This is what the LORD says:
> "Heaven is my throne
>   and the earth is my footstool. . . .
> Has not my hand made all these things,
>   and so they came into being?" (Isa. 66:1–2)

God reigns over all. Let the Lord be glorified that we may see your joy.

Terry C. Muck

Author's Preface

IT HAS BEEN A SPECIAL PRIVILEGE to be able to write a second commentary on the book of Isaiah, one that focuses particularly on contemporary application. This task has proven more arduous than I originally anticipated, and the reader must judge how successful I have been. Nevertheless, it has been a profitable exercise for me and has left me with an even deeper appreciation for the prophet Isaiah and his towering accomplishment. He has written a book that is no less pointed and relevant in its application to the present than when it was first written 2,700 years ago. He has left his mark—and more importantly, God's mark—on the world, and that mark will last until the end of time.

Having said that, I am conscious of how often I have only been able to scratch the surface of the depths contained in it. It is profoundly humbling to be able to get a glimpse of the wonders contained within the words of the prophet and then be able to express them only in part. But I have expressed them as well as I can, and I gratefully leave the result to God.

I want to express my thanks to the trustees of Wesley Biblical Seminary, who granted me a research leave during which the bulk of the writing was completed. I also want to thank Terry Muck and Andrew Dearman, who read the manuscript carefully and made valuable suggestions. The editors at Zondervan, Jack Kuhatschek and Verlyn Verbrugge, were also unfailingly helpful.

Then there were my prayer partners—Sam Biebers, Stuart Kellogg, Daniel Koehn, Keith Megehee, and James Wolheter—whose prayers carried me along through the project.

Finally, I want to acknowledge Karen, my wife and life partner, without whose unfailing love, encouragement, and care none of what I have done would have ever happened.

Abbreviations

AB	Anchor Bible
ABD	*Anchor Bible Dictionary*. D. N. Freedman et. al., eds. 6 vols. New York: Doubleday, 1992.
ANET	*Ancient Near Eastern Texts Relating to the Old Testament*. J. B. Pritchard, ed. 3d ed. Princeton: Princeton Univ. Press, 1969.
BAR	*Biblical Archaeology Review*
BDB	F. Brown, S. R. Driver, and C. A. Briggs. *A Hebrew and English Lexicon of the Old Testament*. Oxford: Clarendon, 1959 reprint.
BHS	*Biblia Hebraica Stuttgartensia*
BKAT	Biblischer Kommentar: Altes Testament
BST	The Bible Speaks Today
BZAW	Beihefte zur Zeitschrift für die alttestamentliche Wissenschaft
CB	The Bible in Contemporary English
CBC	Cambridge Bible Commentary
CBQ	*Catholic Biblical Quarterly*
ConBOT	Coniectania biblica, Old Testament
ETL	*Ephemerides theologicae lovanienses*
EvQ	*Evangelical Quarterly*
FAT	Forshungen zum Alten Testament
FOTL	Forms of the Old Testament Literature
HKAT	Handkommentar zum Alten Testament
ICC	International Critical Commentary
Int	*Interpretation*
ITC	International Theological Commentary
JB	Jerusalem Bible
JBL	*Journal of Biblical Literature*
JETS	*Journal of the Evangelical Theological Society*
JPS	Jewish Publication Society
JSOT	*Journal for the Study of the Old Testament*
JSOTSup	Journal for the Study of the Old Testament Supplement Series
LXX	Septuagint

MT	Masoretic Text
NASB	New American Standard Bible
NCBC	New Century Bible Commentary
NDBT	*New Dictionary of Biblical Theology.* T. D. Alexander and B. Rosner, eds. Leicester, Eng.: Inter-Varsity Press, 2000.
NICOT	New International Commentary on the Old Testament
NIDOTTE	*New International Dictionary of Old Testament Theology and Exegesis.* W. VanGemeren et. al., eds. Grand Rapids: Zondervan, 1997.
NIV	New International Version
NIVAC	The NIV Application Commentary
NLT	New Living Translation
NRSV	New Revised Standard Version
OBT	Overtures to Biblical Theology
OTL	Old Testament Library
POT	De Prediking van het Oude Testament
REB	Revised English Bible
RSV	Revised Standard Version
SBLDS	Society of Biblical Literature Dissertation Series
SBLMS	Society of Biblical Literature Monograph Series
SBLSP	Society of Biblical Literature Seminar Papers
SJT	*Scottish Journal of Theology*
SOTMS	Society for Old Testament Study Monograph Series
ST	*Studia theologica*
TDNT	*Theological Dictionary of the New Testament.* G. Kittel and G. Friedrich, eds. Trans. G. W. Bromiley. 10 vols. Grand Rapids: Eerdmans, 1964–1976.
TDOT	*Theological Dictionary of the Old Testament.* G. Botterweck and H. Ringgren, eds. Trans. D. Green et al. Grand Rapids: Eerdmans, 1974–.
TLOT	*Theological Lexicon of the Old Testament.* E. Jenni and C. Westermann, eds. Trans. M. Biddle. 3 vols. Peabody, Mass.: Hendrickson, 1997.
TOTC	Tyndale Old Testament Commentaries
VT	*Vetus Testamentum*
VTSup	Vetus Testamentum Supplement Series
WBC	Word Biblical Commentary
WTJ	*Westminster Theological Journal*
ZAW	*Zeitschrift für die alttestamentliche Wissenschaft*
ZBK	Züricher Bibelkommentare

Introduction

ACROSS THE YEARS Isaiah has come to be known as "the prince of the prophets." A part of the reason for this title is the possibility that the prophet was a member of the royal family. While there is no indisputable evidence of this, the easy access to the kings that he seemed to enjoy may point in this direction. But the real basis of the claim is the nature of the book known by Isaiah's name. There is a majesty in the book that sets it off from almost any other in the Bible. It contains an unparalleled sweep of theology, all the way from creation to the new heavens and new earth and from utter destruction to glorious redemption.

The book's view of God is equally comprehensive: He is the austere Judge who decrees destruction on a rebellious people, but he is also the compassionate Redeemer who will not cast off a hopeless and despairing people. Nor are these ideas merely presented one after another and then left behind. Rather, they are interwoven in artful ways that suggest the symphonic art that appeared in musical style two millennia after Isaiah. Motifs appear, disappear, and reappear in ways that keep the thoughtful reader involved in an active dialogue with the writer.

Along with this intricacy is a style that moves back and forth from sonorous to lyrical. Chapters 6 and 40 are very different, yet they share the same spare, economical use of words, which makes them both memorable and effective. They have both a power and a beauty that make them unforgettable. Isaiah 52:13–53:12 is a different type of literature, but it is also an example of a style that matches beauty and power.

In many ways the book of Isaiah is the Bible in miniature. Like the Bible, the book has two major divisions, and like the Bible the main theme of the first part is judgment and the main theme of the second is hope. Beyond this, all the main themes of the Bible can be found in Isaiah. Though the Sinai covenant is not mentioned explicitly, it is everywhere assumed. It is the basis of the charges of rebellion, and it is the essential ground of the supposed relationship between God and Israel. The Davidic covenant is mentioned, and it is the foundation of the promises of the Messiah. If the house of David has failed, God's promises have not. Here the whole question of the uniqueness of God vis-à-vis idols is explored more completely than in any other book of the Bible. And it is here that the glory of the Davidic Messiah and the shame of the Suffering Servant are brought together in a way that helps the

New Testament picture of Christ make sense. So whether Isaiah was actually of the royal house or not, it is true that his work, in its theological sweep, towering vision, and powerful language, sets him apart as a prince among the prophets.

Historical Background

ALONG WITH THE princely qualities of the book are several conundrums. One of these is the fact that it seems to be addressed to at least two, and perhaps three, different settings. The first of these is that of Isaiah's own times, from about 740 to 700 B.C. But chapters 40–55 seem to be addressed to the Judean exiles in Babylon between 585 and 540 B.C., and while the evidence is less clear than it seems to be for the preceding two divisions, chapters 56–66 seem to reflect conditions in Judah after the return from exile in 539 B.C.

On the face of it, this seems odd. No other book of the Bible does this. Several speak *about* future times, but no other seems to speak *to* future times as Isaiah does. This is one of the chief reasons why it has become common in scholarly circles to consider that the book is the result of several different authors, with those involved in writing the second two divisions having lived in those times. While it is not impossible that the book is a composite, the book itself seems to make every effort to deny that conclusion, naming only one author throughout and giving no clues as to the life-settings and places of the other supposed authors (see below on Authorship and Date). Nor, if predictive prophecy is granted to be possible, is it out of the question for Isaiah to have understood enough of the general outline of future conditions to have addressed persons in those settings.[1]

But if we grant that Isaiah is responsible for the entire book, why would he have written to future generations as well as his own? Since the Bible itself does not offer an explanation, we cannot give a definitive answer. But there is a plausible possibility. In chapters 6–39, Isaiah is given a sweeping vision of God's absolute superiority over the nations of the earth. All of history is in his hand, and he is able to deliver those who trust him out of the hands of the nations. This was climactically demonstrated in the deliverance of Jerusalem from Sennacherib narrated in 37:36–38. However, Isaiah is permitted to see the future, a time when Judah will not be trusting God in

---

1. It is significant that there is almost no specific historical detail in chapters 40–66 apart from the one glaring exception, the naming of the deliverer, Cyrus. This would be consistent with the historical Isaiah having written these chapters, having a general idea what the future would hold but no specific knowledge. If those chapters were written in those actual times, then we must believe that later editors stripped the details out in order to heighten the impression that Isaiah wrote them.

the face of the Babylonians and when the Babylonians will devastate God's city and remove God's people far from the land he promised to them. What then? Will not future events have invalidated what Isaiah was given for his own day?

Furthermore, Isaiah sees that though there is a return from exile (predicted in the naming of his son Shearjashub ["Only a Remnant Will Return"]), it will be to vastly different conditions from those that pertained before the destruction of the city. Judah will simply be a backwater in the vast Persian Empire. Judah will have no king, no army, and no independence, and it will be faced with a much more subtle danger to their distinctive faith than the outright hostility of the Assyrians and Babylonians, namely, a syncretistic outlook that encouraged them to see their God as only a local manifestation of a universal deity worshiped by all religions.

Is it not possible that God gifted Isaiah with the ability to see the future of his people in order to show them (and us) that God *is still* superior to the nations and their gods (see 40:15–24) even if circumstances and situations are vastly different from those in which the original revelation was given? Is God the Lord of Babylon even if Jerusalem is not delivered out of Babylon's hands? Yes! Is God still the Lord of Judah even if he, because of her sins, has had to drive Judah from the land he promised her? Yes! Is it possible to experience the kingdom of God even if there is no kingdom of Judah? Yes! Is Judah's God the Lord of the nations even if Judah herself is no longer a nation? Yes! If the book had ended at chapter 39, we the readers would have had an incomplete picture of God. We would not have known that God's true lordship of history is not to be found merely in his ability to direct its events, but perhaps even more so in his ability to respond to events in such a way that his original strategy can remain unchanged. Not only is he the King of history; he is also the Redeemer of history.[2]

740–700 B.C.

BETWEEN 900 AND 609 B.C. the nation of Assyria was the single most prominent force, both politically and militarily, in the ancient Near East. Operating from their home base on the middle Tigris River in Mesopotamia, they had spread their domination in all directions, but especially southward to Babylon and the other southern Mesopotamian city-states and westward and

---

2. There is no a priori reason why later authors could not have supplemented the work of the "master" to add these further perspectives. The only problem is that if they did do this, then they have presented their work in such a way as to try to make us believe that they did *not* do it. They have tried to make it appear as if the book is all the work of the prophet Isaiah.

then southward toward Egypt. The small nations on the eastern coast of the Mediterranean Sea stood in the way of this latter advance. Assyria had to go through them to reach the ultimate goal of Egypt because the sea stood on the west and the desert was on the east.

Furthermore, these small nations constituted rich prizes in themselves, having amassed wealth through agriculture, natural resources, and trade. Recognizing the threat, the small nations had formed a coalition to fight the Assyrians at the city of Qarqar in northern Syria in 853 B.C.[3] The outcome of the battle seems to have been inconclusive. The southward thrust of the Assyrian king Shalmaneser seems to have been slowed, but it was by no means stopped since he continued to press southward during the remaining twenty-five years of his reign. His two immediate successors continued the same aggressive policies.

All of this put immense pressure on the kings of Israel and Judah in the century between 885 and 785 B.C. Much of their time and wealth had to be devoted to attempts to deal with the Assyrian threat. But beginning in 782, there were three Assyrian kings who were less aggressive.[4] The third of these died in 745. This meant that for about forty years prior to 745, Judah and Israel had enjoyed a respite. Coinciding with this respite, and perhaps also because of it, both nations enjoyed unusually long and stable reigns. Israel was ruled from 793 to 753 by Jeroboam II, while Judah was ruled from 792 to 740 by Uzziah (Azariah).[5] Since it was possible to devote time and resources to things other than defense, both nations experienced a time of wealth and prosperity unlike anything since the days of Solomon.

But all that came to a crashing close with the accession of a new Assyrian monarch in 745 B.C. This man, Tiglath-Pileser III (2 Kings 15:29, called Pul in 15:19), inaugurated a new period of Assyrian aggressiveness that was to continue right up until the final disappearance of the Assyrian Empire a century and a quarter later. Suddenly everything changed. Now the predictions of imminent destruction of Israel, which Amos and Hosea had made earlier and which had seemed so far-fetched at the time, did not seem far-fetched at all. Undoubtedly the death of Jeroboam II in 753, the almost immediate assassination of his son, and the subsequent chaos of succession contributed to the sense of impending doom. It seems clear that the kingdom of Israel was ruled for at least a dozen years between 752 and 740 by two kings simulta-

---

3. See *ANET*, 278–279.

4. It is interesting to speculate whether the ministry of Jonah may have had anything to do with this.

5. These dates are those of E. H. Merrill, *Kingdom of Priests* (Grand Rapids: Baker, 1987), 320. Other sources, such as J. Bright, *A History of Israel*, 4th ed. (Philadelphia: Westminster, 2000) vary slightly.

neously, with the warlord Pekah ruling in the Transjordan area until he could take complete control in 740.

In Judah also there was a change of kingship at this time, although it was not accompanied by the chaos found in the less-stable north. Here, Uzziah was succeeded in 740 by his son Jotham, who probably had been acting as coregent with his father for some ten years before Uzziah's death.[6] Nevertheless, in spite of a greater stability on the throne, Judah could not help being embroiled in the wrenching crisis. By 740 the region north of the Sea of Galilee had been taken from Israel, and almost all that was left of Syria was the capital city, Damascus.

Desperate for some way of stopping the juggernaut, Israel and Syria conceived of another coalition (2 Kings 16:5–6; Isa. 7:1). None of the small countries on the Mediterranean coast had a hope of standing up against the Assyrians alone, but perhaps together they could at least achieve as much success as they had gained at Qarqar a century earlier. By this time (ca. 735) it appears that Jotham had been forced by a pro-Assyrian group in Judah to accord his son Ahaz a coregency. In fact, Jotham may have been effectively replaced, because Ahaz is the one acting as king at this point.

Undoubtedly, the call for a coalition against Assyria placed Ahaz in quandary as to whether he was a pawn of a pro-Assyrian party. To take a stand against Assyria had serious consequences if the stand proved to be futile. Whatever else the Assyrians were, they were ruthlessly efficient. Their armies showed both a higher level of organization and of armament than had been known previously in the ancient Near East, and their policies were equally well thought out. There was no lenience offered to those who insisted on opposing them, for the simple reason that such lenience might prompt others to run the risk of such opposition. To oppose the Assyrians and fail was to be subjected to as much destruction and terror as the Assyrian mind could conceive and the Assyrian might could carry out. Sieges were costly and time-consuming. If enemies could be convinced to surrender by looking at what previous enemies of Assyria had undergone, it was all to the good.

So Ahaz king of Judah had to weigh his options carefully. If he agreed to go with Pekah of Israel and Rezin of Damascus and they failed, there was no question that he himself would die by torture in as slow and as agonizing a death as possible and that his city would be systematically destroyed and his people scattered across the empire. But if he would not join the coalition, Israel and Syria would attack him; and if they were successful, they would depose him and put someone else on the throne who would be amenable to their plans (someone named "the son of Tabeel," according to Isa. 7:6). There

---

6. See Merrill, *Kingdom of Priests*, 377.

was yet another option: He could actively throw in with the Assyrians and ask them to help him as their vassal.

This latter option is what Ahaz chose. He sent a large sum of money to Tiglath-Pileser and asked for protection from his two enemies (2 Kings 16:7–9). If this seems to us at this distance as though three mice are having a fight and one of them is asking the cat for help, we must remember that Ahaz's political options were limited. But what Ahaz seems not to have taken into account was God. Ironically, the way in which the Bible presents the account is that Pekah and Rezin had already failed in their attempt to take Jerusalem before any intervention from Assyria occurred. If Ahaz had considered God's plans and promises, he might have saved himself a great deal of money.

At any rate, Tiglath-Pileser, perhaps using some of Ahaz's funds, succeeded in capturing Damascus in 732. With this fortress no longer posing a danger in his rear, the Assyrian conqueror was free to push on through northern Israel and on down the coast toward the Philistine cities. Initially Hoshea, Pekah's successor on the throne of Israel, submitted to the Assyrians and paid tribute to them (2 Kings 17:3–4). But, predictably, he wearied of that burden. Thinking he had procured help from the Egyptians, he stopped paying the tribute in 726 or 725. This was early in the reign of Shalmaneser, Tiglath-Pileser's successor, and it was fairly common for vassals to revolt in the early years of a reign, hoping that an emperor would have too many other things to attend to in order to prosecute a rebellion. If that was Hoshea's hope, it was a vain one, because Shalmaneser successfully besieged Samaria and captured it in the year of his death, 722.

By this time yet a third successive coregency seems to have taken place in Judah. This time it appears that the anti-Assyrian party was in the ascendancy and had forced Ahaz's son Hezekiah on him.[7] Hezekiah was sixteen by the time of Samaria's fall and seems to have stepped forward to attempt some sort of rapprochement with the Israelites who remained behind after the deportations (2 Chron. 30:1–11). Perhaps the reality of the Assyrian threat had now come home to the Judeans and Ahaz's influence was on the wane. At any rate, it seems clear that from the outset Hezekiah pursued a

---

7. There is a discrepancy between 2 Kings 18:1 and 2, which does not seem capable of resolution without emending the text. If Hezekiah began to reign in Hoshea's third year (v. 1), that was 729. However, verse 2 says that he was twenty-five years old when he began to reign. Since his father Ahaz was only twenty-four or twenty-five in 729, that is an impossibility. Perhaps verse 2 is referring to 516, when Ahaz died and Hezekiah assumed sole rule. For a helpful discussion of this problem and those related to it, see Merrill, *Kingdom of Priests*, 402–5. Other scholars such as J. Bright, *A History of Israel*, 278, merely assume that Hezekiah began his reign in 715. Even though it solves this problem in a different way from the one accepted here, the best treatment of the chronology of the divided kingdom remains that of E. R. Thiele, *The Mysterious Numbers of the Hebrew Kings*, 3d ed. (Grand Rapids: Zondervan, 1983).

policy that reasserted Judah's dependency on God and a refusal to consider any kind of a surrender to the Assyrians.

This was, of course, a high-risk position, as outlined above. With Samaria gone, the Assyrians, now led by Sargon II, pushed farther south and attacked the Philistine cities on the Mediterranean coast with impunity. By 715 the last of them had fallen. However, Sargon was not able to push immediately ahead to Egypt because for the next ten years he was plagued by revolts and incursions on his northern border, and apart from occasional punitive raids in the south was unable to follow up on his advantage. During this time Hezekiah was able to carry out his religious reforms and to fortify his country. It also appears from the book of Isaiah that there was considerable pressure among Hezekiah's counselors for him to ally Judah with Egypt. Undoubtedly Egypt was pushing hard for this too. They could read the signs as well as anyone else. Sooner or later Assyria would be knocking on their door, and by now only Judah, the remnants of the Philistines, Moab, and Edom were left to stand in the way of that eventuality.

Finally Sargon died in 705, perhaps on the battlefield. He was succeeded by his son Sennacherib, who was shortly (703) faced with a rebellion in Babylon. The leader of this revolt was from Chaldea in extreme southern Mesopotamia. His name was Marduk-apal-idinna (the Bible's Merodach-Baladan, Isa. 39:1). It seems probable that the events described in Isaiah 39 took place some time prior to this revolt as Merodach-Baladan sought to persuade others across the empire to join him in revolt. Whether that is the correct interpretation or not, it is clear that sometime in 703 or 702 Hezekiah led his neighbors in open revolt to the extent of capturing a Philistine kinglet named Padi and imprisoning him in Jerusalem.

Having dealt with the Babylonians, Sennacherib turned his attention to the west and, in the words of Byron, "came down like a wolf on the fold."[8] In short order he brought the hard light of reality to bear on the ephemeral dreams the coalition may have had of actually being able to stand up to the Assyrian might. The promised Egyptian help evaporated, the leading Philistine city of Ekron was captured, and the towns and fortresses of Judah (forty-six of them in all) were captured and destroyed. Only Lachish, southwest of Jerusalem, and Jerusalem itself remained. Hezekiah turned over Padi and sent a large present to Sennacherib, apparently in the hope that Sennacherib would be mollified and return home.

That was not to be the case, however. Sennacherib destroyed Lachish made it clear he was not going home until the rebel city of Jerusalem opened its

---

8. George Gordon, Lord Byron, "The Destruction of Sennacherib," *British Poetry and Prose*, ed. P. Lieder, R. Lovett, and R. Root (New York: Houghton Mifflin, 1928), 774.

gates to him, either willingly or forcibly. He could ill afford to do anything else. There was the military problem. He could not proceed with the attack on Egypt with an enemy stronghold at his rear in position to cut his supply lines. But more importantly, there was the political problem. Hezekiah was the leader of the revolt. Assyria did not allow leaders of revolts to live. If it did, there would be no end of trouble. So Jerusalem had to fall and Hezekiah had to die.

In fact, that is not what happened. Sennacherib does not tell us why. In his own annals, he only boasts that he shut up Hezekiah "like a bird in a cage" and that Hezekiah paid him a huge tribute, agreeing to renew it annually. So Sennacherib returned home and, as far as his records indicate, never campaigned in the west again until his death at the hands of his own sons twenty years later. The door to Egypt, the prize for which Assyria had been straining for almost two hundred years, stood open, and Sennacherib did nothing to go through it. Instead, he was content to fill his palace with huge reliefs of the fall of Lachish. Having been denied the prize, he made do with second or third best. What happened? The Bible gives us the answer in Isaiah 37:36–37. One night most of the Assyrian grand army died at the hand of "the angel of the LORD," and Sennacherib decided he had more pressing business at home.[9]

625–540 B.C.

THE ASSYRIAN EMPIRE eventually reached its Egyptian goal under Sennacherib's successor, Esarhaddon. When Esarhaddon's son, Ashurbanipal, came to the throne in 668, Assyria stood at the apex of its power and glory. Yet within less than twenty years of Ashurbanipal's death in 627 B.C., the Assyrian Empire would cease to exist. What happened? A number of factors were involved, but chief among them was the resurgence of Babylon. Relations between Assyria and Babylon had always been tense, with the Babylonians regularly attempting to break free. For two hundred years Assyria had always been able to regain control, but with Ashurbanipal's death that control was lost irrevocably.

Ironically, Assyria may have contributed to Babylon's success this time by having decisively defeated Babylon's enemy Elam during Ashurbanipal's reign.

---

9. Because Isaiah (along with the parallel account in 2 Kings) immediately follows the destruction of the Assyrian army with the death of Sennacherib and because of certain other issues, some (notably J. Bright) have argued that the biblical account conflates two Assyrian attacks, one in 701 and another in 687. For the most recent defense of this theory see W. Shea, "Jerusalem under Siege, Did Sennacherib Attack Twice?" *BAR* 25 (Nov.–Dec. 1999): 36–44, 64. There are no Assyrian annals known for 689–686, so the theory cannot be tested from that direction. However, the biblical account can stand on its own (see comments on 37:36–38).

At any rate, in the upheavals surrounding Ashurbanipal's succession, a Chaldean general named Nabopolassar took the throne of Babylon and set about driving the Assyrians out. Within ten years he succeeded in this goal and was carrying the fight to the Assyrian homeland. He was aided in this by the Medes, a collection of tribes living in the Zagros Mountains on the eastern border of Mesopotamia. The Assyrians had long spoken glowingly of the warlike qualities of the Medes.

The beginning of the end for Assyria came with the capture and destruction of the city of Ashur in 614. Then in 612 the unthinkable happened. The greatest Assyrian city of all, Nineveh, fell after a siege of only three months. A claimant to the Assyrian throne fled westward with the remnants of the once-mighty Assyrian army. Landing first in Haran, they were ejected from there and fled farther west to Carchemish on the upper Euphrates in what is today Syria. There they were joined by the new Egyptian pharaoh Neco, who was probably trying to keep a weak Assyria alive as a buffer between him and the Babylonians. But in 605 the Babylonian army, now led by Nabopolassar's son Nebuchadnezzar, struck the final blow, destroying both the Assyrian and Egyptian armies.

Following up on his advantage, Nebuchadnezzar immediately marched south, reclaiming the coastal region for Mesopotamian control. Local rulers who for a short time had acknowledged Egyptian rule quickly changed sides. Among them was the Judean king Jehoiakim. He had been placed on the throne by Neco when Neco had deposed Jehoiakim's brother Jehoahaz in 609 (2 Kings 23:33–35). But whatever loyalty Jehoiakim may have felt to his former overlord evaporated when Nebuchadnezzar arrived. Jehoiakim surrendered, agreeing to pay an annual tribute, and gave up to Nebuchadnezzar not only some of the temple treasures but also hostages, among whom were Daniel, Hananiah, Mishael, and Azariah (Dan. 1:1–6).

But Jehoiakim's loyalty to Nebuchadnezzar was as fleeting as had been his loyalty to Neco. After just three years he broke the solemn covenant he had made, apparently hoping that Nebuchadnezzar's other obligations might be more important than the goings-on in faraway Judah.[10] That was not to be the case with an energetic ruler like Nebuchadnezzar. First, he sent various local groups to harass Jehoiakim (2 Kings 24:2; Jer. 35:11), and then he sent the Babylonian army itself. They arrived in 598. It was that year that Jehoiakim died (2 Kings 24:6). It is hard to believe that his dying at just this point was coincidental. This is especially so since his son Jehoiachin was

---

10. It is also possible that Nebuchadnezzar's failure to administer a crushing defeat to Neco at the battle they fought on the border of Egypt in 601 may have encouraged Jehoiakim in his rebellion. See J. Bright, *A History of Israel,* 327.

only eighteen and surrendered the city after only three months. But the Bible does not satisfy our curiosity on the question. At any rate, this time Nebuchadnezzar took Jehoiachin and most of the royal family into captivity along with other leaders and craftsmen (including the young priest Ezekiel). The Babylonian monarch replaced Jehoiachin with his uncle Mattaniah, renamed Zedekiah.

If the picture of Jehoiakim given in the book of Jeremiah is of a hard-eyed opportunist, the picture of Zedekiah is of a waffler who tried to please all sides simultaneously while having no firm convictions of his own. The biblical writers did not even consider him to be the legitimate king. As serious as Judah's spiritual condition was, it is clear from the example of Assyria's repentance in response to Jonah's preaching that if there had come a true national repentance even as late as Zedekiah's time, the city might have been spared and history been quite different. But although Zedekiah was Josiah's son, he was no Josiah. If he even understood the issues that all the great prophets had raised and that Jeremiah was declaring at that very moment, he certainly had no desire to address them. His popularity might have suffered.

Thus, Zedekiah asked Jeremiah for advice privately but was unwilling to support him publicly. The people drifted deeper and deeper into the kind of attitudes and behaviors that would seal their destruction. The picture God had given Isaiah 125 years earlier of a people with blind eyes, deaf ears, and fat, unresponsive hearts had come true with a vengeance. Part of their blindness was that they could not believe the city would fall. After all, they had God's temple, where the holy sacrifices were offered. Beyond this, if God was the God he claimed to be, how could he renege on the promises he had made to their ancestors? So, persisting in injustice, corruption, and violence, the Judean people believed their false prophets, who told them God was pleased with them and would shortly deliver them from the Babylonian threat.

It was in this atmosphere that Zedekiah, listening to counselors who assured him that Egypt would help and fearing a revolt among the people if he continued to tax them to pay the Babylonian tribute, decided to rebel, as his brother Jehoiakim had done before him. One wonders whether he really understood the gravity of what he was doing. Like the Assyrians before them, the Babylonians tended to give people three chances. If there were two rebellions after the initial submission (and there always were), total destruction was the result. This was Jerusalem's second rebellion. The results were entirely predictable. The only question was how soon the Babylonian army would arrive and how long the city could hold out.

The Babylonians began their siege of Jerusalem in 588, and the city was able to hold out for two years. But finally, as it must have done without a divine miracle, the city fell in July of 586. As unthinkable to the Assyrians as the fall of Nineveh had been twenty-five years earlier, the fall of Jerusalem was even more unthinkable to the Judeans. Had God failed? Had they believed lies about his greatness? Were his promises in vain? Had their sin been too much even for God?

All these questions and more must have filled the Judeans' minds as they trudged off into captivity. Many were in bitter despair, believing that everything they had once believed had been proven false. But here and there throughout the group were those who refused to give up hope. We know they did not because somehow they managed to smuggle out copies of the sacred scrolls. Among these was the book of Isaiah, along with the Torah and the writings of the other prophets. How exciting it must have been for those exiles to open Isaiah and to read what is now chapters 40–55 with new eyes, opened by the radically new situation. There they saw that Isaiah, under the inspiration of the Holy Spirit, had anticipated all their questions and had provided them with answers they had never understood before. They did not need to give up hope; God had not been defeated; he had not cast them off; the Babylonian gods were not superior to him.

Undoubtedly the somewhat different approach of the Babylonians to exile from that of the Assyrians helped to promote this renaissance of hope. Whereas the Assyrians had tried to break up national groups by scattering them in various places across the empire (see 2 Kings 17:6), the Babylonians permitted such groups to settle in one place. So the Judeans were placed together in central Babylon near the Kebar River at a place called Tel Abib (see Ezek. 1:1; 3:15). Thus the faithful were able to encourage those whose faith was wavering by getting them into the study of the Scriptures, especially of the prophets. When they discovered that the prophets had foreseen their present situation in varying levels of detail, they were surely moved to see what else the prophets had seen. There they found that the prophets had not only predicted the Exile but also predicted something that had never occurred before—a national return from exile.

Of course, many could not believe such an impossible thing, but their doubt was surely shaken when they heard their contemporary Ezekiel saying the same thing. What was difficult for them to grasp was the truth that God can do new things. They thought that he could not let Jerusalem fall, and when he did, they were sure that it was because he had been defeated and that therefore the ancient promises were nullified. The thought that God might have engineered the destruction of Jerusalem *in order to keep the ancient promises with a purified remnant* (Isa. 4:2–6) was "thinking outside the box," and it is clear both from Ezekiel and Isaiah that most of the exiles were no more able to do that than most of those before the Exile.

By its very nature paganism fosters such "boxed" thinking. The gods are personified natural, social, and psychological forces. They are the result of human thought that seeks to take an often-chaotic world and reduce it to a mental order. Pagan thinkers specifically do not look for the new and unique. Such things are freaks that do not produce order. Rather, they look for the recurring cycles and patterns that are always so. The pagans do not want to go some way they have never been before. That way lies chaos.

This is the basis for the biting satires on the gods that appear in Isaiah, Jeremiah, and Ezekiel. These gods and this way of thinking are a human attempt to get control of life. What good could those things do anybody? Can the creation save the creation from the creation? Not likely! The saving God is the good Creator, who made creation in certain ways but is never bound by those ways. The only thing he is bound by is his own consistent nature. Consistent, yes. Predictable, never. To us fearful humans, frantic to control our little worlds, such a picture is frightening. It means letting go of the familiar and casting ourselves into arms we cannot see, yet believing on the basis of the Word of God and the testimony of those who have gone before that the arms are there, stronger and more loving than anything we could ever imagine on our own.

Some of the exiled Judeans believed what they read in the Scriptures and resisted the temptation to settle down in a new environment and adopt its ways. They refused to give up the ancient promises. They kept their bags packed, spiritually speaking. No better example can be found of these attitudes and behaviors than Daniel and his friends. They refused to be assimilated into the Babylonian culture and religion, looking to the Scriptures for their self-understanding. This is seen clearly when we find Daniel praying for the return from exile on the basis of what he read in the book of Jeremiah (Dan. 9:1–19). As a result, when the man from the east, Cyrus, whom Isaiah had foretold (Isa. 41:2; 44:28–45:6), appeared, these believing Judeans were not surprised. Like Daniel, they had read the Scriptures carefully and knew that the Exile would not last longer than seventy years. So when Cyrus's decree permitting them to go home was made, they were ready.

The so-called Neo-Babylonian Empire looms large for students of the Bible because it was so pivotal in the history of Jerusalem and the Judean people. But actually, it was a brief interlude between the Assyrian and Persian Empires. It was to a great extent a "one-man show." That man was Nebuchadnezzar. When he passed from the scene in 562 B.C., after a forty-three-year reign, the winds that would destroy his work were already blowing. From one point of view the Neo-Babylonian Empire only existed while the Medes caught their breath and recruited a new partner, the Persians. The Medes and an associated group, the Umman-Manda, kept control of the northern part of the old Assyrian Empire. After failing to defeat the Persians who were under the leadership of a half-Median named Cyrus, they joined forces with him. He was able to provide a cohesive leadership that had been lacking, and by 547 he had consolidated his control to the point where he began to move from his northern bases south toward the Babylonian homeland.

In the first seven years after Nebuchadnezzar's death no fewer than three of his descendants took the throne and were removed from it for one reason or another. The man who emerged from all of this was a Babylonian official named Nabonidus, who ruled from 555 until the fall of Babylon in 539. The data about him are somewhat fragmentary; thus, historians vary widely in their estimate of him. Some see him as a scholar and antiquarian who let the crises of the empire go unaddressed. Others see him as a daring and innovative thinker who was overwhelmed by unmanageable realities.[11] In any case, we know that he left Babylon to live in the oasis of Tema for ten years, taking some of the chief deities of Babylon with him. He left a vice-regent named Belshazzar in charge in Babylon.[12]

Whether from Nabonidus's neglect or in spite of his best efforts, Cyrus went from strength to strength. When he finally appeared before Babylon in 539, the city fell to him with hardly a murmur. One of the first things he did was to proclaim that any exiled people who so wished could return home and that the royal treasury would pay for the rebuilding of any damaged temples.[13] The Judeans were ready, and some 50,000 made the long journey, reaching Jerusalem probably in 537 (see Ezra 2:64).

540–500 B.C.

IF THE PROMISES of the prophets had enabled the Judean people to survive the Exile, it is possible that those same prophets made it more difficult to survive the Return. Many of the prophets, in a manner continued by Jesus himself, had a way of telescoping future events together.[14] Thus, the predictions of the messianic age and the setting up of the kingdom of God seemed to follow closely on the predictions of the Return.[15] Since God had proven faithful

---

11. For this view see H. W. F. Saggs, *The Greatness That Was Babylon* (New York: Hawthorne, 1962), 145–52.

12. See Dan. 5 and note that Belshazzar offers to make Daniel *third* in the kingdom (5:7).

13. For Cyrus's report of such activity in the lands east of Babylon, see *ANET*, 316. The text of the proclamation itself is given in a shorter form in 2 Chron. 36:23 and in a longer form in Ezra 1:2–4. The Judeans are the only people we know who returned voluntarily.

14. In Matt. 24; Mark 13; and Luke 21 the destruction of the temple in A.D. 70 seems to be followed closely by the end of the world.

15. E.g., see Isa. 10–11.

in the Exile and then in the Return, surely now the returned exiles could look for all the nations of the world to come flowing to Jerusalem, bringing their wealth with them. Surely a descendant of Jehoiachin would soon ascend the throne of Israel in Judah, there to rule the world in righteousness and peace. Surely Jerusalem was about to become the center of a world empire.

None of these things occurred, however. Judah's condition was not better than before the Exile; in fact, it was worse. At least before the Exile they had had a semblance of independence with their own king, government, and army. And even stripped of much of its golden finery, the temple of Solomon was an impressive structure, fit to be the palace of the God of the world. But now what? They had no king; they had absolutely no independence; they were a subdivision of a division of a Persian region, with their "county seat" being, of all places, in Samaria! Jerusalem was in ruins, and there was neither the wealth nor the incentive to rebuild it. As for the temple of the Lord, when the foundations were laid, it was hard to distinguish the shouts of joy from the cries of those who remembered the glory of the former building (Ezra 3:12). The prospects were so disappointing that the foundations of the new temple lay exposed for sixteen years until the prophets Haggai and Zechariah finally convinced the people to get the task underway again in 520. The rebuilding project was finally completed in 516, twenty years after it began and seventy years after the previous temple had been burned.

In the world around, Persia reigned supreme without a rival. The Babylonians had welcomed Cyrus as a deliverer, much as the people of Ukraine and Belo-Russia welcomed Hitler. But Cyrus proved much more worthy of the acclaim. His proclamation of a return for the exiles was not a fluke. Rather, it was expressive of a new imperial policy, one in which legality, fairness, and generosity would replace terror. The result was a remarkably peaceful two hundred years for the ancient Near East. While it is true that failure to pay the heavy Persian taxes brought retribution again and again, there was little organized rebellion.

When both Assyria and Babylon fell, it was largely due to dissension and revolt from within the empire. That was not to be the case for Persia. Here the quest for legality and fairness had ballooned into a wasteful and elephantine bureaucracy, and the incredible wealth that the empire produced had sapped the original energy and drive that had conquered a world. The result was that when an army of lean and hungry Greeks met a Persian army almost three times larger in battle at Issus in what is now central Turkey in 333, the Persians suffered a defeat from which they never really recovered. After securing the eastern coast of the Mediterranean all the way to Egypt, where he was crowned Pharaoh, Alexander the Great defeated Darius III once again and in 331 captured Babylon, Susa, and Persepolis, burning the latter to the ground.

If the Judeans struggled as to how to define themselves as a people under Persian hegemony, they also struggled with how to define their faith. For all of their history they had thought of Yahweh as standing over against the other gods in competition. It was an either-or struggle. As Elijah said it, "Either Baal or Yahweh is God, and today we will see which one it is" (see 1 Kings 18:22–24). The same continued to be true in Babylon: Is Yahweh God, or is it Bel and Nebo (Isa. 46:1–5)?

But the Persians brought in a different religious policy, just as they did a different foreign policy. Now syncretism ruled the day. It was no longer "my god versus your god." Now it was "the divine has many faces." To you it looks like this; to me it looks like that; but we are both looking at the same divine reality. In many ways this created a more serious threat for the biblical faith than the old either-or confrontation. Now it seemed possible to worship Yahweh and Baal-Shamayim ("the Lord of the Heavens," a Near Eastern title for the Greek god Zeus) at the same time. Now one need no longer endure the stigma of separation and isolation, and equally important, one need no longer worry about whether one was worshiping in the right way or not.

If the Persian premise that all gods and goddesses are manifestations of the one divine essence had been correct, then all of this would have been fine. But of course, that premise is not correct. All the gods and goddesses of the pagan world may indeed have been the manifestation of the same basic understanding of deity, but that understanding is not the same as the one found in the Bible. As noted above, all pagan gods and goddesses are simply personifications of the forces of creation. All of them are built on the premise that there is a basic continuity between all things. Thus, deity can be explained by projecting back from creation. Just as creation is many, so are the gods; just as creation functions in endless cycles, so do the gods; just as creation is determined, so are the gods; just as creation is the result of sexual behavior, so are the gods; just as creation manifests an endless struggle between order and chaos, so do the gods.

But the biblical premise is diametrically opposite. It posits transcendence, with the Creator being radically discontinuous with his creation. Thus, he may not be represented by any created form. He is not many, he is One; he does not function in cycles but acts purposefully; his actions are not determined but are radically free; he is not sexed and does not act in a sexual manner; he is not ethically neutral, containing both order and disorder in himself, but is profoundly ethical. To say that, when the pagan looks at Baal and the Judean looks at Yahweh, they are simply looking at two sides of the same coin is to fail to see the radical nature of biblical religion.

Given both the political and the spiritual factors, it is not surprising that after the burst of energy needed to finish the temple, the former lethargy and apathy seemed to set in again. Clearly, the people were struggling with what is now called a "paradigm shift." How could they continue to maintain the radical uniqueness of God when they had no king and no kingdom and when the whole spirit of the age said that the maintaining of such an idea was not merely passé but unnecessary, a waste of energy?

Along with these problems, Isaiah 56–66 also makes it clear that there were other issues. Was ethical righteousness really so necessary? They had not been delivered from Babylon because of their righteousness but because of God's righteousness, his gracious keeping of his covenant with his people. So why try, especially since we seem regularly to fail in the attempt? It is our birthright as the people of the covenant that guarantees our relationship with God. Thus, at the same time as it was becoming easier and easier to blur the distinction between pagan worship and true worship, it was also easier to say that it was merely your genealogy that made you a member of God's family.

Unquestionably, the strong arguments for the uniqueness of the Lord that appear in Isaiah 40–55 were important to the thinking of the Judeans at this point. Again, Isaiah seems to have understood what challenges the future would hold for the things he had said about God's lordship over the nations in chapters 6–39 and was inspired to address them. Furthermore, chapters 56–66 address the questions of worship, ethics, and internationalism in ways that are consistent with chapters 6–39 but that carry the discussion further in light of the new situation.

The prophet reaffirms the promises of a new messianic kingdom, demonstrating that the earlier promises still hold true. But he also makes it plain that separation is not in order to keep the pagans out. Rather, it is in order to have a distinctive and coherent message to call the pagan *into* from their own darkness. God does not hate the non-Judeans; what he hates is their false religion, which is destroying them. Furthermore, Isaiah makes it plain that there is nothing sacred in the Judean bloodline. A Judean who succumbs to pagan religion and abandons the ethics of the covenant is as detestable to the Lord as any non-Judean would be.

At the same time, while the relevance of the message of Isaiah 56–66 to the Return is clear, some of the characteristic features of the postexilic prophets are missing. Chief among these are the importance of the temple and correct worship, such as appear in Ezekiel, Haggai, Zechariah, and Malachi, as well as in Chronicles, Ezra, and Nehemiah. One way of explaining this difference is that espoused by Paul Hanson, in which he argues that those writings are all by the followers of Ezekiel, whereas the followers of

"Deutero-Isaiah" were visionaries who had no real interest in institutions but were proto-apocalyptists, who looked forward to God's universal kingdom at the end of time.[16] However, since there is no indication elsewhere in the Bible of such competing groups, it seems that another explanation ought to be given consideration—namely, that these chapters were not written in 540–500 and that that issue, which was of great significance to persons of that time, was not in the writer's mind when he wrote.

Authorship and Date

AS MENTIONED ABOVE, the book of Isaiah cites no other author than "Isaiah son of Amoz" of Jerusalem, stating that he received his vision during the reigns of Uzziah, Jotham, Ahaz, and Hezekiah, that is, during the last half of the eighth century B.C. This attribution of authorship appears twice in the book (1:1; 2:1). Many believe that the first is intended to apply to the book as a whole and the second specifically to chapters 2–5. This was the view of the church up until the eighteenth century A.D., when the scholars of the Enlightenment began to insist that all truth claims had to bow at the bar of human reason. Scholars had, of course, long noted the absence of historical references after chapter 39. They had also noted certain stylistic and vocabulary differences between chapters 1–39 and 40–66. They had also commented on the announcement of the name of the Persian emperor Cyrus more than a hundred years before his birth and the fact that chapters 40–66 seemed to be addressed to people of the exilic period. But it remained to the German scholar J. C. Döderlein, writing in 1775, to first propose in print that the present book might consist of a conflation of two different works.[17]

J. G. Eichhorn amplified this idea and gave it further development, asserting that all of chapters 40–66 were written by someone other than Isaiah.[18] This view was increasingly popular in Europe, gaining the support of such eminent scholars as Gesenius.[19] However, the traditional view did not lack for support either. Such notable persons as R. Stier,[20] F. Delitzsch,[21] and the American J. A. Alexander[22] argued forcefully for the single authorship of the

16. Paul D. Hanson, *The Dawn of Apocalyptic* (Philadelphia: Fortress, 1975).

17. J. C. Döderlein, *Esaias* (Altdorfi, 1775).

18. J. G. Eichhorn, *Einleitung in das Alttestament*, 3 vols. (Leipzig: Weidmanns, 1780–1787).

19. W. Gesenius, *Philologisch-kritischer under historischer Kommentar über der Prophet Jesaia* (Leipzig: Vogel, 1821).

20. R. Stier, *Isaias, nicht Pseudo-Isaias* (Barmen: Langewiesche, 1850).

21. Franz Delitzsch, *Kommentar über das Buch Jesaja*, 4th ed. (Leipzig: Dörfflilng & Franke, 1889).

22. J. A. Alexander, *Commentary on the Prophecies of Isaiah* (New York: Scribners, 1846).

book. The influence of these and others meant that there was a certain moderation of tone in the debate in the third quarter of the nineteenth century.

However, this was all to change with the appearance of the commentary of Bernard Duhm in 1892.[23] Much as J. Wellhausen had been able to do with the criticism of the Pentateuch, Duhm was able to take a plethora of theories about the authorship of the book and integrate them into one appealing approach. He proposed that there were not two authors but three, Proto-Isaiah being responsible for large parts of chapters 1–39, Deutero-Isaiah for chapters 40–55, and Trito-Isaiah for chapters 56–66. This proposal, along with others he made in the commentary, seemed to solve the various problems encountered in previous suggestions. As a result, the idea of multiple authorship of the book gained widespread scholarly acceptance.

However, if anyone thought that Duhm's work settled the question of the book of Isaiah's authorship, he was mistaken. A contemporary of Duhm by the name of Hermann Gunkel was proposing a new theory of the composition of ancient literature, based on the research into the origins of German folk literature by a number of researchers, including the Grimm brothers. This theory argued that folk literature was not produced by single authors but was the product of communities, that written literature had a long oral prehistory, and that the particular function of the literary unit in its community required a particular literary form. Although Gunkel was an Old Testament scholar, his application of form-critical methods to the Old Testament did not gain much initial favor. It was only after the method had begun to be used fairly widely in New Testament studies that it began to be applied in the 1920s and 1930s to the Old Testament.

One of the effects of form criticism was to divide books into smaller and smaller units with increasing skepticism about the actual authorship of any of them. This was certainly the result in Isaianic studies. While chapters 40–55 tended to be retained for the supposedly brilliant and spiritual "Deutero-Isaiah," the individual "Trito-Isaiah" disappeared completely with the material in chapters 56–66 considered to be the work of a community in the postexilic period. As for "Proto-Isaiah," or "First Isaiah," his work is largely restricted to portions of chapters 6–12 and 28–31. The rest of chapters 1–39 is a miscellaneous collection coming from various points in the formation of "the Isaiah corpus," a process that was supposed to have gone on more or less continuously from 740 until the Hasmonean period (165 B.C.).

To explain how this process was carried out, an "Isaianic school" was hypothesized. In this hypothesis the disciples of "First Isaiah" began the process of adding to and amplifying the master's works. This process went

---

23. B. Duhm, *Das Buch Jesaja* (Göttingen: Vandenhoeck & Ruprecht, 1892).

on from generation to generation for more than five hundred years. The reason these persons are not named is twofold. (1) They did not consider they were really saying anything different from what the master had said. (2) Apart from "Deutero-Isaiah," the work really was that of a community and not of individuals.[24]

A number of arguments can be lodged against this hypothesis. Above all, it must be said that there is no objective evidence to support it. The earliest text we have is the Isaiah Scroll from the collection at Qumran (1QIsa[a]). This scroll is generally dated to the early first century B.C., and apart from certain minor spelling differences and some text-critical issues, the text is identical to that found in the Hebrew manuscripts of a millennium later. Clearly the text had been in existence long enough to become completely standardized with no hint of any complex redactional process leading to this form. Interestingly, the present chapter 39 ends only two lines from the bottom of a column. If the scribes had any sense of the separation between "First Isaiah" and "Second Isaiah," it would have been easy to leave the last two lines blank and to have started what is now chapter 40 at the top of the next column. But they did not do this. They used the final two lines of the column to begin that chapter.

Another argument against this theory is its dependence on the "Isaianic school," something for which there is no precedent and no evidence. To be sure, Isaiah speaks of sealing his writings and giving them to his disciples for future generations (8:16). But this is far from demonstrating that what he gave them was the equivalent of a dozen chapters that they and fifteen generations of their descendants developed into the present sixty-six chapters. An analogous process would be if Jesus had actually left only enough words and actions to fill out three or four pages in a book and that his disciples then replicated themselves for five hundred years while adding to and amplifying his supposed words and actions until the Gospel of Mark was actually completed in its present form in A.D. 500. The idea is not credible.

Yet another argument that must be lodged against the hypothesis of multiple authorship of Isaiah is the fact that it has not been able to produce any unanimity of results. While the work of Holladay noted above is one example of how the process is supposed to have worked, there would be almost no scholar who would agree with many of the details of his contentions. Although biblical studies are far from being an exact science, it is still true

---

24. For a handy summation of this hypothetical process and a proposal for which parts of the book came from which period, see W. L. Holladay, *Isaiah: Scroll of a Prophetic Heritage* (Grand Rapids: Eerdmans, 1978). For a more recent treatment along the same lines but omitting 56–66, see H. Williamson, *The Book Called Isaiah: Deutero-Isaiah's Role in Composition and Redaction* (Oxford: Clarendon, 1994).

that if a methodology is correct, it ought to yield substantially similar results in the hands of different researchers. In fact, that is not the case with the study of Isaiah. Two commentators who both share a commitment to form criticism and to multiple authorship of Isaiah may vary by as much as three hundred years as to when a particular unit was written.[25] They would disagree just as widely on the literary relation of that unit to those around it. There is something wrong with a methodology that cannot yield more predictable results.

Finally, it must be asked why the supposed authors have intentionally led their readers to believe that the whole is the work of Isaiah ben Amoz of the eighth century B.C., for this is clearly what has been done. The superscription at the beginning of the book can point in no other direction. They want us to believe that this person in the 700s B.C. foresaw what was going to happen to his people over the next several hundred years and conceived a great theological structure to address not only those times but ones further in the future. This conclusion is furthered when we discover that the chief argument for the uniqueness of God over the gods in chapters 41–48 is his ability to specifically foretell the future, something the idols could not and did not do. But if the writers knew at the same time they were making this argument that Isaiah ben Amoz had never foretold what they were saying he had, what does this do to their theological credibility? In fact, they were fabricating false evidence, since Yahweh could no more tell the future than the idols could. The towering theology of the prince of the prophets is in fact built on a foundation of falsehoods, if we accept this hypothesis.[26]

But how are we to explain the data that resulted in the theory of multiple authorship if we do not accept that theory? Some of those data are: addressing future audiences in ways that betray a more than general understanding of what the issues will be in those future times; stylistic and vocabulary differences between various sections; differing theological foci; the lack of any obvious outline; and so on.

Let us begin with the latter. Ancient literature was not characterized by the kinds of unities that the Greek rhetoricians declared were necessary. Rather, they tended to be a grouping together of relatively independent episodes. Classical examples of this form of composition can be found in the Sumerian/Akkadian Gilgamesh Epic and in the Greek *Odyssey*. This feature is said to be characteristic of literature that has an oral prehistory.

---

25. See, e.g., O. Kaiser, *Isaiah 13–39*, trans. J. Bowden (OTL; Philadelphia: Westminster, 1974); and H. Wildberger, *Jesaja*, 3 vols. (HKAT; Neukirchen-Vluyn: Neukirchener, 1982).

26. For a more detailed critique of the theory of multiple authorship, see R. K. Harrison, *Introduction to the Old Testament* (Grand Rapids: Eerdmans, 1970), 764–78. See also the discussions in J. Oswalt, *The Book of Isaiah, Chapters 1–39* (NICOT; Grand Rapids: Eerdmans, 1986), 17–29; and *The Book of Isaiah, Chapters 40–66* (NICOT; Grand Rapids: Eerdmans), 3–12.

Whether this is true or not, the same features can be found in the Bible. While the books of Genesis–2 Kings all show a general chronological organization, and while it may be argued that Genesis–Deuteronomy emphasize one theme and Deuteronomy–2 Kings another closely related theme, it is hard to find a logical outline in any of these books.[27] The feature is even more pronounced in those books known in the English tradition as the Major and Minor Prophets. In several of the books it is possible to identify units of thought, and in many cases readers from diverse perspectives would agree with the identification. So, for instance, Amos 1–2 constitute judgments on the nations, while chapters 3–6 are messages against Israel, and chapters 7–9 are visions of Israel's destruction and restoration. However, it is virtually impossible to discover a logical progression in the thought of the book.

This is true on a grand scale in Jeremiah, where there is even disagreement as to the length of the units of thought. Apart from the call in chapter 1, the hopeful words in chapters 30–32, and the oracles against the nations in chapters 46–51, the commentators cannot agree on what the other units in the book are. Thus, the situation in the book of Isaiah is not something unique. Like all the other prophetic books (with the possible exception of Ezekiel), the material in the book was first given orally and then collected either by the prophet himself or by disciples. As such, the material constitutes a kind of anthology of the prophet's work. Sometimes reports of the prophet's life are interwoven with the things he said. It is probable that differing versions of these circulated even during the prophet's own lifetime.

Again, the Gospels seem to demonstrate the probability of this, as do the differing versions of Jeremiah in the Masoretic Text and the Septuagint. In the case of Jesus, his importance to the Christian community dictated that four authoritative versions of his life and work should be preserved. But in the case of other books, it is apparent that the Judean community fairly quickly recognized one of the versions as having authority, with the rest being discarded. The destruction of Jerusalem in the midst of Jeremiah's ministry and the fragmentation of the community short-circuited this process for that book and left us with two versions extant. In view of these common characteristics of Hebrew prophetic writing, the somewhat miscellaneous character of the book of Isaiah cannot be said to point necessarily to multiple authorship.

The remaining three issues identified above—addressing different audiences, differing vocabulary and style, and differing theological foci—are all part of one set of issues and must be dealt with together. As discussed above

---

27. Notice the same characteristic in the Gospels. It is often noted that there is nothing quite like them in the Hellenistic world. Perhaps that is because the books are replicating a literary style from the pre-Hellenic world.

under the historical background, different parts of the book do seem to be addressed to different audiences. This in itself goes far to explain why there are different theological emphases in these different parts. Different situations require different emphases, and different emphases may well require a different language. Thus, the question must be: Is it possible that one human mind (under the inspiration of the Holy Spirit) could have and would have been able to speak *to* (not *about*) persons in the distant future?

As mentioned above, it seems to me that the different audiences and theology were necessitated by the sweep of the vision given to Isaiah. He had seen a picture of a nation of rebellious, arrogant, and corrupt people being carried away on a Mesopotamian flood called forth by Israel's God (6:1–8:22; 9:8–10:4). Yet he also saw a descendant of Jesse leading a restored remnant of God's people in a kingdom of righteousness and hope (9:1–7; 10:5–11:16). He saw a people who had refused to trust God and were swept away (8:6–8) redeemed and living in hopeful trust (12:1–6). The breadth of this vision could not be confined to his own day, a day in which God had told him that he would be ignored and rejected. If the vision was to have final relevance, it had to find that relevance in people yet unborn.

If these unborn people were to trust the God whom their parents had ultimately refused to trust, then it was imperative that those future generations should know that God can still be trusted even if we have refused him, experienced the results of that refusal, and are in complete despair. Furthermore, when we have dared to believe again and are indeed delivered, it is then that we need to know that trust is useless unless it issues in a life of righteousness. If Isaiah's book had stopped at what is now chapter 39, its effect would have been abortive, both in encouraging faith during the Exile and in providing a vehicle for seeing how the changed situation after the Exile could be reconciled with the preexilic faith.

But what about the significantly different language after chapter 40? It is different, there is no question of that. The Hebrew is both simpler and more lyrical. Some words that were common before chapter 40 may appear rarely or not at all after chapter 40. The differences are significant enough that Yehuda Radday concluded on the basis of a computer-based study that the same person could not have written chapters 7–39 and 40–55.[28] If we argue that Radday's conclusions were based upon certain unproven assumptions about the possible limits of variation in one person's writing, what might account for such a significant difference?

---

28. Y. Radday, *The Unity of Isaiah in the Light of Statistical Linguistics* (Hildesheim: Gerstenberg, 1973). For another computer study that concluded the book is a unity, see L. L. Adams and A. C. Rincher, "The Popular Critical View of the Isaiah Problem in the Light of Statistical Style Analysis," *Computer Studies* (1973): 149–57.

It must be granted that what follows is hypothetical, but it is no more so than the myriad multiple-authorship hypotheses. Sometime after 701, perhaps ten years or more, when Manasseh has joined his father on the throne and it is clear Hezekiah's reforms are not going to last, the elderly prophet is given a vision of the future and of the ways in which what he has taught and believed all his life will relate to that future. The vision is theologically detailed but historically general. It is a vision of the triumph of the transcendent Creator-Redeemer, the Holy One of Israel whom Isaiah has proclaimed, both in history and in the human heart. It is loosely placed within a couple of future historic settings, but it is freed from any specific bonds of a particularized historical setting. I believe this understanding of the origins of the material within Isaiah's life might account for the variations.

If it is possible to answer the questions that have led to the multiple authorship theories, we must also ask whether there is positive evidence supporting single authorship of the book. There is such evidence. One of the more interesting pieces of evidence is the even distribution of the phrase "the Holy One of Israel" throughout the book. This phrase only occurs thirty-one times in the Old Testament, and no fewer than twenty-five of these are in Isaiah, with twelve occurrences appearing in chapters 1–39 and thirteen appearing in chapters 40–55.[29] And when the one occurrence in the Bible of the synonymous "the Holy One of Jacob" at Isaiah 29:23 is factored in, the distribution is exactly even. If we accept multiple authorship, we would have to posit an attempt by the later editors to be sure that the master's favorite term was adequately covered in the later material assigned to him.[30]

And while it is true that there are numerous instances where a word will appear only in chapters 1–39 and not in chapters 40–66, there are also a number of terms that show up in both (or all three) parts of the book *and not elsewhere in the Old Testament*. Again, one would have to assume that someone did a concordance study of the master and inserted his unique words here and there in the later material. This is especially the case where a rare word shows up only once or twice in chapters 1–39 and once or twice in chapters 40–66. That this should happen by chance in a multiple-authorship scheme is unlikely.[31] We would have to suppose that someone discovered the word in

---

29. One of the six occurrences outside of Isaiah is in 2 Kings 19, which is a parallel to Isa. 37, so there are only five independent occurrences: three in Psalms and two in Jeremiah.

30. Alternatively, if we accept Williamson's hypothesis that "Deutero-Isaiah" shaped chs. 1–39, we might think that the phrase originated with him and that he included it when he was rewriting and reorganizing the earlier material. But where does the phrase come from if not out of Isaiah's experience of the Holy One recorded in ch. 6? It originated with Isaiah, not with a hypothetical successor.

31. For a study of these examples see R. Margalioth, *The Indivisible Isaiah: Evidence for the Single Authorship of the Prophetic Book* (New York: Yeshiva Univ. Press, 1964).

one place and then intentionally used it in the later additions simply in order to create the illusion of single authorship.

Another evidence of the single authorship of the book is the absence of specific historical references for the exilic and postexilic periods. When the book of Isaiah is compared to Ezekiel or to Malachi, these differences become obvious. Whereas it is typical among the Hebrew prophets to root their oracles in specific events and circumstances, and whereas this feature is present in chapters 6–39 of Isaiah, there is almost none of this kind of material in chapters 40–66.

Three possible explanations present themselves: (1) The author did not know this information; (2) the author knew it but did not include it; (3) the author originally included it, but it was removed for some reason. If the author of the material was Isaiah, then the facts are easily explicable. Isaiah knew the general circumstances of the exilic and postexilic periods, but apart from the one startling fact of the name of the deliverer Cyrus, he knew no other details. On the one hand, if the author was writing at the time of the events and knew the details, as in the case of Cyrus, there is no obvious reason to make the rest of his presentation so ahistorical. On the other hand, if the details were originally there but were suppressed in all cases but the reference to Cyrus, then we again are faced with editors who want us to believe Isaiah of Jerusalem is responsible for the whole book while they know that is untrue.[32]

Not only are the expected historical details absent, but there are also in chapters 40–66 some hints of an eighth-century setting for the writing of these chapters.[33] Instead of the expected emphasis on the restoration of proper worship in the face of the syncretistic tendencies of the day, there is the kind of diatribe against ritualism that is characteristic of the preexilic prophets. The attacks on the idols are likewise more like that of Jeremiah and his predecessors than they are of Ezekiel and his successors.[34] The concern for the priesthood and its purity, which is characteristic of the postexilic writings, is not found in Isaiah 40–66. While it is possible to hypothesize an anticultic group that existed after the Exile in order to explain these features, that is only necessary if one has already concluded these chapters to have been written in the postexilic period. Apart from that a priori reason, there is no evidence of such a group in any of the biblical books known to be pos-

---

32. B. Childs is one who sees the original details as having been removed to better show the unity of the book. See *Introduction to the Old Testament As Scripture* (Philadelphia: Fortress, 1979), 325–30.

33. See J. B. Payne, "The Eighth Century Background of Isaiah 40–66," *WTJ* 29 (1967): 179–90; 30 (1968): 50–58, 185–203.

34. See R. Vasholz, "Isaiah Against 'the Gods': A Case for Unity," *WTJ* 42 (1980): 389–94.

texilic. A much simpler explanation is that these chapters were written well before the Exile and that while they deal with the theological issues raised by the exilic and postexilic experiences, they do so from within the eighth-century context.

In concluding this section, we must say that there is no a priori reason why God could not have used multiple authors to create a unified work of theology like the book of Isaiah. He is God, and he can do what he likes. But the question is, What does the book itself claim? Here there seems to me to be no question. The book claims to have come through one human mind, that of Isaiah ben Amoz, who lived in the eighth and seventh centuries B.C. and was gifted by God to see the future in such a way that it would forever demonstrate that Yahweh of Israel was not one of the gods. Yahweh's ability to tell the future in detail was the ultimate evidence that he was not a personification of the forces of creation but was the Creator of creation, the One who made it, continued to direct it, and would eventually redeem it.

All of the multiple authorship hypotheses finally undercut this theological point because their underlying rationale is that God *could not* have so inspired Isaiah ben Amoz. It seems to me we cannot have it both ways. If we conclude the theological claims of the book are true, then we cannot avoid the implications of that conclusion for the book's authorship. If we conclude the book was created by a group of persons much later than Isaiah, then we are forced to admit that these persons knew what they were saying was not true but believed it ought to be true and thus tried to create such an account of the book's origins as would make readers believe it was. Such a book may still be an inspiring piece of theological innovation that is of interest to historical theologians, but it has no claims upon those of us who read it 2,700 years later.[35]

Central Themes of the Book of Isaiah

WE NOTED ABOVE that the book of Isaiah is rather like a modern symphony, with themes appearing and reappearing in fascinating harmony. Not only is this true of the themes, it is also true of a number of figures of speech, some of which ought to be mentioned here before we deal with the themes

---

35. One person who is consistent in this way is R. P. Carroll, *When Prophecy Failed: Cognitive Dissonance in the Prophetic Traditions of the Old Testament* (New York: Seabury, 1979). Carroll says Deutero-Isaiah was a failure, predicting things about the return from the Exile that never happened. If the words of chs. 40–66 were not spoken in 555 B.C. but in 690 B.C., the sweeping language is much easier to understand as not being limited to the immediate future after the return from exile.

themselves in more detail. Some of those figures of speech are: trees,[36] high-ways,[37] banners,[38] deserts,[39] gardens and fertile fields,[40] children,[41] and light and darkness.[42] As can be seen from the references given, these figures crop up throughout the book, giving the careful reader a sense of discovery and delight as he or she recognizes the author's craft in recalling an earlier figure and using it in a related, but amplified, way.[43] On the thematic level, as with the figures, a recurring feature is the pairing of opposites, such as judgment and hope, servanthood and kingdom, trust and rebellion, and arrogance and humiliation. Other important themes are the uniqueness of Yahweh, righteousness, and the nations.[44]

Judgment and Hope

FROM THE OUTSET of the book these two themes are interchanged. The interchange appears first in chapter 1, where the accusations of 1:1–15 give way to a promise of restoration if there is genuine repentance (1:16–20). The interchange occurs again in 1:21–27, with 1:21–24 detailing the perversion of the leaders and the destruction that must follow, but with 1:25–27 telling us that the destruction is for the purpose of purification. Finally, chapter 1 ends on the note of accusation with which it began (1:28–31). On a larger scale, the interchange continues through the introduction (chs. 1–5), with chapter 1 being primarily an announcement of judgment; 2:1–5 a promise of hope; 2:6–4:1 reverting to announcement of judgment; 4:2–6 a promise of hope; and 5:1–30 an announcement of imminent judgment. The pattern is then repeated in the book as a whole, with chapters 7–39 giving primary emphasis to judgment and a minor empha-

---

36. See 1:29–30; 2:13; 6:13; 10:33–34; 29:17; 32:15, 19; 37:24; 44:14, 23; 55:12; 57:5; 60:13; 61:3.

37. See 2:3; 7:3; 11:16; 19:23; 35:8; 40:3; 49:9, 11; 57:10, 14; 59:7–8; 62:10.

38. See 5:26; 11:10–12; 13:2; 18:3; 30:17; 49:22; 62:10.

39. See 5:6; 6:11–12; 32:14; 34:13–17; 41:18–19; 43:20; 48:21; 50:2; 64:10.

40. See 29:17; 32:15; 35:1–7; 41:18–19; 51:3; 65:3, 10; 66:17.

41. See 1:4; 3:12; 9:6; 11:8; 26:17; 37:3; 49:19–21; 54:1–3; 66:7–12.

42. See 2:5; 5:20, 30; 8:22; 9:2; 26:19; 29:18; 30:26; 42:6–7, 16; 45:7; 49:9; 51:10; 58:8, 10; 59:9–10; 60:1–3, 19–20.

43. Adherents to a multiple-authorship theory explain this phenomenon as an example of intertextuality, assuming that later editors are consciously alluding to earlier elements in the "Isaianic tradition." See, e.g., B. Sommer, *A Prophet Reads Scripture: Allusion in Isaiah 40–66* (Stanford, Calif.: Stanford Univ. Press, 1998).

44. For an extended treatment of some of these themes, see J. Oswalt, "Key Themes in the Book of Isaiah: Their Relevance for Christian Theology," in *The Newell Lectureships*, ed. T. Dwyer (Anderson, Ind.: Warner, 1996), 3:13–90, 202–11. See also "Isaiah: Theology of," in *NIDOTTE*, 4:725–32; idem, "Isaiah," in *NDBT*, 217–22.

---

sis on hope, while the major emphasis of chapters 40–66 is hope with a secondary emphasis on judgment.

What is the point of this interchange, especially as it is laid out for us in the introductory chapters? Isaiah's point seems to be that if there is to be hope for the nation, it is only through judgment. To be sure, as chapter 1 indicates, if there were a genuine turning to God as evidenced in a changed way of treating one another, judgment could be avoided. However, as Isaiah's call experience made plain to him, there was no likelihood of genuine repentance for this people. Therefore, if there was to be any hope for them to become a clean and bright lamp (4:2–6) through whom the nations could be blessed (as per the promise to Abraham, and in 2:1–5), it was only *through* judgment.

Obviously this was difficult for the Judean people to grasp. They had the ingrained idea that it was *either* judgment *or* hope. After all, God had made all these promises to them. They were his chosen people and no one else. They were the custodians of his holy city and his holy temple. If judgment came in the form that some of the prophets were talking about—destruction of the city and the temple, and even of some part of the people—then all the promises of God were null and void. Thus the only hope was to avoid judgment. To all of this Isaiah said a resounding no. The promises of God would only be realized through fire. Just as the unclean lips of the man Isaiah could only be used to proclaim the holiness of God to his people after they had been purged with fire (Isa. 6), so the unclean lips of the nation were going to have to be purged with the cleansing fires of judgment if the nation could ever proclaim those promises of God to the nations of the world.

If the people of Isaiah's day had difficulty believing there was hope beyond judgment, it is clear from the book that the people of the exilic period would have difficulty believing in hope after judgment. For them the impossible had occurred. As far as they could see, all was lost. God had either abandoned them or they had been defeated by the Babylonian gods. The holy city and temple were forever gone. The priesthood was defiled and could never be cleansed. As much as the pagans had difficulty imagining anything other than what had always been, so did the Judeans. They could not imagine that God was so creative that he could do something completely new to keep the ancient promises.

Thus, the prophet has to keep calling on them to believe what God says he will do for them, to listen to the promises he makes of redemption and restoration. Like their ancestors, they really could not believe that judgment is never God's intended last word but that his intention is to use judgment to bring about lasting hope.

The message of judgment and hope goes through a third permutation when it is addressed to the postexilic audience. Here the danger is that the restored Judeans will believe that hope realized removes the possibility of judgment. Since they have been restored through no effort or merit of their own, there is a serious possibility they will therefore believe that they can continue to experience the blessing of God while living lives of ritual purity and social wickedness. Here the prophet has to tell them that this is not the case. Yes, God has restored them, and yes, they are in line to experience the fulfillment of the kingdom of God. But that does not remove the possibility of further judgment. In fact, an obedient foreigner or eunuch is more a child of the kingdom than a pure-bred Judean who is living in sin. Yes, it is true that judgment is not God's intended last word. But unless people repent and live godly lives by the Spirit's power, it *will* be his last word.

Servanthood and Kingdom

AS MENTIONED ABOVE, the introductory chapters present the reader with a dilemma. How can the proud, rebellious, polluted, and ultimately desolate Israel that is described in Isaiah 1; 2:6–4:1; and 5 ever become the pure, submissive, and abundant repository of the word of God for the nations described in 2:1–5 and 4:2–6? Isaiah seems to offer his own experience as a solution to this dilemma. Just as his unclean lips were cleansed so that he could declare the word of God to the nation, so the nation's unclean lips could be cleansed so that it could declare God's word to the nations. Israel could become the servant of God to fulfill that role.

This is made explicit in chapters 40–66, but it is implicit in chapters 1–39 as well. In chapter 6 the beginning of Isaiah's commissioning into God's service is a vision of God and of himself that makes his condition clear. Without that accurate picture there is no hope of ultimate cleansing. The same thing happens to Israel in chapters 7–39. Here the nation is given a vision of the glory and greatness of God that demonstrates the trustworthiness of God. This is the essential basis for servanthood. Unless we can trust the Master in every respect, there is no hope of our laying aside our pride and putting on the towel of servanthood.

The first lesson in the relationship between servanthood and kingdom is given in the picture of the servant-king in chapters 7–12. These chapters deal with the Assyrian crisis of 735 B.C. Here Judah is threatened not only by her neighbors, Israel and Syria, but ultimately by the Assyrian colossus. Visions of oppression, domination, and terror rear up on every side. Within Judah, the house of David is terrified, shaking like leaves in the wind. What does Judah feel she needs? A king who will be stronger, crueler, and more implacable than any other! And what is the vision Isaiah gives? A vision of a child (9:6)! He sees a child-king who will be wise, perceptive, and righteous, a child who will bring in a kingdom where no one hurts or destroys (11:9; see also 65:25). God's solution to the cruelty and oppression of the world is not to be more cruel and oppressive, but, as 52:13–53:12, the last of the so-called Servant Songs, shows, it is to take that cruelty and oppression into himself and give back love. This is ultimate power. A similar view of the servant-king appears in 16:5 and 32:1–5.

The way in which the two Davidic monarchs Ahaz and Hezekiah are contrasted in chapters 7–39 reinforces this idea of servant king. In chapters 7–8 Ahaz is depicted as trusting in the power of the world to deliver him, refusing to submit his plans and ways to God. The result is destruction. In contrast, chapters 36–38 show Hezekiah submitting himself to God and calling on his people to do likewise. The result is deliverance, both for the nation and for Hezekiah personally. Ahaz, who speaks pious words but refuses to bow in the servant posture, is contrasted with Hezekiah, whose prayer shows an overriding concern for the honor and name of his Lord (37:16–20). Thus, chapters 7–39 depict a God who has the power to care for his servants and the compassionate heart to actually do so.

The kingly servant is presented especially in chapters 40–55. That he is the king is shown in the functions ascribed to him. Both in 42:1 and 49:6 it is made plain that this Servant of the Lord will do the very things said of the Messiah in Isaiah 9–11; 16; and 32. He will bring justice and salvation to the nations. Yet, how will he do this? He will do it by laying aside the robes of pomp and royalty. He will submit to cruelty and abuse; he will be discouraged and despairing; he will finally give his life. He will become the Servant of both Israel and the world. In so doing he will become the ideal Israel (49:3), who makes it possible for the actual Israel to become the servants they were chosen to be. He becomes both the motive and the means whereby Israel can, out of the fires of judgment, fulfill its calling.

The motivation to servanthood is the unmerited grace of God in restoring his people to himself after they have brought destruction and rejection on themselves and his willingness to use them as his evidence in his legal suit against the gods (e.g., 43:8–13). This gracious refusal to cast them off provides the motivation to exercise the trust that was so amply demonstrated and explained in chapters 7–39. But how can God do this? How can God take sinful Israel back? How can sinful Israel become servant Israel? The means is the Servant. In his atoning death he provides the means whereby both love and justice can be satisfied (53:10–11).

But the ministry of the king is not exhausted in chapters 1–55. What about these servants when they are restored to their land? It was not the power of Babylon that sent them into exile. It was the pervasiveness of their sin and unrighteousness. What is to be done about that behavior? Is the only power of the kingly servant's death to forgive sin? Can the servants of the Holy One continue in sinful living? The answers to such questions are found in chapters 56–66, which talk about the character of servanthood. Here, on the one hand, God makes it clear that grace is not a justification for unrighteous living. He expects his servants to live righteous lives. But, on the other hand, the servants confess their inability to live the kind of righteousness God calls for. They cannot produce the light for which the world yearns.

What is to be done? Once again, the answer is the Servant. But this time he is presented as the mighty Warrior (59:15b–21; 63:1–6). The enemies he destroys are no longer the oppressive nations. Babylon is gone, and Persia is not a threat to God's promises. No, the enemy that the Warrior attacks with implacable fury is the enemy of sin in the hearts of the servants. As a result of his work, the light of God dawns on his people, and all the nations are drawn to it (chs. 60–62), just as 2:1–5 predicted. Interestingly, at the center of chapters 60–62, between the two Warrior passages and at the center of chapters 56–66, we have one more view of the Spirit-anointed Servant (61:1–3). Here he is not the terrifying Warrior, but One who speaks comfort and peace. In other words, *servant* is his nature while *warrior* is one of his roles. Nevertheless, he makes it plain that his function is to make persons "oaks of righteousness" (61:3). Whether it be by quiet persuasion or terrifying glory, he intends to make the servants of God like God.[45]

Trust and Rebellion

As MENTIONED ABOVE, trust is a major theme of chapters 7–39. Interestingly, rebellion is a major theme in chapters 40–66, which are usually associated with hope.[46] The connection between the two is established in chapter 1, where the people are identified as rebels no less than five times (1:2, 5, 20, 23, 28). They are clearly told the contrasting results of these two behaviors in 1:19–20: Be willing and obedient and eat the best of the land, or rebel and be eaten by the sword.

After chapter 1, specific occurrences of terms for rebelliousness are scattered (3:8; 24:20; 30:1; 31:6; 36:5), but the last one is the most telling. The Assyrian officer stands outside the walls of Jerusalem demanding the surrender of the city. Speaking for the Assyrian king he says, "On whom are you

---

45. For further discussion, see J. Oswalt, "Righteousness in Isaiah: A Study of the Function of Chapters 56–66 in the Present Structure of the Book," in *Writing and Reading the Scroll of Isaiah*, ed. C. Broyles and C. Evans (Leiden: Brill, 1997), 1:177–92.

46. Words connoting rebellion occur some twenty times there (out of a total of thirty-one in the book as a whole). A variety of Hebrew terms are used. Among the roots used are *pšʿ, mrh, mrd, srr,* and *srh.*

depending, that you *rebel* against me?" We can either trust the nations and rebel against our true Lord, or we can trust the Lord and repudiate all the false alliances that cannot supply what they promise.

This is the way in which chapters 7–39 develop the theme of trust. Chapters 7–12 and 36–39 stand in contrast to each other at the beginning and end of the unit. In chapter 7 Isaiah challenges Ahaz to trust God instead of the nations. Ahaz refuses to do this, choosing instead to trust his worst enemy, Assyria. Isaiah says that Assyria will turn on Judah and destroy it, but that after the destruction has come God will restore his people again under the leadership of a Davidic monarch who will value the well-being of his people above his own skin. Thus, the real trustworthiness of God will be demonstrated (see 12:1–3). Chapters 13–35 explore whether it is God or the nations who is supreme. In various ways these chapters assert the lordship of Yahweh over the nations, concluding in chapters 34–35 that if we trust the nations, we will end up living in a desert, but that if we will turn to God even then, he can make that desert blossom like a rose.

After those lessons Ahaz's son Hezekiah is put to the test again. Now Isaiah's prediction to Ahaz has come true: Assyria is destroying the land and is about to complete the task by taking Jerusalem. Will Hezekiah pass the test his father failed? The answer is "yes, but." In the crisis of the Assyrian threat, Hezekiah dares to defy the Assyrians and trusts God, and he is delivered. So also when he is fatally ill, he turns to God and is delivered. But in the much more subtle crisis when the Babylonian ambassadors come to congratulate Hezekiah after his recovery (ch. 39), he fails, parading his wealth and armaments instead of giving the glory to God. The Ahaz unit begins in no trust and ends in joy, whereas the Hezekiah unit begins in trust and ends in grief, with Isaiah predicting the Babylonian conquest.

What happened? Perhaps the point is this: Hezekiah has provided the positive illustration for the previous lessons: God can be trusted. At the same time, he provides a negative illustration that has a foreboding of the future: Trust is a way of life, not a one-time panacea. At various points the people of Judah turned back to God, yet these moments of trust did not become the settled pattern of their lives. So chapters 7–39 have taught the truth theoretically. All that needs to be said on the subject has been said, and its truth has been amply demonstrated. Yet the lesson has not been applied in an ongoing practical way. Hezekiah illustrates both of these points.

What can actually motivate the servants of the Lord to make trust a way of life, to lay aside the pride and self-interest in a life-changing trust? This was already intimated in 12:1–3. When God delivers his people from the justly deserved consequences of their sin, they will turn to him in trust. But will they actually do so, or will they persist in rebellion? This is the burden of chapters 40–66 in their twenty references to rebellion. God has forgiven their rebellions and will continue to forgive those who turn away from that rebellion to put their trust in him.

But *will* they turn away? Their fathers were rebels, and they themselves are rebels. The sin problem is not merely wrong acts but a way of thinking about and relating to the supreme Lord of the universe. If we will relate to him in submission and trust, all the treasures of heaven are ours. But if we will not, then the day will come when those who do trust him will see the destruction of us who persist in revolt (66:24). Thus the book ends on the same note with which it began: Surrendering to the Creator-Redeemer in trust is the height of wisdom, whereas rebellion against him is the height of folly.

Arrogance and Humiliation

THIS PAIR OF themes is closely related to the previous one. The primary reason for not submitting to God in trust is human pride, and the primary reason for trusting the nations instead of God is the power and glory of the nations. But human pride, power, and glory are all illusory. They are derived from the only One in whom true power and glory reside. As Isaiah heard in his inaugural vision, "the whole earth is full of his glory." If there is any glory in the world, says Isaiah, it is derived from the Creator of the world. Thus, for humans to arrogate that glory and act as if it was their own rather than a gift is to be living a lie. And like all lies, it must inevitably betray its perpetrators.

No place in the book is this more powerfully presented than in 2:6–4:1. Here the prophet shows how all attempts to exalt ourselves are doomed to fail. In fact, the very attempt to exalt ourselves will be the cause of our humiliation. This is profoundly true, because by denying that there is a Creator who is sovereign over us, we make ourselves the most significant beings in the universe. And if we are the most significant beings in the universe, then there *is* no significance in the universe. This is the story of the Enlightenment in the West. We placed human reason on the throne in the nineteenth century, and it led us to bloody trenches, death camps, and addiction to mindless pleasures in the twentieth century. Isaiah saw this 2,500 years ago when he cried out, "The eyes of the arrogant man will be humbled, and the pride of men brought low; the LORD alone will be exalted in that day" (2:11; cf. 2:17); and, "Stop trusting in man, who has but a breath in his nostrils. Of what account is he?" (2:22).

These themes recur throughout the book. God alone is high and lifted up, and everything else will be brought down. In this respect idolatry is mocked relentlessly. The attempt to exalt humanity by making God in our image is utterly ridiculous. In fact, it makes humanity worthless (41:24; 44:9). By contrast, God delights to exalt those who recognize the truth of existence and gladly humble themselves before him. The prototype of this is the Servant who humbles himself even to death, but whom God declares to be high and lifted up, like himself (52:13; cf. 6:1). In the same way 57:15 says that the Lord dwells in the high and holy place *and* with the humble and lowly. Like some of the other themes, this one is brought to a climax in chapters 56–66, where those who attempt to exalt themselves through ritualistic religion and pious behavior are treated with contempt, while those who take the lower place, humbly attempting to obey God's covenant in its full implications, are commended and encouraged (see esp. 65:11–16).

The Uniqueness of Yahweh

NO BOOK IN the Bible treats this theme as forcefully as does Isaiah. From beginning to end the idea that God can be compared to the gods of the nations is ridiculed. He alone is exalted. There is no other. As already noted, this point is first made in chapter 2, where it is said that to worship such things is like worshiping bats and moles. It reduces a person to the rocks and holes of the earth. This would have been especially poignant since the gods were typically worshiped on the mountaintops and other high places. But as was said on the previous theme, the Lord is the only One high and lifted up.

This attack on the idols continues throughout the book. In chapter 19 Egypt's supposed wisdom is denigrated because of its worship of idols. In the conflict between Hezekiah and Sennacherib, it all comes down to whether the Assyrian emperor can treat Yahweh just as he has treated the gods of the other nations. Hezekiah rightly understands that the issue is not whether Judah can escape from the oppressor's clutches, but whether Judah's God is a different order of being from pagan gods. In the outcome, the answer is clear: Yahweh is not one more of the gods. Rather, he is the One who brought Sennacherib to Judah and who can send him home again.

But what if there should come a time when the Lord would not deliver his people from some other oppressor, such as the Babylonian Nebuchadnezzar? Would that not disprove the whole point of the argument made so carefully in chapters 7–39? Would it not show that God may be superior to some gods, but not all? Anticipating that development and those questions, Isaiah answers them in advance. He represents the Lord as calling the Babylonian gods into court and challenging them to bring evidence proving that they are gods. He challenges them to explain past events and how those events will work out in the future. Then he sharpens the challenge, calling on them to show that even once they had specifically and correctly foretold a future event. And the captive Judeans are to be God's witnesses that he had indeed done that very thing in predicting the Exile, naming the deliverer and predicting a return from exile.

The point here is profound. The gods have no hope of doing this because they are a part of the cosmic system. Thus, they cannot have any idea where the system came from or where it is going. They are unable to foretell the events of history because they are a part of those events. But if there were a Creator who was not a part of the system, he could reveal his purpose in creating and what the final end of the creative process would be. Furthermore, he could direct the evolution of history, intervening in it at will. That is, of course, exactly what Isaiah claims. The God of Israel is the sole Creator of the universe, the Lord of history. Much the same point is made in chapters 24–27, although in a more poetic and less didactic fashion.

All of this means that it is foolish to be seduced by the glory of the nations into rebelling against God. Rather, God's servants are meant to submit to him trustfully and declare the glory of the only God to the nations. This is so because as the sole Creator, he is the sole Redeemer. When creation has lost its way, seeking its own glory and in so doing ensuring its own destruction, it is only the Creator of the system who can redeem the system. Certainly no idea or form created by the human mind can deliver us. When put that way, the idea is laughable. Can a person who has blundered into quicksand save himself by pulling up his feet? Of course not. Help must come from outside, or there is no hope. Isaiah declares that the Creator of the universe is a God of steadfast love, who can save us from ourselves and will, if we would only allow him.

The Nations

WE HAVE ALREADY spoken in some detail about the nations in connection with the other themes, but they are significant enough that they deserve special attention. As in the case of many other themes, Isaiah brings together in one book many of the things said about the nations elsewhere in the Old Testament. The result is a wholistic treatment not found elsewhere.

From the outset Isaiah insists that Israel has a responsibility to the nations. The nations are to learn the intentions and ways of the Creator by means of God's people. The placement of this teaching in chapter 2 almost at the beginning of the book highlights its importance to the writer. That importance is further underlined by the theme's appearance in the final chapter. There it is said that some of the remnant will be sent to the nations of earth to tell them whose glory it is that fills the earth, and some from those nations will come to bow down to God in surrender and trust. This is like the picture painted in chapter 25, where all nations are called to a feast prepared by

God in which he will remove the shroud of death from the faces of all peoples (25:6–8). The response of the nations there is much like that of redeemed Israel reported in 12:1–3: "Surely this is our God; we trusted in him, and he saved us. This is the LORD, we trusted in him; let us rejoice and be glad in his salvation" (25:9).

But between the announcement of the responsibility and its achievement, there are many slips. Instead of trusting God, Israel trusts the nations. She sees the glory of the great empires and forgets the glory of God. The inevitable result is destruction by the very nations who were trusted (8:5–10). Whatever we trust in place of God must inevitably betray us. But God is supreme over the nations. As the prophet says in chapter 40, to him the nations weigh less than the dust on the scales; they are less than a drop of water in a bucket. And because Israel's God is supreme over the nations, all of them must come to his judgment bar (chs. 13–23; 47). Isaiah asks Israel in a rhetorical way why they would be overawed by nations who must give an account of themselves to Israel's God. Furthermore, how could they think that the nations could save them when the nations themselves must look to Israel's God as their only Savior? Why depend on horses and chariots from Egypt when they can have the Spirit of God (31:1–3)?

Having refused to trust the nations and thus having become captive to the nations, the Judeans must eventually be driven back to trusting in God. When they do so, they will find that God can deliver them from the nations. Even mighty Babylon will not be able to hold them. They will return home with shouts of joy. And the nations will not only release them but will actually *bring* them home, as the nations come to worship Israel's God (60:14). Those nations who refuse to worship the one God in Jerusalem will be forced to serve God's people. The tables will be completely turned, with the former masters now becoming the servants and the former servants becoming the masters.

However, it is plain that this is not the end of the story of Israel's relations with the nations. God intends to remove the shroud of death from the face of all the peoples, and Israel's responsibility is to make that a possibility by declaring God's glory and saving power to all the world (12:4–5; 66:19–23).

Righteousness

THE MASCULINE AND feminine noun forms of the Hebrew root commonly translated "righteous" (ṣdq) appear in the book of Isaiah sixty-one times (cf. twelve occurrences in Jeremiah, twenty-two in Ezekiel). Clearly, this is an important idea for the writer. Moreover, the terms are spread fairly evenly throughout the book. This means it has importance for all three of the theological emphases the book contains. As is the case with several of the other themes, this one is given special prominence in chapter 1, occurring three times between verses 21 and 27. This point continues to be made throughout the first part of the book: God expects his people to live righteous lives; if they do not, judgment will come upon them *in order that* they may be purified and live such lives (1:21, 26, 27).

Five words with the *ṣdq* root occur in chapters 32–33, where it said that righteousness will characterize the messianic kingdom in which the Spirit is poured out. Isaiah 33:14–16 is particularly instructive in that it makes it plain this is not a forensic or judicial righteousness but one that represents a specific kind of behavior:

> "Who of us can dwell with the consuming fire?
>   Who of us can dwell with everlasting burning?
> He who walks righteously
>   and speaks what is right,
> who rejects gain from extortion
>   and keeps his hand from accepting bribes,
> who stops his ears against plots of murder
>   and shuts his eyes against contemplating evil—
> this is the man who will dwell on the heights. . . ."

Yet the people of Isaiah's day and after did not achieve that standard. The result was as God had predicted: destruction. But this leaves an unanswered question for those on whom the destruction would fall: "Since we have failed to be a righteous people and have brought God's just wrath upon us, how can there be any hope for us?" Again in this case, as with several of the other themes of the first part of the book, God seems to have inspired Isaiah to address that question, which future readers would have.

In chapters 40–55 "righteousness" undergoes a dramatic change. It is no longer the righteousness of the people that is in focus but the righteousness of God. How can a people who have utterly failed to be righteous hope to receive the blessing of God's continued promises? *Only through God's righteousness.* But what is God's righteousness in regard to his captive people? Here it is important to recognize that "righteousness" in the Bible is more than a synonym for "justice." God had treated the people justly in delivering them over into the hands of the Babylonians. The Israelites had broken their solemn covenant with God again and again. Many years earlier Moses had warned them that such behavior would result in their being evicted from God's land, which they only held in trust. If righteousness was nothing more than justice, that would have been the end of any relation between them and God.

But righteousness is more than mere justice. It is to act in the "right" way. What is the "right" way for the God of all compassion to act? It is to have mercy, to be loyal to his subjects when they have not been loyal to him, to keep his promises when there is no more legal reason to do so. Thus, God could not in righteousness leave his people in captivity. Did they deserve to be delivered? No. Did they change and live such righteous lives that God was compelled to deliver them? Not at all. Ezekiel makes this plain in Ezekiel 36 when he says God is not delivering them for their sakes, as though they deserved such deliverance (36:22; see also Isa. 46:12). No, they will be delivered solely as an expression of the righteousness of God.[47] They will be accounted righteous because of the righteousness of God coming to them through his righteous Servant (Isa. 53:11). The only prerequisite was that they believe God's promises and take advantage of his offer of deliverance when it came.

But what does this mean for the life of God's servants? A deadly conclusion could be drawn from the sequence recounted above. The reasoning would go something like this: It is impossible for me to achieve God's standard of righteousness in my behavior; if I depend on my performance to maintain a relationship with him, I will fail, and there is nothing but judgment and destruction ahead for me; God has delivered me from that judgment solely as an expression of his own righteousness; *therefore, it does not really matter whether my life is characterized by righteousness or not; I should espouse it and work toward it, but all the time knowing that I cannot achieve it and that it does not really matter in the end.* Those familiar with the book of Romans will know that it is precisely this line of reasoning that Paul attacks in chapters 6–8 of that book. The conclusions he draws are remarkably similar to those found in the book of Isaiah.

In chapters 56–66, there is an interesting blend of the two uses of righteousness seen in chapters 1–39 and 40–55 respectively. On the one hand, the prophet makes it clear in no uncertain terms that God's standards for the behavior of his servants have not changed from that put forward in the first section. God's servants are to have ethics like his, period. Note 56:1, "Maintain justice and do what is right." This is not a forensic or judicial righteousness, where we are accounted righteous regardless of our behavior. Furthermore, if there were any remaining question, it is immediately dispelled in the shocking illustration that the prophet uses in the immediately following verses (56:3–8). Who is the true servant of God? A restored descendant of Abraham who has been delivered by the grace of God and is reveling in

---

47. Because "the righteousness of God" is expressed in his deliverance and is often treated as a synonym of salvation (e.g., 51:5), some modern translations (e.g., RSV, NRSV) actually translate "righteousness" in Isa. 40–55 with such terms as "deliverance" or "vindication."

his or her imputed righteousness? No, it is a foreigner or a eunuch who lives a life of obedience to the covenant of God. In the Torah, foreigners and eunuchs might not even enter the temple, let alone participate in the covenant, so the prophet is clearly using shock tactics to underline his point. The marks of servanthood are a life of righteousness like God's (so Rom. 6).

But here we are between the proverbial irresistible force and immovable object. God requires us to be righteous, yet experience shows us we cannot be righteous on his standards. This poignant dilemma is represented twice in this section: in 56:9–59:15a and again in 63:7–65:16. In both of them, the prophet takes up the voice of the people and laments as one of them over their persistent inability to do what is required of them. Far from bringing the light of God's righteousness to the nations, they grope in self-induced darkness (see esp. 59:9–15a). Here we are reminded irresistibly of Romans 7, where Paul in the same way takes up the lament of his reader over the inability to do what is right.

So what is to be done? Are the servants of the Lord condemned to a life of frustration, giving assent to God's requirements for righteousness in their minds, while all the time doing the very things they know God hates? Not at all! Here Isaiah artfully blends together the points of chapters 1–39 and 40–66. How are we to fulfill the righteousness called for in chapters 1–39? By means of the righteousness of God, which was revealed in chapters 40–55. God himself will defeat the enemy of sin and enable us to live lives of righteousness before the world. To be sure we cannot do this in our strength, and any attempt to do so is simply to relapse into pride and arrogance. But those who humbly admit their helplessness and cast themselves on the provision of God in Christ will be able to live the kind of life God requires. Here we come to Romans 8.

As mentioned above, it is the divine Warrior who comes to defeat this last enemy (59:15b–21; 63:1–6). He must do this work alone, there being none to help him; but having done it as an expression of his own righteousness, it is now possible for the light of the Lord to shine forth on the world through his servants (61:1–62:12). Isaiah 63:1–6 especially uses the defeat of the nations as a figure for the victory of the Warrior. Both the historical and literary context make it clear this is a figure of speech. Historically, this material is addressed to the returnees who have already been delivered from the nations; Edom, the specific subject, has already been destroyed and poses no threat to Judah at this time. No, the enemy is the sinful behavior of the servants, which prevents them from being the light-bearers God intends.

The literary structure of this section (chs. 56–66) further underlines this point. It is arranged in what is known as a chiastic format. That is, the units at the beginning and end of the section parallel each other, the next units inward parallel each other, and so forth until the climactic unit is reached in the center. In this case the outer units speak of faithful and believing Gentiles (56:3–8; 66:18–24); the next units deal with the inability of God's people to do righteousness (56:9–59:15a; 63:7–66:17); the next contain the announcement of the divine Warrior's victory over the enemy (59:15b–21; 63:1–6); the next describe Jerusalem's light to the world (60:1–22; 61:4–62:12); and the climactic one (61:1–3) presents the Messiah, the servant king, who delivers his followers and defeats their enemies, *so that* they may be "oaks of righteousness . . . for the display of his splendor."

The Relevance of the Book of Isaiah Today

LIKE ALL THE books in the Bible, Isaiah has a remarkable relevance to all times and circumstances. One of the evidences that the Bible is the revelation of God is this amazing combination of timeliness and timelessness. Persons from diverse cultures, economic circumstances, and time periods pick it up and find it speaking directly to them. Obviously, some books will speak more forcefully in some times and settings, and others in others. But the impact of the whole is always remarkable.

Because of both its breadth and its depth, Isaiah is even more perennially relevant than some other books, such as Obadiah or Nahum, which tend to be "one-issue" books. Isaiah has something for everyone. What does not speak to one person will be powerfully meaningful to another, and something one may have glossed over at one point in his or her life springs off the page in another. Here I want to point out some of the things in Isaiah that I believe have special significance for the present day.

The Uniqueness of Yahweh

I DO NOT BELIEVE there is any question that this concept is the most significant for our day. We live in an age where exclusivism of any sort is close to being the unpardonable sin. Tolerance is the rule of the day, except that intolerance of those who insist on the possibility of absolute truth is not only permitted but encouraged. Syncretism is encouraged so that it is understood that all religions are equally valid as expressions of each worshiper's personal preference. What is masked in all of this is that it represents an adoption, whether conscious or unconscious, of a worldview that has profound consequences for human life.

In fact, all of the myriad ways of thinking about reality can be grouped into just two categories: Either ultimate reality is an intrinsic part of the psycho-socio-physical universe, inseparable from it, or ultimate reality is somehow separate from, other than, that universe. All of the religions of the ancient world except one, and all the religions (and philosophies) of the modern world except three, fall into that first category. "God," whatever "god" may be, is the world as we know it; there is nothing else. What are the implications of such a view? They are strikingly similar around the world, because we are explaining ultimate reality by analogy with this world. Some of those implications are these:

1. There is no ultimate meaning in life. Our existence is an accident. Thus humans are finally without value.
2. There is no goal in life. We came from nothing, and we go to nothing. The only law is survival for the maximum time possible.
3. Conflict between destructive forces (evil) and constructive forces (good) is both endless and inevitable.
4. Ethics are always relative. The only enduring "good" is a maximum of comfort, pleasure, and security.
5. Self-interest is paramount.
6. In view of the preceding, the acquisition and use of power is of maximum importance.
7. Because there is an element of spirit power that is beyond physical manipulation, we must find "spiritual" ways to tap into that power. Since the entire universe is connected, it is possible through use of correct technique to become identified with those spirit powers and have their power at one's own disposal.
8. Human behavior is largely determined by forces outside of human control or understanding. Furthermore, the only reason for recording behavior is self-serving, so careful attention to actual events is insignificant. Therefore, history writing as an attempt to understand human behavior is both fruitless and pointless.

In all the ancient world, there was only one people who systematically and consistently denied all of the above: the Israelites. Sometimes a people might deny one or two for a period of time, but inevitably they fell back into the overall system. But the Israelites did not. They too felt the tug of this way of looking at reality, and again and again they adopted one or another of its implications. Yet they were always called back until, in the postexilic era, the opposing tenets to every one of these began to become second nature to them. What are these opposing tenets?

1. We were created in the image of a good and consistent God to be the stewards of his creation under his lordship. Therefore, human life is of ultimate value.

2. We are called to share the character of God, and yet we can choose not to. Thus it is possible both to progress toward and regress from the ultimate goal of experiencing his life.
3. The Creator is the Good. There is no conflict in him. Evil is not a cosmic reality but simply the absence of the Good in our lives.
4. The character of the Creator is the absolute standard of ethics, against which all behavior may be measured.
5. Surrender of one's self-interest into the care of the Creator is the most personally beneficial thing one can do.
6. Acquisition of right standing with the Creator is the most important thing one can do.
7. The attempt to gain spiritual power through the use of technique apart from submissive, obedient relationship is strictly forbidden.
8. Human behavior can be evaluated according to a consistent standard. Furthermore, it is possible to record that behavior with accuracy and integrity. Therefore, history writing is an important key to understanding human behavior.

Why did the Hebrews alone stubbornly hold to these concepts, which became the foundation of all of Western culture? It is because they held a different view of reality from all their contemporaries. They alone believed that God is not the world. They alone believed that deity, humanity, and nature are not all parts of one indivisible whole. That view is nowhere better expressed in the Bible than in Isaiah. The technical term for this concept is *transcendence*. If God is the ultimate reality behind all things, then there is only one such reality. And if there is only one reality who created the world as an expression of his will and purpose, then to give ultimate obedience to anything else is ultimate disaster.

Such a being cannot be manipulated by means of any created thing; to even think of it is laughable. So how do we acquire his power so that we can meet our needs? That is just it: We cannot. We must entrust the satisfaction of our needs into his hands, believing that he really is true and good and that we are precious to him. That has been the sticking point with humans ever since our first mother and father. We are afraid to entrust our fragile selves into our Maker's hands. We believe the lie the first rebel told them and us: God is not for you; he wants to use you to satisfy his own self-interest. Fearing to surrender, we create gods in our image, foolishly believing the lie that somehow we can gain power to use for ourselves and never have to surrender.

If the Western world is to survive, we must recover our spiritual roots in the Bible, and there is no book in the Bible that makes those roots more clear than does Isaiah. Somehow we must remind ourselves that the "inclusive" worldview will not help us to become more human but less. To be sure, there is a sinful "exclusivism" that is nothing more than arrogance. That is not biblical faith. Nevertheless, the only basis for human worth is in the biblical understanding that all of us share the image of the one Creator. To embrace some wooly-headed syncretism is not to come closer to righting the wrongs of the world; it is to lose the very basis for saying there is a right and a wrong. In that world the only right is the will of the person who can shout the loudest and hit the hardest. That is not the way of hope.

But suppose, as some think, the battle for the soul of the West is already lost. If so, it becomes doubly imperative for contemporary believers to know the truths of Isaiah. When we are called "bigots" and "closed-minded," we must know in our own souls why that is not the case. And when it becomes expensive and inconvenient to maintain this faith, we need to be able to know why we should maintain it anyway. There are no better resources for this than the ones we find in the book of Isaiah.

Servanthood

WE LIVE IN an age that, because of its abandonment of the biblical worldview, has made status, position, and power the absolute good. A major function of education has become not the acquisition of knowledge but the enhancement of self-esteem. The irony in all of this, as was argued above, is that in the unbiblical worldview, humanity has no significance whatsoever. We are an electrochemical accident. Thus, the more we cut ourselves off from the transcendent Creator, the less significant we become. The result, as is clearly seen in Camus, Sartre, and Kafka, is a downward spiral of despair. The more we try to puff ourselves up by cutting ourselves off from God, the less there is to puff up.

How desperately we need to hear the words of Isaiah, who tells us that the way to significance is not through arrogance but through humility, not to demand that others serve us but to serve others. How much we need to recover from Isaiah the prototype for what the apostle Paul called "the mind of Christ." This "mind" or attitude is almost completely foreign to us fearful children of Adam and Eve. We are so afraid of loss, of discomfort, of pain that we will sacrifice almost anything, or anyone, to avoid them. Yet, as Isaiah shows us, the way to real power is through powerlessness.

If we are to believe that, we need to be steeped in Isaiah's teaching. We need to be reminded again of the folly of depending on human glory for anything lasting. We need to hear again that God can be trusted—trusted enough to lay down our own foolish pride. We need to be motivated in deep ways by the realization that the sole Creator of the universe, the just Judge, the betrayed Father, has not cast us off but has chosen us to be the evidence to the world that he alone is God. We need to learn again that his honor before the world is so precious that it is worth any price to him to find a way to renew his character in us.

How desperately modern Christians, who have allowed their ways of thinking to be reshaped according to the wrong model, need to allow Isaiah's view of servanthood to reshape our outlook. The cross is still foolishness to the Greeks. To win is to lose? To lose is to win? To die is to live? To live is to die? To rise is to fall? To fall is to rise? To take the lowest place is to sit with the King? To take the highest place is to sit in the dust? Come on! Yet, as we who have found God in Christ know, all that is absolutely true. But how are we going to believe that unless we consciously allow our minds to become saturated with that point of view? If we do not, the other understanding of reality will take us by default.

The Lord of History

CONSIDERED SIMPLY AS a philosophy, transcendence has some serious weaknesses. This is why, apart from perhaps Confucius and Aristotle, it has rarely been considered seriously by philosophers. In the first place, anything that is utterly removed from the psycho-socio-physical universe would have no contact with that universe and could not communicate with it. Thus, transcendence would seem to be an interesting and perhaps useful mental construct, but it would have no relevance to everyday life.

Both the Greeks and Confucius sought for a way around this by positing the existence of certain norms in life that reflect the activity and nature of this transcendent element, which Aristotle called "the Unmoved Mover" and Confucius called the "Tao" or "Way." Why is it that no culture where everyone lies or everyone steals can long survive? Is it not because there is a single, transcendent originating force behind all cultures? This argument seems to have been more persuasive in China than it was in Greece, because the following of "the Way" became a major cultural force through a great part of China's history, whereas this way of thinking had largely died out in Greece by the beginning of the Roman period. But even in China the Tao had no means of intervening in the life of the world to right any wrongs that might be there.

This highlights the second serious weakness of transcendence: the necessary impersonality of the originating force. One of the characteristics of human personality is its transitoriness. Our moods flit back and forth like hummingbirds. So do our affections and even our convictions. Surely the element from which all things extend and which forms the foundation of all that is could not have those characteristics. Furthermore, that force must of necessity be completely unconcerned with our response to it. It determines all things and is not itself determined by anything. All of this is much too ethereal and cerebral for most people caught up in the business of daily life, trying to survive for another day.

The other worldview, that of continuity, seems to offer a much more useful and practical way of understanding the way things are. Here the forces of the universe are given personalities on the analogy with us humans. But a study of mythology convinces one that the forces are forces still, only wearing masks that give them the illusion of personality and approachability. But behind the masks they are just as inscrutable and implacable as any "Unmoved Mover." What the overlay of human personality does give them is an element of capriciousness and arbitrariness that is not good news.

So how do we arrive at the biblical view, which is definitely not the worldview of continuity, but neither is it the same kind of transcendence as has just been described? If we ask the Hebrews where they got their concept of God, they will tell us that they did not get it either by extrapolating from this world or by logical deduction. Instead, they tell us of a God who broke into their experience, revealing a distinct will for their behavior and calling them to submission and obedience. They tell us of a God who interacted with them in their choices and in the consequences of those choices, revealing a complex and many-faceted personality.

How can we ever find God, if he is truly transcendent? The answer is that we cannot. As the New Testament says it, "No one has ever gone into heaven" (John 3:13). On this score the philosophers are right. But suppose the philosophers' logic is too limited. Suppose the transcendent One can retain his otherness while intersecting his world at any point and in any time. And suppose the problem of personhood is ours and not his. Suppose it is possible to be fully personal and yet entirely self-consistent. Suppose it is possible to interact deeply and faithfully with other persons and never yet vary from what One is in Oneself. This changes the question of knowing completely.

If such a being chose to, he could come to us, somehow translating himself into terms we could comprehend. For the One who spoke the universe into existence, that kind of translation should not be so hard. But what language should he use? Should he use the language of nature? How can he? How can nature convey personhood? How can nature convey an intended will? How can nature convey the necessity of surrender and obedience? How can nature convey ethical absolutes that are a concomitant of a loving, committed relationship? The language God chose was the language of human interrelationships, the language we call history. Why is it that the earliest examples of extended works of history are found in the Hebrew Bible?[48] It is because that is the arena in which God chose to make himself known. In the arena of human relationships, choices, and decisions, God revealed his nature and character and the nature of reality to his people.

The Hebrews would deny that their creation of historical narrative betrayed any special perception on their part. Rather, they would tell us that God simply broke in upon them and called them to make certain choices, telling them what would be the consequences of the various choices. When they discovered that those consequences did follow, we can imagine that they said to themselves: "It would be a good idea to record this so that when we come this way again, we won't make the same mistakes again." That was precisely what God wanted. How could he teach them a complicated truth like monotheism, especially when all their more brilliant neighbors were polytheists? He could call them into a historical covenant relationship, whose first stipulation was that they must worship him alone. How could he teach them he was not a part of this world, an even more complex idea? He could make it a covenant stipulation that they not make or worship idols. How could he teach them that there are absolute ethics? By requiring them to emulate the character of the one transcendent deity. Thus, their own historical experience became the basis for their knowledge of God.

All of this is portrayed for us in the book of Isaiah. There we see the truth of God being worked out in Israel's experience. Religion is not about mystic rites. Rather, it is about what you are going to do about the Assyrian threat. It is about how you treat the poor and downtrodden. It is about how you represent yourself and your God to foreign ambassadors. It is about how you continue to function when your entire life has fallen in on you, largely as a result of your own stupid choices. Religion is about ethics in daily life. This is the truth that is always in danger of being lost, and it is especially in danger now as the West progressively cuts its Christian moorings and all unconsciously drifts off into a pagan sea.

The study of history is dying around us. Why? Because such a study must believe that real choices are possible, that real progress toward a worthwhile goal may be made, and that there is a single overarching standard by which those choices may be evaluated and by which progress may be judged. Without these—and biblical transcendence is the only basis for them—the whole reason for studying the past at all is lost. The only thing that matters is me,

---

48. It is fashionable today to say that Hebrew history writing only originated in the fourth or third centuries B.C., at about the same time the Greek historians Thucydides and Herodotus were writing and for the same (basically inexplicable) reasons. However, there is no objective evidence to discount the clear claims of the Hebrew text.

now. Who cares what some old dead people did? As for learning from them, that's crazy. We all do what we have to do. The past is gone, and the future will be more of today, only maybe worse.

So what can counter these tendencies? A strong dose of the truth of Isaiah, that there is a God who is at work in the corporate history and in our individual histories. We can know him in the daily experiences of life, as the Israelites did. Knowing him in that way, we can then recover for ourselves, and maybe for our culture, the reality that human choices matter, that we are headed somewhere, and that the transcendent God is calling us to go with him.

Realized Righteousness

ONE OF THE chief values of studying the New Testament in the context of the Old is the corrective value of the Old. Many of the weaknesses in the church today are a result of misreading the New Testament because of ignorance of the Old Testament. For instance, the excessive individualism and privatism of the modern evangelical church is only possible if one is almost wholly ignorant of the Old Testament. To be sure, the Old Testament cannot be read alone. To do so is to fall into the opposite ditch from the one into which exclusive New Testament readers fall. By reading the Old Testament alone, one can easily miss the love of God that is clearly there and come to see him only as an austere and implacable Judge. But when the two Testaments are read together, there is a wholistic, invaluable presentation of the truth.

Because Isaiah sums up so many of the Old Testament teachings, it is especially helpful in achieving a balanced theology. One of these areas of balance desperately needed today is in the area of *realized righteousness*. Modern evangelical theology has become dangerously one-sided, and this is especially apparent in American public life. At the same time that evangelicalism has become the dominant expression of Christian faith in America, public morality has collapsed. Is this only coincidental? I fear not. Reacting against the loss of a concept of personal salvation in the so-called mainline churches and an increasingly cultic mentality in the holiness movement, evangelical theology in the first half of the twentieth century put increasing emphasis on "imputed righteousness." That is, God calls us righteous because we have accepted the saving work of Christ on the cross. There was a strong reaction against "works righteousness" with its suggestion that one could somehow earn merit with God by doing good things. This understanding can be wonderfully freeing. We don't have to wonder whether our behavior is good enough to deserve a relationship with God; we can know we are his simply because we have accepted his offer of eternal life in his Son. This is genuinely good news.

But the problem with this overemphasis on "subjective righteousness" is that it cuts the nerve of "objective righteousness." The believer can easily feel that in the end his or her actual behavior is of little significance. If this is then coupled with a false idea of the security of the believer, the effect can be pernicious. We can essentially live in conscious sin, secure in the fact that God sees us as righteous and that we can never lose our salvation. Thus, we see persons in the highest offices in the land claiming to be "born-again Christians" while living lives of conspicuous immorality and showing neither remorse nor repentance when caught. How we need to hear Isaiah's excoriation of such behavior! The people of God must manifest the life of God or give up the right to be called the people of God.

As always, the truth has two sides, and Isaiah makes this masterfully clear. On the one hand, it is true that in ourselves we are incapable of being righteous on the standard required of us by God. We are doomed to failure and deserve the condemnation that comes on that failure. We cannot bring ourselves to God by ourselves, and the failure of the good Hezekiah underlines that point. If we are ever to have a relationship with God, it must be on the basis of his grace alone. He must come to us as he did to the captive Judeans with words of comfort and grace, assuring us that he has not cast us off and that he has provided a means through his Servant whereby we may be restored to a life-giving relationship with our Father. That is one side of the truth, a side that dare not be lost.

But there is another side that equally dares not to be lost. This is the truth relating to the whole purpose of salvation. Why does God bring us into a relationship with him? A truncated view based on a misreading of the New Testament alone would say that it is so we can spend an eternity of bliss praising our Savior. This is an incredibly self-serving picture, both from a human and divine point of view. That is not, however, the New Testament teaching, as becomes clear when we read the two Testaments together. God calls us into a relationship with him so that his original purpose may be realized for us. What is that purpose? *That we might share his character with us.* This is obvious from the covenant. God's purpose in giving the covenant is so that the people might be holy as he is holy. Such holiness is not a cultic thing but a way of treating the world and other people.

As discussed above, Isaiah represents this point in a powerful way in chapters 56–66, where he synthesizes the demand for righteousness from chapters 1–39 with the offer of free grace in chapters 40–55. In chapters 56–66, Isaiah, much as Paul does in his letters, asks what that grace was for. Was it in order that God's people should revel in their chosenness while engaging in religious practices that were self-serving and ultimately perverse? Of course not! It was in order that they should live lives of justice and righteousness and in so doing become a lamp through which God's light should shine on the nations.

But how is that possible, given a long history of failure? It is possible through the same grace that restored you to a relationship with God in the first place. The demand is from God, but so is the provision. Clearly Isaiah is not promoting some arrogant claim to having arrived spiritually. Nor is he suggesting that the believer's relationship with God is ever on any basis but divine grace. But he is saying that if a believer is not a conduit for the Holy Spirit's righteousness (32:15–16; 44:1–5), then he or she is missing a large portion of what the grace of God came to do.

Outline of Isaiah

I. Introduction: God's Servants, Now and Then (1:1–5:30)
   A. God's Denunciation, Appeal, and Promise (1:1–31)
   B. The Problem: What Israel Is Versus What She Will Be (2:1–4:6)
      1. The Destiny of the House of Jacob (2:1–5)
      2. The House of Jacob Forsaken (2:6–4:1)
      3. Israel Restored (4:2–6)
   C. A Harvest of Wild Grapes (5:1–30)

II. A Call to Servanthood (6:1–13)

III. Lessons in Trust—the Basis of Servanthood (7:1–39:8)
   A. God or Assyria? No Trust (7:1–12:6)
      1. Children, Signs of God's Presence (7:1–9:7)
      2. Measured by God's Standards (9:8–10:4)
      3. Hope for Restoration (10:5–11:16)
      4. The Song of Trust (12:1–6)
   B. God: Master of the Nations (13:1–35:10)
      1. God's Judgment on the Nations (13:1–23:18)
      2. God's Triumph over the Nations (24:1–27:13)
      3. The Folly of Trusting the Nations (28:1–33:24)
      4. Trusting God or the Nations: Results (34:1–35:10)
   C. God or Assyria? Trust (36:1–39:8)
      1. The Assyrian Threat (36:1–37:38)
      2. The Human Limits of Trust (38:1–39:8)

IV. The Vocation of Servanthood (40:1–55:13)
   A. Introduction: The Servant's Lord (40:1–31)
   B. Motive for Servanthood: Grace (41:1–48:22)
      1. The Servants of the Lord: His Witnesses (41:1–44:22)
      2. The Lord Delivers His Servants (44:23–46:13)
      3. The Lord's Testimony (47:1–48:22)
   C. Means of Servanthood: Atonement (49:1–55:13)
      1. Anticipation of Reconciliation (49:1–52:12)
      2. Revelation of the Means of Reconciliation (52:13–53:12)
      3. Invitation to Reconciliation (54:1–55:13)

Select Bibliography

Commentaries

Achtemeier, E. *The Community and Message of Isaiah 56–66: A Theological Commentary*. Minneapolis: Augsburg, 1982.

Alexander, J. A. *Commentary on the Prophecies of Isaiah*. New York: Scribners, 1846.

Beuken, W. A. M. *Jesaja II-III*. POT. 4 vols. Nijkerk: Callenbach, 1979–89.

Calvin, John. *Commentary on the Book of the Prophet Isaiah*. Trans. W. Pringle. 4 vols. Grand Rapids: Eerdmans, 1948 reprint.

Cheyne, T. K. *The Prophecies of Isaiah*. 3d ed. 2 vols. New York: Whittaker, 1895.

Childs, Brevard S. *Isaiah*. OTL. Louisville: Westminster John Knox, 2001.

Clements, Ronald E. *Isaiah 1–39*. NCBC. Grand Rapids: Eerdmans, 1980.

Delitzsch, Franz. *Commentary on Isaiah*. Trans. James Denney. 3d ed. 2 vols. New York: Funk & Wagnalls, n.d.

Duhm, Bernard. *Das Buch Jesaja*. BKAT. Göttingen: Vandenhoeck & Ruprecht, 1892.

Fohrer, Georg. *Das Buch Jesaja*. ZBK. 2 vols. Zürich: Zwingli, 1960–67.

Gray, George B. *A Critical and Exegetical Commentary on the Book of Isaiah I-XXVII*. ICC. Edinburgh: T. & T. Clark, 1912.

Hanson, Paul D. *Isaiah 40–66*. Louisville: John Knox, 1995.

Kaiser, Otto. *Isaiah 1–12: A Commentary*. Trans. J. Bowden. OTL. 2d ed. Philadelphia: Westminster, 1983.

_____. *Isaiah 13–39: A Commentary*. Trans. J. Bowden. OTL. Philadelphia: Westminster, 1974.

Kissane, E. J. *The Book of Isaiah*. Dublin: Browne & Nolan, 1926.

Knight, G. A. F. *The New Israel: A Commentary on Isaiah 56–66*. ITC. Grand Rapids: Eerdmans, 1985.

_____. *Servant Theology: A Commentary on Isaiah 40–55*. ITC. Grand Rapids: Eerdmans, 1984.

Leupold, H. *Exposition of Isaiah*. 2 vols. Grand Rapids: Baker, 1963–71.

Mackenzie, John. *Second Isaiah*. AB 20. Garden City, N.Y.: Doubleday, 1968.

Motyer, J. Alec. *The Prophecy of Isaiah: An Introduction and Commentary*. Downers Grove, Ill.: InterVarsity Press, 1993.

_____. *Isaiah: An Introduction and Commentary*. TOTC. Downers Grove, Ill.: InterVarsity Press, 1999.

Muilenberg, James. "The Book of Isaiah: Chapters 40–66." Pages 381–772 in *The Interpreter's Bible*, vol. 5. Nashville: Abingdon, 1956.

Oswalt, John N. *The Book of Isaiah: Chapters 1–39.* NICOT. Grand Rapids: Eerdmans, 1986.

———. *The Book of Isaiah: Chapters 40–66.* NICOT. Grand Rapids: Eerdmans, 1998.

Pieper, A. *Isaiah II: An Exposition of Isaiah 40–66.* Trans. E. Kowalke. Milwaukee: Northwestern, 1979.

Scott, R. B. Y. "Introduction and Exegesis of the Book of Isaiah, Chapters 1–39." Pages 156–381 in *The Interpreter's Bible*, vol. 5. Nashville: Abingdon, 1956.

Seitz, Christopher. *Isaiah 1–39.* Louisville: John Knox, 1993.

Skinner, John. *The Book of the Prophet Isaiah.* CBC. Cambridge: Cambridge Univ. Press, 1925.

Smith, G. Adam. *The Book of Isaiah.* 2 vols. Rev. ed. Expositor's Bible. London: Hodder & Stoughton, 1927.

Watts, John D. W. *Isaiah 1–33.* WBC 24. Waco, Tex.: Word, 1985.

———. *Isaiah 34–66.* WBC 25. Waco, Tex.: Word, 1987.

Westermann, Claus. *Isaiah 40–66, A Commentary.* Trans. D. Stalker. OTL. Philadelphia: Westminster, 1969.

Whybray, R. N. *Isaiah 40–66.* NCBC. Grand Rapids: Eerdmans, 1975.

Wildberger, Hans, *Isaiah 1–12, A Continental Commentary.* Trans. T. Trapp. Minneapolis: Fortress, 1990.

———. *Isaiah 13–27, A Continental Commentary.* Trans. T. Trapp. Minneapolis: Fortress, 1997.

Young, E. J. *The Book of Isaiah.* 3 vols. NICOT. Grand Rapids: Eerdmans, 1964–1972.

Monographs on Isaiah

Allis, Oswald T. *The Unity of Isaiah: A Study in Prophecy.* Philadelphia: Presbyterian & Reformed, 1950.

Broyles, Craig C., and Craig A. Evans, eds. *Writing and Reading the Scroll of Isaiah: Studies of an Interpretive Tradition.* 2 vols. Leiden: Brill, 1997.

Clements, R. E. *Isaiah and the Deliverance of Jerusalem: A Study in the Interpretation of Prophecy in the Old Testament.* JSOTSup 13. Sheffield: JSOT Press, 1980.

Clifford, R. J. *Fair Spoken and Persuading: An Interpretation of Second Isaiah.* New York: Paulist, 1984.

Conrad, Edgar W. *Reading Isaiah.* OBT. Philadelphia: Fortress, 1991.

Darr, Katheryn Pfisterer, *Isaiah's Vision and the Family of God.* Louisville: Westminster John Knox, 1994.

Erlandsson, S. *The Burden of Babylon: A Study of Isaiah 13:2–14:23*. ConBOT 4. Lund: Gleerup, 1970.

Gowan, D. *When Man Becomes God: Humanism and Hubris in the Old Testament*. Pittsburgh: Pickwick, 1975.

Hanson, Paul D. *The Dawn of Apocalyptic*. Philadelphia: Fortress, 1975.

Hayes, John H., and S. A. Irvine. *Isaiah, the Eighth Century Prophet: His Times and His Preaching*. Nashville: Abingdon, 1987.

Johnson, Dan G. *From Chaos to Restoration: An Integrative Reading of Isaiah 24–27*. JSOTSup 61. Sheffield: JSOT Press, 1988.

Margalioth (Margulies), Ruth. *The Indivisible Isaiah: Evidence for the Single Authorship of the Prophetic Book*. New York: Yeshiva Univ. Press, 1964.

Melugin, Roy. *The Formation of Isaiah 40–55*. BZAW 141. Berlin: de Gruyter, 1976.

Mettinger, T. N. D. *A Farewell to the Servant Songs: A Critical Examination of an Exegetical Maxim*. Scriptura Minora 13. Lund: Gleerup, 1983.

Miscall, Peter. *Isaiah*. Sheffield: JSOT Press, 1993.

North, Christopher R. *The Suffering Servant in Deutero-Isaiah: An Historical and Critical Study*. Oxford: Oxford Univ. Press, 1948.

Oswalt, John N. "Key Themes in the Book of Isaiah: Their Relevance for Christian Theology." Pages 1–90 in *Newell Lectureships*, vol. 3. Ed. T. Dwyer. Anderson, Ind.: Warner, 1996.

Seitz, Christopher, ed. *Zion's Final Destiny: The Development of the Book of Isaiah: A Reassessment of Isaiah 36–39*. Minneapolis: Fortress, 1991.

_____, ed. *Reading and Preaching the Book of Isaiah*. Philadelphia: Fortress, 1988.

Staton, Cecil P., ed. *Interpreting Isaiah for Preaching and Teaching*. Greenville, S.C.: Smyth & Helwys, 1991.

Vermeylen, J. *Du prophète Isaïe à l'apocalyptique: Isaïe i–xxxv, miroir d'un demi-millénaire d'expérience religieuse in Israël*. Paris: Ledoffre, 1977.

Webb, Barry. *The Message of Isaiah: On Eagles' Wings*. BST. Leicester: Inter-Varsity Press, 1996.

Wolf, Herbert M. *Interpreting Isaiah: The Suffering and Glory of the Messiah*. Grand Rapids: Zondervan, 1985.

Isaiah 1:1–9

THE VISION CONCERNING Judah and Jerusalem that Isaiah son of Amoz saw during the reigns of Uzziah, Jotham, Ahaz and Hezekiah, kings of Judah.

² Hear, O heavens! Listen, O earth!
    For the LORD has spoken:
"I reared children and brought them up,
    but they have rebelled against me.
³ The ox knows his master,
    the donkey his owner's manger,
but Israel does not know,
    my people do not understand."

⁴ Ah, sinful nation,
    a people loaded with guilt,
a brood of evildoers,
    children given to corruption!
They have forsaken the LORD;
    they have spurned the Holy One of Israel
    and turned their backs on him.

⁵ Why should you be beaten anymore?
    Why do you persist in rebellion?
Your whole head is injured,
    your whole heart afflicted.
⁶ From the sole of your foot to the top of your head
    there is no soundness—
only wounds and welts
    and open sores,
not cleansed or bandaged
    or soothed with oil.

⁷ Your country is desolate,
    your cities burned with fire;
your fields are being stripped by foreigners
    right before you,
    laid waste as when overthrown by strangers.
⁸ The Daughter of Zion is left
    like a shelter in a vineyard,

> like a hut in a field of melons,
> like a city under siege.
> ⁹ Unless the LORD Almighty
> had left us some survivors,
> we would have become like Sodom,
> we would have been like Gomorrah.

THE OPENING NINE verses of Isaiah introduce the author and time of composition and summarize the charge of God and also of Isaiah against the people of Judah. As such, the verses open both the book and the introductory section (chs. 1–5). Many commentators believe that these chapters were put together after the rest of the book for the express purpose of introducing the finished whole.[1] The unusual position of the prophet's call in chapter 6 may well support this contention. However, unless the "Branch of the LORD" in 4:2 refers to the Messiah, the absence of that theme does raise questions about chapters 1–5 having been consciously composed as a book introduction. It seems more likely that certain pieces were collected to introduce the main judgment–hope theme without trying to summarize everything in the book.

Verse 1 identifies the author of what follows and the time period in which he wrote. We know nothing more of Isaiah ben Amoz than what is mentioned in the book, though his easy access to the kings has suggested he may have been of royal blood.[2] The dates of the four kings mentioned extend from approximately 690 B.C. to 590 B.C., but chapter 6 makes it plain that Isaiah's ministry only began in the last year of King Uzziah, about 640 B.C. Jewish tradition has Isaiah being put to death by Manasseh, but there is no independent confirmation of this.[3]

The charges are those of rebellion (v. 2) and corruption (v. 4), which have resulted in desolation. Isaiah concludes (v. 9) that only because of the mercy of God does the land continue to exist at all. Verse 2 begins with formal-sounding language as God calls the heavens and earth to witness his charges. This is reminiscent of Deuteronomy 4:26, where Moses called heaven and earth to witness the promise that if the people persisted in sin, they would

---

1. Expressed succinctly in D. R. Jones, "The Tradition of the Oracles of Isaiah of Jerusalem," *ZAW* 69 (1955): 226–46.

2. For the history of this theory, see J. Alexander, *The Prophecies of Isaiah* (Grand Rapids: Zondervan, 1975), 10.

3. For further discussion of date, authorship, and composition, see the introduction.

be expelled from the land of promise. Obedient nature is thus called upon to witness what God says about rebellious humanity.

This theme of obedient and responsive nature continues in verse 3, where Israel is said to be less intelligent than an ox or an ass that at least knows where the barn is. Israel does not know as much and persists in turning its back on its good Master even when its turning away results in its being beaten (v. 5).

In 1:5–8 Isaiah uses two graphic figures to depict the nation's spiritual condition. The first (vv. 5–6) is that of a bruised and wounded body that is left untended; the second (v. 8), that of an abandoned hut in a harvested field. The harvesters are gone, and the winter winds have blown away most of the odds and ends used to build the hut. That is what Israel is like. Yet for all of this, it seems Israel cannot put two and two together and come up with four. If only they would turn back to the Lord, he would gladly restore the blessings he had formerly showered on them. But it is a sign of the depth of their rebellion that even with the evidence of judgment all around them, they will not turn back.

AT ITS HEART, this passage is about rebellion and ignorance—*rebellion* that brings about certain consequences and the *failure* to see the connection between an action and its consequences. Rebellion (*peša'*) is at its heart a refusal to recognize boundaries. But by what right does "the Holy One of Israel" establish such boundaries (v. 4)? There are four reasons stated or implied in the passage.

(1) The first is that there is only one Holy One. In the ancient world, "the holy" defined that which pertained to deity. For Isaiah there was only *One* who could be defined as holy. The things that Israel's pagan neighbors worshiped were certainly not holy. In fact, they were abominations (44:19). Thus, if there is only one real deity in the universe, that deity certainly has the right to draw some lines for the rest of the universe.

(2) The Holy One is the Creator. He is the One who set up the boundaries of earth and heaven. Does he not have a right to establish boundaries for humans as well?

(3) Next is the right of the covenant Lord. God has entered into a covenant relationship with humans. He has committed himself to us and in turn calls us to commit ourselves to him.

(4) There is the right of the Father. Humans are not merely objects to God, nor are we merely subjects. We are his children (1:2), whom he loves and cares for. If he establishes boundaries, they are finally established out of love. When we rebel, it is against the only God, the sole Creator, the covenant Lord, and the heavenly Father.

Rebellion has consequences. Consequences for spiritual choices are as certain as consequences for physical choices. Just as a bruised and wounded body will die if left untended, and just as a lean-to will be blown down if not constantly maintained, so if we rebel against the Creator of the universe and reject his ways, spiritual corruption and death will follow. As intelligent human beings, we should be able to work that equation. Animals seem to know what is best for them, yet humans do not.

WE HUMANS ARE an interesting lot. When we are offended, we want instant justice. But when we offend, we want complete mercy. We demand consequences when they are in our favor, but we want to avoid consequences when they are not. Beyond that, while we cannot deny there are largely inescapable consequences for physical behavior, we insist there are no comparable consequences for spiritual behavior. We are not offended by the "law" of gravity. We do not feel that our essential freedoms have somehow been infringed upon by the fact that if we jump off a forty-story building, we will do irreparable damage to ourselves. Yet if someone has the nerve to suggest that there might be comparable "laws" in the spiritual realm, such a person is treated as if he or she is profoundly evil.

Personal freedom has become an absolute good in the modern world, regardless of the obviously tragic results when it is pushed to its extremes. Studies show that the one common denominator in delinquency is the absence of a father. Yet males continue to imagine that they can father children whenever and wherever they like without consequences. At the same time, adults imagine they can have sex without restraints because they can always kill the unwanted consequences. Others among us imagine that they can acquire an endless string of material goods without any impact on their sense of priorities in life.

But Isaiah tells us there are standards for spiritual behavior that are just as consequential as those in the physical world. They have been established by the Creator of the universe and are never broken, only crashed up against. It is the Christians today who need to recover this truth, both for ourselves and for our children. We live in a society whose hostility to any kind of spiritual norms is so deep-seated and so pervasive that it comes out on every hand. We are in danger of imbibing it without even being aware of it, and our children more so. We must tell ourselves again and again that the Holy One has not created the law of marital fidelity any more arbitrarily than he has the law of gravity. Both of these laws simply describe the way he made us to function.

To require a railroad engine to stay on its tracks is not some infringement of its basic rights; it is merely to define the circumstance under which that machine must operate if its potential is to be realized. We must recover this kind of basic arithmetic of life. Why is it, for example, that all organized societies forbid lying? It is because for some reason no society where everyone lies can long exist. And why is that? Does it not argue that it reflects the nature of a creation where integrity (oneness) is a physical, emotional, and spiritual necessity? Yet our society has made pleasing oneself the absolute good when it says, "Oh, everybody lies once in a while. Don't be so narrow." But we hear Isaiah saying, "Why do you want to keep on smashing into that brick wall? God does not prohibit lying because he is some heavenly killjoy, but simply because that is the way he has made the world."

This underlines the necessity of the biblical doctrine of God. Is there a being in the universe who has the right in his essence (the Holy One), his nature (Father), his actions (Creator), and his relationships (covenant Lord) to define the terms of our life? If so, rebellion is not merely the assertion of our right to be self-determining, but it is an offense against the very nature of our existence. But we ask, is this not merely to reduce us to robots who mindlessly follow the program that determines their behavior? And the answer is clearly no. Given the character of God as defined in the Bible and particularly in Isaiah, the alternative to rebellion is not mechanical obedience. For God has not prescribed every action for us. He has merely defined the outer limits beyond which we may not go without hurting ourselves. Just as the law of gravity does not render us mindless robots, neither does the law forbidding stealing.

Interestingly, some states in the United States still have laws on their books defining what sexual positions between a husband and wife are legal. There is nothing like that in the Bible. Live creatively within the general limits the Creator-Father has defined for you and there will be health, productivity, and joy.

Isaiah 1:10–20

¹⁰ HEAR THE WORD of the LORD,
   you rulers of Sodom;
listen to the law of our God,
   you people of Gomorrah!
¹¹ "The multitude of your sacrifices—
   what are they to me?" says the LORD.
"I have more than enough of burnt offerings,
   of rams and the fat of fattened animals;
I have no pleasure
   in the blood of bulls and lambs and goats.
¹² When you come to appear before me,
   who has asked this of you,
   this trampling of my courts?
¹³ Stop bringing meaningless offerings!
   Your incense is detestable to me.
New Moons, Sabbaths and convocations—
   I cannot bear your evil assemblies.
¹⁴ Your New Moon festivals and your appointed feasts
   my soul hates.
They have become a burden to me;
   I am weary of bearing them.

¹⁵ When you spread out your hands in prayer,
   I will hide my eyes from you;
even if you offer many prayers,
   I will not listen.
Your hands are full of blood;
¹⁶   wash and make yourselves clean.
Take your evil deeds
   out of my sight!
Stop doing wrong,
¹⁷   learn to do right!
Seek justice,
   encourage the oppressed.
Defend the cause of the fatherless,
   plead the case of the widow.

¹⁸ "Come now, let us reason together,"
   says the LORD.

"Though your sins are like scarlet,
 they shall be as white as snow;
though they are red as crimson,
 they shall be like wool.
¹⁹ If you are willing and obedient,
 you will eat the best from the land;
²⁰ but if you resist and rebel,
 you will be devoured by the sword."
               For the mouth of the LORD has spoken.

ISAIAH FOLLOWS HIS opening charges by presenting two alternate ways of dealing with Israel's alienation from God, a wrong way and the right way. The wrong way, the way of hypocritical ritual, is described in 1:10–15; the right way, the way of repentance and changed living, is described in 1:16–17. Finally, the alternatives are summed up in 1:18–20. If we take the right way, we will enjoy blessing; if we take the wrong way, we will be destroyed.

One of the interesting features of the book is its transitions. For those who espouse multiple authorship, this is taken to be a sign of the way in which later editors have done their work. But it may also be an indication of a single mind at work, linking one thought to another. In this case, the link is the use of Sodom and Gomorrah in both verses 9 and 10. In verse 9, the author says that it is only because of the mercy of God that Israel and Judah have not already been destroyed like Sodom and Gomorrah were. In verse 10 he reinforces the comparison by calling the people he is addressing "rulers of Sodom" and "people of Gomorrah." If the people of Israel think they are immune from judgment because they are God's chosen people, they must think again. If their behavior is no different from that of the world, their fate will be no different either.

But the Israelites think they are entitled to favorable treatment because they have God's revealed way of doing offerings. If they will just do all the rituals more carefully, they think, God will have to avert the coming judgment and give them his blessings. God responds to such an idea with dripping scorn in verses 11–15. He does not want any more sacrifices and takes no pleasure in them (v. 11). Verse 12 is a rhetorical question whose answer has him saying he never asked for them to come before him in this way. Their gifts are worthless, their incense an abomination, and their worship services evil (v. 13). In fact, the whole thing has become too much for him to bear any more (v. 14). They may as well stop lifting their hands to him in prayer, because he won't even look at them, let alone listen to their prayers. Clearly, if God's people intend to take the way of increased religiosity as the way of solving their problems, they are taking a dead-end street.

Why? A clue appears in verse 15. "Your hands are full of blood." There is perhaps a bit of double entendre here. Yes, their hands are full of the blood of sacrifice, but they are also full of the blood of the innocent, whom they have abused or in whose abuse they have been implicated. God will not hear their prayers because their prayers are not matched by godly lives. They want God to bless them while they are the source of destruction and curse for those around them.

This becomes explicit in verses 16–17. The covenant in which the sacrificial laws appear is the same covenant where ethical treatment of one's neighbors is required. It is not possible to have the one and not the other. We cannot persist in evil deeds and expect ritual to deliver us from the consequences of those evil deeds. What God wants is right and just behavior, especially toward those who are helpless to demand such behavior on their own behalf: the oppressed, the fatherless, and the widow. Here is the true evidence that a person "knows" the Lord. Anyone can perform rituals, but the person who acts like God is the person who has entered into a life-changing relationship with him, and that is clearly what God wants.

In verse 18 the reader is called to argue the case with God ("reason together" is a little weak). God is challenging us to do our best thinking. If one way of acting (rebellion and stubbornness) brings destruction (v. 20) and another (submission and changed living) brings not only forgiveness and restoration (v. 18) but all the blessings of life (v. 19), which choice makes the best sense? It seems as though even an ox or a donkey could figure that out (cf. 1:3)!

SINCE WE NO LONGER offer sacrifices and most of us do not burn incense in our worship services, it may appear on first glance as if 1:10–15 have only limited relevance for modern readers. However, what this paragraph is talking about is very relevant—the human tendency to use religious behavior as a means of manipulating God for our own benefit. Around the world, this is the function of ritual, because it is believed, sometimes consciously and sometimes unconsciously, that by performing such actions we can force God to do certain things.

This is very conscious in the worldview of continuity wherein actions performed in the human realm must of necessity be replicated in the divine realm and then in the natural realm. This is a great part of the appeal of ritualistic religion; it gives the worshiper the feeling of being in control and being able to procure for oneself the benefits one seeks. This was certainly the appeal of such behavior to the Hebrews. By contrast, treating other people, especially people weaker than we, in just and right ways seems to have no religious efficacy at all. It does not put God in our debt and seems to have no capacity for manipulating him. Perhaps we might earn some favor with him, but that is a precarious basis for trying to placate his anger. It requires that we simply surrender to him and trust him to keep his Word, a frightening position in which to put oneself.

But this is precisely the consequence of God's transcendence: He cannot be manipulated by any human activity. We cannot in some mechanical way force God to do something. He is not continuous with this world, and nothing done here requires him to do anything. But how, and why, does treating the poor justly and rightly have any impact on our standing with God? For the Israelites it was because God required it in his covenant with them. If they were to experience the blessings their covenant Lord offered, then they had to agree to treat one another in ethical ways.

Why? Because this was his will, expressing his own nature and character. If God's people wanted to walk with him, they had to agree to act like him. This is where the connection lies for modern believers. Like the old covenant, which was written on tablets of stone, the new covenant, which is written on our hearts, calls on us to share the character of God. He offers us his favor; we cannot force him to give it to us. But if we are to receive that favor, we must be in the right kind of relationship to receive it. We cannot receive it if we refuse to walk in his way.

But were not the sacrifices part of the covenant requirements too? Yes and no. The requirements of the covenant are given in Exodus 20–23. In those chapters the statements about worship and sacrifice are general, while the ethical demands are detailed.[1] The so-called "Manual of Sacrifice" only appears after the segment on the tabernacle (Ex. 25–40), and almost all the sacrifices described there (Lev. 1–7) have to do with unintentional sin. This placement and content are significant. The sacrificial system was not given for the purpose of procuring God's favor but as a means whereby those who have accepted God's grace and are keeping the covenant and enjoying the presence of God may continue to do so in spite of their unintentionally falling short of perfect performance. To attempt to use sacrifices to cover

---

1. Note that there is nothing at all about sacrifice in the summary of the covenant requirements, the Ten Commandments. The only thing close is the fourth commandment regarding the Sabbath.

intentionally breaking the covenant of God was a terrible violation of what the covenant was all about.

Religious actions were to be a symbol of the heart condition. If the heart was not in an obedient and submissive posture before God, then all the sacrifices in the world would accomplish nothing. Nowhere in the Old Testament is this more clearly stated than in Psalm 51, where we read that God does not desire sacrifices; rather, the sacrifice he desires is the one of the broken and contrite heart. So why did he require sacrifices? Because we humans need a way of symbolizing spiritual realities. Trying to make the symbol stand in place of the reality is sin.

THERE IS NO QUESTION that we today are as guilty of trying to use religious behavior to manipulate God as any Israelite was. How easy it is to think that when we go to church regularly, read the Bible, pray, tithe, and don't engage in substance abuse, God somehow owes us something. Moreover, how easy it is to think that when we have done all these things, God could hardly expect more from us. Look at all the heathen around us who do not do any of these things. God should be grateful to have such faithful servants as us, we think. Then, when difficulties come to us, we are angry at God, accusing him of being unfair after all we have done for him.

In fact, it is easy for these behaviors to become substitutes for real biblical faith. Real biblical faith, as both the Old and New Testaments show, lies in surrender and obedience as manifested in how we treat one another. Certainly Jesus' statement in John 13:35 is not meant to be all-inclusive. Nevertheless, its import is clear: "By this all men will know that you are my disciples, if you love one another." It is not by our religious behavior but by our love. Paul makes the same point in 1 Corinthians 13. Note too that when the apostle describes the fruit of the Spirit in Galatians 5:22–23, he does so in entirely relational language.

As with the Israelites, our worship practices and religious activities are intended to be symbolic of deeper realities. There is no necessary connection between these and the realities. But there *is* a direct connection between those realities and our ethical behavior. We can be very religious and yet be living our lives for ourselves. We can give the appearance of obedience and yet be living a self-centered life that is nothing but rebellion.

In contrast, it is unlikely that a person will manifest consistent integrity, compassion, and self-denial in his or her dealings with others, especially those who can never repay what is given them, unless that person has surrendered to the love and grace of the God of the Bible. When we do meet persons who are acting in these ways but who give no testimony of faith, in almost all cases there is a Christian source of such behavior in a previous generation. But the point is this: God says that what we *must* show if we are to experience his favor is evidence of his life within us. Religious and cultic activity in the absence of a changed life is *not* such evidence.

Isaiah 1:21–31

²¹ SEE HOW THE faithful city
    has become a harlot!
  She once was full of justice;
    righteousness used to dwell in her—
    but now murderers!
²² Your silver has become dross,
    your choice wine is diluted with water.
²³ Your rulers are rebels,
    companions of thieves;
  they all love bribes
    and chase after gifts.
  They do not defend the cause of the fatherless;
    the widow's case does not come before them.
²⁴ Therefore the Lord, the LORD Almighty,
    the Mighty One of Israel, declares:
  "Ah, I will get relief from my foes
    and avenge myself on my enemies.
²⁵ I will turn my hand against you;
    I will thoroughly purge away your dross
    and remove all your impurities.
²⁶ I will restore your judges as in days of old,
    your counselors as at the beginning.
  Afterward you will be called
    the City of Righteousness,
    the Faithful City."

²⁷ Zion will be redeemed with justice,
    her penitent ones with righteousness.
²⁸ But rebels and sinners will both be broken,
    and those who forsake the LORD will perish.

²⁹ "You will be ashamed because of the sacred oaks
    in which you have delighted;
  you will be disgraced because of the gardens
    that you have chosen.
³⁰ You will be like an oak with fading leaves,
    like a garden without water.

³¹The mighty man will become tinder
    and his work a spark;
both will burn together,
    with no one to quench the fire."

THE PROPHET RETURNS from his call to repent to a description of the present (1:21–24) and to what the consequences of the present will be in the absence of repentance (1:25–31). He puts those consequences in perspective by saying that while the coming judgment will have a purging and renewing effect on the nation as a whole, individual sinners should not take false comfort from that. If they do not repent, they will be burned up like tinder.

The prophet describes the present situation in a series of contrasts between what the Lord intended and what he actually got. He intended faithfulness and got harlotry; he intended righteousness and got murder. Instead of silver he got dross; instead of pure wine, tasteless dilution. Instead of rulers he got rebels; instead of defenders of the helpless, takers of bribes. Here is the same definition of true religion as given above. True religion is to be faithful to God as demonstrated in a right and just treatment of others. It is not to be a dilution of godly and self-serving principles but a pure distillation of the former. Those in authority are to see themselves as responsible to God for their care of the helpless and not in positions of privilege, where they may enrich themselves.

It is apparent that God's people considered themselves in a position of privilege. God had chosen them and promised to bless them. Indeed, he had blessed them. They had risen from a nation of slaves to become one of the significant empires in the ancient world. They had God's law, God's temple, God's city, God's land. God had a special commitment to protect them from any and all enemies. How it must have stung when Isaiah said that they were *not* God's favorites but his enemies, on whom he would be avenged (1:24)!

But God's judgment is never intended to be his last word.[1] If the nation has become his enemies for the moment, that has not changed his ultimate intention for them. Thus, he does not intend to destroy Israel but to refine her. As the silver is melted in the crucible, so God intends to melt down the nation in order to "remove all your impurities." The fires of the Exile will be terrible and painful, but in giving his people over to that fate God is not

---

1. For a fuller discussion, see "Judgment and Hope" in the central-themes section of the introduction.

abandoning them. Instead, he will use those fires to restore to Israel the kind of leadership they once knew in order that Jerusalem could indeed fulfill God's intention for it and become "the City of Righteousness, the Faithful City" (1:26).

Verse 27 shows an interesting double usage of "justice" and "righteousness." On the one hand, it is the justice and righteousness of God that will accomplish the ultimate redemption of Zion. But on the other hand, that justice and righteousness is available because people have repented of their own unjust and unrighteous behavior and have reaffirmed their willingness to emulate God's behavior.

This segment introduces a prominent theme of the book, that of "Lady Zion." While it is true that in the conventions of Semitic languages, cities were feminine by definition, more than that seems to be taking place here. In many ways Zion is seen to be the wife of Yahweh. The same imagery is to be found in Hosea (e.g., Hos. 9:1–2; etc.) and Ezekiel (e.g. Ezek. 16:8–19; etc.). Yahweh has betrothed himself to this lady, and he expects faithfulness and loyalty in return. Sadly, that is not the case. Zion has turned her back on her husband and has sold herself into harlotry. Not only has she entered into alliances with other nations; she has also entered into alliances with the gods of those nations. Yet in spite of that, God's love for his bride has not changed. He intends to find a way to woo her back to himself (Isa. 49:15–21; 66:7–11; cf. Hos. 2:14, 19–20).

One of the characteristics of Isaiah is that no matter how promising his oracles of salvation may be, he never lets them give his audience a false comfort. The good news is only available to those who make a radical turnaround. The certainty of future hope is no justification for continuation in rebellion. In the present passage, those who persist in their rebellion *will* be destroyed (1:28); those who forsake the covenant they made with the Lord will have no hope.

Both the condition and the actions of these rebels are illustrated with the first occurrence of one of Isaiah's favorite images: trees. Sometimes it is difficult to know when the prophet is using such graphic elements as these literally and when he is using them figuratively. For instance, 1:29 may describe the literal actions of the rebels in worshiping idols. Oftentimes the idol sanctuaries were located in groves of trees. But 1:30–31 are clearly figurative. The proud rebels may think of themselves as towering trees, but if so, they are trees that have no water. In fact, they are just tinder waiting for the first spark to ignite and destroy them in a moment. This suggests that even 1:29 may be figurative, with the groves and gardens there being figurative of human pride and glory. In any case, the point is that the future promise for Zion should offer no comfort for those who will not repent.

Bridging Contexts

IF WE ASK what is the message of these eleven verses, three thoughts should be highlighted. (1) The first is the nature of true religion. Isaiah's perspective on this is much the same as that found in Deuteronomy, Micah, or James. Deuteronomy 10:12–13 instructs us "to fear the LORD your God, to walk in all his ways, to love him, to serve the LORD your God with all your heart and with all your soul, and to observe the LORD's commands and decrees." Micah 6:8 says it is "to act justly and to love mercy and to walk humbly with your God." In James 1:27, the author calls us "to look after orphans and widows in their distress and to keep oneself from being polluted by the world."

In other words, true religion involves two components: an affective one and a volitional one, a relational one and a performative one. We must have a love relationship with God that separates us from the world and changes the way we live, especially in respect to the helpless. What none of them suggest is that true religion is primarily a forensic position.

(2) God wishes even well-deserved judgment to have a positive effect. God never considers judgment to be an end in itself. As Psalm 30:5 has it, "His anger lasts only a moment, but his favor lasts a lifetime." We do not serve a God whose justice is like a steel trap: Do what is wrong, reap the consequences, and that is that. No, if God finally permits judgment on his people (and look how long he deferred it), even then he does not intend the fire to destroy but to purge, to purify. In the end, this was corrupt Judah's only hope. If they had been allowed to continue in their sin, they would have drifted off into just one more example of paganism. If they were ever to be God's people, bearers of his light to the nations, then the fire was inescapable.

(3) Finally, Isaiah reflects on the danger of false security—his first occurrence of this recurring theme. This prophet is clearly concerned that when he prophesies good things for the future, the people will relax and conclude that they do not need to give attention to their terrible present behavior. This is one of the differences between a false prophet and a true prophet. The false prophet lulls his hearers into believing that all is well and that they do not need to deal with their persistent sinning. It is the ministry of encouragement run amok. The true prophet cares enough for his people to tell them what they don't want to hear. So Isaiah continually tells the people that the fact God will keep his promises to the descendants of Abraham and not let them be erased from the earth is no guarantee for any individual Israelite. They must repent from their sins now, or they will have no part in those promises.

Contemporary Significance

MUCH OF CONTEMPORARY evangelical theology constitutes a reaction against the so-called "social gospel" of the late nineteenth and early twentieth centuries. That "gospel"—that we should concentrate less on personal piety and more on changing the sinful structures of society—was itself a reaction against some of the excesses of the last half of the nineteenth century in which there was an almost neurotic fixation on personal holiness and personal spiritual experience. In the 1920s and 1930s the social gospel reigned supreme, and fundamentalists responded by saying that all that was necessary to reform society was to save individuals.

Carl F. H. Henry addressed what he believed was the overreaction in evangelical circles with his landmark book, *The Uneasy Conscience of Modern Fundamentalism*.[2] But that book is now more than fifty years old, and we need to hear its message again. Evangelicals as a group have moved out of the upper-lower class and are now largely in the upper-middle and in some cases in the upper class.[3] Yet attempts to assist the helpless and the broken and our involvement in efforts to secure justice and righteousness in our society have not kept pace.

J. Edwin Orr, a student of revival movements, said in a lecture given at Asbury Theological Seminary in the late 1970s that he wondered if "the Jesus Movement" of that decade should really be classed as a revival. His reason for wondering was that all other revivals were immediately followed by social reform, but he saw no evidence of such a thing happening in this case. The succeeding two decades have sadly borne out his fears. With only a few exceptions, the 1980s and 1990s have not seen the evangelical church addressing the great issues of our day. Instead, we have been right in the midst of what Malcolm Muggeridge called "the Gadarene plunge" of our society into wealth, pleasure, and comfort.

So what should be our attitude in all of this? For almost two hundred years Christendom has been a dominant force in the West, especially in America. Now we see the church increasingly marginalized as a force to change society, even losing its ability to maintain its own identity. What should be our attitude? Surely Isaiah would say that we ought not to be trying to increase our power and influence. Nor should we be wringing our hands and crying, "All is lost." Rather, we should each be looking inward at our own lives and outward at a lost and broken world, confident God does

---

2. C. F. H. Henry, *The Uneasy Conscience of Modern Fundamentalism* (Grand Rapids: Eerdmans, 1947).

3. M. Hamilton, "We're in the Money," *Christianity Today* 44 (June 12, 2000): 36–43.

not intend to harm us but aware he demands purity, selflessness, and love in all our relationships.

We should, of course, live courageously and self-forgetfully, knowing that the church will survive. Furthermore, we should not be discouraged when difficulties come. Whether we deserve them or not, God's good purpose is not to destroy us but to purify us. But neither dare we live in false confidence. The scriptural adage that "the soul that sins will die" is still true. We should allow the Holy Spirit to purify us, and then we should lose ourselves in service to others.

Isaiah 2:1–5

THIS IS WHAT Isaiah son of Amoz saw concerning Judah and Jerusalem:

² In the last days

the mountain of the LORD's temple will be established
as chief among the mountains;
it will be raised above the hills,
and all nations will stream to it.

³ Many peoples will come and say,

"Come, let us go up to the mountain of the LORD,
to the house of the God of Jacob.
He will teach us his ways,
so that we may walk in his paths."
The law will go out from Zion,
the word of the LORD from Jerusalem.
⁴ He will judge between the nations
and will settle disputes for many peoples.
They will beat their swords into plowshares
and their spears into pruning hooks.
Nation will not take up sword against nation,
nor will they train for war anymore.

⁵ Come, O house of Jacob,
let us walk in the light of the LORD.

Original Meaning

AFTER THE GRIM ending of chapter 1 and indeed the generally grim tone of that entire chapter, these verses come as a shock. They do not speak of the stubborn and rebellious Israelites worshiping in the groves of their self-adoration. Instead, we have all the nations streaming to "the mountain of the LORD"—that is, to his house, his temple, in Zion—to learn his ways. They go there because that is the place where God's Torah (NIV "law") and word go forth.

It is not clear why there is a second attribution of authorship in verse 1. Many believe that whereas the attribution in 1:1 is identifying Isaiah as author of the book as a whole, this one is specifically identifying him as responsible for chapters 2 through 5.[1] This is more interesting since 2:2–4 is identical to Micah 4:1–3, and the verses seem to fit more naturally into their context in Micah than they do here. Perhaps the piece was something that existed independently, and both prophets made use of it.[2]

While the temple in Jerusalem was located on a hilltop, it was not the highest hill in the area, with even the neighboring Mount of Olives being higher. So what is the significance of the repetition of "mountain" with regard to the temple in these verses? Probably it has to do with the ancient belief that the gods lived on the high mountains. So Zeus was thought to live on Mount Olympus in Greece and Baal on Mount Cassius in northern Syria. What this text is saying is that while Zion may not be the highest of the mountains, it is still *the* mountain where the one true God is to be found. This is the mountain where humanity should seek God.

The reason they should do so at this place is because this is where God has revealed his ways to humans. Moreover, they are the same ways in which humans are expected to walk. In his Word, God has given instructions (*torah*) on how to walk in his ways. Thus, the nations do not come to Jerusalem for power or mystical union with the divine but in order to learn how the Creator intends his creations to live.

When the nations walk in God's ways, they will be submitting to his lordship. The concept of "judgment" in Hebrew (*šapat*, 2:4) is larger than the parallel idea in English. In English it has to do primarily with the administration and enforcement of the law codes. While that is one part of the idea in Hebrew, there is much more to it. It involves the administration of the world, the establishment of governmental order. Thus, the expected outcome of God's Word among the nations is harmony. The One who created the world order will now put that order into practice, and just as individuals who submit to God no longer need to resort to violence in order to have their needs met, neither will the nations.

Some ask when Isaiah anticipated that this pilgrimage to Jerusalem would take place. But that might be the wrong question. Perhaps he is merely making a theological point about the universal significance of the truth that had been revealed to Israel. It may be that he did not have in mind one particular event; rather, he foresaw many ways in which the message of the Torah could and should have impact on the world around.

It is not just any god who is doing this, but the "God of Jacob" (2:3). He is the God who has revealed himself in the context of the history of a

---

1. The Heb. "the word that Isaiah saw" does not require that all the following words originated with him, but it does argue that he put it into the present form.

2. For a fuller discussion of these issues, see Oswalt, *Isaiah 1–39*, 113–14.

particular people. He has condescended to become involved in the specifics of their lives in order that the world may know him and be redeemed. If that is true, then there is all the more reason why the family ("house") of Jacob (2:5) should walk in the light of the Lord. Thus, Isaiah produces another appeal for the people of Israel to live up to the truth that has been given them—the mission entrusted to them. If it is true that even the Gentiles will one day seek out God's ways so that they can walk in them, surely God's chosen people ought to be walking in those ways now.

IT IS OFTEN DEBATED whether Israelite religion was a "missionary religion," but passages such as this show that it was at least a universal religion. The writers of the Bible did not believe the Lord was a local deity on a par with Baal or Chemosh. They believed that he was the God of the whole world. Although this passage does not specify that the Hebrews were to actively reach out to the Gentiles, both Micah and Isaiah, by their use of these verses, make it plain they did believe God's "ways," as manifested in the Torah, were for all people and not just for themselves. The ethical standards of the covenant are the standards of the entire earth, because the God of Zion is the Creator of the earth and his character has been built into it. Living by those standards will produce a health, both physically and relationally, that will draw people to them. And if those standards are followed in public life and private life by all peoples, wars will cease.

THERE ARE TWO DANGERS with a passage like this. One danger is to take it too seriously, and the other is not to take it seriously enough. The danger of taking the passage too seriously is that we try to produce such a society here and now. Thus, across the centuries there have been attempts to create utopian societies where conflicts cannot occur. All of these have inevitably failed. But the danger in these failures is that we then simply relegate these promises to "the Millennium," thereby dismissing ourselves from any responsibility to see them fulfilled in any real way now.

So what is a middle way between these extremes? First of all, we must not lose sight of the universal character of the biblical faith. Today, we have come full circle from Isaiah's day. In his day it took a great deal of courage to say that *all* the nations would one day worship Israel's God. There were so many great deities in the world; how could the people of this little country of Judah dare to proclaim that their God is the one true God whom all would worship and that his ways are the ways in which all should walk? But they did proclaim such a thing. Because of their faithfulness, by the end of the nineteenth century A.D. it did not seem at all unlikely that the whole world would hear the good news of the God and Father of the Lord Jesus Christ in that generation.

Then came the twentieth century and the terrible spectacle of the Christian nations of Europe and America destroying one another in two world wars. And now we have come to the place where the very idea of Israel's God being the God of the whole world seems arrogant to many people, and the idea that there is a universal ethical standard is unthinkable. Christians too have been infected by this idea. We don't want to be thought arrogant and demanding. As a result, the numbers of young people giving themselves to foreign missions as a lifelong vocation has dropped alarmingly, as has giving money to fund such enterprises.

So what must we do? (1) We must reaffirm the truth of these promises: God is the God of the whole world. What is more, he is the *only* God of the whole world. We must not allow the world to define our faith for us. Persons who can see a tree are not arrogant to correct the misperceptions of a tree on the part of someone who is blind. Neither are those who have received the revelation of God arrogant to tell someone who has not received it what is the true nature of life.

(2) As Isaiah pleaded with his people, we must put God's ways into practice in our own lives. We must start living lives of grace and nonviolence. We must start reaching out to the poor and the helpless. We must give up our lust for riches and power. Mother Teresa is a shining example. Was she able to stem the tide of sin in Calcutta? Reverse the mortality rate? Bring in utopia? No, to all three questions. Nevertheless, she was faithful in her day, and because of her many people from the world have been impressed to look more carefully at the ways of her God.

Isaiah 2:6–4:1

❦

⁶ YOU HAVE ABANDONED your people,
   the house of Jacob.
 They are full of superstitions from the East;
   they practice divination like the Philistines
   and clasp hands with pagans.
⁷ Their land is full of silver and gold;
   there is no end to their treasures.
 Their land is full of horses;
   there is no end to their chariots.
⁸ Their land is full of idols;
   they bow down to the work of their hands,
   to what their fingers have made.
⁹ So man will be brought low
   and mankind humbled—
   do not forgive them.

¹⁰ Go into the rocks,
   hide in the ground
 from dread of the LORD
   and the splendor of his majesty!
¹¹ The eyes of the arrogant man will be humbled
   and the pride of men brought low;
 the LORD alone will be exalted in that day.

¹² The LORD Almighty has a day in store
   for all the proud and lofty,
   for all that is exalted
   (and they will be humbled),
¹³ for all the cedars of Lebanon, tall and lofty,
   and all the oaks of Bashan,
¹⁴ for all the towering mountains
   and all the high hills,
¹⁵ for every lofty tower
   and every fortified wall,
¹⁶ for every trading ship
   and every stately vessel.
¹⁷ The arrogance of man will be brought low
   and the pride of men humbled;

the LORD alone will be exalted in that day,
¹⁸   and the idols will totally disappear.

¹⁹ Men will flee to caves in the rocks
    and to holes in the ground
from dread of the LORD
    and the splendor of his majesty,
    when he rises to shake the earth.
²⁰ In that day men will throw away
    to the rodents and bats
their idols of silver and idols of gold,
    which they made to worship.
²¹ They will flee to caverns in the rocks
    and to the overhanging crags
from dread of the LORD
    and the splendor of his majesty,
    when he rises to shake the earth.

²² Stop trusting in man,
    who has but a breath in his nostrils.
    Of what account is he?

^{3:1} See now, the Lord,
    the LORD Almighty,
is about to take from Jerusalem and Judah
    both supply and support:
all supplies of food and all supplies of water,
²   the hero and warrior,
the judge and prophet,
    the soothsayer and elder,
³ the captain of fifty and man of rank,
    the counselor, skilled craftsman and clever enchanter.

⁴ I will make boys their officials;
    mere children will govern them.
⁵ People will oppress each other—
    man against man, neighbor against neighbor.
The young will rise up against the old,
    the base against the honorable.
⁶ A man will seize one of his brothers
    at his father's home, and say,
"You have a cloak, you be our leader;
    take charge of this heap of ruins!"

⁷But in that day he will cry out,
  "I have no remedy.
I have no food or clothing in my house;
  do not make me the leader of the people."

⁸Jerusalem staggers,
  Judah is falling;
their words and deeds are against the LORD,
  defying his glorious presence.
⁹The look on their faces testifies against them;
  they parade their sin like Sodom;
  they do not hide it.
Woe to them!
  They have brought disaster upon themselves.

¹⁰Tell the righteous it will be well with them,
  for they will enjoy the fruit of their deeds.
¹¹Woe to the wicked! Disaster is upon them!
They will be paid back for what their hands have done.

¹²Youths oppress my people,
  women rule over them.
O my people, your guides lead you astray;
  they turn you from the path.
¹³The LORD takes his place in court;
  he rises to judge the people.
¹⁴The LORD enters into judgment
  against the elders and leaders of his people:
"It is you who have ruined my vineyard;
  the plunder from the poor is in your houses.
¹⁵What do you mean by crushing my people
  and grinding the faces of the poor?"
                    declares the Lord, the LORD Almighty.

¹⁶The LORD says,
  "The women of Zion are haughty,
walking along with outstretched necks,
  flirting with their eyes,
tripping along with mincing steps,
  with ornaments jingling on their ankles.
¹⁷Therefore the Lord will bring sores on the heads of the
       women of Zion;
  the LORD will make their scalps bald."

[18]In that day the Lord will snatch away their finery: the bangles and headbands and crescent necklaces, [19]the earrings and bracelets and veils, [20]the headdresses and ankle chains and sashes, the perfume bottles and charms, [21]the signet rings and nose rings, [22]the fine robes and the capes and cloaks, the purses [23]and mirrors, and the linen garments and tiaras and shawls.

> [24]Instead of fragrance there will be a stench;
> > instead of a sash, a rope;
> instead of well-dressed hair, baldness;
> > instead of fine clothing, sackcloth;
> > instead of beauty, branding.
> [25]Your men will fall by the sword,
> > your warriors in battle.
> [26]The gates of Zion will lament and mourn;
> > destitute, she will sit on the ground.
> [4:1]In that day seven women
> > will take hold of one man
> and say, "We will eat our own food
> > and provide our own clothes;
> only let us be called by your name.
> > Take away our disgrace!"

EVEN MORE ABRUPTLY than 2:1–5 after Isaiah 1, these verses are a radical shift from the hopeful note of 2:1–5. As noted at the end of chapter 1, Isaiah is clearly concerned that no one fails to deal with present sins because of a false security in the certainty of future hope. Whatever good the future may hold, the present is dark indeed. At the center of that ominous present is human arrogance—and that is the theme that unites 2:6–4:1.[1]

But the theme is not merely arrogance; it is the humiliation that arrogance necessarily brings upon itself. Because Israel and Judah have been seduced by human power and glory and have consequently abandoned the Creator in whom the only true glory exists, they are doomed to be terribly

---

1. The fact that there is a common theme need not preclude the unit's possibly being made up of smaller units that were originally composed separately. See most recently the discussions in B. Childs, *Isaiah* (OTL; Louisville: Westminster John Knox, 2001), 28–37, and C. Seitz, *Isaiah 1–39* (Louisville: John Knox, 1993), 40.

humiliated. The theme is addressed in three sections. In the first (2:6–22) is a general statement of the principle. The second (3:1–15) is a specific illustration of the principle, while the third (3:16–4:1) is an even more specific illustration.

General Statement of the Principle (2:6–22)

THIS SECTION IS marked by the repetition of a refrain in verses 11 and 17. While there is a slight variation in wording between the two,[2] the import of both is the same: Human "height"[3] is an impossibility in view of the sole glory of God. He alone is "high and exalted" (6:1), and any attempt on our part to claim some of that glory for ourselves is doomed to fail. The chapter ends with a grim conclusion: Why would anyone put ultimate trust in humanity when every human being is only one breath away from extinction?

Verses 6–10 begin with a sharp contrast to 2:5. There the "house of Jacob" was called to walk in the ways of the Lord, since the day is coming when all the nations of earth will be seeking those ways. But here Isaiah says God has abandoned the "house of Jacob" because instead of being filled with the ways of the true God, they are full of human wisdom (v. 6), human wealth and power (v. 7), and human-made idols (v. 8).[4] None of these can stand up for a moment against the true splendor of the universe that exists in God alone, so the result is that those who trust in such things must be humiliated (vv. 9–11).

The first colon of verse 6 does not actually specify what it is from "the East" that fills the house of Jacob, but the appearance of those who practice "divination" in the second colon suggests the idea of "superstitions." The East was understood as the origin of wisdom and learning ("east" and "antiquity" are derived from the same root: *qdm*). Undoubtedly the complex religious thought of Mesopotamia had a terrific appeal over against the simple and austere religion of Yahweh.

Not only have the Israelites filled themselves with the world's learning; they have filled themselves with the world's values: wealth and power. In Isaiah's time "horses" and "chariots" represented the most powerful weapons of war available. For a king to have a large chariot force was a sign of his wealth and power. This is why God forbade their multiplication in Deuteronomy 17:16 and why Solomon's disobedience (1 Kings 10:28) was so serious.

---

2. The verbs are reversed in the first two cola, and "eyes" is missing from the first colon in v. 17.

3. Both of the Heb. words used for arrogance here are derivatives of roots meaning "high, lofty" (*gbh, rwm*).

4. Verse 6 begins with a Heb. *ki*, which may indicate a causal connection with v. 5 (cf. NASB, "walk . . . because . . . abandoned"), but it can also be an asseverative with the force of "indeed," as the NIV seems to construe it.

Placing a premium on human wisdom and human values issues in human self-worship, and the outcome is idolatry—conceiving of the divine in human terms. Again and again throughout the book, Isaiah mocks the practice of idolatry as the use of human hands to make gods and questions how something made by us can possibly take care of us (17:8; 30:22; 40:18–20; 44:9–10; 46:5–7). Putting our trust in the creation instead of the Creator and trying to elevate ourselves to the place of God can only result in humiliation when the true God is revealed.

The cryptic injunction "Do not forgive them" at the end of verse 9 can be understood in different ways. It may be the prophet's cry to God not to be too gracious to these people who have filled themselves with all the wrong things. But it may also be his injunction to other humans not to let fellow humans too easily out of the consequences of their self-exaltation.[5]

Verses 12–18 amplify this theme of the Lord's sole glory by contrasting him with every "high" thing in creation. That includes trees (v. 13), mountains (v. 14), fortifications (v. 15), and beautiful, tall-masted ships (v. 16). Nothing in all creation can compare to the Lord. He is another order of being altogether. So how can mere humans and the gods they have created hope to stand up to him (vv. 17–18)?

All this is brought to a blistering conclusion in verses 19–22. The prophet declares that those things that human hands created and human minds pronounced holy will be hastily cast away when he who is truly holy is revealed. They will not merely be cast away but will be cast away to "the rodents and bats," the most unclean of animals. Those who tried to make themselves as tall as the trees or as high as the mountains will be cowering under the rocks, seeking the lowest holes in which to hide from the One who is truly lofty (see Luke 23:30). The study of opposites in the section is thus brought to its climax. Our attempt to make humanity holy actually ends up making us unclean, and our attempt to give ourselves significance renders us worthless. Why would the Israelites put their trust in something worthless and unclean when they can put their trust in the living God?

Illustration of Human Arrogance (3:1–15)

THIS SECTION ILLUSTRATES the theme of arrogance producing humiliation by looking at the leadership of Judah. While it is possible that several originally independent pieces have been put together here (vv. 1–4, 5–7, 8–15), the use of the same terms for God in the opening and closing verses ("the Lord, the LORD Almighty") and the continued attention to leadership argue

5. See Oswalt, *Isaiah 1–39*, 124.

that the collection is not an accidental one. It begins with the assertion that the things Judah has trusted in apart from God will be removed. Not only will this include the obvious things such as food and water (v. 1), but even more significantly (on the basis of the amount of space given), all the great leaders from "warriors" (v. 2) to "enchanters" (v. 3) on whom Judah has depended. They have trusted in mere breath-filled humans (2:22), and now they will be deprived of such leadership. This is not merely because to place such trust in them was wrong in the first place, but also because the leaders have failed in their responsibilities (3:13–15).

The Judeans have idolized the great men, somehow believing that such people will deliver them from their difficulties. But God is going to deprive the people of their false security (3:1–3). Instead of great men, mere "boys" will be their leaders (3:4), people lacking either the maturity or the moral authority to administer the nation in a just way. The result will be anarchy, with violence undermining the last vestiges of order (3:5).

It is probable that Isaiah has in mind here typical conditions following the defeat of a nation and the exile of its leaders and craftsmen. They are certainly similar to the conditions described in Jeremiah 40–42. The connection with exile is further reinforced by the vignette in Isaiah 3:6–7. Since no one with natural leadership skills is left to govern "this heap of ruins," even the possession of a cloak (as a badge of office?) will be considered all that is necessary to assume a leadership position—but such a person will not take the job. This is how far, the prophet says, we are going to go in humiliation after having exalted our great men so high.

The connection of the forgoing with 2:6–22 is underscored by 3:8–9. Judah's sin is arrogance. They have defied "the eyes of his glory" (lit.; NIV "his glorious presence"), which reminds us immediately of the "eyes of the arrogant" in 2:11. God's eyes are the only ones that can be legitimately lifted up over the world, and to defy him by lifting up our eyes is foolish. Ultimately, it is to commit the sin of "Sodom" and Gomorrah, which was not first of all sexual sin but the insistence of the residents that they had the right to determine right and wrong for themselves. The only result of such pride is "disaster."

Verses 10–11 underline the cause-and-effect nature of relations with God. He is not arbitrary in his judgments. If "woe" comes upon the wicked, the righteous need to know that "it will be well with them." As in the physical world, so it is in the spiritual world. We have been made to operate within certain parameters. If we do so, we may expect positive results. If we choose to live outside those parameters, we should not be surprised if negative results follow.

Verses 12–15 detail God's judgment on the leaders whom Judah has idolized. Why will they be removed? Why will they be taken into captivity? Why will their nation be humiliated? The simple answer is that they are not great men at all. They may appear so, and the people may praise them as if they are, but their behavior makes it plain that they are not qualified to lead. They are "youths" and "women," two categories of persons who in that society had neither the training nor the status to give leadership. These elders of the people oppress the poor, "grinding" their "faces" in the dirt. Instead of denying themselves to tend the Lord's "vineyard," the nation of Judah, they have "ruined" it with their greed for gain and their lust for power.

Another Illustration of Human Arrogance (3:16–4:1)

THIS THIRD SECTION on human arrogance is the most graphic of all. Most commentators believe it is addressed to the wealthy women of Judah and Jerusalem.[6] And it may have been, originally. However, in the context in which it now occurs, I believe it is being used to symbolize the nation as a whole.[7] This conclusion is reinforced both by the use of "women [lit., daughters] of Zion" in 4:4 and by the way in which Zion is personified in 3:25–26. The nation is compared to a beautiful and haughty woman, whose whole attention is given to appearance and image. Zion has sought to exalt herself with every kind of accouterment and ornament. She glances at potential lovers from behind her veils and fans.

Once again, the prophet presents the contrast in the strongest terms. The arrogant heads will be bowed in shame, the beautiful hair shaved off to reveal sores seeping pus (3:17). All the beautiful clothing will be stripped off and replaced with a strip of burlap and a piece of rope (3:24). The city will be reduced to utter destitution.

In 4:1 the prophet gives the final graphic illustration of humiliation. In that society it was a great shame for a woman to have no family connections. Yet Isaiah foresees a day when so many of the men have died in plague or been killed in war that there are not enough fathers and husbands to go around. In utter humiliation, seven women will beg one man to give them his name with no obligation on his part at all. Here is the final degradation of human pride.

---

6. See, e.g., R. E. Clements, *Isaiah 1–39* (NCBC; Grand Rapids: Eerdmans, 1980), 50.

7. "Women of Zion" in vv. 16 and 17 is lit. "daughters of Zion," a phrase that only occurs elsewhere in 4:4 and Song 3:11. The singular "daughter of Zion" is used in Isaiah (1:8; 10:32; 16:1; 37:22; 52:2; 62:11) as well as in Jeremiah, Lamentations, Micah, Zephaniah, and Zechariah to denote Jerusalem itself. Furthermore, the villages surrounding a city are sometimes referred to as its "daughters" (see Jer. 49:2–3, where the villages around Rabbah are called its "daughters," and then the "daughters" of Rabbah are told to weep).

Bridging Contexts

THE BASIC MEANING of this passage needs little translation to make it applicable to the modern setting. The central issue is the human instinct to exalt ourselves in a number of ways, whether it be wealth, education, political power, military power, beauty, religion, or whatever. We do this because of our fundamental insecurity. When we face reality, we know we are but a breath, here one moment and gone the next (2:22). But beyond our transitoriness, there is a more serious problem—our sin. We may not choose to call it that. We may prefer "mistakes," "shortcomings," "failures," or some other softer term. But the fact is that there is an almost universal awareness among humans of having fallen short of our potential.

It is interesting that there are no public school programs designed to lower students' falsely high self-esteem. No, the sense of failure and worthlessness seems ingrained in all of us. This is, of course, to be expected if the account in Genesis 3 is true. We are alienated from the true source of permanence and meaning in our lives and are thus doomed to replicate the tragedies of those first generations. But instead of seeking to come penitently to our Creator and seek the forgiveness (2:9) of the Judge of the universe, human beings seek to build themselves up in all the ways described here. The problem with all of these attempts is that they cannot achieve what they promise. Every attempt to make ourselves significant on our own is rendered helpless by the fundamental fact of our mortality.

Contemporary idolatry. We may be inclined to think that the diatribe against idolatry here has little relevance to those of us in the West at present. However, we must remember that idolatry is a state of mind before it is a religious practice—that state of mind that believes it can guarantee security through the manipulation of this world. This idea rests on two false premises: that the guarantee of my security is the most important aim in life, and that that security can be maintained through the powers of this world.

Both of those are false because they make creation primary. They exalt creation to the place reserved for the Creator alone. The most important aim is to be rightly related to the Creator, who alone can hold us securely. For most of the last two centuries we in the West have believed these premises but have insisted that there is no spiritual component to creation. We have believed that the powers we had to manipulate in order to guarantee our security were inanimate and material. But that has not made us any the less idolaters than our pagan predecessors. We have exalted creation to the heights and have placed ourselves and our capacity for reason at the very center of it. We have said that we are ultimate and that there is nothing more important than us and the achieving of our goals.

Now, however, having conquered the powers of nature to a degree unimaginable even a hundred years ago, we are discovering that we have still not made ourselves secure in the ways we expected to. We are discovering that there is something more to reality than just the physical and material. But we do not wish to bow down to that spiritual reality. So, in order to give ourselves the feeling of being able to control it, we are imagining it on our own terms. This is nothing more than the people of the ancient Near East did five thousand years ago. To try to imagine the universe with ourselves at the center of it is to become idolaters.

Idolization of human leaders. Just as idolatry is one logical effect of the attempt to make the achievement of human needs primary in the world, so is the idolization of human leaders. One aspect of this is what is known as projection. Wanting to be great ourselves, we admire those who have achieved what we think of as ultimate. But another aspect grows out of the realization that we cannot achieve our goals of wealth, pleasure, comfort, and power by ourselves. There must be some political order and stability if those goals are to be achieved. Therefore, we exalt the strong leader who seems able to guarantee those conditions. But what we are doing in those cases is giving a human the position of God. The end is predictable: The human who is given power and adulation wants more of those; there can never be enough.

The next step is oppression as the leader makes himself and his desires the end of everything. The final step, then, is the need of the people to destroy the leader. Again, there are two aspects to this: Not only is there the desire to be free of the oppression, but there is also the awareness that the one whom we expected to be God for us has failed us. We have placed him in an impossible position: He can never possibly provide for us the things we demand of him, so he must be destroyed.

ULTIMATE REALITY. Some would claim that the roots of our present intellectual disaster extend all the way back to Aquinas with his separation of reality into nature and grace, or nature and supernature.[8] This had the effect of separating God from the material and physical world and of removing him from normal history. From that time on, God has been moved more and more to the periphery of things. In the eighteenth century, human reason was lifted to the level of court of last resort. If something was not rational, it did not exist. Immanuel Kant sought to make a

---

8. See, e.g., F. Schaeffer, *Escape From Reason* (Downers Grove, Ill.: InterVarsity Press, 1968).

place for God by arguing that real value is beyond reason, but he only succeeded in separating fact and meaning in such a way as to make meaning almost wholly subjective. This ultimately led Friedrich Nietzsche to declare that the whole concept of God is not only useless but pernicious, because it tends to confuse and dilute the real meaning of life, which is the will to power.

All of this movement of European thought led in one direction, that of making humans and their desires and goals ultimate reality. If there is a God at all, he is removed from everything necessary to the functioning of ordinary human life. But the end of this type of thinking had already been discovered in the ancient Near Eastern religions. If there is no reality outside of the cosmos, then all reality may be defined in terms of our experience. That means reality is to be understood by analogy with this world. The gods are humans, only larger in every way. They are better than we, but worse than we. They are more generous than we, but more petty than we. They are more disciplined than we, but more debauched than we. Humanity is the measure of reality. And what was the result of that thinking in the ancient pagan religions? Humans themselves became worthless. The human race was an afterthought, without real significance or value, and individual humans were less than nothing.

This same thing has happened in Western thought. If all of reality is defined in terms of humanity, if we are the highest order of being, then reality is meaningless because we have no meaning in ourselves. This is nowhere clearer than in the movement of existentialism that emerged after World War I and has finally taken root in popular consciousness. Prior to that global catastrophe, it was possible to argue that inanimate nature was necessarily progressing to higher and higher forms, of which humanity was the highest yet to appear. That was a key idea in the thinking of Marx and Engels, who argued that if the means of production were forcibly redistributed among the masses, true equality among humans would necessarily emerge.

But after Ypres and the Somme, the idea of inevitable human progress became laughable. When science and human reason had been used to devour a whole generation of European youth, the idea of the inevitable upward progress of the human race could only be maintained under the harshest of human tyrannies, as in Russia. In freer Western Europe, the logical consequences of the Great War have been inescapable: There is no meaning in existence; humanity is all there is and humanity is nothing. But the terrible irony of life is that we humans must have something beyond ourselves to live for! So, the existentialist philosophers argued that we must each create our own pattern of meaning, all the time knowing that there is no meaning. This, of course, means that no one can claim that his or her system of meaning is *the* meaning of life; there is no such thing. Thus today, although the person on the street cannot explain the philosophical basis for his or her ideas, it is still obvious that existentialism has come to rule the day.

True humility. This is exactly what Isaiah is talking about here. We as humans have sought to arrogate for ourselves the place of God in the universe. We have said that the fulfillment of our personal needs is ultimate, and we have understood with Nietzsche that the only way to do that is to gain power for ourselves. But that way is disaster. If we are the greatest beings in the universe, then there is no meaning in the universe and Death is the lord of all. Whatever we may achieve, he stands at the end of the road, laughing at all our pretensions. Why should we pay any attention to humans? Of what worth is a blob of protoplasm? In our attempt to exalt ourselves, we have in fact reduced ourselves to nothing. The apostle Paul also saw this clearly, as he testifies in Romans 1:21–32: Refusing to submit thankfully to God, we are reduced to worshiping our appetites and representing the divine with the basest forms of earth.

What should we have done? Although it is not explicitly stated here, it is still appropriate to mention it in this context. We should have done the very opposite. We should have admitted that our needs are not primary but that a relationship with our Creator is. We should have submitted our needs to him, recognizing that he is Lord of all. We should have recognized that he has entered into our time and space, ultimately in Jesus Christ, and has thus given that time and space eternal meaning. Even more, we should acknowledge that by taking on our form, God has given humanity ultimate worth.

Thus, if instead of trying to make ourselves God in order to take care of ourselves, we submit to God and allow him to care for us, we will find ourselves lifted to the place of sons and daughters of God. Trying to take his place, we become nothing, but allowing him to be exalted alone, we become the princes and princesses of the universe. This is what Peter means when he says, "Humble yourselves, therefore, under God's mighty hand, that he may lift you up in due time" (1 Peter 5:6).

It is important to think about the real meaning of humility in this context. Too often we think of humility as "feeling bad about yourself," or at least pretending to! Thus, we have the common phrase "false humility." But in fact, that is not what humility is at all, as this passage in Isaiah makes clear. The opposite of self-exaltation is not self-denigration. Too often that is simply an attempt to garner sympathy for oneself, an attempt to get others to say good things about us. No, true humility is to refuse to put oneself in the place of God. It is to know oneself as a child of God, to know one's place in God's economy, and to know one's worth in his sight. Knowing these, it is possible not to need to call attention to oneself.

That is true humility: self-forgetfulness. It is the ability to go about the tasks God has given, secure in his love and his valuing, without wondering if others appreciate us as much as they should. It is the ability to see others being praised and not need to belittle them, either silently or aloud, in an effort to make oneself look good by comparison. To paraphrase a popular saying: "Humility is to know there is a God, and to know you are not him!"

Proper approach to leadership. A third concern this passage addresses is the proper approach to leadership. As mentioned above, the human tendency is first of all to idolize human leaders. It is to place them on a pedestal, giving them all the attributes we want them to have for our sakes. We see in them what we would like to have and be, and we expect them to give us what God alone can give: meaning, worth, and security.

This is a sure recipe for failure. We are placing our leaders in impossible positions when we treat them in this way. We are asking them to be God for us, and this is something they can never be. What happens then is predictable. When leaders fail, as fail they must, we turn on them and demand their heads. Having expected them to be God for us, we are unable to let them be anything less than the perfect leader. The often merciless criticism that follows is another part of the pattern: We exalt ourselves by belittling the "great" ones.

Under such oscillating adulation and criticism our leaders typically crack. The break often manifests itself in one of two ways, both closely related. The one way is the way of oppression. Believing the adulation they have received and writhing under the criticism, they take the way of power. They assert a right to dictate to the followers the way they should go, and as leaders, they take the right to make use of the followers to serve their own ends. If people don't like it, that's too bad! "After all, I have given them so much!"

The other break is a moral break. Here the erosion is more subtle. The leader is conscientious in trying to meet the needs of the followers, but he or she increasingly feels the impossibility of what is being demanded. The strain mounts, and when it is coupled with an unreal level of adulation, the stage is set for collapse. It may have to do with sexuality, or money, or substance abuse, but the break comes.

What is the biblical way of leadership, particularly as displayed here? As is obvious, it is a two-way street, involving both the followers and the leader. (1) The people must surrender themselves and their needs to God. They must stop looking to any human, themselves or another, for what only God can provide. (2) They must allow their leaders to be fallible. I do not mean morally fallible, but in their performance as leaders. The people have a right to expect their leaders to be exemplary, both as persons and as believers, but they do not have a right to ask their leaders to fill the place of God in the lives of their followers. (3) They must not give to any human the adulation that is due to God alone. Leaders must be respected, if only for the position they hold, but they must not be worshiped. (4) They must be aware that a spirit of constant criticism of a leader is a sure sign of an unsurrendered spirit in the critic. The attempt to belittle another is a certain indicator of an inner need to exalt oneself.

As for leaders, it is clear that they should never believe the adulation that people give them. Here, it is not so important how one responds to such fulsome praise on the outside as it is on the inside. Once again, the condition of one's own soul is critical. If you know your own fallibility and how desperately you need God, and if you have genuinely surrendered your destiny to God, you can offer up all the praise to God at the end of the day with a smile.

At the same time, these conditions will not allow the criticism to destroy you. You know you are not in this to please yourself but God. Thus, even though cruel comments hurt, you can look at what is said with a somewhat objective eye, not rejecting them outright but neither taking them too deeply to heart. In it all, you know, as Moses did in Exodus 32:11 or Paul in 1 Corinthians 3:5–9, that these are not your people but God's. Like the good shepherd, you do not have the right to use the flock for your purposes but are expected to lay down your life for God's purposes in them (John 10:10– 11). In the end, the question for the leader is the same as it is for those being led: Who supplies my needs? If we have genuinely surrendered our needs to God, we will be armored against the temptations to satisfy the lust of the flesh, the lust of the eyes, and the pride of life for ourselves (1 John 2:16).

Isaiah 4:2–6

I N THAT DAY the Branch of the LORD will be beautiful and glorious, and the fruit of the land will be the pride and glory of the survivors in Israel. ³Those who are left in Zion, who remain in Jerusalem, will be called holy, all who are recorded among the living in Jerusalem. ⁴The Lord will wash away the filth of the women of Zion; he will cleanse the bloodstains from Jerusalem by a spirit of judgment and a spirit of fire. ⁵Then the LORD will create over all of Mount Zion and over those who assemble there a cloud of smoke by day and a glow of flaming fire by night; over all the glory will be a canopy. ⁶It will be a shelter and shade from the heat of the day, and a refuge and hiding place from the storm and rain.

Original Meaning

AS WAS THE case in moving from Isaiah 1 to 2:1–5, so here there is no transition between the negative words of 2:6–4:1 and these much more positive words. In fact, the contrast between these two sections is heightened by the fact that both 4:1 and 4:2 begin with "in that day," a reference to the future. In 4:1 the future is grim, as Jerusalem is humiliated. But in 4:2 the future is bright, as God promises abundance in place of desolation and cleansing in place of blood and filth. God does not intend to leave his people in the consequences of their sins.

Commentators are divided as to the intent of the phrase "the Branch of the LORD" (4:2). Some take it to refer to the Messiah, as in Jeremiah 23:5; 33:15 and Zechariah 3:8; 6:12.[1] Others argue that the immediate context of Isaiah 4:2 suggests that it is the land itself that is being talked about.[2] However, the overall context of 4:2–6 seems to argue against a too-literal understanding. There is a clear eschatological tone that calls for an understanding of the phrase in that light.[3] The kind of cleansing and purification being

---

1. So J. A. Motyer, *The Prophecy of Isaiah: An Introduction and Commentary* (Downers Grove, Ill.: InterVarsity Press, 1993), 65; E. J. Young, *The Book of Isaiah*, 3 vols. (NICOT; Grand Rapids: Eerdmans, 1964–1972), 1:173–75.

2. So Clements, *Isaiah 1–39*, 59; see also Calvin.

3. So Childs, *Isaiah*, 35–36; Seitz, *Isaiah 1–39*, 42.

described here can only take place in the context of the fulfillment of the messianic promises.

The promises here are not in place of judgment but through it. The "survivors" (4:2) are the remnant left after the "fire" of judgment (4:4) has done its work. There are three results of that raging firestorm (NIV, "spirit ⌊or wind⌋ of fire"). (1) The people will be "holy" (4:3); that is, they will belong to God alone and will reflect the character of their owner (see Ex. 19:6; Lev. 22:32). (2) They will be cleansed of their "filth" and "bloodstains," that is, the accumulated guilt of all their sins (4:4). (3) They will experience the presence of God not as a threat but as a blessing (4:5). By his presence ("the glory"), he will provide the very security for which they had turned to idols. The imagery of the "cloud . . . by day" and "fire by night" is reminiscent of that used in Exodus (Ex. 40:38). In short, Isaiah sees the messianic kingdom as a return to what the Exodus was meant to produce.[4]

WHAT ARE WE to make of the abrupt shift after 2:22–4:1? At the least, it is underlining again the fact that God does not intend judgment to be his last word. If it is true that there are certain inevitable consequences that follow sinful choices, it is also true that God can take us through those consequences and bring us out on the other side without the consequences having annihilated us. Judgment is not intended to destroy but to cleanse. The only issue is whether we will be among those who allow the judgment to do its cleansing work.

This passage also speaks of the unchanging nature of God's plans for his people. From the Exodus onward, it is plain that God's ultimate goal is to live among his people and, in fact, not merely among them but in them. He means to provide the security, the comfort, the well-being that we so desperately crave. This is why the climax of the book of Exodus is not the crossing of the Red Sea or the sealing of the covenant, but rather the moment of God's glory filling the tabernacle (Ex. 40:38).

However, if God is to dwell among us—indeed, in us—two things must happen. (1) There must be a means of cleansing us from the accumulated guilt of the past. God cannot live in a filthy temple. That is what Leviticus 1–9 is about. (2) God's character must somehow be replicated in us. As Amos says it, two cannot walk together unless they be agreed (Amos 3:3). That's what Leviticus 10–27 is about.

---

4. Ezekiel has the same perspective (see, e.g., Ezek. 36:27–28).

IN THIS DAY when Christianity is often preached as a get-rich-quick scheme, we need to hear Isaiah's words with clarity. Too easily when difficulties come upon us, we think that God has abandoned us or that the devil is oppressing us. In many of these cases, the adversity is the judgment of God. We have sinned in our lust for comfort, pleasure, and security, and we are now experiencing those results. But it is not a cruel God who brings those things upon us, and it is not a rejecting God who abandons us to the fire. Rather, it is a loving God who sees no other way to bring us to the place where he can live in us.

The fact is, God is not too concerned whether we are happy or not. But he is very concerned over whether we are holy.[5] We can be happy and on our way to hell. But if we are holy, it is only because the Holy One is at home in his temple, our hearts. So we ought to take a long look at adversity and ask what Jesus the Branch means to burn out of us so that he can take us into his tabernacle, where he abides with the Father.

We should also recognize that comfort, pleasure, and security are all by-products, not ends in themselves. If we make those things primary, we *will* become idolaters, and we will lose those things even as we seize them. But if we make God's presence and his character primary, then comfort, pleasure, and security will fall on us all unawares. But they will be when and where God chooses, and that will be enough because we know he is all we need and that all those other things may come and go as they will. We can live that way because we know that he has no desire to deprive us but seeks, even in the fire, to do us good.

5. O. Chambers, *My Utmost for His Highest* (New York: Dodd, Mead, 1957), 245.

Isaiah 5:1–30

❦

¹ I WILL SING for the one I love
    a song about his vineyard:
My loved one had a vineyard
    on a fertile hillside.
² He dug it up and cleared it of stones
    and planted it with the choicest vines.
He built a watchtower in it
    and cut out a winepress as well.
Then he looked for a crop of good grapes,
    but it yielded only bad fruit.

³ "Now you dwellers in Jerusalem and men of Judah,
    judge between me and my vineyard.
⁴ What more could have been done for my vineyard
    than I have done for it?
When I looked for good grapes,
    why did it yield only bad?
⁵ Now I will tell you
    what I am going to do to my vineyard:
I will take away its hedge,
    and it will be destroyed;
I will break down its wall,
    and it will be trampled.
⁶ I will make it a wasteland,
    neither pruned nor cultivated,
    and briers and thorns will grow there.
I will command the clouds
    not to rain on it."

⁷ The vineyard of the LORD Almighty
    is the house of Israel,
and the men of Judah
    are the garden of his delight.
And he looked for justice, but saw bloodshed;
    for righteousness, but heard cries of distress.

⁸ Woe to you who add house to house
    and join field to field

till no space is left
and you live alone in the land.

⁹The LORD Almighty has declared in my hearing:

"Surely the great houses will become desolate,
the fine mansions left without occupants.
¹⁰A ten-acre vineyard will produce only a bath of wine,
a homer of seed only an ephah of grain."

¹¹Woe to those who rise early in the morning
to run after their drinks,
who stay up late at night
till they are inflamed with wine.
¹²They have harps and lyres at their banquets,
tambourines and flutes and wine,
but they have no regard for the deeds of the LORD,
no respect for the work of his hands.
¹³Therefore my people will go into exile
for lack of understanding;
their men of rank will die of hunger
and their masses will be parched with thirst.
¹⁴Therefore the grave enlarges its appetite
and opens its mouth without limit;
into it will descend their nobles and masses
with all their brawlers and revelers.
¹⁵So man will be brought low
and mankind humbled,
the eyes of the arrogant humbled.
¹⁶But the LORD Almighty will be exalted by his justice,
and the holy God will show himself holy by his
righteousness.
¹⁷Then sheep will graze as in their own pasture;
lambs will feed among the ruins of the rich.

¹⁸Woe to those who draw sin along with cords of deceit,
and wickedness as with cart ropes,
¹⁹to those who say, "Let God hurry,
let him hasten his work
so we may see it.
Let it approach,
let the plan of the Holy One of Israel come,
so we may know it."

²⁰ Woe to those who call evil good
    and good evil,
  who put darkness for light
    and light for darkness,
  who put bitter for sweet
    and sweet for bitter.
²¹ Woe to those who are wise in their own eyes
    and clever in their own sight.

²² Woe to those who are heroes at drinking wine
    and champions at mixing drinks,
²³ who acquit the guilty for a bribe,
    but deny justice to the innocent.
²⁴ Therefore, as tongues of fire lick up straw
    and as dry grass sinks down in the flames,
  so their roots will decay
    and their flowers blow away like dust;
  for they have rejected the law of the LORD Almighty
    and spurned the word of the Holy One of Israel.
²⁵ Therefore the LORD's anger burns against his people;
    his hand is raised and he strikes them down.
  The mountains shake,
    and the dead bodies are like refuse in the streets.

  Yet for all this, his anger is not turned away,
    his hand is still upraised.

²⁶ He lifts up a banner for the distant nations,
    he whistles for those at the ends of the earth.
  Here they come,
    swiftly and speedily!
²⁷ Not one of them grows tired or stumbles,
    not one slumbers or sleeps;
  not a belt is loosened at the waist,
    not a sandal thong is broken.
²⁸ Their arrows are sharp,
    all their bows are strung;
  their horses' hoofs seem like flint,
    their chariot wheels like a whirlwind.
²⁹ Their roar is like that of the lion,
    they roar like young lions;
  they growl as they seize their prey
    and carry it off with no one to rescue.

³⁰ In that day they will roar over it
    like the roaring of the sea.
And if one looks at the land,
    he will see darkness and distress;
    even the light will be darkened by the clouds.

IN CHAPTER 5 Isaiah brings his introduction to a close. Once again, without transition, the tone shifts from hope to judgment. Once again, as real as the future hope may be, the prophet wants his readers to know that apart from a radical change of behavior, the only way for that hope to be realized is through the fire. The chapter divides fairly clearly into three sections. (1) The first is another graphic illustration, that of a vineyard that despite the farmer's careful work produces only bitter grapes (5:1–6). (2) Next is the explanation of the illustration, in which the prophet declares that Israel is the vineyard, God the farmer, and the bitter grapes Israel's sinful behavior (5:7–24). (3) The conclusion (5:25–30) states that the enemy nations are being called in to destroy Israel, just as the wild animals were called in to destroy the useless vineyard.

The Vineyard (5:1–6)

THROUGHOUT THE BOOK Isaiah makes use of illustrations to bring his point home. We have already seen a number of brief examples, such as the wounded body and abandoned lean-to of chapter 1. We have also seen a longer example in 3:16–4:1, where Jerusalem is compared to a beautiful and haughty woman. Here, in one sense, the author sums up everything he has said thus far in one powerful image. This image of the vineyard would have special poignancy for the Judean audience that Isaiah is addressing, because grapes is the crop that grows best in Judah.

But, as the illustration makes plain, a grape crop demands a great deal of preparation and care. The land must first be cleared of other plants and then of the rocks that the Judean hillsides produce in abundance (v. 2). This is the work of an entire year. Then the finest vines that one can afford must be purchased and carefully set out. During that second year the cleared rocks must be built into fences and watchtowers in order to keep out marauders, both four-footed and two-footed. Finally, in the third year, the fruit of all the previous labor is ready.

It is easy to imagine the Judean farmers being right with the speaker as they anticipate the sweet harvest. And it is also possible to imagine their outrage when they are told that for all that effort, the outcome is only bitter grapes (v. 2). So when Isaiah announces that he is going to tear down the wall and let the wild animals in and even pray the heavens to stop raining on that vineyard (vv. 5–6), we can imagine the hearers shouting, "Yes, do it!"

Explanation of the Vineyard (5:7–24)

BUT LIKE THE religious leaders to whom Jesus told the story of the wicked tenants (Luke 20:9–19), the hearers suddenly realize Isaiah is talking about them: "The vineyard of the LORD Almighty is the house of Israel." In the succeeding verses Isaiah tells his hearers what those bitter grapes are. He begins with a general statement in verse 7 and then gives the specifics in a series of "woes" in verses 8–24. Verse 7 contains two wordplays in Hebrew that are not apparent in English. The word for "bloodshed" (*mišpaḥ*) sounds like the word for "justice" (*mišpaṭ*), and the word for "cries" (*ṣᵉᶜaqah*) sounds like the word for "righteousness" (*ṣᵉdaqah*). Thus the poet underlines the contrast between what was expected and what was actually received.

Five specific behaviors are condemned in verses 8–24, each introduced with the word "woe." This is a word associated with funerals. A slightly more contemporary, though still archaic equivalent, would be "alas." "Woe" is a word that speaks of sorrow, regret, and anger. A death lies ahead, all the more tragic because it is so unnecessary. The woes describe the sins of the people in relation to the kinds of lives God had called for them to live in the Sinai covenant. These sins include greed (vv. 8–10), self-indulgence (vv. 11–17), cynicism (vv. 18–19), moral perversion (v. 20; also v. 21), and social injustice (vv. 22–24).

Although there is an overall conclusion to the chapter in verses 25–30 (where the consequences of these actions are spelled out), several of the woe passages also include a statement of consequences. The most prominent of these is found in verses 13–17, but they also appear in verses 9–10 and 24. Clearly the people feel as if they can live in all these ways and still escape the consequences because of their relation to God. But Isaiah is saying that is foolish. There are consequences in life. Just as the vineyard of bitter grapes will be destroyed because of what it produced, so will Israel.

Greed. The particular expression of greed addressed in verse 8 is greed for bigger houses and more land. The rich man buys more and more land, dispossessing the former owners one by one until at last he lives alone on a vast estate, with the former owners as his serfs. This kind of sin was particularly offensive to God because in the covenant God retained ownership of the land, giving it in the form of grants to his servants. These grants were not absolute possessions to be disposed of at will, but they were to be maintained in the respective families for all time.¹ This not only reinforced the idea of dependence on God, but it also guaranteed both a sense of worth and a means of subsistence for the small landowner.

In verses 9 and 10 God announces a punishment that fits the crime. Just as the rich man has dispossessed others, he will be dispossessed, and all the land he has acquired will produce almost nothing. Undoubtedly, the Exile is in view here, as it is throughout the chapter.

Self-indulgence. The "bitter grape" given most attention is the one of self-indulgence (vv. 11–17), and much of the passage is the announcement of judgment on this behavior. The real issue here is one of attention. Clearly, the God of the Scriptures is not opposed to physical pleasure. Isaiah himself depicts the final scene of history as a vast banquet that God has prepared for all peoples on earth (25:6). This idea is continued in the New Testament with the wedding feast of the Lamb (Rev. 19:7–9). So this is not an attack on all physical enjoyment. Rather, it is attacking the paying of attention to these things as if they are the only things that matter. Instead of paying primary attention to God and his "work" (Isa. 5:12), they are giving that attention to things that are all passing away.

Once again, the punishment fits the crime. As these wealthy and noble people have focused on what goes down their throats, the day will come when nothing goes down (v. 13). And just as they have opened their mouths wider and wider to take in more, so death will open its mouth yet wider still and suck them all down.² It is clear that the wealthy and mighty are especially in view because verses 15–16, using language directly reminiscent of 2:6–22, speak of the humiliation of the arrogant, while the greatness and holiness of God is manifested in his justice and righteousness. Verse 17 depicts the sheep that once provided the expansive meals for "the rich," now feeding quietly among the "ruins" of the banqueting halls of the rich.

Cynicism. From the more "fleshly" sins of greed and indulgence, the prophet proceeds to the underlying attitudes that both precede and follow the sins of the flesh. The first of these attitudes is cynicism that dares God to take action (vv. 18–19). The precise meaning of the phrase "cords of deceit" is not clear, but the general intent is. These are people who delight in sinning, who seek out ways to do it more aggressively, all the while insisting that if such a course of action was so bad, the great God, this

---

1. See Lev. 25:23–30; Num. 27:1–11.
2. The Heb. word translated "grave" here is *šᵉʾol* (often written in English as "Sheol"), which refers to the underworld. The Old Testament does not have a fully developed view of the afterlife. It is generally not viewed as a place of reward but as a shadowy, dusty place where the spirits of the dead exist (cf. Isa. 14:9–11). See E. Merrill, "שׁאוֹל," *NIDOTTE*, 4:6–7.

"Holy One of Israel" Isaiah keeps going on about, will certainly take some action against it. In the meantime, they intend to keep right on pleasing themselves at all costs.

Moral perversion. The fourth woe (vv. 20–21) takes the situation one step further. Now it is not merely daring God to condemn sin. Rather, it is declaring that there is no such thing as sin, that in fact what was previously declared to be wrong is actually right and that what has been considered right is actually wrong. Such persons have dismissed God from the picture entirely. They are so wise that they can make up their own morality. Oddly enough, this new morality takes the shape of direct opposition to what had been God's standards. It is not a matter of simply picking and choosing, but a specific contraversion of what had been declared right and wrong. This suggests that what is going on is not merely asserting one's right to choose one's own moral conventions, but is rather a revolt against any moral authority at all.

Social injustice. The final woe (vv. 22–24) comes back to matters of practice and, in so doing, links all of the sins together. The prophet speaks ironically of those who are great at what does not matter (mixing drinks) and therefore neglect what does matter—justice. The nobility of Judah, instead of standing up for truly noble causes, have turned to ignoble pursuits. They give prizes not to those who defend the helpless but to those who can drink the most liquor before going under the table. They are small in the great things and great in the small things.

This is not accidental. If the goal of one's life is to take care of oneself, then serving one's own appetites and perverting justice in order to do so are as logical as any mathematics. What has happened? The people have rejected the instruction (NIV "law," Heb. *torah*) of the One being who stands outside of time and space, the One being in the universe who has the right to be called "Holy," the One who has yet condescended to give himself in covenant to Israel (v. 24b). That is, the people have rejected the instruction of the One being in the universe who is in a position to give such instructions. The only permanence humans have is in relation to the transcendent Creator, so it should not be surprising to them if, having rejected him, they are swept away like dry grass in a brush fire (v. 24a).

The Calling of the Enemy Nations (5:25–30)

IN THESE CLOSING VERSES of chapter 5, the intimations of exile in the preceding verses are brought together and made explicit. The vineyard has produced the bitter grapes of greed, self-indulgence, cynicism, moral perversion, and social injustice, and there is nothing left but to tear down the walls and call the animals in to trample the useless vines and strip off their leaves. Isaiah makes it clear that the coming destruction is not merely because the Mesopotamian powers of Assyria and Babylon are so great. In one way their greatness and power has nothing to do with it. No, it is not these military and political powers to which Israel must come to terms. It is God's moral character.

To underline this point, Isaiah uses a refrain he will repeat again several times in 9:8–10:4: "For all this, his anger is not turned away, his hand is still upraised" (5:25b). Why are these great powers coming? Merely as an expression of their own imperial ambitions? No, they are instruments in the hands of God, being used to enforce the logical consequences of a continued pattern of covenant-breaking. They come in response to his signal "banner"; they respond to his "whistle" like obedient dogs (5:26).

In 5:27–29 Isaiah uses short, terse couplets to create a sense of urgency and impulsion. The great army comes on with unstoppable speed. Everything is in readiness, every weapon ready to be used against these people who have become God's enemies (1:24). They had claimed for themselves the right to say what was light and what was darkness. Now they will be treated to the folly of such claims, when genuine light becomes genuine darkness (see 8:20–22 for the same thought).

THE POWER OF STORY. What we find in this chapter is the power of the well-told illustration. That power disarms us. When someone tries to make a point to us, we already have our guard up, thinking about the ways this idea might apply to us in uncomfortable ways. But with stories we lower our guard and simply enter into the experience. Sometimes we find ourselves forced to embrace ideas we never would have otherwise. That is what happened to David when Nathan told him the story of the poor man and his one lamb (2 Sam. 12:1–6). All the justifications David had created for his outrageous immoral behavior were blown away in an instant. The religious leaders of the Jews had the same experience when Jesus told the story of the wicked tenants. They had unconsciously admitted the logic of the argument before they realized there was an argument going on.

The point here is that we do not belong to ourselves. We are the workmanship of someone else. If that is so, that someone else had some purpose in mind for us when he worked on us. And if *that* is so, that person has a right to expect that his workmanship will yield the results he planned. If it does not, he has the right to do with his work whatever he chooses. The real issue, then, is whether we are the work of someone other than ourselves.

The Hebrews admitted this point, at least officially, but in practice many of them acted as if that were not so. So Isaiah is seeking to get them to recognize the illogical position in which they are living. If there is a God and if he is the sole Creator of the universe, then he has the right to expect us to live in accord with his purposes and character, especially if he has revealed them to us in the context of a mutual covenant.

Sins of the flesh and sins of the spirit. The particular behaviors that Isaiah chooses as expressions of the "bitter grapes" in Israel's life seem significant. They begin and end with social injustice. The astounding truth of the covenant is that how we treat each other is perhaps the most significant indicator of our relationship to God. This can be seen in the shape of the Ten Commandments, in which only four have to do with obviously "religious" behavior whereas fully six are behaviors that no one in the ancient world would have said have anything to do with one's relationship to the divine. But for God they do. If we are to be in a relationship with him, we must agree to treat one another fairly and with fundamental respect, recognizing that a person's life, possessions, reputation, and marriage are inviolable. This is so because God is a person and this is how he treats persons. If we are to be in a relationship with him, we must act as he does.

But how is such a thing possible in a world of limited resources? Only if we have committed our needs to a just and loving heavenly Father. Thus, all of the sins identified here have to do with the failure to admit that there is someone outside of ourselves who has the right to establish the parameters of our existence. It begins with simple greed, the desire for more, coupled with the failure to recognize that our desires are fundamentally insatiable and that the only way to control them is a conscious decision to stop. This is directly related to self-indulgence. If there is truly no one superior to our desires, then who can say when enough is enough? Comfort, pleasure, and security are absolute goods, and whatever seems to increase them cannot be spoken against.

But the more or less unconscious sins of greed and self-indulgence (sins of the flesh) grow out of a deeper attitudinal sin (sins of the spirit). These sins are the crystallization of what is implicit in greed and self-indulgence: My needs are all-important, and I have an absolute right to meet them as I see fit. The cynicism about God emerges as it becomes clear there is a conflict between what I want and what God's revealed will is. If there is no submission of my needs and myself to God at that moment, cynicism about him is the logical next step: "If God doesn't like what I am doing, let's see him stop it."

The next step is equally logical. It is the insistence that I have the right to determine for myself what is right and wrong. No one knows my needs better than I do myself, so if the will of this so-called God is contrary to my needs as I feel them to be, that will must be false. It is not God's will at all, but the will of some other humans who are trying to use their power to frustrate me. If the biblical understanding of the perversion of the human capacity to form images is correct (Gen. 6:5), then it should come as no surprise that when humans create a moral system of their own, it is diametrically opposite to what the Bible identifies as God's moral system, calling right what he calls wrong, and vice versa.

The direct linkage of self-indulgence and social injustice in 5:22–23 demonstrates an important connection. There cannot be social justice until some persons decide that the meeting of their personal needs must be secondary to having the basic needs of others met. This will never happen until such persons come to the realization that God wishes to meet their needs and can do it better for them than they themselves can. Furthermore, they must commit themselves to the values of God, the builder of the vineyard. This God considers persons to be of absolute worth, and those who belong to him must see persons in a similar light.

The logic of life. Another truth that this passage underlines is the logic of life. This idea is not unique to this place in the book of Isaiah. Indeed, it is a theme that runs especially through chapters 1–39. But it is important to recognize it here. As mentioned earlier, we humans have a peculiarly warped view of the cause-and-effect relationship. We want the relationship to be ironclad when we consider it to work in our favor. But when it works against us, we are incensed. If we are obedient, we expect to be blessed, but if we are disobedient, we expect to be excused.

Isaiah is at pains to disabuse the Israelites of this idea. We cannot break the laws of nature and avoid the effects of that breaking. Neither can we avoid the effects of breaking the laws of the spirit. We were made to live in certain ways, and if we do not live in those ways, the results are predictable. Is there mercy upon genuine repentance? Of course. But has a person who consistently repeats the same sins ever genuinely repented? The Israelites expected to live lives of continuing disobedience, perform certain expensive rituals, and have mercy become the norm (see chapter 1 and the comments there). Isaiah says that is not the way it works.

Lordship of history. The final truth in the passage is God's lordship of history. It is fairly easy for us who have lived in a superficially Christian culture all our lives to give lip service to this idea. However, for Isaiah and the other prophets it was positively revolutionary. It was not that the God of these two little countries, Israel and Judah, on the Mediterranean coast was going to fight it out with the gods of the great empires and come out as the top god. That would have been remarkable enough (and that is what the false prophets asserted). Rather, the true prophets asserted that Yahweh was *already* the Lord of those other countries (their gods being no gods at all), and he was using those nations to accomplish his disciplinary purposes among his people. Given the relative size and circumstances of Israel and Judah compared to Assyria and Babylon, this was an incredible leap of faith. Yet because of it, when the predicted destruction came, the believers were able to survive, knowing that far from having been defeated, Yahweh was behind all of what had happened.

 THE CRISIS OF WORLDVIEW. The Christian church today faces a crisis of major proportions. It is a crisis of worldview. Various thinkers, from Francis Schaeffer to Charles Colson,[3] have alerted us to its coming, but it is now upon us. The issue is as new as today and as old as time. It is the question: Is there any meaning to life outside of myself and the meaning I give it? Our culture has come to the very concerted conclusion that there is not.

The implications of this conclusion are all around us, and they are profound. Like the ancients we recognize the obvious: A culture where lying and stealing are the norm cannot survive. So we give lip service to the prohibition of such behaviors. However, the fact is that a little judicious lying and stealing can help me meet my needs. So a whole society says one thing and does another. For two centuries a Christian ethic has dominated America. That is, we have obeyed the laws of the land because we believed that they fairly represented the laws of the Creator and Savior. We had an allegiance to something outside of ourselves, and so we obeyed the laws even when no one else was looking and even when it was not convenient. We became an unusually law-abiding people, and people from other countries still comment on the fact.

But all that is rapidly changing. We have lost the idea that there is a God outside of myself to whom I owe obedience. As a result, we increasingly obey the laws of the land selectively. We obey only those laws that we think will benefit us individually and those we are forced to. But we have a hard time seeing the personal benefit in most laws, so we are becoming increasingly lawless, because there is not enough force in the world to make a nation of people obey if they do not want to obey. Tragically, we cannot see that we are enjoying the benefits of our ancestors' choices and that the way we are choosing will

---

3. F. Schaeffer, *The God Who Is There* (Chicago: InterVarsity Press, 1968); C. Colson, *Kingdoms in Conflict* (Grand Rapids: Zondervan, 1987).

destroy those very benefits. We think we can gain more comfort, pleasure, and security by serving ourselves at all costs, when in fact the comfort, pleasure, and security we now enjoy are the result of persons who, in obedience to God, voluntarily limited their self-interests in the interest of others.

The challenge to the church is that this kind of thinking is creeping in among us as well. Studies show that Christian teenagers are almost as likely to cheat as are non-Christians. So also more than half of them think that there are no absolute moral standards.[4] Divorces among evangelicals now exceed the national norm.[5] What has happened? We are slowly losing our grip on the idea that there is a Creator whose character is absolutely consistent and who has created humans in his image. We are losing the idea that this Creator has built into his universe certain spiritual principles that are as unchangeable as any of the natural principles.

How has this happened? We are losing the idea of the authority of the Bible.[6] In the end, there are only two ways of knowing. Either we learn from our experience, or we have information given us that is outside our experience. If God is other than the cosmos, we can never discover him from within our own experience. All we will find is ourselves. So if God wishes to be known by us, he will have to reveal himself to us. Is there any reason to think he has done this? Yes, there is. The Bible is unique in all the world.

This is not the place to go into all the arguments supporting that claim, but consider one example: The Old Testament contains the origins of monotheism as a thorough-going doctrine (see the introduction under "The Uniqueness of Yahweh"). The three monotheistic religions in the world— Christianity, Judaism, and Islam—all go back to that single source. The same is true of many other doctrines. There is no adequate explanation of them apart from the one the Israelites give us: revelation.

Now the church in the West is locked in a do-or-die struggle. Of course the church will survive; that is a given. But will the church *in the West* survive? It will not if we allow the authority of the Bible to be taken from us. That is our only reason for existing. Why is greed wrong? Why is self-indulgence wrong? Why is it wrong to make up our own moral code? Why is it wrong to deprive the poor of justice? In the end, there is only one answer. They are wrong because the one Creator of the universe says so. They are wrong because that is not the way he acts and because he did not make us to act in those ways.

No other argument is sufficient. All of the utilitarian arguments will fall

---

4. J. McDowell and B. Hostetler, *Right From Wrong* (Dallas: Word, 1994), 8–9.

5. G. Barna, *Boiling Point: It Only Takes One Degree* (Ventura, Calif.: Regal, 2001), 42.

6. Donald Bloesch, "Whatever Happened To God," *Christianity Today* 45 (Feb. 5, 2001): 54.

short. Why shouldn't I grab all I can? The commercials tell me I owe it to myself, and after all, life is short. You only go around once, and then the lights go out. Why shouldn't I lie? It pays off better than the truth does most of the time. To be sure, it makes life a little more challenging because you have to remember which lie you told to which person, but then nobody said life was easy. And as for the helpless, well, we will take care of them because they have their "rights." But those "rights" mean nothing when they conflict with convenience (the unborn) or expense (the aged).

In the end, unless the authority for moral behavior lies beyond ourselves, wrong will rapidly become right, and right will become wrong, as we see happening apace in our society. So insistence that homosexual behavior is wrong becomes an act of hatred or fear. The "nuclear family" is said to be one of the main sources of paranoia and oppression.[7] Self-sacrifice is stupid, and marital faithfulness is banal, if not hypocritical.

Thus, it is incumbent on the church to reaffirm and strengthen our commitment to the authority of God's revelation. If we compromise on this issue, we will have lost our reason to exist. The salt will have lost its saltiness indeed (Matt. 5:13), and we will deserve the logical conclusion Jesus declared: being thrown out.

Submission and sacrifice. Fundamental to this entire discussion is the issue of submission. In his book *Before Philosophy* Henri Frankfort says that the Hebrews replaced the pagan myth of nature with the myth of the will of God.[8] We may argue with him over his definition and use of the term *myth* (he basically means "religious system"), but his observation is acute. The religions of the peoples surrounding Israel saw the meaning of life in the recurring cycles of nature, where there was neither purpose nor goal but only the exercise of power. But the Israelites understood that God had a purpose for human life outside of those recurring cycles and that it had to do with how they lived their lives. This is the same point that the apostle Paul makes in the well-known opening sentences of Romans 12:1–2:

> Therefore, I urge you, brothers, in view of God's mercy, to offer your bodies as living sacrifices, holy and pleasing to God—this is your spiritual act of worship. Do not conform any longer to the pattern of this world, but be transformed by the renewing of your mind. Then you will be able to test and approve what God's will is—his good, pleasing and perfect will.

---

7. It is interesting to see the regression in the depiction of the family on television from *Ozzie and Harriet* to *Leave It to Beaver* to *All in the Family* to *The Simpsons* to *Seinfeld* and *Friends*, where the family ultimately disappears. Cynicism has become the norm.

8. H. Frankfort, *Before Philosophy* (Chicago: Univ. of Chicago Press, 1949), 244.

God has an intentional will for his people. He intends that they live in a certain way that is the result of a spiritual decision affecting how they conduct their bodies. This decision involves sacrifice, the conscious giving up of something to God, and it will lead them to live in ways that are contrary to the way the rest of the world lives. Paul is saying nothing here other than what is found throughout the entire Old Testament. The difference for Paul is that now a whole new motivation for the sacrifice has been revealed: the incredible self-sacrifice of God on our behalf in his Son.

But exactly what is it that we are to sacrifice? What is the something we are to give up to God? Genesis 2 makes it perfectly clear. We are to surrender two things: our right to decide what is right and wrong for us, and our right to supply our own needs for ourselves. Because our first mother and father refused to make that surrender, what Paul calls "the pattern of this world" was firmly established. It is the pattern of pleasing myself by satisfying my desires at all costs and of determining what is right and wrong for me on the basis of what I believe will most nearly achieve that satisfaction.

By contrast, we see another way in the stories of the patriarchs Abraham and Joseph (Gen. 12–50). If we surrender the supplying of our needs to God, we will no longer need to be grasping, self-serving people. We see an Abraham voluntarily giving up the best land to his nephew Lot (13:5–12), and we see a Joseph who chooses to be chaste under enormous pressure (39:8–9) and who is delivered from hating his brothers for what they did to him (50:17–21). Here is the victory over greed, self-indulgence, cynicism, moral perversion, and social injustice. We surrender our lives to God, knowing that he will supply our truest needs in better ways than we ever can, as we submit to his will and walk in it.

In this walk, however, we must be careful not to demand immediate results. For instance, Isaiah spoke of the logical consequences that follow from disobedience to God's will. But while the exile of Israel occurred within Isaiah's lifetime, the exile of Judah did not actually occur for another 150 years. It would have been easy for some of those to whom Isaiah was speaking to retort that if there are such logical consequences to sin, where were they? In fact, that may be exactly what prompted the people referred to in 5:18–19 to say what they did.

The writer of Psalm 73 seems to have had a similar experience when he was moved to ask why the wicked seemed always to prosper. In that case, as well as in Jesus' parable of the wheat and the weeds, the answer is to take the long view. So in Psalm 73 the writer says that he was saved from betraying God's people (denying God's moral logic) by taking the long view and seeing the final destiny of the wicked from God's perspective (73:15–17). Jesus says much the same thing when he says that the weeds will be permitted to flourish until the final harvest, when they will be separated out and cast into the fire (Matt. 13:24–30).[9] There are consequences to sin, but they are administered in God's time, not ours. Thus, we must not only surrender our needs to God as we choose to live within his will, but we must also surrender the outcomes to God, secure in the knowledge that those outcomes are certain, but they are in his time.

9. See also Mal. 3:14–4:6.

Isaiah 6:1–13

I N THE YEAR that King Uzziah died, I saw the Lord seated
on a throne, high and exalted, and the train of his robe
filled the temple. ²Above him were seraphs, each with six
wings: With two wings they covered their faces, with two they
covered their feet, and with two they were flying. ³And they
were calling to one another:

> "Holy, holy, holy is the LORD Almighty;
> the whole earth is full of his glory."

⁴At the sound of their voices the doorposts and thresholds
shook and the temple was filled with smoke.

⁵"Woe to me!" I cried. "I am ruined! For I am a man of
unclean lips, and I live among a people of unclean lips, and
my eyes have seen the King, the LORD Almighty."

⁶Then one of the seraphs flew to me with a live coal in his
hand, which he had taken with tongs from the altar. ⁷With it
he touched my mouth and said, "See, this has touched your
lips; your guilt is taken away and your sin atoned for."

⁸Then I heard the voice of the Lord saying, "Whom shall I
send? And who will go for us?"

And I said, "Here am I. Send me!"

⁹He said, "Go and tell this people:

> "'Be ever hearing, but never understanding;
> be ever seeing, but never perceiving.'
> ¹⁰ Make the heart of this people calloused;
> make their ears dull
> and close their eyes.
> Otherwise they might see with their eyes,
> hear with their ears,
> understand with their hearts,
> and turn and be healed."

¹¹Then I said, "For how long, O Lord?"
And he answered:

> "Until the cities lie ruined
> and without inhabitant,

until the houses are left deserted
    and the fields ruined and ravaged,
[12] until the LORD has sent everyone far away
    and the land is utterly forsaken.
[13] And though a tenth remains in the land,
    it will again be laid waste.
But as the terebinth and oak
    leave stumps when they are cut down,
    so the holy seed will be the stump in the land."

AS I STATED in the introduction (see Authorship and Date), I believe the first six chapters of the book are not in chronological order of their writing. Rather, they have been placed in this order so that Isaiah can make a theological point: If the "people of unclean lips" (6:5) can have the same experience that he, the "man of unclean lips" had, then the dilemma Isaiah sees in Israel, and which he expresses in chapters 1–5, can be solved. That dilemma is: How can the present corrupt, rebellious Israel (as expressed in Judah), defying God's instruction, ever become the promised clean, obedient Israel from whom all the nations will learn that instruction? By placing his call narrative in the unusual place where it is, Isaiah is holding it up as a model. Just as he was enabled to bear God's message to his people, so, by the same process, Israel will be enabled to bear God's message to the world.

This narrative is tightly organized, without a single wasted word. It begins with a vision of God (6:1–4), in which his majesty, transcendence, and holiness are emphasized. There follows Isaiah's cry of dereliction, in which he testifies to the terrible self-knowledge that has come because of the vision (6:5). He recognizes that what separates him from God is not finitude but moral corruption, and he knows that such corruption cannot coexist with the God who has been revealed to him. But, amazingly, God is not willing for Isaiah to be destroyed, because one of God's flaming ministers comes to the prophet with a blazing coal from the altar. With it he cauterizes Isaiah's lips and pronounces him clean (6:6–7). Only then is the voice of God heard asking in a rather off-handed way who might be willing to carry a message for him.

Isaiah, exulting in the new-found cleanness of his lips, makes himself available to go (6:8), and God responds with a shocking commission: Isaiah is to speak a message that will harden the people's hearts and prevent them from being healed (6:9–10). When Isaiah asks how long he is to go on preaching in this way (6:11a), God's response is even more frightening. He is to preach until the whole nation is like a field of burned-out stumps (6:11b–13). But at the very end of verse 13, there is an enigmatic glimpse of hope when it is said, "the holy seed will be the stump in the land."

The passage contains a number of exegetical issues that can only be touched on here.[1] First of all, it should be noted that the careful dating of the experience cannot be accidental. In a document this terse, no merely casual information is included. So why is it significant that Isaiah's call occurs in the year King Uzziah dies? I believe it is because it is with Uzziah's death that Judah's truly hopeless situation emerges.

The date is approximately 740 B.C. By this time the Assyrian emperor Tiglath-Pileser III has clearly established himself as a military conqueror to be feared. But it seems likely that for Judah, as long as the powerful Uzziah was on the throne (even with his son Jotham acting as the front man), the immediacy of the threat was blurred. But when Uzziah was removed from the scene, the danger could no longer be ignored. Jotham was no strong man, and possibly Jotham's son Ahaz was already under the control of a pro-Assyrian party in the government. What could possibly be done? Isaiah's vision, at least for him, was a reorienting of his moral compass. The king was dead? Who is the king in this world anyway? "My eyes have seen the King, the LORD Almighty!" (6:5).[2]

As already noted, the images and language used to describe God emphasize majesty ("seated on a throne"), transcendence ("high and exalted," "the train of his robe filled the temple," "the temple was filled with smoke"), and holiness ("Holy, holy, holy"). In the ancient Near East "holy" was not used especially widely, and when it was used, it was not given special prominence. It merely denoted that which sets deity, and that which belongs to deity, apart from the common. It had no moral connotations—and could not, given the variety of moral behaviors among the gods.

But for the Hebrews, the idea of the holy was decidedly different. Beginning with Exodus 6:3 and continuing on through 19:6 and throughout the entire Old Testament, the word "holy" is given special prominence in describing Israel's God, occurring in all its forms more than eight hundred times. This is as it should be, for the people of Israel had learned that there is only one being who is truly other than this world, and they had learned that it was his character, even more than his essence, that set him apart from us humans.

This is why Isaiah knew there was no hope for him once he had heard the seraphs describe the Lord as the absolutely Holy One (the triple "holy"

---

1. See Oswalt, *Isaiah 1–39*, 170–91 for a full discussion.

2. The title "the LORD Almighty" is a favorite of Isaiah's as well as several of the other prophets. Literally it is "the LORD of Armed Hosts" and denotes Yahweh as the leader of a mighty heavenly army. Thus it speaks of God's incomparable power (see 2 Kings 6:17).

expresses the superlative). He knew that his character was utterly unlike that of the Holy One. If there were any question whether "unclean" had moral connotations (after all, altars and ceremonial vessels could be "unclean" too), all doubt is dispelled when, after touching Isaiah's lips with the coal, the seraph pronounces that Isaiah's "guilt" has been "taken away" and his "sin atoned for."

But why does Isaiah say that his lips are unclean? Why not his heart? Two suggestions may be offered. (1) It may be that the lips are being referred to as the evidence of what is really in the heart.[3] What is actually emerging in Isaiah's life shows that whatever he might say about his heart, it is unclean. James refers to the "tongue" in this way (James 3:9–12), as Jesus also does the "mouth" (Matt. 15:18). (2) But a related possibility is that having just heard the golden tones of the seraphs, Isaiah knows that his lips, having been used to praise himself, put others down, and generally serve his own ends, could never be used in such holy service. This relates closely "the tongue" to the whole idea of commissioning and seems the most likely use here, insofar as it to some extent includes aspects of the first possibility.

Isaiah sees his situation as being so hopeless that he does not even bother to ask for cleansing or deliverance. But here he underestimates the grace of God. God has not given him this vision in order to annihilate him, and he does not bring the fire in order to destroy the offending lips. Rather, as would be true for the nation, he brings these terrifying things into the prophet's life in order that, having seen the truth of God and of himself and having received the gracious provision of cleansing fire, he might be delivered into his true vocation.

The tone of the divine question deserves some comment. Isaiah 6 is the only instance of a prophetic calling where there is no direct call. There is no obvious explanation why this is so. It may be that the especially difficult nature of the assignment called for a volunteer rather than a conscript, but none of the true prophets had an easy assignment. At any rate, the prophet's experience of the divine grace clearly puts him in a position where he wants to be of service to this holy Sovereign of the universe.[4]

But note the surprising nature of the commission. Does God truly not want his people to be healed? Has he predestined them for destruction? That would surely be a misreading of the book as a whole. God clearly does want

---

3. The technical literary device used here is *metonymy*, where the name of one part is used to designate the whole.

4. The "us" in 6:8 may refer to the heavenly council (see Jer. 23:18–22). However, it is important to distinguish this from the "divine council" of the pagan religions. There all the gods and goddesses come together to make decisions. The high god may "chair the meeting," but his wishes are as often as not overruled. This is not the biblical picture. There the angels, called the "sons of God" in Job 1:6, like the seraphs here in Isaiah, exist simply to do the bidding of the One alone who can be called God.

to heal his people and promises to do so. If nothing else, the promises of chapters 2 and 4 make that clear. But those promises are not alone. They are representative of many other promises throughout the book.

So what could Isaiah 6:9–10 possibly mean? Perhaps the point is this: Suppose Isaiah had chosen to be among the false prophets; suppose he had preached a message of affirmation and encouragement that did not address the people's sin directly. It is possible he could have gained a large number of followers, people who were "healed" and convinced that they ought to make more of a place for "God" in their lives. But would this superficial healing have any long-term effects on the destiny of the nation? Only detrimental ones! And we can be sure we would never have heard of that Isaiah.

Rather, Isaiah is called upon to preach a message that, given the already-hardened hearts of his generation and several of the following, will only push them farther away from God. But some will turn, among them faithful followers of Isaiah, who will preserve his words until the day when the cauterizing fires of the Exile fall and there will finally be a generation willing to listen. Then real healing will result, and the stage will be set for the promised Messiah to come. So Isaiah's calling is not to success as the world counts success, but to faithfulness. And because he accepts that difficult commission, we still read his book twenty-seven centuries later.

This understanding also illuminates the enigmatic final sentence of the narrative. The only hope of healing for these people is in near total destruction. It is only when all is lost that a scrap of hope appears. There is no other way. If these people are allowed to continue as they are, there really is no hope. Their religion is already half-pagan, and if they are allowed to continue, they will ultimately be completely pagan and all of the revelation will have been for nothing.

But God is not going to allow that to happen, either to his revelation or to his people. So the cleansing must be frighteningly thorough. But afterward, when the forest has been felled and even the remaining stumps have been burned, one of those stumps will still have life in it. There seem to be two possible referents for "holy seed." One is to the Messiah. The promises of Genesis 3:15 and 22:18 seem to point in this direction. Also the references to tree parts to describe the Messiah in Isaiah lends support ("branch," *ṣemaḥ* [4:2]; "shoot," *ḥoṭer*, and "branch," *neṣer* [11:1]). However, the fact that the word rendered "stump" in "stump of Jesse" in 11:1 is *šereš* instead of the *maṣṣebah* as here in 6:13 prevents us from saying that the connotation of Messiah is certain. The other possibility seems slightly more likely, that it refers to the remnant, the people of God. The recurring use of "seed" to refer to Abraham's descendants in Genesis supports this idea. In any case, there is hope that the nation will survive in some way.

Bridging Contexts

THE OVERALL MESSAGE of this narrative needs little translation to make it intelligible for our day. However, there are a few points that should be commented upon. (1) The pattern of the events is important. The process of becoming a servant of God begins in our recognition of the hopelessness of our situation. It continues in an adequate recognition of the character and nature of God. That will necessarily result in a shattering recognition of the impossible gulf between us and God—the gulf of our sinfulness. But that makes it possible to recognize and receive the incredible and undeserved grace of God that cleanses us. Then at long last we are ready to get a glimpse of the heart of God and to offer ourselves to him in service. But that experience of grace is not in order that we can win the praise of humans or even necessarily to fulfill our own dreams. It is in order that we can be faithful to the call of God no matter where it takes us. Far too many sermons on Isaiah 6 end at verse 9 with "Here am I. Send me." To be faithful to the full intent of the chapter, we must preach the entire passage.

(2) A second issue is the meaning of the phrase "the train [or hem] of his robe filled the temple" (6:1). If just the hem of his garment filled the temple, then how big was the throne? And how big was the One sitting on the throne? In other words, words fail to describe the greatness of this God. They can rise no higher than the hem of his robe. This is analogous to the words of the elders in Exodus 24 when they return from feasting with God on the mountain and report that "under his feet was something like a pavement made of sapphire, clear as the sky itself" (Ex. 24:10). Words stop at the pavement. God is utterly outside our categories. To try to describe him in terms of the created world is always to fail. That is why it was necessary for him to translate himself into our terms and come to us as one of us—Jesus Christ.

(3) Throughout the Bible, fire is the symbol of God. The flaming swords of Genesis 3 symbolize his unapproachable holiness that forever barred sinful Adam and Eve from going back to the simple fellowship they once knew. On Sinai, it was a bush that was burning but not consumed. Later it was the fire descending on the mountain. Then it was the fire blazing forth and consuming Nadab and Abihu (Lev. 10:1). There was the fire of Gideon's torches and the fire that fell from heaven, consuming Elijah's sacrifice on Mount Carmel. Fire is destructive, yet cleansing; it is frightening, yet fascinating; it turns mass into energy; what it consumes it leaves dark, but in the process makes light.

In this context it is probable that the word "seraph" connotes "burning one."[5] God's very ministers are flames. Thus, it is entirely appropriate that it

---

5. See R. Wakely, "שׂרף," *NIDOTTE,* 3:1290.

is fire that touches Isaiah's lips. It is not merely that sin must be consumed in his life and that the instrument he would use to declare God's Word must have the dross burned out of it. Rather, it is an encounter with the very person of God himself. Thus too, it is not at all surprising that Isaiah later asks, "Who of us can dwell with everlasting burning?" (Isa. 33:14; see also 10:16; 30:27).

Apparently it was not a major issue to Isaiah which altar the coal came from. It may have been the incense altar before the Most Holy Place. But from what we know of the means of God's grace in the New Testament, it is tempting to think of the coal that touched his lips as a piece of charred, smoking lamb's flesh from off the altar of sacrifice.

SEEING GOD AND SERVING GOD. It is foolish for us to think that we can somehow serve God until we have come to the end of ourselves. As long as we think there is some hope of a human solution to our problems, there is little chance of our genuinely seeing God. Nor is there hope for any of us becoming servants of the living God without there first being an adequate understanding of who he is. As long as I think that I can solve my problems (with a little help from God, of course), then I am the sovereign and he is the servant.

This is the position in which Jacob was between Genesis 28 and 32. Yes, he had seen God in the dream and had gotten a glimpse of both his transcendence and his immanence. But still it is clear that God is only an adjunct to Jacob's plans. It is only when Jacob comes to the end of himself in Genesis 32 that he understands that God is not an adjunct but is Jacob's only hope. It is no accident that having seen God face to face, Jacob can step out in front of his family to meet his fate and see not an enemy, a competitor, a rival in his brother, but "the face of God" (Gen. 33:10).

Only when we come to the end of ourselves are we ready to see God, and that vision is absolutely essential to genuine service. Many years ago J. B. Phillips wrote an influential little book entitled *Your God Is Too Small*.[6] The title says it all. Phillips argued that especially evangelicals with their correct stress on the reality of an intimate, personal relationship with God are in danger of creating a God who exists only to serve them. In the ensuing fifty years since that book appeared, the trend has gone, if anything, in the opposite way from the one Phillips was arguing for. We have made God our "good buddy" in the sky, or a blind, half-senile grandfather who says, "Oh, that's ok, honey," when we mess up. So much of our worship is ultimately about us and the good

6. J. B. Phillips, *Your God Is Too Small* (New York: Macmillan, 1962).

feelings we get when we envision ourselves in the television eye lost in a paroxysm of praise.

As a result, God's grace has become horribly cheapened. It is something he all but owes us, since he knows that basically all of us are pretty good people who just can't help messing up once in awhile. How we need a vision of the blazing holiness of God. How we need to be crushed under the awareness of a Being who is greater than the entire known universe (which is one meaning of "the whole earth is full of his glory," 6:3). How we need to come face to face with a white-hot moral perfection in the presence of which sin cannot even exist. Will "Boomers" and "X-ers" sit still for this? What generation ever has? So will we be like Isaiah, or will we become one of the false prophets?

In part, the answer to that question depends on whether we ourselves have ever had such an experience of God. Should we expect something as Isaiah had? Of course not. God is infinitely creative and hates doing the same thing twice. But we can expect that God wishes each of us to confront the truths about him as Isaiah did.

When we have seen God in that way, we will know that God owes us nothing. We are not "basically nice folks with an unfortunate tendency to mess up." We are proud, arrogant, self-centered, perverse, cruel, violent rebels in whom the stain of sin and sinfulness goes down to the last atom in the last molecule. We do not just "mess up." We "sin" (6:7). That is, we consciously and unconsciously miss the targets God has set up for his creatures. And that sin (Heb. *haṭṭaʾh*) is a result of an inner twistedness (Heb. *ʿawon*) that is both the cause ("iniquity," see 53:6; 61:8) and the result ("guilt," 6:7) of sin. We no more have the "right" to God's love than a bale of hay has the "right" to live in a blast furnace. "Rights" don't enter into the question; the two things are simply utterly incompatible.

There is a strong likelihood that until we come to an understanding of ourselves like this, we will treat the grace of God—his unfailing, undeserved love—as a throwaway item: "Of course God loves me; that's his job." No, it is not his job. It is an unimaginable, unexpected, and, indeed, unnecessary wonder of the universe. If we see God as he is and ourselves as we are, then like Isaiah, it will not even occur to us to ask for continued life. Obviously, it is an impossibility. However, to the eternal praise of God, it is not an impossibility. God has found a way, amazing as it is to think of, to satisfy both his holiness and his love.

Clearly, Isaiah was never able to escape the wonder of this all his life, and we should never do so either. What is that way? Whatever altar the burning coal may have actually come from, we know that the way was the cross. God's death became the means of our life. Here the connection between Isaiah 6 and 53 is unmistakable. How could God possibly restore his people to himself? Yes, they had suffered double for their sins (40:2). But what does that accomplish? Does punishment restore relationship? No, it only satisfies justice—and the only real punishment for sin is death. So how can God keep from simply wiping his people—including us—off the face of the earth? The answer is the Servant who gives his life for his Father's, and his own, loved ones. Does this story grow old and boring for some of us? Do we often think that God is asking too much of us? What does that say about our grasp of what it is Christ has done for us?

If we have the kind of wonder at God's grace that Isaiah had, we will not have to be compelled into his service. Have you ever heard anyone testify that he or she had always wanted to be a preacher of the gospel but that God had forced this person to become an orthodontist? I have not. But we have all heard many people tell how they were dragged kicking and screaming into the Lord's service. Why is that? I suspect it is because we have grown up never really feeling the wonder of having been forgiven of our sins and given new life.

Our Christian calling. And what are the servants of God called to? We need a strong dose of Isaiah 6 to counter the "prosperity gospel" of these days. Which of the true prophets were wealthy and comfortable? Where was the palace Jesus Christ lived in on earth? Which of the apostles died in his own bed? It is amazing that contemporary followers of Jesus and the apostles and prophets can speak of their Christianity as though it were a stock investment. Jesus did not call his followers to take up their portfolios and follow him. Neither did the Father of the Lord Jesus call Isaiah to worldwide success with millions of followers trailing after him wide-eyed, pressing cash contributions upon him.

Where are the Christians today who will leave their worship palaces and their luxury automobiles and their stock options to take up the cross of Christ even in sacrificial giving to the cause of Christ? Where are the young people who will stop looking for careers in sports and entertainment and rather choose, like the gifted cricket player C. T. Studd, to become nobodies in order to tell the broken and the outcast of the holy God who has died for them because he loves them?[7] Of course there are such persons today, and there will be until the Lord returns. But in Christian America there are not enough. The fire has not touched our lips so that we can taste the candy better. Nor has it touched our lips so that we can become golden-tongued orators. Rather, the burning sacrifice of Christ has been laid on us so that we too will be able to lay down our lives for the gracious God and for those who will hear whenever that becomes possible.

---

7. See J. Erskine, *Millionaire for God: The Story of C. T. Studd* (London: Lutterworth, 1968).

That was the kind of faithfulness that marked the apostles. It comes as a surprise to many people to learn that the portion of Isaiah that is quoted most often in the New Testament is Isaiah 6:9—10, the passage about the deafening, blinding, hardening effect of Isaiah's preaching.[8] Clearly the apostles found the experience of Isaiah helpful in making sense of their own. It seems that the more they preached Jesus, the more their own people turned away from him. The more they called for repentance, the more the Jewish people refused to listen. In that sense, they were failures.

Yet this did not cause them to lose hope. They knew the grace they had received, and they knew the call of God on their lives. So, like Isaiah, they were "prepared in season and out of season" (2 Tim. 4:2) to declare God's truth, confident that those who should listen would listen. This is the mandate of modern servants of God as well.

---

8. Matt. 13:14—15; Mark 4:12; Luke 8:10; John 12:40; Acts 28:26—27.

Isaiah 7:1–25

WHEN AHAZ SON of Jotham, the son of Uzziah, was king of Judah, King Rezin of Aram and Pekah son of Remaliah king of Israel marched up to fight against Jerusalem, but they could not overpower it.

²Now the house of David was told, "Aram has allied itself with Ephraim"; so the hearts of Ahaz and his people were shaken, as the trees of the forest are shaken by the wind.

³Then the LORD said to Isaiah, "Go out, you and your son Shear-Jashub, to meet Ahaz at the end of the aqueduct of the Upper Pool, on the road to the Washerman's Field. ⁴Say to him, 'Be careful, keep calm and don't be afraid. Do not lose heart because of these two smoldering stubs of firewood—because of the fierce anger of Rezin and Aram and of the son of Remaliah. ⁵Aram, Ephraim and Remaliah's son have plotted your ruin, saying, ⁶"Let us invade Judah; let us tear it apart and divide it among ourselves, and make the son of Tabeel king over it." ⁷Yet this is what the Sovereign LORD says:

"'It will not take place,
  it will not happen,
⁸for the head of Aram is Damascus,
  and the head of Damascus is only Rezin.
Within sixty-five years
  Ephraim will be too shattered to be a people.
⁹The head of Ephraim is Samaria,
  and the head of Samaria is only Remaliah's son.
If you do not stand firm in your faith,
  you will not stand at all.'"

¹⁰Again the LORD spoke to Ahaz, ¹¹"Ask the LORD your God for a sign, whether in the deepest depths or in the highest heights."

¹²But Ahaz said, "I will not ask; I will not put the LORD to the test."

¹³Then Isaiah said, "Hear now, you house of David! Is it not enough to try the patience of men? Will you try the patience of my God also? ¹⁴Therefore the Lord himself will give you a sign: The virgin will be with child and will give

birth to a son, and will call him Immanuel. [15]He will eat curds
and honey when he knows enough to reject the wrong and
choose the right. [16]But before the boy knows enough to reject
the wrong and choose the right, the land of the two kings you
dread will be laid waste. [17]The LORD will bring on you and on
your people and on the house of your father a time unlike any
since Ephraim broke away from Judah—he will bring the king
of Assyria."

[18]In that day the LORD will whistle for flies from the distant
streams of Egypt and for bees from the land of Assyria. [19]They
will all come and settle in the steep ravines and in the crevices
in the rocks, on all the thornbushes and at all the water holes.
[20]In that day the Lord will use a razor hired from beyond the
River—the king of Assyria—to shave your head and the hair
of your legs, and to take off your beards also. [21]In that day, a
man will keep alive a young cow and two goats. [22]And
because of the abundance of the milk they give, he will have
curds to eat. All who remain in the land will eat curds and
honey. [23]In that day, in every place where there were a thousand vines worth a thousand silver shekels, there will be only
briers and thorns. [24]Men will go there with bow and arrow, for
the land will be covered with briers and thorns. [25]As for all the
hills once cultivated by the hoe, you will no longer go there
for fear of the briers and thorns; they will become places
where cattle are turned loose and where sheep run.

STRUCTURE OF ISAIAH 7–12. One of the difficult
features of Isaiah is deciding whether transitional
passages should be assigned to the previous section or to the following one. This is true for chap-
ter 6. In one sense it is the logical conclusion of chapters 1–5, providing the
answer for the question implicit in those chapters. But in another sense it is
the opening chapter not only of the next section (chs. 7–12) but of the
entire division (chs. 7–39).

As I mentioned in the introduction, all of these chapters are united by the
theme of trust in God instead of human nations. Chapters 7–12, which discuss the consequences of refusal to trust in a specific historic setting, are
directly paralleled by chapters 36–39, where God's trustworthiness is demonstrated in a subsequent and related historic setting. The prophet is attempting to present his people with the vision of God that has come to him, which

is the foundation of all true servanthood. This God, the Holy One of Israel, is great enough and wise enough and transcendent enough that he can be trusted. If Israel can only get that vision of Yahweh, there will be hope for them. But as the Lord predicted, Isaiah's message falls on deaf ears, and his vision is unintelligible to blind eyes. Yet Isaiah is faithful, and all later history is the benefactor of his faithfulness.

In chapters 7–12 the predicted rejection of Isaiah's message is immediate. King Ahaz would rather trust his ultimate enemy Assyria to deliver him from his troubles with Israel and Syria than he would risk trusting God. To this, Isaiah replies with the sign of Immanuel—God with us (7:14–15). Whether Ahaz admits it or not, God is with Israel, and that is not good news if Israel rejects him. So in 7:16–8:22 the prophet talks about the tragic consequences of trusting your worst enemy while trying to leave the transcendent God out of the equation of your life.

Yet, as has been said frequently already, God's ultimate purpose is not destruction. If fearful, distrusting humans have brought darkness on themselves (8:21–22) and if God has let that darkness come, he still does not intend to leave them there. Thus, in chapter 9 the prophet announces that in the very place where the Assyrian depredations started—that is, Galilee—there will God's light dawn. It is the light of a child-king, a descendant of David, who will rule in justice and peace. So there is a double reason to trust God: (1) He is God and there is no other; (2) when we rebel against him, refusing to trust him, and when we reap the results of such a foolish choice, God comes in mercy to deliver. Surely, such a God should be trusted (see 12:1–3).

Thus, Isaiah says in 9:8–10:4, it is not Israel or Syria, nor even Assyria, with which Judah must come to terms. It is the holy God. And what is it about the holy God we must come to terms with? Is it his power, or his sovereignty, or even his will for history? It is none of these. Instead, it is his moral character. If we are not living in keeping with that moral character, we are out of his will and out from under his protection. But if we choose to live in that obedient covenant relationship with him, we need fear nothing.

That is the theme of 10:5–34. In the end, Assyria need not be feared because that mighty empire is only a tool in the hand of Judah's covenant Lord. The Assyrians may arrogantly think that they rule their own destiny, but they do not. The day will come when God will cut them down like a mighty forest. Then he will set up that kingdom promised in 9:1–7. There a Spirit-filled Messiah will rule a "peaceable kingdom," where none will hurt or destroy (11:1–16), and at that time all those exiled to the ends of the earth will return (11:12).

Chapter 12 is a reflection on what all this means about the trustworthiness of God. Surely the God who will not give his people up to final destruction but will deliver them and set them up in a kingdom of the true Davidic monarch can be trusted. More than that, surely his glorious exploits should be told to all the earth.

Isaiah 7:1–8:22 forms the first unit of thought in chapters 7–12. They deal with the immediate, tragic consequences of Ahaz's refusal to trust in God and his turning to Assyria for help. Within this unit, it is possible to further subdivide 7:1–25 from 8:1–22. Chapter 7 presents Isaiah's call for trust (vv. 1–9) and the sign of Immanuel (vv. 10–25). Chapter 8 addresses the effects of Ahaz's bad choice in greater detail.

The Call to Trust (7:1–9)

WHILE WE DO NOT KNOW the precise date of the events described in these verses, it seems probable that they occur about 735 B.C., about three years before the conquest of Damascus in 732 and thirteen years before the destruction of Samaria in 722 (see comments on 7:15 and 8:4). We do not know the specific reason why Syria and Israel are attacking Judah. However, it seems probable that they are attempting to force Judah to join a coalition with them against the Assyrians. It appears that Hezekiah did something similar to the Philistines in 705, when he led a revolt against Sennacherib.[1] It is also possible that Ahaz has already allied himself with the Assyrians, and the kings of Syria and Israel are seeking to punish him for this. (Ahaz calls himself the "servant and vassal" of Tiglath-Pileser when he asks for help in 2 Kings 16:7.)

At any rate, the two neighboring kingdoms are attacking Judah with the express purpose of deposing Ahaz and putting someone named Tabeel on the throne in his place (7:6). It is little wonder that Ahaz and his courtiers are so frightened; they are like "trees . . . shaken by the wind" (7:2).

The exact location of "the aqueduct of the Upper Pool on the road to the Washerman's Field" (7:3) is unknown. But it is evidently just outside the city walls and close enough so that someone standing there and speaking in a loud voice can be heard by those sitting on the wall. We know this because this is the same place where the Assyrian officer stood and demanded the city's surrender thirty-four years later (36:2, 11–15). Most likely Ahaz is looking over the city's water supply in preparation for the coming siege. While there were no fool-proof procedures for breaking into a well-defended, walled city, it was possible to force such a city to surrender if its water supply could be cut off. Ahaz wants to be sure that such a thing does not happen.

Throughout chapters 7–11 children are important figures, and this is especially true in chapters 7–8, where three children are presented, all with

---

1. See *ANET*, 287b.

names symbolic of what Isaiah is predicting. At least two of them are Isaiah's own children. The first is presented here, accompanying his father to confront the king (7:3). This child's name is Shear-Jashub, which means "only a remnant will return." We may wonder if the child was born after the call experience in Isaiah 6, when God gave Isaiah the awareness that the only hope for the future was in a remnant.

At any rate, if Isaiah introduces his son to the king, the conversation may have started off on a rather grim note! However, with God there is always hope. Whatever the more distant future may hold, that does not precondition Ahaz's choices. He can choose to live and act faithfully in his own time and in so doing experience the blessing of God both on his own life and on the life of his kingdom. That is what Isaiah has come to plead with Ahaz to do.

The prophet addresses the king's fearfulness, telling him that it is not necessary (7:4–9). He uses no less than four different terms in verse 4 to address this fear: The king must keep watch ("be careful") over his emotions ("keep calm") and not "be afraid"; fear should not cause his heart, the center of thought, will and action, to grow weak ("lose heart"). The reason Ahaz need not quake in fear is that Rezin of Damascus and Pekah of Samaria[2] do not really pose a threat. For all their bluster they are unable to do anything (7:1). They are just like the burned-out ends of logs remaining around the edges of the campfire when the real fire has gone out. They may still be "smoldering," but there is no genuine fire there, and Ahaz need not fear them.

In the end it does not matter what Rezin and Pekah say (7:5–6). It only matters what the "Sovereign LORD" (lit., "the Lord Yahweh") says, and he says that their threats will amount to nothing. In fact, in "sixty-five years" the northern kingdom of Israel (symbolized here by the dominant tribe in the north, "Ephraim") will not even exist as a people. It is not clear what this sixty-five years refers to. Probably it is a way of saying that within one person's lifetime (by about 670 B.C.) the deportations of the Israelites (beginning in 722) and the importing of groups from other areas in the empire will have completely diluted the genetic heritage of those remaining in the home area of the northern kingdom (this was the Samaria of the New Testament). Far from being a dominating kingdom, they would not even be a people.

Isaiah concludes his appeal to trust God and not to give way to fear with an aphoristic challenge that uses a Hebrew wordplay. He uses two forms of the root ʾmn, which means "to be firm, stable." He says, "If you do not *stand firm in your faith* [ʾmn], you will not *stand at all* [ʾmn]." That is, "if you do not 'make

---

2. The fact that Pekah is regularly called "the son of Remaliah" is probably a way of stressing that Pekah has usurped the throne of Israel. His father Remaliah was not king before him.

firm' (believe), you cannot 'be firm.'"[3] The NIV captures the idea fairly closely. Unless Ahaz puts his faith in God and what God has said through his prophet, then he will have to give way to fear. But if he will firmly believe in God, then he can stand in quiet confidence no matter how desperate the immediate circumstances may appear.

The Sign of Immanuel (7:10–25)

GOD TAKES AHAZ a step further by offering him a sign to prompt faith. It can be of any magnitude that Ahaz likes: high as heaven or deep as hell. In other words, God is asking Ahaz to be daring in reaching out to him in faith. In some ways, this is Ahaz's last chance. Had he picked up the challenge at this point, who can say how his own story and the story of his nation might have been different? That may be one explanation for the extreme nature of the offer: God is "pulling out all the stops" to try to move the Judean king to faith.

But Ahaz refuses the challenge (7:12). Maddeningly, he does so with an appeal to piety. He says that to ask God for a sign would be to test God, something forbidden in the Torah (Num. 14:22; Deut. 6:16). But the testing referred to in the Torah is not believing God's promises! To obey the command of God and step out in faith in his promises is nothing like the rebellions in the desert, where the Israelites doubted God's goodness and essentially dared him to do what he had said he would. Ahaz's supposed piety is only a mask for the same kind of unbelief.

Isaiah clearly recognizes this as he responds with frustration (7:13). Ahaz has already tried his people's "patience," perhaps with the huge tribute he has sent to Tiglath-Pileser (2 Kings 16:8). Now he is trying the patience of God. It is one thing for the people to wonder how much longer they must put up with this pro-Assyrian king, but things move to an entirely different level when God begins to wonder how much longer he must put up with that king. Such a king is on thin ice indeed.

So God says he will give Ahaz a sign anyway. The sign that Isaiah offers (7:14) has provoked endless controversy, largely because of Matthew's identification of its fulfillment in Christ (Matt. 1:23). If it were not for this fact, there appears to be little in the sign itself to arouse such emotion. On the surface the sign seems to be that before a child conceived at the time of the saying is twelve years of age, the two nations that so frighten the house of David will be destroyed (7:16).

---

3. Note that both of the verbs are plural, indicating that it is not only Ahaz who is being called upon to exercise faith here. The fact that 7:13 is addressed to "the house of David" suggests that Isaiah is calling the whole royal family into judgment.

However, there are three factors in the sign itself that raise some question about this apparently straightforward interpretation. (1) God himself urges Ahaz to ask for a remarkable sign. On the surface there seems nothing remarkable about the sign that God actually gives. (2) The second unusual feature is the choice of the word used to identify the mother of the child. The word used is not the normal one for "woman" (*ʾiššah*) or "girl" (*naʿarah*), but a relatively unusual one meaning "young woman of marriageable age" (*ʿalmah*). When we discover that the LXX translates the word with "virgin" (*parthenos*), the mystery is deepened. (3) Finally, the choice of a name for the child is a bit strange since its immediate relevance to the historic situation is not clear, whereas there is a direct relevance in the names of the other two children mentioned (Shear-Jashub [7:3]; Maher-Shalal-Hash-Baz [8:3]). The mention of this second child highlights another oddity. The verbs describing the conception, birth, and naming of that child there are the same as those in 7:14.

Taken together, all of these suggest that there is more going on in this sign than meets the eye and that Matthew has not merely (mis-)appropriated some ancient text for his own purposes, as some modern commentators suggest he did.[4] I believe that the sign as originally given had a single meaning but a double significance. Its meaning is that God is with us and we need not fear what other human beings may do to us. The first significance is for Ahaz's own day. He need not go to Assyria because God is with Judah.

But is that just a sentiment? Is it just a theological assertion, or is it based on fact? Is God *really* with us? The answer to the question is "yes." God has come to take up residence with us as one of us. How has that fact been accomplished? By giving him a human mother but no human father. This is the reason for the use of the ambiguous word *ʿalmah*. In its first significance the virginity of the mother at the time of the announcement of the sign is all that is being intended. Thus, the typical word for "virgin" (*bᵉtulah*) is not used; it would have called too much attention to itself. Yet for the real significance of the sign to be realized, the virginity of the mother at the time of the birth is critical. Thus, the common words for "woman" or "girl" cannot be used.[5]

The fact that *ʿalmah* has the definite article suggests that Isaiah is identifying a particular woman. Some have suggested that this is a wife of Ahaz, who will be the mother of Hezekiah.[6] There are two difficulties with this pro-

---

4. Cf. G. Gray, *A Critical and Exegetical Commentary on the Book of Isaiah I–XXVII* (ICC; Edinburgh: T. & T. Clark, 1912), 133–36.

5. For a full discussion of these issues, see Oswalt, *Isaiah 1–39*, 209–13. On the possibility that in the first significance of the sign "Immanuel" and "Maher-Shalal-Hash-Baz" are the same person, see comments on 8:1–3.

6. See Watts, *Isaiah 1–33* (WBC 24; Waco, Tex.: Word, 1985), 1012.

posal. One is the unlikelihood that Hezekiah could have been born as late as 734 B.C., especially if the 726 date for his accession is accepted. The other is the use of the word ʿalmah itself. There seems to be no reason to use it if the referent is to the queen or a member of the harem. They are already married, and the word does not appear to be used elsewhere of an already-married woman. Another possibility, and one that seems more likely to me in the light of 8:1–3, is that Isaiah is referring to the young woman he is about to marry, who is standing there in the crowd.[7]

At any rate, before this child who is shortly to be conceived is able "to reject the wrong and choose the right" (7:15–16), Syria and Israel will be destroyed. This phrase most likely refers to the age of accountability, the time when, in later parlance, a boy became a "son of the commandment."[8] Although this is now considered to occur at age twelve, there is no precise statement of the age in the Bible. As mentioned above, this suggests that the encounter narrated here takes place by 735 B.C., some twelve or thirteen years before the fall of Samaria and the final destruction of the northern kingdom of Israel.

Commentators are divided as to the significance of the two statements about eating "curds and honey" (7:15, 22). Some see it as a reference to deprivation, since the context of 7:22 suggests the destruction and depopulation of the agricultural land. In other words, all that will be left to eat will be a little curdled milk and some honey. However, while it is correct that 7:23–25 do depict agricultural disaster, the reference itself may have an ironic twist. Typically, curds and honey were the food of royalty, but Isaiah seems to be saying that there will be so few people left in the land after the Assyrian incursions that they will be able to eat like kings on what is left (7:21–22).

In this light, the sign has a double implication. On the one hand, the young boy will see a day when Judah will no longer need to fear either Syria or Israel; they will be gone. But on the other hand, they will have been replaced with something infinitely worse: rampaging Assyria (7:17, 20). In the nearly two hundred years since the division of Solomon's kingdom, there had been no major political changes on the east coast of the Mediterranean. Now all that is to change dramatically as Assyria wipes out nation after nation in a matter of about fifty years (7:17).

Thus, the child is a sign that God is with Judah in two ways, one positive and the other negative. Since God is with them, they need not fear their two small neighbors. But since they have refused to trust God and have instead

---

7. If this suggestion is correct, Isaiah would be a widower at this point, the mother of Shear-Jashub having died.

8. Cf. Gen. 2:17; Deut. 1:39; Isa 5:20.

put all their trust in their worst enemy, they are going to find out what a disastrous mistake that is. To leave God out of the equation of their lives and their planning because of fear is to fall prey to a far worse fear. Ahaz has acted as though God is not and Assyria is, and that is a foolish course of action. It is God's presence that must be accounted for in every decision. Because Ahaz is trusting something else in place of God, he will discover God who *is* with us, bringing the very thing he has trusted against him (7:18–19).

THE LONG VIEW AND THE SHORT VIEW. These verses speak of the difference between the long view (God's) and the short view (ours). The short view will always plunge us into fear and instability, just as it did Ahaz. Ahaz could only see the immediate danger and therefore thought that he had to find a way out by entrusting himself to what was a much greater danger—Assyria. If he had taken the time to listen to God's perspective on the matter, he would have known that the extreme measures he thought he had to take were in fact unnecessary. Because he refused to do what Isaiah urged him to do (i.e., trust God and look at the situation from God's perspective), he was ruled by fear and made a bad decision. Decisions made out of fear will almost always be bad ones. Decisions that grow out of the calmness borne of explicit trust, however, can be thoughtful and reasoned.

Piety and faith. Ahaz demonstrates a profound truth: Piety is not the same as faith. Piety is the appearance of religion while trust in God is the substance of religion. Ahaz does not have the substance and tries to cover this up with a veneer of appearance. Jesus condemned the Pharisees for the same sin. They tithed and prayed and gave charity to the poor, but it was all a show. They were worshiping themselves being pious. True piety follows as a result of trusting in God. There are certain behaviors that reflect a life given over completely to him. To say we trust God and yet refuse to obey his commands is a contradiction in terms. True, it is possible to have genuine trust in God and lack certain evidences of piety, but it is *not* possible to have genuine piety while lacking genuine trust in God.

On the surface of it, the Immanuel sign seems odd. It was not fulfilled in the short term until several years into the future, and it was not fulfilled in the long term for seven hundred years! We should note that most of the kinds of signs offered by God in the book of Isaiah, and indeed in the Old Testament, were not designed to create faith. That is, they were not some supernatural act that made unbelieving people believe on the spot. Rather, they were typically events occurring in the future that would confirm that the faith exercised in the past was correct.

Faith is always faith. It is a step into the unknown. There will be evidence to support it, but there is never advance proof, so that we may take the step of "faith" with no risk attached. That is not faith.

This was the problem with the religious leaders in Jesus' time. They wanted "signs" that would create faith where there had been none, as they understood the signs of the Exodus to have done. As a matter of fact, the Exodus signs did not create faith; witness the entire generation who had seen the Exodus signs dying in the desert, convicted by the failure of their faith to go up and receive the Promised Land. Signs *confirm* faith; they do not create it. That is why Jesus would only give the "sign" of his resurrection (Matt. 12:39; John 2:19). To those who did not believe previously, the resurrection was merely an embarrassment to be explained away. But for those like the disciples, who had already committed themselves to him, the resurrection was a wonderful confirmation of their faith.

The genuineness of predictive prophecy. One of the issues at stake in the Immanuel prophecy is the genuineness of predictive prophecy. It is an axiom of many modern biblical scholars that Bible writers had no more access to the future than any normally perceptive person has today. This means two things: (1) Writings that claim to predict the future were actually written at the same time or even after the events they claimed to predict, and (2) later writers who saw the fulfillment of prophecy in events in their own times were simply making creative appropriation of ancient writings that actually had no reference to future events.

The biggest problem with this view is that it flies directly in the face of the biblical claims. Some who hold such a belief are at least consistent and admit that the Bible has no revelatory value. But what about those who accept those arguments and yet still say the Bible has authority for the Christian church? What authority? The authority of false claims and misreadings? There is no easy middle ground. I will develop this argument in more detail later in this commentary where Isaiah makes it the lynchpin in his argument for the incomparability of Yahweh (see comments esp. on 43:8–13). Suffice it to say here that if there was no intention to speak of the Messiah in Isaiah 7:14, then Matthew is guilty of misusing evidence in his claim that this proves Jesus of Nazareth was the promised Messiah of the Old Testament. If that is so, much of the New Testament claim for the identity of Jesus must be discarded.

At the same time, we should not push the evidence to say more than it does. To say that Isaiah expected a literal fulfillment of "God with us" in the flesh at some future date is not to say that he had anything like a full understanding of the details of Jesus Christ's life. In fact, apart from what was directly revealed to him, he may have had many incorrect expectations for the Messiah. Thus, to say that the book of Isaiah contains many predictions of the coming Son of David that were given as specific predictions and were legitimately interpreted as such by New Testament writers is not to say that the Old Testament prophets had anything like a complete picture. This is the point of Peter's comment in 1 Peter 1:10–12, that the prophets would have loved to see what the people of the first century A.D. saw.

The idea of God's being "with" people is a prominent one in the Old Testament. From the Garden of Eden (Gen. 3:8) to Isaac (26:28) to Joseph (39:2–3) to the tabernacle (Ex. 40:38) to Gideon (Judg. 6:12–13) to David (1 Sam. 18:12, 14) to Asa (2 Chr. 15:9) to Hezekiah (2 Kings 18:7) and to Ezra (Ezra 1:3), the presence of God with his people is the heart of the Old Testament experience. God is not a force or a principle but a person—and a person who wishes to be personally present with his creatures. That presence is protection; it is fulfillment; it is sustenance. When he is not with us, the result is disaster (Num. 14:43). But if he is with us, then life cannot only be endured, it may be triumphed over. But that presence is not only a metaphor; it is a reality. God has taken on himself our flesh, and in that flesh he has taken even our sin into himself. This is why the enfleshed God is to be called "Immanuel"—"God with us."

DECISION-MAKING TIME. We live in a day when good decisions are harder and harder to come by. Thirty years ago the Swedish economist Staffan Linder predicted that as we in the West became more and more productive and therefore had more and more things to consume, time, a fixed commodity that cannot be increased, would become more and more precious.[9] Thus, such time-consuming occupations as relationship-building, romance, child-rearing, and caring for the elderly would have to be radically streamlined, with the latter two being farmed out to the least productive (least expensive) elements in the society. His predictions have proved frighteningly prescient.

Linder made the same observation concerning decision-making. In a society where it is cheaper (less time-consuming) to make something new than to repair something defective, Linder said we would simply make snap decisions and throw away the results of our bad decisions. So we witness the abortion epidemic today. Shall we take a lot of time to get to know one another, and shall we carefully guard our sexuality for the one to whom God guides us? Of course not. That is much too slow. Simply jump into the beds

---

9. Staffan Linder, *The Harried Leisure Class* (New York: Columbia, 1970).

of partner after partner in the hope that one of them will turn out to be Ms. or Mr. Right. Pregnancies? Just throw them away.

Surely there are some decisions that can be made quickly. This is not an argument for paralysis. We can spend so long debating the merits of the alternatives that we never do anything. Rather, this is a plea that we consider the direction of God in our lives as something worth any amount of time we put into it. To do otherwise is to run the risk of deciding for all the wrong motives: self-aggrandizement, fear, passion, or greed.

We need to seek God's Word—something Ahaz did not do. We need to seek it in the Scriptures, in the counsel of godly elders, in the nature of the circumstances, and in our own hearts. What we must avoid at all costs is what Ahaz did, deciding what we want and then asking God if he could not please bless what we want. We need to come to him at the beginning of the process and ask his will with the blankest page possible. When we have the confidence of his word on the subject, we can then go forward with a clean conscience, a courageous heart, and a confident step. If we live in trust in God, even if we do not have a prophet who can tell us exactly what the future holds, we can live in the kind of watchful quietness Isaiah urged upon Ahaz and thus make decisions that are not emotional knee-jerks but thoughtful and reasoned responses.

Piety and faith. Ahaz demonstrates the real danger of piety without faith. It is to have the form of godliness (2 Tim. 3:5) while missing the substance of the relationship. Piety is the by-product, not the end product. Is going to church good? Is having daily devotions good? Is avoiding lust, greed, and self-indulgence good? Is moderate, inoffensive speech good? Is regular, significant giving to the cause of Christ good? Is integrity in all one's dealings good? The answer to all of these is "of course." But are any of them faith in God? The answer is "no."

In fact, these things can be deadly substitutes for faith in God. If I rely on any of these to give me standing with the eternal, holy God, I am building my house on the sand (Matt. 7:26–27). Faith in God is a radical, soul-encompassing surrender to the love of God demonstrated to us in "God with us"—Immanuel. If we are genuinely walking in such a trust relationship, then we will do all those things listed above. But they will be expressions of the relationship with Immanuel, not substitutes for it, as was the case with Ahaz.

At the same time these kinds of actions are valid fruit of a life in God. If they are not present—that is, if I have no love for worship with the people of God, if my mouth is flippant and coarse, if I am ruled by destructive habits, if I use my money first for myself and toss a crumb to God now and then—observers may justly wonder whether I know God at all. So the two are concomitants of each other. But it is the radical faith that is the root, with piety being only the fruit.

God with us. What does it mean for us today that "God is with us"? This is one of the most profound truths in all of Scripture—profound because of the nature of the biblical God. It was not a big thing in the ancient Near East to say that one of the gods was with someone. After all, the gods were a part of the universal system. Just as the air was "with" them, so were the gods. But the biblical God is not part of the universal system. He stands outside of that system. This was one problem the Greek philosophers wrestled with. If there is such a being, then of necessity that being must be utterly separated from his creatures. He could have nothing to do with them because if he did, they would be affecting him, and that could not be.

The Bible does not solve this problem for us; it simply asserts that it is not a problem. God is absolutely other than we, *but* this supreme, all-powerful, all-good, all-caring One is able to enter into fully personal relationships with each of his creatures. This was true throughout the Old Testament, where to say God was with someone was almost synonymous with saying that person was full of the Spirit of God (see Gen. 39:23; 41:38—39). Evidently the Spirit is the agent through whom we experience the presence of God in our lives.

But with the coming of Christ the reality of God's "withness" has taken on a new dimension. Prior to the Incarnation there was a sense in which God could only be alongside us. Now he is able to be *in* all of us in ways that were limited to a select few in Old Testament times. This is what Jesus had in mind when he said that the Spirit was with the disciples and would be in them (John 14:17). His tabernacle is no longer in the center of the camp but in the human heart itself. This means we can walk without fear. If God is in us through the power of the Holy Spirit, then neither the condemnation of our past sins nor the power of present temptation can defeat us. If God be for us, who can be against us (Ps. 56:9; Rom. 8:31)? Nothing that any earthling can do to us can ultimately hurt us, because Immanuel has conquered death. If God is with us, we can dare to have integrity in our dealings with one another and with the world. There is no loss that can overcome the power of the cross of Christ to redeem it.

"God is with us" would be a great truth even if Christ had not come. But it would only be partial in its hope. There would always be the grave, the single most inescapable reality of human experience, the one reality the immortal God could not share or remove if he is just. But God in Christ has gone with us all the way. He has gone with us all the way into the tomb. And having gone in with us, he can bring us out with him. Immanuel!

Isaiah 8:1–22

THE LORD SAID to me, "Take a large scroll and write on it with an ordinary pen: Maher-Shalal-Hash-Baz. ²And I will call in Uriah the priest and Zechariah son of Jeberekiah as reliable witnesses for me."

³Then I went to the prophetess, and she conceived and gave birth to a son. And the LORD said to me, "Name him Maher-Shalal-Hash-Baz. ⁴Before the boy knows how to say 'My father' or 'My mother,' the wealth of Damascus and the plunder of Samaria will be carried off by the king of Assyria."

⁵The LORD spoke to me again:

⁶"Because this people has rejected
    the gently flowing waters of Shiloah
and rejoices over Rezin
    and the son of Remaliah,
⁷therefore the Lord is about to bring against them
    the mighty floodwaters of the River—
    the king of Assyria with all his pomp.
It will overflow all its channels,
    run over all its banks
⁸and sweep on into Judah, swirling over it,
    passing through it and reaching up to the neck.
Its outspread wings will cover the breadth of
        your land,
    O Immanuel!"

⁹Raise the war cry, you nations, and be shattered!
    Listen, all you distant lands.
Prepare for battle, and be shattered!
    Prepare for battle, and be shattered!
¹⁰Devise your strategy, but it will be thwarted;
    propose your plan, but it will not stand,
    for God is with us.

¹¹The LORD spoke to me with his strong hand upon me, warning me not to follow the way of this people. He said:

¹²"Do not call conspiracy
    everything that these people call conspiracy;

do not fear what they fear,
     and do not dread it.
¹³ The LORD Almighty is the one you are to regard as holy,
     he is the one you are to fear,
     he is the one you are to dread,
¹⁴ and he will be a sanctuary;
     but for both houses of Israel he will be
a stone that causes men to stumble
     and a rock that makes them fall.
And for the people of Jerusalem he will be
     a trap and a snare.
¹⁵ Many of them will stumble;
     they will fall and be broken,
     they will be snared and captured."

¹⁶ Bind up the testimony
     and seal up the law among my disciples.
¹⁷ I will wait for the LORD,
     who is hiding his face from the house of Jacob.
I will put my trust in him.

¹⁸ Here am I, and the children the LORD has given me. We are signs and symbols in Israel from the LORD Almighty, who dwells on Mount Zion.

¹⁹ When men tell you to consult mediums and spiritists, who whisper and mutter, should not a people inquire of their God? Why consult the dead on behalf of the living? ²⁰ To the law and to the testimony! If they do not speak according to this word, they have no light of dawn. ²¹ Distressed and hungry, they will roam through the land; when they are famished, they will become enraged and, looking upward, will curse their king and their God. ²² Then they will look toward the earth and see only distress and darkness and fearful gloom, and they will be thrust into utter darkness.

THIS CHAPTER IS a continuation of the Immanuel sign and its implications, introduced in chapter 7. As will be discussed below, there is good reason to think that Isaiah's son Maher-Shalal-Hash-Baz, who is introduced here, was the first fulfillment of that sign. He represents the negative impact of God's presence that results when both king and people have reckoned without that presence.

The material is presented in two sections. In 8:1–10, the circumstances of the child's birth are given and the significance of his name explained. The second section (8:11–22) deals more specifically with what Isaiah's response to the people's blindness is supposed to be (vv. 11–18) and with the manifestations and outcomes of that blindness (vv. 19–22).

Birth of Child and Significance of Name (8:1–10)

WHILE IT IS not clear what the specific intent of writing on "a large scroll" with "an ordinary pen"[1] is, the general intent seems clear enough, especially in light of the witnesses. Isaiah is to write down the child's name even before he is conceived as an evidence of predictive prophecy. This may be taking place before Isaiah marries the mother of Maher-Shalal-Hash-Baz.[2] Heathen gods cannot tell the future since they are as much imprisoned in time as humans are. But God stands outside of time and can declare what is to happen before it happens.

The language of 8:3 (she conceived and bore a son) is similar to that of 7:14 except for the change in tenses. This suggests that the two verses may be referring to the same event. Furthermore, the nature of the sign is the same as that given in 7:15–17 (she will conceive and bear a son). Before the child reaches a certain age, the two nations Ahaz so much dreads will be helpless to do any harm to Ahaz and his nation. When these are coupled with references to Immanuel in verses 8 and 10, it seems to me that there is a strong case for identifying Maher-Shalal-Hash-Baz with the first fulfillment of the Immanuel sign.

If this is so, the child will not be able to speak clearly before Damascus and Samaria have been plundered. If the encounter between Ahaz and Isaiah occurred sometime in 735 B.C. (see comments on 7:1, 15), this expression of the sign points to the destruction of Damascus in 732 B.C. and the stripping away of almost all Israel's territory outside of the areas of Ephraim and Manasseh, which occurred at about this time. It also appears that both Rezin and Pekah died in 732. Thus, if the sign was given in 735, the child would have been born sometime in 734 and would not be speaking clearly by 732, when the sign was fulfilled.

Verses 6–10 encapsulate Isaiah's (and God's) perspective on history. The nations come and go at God's command and serve his plan being worked out through his people. God is with Israel; thus, if Israel tries to live as if that were not so, there will be tragic consequences (vv. 6–8). At the same time, the

---

1. Lit., "the pen of a man."
2. If the supposition is correct that Maher-Shalal-Hash-Baz is the initial fulfillment of the Immanuel sign, then the "young woman of marriageable age" mentioned in 7:14 (see comments on 7:10–25) is not yet married to Isaiah and is not the mother of Shear-Jashub (7:3). Perhaps that child's mother has died. See Oswalt, *Isaiah 1–39*, 219–23, and references there.

nations must never forget that they are but instruments in the hand of the Holy One of Israel. If they think they can wipe out his people in order to achieve their own geopolitical goals, they are mistaken, because God *is* with his people and will achieve his goals through them, regardless of what any other nation on the face of the earth does (vv. 9–10).

As already noted, this fulfillment of the Immanuel sign has a primarily negative aspect. Because Israel and Judah have rejected the presence of the living God, "quick to the plunder, swift to the spoil."[3] Not only is this true for Syria and Israel but for Judah as well. They have rejected the Lord, the "gently flowing waters of Shiloah" (8:6), in favor of Assyria, "the River" (Euphrates) (8:7). As a result, that river will all but drown them (8:7–8). The meaning of "rejoices over Rezin and the son of Remaliah" is not clear, since Isaiah 7 speaks of being terribly afraid of these two kings. Perhaps in this context the meaning is that the Judeans are rejoicing over the apparent success of their alliance with Assyria in destroying their two enemy neighbors.

But such rejoicing will be short-lived. Although God's help seems like nothing but a spring while Assyria looks like a great river, that river can quickly "overflow its . . . banks," and the edges ("channels") of its floodwaters will reach to the farthest corners of the land. Of course, this is exactly what happened some thirty years later when the Assyrian king Sennacherib came against Judah (Isa. 36–37). Any alliance with Assyria was like an alliance with Nazi Germany. They were simply waiting for the day when they could take you too, as Stalin learned to his chagrin in 1941.

But whose land is it that Assyria is going to flow over into? Assyria's? No, Immanuel's (8:8). Here the other side of the sign comes out. If failure to take account of God's presence will bring the swift plundering of the land, that cannot change the fact that it is still the land of "God-with-us." Isaiah addresses the implications of this fact in powerful poetic lines in 8:9–10. He changes what we think of as a normal sequence of events and shocks us with it. Why does one "raise the war cry" or "prepare for battle"? To shatter the enemy, of course. But Isaiah says the result will be the shattering of those who have given the cry, of those who made the preparations. Why does one "devise . . . strategy" or "propose [a] plan"? In order to ensure success. But Isaiah says the strategy and the plan will result in failure. Why? Because like Ahaz, the nations have left out one tiny, but huge, factor: "God is with us."

The People's Blindness and Its Consequences (8:11–22)

WHAT IS TO BE Isaiah's response to all of this? How is he to react to the swirling intrigues all around him? Undoubtedly Jerusalem in 735 B.C. was

---

3. This is the meaning of Maher-Shalal-Hash-Baz (see NIV text note).

like a pot on the boil. Not only was there a resurgent Assyria to worry about; there was the nearer problem of Syria and Israel. Everybody must have had a theory about what was really going on, and everyone had an opinion about what should be done.

In the middle of this whirlpool, God comes to Isaiah with specific instructions. In the first place, he is not to lose his focus on God. He should not be swept off his feet with the latest "conspiracy" theory, and he should not fall into the trap of fear. Unlike his contemporaries, he should not be spending time creating fanciful, unfounded explanations of "what is *really* going on," arising out of the terror of uncontrollable events. Instead, he should focus his attention on serving and pleasing the God in whose hands our destinies reside. The attention to "fear" in 8:12—13 is important. The fear of the unknown is a defiling kind of fear,[4] but the "fear of the LORD" is clean (see Ps. 19:9). This phrase describes a way of life that pays primary attention to learning and obeying the ways of the only one who can truly be called "holy" (Isa. 8:13).

God tells Isaiah that if he gets his attention focused properly, God will be a "sanctuary" (8:14) for him. Regardless of what may be happening all around, the one focused on living for God and pleasing him in all things will have a place of security and confidence. The Holy One will provide a holy place ("sanctuary"; Heb. *miqdaš*), where the one who has focused on God will be at peace. But those who refuse to give God that central place in their lives will find that instead of being a rock of refuge, he will be a "stone" in the road to "stumble" over (8:14).

Here we come again to the dual significance of "God is with us." God's presence is the one inescapable fact of human life. We *will* encounter him in one way or another. Those who make a place for him find him to be the glue that holds everything together. Those who ignore him find their lives to be askew and cannot understand why. They have left out the most crucial factor in the equation of their lives, so that everything will always be unbalanced. The Lord God is either a sanctuary to dwell in or a stone to stumble over. Both Israel and Judah have chosen the latter way. Choosing to pay only ritual attention to God, they are prey to every new fear that comes along. And being prey to their fears, they make all the wrong decisions.

So what should Isaiah do in such a climate? Shall he simply give up in frustration? Or shall he keep hammering away at a people who cannot even understand what he is talking about? The answer is the middle way (8:16—17). He should not give up declaring God's word, but he should do it

---

4. Note the tendency to lose control of the bladder and bowels in the presence of sudden terror.

particularly to disciples who will "bind up" (i.e., treasure) those words for another day when God's face will no longer be hidden from his people. Here Isaiah is a model of the very thing he is calling his people to do. Although he does not see the results he would like to see, still he will be faithful to God and to his calling, trusting God to fulfill his promises in his own way and time.

It is important here to note the synonymous relation between "wait" and "trust" (8:17) in this book and elsewhere in the Old Testament. True trust always involves an element of waiting. It means believing in results that we cannot see. A determination to have the results I want now is a major sign of an inability to trust.

In 8:19–22 we read what happens when people refuse to trust and obey God. They have God's word given to them in the Torah and the Prophets, yet they refuse to consult it. They prefer instead to consult the dead! They go to "mediums and spiritists," whose bizarre and mysterious mutterings are so much more interesting than the austere commands of God to treat one another in holy ways. The result is "distress and darkness" (8:22), which is hardly surprising. What can the creation tell creatures about the meaning and destiny of life? Only, as the philosopher said, that life is short and brutish. Neither nature ("the earth" [8:22]) nor politics ("the king" [8:21]) nor religion ("their God" [8:21]) will be able to shed any light. They have been trusting all these other things instead of the revealed God, and all of them have failed.

Bridging Contexts

DECEPTION AND FALSE HOPES. Verses 1–10 demonstrate that in this world appearances can be deceptive. Although God's help often seems pitifully small in comparison with what the world seems to offer, we should not be deceived. In the end, what seemed so small is destroying what seemed so great (8:9–10). A recurring truth in this part of the book is that God's weakness is greater than all human strength. Therefore he can be trusted, and we should not be deceived by the ephemeral glory of the nations of earth. It is all passing away, faster than we can imagine.

The section is also about the inevitable failure of false hopes. Humans were made with a capacity for trust. But that capacity was intended to find its ultimate residence in the One who does not change, the One who stands outside of time. If we have learned to do that, we will be able to trust those who are less than God, knowing that they may very well fail us, but knowing that if that should happen, all will not be lost. But when we refuse to trust God and instead place ultimate trust in creation, we are doomed to disappointment. When we put anything created in the place of God, it *must* fail, because we are asking something of it that it cannot possibly produce.

Focus on God. Humans have an incredible need to explain matters even when we do not have the data to do so. So we create explanations, which usually involve bad motives on the part of the participants. In the process of creating our conspiracy theories, we become so attached to them that even when the correct data emerges, we would rather believe our theories than the facts. Isaiah calls his people—and us—to focus on God and not on our own, usually spurious, explanations of events. We do not have all the data we need to provide adequate explanations. But we do have all the data we need on what it takes to please God. So Isaiah's word is to focus on what we know and leave what we don't know well enough alone.

It is often suggested that "the fear of the LORD" is an Old Testament concept that modern Christians can do without. After all, 1 John 4:18 says that "perfect love drives out fear." In other words, so the reasoning goes, if you fear God, then you must not really love him. But we need to remember that Jesus says almost the same thing as Isaiah: "Do not be afraid of those who kill the body but cannot kill the soul. Rather, be afraid of the One who can destroy both soul and body in hell" (Matt. 10:28). So what is the proper "fear of the LORD"? The fear of the Lord is awe-filled obedience to the Holy One, who has only to look at us to dissolve us but who instead has loved us and given himself for us. It is to put pleasing him before any other concern in our lives, being fully aware that our relationship to him is the *only* factor in life that will determine our destiny.

God will be a force in our lives in one way or another. He will either be a positive force or a negative one. He cannot be avoided. Either he will be the sanctuary we rest in secure from everything the world can throw at us, or he will be the thing we keep stumbling over. When he is left out of life, life does not work right. Relationships do not work. Laughter does not work. Work does not work. Stimulation does not work. This is the point of Genesis 3:16–19. It is not that a cruel God decided to make everything frustrating to Adam and Eve. Rather, life was made to function with God at the center of it. When we take him out and put ourselves at the center, life simply does not work.

Isaiah models an important principle of ministry that Jesus modeled as well. While he did not stop speaking to the masses and to the political leaders, he concentrated his ministry on a few disciples who were able to receive what he was saying and to transmit it faithfully to succeeding generations.[5] In this way, he had the satisfaction of seeing some success while keeping the

---

5. This model has perhaps been best expressed in modern times by Robert Coleman in his classic *The Master Plan of Evangelism* (Old Tappan, N.J.: Revell, 1956). See also Allan Coppedge, *The Biblical Principles of Discipleship* (Grand Rapids: Zondervan, 1989).

claims of God before the nation and seeking any who might wish to join his followers. Modern youth ministry has picked up this model and is using it with success.

Control over the future. The message of 8:19–22 is self-evident. If God is left out of life's equations, then we must resort to other means in order to feel as if we have some control over life's forces. There is a deep need in us to feel we have some knowledge of, and control over, the future. If the creator God of the Bible is rejected, then we will have to consult other means, and often it is the dead who are considered to have both some interest in their descendants and some access to the world of the spirits. But in fact, the dead know nothing, and the result is a deeper darkness of fear and superstition, as the practitioners of these spiritualist cults resort to sleight of hand, mysterious rites, and then spirit-possession in an attempt to hold their clients.

SUPREME POWER. In our own times we have seen ample evidence of the futility of trusting in human glory instead of in God. Who could have believed in 1875 that in just seventy-five years the mighty British Empire would be dismembered and in ruins? It seemed more eternal than God. But the poet Laureate Rudyard Kipling, asked to compose a poem for Queen Victoria's Diamond Jubilee, saw that reality clearly and wrote a somber piece fittingly called "Recessional." One of its stanzas says:

> Far-called, our navies melt away
> On dune and headland sinks the fire;
> Lo, all our pomp of yesterday
> Is one with Nineveh and Tyre!
> Judge of the Nations, spare us yet,
> Lest we forget—lest we forget!

And the final one says:

> For heathen heart that puts her trust
> In reeking tube and iron shard—
> All valiant dust that builds on dust,
> And guarding, calls not Thee to guard—
> For frantic boast and foolish word,
> Thy mercy on Thy people, Lord![6]

---

6. Rudyard Kipling, "Recesional," *British Poetry and Prose*, ed. P Lieder, R. Lovett, and R. Root (New York: Houghton Mifflin, 1928), 1341.

Kipling saw correctly that it is God who is eternal, not the British Empire. Will any of us in the United States today, supreme in the world and unchallenged in its power, see the same?

More recently, who could have predicted in 1980 that within a decade the mighty Soviet Union that President Reagan so aptly named the "evil empire" would be reduced to a group of small struggling states looking to the West for investment just so they could produce basic needs? Who could have imagined the scene of Western Christian youth handing out Bibles on the streets of Russian cities being almost trampled as people who had been trained as atheists rushed to get a copy? God is still "the gently flowing waters of Shiloah," but those waters are mightier than all the rivers of human dominion.

God at work in history and in our lives. It is interesting to watch the fascination of modern people with so-called "conspiracy theories of history," such as the theories about the assassination of President Kennedy. There are those who seem to know exactly what happened, except that there are others who know it also and know something different. My experience as a college president taught me that many people prefer a twisted explanation of some event to the simple truth.

But Isaiah calls us to give up the fascination with "what really happened." He calls us to believe that God is at work in history and that we can trust him to work all things together for the good of those who are called according to his purpose (Rom. 8:28). We need not worry about who really did this or why. This is not to say we should take no interest in current events, but it is to say that we need not be consumed with anxiety over these events and their causes and outcomes. We should focus on pleasing God, and then we can walk in quiet confidence with him.

The fear of God. Today we do not hear much about the fear of the Lord. In a "feel-good" age we want to hear that God loves us no matter what we do and that he will never leave us or forsake us. Both of those sentiments are profoundly true, and without them there would be no gospel for us to proclaim. However, the corollary that is often drawn from these truths is profoundly untrue, namely, that since God's love is unconditional and since he will not forsake us, therefore how we behave is fundamentally unimportant. Of course, we think, we need to try to do our best, but since we will always sin anyway, we need not expect too much of ourselves. How far this thinking is from the perspective of Isaiah. God tells his people to stop worrying about what the Assyrians and the Syrians and the Israelites are going to do and to start worrying about what *he* is going to do!

This is not just some legalistic Old Testament idea. As noted above, Jesus echoes almost the same words. This is not to say that we should live in shivering terror that God is suddenly going to kill us because he has decided he does not like the way we are acting. Jesus goes on to say that we are worth more to God than the sparrows or the lilies he cares for so prodigally. So what does "fear of the LORD" mean for us? It means we have to reorder our priorities. Instead of asking how we can please ourselves, we must ask how we can please God. Instead of spending all our time worrying about how to take care of ourselves, we ought to be asking how well we are living the life of the One who called us to be holy as he is holy (1 Peter 1:15—16). If we pay attention to this—the main thing—we can trust God to care for us in far better ways than we can ourselves.

Dr. Ben Hayden, pastor of First Presbyterian Church in Chattanooga, Tennessee, tells the story of a businessman whose company built landing craft for the military. A young government inspector let the businessman know that it was standard practice to pay the inspector under the table. The businessman told the inspector, "Son, I can't do that. You see, I fear God, and that's not right." The inspector persisted, pointing out that he would allow the boats to be built much more cheaply than specified if he were paid off. But the businessman also persisted. A few days later the inspector rejected an entire batch of boats, and he told the businessman that either he would be paid or he would destroy the company. The businessman replied, "Son, I fear God, and that means I don't fear you." In the upshot, the company was pushed almost to liquidation but was saved at the last minute by an order for boats from another country, which had come upon some of the rejected boats at surplus and was impressed by their quality. If we fear God, we do not need to fear anything else.

Thus, God will either be our sanctuary or the stumbling block we keep falling over. This is much like the sun as described in Malachi 4. God will rise on us in the last day like the relentless Middle Eastern sun. But his effect on us will be determined by our condition. It is the same sun, but its heat affects stubble and a flesh wound in two very different ways. It sucks the last drops of moisture out of the stubble and effectively brings its life to an end. But that same sun seems to suck the infection out of the wound and speed its healing and restoration. The sun has not changed, only the conditions of those the sun's rays strike are different. It is the same with us. God does not change. He does not love one and hate another. He loves everyone and does not will that anyone should be lost (Matt. 18:14; 2 Peter 3:9).[7] It is up to us how we experience God. If we focus on him and on living his life in the power of the Holy Spirit, we will find that nothing the world can throw at us need disturb our peace in any final way.

---

7. Mal. 1:2—3 is not talking about the eternal destinies of the individuals Jacob and Esau. The prophet is speaking of God's differing responses to the nations of Israel and Edom.

It was an experience of such peace that convinced the Anglican missionary John Wesley, who was on his way to convert Indians in America, that he himself was not converted. He was on board a ship for America when a major storm struck. Wesley was terribly frightened and astounded to discover that some Moravian missionaries on board the ship were continuing a worship and prayer service in total serenity. When he asked them later if they were not afraid, they assured him that they knew their lives were in God's hands and trusted him whatever the outcome. This is reminiscent of Shadrach, Meshach, and Abednego thousands of years earlier (Dan. 3:16–18). Get God in the right place in our lives and he is an impregnable sanctuary.

But if we do not get him in the right place, it is not simply that we do not have the blessing of his security. Rather, the failure to take account of him in life means that he becomes a genuine hindrance to all we undertake. It is customary in modern culture to lament the absence of God. The play *Waiting for Godot* presents with mind-numbing force the triviality and pointlessness of a life where one is constantly waiting for "Godot" to show up, something "Godot" never does. The playwright, Samuel Beckett, seems to be saying that we should stop this foolish looking for "Godot" and get on with trying to put together the pieces of life without him. But Beckett does not seem to realize that life is not so simple. It is not that we in the West want God but cannot find him. Rather, we have constructed a model of reality that we think effectively excludes God.

But we cannot exclude the Father from his universe. So we keep stumbling over him as we try to fill the God-shaped vacuum in our souls with possessions, pleasures, diversions, work, and power. In so doing we try to make creation serve us and fill the place of God in our lives. But no created thing can do that. No human relationship can do it. When we demand that someone else give us total allegiance, it does not work. Pleasure cannot do it. When we ask some pleasure to give us total joy, it does not work. Work cannot do it. When we ask work to give us complete fulfillment, it does not work. What are we doing? We are falling over God.

But perhaps someone says, "Hey, it seems to work pretty well for some people, if I believe half of what television depicts." Perhaps, but even when life without God seems to work fairly well, who stands beckoning at the end of the way? It is life's most inescapable reality, Death, and he mocks everything in a world without God. In the end, Death mocks all our attempts to make life work without God (Ps. 73:13–20; Eccl. 9:3). So the choice is ours: Will God be our sanctuary or our stumbling block?

The secret of contentment. Many people in the West today have chosen to make God their stumbling block. We have accepted the dictum of Reason Triumphant that there is nothing in life except the physical and material.

Never mind that Reason is speaking outside its competency; we have accepted it. We have attempted to jettison the realities of the spiritual world and to function merely as if we were "naked apes," as one book title has put it.[8]

But a strange thing has happened to us superior Westerners. We have discovered that incredible physical and material wealth has not made us a happier, more contented people. Instead, we have found something strangely missing. Of course, that something is God. But we have not turned back to that old-fashioned biblical God of our ancestors. No, we have turned to something much more "modern" and "scientific"—the horoscope, the occult, and the mother goddess. Much too educated to believe in miracles, we swallow with alacrity the most amazing hodge-podge of superstition and paganism. Then we are surprised at the rapid increase of spiritual darkness all around us. God has become the stumbling block, and we are falling all over him. The only question is how far he will have to let us fall before we finally get the picture.

---

8. Desmond Morris, *The Naked Ape* (New York: McGraw Hill, 1967).

Isaiah 9:1–7

NEVERTHELESS, THERE WILL be no more gloom for those who were in distress. In the past he humbled the land of Zebulun and the land of Naphtali, but in the future he will honor Galilee of the Gentiles, by the way of the sea, along the Jordan—

²The people walking in darkness
  have seen a great light;
on those living in the land of the shadow of death
  a light has dawned.
³You have enlarged the nation
  and increased their joy;
they rejoice before you
  as people rejoice at the harvest,
as men rejoice
  when dividing the plunder.
⁴For as in the day of Midian's defeat,
  you have shattered
the yoke that burdens them,
  the bar across their shoulders,
  the rod of their oppressor.
⁵Every warrior's boot used in battle
  and every garment rolled in blood
will be destined for burning,
  will be fuel for the fire.
⁶For to us a child is born,
  to us a son is given,
  and the government will be on his shoulders.
And he will be called
  Wonderful Counselor, Mighty God,
  Everlasting Father, Prince of Peace.
⁷Of the increase of his government and peace
  there will be no end.
He will reign on David's throne
  and over his kingdom,
establishing and upholding it
  with justice and righteousness
  from that time on and forever.
The zeal of the LORD Almighty
  will accomplish this.

CHOOSING THEIR OWN way rather than God's way, trusting in human glory rather than in God, the nation has plunged itself into darkness. Instead of having the protective canopy over them and being guided by the pillar of cloud and lighted by the pillar of fire (4:6), they are in confusion and darkness, the prey of the very nations they trust in. But that is not where God intends to leave them. In the very areas where the Assyrian conquests began, there God promises that the light will dawn. The people of Israel have done nothing to deserve this; it is nothing but God's grace.

The Assyrian conquests began in the tribal territory of "Zebulun" and "Naphtali," which extended from the Jezreel Valley northward to the foot of Mount Hermon. A major part of that area is what is known today as the Huleh Valley. The Jordan River flows through this valley before emptying into the Sea of Galilee. Not only was this a lush agricultural area, it was also the place through which the main trade route from Mesopotamia to Egypt ran ("the way of the sea"). Thus, it is easy to see why it was high on the priority list for conquest. But God is greater than Assyria, and he promises that just as these people have experienced the grief and despair of conquest, they will also experience the joy and triumph of victory (9:3–5). As Gideon defeated Midian in the Valley of Jezreel (Judg. 7), so God will defeat Israel's enemies in that same place.

But how will God accomplish this great feat? Through the birth of a child (9:6)! For the third time in as many chapters, the birth of a child is filled with great portent. In 7:14 the child's birth was a sign that it was unnecessary for Judah to trust in Assyria for deliverance from Syria and Israel. In 8:3 the child's birth was a sign of the same thing, but also that the misplaced trust was going to result in disaster for the nation of Judah. Now this birth carries the message another step forward. Out of the disaster God will yet bring final victory. The repetition of birth and the close connection in the meaning of the three signs argues that all three are expressions of Immanuel.[1] Maher-Shalal-Hash-Baz was the immediate fulfillment of the sign, and this child is its ultimate fulfillment. God will keep his promises both to Israel and to the house of David (9:7).

But who is this child? The titles given argue forcefully against its being any human, such as Hezekiah. No Israelite or Judean king was ever identified as "Mighty God."[2] Clearly the person being referred to here is the

---

1. For further discussion on the connection of this sign to Immanuel, see Young, *Isaiah, 1–18*, 329–31.

2. See Motyer, *The Prophecy of Isaiah*, 102–5, for a discussion of the titles.

promised Messiah, who will reign over God's people with a kind of justice and righteousness that no mere human descendant of David ever achieved.[3] Furthermore, the government and the social and personal integration ("peace," Heb. *šalom*)[4] he will produce will be eternal (9:7). This is not Hezekiah or any other merely human son of David.

THIS PASSAGE TEACHES several things about both the character and purpose of God and about the ultimate significance of Immanuel. (1) It teaches initially about God's grace. If God has "humbled" a person or a nation, it is for the final purpose of giving that person or nation "honor" (9:1). He brings us down only because, given our sinfulness, that is the only way he can raise us up. He does not ever wish simply to destroy. In some cases that is the final result, but not because God wishes it to be so. God wants light, joy, abundance, liberty, and cessation of hostility (9:2–5)—not only for his own people but for all people (25:6–9).

(2) This passage also teaches some rather startling things about the nature of the Messiah. We can imagine Isaiah asking God just what the things he has been inspired to say mean. We are told that the Messiah will come as a child. God's answer to the oppression and hostility of this proud and cruel world is not to come as a jack-booted warrior to smash the opposition. Somehow, although we are not told how here, he will shatter "the yoke that burdens" his people without becoming a greater oppressor than the enemy.

(3) We are also told this Messiah will be a son, although we are not told whose son he is. He will be the Mighty God, but he will reign from David's throne. And although David's throne is in Jerusalem, yet his light will dawn in Galilee (cf. Matt. 4:14–16). Nor will these events be of a casual sort, for it will all be accomplished through the passionate involvement ("zeal") in earth's affairs by the transcendent One, the Lord of heaven's armies ("LORD Almighty"). Taken together these various statements seem incapable of resolution. But of course they have been resolved, and we know how.

---

3. Although Childs (*Isaiah*, 80–81) grants that the passage may have had some other historical referent originally, he insists that in its present setting it must be understood in a messianic way.

4. The English word "peace" only partially reflects the meaning of *šalom*. The word involves putting back together what had been divided. Thus it speaks of much more than merely the absence of hostilities. See Philip J. Nel, "שלם," *NIDOTTE*, 4:130–35.

Contemporary Significance

"GOD WITH US" has its foundations, both in theology and as a historical fact, in these verses. If the God who is inescapably present in our lives were a demon or a monster, this affirmation would be one of endless terror. Even if he were only implacably just, his presence would not be a blessing to us unless we were somehow able to live without mistake, error, or sin at all times. But the good news is that the God who is with us is a God who wants to turn our darkness into light, our conflict into *shalom*, our loss into abundance, our despair into joy. The One who rides with passionate desire at the head of the hosts of heaven ("LORD Almighty"; lit., "Yahweh of hosts") has a passionate desire to do good to all people. If a God like that is with us, that is good news to all eternity.

But how can he be with us? If he is transcendent, if he is morally perfect, if he is infinite, if he is eternal, how can he be with us who are created, sinful, finite, and mortal? Surely he can only be with us in a metaphorical way, because the barriers are too great to be crossed. If that is all the phrase can mean, then it is a very hollow one. But this passage sets the stage for the most astounding event in history. The transcendent becomes one of the created; the morally perfect experiences what it is to have sinned;[5] the infinite becomes finite; the immortal experiences mortality.[6] He is with us!

The "child" born of the virgin is the son of David, but he is also the Son of God. The bulk of his ministry was in Galilee, but he was "enthroned" on a cross in Jerusalem. By taking into himself the sin and oppression, the horror and tragedy of this world, he was able to give back righteousness and freedom, hope and fulfillment. In fact, we may argue that it is hard to think of another way in which the apparent contradictions of Isaiah 9:1–7 could have been resolved than in the way in which they actually were in Jesus Christ. The contemporary significance of this passage of Scripture comes down to this: Have we allowed the Child-King to take over the government of our lives? Only then can we know the benefits of God with us. We cannot have the light, the honor, the joy, the abundance, the integration that he offers in any other way.

---

5. I do not mean that he committed sin; the New Testament is very clear he did not (2 Cor. 5:21; Heb. 4:15). But it is equally clear that he experienced what it is to have sinned, not objectively but subjectively (Isa. 53:6; Mark 15:33).

6. While it is tempting to relate Christ's death to "the land of the shadow of death" (9:2), there seems to be little direct explicit connotation of death in the Heb. word *ṣalmawet* (see the NIV note "or *land of darkness*"; see also James D. Price, "צלל," *NIDOTTE*, 3:809).

Isaiah 9:8–10:4

⁸ THE LORD HAS sent a message against Jacob;
  it will fall on Israel.
⁹ All the people will know it—
  Ephraim and the inhabitants of Samaria—
who say with pride
  and arrogance of heart,
¹⁰ "The bricks have fallen down,
  but we will rebuild with dressed stone;
the fig trees have been felled,
  but we will replace them with cedars."
¹¹ But the LORD has strengthened Rezin's foes against them
  and has spurred their enemies on.
¹² Arameans from the east and Philistines from the west
  have devoured Israel with open mouth.

Yet for all this, his anger is not turned away,
  his hand is still upraised.

¹³ But the people have not returned to him who struck them,
  nor have they sought the LORD Almighty.
¹⁴ So the LORD will cut off from Israel both head and tail,
  both palm branch and reed in a single day;
¹⁵ the elders and prominent men are the head,
  the prophets who teach lies are the tail.
¹⁶ Those who guide this people mislead them,
  and those who are guided are led astray.
¹⁷ Therefore the Lord will take no pleasure in the
      young men,
  nor will he pity the fatherless and widows,
for everyone is ungodly and wicked,
  every mouth speaks vileness.

Yet for all this, his anger is not turned away,
  his hand is still upraised.

¹⁸ Surely wickedness burns like a fire;
  it consumes briers and thorns,
it sets the forest thickets ablaze,
  so that it rolls upward in a column of smoke.

¹⁹ By the wrath of the LORD Almighty
> the land will be scorched
and the people will be fuel for the fire;
> no one will spare his brother.
²⁰ On the right they will devour,
> but still be hungry;
on the left they will eat,
> but not be satisfied.
Each will feed on the flesh of his own offspring:
²¹   Manasseh will feed on Ephraim, and Ephraim
>   on Manasseh;
together they will turn against Judah.

Yet for all this, his anger is not turned away,
> his hand is still upraised.

¹⁰:¹ Woe to those who make unjust laws,
> to those who issue oppressive decrees,
² to deprive the poor of their rights
> and withhold justice from the oppressed of my people,
making widows their prey
> and robbing the fatherless.
³ What will you do on the day of reckoning,
> when disaster comes from afar?
To whom will you run for help?
> Where will you leave your riches?
⁴ Nothing will remain but to cringe among the captives
> or fall among the slain.

Yet for all this, his anger is not turned away,
> his hand is still upraised.

WITH ISAIAH 9:7 the so-called "Book of Immanuel" closes, but the theological reflection on Ahaz's refusal to trust does not. As we saw throughout chapters 1–5, Isaiah keeps calling his hearers back from the beautiful promises of the future to the grimmer realities of the present. So here he is at pains to remind the Judeans that it is not Assyria with whom they must come to terms but the Holy One of Israel. Assyria will not determine Judah's final destiny, but Yahweh will; thus, they must look to their relationship with him.

The prophet addresses this first in 9:8–10:4, where he points out to the Judeans that their trouble is not because of Assyria's greatness but because God's hand of punishment is raised against them. This means that a day will come when Assyria's task is finished, and in that day, in view of Assyria's overbearing pride, God's hand will be raised against Assyria as well (10:5–34). With God's lordship of history established, the prophet then turns to a discussion of the events at the end of history, the messianic kingdom (11:1–16). This is followed by the beautiful two-part hymn of chapter 12, which closes the subdivision by praising God for his trustworthiness.

Isaiah 9:8–10:4 has four stanzas, each of which closes with the refrain already encountered in 5:25: "Yet for all this, his anger is not turned away, his hand is still upraised."[1] It is not Assyria's anger but Yahweh's that must be dealt with. The four charges God lodges against Israel, as in chapter 1, all have to do with ethical behavior, with the covenant providing the background.

The first charge (9:8–12) is arrogance; instead of humble submission to their covenant Lord, the Israelites attempt to exalt themselves. The result, as in 2:6–4:1, will be humiliation. The second charge (9:13–17) is adulation of great men instead of turning back to the Lord. Thus, the whole nation will suffer. The third charge (9:18–21) is the lack of brotherly love. Having forsaken their covenant Lord, the various tribes attack each other in a bloodbath reminiscent of the final three chapters in the book of Judges. The final charge (10:1–4) describes the social injustice that is inescapable in a society where everyone is looking out for himself or herself alone.

These are the reasons the Assyrians are coming. Change these, and history itself will change. But fail to address these, and even if there might no longer be an Assyria on the scene, God will use another punishment to deal with his people.

Arrogance (9:8–12)

THE FIRST OF the charges is specifically focused on the northern kingdom of Israel. By this time that kingdom is in the final decade of its existence. Yet these Israelites are insisting with the kind of unreality born of desperation that they can still "pull it out." The words of Amos and Hosea calling for repentance, confession, and a humble admission of sin have fallen on deaf ears. So "Rezin's foes" (the Assyrians) as well as Israel's former allies, "the Arameans" (the Syrians), and their perpetual enemies, the Philistines, will all be brought against them by their former covenant Lord, Yahweh.

---

1. Critics have sought to show that 9:8–10:4 and some part of chapter 5 were originally part of the same poem, but as Motyer cogently points out, there has been no agreement among the host of proposals that have been made (*Prophecy of Isaiah*, 112). It is best simply to allow an artist to use a favorite theme in different ways and different places.

The phrase "his hand is still upraised" can be understood in one of two ways. It may be a judicial figure of speech, with the judge raising his hand to pass judgment. But it was common in the ancient Near East (apparently originating in Egypt) to represent the king holding a mace in his raised hand beating down his enemies; this seems the more likely intention here. Israel (and Judah) have become God's enemies (cf. 1:24).

Adulation of Great Men (9:13 – 17)

WHEN GOD, WHO is the true source of glory, is forsaken, the natural substitute is human leaders. These leaders are praised as those who can somehow achieve superhuman things. Inevitably they fail, for too much is being asked of them. In language reminiscent of chapter 3, God says that he will deprive Israel and Judah of all such false leaders. The same phrase "head and tail . . . palm branch and reed" occurs in 19:15, where it refers to the leadership of Egypt. This may have been a proverbial way of speaking of totality, something like "front to back, top to bottom."

It does not matter who these leaders are, whether they are social, political, or spiritual (9:15); they will all be swept away. As a result of their leadership the land has become so corrupt that no one, neither the strongest ("the young men") nor the weakest ("the fatherless and widows"), will be in a position to claim any special favors from God.

Lack of Brotherly Love (9:18 – 21)

IN THIS STANZA, as in the previous one, there is a sense in which the anger of the Lord speeds along the destruction that a particular sin has set in motion. Here the breakdown of social structure as a result of sin is burning up the land (9:18), and God's righteous judgment adds tinder to the flame (9:19). As the terrific pressure of Assyria's demand for tribute mounts higher and higher, everyone scrambles to save his or her own neck; if that means robbing your neighbor or even your brother, then so be it.

Ultimately, as the final siege begins, the devouring of one's "own offspring" ceases to be metaphorical and becomes a horrible, literal fact (9:20). In a world where self reigns supreme, no one is safe. In the kingdom of northern Israel, the two dominant tribal groups were Ephraim and Manasseh. Here they are shown destroying each other, and in their frenzy of self-destruction, they turn on their brother tribe to the south: Judah (9:21), as Pekah had done (7:1).

Social Injustice (10:1 – 4)

IN A WORLD characterized by human arrogance, adulation of human leaders, and mutual destruction by the various elements of society, justice becomes a rarer and rarer commodity, with the poor and the helpless being least able to secure it. That is what is described in this final stanza. God's particular anger is reserved for those who consciously use the legal system to oppress the poor and make themselves rich (10:1–2). But God says that all those riches will do no good when the enemy comes. There will not be enough "riches" to deliver them from captivity.

PRIDE. The problem of human pride is a perennial one. It is the deepest and most serious of human sins. It is as much a problem for those with low self-esteem as for those with a superiority complex. In fact, it may be a more serious problem for the former. It is not as much the looking down on others from some lofty height as it is the self-absorption that is passionately concerned to make oneself look good.

That can be seen in the present passage. Israel is in serious trouble. They have lost large areas of their land already. They have experienced significant destruction. But in their concern to look good, they assure themselves and any who will listen that they can "come back." It is pride that prevents people from a realistic assessment of themselves and a humble turning to God for help, strength, and guidance.

Adulation. Isaiah 9:13–17 is about the consequences in political and social life when people do not recognize the lordship of God. They expect the leaders to give them the security and meaning only God can give. Moreover, the leaders believe the adulation the people give them. Thus, the leaders lead for their own position and power, saying what they think the people want to hear ("teach lies") instead of what may be unpopular but necessary for the public good.

Self-interest. A further consequence of refusing to acknowledge God is social breakdown as a result of ravaging self-interest (9:18–21). As individuals put their own self-interests first, they begin to associate those self-interests with their own affinity groups, whether kinship or otherwise. The result is that these groups no longer have a concern for the greatest good of the people as a whole. Rather, they conceive the good on an ever-narrower scale—that which we want. Unable to see anything from a larger divine perspective, they see every other group as a potential threat to be minimized as decisively as possible.

Social injustice. In the end social injustice for personal gain is a self-defeating process. The gains achieved are only temporary, and those who make them will soon be deprived of them. Why? Because God values persons for themselves, not for what they can contribute to someone's financial plan.

People are not merely counters on a board, and any attempt to use them in that way is contrary to the reality God has created. To be sure, it may be possible to oppress the weaker or less-fortunate members of society and take advantage of them for many years. After all, the capture of Jerusalem was not to take place for more than 125 years after these words were uttered. Nevertheless, sooner or later, according to this passage, there will be a reckoning.

GOD'S ANGER. WHEN we think of God's anger, we must avoid several things. (1) We must avoid thinking: "Oh, that's just an Old Testament misunderstanding of things. We know better now. Since Jesus, we know that God is really a God of love." (a) This fails to recognize that when the church affirmed the authority of the Old Testament, it testified that the Old Testament is equally inspired with the New. (b) God's anger and love are found in both Old and New Testaments. Jesus himself became terribly angry on several occasions. (c) If we allow God to be passionately involved with his creation in a positive way and call that "love," we must also allow that the same passionate involvement might express itself in the negative way known as "anger." The two terminologies express two sides of the same phenomenon.

(2) We must also avoid thinking that whenever we suffer, God must be angry at us. If a drunk driver swerves onto the sidewalk and kills my child, that is not a sign God is angry at me.

(3) Finally, we should also avoid the idea that the anger of God in the Bible is simply a metaphor for the cause-and-effect nature of existence, similar to the unpleasant consequences we may experience. Take gravity, for example. Falling is just the way things are. The ground is not angry at you if you step out of a twenty-third-story window and fall to the ground. The problem with reducing God's anger to mere cause and effect in this way is that it removes God from the personal involvement with his creation that is so much at the heart of the biblical experience.

The truth involves some of each of the three positions mentioned above. There is a difference between God's love and his anger. He *is* love, and he *gets* angry. That is, his love is a part of his being. Thus, he is not some tyrant with a hair-trigger temper. The one constant description of God in the Old Testament is that he is full of compassion and slow to get angry (Ex. 34:6; Num. 14:18; Neh. 9:17; Ps. 86:15; etc.). At the same time, he does care *very* deeply about what we do to ourselves, just as any good and responsible father cares about what his children do to themselves. So he *does* get angry when people destroy their own potential and violate the personhood of those around them.

Furthermore, there *is* a sense in which the spiritual world is made just like the physical world. There are certain behaviors that fit in perfectly with the ways in which we are made and will lead to abundance and satisfaction, and there are other behaviors that will lead to destruction. If we choose those ways consciously or unconsciously, there are deadly consequences, not because some arbitrary divine monster has said, "I'm going to get you for that!" but simply because we have violated the terms of our creation.

So, does God get angry? Yes he does, but it is not the selfish anger of a fallen human. Nor is it the temper tantrum of an imperious heavenly monarch who will not permit his lowly subjects to do what they want. It is the heart-broken response of an Artist who watches his artistic creations doing things that are not only a violation of his original dream but are a violation of their very natures.

Self-respect and pride. Where is the line between "decent self-respect" and pride, or between "healthy self-esteem" and self-conceit? The answer is deceptively simple. It all depends on what the "self-respect" or "self-esteem" is based. If it is based on placing ourselves at the center of our world, as modern society recommends, then it is deadly. Such an attitude is nothing other than pride and conceit, because we are trying to make ourselves the basis of our own existence, and that is not possible in this world God has made. To say "I am somebody important, because I say so" is ridiculous.

As charming as the story "The Little Engine That Could" may be, saying "I think I can, I think I can" does not create the ability to do something. We are not complete in ourselves. Only when we surrender to the love of God and learn that we are worth the life and death of the Prince of Peace will we discover how much we are really worth. Only when we have admitted that in ourselves dwells no good thing (Rom. 7:18) will we be able to know those inner resources that enable us to say, "I can do everything through him who gives me strength" (Phil. 4:13).

A note to leaders. Unless leaders constantly acknowledge their dependence on God, the tendency to the demonic is present. The leaders themselves will believe the adulation that fallen humans will heap on them. Then they will begin to believe that they have a right in themselves to positions of prominence and power. Soon they are governing not for the governed but for themselves. Their actions are tailored as to how best to maintain themselves in power. They are unwilling to take right positions that might be dangerous to their power. Instead, they govern by polls, trying to decide where the people are going and then running to get in front of the crowd. As a result, the leaders "mislead," and those who are "led" are "led astray" (cf. 9:16).

Love. Jesus' words in John 13:35 do not lose their shocking power. What is the distinctive mark that shows which people are his disciples? Is it sound doctrine, evangelistic fervor, or joyous worship? No, it is none of these. "By this all men will know that you are my disciples, if you love one another." The distinctive sign of discipleship is mutual love. All of the New Testament writers pick this up—Paul ("You yourselves have been taught by God to love each other," 1 Thess. 4:9), John ("Dear friends, let us love one another, for love comes from God," 1 John 4:7), and Peter ("Love the brotherhood of believers," 1 Peter 2:17).

Speaking negatively, Paul sounds a note much like the one here in Isaiah: "If you keep on biting and devouring each other, watch out or you will be destroyed by each other" (Gal. 5:15). One of the things legendary about the church of Jesus Christ is "church fights." This is not to say it is never right to have heated disagreements. When heresy is in the air, truth must be contended for. The prophets themselves are evidence of that. But sadly, most "church fights" have nothing to do with biblical faith. They too frequently have to do with "my way or no way" on some issue relating to style, decoration, or habit. What this betrays all too clearly is an absence of surrender of my will to Christ. To love one another as Christ loved us is to nail my way to the cross for your sake. There is no other way to avoid "biting and devouring" one another.

Social injustice. One of the problems many of us face when we are confronted with the fact of social injustice is that we do not sense any direct involvement in such practices. We are not foreclosing on the mortgage of a widow; we are not requiring an orphan to work for us with no pay; we are not taking payoffs from the lawyer of a crook to deny the claims of a small-time plaintiff. So how do we respond to a passage such as Isaiah 10:1–4?

(1) First, we need to be sure that it is really true that we are not involved in oppression of those more helpless than we. What about my students? As a professor I am in a position of power over them. Am I putting them down in some way for my own convenience? What about help at home? Am I gouging those who work for me on the lawn or in cleaning or in childcare? Or am I generous? What about those I supervise in the office? Do they feel taken advantage of by me? (2) Am I involved in institutions that profit from oppression? When is the minimum wage the wrong wage? (3) Positively, each of us needs to ask what we can do to address injustice where we live. It may be little enough, but it will be something—and that is better than nothing.

Isaiah 10:5–34

[5]"WOE TO THE Assyrian, the rod of my anger,
    in whose hand is the club of my wrath!
[6]I send him against a godless nation,
    I dispatch him against a people who anger me,
  to seize loot and snatch plunder,
    and to trample them down like mud in the streets.
[7]But this is not what he intends,
    this is not what he has in mind;
  his purpose is to destroy,
    to put an end to many nations.
[8]'Are not my commanders all kings?' he says.
[9] 'Has not Calno fared like Carchemish?
  Is not Hamath like Arpad,
    and Samaria like Damascus?
[10]As my hand seized the kingdoms of the idols,
    kingdoms whose images excelled those of Jerusalem
        and Samaria—
[11]shall I not deal with Jerusalem and her images
    as I dealt with Samaria and her idols?'"

[12]When the Lord has finished all his work against Mount
Zion and Jerusalem, he will say, "I will punish the king of
Assyria for the willful pride of his heart and the haughty look
in his eyes. [13]For he says:

  "'By the strength of my hand I have done this,
    and by my wisdom, because I have understanding.
  I removed the boundaries of nations,
    I plundered their treasures;
    like a mighty one I subdued their kings.
[14]As one reaches into a nest,
    so my hand reached for the wealth of
        the nations;
  as men gather abandoned eggs,
    so I gathered all the countries;
  not one flapped a wing,
    or opened its mouth to chirp.'"

¹⁵ Does the ax raise itself above him who swings it,
    or the saw boast against him who uses it?
As if a rod were to wield him who lifts it up,
    or a club brandish him who is not wood!
¹⁶ Therefore, the Lord, the LORD Almighty,
    will send a wasting disease upon his sturdy warriors;
under his pomp a fire will be kindled
    like a blazing flame.
¹⁷ The Light of Israel will become a fire,
    their Holy One a flame;
in a single day it will burn and consume
    his thorns and his briers.
¹⁸ The splendor of his forests and fertile fields
    it will completely destroy,
    as when a sick man wastes away.
¹⁹ And the remaining trees of his forests will be so few
    that a child could write them down.

²⁰ In that day the remnant of Israel,
    the survivors of the house of Jacob,
will no longer rely on him
    who struck them down
but will truly rely on the LORD,
    the Holy One of Israel.
²¹ A remnant will return, a remnant of Jacob
    will return to the Mighty God.
²² Though your people, O Israel, be like the sand by the sea,
    only a remnant will return.
Destruction has been decreed,
    overwhelming and righteous.
²³ The Lord, the LORD Almighty, will carry out
    the destruction decreed upon the whole land.

²⁴ Therefore, this is what the Lord, the LORD Almighty,
says:

"O my people who live in Zion,
    do not be afraid of the Assyrians,
who beat you with a rod
    and lift up a club against you, as Egypt did.
²⁵ Very soon my anger against you will end
    and my wrath will be directed to their destruction."

²⁶ The LORD Almighty will lash them with a whip,
    as when he struck down Midian at the rock
        of Oreb;
  and he will raise his staff over the waters,
    as he did in Egypt.
²⁷ In that day their burden will be lifted from your shoulders,
    their yoke from your neck;
  the yoke will be broken
    because you have grown so fat.

²⁸ They enter Aiath;
    they pass through Migron;
    they store supplies at Micmash.
²⁹ They go over the pass, and say,
    "We will camp overnight at Geba."
  Ramah trembles;
    Gibeah of Saul flees.
³⁰ Cry out, O Daughter of Gallim!
    Listen, O Laishah!
    Poor Anathoth!
³¹ Madmenah is in flight;
    the people of Gebim take cover.
³² This day they will halt at Nob;
    they will shake their fist
  at the mount of the Daughter of Zion,
    at the hill of Jerusalem.
³³ See, the Lord, the LORD Almighty,
    will lop off the boughs with great power.
  The lofty trees will be felled,
    the tall ones will be brought low.
³⁴ He will cut down the forest thickets with an ax;
    Lebanon will fall before the Mighty One.

IF THE PEOPLE of Israel recognize that it is the Lord with whom they must come to terms and not the nations, if they realize that their destiny is determined by their obedience to the covenant and not by their relations to the nations, God will deliver them from the nations among whom he has abandoned them. This point is expressed with colorful force in this section.

Isaiah 10:1—4, the immediately preceding stanza dealing with social injustice, began with the funeral cry, "Woe!" Verse 5 begins with the same word, but now it is directed toward the instrument God had used to punish Israel's and Judah's sins: the nation of Assyria. This is God's way of showing two things. (1) The promised destruction by Assyria is temporary and not permanent. God is not going to wipe out his people, letting Assyria run roughshod over them. (2) Assyria is not operating on its own. It may think so, but it is not. However great the Assyrian power, it operates only under God's sufferance. It only serves God's purposes. Once those purposes have been served, Assyria will be subject to the same moral scrutiny as any other nation. Just because that nation has been God's tool does not mean its people can live without any accountability to their Creator. In fact, they deny such accountability, insisting that they are the product of their own hands. Thus, they are one more expression of the creaturely pride that has such deadly effect on God's creatures (see 2:6—4:1; 13—14).

A Message Against Assyria (10:5–19)

ASSYRIA IS THE "rod" that is held in God's upraised hand (9:12, 17, 21; 10:4), and it is raised up to punish "a godless[1] nation." As with the charge that Judah and Israel had become God's enemies (1:24—25; 10:3), so this word must have seemed unjust to many. Surely the Assyrians are the ones who are "godless" and perverse. But the fact is, the Israelites have been given the covenant of God, and the Assyrians have not. The people of God know better, yet they pervert their way by turning their backs on the truth revealed to them. The Assyrians would certainly disdain the idea that they are no more than a tool in the hand of the God of the little, despicable nations of Israel and Judah. Their "purpose" (10:7) is not to obey Yahweh but to conquer and "destroy" as many nations as possible. In other words, they recognize no purpose in life but their own will to power.

This idea is expressed in the quotation put in the mouth of the Assyrian king in 10:8—11. The language is reminiscent of 37:10—13. The king has no qualms about saying that he is superior to everything on earth, including all its gods. He is so great that even his "commanders" are the equivalent of the kings of other lands. He is truly the king of kings.

The first four cities mentioned in 10:9 were all fortress cities in northwestern Syria, outposts of "Damascus." But fortresses or not, the tyrant says

---

1. The verb *ḥnp* has the sense of "to profane" or "to pervert" (see, e.g., Num. 35:33; Isa. 24:5), thus "godless" may not be the best rendering for the noun. The KJV rendering of "hypocrite" or "hypocritical" (based on one way the LXX translates the noun) may be appropriate in some cases. In others, such as here, "perverse" might be better. See R. E. Averbeck, "חָנֵף," *NIDOTTE*, 2:206—9.

he has treated them all alike, destroying them. Nor have Damascus and Samaria escaped his grasp. Moreover, since far finer idols than those in Samaria and Jerusalem have not been able to save their lands from the Assyrian king, and since he has in fact already taken Samaria and its gods, why should he think of himself as the lackey of Jerusalem's God? He is superior to that God and will do to Jerusalem whatever he wants.

But as Isaiah points out, the king of Assyria is not superior to Jerusalem's God. Whatever he thinks, he is coming against Jerusalem with only one task: to carry out the "work" God has for him to do "against Mount Zion." When Jerusalem's punishment is complete, at least for the moment, Assyria's punishment will begin (10:12). That punishment will be because of Assyrian "pride," which is expressed in another quotation from their king (10:13–14). The prominence of "hand" seems significant in these two verses. That king does not recognize that he is a tool in the hand of God. Rather, he boasts that it is his "hand" that has captured the nations and their wealth, his "hand" that has looted the nations as though they were nests of "abandoned eggs." No one even dared to flap "a wing" to protest his plundering.

But Assyria is not acting independently, despite their thinking. They are but tools in the hand of Yahweh. There are two figures used in 10:15. The first involves lumbering tools, the "ax" and the "saw," while the second set are tools of warfare or oppression, the "rod" and the "club." God said he would cut down the "forest" of Judah's pride (6:13), and Assyria is the "ax" in God's hand to accomplish that task. God also said that he would punish his people for their sin (5:25), and Assyria is the instrument of that punishment.[2] But Assyria does not admit that it is not ultimate and thinks, foolishly, that it moves itself.

Because Assyria refuses to recognize the truth, God will turn the tool over to destruction. The "flame" (10:16) of God's holiness, which was once turned on Israel (6:11–12), will be turned on those who refuse to admit that there might be One superior to them. When Israel turns and recognizes who their true "Light" is, that light will blaze against their enemies and not against them. The metaphors of field and forest are used again to convey the idea of glory destroyed (10:17–19). Not only the least in Assyria ("thorns" and "briers") but also the greatest ("forests and fertile fields") will be consumed— and all "in a single day." This most likely refers to the destruction of the Assyrian army in 701 B.C. (see 37:36–37). When 185,000 died in a single night (note "a wasting disease" in 10:16), Sennacherib had only a "few" soldiers ("trees of his forests," 10:19) left to accompany him on a hasty departure to his homeland.[3]

---

2. See Isa. 9:4 and 10:24 for the same word pair for "club" and "rod."
3. Note yet another reference to a "child" in this section (7:1–12:6) in 10:19.

A Remnant Will Survive (10:20–23)

"IN THAT DAY" is an expansive term referring to any future time of God's judgment and/or restoration.[4] Thus, it is not necessary to refer it directly to the events of 701 B.C. nor even to the events of 620–609 B.C., when Assyria was finally destroyed. Rather, here it speaks of that future time when all the punishment at the hands of the nations will be over and the purified "remnant" of God's people (see 4:2–6) will be brought home.

The prophet utilizes the name of his son Shear-Jashub ("only a remnant will return") to do two things here. (1) He wants to assure his hearers that no matter how great Assyria (and later Babylon) may be, they will not be able to destroy God's people. After all, they are only tools in God's hand and can do no more than he gives them permission to. Since God is gracious and compassionate, a remnant will survive.

(2) However, *only* a remnant will survive, and the prophet stresses this with his recurring use of the word "remnant." As is typical of this part of the book, Isaiah is trying hard to guard against false expectations. No one should get so focused on the future survival as to forget the terrible judgment that precedes that survival. Thus, he insists to his hearers that even though the destruction will not be complete, it will be thorough. It has been so "decreed" (10:22).

But the remnant will be different from their predecessors in at least one respect. They will no longer "rely on" (10:20), or trust, their worst enemy before they will trust "the Holy One of Israel." In that coming day when a handful of survivors return to the land from which they have been exiled, they will learn the lesson of trust that Isaiah 7–39 focuses on.[5]

The Lord's Protection of His People (10:24–34)

IN VIEW OF the fact that Assyria will be judged and that a remnant of the nation will survive, "therefore" (10:24) the people of Judah should not live in fear of Assyria. Their foreign policy and their spiritual outlook should not be shaped by either the offers or the threats of that great power. When God's purposes for using Assyria are complete, Assyria will disappear from the scene, and the Judeans should make their plans with that fact in mind. As Isaiah earlier said to Ahaz, no emergency action is necessary. While it is difficult to know what "very soon" (10:25) implies in the divine timetable, it is tempting to conclude that this refers to the destruction of the Assyrian army

---

4. See R. Hiers, "Day of the Lord," *ABD*, 2:82–83.

5. For a study of the remnant, see G. Hasel, *The History and Theology of the Remnant Idea from Genesis to Isaiah*, 2d ed. (Berrien Springs, Mich.: Andrews Univ. Press, 1975).

mentioned above and the removal of any serious threat to Judah's existence on the part of the Assyrians.

In 10:26 the prophet turns to two experiences from the past as confirmation of the Lord's power to protect his people from massive threats. Whether it was the multitude of Midianite troops led by Oreb (Judg. 7:25) or Egypt's chariot corps, the finest in the world at the time of the Exodus (Ex. 14:26; 15:4), neither was any match for the power of the "Lord Almighty" (lit., "Yahweh of armies"). Because of that, the heavy "yoke" of oppression that the Assyrian kings used to boast about putting on the necks of conquered peoples will be "broken" off (10:27).

One example of such boasting appears in the annals of Sargon II, where he says, "[I] imposed upon them the yoke of Ashur, my lord."[6] There is some question about the proper reading of the last phrase in 10:27, both because the meaning of the Hebrew is obscure and the versions have a number of different readings.[7] If the Hebrew is correct, then the idea is that the ox is so well fed that its neck becomes so fat it breaks the bow that holds the yoke in place.

Verses 28–34 have occasioned a great deal of scholarly discussion, primarily over whether they describe a literal historical event. Those who believe there were two attacks by Sennacherib on Jerusalem suggest that this may describe the route taken by the Assyrian army when it attacked Jerusalem a second time (about 687 B.C.).[8] However, the "two-attack theory" is only a theory, for there is no evidence to support it. Furthermore, it is hard to imagine a major army actually using the route described here. It is not the main route and would be difficult for a small troop to navigate, let alone a large one. Thus, it seems better to understand this material as another of Isaiah's word pictures.[9]

"Aiath," the first village mentioned, is about fifteen miles north of Jerusalem, and "Nob" is on the slopes of Mount Scopus, overlooking Jerusalem on the north. The route described diverges from the normal one that begins to the north of Jerusalem and travels instead down the east side of the ridge line. Probably the reason for this is to express the almost unstoppable approach of the enemy army. It does not matter that the route is rugged and filled with

---

6. *ANET*, 285b.

7. The lxx has "broken from off your shoulder"; the Targum, "the nations will be destroyed before the Messiah"; the Syriac, "broken because of your strength."

8. See J. Bright, *A History of Israel*, 3d ed. (Philadelphia: Westminster, 1981), 286–88, 298–309; W. Shea, "Jerusalem Under Siege: Did Sennacherib Attack Twice?" *BAR* 25/6 (Nov.–Dec. 1999): 36–44, 64; M. Cogan, "Sennacherib's Siege of Jerusalem: Once or Twice?" *BAR* 27/1 (Jan.–Feb. 2001): 40–45, 69.

9. So also Childs, *Isaiah*; Motyer, *Prophecy of Isaiah*.

obstacles—on they come! In less than two days they have traversed the rugged terrain and are shaking their fists at the apparently doomed city. This is a metaphor for Assyria. On they have come year after year. Nothing can stop them. Judah must come to terms with them or be destroyed.

But Isaiah tells his hearers they should look at another reality. For at the moment when the Assyrian ax believes it will topple the Judean tree, Judah's God turns the ax upon the ax! In a moment a forest as mighty as that covering the Lebanon mountains falls to the ground.[10] Human pride cannot stand before the true "Mighty One" (*ʾaddir*; note the similar *ʾabbir*, "a mighty one," in 10:13, which is what the Assyrian king called himself). The true Mighty One is the One whom Judah should be relying on, not on the ax in the Mighty One's hand.

VERSES 5–19. These verses are about the lordship of God over history and the need to keep a true perspective. This is more difficult in the modern setting when we do not have inspired prophets who can tell us exactly what each entity of history is about, but the central message is no less true. No nation stands on its own. Every nation is subject to God, and every nation is serving God's ultimate purposes.

This has implications for the nations: Whenever a nation begins to believe it is superior to God and can do what it wishes, we may be sure that nation's end is soon to come. But it also has implications for individual believers. We should neither be paralyzed by the nations in their power and glory, nor should we put any ultimate degree of trust in them. God is supreme over the nations, and he is the One we should fear and the One in whom we should trust.

This section also describes the nature of human pride. The Assyrian king makes no appeal here to his gods as he makes his claims. He feels he is superior to the gods of all his enemies. In the end pagan religion exists to serve human needs. This means that while lip service may be given to the gods, in fact what is supreme is the human ego. It is this that must be preserved at all costs, and at the bottom of everything the gods are only devices created to serve the ego. If one set of gods does not accomplish what is needed, it can easily be discarded and a new set put in place. The repetition of the first-person pronouns in these verses underlines this point—no less than

---

10. The use of this particular imagery suggests another conscious play on Assyria's boasting. Their kings were fond of saying how they had cut down the forests of Lebanon, both to make a path for their armies and to decorate their palaces. Now they themselves will be cut down. See also Ezek. 31, where an entire chapter is given to the metaphor of Assyria as a great cedar in Lebanon.

thirteen occurrences here. So the question arises: Am I at the center of my world, or is there some other center?

Finally, we must be careful not to take credit for what God has done through us. It was this sin that kept Moses out of the Promised Land (Num. 20:12): "Because you did not trust in me enough to honor me as holy in the sight of the Israelites, you will not bring this community into the land I give them." What had Moses done? It was not merely a matter of striking the rock instead of speaking to it. He had led the Hebrews to believe that he had the power in himself and his magic staff to produce water for them: "Listen, you rebels, must we bring you water out of this rock?" (20:10). Instead of making it clear that God alone is the Holy One whose transcendent power and endless love supply all human needs, the ax pretended it could swing itself. If this Moses had led the people into the Promised Land dry-shod across the Jordan, they would have been worshiping him inside of a year. God had no choice but to keep him from entering.

Verses 20–23. Keeping both emphases of hope and judgment before our eyes is difficult. Isaiah's constant attempt to keep the two in balance is a reminder of this. If the only word heard is judgment, people tend to lose heart and give up. But if the only word they hear is certain hope, there is a strong tendency to "let up" in the matters of daily obedience and accountability. So, while the body of this poetic stanza relates to the certainty of a remnant returning, the prophet is at pains to remind his readers that *only* a remnant will return, and this will not preclude judgment but will follow it. As Peter says, judgment begins with the household of God (1 Peter 4:17).

A second important point in this stanza is the idea of "the remnant." From Genesis on, the Scriptures portray the concept of a handful maintaining the faith while the masses go to perdition. It is explicit with the family of Noah in the Flood and implicit with the family of Abraham following the Tower of Babel. It is explicit with Sodom and Gomorrah, and while the number of those entering the Promised Land is as great as the number of those who left Egypt, it could have reasonably been expected to be a good deal greater, given geometric progression. In fact, the second generation is a remnant. Again and again throughout the history of Israel, the continuation of the faith seems to hang by a shoestring, such as the boy Samuel when the priesthood was deeply corrupted, or the boy David when the entire army of Israel was cowed before the giant. In other words, despite the fact that biblical faith is a community faith, it is not a mass faith. That is, faithfulness always is intentional and accountable, and that often comes down to a handful.

Another point that should not be overlooked is the issue of trust. Why do we tend to put our trust in the wrong things, as Judah did in Assyria? Surely the answer in that situation was that it seemed the only thing to do.

The situation was desperate. Israel and Syria were on the march and might even be minded to do away with the Davidic dynasty. Something had to be done. Furthermore, Assyria loomed in the background and would eventually have to be faced. Perhaps a direct approach would curry favor with the monster and also dispose of the two vicious neighbors. Trust God? That always seems so intangible. But more than that, it always starts with the surrender of my ability to take care of things in my way for myself. There is the sticking point: surrender. We do not want to give up our own way and our own estimation of what we really need.

Verses 24–34. Two points need emphasis here. The first is the importance of memory. Isaiah reminds the people of two of the great deliverances they had experienced in the past: Egypt and Midian (vv. 24, 26). The lesson is plain: If God could deliver from those mighty powers, he can deliver from Assyria as well. God wants us to learn certain principles from the past that have universal implications. That is different from the pagan approach to the past, which is focused on the now, and the past is used primarily in a ritualistic way. That is, if one does all the same things now, then all the good things that happened then will be repeated. That is not the biblical way. God rarely does the same thing twice. But there are principles we can learn from the past that may be applied to new situations where the same kinds of issues are in play. That is what Isaiah is calling for: new choices made in the light of old truths.

The second truth is that human power is no match for divine power. Again, this calls for a perspective beyond now. It is one thing to assert that God is greater than any human nation, but it is another actually to be able to base one's behavior on such an idea. To do that we must be able to draw on evidence from the past as well as on our own personal experiences. Here Isaiah is saying that his own experience of the greatness and goodness of God confirms his belief that God will not allow the arrogance of any human nation to stand, especially when that arrogance leads such a nation to believe it can destroy others with impunity. There is a bar of judgment above even the greatest of nations, and every nation would do well to remember that fact.

GOD'S LORDSHIP OVER HISTORY AND HUMAN PRIDE. When we think of God's lordship over the nations today, we naturally think of the way in which he has humbled the Russian empire in the last ten years. Marx's famous line, "Religion is the opiate of the people," has come back to haunt his successors who built their whole regime on the official attempt to remove the very idea of God from life. The result is, as one Russian official put it to a friend of mine, "We have stared into the very face of evil, and it has seared our minds." Any nation that attempts to put itself in the place of God cannot survive.

But there is an earlier example in the lifetime of many of us that must not be overlooked. That is Nazi Germany. The parallel to what Isaiah is talking about here is startling enough that many do not like to bring it up. But the fact is that the Holocaust[11] may well be seen as a modern parallel to the Exile. Then, as now, a mighty power set itself to destroy the people of God. In the case of Assyria and Babylon, they were allowed to succeed to the extent they did only because God permitted it as a source of discipline and punishment for the unbelief of those people. May this perhaps be the case with Nazi Germany? Yet if Germany was a tool in the hand of God, it certainly did not see itself as such. Like Babylon and Assyria, it saw itself as supreme in itself, with the power and therefore the right to destroy whomever it wished. But like Assyria and Babylon, Germany was terribly destroyed, and God's Jewish people not only survived but prospered. No nation can set itself up as superior to God and survive.

Will the United States learn this lesson? What is it that God wants to do through us in the world today? Will we make any serious attempt to discover that? And if we do, will we carry out our tasks in humility, recognizing the terrible risks of pride? The history of nations in the Christian West is not encouraging in this respect. One after another has come to power proclaiming its dependence on God, and one after another has exited the scene in disgrace, having come to believe that they were ultimate in themselves.

What will Christians learn from this? Surely we should learn that no nation is God. It may be a tool in the hand of God, but it is only a tool. As soon as it begins to arrogate his place, it is marked for destruction. Thus, we may love our nation and be grateful for it, but the idea of "my nation, right or wrong" can never be ours.

Pride is the ultimate enemy, both of nations and of individuals. The tendency is to focus on ourselves as both the source and end of our lives. This is what Paul talks about in Romans 1:21: "For although they knew God, they neither glorified him as God nor gave thanks to him." Having put ourselves in the place of God, we then create a religious system to support such a reversal of reality. The end is the worship of the creation as an act of self-worship. God is made in our image and can be changed as necessary to support that image. This is why secularism has such appeal today. It seems to relieve us of any need to go outside of ourselves for an object of worship. But this is also the ultimate downfall of secularism: We *must* worship something

---

11. The term *Holocaust* is an English transliteration of the Hebrew term usually translated "whole burnt offering." Jews today see themselves as having been sacrificed for the sins of the world.

outside of ourselves to give ourselves any sense of significance. Thus, having already rejected a God who calls for surrender, the modern descent into the occult is wholly predictable.

It is remarkably easy to take credit for God's actions in one's life. As just noted, all we have to do to begin the slide into eventual paganism is to live without a continually thankful attitude. This is a problem both for those who are successful and for those who are not. Those who are successful come to take their abilities and achievements for granted. Perhaps this is what happened to Moses. He was used to succeeding in moments of crisis and may have come unconsciously to believe that his powers were his own. He forgot that he was only a tool in the hand of God. He forgot to cultivate a thankful attitude.

The same is even more true for those who do not see themselves as successes. Why give thanks for failure? But the fact is, all of us are tools for God's service, whether we see the results or not. So, when we pray for something and it occurs, it is easy to say, "Well, I had that coming," and in so doing give the impression that it was something we earned and deserved instead of its being an evidence of God at work through us.

The security of the believer. One of the great issues in the evangelical church is the security of the believer. Churches that have been more influenced by Calvinist theology tend to preach "eternal security" even when they have rejected Calvin's previous four points, which led to that teaching as a logical necessity. All too often holy living is neglected because heaven is certain. By contrast, churches that have been more influenced by Arminius have tended to preach a kind of "eternal insecurity," in which a believer's eternal state depends on whether or not the most recent sin has been confessed. Their tendency is to focus on one's behavior rather than on one's relationship to the Savior.

These issues seem to be the very ones underlying a passage such as this one. On the one hand, Isaiah is intent on assuring the people that the future of the nation is secure. Israel will survive; the Mesopotamians will not be able to achieve their murderous desires. That means the people can live confidently. They do not need to surrender their trust in God in order to secure the outcome. Nevertheless, that confidence in the future must never be allowed to make them think their present behavior will not have consequences. That the future of the nation is secure does not mean individual Israelites can sin with impunity.

This has two implications. (1) The first has to do with the church. The church will survive. It is the bride of Christ, and Christians need have no fears on that score. As someone has said, "I've read the last chapter in the Book! We win!" But that does not mean that every individual associated with the church is thereby guaranteed a place in heaven. Unless we live lives that show that we are truly "remaining" (KJV "abiding") in Christ, we will be thrown into the fire and burned (John 15:5–6).

(2) But there are also implications for the individual. If we have entered into a personal relationship with Christ, we can know that we will be kept by him (John 10:28–29). We need not live in a constant state of anxiety as if the continuation of that relationship depends on our performance. It does not; it depends on our continued faith, and he will make that continued faith possible. But the danger comes in our conception of faith. For many, belief in Christ is primarily assent to a certain set of ideas. That is, it is a kind of mental gymnastics. But that is not true. Faith in Christ is primarily a way of living. If I think that I can live a life where I and my desires and my way are the central focus and still expect to have eternal life merely because at a junior high retreat somewhere I accepted Christ, and I go to church somewhat regularly now, I am not merely deluded, I am lost. If the apostle Paul had to say, "No, I beat my body and make it my slave so that after I have preached to others, I myself will not be disqualified for the prize" (1 Cor. 9:27), none of us can live as though personal holiness is only a position and not a reality.

The remnant. The concept of the remnant tends to go in and out of fashion, depending on the state of the church at a given time. When the church has been strong and moving forward, the emphasis has tended to be on the idea of participating in the coming kingdom of God. But when the church has felt persecuted and was in a state of little or no growth, the "remnant" theology has tended to be more popular. Some of both emphases are probably needed in every time. In a time of growth and seeming power, we need to ask whether we are producing more chaff than wheat and whether there is fruit here that will stand a blasting drought. At the same time, when the situation is difficult, the "remnant" must remember that they are the representatives of a kingdom that cannot fail.

There are two great dangers in a "remnant mentality," closely related to each other. (1) One may be called "ghetto-ization." That is, those who believe themselves to be the righteous remnant will withdraw into a protective cocoon secure in their own righteousness and so cease to have the effect of salt and light in the world that Jesus commanded us to have (Matt. 5:13–16). (2) The other danger is self-pity. Here we take on a kind of "hang-dog" mentality, where we are always feeling sorry for ourselves as the last vestiges of whatever God is trying to do. But if we are secure in the promises of God and rely on God and not on human power, our own or that of the state, we can dare to live in the open with quiet confidence and humble joy.

Believers in the former Eastern bloc countries are shining examples of this truth. While they did not go out of their way to provoke confrontation, neither did they avoid it. They lived their lives before God, seeking to love everyone, even those who counted themselves their enemies. The state tried to isolate them, but it never truly succeeded. They were truly the remnant, yet many of them did not succumb to a remnant mentality.

Memory. The place of memory in the Bible is important. This is partly so because of the importance given to human history in the Bible. Alone of all the world's holy books, the Bible declares that God has made himself known in ongoing human relationships. Therefore, it was of utmost importance to record the details of those relationships with honesty and accuracy and to record the inspired interpretations of the meaning of those relationships. This is why words associated with memory are so important in a book such as Deuteronomy (e.g., Deut. 4:10; 5:15; 7:18). God had done some things in Israel's experience that demonstrated the central truths of human (and divine) existence. He did not reveal himself in disembodied aphorisms but in the raw stuff of daily life. He did not only say that he was dependable; he showed it. In fact, he showed it before he said it (as in the Abraham narrative). Therefore, when God called his people to believe in him, there was evidence in life to support that call.

The same must be true for us. If we are to keep the faith in times of stress, difficulty, and perhaps real persecution, there must be a solid block of memory in our minds. First, we must remember sacred history. It is not accidental that we teach our children "Bible stories." God has once for all intercepted human life and given us the final word on how we are to interpret our own lives in that regard. As the Israelites did, we are to remember the Exodus and the Conquest and the tragedy of the judges. Those events are our history too. Beyond this we can also remember the life, death, and resurrection of our Lord and the stirring narrative of the founding of the church.

Then there is our personal history. We dare not succumb to a kind of spiritual Alzheimer's disease. We need to recount to ourselves and our families the ways God has intervened in, provided for, guided, and sustained our lives. When our spiritual memory is intact, so is our spiritual identity. With a secure spiritual self-identity, we can look with perfect confidence at the various Assyrias that cross our paths, able to learn whatever lessons of discipline or correction God wants for us, but also able to see their certain doom in the end.

In the 1970s Joseph Tson, a Romanian pastor, heard a Voice of America broadcast enumerating all of the failed promises of Marxism, and he immediately thought of all the promises of the Christian faith that have come true. He has said that in that moment he knew Communism could not survive and that he and other Christians should begin preparing for the day of its collapse. We might marvel at such vision, but the fact is, Tson was a man with a memory, and because of that memory, he could see the future when others could not.

Isaiah 11:1-16

¹A SHOOT WILL come up from the stump of Jesse;
   from his roots a Branch will bear fruit.
²The Spirit of the LORD will rest on him—
   the Spirit of wisdom and of understanding,
   the Spirit of counsel and of power,
   the Spirit of knowledge and of the fear of the LORD—
³and he will delight in the fear of the LORD.

  He will not judge by what he sees with his eyes,
   or decide by what he hears with his ears;
⁴but with righteousness he will judge the needy,
   with justice he will give decisions for the poor of
    the earth.
  He will strike the earth with the rod of his mouth;
   with the breath of his lips he will slay the wicked.
⁵Righteousness will be his belt
   and faithfulness the sash around his waist.

⁶The wolf will live with the lamb,
   the leopard will lie down with the goat,
  the calf and the lion and the yearling together;
   and a little child will lead them.
⁷The cow will feed with the bear,
   their young will lie down together,
   and the lion will eat straw like the ox.
⁸The infant will play near the hole of the cobra,
   and the young child put his hand into the viper's nest.
⁹They will neither harm nor destroy
   on all my holy mountain,
  for the earth will be full of the knowledge of the LORD
   as the waters cover the sea.

¹⁰In that day the Root of Jesse will stand as a banner for the peoples; the nations will rally to him, and his place of rest will be glorious. ¹¹In that day the Lord will reach out his hand a second time to reclaim the remnant that is left of his people from Assyria, from Lower Egypt, from Upper Egypt, from Cush, from Elam, from Babylonia, from Hamath and from the islands of the sea.

¹²He will raise a banner for the nations
    and gather the exiles of Israel;
he will assemble the scattered people of Judah
    from the four quarters of the earth.
¹³Ephraim's jealousy will vanish,
    and Judah's enemies will be cut off;
Ephraim will not be jealous of Judah,
    nor Judah hostile toward Ephraim.
¹⁴They will swoop down on the slopes of Philistia to the west;
    together they will plunder the people to the east.
They will lay hands on Edom and Moab,
    and the Ammonites will be subject to them.
¹⁵The LORD will dry up
    the gulf of the Egyptian sea;
with a scorching wind he will sweep his hand
    over the Euphrates River.
He will break it up into seven streams
    so that men can cross over in sandals.
¹⁶There will be a highway for the remnant of his people
    that is left from Assyria,
as there was for Israel
    when they came up from Egypt.

Original Meaning

HERE COMES THE final evidence of God's trustworthiness. Although the house of David in the person of Ahaz has failed to trust the Lord in the crisis brought on by Israel's and Syria's attack and has thus brought disaster on the nation of Judah, God will not allow that disaster to be his final word. Instead, as promised briefly in 9:1–7, he will one day bring a true descendant of the house of Jesse to rule over his people. Instead of the cowardly shepherd who depends on force to secure his kingdom, this One, filled with the Spirit of God, will rule with fairness and justice and will bring about true *šalom*.

The Coming Descendant of Jesse (11:1–9)

WHY IS THE MESSIAH here attributed to the family line of Jesse and not more directly to that of Jesse's son David? Perhaps the point is that this new David will spring up as a new beginning, just as the first one did.[1] Or perhaps it is

---

1. So Motyer, *Prophecy of Isaiah*, 121.

intended to point beyond royal Jerusalem to the humble origins of the dynasty in Bethlehem.[2] At any rate it serves to underline a certain discontinuity with the present representatives of the house of David. The One who is coming will not be merely one more descendant of the royal line that is now so thoroughly besmirched; rather, he will spring from the very roots of that dynasty.

The forestry imagery that has played such a prominent role in these early chapters continues here. The prophet sees the forest of Israel's pride having been thoroughly cut down and burned, as prophesied in chapter 6. In its place grew up the mighty forest of Assyria. But now that forest too has been cut down (as ch. 10 predicted). In this field of burned-out stumps, as suggested in 6:13, a green "shoot" is springing up from one of the stumps. It is a "branch" coming from the original "root."[3] Although the tree of Davidic pride has been cut down and burned, there is still life in the original root, a life that resides finally in the faithfulness of God (cf. 2 Sam. 7).

This descendant of Jesse will rule with a different spirit than that which characterized too many of the previous descendants. It will be the Spirit of the Lord. Throughout the Old Testament when someone is marked by a different kind of ability and motivation than what normally characterizes humans, this is the language that is used. It extends from Joseph (Gen. 41:38) through Bezalel (Ex. 31:3) and Othniel (Judg. 3:10) and David (1 Sam. 16:13) to Micah (Mic. 3:8) and the other prophets. The Spirit of the Lord is the means by which God's people will be able finally to keep their covenant with God (Ezek. 36:27). Thus, the Messiah will not rule in the power and the motivation of the fallen human spirit but by the life and breath of God himself.

As a result, his reign will be characterized by "wisdom," "understanding," "counsel," "power," "knowledge," and "the fear of the LORD"—all the characteristics lacking among God's people (1:3) but found wherever God is truly present (Prov. 9:10; Isa. 33:6). This kind of true understanding will not be an intellectual grasp of certain facts but that kind of wisdom that springs from an experiential knowledge of the One who is true. The repetition of "the fear of the LORD" in 11:2–3 underlines this point. The problem with too many of the Davidic monarchs who ruled Judah and all of the kings of Israel is that they did not rule out of a chief concern for obeying, pleasing, and glorifying God, which is what this phrase means. Instead, the chief concern of too many was with maintaining their own power. This ruler will be different.

---

2. So Watts, *Isaiah 1–33*, 171; see also Childs, *Isaiah*, 102.

3. Heb. *ḥoter* ("shoot") occurs only here and in Prov. 14:3, while *neṣer* ("branch") only occurs here and in 14:19; 60:21; Dan. 11:7. Neither term has a particularly messianic connection.

How different he will be becomes clear in 11:3–5. He will not "judge" on the basis of appearances or of image. He will not "decide" on the basis of what the outcome of the case might mean to him. He will not be biased in favor of the rich and powerful. Instead, he will concern himself with what is right[4] according to the unchanging standards of the One who is Right. The "justice"[5] he dispenses will connect with the regulations for life designed by the Creator. As a result the "poor" and the "needy" will no longer be at a disadvantage with the rich. Nor will the powerful escape if they are among the "wicked." His words will be more powerful than the mightiest "rod" some other king might brandish to try to enforce his will, and the "breath" (*ruaḥ*, "spirit") of his lips will not only pronounce the sentence of the "wicked " but actually kill them.

How will all this be possible? Because "righteousness" and "faithfulness" will be at the very heart of this person's existence. The English translations tend to obscure the imagery used in 11:5, but the sense is that these characteristics are the Messiah's most intimate garments, his underclothing. When you strip away everything else, what do you find? A continuing concern to be right with all that is right and to be true to all that is true in God's universe. Can such a king be trusted? Will he have an inescapable personal authority? By all means!

The result of this kind of leadership will be peace—not merely the cessation of hostilities but the unification of that which was formerly divided. The imagery used to convey this point in 11:6–9 has captured thinkers and artists across the centuries. Isaiah depicts the very opposites of aggressiveness and helplessness living together in harmony. Wolves, leopards, lions, and bears are together with lambs, goats, calves, and cows. Perhaps the most shocking image of all is the one of a baby playing in a nest of deadly snakes.

Should these images be taken literally? Many have believed so and have seen these things to be characteristic of the millennial reign of the Messiah predicted in Revelation 20:1–6. If so, it will truly be a new heaven and new earth (see 65:17), for a lion as now constituted can neither chew nor digest "straw like the ox" (11:7). Others have argued that this imagery speaks of an equally dramatic change in human nature, where the aggressiveness and cruelty that are so much a part of us will be forever changed (11:9). This latter change has already been effected in part, and we may look forward with joy to its final fulfillment. The means by which this will be accomplished is cited

---

4. "Righteousness" (*ṣedeq*) is right behavior, implying absolute standards by which such behavior can be judged.

5. "Justice" (lit., "with uprightness"; Heb. *mîšor*, from the root *yšr*), that is, "in an upright, straight way." In the Hebrew mind, justice is more than legal equity; it is that divine order by which all things are rightly governed.

in the final colon of 11:9: "The earth will be full of the knowledge of the LORD as the waters cover the sea."

In this verse we return to the opening theme of 11:2, true knowledge. The Israel that was too stupid to know where the barn was, spiritually speaking (1:2–3), will now have true knowledge of reality and will be able to act accordingly. The Hebrew language does not recognize any distinction between knowledge that is an accumulation of information and knowledge that is personal acquaintance. For the Hebrews, all true knowledge is based on experience. Therefore, when the prophet speaks here about "knowledge of the LORD," he is not speaking primarily of knowledge *about* the Lord but of insight into reality born of a close and intimate relationship with him. The Messiah will make it possible for all people to know God intimately.[6]

The Messiah As the Banner (11:10–16)

AS GOD PREVIOUSLY ran up a "banner" (5:26) to call the enemy nations to come and destroy his people, now the Messiah is a "banner" (11:10, 12) calling the nations to himself (see 2:1–5), with the express purpose of restoring his people to their homeland. The places cited in 11:11 emphasize the worldwide nature of this return. They will come from the far south ("Cush"), the far east ("Elam"), the far north ("Assyria"), and the far west ("the islands of the sea"). The phrase "the four quarters of the earth" in 11:12 expresses the same idea. There is no part of the earth too far away for God's "hand" to reach.[7]

The precise intent of "a second time" in 11:11 is not clear. Perhaps the first time was the Exodus from Egypt, so that the return from the Exile constitutes a kind of second Exodus. But the worldwide extent of the Dispersion was greater than anything that happened between 722 and 586 B.C., and the return in 538 B.C. was only from Babylon and not from these other lands. This invites us to consider that the "second time" may point to a second return from exile.[8] The fact that this return from the nations figures again in chapters 60–61, which seem to be addressed to people after the return in 538 B.C., adds support to this understanding.

This part of the book (Isa. 7–12) started with the hostility of the northern kingdom (here identified by the primary tribe of that area, "Ephraim" [11:13]) toward Judah. Now the prophet envisions a day when that hostility, stretching back to the division after Solomon's death and even further (see

6. Note also 53:11, which says that the "knowledge" of the Suffering Servant "will justify many."
7. Cf. the Assyrian king boasting that his hand has reached into the "nests" of the nations to gather up all their wealth (10:13–14).
8. So *Young, The Book of Isaiah,* 1:395–96; Motyer, *Prophecy of Isaiah,* 125–26.

2 Sam. 2:1–11), will be permanently healed. The division between Samaria and Judea at the time of Christ was one continuation of that hostility. When Christ drew some of the Samaritans to himself (John 4), he was beginning to bridge the gulf; we await the final bridging to occur when Christ's kingdom is fully realized.

Instead of fighting among themselves, the unified people of Israel will be able to mount an effective offense against the historically hostile nations on the east side of the Jordan: Ammon to the north, Moab in the center, and Edom to the south (11:14). No longer will these peoples be able to attack the Israelite people at will.

Again in 11:15 it is unclear how literally the prophet intends these figures to be taken, but the point is clear. There will be no effective barrier to the return of his people either from the south ("the gulf of the Egyptian Sea," i.e., the gulf of Suez) or from the north ("the Euphrates River"). In language reminiscent of the Exodus, Isaiah speaks of a wind drying up the waters (cf. Ex. 14:21) and of crossing a riverbed dry-shod (cf. Josh. 3:17). Isaiah 11:16 continues the imagery of ease of travel with the first use of the motif of "highway" in this book.[9] Here the allusion to the Exodus becomes explicit, and it is clear that symbolism is intended since there was no literal highway through the desert for the people of the Exodus.

Bridging Contexts

VERSES 1–9. These verses are speaking of the characteristics of the kingdom of God. God keeps his promises, although not always in the way we might envision him doing so. The Jews of the New Testament era were certain that the promises of a descendant of David ruling over Israel meant that a literal political/military leader would rule over them and defeat their political/military enemies. Thus, when God kept his promise in another way, they had a difficult time making the changeover. We might say that they should have been prepared for a more spiritual emphasis in the messianic kingdom if we look at the type of language used here and elsewhere. However, we cannot be too hard on them, especially since they viewed themselves as the "poor" (11:4) whom the Messiah would vindicate when he destroyed the "wicked" (11:4), their oppressors, with fire from his mouth.

But it is instructive to modern-day readers, who should read prophecy with a bit more humility and a bit less certitude that they know exactly how the

---

9. See also 19:23; 35:8; 40:3; 62:10, all of which are in the context of redemption and restoration.

predictions are going to be fulfilled. In particular we need to read prophecies like this with more of an eye on their spiritual teaching and less on the mechanics of their fulfillment. Thus, this passage speaks about the basis of true knowledge in the fear of the Lord, about the power of the Word of God, and about the hope for the healing of humanity's aggressive and oppressive instincts.

Verses 10–16. This prophecy of the return of God's people to their land perhaps speaks to the opposite tendency of that just mentioned. If we need to be careful not to interpret predictions overly literally, we need also to leave a place for literal fulfillment. For centuries the church understood itself to be the spiritual successor to the people of Israel and saw all the promises as having a spiritual fulfillment in the life of the church. Thus, when Jews began to return to Israel in the last part of the nineteenth century and that return became a flood after World War II, many Christians were taken by surprise. Again, it is too easy to say they should not have been surprised, given Paul's rather clear statement in Romans 9–11 about the old stock not having been rejected. It is always much easier to see where we have been than where we are going. So, bald assertions that a certain passage can *only* have spiritual significance ought to be held suspect.

 A MILLENNIAL KINGDOM. It seems plain to me that just as there will be a literal return of Christ, there will also be a literal new heaven and new earth over which Christ will reign; it is to that kingdom that this chapter is looking forward. Apart from the explicit biblical statements, I believe the logic of creation calls for a time when God's creatures will experience creation as it was meant to be. Whether that reign will be a literal thousand years, as Revelation 20:1–5 has it, I am much less certain. The reason for that uncertainty is that the round number "thousand" is only exceeded in Hebrew numerology by "ten thousand" as a really large number (cf. 1 Sam. 18:7). We today might talk of "millions" and "billions," respectively. So this reign of Christ will be for a very long time until the creation is brought to its logical fulfillment.

That the church is going to bring in the kingdom described here even symbolically seems less and less likely. If it may be argued that the Christian "kingdoms" have been somewhat more enlightened and humanitarian than the non-Christian ones, it is still true that the two great blots on human history, World Wars I and II, were either centered in, or had their origins in, Christian Europe. Too often human aggression and oppression have been justified in terms of the Christian Bible. So we look to a day yet to be when "they will neither hurt nor destroy in all my holy mountain" (11:9), and we look to a power not our own to bring that to pass.

The present kingdom. At the same time, this is not an excuse for Christians to sit on their hands and wait for *deus ex machina* to come and deliver us from this mess. Clearly Christ's kingdom has both come and is yet to come.[10] In the sense I have just been speaking of, it is yet to come. But in another sense it has come. The Holy Spirit is available in his fullness to every believer, and he will enable us to know God in a way that changes our individual behavior. That the sinful nature in humanity has proven much more intractable than the church has believed in its more optimistic moments does not justify each of us avoiding full participation in all that Christ died to make available to us.

We can know God in ways that will forever change our thinking and acting, and that change can affect our communities in positive ways. We can participate with Christ as he seeks to bring right to the needy and justice to the poor. We can surrender our "rights" to him and thus any need to aggressively claim what is ours for ourselves, knowing he will supply our needs better than we ever can ourselves (Eph. 3:20–21; Phil. 4:19).

In our own times we have seen the beginning of the fulfillment of the promises of this chapter as the Jewish people have been gathered into Israel from all over the world. Furthermore, it is interesting that the kingdom of Jordan, which encompasses ancient Ammon, Moab, and Edom, is at peace with Israel. To be sure, most modern Israelis give God no credit for their return, which is a dangerous position for them to be in. However, it is obvious that God is not finished with his plans for his people, and we may look forward with excitement to see exactly how he will fulfill his promises.

---

10. This is the thesis of O. Cullmann in his *Christ and Time: The Primitive Christian Conception of Time and History*, trans. F. Filson (Philadelphia: Westminster, 1964).

Isaiah 12:1–6

IN THAT DAY you will say:

"I will praise you, O LORD.
>Although you were angry with me,
your anger has turned away
>and you have comforted me.
²Surely God is my salvation;
>I will trust and not be afraid.
The LORD, the LORD, is my strength and my song;
>he has become my salvation."
³With joy you will draw water
>from the wells of salvation.

⁴In that day you will say:

"Give thanks to the LORD, call on his name;
>make known among the nations what he has done,
>and proclaim that his name is exalted.
⁵Sing to the LORD, for he has done glorious things;
>let this be known to all the world.
⁶Shout aloud and sing for joy, people of Zion,
>for great is the Holy One of Israel among you."

Original Meaning

THIS BEAUTIFUL TWO-PART hymn concludes the first subdivision of chapters 7–39. Isaiah has challenged Ahaz to trust the Holy One of Israel, who has revealed himself to Isaiah. When Ahaz rejected that invitation and the offered sign of God's presence with his people, Isaiah announced that what Ahaz had trusted in place of God—Assyria—would turn on Judah and destroy it. But, demonstrating how genuinely trustworthy God is, the prophet then declared that God would give light in place of Judah's self-induced darkness—light in the form of a descendant of David who would be "God with us." Furthermore, once Israel faced the fact that it was God who controlled her destiny and not Assyria, God would demonstrate that truth by destroying arrogant Assyria and bringing about a messianic kingdom of peace peopled not only with his own people but also with representatives of all the nations. Should such a God be trusted? Absolutely!

That is just the response we find in 12:1−6. God should be trusted simply because he is God, but how much more he should be trusted when we realize that he himself has turned his righteous anger to "comfort" or encouragement. As on the shores of the Red Sea, the people can say what they have learned about God: He is "strength," he is "song," he is "salvation." Who would not trust such a God as this? Drawing "water from the wells of salvation" is not only to avail oneself of the deliverance God has offered, but it is also to live out the implications of that salvation in obedience and witness, as Psalm 116:13−14 makes clear.

Just as the elements of hope in the introduction (2:1−5; 4:2−6) led us to believe, the immediate results of redemption and salvation (12:1−3) are witness to the nations (12:4−6). The same thing is true in microcosm in the prophet's own call. He was not cleansed so that he could enjoy the condition of being cleansed but so that he could declare God's word to the people.

Verse 4 gives a short course in the behavior of the believer: thanks, prayer, and witness. The witness is to what God "has done" and to the obvious conclusion: There is no one with a character ("name") so high and holy as his. The witness is in the form of a song. Works like those the Holy One has performed cannot be proclaimed with a long face. They must be sung "to all the world" (v. 5).

THIS CHAPTER IS BRIM-FULL of evangelical theology. God is the One who initiates salvation. There is nothing that Israel did to earn God's grace toward them. If there was to be reconciliation, it would have to come from God. Trust (or faith) does not produce reconciliation but is a response to the reconciliation announced. As such, it is the only adequate response. When God himself has satisfied his own justice and invites us to trust him, what else can we do?

This means that our response must finally issue in songs. No other form of human expression so captures the whole human psyche as does singing. Furthermore, there is a continuity in the songs of Zion that flows from the shores of the Red Sea to the shores of the "glassy sea" around which all the saints will gather:

> You are worthy to take the scroll
> and to open its seals,
> because you were slain,
> and with your blood you purchased men for God
> from every tribe and language and people and nation.

You have made them to be a kingdom
   and priests to serve our God,
and they will reign on the earth. (Rev. 5:9–10)

CHRISTIANS TODAY WHO THINK about this chapter cannot help but reflect on the work of Christ. Paul says, "In Christ God was reconciling the world to himself" (2 Cor. 5:19 RSV). That says it all. God reconciled us to himself through his own work on the Cross. Reconciliation is by nature a two-way street, but not in this case. There was nothing we could offer to God in the way of negotiation. We were condemned sinners, estranged from God and alienated from life (John 3:18; Eph. 4:18; Col. 1:21). But God found a way to satisfy his own justice in that Christ has died in our place. In place of judgment he has come to offer us encouragement.

It is no accident that the Holy Spirit is called the "Comforter" in King James English. Unfortunately the word "comfort" has become so watered down that we can no longer use it in contemporary translations. But "comfort" in its original sense is exactly what God the Holy Spirit has come to do for us. He has come to enable us to stand before the Accuser and know ourselves forgiven. He has come to tell us all is not lost when we have failed again. He has come to enable us to stand before a mocking world with love and fortitude. None of this is in us but is in the power of Christ's cross and resurrection.

The story is told that in the late 1940s when the Indian constitution was being debated, an article prohibiting proselytization was proposed. But one legislator, who was not a Christian, rose and said that would involve them in self-contradiction. When asked why, he pointed out that they had already adopted an article guaranteeing freedom of religion and said that Christians *had to* seek converts; it was a part of their religion! The article prohibiting proselytization failed. Not only is this a characterization of Christianity, it is true of biblical religion as a whole (note Jesus' comment about the Pharisees' zeal for converts, Matt. 23:15). If God is the sole Creator of this world and if after we have alienated ourselves from him, he has found a way for us to come home again, that is news the whole created world needs to hear. How can we keep silent?

Isaiah 13:1–22

🌿

AN ORACLE CONCERNING Babylon that Isaiah son of Amoz saw:

² Raise a banner on a bare hilltop,
   shout to them;
beckon to them
   to enter the gates of the nobles.
³ I have commanded my holy ones;
   I have summoned my warriors to carry out my wrath—
   those who rejoice in my triumph.

⁴ Listen, a noise on the mountains,
   like that of a great multitude!
Listen, an uproar among the kingdoms,
   like nations massing together!
The LORD Almighty is mustering
   an army for war.
⁵ They come from faraway lands,
   from the ends of the heavens—
the LORD and the weapons of his wrath—
   to destroy the whole country.

⁶ Wail, for the day of the LORD is near;
   it will come like destruction from the Almighty.
⁷ Because of this, all hands will go limp,
   every man's heart will melt.
⁸ Terror will seize them,
   pain and anguish will grip them;
   they will writhe like a woman in labor.
They will look aghast at each other,
   their faces aflame.

⁹ See, the day of the LORD is coming
   —a cruel day, with wrath and fierce anger—
to make the land desolate
   and destroy the sinners within it.
¹⁰ The stars of heaven and their constellations
   will not show their light.
The rising sun will be darkened
   and the moon will not give its light.

[11] I will punish the world for its evil,
    the wicked for their sins.
I will put an end to the arrogance of the haughty
    and will humble the pride of the ruthless.
[12] I will make man scarcer than pure gold,
    more rare than the gold of Ophir.
[13] Therefore I will make the heavens tremble;
    and the earth will shake from its place
at the wrath of the LORD Almighty,
    in the day of his burning anger.

[14] Like a hunted gazelle,
    like sheep without a shepherd,
each will return to his own people,
    each will flee to his native land.
[15] Whoever is captured will be thrust through;
    all who are caught will fall by the sword.
[16] Their infants will be dashed to pieces before their eyes;
    their houses will be looted and their wives ravished.

[17] See, I will stir up against them the Medes,
    who do not care for silver
    and have no delight in gold.
[18] Their bows will strike down the young men;
    they will have no mercy on infants
    nor will they look with compassion on children.
[19] Babylon, the jewel of kingdoms,
    the glory of the Babylonians' pride,
will be overthrown by God
    like Sodom and Gomorrah.
[20] She will never be inhabited
    or lived in through all generations;
no Arab will pitch his tent there,
    no shepherd will rest his flocks there.
[21] But desert creatures will lie there,
    jackals will fill her houses;
there the owls will dwell,
    and there the wild goats will leap about.
[22] Hyenas will howl in her strongholds,
    jackals in her luxurious palaces.
Her time is at hand,
    and her days will not be prolonged.

As NOTED IN the introduction, Isaiah 7–12 and 36–39 are "bookends," dealing with the different ways in which two Judean kings, Ahaz and Hezekiah, approach the problem of trust in God in the face of serious military/political threats to their kingdom. But what lies between in the intervening chapters? We might call them "Lessons in Trust."

It is as though the student has failed the examination in chapters 7–12. So before this student is allowed to take the examination again in chapter 36, some tutoring is necessary. The tutoring falls into three sessions: chapters 13–23; 24–27; and 28–33, with a wrap-up in 34–35. Here are some of the subjects covered in the tutoring sessions:

- Why trust the nations when they are under judgment from God (chs. 13–23)?
- Why trust the nations when all of history is in our God's hands (chs. 24–27)?
- Those who counsel you to trust flesh and blood instead of the Spirit of God are fools (chs. 28–35).

Once these lessons have been presented, it will be time to take the test again, but this time, as the prophet has foretold, for much higher stakes: not merely for the survival of the Davidic dynasty but for the very survival of the nation.

The material in chapters 13–23 fits a category found in several of the prophets: oracles against the nations (see esp. Jer. 46–51; Ezek. 25–32, but note also Obadiah and Nahum, which are each composed of a single such oracle—Obadiah against Edom and Nahum against Assyria). In general these oracles are God's way of saying that just because he chooses to use the pagan nations as his tool to judge disobedient Israel and Judah does not mean those nations are going to escape judgment for their sins. Israel will be restored after disciplinary punishment, but some of these nations are going to disappear from the face of the earth.

As I have already said, the oracles against the nations have been placed at this point in the book of Isaiah to emphasize the foolishness of trusting in the nations, something Ahaz has done and Hezekiah will be tempted to do. They may also be at this place to underline the certainty of the promises of restoration made in chapter 11. The nations will not be able to hold their captives because God will certainly judge them. The particular nations marked for judgment are Babylon (13:1–14:23; 21:1–10 [and Assyria, 14:24–27]), Philistia (14:28–32), Moab (15:1–16:14), Damascus (Syria, 17:1–14), Cush (Nubia and Ethiopia, 18:1–7), Egypt (19:1–20:6), Dumah (Edom? 21:11–12), Arabia (21:13–17), Jerusalem (Judah, 22:1–25), and Tyre (23:1–18). There is no obvious reason for this particular selection or this particular arrangement, although scholars have tried valiantly to find one.[1] About the most one can say is that it is an inclusive list, covering the whole ancient Near Eastern world (omitting only Ammon), beginning with the great commercial power in the east, Babylon, and concluding with the great commercial power in the west, Tyre.

Address Against Babylon (13:1)

THE FACT THAT the first oracle (chs. 13–14) begins with Babylon, which was not a world power in Isaiah's lifetime, is often taken to be proof of the late date of the book. According to this argument, the later editors of the book, realizing that it was Babylon to whom Judah fell and not Assyria, inserted this oracle at this point. But the opening lines of chapter 13 seem to have been designed precisely to counter such a conclusion. We are told that "Isaiah son of Amoz," not some later editor, saw this oracle against Babylon. Either this is a truthful statement or a deception. If it is a deception, then the reliability of the other things that are said in the book, including its theological claims, are all in question.[2] The final chapter of this division (ch. 39) shows that Isaiah clearly understood Babylon as the enemy to whom Judah would finally fall.

If we grant Isaiah enough perspicuity to know that Babylon was Judah's real enemy, then it is not too much to believe that God could have inspired this oracle, especially since it contains many features that were perennially true of Babylon.[3] Even during the time of the Assyrian Empire, Babylon was the center of culture and civilization in the Mesopotamian valley and indeed in the entire Near East. Thus, it is fitting to begin a series of judgments against human power and glory with an oracle against Babylon.[4]

When compared with the other oracle against Babylon in 21:1–10, chapters 13–14 have a much more universal flavor. The very stars and constellations are darkened (13:10), the whole world is punished for its arrogance

---

1. For an involved suggestion concerning the arrangement, see Motyer, *Prophecy of Isaiah*, 131–34.

2. Childs, *Isaiah*, 124, simply dismisses the claim of authorship by saying it indicates "a redactional strategy." This does not answer the questions of authenticity and integrity raised by the statement.

3. On this point, see S. Erlandsson, *The Burden of Babylon: A Study of Isaiah 13:2–14:23* (Lund: Gleerup, 1970). Seitz, *Isaiah 1–39*, 131–32, admits this as a possibility but says the material was later "enriched."

4. Note that the "oracle" against Assyria (14:24–27) is contained within this one, with no special introductory rubric of its own. This suggests again that "Babylon" here represents all the ancient Mesopotamian cultures.

and haughtiness (13:11[5]), and the "heavens" and "earth" will be shaken. The king of Babylon (ch. 14) is also clearly much more than one particular ruler, although Sargon II of Assyria may have provided the model (see comments on 14:16–21). Clearly this figure represents all creaturely pride that believes it can contend with God for rule of the world. Thus, the introductory oracle uses Babylon to represent the pride and glory of all creation and to argue that at its greatest and highest, there is no reason to trust any such creatures, because the Lord God will bring them all down into the dust.

The Terror of Coming Judgment (13:2–8)

IN THIS STANZA the terror of the coming judgment is emphasized. Once again (cf. 5:26), a signal "banner" is run up to call the various nations to come against God's enemy in judgment (13:2; see 5:26). But these armies come from the very "ends of the heavens" (13:5). This is not a merely historical judgment but an eschatological one. Furthermore, there is no question who is the effective cause of this uproar. It is "I," "the LORD Almighty,"[6] "the Almighty."[7] Even the mightiest and most glorious of earth's nations is no match for the God who has placed his name on Jerusalem. Against him there will be no mighty blows, only limp hands and melted hearts (13:7). Nor will there be any arrogant looks, only the red faces of shame and disgrace (13:8).

The Sin of Pride (13:9–13)

AS SEEN IN the earliest chapters of Isaiah, the greatest of all the sins of creation is the sin of pride. For those who depend for their very existence on the continued grace of a loving Creator to act as if they are somehow ultimate is the worst trespass upon reality imaginable. Oftentimes, the pagan deification of humanity expresses itself in the fiction that the gods, made in human form, are the stars. In fact, says Isaiah, the opposite is true. Far from the stars being the guarantee of our lordship of creation, they are the dutiful servants of the Almighty, and they will not escape the cataclysms when he punishes rebellious earth. He will darken them and shake them (13:10, 13).

The Collapse of Power (13:14–22)

ISAIAH NOW TAKES up a somewhat more historical note, although the language still retains a distinctly universalistic tone. Verses 14–15 describe the breakup of the collection of city-states out of which every ancient empire was

---

5. See also 13:5, 9, which the NIV translates "the whole country" and "the land." In both cases, and especially the latter, I believe "earth" would be a better translation.

6. Lit., "Yahweh of hosts."

7. Heb. *šadday.*

crafted. As the central power began to collapse, it was quickly every city ("native land") for itself, as everyone rushed to get some modicum of protection. But, in fact, there would be no protection, for the strongest of men could not save his wife, his children, or his possessions (13:16).

The "Medes" were a warlike people from the Zagros Mountains east of the Tigris River (in what is today Iran). They seem to have loved fighting more than ruling, for they were successively allied with Assyria, Babylon, and Persia. Only the Greeks under Alexander proved their match, and even the Greeks spoke of the Medes with a certain degree of awe. Here (13:17), with prophetic inspiration, Isaiah recognizes that the Medes are the ones who will undo the Mesopotamian power as they first join Babylon to destroy Assyria and then join the Persians to wipe out Babylon. Neither the strong ("the young men") nor the weak ("infants," "children," 13:18) will receive any quarter from them, so that Babylon's destruction will be complete (13:19–22).

Although the Medo-Persian conquest of Babylon did not signal the city's immediate demise, it did signal the beginning of the end. The Persians had dual capital cities in Susa in Persia and Ecbatana in Media, while the successors of Alexander made their capitol in Antioch of Syria. Thus, the greatest city in the ancient world went into a slow decline so that in the eighteenth century A.D., even its location was unknown. Isaiah's prophecy about its becoming a haunt of "hyenas" and "jackals" (13:22) came true with a vengeance. Was it the glory of the world? Listen to the owls hooting in its windows and the goats bleating as they jump over the stumps of its walls!

Bridging Contexts

ON THE SURFACE, Isaiah seems to be picking an uneven fight. What can the God of tiny little Jerusalem do to mighty Babylon? Of course Isaiah knows something that the rulers of Babylon do not. The Holy One of Israel is the sole God of the whole world, the Creator and Sustainer of the universe. Yes, it *is* an uneven fight, but in the exact opposite direction from what the Babylonians may be thinking.

Many years after Isaiah, when Babylon was at the height of its power, the God of the exiled Judeans humbled Nebuchadnezzar, the mightiest Babylonian king of all time, to eat grass like an ox (Dan. 4:24–35). The words that Nebuchadnezzar spoke at the end of that experience are true then and now (see 4:34b–35):

> His dominion is an eternal dominion;
>   his kingdom endures from generation to generation.
> All the peoples of the earth
>   are regarded as nothing.

He does as he pleases
　　with the powers of heaven
　　and the peoples of the earth.
No one can hold back his hand
　　or say to him, "What have you done?"

Compared to the glory of the Creator and Sustainer of the universe, the glory of the greatest Babylon that the earth can produce is only dust and ashes.

John the Revelator said much the same thing six centuries after Nebuchadnezzar, when he depicted the Babylon of his day, Rome, as a gorgeous prostitute to whom all the great of the earth came. Yet, using language that clearly combines that used to describe Babylon here and Tyre in Isaiah 23, the prophet writes that all her wealth and power will come to nothing:

"Fallen! Fallen is Babylon the Great!
　　She has become a home for demons
and a haunt for every evil spirit,
　　a haunt for every unclean and detestable bird.
For all the nations have drunk
　　the maddening wine of her adulteries.
The kings of the earth have committed adultery with her,
　　and the merchants of the earth grew rich from her excessive
　　　　luxuries. . . .
'Woe! Woe, O great city,
　　O Babylon, city of Power!
In one hour your doom has come!'" (Rev. 18:2–3, 10)

Today, all that remains of ancient Rome is a collection of impressive ruins. "Eternal Rome" did not last for even a thousand years. More recently, the world-spanning British Empire, on which "the sun never set," was more presciently described by Rudyard Kipling when he said, "Lo, all our wealth of yesterday is one with Nineveh and Tyre."[8]

IT IS ALL TOO EASY to be blown away by the glory of this world. We see the glamour of the movie stars; we see the power that wealth gives; we see aircraft carriers and intercontinental ballistic missiles, and we think, "Ah, there is reality." But that is not where glory

---

8. A part of Kipling's "Recessional."

resides. Isaiah heard the seraphim correctly when they sang, "The whole earth is full of his glory."

Imagine if New York City, arguably the most glamorous and powerful city on the earth, were struck with a nuclear attack this afternoon. What would all the glamour and power be worth in one millisecond? Exactly nothing. Isaiah knows nothing about nuclear physics, but he knows about a God to whom earth's mightiest nuclear explosion is less than a sneeze. What is the fusion of a few atoms of uranium to the One who spoke a word of command and the "Big Bang" occurred?

Yet we all, like the ancient Hebrews, persist in trusting everything else before God. We give our allegiance to flesh and blood, to physical things, as though they can give us significance and worth. In fact, they are all passing faster than we can imagine. In childhood the days seem to stretch on and on forever, and the month of December takes several years to pass—or so it seems. With the passing of years, the days begin to fly by, and we begin to see that some things we thought were so important will shortly be gone.

So wisdom asks: What will survive the wreck of all human accomplishments? It is not the works of humans, amassed by cleverness and oppression. Nor is it even our finer works of art and culture. In the end, while they may survive their creators, they are as fragile as we are. One day the finest cathedrals will fall, as did Solomon's temple. One day, the Mona Lisa will crumble into dust. If we trust our power, someone will emerge more powerful than we; if we trust our intelligence, someone will emerge smarter than we; if we trust our creativity, someone will emerge more creative than we; if we trust our allies, they will one day run away before an enemy mightier than we, and they may even become the enemy themselves.

Whence comes this endless string of supersedence? It comes from the fact that we are neither self-originating nor self-authenticating. Thus, it is foolish to trust in humanity that has breath in its nostrils (2:22). Rather, we should be looking to the eternal, which will not pass away. We may love our country and grieve over the unmistakable signs of its demise that are all around us. But if we put our hope in its eventual recovery and success, that is a vain hope. Yes, God may give us a revival, and we may have years to come. But the end is inevitable. Why trust the veil when we may trust him who is behind the veil and will assuredly one day pull that veil to the ground?

Once again, Christ's words come to mind: "Therefore everyone who hears these words of mine and puts them into practice is like a wise man who built his house on the rock" (Matt. 7:24). If we put our trust in God and give our lives to finding out his nature and purposes, that will endure whatever crashes time may bring on us. Nations may—indeed, will—fall, but we can stand. The apostle Peter said it well when he said,

> Therefore, my brothers, be all the more eager to make your call-
> ing and election sure. For if you do these things, you will never fall,
> and you will receive a rich welcome into the eternal kingdom of our
> Lord and Savior Jesus Christ. (2 Peter 1:10–11)

While the "these things" he is talking about may be our calling and election,
it is more likely that he is referring to the "these things" in verses 8–9 (NIV
"these qualities" in v. 8, "them" in v. 9), namely, the virtues of faith, goodness,
knowledge, self-control, perseverance, godliness, brotherly kindness, and
love. These will endure because they are the very qualities of God. If we, in
response to his grace, have given our lives to pursuing him, we too will
endure (John 12:25–26).

Isaiah 14:1–27

¹ THE LORD WILL have compassion on Jacob;
　　once again he will choose Israel
　　and will settle them in their own land.
　Aliens will join them
　　and unite with the house of Jacob.
² Nations will take them
　　and bring them to their own place.
　And the house of Israel will possess the nations
　　as menservants and maidservants in the LORD's land.
　They will make captives of their captors
　　and rule over their oppressors.

³ On the day the LORD gives you relief from suffering and
turmoil and cruel bondage, ⁴ you will take up this taunt against
the king of Babylon:

　How the oppressor has come to an end!
　　How his fury has ended!
⁵ The LORD has broken the rod of the wicked,
　　the scepter of the rulers,
⁶ which in anger struck down peoples
　　with unceasing blows,
　and in fury subdued nations
　　with relentless aggression.
⁷ All the lands are at rest and at peace;
　　they break into singing.
⁸ Even the pine trees and the cedars of Lebanon
　　exult over you and say,
　"Now that you have been laid low,
　　no woodsman comes to cut us down."

⁹ The grave below is all astir
　　to meet you at your coming;
　it rouses the spirits of the departed to greet you—
　　all those who were leaders in the world;
　it makes them rise from their thrones—
　　all those who were kings over the nations.
¹⁰ They will all respond,
　　they will say to you,

"You also have become weak, as we are;
    you have become like us."
[11] All your pomp has been brought down to the grave,
    along with the noise of your harps;
maggots are spread out beneath you
    and worms cover you.

[12] How you have fallen from heaven,
    O morning star, son of the dawn!
You have been cast down to the earth,
    you who once laid low the nations!
[13] You said in your heart,
    "I will ascend to heaven;
I will raise my throne
    above the stars of God;
I will sit enthroned on the mount of assembly,
    on the utmost heights of the sacred mountain.
[14] I will ascend above the tops of the clouds;
    I will make myself like the Most High."
[15] But you are brought down to the grave,
    to the depths of the pit.

[16] Those who see you stare at you,
    they ponder your fate:
"Is this the man who shook the earth
    and made kingdoms tremble,
[17] the man who made the world a desert,
    who overthrew its cities
    and would not let his captives go home?"

[18] All the kings of the nations lie in state,
    each in his own tomb.
[19] But you are cast out of your tomb
    like a rejected branch;
you are covered with the slain,
    with those pierced by the sword,
    those who descend to the stones of the pit.
Like a corpse trampled underfoot,
[20]   you will not join them in burial,
for you have destroyed your land
    and killed your people.

The offspring of the wicked
    will never be mentioned again.

²¹ Prepare a place to slaughter his sons
    for the sins of their forefathers;
they are not to rise to inherit the land
    and cover the earth with their cities.

²² "I will rise up against them,"
    declares the LORD Almighty.
"I will cut off from Babylon her name and survivors,
    her offspring and descendants,"
                               declares the LORD.

²³ "I will turn her into a place for owls
    and into swampland;
I will sweep her with the broom of destruction,"
    declares the LORD Almighty.

²⁴ The LORD Almighty has sworn,

"Surely, as I have planned, so it will be,
    and as I have purposed, so it will stand.
²⁵ I will crush the Assyrian in my land;
    on my mountains I will trample him down.
His yoke will be taken from my people,
    and his burden removed from their shoulders."
²⁶ This is the plan determined for the whole world;
    this is the hand stretched out over all nations.
²⁷ For the LORD Almighty has purposed, and who can
        thwart him?
His hand is stretched out, and who can turn it back?

Original Meaning

ISAIAH 14 CONTINUES the general pronouncement of judgment on creaturely pride, using Babylon as a vehicle. Here, after some words of encouragement to Israel (vv. 1–4a), Isaiah focuses on the downfall of the so-called "king of Babylon" (vv. 4b–21). The section on Babylon then closes with a statement from God on what it is he is doing to the Mesopotamian powers (vv. 22–27).

Students of this passage have long been aware that much more than some individual human monarch is being talked about. Just as in Ezekiel 28, where the fall of the "king of Tyre" is discussed,[1] the language is much too sweeping

---

1. See also Ezek. 32, where the arrival of the pharaoh in hell has a number of similarities to this passage.

and expressive to be talking only about one human being. As a result, some of the church fathers understood this passage and Ezekiel 28 to be primarily talking about Satan (see esp. Isa. 14:12–15). John Milton drew on this exegesis for his epic poem, *Paradise Lost*. However, the great expositors of the Reformation, Luther and Calvin, do not support this latter interpretation, arguing that the passage is discussing human pride, not angelic pride. We actually know very little about Satan's origins from the Bible, especially if Revelation 12:8–9 are discussing events at the end of time and not those before time began. Jesus tells us that he saw Satan fall (Luke 10:18), but beyond that we have little other information.

It is generally agreed that the poem in Isaiah 14:4b–21 is one of the finest in the Hebrew language. The four stanzas are set up as a "lament," a song mourning the death of someone, with the typical meter of a lament and much of the typical vocabulary. The first stanza (vv. 4b–8) considers earth's reaction to the death; the second (vv. 9–11), the underworld's response; the third (vv. 12–15), heaven's perspective; finally (vv. 16–21), a return to contemplate the dead person's tragic fate on earth. But this is not a typical lament. Far from it! It is a biting parody of a lament. Instead of expressing grief over the death of the tyrant, it expresses both delight and satisfaction. Death is welcomed as the leveler of the tyrant's proud and oppressive ambition.

Words of Promise to Israel (14:1–4a)

BETWEEN THE ANNOUNCEMENT of the destruction of Babylon in chapter 13 and that of Babylon's king in chapter 14 are words of promise to Israel. If rejection and implacable judgment by God lie in the future for the descendants of Jacob, those are not God's final word. For further out in the future, beyond those realities, lie still greater realities: divine "compassion" and a reaffirmation of God's choosing of them to be his own people. If it is true that the land will one day spit them out (cf. Lev. 18:28), it is also true that beyond that day is another day when God will once more "settle them in their own land." Once more the prophet affirms that the coming destruction is not because the Mesopotamian powers are so great that God cannot stop them. No, those powers are mere tools in his hand, and once their work is finished, they too will come in for judgment while Israel will be restored to all the promises.

Not only will Israel be freed from the onerous grip of the nations, but either the nations must become partners with Israel (as in 2:2–5) or they will have to submit to the rule of Israel (14:1b–2)! If the oppression of the tyrants seems endless, Israel must remember that such rule is strictly limited and that someday the tables will be radically turned. How exciting it must have been for the Judean exiles as they recognized the arrival of Cyrus whom

Isaiah had predicted and so knew that the hour for the overthrow of the Babylonian tyrant had arrived, the hour when they could sing Isaiah's song not as a prediction but as a fact. The faithful among them had sung it secretly in daring hope, but now it could be sung openly, as 14:3–4a promised.

Rest for People on Earth (14:4b–8)

A TYPICAL LAMENT might begin by saying how earth's inhabitants are struck over the news of the departed's death. But here the poet tells in anticipation how grateful the people on earth are to have "rest" (v. 7) from the repeated blows of the oppressor's rod (vv. 5–6). The Lord "has broken the rod." What good news! In the years between 855 and 555 B.C., we almost lose count of the number of times a rampaging Mesopotamian army devastated Israel and Judah. What good news to know that the hammer blows are over.

Nor is it just human beings who are glad to know that the reign of terror is over. The whole creation, including the trees, are glad (v. 8). Isaiah here seems to show an awareness of the writings of the Assyrian kings, who regularly boasted how they cut down the mighty forests of Lebanon both for lumber for their engines of war and also for the beautification of their palaces and temples. Human pride sees both humans and nature as fodder to be consumed in support of its towering pretensions, so even nature breathes a sigh of relief when the news of that pride's death is announced.

The Underworld (14:9–11)

THE PICTURE CHANGES from the earth to the underworld (NIV, "the grave"; Heb. *šᵉᵓol*[2]). In place of the peace and quiet that the tyrant's death has brought to the earth, the underworld is in an uproar. All the kings have been sitting on their thrones. Now they rise, stretching their necks to get a glimpse of this newcomer. He is the one who sneeringly sent them on their way to this grim and dusty place, and now he has come to join them! In the end he is no stronger than they were. He could no more prevent his death than they could theirs.

Verse 11 is a masterpiece of sarcasm and irony. We see a funeral celebration where a gorgeously bedecked bier is carried past with "pomp" and with lovely music played by "harps" and other instruments. "Beautiful," we say. Then the picture suddenly changes. All is deathly still, and we see that the beautiful bier and its coverings are nothing but a writhing mass of "maggots." Human pretension is no match for the grim reality of death and decay.

---

2. For a discussion of this term in its Old Testament context, see Oswalt, *Isaiah 1–39*, 318 n. 15.

A Message from Heaven (14:12–15)

THE PICTURE CHANGES AGAIN, this time to heaven. What has this world emperor sought to do in his towering egotism? In effect, he has tried to take the place of the Holy One. The language here has intriguing overtones of several ancient stories about both human and divine hubris, and scholars have expended a good deal of energy seeking for the original poem that the prophet supposedly makes use of. There seems to be a scholarly antipathy to the idea that anything in the Bible could be original. However, the search has not paid off, and it still seems as if Isaiah has taken a number of themes familiar to his hearers and woven them together into a new creation to make his unique theological point.[3]

In verses 13–14, the egotist has made four boasts about what he will do: He will rule above even the stars; he will sit on the highest mountaintop, from which the king of the gods rules; he will ascend into the highest heaven ("above the tops of the clouds"); and he will become equal to God himself.[4] Isaiah recognizes that when we make our own selves the most important thing in our world, we are usurping the rightful place of God. But this man, who thought to make himself equal to God, is mocked by death, which has taken him from the "heights" (v. 13) of his own pretensions to the "depths of the pit" (v. 15) in one terrible moment.

The Tragedy of the Fallen King (14:16–21)

THE FINAL STANZA of the poem contemplates the tragedy of this mighty man. He is said to have suffered an ignominious death and to have left behind no children. It may be that the original poem ended at verse 20a, with verses 20b–21 added later, since the inclusion of this material makes the stanza significantly longer than the first two. But it must be admitted that Western ideas of literary symmetry may be different from those of the Hebrews.

As was said in the opening discussion at the beginning of chapter 13, no single individual is being addressed here. This "king of Babylon" is a composite of all the proud, despotic kings who have ruled on the earth. However, one of the prouder and more despotic ones was Sargon II of Assyria, who ruled from 721 until 705 B.C. While we cannot say for certain, it seems likely he was the one Assyrian emperor who died on the battlefield. We do know that after his death, there was what one author calls a "general defection and

---

3. For a concise review of the claims, see Childs, *Isaiah*, 126. See also Oswalt, *Isaiah 1–39*, 321–22.

4. In Canaanite mythology the king of the gods is called *El*, which is the word translated "God" in v. 13; the word *Elyon*, translated "Most High" in v. 14, is often added to the name of the god Baal in that same mythology.

rebellion" that took Sargon's son Sennacherib a number of years to quell.[5] It is also interesting that Sennacherib was killed by his own sons, who were in turn slaughtered by the eventual successor to the throne, a usurper named Esarhaddon. Thus, Sargon and Sennacherib together may have provided models for this stanza.

Verses 16–20 show people staring at the mangled corpse of the tyrant lying in a heap of other corpses in a pit (see esp. v. 19). This agrees with the idea of a battlefield death. Instead of a dignified death and an honorable burial, the corpse is abandoned in the field, perhaps in a hasty retreat. But again, we need to remind ourselves that this is not a historical narrative but a poem about human pride, so we should not work overly hard to make everything consistent. The point is one of final and complete humiliation for the most vaunting arrogance. Far from being equal to God, this king is not even equal to the other kings he has killed. They at least have their own tombs; pride has none. It is thrown away, as it was customary to throw away a miscarried fetus.[6]

But not only does the proud king have no decent burial, neither does he have any continuing dynasty. Verses 20b–21 express the hope that the oppressor will have no offspring to carry on his name. Thus his destruction is complete. He has neither a memorial in stone nor one in flesh. His very memory is blotted out. This is entirely fitting, for his pride has not only destroyed the lands of others (v. 17), it has destroyed his own land as well (v. 20). This is the end of the pride that says it will sit on the throne of God: absolute and complete destruction.

Conclusion (14:22–27)

THE CONCLUSION OF the two-part oracle against "Babylon" and its king also takes two parts. The first (vv. 22–23) is more general, while verses 24–27 form a specific example. As we saw in 2:6–4:1, this is a characteristic feature of the composition of the book.

In 14:22–23 the thought of the immediately preceding verses is continued and expanded. Not only will the king of Babylon have no offspring and thus no living memorial, neither will Babylon itself. As noted in the comments on Isaiah 13, the city is to be forgotten completely and to become merely a haunt for animals of the night and of the swamp.

In 14:24–27, the prophet gives a specific example of this destruction of Babylon, namely, the coming downfall of Assyria. The fact that there is no

---

5. A. L. Oppenheim, *Ancient Mesopotamia* (Chicago: Univ. of Chicago Press, 1964), 169.
6. "Rejected branch" (v. 19) is lit. "abominable branch," which must be a figure of speech. Two of the ancient versions translate it with "miscarriage."

introductory "oracle" formula here gives us a clue that this is not a separate oracle against Assyria but should be read as a conclusion to the "Babylon" oracle.[7] Assyria represents all the Mesopotamian powers subsumed under the head "Babylon," which have exalted themselves to the heights and must therefore eventually go down into the pit. Any person or nation that lifts itself up against the "plan" and "purpose" of God (14:24, 26–27) marks itself for destruction.[8] Verse 25 seems to refer to the destruction of Sennacherib's army in Judah in 701 B.C. (as described in 37:36). Whatever the mighty Assyrian king may have planned in his pride to do to Jerusalem (10:7) means nothing compared to the plans of God.

PRIDE. When we think of human pride, we think first of all of the will. It is the human will that has gone astray, that reverses the words of Jesus (Mark 14:36) and says, "Not *thy* will but *mine* be done." For what is human pride except an attempt to set ourselves up in the place of God in our world? Notice the five recurrences of the pronoun "I" in 14:13–14. Pride is to place myself and my will at the center of creation.

One of the most telling descriptions of this pride in recent literature is found in C. S. Lewis's book in the Narnia series *The Magician's Nephew.* The first description of pride is seen in the magician and his complete focusing on himself and what he is trying to do. His nephew, Digby, is nothing but a pawn for his uncle's researches. But the more chilling picture is found when Digby and his friend Jill arrive by magic in the world of Charn. This world seems completely dead and empty. Yet obviously it was once a place of great culture and civilization. The children make their way into a great crumbling palace and into a long hall filled with statues seated on thrones. The earliest statues are of people who seem energetic and approachable. But as the children proceed down the line of statues, they notice how each one seems greater and haughtier and more terrible than the previous one.

Finally they come to the last one, a great queen grander and more terrifying than all the rest. In the center of the room is a table with a crystal bell on it, and Digby, against Jill's advice, cannot resist ringing it. When he does, all the statues crumble to dust except the last one, and she, Queen Jadis, comes to life, standing before the children in all her commanding splendor.

---

7. So Childs, Seitz, and others.
8. On the plan of God, see also 19:12; 22:11; 23:8–9; 25:1; 37:26; 46:10–11; 48:14; 55:11.

She is disappointed to find that her last summons upon dying has only brought a child to restore her to life, and she is contemptuous to discover that they do not even know that is why they have come.

So she tells them the story of Charn. The long line of kings and queens of Charn had come down to Jadis and her sister, who struggled for the throne of the kingdom. Having devastated their world with their wars, it finally appeared that the sister had won and that Jadis would have to bow. But that she refused to do. She knew a secret word that would instantly kill everyone on Charn but would one day restore her to life to rule the dead planet alone. Rather than bow to her sister, she chose to speak that word. That is pride, and we think of the words John Milton puts in Satan's mouth in *Paradise Lost*: "Better to rule in Hell, than serve in Heaven."

Another telling reflection on these truths is found in Shelley's sonnet "Ozymandias," allegedly composed while looking at the fallen statue of the great Egyptian Pharaoh Ramesses in the Nubian Desert. The final lines read,

> "My name is Ozymandias, king of kings:
> Look on my works, ye Mighty, and despair!:
> Nothing beside remains. Round the decay
> Of that colossal wreck, boundless and bare
> The lone and level sands stretch far away.[9]

This poem beautifully sums up Isaiah's comment on pride because it reflects not only the destructive nature of pride but also its essential silliness. How can humans who die think they can play God? That mortals think they can give their petty activities eternal worth when they will one day leave all of their achievements behind to succumb to inevitable decay and destruction is amazing. Death is the great leveler—the bane of the arrogant and the hope of the oppressed.

The Chase, a film starring Dennis Weaver, sums up this message of death's deliverance in a powerful way. It tells the story of the driver of a car who inadvertently cuts off a huge tractor-trailer truck while passing it. For reasons the viewer never learns, the driver of the truck goes berserk and takes it upon himself to force Weaver into a crash that will probably kill him. He rear-ends the car several times and tries to force Weaver off the road on a couple of other occasions. So Weaver tries to outrun the truck, but his car is a small, underpowered compact, and he cannot seem to get away. When he does once and stops in a roadside diner to let the crazy man go on past, he comes out of the diner to find the truck waiting for him.

---

9. P. Shelley, "Ozymandias," *British Poetry and Prose*, ed. P. Lieder, R. Lovett, and R. Root (New York: Houghton Mifflin, 1928), 813.

Finally, in complete desperation, Weaver turns up a small gravel road on a mountainside, knowing it may be a dead end but not knowing where else to go. He skids around a hairpin curve, almost losing control and going off a cliff, which is exactly what the truck does do, hurtling over the edge to crash far below. Weaver coasts to a stop and slowly backs up. He gets out of the car and walks cautiously to the edge, clearly fearful that somehow, against all odds, the monster is going to come roaring up over the edge. But it does not, and the final scene shows Weaver, completely exhausted, sitting on the edge of the cliff tossing pebbles at the wreck below, emitting sounds somewhere between a sigh and a chuckle. Death finally spells the end to the aggressive pride of humanity.

The plan and purpose of God. There is one other important thought in this material that bears mentioning here: the idea of the plan and purpose of God (14:24–27). Here again, there is a contrast highlighted. The Assyrian king had his plans, but they were not God's plans (cf. 10:6–8). This theme recalls Proverbs 19:21: "Many are the plans in a man's heart, but it is the LORD's purpose that prevails." This brings us full circle to the thought that opened this section: the human will. The reason why the exaltation of the individual human will is so foolish is that God has a plan and purpose for each of us.

This is not to say that there is some immense blueprint for all of existence in some vast chamber in heaven. Nor does it mean that each of us has but one chance to "get it right," which, if we fail, will forever doom us to second best. The blueprint image has some utility, but it is only an image and thus has serious limitations. God is so creative that he is able to continually revise his tactical plans without ever altering his final strategic goal. The point is that since the Creator has a purpose, it is perfectly foolish for any of us to exalt our will against his. That way is frustration, danger, and endless loss.

PRIDE AND HUMAN WILL. In our own day, who could better represent the "king of Babylon" than the two greatest murderers of all time: Adolf Hitler and Joseph Stalin? Each in his own way expected to leave behind him an empire that would encompass the world. And because of his towering pride, each one believed in his absolute right to destroy every single human being who in any way seemed to thwart the arrogant vision. Each one was willing to reduce not only the world, *but his own kingdom* (v. 20), to destruction if necessary to achieve his goals. How the oppressed of the world breathed a sigh of relief when each of these monsters, correctly termed, died. Their pride was brought down into the dust,[10] and their particularly vicious cruelty no longer existed on the earth.

Both of these men had been influenced by the German philosopher Friedrich Nietzsche. Nietzsche despised Christianity because he claimed it "feminized" men. It robbed males of their native aggression, impatience, cruelty, and discourtesy and replaced those "virtues" with passivity, meekness, and sensitivity. In so doing, he argued, Christianity robbed males of the one essential for greatness, the will to power. The terrible fruit of Nietzsche's philosophy can be seen in the events of the Russian Revolution and World War II. He wanted the human race to stand forth in all its terrible glory. But in fact, he was only romanticizing sin, and sin cannot be romanticized in the end. As the apostle Paul says (Rom. 6:21, 23), the only fruit sin bears is death, and *Romeo and Juliet* to the contrary, death is not romantic. It is simply sordid and awful.

That is especially clear in the horrifying photographs of death coming out of World War II. Whether it be the stacks of emaciated corpses at Auschwitz or the maggots crawling on the body of the American soldier lying face down in the sand on the beach of Tarawa, we have seen death as it is, and there is nothing romantic about it.

Nietzsche was also wrong about Christianity and the sexes. Kindness, gentleness, patience, and generosity are not distinctly feminine. To be sure, these virtues may express themselves somewhat differently in males than in females, but they are no more innate in women than in men. In fact, what we are seeing today is that women can be more brutal, aggressive, and coarse than men if they choose to be. If sin is not romantic, neither is it gender specific. Manipulative passivity is neither feminine nor Christian. It is the sinful response to apparent powerlessness and is manifested as much by men as by women in comparable circumstances.

But if manipulative passivity is not the answer to powerlessness, what is? Nietzsche said that it was to be more aggressive than the oppressor, to seize power by sheer force of will, and failing that to die with one's back in the corner snarling defiance at one's killers. William Ernest Henley, dying of tuberculosis, penned a poem in this vein that is a favorite among sophomores of all ages. The first two stanzas are as follows:

> Out of the night that covers me,
> Black as the pit from pole to pole,
> I thank whatever gods may be
> For my unconquerable soul.

---

10. The ignominious death of Hitler, in particular, shows some startling parallels to Isa. 14:16–20a.

In the fell clutch of circumstance
I have not winced nor cried aloud.
Under the bludgeonings of chance
My head is bloody, but unbowed.[11]

The tragedy for both Nietzsche and Henley is that they are diametrically wrong. It is the will to power, the unconquerable soul, that is at the root of all the problems of the human race. Pride kills, as Isaiah 14 says so eloquently. It kills those around it who cross its will, and finally it kills itself as it plunges down in a deadly spiral where in the end it exists for itself alone.

This is a fact of human existence that we refuse to learn. Why is it a fact? A thousand hypotheses could be put forward, but the simplest one is the one given to us by our Creator in his revelation. The answer is that he is ultimate and we are not. Any attempt to make ourselves ultimate has results that are just as predictable as are the results of jumping off a tall building. We have been made to reflect the glory of the only God. If a mirror says, "No, I will reflect only myself" and pulls down all the shades and turns the lights off, it should not be surprised to discover there is nothing to reflect. The mirror has violated the terms of its creation. So it is that when we humans say, "I will live only for myself," we should not be surprised to discover that there is no life to be lived.

Surrendering our will to Christ. This means that the answer to powerlessness is not to try to seize power for ourselves and, failing the attempt, to die snarling. Rather, it is to surrender even our powerlessness to our heavenly Father and to find in him the power to "do all things" (Phil. 4:13 NASB). Here is power, when the oppressor cannot make us hate him or her. Here is power, when the victim need not hide behind victimization but finds his or her identity in rising above that grief to heights of generosity, forgiveness, and love. Here is power, when a raw deal is triumphed over with grace and self-forgetfulness.

But how are such things possible? How exactly do we surrender our powerlessness? We see it in Christ's words, "Not *my* will, but *thine* be done." The divine-human problem is a problem of the will, and until Christians have consciously surrendered their will to Christ their Lord or, in Paul's words, "have been crucified with Christ" (Gal. 2:20), their own pride will keep defeating them. Paul makes it clear that a death is involved. We do not get up each day asking whether we think we might like to surrender our will today. This is a radical, even violent, decision that is of a once-for-all nature. Of course, its implications must be worked out every day, but it is not a new

---

11. W. Henley, "Invictus," *The Best Loved Poems of the American People*, ed. H. Felleman (Garden City, N.Y.: Garden City Books, 1936), 73.

decision every day. Neither is it something we do on our own; rather, it is something we give the Holy Spirit permission to do.

But someone will say, "Surely, a little self-respect is a good thing. We can't go around all the time saying, 'Oh, I'm not worth anything.'" No, we cannot, and God does not expect us to. However, much of the modern "self-esteem" movement is simply a failed attempt to counteract the effects of the increasing self-centeredness of this society. As parents have increasingly focused on their own needs and desires, children have been left in the dust. Children are incredibly perceptive, and they know what they are worth to their parents. Parents may shower the children with expensive toys and give them a few minutes of the misnamed "quality time" every day or so. But the child knows that he or she is really only one more of their parents' acquisitions—and a rather bothersome one at that. The child makes no real contribution to the family and knows it.

So how does society try to cope with this crisis? By encouraging parents to scale back on their wants and desires in order to be able to devote more time to integrating the child into the family? Never! The society instead tries to get children to say to themselves "I have worth!" To whom? Not to the only people who count. Instead, we are trying to counter the effects of an epidemic of self-centeredness with more self-centeredness. In a fallen world, the only hope for rediscovering the secret of individual worth is to discover how much we are actually worth to our heavenly Father. He was willing to die in our place. He not only loves us, he likes us! The sense of worth that springs from that knowledge is the furthest thing in the world from the kind of proud, lonely self-love that shouts to a deaf universe, "I am somebody!"

The apostle Paul sums up what I have just been saying in the well-known passage in Romans 12:1–2:

> Therefore, I urge you, brothers, in view of God's mercy, to offer your bodies as living sacrifices, holy and pleasing to God—this is your spiritual act of worship. Do not conform any longer to the pattern of this world, but be transformed by the renewing of your mind. Then you will be able to test and approve what God's will is—his good, pleasing and perfect will.

The sacrifice of Christ and the gift of the Holy Spirit ought to motivate us in a certain direction. That direction is expressed in three phases: the sacrificial surrender of our bodies to God, which will be the expression of a transformed way of thinking from that of the world, which has as its goal both the experiencing of, and the saying yes to, God's complete will in our lives. Surrender leads to life; pride leads to death.

Isaiah 14:28–32

THIS ORACLE CAME in the year King Ahaz died:

29 Do not rejoice, all you Philistines,
   that the rod that struck you is broken;
from the root of that snake will spring up a viper,
   its fruit will be a darting, venomous serpent.
30 The poorest of the poor will find pasture,
   and the needy will lie down in safety.
But your root I will destroy by famine;
   it will slay your survivors.

31 Wail, O gate! Howl, O city!
   Melt away, all you Philistines!
A cloud of smoke comes from the north,
   and there is not a straggler in its ranks.
32 What answer shall be given
   to the envoys of that nation?
"The LORD has established Zion,
   and in her his afflicted people will find refuge."

Original Meaning

ALTHOUGH THE DATES for the end of Ahaz's reign and the beginning of Hezekiah's are complicated by apparently contradictory datings in 2 Kings 18, it seems probable that Ahaz died in 716 B.C. and that Hezekiah either began to reign then or assumed full regnancy after having been coregent for some time.[1] But it is not clear what the significance of Ahaz's death is for the meaning of this oracle. It is possible that the date has no significance for the interpretation of the judgment on Philistia, but since there are only three datings in Isaiah (6:1; here; 20:1), that does not seem likely.

---

1. Second Kings 18:1, 9–10 place the beginning of Hezekiah's reign in 727 B.C. before the fall of the northern kingdom. Yet v. 13 says that Sennacherib's attack, which can be dated securely in 701 B.C., occurred in Hezekiah's fourteenth year. Perhaps there was a coregency with his father Ahaz until 716, but elsewhere in Kings the first year of a coregency is counted as the king's first year of rule, meaning that we would expect 18:13 to say that Sennacherib's attack occurred in Hezekiah's twenty-sixth year. For a full discussion of the problems, see E. Thiele, *The Mysterious Numbers of the Hebrew Kings*, 3d ed. (Grand Rapids: Zondervan, 1983), 132–40.

Nevertheless, the connection is unclear. If Ahaz had been a threat to the Philistines, it would be natural to say he was the broken rod who had struck the Philistines. But that is not the case. If anything the reverse was true, for 2 Chronicles 28:18 indicates that Ahaz lost several cities to the Philistines. Perhaps the date is significant because the Philistines had revolted against Assyria at this time and were urging the new king Hezekiah to join them because Assyria, "the rod that struck [us,] is broken." In 715 B.C. Sargon of Assyria was still trying to regain full control of the empire after his accession in 721, and the Philistines may have taken this prolonged struggle as a sign of weakness. If that is correct, Isaiah quickly disabuses them of such a false notion. In fact, Assyria's period of greatest strength is still in its youth and will continue to grow for another sixty years. Like Moses' staff, this "rod" will turn into a "snake," and the snake will give birth to a venomous "viper" (Isa. 14:29).

Verses 30 and 32 strengthen the suggestion that the Philistines are inviting the Judeans to join them in revolt. To this proposal, Isaiah answers that the Lord will take care of Judah without any help from the Philistines. Here again is the trust issue. Will Judah trust the nations or the Lord? They need not ally themselves with the Philistines because the Judeans are the flock of God, and he will tend them (14:30; see also 40:11). In fact, the great Philistines themselves will be consumed by a "cloud of smoke ... from the north" (14:31). This refers to the Assyrian armies coming south along the coast. Since "the LORD has established Zion," an alliance with a soon-to-be-destroyed neighbor is hardly necessary.

THE ISSUE HERE is the folly of turning away from that which is secure to depend on what is failing. The Lord's help often seems so intangible while the material and physical seems so real. Today as in ancient times, we need prophets who will help us see the real fragility of what seems on the surface to be so strong.

THE CHURCH TODAY is often in the position of Judah. We feel beleaguered on every hand, and we look for allies. Unfortunately, the allies to whom we are tempted to turn are weaker than us and in some cases are actually our enemies, just as Philistia was to Judah. We feel we need a large new facility and turn to a fund-raising consultant who has only veneered over the most cynical and manipulative methods of the world with a layer of superficial "spirituality."

Yet it is "Zion" that will survive when all the world's institutions are gone. Is it wrong "to spoil the Egyptians," to raid the world for its best products? No, but the history of the church's attempts to do this is a pretty sorry one. All too often we discover that the world's "best products" carry with them understandings of reality that are alien to everything the church stands for. All too often the subtle assumption on which these methods and approaches is based is that "God helps those who help themselves." Count Bismarck is reported to have said, "God is on the side of the big battalions." That is the world talking. The Bible says "Trust in the LORD with all your heart and lean not on your own understanding" (Prov. 3:5). That is what Isaiah is saying.

A N ORACLE CONCERNING MOAB:

Ar in Moab is ruined,
    destroyed in a night!
Kir in Moab is ruined,
    destroyed in a night!
2 Dibon goes up to its temple,
    to its high places to weep;
    Moab wails over Nebo and Medeba.
Every head is shaved
    and every beard cut off.
3 In the streets they wear sackcloth;
    on the roofs and in the public squares
they all wail,
    prostrate with weeping.
4 Heshbon and Elealeh cry out,
    their voices are heard all the way to Jahaz.
Therefore the armed men of Moab cry out,
    and their hearts are faint.

5 My heart cries out over Moab;
    her fugitives flee as far as Zoar,
    as far as Eglath Shelishiyah.
They go up the way to Luhith,
    weeping as they go;
on the road to Horonaim
    they lament their destruction.
6 The waters of Nimrim are dried up
    and the grass is withered;
the vegetation is gone
    and nothing green is left.
7 So the wealth they have acquired and stored up
    they carry away over the Ravine of the Poplars.
8 Their outcry echoes along the border of Moab;
    their wailing reaches as far as Eglaim,
    their lamentation as far as Beer Elim.
9 Dimon's waters are full of blood,
    but I will bring still more upon Dimon—

a lion upon the fugitives of Moab
and upon those who remain in the land.

16:1 Send lambs as tribute
to the ruler of the land,
from Sela, across the desert,
to the mount of the Daughter of Zion.
2 Like fluttering birds
pushed from the nest,
so are the women of Moab
at the fords of the Arnon.

3 "Give us counsel,
render a decision.
Make your shadow like night—
at high noon.
Hide the fugitives,
do not betray the refugees.
4 Let the Moabite fugitives stay with you;
be their shelter from the destroyer."

The oppressor will come to an end,
and destruction will cease;
the aggressor will vanish from the land.
5 In love a throne will be established;
in faithfulness a man will sit on it—
one from the house of David—
one who in judging seeks justice
and speeds the cause of righteousness.

6 We have heard of Moab's pride—
her overweening pride and conceit,
her pride and her insolence—
but her boasts are empty.
7 Therefore the Moabites wail,
they wail together for Moab.
Lament and grieve
for the men of Kir Hareseth.
8 The fields of Heshbon wither,
the vines of Sibmah also.
The rulers of the nations
have trampled down the choicest vines,
which once reached Jazer
and spread toward the desert.

Their shoots spread out
  and went as far as the sea.
⁹So I weep, as Jazer weeps,
  for the vines of Sibmah.
O Heshbon, O Elealeh,
  I drench you with tears!
The shouts of joy over your ripened fruit
  and over your harvests have been stilled.
¹⁰Joy and gladness are taken away from the orchards;
  no one sings or shouts in the vineyards;
no one treads out wine at the presses,
  for I have put an end to the shouting.
¹¹My heart laments for Moab like a harp,
  my inmost being for Kir Hareseth.
¹²When Moab appears at her high place,
  she only wears herself out;
when she goes to her shrine to pray,
  it is to no avail.

¹³This is the word the LORD has already spoken concerning Moab. ¹⁴But now the LORD says: "Within three years, as a servant bound by contract would count them, Moab's splendor and all her many people will be despised, and her survivors will be very few and feeble."

Original Meaning

THE ORACLE AGAINST Moab takes a very different tone, at least on the surface, from the ones against Babylon and her king. There, even though the oracle against the king took the form of a lament, there was no question that the prophet, speaking for Judah and Israel, took delight in the destruction of the proud oppressor. Here there seems to be genuine sorrow over the coming destruction of Moab.[1] Perhaps this is because there was an unusually close relationship between Judah and Moab. The book of Ruth clearly illustrates this relationship. Not only did Naomi and Elimelech have no problem about resettling in Moab when a famine struck Judah, neither did Boaz seem to have any qualms about marrying the Moabitess Ruth after she converted to the worship of Yahweh.

---

1. See B. Jones, *Howling over Moab: Irony and Rhetoric in Isaiah 15–16* (SBLDS 157; Atlanta: Scholars Press, 1996), for an alternate interpretation. Jones feels that the weeping here is ironic, just like the lament in ch. 14.

At any rate, Isaiah 15 has no less than twelve occurrences of words for weeping, crying out, and lamenting (vv. 2, 3, 4, 5, 8). All but one of these occurrences speak of the Moabites weeping for the death and destruction being brought upon them. The one exception is found in verse 5, where Isaiah says, "My heart cries out over Moab." If this is not ironic, then the prophet is empathizing with the Moabites over the terrible losses they are suffering.[2] In chapter 16 the same pattern appears, although less emphasis is placed on grieving in that chapter. There Moab's wailing is mentioned in 16:7, while 16:9 reads, "I weep, as Jazer weeps," and 16:11, "My heart laments for Moab." It is tempting to see the person being referred to here as God, since he is clearly the referent in verse 10.

With the exception of Kir (15:1), the towns and villages mentioned in 15:1–4 all are found in the northern part of Moab, the area given to the Israelite tribes of Gad and Reuben (Num. 32:34–38). The mention of Ar in the north and Kir[3] in the south in Isaiah 15:1 gives that verse a certain comprehensive scope that enables it to function as an overall introduction. Verse 8 may have a similar kind of pairing, with Eglaim being near the northern border of Moab and Beer (Well of) Elim near the southern border. However, these two locations are much less firmly fixed than those in 15:1.

Although several of the sites mentioned in 15:5–8 are unknown, those that are known are in the southern part of Moab, south of the Arnon River. This north-to-south movement would have been characteristic of the flight of the Moabites southward before a marauding army heading south along the King's Highway from Damascus. The gods of Moab have failed (15:2), and the military men are helpless (15:4). Unless 15:6 is to be understood as figurative, nature has failed as well, for when the "fugitives" (15:5) reach the "waters of Nimrim" at the southern end of the Dead Sea, they find no water for themselves or the flocks they are trying to take with them—the "wealth" (15:7) of Moab. Thus, there was nothing else to do but to keep on pushing southward to the "Ravine of the Poplars," which is probably a reference to the Zered River, which formed the border between Moab and Edom.

"Dimon" in 15:9 is problematic because no such place is known. Dibon, on the other hand (cf. 15:2), was very well known as both a political and religious center. St. Jerome was the first to propose that there was either an intentional or an unintentional interchanging of the labial *b* in "Dibon" for the labial *m*. The fact that the Hebrew word for "blood" is *dam* could explain either kind of interchange. If that suggestion is correct, then Dibon, the bloody city, is

---

2. Note that there is no such empathy in the announcement of judgment on Moab in 25:10–12, so if this interpretation is correct, these feelings are by no means unchanging.

3. Probably Kir Hareseth (see 16:7, 11).

standing for Moab, the part for the whole. The point of verse 9 is clear: In the end there is no place Moab can flee from the judgment of God.

If the southward flight suggested in chapter 15 is correct, it would be natural for the fugitives to have sought refuge in Edom. But in fact, that is not the case. The prophet knows that Moab's only hope is in the Lord and in the Messiah he has promised. Again we are reminded of the function of these prophecies against the nations. Should Israel and Judah trust in the nations in the face of the Assyrian threat? Why should they do that when the only hope the nations have is the same hope Israel and Judah have, namely, the God of Jerusalem?

Isaiah 16:1—4a are the cries of the refugees for help. Verse 1 is perhaps the counsel they give to one another. Earlier Moab had had to provide sheep and lambs for the kings of Israel (2 Kings 3:4), so it would be natural for them to think of giving "lambs" as a gift to the king in Jerusalem ("the mount of the Daughter of Zion"). During biblical times the water level in the Dead Sea sometimes fell low enough that it was possible to ford the sea south of its midpoint and then to proceed up to Jerusalem through the "desert" of Judah. In any case the "refugees" beg permission to "hide" in Judah from the "destroyer," the plundering enemy (Isa. 16:3).

In 16:4b—5 Isaiah takes an opportunity to speak about the ultimate trust not only for the Moabites but for the whole world. This short statement is reminiscent not only of 11:1—16 but also of 9:1—7. Although his appearing will come long after this time when the Moabites are fleeing the Assyrians, a "man" will come out of "the house of David" and bring an end to oppression, destruction, and aggression. His throne will not be established on those rotten foundations but on the sure foundations of "love" and "faithfulness," the two chief characteristics of the Holy One of Israel.[4] As a result, his government will be characterized by "justice" and "righteousness."[5] Neither the Judeans nor the Moabites will survive to see him. Nevertheless, persons in both groups can put their trust in the God who made such a promise in their own day.

As he has already done several times in the book, Isaiah once again follows a familiar pattern: After a glimpse of that bright future hope, which should give people the basis for living lives of trust in dark hours, the prophet swings back to the grim present realities (16:6—13). Far from exercising humble trust, Moab is characterized by "pride" (v. 6) and idolatry (v. 12). She trusts herself and the gods she has made in her own image. The results are predictable for

---

4. The Heb. words here are *ḥesed*, and *ʾemet*, words with rich theological content stressing the undeserved nature of the love involved and the absolute stability of God's promises.

5. The Heb. words are *mišpaṭ* and *ṣedeq*, which have the connotations of true order and right activity.

anyone who has read thus far in the book: humiliation, exhaustion, and loss. Those who attempt to exalt themselves only ensure their eventual downfall, and those who labor to manipulate the forces of this earth for their own sakes only exhaust themselves in futility.

Moab has been like a lush spreading vine. It spread northward all the way to Jazer in the land of Ammon, to the edges of "the desert" on the east, and to the shores of the "sea" (the Dead Sea) on the west. But now the beautiful vine has been trampled down and broken. The shouting and laughter that accompanied an abundant harvest "have been stilled" (v. 9) and "put [to] an end" (v. 10). They have been replaced with moaning and wailing.

Isaiah 16:14 commits the prophet to a test. He asserts that within three years of these words having been uttered, calculated as carefully as an indentured servant would calculate the days remaining on his servitude, the predictions will be fulfilled. There was a major destruction of Moab by the Assyrians in 715 B.C., so these words may have been first spoken in 718 B.C. In any case, the prophet is not merely speaking in generalities; he is speaking for the God of truth, who is the Lord of history, and he dares to stake both his reputation and God's on the fulfillment of what he says will happen.

THE TWENTIETH CENTURY has given us numerous examples of the refugee experience, with people streaming out from the glorious cities of Europe or straggling out of a burning village in Vietnam. Photography has made the reality all the more vivid. I think particularly of three photographs. The first is of a woman in a long line of people fleeing the blitzkrieg in northern France. She is pushing a baby buggy filled with a strange collection of things: some clothes, a lamp, a book or two, and a lot of odds and ends. Her face is almost completely expressionless, but the tears are literally streaming from her eyes.

The second photograph is also from northern France. It is of a seemingly endless line of vehicles of all sorts abandoned by the side of the road. Clearly the tide of war had overtaken the persons involved, and they had left everything to run for their lives. There are luxury cars and farm carts with the horses dead in the shafts; there are milk trucks and children's wagons; there are bicycles and tractors. Falling out of all of them and scattered about on the ground, probably hurriedly pillaged by the soldiers, is all the detritus of life: clothes, books, paintings, furs, trinkets, everything we work so hard to acquire—all lost.

The third photograph is of a group of villagers on the steppes of Russia in the 1930s. The sky overhead is dark and threatening. All around them, stretching to the horizon, is a flat, empty plain. Behind them, almost at the horizon, is a towering black column of smoke. Their homes and everything they possessed, except for the clothes on their backs, are going up in that smoke. On their faces is anguish and raw fear. They have been turned out into this empty landscape to die, and die they will—sooner rather than later.

 THERE IS NO HOPE in our achievements, whether they be the refined culture of Europe or the rough accoutrements of a village on the steppes. None of our accomplishments can save us from the brutality of humans run amok. Even if our lives are lived out in peace, cruel Death will make us all refugees in the end, leaving all we have on the road to be pillaged by those who come after us.

We may be justly proud of the things we have done, but if that is the source of our eternal hope, our hope is small indeed. Perhaps the pyramids of Egypt will endure to the end of time, but what do they tell us about their builders? Next to nothing. We marvel at the intelligence that planned them, at the organization and effort that built them, at the immensity of the egos that demanded them, but there is nothing else. If Khufu was ever buried in the Great Pyramid, then every last thing he intended to endure to eternity, including his mummified body, has been stripped away. The burial chamber contains only one object, a huge, empty sarcophagus. Khufu is one more refugee on the road of eternity, having left all his possessions behind.

It is the same for us, whose accomplishments are a lot less stupendous than those ancient Egyptians. What will we leave behind when we take the road? Everything! And it will soon be scattered to the four winds. All our efforts to gain control of our environment, whether it be home or office or love of life, will only end in a final exhaustion. Later in this book, Isaiah says it eloquently, "Why [do you] labor on what does not satisfy?" (55:2). Like the Moabites, we tend to look in all the wrong directions for our hope. Then, when the world falls apart, as fall apart it must, there is nothing left but to wail, for all that is lost.

But in their extremity the Moabites did make one right move. They turned to Judah and not to Edom. Was it mere expedience? Did they recognize that Judah, for whatever reason, was in a more defensible position than Edom? Or was it more than that? Did they recognize that Judah's God, Yahweh, was a different order of being than Chemosh and Molech? Did they recognize that Yahweh had both the power and the grace to deliver his people and those who allied themselves with them? In view of the rest of chapter 16, it does not seem likely their understanding was nearly that deep.

The same is true today. Many turn to the church for reasons they themselves understand poorly. Perhaps they want their children to have some "training in morality." Perhaps they have some vague childhood memories of people who seemed happy and fulfilled. Perhaps life has dealt them a series of crushing blows, and they have nowhere else to turn. Perhaps they just think it's a "good thing." Whatever the reasons, as Isaiah had only one word for the Moabites, so the church today has finally only one word to say to these "refugees." We may offer them programs to meet their "felt needs." We may help them get back on their feet again. We may offer them education and guidance. But in the end, the only final hope is to be found in the "man" of Isaiah 16:5—the man, Jesus Christ. Only in his eternal kingdom is there true freedom and justice.

That is so because his kingdom lasts forever. In this world the only certainty is death and loss. But in the goodness and light and fertility that may be found in the world, we see the promise that death and loss are not intended to be the final realities. So, if we help people to put shattered lives back together and that is all we do, we have only staved off the final loss for a few more days or years. But if we bring them into the throne room of heaven and help them to bow in submission before the Lamb slain from the foundation of the earth, we have given them a surety against all loss for all time.

That hope is not in our accomplishments but in his. He has forever solved the problems of justice and freedom by taking into himself the consequences of all our pride and idolatry, which have produced wrong and oppression. In place of the world's seemingly endless tears and loss, he has given joy and abundance. If we wait for a day yet to come to see him enthroned in all his glory, we can still live our days here on earth with confidence and rest.

Isaiah 17:1–11

A<small>N ORACLE CONCERNING</small> D<small>AMASCUS</small>:

"See, Damascus will no longer be a city
   but will become a heap of ruins.
² The cities of Aroer will be deserted
   and left to flocks, which will lie down,
   with no one to make them afraid.
³ The fortified city will disappear from Ephraim,
   and royal power from Damascus;
the remnant of Aram will be
   like the glory of the Israelites,"

                        declares the L<small>ORD</small> Almighty.

⁴ "In that day the glory of Jacob will fade;
   the fat of his body will waste away.
⁵ It will be as when a reaper gathers the standing grain
   and harvests the grain with his arm—
as when a man gleans heads of grain
   in the Valley of Rephaim.
⁶ Yet some gleanings will remain,
   as when an olive tree is beaten,
leaving two or three olives on the topmost branches,
   four or five on the fruitful boughs,"

                        declares the L<small>ORD</small>, the God of Israel.

⁷ In that day men will look to their Maker
   and turn their eyes to the Holy One of Israel.
⁸ They will not look to the altars,
   the work of their hands,
and they will have no regard for the Asherah poles
   and the incense altars their fingers have made.

⁹ In that day their strong cities, which they left because of
the Israelites, will be like places abandoned to thickets and
undergrowth. And all will be desolation.

¹⁰ You have forgotten God your Savior;
   you have not remembered the Rock, your fortress.
Therefore, though you set out the finest plants
   and plant imported vines,

> [11] though on the day you set them out, you make
> them grow,
> and on the morning when you plant them, you bring
> them to bud,
> yet the harvest will be as nothing
> in the day of disease and incurable pain.

THERE IS CONSIDERABLE debate over the structure of the materials in Isaiah 17 and 18, for two principal reasons. (1) There is no oracle formula at the beginning of chapter 18. All of the other judgments pronounced against specific nations in this section begin with the words "an oracle[1] concerning," with the name of the nation following. But chapter 18 begins with the words, "Woe to the land of whirring wings along the rivers of Cush [Ethiopia]." (2) Moreover, the materials between 17:12 and 18:7 do not sound at all like a judgment on a specific nation. Rather, they speak of the sovereignty of God over all nations. The fact that 17:12 begins with "Woe" (NIV, "Oh"), as 18:1 does, seems to further support the idea that 17:12–18:7 forms a single thought unit (although these verses may have been originally separate literary units).

The fact that 17:1–11, although labeled "an oracle concerning Damascus," is actually largely addressed to Israel may explain why 17:12–18:7 is appended to the oracle. It was the attack of Israel and Aram on Judah that precipitated this entire crisis of faith and trust. It was because Judah turned to the nations of the world for its help in that moment instead of to God that the whole issue of the judgment of the nations is being discussed in chapters 13–23. Thus, it may be that the prophet sees the mention of Aram and Damascus as a good opportunity to recap the larger truth that these chapters are illustrating: All the nations of the world are subject to Yahweh, so Judah should neither fear nor trust any of them.[2]

Isaiah 17:1–3 speaks of the fall of Aram (Syria). The nation is represented by its capital city, Damascus (v. 1), and by the city of Aroer (v. 2), which was located on the Arnon River in Moab at the farthest southern extent of Aram's control. These cities will be reduced to "ruins," where "flocks" will feed. In

---

1. The Heb. word is *maśśaʾ*, lit., "burden."

2. Childs (*Isaiah*, 135–36) says that M. Sweeney (*Isaiah 1–39* [FOTL 16; Grand Rapids: Eerdmans, 1996], 252–65) has "finally made sense" of chapters 17 and 18, but neither he nor Sweeney really succeed in explaining the unity of thought in the passage. In my judgment Motyer (*Prophecy of Isaiah*, 155–63) is much more successful at explaining how the various ideas fit together.

verse 3 the reader is prepared for the change of subject to Israel in verse 4 by the mention of "Ephraim" and by the statement that Aram's glory will be as fading as that of Israel.

The fading glory of "Jacob" then becomes the main topic in the rest of the segment (17:4–11). It begins with an extended comparison of Israel's fate to that of a harvested field or orchard (vv. 4–6). Just as only a few stray stalks are left in a grain field or a few wizened or unripe fruits are left on the trees, so there will only be a remnant left of all that Israel once boasted of. As in the name of Isaiah's son, Shear-Jashub (see comments on 7:1–3), the concept of the remnant is double-edged: Hardly anything of the nation will remain, though there *will* be something left.

Thus, 17:7–8 speak of that future day when the Israelites will be purified by judgment and will turn their backs on their idols.[3] The key emphasis is on worshiping "their Maker" (v. 7) instead of what "their fingers have made" (v. 8). Idolatry is a reversal of reality. Why should we worship our own works? Should we not rather worship the One who made us?[4] According to these verses, a day will come when the remnant will finally abandon idolatry. This, of course, had occurred by the time of Christ, when the Jews had become almost fanatically anti-idolatrous.

In 17:9–11 Isaiah once more demonstrates his familiar pattern. Yes, there is the hope that in the future the trust in the human creatures of idolatry will be abandoned. But between then and the present, there is the awful reality of judgment. Like the cities of Aram, the cities of Israel will be "abandoned" and desolate (v. 9). Why? Because they have "forgotten God," who is the only hope for deliverance and refuge (v. 10). Instead of trusting the one who delivered them from Egypt and gave them the good land in which they live, they trust in their own strength and cunning.

Isaiah 17:10b–11 express this again (like 5:1–7) in imagery that is familiar to these largely agricultural people. They have done everything that their human strength can do. They have purchased the finest "imported" vines (v. 10b), perhaps an allusion to alliances with foreign nations. But even if they are such skillful agrarians that they could cause the plants to bud and bear fruit in a single day (something they obviously cannot do), the harvest would be worthless. Judgment is coming and cannot be averted by human skill. The best of human effort is not enough to solve the human problem. Someday the remnant of Israel will learn that fact.

---

3. "Asherah poles" apparently refer to groves of poplar trees that were dedicated to the worship of the Canaanite fertility goddess. Recent archaeological discoveries have shown that some apostate forms of the worship of Yahweh saw her as his consort.

4. This is a frequent theme in the book (see 2:8; 40:19; 44:9–11).

IT IS AMAZING HOW OFTEN religion based on human effort degenerates into the crudest fascination with sexuality. It was true in Canaan, it was true in Ephesus, it was true in Rome, and it is true today. The harvest we reap is one of disease, degeneration, and perversion.

But if we think about the issues more closely, it is perhaps not so amazing after all. Once we have abandoned the worship of the Maker, there is only one outlet for our inveterate need to worship something outside of ourselves. We must worship what we have made. But whence comes creativity? Ultimately, we worship the creative powers within ourselves. And since mere creativity as a concept is far too abstract and bland and since we who were made to worship the Transcendent One cannot live without mystery, the mystery of sexuality comes to rule our lives.

Another truth this passage teaches is one that occurs again and again in Isaiah. Yes, the coming judgment will be severe, but God has as his goal not the destruction of the nation but its purification. There will be a remnant, and that remnant will learn the lessons of destruction. They will recognize their own responsibility for the disaster and will turn back to God, looking to him and not to the products of their own skill and creativity. They will recognize that God has not failed them but that their own efforts to save themselves have.

THE EPIDEMIC OF PORNOGRAPHY today is a contemporary manifestation of the age-old problem. Having forgotten our Maker and what he teaches us about the surrender of our needs to him for him to supply, we become lost in self-indulgence, lack of discipline, and a spiraling inability to find stimulation in the normal and ordinary. Thus, we descend into more of the bizarre and destructive until a normal and healthy sexual experience becomes impossible. Then we hear the media "poohpoohing" these concerns as merely the censorious pratings of prudes, people who want to abridge the "first amendment rights" of others.

It is tragic that millions of dollars can be raised to combat pollution of the physical environment while the much more serious pollution of the spiritual environment proceeds apace with influential voices raised to defend it. Those who work with young boys know what is happening around us and are not at all surprised at the geometric rise in sexual violence in our society. The idea that "free expression" will solve all our societal ills is one result of having forgotten God. It is one thing for a person to have the right to express his or her opinions, even if those opinions are wrong or perverse. It is quite another thing for a person to have the right to market those "opinions" to the vulnerable, making huge fortunes while destroying the fabric of the society.

To paraphrase the prophet, we may be able to import the finest digital technology and use the most professional skills in photography, we may have a website up in a day and have ten thousand "hits," we may make millions of dollars, but "the harvest will be as nothing in the day of disease and incurable pain." Instead of a society that is genuinely fruitful, because people are turned outward and are able to sublimate their desires to accomplish worthwhile goals, we will have a society that is wholly given over to pleasing itself and is ultimately barren.

Isaiah 17:12–18:7

¹² OH, THE RAGING of many nations—
    they rage like the raging sea!
  Oh, the uproar of the peoples—
    they roar like the roaring of great waters!
¹³ Although the peoples roar like the roar of surging waters,
    when he rebukes them they flee far away,
  driven before the wind like chaff on the hills,
    like tumbleweed before a gale.
¹⁴ In the evening, sudden terror!
    Before the morning, they are gone!
  This is the portion of those who loot us,
    the lot of those who plunder us.

^{18:1} Woe to the land of whirring wings
    along the rivers of Cush,
  ² which sends envoys by sea
    in papyrus boats over the water.

  Go, swift messengers,
  to a people tall and smooth-skinned,
    to a people feared far and wide,
  an aggressive nation of strange speech,
    whose land is divided by rivers.

  ³ All you people of the world,
    you who live on the earth,
  when a banner is raised on the mountains,
    you will see it,
  and when a trumpet sounds,
    you will hear it.
⁴ This is what the LORD says to me:
    "I will remain quiet and will look on from my
        dwelling place,
  like shimmering heat in the sunshine,
    like a cloud of dew in the heat of harvest."
⁵ For, before the harvest, when the blossom is gone
    and the flower becomes a ripening grape,
  he will cut off the shoots with pruning knives,
    and cut down and take away the spreading branches.

⁶They will all be left to the mountain birds of prey
    and to the wild animals;
the birds will feed on them all summer,
    the wild animals all winter.

⁷At that time gifts will be brought to the LORD Almighty

from a people tall and smooth-skinned,
    from a people feared far and wide,
an aggressive nation of strange speech,
    whose land is divided by rivers—

the gifts will be brought to Mount Zion, the place of the Name
of the LORD Almighty.

AS MOTYER CORRECTLY notes, whatever the original settings of 17:12−14 and 18:1−7 may have been, they now function together to address the topic "who actually rules the world and whose purposes will in the end be accomplished?"[1] According to 17:12−14, it is unnecessary to become frightened because of the raging of the nations, for they will soon be gone. Isaiah 18:1−3 says that instead of envoys coming from the Ethiopian king of Egypt to invite Judah to join a coalition against Assyria, envoys should go to the Ethiopians to tell them what God says. A direct message from God appears in 18:4−7. While the nations roil about like the waves of the sea, God quietly waits and will take action at just the right moment, cutting off the oppressing nations and leaving their corpses on the mountains.

The Raging of the Nations (17:12−14)

IN LANGUAGE REMINISCENT of Psalm 46, the prophet compares the nations to the raging sea. The waves crash and roar with frightening power, and it seems as though they are the ultimate reality with which we must come to terms. But in fact, that is not the case. As Psalm 2 says, it is the One who sits in the heavens who is the ultimate reality. Before his breath, the nations are no more substantial than bits of "chaff" or a rolling "tumbleweed" (Isa. 17:13; see also 11:4). They have their day, but suddenly night falls, and in the morning nothing is left of what seemed so enduring (17:14).

In other words, Isaiah is attempting to get his people to focus beyond apparent realities and onto the One who is reality in himself. The nations may

1. Motyer, *Prophecy of Isaiah,* 160.

plan to "plunder" and "loot" God's people, but whatever they may think, they do not control their own destinies (cf. 14:24–27).

Messengers for Cush (18:1–3)

ABOUT 740 B.C. the Ethiopian Piankhy (also known as Piye) took over Egypt from the previous Libyan rulers. He along with his successor Shabako (715–702) brought a new energy to Egyptian affairs. Most likely both of them attempted to cement alliances with various surrounding countries in order to counter the Assyrian threat posed by both Sargon and Sennacherib.[2] We can imagine the stir made in Jerusalem by the tall, regal-looking Ethiopian envoys,[3] who came up the Mediterranean coast in their strange "papyrus" craft (18:2). But Isaiah says that envoys should instead go to Ethiopia[4] to tell them to beware of the true Ruler of the world. It is his battle flag and his war trumpet for which they should be on the alert (18:3).

A Message from God (18:4–7)

COMPARED TO THE marching of armies and the comings and goings of ambassadors, God's activity often seems unnoticeable. But in a masterful way the prophet reminds his hearers that just because something does not draw much attention to itself does not mean it is powerless.

He uses two comparisons to make his point: the sun and the dew (18:4). Neither comes with fanfare or pageantry; they are simply present and inescapable. So is God. And in his harvest he will cut down the enemy nations like unproductive branches on a vine (18:5–6). He is the reality, not they. This means that instead of the Judeans giving the Ethiopians a large sum of money for their help, the Judeans should remember that the day will come when the Ethiopians will be giving gifts to the God of Jerusalem (18:7; cf. 2:1–3; 60:10–14).

IN THE MIDST of earth's struggles, it is sometimes hard to believe that God is really on the throne. For instance, suppose a modern-day Isaiah had stood up on the streets of London in the spring of 1942 and said that Germany and Japan, who at that moment ruled fully half the world between them, would be completely powerless in just a little

---

2. For the most current thinking on this period on Egyptian history, see I. Shaw, ed., *The Oxford History of Ancient Egypt* (Oxford: Oxford Univ. Press, 2000), 352–68.

3. Note that Piankhy ruled Upper (southern) Egypt and all of Nubia.

4. "The land of whirring wings" apparently refers to the many insects found in the swampy areas along the upper Nile.

over three years. He would probably have been laughed to scorn. Yet he would have been completely correct. Despite the energy, intellect, and military power of those two great nations, they were swept away. God is the one reality who does not change or fade away. He is the One with whom we must come to terms.

IN PSALM 2:1–4 we read these words,

> Why do the nations conspire
>   and the peoples plot in vain?
> The kings of the earth take their stand
>   and the rulers gather together
against the LORD
    and against his Anointed One.
"Let us break their chains," they say,
    "and throw off their fetters."

The One enthroned in heaven laughs;
    The Lord scoffs at them.

The nations of the earth may take many drastic steps to elevate themselves to positions of absolute power. But God has kept that power for himself, and all the efforts by the nations will be as futile as a two-year-old's straining against the restraints in a car-seat. To the child this is a matter of serious rebellion. To the adults looking on, it is merely laughable. Psalm 46:6 makes a similar point: "Nations are in uproar, kingdoms fall; he lifts his voice, the earth melts."

Created beings are not the final reality; only the Creator is. We may see the nations of earth boiling about. We grow anxious as we see kingdoms fall. But the psalmist and Isaiah invite us to remember that all the power of the nations is derivative. Despite anything they do, the basic conditions of life are unchanged. But God is the One who established those conditions. Having brought the universe into existence with a word, he can just as easily put it out of existence with a word (cf. Isa. 11:4; Rev. 19:15). That is indeed power—power the nations of the earth can only dream about (cf. Isa. 40:15–17.)

When we think of the prediction that the Ethiopians will come to Jerusalem bearing gifts to the Lord Almighty (18:7), we remember the Ethiopian eunuch who received the Christian interpretation of Isaiah 53 in Acts 8:26–39 and became a believer. He represents all those other nations who have brought their gifts to God in Jerusalem, both before the birth of Christ and even more since. Isaiah has the long view that sees the reality behind what the other people of his day only imagine to be reality.

Isaiah 19:1–20:6

❦

A N ORACLE CONCERNING EGYPT:

See, the LORD rides on a swift cloud
    and is coming to Egypt.
The idols of Egypt tremble before him,
    and the hearts of the Egyptians melt within them.

2 "I will stir up Egyptian against Egyptian—
    brother will fight against brother,
    neighbor against neighbor,
    city against city,
    kingdom against kingdom.
3 The Egyptians will lose heart,
    and I will bring their plans to nothing;
they will consult the idols and the spirits of the dead,
    the mediums and the spiritists.
4 I will hand the Egyptians over
    to the power of a cruel master,
and a fierce king will rule over them,"
    declares the Lord, the LORD Almighty.

5 The waters of the river will dry up,
    and the riverbed will be parched and dry.
6 The canals will stink;
    the streams of Egypt will dwindle and dry up.
The reeds and rushes will wither,
7   also the plants along the Nile,
    at the mouth of the river.
Every sown field along the Nile
    will become parched, will blow away and be no more.
8 The fishermen will groan and lament,
    all who cast hooks into the Nile;
those who throw nets on the water
    will pine away.
9 Those who work with combed flax will despair,
    the weavers of fine linen will lose hope.
10 The workers in cloth will be dejected,
    and all the wage earners will be sick at heart.

¹¹ The officials of Zoan are nothing but fools;
　　the wise counselors of Pharaoh give senseless advice.
How can you say to Pharaoh,
　　"I am one of the wise men,
　　a disciple of the ancient kings"?

¹² Where are your wise men now?
　　Let them show you and make known
what the LORD Almighty
　　has planned against Egypt.
¹³ The officials of Zoan have become fools,
　　the leaders of Memphis are deceived;
the cornerstones of her peoples
　　have led Egypt astray.
¹⁴ The LORD has poured into them
　　a spirit of dizziness;
they make Egypt stagger in all that she does,
　　as a drunkard staggers around in his vomit.
¹⁵ There is nothing Egypt can do—
　　head or tail, palm branch or reed.

¹⁶In that day the Egyptians will be like women. They will shudder with fear at the uplifted hand that the LORD Almighty raises against them. ¹⁷And the land of Judah will bring terror to the Egyptians; everyone to whom Judah is mentioned will be terrified, because of what the LORD Almighty is planning against them.

¹⁸In that day five cities in Egypt will speak the language of Canaan and swear allegiance to the LORD Almighty. One of them will be called the City of Destruction.

¹⁹In that day there will be an altar to the LORD in the heart of Egypt, and a monument to the LORD at its border. ²⁰It will be a sign and witness to the LORD Almighty in the land of Egypt. When they cry out to the LORD because of their oppressors, he will send them a savior and defender, and he will rescue them. ²¹So the LORD will make himself known to the Egyptians, and in that day they will acknowledge the LORD. They will worship with sacrifices and grain offerings; they will make vows to the LORD and keep them. ²²The LORD will strike Egypt with a plague; he will strike them and heal them. They will turn to the LORD, and he will respond to their pleas and heal them.

²³In that day there will be a highway from Egypt to Assyria. The Assyrians will go to Egypt and the Egyptians to Assyria. The Egyptians and Assyrians will worship together. ²⁴In that day Israel will be the third, along with Egypt and Assyria, a blessing on the earth. ²⁵The LORD Almighty will bless them, saying, "Blessed be Egypt my people, Assyria my handiwork, and Israel my inheritance."

²⁰:¹In the year that the supreme commander, sent by Sargon king of Assyria, came to Ashdod and attacked and captured it—²at that time the LORD spoke through Isaiah son of Amoz. He said to him, "Take off the sackcloth from your body and the sandals from your feet." And he did so, going around stripped and barefoot.

³Then the LORD said, "Just as my servant Isaiah has gone stripped and barefoot for three years, as a sign and portent against Egypt and Cush, ⁴so the king of Assyria will lead away stripped and barefoot the Egyptian captives and Cushite exiles, young and old, with buttocks bared—to Egypt's shame. ⁵Those who trusted in Cush and boasted in Egypt will be afraid and put to shame. ⁶In that day the people who live on this coast will say, 'See what has happened to those we relied on, those we fled to for help and deliverance from the king of Assyria! How then can we escape?'"

THIS ORACLE CONCERNING Egypt falls into three parts. The first part (19:1–15) predicts Egypt's fall, showing that none of the great gifts that this nation has historically relied on can save her from the coming judgment. The second part (19:16–25) speaks of the way in which after judgment, Egypt will one day turn to worship Israel's God. The third part (20:1–6), true to form, reverts to the present and the certainty of Egypt's judgment. In all of this the reiteration of the theme of this part of the book is clear. Why would one trust Egypt since she cannot save herself and since she will one day turn to worship the very God Israel is now fearing to trust?[1]

Prediction of Egypt's Fall (19:1–15)

THIS FIRST POEM falls into three stanzas of nearly equal length: verses 1–4, 5–10, and 11–15. Each stanza deals with a different feature of Egypt in which

---

1. For further discussion on this point in this context, see Oswalt, *Isaiah 1–39*, 366–86.

the Egyptian people might be inclined to trust: the gods of Egypt, the Nile (the river of Egypt), and the fabled wisdom of Egypt. Each of these is shown to fail, leaving the Egyptians disgraced and despairing.

Isaiah 19:1–4. In several places Israelite writers appropriate the imagery of the Canaanite storm god Baal to say that the Lord rides upon the clouds (e.g., Deut. 33:26; Ps. 68:4; 104:3). So here it is not the Assyrian armies from the north whom the Egyptians should fear, but the God from the north, whose chariots are the clouds (Isa. 19:1). Compared to him, the multitudinous "idols" of Egypt (19:1, 3) are utterly helpless.

Certainly Egypt was the most polytheistic of all the peoples of the ancient Near East; they compare favorably for sheer number of gods with modern Hinduism. But all those gods, along with the spiritist practices associated with the polytheistic worldview, are helpless before the living God. They cannot prevent the kind of anarchy that historically occurred in Egypt when the central government collapsed (19:2). The Egyptians were an orderly people who hated change of all sorts. As a result, when rapid change came, they tended to "lose heart" (19:3), and order quickly gave way to disorder. Many possibilities exist for the identity of the "cruel master" of 19:4, from Piankhy the Ethiopian to Ashurbanipal the Assyrian, but the point is that this person will only rule at the sufferance of Yahweh, the God of Israel.

Isaiah 19:5–10. The Egyptians referred to their land as "the gift of the Nile." That is literally true. If it were not for the Nile River, Egypt would be simply an eastern extension of the Sahara Desert. For centuries the Nile has with clocklike regularity brought irrigation water and new topsoil to the land. Because of that water and fertility, the land has produced abundant crops, which in turn have made possible the leisure necessary to develop a high culture. In addition to its agricultural significance, the river has been a route of commerce and a military highway. Thus, Egypt and the Nile are inseparable.

But Isaiah says that it is foolish to put one's trust in any natural resource, even one as dependable as the Nile. Thus, he envisions a day when the mighty river will run dry, along with all the activities dependent on it: agriculture (19:7), fisheries (19:8), and flax-making (19:9–10).

Isaiah 19:11–15. Even more than its complex religion and its mighty river, Egypt was known in the ancient world for its wisdom and culture. But Isaiah says all of that will prove helpless in the face of God's plan. Although a connection cannot be proven, it is tempting to think that there is an allusion to the Joseph narrative in the inability of all the Egyptian wise men to tell the pharaoh what the Lord has "planned" for Egypt (19:12). Since they cannot even do that, Isaiah wonders how they dare to call themselves "wise" (19:11).

The language of 19:14 is like that found in chapter 28, where the prophet condemns the leaders of Judah for giving foolish counsel (cf. 28:7–8). Isaiah 19:15 uses the same language as 9:14 to describe the leadership of the land. As there, "head or tail, palm branch or reed" are figures of totality, like the English "top to bottom." Egypt's entire collection of counselors is helpless to discern what Israel's God is going to do with them and their land.

Egypt's Coming Worship of God (19:16–25)

THERE ARE NOT only negative reasons why Egypt should not be trusted, but there is also a positive reason why trusting in Egypt is foolish: The Egyptians will one day turn to Judah's God! Four different prose statements are made here, each headed by the phrase "in that day" (19:16, 18, 19, 23). This phrase does not refer to some specific twenty-four-hour period but to a more general time in the future. A good English equivalent is "at that time."[2]

At certain points in the future events will take place in God's providence that will forever alter the outlook of Egypt. The Egyptians will move from fear of the judging God to trust in the delivering God whom Judah now hesitates to trust. It is not necessary to believe that all these events will occur at the same time or even in the sequence given here. The prophet is only saying that future events will vindicate the counsel he is giving to Judah.

Verses 16–17 form a transition in that they are in the prose form of what follows, while their message is more like that of 19:1–15. Once more Isaiah emphasizes the "plan" of God (19:12, 17). "Plan," "counselors," and "advice" (19:11) all share the Hebrew root *y's*, so there is probably an intentional play on the foolish "plans" that the unwise counselors of the pharaoh have given. Because of that foolish counsel, the Egyptians will be plunged into terror when the God of Judah acts. Because it is Judah's God who is at work, the very name of Judah will frighten the people of Egypt.

But just as God's ultimate goal is not to destroy his people, neither is it his ultimate goal to destroy the people of Egypt. Isaiah 19:18–25 shows that his ultimate purpose is to bring them to worship him together with Israel and Assyria. This is an amazing thought, showing the truly universal character of Old Testament religion. Although at various points Judah is spoken of as triumphing over such perennial enemies as Egypt and Assyria, that is not the end of the story. The ultimate vision of the Hebrew prophets, first seen in Isaiah 2 (and in Mic. 4), is that Israel will be a blessing to the nations as it

2. See the discussion of *yom* in *Theological Lexicon of the Old Testament*, ed. E Jenni and C. Westermann, trans. M. Biddle (Peabody, Mass.: Hendrickson, 1997), 2:526–39. The phrase actually occurs a second time within each of the third and the fourth statements (19:21, 24), so that there are no less than six occurrences in these ten verses.

leads them to the one true God. All the peoples will worship him together (see also 25:6–9).

The hope of Egypt is expressed in three movements. (1) Several cities[3] will speak Hebrew ("the language of Canaan") and swear allegiance to the Lord (19:18). If the emendation accepted by many scholars is correct,[4] one of the five cities will actually be the home city of the cult of the sun god, Re.

(2) The Lord will be worshiped in Egypt, with an "altar" in the center of the land and a "monument" on the border (19:19). Probably not just one altar and one memorial are in Isaiah's mind here; rather, these represent many worship centers where, like Abraham (Gen. 12:8) and Jacob (28:18), the building of an altar or the setting up of memorial pillars was a way of acknowledging God's presence and of thanking him for his care.

The language of Isaiah 19:20–22 appears to have been consciously chosen to demonstrate that Egypt will share the same kind of relationship with the Lord as Israel did. They will be subject to the same kinds of divine discipline ("oppressors," v. 20; "plague," v. 22), and they will have available to them the same kinds of divine deliverance ("savior," v. 20; "heal," v. 22). He will reveal himself to them, and they will "acknowledge" (lit., "know") him.

(3) The final expression of God's positive plans for Egypt is, if anything, even more shocking than the previous two. He is not merely going to deliver Egypt and Israel from the Assyrian oppressors, he is going to join the three countries together in the common worship of the Lord! Egypt and Assyria will travel back and forth to one another's countries, not to attack one another or to strike shrewd business deals but to worship Israel's God.[5] Between the two poles of northeast (Assyria) and southwest (Egypt), Israel will fulfill the function that God promised to Abraham for his descendants (Gen. 12:3). They will be a blessing to the world, a means whereby the blessings of God can come to all peoples, a means whereby the election of Israel is extended to everyone ("Egypt my people, Assyria my handiwork," Isa. 19:25).

---

3. The significance of the number five is unclear. Motyer, *Prophecy of Isaiah*, 168, notes that the number is used in 17:6 and 30:17 to express the idea of "a few." H. Wildberger, *Isaiah 13–27: A Continental Commentary*, trans. T. Trappe (Minneapolis: Fortress, 1997), 270–71, has a detailed discussion of the possibilities and concludes that the author wrote during the postexilic period and knew of five specific cities where there was a significant Jewish presence. But the text is not speaking of Jewish communities in Egyptian cities.

4. Most editions of the Masoretic Text reads *'ir haheres* ("city of destruction"), but a few Hebrew MSS, 1QIsaᵃ, and some other versions read *'ir haheres* ("City of the Sun"), that is, Heliopolis (see NIV text note). It is easy to see how an error in copying could have occurred.

5. Here the theme "highway" occurs once again (cf. 11:16; 33:8; 35:8; 40:3; 49:11; 62:10). As a theme it expresses the removal of separation and alienation. There was a great highway connecting Assyria and Egypt, but this is speaking of reconciliation and not heavy construction.

Certainty of Egypt's Judgment (20:1–6)

THIS FINAL SECTION represents two of the common features of the prophecy of Isaiah: following up hopeful promises of the distant future with a discussion of coming judgment in the near future, and a graphic illustration of a point just made in a more discursive form. Isaiah is called to act out the coming defeat and exile of Egypt. Why would Judah want to trust a nation that will shortly fall to the enemy from whom they are promising to protect Judah?

There is uncertainty whether Isaiah is fully nude during this three-year period. The Hebrew word (NIV, "stripped") can connote either full or partial nudity, such as only wearing a loincloth, which would leave the "buttocks bared" (20:4). It is hard to imagine that the Judean community would have permitted full nudity for this long a period, though perhaps prophets were permitted kinds of behavior that would be otherwise forcibly prohibited. In any case, Isaiah is acting out what is going to happen when the Assyrians strip the captive Egyptians and march them off into captivity. Not only will Egypt fail those who trust in her, as Ashdod did, but she will ultimately not even be able to save herself.[6]

This is the only recorded example of Isaiah's performing symbolic actions, something more common in certain of the other prophets, notably Ezekiel (see Ezek. 4:1–17; 5:1–4; 12:1–20; see also Hos. 1–3). These actions reflect a peculiarly Hebrew understanding of the relation between symbol and reality. In the pagan view of the continuity of all things (see comments in the introduction), the symbol and the reality were identical. Thus, what was done to the symbol was necessarily done to reality. To act something out was to bring it to pass. By contrast, in Greek philosophical understanding, which has shaped modern thinking, there is no necessary relation between the symbol and the reality. Symbols may be freely alternated in whatever way seems to aid communication, and the reality is not affected in any way.

The biblical understanding stands somewhere between these extremes. While the symbol is not identical with reality, it does "partake" of the reality. Thus, certain symbols have a uniquely powerful ability to depict and evoke a given reality. As such, they cannot be freely alternated with other symbols. But at the same time, there is never the sense that because the prophet has performed some symbolic action, the corresponding reality *must* occur. The symbol has evocative power, not causal power. The law of transcendence has forever broken that understanding of causation.

---

6. The events described here took place between 714 and 711 B.C. The Egyptians had persuaded the people of Ashdod to revolt against the Assyrians. But the Assyrians recaptured the city, and when the king fled to Egypt for asylum, the Egyptians gave him up to the Assyrians. For a fuller discussion of this incident, see Oswalt, *Isaiah 1–39*, 382–84.

The repetition of words for "trust" in the final two verses of this passage remind us again that the central issue throughout this section (chs. 13–23) continues to be the fallacy of trusting the nations instead of the Lord.

Bridging Contexts

THIS PASSAGE IS about three things: the inadequacy of all the things of earth when it comes to giving full meaning to life, God's intention to save the whole earth, and the inevitable failure of all false hopes.

The inadequacy of the things of earth. There are three things we are tempted to trust when it comes to making sense of life: human wisdom, the natural environment, and the spirit world. Each of them is rooted in the creation and therefore each is drastically limited. But if we have rejected the possibility of a transcendent Creator, they are the best we have. Idolatry is in essence a combination of all three as it uses the best of human intelligence to imagine how the spirit world and the natural environment are interrelated. Specifically, this interrelationship is imagined in such a way as to maximize the human control of these forces. In doing so, we think that will give us the maximum of security, pleasure, and comfort.

But in the end such control is only possible if the worldview of continuity is correct. In this view all things that exist are part of each other. Thus, what is done in the human realm is automatically replicated in the divine and natural realms unless the demonic has somehow ruptured the links. The Bible tells us this is a false premise. God is not the world, and what is done here does not automatically affect him. Furthermore, there is a break between the human world and nature. Humans are not apes with the capacity for speech. We are uniquely created.

Thus, unless the Creator reveals the meaning of life to us, it is beyond our capacity to either find it or to create it. Our capacity will lead us in exactly the wrong direction, the direction of continuity, when the truth is transcendence. Thus, as Isaiah says, our wisdom becomes foolishness, nature regularly turns on us, and the spirit world is increasingly peopled with figures of horror and terror who cannot help us, only hurt us.

Salvation for the entire earth. If it is surprising that little Judah insists that its God is the only God in all the earth, it is even more surprising to discover, as here, that they also believe their God intends to save the whole earth. Other nations who believed their god was superior to all the others typically spoke of that god as dominating all the earth and making his own particular people rulers of the whole thing. Thus, it is not surprising to find some of those sentiments present in the Old Testament; it would be more surprising if we did not. That attitude was simply part of the mental furniture of that day and time.

But what *is* surprising is the idea that the eventual purpose of God's rule is not domination but salvation. This view is consistent with the revelation of God the Hebrews have received. This sole God of all the earth is not like the other gods, who were self-serving and petty; he is self-giving and gracious. Since he is the only God, he will treat all peoples who repent, even Egyptians and Assyrians, in the same way as he has treated his own people.

The failure of false hopes. The haunting popular song of the 1970s "Is That All There Is?" illustrates the third theme of this passage. The singer speaks of the anticipation of love, freedom, and accomplishment, but she is always disappointed with the reality, saying in each case, "Is that all there is?" In the end, she contemplates suicide but is afraid to carry it out, because she is afraid she will end up saying once more, "Is that all there is?"

Somehow in this world, the reality usually falls short of the expectation. Why? As Blaise Pascal has said, there is a God-shaped vacuum in each of us, and when we attempt to fill that vacuum with anything less than God, the result must always be disappointing.[7] But if that vacuum is filled with its rightful resident, we will stop expecting earthly things to fill the void and will be able to enjoy each of them for their limited selves. There is great joy in learning; there is great joy in nature; there is great joy in spiritual experience—but only when none of them is made ultimate.

FULFILLMENT OF PROPHECY. This is a convenient place to talk about the fulfillment of prophecy. How much of what Isaiah says about Egypt (and the other nations) should we expect to be literally fulfilled? At the outset, let me lay down some important parameters.

(1) If there is a transcendent God who reveals himself in history, then the possibility of genuine predictive prophecy must be allowed for.[8] Most of modern scholarship, operating on the premise of uniformity, denies such a possibility. Uniformity presupposes that whatever happens today has always happened this way, and we interpret the past in the light of the processes we see happening in the present. Note glacial dating in archaeology as an example. The deposits of various ice ages can be detected, especially in Europe. A system of dating has been developed based on the assumption that glaciers have always grown and contracted at the same rates they do today. Inter-

---

7. B. Pascal, *Pascal's Pensées*, trans. W. Trotter (New York: Dutton, 1958), 113.
8. More will be said on this in the comments on chs. 41–45.

estingly, increasing numbers of secular scientists now accept the likelihood that there were periods of sudden and catastrophic changes on the earth, but that has done little to change the faith of scholars in the theory of uniformity.

When uniformity is applied to prophecy, the results are obvious. Is there anyone today who genuinely knows the future? No. There are many who claim to do so, but when they and their predictions are scrutinized carefully, the results are always disappointing. They are either flatly wrong, or they miss the really big events (what fortune-teller predicted the break-up of the Soviet Union more than a few months in advance?), or they are so ambiguous as to be meaningless. People only know things after they have happened. So, on the basis of uniformity, it is said that this is the way things have always been. The biblical prophets were supposedly no different from anyone today. Contemporary events gave the "prophets" ideas, and the "prophets" tried to make it appear that God had predicted the event before it actually occurred.

But the Bible is premised on something other than uniformity. If the Bible is right at all, then there was a history of salvation when God was uniquely active in the world. He intervened in that period in unique ways to disclose himself to the world. The culmination of that disclosure was in Jesus Christ. Thus, the books that give the authoritative interpretation of Jesus' life, death, and resurrection are the culmination of that process of self-disclosure. To say that there has never been any other kind of self-disclosure by God than the type that occurs now is to disbelieve what the Bible claims about itself and the process that brought the Bible about. If one grants the truth of the biblical teaching about God and about the way in which he revealed himself, then genuine predictive prophecy must be considered to be a possibility. This means it is impossible to dismiss the reference to the five cities speaking the "language of Canaan" as a postexilic reference to the Jewish communities that existed in Egypt at the time of the writing.

(2) The second parameter is on the opposite end. This one has to do with understanding the purpose of prophecy. Prophecy is not given so that those hearing it can map out a timetable of future events. That was what pagan prophecy sought to do. Biblical prophecy is different. In the Bible prediction is put into a context that radically changes the significance of the prediction. Biblical prophecy is a call to obey God revealed in the terms of the covenant. In this new context prediction has two purposes: to verify that the God who is calling for obedience is indeed the God of the universe, who knows all things and is worthy of obedience, and to give confidence to the listeners that they can dare to obey because this God has the entire future in his hands.

Thus, much of the modern fascination with biblical prophecy is foreign to the purposes for which the prophecy exists. Instead of promoting moral obedience and social justice, it promotes spiritual elitism and arrogance. It also promotes a certain "slipperiness." It is fascinating to watch people who have been "interpreting" biblical predictions for thirty years or more keep readjusting their interpretations as time passes. Their continued ability to draw crowds is primarily a testimony to the interpreter's facile imagination and the gullibility of many Christians. The fact is that the biblical data are complex enough that an imaginative and diligent student can create a plausible case for almost any scenario.

(3) This latter point establishes the need for a third parameter, to be established in the center. It is dangerous to attempt to define in advance exactly how a biblical prediction is going to be fulfilled. For instance, it would have been natural for someone reading Micah 5:2 to say that the Messiah would have to be born and raised in Bethlehem. This may have been partly behind Nathaniel's remark, "Can anything good come from [Nazareth]?" (John 1:46). How can Jesus be the Messiah if he comes from Nazareth? Everybody knows the Messiah comes from Bethlehem. Was the scriptural prediction incorrect? No, but it was not fulfilled as one might expect. This means that we need to be both open and tentative about how scriptural prophecy is going to be fulfilled and about how literally it will be fulfilled.

Thus, shall we expect at some point in the future to hear of five Egyptian cities where Hebrew is the official language? Shall we expect an altar to the living God to be erected there and a superhighway extending from Cairo to Baghdad by way of Tel Aviv? To all of these I answer, "I don't know"—and you should be suspicious of anyone who says he or she does know.

Will the promises recorded here be fulfilled? Yes, they will. In fact, from one point of view they already have been fulfilled. For the first half of the first millennium, Egypt was one of the major centers of Christian, that is, biblical, faith. Believers from Egypt and Mesopotamia journeyed to Jerusalem to worship the God of the Bible. Perhaps there will be a more literal fulfillment yet to come. But we should be careful to avoid two extremes. On the one hand we should not say that the only possible fulfillment is a literal one according to my, or my group's, definition of "literal." On the other hand, we should not say that the spiritual teaching of these predictions is all that is important. If God is God, then history is still his arena to act in as he chooses.

Conflict in worldviews. This oracle in Isaiah 19–20 highlights the conflict between two worldviews: the biblical one and the pagan one. For many years, we in the Western world have argued that there are three worldviews: the transcendent, the pagan, and the a-religious. We have argued that it is possible to take a purely mechanistic view of life without taking into account the spiritual. But the ancient Egyptians and Mesopotamians were more acute observers than we. They understood that there is a spiritual component in existence that cannot be ignored. The only issue is how to relate to it. The pagan view says we can relate to the spiritual realm through magical manipulation and participation. But this view has a number of deadly implications, all of which become clearer and clearer as we in the West fall back into it.

Paul's insight in Romans 1 cannot be improved upon. He demonstrates the inevitable confusion that comes to the one who refuses to recognize that there is a God outside of himself or herself who cannot be manipulated by anything he or she does. Once we deny God is outside of the world, then the only alternative is that the divine *is* the world. That in turn means that the world is without purpose or goal and that we can never transcend the cycles of existence. Individuals no longer matter and the only wisdom is utilitarianism: "If it works, it's good." There is no morality except power, and salvation is nothing more than self-actualization. The thought that one can transcend one's background or conditioning is not only laughable, it is evil.

By contrast, transcendence speaks of a world where we can move forward out of the conditioning of the past into a bright new day where potentials can become reality. We are not locked into the past, nor are we doomed to repeat its failures. By surrendering to and trusting the God who is not the world, we can overcome the world (cf. 1 John 5:4–5). Not only can we know the way we were meant to live, we can find grace through surrender to live that life. The wisdom of paganism in its worship of nature and its deification of humanity has failed and will continue to fail. But the God who is beyond time and space yet is everywhere present will be worshiped from sea to sea.

Coming to God. One of the consequences of the loss of the transcendent vision is the assertion that all roads lead to God. Of course, if the world is god and if there is no such thing as divine self-revelation, that is manifestly true. But both of those premises are false, profoundly false. The Bible is the most inclusive book in the world, but it achieves that distinction by being the most exclusive one. Can the Egyptians find God? Can they worship at his feet? Or is he the exclusive possession of the Israelites? No, he is not the possession of the Israelites. The gospel word "Whoever will may come" is gladly, gloriously true. Christ has died for all persons everywhere; he is "not wanting anyone to perish" (2 Peter 3:9).

But *how* do they come? Here is the issue. Do they come in their own way, or do they come in God's way? The Christian community today is in grave danger of losing its missionary zeal through a misguided desire not to appear too exclusive. Since the only sin left in a permissive society that has lost the capacity to say no is intolerance, Christians are regularly called sinners, and we don't like it.

But misguided tolerance is deadly. How exclusive is electricity? Completely! You either relate to it on its terms or you die. Is electricity therefore a curse? Of course not! It is an incredible blessing, but only if you relate to it on its terms. The same is true for God. We relate to him on his terms, and he in his grace has allowed us to know what those terms are. This is what the whole sacrificial system was designed to teach. God wants to live in our midst, but given our sinful nature and his holy nature, that is not possible unless God makes a way and reveals that way to us, and we choose to walk in that way.

If you saw a little boy running to pick up a bare electric wire and the only way to stop him from touching it was to tackle him and knock him down, would you do it? Of course! But how intolerant and how cruel! The child does not mean any harm, and after all, your way of relating to electricity is just your own narrow idea. I think the analogy is clear. Everything depends on the truth of the Bible. If God is not transcendent and holy, if he is just the world, then there is no salvation from ourselves; we came from nothing and we go back to it. There is no right and wrong, and all so-called moralities are simply power plays. But if God *is* transcendent and holy, if he does want to relate to us in order to give us eternal life, and if we can only relate to him on his terms, then Christians must get out into the world with renewed zeal and joy.

This latter truth helps us to understand why God required Isaiah to do such a degrading thing as walking among his people either nude or seminude for three years. We are offended at a God who would demand such a thing of his faithful servant. The same thing applies when we think of Ezekiel, who was also called to act out various kinds of degrading things, such as cooking food over a fire of manure. Why would God call for this? Surely it wasn't necessary to go to such extremes!

It all depends on how seriously you take God and his Word. How important was it that the Judeans, and particularly Hezekiah, learn not to trust Egypt and instead trust God? Was it more important than Isaiah's dignity? Or was it just a matter of personal preference whether to obey God? Was it a matter of life and death for Judah? It certainly was. And it may be argued that because of Isaiah's willingness to be faithful to God, Hezekiah did trust God and Judah gained another 115 years of life.

How seriously do I take the condition of the people around me? Seriously enough to be thought a fool or a little "cracked" if that will reach them? Of course, bizarre behavior for its own sake is not a virtue. It will do damage to the gospel. But every one of us who is a believer has to be ready to make the claims of the gospel visible in the most powerful way possible.

Isaiah 21:1–17

※

AN ORACLE CONCERNING the Desert by the Sea:

Like whirlwinds sweeping through the southland,
an invader comes from the desert,
from a land of terror.

² A dire vision has been shown to me:
The traitor betrays, the looter takes loot.
Elam, attack! Media, lay siege!
I will bring to an end all the groaning she caused.

³ At this my body is racked with pain,
pangs seize me, like those of a woman in labor;
I am staggered by what I hear,
I am bewildered by what I see.
⁴ My heart falters,
fear makes me tremble;
the twilight I longed for
has become a horror to me.

⁵ They set the tables,
they spread the rugs,
they eat, they drink!
Get up, you officers,
oil the shields!

⁶ This is what the Lord says to me:

"Go, post a lookout
and have him report what he sees.
⁷ When he sees chariots
with teams of horses,
riders on donkeys
or riders on camels,
let him be alert,
fully alert."

⁸ And the lookout shouted,

"Day after day, my lord, I stand on the watchtower;
every night I stay at my post.

⁹Look, here comes a man in a chariot
  with a team of horses.
And he gives back the answer:
  'Babylon has fallen, has fallen!
All the images of its gods
  lie shattered on the ground!'"

¹⁰O my people, crushed on the threshing floor,
  I tell you what I have heard
from the LORD Almighty,
  from the God of Israel.

¹¹An oracle concerning Dumah:

Someone calls to me from Seir,
  "Watchman, what is left of the night?
  Watchman, what is left of the night?"
¹²The watchman replies,
  "Morning is coming, but also the night.
If you would ask, then ask;
  and come back yet again."

¹³An oracle concerning Arabia:

You caravans of Dedanites,
  who camp in the thickets of Arabia,
¹⁴ bring water for the thirsty;
you who live in Tema,
  bring food for the fugitives.
¹⁵They flee from the sword,
  from the drawn sword,
from the bent bow
  and from the heat of battle.

¹⁶This is what the Lord says to me: "Within one year, as a servant bound by contract would count it, all the pomp of Kedar will come to an end. ¹⁷The survivors of the bowmen, the warriors of Kedar, will be few." The LORD, the God of Israel, has spoken.

AS MENTIONED AT the beginning of this section on the oracles against the nations (Isa. 13–23), it is difficult to know whether there is an intentional order. It does seem possible to see certain groupings. We began with the Mesopotamian powers of Babylon and Assyria (chs. 13–14) and then moved to the neighbors Philistia, Moab, Aram, and Israel (chs. 14–17). Chapter 18 formed an interlude chapter, where Ethiopia was used to focus on the lordship of Yahweh over all nations. Then came the oracle against Egypt (chs. 19–20).

But what about the remaining chapters? Some scholars believe that the four oracles in chapters 21 and 22 should be considered together,[1] but the reasons given vary. Most comment on the prophet's clear sense of grief over what he sees happening. Many also observe the enigmatic titles of the first, second, and fourth oracles. I have proposed that the first refers to Babylon, while the second, third, and fourth all refer to Arabia, who will be failed by it.[2]

The Desert by the Sea (21:1–10)

THE TITLE OF this oracle is a puzzle. Literally it is "the burden of the desert of the sea." Clearly, that is a contradiction in terms: The desert is not wet, and the sea is not dry. So what is the writer intending to convey? Verse 9 suggests that the subject is Babylon, so why use this obscure title? Furthermore, if the subject is Babylon, what destruction is being talked about? The mention of Elam and Media (21:2) suggests the final destruction in 540 B.C., because prior to that time the Medes were allies of Babylon, not enemies. Yet the general time frame of this section (chs. 13–23) seems to be relating to events closer to Isaiah's own time. So perhaps the prophet is telescoping together several destructions, beginning with those near his own time and culminating in the Persian conquest—all to argue the folly of trusting Babylon.

But that still leaves unanswered the question of the title. The most likely possibility is that it is a play on the name of Merodach-Baladan's (39:1) homeland in extreme southern Mesopotamia, "the Sealand." Is the great Babylonian rebel in a position to offer Judah any help? Yes, just about as much as a desert might offer![3]

---

1. Scholars as diverse as Delitzsch, *Commentary on Isaiah*, trans. J. Denney, 3d ed., 2 vols. (New York: Funk & Wagnalls, n.d.), 343–44, and Seitz, *Isaiah 1–39*, 157–59, have taken this position. Motyer, *Prophecy of Isaiah*, 171–72, also includes ch. 23, primarily for reasons of atmosphere.

2. Oswalt, *Isaiah, 1–39*, 388–90.

3. It is also possible that *yam* ("sea") is a corruption or an original masc. pl. ending on "desert." The word is missing from the LXX (though it is present in both the Vulgate and the Syriac).

Verses 1–2 depict the suddenness of destruction. Like a whirlwind in the "southland" of Judah, the destruction will sweep in. Babylon's power, like Assyria's before it, will be built on betrayal and plunder. But the day will come when the tables will be turned. Both "Elam" and "Media" were occasionally allies of Babylon, and both turn against her at various points. This is always the story when power and self-interest are the guiding principles of life, and Isaiah sees nothing but tragedy in store for those who build on them.

Probably the best explanation for the grief that racks Isaiah in 21:3–4 is that he is lamenting for those who put their trust in Babylon and will be destroyed when that trust fails (see 22:4). But he may also be experiencing vicariously the grief of those who are tortured and taken into exile. They hope for the end of the day of battle and struggle, but at the end of the day, as "twilight" falls, it is not a twilight of respite from battle but a twilight of defeat, leading into a night of "horror" (21:4). The Babylon whom they trust now to deliver them from Assyria will eventually become the oppressor who destroys them before it itself is conquered.

Verse 5 reminds the reader of the scene in Daniel 5, where Belshazzar is feasting in Babylon while the enemy is at the gates. The scene of feasting is quickly changed to one of frantic preparation for war ("oil the shields"), but the preparation is far too late.

While the overall sense of 21:6–9 is clear enough—that is, look for the message to come that "Babylon has fallen"—the specific significance of the repeated references to chariots and teams of horses is not. Perhaps they are suggestive of the fleeing, defeated remnants of an army who bring with them the first intimations of the defeat. Like Ezekiel later (Ezek. 3:17; 33:1–7), Isaiah is to be a watchman for his people to warn them of what lies ahead if they persist in disobeying God. The idols of Babylon cannot deliver their own land, so how can they deliver those outside of Babylon who trust in them?

Verse 10 continues that thought. The people of Judah are like grain "crushed on the threshing floor." The oxen have been driven around and around on the heap of grain, pulling a heavy sled behind them. The stalks and husks have been crushed and the kernels of grain separated. Soon the whole mass will be tossed in the air with winnowing forks so that the chaff can be blown away. Clearly, that is what the Judean people feel like. They have been crushed under the sled of Assyria, so it looks as if Babylon offers a ray of hope. But Isaiah, the watchman, sees a false hope. Babylon is no more able to help than any other nation on earth.

The "Dumah" Oracle (21:11–12)

THIS TWO-VERSE ORACLE is a puzzle. The message seems to concern Edom ("Seir," 21:11), but it is addressed to the Arabian oasis Dumah, which was about three hundred miles southeast of Jerusalem.[4] This oasis was at the intersection of the east-west trade route from Babylon to Edom and Egypt, and the north-south route from the Red Sea to Palmyra. Undoubtedly, the fate of Babylon is of great concern to Dumah, and farther west to Edom. In view of the fact that the third oracle in this cycle clearly concerns the Arabians and the other great oasis of Tema, it seems best to retain the reference to Dumah.

But what of the message itself? Perhaps the thought is that even the Edomites turn to Isaiah, the Judean "watchman," to see what is happening in the east. Because of his God he is able to see the future in ways the ordinary "seer" cannot. But if that is the case, the message given is a rather enigmatic one. In 21:4, the speaker admitted that the longed-for twilight had not produced relief. Now the prophet seems to be saying that the longed-for dawn may not be a relief either, for night will swiftly follow it. This may refer to the Assyrian "night" ending, but a Babylonian "night" following it in swift succession. It may also speak of the coming defeat of Sennacherib in 701 B.C. ("dawn"), but the subsequent destruction of Babylon in whom Judah is trusting in 689 B.C. ("night").

An Oracle on Arabia (21:13–17)

OF THE SUCCESSION of four oracles in Isaiah 21–22, this third one is the only one that appears to have a straightforward title. It is addressed to the "Arabians" who lived in the desert between Babylon and Judah. The oasis of "Tema" was located about two hundred miles south of Dumah on the road to the Red Sea, and Dedan is about ninety miles south of Tema. Both are located in an area of northwest Arabia known as Kedar (21:16). Tema is significant because this is where the last king of Babylon made his headquarters for most of his reign. While he was there, his son Belshazzar was viceregent in Babylon.

It is not clear who the "fugitives" mentioned in 21:14 are. Perhaps they are Babylonians fleeing the destruction of their city. Or they may be fugitives from Dumah, fleeing southward away from the conflagration spreading outward from southern Mesopotamia. But 21:16–17 make it clear that Kedar itself will not escape the disaster. War will overtake them "within one year" of this pronouncement having been made, and their armies will be decimated. All this is certain because Israel's God "has spoken."

---

4. The situation is further confused because the LXX reads "Idumea" (Edom) in the title. Some see "Dumah" as simply an anagram of Edom, but why that would be done is unclear. See Wildberger, *Isaiah 13–27*, 328–29, 331–37 for an exhaustive discussion of the issue.

ONE OF THE classic examples of the failure of a web of deceptive alliances in our time is the story of Russia and Germany. One of Hitler's greatest fears growing out of World War I was of a "two-front" war. So, in order to secure his eastern flank while campaigning in the west, he concluded what must surely be one of the most cynical alliances of all time. Knowing that he would one day attack Russia (already having said so in his *Mein Kampf*), he still got Russia to agree to a nonaggression pact. For his part, Stalin was frightened of the rapidly growing German war machine and congratulated himself for having effectively stopped it at his borders.

Both of these pirates had built their empires on lies and looting, and now they were announcing their "mutual understanding and trust." It is amazing that Stalin could not see what sort of person Hitler was after all the promises he had broken from Czechoslovakia onward, but perhaps the Russian tyrant thought he saw a kindred spirit in the man. It may also be true that Stalin was afraid of his remaining generals (after the purges of 1937–1938) amassing power within the country if he permitted a great buildup in the armed forces, and he thought he could avoid such a buildup with the pact.

In any case, once Hitler felt the west was secure, he turned to gobble up the great wheat fields of Byelo-Russia and the Ukraine, sure that a cowed Stalin would hide behind the Urals and sue for peace. But if Stalin misread Hitler, so did Hitler misread Stalin. Hitler did not know that he had kicked a bulldog. The former Orthodox priest had pursued his goals of absolute power for twenty years with incredible tenacity and stubbornness, and those traits would serve him well in "The Great Patriotic War." Both men thought that they had put something over on their neighbor that would be to their own advantage. But in the end, both countries were devastated.

That is the picture here. Whoever trusts in deception and betrayal to build his kingdom must eventually watch that kingdom being torn down by the very traits that built it in the first place. Trusting Babylon was an exercise in self-deception.

PROMISES AND SELF-INTEREST. These three oracles speak of the sovereignty of God, the folly of trusting in human power, and the fickleness of human promises. The believer today must constantly remind himself or herself of these truths. We must think about these things from our own point of view. Are people depending on us? Why? Have we, like Babylon, made promises to people that are chiefly for the purpose of getting them involved in "our agenda"? Are we only interested in using them for our own advantage? Have we made promises to them that we either cannot or do not intend to keep?

These are serious questions. One of the reasons they are so serious is because of the immense capacity for self-deception that human self-interest provokes. Needing to take care of ourselves, we easily justify questionable behaviors because of that "worthwhile" end. Parents can make promises to children, spouses can make commitments to spouses, church members can make promises to other church members—and all the time those promises are only devices to promote our own self-interest. I do not care about my child's development; I only want peace from his constant nagging, or I want her to think well of me. I promise to love, honor, and cherish until death, when what I really want is a beautiful wedding, or the sense of having exclusive right to the other person, or the satisfaction of having beat out the competition. I promise to be faithful as a church member, but only so long as it does not interfere with other, more enjoyable activities. As a result, when keeping the promises requires me to deny myself in some way, as it always will, the promises, like Babylon's, turn out to be useless. Since the very reason I made the promise was for self-interest, as soon as keeping the promise conflicts with self-interest, there is no contest.

At the same time, we need to be realistic about the promises of others to us. In many cases their commitments to us will be just as self-serving as ours were to them. If we look for any ultimate security in human commitments or human institutions, we need to be prepared for disappointment. This is not only true because of the self-interest problem but also because of human limitations. If there are mighty human weapons to be used on our behalf, there are even mightier ones to be used against us. Humanity simply cannot provide the kind of ultimate security we are looking for. The result is not only disappointment but often cynicism and embitterment.

What is the solution for both of these cases? How can we become truly trustworthy in our relations with others, and how can we avoid the embitterment of failed trust? We need to surrender our self-interest into the hands of the sovereign God. We need to stop trusting others to supply what only God can provide, and we need to stop trying to supply our own needs out of our own resources and turn instead to God in a genuine self-denying trust. If I have come to know that God is infinitely trustworthy and if I have abandoned my self-interest into his hands, I can become trustworthy myself. My promises are not to get but genuinely to give. And if others take advantage of my promises, as they frequently will, given the human condition, I can remain faithful knowing that I have resources to turn to that are not dependent on what others may do.

Here is the secret of "sweet" saints over the centuries of the Christian church. Have they never been disappointed by broken promises or failed trusts? Of course they have, and maybe more than the rest of us because they are so prodigal with their kindnesses. But they have put their weight down on God and not on humans. Thus, if the human branch beneath them breaks, they can still sing, knowing they have wings to fly.

All this depends on the sovereignty of God displayed in the final phrase of 21:17. If there is a sovereign God who can reveal himself and his will to human beings, then there is a divine resource we can turn to in the midst of trouble and uncertainty. Furthermore, if that God is loving, faithful, and good, we who abandon ourselves into his care need not fear any final loss, on either side of the grave. But everything depends on the validity of this revelation. If God is one degree less than what the Bible claims him to be, either in his power or his character, then we are without hope. But the testimony of the Bible and of the saints coincides. The One Holy Being in the universe is all-powerful and all-loving. We can trust him (see Matt. 6:26–30; Rom. 5:8).

This is the message Isaiah is trying to get his compatriots to hear: God is faithful and humans are not. Humans will fail you, so if you abandon your trust in God to trust in the nations of the earth, prepare for disappointment (21:3–4; see also Ps. 56:1–4). But if you have put your trust in God, you can be faithful even to those who fail you because, like Christ, you will have "food" to eat that no one else knows of (John 4:32–34).

Isaiah 22:1–25

❦

A N ORACLE CONCERNING the Valley of Vision:

What troubles you now,
   that you have all gone up on the roofs,
² O town full of commotion,
   O city of tumult and revelry?
Your slain were not killed by the sword,
   nor did they die in battle.
³ All your leaders have fled together;
   they have been captured without using the bow.
All you who were caught were taken prisoner together,
   having fled while the enemy was still far away.
⁴ Therefore I said, "Turn away from me;
   let me weep bitterly.
Do not try to console me
   over the destruction of my people."

⁵ The Lord, the LORD Almighty, has a day
   of tumult and trampling and terror
   in the Valley of Vision,
a day of battering down walls
   and of crying out to the mountains.
⁶ Elam takes up the quiver,
   with her charioteers and horses;
   Kir uncovers the shield.
⁷ Your choicest valleys are full of chariots,
   and horsemen are posted at the city gates;
⁸   the defenses of Judah are stripped away.

And you looked in that day
   to the weapons in the Palace of the Forest;
⁹ you saw that the City of David
   had many breaches in its defenses;
you stored up water
   in the Lower Pool.
¹⁰ You counted the buildings in Jerusalem
   and tore down houses to strengthen the wall.
¹¹ You built a reservoir between the two walls
   for the water of the Old Pool,

> but you did not look to the One who made it,
> or have regard for the One who planned it long ago.

¹²The Lord, the LORD Almighty,
> called you on that day
to weep and to wail,
> to tear out your hair and put on sackcloth.
¹³But see, there is joy and revelry,
> slaughtering of cattle and killing of sheep,
> eating of meat and drinking of wine!
"Let us eat and drink," you say,
> "for tomorrow we die!"

¹⁴The LORD Almighty has revealed this in my hearing: "Till your dying day this sin will not be atoned for," says the Lord, the LORD Almighty.

¹⁵This is what the Lord, the LORD Almighty, says:

> "Go, say to this steward,
> to Shebna, who is in charge of the palace:
¹⁶What are you doing here and who gave you permission
> to cut out a grave for yourself here,
hewing your grave on the height
> and chiseling your resting place in the rock?

¹⁷"Beware, the LORD is about to take firm hold of you
> and hurl you away, O you mighty man.
¹⁸He will roll you up tightly like a ball
> and throw you into a large country.
There you will die
> and there your splendid chariots will remain—
> you disgrace to your master's house!
¹⁹I will depose you from your office,
> and you will be ousted from your position.

²⁰"In that day I will summon my servant, Eliakim son of Hilkiah. ²¹I will clothe him with your robe and fasten your sash around him and hand your authority over to him. He will be a father to those who live in Jerusalem and to the house of Judah. ²²I will place on his shoulder the key to the house of David; what he opens no one can shut, and what he shuts no one can open. ²³I will drive him like a peg into a firm place; he will be a seat of honor for the house of his father. ²⁴All the

glory of his family will hang on him: its offspring and offshoots
—all its lesser vessels, from the bowls to all the jars.

²⁵"In that day," declares the LORD Almighty, "the peg driven
into the firm place will give way; it will be sheared off and will
fall, and the load hanging on it will be cut down." The LORD
has spoken.

THIS APPEARS TO BE the fourth of the oracles in the
sequence beginning with the oracle "concerning
the Desert by the Sea" in 21:1. Like two of the
other three, its title is enigmatic, and it is also
marked by the prophet's grief over what he sees as about to take place (21:3–
4; 22:4, 12). Given these two similarities and recognizing that the second and
third oracles seem to be related to the fall of Babylon, most likely this one is
related in the same way. Judah is rejoicing in the help that Babylon can give
in the fight against Assyria, but Isaiah weeps as he sees that not only will Babylon give no help, but it will eventually be the cause of Judah's destruction.

The Valley of Vision (22:1–14)

THE STRANGE TITLE of the oracle ("The Valley of Vision") is reminiscent of the
title for the oracle against Babylon in 21:1. Like that one, it seems to involve
contradictory ideas to make its point. A valley is not where one goes to get
a long view of things. In fact, it is the exact opposite; it is a place where you
cannot see. It seems plain from the rest of the oracle that it is addressed to
Jerusalem, but why describe it so strangely? Perhaps the prophet is condemning the Judeans precisely for their lack of vision. They claim to know
God and his ways, but their behavior makes it appear they do not. Instead
of standing on a mountaintop where they can see clearly, they are in the
bottom of a valley, having lost all perspective on reality and what it means.
In fact, they have become like one more of the pagan nations on whom
judgment is being pronounced in this section of the book.

There is considerable uncertainty among scholars as to the events being
referred to in these verses. The references to strengthening defenses (22:8–
11) suggest either the coming of Sennacherib in 701 B.C. or the final siege
of Jerusalem begun in 588 B.C. However, the references to rejoicing and revelry (22:2, 13) are difficult to integrate into either of those events. Also, Eliakim, not Shebna, was prime minister ("in charge of the palace," 22:15) in 701
B.C. This suggests another possibility, the attack of Sargon on the Philistine
city of Ashdod in 711 B.C. (cf. 20:1). This must have been a frightening event
for the Judeans, certainly frightening enough to provoke a strengthening of

the defenses. But after taking Azekah, another Philistine city, the Assyrians withdrew. That surely would have occasioned a time of rejoicing. It also would seem to confirm any encouragement to revolt that the Babylonian envoys may have given to Hezekiah in their visit at about this time (see comments on ch. 38 for the date of the events in chs. 38–39).

All the inhabitants of "the Valley of Vision" can see is short-term relief (22:1–2). They cannot see the longer view that the prophet has, namely, the events just before the fall of Jerusalem, when King Zedekiah fled from the city with his bodyguard only to be captured near Jericho. Thus, the people are rejoicing at the moment over a short-term lifting of the Assyrian threat, while the prophet sees how this whole episode will end 125 years later and weeps "bitterly" over that reality (22:4). He sees what they cannot.

Verses 5–7 probably continue Isaiah's view of the distant future, when the besieging armies will be camped around the city, filling the Kidron Valley on the east and the Hinnom Valley on the south. Among the Babylonian armies will be mercenary soldiers from "Elam" and "Kir" (possibly Media). In that hour there will be no more rejoicing in "the Valley of Vision" but only "tumult" and "terror."[1]

In 21:8–14 the prophet makes his pronouncement against "the Valley of Vision." Note the recurrence of verbs for seeing in verses 8, 9, and 11. Temporal "realities" have been looked at instead of eternal ones. It is not clear who the repeated "you" is in verses 8–12. It is probably Hezekiah, because we know he strengthened the walls of Jerusalem and had the famous tunnel dug to bring water from the spring of Gihon to the pool at the foot of the old city (2 Chron. 32:1–5); if so, he is not named. Moreover, we should note that although the first verb of the succession of second-person verbs is singular (Isa. 22:8),[2] the rest are plural (22:9–11). Perhaps the point is that Hezekiah is not himself responsible for the misplaced priorities, but that it is the people at large and the royal counselors, like Shebna (22:15–19), who paid no attention to the real causes of the coming disaster. Both the books of Kings and Chronicles suggest that Hezekiah himself had his priorities in the right order (2 Kings 18:1–8; 2 Chron. 29:1–31:21).

Jerusalem exists as the capital city of Judah only because of the grace and power of God (Isa. 22:11). He was not only the One who gave the city to David against all the odds (2 Sam. 5:6–10), he was also the One who gave the entire land to his people (Josh. 1:2; etc.). So since Israel had not taken either the city or the land in their own strength, it is foolish to think they can

---

1. This understanding of vv. 2–7 represents a change from the position taken in Oswalt, *Isaiah 1–39*, 410, where I proposed the material all related to the recent past.

2. The LXX makes it plural like all the rest.

keep them in their own strength. The land is a covenant gift from their covenant Lord. Thus, the most important thing to do in a moment of danger and threat is to be sure that they are acting within the covenant Lord's will and that their relationship with him is intact so that they can continue to receive the promised blessings of the covenant.

But that is precisely what they are not doing. They are acting as if the most important things they can do are the human things they do for themselves, such as tearing down the houses that are crowded against the insides of the walls, so that the building materials can be used to "strengthen the wall" (22:10) and also so that troops can easily be rushed to any point where an attack is being made.

In fact, Judah's relations with God are in anything but good repair. They congratulate themselves that they are not corrupt as the northern kingdom of Israel had been, and so they believe they have survived because of their merits when Israel fell. But Isaiah and the other prophets see clearly that all the same trends are at work in Judah that so tragically affected Israel. Furthermore, if those trends are not reversed, Judah will become as corrupt as Israel and will go the same way in the end. When that end did come in the 580s B.C., Ezekiel said that Judah and Israel were like two whoring sisters and that in the end Judah was even more deserving of punishment than Israel (Ezek. 23).

It is for this reason that God is calling for weeping and wailing (22:12). This is no time for self-congratulation and partying. It is a time for bitter repentance and for pleading with God for mercy. It is a time for careful self-reflection and for amending their ways where those ways have varied from God's ways. There is still hope for Judah, if they will only learn the lessons of the times.

But all the indications are that they have neither the interest nor the attention to learn those lessons. Thus, since the people will not weep and wail over their sins, it falls to the prophet to do it (22:4). He sees that apart from confession, repentance, and the attendant mercy of God, there is no possibility for the sins of the nation to be "atoned for" ("covered over," 22:14), and that is a source of terrible grief for him. Where there is confession and repentance, that mercy is always available, as the book of Jonah makes abundantly clear; but apart from that kind of humble turning to God, even he is powerless to bring his mercy to bear on the situation.

A Picture of Two Men (22:15–25)

As we have already seen earlier in Isaiah, one of its features is the use of graphic illustration. We first saw it in chapter 3 and most recently in chapter 20. After a discourse, the prophet's point is reinforced with a concrete picture of what has just been said. Here the picture takes two parts, revolving around two different men. The first illustration (22:15–19) is negative, while the second (22:20–25) is more positive.

As is clear from chapter 36, where the embassy to the Rabshakeh of Assyria is headed by the "palace administrator" (the same Heb. phrase translated "in charge of the palace" here), this position has sweeping responsibilities. In fact, there is reason to think that it is analogous to the task of "prime minister."[3] Thus, Shebna carries great responsibility for the well-being of the country, both spiritually and materially. But his priorities are misplaced. Instead of denying himself for the good of the country, he is building himself a fine rock tomb. Instead of losing himself in order to bring life to his country, he is trying to make sure he will be remembered in death! When he should be thinking about the life of others, he is focusing all his attention on his own death.

There are many fine rock-cut tombs in the hillside on the east side of the Kidron Valley directly across from the lower part of old Jerusalem, which was the main part of the city at that time. It is easy to think of the prime minister driving one of his "splendid chariots," one of the "perks" of his office, out to see how the work was coming. The fine tomb would be there for all future generations to see how important and significant Shebna had been. But when he arrives at the site, he finds an unwelcome visitor, the prophet Isaiah. Isaiah tells Shebna that far from being important and significant, he is a "disgrace to [his] master's house" (22:18). Instead of being memorialized before all the people, he will be wadded up and thrown away like an old rag (22:17–18). We do not know Shebna's ultimate fate, but the reference to "a large country" (22:18) leads us to wonder whether he may have died as a hostage in Assyria.

In the short term, Shebna will have his office taken from him and given to another (see 22:19–25). We can imagine that for a person like Shebna, the tokens of importance were significant to him. Thus, to have his official uniform ("robe" and "sash," 22:21) taken from him and given to another will be terribly humiliating. We cannot help but think of 2:6–4:1 here, which speaks of the inevitable humiliation that comes to those who exalt themselves.

It is not known whether the "key" referred to in 22:22 is only a figure of speech. Perhaps it is a symbolic badge of office, or it may actually have been a key to the palace. In any case, it represents absolute authority to determine who will have an audience with the king and who will not. Unlike Shebna, who is only concerned for himself, Eliakim will be concerned for the peo-

---

3. See S. Layton, "The Steward in Ancient Israel: A Study of the Hebrew (ʿašer) ʿal-hab-bayit in Its Near Eastern Setting," *JBL* 109 (1990): 633–49.

ple under his charge and will act as a "father" (22:21) to them. That is, he will be concerned about their welfare before his own and will work for them, not himself. The reference to "the house of David" may also be significant. It suggests that Eliakim's interests are not merely for temporal affairs, as symbolized by the "house" (i.e., the palace). Rather, they are for the larger spiritual matters that ought to be concerning the court, the "house" of David.

But there is a danger that can befall anyone who is truly responsible and reliable. That danger is spelled out in 22:23–25. Such a person becomes so dependable that people rely too much on him. Like a good, strong "peg" in the wall, everything imaginable, and some things unimaginable, get hung on such a person. A weak or broken peg we do not put so much upon. But the one that is obviously strong and reliable we hang everything on. In this case, there seems to be a suggestion that Eliakim's family will become a special burden to him (22:23–24). This is still a feature of Near Eastern culture. If one member "makes good," he is expected to care for and make a place for all the rest, even the ne'er-do-wells and the hangers-on.

Sadly, however, even the best of us often cannot endure such pressure forever. That seems to be what Isaiah is predicting for Eliakim. Eventually, he will crack under the strain, and all that has been dependent on him will come crashing down (22:25). That such a thing will happen in that setting is entirely predictable. The people have rejected divine resources and are trusting in humans instead. Most humans fail their trust, and thus if one turns out to be unusually trustworthy, the loads are simply piled on. But no human can bear what is meant to be rolled onto the Lord (Ps. 37:3–6). Even the best person will break under those circumstances.

Bridging Contexts

IT IS SAID that the last nights of Berlin in April of 1945 were marked by revelries and parties. The Berlin Philharmonic Orchestra played Wagner's *The Twilight of the Gods*. There was a general air of "Let's eat and drink, for tomorrow we die." The inflated promises of National Socialism to bring in the millennium—the thousand-year *Reich*—had disappeared in dust and ashes. The Russian army was on the Oder River, just a few miles to the east, and to the west, German soldiers were surrendering in the thousands to the victorious Allies. The war was lost. But instead of national repentance or even reflection, there was only an attempt to forget in waves of artificially induced giddiness.

From one point of view, such a response is not surprising. What was there to repent of? The Kaiser's army in World War I had at least made a pretense of trusting in God, as their uniform belt buckles had stamped on them "Gott

Mit Uns" (i.e., "God With Us"). Hitler's armies made no such pretense. They had abandoned the Christian God Nietzsche accused of turning men into old women and had tried to revive the harsh gods of Norse and Germanic legend. But their real god was simply the god of power. Now cruel fate had turned against them, and the fickle god of power had gone off to fawn on their enemies. What's to repent of?

For starters, there were an estimated fifty million people dead, including six million Jews. The culture and spirit of Europe lay in ruins, with the spirit in particular hard-pressed ever to recover. Germany, the land of Luther, had, like Judah many years before it, become a "Valley of Vision," where a glorious past of spiritual insight had been forfeited and the claims to see true reality were in fact a mockery.

PLANS AND PRIORITIES. This passage of Isaiah is about priorities. There is nothing wrong with making preparations for certain eventualities, nor is there anything wrong with using our strengths and abilities to care for ourselves. The book of Proverbs is clear that those who are lazy and careless are fools. They have not made adequate preparations for the day of trouble, and when it falls on them, they are helpless. By contrast, those who are wise have carefully planned their lives and will carry out those plans. Note Proverbs 24:30–34; 27:23–27:

> I went past the field of the sluggard,
>> past the vineyard of the man who lacks judgment;
> thorns had come up everywhere,
>> the ground was covered with weeds,
>> and the stone wall was in ruins.
> I applied my heart to what I observed
>> and learned a lesson from what I saw:
> A little sleep, a little slumber,
>> a little folding of the hands to rest—
> and poverty will come on you like a bandit
>> and scarcity like an armed man.
>
> Be sure you know the condition of your flocks,
>> give careful attention to your herds;
> for riches do not endure forever,
>> and a crown is not secure for all generations.
> When the hay is removed and new growth appears
>> and the grass from the hills is gathered in,

> the lambs will provide you with clothing,
>> and the goats with the price of a field.
> You will have plenty of goats' milk
>> to feed you and your family
>> and to nourish your servant girls.[4]

So what is the problem here in Isaiah? Plans and preparations have been made without first seeking God's guidance and blessing. Proverbs is also insistent that the outcome of all our plans is in the hands of God. "A man plans his course, but the LORD determines his steps" (Prov. 16:9); "the horse is made ready for the day of battle, but victory rests with the LORD" (21:31).[5] How seriously do we seek God's plans before we make our plans? How easily do we work everything out our way and then casually ask God to bless it?

But even more seriously, do we pay more attention to our relationship to the Lord than we do to our plans and preparations? This was the problem in Isaiah's day, and it remains so in ours. The plans may have been fine, but how can God bless them when the people making them are self-serving covenant-breakers? That is the problem with the rich farmer in Jesus' parable in Luke 12:16–21. He does not pay attention to the main issue in life:

> "'And I'll say to myself, "You have plenty of good things laid up for many years. Take life easy; eat, drink and be merry."'
>
> "But God said to him, 'You fool! This very night your life will be demanded from you. Then who will get what you have prepared for yourself?'
>
> "This is how it will be with anyone who stores up things for himself but is not rich toward God." (Luke 12:19–21)

In Isaiah's day, it was a leadership problem. The Judean leaders were worrying about walls and water supplies when they should have been worrying about sin. How much easier it is to plan for increased facilities in a church than it is to deal with the spiritual deadness in the congregation. How much easier it is to plan additional programs for speaking to postmoderns than it is to speak out against rampant materialism. Thus, the physical plant may be increasing and the numbers in the congregation may be growing while the members of the church are drifting further and further from God. Like the Judeans or the rich farmer, we are "fat and happy," rejoicing in our blessings, going from one party to another, chiding the saints among us for their long faces and sour attitudes, never hearing the Lord saying to us, "You fools!"

---

4. See also Prov. 10:4; 12:11, 24, 27; 14:1, 23; 15:22; 18:9; 19:15; 20:4, 18; 21:5; 22:29; 24:3–4; 31:12–29.

5. See also Prov. 16:1; 19:21; 21:2.

What does it mean to be an Eliakim rather than a Shebna? Above everything else, it means that we have gotten ourselves off our hands. That's the difference between a David and a Saul, or a Jesus and a Judas. The second person in each of these pairs was always looking out for himself. He was worried about his image, about what other people thought of him, about how he was going to supply his needs, and about how people would remember him. These were the last things the first person in each pair worried about.

I am convinced that these are the kinds of things Jesus had in mind when he said we must become like little children to enter the kingdom of heaven (Matt. 18:3–4). There are a number of things about children that are not heavenly: They are ignorant and naïve; they can be petty and selfish; and if you are a parent, you know they are not innocent. But, by and large, they lack self-consciousness. It does not occur to them to worry about how they are appearing to others. Status means nothing to them. But how quickly that changes as we grow up. We become absorbed not with reality but with image. We are consumed with a need for approval and position, and all too often with the approval of the wrong people and the positions that are worthless.

That was Shebna. He had achieved the highest position in the land after the king, and he was using that position to build a memorial for himself. He was laboring for what did not really matter, and as a result his only real memorial is the one of disgrace found in Isaiah 22. We can go down that road too unless we make that kind of total self-renunciation where in the end we care for nothing but the approval of God. In his sermon "The Weight of Glory," C. S. Lewis says that it matters little what we think of God, but it matters to all eternity what God thinks of us.[6]

That is the kind of person we see in Eliakim. Like Christ, he will care more for the welfare of others than he does for his own. And like Christ, his greatest joy will be to make it possible for people to enter the throne room of the King. He will be seeking God's grace so that he can be responsible, reliable, and true in the cesspool of court intrigue. He will be concerned for the needs of others above his own to the extent that he will shoulder loads that are really too heavy to carry. But he will carry them, not because he constantly needs to prove to himself that he is indispensable or that he is really somebody, but because he does not want others to have to bear those loads.

Nor do such burdens need to break us in the end, as they apparently did Eliakim. To be sure, health may break, not because we have abused our bodies but simply because the reed we were given at birth was weaker than the one given to some others. But even in a broken body, our spiritual health may

---

6. C. S. Lewis, *The Weight of Glory* (Grand Rapids: Eerdmans, 1949), 10.

be radiant and robust, in spite of our carrying impossible loads. If we have learned how to carry those loads to the Master and leave them there, we will not be broken by what we are called to shoulder for the sake of others.

This is the opportunity Christ offers each of us. We may chose to be Eliakim or Shebna. We may focus on the temporal or the eternal. If we focus on the temporal, we and all our works will perish with the temporal. If we choose the eternal, then none of our temporal works will ever be lost (Rom. 8:13). Furthermore, like Eliakim and the apostles after him, we will be given the authority to open the doors of heaven for those who will never get in otherwise (Matt. 16:19; cf. also Rev. 3:7). More frighteningly, we will have the authority to close the doors for those who are trying to get in for all the wrong reasons. There is power, but it is only gotten by renouncing power and all its trappings.

Isaiah 23:1–18

AN ORACLE CONCERNING TYRE:

Wail, O ships of Tarshish!
   For Tyre is destroyed
   and left without house or harbor.
From the land of Cyprus
   word has come to them.

2 Be silent, you people of the island
   and you merchants of Sidon,
   whom the seafarers have enriched.
3 On the great waters
   came the grain of the Shihor;
the harvest of the Nile was the revenue of Tyre,
   and she became the marketplace of the nations.

4 Be ashamed, O Sidon, and you, O fortress of the sea,
   for the sea has spoken:
"I have neither been in labor nor given birth;
   I have neither reared sons nor brought up daughters."
5 When word comes to Egypt,
   they will be in anguish at the report from Tyre.

6 Cross over to Tarshish;
   wail, you people of the island.
7 Is this your city of revelry,
   the old, old city,
whose feet have taken her
   to settle in far-off lands?
8 Who planned this against Tyre,
   the bestower of crowns,
whose merchants are princes,
   whose traders are renowned in the earth?
9 The LORD Almighty planned it,
   to bring low the pride of all glory
   and to humble all who are renowned on the earth.

10 Till your land as along the Nile,
   O Daughter of Tarshish,
   for you no longer have a harbor.

¹¹ The LORD has stretched out his hand over the sea
   and made its kingdoms tremble.
He has given an order concerning Phoenicia
   that her fortresses be destroyed.
¹²He said, "No more of your reveling,
   O Virgin Daughter of Sidon, now crushed!

"Up, cross over to Cyprus;
   even there you will find no rest."
¹³ Look at the land of the Babylonians,
   this people that is now of no account!
The Assyrians have made it
   a place for desert creatures;
they raised up their siege towers,
   they stripped its fortresses bare
   and turned it into a ruin.

¹⁴ Wail, you ships of Tarshish;
   your fortress is destroyed!

¹⁵At that time Tyre will be forgotten for seventy years, the
span of a king's life. But at the end of these seventy years, it
will happen to Tyre as in the song of the prostitute:

¹⁶"Take up a harp, walk through the city,
   O prostitute forgotten;
play the harp well, sing many a song,
   so that you will be remembered."

¹⁷At the end of seventy years, the LORD will deal with Tyre.
She will return to her hire as a prostitute and will ply her
trade with all the kingdoms on the face of the earth. ¹⁸Yet her
profit and her earnings will be set apart for the LORD; they
will not be stored up or hoarded. Her profits will go to those
who live before the LORD, for abundant food and fine clothes.

Original Meaning

WE COME NOW to the last of Isaiah's oracles
against the nations (chs. 13–23). As we said at
the outset, these oracles serve two purposes in
the present structure of the book. (1) Isaiah
promised in chapter 11 that although Judah's persistent trust of the nations
instead of God will result in destruction of the nation and captivity among

the nations, God will one day restore the people from that captivity. The question such a promise raises is whether God is really capable of doing that. The oracles against the nations demonstrate that the God of Israel knows the future of each of the nations and that they are ultimately accountable to him. They are in his hand, not he in theirs, as is true of the idols. Therefore, he can deliver his people whenever he chooses.

(2) These chapters also introduce a subdivision of the book I have labeled "Lessons in Trust" (chs. 13–35). In these chapters Isaiah is seeking to show Hezekiah and his generation the foolishness of trusting the nations and the great wisdom of trusting the Lord. The first part of that subdivision, the oracles against the nations, raises the question: "Why would you trust any of the nations instead of the Lord when all the nations are subject to him and some of them will actually turn to him in faith before history closes?"

The last oracle is addressed to Tyre, the great Phoenician (Canaanite) seaport located on the east coast of the Mediterranean Sea, about one hundred miles northwest of Jerusalem. As Babylon, with which the series began, was the great commercial power on the east of the ancient Near Eastern world, Tyre was the commercial power on the west. The Phoenicians, living roughly where the modern nation of Lebanon is located today, were pretty much forced to become a seafaring nation by their geography. The Lebanon mountain range runs parallel to the coast at this point, with fingers of the range extending right to the water's edge. This means that both east–west and north–south travel by land is difficult.

But this geography also means that in the bays created by the fingers of the mountain range were some excellent ports. When we remember that in ancient times the Lebanon mountains were covered with forests, it becomes easy to see how the Phoenicians got into the business of freighting lumber first to lumber-starved Egypt and then to other parts of the ancient world. From there, Phoenician mastery of the Mediterranean Sea seemed limitless. We remember that Carthage, which battled Rome for supremacy in the third and second centuries B.C., was a Phoenician colony. Sidon, located about twenty-five miles north of Tyre, was another important Phoenician port. These two cities vied with each other for control of the trade. The present oracle seems to include Sidon in the judgment along with Tyre (23:2, 4, 12). Tyre, being closer to Israel, was more important to Israel for trade.[1]

Tyre's Destruction (23:1–14)

ISAIAH BEGINS HIS discussion of Tyre's destruction with the word reaching the merchant ships homeward bound from the West. The exact location of

1. See H. Katzenstein and D. Edwards, "Tyre," *ABD*, 6:686–92.

"Tarshish" is unknown, though many scholars place it in Spain at Tartessus.[2] When Tyrian ships stop over at "Cyprus," they hear the news that they have no home port to return to. The reference to "the island" in 23:2 is a recognition that Tyre consisted of both a mainland city and an offshore island, with the harbor between the two. Verse 3 notes that Tyre was a shipper for Egyptian "grain." The "Nile" Valley ("Shihor" is probably one of the Delta branches) produced much grain that was of no use to the Egyptians unless they sold it. For shipping it elsewhere they were dependent on the Phoenicians. One of the reasons the Romans were so anxious to gain control of Egypt many hundreds of years later was to get control of the grain source on which Rome itself had come to depend.

In 23:4 the Canaanite sea god Yam cries out like a parent bereft of children. Tyre, his foremost child, is gone, and it is as though he has never had any children. When the word reaches "Egypt" (23:5), the Egyptians "will be in anguish," not only because they have lost their trading partner but also because they know that with the loss of one more country lying between them and the conquerors from Mesopotamia, their own time of terror is drawing nearer.

Verses 6—12 are addressed to the Phoenician colony of Tarshish as the Lord calls on them to think about the implications of what has happened. Tyre was a "city of revelry" (23:7), a place of wealth and pleasure. It was also an "old" city, a mother city that had given birth to Tarshish and probably more colonies that we do not know of now (23:7). These colonies were so powerful and wealthy that each had its own king, authorized by the mother city. Tyre's merchants had become so wealthy that they were no longer considered businessmen but rather were a part of the nobility (23:8).

Yet Isaiah sees the day when all of that will come to a screeching halt. The revelry will cease (23:12), and Tarshish will have to become self-subsistent, since the Egyptian grain will no longer be available (23:10).[3] What possibly explains this terrible coming disaster? The answer is to be found in the recurrence of two of Isaiah's favorite themes: the plan of Yahweh[4] and the humbling of the proud.[5] Tyre will not fall by accident or because of the superior

---

2. These ships are also referred to in 1 Kings 10:22; 22:48; Ps. 48:7; Isa. 2:16; 60:9; Ezek. 27:25; Jonah 1:3. They may have originally been ore-carriers (Semitic *ršš* means "to melt"), but ultimately the name came to be used for any large trading ship.

3. The meaning of the Heb. of v. 10 is uncertain. A lit. translation would be: "Go over your land like the Nile, daughter of Tarshish, there is no more strength." The NIV reading is based on the LXX. The meaning may be that with Tyre's constraint gone, the colonies can do what they like (see Motyer, *Prophecy of Isaiah*, 191).

4. See 5:26; 9:11; 10:6; 14:26; 19:12; 37:26; 41:2; 45:1; 46:10—11.

5. See. 2:11, 17; 4:2; 5:15—16; 13:19; 14:12—20; 28:1—6; 60:15.

might of the Assyrians, the Babylonians, or the Greeks. It will fall according to the eternal purposes of the Holy One of Israel.

As I have remarked elsewhere, this takes incredible faith on the part of the prophet. There seems little evidence to support such an outlandish claim. Yet God said it, and that was enough for Isaiah. Nor were the plan and purpose of God's merely arbitrary. He had not just taken a disliking to Tyre and decided to destroy it. Rather, like all the other pagan nations (including Judah, cf. ch. 22), Tyre exalted itself against the Creator (23:9). It promulgated a lie that humans can supply their own spiritual needs and can shape deity in the image of humanity.[6] In the end pride is what destroys the human race, and God's hand is extended against pride in all its forms (see also 5:25; 9:12, 17, 21; 10:4).

As Childs points out, the RSV (and NRSV) rendering of the second and third clauses of 23:13 is attractive: "This is the people; it was not Assyria." That is, the prophet (or in Childs's view, a later editor) points out that Tyre was not destroyed by the Assyrians of Isaiah's own time but by the later Babylonians under Nebuchadnezzar. However, that rendering is not grammatically defensible, and the rendering of NIV and several other modern translations is correct. The reader is invited to compare the fate of Babylon with that which is coming to Tyre.[7] Sargon brought heavy destruction on the city of Babylon in 710 B.C. and Sennacherib even greater in 689 B.C. Thus, the two cities that begin and end the sequence of oracles are brought together here. Neither will escape the judgment planned by God.

Tyre's Turning to the Lord (23:15–18)

LIKE EGYPT EARLIER (19:18–25), Isaiah foresees a day when Tyre will turn to the Lord. This message is set apart from the preceding verses not only by its content but also by it prose format. While the general point is clear enough—that Tyre's profits will be given over to the Lord—some of the precise points are unclear. For instance, it is not clear what the seventy-year period in 23:15 refers to.[8] Perhaps it is simply an indefinite time of punishment, with seventy referring to completeness. In any case, after this time of eclipse the Lord will permit Tyre to regain some of its former eminence. Once again it will sell itself to the merchants of the world in order to gain a profit (23:17).

Commentators have struggled with the idea of a prostitute's profits being given over to the Lord, since this is specifically prohibited in Deuteronomy

---

6. Notice that the king of Tyre is described in similar language in Ezek. 28:1–19, also similar to that used to describe the king of Babylon in Isa. 14.

7. Childs, *Isaiah*, 168–69.

8. Motyer (*Prophecy of Isaiah*, 193) believes it refers to the period between Sennacherib and the rise of Nebuchadnezzar. See Oswalt, *Isaiah 1–39*, 435–36, for some other options.

23:18. Various solutions have been offered, none of which fully resolve the problem. It may be that the prophet is simply continuing to use prostitution as a symbol for trade, as elsewhere in the prophets. But there is nothing intrinsically sinful about trade, and its profits may be given over to the Lord without shame. In any case, the point is clear: Why fear or trust Tyre instead of the Lord, when the Lord holds Tyre's fate in his hands?

THIS CHAPTER SPEAKS of the dismay of colonies and clients as the mother city comes to destruction. We may think of the struggles of some of the members of the British Commonwealth as they have tried to find their own way after the collapse of the British Empire. Their relations and their trade had been largely coordinated by the mother country, and when that influence was dissipated at the end of World War II, a number of the former colonies found themselves struggling in a new world where the rules were all different.

On a more personal level, we can see the destructive nature of the relationship that psychologists have come to label *codependency*. It used to be thought, for instance, that all the fault was on the side of an alcoholic husband. We thought of the poor, long-suffering wife who had to put up with her husband's constantly "falling off the wagon." Then we were surprised to learn that after that man's death, she married another one just like him. What happened? In fact, she had become just as dependent on the husband's failings for her sense of identity as he had been on her for continually taking him back and drying him out again. And because from one point of view she needed his failings to support her own need for being abused and unappreciated, she was unwilling to force her husband to take some of the hard steps necessary to take responsibility for himself and overcome the addiction. To become ultimately dependent on anything other than God is finally destructive, even if it appears that we are not dependent.

STEWARDSHIP OF WEALTH. Whereas Babylon's love was for glory and military power, Tyre's love was for money and the luxury and influence it could buy. As the playwright said, "Diamonds are a girl's best friend"—and Tyre would have echoed that sentiment. The strange thing about money is that there is never enough. No matter how much we get, we always want more.

Few would admit to loving money for itself. This brings up pictures of Silas Marner living in one or two filthy rooms continually counting and recounting his gold coins. That is definitely not a "cool" picture. But it is difficult to separate the money from what we think it can buy. How big a house is big enough? How many cars are enough? How many television sets? How much clothing? And how much do we need for a "comfortable" retirement? The idea of moderation has gone out of fashion. What are we looking for? Comfort, pleasure, and security—the things humans have been looking for since the beginning of time. And what will give these to us? Money, lots and lots of money, the more the better!

In other words, we are little different from Tyre. We have allied ourselves, both personally and nationally, with the sources of wealth. We have forgotten or ignored Jesus' words in Mark 10:24–25 about how hard it is for a rich person to enter the kingdom of heaven:

> The disciples were amazed at his words. But Jesus said again, "Children, how hard it is to enter the kingdom of God! It is easier for a camel to go through the eye of a needle than for a rich man to enter the kingdom of God."

Why is it so hard for the rich to enter the kingdom of God? Because they have found another source of trust besides God. Their allegiance has been given to another kingdom. And this can happen all too unconsciously. We start out as servants of God, but he blesses us with wealth, and all too easily we slip from one kingdom to another. No longer is our trust in the God who cares for us. Now our trust is in the money we have, which will secure us against all pain, discomfort, and insecurity. Then when God calls us to give it up, as he did the young man in the Gospel account, we cannot do it.

But the money is the Lord's, not ours. There is the fatal error. We keep thinking how generous we are by allowing the Lord to have 10 percent of our money. But John Wesley had it right in his sermon on money when he said that we have it backward. Wesley said that for the Christian, all our money is God's. The only issue is how much of God's money we are going to spend on ourselves.[9] As the Tyrians were to find out, their money was not theirs; whoever was stronger than they were could take it all away, and nothing they could do would stop it. Tyre's wealth was a gift from the God of Israel, and in the end the best thing they could do was to give it back to the One who had given it to them in the first place.

Wesley has some timeless advice on the stewardship of wealth. Although he himself had a number of ascetic tendencies, he was no ascetic. He believed

---

9. J. Wesley, *The Standard Sermons of John Wesley* (London: Epworth, 1964), 2:326.

that a person should amass as much wealth as honesty, integrity, diligence, and brotherly love would permit. But this wealth was not to be squandered on oneself or one's family in what he called "dainties" or "delicacies." Rather, it should be used to advance the kingdom of God in us and in those around us. On these grounds he proposed that we should be guided by four principles:

(1) In expending this, am I acting according to my character? [That is,] am I acting herein, not as a proprietor, but as a steward of my Lord's goods?

(2) Am I doing this in obedience to his Word? In what scripture does he require me so to do?

(3) Can I offer up this action, this expense, as a sacrifice to God through Jesus Christ?

(4) Have I reason to believe that for this very work I shall have a reward at the resurrection of the just?[10]

Of course, these could be made a straitjacket that would deliver us into bondage. But few American Christians are too narrow in their conception of the relation of money to our faith. We are more likely to err on the other side. We gain all we can, but then we expend the mass of it on ourselves in ways that cannot help but anger a holy God whose heart bleeds for a lost and hurting world. If we are to learn the lesson of Tyre, we must learn to let go of our wealth and relearn the reality of trusting God. Like them, we need to learn that actually we are working for God and that all our money is "set apart [i.e., holy] for the LORD" (23:18).

---

10. Ibid., 325

Isaiah 24:1–23

¹ SEE, THE LORD is going to lay waste the earth
    and devastate it;
  he will ruin its face
    and scatter its inhabitants—
² it will be the same
    for priest as for people,
    for master as for servant,
    for mistress as for maid,
    for seller as for buyer,
    for borrower as for lender,
    for debtor as for creditor.
³ The earth will be completely laid waste
    and totally plundered.
                    The LORD has spoken this word.

⁴ The earth dries up and withers,
    the world languishes and withers,
    the exalted of the earth languish.
⁵ The earth is defiled by its people;
    they have disobeyed the laws,
  violated the statutes
    and broken the everlasting covenant.
⁶ Therefore a curse consumes the earth;
    its people must bear their guilt.
  Therefore earth's inhabitants are burned up,
    and very few are left.
⁷ The new wine dries up and the vine withers;
    all the merrymakers groan.
⁸ The gaiety of the tambourines is stilled,
    the noise of the revelers has stopped,
    the joyful harp is silent.
⁹ No longer do they drink wine with a song;
    the beer is bitter to its drinkers.
¹⁰ The ruined city lies desolate;
    the entrance to every house is barred.
¹¹ In the streets they cry out for wine;
    all joy turns to gloom,
    all gaiety is banished from the earth.

¹²The city is left in ruins,
      its gate is battered to pieces.
¹³So will it be on the earth
      and among the nations,
   as when an olive tree is beaten,
      or as when gleanings are left after the grape harvest.

¹⁴They raise their voices, they shout for joy;
      from the west they acclaim the LORD's majesty.
¹⁵Therefore in the east give glory to the LORD;
      exalt the name of the LORD, the God of Israel,
      in the islands of the sea.
¹⁶From the ends of the earth we hear singing:
      "Glory to the Righteous One."

   But I said, "I waste away, I waste away!
      Woe to me!
   The treacherous betray!
      With treachery the treacherous betray!"
¹⁷Terror and pit and snare await you,
      O people of the earth.
¹⁸Whoever flees at the sound of terror
      will fall into a pit;
   whoever climbs out of the pit
      will be caught in a snare.

   The floodgates of the heavens are opened,
      the foundations of the earth shake.
¹⁹The earth is broken up,
      the earth is split asunder,
      the earth is thoroughly shaken.
²⁰The earth reels like a drunkard,
      it sways like a hut in the wind;
   so heavy upon it is the guilt of its rebellion
      that it falls—never to rise again.

²²In that day the LORD will punish
      the powers in the heavens above
      and the kings on the earth below.
²²They will be herded together
      like prisoners bound in a dungeon;
   they will be shut up in prison
      and be punished after many days.

²³ The moon will be abashed, the sun ashamed;
   for the LORD Almighty will reign
   on Mount Zion and in Jerusalem,
   and before its elders, gloriously.

WE TURN NOW from the particularities of the oracles against the nations to a more general treatment of Yahweh's control of time and space and thus his ultimate trustworthiness. The general treatment extends from chapters 24 to 27. In chapters 13–23 the nations could be thought of as the main actors with the Lord in the position of reacting to them. Thus, one could get the idea that the nations are somehow originators of the events of history. Chapters 24–27 correct that impression. God is the sovereign actor on the stage of history. All things come from him, and all things must eventually return to him. He created time, and he will bring it to an end.

Because these chapters focus especially on the end of time, they are sometimes referred to as "Isaiah's Apocalypse." However, a comparison with Daniel, the intertestamental Jewish apocalypses, and the book of Revelation demonstrates that this material is not really in the genre of apocalypse. It lacks the fantastic imagery, color, and numerology that tend to characterize that genre. At the most it might be called preapocalyptic. It is certainly eschatological, in that it deals with the last things, but it lacks the kind of mysterious imagery that needs a special revelation in order to understand its significance.[1]

There are two recurrences that run throughout the four chapters. There is also a measure of contrast in the recurrences. (1) The first is of songs and singing. The contrast is between the silenced songs of the ruthless (24:8–9; 25:5) and the jubilant songs of the redeemed (24:14, 16; 26:1, 19; 27:2). (2) The other is of city, with a contrast between the city of the ruthless (24:10, 12; 25:2–3, 12; 27:10), which is destroyed, and the city of God (26:1, also referred to as "this mountain," 25:6, 7, 10; 27:13), which is redeemed and secure. The line of thought in the chapters moves from the destruction of the "earth" (ch. 24) to the promise of restoration for God's people (ch. 27). Between these two poles is the dramatic assertion that God's deliverance is not only for his own people but for all nations who will turn to him (ch. 25). Chapter 26 is both an assertion of trust in God and a prayer for him to deliver a people helpless to deliver itself.[2]

---

1. See J. Oswalt, "Recent Studies in Old Testament Apocalyptic," in *The Face of Old Testament Studies*, ed. D. Baker and B. Arnold (Grand Rapids: Baker, 1999), 369–90.

2. There is no agreement among critical scholars as to the date, authorship, or composition of these chapters. For an exhaustive treatment of the issues, see Wildberger, *Isaiah 13–27*, 439–67. See also Oswalt, *Isaiah 1–39*, 441–43.

Like chapter 6, chapter 24 can be understood either as part of what precedes it or of what follows it. In that sense, it is an excellent transitional piece. This chapter does give a general summary to what was said in particular detail in chapters 13–23: The entire earth is under God's judgment. The fact that chapters 13–14 open the section with something of a worldwide focus lends further support to that idea. Indeed, if chapters 25–27 did not follow chapter 24, there would be no question that it was intended to be read as a conclusion to chapters 13–23. However, those chapters do follow, and that makes it more difficult to include chapter 24 in a unit with the preceding chapters. As already noted, the recurrence of "city" and "song" unites it to chapters 25–27, as does the central focus on the Lord's activity. Thus, it seems best to read chapter 24 with chapters 25–27 but to recognize that the entire block of material has been inserted here in order to put chapters 13–23 into a worldwide context.[3]

The Destruction of the Earth (24:1–13)

THERE CAN BE NO question of the focus of chapter 24: the destruction of the "earth." The word "earth" occurs no less than sixteen times in these twenty-three verses.[4] Nor is there any question as to who will bring this destruction about: the Lord (24:1, 3, 21). Verses 1–3 underline the universal nature of this judgment. Everyone will be subject to it, and no one will be exempt. This is established in verse 2 with the use of complimentary pairs, such as "priest" and "people" or "mistress" and "maid." Neither gender, nor rank, nor function will permit any to escape what God is bringing on the earth.[5]

But why is this destruction coming? Is it the result of divine pique or the need to demonstrate divine power? Neither. Instead, it is the result of the choices that earth's inhabitants have made. Verses 4–13 use one of the common images of this early part of the book to make this statement: the vine (cf. 5:1–7; 16:8–10; 27:2–6). The earth "dries up" and "withers" (24:4) like a vine (24:7). All the merry-making associated with the wine

---

3. Seitz is representative of a number of scholars who, while not believing that the same writer is responsible for chs. 13–23 and chs. 24–27, still see the materials as having been intentionally put in sequence by a later editor (*Isaiah 1–39*, 172–75). Motyer has developed an intricate chiastic structure uniting chs. 24–27, but it is perhaps a bit too intricate (*Prophecy of Isaiah*, 194–95).

4. Watts, *Isaiah 1–33*, 320–21, contends that Heb. *ʾereṣ* should be translated "land" throughout, taking the chapter to refer to the destruction of Israel by Assyrian armies. But apart from his idiosyncratic understanding of the way this segment is structured, one would not naturally think of such a rendering here.

5. Like 14:4–21, this chapter is a fine example of Hebrew poetry. It is esp. noteworthy for the alliteration and assonance that characterize it.

harvest and the making of the first new wine is stilled. Why? Because earth's inhabitants have "disobeyed the laws" of life. They have "broken the everlasting covenant" (24:5).

At first glance this language seems strange. References to "laws," "statutes," and "covenant" sound much like language regarding Israel, but this is not Israel, it is the world. What is the point? How can the inhabitants of the earth be held accountable for what was exclusively revealed to the Israelites? In fact, like Paul in Romans 1, Isaiah insists that apart from the Sinai covenant, there are laws that God the Creator has written on the human conscience. Thus, he will not admit any argument of ignorance as justification for sin.

Implicit here is the understanding that humans know enough to behave better than they do. There are common standards of human behavior; if we violate them, we do so to our own destruction. The "covenant" referred to here may be the Noachic covenant of Genesis 9:1–17 with its prohibition of bloodshed. Here again is an understanding between the creature and the Creator that is not dependent on special revelation. Rather, it has been passed down through the ages as common human heritage.

Thus, judgment is not coming on the earth because the gods have decided that humans are too noisy, as in the Sumerian flood story, or because one god has flown into a rage at a petty slight, as is the case in some other myths. Destruction is coming because humans have violated the terms of their creation. Israel's God is the Creator of all the nations, and they are accountable to him, and him alone. One of the features of covenants was the custom of the parties calling down curses on themselves for failure to keep the covenant. That is what has happened to earth's inhabitants: They are under a "curse" and bear "guilt" for what they have done (24:6).

Dried up like a vine cut off from its roots, the "city" of earth (24:10, 12) lies silent and desolate. The forced and artificial gaiety induced by alcohol (24:7, 9, 11) vanishes like a vapor before the awful realities of judgment and destruction. Despite the effort of some commentators to argue that a specific city (e.g., Jerusalem or Babylon) is intended in these references, it seems clear that this is not the case. Rather, the earth as a whole is treated under the image of "city."[6] It is easy to see why this might be the case. The city offers wealth, glamour, excitement, pleasure, intrigue, and power—all the things humans are prone to sell their souls for. But as mighty and alluring as the city of earth is, a day of harvest is coming when all the fruit will be stripped off and nothing will be left of all the riches that earthlings thought were their own (24:13).

---

6. So, e.g., Seitz, *Isaiah 1–39*, 174–75.

A Dramatic Contrast (24:14–18a)

THESE VERSES ARE something of a riddle because of the dramatic contrast between verses 14–16a and verses 16b–18a. Either one by itself can be justified in this passage without difficulty, but their juxtaposition causes a problem. The first segment speaks of overflowing shouts of "joy" coming from the ends of the earth because of the "glory" and "majesty" of the Lord. That is not out of place as a response to the righteous judgment of God (cf. 30:29–33). But this is immediately followed with an unidentified "I" (the prophet?) protesting that he is wasting away because of the "treachery" and "terror" that characterize the earth.

What are we to make of this? The great variety of proposals and even the number of different readings in the versions prohibit any degree of dogmatism. But it seems most likely to me that the first segment is the cry of joy from those who have been oppressed by the evil earth-city. They are looking joyously at the end of the story. But the prophet cannot move so quickly beyond the present dark realities. He sees all the horrors that must take place before that final resolution, and he is stricken by them. We have seen this feature elsewhere in this book, beginning as early as the end of chapter 1. The prophet will not let the joyful promises of the future hide the awful present realities that must be dealt with before the promises can be realized.[7]

The Entire Creation Subject to God (24:18b–23)

THE IMAGERY OF 24:18b–20 is reminiscent of the description of the Flood in Genesis 6. The heavens open up, and such a weight of water pours out that the earth is literally torn apart under it. The solid earth, which seems so enduring, shakes, "reels," and "sways." But the water is only an image. The real weight that crushes the earth is the "guilt of its rebellion" (Isa. 24:20). Again the issue is clear, as it has been from the earliest verses of the book: the human problem of rebellion against God. We refuse to bow to the Lord of glory. He defined the terms of our existence when he created us, but we refuse to abide by those terms. As a result, creation itself is marred (Gen. 3:17–19) and must eventually be replaced (Isa. 65:17).

Isaiah 24:21–23 expand the theme from the earth to the entire creation. People in the ancient world considered the "powers in the heavens"

---

7. This is similar to the position taken by D. Johnson, *From Chaos to Restoration: An Integrative Reading of Isaiah 24–27* (JSOTSup 61; Sheffield, JSOT Press, 1988). Motyer, *Prophecy of Isaiah*, 202, argues against this position by saying that unlike 22:4, where the prophet refused to partake in false revelry, this is true praise that he can only affirm. I do not believe this is the issue. Rather, it is the point already noted: a refusal to let future joy obscure present reality.

(24:21)—that is, the stars, the sun, and the moon—to be deities. But the God of Israel insists they are not. They are just as much subject to his power and to his creation laws as any king on earth is (cf. 40:26). If God chooses, he can turn off their light and shut them up in a dark "dungeon" (24:22). Their light is not eternal. It came on once, at the word of God (Gen. 1:3, 14–19), and he can easily turn it off again. In fact, compared to the light of the eternal, uncreated One, "the LORD Almighty," their light is something to be ashamed of (Isa. 24:23; see also Joel 2:31; Matt. 24:29; Rev. 6:12–13).

This final verse of Isaiah 24 provides a transition to chapter 25. All the powers in creation that may have claimed lordship, whether divine or human, have been put down; there is only One who has the right to be called King of the universe. Where will be the seat of his rule? On some distant star? No, he will rule on "Mount Zion," and the "elders" of "Jerusalem," persons who are condemned elsewhere in the book (1:23; 3:14; 9:15), will be his courtiers (see also Rev. 4:4, 9–11). Thus, we are prepared for the shift to hope that occurs in the following chapter.

ANCIENT COSMOLOGY—AND MODERN. For the ancient pagans the cosmos was unchanging. The heavens and the earth were the parents who had engendered us, and they would go on forever. To be sure, they had had a beginning because all life has beginnings, but they had existed forever in the chaotic matter that is the eternal stuff. The idea of progress or development was foreign to the Canaanites and the other neighbors of the Hebrews. There is change, of course, but the change is always repeating itself. So humans are constantly changing from infancy to childhood to adulthood to senescence, but the human race is going nowhere. The same is true for nature and for the gods: Change is only an endless cycle, repeating the same things again and again.

Thus, the ancients could not think of a time when the cosmos would cease to exist or would exist in a radically changed form. Thus, the system of nature was the given that the ancients started with when trying to imagine deity. It was the cosmos and its characteristics that determined who the gods were and what they looked like. To be sure, the gods were supposedly the ones the earth reflected, but it was the characteristics of earth that defined the nature and characteristics of the gods.

The modern conceptions of reality are not much different. True, we have depersonalized the cosmos, but one wonders how long that will remain so, given the significant voices around us (including many in the church) arguing for the need to recapture the "spiritual" side of nature. But apart from that depersonalization, modern concepts do not form much of an advance over those we first see among the ancient Sumerians in the lower Mesopotamian valley five thousand years ago. Like them, many believe that matter has always existed, first in an "undifferentiated" (chaotic) form. Like them, many believe that matter predates spirit and that spirit has emerged from matter. Like them, many believe that the cosmos is eternal.

For much of the last century cosmologists believed in a "steady state" universe, where no real change occurred. Recently, with the Hubble telescope in space, many scientists have concluded that the Sumerians were right. Our present universe had a beginning when eternal matter finally contracted to the point of critical mass and exploded in the "Big Bang." Since that beginning, the universe has been constantly changing. But like the thoughtful people of the ancient Near East, they believe the change is not leading anywhere. The universe will expand to a certain point and then fall back in on itself and start all over again—just as human beings do.

Perhaps this will help us to see just how radical the biblical claim is, both then and now. Far from having his characteristics determined by the constantly cycling cosmos, the God of the Bible is the Lord of the cosmos. Far from the earth determining his characteristics, he has set the standards for earth, standards it does not reach! That is significant. Where do such standards come from? Not from the earth, because the earth does not live in the way God calls for. Is it possible that the direction of biblical religion is just what it claims—revelation from the One who made the earth? I do not believe there is any other satisfactory explanation for this phenomenon.

Thus, the idea that God could destroy the earth and put the sun, moon, and stars in a dark dungeon was a shocking idea in the ancient world. The thought that he could interrupt the endless cycles of time and do a new thing such as had never occurred before was unthinkable. It flew in the face of every cherished truth that the greatest thinkers of earth thought they knew. But such is biblical revelation, as testified by Isaiah here.

CLOSING THE CURTAIN ON EARTH'S STAGE. The truth of this chapter still flies in the face of what cosmologists are sure they know. When the well-known astronomer Carl Sagan was dying of cancer and Christian believers wrote to him, telling him they were praying for him, he responded kindly, thanking them for their concern but insisting that there is nothing beyond the physical universe. To believe that there is a reality outside of the limitations of our experience and knowledge is still too much for us.

Yet that is exactly what the Bible says. It insists that God existed before the universe did and that he brought it into existence as part of a prior plan. (The refrain, "God saw that it was good" presupposes a plan to which the result conforms.) Furthermore, God had a plan for the conduct of the earth: Humans, who shared his holy character, were to cultivate it so that it could reach its highest potential for blessing. Now, although that plan has not changed, sin has entered the picture, and it constantly frustrates the plan. Thus, the earth as it now exists does not define the character and nature of God. He is other than the earth, both in essence and in character.

One evidence of this can be found in the law codes of every civilization, both ancient and modern. To pick just two, why does every civilization prohibit lying and stealing? Someone may say, "Well, that's obvious! There can be no civilization where everybody lies and steals. Existence maybe, but not harmonious civilization." But that is precisely my point. Why can there be no civilization where everybody lies and steals? It is not because not lying and not stealing are our normal way of behaving. The opposite is the case. No one ever had to teach a child to lie or to steal. What we have to struggle hard to do is to teach our children to tell the truth and to share. So if truthtelling and respecting the possessions of others is a necessity for the existence of a harmonious social organization and yet are not things we "naturally" do, what else can we conclude but that these behaviors are determined not by our natures but by the nature of the One who created us? There is One outside of our existence whose character is not reflective of ours.[8]

So what is God to do with a creation that has gone badly astray from its original purpose? He could simply destroy the earth and start over again. But Jesus' parable of the wheat and the weeds (Matt. 13:24–30) succinctly shows us that is not what God wants or intends. Both his justice and his mercy come into play. He will not destroy the weeds until the wheat has had a chance to grow and mature.

We may also think of God's words to Abraham in Genesis 15. He could not give the land of the Canaanites to Abraham's descendants until the "sin of the Amorites [Canaanites] has ... reached its full measure" (Gen. 15:16). It would be unjust to destroy the nation until its sin had reached irreparable proportions. That seems to be the case with humanity as a whole and the cosmos it has infected: God will not bring the world to its end until the full harvest of both sin and righteousness has been reached. As we look at the horrors of the twentieth century, we may wonder just how much longer we can possibly have, and we may question with a shudder what the sins of the future will be like if those of the past century were not the "full measure."

---

8. For more of this argument, see C. S. Lewis, *The Abolition of Man* (Macmillan: New York, 1947).

But until the end comes, we must continually relearn the lessons of this chapter. Especially as we grow older, it becomes easier and easier to believe that this world is all there is. Yes, we may mouth the words of faith and even tell ourselves we believe them, but we more and more act as if this world is our true home and that this world defines God. Children do not have this problem. Wordsworth expressed it this way:

> Our birth is but a sleep and a forgetting:
> The Soul that rises with us, our life's Star
> Hath had elsewhere its setting
> And cometh from afar:
> Not in entire forgetfulness,
> And not in utter nakedness,
> But trailing clouds of glory do we come
> From God, who is our home:
> Heaven lies about us in our infancy![9]

The child has no difficulty believing in the invisible, and that is no accident. He or she has not been long enough in a body to have his or her spirit become confined. But such thinking is profoundly subversive in the modern age, with its conviction that matter precedes spirit. If we believe the Bible, we must know that Wordsworth is correct, and we must do everything in our power to counteract that conviction, which Paul titles with the catchall term "the flesh" (*sarx*). *Sarx* is a compound of two attitudes: (1) that satisfying bodily desire is really all that matters in life, and (2) that I am the only one who can really satisfy my desires, and I have an absolute right to do so.

These two together constitute *sarx*.[10] Paul says that the only way to deal with this double attitude is by death (Col. 3:5). We must die to it both in a once-for-all manner and in daily renunciation of it. Something as simple as daily personal worship is profoundly helpful in keeping us oriented to the truth that this world and the material things in it are not eternal. Only God is eternal, and he will one day bring down the curtain on earth's stage. It will be too late to get ready for that day when it arrives. Either we are ready every day, or we are not ready at all.

---

9. William Wordsworth, "Ode: Intimations of Immortality."

10. The NIV, in a worthy attempt to give *sarx* when used in this way some meaning for the modern reader, often translates it as "the sinful nature" (cf. Rom. 8:5). I am afraid this often obscures the sense as much as reveals it, but there are not many good alternatives.

Isaiah 25:1–12

¹ O LORD, YOU are my God;
   I will exalt you and praise your name,
for in perfect faithfulness
   you have done marvelous things,
   things planned long ago.
² You have made the city a heap of rubble,
   the fortified town a ruin,
the foreigners' stronghold a city no more;
   it will never be rebuilt.
³ Therefore strong peoples will honor you;
   cities of ruthless nations will revere you.
⁴ You have been a refuge for the poor,
   a refuge for the needy in his distress,
a shelter from the storm
   and a shade from the heat.
For the breath of the ruthless
   is like a storm driving against a wall
⁵   and like the heat of the desert.
You silence the uproar of foreigners;
   as heat is reduced by the shadow of a cloud,
   so the song of the ruthless is stilled.

⁶ On this mountain the LORD Almighty will prepare
   a feast of rich food for all peoples,
a banquet of aged wine—
   the best of meats and the finest of wines.
⁷ On this mountain he will destroy
   the shroud that enfolds all peoples,
the sheet that covers all nations;
⁸   he will swallow up death forever.
The Sovereign LORD will wipe away the tears
   from all faces;
he will remove the disgrace of his people
   from all the earth.
                              The LORD has spoken.

⁹In that day they will say,

   "Surely this is our God;
      we trusted in him, and he saved us.

This is the LORD, we trusted in him;
  let us rejoice and be glad in his salvation."

¹⁰The hand of the LORD will rest on this mountain;
  but Moab will be trampled under him
    as straw is trampled down in the manure.
¹¹They will spread out their hands in it,
  as a swimmer spreads out his hands to swim.
God will bring down their pride
  despite the cleverness of their hands.
¹²He will bring down your high fortified walls
  and lay them low;
he will bring them down to the ground,
  to the very dust.

AS I HAVE SAID previously, the book of Isaiah makes it clear that judgment and destruction are never God's intended last words. Rather, he intends that those harsh words will pave the way for the happier words of hope and redemption. This is the case in Isaiah 24 and 25. From the silence of the shattered city, we move to the joy of a feast where the host is the Lord.

Initially, the note of praise sounds like the praise we expect from redeemed Israel. Her Lord has been faithful to his promises and has "done marvelous things" (25:1). He has completely destroyed the "city" of the wicked and the oppressors (25:2) and in so doing has become a "refuge for the poor . . . [and] the needy"[1] from "the breath of the ruthless" (25:4–5). But in 25:3 is the hint of a significant addition to this picture. The guests at the coronation feast are not merely the people of God rejoicing in their deliverance from "the strong peoples" and "the ruthless nations." In fact, representatives of those very peoples are present at the feast as well, honoring and revering (lit., fearing) the Lord. Redemption and deliverance are not for Israel alone but for all peoples who turn to God in faith and humility.

This theme is developed in 25:6–9. There is no sense in which God glories in the destruction of the wicked (cf. Ezek. 18:23; 33:11). He does not wipe his hands with a sigh of relief and say, "I'm glad that's over." If judgment

1. In many ways, these two terms *poor* and *needy* are the antithesis of *arrogant* and *self-sufficient*. Thus, they speak at least as much about attitudes of humility and dependency as they do about financial or material want. See also 11:4; 14:30; 32:7; 41:17; cf. Ps. 40:17; 109:22; Matt. 5:3.

and destruction cannot be avoided in the end in the name of justice, that is not what God wants to do. Rather, he wants to invite "all peoples" (Isa. 25:6) to his feast. Nor is the "all" merely accidental, for it is repeated no less than four more times in 25:7–8. The author wants us to know that everyone on earth is invited to the celebration.

What is the occasion of that celebration? Oftentimes a king would hold a great feast at a time when he wished to make a special pronouncement. That is the case here. At this great feast where the very finest of foods (25:6) have been put before his guests, the host announces a new dispensation. The "death" that has ruled the earth since Adam and Eve, drenching it with tears, is going to be swallowed up. The "shroud" that has covered "all nations" will be removed (25:7), and the tears that have stained every face will be wiped away (25:8). No longer will there be a division between those who believe in the one God ("his people") and those who do not. Rather, it will become apparent that the faith the Israelites put in God, which seemed so misplaced to the idol worshipers (a "disgrace"), was in fact the truth (25:8). The Holy One of Israel is the one God of the whole earth. When he finally declares the rule of death to be at an end, his sole lordship will become crystal clear.

Verse 9 emphasizes once again the overarching theme of chapters 7–39: the trustworthiness of God. If the nation of unclean lips (cf. 6:5) is to bear a message of hope and redemption to the world, then, like the prophet of unclean lips, they must have a revelation of the supremely trustworthy character of God. So at the great feast in Mount Zion, what will "they"—not only Israel but also the redeemed from all peoples—say? "Surely this is our God; we trusted[2] in him, and he saved us." In other words, they will praise God for his trustworthiness.

God can be trusted when nothing and no one else on earth can. If we trust the nations of humanity instead of God, they will turn on us and destroy us. But why should we trust them in the first place? They are all subject to God and will be judged at his bar of judgment. They cannot save us if they would. Their only hope is the same as ours: the trustworthiness of God.

But the thought of this unit does not end on this glorious note. Instead, it turns to a stunning contrast—so stunning that some commentators argue it does not belong here.[3] However, it does fit with the characteristic we

---

2. The Heb. word here is *qwh*, lit., "to wait." But this waiting in not merely a marking of time. Rather, it is a refusal to rush ahead with one's own solution to the problems at hand and a confident expectation that God will solve the problem in his own way and in his own time. See Jenni and Westermann, *Theological Lexicon of the Old Testament*, 3:1126–32.

3. See Wildberger, *Isaiah 13–27*, 455, 538–41. He believes that 25:9–10a speaks exclusively of Israel's salvation and that a later person, who had been somehow deeply hurt by Moab, decided to insert 25:10b–12 specifically to show the difference between Zion and Moab. See

have already seen several times in the book (as recently as 24:14–16), namely, the prophet's tendency to turn back from glorious promises of the future to the grim realities of the present. Furthermore, we have noted his penchant for graphic illustrations of a point, and this segment is nothing if not graphic.

If this understanding of the material is correct, what point is being made? It is similar to the one made in Exodus 34:6–7:

> The LORD, the LORD, the compassionate and gracious God, slow to anger, abounding in love and faithfulness, maintaining love to thousands, and forgiving wickedness, rebellion and sin. Yet he does not leave the guilty unpunished; he punishes the children and their children for the sin of the fathers to the third and fourth generation.

Yes, God is merciful and compassionate, slow to get angry, and quick to forgive. But no one dare presume on that grace to live a profligate life, assuming God will not notice. Sin *will* be punished, and its deadly consequences will not be immediately curtailed.

That is the point being made here. Yes, God intends to make his salvation available to all persons from all nations. He intends to remove the shroud of death from all people, not just those he chose as his own. But there is *one* qualification. Those benefits are available to all who abandon their trust in themselves or in any other created thing; they are not available to those who persist in "pride" (25:11) or who trust in their own mighty achievements (25:12). So if the end of time will be marked by a great feast where God's blessings will be made available to all, it will also be marked by terrible destruction on those who refuse to turn to God in trust. Destruction is not God's intended last word, but we have the choice of making it his last word.[4]

The language of 25:10b–11 is difficult, so it is not possible to be sure about some of the imagery. The general picture, however, is clear. Moab, representing all who oppose ultimate reality, instead of having the shroud of death removed from his face, finds himself face down in a barnyard of liquid manure.[5] If the NIV reading "under him" is correct,[6] then the contrast between those who trust God and those who refuse to do so is made more explicit. The former experience his hand of blessing upon them (25:10a)

---

also Watts, *Isaiah 1–33*, 334–35, who believes this section is being held up as a specimen of the littleness of Jerusalem as opposed to God's attention to the "weighty matters."

4. Seitz, *Isaiah 1–39*, 191–92, expresses these ideas eloquently.

5. For somewhat similar imagery, see Mal. 2:3, where God says he will spread the manure of their sacrifices on the faces of the corrupt priests. See also Phil. 3:8, where Paul calls all his former, proud achievements manure (NIV "rubbish").

6. Another possibility is "in his place."

while the latter are "trampled" under his feet (25:10b). They will "spread out their hands" to swim in the manure, but despite all their skills,[7] they will be unable to save themselves.

As in 24:20, the weight of the guilt of rebellion is simply too heavy. All the human achievements in which we are inclined to trust will be brought down into the "dust." We should not think that "Moab" is worse than any other nation here. They have simply been singled out to represent the rest of the proud human race that refuses to recognize the right and authority of their Maker.[8] Edom is used in the same way in Isaiah 34 as the conclusion to chapters 13–33.

PERSONS WHO TRAVEL to Israel are often disappointed to find that Jerusalem is not located on the highest mountain in the area. They have read passages like this one, where Jerusalem is repeatedly referred to as "this mountain," and have formed certain expectations. But the point of this reference is a symbolic one. In the ancient world mountains were considered to be the homes of the gods. So Mount Olympus in Greece or Mount Cassius in Syria was felt to be an especially holy place. Here God is saying that there is really only one "holy mountain," the place where he, the sole Creator of the universe, has chosen to place his name. Thus, we read elsewhere that Jerusalem will be made the highest of the mountains (cf. Zech. 14:10), and Isaiah speaks not only here but on three other occasions about all the nations coming to worship God on the "holy mountain" of Jerusalem (2:3; 27:13; 66:20). Thus, Jerusalem's prominence is not a geographic one but a spiritual one.

Many modern Western, largely urbanized readers will find the language of 25:10–12 concerning Moab shocking and disgusting. At the same time, such people can munch on popcorn while watching horror movies where the blood seems almost to flow out of the movie or television screen. The people of biblical times would find that shocking. While it is important to recognize that there was a shock value intended in this description, we must also remember that rural people of all times and places can be matter-of-fact about some of the grosser and cruder elements of life that tend to send more urbanized people reeling. What biblical people find truly shocking is the casual and thoughtless brutality that all too often characterizes urban life.

---

7. NIV "cleverness." Another possibility is "struggles."
8. It is perhaps significant that in the oracles against the nations "pride" is specifically attributed to Moab (16:6). This fact may have prompted its use here.

DEATH AND RESURRECTION. This chapter puts the choices that face the human race in bold relief. No matter what we may have done to one another, if we will turn to God in trust, there is hope for us. Death, the last enemy, has been conquered. But if we insist that we need no redemption, that we can take care of ourselves, God himself will assist the death angel as he carries us off.

This passage has one of the clearest teachings on resurrection in the Old Testament. As such it speaks to the greatest issue in the modern world—the issue of death. Given the insistence today that this world and this life are all there is, death makes a mockery of the whole thing. All our achievements and accomplishments, all our struggles and pain, are meaningless because, as the Preacher says, we all die, the saint and the sinner, the winner and the loser together (Eccl. 9:3–4). Death takes away the possibility of individual human significance. The only alternative is to say that humanity will go on after I die and that therefore I have some significance as a part of the race. But that is my only significance, and a very small one.

This is, of course, exactly where paganism enters. Individuals do not count for anything. It is only as they conform to some ideal conception of humanity that they matter at all. Our individual differences are erased in death and so are insignificant. The one small hope that our individuality might survive is if ancestor worship can be sufficiently inculcated.

Death not only destroys the idea of individual worth, it also destroys the idea of moral values. What does it matter what you or I do, since death is going to get us all in the end? The only thing that matters is a maximum of comfort, pleasure, security, and power so that I can escape death as long as possible.[9] If this world is all there is and death marks the end of any mean-ingful existence, then there is no right or wrong, and no activity has any real meaning. But because our silly spirits crave meaning, we each have to cre-ate it in any way we can, all the time knowing that the meaning we are cre-ating is itself meaningless. This is where the "existentialist" philosophers arrived in the middle of the last century, and their thinking has filtered down to the average person today.

But this chapter and its fulfillment in the New Testament tell us that the existentialist idea is false. We have not been created for death but for life. Death has lost its sting, and the grave has been robbed of its victory (1 Cor.

---

9. Note the irony here. There is no individual worth, but my individual existence is all I have and every scrap of my energy must be devoted to that. Thus, paganism knows noth-ing of individual self-sacrifice for the community good, something that the biblical doctrine of individual resurrection makes possible.

15:55). God the Father has defeated death forever in the death and resurrection of his Son, Jesus Christ. To be sure, we await the final day when the King will make his promised pronouncement and death will cease to be. But until then we can live in the assurance that we do have individual significance and that death cannot destroy that. Furthermore, we can know that trust in God and renunciation of our pride are ultimate values that will make all the difference in whether we conquer death or death conquers us.

When will that pronouncement occur? The book of Revelation gives us more details. The feast of the King portrayed here will be the wedding supper of the Lamb (Rev. 19:7−9). It is the feast of the Lamb because it is through his death and resurrection that death is conquered. This imagery extends back to Exodus, when a lamb's death made it possible for the firstborn of Israel to escape death in Egypt (Ex. 12:12−13). So it is not accidental that Jesus instructed those who follow him to eat his flesh and drink his blood (John 6:53−56). He was consciously associating himself with the Passover lamb. But because death could not conquer him and the Father has raised him to new life, "the Lamb who was slain" (Rev. 5:12; cf. 13:8) is alive to be both host and groom at the last day.

Immediately following the announcement of the wedding supper of the Lamb in Revelation 19 is a discussion of the conquest of death, culminating in the statement in 20:14 that "death and Hades were thrown into the lake of fire," and in 21:4 that "there will be no more death or mourning or crying or pain, for the old order of things has passed away." It is significant that the imagery of Christ changes from Lamb to Conqueror immediately after the announcement of the wedding supper. He rides on a white horse (19:11) and leads the armies of heaven (19:14) to a great battle, which is called "the great supper of God" (19:17), when the vultures eat the corpses of those who have opposed the King (19:21).

We think here immediately of what Isaiah said about Moab. Death will be conquered and destroyed, but those who refuse the offer of the Lamb will be met by the Conqueror and will go down to a worse fate than death, namely, "the second death" (Rev. 2:11; 20:6, 14; 21:8). God offers deliverance from death to all, but those who refuse his offer will find an eternity of torment.

Isaiah 26:1–27:1

IN THAT DAY this song will be sung in the land of Judah:

> We have a strong city;
>> God makes salvation
>> its walls and ramparts.
> ² Open the gates
>> that the righteous nation may enter,
>> the nation that keeps faith.
> ³ You will keep in perfect peace
>> him whose mind is steadfast,
>> because he trusts in you.
> ⁴ Trust in the LORD forever,
>> for the LORD, the LORD, is the Rock eternal.
> ⁵ He humbles those who dwell on high,
>> he lays the lofty city low;
> he levels it to the ground
>> and casts it down to the dust.
> ⁶ Feet trample it down—
>> the feet of the oppressed,
>> the footsteps of the poor.

> ⁷ The path of the righteous is level;
>> O upright One, you make the way of the righteous
>>> smooth.
> ⁸ Yes, LORD, walking in the way of your laws,
>> we wait for you;
> your name and renown
>> are the desire of our hearts.
> ⁹ My soul yearns for you in the night;
>> in the morning my spirit longs for you.
> When your judgments come upon the earth,
>> the people of the world learn righteousness.
> ¹⁰ Though grace is shown to the wicked,
>> they do not learn righteousness;
> even in a land of uprightness they go on doing evil
>> and regard not the majesty of the LORD.
> ¹¹ O LORD, your hand is lifted high,
>> but they do not see it.

Let them see your zeal for your people and be put to shame;
    let the fire reserved for your enemies consume them.

[12] LORD, you establish peace for us;
    all that we have accomplished you have done for us.
[13] O LORD, our God, other lords besides you have ruled
        over us,
    but your name alone do we honor.
[14] They are now dead, they live no more;
    those departed spirits do not rise.
You punished them and brought them to ruin;
    you wiped out all memory of them.
[15] You have enlarged the nation, O LORD;
    you have enlarged the nation.
You have gained glory for yourself;
    you have extended all the borders of the land.

[16] LORD, they came to you in their distress;
    when you disciplined them,
    they could barely whisper a prayer.
[17] As a woman with child and about to give birth
    writhes and cries out in her pain,
    so were we in your presence, O LORD.
[18] We were with child, we writhed in pain,
    but we gave birth to wind.
We have not brought salvation to the earth;
    we have not given birth to people of the world.

[18] But your dead will live;
    their bodies will rise.
You who dwell in the dust,
    wake up and shout for joy.
Your dew is like the dew of the morning;
    the earth will give birth to her dead.

[20] Go, my people, enter your rooms
    and shut the doors behind you;
hide yourselves for a little while
    until his wrath has passed by.
[21] See, the LORD is coming out of his dwelling
    to punish the people of the earth for their sins.
The earth will disclose the blood shed upon her;
    she will conceal her slain no longer.

²⁷ʲ¹In that day,

> the LORD will punish with his sword,
>> his fierce, great and powerful sword,
> Leviathan the gliding serpent,
>> Leviathan the coiling serpent;
> he will slay the monster of the sea.

CHAPTERS 26 AND 27 (both are labeled as songs, 26:1; 27:2) seem to reflect on chapters 24 and 25. Chapter 26 focuses on the way in which the city perceives itself and its role in the world in the light of who God really is. Thus, it becomes an affirmation of trust and a call for God to demonstrate his sovereignty through his people. Chapter 27 concludes the section with a promise of return and restoration for Israel, making special use of the imagery of a vineyard.

As chapter 26 is now constructed, there are three units of thought: thanks for God's deliverance (vv. 1–6), dependence on God (vv. 7–19), and promises to the faithful (26:20–27:1).[1] The second segment (26:7–19) seems to begin on a positive note of trust in God but then moves to a more negative confession of failure to have made a real difference in the world. It is difficult to ascertain whether there is a single line of thought or whether several related thoughts have been brought together.

Thanks for God's Deliverance (26:1–6)

THE OPENING SONG of thanks picks up themes from chapters 24–25. Instead of the silent and ruined city of the earth (26:5), there is now the city of God, peopled with the faithful singing his praises (26:1–2). This city has the "salvation" of God for "walls," making it plain that it is a state of mind more than a geographical place. Instead of the closed gates of a city fearful of attack, it has the open gates of confidence. But the gates are not open to everyone. They are open to those who choose to live in the ethical righteousness of the covenant. As in Psalm 15:1–5; 24:3–10; 118:19–20, the key is not ritual purity but a kind of behavior that mirrors that of the King. One is able to behave in this way because of a complete inner integrity (Heb. *šalom*) that stems from complete dependence on God: "trust" (Isa. 26:3).

---

1. While there is broad scholarly support for this division, there is almost no agreement on the details. See Oswalt, *Isaiah 1–39*, 469–70, n. 9. Motyer, *Prophecy of Isaiah*, 212, offers an intricate four-part chiastic structure. But the parallel structure seems to break down in the center sections. Isa. 27:1 is included with 26:20–21 because its content agrees more closely with those verses than it does with 27:2–11. See the discussion below.

Once again, the main theme of this entire subdivision (chs. 7–39) is trust in the Lord, not in the nations. This trust is eminently justified because the Lord is as secure as a "rock" that is "eternal" (26:4) and because he will bring the "lofty city" of earth down into the dust (26:5–6). The Lord is the eternal Rock, whereas the city, the symbol of all earthly power, is crushed into dust. Ultimately, the city will be brought down by the very people who were oppressed by it. God puts the high and the mighty under the humble and lowly. Since the meek will inherit the earth (Ps. 37:11), it makes no sense to put one's faith in the mighty of the earth.

Dependence on God (26:7–19)

IN 26:7–11 THE prophet asks God to speed that day of retribution. He begins by talking about the "path" or way of life on which God calls the "righteous" to walk. It is not crooked or misleading. It is not filled with snares and traps. Instead, it is "level" and "smooth" (26:7; cf. Moses' words in Deut. 10:12). God does not ask his people to do things that are bizarre or hurtful to themselves. He only asks them to live in the way they were made for.

The righteous gladly accept the way of God's "laws" (*mišpaṭim*, "regulations") for two reasons. (1) It is the way in which believers express trust ("wait") in the Lord. They do not say they trust God and then rush ahead to take care of themselves in ways that violate God's desires, his regulations for fruitful living. (2) God's honor and reputation have become the believers' deepest desire (26:8).[2] They want to live in a way that will bring honor to him and not disgrace.

This thought is deepened in verse 9. "Morning" and "night" the believer's passionate longing is for God. But the context makes it clear that it is not merely an emotional feeling that is wanted. Rather, it is the manifestation of God's character in one's life. The repetition of *mišpaṭim* (NIV "judgments") in this verse makes this clear. What Isaiah is praying for is the expression of God's regulations both in individual human lives and on the larger world scene. He is longing for the ethical evidence of God's presence to be unmistakably seen, because this is the only way "the people of the world" will learn what is right.

Verses 10–11 express a profound truth. In the absence of repentance, "grace" may be actually counterproductive. Unless the "wicked" experience the results of their having broken God's just regulations for life, his "judgments," they will persist in "doing evil." If they do not experience the consequences of their behavior, they will see no reason to change. The good of others means nothing to them. Thus, the prophet calls on God to demon-

---

2. Lit., "the desire of the *nepeš* [self]" (NIV, "desire of our hearts").

strate his justice to the wicked nations by redeeming his "people." To be sure, many of God's people have sinned and brought God's wrath on themselves, as expressed through conquest by the nations. But the nations have not seen it in that way. They believe they have conquered Israel and Judah simply through their own power and glory, taking whatever they wanted in spite of the Lord (cf. Ezek. 36:18–20). Sooner or later, Isaiah says, God must demonstrate to the world that this is not the case. He must rise up against the wicked on behalf of his people and make the consequences of sin clear.

Verses 12–18 reflect further on this thought. The people have been unable to accomplish God's work in the world, and they call on him to demonstrate his delivering power there. This reflection begins with a testimony of his grace on their behalf in the past (26:12–15). Perhaps it is the period of the judges that is especially in the writer's mind, when God delivered his people from so many different overlords.

Verse 12 is a beautiful affirmation. God is the One who has done everything for his people. He has made it possible for them to have true "peace" and to accomplish significant things. Apart from his grace and goodness, they would have been just one more insignificant people group in the ancient world.

Verses 13–15 then particularize what God has done in and though his people. He has delivered them from various peoples who have ruled over them at one time or another. Those people no longer have a "name" (i.e., an honorable memory, a reputation) in Israel,[3] but God's "name" continues to be honored through all time among his people. The reason is that although Israel's enemies have made numerous attempts to wipe out the "nation" and enslave its people, God has frustrated them and "enlarged the nation" in spite of them. None of this is to the glory of Israel and its kings; it is all to the "glory" of God (26:15).

Verses 16–18 continue the previous theme, but the focus changes from the might of God to the helplessness of the people. Verse 16 is difficult, but the basic point seems to be that the people recognize that when the nations triumphed over them, it was because of God's "discipline," not because of the power of the nations.[4] They were helpless under that punishment. Like a woman with a false pregnancy, who goes into labor but has nothing to deliver, they struggled and struggled but were unable to deliver themselves or anyone else.

---

3. But cf. 54:4–5, where Isaiah asserts that even these can have a "name" if they will choose to keep God's covenant.

4. See the discussion in Oswalt, *Isaiah 1–39*, 483–84, n. 42. I prefer to read the verse "O LORD, in distress they were constrained by you; in straits, they were humbled by your discipline upon them."

This last thought in verse 18 is an interesting one. We would expect it to say that they were unable to save themselves from the oppression of the world. But in fact the actual statement in both parts of the parallel appears to be that they have been unable to bring salvation into the world.[5] The prophet is perhaps reflecting here on Israel's larger mission to be a blessing on the nations. This, of course, first appeared in God's promises to Abraham (Gen. 12:3). But, as we have seen, it is also a significant part of Isaiah's own message, which may explain its presence here. Not only does he long to see God's justice applied to the world in regard to Israel (26:9–11), he also wants to see God's salvation made available to the world through Israel.

Verse 19 is another example of a transition in Isaiah that can be read either with the preceding material or the following. In one sense it concludes what has just been said. In verse 18, the prophet, speaking for the people, has confessed their impotence in carrying out God's program in the world. They have failed him and been forced to submit to the discipline of destruction by the nations. They have been unable to recover from that discipline on their own. They are helpless, laboring as in childbirth but to no effect. But in verse 19 the prophet, speaking for God, tells them not to despair. Though years have passed and many of the faithful have died, with no effect either on the nation and the world, death does not have the last word; God does.

As in chapter 25, resurrection is seen as the final answer to all of earth's questions. If it were true that death conquers all, there would be no reason to live a life faithful and committed to God; it would make so little difference in the outcome of world events. But death does not conquer all. Those who have gone down into "the dust" in death "will rise." "The earth" will give up the "dead,"[6] and then it will be demonstrated that the life of faith was not in vain.[7]

---

5. The correctness of this observation depends on how the Heb. of the final colon is translated. The lit. reading is, "Nor have the inhabitants of earth fallen." The NIV, in view of the context, takes this to be a reference to the "dropping" (birthing) of a baby. If so, this is the only place in the Old Testament where the phrase is used in this way. Usually, the connotation is to "fall" in battle. The NRSV and REB both support the idea of birth.

6. The lit. Heb. is, "The earth will cause the slack ones to fall." As in my comments on v. 18, it is not certain that "fall" in these two places connotes birth (as per NIV). The earth has been holding these people captive, so it may be that the idea is that the earth will let them drop from its jaws (see v. 21).

7. The reference to "dew" in connection with light ("morning") and "earth" suggests the possibility that Isaiah is consciously making use of some of the language of Canaanite myth. In certain of those myths dew and earth are two maidens who appear with a third, who is a daughter of light. See comments on 27:1 for further discussion of this reuse of mythical language.

Promises to the Faithful (26:20–27:1)

BUT IT IS also possible for verse 19 to be read with verses 20–21. In view of the promise of the resurrection, the people do not need to fear that God has forsaken them in his "wrath" (v. 20). Instead, they can trust in his protective covering until his judgment on the nations, the judgment they requested (26:9–11), has passed. There are allusions here to both Noah (Gen. 6:13–14) and the Passover (Ex. 12:21–24). God will take care of his own and protect them from final harm.

But again, as in 25:10–12, there will be a final judgment. The assurance of protection for the faithful and a resurrection to new life cannot obscure the fact that the iniquity (NIV "sins") of earth's "people," that inner twisted sinfulness that ultimately expresses itself in murder (lit., "its bloodshed"), will not go unpunished. God will demonstrate to "the people of the earth" the very things called for in the earlier verses of the chapter. He will show that he is the One who has set the terms of existence. Just as we find at the end of the book (Isa. 66:24), grace does not wipe out justice. Those who will not use grace to enable themselves to turn about and live according to God's regulations will find that justice is inescapable.

Isaiah 27:1 is another slippery transitional verse. It could introduce what follows in 27:2, as is indicated by the chapter break in the Hebrew (followed by the English versions). If so, it introduces the destruction of all opposition so that God can truly protect his vineyard. But at the same time, it can serve as a graphic illustration of what was just said in 26:21, something we have seen Isaiah do several times previously (3:16–4:1; 5:1–25; 25:10–12). The repetition of the verb "punish" in both 26:21 and 27:1 supports this idea. There also seems to be a more direct similarity of thought between these two verses than between 27:1 and 27:2–11.

The illustration that is used in 27:1 is almost certainly taken from Canaanite mythology, in which the chaos monster is a sea serpent named Leviathan. Leviathan is destroyed by one of the gods so that order can prevail. This is one form of a story that was widely known all over the ancient Near East, with actors having different names but with the same plot. Isaiah is not endorsing the worldview of those myths here. Rather, he is simply making use of emotive images familiar to many in his audience to make his point, much as we today might say, "He is as strong as Hercules," without thereby indicating we believe in the Greek myth.[8]

In this graphic illustration, Isaiah says that no enemy can defeat God's plan and purposes. His people do not need to fear that somehow in the end all

---

8. For a fuller discussion, see Oswalt, *Isaiah* 1–39, 490–91, and the notes there.

they have believed and lived for will fall to the ground. God has already won the victory, and we only await its final consummation.

Bridging Contexts

PERSECUTION. Perhaps in our day there is no more similar context to what is being talked about here than that of the persecuted church around the world. We in the West have known little of what it means to say "other lords besides you have ruled over us, but your name alone do we honor" (26:13). But Christians who have endured persecution under Communist regimes and in Islamic countries resonate clearly with such a statement. The few stories we hear are inspiring. When all the evidence seemed to be that evil had won and faith had been vanquished, these people refused to surrender, and because of them God was able to continue to build his kingdom.

In the Soviet Union, the Methodist church largely disappeared. Only in Estonia did Methodist congregations survive. When we ask the Methodists in Estonia today how that happened, they tell the story of a Methodist superintendent who was required under pain of imprisonment in Siberia to sign over the deeds of his churches to the Russian conquerors. But he refused to do so, saying that they were not his churches but God's and that God's property could never belong to the state. When he was removed, several of the young pastors said to themselves, "If he can be faithful unto death, we can too."

Thus, even though their buildings were taken from them by force, these young men did not give up their callings. They continued to shepherd their flocks in little, out-of-the-way, rented rooms amidst harassment, ridicule, and want. They believed what Isaiah said about the ultimate triumph of God. And by God's grace some of them have lived to see a measure of that triumph. In Pilsen in the Czech Republic, a church was taken by the government and turned into a school for atheism. But in the early 1990s the building was returned to the remnants of the former congregation. What a thrill it is to stand in a former hall of atheism and hear several hundred predominantly young people singing the praises of the true owner of the building.

A similar story can be told in Romania. There, although Christian congregations were allowed to retain their buildings, it was always under great duress. No Christian meeting or any kind of witness was allowed outside of the unmarked church buildings. No Christian was permitted to be in any profession or to attend university. If you wished to be a clerk or a day laborer, then go ahead and confess Christ as your Savior. Pastors were required to meet with a secret police agent each week and prove that what had been preached the previous Sunday was not in any way subversive. They were effectively isolated from each other because it was known that some of them were inform-ers, but no one knew who these informers were. Nevertheless, these pastors endured the hardships and were faithful, refusing to believe, despite the appar-ent triumph of state-sponsored atheism, that God was defeated.

Although these pastors endured all kinds of deprivation, God honored them. The churches were full to overflowing. One church, prohibited from expanding and intentionally surrounded by high-rise apartment buildings, simply removed their windows and placed high-powered amplifiers in the openings. People all around went to church! To be in one of those packed churches in the dead of winter, when most of the congregation had walked long distances through the snow and cold to be there, and to hear them sing and pray was a never-to-be-forgotten experience. Like the people in Isaiah 26, they had doubts and fears. They wondered if it was still possible that their faith was in vain and that the deprivations they had endured were for noth-ing. Yet they persevered, believing in the resurrection and God's eventual tri-umph over evil in every form, both personal and institutional.

CULTURAL CHANGES. This chapter is about per-severance in spite of hardship and uncertainty. We in the West know little of this. For two hun-dred years we have experienced a rarity on the face of the earth: a culture profoundly influenced by Christian ethics from top to bottom. To be sure, there was plenty of corruption. But when such was revealed, it was not winked at or taken for granted. It was reviled and rooted out as best as possible. As a result, we have inherited a culture where cour-tesy and respecting God's law are givens.

Now, however, since the cultural upheavals of the 1960s and 1970s, when parents began to abdicate their responsibilities and when the Jesus Movement produced a "feel-good" revival instead of a moral renovation, all that heritage is being fast eroded. Christians are finding themselves more and more mar-ginalized while cultural gurus spend millions of foundation dollars (often earned by hard-working evangelicals) trying to find out what is the missing glue that once held American society together.

How shall Christians respond to circumstances like these? One of the common ways is to develop a fascination for the "end times." The current popularity of the "Left Behind" series is one example of such fascination.[9]

---

9. Timothy LaHaye and Jerry Jenkins, *Left Behind* (Carol Stream, Ill.: Tyndale, 1995). To date no less than eight subsequent books have appeared in the series, each of them an instant bestseller on national lists.

There is a degree of escapism involved because it is hard to keep one's focus when we are neither popular nor overtly persecuted. So we fantasize about a time when everything will be perfectly clear, when the lines will be drawn so that everyone can see them. But these verses in Isaiah are written for just such an ambiguous time as ours, when the lines are not clear. Their prescriptions are just what we need today. They tell us to do five things: Trust God in an active way; honor God's name alone; believe God can do what we cannot; do not let go of the resurrection; and focus on the real enemy.

Trusting God as a way of living. What does it mean to "trust God"? Most of us think of it first as an attitudinal thing. To trust God is not to be anxious. That is surely true. Verse 3 says if our *yeṣer*, our capacity for imagining, rests on God, we can know perfect peace. In many cases we find it difficult to trust God because our imaginations have been filled with anything else but God. We have allowed the culture around us, through the media domination, to saturate our vision. The result is that many of us know nothing of inner serenity. The scriptural admonition, "Do not be anxious about anything" (Phil. 4:6), becomes almost laughable. We are anxious about everything, most of it far beyond our control.

What must we do? We must first of all guard much more closely what we let into our minds. Paul followed up the admonition just quoted with a further one, "Finally, brothers, whatever is true, whatever is noble, whatever is right, whatever is pure, whatever is lovely, whatever is admirable—if anything is excellent or praiseworthy—think about such things" (Phil 4:8). This does not mean we hide our heads in the sand from the opposite of such things. But it does mean we do everything in our power to keep those opposite things from filling our heads. This begins at home. Are our homes places of quiet, beauty, and serenity? Hardly! Many of our homes are places of frantic activity, where cluttered minds reveal themselves in cluttered living spaces. When will Christians admit that we are countercultural and begin to embrace that reality?

But Isaiah 26 also helps us to realize that trusting God has a less cerebral side. Verse 8 instructs us to "wait" for God by "walking in the way of your laws." On the surface, this seems counterintuitive. "Walking" and "waiting" seem contradictory. However, as I pointed out on 25:9, the biblical concept of "waiting" is a way of thinking. It is not doing nothing, but it is doing what you know is right while refusing to run ahead of God to try to solve your problems for yourself. In other words, to trust God is to obey him by following his regulations for life. This is what the writer of the Proverbs is talking about when he says in Proverbs 3:5–6:

> Trust in the LORD with all your heart
> > and lean not on your own understanding;
> in all your ways acknowledge him,
> > and he will make your paths straight.

To trust God is to show we know him in our "paths," that is, by the way we live. We trust God when we are honest in situations where it would be to our advantage to cheat. We trust God when we refuse to break faith with our wife by flirting with a pretty girl who is obviously interested. We trust God when we give valuable time to work for the poor. We wait for the Lord, believing that he will act in our behalf in his own best time, by obeying his *mišpaṭim*, his regulations for life, and not making up our own to serve ourselves as we go along.

In this respect it is important to remind ourselves who those people are who live in the security of the walls of salvation. Who will go through the open gates of God's city? It is the righteous nation that keeps faith (26:2). Note Psalm 15:

> LORD, who may dwell in your sanctuary?
> > Who may live on your holy hill?
>
> He whose walk is blameless
> > and who does what is righteous,
> who speaks the truth from his heart
> > and has no slander on his tongue,
> who does his neighbor no wrong
> > and casts no slur on his fellowman,
> who despises a vile man
> > but honors those who fear the LORD,
> who keeps his oath
> > even when it hurts,
> who lends his money without usury
> > and does not accept a bribe against the innocent.
>
> He who does these things
> > will never be shaken.

There are two pitfalls to be avoided here. (1) One is the idea that we can earn a place in the city of God by our excessive righteousness. The Bible is clear from beginning to end that this is impossible. The idea that we can is a pharisaic misreading of the Old Testament. Paul turns to the Old Testament for a host of references to support his statement in Romans 3:10 that "there is no one righteous, not even one." There is only one key to the divine city—the blood of the Lamb (Rev. 5:9–10).

(2) The other pitfall is a mirror image of the first, a pitfall that American evangelicals and our offspring in two-thirds of the world are in danger of falling into. It is the one Paul tries to guard against in Romans 6–8: "Shall we go on sinning so that grace may increase?" (6:1). There is only one appropriate response to the grace of God in Christ, namely, to allow the Holy Spirit such free rein in our lives that we cease to "walk in the flesh" (Rom. 8:4, NIV "live according to the sinful nature"). We evangelicals are in great danger of saying that since we are saved by grace alone, it does not really matter if we sin a little. No part of the Scripture supports this.

The apostle John agrees with Paul in his statement that Christians have ceased habitual sinning (1 John 3:6). This verse has terrified many a young Christian who has not learned what it means to make a full surrender to the Holy Spirit in faith. But it is not meant to be a word of terror but of hope. Our hands have been cleansed by the blood of Jesus, and they can remain clean through the power of the Holy Spirit.

Honor God's name alone. Verse 13 says that although others have ruled over God's people, the people have honored God's name. Though that certainly was not true of all of them, it was true for the remnant. And because they put the honor of God's name above everything else, God was able to triumph through them. This must be our attitude as well.

But how can we do that? One way is to be sure that he gets the glory for his achievements in us. Moses was not permitted to enter the Promised Land because he made it appear as if it was his own power that produced water out of the rock (Num. 20:10). He did not sanctify, or give honor to, the name of the Lord. This reminds us that God's "name" is not his label. Rather, it is his nature, his character, his reputation.

Another way we honor the name of the Lord is by demonstrating that he is able to deliver us from whatever may come upon us. God tells the people in Ezekiel 36:20 that they have "profaned my holy name" by going into captivity and giving the Babylonians an opportunity to say, "These are the LORD's people, and yet they had to leave his land." All we have to do to profane God's name is to make it appear as if he is helpless to deliver us. Because the people sinned against God and brought his well-deserved wrath on them, they gave God's enemies an opportunity to say that God could not deliver them.

Thus, the main way to honor God's name is not by raising our hands and singing songs of praise. We do it chiefly when our lives show that he alone is the Holy One and that he is like no one else. This is what we pray for when we repeat the second clause of the Lord's Prayer: "Hallowed be your name" (Luke 11:2). We are asking God to assist us in demonstrating his character in everything we do and say. This is what it means to "honor God's name."

Believe God can do what we cannot. The book of Malachi was written for a time such as ours. The prophet was preparing God's people for that long interlude we now know as "the intertestamental period" (between 400 B.C. and the coming of Christ). All the revelation necessary to prepare for the coming of Christ was concluded with Malachi's prophecy, and now a period of four hundred years would ensue before all the circumstances were right for that coming. During most of that time, the Jews had little control over their political destiny, being ruled by one great power and then another. The glowing promises of the prophets for the time after the Exile had not come true. Already the kinds of jibes reported by Malachi were being said: "Where is the God of justice?" (Mal. 2:17), and "It is futile to serve God" (3:14). And they would only be said more loudly in some quarters in the days to come.

What is Malachi's (and Isaiah's) prescription? It is to rest in the Lord's ability to do what we cannot do and not to give up believing that he will act (see Isa. 26:11, 20–21). Malachi writes in Malachi 3:16–18:

> Then those who feared the LORD talked with each other, and the LORD listened and heard. A scroll of remembrance was written in his presence concerning those who feared the LORD and honored his name.
>
> "They will be mine," says the LORD Almighty, "in the day when I make up my treasured possession. I will spare them, just as in compassion a man spares his son who serves him. And you will again see the distinction between the righteous and the wicked, between those who serve God and those who do not.

In a time when God seems to be doing nothing, believers need to be encouraging one another with the evidence of God's faithful activity in the past and with all the promises that he will not leave us. We refuse to succumb to the temptation to take things into our own hands and instead persevere in faithful living, trusting God to do what we cannot as we trust him.

Hold fast to the resurrection. The key in all of this is the resurrection. If we did not have this certainty, we would be forced to demand that God act "now." But we do not need to make such demands. This is John's point when he has Christ saying, "Be faithful, even to the point of death, and I will give you the crown of life" (Rev. 2:10). If the only rewards for a life of faithfulness are here, then we cannot afford a life of peaceful trust; we must "make it happen." But if the real rewards are on the other side of death, we can well afford such a life. If we have not "brought in the kingdom" as the people confess not to have done in Isaiah 26:18, but we have trusted Christ by living a life of obedience and faith that honors him, we can live confidently, knowing that death has no final ability to hurt us.

As I said in the comments on chapter 25, however, the resurrection awareness is something that must be cultivated, especially in our culture where maintenance of life has become almost cultic. We need periodically to rehearse for ourselves the words of the old spiritual, "This world is not my home, I'm just a-passing through." With the strains of heaven playing in our ears, we can live for God, even if we do not see all the promises fulfilled to our own satisfaction. We know that death has been defeated and that life will win in the end.

Focus on the real enemy. One serious danger in times of uncertainty and ambiguity is to begin looking for enemies, for those whom we can blame for our troubles. In times like the present, the church has often been wont to turn to the spirit world and blame the demonic for our difficulties. Isaiah's reference to "Leviathan" (27:1) may be an expression of such a thing. Many see "Leviathan" as a code name for Satan. After all, the book of Revelation depicts "an enormous red dragon" (Rev. 12:3) as the enemy of the "woman" (12:1–2, 4–6), who is often identified with the church. But we must be careful at this point. The Bible is clear from beginning to end that the real enemy of God and of his people is not a rebellious spirit being.

Yes, there is such a being, and he opposes God and his people (1 Peter 5:8). But he is not responsible for the existence of sin in the world. Our first mother and father chose to sin against God of their own free will (Gen. 3:6). The snake only asked a leading question and told a lie about God's character. The enemy that God must destroy in the world is moral evil, and that chiefly in ourselves. We must be careful not to excuse immorality of every sort in ourselves ("after all, I'm only human") while becoming engrossed in "spiritual warfare."

Isaiah 27:2–13

I N THAT DAY—

"Sing about a fruitful vineyard:
3   I, the LORD, watch over it;
     I water it continually.
I guard it day and night
     so that no one may harm it.
4   I am not angry.
If only there were briers and thorns confronting me!
     I would march against them in battle;
     I would set them all on fire.
5 Or else let them come to me for refuge;
     let them make peace with me,
     yes, let them make peace with me."

6 In days to come Jacob will take root,
     Israel will bud and blossom
     and fill all the world with fruit.

7 Has the LORD struck her
     as he struck down those who struck her?
 Has she been killed
     as those were killed who killed her?
8 By warfare and exile you contend with her—
     with his fierce blast he drives her out,
     as on a day the east wind blows.
9 By this, then, will Jacob's guilt be atoned for,
     and this will be the full fruitage of the removal
          of his sin:
When he makes all the altar stones
     to be like chalk stones crushed to pieces,
no Asherah poles or incense altars
     will be left standing.
10 The fortified city stands desolate,
     an abandoned settlement, forsaken like the desert;
 there the calves graze,
     there they lie down;
     they strip its branches bare.

¹¹When its twigs are dry, they are broken off
    and women come and make fires with them.
For this is a people without understanding;
    so their Maker has no compassion on them,
    and their Creator shows them no favor.

¹²In that day the LORD will thresh from the flowing
Euphrates to the Wadi of Egypt, and you, O Israelites, will be
gathered up one by one. ¹³And in that day a great trumpet
will sound. Those who were perishing in Assyria and those
who were exiled in Egypt will come and worship the LORD on
the holy mountain in Jerusalem.

IN THE EARLIER CHAPTERS in this subdivision (Isa. 24–27), which celebrate God's lordship over history, the songs are those of drunkards trying to forget (24:9), or of ruthless triumph (25:5), or praise for God's security (26:1). The present song is a more intimate one. It praises God for delivering his people and celebrates his personal relationship with them. In this sense it forms the conclusion of the four chapters. The first and second songs (chs. 24 and 25) declare universal judgment and universal salvation. In the third (ch. 26), the people proclaim their trust in God, but they also confess their inability to deliver themselves and fulfill their ministry in the world. Now, God confirms his promise to deliver them.[1]

Here we have the opposite picture from the one we saw in chapter 5. There God called in the wild animals to destroy the vineyard of bitter grapes, his nation. He tore down the walls and left it to "briers and thorns" (5:6). Now we see the "vineyard" from the other side. God says he is "not angry," and he wishes that there were "briers and thorns" for him to contend with (27:4), so that he could chop them down and burn them. But in a mixing of metaphors, he says the thorns and briers (evidently the nations) could come and "make peace" with him (27:5). In any case, the vineyard of "Jacob" is going to be so fruitful that it will fill "the world with fruit" (27:6).

What accounts for this radical shift? Surely God *was* angry with his people, angry enough to destroy them. Yet here he talks as if those words had

---

1. The entire chapter is written from a postexilic perspective. For many, this proves that the material could not have been written before that time. However, if we grant any possibility of genuine predictive prophecy, that need not be the case. The prophet is making a case in the 700s B.C. for the trustworthiness of God. A necessary part of that argument is that when Israel has brought disaster on itself by its refusal to trust, God will prove just how trustworthy he is by his gracious deliverance of them.

never been said. Verses 6–11 explain the matter. God did not bring destruction on Israel for the purpose of annihilating his people, his vineyard. If they want to see that kind of destruction, let them look at those whom God used as tools to strike the punishing blows (27:7).

Yes, God had indeed driven Israel out, like a tumbleweed before a driving windstorm (27:8). But his purpose was not annihilation but cleansing. That point comes clear in 27:9, where God says that the fruit of the "removal of his sin" will be the destruction of idol worship. The Hebrew of the verse is obscure, so that we do not know the means by which "Jacob's guilt [will] be atoned for," but the result is clear. Out of the fires of the Exile, the idolatry that was the obvious sign of disloyalty to the covenant Lord will be done away with.[2]

There is a clear causal connection between 27:9 and 10 in the Hebrew. Verse 10 begins with *ki* ("because"). This shows we must at least read verse 9, if not verses 7–9, with verses 10–11. But what that connection portends is not entirely clear because the identity of "the fortified city" is not spelled out. Elsewhere in this section this city seems to represent the oppressors of God's people (25:2).[3] If that is the case, it seems to me the most natural reading is that when the "fortified city," a "people without understanding," is destroyed, Israel will be set free by God's grace and will respond with renewed obedience to the covenant.

The other alternative is that there has been a shift of metaphor and that "the fortified city" is now a reference to Jerusalem, which it would be natural to assume in the immediate context.[4] The phrase "without understanding" also sounds much like what is said of Israel in 1:3. In this case, the passage is restating the point in 27:8 as to why the destruction was needed. On balance, and without a sign that the metaphor has been shifted, I tend to side with the former of the two understandings.[5]

Isaiah 27:12–13 cap the Lord's promises to his people. The writer begins with the metaphor of harvest. The Lord will not allow one kernel of grain or one olive to be lost but will diligently gather them all from the distant borders of the land—the "Euphrates" in the north and the "Wadi of Egypt"[6] in

---

2. "Asherah poles" were perhaps poplar groves surrounding the altar to Asherah, a Canaanite fertility goddess. They appear to have been symbols of the goddess.

3. So among recent commentators, Motyer, *Prophecy of Isaiah*, 224–25; Seitz, *Isaiah 1–39*, 198–200; Childs, *Isaiah*, 198. But Seitz and Childs arrive at radically differing interpretations: to Seitz, the passage demonstrates that the pagan worship of the world can be atoned for; to Childs, it demonstrates that there is no universal salvation in the Old Testament.

4. Watts, *Isaiah 1–33*, 349–50, is an example of this position among recent commentators.

5. A third alternative is espoused by Wildberger, *Isaiah 13–27*, that the reference is to Samaria, noted for its idolatry.

6. The historical southern border of the Promised Land (Josh. 15:47), approximately where the southern border of Israel is today.

the south. The same point is made with a different metaphor, the trumpet call of muster for battle, in verse 13. The "exiles" from north and south are called to "worship the LORD on the holy mountain," where the last great feast is to be held (25:6–8).

IF FEW OF US have vineyards today, many of us are familiar with *This Old House*. We might think of what God is saying here along those lines. God just wishes that some termites would show up in the old house. How he would delight in rooting them out and repairing the damage they have done. The new work would be better than the original. Or what about tearing out some old plumbing and wiring? God would love to lavish attention on the old place. In the end you would hardly recognize it from what he started with. Why would he do it? To sell it and make a lot of money? Never! He would pour so much of himself into the work because that is where he wants to live.

We continually have to remind ourselves that idolatry is not first of all the making of figures of gods and goddesses. It is an attitude, the attitude that I must find a way to manipulate the forces in control of the universe to satisfy my needs. The statues, then, are simply a way to visualize those forces and make them amenable to my control.

But the statues are only symptoms. It is possible to have the attitude of an idolater and never think of making an idol. Whenever I try to satisfy my needs for myself by manipulating the elements of the creation, I am succumbing to idolatry. God calls us to surrender our needs to him and to trust him to meet those needs in his ways. Usually he will meet them through our talents and abilities, but it is the attitude with which we do it that makes all the difference.

GOD'S ACTIONS IN our lives today continue to be not for the purpose of destruction but for refinement. If trouble and adversity have come our way, our attitude about God will make all the difference in how we receive them. If we think of God as passionately loving "the old house" that we are, then the ripping of the saw and the crashing of the hammer will still be painful but much easier to bear. But if we think of him as the implacable judge determined to wring the last ounce of retribution out of us, the blows will be heavy indeed.

It is also important to keep the lesson of Job in mind. Adversity and trouble do not have easy explanations, and sometimes to give easy explanations in a glib manner can do more damage than the trouble itself. Job's "comforters" would have done much better to remain silent than to give faulty explanations concerning what they knew nothing about.

What we should do is to use difficulty as an opportunity. Is there something that has come between me and God? Has my loyalty to my covenant Lord become diluted? Has my surrender to him and my trust become less than total? If the answer to any of these is "yes," then there is only one option: godly sorrow, repentance, and flinging oneself on his divine grace. This was Paul's goal in calling for the expulsion of an immoral man from the church in Corinth. It was not punishment but the hope that hardship would bring about restoration (1 Cor. 5:5).

If there is no conviction from the Holy Spirit that a certain suffering is deserved, then the admonition of Peter is appropriate:

> Dear friends, do not be surprised at the painful trial you are suffering, as though something strange were happening to you. But rejoice that you participate in the sufferings of Christ, so that you may be overjoyed when his glory is revealed. (1 Peter 4:12–13)

This is not easy for us who are tempted to avoid pain at all costs. But we must realize that God does not have destruction in mind when he allows suffering to come across our path. If it is not for discipline, it may well be for a testimony of his grace in the conflict with evil. At any rate, we can know that just as Christ's sufferings led to his glory, so may ours (1 Peter 5:10), for God's final purpose is to lead us beyond judgment to the final ingathering.

Isaiah 28:1–29

¹ WOE TO THAT wreath, the pride of Ephraim's drunkards,
   to the fading flower, his glorious beauty,
 set on the head of a fertile valley—
   to that city, the pride of those laid low by wine!
² See, the Lord has one who is powerful and strong.
   Like a hailstorm and a destructive wind,
 like a driving rain and a flooding downpour,
   he will throw it forcefully to the ground.
³ That wreath, the pride of Ephraim's drunkards,
   will be trampled underfoot.
⁴ That fading flower, his glorious beauty,
   set on the head of a fertile valley,
 will be like a fig ripe before harvest—
   as soon as someone sees it and takes it in his hand,
   he swallows it.

⁵ In that day the LORD Almighty
   will be a glorious crown,
 a beautiful wreath
   for the remnant of his people.
⁶ He will be a spirit of justice
   to him who sits in judgment,
 a source of strength
   to those who turn back the battle at the gate.

⁷ And these also stagger from wine
   and reel from beer:
 Priests and prophets stagger from beer
   and are befuddled with wine;
 they reel from beer,
   they stagger when seeing visions,
   they stumble when rendering decisions.
⁸ All the tables are covered with vomit
   and there is not a spot without filth.

⁹ "Who is it he is trying to teach?
   To whom is he explaining his message?
 To children weaned from their milk,
   to those just taken from the breast?

¹⁰ For it is:

    Do and do, do and do,
    rule on rule, rule on rule;
    a little here, a little there."

¹¹ Very well then, with foreign lips and strange tongues
    God will speak to this people,
¹² to whom he said,
    "This is the resting place, let the weary rest";
  and, "This is the place of repose"—
    but they would not listen.
¹³ So then, the word of the LORD to them will become:

    Do and do, do and do,
    rule on rule, rule on rule;
    a little here, a little there—
  so that they will go and fall backward,
    be injured and snared and captured.

¹⁴ Therefore hear the word of the LORD, you scoffers
    who rule this people in Jerusalem.
¹⁵ You boast, "We have entered into a covenant with death,
    with the grave we have made an agreement.
  When an overwhelming scourge sweeps by,
    it cannot touch us,
  for we have made a lie our refuge
    and falsehood our hiding place."

¹⁶ So this is what the Sovereign LORD says:

    "See, I lay a stone in Zion,
    a tested stone,
  a precious cornerstone for a sure foundation;
    the one who trusts will never be dismayed.
¹⁷ I will make justice the measuring line
    and righteousness the plumb line;
  hail will sweep away your refuge, the lie,
    and water will overflow your hiding place.
¹⁸ Your covenant with death will be annulled;
    your agreement with the grave will not stand.
  When the overwhelming scourge sweeps by,
    you will be beaten down by it.
¹⁹ As often as it comes it will carry you away;
    morning after morning, by day and by night,
    it will sweep through."

The understanding of this message
will bring sheer terror.
[20] The bed is too short to stretch out on,
the blanket too narrow to wrap around you.
[21] The LORD will rise up as he did at Mount Perazim,
he will rouse himself as in the Valley of Gibeon—
to do his work, his strange work,
and perform his task, his alien task.
[22] Now stop your mocking,
or your chains will become heavier;
the Lord, the LORD Almighty, has told me
of the destruction decreed against the whole land.

[23] Listen and hear my voice;
pay attention and hear what I say.
[24] When a farmer plows for planting, does he plow
continually?
Does he keep on breaking up and harrowing the soil?
[25] When he has leveled the surface,
does he not sow caraway and scatter cummin?
Does he not plant wheat in its place,
barley in its plot,
and spelt in its field?
[26] His God instructs him
and teaches him the right way.

[27] Caraway is not threshed with a sledge,
nor is a cartwheel rolled over cummin;
caraway is beaten out with a rod,
and cummin with a stick.
[28] Grain must be ground to make bread;
so one does not go on threshing it forever.
Though he drives the wheels of his threshing cart over it,
his horses do not grind it.
[29] All this also comes from the LORD Almighty,
wonderful in counsel and magnificent in wisdom.

IN CHAPTERS 28–33 the prophet continues the
lessons in trust that have characterized the material from chapter 13 onward. Having established
God's sovereignty over the nations both in partic-
ular (chs. 13–23) and in general (chs. 24–27), Isaiah now returns to particular
situations in Israel and Judah that illustrate the folly of trusting the nations
instead of the King who had been revealing himself through the prophet.

Because refusal to trust in God will only lead to destruction, Isaiah begins
several of the sections with the funeral word "woe" (28:1; 29:1, 15; 30:1;
31:1; 33:1). It is possible to consider the material in groups of two chapters
each. Chapters 28–29 deal with a problem that is exacerbated by the foolish, drunken leaders; chapters 30–31 critique the proposed solution: dependence on Egypt; and chapters 32–33 present the true solution: reliance on
the true Leader, the righteous King.

Most of these chapters are focused on Judah, as might be expected since that
is Isaiah's home. However, chapter 28 begins with a woe addressed to "Ephraim,"
that is, northern Israel. It is unclear just how far this address continues. Clearly,
by 28:14 the focus has shifted to Jerusalem, and the prophet does not specifically return to Israel after that. However, most of what is said after 28:14 is still
relevant to the northern kingdom since it has entered its final death throes.

This material seems to relate to events somewhat later than those recorded
in chapters 7–8. They also apparently precede the events of chapters 36–37.
Thus, they fall roughly between 730 and 705 B.C. When it became clear that
the northern kingdom was going to fall to Assyria and that Ahaz's "alliance"
with Assyria was as worthless as Isaiah had predicted, the only human hope
left was Egypt. No other country in the area had the wealth or resources to
mount an army of sufficient size to stand up to the Assyrians. But to Isaiah,
trusting Egypt is as foolish as trusting Assyria. Although it is unlikely that
Egypt will turn on Judah as Assyria had, they are still only flesh and blood
(31:3) and can offer nothing like the help that the King can.

Chapter 28 has four subunits: verses 1–6, 7–13, 14–22, and 23–29. There
is a question whether verses 7–13 relate more closely to verses 1–6, as I tend
to read it, or to verses 14–22, as Motyer does.[1] It is a question of whether
the pronouncement against Ephraim is continuing in these verses or whether
it has already shifted to Judah and Jerusalem.

Pronouncement Against Ephraim (28:1–6)

THROUGHOUT THIS STANZA, there is a play on "wreath." This is the circlet of
flowers or vines worn on the head of champions or revelers. The same

---

1. Motyer, *Prophecy of Isaiah*, 229–30.

practice existed in the Greek and Roman cultures. The drunken partygoers in Samaria wear these wreaths on their heads as they try to forget the terror facing them. At the same time the battlements of the city sitting on its hilltop at the "head" of the "valley" (28:1, 4) give it the appearance of one of these wreaths. But Isaiah sees a day when all these wreaths, both the real and the symbolic, will be thrown to the ground and trampled. The "pride" of the northern kingdom is going to be snatched up like a ripe "fig" (28:4).

In contrast, there is another "wreath," the Lord himself (28:5). He will be the source of beauty and glory for those who have abandoned their own pride in glad submission to him. He will give "justice" to the judges and "strength" to the soldiers (28:6). The mention of "crown" in verse 5 puts the issue in a clear light: Who is the King, the drunken political leaders or "the LORD Almighty?"

Continuing Pronouncement Against Ephraim (28:7–13)

THE OCCURRENCE OF "also" in 28:7 makes me believe that these verses continue to be addressed to the northern kingdom. Verses 1–4 spoke of the political leaders and the nobility, whereas verses 7–8 show that the priests and prophets are no better off. They too are besotted with the attempt to please and satisfy themselves. Undoubtedly, alcohol abuse is a problem for them, but it is only a symptom of their deeper problem, an unwillingness to surrender their needs and desires to the Lord (cf. also Mal. 2:1–9).

The result is that those who should be giving clear guidance and teaching in that desperate hour are "befuddled" and staggering around in a stupor. The "tables" (28:8) may be tables at which the priests sit to give judgment, or they may be the mats around which the partygoers sit. In any case, Isaiah says they "are covered with vomit," expressing the depths of his disgust with what is taking place.

Verses 9–10 express the mockery of these religious leaders for the true prophet. "Who does he think he is," they say, "treating us like little children?" Of course, childishness is just what alcohol does to a person, but it makes them unable to recognize the fact. They denounce the repetitive simplicity of the prophet's teaching, clearly wanting something more nuanced and ambiguous as befits their supposedly sophisticated understanding.[2]

---

2. The meaning of the Heb. is a matter of debate. It is *saw lasaw, saw lasaw, qaw laqaw, qaw laqaw*. Some of the suggestions are that they are a meaningless babble, part of a device to teach the Heb. alphabet, or baby talk used by parents when teaching a child to walk. The NIV is based on the idea that *saw* is a shortened form of *miswah*, "commandment," and *qaw* is the word for "measuring line" or rule (see v. 17). See Oswalt, *Isaiah 1–39*, 512, n. 36, for a fuller discussion of the alternatives.

The prophet responds in 28:11–13 by saying that since this is what they think they are getting, it is exactly what they *will* get, only from other lips than his. Since they refuse God's invitation to rest in him by abandoning their petty pride and demeaning pleasures, they will learn his truth through "foreign lips and strange tongues." In other words, the Assyrians will teach them that what the prophet said is true. Then the demands of the conquerors will *really* be repetitively simple. If the people will not learn the easy way of faith, then they must learn the hard way of experience: "They will go and fall backward" (28:13).

A Message to the Leaders in Jerusalem (28:14–22)

THE FOCUS NOW shifts to the leaders in Jerusalem. With the opening "therefore" the prophet calls them to pay attention to what has been said to the northern leaders and perhaps learn something from his message to them. Judgment is imminent in the north, and it is not at all clear that they will escape it in the south. If they continue in their present ways, they will not escape. It is unclear whether 28:15 represents an actual quote from the Judean leaders or a sarcastic restatement of their words by the prophet. I tend to think the latter because it is hard for me to imagine that people would actually say they have made a lie their refuge.

"Scoffers" (28:14) is perhaps the most serious Old Testament epithet Isaiah could apply to these leaders. A "scoffer" is someone who not only rejects the truth but also makes light of it.[3] Like the leaders in the north, these Judean scoffers have laughed at the foolishness of trusting God and have made their cynical covenants "with death." Probably this is a reference to an alliance with Egypt.[4] They believe that it will guarantee life for them and their nation when Assyria, "the overwhelming scourge," comes. In fact, Isaiah says, their covenant is going to bring the very opposite—death.[5] They have allied themselves with a "lie," the idea that human power is a better means of protecting oneself than God's power.

God's response to the "covenant of death" appears in 28:16–19b. He begins by asserting once again that he alone is trustworthy. The "tested stone" (v. 16) is the opposite of the "lie" on which the leaders have built their "refuge" (v. 17). Its measurements are the "justice" and "righteousness" of

---

3. See Prov. 1:22; 29:8. See also "mockers" in Ps. 1:1; Prov. 21:24; 22:10; Isa. 29:20.

4. It is also possible that this refers to the Canaanite god Mot, "Death," suggesting that the leaders have entered into some sort of a contract with Death to protect them from his scourge.

5. The prophet may also be alluding to the importance of Osiris, the underworld deity, in Egyptian religion.

God, and it can stand whatever shocks might come to it. Anyone who builds on it "will never be dismayed"; that is, they can be calm and deliberate, experiencing the "repose" promised in verse 12. The "stone" is probably to be understood as an agglomeration of all the elements of God's trustworthiness. When any other trust is measured against him, its faultiness becomes apparent at once, as is the case with the "covenant with death" (v. 18).

In 28:17c–19b God declares that the "hiding place" the leaders have so craftily built is going to be swept away like a hut in a windstorm. Far from being safe from the "overwhelming scourge" (v. 15), they are going to be totally swept away by it (v. 18). The foolish attempt of these Jerusalem leaders to protect themselves from it will actually make it the more dangerous to them. Moreover, the flood will not come just once but again and again ("morning by morning"). This is an accurate reflection of the Assyrian tactics, as they came back to an area again and again until it was completely destroyed.

Isaiah 28:19c–22 give us the prophet's reflection on the Lord's words. Anyone who truly understands this message should be terrorized by it, for there will be no place to hide. Verse 20 is perhaps a popular proverb expressing this idea. The Egyptian alliance will not be big enough to do them any good when God sets to work. And that is just the point, for it is not Assyria that is the "overwhelming scourge" (28:15, 18); rather, it is the Lord. He is the One with whom the scoffers have to do, and he is a far more serious enemy than even Assyria.

Just as the Lord struck down the Philistines with a flood at "Mount Perazim" (28:21; cf. 2 Sam. 5:20) and scattered the Canaanites with hail in the "Valley of Gibeon" (Isa. 28:21; cf. Josh. 10:11), so now he will treat his own people like those enemies (cf. Isa. 1:24). Because of that, it will be "a strange work" (28:21). But it will be a necessary one if there is to be any hope of redemption for the people. Thus, the scoffers had better "stop [their] mocking" (28:22) of the word of God and had better start listening to what "the Lord, the LORD Almighty" (lit., "the Lord, Yahweh of heaven's armies") is actually saying.

Illustration from the World of Agriculture (28:23–29)

ONCE AGAIN, ISAIAH closes his message with a graphic illustration. He has been talking about the word of God, to which the scoffers and drunkards refuse to listen. He has been saying that there is a set of simple cause-and-effect principles that rule the spiritual world, which if they are flouted will result in disaster. In these verses the prophet seeks to illustrate his point from the world of agriculture.

The least-educated farmer knows that there are some things you do and some things you don't. "Listen and hear my voice" (28:23) has overtones of wisdom literature, with which the royal counselors would be familiar. Also, the comparison of one activity, royal counsel, with another, farming, is characteristic of wisdom literature. A farmer knows that there are certain appropriate ways to do things. He does not keep on plowing forever, as though that were an end in itself. When he plants, he does not mix up all the different seeds together. Each has to be grown separately. When he threshes, he uses appropriate tools to the size of the grain involved. To use a heavy threshing sledge or a stone roller on the tiny "caraway" and "cummin" seeds would crush them to dust. Instead, he uses a jointed "stick" called a "flail" in English. Neither does one use a threshing sledge to grind up the grain for flour. There are other tools for that.

In each of these cases, Isaiah says these peasants have learned these principles from God, the Creator. His natural revelation has taught them how life works. Why cannot these wise counselors, who have the benefit of both natural and special revelation, be as intelligent as an uneducated peasant when it comes to understanding that God can be trusted and humans cannot?

 SAMARIA THE WREATH. As mentioned above, Samaria sat on a hilltop at the head of a fairly broad valley that sloped gently up from the Mediterranean coastal plain. With its crenelated walls ringing the hilltop, it looked like the wreath worn by victors or revelers. When Omri, king of Israel, moved his capital there from Tirzah, a much more secluded interior site, he was expressing in a physical way that the northern kingdom had "come of age." They no longer needed to be worried about their security, and they were no longer to be an isolated, parochial state. They would take their place in world affairs, because just at the foot of Samaria's valley, about ten miles away from the city, ran the great international highway connecting Egypt and Mesopotamia.

Under Omri's son Ahab, the city's glory grew. Amos mentions (Amos 6:4) the people of Samaria stretching themselves out on couches inlaid with ivory, and archaeological discoveries from the time of Ahab have shown fine inlaid ivory work in the city. The wealth and beauty of Samaria were clearly a source of pride for the people of the northern kingdom. But Isaiah says that that beautiful "wreath" will be thrown down to the ground, as indeed it was by the Assyrian kings Shalmanezer and Sargon in 722/721 B.C. Although Herod the Great rebuilt it, naming the new city Sebaste, it never regained the glory of the Israelite period; it is abandoned today.

Ephraim. The two dominant tribes in the northern kingdom were Ephraim and Manasseh. Although Manasseh was initially given a much larger share of land than Ephraim, Ephraim's was almost entirely in the hill country and was more easily conquered from the Canaanites than Manasseh's. This may explain why Ephraim was generally the more influential of the two and why it is frequently used in the Bible as a synonym for the entire northern kingdom. Its territory extended from about six miles north of Jerusalem to the foot of Mount Gerizim, about eighteen miles, and from the top of the Jordan Valley on the East to the coastal plain on the west, about twenty-five miles. Even though Samaria was actually located in the territory of Manasseh, it is referred to as the capital of Ephraim in Isaiah 7:9 (see also 9:9; Hos. 7:1; Obad. 19).

Foreign lips. Although almost all the languages spoken in the ancient Near East were in the Semitic family (with the exceptions of Egyptian and Hittite), they were enough different from each other that they were unintelligible to native speakers of one language who had not made a specific study of the other language. This would be analogous to French, Spanish, and Italian today (all rooted in Latin). The result is that even though the Assyrian language shares much of the same phonetic structure as Hebrew and even some of the same vocabulary, it would still sound like gibberish to the average Israelite.

To bridge the language problem in its empire, Assyria promoted the use of Aramaic, the language of Syria, as a common language.[6] This may have been both for geographic and linguistic reasons. Geographically, Syria lay close to the midpoint of the empire, and linguistically Aramaic lies somewhat between two of the main branches of the Semitic system, Eastern and Northwestern.

Farming. In the narrow valleys of the Judean and Ephraimite hill country, farming was generally a subsistence affair. People lived in villages and then walked out to their plots of ground. The plow was usually a metal-pointed stick, pulled by oxen if one was rich or by another human if one was poor. This broke up the earth to a depth of three or four inches. Then the clods were broken up with a harrow, a framework of logs with metal spikes driven down through them, again pulled by animals or humans. The fields were divided into smaller plots, sometimes separated from each other by hedges of thorns or just by pathways.

The chief grain crops were wheat and barley, with the finer condiment grains of caraway and cummin grown in smaller, separate areas. At harvest

---

6. Note that the embassy from Hezekiah asked the Assyrian representative to make his demand for surrender in Aramaic (36:11), but the speaker insisted on using Hebrew so the common people could understand the threat.

time the grains were cut with wooden sickles having metal or stone teeth set in them. The grain was then piled in heaps in a flat open area, where heavy threshing sledges or stone rollers could be pulled around and around on top of the heap until the kernels of grain had been separated from the straw and chaff. Then on a windy day, the whole mass was tossed in the air with baskets or with basket-shaped winnowing forks. The chaff would be blown away and the heavier grain would fall back to the ground to be gathered up and stored. The finer seeds would be separated from the straw and chaff with a jointed stick before being winnowed.

ALCOHOL. This chapter highlights the problem of alcohol. After the failed experiment of Prohibition, to which the American church gave so much of its energies, the church has become almost silent on the subject of alcohol. Part of this may be due to the increasing sophistication of young evangelicals, the impression successfully promoted by the media and the alcohol industry that drinking is sophisticated, and the notion that binge drinking is fun and funny. Today in America, despite all the attention given to drug abuse, addiction to alcohol is an even more serious problem. While it may be true that alcoholism has a genetic basis, it is also true that one can never become an alcoholic if one never begins drinking alcohol in the first place.

In the ancient Near East, with the problem of water contamination and the difficulty of procuring water in many places, wine and beer were often necessities, both for water purification and as a water substitute. Today, that is not an issue. We have clean water available in abundance, and there is no good reason to drink alcohol. Instead, it is seen today as a recreational drink. But it is recreation that comes at a terrible price. Despite the imposition of "zero tolerance" for drunk-driving offenses and the worthwhile efforts of Mothers Against Drunk Driving, deaths from driving while under the influence continue to mount. One state policeman told me that if drunk driving were eliminated, more than 50 percent of highway fatalities would be prevented.

We in the church need to renew our stand against the drinking of alcohol. Total abstinence is now regarded as some sort of fringe radicalism. We need to assert again that abstinence is a wise and reasonable course, one that will lead to health and well-being. Of course, it is possible to use alcohol in moderate ways, but why should it be necessary for the Christian? Some assert that it is a way of showing Christian freedom. But why should freedom be shown in a potentially destructive way? Why not show our freedom by demonstrating that artificial stimulation is not necessary, that it is possible to relax and have a good time without taking a substance into our bodies that lowers God-given inhibitions and provides unnecessary calories? At the least, we must reopen the discussion in the church and face the crisis in a biblical way. We must also do everything we can to help raise the awareness of this threat for our young people before an increasingly hedonistic culture carries them off.

The simplicity of the gospel. One of the charges that the drunken leaders of Israel and Judah lodged against Isaiah was that he was treating them like children. He was saying such simple things to them. We get a sense of that in the story of Naaman, the Syrian general, and Elisha (2 Kings 5:1–14). Naaman wanted some mysterious rituals performed on him for healing; he did not want to do something as simple as dipping himself in the Jordan.

This was also the case with the early preachers of the gospel of Christ. When we look at the sermons the apostles preached in the book of Acts, we see models of simplicity and clarity (cf. Acts 2:14–36; 17:22–31). Certainly the messages have been abridged and condensed, but still there is little that smacks of erudition and intellectual complexity. The reason for this is obvious. While Christian theology has provided more than its share of intellectual complexity, the central core of its truth is simple. Nowhere is this more obvious than in the so-called "plan of salvation." In five simple statements taken from Scripture, the essentials can all be laid out:

1. All humans are estranged from God by their sin. "For all have sinned and fall short of the glory of God" (Rom. 3:23).
2. The result of sin is eternal death, but that is not God's desire. "For the wages of sin is death, but the gift of God is eternal life in Christ Jesus our Lord" (Rom. 6:23).
3. We may receive God's gift of eternal life by faith. "For it is by grace you have been saved, through faith—and this not from yourselves, it is the gift of God—not by works, so that no one can boast" (Eph. 2:8–9).
4. We exercise faith by repenting from our sins and accepting what Christ has done for us. "If we confess our sins, he is faithful and just and will forgive us our sins and purify us from all unrighteousness" (1 John 1:9); "if you confess with your mouth 'Jesus is Lord,' and believe in your heart that God raised him from the dead, you will be saved. For it is with your heart that you believe and are justified, and it is with your mouth that you confess and are saved" (Rom. 10:9–10).
5. We are enabled to live a new life of victory over sin. "Therefore, if anyone is in Christ, he is a new creation; the old has gone, the new

has come" (2 Cor. 5:17); "for we know that our old self was crucified with him so that the body of sin might be done away with, that we should no longer be slaves to sin" (Rom. 6:6).

All of this is "a stumbling-block to Jews and foolishness to Gentiles" (1 Cor. 1:23). That is, to those who insist on justifying themselves before God by their own spiritual achievements, this simple message is offensive because it says they are sinful and cannot solve the problem for themselves. Undoubtedly, this was the same reaction the leaders of Israel and Judah had to Isaiah: "How dare you say we are sinful by indulging ourselves a little (hic) and by trying to work out sensible arrangements with our neighbors instead of doing a perfectly foolish thing like trusting in God. Who do you think we are, children?"

The message of the gospel was "foolishness" to the educated Gentiles, who were also trying to save themselves by their own efforts—in the case of the Corinthians, by intellectual prowess. They had imagined an evil world that was the result of a succession of creators, each a bit more corrupt than the last. Thus, to get to the "Good," the real originator of the world, it was necessary to work one's way up through the angelic "creators" with a whole host of passwords and special rubrics. This deliciously complex intellectual structure gave endless fascination. It also was a way of separating the true elite from the raw crowd. Only the select few could master this system and demonstrate a true mastery of the spirit over the evil body.[7] What foolishness the gospel of Christ seemed to the Greek intellectuals. How hard it was to accept that all the arduous study of arcane knowledge did not put them ahead of the ditch-digger, who knew nothing but the cross of Christ. Furthermore, to believe that one could somehow be identified with Christ in his death and that that was more important than intellectual attainment was plain foolishness!

This idea—salvation by one's own effort, either in spiritual activity or in intellectual accomplishments—is a continual alternative to the simplicity of the Christian message. We must constantly be on guard against it. We must reiterate the message and make plain just how it flies in the face of the world's wisdom. This is what Paul says he decided to do when he arrived in Corinth:

> Where is the wise man? Where is the scholar? Where is the philosopher of this age? Has not God made foolish the wisdom of the world? For since in the wisdom of God the world through its wisdom did not know him, God was pleased through the foolishness of what was preached to save those who believe.... For I was resolved to know nothing while I was with you except Jesus Christ and him crucified. (1 Cor. 1:20–21; 2:2)

---

7. See K. Rudolf, "Gnosticism," *ABD*, 2:1033–40.

If this brings the scorn of the world on us, so be it. But the simplicity of the Cross is also the power of the Cross. Just as Isaiah's simple message was the one that has endured across the centuries, so it is the message of the Cross that will endure, when all the sophisticated (and often debauched) alternatives to it have expired. Isaiah expresses this enduring quality with his language of the "tested stone," the "cornerstone." A building can only stand straight and true if it is on a proper foundation. The New Testament writers understood Isaiah as referring here to the Incarnation (Rom. 9:33; 10:11; 1 Peter 2:6). In Jesus Christ, God has forever demonstrated his love, his trustworthiness, his saving righteousness, and his justice.

The nature of God's requirements. When Isaiah appealed to the practices of the farmer, he was making a profound point, namely, that the Creator has made the world according to certain principles that can be discovered without a great deal of effort. The uneducated peasant has been taught these principles by God. We may argue that God had nothing to do with such principles; they are simply common sense. But Isaiah would answer, "Where do you think common sense came from? Did you create it?" Naturally, the answer to that question is no. In other words, as we live in the world and observe its causes and effects, we learn that certain things are so. We may not know why they are so, but we can see that they are. If you thresh caraway with a stone roller, you will crush the tiny seeds. Why is it that way? Well, it just is.

This point is just as distasteful today as it was in Isaiah's day. There are spiritual principles that are as simple and ironclad as physical ones. The pagans of Isaiah's day had observed these and had written them into their civil law codes. They knew that no human society could survive where lying, stealing, murder, and adultery occurred with any regularity. The pagan cultures, with no real concept of transcendence and thus no true doctrine of creation, could not explain it, but they recognized it to be so. Thus, such behaviors were forbidden in all the legal codes of the ancient Near East. It waited until biblical revelation for the explanation to be made clear.

The Creator is a God of truth, integrity, love, and faithfulness, and thus his creation reflects that character. The Sinai covenant shows that living according to the standards of truth, integrity, love, and faithfulness is not simply a utilitarian choice but is an act of glad submission to the Creator. This is why Moses could say:

> And now, O Israel, what does the LORD your God ask of you but to fear the LORD your God, to walk in all his ways, to love him, to serve the LORD your God with all your heart and with all your soul, and to observe the LORD's commands and decrees that I am giving you today for your own good? (Deut. 10:12–13)

In other words, obedience to the covenant did not require some strange, occult activities outside of human experience. It involved nothing other than living out the lifestyle that others had discovered before them, but doing it for the sake of the love of God.

Modern legal theory is deeply opposed to the idea of "natural law." We are passionately committed to the idea that we can make up laws of human and social behavior as we go and that these laws are nothing but our own creations. To admit that we cannot do so is to admit that we are not ultimate in the world, and that we will not permit. Isaiah would merely shake his head and point to the farmer. Are there "natural laws" in nature? he would ask. If so, why would we think there are none in the rest of the natural world, that is, the world of the spirit?

Isaiah 29:1–14

¹WOE TO YOU, Ariel, Ariel,
    the city where David settled!
  Add year to year
    and let your cycle of festivals go on.
²Yet I will besiege Ariel;
    she will mourn and lament,
    she will be to me like an altar hearth.
³I will encamp against you all around;
    I will encircle you with towers
    and set up my siege works against you.
⁴Brought low, you will speak from the ground;
    your speech will mumble out of the dust.
  Your voice will come ghostlike from the earth;
    out of the dust your speech will whisper.

⁵But your many enemies will become like fine dust,
    the ruthless hordes like blown chaff.
  Suddenly, in an instant,
⁶   the LORD Almighty will come
  with thunder and earthquake and great noise,
    with windstorm and tempest and flames of a devouring fire.
⁷Then the hordes of all the nations that fight against Ariel,
    that attack her and her fortress and besiege her,
  will be as it is with a dream,
    with a vision in the night—
⁹as when a hungry man dreams that he is eating,
    but he awakens, and his hunger remains;
  as when a thirsty man dreams that he is drinking,
    but he awakens faint, with his thirst unquenched.
  So will it be with the hordes of all the nations
    that fight against Mount Zion.

⁹Be stunned and amazed,
    blind yourselves and be sightless;
  be drunk, but not from wine,
    stagger, but not from beer.
¹⁰The LORD has brought over you a deep sleep:
    He has sealed your eyes (the prophets);
    he has covered your heads (the seers).

¹¹For you this whole vision is nothing but words sealed in a scroll. And if you give the scroll to someone who can read, and say to him, "Read this, please," he will answer, "I can't; it is sealed." ¹²Or if you give the scroll to someone who cannot read, and say, "Read this, please," he will answer, "I don't know how to read."

¹³The Lord says:

"These people come near to me with their mouth
    and honor me with their lips,
    but their hearts are far from me.
Their worship of me
    is made up only of rules taught by men.
¹⁴Therefore once more I will astound these people
    with wonder upon wonder;
the wisdom of the wise will perish,
    the intelligence of the intelligent will vanish."

THIS SECOND "WOE" is addressed to Jerusalem, as is apparent from its being called "the city where David settled" (29:1). However, it is also called "Ariel," and the explanation of this word is not given. One possible meaning of the word is "altar hearth," which is the most probable explanation (so NIV, 29:2; see Ezek. 43:15). This would fit in with the general emphasis of the passage on the cultic activity that took place at Jerusalem (29:1, 13).

A second matter of scholarly debate is the presence of a sizeable section of promise (29:5–8) in what seems on the surface to be a judgment oracle. Many scholars believe these verses to be a later insertion.[1] However, this presupposes that the original book was only words of judgment. Yet one of the central themes of Isaiah as it now exists (see the introduction) is the interplay of hope and judgment. To suggest that this entire interplay is secondary, imposed on whatever the original book may have been, is asserting too much.[2] Here, as we have seen so many times before in the book, we

---

1. See, e.g., Clements, *Isaiah 1–39*, 236–37.

2. Childs, *Isaiah*, 215–17, appears to argue for the unity of the material, but he does not make it clear exactly how or when it received this unified form. Presumably, since he accepts the scholarly consensus of a long editorial process that brought the book to its present form, there were preexisting pieces of material that have now been combined into a "unity." If that is his position, I do not believe his attempt to save the literary unity of this

have the movement from judgment (29:1–4) to hope (29:5–8) and back to judgment again (29:9–14). Judgment is not final, hope is. But the reality of the coming hope must not divert the hearers from the reality that apart from genuine repentance, judgment is the inescapable route to hope.

As in Isaiah 1, Jerusalem's problem is that they believe they have immunity from judgment because they have the true cult of Yahweh (29:1, 13). But as there, Isaiah says this worship is worthless because it is not from the heart (29:13). He even goes so far as to say that what they are doing is not revealed but is made up by men. That must have been shocking in view of the pre-scriptions for worship in the Torah. Probably his point is that since their "hearts" are not devoted to God, all they are really responding to is human demands; they are not really worshiping. Therefore, Jerusalem is no more immune from destruction than Samaria. The fact that they are not officially worshiping idols hardly enters into the equation. They too are trying to manipulate God with cultic activity, not worshiping as an expression of covenant love.

Verse 2 suggests that all of Jerusalem will become an altar hearth on which the people themselves will become the sacrifice. Like the Canaanites, whose persistent sinning meant that in the end they were "devoted" (Josh. 6:17) to the Lord as an offering by the Israelites, the Israelites themselves will be on the altar. We must either accept God's substitute with genuine repentance and faith or become the sacrifice ourselves. Note that there is no mention of Assyria here; God is the enemy who besieges the city (Isa. 29:3).

Verse 4 is perhaps an allusion to the worship of the dead and to spiritism (see 8:19; also comments on 28:1–29). While priding themselves on their pure worship, the people of Jerusalem and Judah are secretly engaging in many pagan practices. Ezekiel's vision of what was taking place in the tem-ple in his own day (Ezek. 8–9), some 125 years later than Isaiah, argues that similar practices were going on for some time. Like the mediums and spiri-tists, the captives of Judah will be mumbling and whispering as they lie in the "dust" beneath the tyrant's boot.

But because it is God, not Assyria, who puts his people into the dust, it is also God who can make Jerusalem's enemies as insubstantial as "fine dust" (29:5). If Assyria had devastated God's land against his wishes, God would be unable to deliver his people. But as it is, he can deliver them whenever he chooses and can blow the mighty nations away like so much "chaff." In fact, before God that is all the great nations are. They appear so weighty and ter-rifying, but before God they are as thin and as vaporous as a "dream" (29:7;

---

passage, or of the book as a whole, succeeds. If the final form of the text results in a dif-ferent intent from that of the original author(s), then we must bear both those differing intents in mind when we interpret the material.

see also 40:15–17). The nations think that they can devour Jerusalem and wipe her off the face of the earth. But that is only a dream on their part (29:8). Little do they know that Jerusalem will be drawing pilgrims from all over the earth thousands of years after the capitals of those nations have ceased to exist.

But the tragic reality is that all of this is as unintelligible to the Judeans as it is to the Assyrians (and later to the Babylonians). They are all equally "blind" (29:9) to the reality of the Lord's work. In verses 9–10 the interplay of causation is significant. The people have blinded themselves, yet at the same time God has made the prophets unable to see the truth. We may endlessly debate which of these comes first, but the fact is that nothing happens apart from both those causes. As a result, the word of God ("this whole vision") is a closed book to God's people (29:11–12). From God's side it is sealed up and cannot be opened; from the human side, it cannot be read when it is opened.

Consequently, Jerusalem's religion has become only a performance with themselves as the audience. There is no real connection between the worshipers and the One being worshiped. They go through the motions with no expectation of any real encounter with the living God. Their religion has lost all sense of wonder. So God says he *will* encounter them with wonders (29:14), but the clear implication is that it will be the wonder of the God they thought they had under their control suddenly bursting forth to become their enemy (cf. 28:21). All the "wisdom" of the counselors and leaders who urge reliance on Egypt will be proven false.

VERSE 3 DESCRIBES siege warfare. In the days before the invention of gunpowder, there was no sure way to break into a walled city. In most cases, apart from treachery inside the city, there was no alternative to a long siege. The besieging army encircled the city with armed camps. Sometimes they actually built a wall around the city outside of its own walls, in order to be sure that no one could get out or in to bring supplies or arms of any sort into the city. Moreover, to try to shorten the time of the siege, attempts would be made to break into the city. Because the cities were usually built high atop natural hills or on mounds of debris from previous destructions, it was necessary to build ramps of earth up which battering rams ("siege machines") could be pushed to try to breach the walls.

Another device used was prefabricated "towers," which could be moved up the ramps quickly and erected against the walls. Attackers on these towers could prevent defenders from attacking those operating the battering rams, and they could also use the towers as a means to get over the walls and down into the city. To make the same point today, God might say that he will bring his helicopter gunships, his main battle tanks, and his ballistic missiles against us. It is a terrible thing to have the God you think is your "rabbit's foot" turn out to be the main armament arrayed against you.

TRUE WORSHIP. Since Hebrew worship was similar in form to that of the pagans, it was easy for the Hebrews to fall into a pagan understanding, namely, that because certain human activities have been performed, the gods must do certain things. This rests on the worldview of continuity, which holds that the human, divine, and natural realms are continuous, so that what takes place in one realm is duplicated in the others. Thus, the attitude of the worshiper's heart has no real effect on the efficacy of the ritual performed. The key is to do the ritual correctly so that the maximum linkage with the divine world can be maintained. The result is that the activity has much more to do with manipulation than with worship. Because I have given God a very expensive gift, he is obligated to bless me; or because the lamb and I have become continuous through the ritual, God thinks I have died and will not punish me for my sins anymore.

Again and again the Old Testament speaks out against such an idea. God is transcendent; that is, he is radically discontinuous from this world. Thus, he cannot be manipulated through anything done in this world. He forgives through his grace alone because of the death of Christ, and the giving of a lamb is only a symbol of true repentance and faith. Apart from these, offering a lamb is worse than useless. Isaiah says such an offerer might as well break the neck of a dog and offer it to God (66:3). No place is this truth stated more plainly than in Psalm 51:16–17:

> You do not delight in sacrifice, or I would bring it;
>> you do not take pleasure in burnt offerings.
> The sacrifices of God are a broken spirit;
>> a broken and contrite heart,
>> O God, you will not despise.

Although we today no longer offer blood sacrifices, we run the same danger as the people in Old Testament times. That is, because we have performed certain religious activities, we believe God must do our will. We have prayed long and fervently; therefore, God must heal our child. We have gone to church every Sunday for months; therefore, God must give us a good job. We have read the Bible and prayed every day for weeks; therefore, God must lift our depression. These are not acts of worship but attempts at manipulation. We do not want God in our lives; we want what he can do for us.

But worship is not utilitarian; rather, it is a free expression of praise and thanks. By graciously freeing us from the condemnation of our sin and making it possible to live a life of holiness, God has already done many times more than we can ever deserve. Of course, he wants to bless us even further, but all too often our attempts to use him, while still maintaining control of our lives, only serve to block the very blessing he wants to give.

Hearing the Word of God. Verses 10–12 speak of a situation where the Word of God is unintelligible to a person, defining a dual responsibility for that situation. On the one hand, God has blinded the eyes of the prophets—the scroll "is sealed." On the other hand, it is a human problem—"I don't know how to read."

The same situation applies today. First there is a spiritual problem. In Isaiah's time, the prophets did not want to hear God's Word. Instead, they wanted some encouraging omen to give to the king or in order to get paid a handsome fee. So God blinded their spiritual eyes and took his Word away from them. Similarly, if we try to read the Bible just for intellectual enrichment without first surrendering ourselves to its ultimate author to do what he says, we will find it a closed book. It will be as dry as dust and just as boring. Note Paul's words: "The sinful mind is hostile to God. It does not submit to God's law, nor can it do so" (Rom. 8:7). But if we have fallen in love with the Author and long to know him better, it is amazing how the Scriptures open up. The story of a new convert to Christ suddenly discovering how marvelous the Bible is can be multiplied thousands of times.

But there is also a human component in the reading process. Unless we have prepared ourselves to read, we may miss volumes of what God is trying to say to us. This story is also multiplied: After some months of reading the Bible, the new convert still finds great joy in it but begins to discover more and more that he or she does not understand. What is the problem? It is that the Bible was not just dropped from heaven. Rather, God's Word has come to us through specific people who lived in specific times and places and used language in certain ways. Just as we need to learn about a new person we meet if we are really to understand what he or she is saying, so we need to prepare ourselves to understand the Bible. We need to learn about the backgrounds and settings of the biblical writers, and we need to learn how they used language.

If we learn a basic method of Bible study and purchase a small library of Bible reference tools (many now available in electronic form), we will have fulfilled our side of the equation. If the Holy Spirit unseals the book to our regenerated hearts and if we have trained ourselves to read it, it will be an unending source of life and truth. If not, it will be a sealed scroll that we cannot read, and destruction will come on us all the more unawares.

Isaiah 29:15–24

❦

¹⁵ WOE TO THOSE who go to great depths
    to hide their plans from the LORD,
who do their work in darkness and think,
    "Who sees us? Who will know?"
¹⁶ You turn things upside down,
    as if the potter were thought to be like the clay!
Shall what is formed say to him who formed it,
    "He did not make me"?
Can the pot say of the potter,
    "He knows nothing"?

¹⁷ In a very short time, will not Lebanon be turned into a
        fertile field
    and the fertile field seem like a forest?
¹⁸ In that day the deaf will hear the words of the scroll,
    and out of gloom and darkness
    the eyes of the blind will see.
¹⁹ Once more the humble will rejoice in the LORD;
    the needy will rejoice in the Holy One of Israel.
²⁰ The ruthless will vanish,
    the mockers will disappear,
    and all who have an eye for evil will be cut down—
²¹ those who with a word make a man out to be guilty,
    who ensnare the defender in court
    and with false testimony deprive the innocent of justice.

²²Therefore this is what the LORD, who redeemed Abraham,
says to the house of Jacob:

    "No longer will Jacob be ashamed;
        no longer will their faces grow pale.
    ²³ When they see among them their children,
        the work of my hands,
    they will keep my name holy;
        they will acknowledge the holiness of the Holy One
            of Jacob,
        and will stand in awe of the God of Israel.
    ²⁴ Those who are wayward in spirit will gain understanding;
        those who complain will accept instruction."

THIS THIRD "WOE" is like the second (29:1–14) in that it is composed of both judgment (29:15–16) and hope (29:17–24). If we think about the situation, we can imagine why the promises of future redemption are necessary to the prophet's argument. He is calling on the Judeans to "wait" (see 30:15–18) for God's deliverance and not to rush off to Egypt for help, as the royal counselors are urging. Their counsel is foolish because it is unnecessary. God can be trusted to deliver his people. Indeed, the deliverance is assured, either on this side of judgment if there is genuine repentance and trust, or on the other side, if trust is refused. God is trustworthy.

The first and second woes were more general, aimed at the leadership at large. The fourth and fifth (31:1–9; 33:1–6) are more specific, focusing particularly on the counsel to trust Egypt. This third one is transitional, speaking not so much of the content of the counsel as its manner. The prophet accuses the counselors of trying to hide their counsel. In trying to hide their plans "from the LORD," they are probably trying to hide it from his prophet. Undoubtedly, by this time Isaiah's (and the Lord's) position on placing trust in human nations is well known.

Nevertheless, the royal counselors, spiritually blind as they are, have made up their minds that an alliance with Egypt is what is needed. They have made their "plans" secretly, without consulting the Lord's prophet, foolishly hoping he will not find out. False hope! Isaiah says this is like the pot telling the potter how to do his work (29:16). They have things "upside down." It is the Maker who determines how a thing is made and not the other way around.

The promises made in 29:17–24 are more far-reaching than for mere physical restoration. They deal primarily with the spiritual needs of the nation. They promise a day when the kinds of attitudes and behaviors that have brought the nation to this dark day will be radically changed. In this regard, they are like the promises associated with the coming of the Spirit in 32:15–17. As there, the nation is seen as a spiritual desert that is transformed into a lush, "fertile field" (29:17). The progression there from desert to field to forest suggests that "Lebanon" here refers to the barren tops of the Lebanon mountain range, where nothing could grow. In that coming day, the "blind" and "deaf" (cf. 6:9–10) will see and hear.

The reference to the "scroll" (29:18) connects the thought back to 29:11–12. No longer will the Word of God be closed to God's people. Verses 19–21 deal with the social results of this restored sensitivity to God's leading and will. Those who are usually oppressed (the "humble" and the "needy") will be rejoicing in "the Holy One of Israel" (the sovereign Redeemer) because all the oppressors (the "ruthless," the "mockers," and those looking for a chance to do "evil") will be "cut down." Verse 21 identifies the oppression as judicial oppression, where the machinery that should be used specifically to protect the helpless is turned around to crush them. That kind of reversal is especially despicable to God (cf. Prov. 28:21; Amos 5:10, 12).

Isaiah 29:22–24 gives the results of all of this, as signaled by the opening "therefore." Gracious redemption will result in holy living and a transformed attitude towards God's truth. Redemption is expressed in a figure that appears frequently in the last section of the book: many children (cf. 54:2–3; 66:7–11). God will not allow his promises to Abraham to fail. The nation will not be wiped out. Furthermore, a day will come when the nation can hold up its head in joy, as God delivers her. Gone will be the shame of defeat. In response to that deliverance, there will be a new willingness to live God's life.

This is, of course, covenant language. Those who are in covenant with God are committed to replicating God's holy character, his "name" (29:23), in their own behavior. Their defeat and exile have profaned God's name (Ezek. 36:20), but God promises that he will make them able to demonstrate his holiness. The continuity of the promises from Abraham (Isa. 29:22) through Jacob (29:23) and on up to Isaiah's own day is emphasized by the variation in the typical title from "the Holy One of Israel" to the more personal "the Holy One of Jacob." No longer will the descendants of Jacob take "the Holy One" for granted, but they will tremble before him (NIV "stand in awe of").[1] The upshot of this will be a new sensitivity to the Word and will of God. Instead of the stubbornness, willfulness, and general hardheadedness that tend to characterize all humans, not just Israel, there will be a grasp of "understanding" and a genuine teachability.

Bridging Contexts

THE JEWS. The promise that "when they see . . . their children," the people of Israel will "keep my name holy" (29:23) sounds strange to us in a day of population explosion and concern about overcrowding of the planet. But in biblical times, as up until the last century, child mortality was high. Only a small percentage of children lived past age ten. When such a high child mortality rate was coupled with famine and warfare, it was possible for a people to simply cease to exist. We can look at the Mayan civilization in this hemisphere or the Ankor Wat people in

---

1. The Heb. word is *'araṣ*, "to be in dread of, be terrified," a stronger word than the typical *yara'*, "to fear."

Myanmar as examples of this. God here promises that he will not let that happen to Israel. Their children will live and multiply. Those children will be sources of labor for the family and a guarantee of care for the parents in their old age. As a result, Israel will survive as a people.

We can look around us and see that promise fulfilled today. How is it that the Jewish people still exist after thousands of years of hatred and unjust treatment? There are no satisfactory human answers to that question. By all the evidence, they should have ceased to exist long ago. But God has promised, and his promises do not fail!

Israel's legal system. In the NIV, Isaiah 29:21 speaks of "the defender in court." The Hebrew is "the one who seeks justice in the gate." So far as we know, there was no organized legal system in Israel such as we know today. "Judges" were more those who demonstrated and enforced God's rule in the world than those who interpreted and enforced a written code of laws. That task seems to have fallen to the priests (cf. Num. 5:30; Jer. 18:18; Mal. 2:7). In matters of civil law, it was the "elders," many of whom may have been old men retired from active life, who seem to have been given the responsibility to see that justice was done (cf. Ruth 4:1−12). These old men could most easily be found sitting in the main city gate.

These "gates" were actually multichambered gatehouses. In and around these gatehouses much of the activity of the city took place. The old men could sit in the shade inside the gatehouse and observe with interest the bustle around them. A person seeking redress for some injustice could come here seeking support for his case from the elders. Although there is no evidence that the decision of the elders was legally enforceable, it is clear their opinion carried great social weight. Someone who flaunted them could find himself unable to do any more business in the town. Sadly, this verse and others like it suggest that then, as now, the system could be "bought" and that the elders' opinions were not always impartial. To the God whose judgments are impartial, that situation is intolerable.

FROM THE BEGINNING of time we as human beings have been trying to hide our real intents and feelings from God. We remember Adam and Eve hiding in their sin in the garden, as though God would not know where they were (Gen. 3:8). We remember Jacob hiding under a cloud of arrogance and self-sufficiency when God found him asleep in the desert (Gen. 28:16−17). We remember the disciples hiding their fear and uncertainty with a step back into the old life on a fishing expedition on the sea of Galilee (John 21:2−3).

Of course, God always finds us. He is our Maker, so he knows exactly how his pots are made (see Jer. 18:1–17; Rom. 9:20–21; 15:21). He finds the disobedient, he finds the proud, he finds the fearful. He does not exist for us, but we for him, so we cannot turn him off at will. How foolish, then, not to bring our plans to him for his approval and correction. Or better yet, why not come to him to find out what his plans are for us? After all, he made us for a purpose, so perhaps it would be a good idea to try to find out that purpose.

Sometimes he gives us a long view, as he did with Isaiah and the Messiah. Sometimes he will unfold a life-calling in a moment. But equally often, it is simply the next step, which if we will follow leads to the next step and the next step until finally we come to some hilltop. We can then look back with wonder at the way he has led us. How sad when we stop our ears and say to our Maker, "You don't know what's best for me! I do, though, so I won't listen to you." How much better to say with Paul, "But my life is worth nothing unless I use it for doing the work assigned me by the Lord Jesus" (Acts 20:24, NLT).

When God has found us, disciplined us, and, if we will let him, through repentance and faith restored us to himself, what does he want to happen in us? The text says of the restored Israelite people that they will sanctify the Holy One of Jacob (NIV, "acknowledge the holiness of the Holy One of Jacob"). To "sanctify" is to make holy. But how is it possible to "sanctify" the only truly Holy One in the universe? What can we possibly do to make him any more holy?

Of course, the answer is that we cannot make him more holy. So what does the phrase mean? From a negative perspective, Moses' experience gives us the answer. The people had demanded water, and God had told Moses to speak to a nearby rock that would then pour out water. But Moses went out and said, "Listen, you rebels, must we bring you water out of this rock?" and he struck the rock twice with his staff (Num. 20:10–11). Moses had made it appear that with his magic staff he could produce water on demand. God's response was that Moses did not "sanctify my name" (NIV "honor me as holy," 20:12). Moses had a golden opportunity to demonstrate that there is only one Holy Being in the universe: all-powerful, absolutely other, and completely loving. Instead, Moses took the opportunity to make himself look good.

So how do we sanctify the Lord? We do it by glad obedience. We demonstrate through holy lives just how holy God is. We do it by surrendering our glory to his. After all, we cannot save the world. If people look to us as though we were the Savior who can solve all their problems, they are going to be vastly disappointed. So God promises his people a day when they would be able to gladly and completely obey his Word. It will not be any honor to them, but all honor goes to God. This is, of course, exactly what the covenant calls for: "Be holy because I, the LORD your God, am holy" (Lev. 19:1). God's people will demonstrate God's holy character by living out that holy character in their personal lives.

There was only one catch: They cannot seem to do it. To a large extent, the Old Testament is the story of Israel's failure to be a holy people. Here in Isaiah God promises that the day will come when they can actually fulfill the demands of the covenant. We now live in that day. The Holy Spirit is available to each of us to do what the old covenant could not do. It could tell the Israelites to live holy lives, but it could not enable them to do it. But now, as Paul tells us in Romans 8:3—4,

> For what the law was powerless to do in that it was weakened by the sinful nature, God did by sending his own Son in the likeness of sinful man to be a sin offering. And so he condemned sin in sinful man, in order that the righteous requirements of the law might be fully met in us, who do not live according to the sinful nature but according to the Spirit.

In other words, through what Christ has done for us in forgiving the sin of the broken covenant and in giving us his Spirit, it is now possible for us to fulfill all the "righteous requirements of the law" in real life. It is possible for us to "sanctify the Holy One" by demonstrating his holiness in our lives, just as Isaiah promised.

Isaiah 30:1–33

¹ "Woe to the obstinate children,"
   declares the Lord,
 "to those who carry out plans that are not mine,
   forming an alliance, but not by my Spirit,
   heaping sin upon sin;
² who go down to Egypt
   without consulting me;
 who look for help to Pharaoh's protection,
   to Egypt's shade for refuge.
³ But Pharaoh's protection will be to your shame,
   Egypt's shade will bring you disgrace.
⁴ Though they have officials in Zoan
   and their envoys have arrived in Hanes,
⁵ everyone will be put to shame
   because of a people useless to them,
 who bring neither help nor advantage,
   but only shame and disgrace."

⁶ An oracle concerning the animals of the Negev:

Through a land of hardship and distress,
   of lions and lionesses,
   of adders and darting snakes,
 the envoys carry their riches on donkeys' backs,
   their treasures on the humps of camels,
 to that unprofitable nation,
⁷   to Egypt, whose help is utterly useless.
 Therefore I call her
   Rahab the Do-Nothing.

⁸ Go now, write it on a tablet for them,
   inscribe it on a scroll,
 that for the days to come
   it may be an everlasting witness.
⁹ These are rebellious people, deceitful children,
   children unwilling to listen to the Lord's instruction.
¹⁰ They say to the seers,
   "See no more visions!"
 and to the prophets,
   "Give us no more visions of what is right!

Tell us pleasant things,
  prophesy illusions.
[11] Leave this way,
  get off this path,
and stop confronting us
  with the Holy One of Israel!"

[12] Therefore, this is what the Holy One of Israel says:

"Because you have rejected this message,
  relied on oppression
  and depended on deceit,
[13] this sin will become for you
  like a high wall, cracked and bulging,
  that collapses suddenly, in an instant.
[14] It will break in pieces like pottery,
  shattered so mercilessly
that among its pieces not a fragment will be found
  for taking coals from a hearth
  or scooping water out of a cistern."

[15] This is what the Sovereign LORD, the Holy One of Israel,
says:

"In repentance and rest is your salvation,
  in quietness and trust is your strength,
  but you would have none of it.
[16] You said, 'No, we will flee on horses.'
  Therefore you will flee!
You said, 'We will ride off on swift horses.'
  Therefore your pursuers will be swift!
[17] A thousand will flee
  at the threat of one;
at the threat of five
  you will all flee away,
till you are left
  like a flagstaff on a mountaintop,
  like a banner on a hill."

[18] Yet the LORD longs to be gracious to you;
  he rises to show you compassion.
For the LORD is a God of justice.
  Blessed are all who wait for him!

¹⁹O people of Zion, who live in Jerusalem, you will weep no more. How gracious he will be when you cry for help! As soon as he hears, he will answer you. ²⁰Although the Lord gives you the bread of adversity and the water of affliction, your teachers will be hidden no more; with your own eyes you will see them. ²¹Whether you turn to the right or to the left, your ears will hear a voice behind you, saying, "This is the way; walk in it." ²²Then you will defile your idols overlaid with silver and your images covered with gold; you will throw them away like a menstrual cloth and say to them, "Away with you!"

²³He will also send you rain for the seed you sow in the ground, and the food that comes from the land will be rich and plentiful. In that day your cattle will graze in broad meadows. ²⁴The oxen and donkeys that work the soil will eat fodder and mash, spread out with fork and shovel. ²⁵In the day of great slaughter, when the towers fall, streams of water will flow on every high mountain and every lofty hill. ²⁶The moon will shine like the sun, and the sunlight will be seven times brighter, like the light of seven full days, when the LORD binds up the bruises of his people and heals the wounds he inflicted.

> ²⁷See, the Name of the LORD comes from afar,
>> with burning anger and dense clouds of smoke;
> his lips are full of wrath,
>> and his tongue is a consuming fire.
> ²⁸His breath is like a rushing torrent,
>> rising up to the neck.
> He shakes the nations in the sieve of destruction;
>> he places in the jaws of the peoples
>> a bit that leads them astray.
> ²⁹And you will sing
>> as on the night you celebrate a holy festival;
> your hearts will rejoice
>> as when people go up with flutes
> to the mountain of the LORD,
>> to the Rock of Israel.
> ³⁰The LORD will cause men to hear his majestic voice
>> and will make them see his arm coming down
> with raging anger and consuming fire,
>> with cloudburst, thunderstorm and hail.

³¹ The voice of the LORD will shatter Assyria;
    with his scepter he will strike them down.
³² Every stroke the LORD lays on them
    with his punishing rod
  will be to the music of tambourines and harps,
    as he fights them in battle with the blows of his arm.
³³ Topheth has long been prepared;
    it has been made ready for the king.
  Its fire pit has been made deep and wide,
    with an abundance of fire and wood;
  the breath of the LORD,
    like a stream of burning sulfur,
    sets it ablaze.

THIS CHAPTER CONTAINS the fourth "woe" message between chapters 28 and 33. It is the first of two aimed specifically at the alliance with Egypt that the royal counselors are urging. Here Isaiah speaks more pointedly of the foolishness of such a course, for Egypt cannot offer any real help. She is a toothless dragon (30:1–7). Thus, because Judah has rejected the true help offered by God, they will be devastated, as though a high wall suddenly collapsed. They will be left like a tattered flag on a hilltop. God will have to wait until they come to their senses (30:8–18). When they do, he promises redemption and restoration for his people (30:19–26) and defeat for all their enemies (30:27–33).

Thus, once again we see a reiteration of the great themes of the first part of Isaiah's book. There is the poignant appeal to trust God, a promise of judgment on those who so stupidly rebel against God by trusting human nations instead of him, but then the assertion that after the judgment has come, there will yet be hope for those who turn to him.

Foolishness of Looking to Egypt (30:1–7)

THIS SECTION IS composed of two parts: The first (30:1–5) states the foolishness of trusting Egypt; the second (30:6–7) illustrates this message. Verse 1 is reminiscent of 1:2 as it speaks of "obstinate [or rebellious¹] children." God has carefully reared them, but they refuse to follow his ways (see Ezek. 16).

---

1. The Heb. root is *srr*, "to be stubborn." It occurs also in 1:23, "your rulers are rebels," and in 65:2, "an obstinate people." This distribution is significant since there are only seventeen occurrences of the word in the Old Testament.

They do not consult their Father for his counsel and advice but hastily make their own "plans" (Isa. 30:1) to serve what they think are their own best interests. Because they are "wayward in spirit" (29:24), they refuse to be led by God's Spirit (cf. 63:10–11). As a result, they do the very thing they are forbidden to do: go back to Egypt (cf. Deut. 17:16).

Admittedly, allying themselves with Egypt makes a good deal of sense from a human point of view. No other nation offers any hope of "protection" to Judah. On the surface, Egypt is large enough and powerful enough to be like a large palm tree, whose fronds offer "shade" (30:2) from Assyria's blazing sun. But God sees things differently. He sees that there is nothing behind the beautiful facade. There may be impressive "officials in Zoan" (30:4), the town in the northeastern Nile Delta where the Hebrews were once enslaved (Ps. 78:12, 43), and there may be persuasive "envoys" in "Hanes" (perhaps Heracleopolis, north of Memphis),[2] but there is nothing substantial behind the facade. The great palm tree is rotten in the center. Egypt cannot give any true help. Everyone who puts their trust in Egypt will be disgraced ("put to shame," 30:5).

This idea of Egypt's helplessness is illustrated in a two-verse (30:6–7) "oracle" or "burden" (Heb. *maśśa'*). Isaiah pictures a caravan struggling through a terrible desert, filled with hardships and dangers. This sounds like the Sinai Desert. Perhaps the Assyrian presence on the Philistine plain has already made the direct approach down the coast to Egypt too risky. This caravan is carrying "riches" and "treasures" to Egypt. The mention of "envoys" suggests that this is a diplomatic mission and that the caravan is carrying a large payment for the Egyptian "help."[3]

But in fact, says Isaiah, all the struggle and hardship as well as the great expense are in vain. Egypt really can offer no help; they are "unprofitable." In a final touch of sarcasm, Isaiah creates an oxymoron to describe Egypt. She is "Rahab the Do-Nothing." Rahab is another name for the chaos monster (see comments on "Leviathan," 27:1), that terrifying dragon who is always threatening to destroy the order on which human life depends. But *this* Rahab is far

---

2. It is not clear whether the officials and envoys are Judean who have gone to Egypt or Egyptians. If the former, then the people are saying, "See, the Egyptians have received us everywhere from north to south." If the latter, then perhaps the new Nubian dynasty has succeeded in establishing its hegemony of the entire land of Egypt, both delta and river valley. Young, *The Book of Isaiah*, 2:338–39, seems to take the officials as Egyptians and the envoys as Judeans.

3. This is, of course, exactly what Ahaz did with Assyria, paying them a large amount of money for their "help" (2 Kings 16:7–9). It is significant that Hezekiah is not accused of doing the same thing his father did here. Perhaps this alliance is made with Egypt against his will. Seitz, *Isaiah 1–39*, 215–17, discusses the issues carefully but does not really resolve them.

from terrifying. In fact, all she does is sit in one place, not threatening anyone.[4] She is a toothless old monster, too lazy to move.

Judah's Coming Devastation (30:8-18)

ISAIAH NOW PRONOUNCES judgment on the Judeans, who are again called "rebellious people, deceitful children" (30:9). He begins by describing their attitude (30:8–11) and then turns to the specific announcement of the judgment caused by that attitude (30:12–14). Then in a third section (30:15–18), he details what God has invited them to do, what will be the results of their refusal to accept his invitation, and what he must do in response. Most commentators take verse 18 with the third section of the oracle (30:19–26), since this verse has a hopeful tone. However, I believe it is really the conclusion of the judgment messages, as I will try to show.[5]

In 30:8 Isaiah offers the purpose of writing down prophetic words, so that when the predictions came true, people will know it (cf. 8:1, 16; 29:11, 18). He defines the rebellion of the people more clearly. Not only are they unwilling to consult with God when forming their plans, they do not want to hear "the LORD's instruction" (30:9) or "what is right" (30:10). Instead, they ask the prophets to say pleasant things to them. They do not want Isaiah to confront them. Undoubtedly they do not actually ask for "illusions" (30:10), but Isaiah says that is what they are actually asking for when they demand that he stop telling them about "the Holy One of Israel."

Ironically, Isaiah's response to that demand is to tell them "what the Holy One of Israel says" (30:12). The text emphasizes the causal connection between the people's actions and the coming destruction, both with the opening "therefore" and with the subsequent "because." They have "rejected" the truth that God alone can be trusted and instead have trusted in "oppression" and lies, grinding the poor to get money to pay Egypt for its worthless help. As a result, their destruction will come as suddenly as a collapsing wall.

We can imagine a wall whose stones have been leaning a bit more each year, with the result that people have simply gotten used to it. But then one day the center of gravity is passed and in an instant it comes down. So it will be with Assyria. For years Assyria has been threatening, but then the day will suddenly come when Assyria will devastate the land. There will be nothing left. Judah will be like a smashed pot with the pieces so small that they will be useless for any other tasks.

---

4. There are three Heb. words in the phrase. Lit. translated, they read "Rahab are they—sitting." If the second and third words are combined into one, the translation would be "Rahab the one who sits" (cf. *BHS*).

5. See also Seitz, *Isaiah 1–39*, 219.

God has told them again and again the prescription for their condition. They must turn back to him in "repentance" and "rest" in him (30:15). In quietly trusting him instead of frantically rushing around trying to solve their problems for themselves, they will find both "salvation" and "strength." But the patient has refused the physician's prescription.

Isaiah 30:16 offers a strong contrast with 30:15. Instead of quietness and trust, there will be rapid flight. There is only one problem with that course of action: The "pursuers" will be swifter yet. If the people rested in God, flight would not be necessary. But because they have refused to trust him, flight will not be enough. Once it becomes apparent that their strength is not enough, retreat will turn into headlong rout, with a "thousand" running from "one," for they will have no inner resources to face any other alternative than victory. As a result, they will be as forlorn as a tattered flag whipping in the wind, with nothing but corpses surrounding it (30:17).

So what is God's course of action in the face of this reality? Will he wash his hands of them? Will he abandon them in a fit of well-justified rage? No, in one of the greatest statements in all of Scripture, he says that since Israel will not wait for (trust in) him, he will have to wait (NIV "longs") to be gracious to them. He "rises" from his throne—not to bring final destruction but to show "compassion." Because he is a "God of justice," those "who wait for him" will never be disappointed. Those who wait for the nations will be disappointed again and again because they are serving themselves and not the causes of right and truth. But God will unfailingly do what is right, and we can depend on him, no matter what. Thus, Isaiah presents the picture of the Creator of the universe patiently standing, waiting for us to discover what fools we have been and to turn back to him to receive the grace and compassion that are in his fatherly heart.[6]

Promises of Redemption of God's People (30:19–33)

THIS LAST SECTION details what will happen when the Israelites finally come to their senses and turn back to God. Three kinds of promises are made: The first one (30:19–22) involves spiritual regeneration; the second one (30:23–26) speaks of the physical blessings God intends to pour out on his people; the final one (30:27–33) prophesies defeat for all of Israel's enemies, particularly Assyria.

---

6. While there is no question that 30:18 is a transitional statement, I believe it is better seen as a conclusion to 30:8–17 than an introduction to 30:19–26. In part, this is because of the two occurrences of "therefore" (NIV "yet," "for") in this verse, which clearly signal a conclusion. It is because Israel has refused to wait and must undergo destruction that God must wait to be gracious to his people.

(1) In chapter 6, God said that Isaiah's ministry would simply contribute to the blindness, deafness, and "fat-heartedness" of the people. Perhaps the starkest expression of that condition was the demand that Isaiah stop confronting them with the Holy One of Israel (30:11). But Isaiah sees a day coming when all of that will be changed. The people will "cry" out to God, and he will "answer" them with grace (30:19). The people will no longer be driven from him by "adversity" and "affliction." Rather, their spiritual eyes will be open to see all that he is teaching them through these experiences (30:20).[7]

No longer will they be like a stubborn mule, refusing to turn even when the bit is jerked in the mouth. Now their spiritual ears will be so sensitive they will only need the merest whisper in their ear to turn them to the right or the left (30:21). This will result in a despising of all the expensive idols on which they have lavished such attention and which have meant so much to them. They will be disgusted at the very thought of worshiping such things (30:22).

(2) Verses 23–26 are closely related to the first promise. One of the reasons for worshiping idols was, and is, to secure physical blessings. Here God promises that when his people are responsive to him and have stopped their attempts to manipulate the physical, social, and spiritual world to their own advantage, he will give all those blessings freely. Verses 23–24 express the blessings in agricultural terms. The rain will come at its appointed times, and the harvests will be so plentiful that even the work animals will have food to eat by the shovel-full.

Verses 25–26 contrast "slaughter" with "healing." This may refer to earth's final battle in which Israel's enemies are finally destroyed and Israel, though wounded, triumphs (cf. Zech. 14:1–4; Mal. 4:1–2). It may also refer to the destruction of pride, both that of Israel and the world, because height, barrenness, and darkness are associated with pride elsewhere in the book (2:12–17; 8:21–22; 47:5). In any case, barrenness will be replaced with abundant water, and darkness will be replaced with incredible light. God is the One who gives blessing.

(3) In the final promise (30:27–33), Isaiah recalls the counselors urging an alliance with Egypt because they say that is the only hope for deliverance from the rapacious Assyrians. Isaiah says that if the Judeans want deliverance, they should be looking at God, not Egypt. As in 30:23–26, the language has a certain "end of history" flavor. It is highly emotive and loaded with

---

7. While *moreyka* may be "your teachers," as per NIV, the form may also be a singular, as per NRSV. The idea that it is God who is this teacher seems to fit the context best. See also Motyer, *Prophecy of Isaiah*, 250.

vivid imagery. Yet verse 31 makes it clear that the ultimate subject of God's wrath here is Assyria. This should make us cautious about what passages we assign as "end-time" promises.

Perhaps the reason for the unusually vivid language here is to convince the hearers of the certainty of the promises. After all, Assyria is the mightiest force on earth, and Judah is small and weak in comparison. So perhaps Isaiah is inspired in this way to try to help the people see that this is not a contest between Judah and Assyria but between Assyria and the most overwhelming Being in the universe. In any case, God promises not just a slap on the wrist for those who oppose him—and in opposing him, opposing reality itself. They will be carried off in a flood (30:28); they will be consumed with fire (30:27, 30, 33); they will be pummeled with hail and pelting rain (30:30); they will stagger under repeated, terrific blows (30:30, 31, 32); they will finally be hurled into the place of endless burning (30:33).[8]

In all of this, one recurring feature is a reference to the Lord's mouth, breath, and voice (30:27, 28, 30, 31, 33). Just as his word is life and health to those who respond to it, it is sudden, terrible death to those who reject it.[9] In Malachi, the same sun that heals the wounded is the one that draws the last moisture from the chaff (4:1–2).

ALLIANCES. Insofar as America today is not, as a nation, the chosen people of God, these passages on trusting the nations do not have the same political relevance to us as they did for Judah. However, the principles remain relevant for Christians. We must ask ourselves why we are entering into dependent relations with people or institutions and what such people or institutions can really offer us.

In the eighth century B.C., Egypt was long past its prime. After about 1000 B.C. it was never again a dominant force in the ancient Near East. After its heyday, Egypt was ruled first by the Libyans from the west. After that, it was ruled by Nubians from the south; they were the ones ruling at this time. The native Egyptians seemed to lack either the energy or the initiative to rule on their own. Thus, Egypt appeared to be powerful but really was not. We do not know how obvious that was, although the Assyrians seemed to recognize it (cf. the field commander's remarks in 36:6). In any case, those with

---

8. "Topheth" was probably located in the Hinnom Valley south and west of Jerusalem. It is referred to as the place where children were burned in sacrifice to the Ammonite god Molech (2 Kings 23:10; Jer. 7:31–32; 19:6, 11–14; see also Ezek. 23:37–39).

9. See also Isa. 11:4; Job 4:9; Ps. 18:8; Ezek. 21:31; 2 Thess. 2:8; Rev. 19:15.

spiritual discernment recognized the situation. Isaiah saw it in the 700s B.C. and Jeremiah in the 600s.

That is the kind of discernment we need. Are those on whom we are tempted to rely just as weak as we are, though giving a good appearance? Do they have our best interests at heart or only their own? Are we relying on them as a way to avoid the risk of trusting God? Have we sought the guidance of those with spiritual discernment concerning the relationship? Have we sincerely sought God's guidance? In many cases destructive relationships are clear to others around us. Our problem, like the Judeans, is that we are afraid to let go of "the splintered reed" (36:6) and so do not allow ourselves to look at the situation with true discernment. If we would first let go of it mentally and spiritually, God would open our eyes to its dangers.

True and false prophecy. Strikingly, the main difference between true and false prophecy was that false prophets said nice things about their hearers. They said things their hearers wanted to hear. They spoke of peace and prosperity and of God's certain deliverance. The true prophets spoke of these things as well, but they were always in the context of repentance and changed behavior. Those features were notably absent from the preaching of the false prophets. For them the "good news" was unconditional. This is what Isaiah means when he says that people are asking him to "prophesy illusions" (30:10). They are asking him to promise good consequences without appropriate causes.

This is an increasing problem today. Children are not being taught about consequences in life. You can do whatever you like and never have to pay. "Self-esteem" has nothing to do with performance and behavior. Thus, it is emerging that some of the people with the highest self-esteem are thieves and crooks. The triumph of "feel-good" psychology is killing us, because all of this is an illusion. There are consequences in life, and those in the public eye who teach otherwise are the modern equivalent of the false prophets. They tell us that we can have everything we want with no responsibility for the outcome. One of the tragic examples of this trend is the epidemic increase in male irresponsibility for the children they have fathered. The social costs of this phenomenon are only beginning to be felt. We need prophets who will declare "what is right" and not what a sinful people want to hear.

The dangers of false confidence. Isaiah says that because Judah has refused to trust in God and is choosing instead to depend on Egyptian horses, a thousand Judeans will flee (on those swift horses) from one Assyrian. Because they trust in the wrong things, when those things fail, they will be completely undone.

A similar thing happened outside of Washington, D.C., in 1861. The Union Army had convinced itself that they could dispose of the ragtag

Confederate Army in short order. After all, they had smarter uniforms and more up-to-date equipment, and they were better drilled. As a matter of fact, however, they knew little about discipline, determination, and courage— things the Southerners had a good deal of. In the battle, it quickly became apparent that in terms of raw fighting skill, the northern army was badly outclassed. Soon setbacks were turned into defeats, defeats to retreats, and the retreats turned into headlong flight. The picnickers who had come out to watch the "jolly fight" led the rush back to the defenses of Washington.

If we place our confidence in the wrong things, adversity and difficulty will destroy us. We will have no resources to meet them. But if our confidence is in God and not in ourselves, these things will only drive us closer to him. We know that he will not fail us, so we can be faithful, even to death. That kind of fortitude means that defeats do not turn into routs. We can fall back to a new line of defense and fight it out with courage, knowing that God is at our back. The Judeans had forfeited that knowledge by turning to Egypt, just as the overconfident Yankees had trusted in their own superiority.

Apocalypse. In this section of his prophecy, Isaiah blends the vivid imagery often associated with prophecies of the end times with the more prosaic language usually associated with discussions of the present. This blending can be confusing. What is he really talking about—now or then? But the blending can also be helpful because it reminds us that we live in two times: that which is and that which is to come. The vivid and colorful language is not created by end-time thinking, but rather the thinking is often best expressed with that kind of language. As they look out into the future and contemplate distant and cataclysmic events, the writers can usually best express their points with that kind of sweeping and gripping expression.

But that same kind of expression can also be useful for other purposes, as seems to be the case here, where Isaiah is trying to show the true nature of the enemy Assyria has roused against herself in the Lord. Furthermore, we must be careful in our interpretation of such language. To interpret it overly literally is to run the danger of missing the spiritual points being made by the images. In this case, I believe it is wrong to look for a day when God's people will use tambourines to beat out the rhythm of God's blows on their enemies. The point is to promise that our enemies are God's enemies and that we may rejoice, both now and in the future, in God's defeat of them. The question should not be precisely when these events will occur. Rather, does the confidence that God will defeat my enemies cause me to live in constant trust in him now?

RETURNING TO EGYPT. For the Judeans, their attempt to solve the Assyrian problem for themselves led them back into the very thing God told them not to do, to go back to Egypt, in spirit, at least (see also Hos. 7:11; 9:1–6). Ultimately, of course, some of them returned physically (Jer. 42–43). The same is often true for us. Our attempts to take care of ourselves lead us back into the very things from which God has delivered us in the first place. Why is that?

The writer to the Hebrews refers to this as "the sin that so easily entangles" (Heb. 12:1). There are areas of our lives where we are particularly susceptible to temptation. When we refuse to trust God in some other area of our lives, perhaps one that appears totally unrelated, we effectively take ourselves out from under the protection of God and throw ourselves open to that old area of weakness. Oftentimes, we are weak there precisely because it is something that seems to offer us the pleasure or security or significance we think we must have. When we learn to trust God for these things and to find them in his ways, not ours, then we experience deliverance from the bondage of those old sins. But when we refuse to trust God in any area, we have cut off the power source and are thrown back onto all our old resources. So it is not surprising that we are defeated at precisely the same points as we were before.

Exchanging God's shadow for a man's. In the Near East, the importance of shade cannot be overemphasized. In many cases, shade from the searing rays of the sun is the difference between life and death. The sun is so direct and so hot that a person can become seriously dehydrated before he or she is aware of danger. So certain psalms refer to God as One who offers protection under his "shade" or his "shadow." The shade may be cast by his outstretched wings (Ps. 17:8; 36:7; 57:1; 63:7), a symbol of protection as the parent bird shelters the chicks. But on two occasions God himself casts the shadow in which the believer rests:

> He who dwells in the shelter of the Most High
>   will rest in the shadow of the Almighty. (Ps. 91:1)

> The LORD watches over you—
>   the LORD is your shade at your right hand;
> The sun will not harm you by day,
>   nor the moon by night. (Ps. 121:5–6)

God's "shade" is an important figure for Isaiah, and we can understand why, with his emphasis on trust.[10] To him it is almost unimaginable that the people

---

10. Isa. 4:6; 16:3; 25:4; 32:2; 49:2; 51:16.

of Judah will exchange God's shadow for that of a human being. How can they choose to look to Pharaoh for the protection only God can give? Yet we are prone to the same thing. Of course it is appropriate to place a certain degree of trust in other humans. We trust our spouse; we trust our employer; we trust our pastor. But if those are the ultimate places where we seek shelter from the world, to the point that we exclude God from the picture, we are in for a terrible disappointment, for even the best of humans will fail us.

They will fail us especially if we put them in the place of God in our lives. Any time we expect humans to give us what only God can, we are setting them up to fail because we are asking too much of them. By contrast, if we have come to the place where God is genuinely the shelter under which we live, we will not be crushed when humans fail us. Because we, living under the protection of God, will be able to be more trustworthy, many of our human relations will be too. But we must have the order right: God first, all others second.

In this regard, it is important to think about the reasons God will not let us put our trust in certain persons or institutions. Why was it wrong for Judah to make an alliance with Egypt? Could not that have been God's way of delivering his people from Assyria? Later on, he did use Persia as the means of delivering the exiles from Babylon (much to the apparent surprise of some; see below on ch. 45). So there certainly does not seem to have been anything *intrinsically* wrong with God's using Egypt in a similar way.

The chief problem is that the Judeans were making their plans without consulting God. They did not look to Egypt as God's way of delivering them. Instead, they looked to her as *their* way of delivering *themselves*. It is possible that if they had come to God obediently and submissively, he would have sent them in that direction. But sometimes God refuses to let us go in an obvious direction precisely because it keeps us from trusting him.

This may have been the case with Paul and Silas. When they were on their missionary journey through Asia Minor, the obvious path for them was to make a circle back to the east through Bithynia toward their home base in Antioch (Acts 16:6–10). After all, they had been successful in Asia Minor; they had learned "how to do ministry" there. Why not continue to minister in that region and build on that success? To go into the Greek homeland seemed fraught with danger. They had not done this before; they had no base of support there; they were not familiar with the area. But that is where God was sending, and they were obedient.

Since Paul and Silas were obedient, God blessed their ministry. As a result, the world is different. In other words, the principle for us is to start with obedient openness to God, always being aware that he may take us outside our "comfort zone" and put us in a place where we are driven back on him alone.

He may use the obvious, but possibly he will use something not at all obvious so that when he delivers us, it will be clear that he did it and no one else.

The character of preaching. One contemporary issue that this passage raises has to do with the nature of preaching. We are told today that people in the "postmodern age" will not sit still for "judgmental preaching." Isaiah shows us that this is hardly a postmodern phenomenon! It has been with us for 2,700 years. It is a human condition and not associated with any one age.

When Paul spoke to his disciple Timothy about people having "itching ears" and not being willing to sit still for "sound doctrine" (2 Tim. 4:3), he was not speaking about the twenty-first century in the United States. He was talking about the human race in all times and places. People have always wanted to hear good things about themselves and to have their natural inclinations affirmed. There is nothing new in that. If we tailor our preaching to such inclinations, we run the danger of falling in with the false prophets, who did the same thing in Israel and Judah long ago. The great danger is that we get converts who have never truly repented (see below). Instead, they merely add one more item to their portfolio of "life options."

There are two tragic results from this situation. (1) There is no real change of behavior. The "adherent" is just as materialistic and self-centered as before, with no real commitment to the life of the church or the life of faith. They may know something about "commitment," and they may know a veneer of Christian language, but they know nothing about surrender. (2) Such people are powerless when it comes to life's crises. They have no anchor and no resources for facing a crisis with spiritual vitality.

As a result, we have rapidly growing churches but no real salt and light in the society. Some insist that we can first draw people in and later help them to understand the moral demands of the Christian life. But if we do that, we will find the crowds rapidly disappearing. It is easy to gain "adherents," but making "disciples" is another thing. Jesus said that unless people are willing to leave everything in their past lives behind, they cannot be his disciples.

This is not to say we must feed people a steady diet of harsh and bitter condemnation. That is not the way of the Bible or the way of Christian faith. The idea of a message of "good news" is an Old Testament idea before it was a New Testament one (cf. Isa. 52:7; 61:1), and Isaiah's consistent coupling of judgment and hope (including this chapter) shows that this is not the way. But he *did* begin by shedding the stark light of God's holiness on what was taking place in the people's lives. Furthermore, he consistently showed how the hope for them was not that they could escape judgment but that God would not stop with judgment on them. Some of us need to regain the courage of an Isaiah who when told to "stop confronting us with the Holy One of Israel" responded by saying, "This is what ... the Holy One of Israel ... says" (30:15).

The connection between repentance and rest. The point just made is underlined by the appeal of God to the people, "In repentance and rest is your salvation" (30:15). Both concepts are important, and each is integrally related to the other. There is no real rest (complete dependence on God) without repentance, and there is no real repentance that does not issue in rest.

The fundamental idea behind repentance in the Old Testament is to turn around or to turn back.[11] It is to stop going in the direction you were, namely, one of self-dependence and self-pleasing, and to turn away from that life to one of depending on God and pleasing him. To talk about resting in the Lord while still keeping hold of one's life and its direction is a contradiction in terms. By the same token, to stop committing certain sins and to "clean up one's act" merely for the sake of avoiding punishment is not to turn back to God. It is only to turn away from sin and may be just as selfish as any other act.

The New Testament development of the idea, as expressed in the term *metanoia*,[12] is the same. To repent is to turn about mentally, spiritually, and behaviorally. It is not surprising that Jesus in his ministry began with a call for repentance: "Repent, for the kingdom of heaven is near" (Matt. 4:17); "the kingdom of God is near. Repent and believe the good news" (Mark 1:15); "I have not come to call the righteous, but sinners to repentance" (Luke 5:32). Unless we reject the old king, ourselves, and his ways, sin, there is no way we can come into the kingdom of God.

Just as the Old Testament put the correct relationship with God within the context of absolute loyalty to a covenant king, the New Testament calls us to turn from loyalty to ourselves and become the glad subjects of heaven's King. If we find real trust difficult, perhaps it is because there has never been a real change of king in our lives. The idea that we can have the benefits of the kingdom without turning away from our own kingship is a fallacy.

The limits of our resources. When we try to have God's way and our way, as the Judeans did, we effectively say that our way is better. So the Judeans believed that they could depend on their own strength and cunning to deliver them from their difficulties (30:16). There is only one problem with that, as Jacob discovered. For all his life up until he met his uncle Laban, Jacob had always been able to outthink and outmaneuver everyone around him. Perhaps that is why, when he met God in the dream, he did not actually submit to him but instead tried to strike a deal (Gen. 28:20–22). Fortunately, God is patient, and he was willing to work with Jacob as he found him. This was a good thing for Jacob because in Laban Jacob met a man who could outthink and outmaneuver him. If it had not been for God, Jacob would have disap-

---

11. See J. A. Thompson and Elmer A Marten, "שׁוּב," *NIDOTTE*, 4:55–59.
12. See E. Würthwein, "μετανοέω, μετάνοια," *TDNT*, 4:975–89.

peared from the pages of history, being merely one more of a shrewd man's conquests.

If we depend on our strength and cunning, there will always be someone stronger and more cunning than we are. That is the message Isaiah gives to his people, and it is the message he gives to us. Depend on your resources and you *will* meet someone with more resources than you. But if you will depend on God's resources, you can be sure that you will never meet anyone with more than your heavenly Father makes available to you. When Paul said, "I can do everything through him who gives me strength" (Phil. 4:13), he was expressing this principle. He stopped trusting in his own accomplishments and discovered that God's resources are endless.

The twofold nature of blessing. In Isaiah 30:19–33 Isaiah emphasizes the key principles of divine blessing. These principles are important for our day. The key point is that blessings are both spiritual and material and that they are inseparably so. It seems today that Christians are either in one ditch or the other. Some contend that the Old Testament promises of physical blessing are all symbolic, referring to the spiritual blessings of the Christian life. Others say that all the promises of the Scripture are to be taken literally, so that the Old Testament promises of riches and abundance are for us today.

I believe there is a middle way between these two extremes. One of the problems with the latter position is that it often sounds like another form of the idolatry that Isaiah says the true believer will despise (30:22). We serve God in order to become rich; we meet certain conditions he lays down so that we can get his blessing. This is simply Christian paganism. When we look at Christ and the apostles, we do not see rich men doing certain religious things so they can get a payoff. In fact, Christ tells his disciples to reject such ideas. The Beatitudes that begin the Sermon on the Mount specifically repudiate what the world (and some Christian preachers) call blessing (Matt. 5:1–12). As Isaiah says in Isaiah 30:19–22, blessing is a matter of a transformed heart that can take adversity and affliction and see God's hand in them.

But it is also true that God the Father wants to give good things to his children. To say that all the Old Testament promises are only symbolic is to miss the fact that God made humans both material and spiritual and that to restrict the promise of Genesis 1:27 to only one of these aspects is to arbitrarily eliminate one part of his creation. When we repent of the way of trying to supply our needs for ourselves, commit those needs to him in self-denying trust, and delight to serve him for love, two things will happen. (1) We will be living in a way where there is no longer any blockage against all the good things God wants to give us. (2) We will be able to see everything that comes to us as what it really is: an incredible, undeserved blessing from God.

The truth is that for those who seek physical blessings, there is never enough, even in incredible abundance. But for those who seek God, they are able to receive everything that comes from his hand for just what it is, an undeserved blessing. They have learned the truth of his Word, "I shall not be in want" (Ps. 23:1)—and that is enough, because he is enough.

Living in the kingdom. Isaiah 30:27–33 combines the "now" and the "not yet" in an important way. It expresses another aspect of the point just made. We experience the blessings of today, but all the time knowing that there are incredibly greater blessings to come on the other side of the grave. Ironically, the pagan view, having imagined that the invisible world is just like this one, only bigger in every way, ends up devaluing this world, the very model used to construct the other one. The invisible world is the real one, and this one is only a dim reflection of it.

The modern secular view denies that there is any other world than this one. This physical-material world is all there is. But again, the result is to make this world valueless. It came from nowhere and it is going nowhere. So nothing really matters except personal survival—and the sure fact of death makes even that continued survival pointless.

The biblical worldview is markedly different. It insists that this is a real world, where real decisions of great consequence are to be made. The Old Testament in particular hammers this point. We are not conditioned by a fate determined in that real, unseen world. We may choose to make our lives here and now better, or we may choose to make them worse. But why is this world real? Because it is the product of the invisible Creator, and that leads us to the realization that as real as this world is, it is only part of a larger reality that includes the unseen world.

Thus, Christians live in two worlds. We live here and now and confront the Assyrias of everyday life. We seek to live as obedient subjects of the kingdom of God this very day. But at the same time we know that there is more to come. Just because Assyria is defeated today does not mean that there are no more Assyrias ahead. And we see a world where the kingship of the Creator is not yet fully worked out. So we live faithfully and confidently today, looking to the last day when all God's enemies will be defeated forever and when he, the slain lamb, will ascend his throne and rule his happy subjects forever.

In the same way, we can experience God's kingship in our lives and in our relationships today, but we look for the day when his kingdom will come in all its fullness and his righteous rule will extend throughout all his creation for all time. So we do not devalue this life as we look to the next one, for we know that it is not a different reality than this one, only a fuller one.

Isaiah 31:1–9

¹ WOE TO THOSE who go down to Egypt for help,
who rely on horses,
who trust in the multitude of their chariots
and in the great strength of their horsemen,
but do not look to the Holy One of Israel,
or seek help from the LORD.
² Yet he too is wise and can bring disaster;
he does not take back his words.
He will rise up against the house of the wicked,
against those who help evildoers.
³ But the Egyptians are men and not God;
their horses are flesh and not spirit.
When the LORD stretches out his hand,
he who helps will stumble,
he who is helped will fall;
both will perish together.

⁴ This is what the LORD says to me:

"As a lion growls,
a great lion over his prey—
and though a whole band of shepherds
is called together against him,
he is not frightened by their shouts
or disturbed by their clamor—
so the LORD Almighty will come down
to do battle on Mount Zion and on its heights.
⁵ Like birds hovering overhead,
the LORD Almighty will shield Jerusalem;
he will shield it and deliver it,
he will 'pass over' it and will rescue it."

⁶Return to him you have so greatly revolted against, O Israelites. ⁷For in that day every one of you will reject the idols of silver and gold your sinful hands have made.

⁸ "Assyria will fall by a sword that is not of man;
a sword, not of mortals, will devour them.
They will flee before the sword
and their young men will be put to forced labor.

357

⁹Their stronghold will fall because of terror;
    at sight of the battle standard their commanders
       will panic,"
declares the LORD,
    whose fire is in Zion,
    whose furnace is in Jerusalem.

CHAPTER 31 SAYS many of the same things that were said at greater length in chapter 30. However, if the chapter break were eliminated and chapters 31 and 32 were combined into one, the new chapter would be about the same length as chapter 30, and that may be what the author or editor intended, since the present chapter 32 is the only one in this section (chs. 28–33) that does not begin with "woe."[1] The present chapter structure probably reflects the fact that beginning with 32:1 there is a new emphasis on the coming King.

Chapter 31 has two sections. Verses 1–3 include the fifth of the woes in this subdivision of the book. As such, it brings the sequence to a kind of a climax. The woe in 28:1 was against the drunken leaders in Ephraim; in 29:1 it was against those in Jerusalem who depended on cultic righteousness; in 29:15 it was against those who tried to hide their counsel from the Lord; in 30:1 it was against "obstinate children" who would not bring to the Lord their plans to make an alliance with Egypt. The present "woe" is specifically against "those who go down to Egypt for help." Thus, the climax (or the nadir) has been reached. Drunken leaders who focus on the wrong things have given ungodly advice that rebellious people have adopted without consulting God.

The result is now baldly stated: They have chosen to trust men and horses instead of "the Holy One of Israel."[2] They have chosen to trust the creation rather than the Creator. This is foolish, as 31:2–3 explains. God is just and will not let those who reject him in order to do evil escape. There is a just order in the world, and to overlook it is a bad mistake. Furthermore, the idea that "flesh" and blood can outface "spirit" is ridiculous. When God raises his fist ("stretches out his hand"[3]), whatever puny help Egypt might offer will be useless. If God chooses to use Assyria to punish his people, there will be nothing in the world the Egyptians can do about it.

---

1. Motyer, *Prophecy of Isaiah*, 253–54, analyzes the material in this way.

2. The thirteen uses of the phrase "the Holy One of Israel" in chs. 1–39 (including the one "Holy One of Jacob" in 29:23) tend to emphasize God's transcendent power and glory. Thus, to trust in flesh and blood, as here, instead of him is complete nonsense.

3. See 5:25; 9:12, 17, 21; 10:4; 14:26, 27; 23:11.

Up to here, Isaiah has been counseling the Israelites not to trust Egypt because Egypt cannot help. In 31:4–9, he develops the other side of the argument: Trust the Lord because he is the only One who can deliver you. He makes three points: God will defend Jerusalem (vv. 4–5); turn back to him and away from idols (vv. 6–7); Assyria is no match for the Lord (vv. 8–9).

Some understand 31:4 to be negative, with God attacking Jerusalem.[4] However, the undoubted positive point of 31:5 argues that "the lion" has come to attack *the enemies of Jerusalem* and cannot be "frightened" off by anything. It is unnecessary to find an equivalent for "the shepherds." The point is simply that the Lord cannot be diverted from his gracious purpose. Verse 5 uses another image from nature to depict the Lord—as a mother bird hovering over her nest, seeking to distract the attacker or, if necessary, to give her own life to protect the nestlings.

Since these promises of the Lord's care are assured, how should Israel respond? Surely they should cease their revolt against God's lordship and "return" to obeying him (31:6). It does not matter how much time and money they may have invested in their "idols" or how beautiful they may be. The fact is that the images and the gods they represent are a human creation. They have been made with "sinful" human "hands." How can such creations save humans? When it comes down to the bottom line of life or death, what are those things compared to the Creator?

Just as 31:1–3 is the most specific in denouncing the counsel to trust Egypt, so 31:8–9 is the most specific in promising deliverance from the Assyrian threat. The promise that they "will fall by a sword that is not of man" (v. 8) surely sounds like what is described in 37:36, when 185,000 Assyrian soldiers died in one night. Again, Isaiah's main point is that it is much wiser to trust God than Egypt in the face of the Assyrians. The Assyrians will put the Egyptians to flight, but God will put the Assyrians to flight. God is the flame that burns in "Zion," and anyone who puts a hand in that "furnace" will likely get burned.

WHERE IS OUR TRUST? In the ancient Near East at this time, the horse and chariot were something like the "ultimate weapon." When the horse, with its speed and stamina, was hitched to a light two-wheeled chariot on which were a two- or three-man crew, the results could be devastating to unprepared foot soldiers. Along with the driver, there was at least an archer with a powerful compound bow. In some cases there was

---

4. Young, *The Book of Isaiah*, 2:377–78.

also a spearman, who could provide additional offensive power as well as defense in tight situations.

These were the elite troops in the armies of the time. They were, of course, expensive to obtain and to maintain. Horses are much more temperamental and delicate than donkeys or other beasts of burden. Furthermore, the chariots, in order to strike the right balance between light weight and durability, had to be carefully crafted and were in constant need of repair. But they were so desirable that even countries like Judah, whose hills and valleys meant chariotry was of limited usefulness, felt they had to have a chariot force.[5]

At this time, another use of the horse was also emerging, perhaps pioneered by the Assyrians. That was cavalry. Here mounted, well-disciplined troops could have a greater massed effect and even more mobility than chariots . The Assyrian field commander's sarcastic comment in 36:8 about the Assyrian king providing Judah with horses if they had men to ride them might be a way of saying that they were not trained in this latest tactical skill.

Today we look for defense to other kinds of armaments: shell-proof tanks and stealth aircraft and laser-guided missiles. But where is our defense? At the turn of the last century, rifled artillery was the latest thing. But Rudyard Kipling thought along Isaiah's lines when he wrote:

> For heathen heart that puts her trust
> In reeking tube and iron shard
> All valiant dust that builds on dust
> And, guarding, calls not Thee to guard,
> For frantic boast and foolish word,
> Thy mercy on thy people, Lord![6]

Nations in a fallen world may need weapons of defense, yet the question still is: Are those the things that give us confidence? Does sleeping with a pistol under my pillow mean I don't have to trust God for my life? What does it mean to trust God and not armaments? Americans have traditionally been uncomfortable maintaining a large peacetime army. As a result, the two world wars caught us unprepared. Yet is that not better than spending a fortune on "valiant dust"? There are no easy answers to these kinds of questions, but we must still ask them, both nationally and personally. What is it I am trusting in?

---

5. A part of Solomon's income was as an arms dealer, purchasing horses from Asia Minor and chariots from Egypt and selling the resulting units to the neighboring countries (1 Kings 10:28–29).
6. From Kipling's "Recessional."

FULFILLMENT OF PROPHECY. The statements here about God's shielding Jerusalem (31:5) and about his furnace being Jerusalem (31:9) raise questions for us about the appropriate attitude Christians should take toward Jerusalem and Israel today. For many centuries Christians taught that the church was the new Jerusalem and that the Old Testament promises no longer have relevance to the physical place. That changed somewhat during the Crusades, when it was felt to be a sin to leave the Holy Land and Jerusalem in the hands of the Muslims. But after the failure of the Crusades, something of the old attitudes were restored.

In the nineteenth century, however, two things changed that dramatically. (1) One was the rise of Zionism, the conviction among Jews that they would never be secure until they had their own homeland back. (2) The other was the rise of Darbyism or dispensationalism, which took a literal approach to all biblical prophecy. These two together have given a new surge of conviction to the belief that the land of Israel and the city of Jerusalem deserve special care from Christians.

My approach to this question is similar to the one I advocated in the previous section with regard to blessing. I believe there are two extremes to be avoided. On the one hand, it is true that God's ultimate goals with the human race are spiritual. Thus Paul can say that the true children of Abraham are those who are the descendants of Abraham's faith, not his physical body (Gal. 3:6–9). Thus, it does not follow for us to say that we must always defend the actions of modern Israelis, many of whom profess no faith at all, much less the faith of Abraham.

On the other hand, Paul can say that God has not rejected his people but will one day graft them back into the stock from which they have been cut off (Rom. 11:24). This tells us that God still has an interest in that physical people and, by extension, in the land he promised to them. Thus, I believe it is still true to say that for anyone to seek to wrest Jerusalem from the hand of the God of the Bible is to invite serious consequences on themselves. However, while I believe that God's promises for physical Israel will be fulfilled, I suspect they may be fulfilled in very different ways than a simplistic, literal reading of the Bible would suggest. The Jews in Jesus' day read the prophecies of the Messiah in that way and were almost completely unprepared for the way in which they were actually fulfilled. We need to be reading the text with faith and yet openness; God is still the Creator, who loves to do things in new ways.

Isaiah 32:1–8

[1] SEE, A KING will reign in righteousness
 and rulers will rule with justice.
[2] Each man will be like a shelter from the wind
 and a refuge from the storm,
 like streams of water in the desert
 and the shadow of a great rock in a thirsty land.

[3] Then the eyes of those who see will no longer be closed,
 and the ears of those who hear will listen.
[4] The mind of the rash will know and understand,
 and the stammering tongue will be fluent and clear.
[5] No longer will the fool be called noble
 nor the scoundrel be highly respected.
[6] For the fool speaks folly,
 his mind is busy with evil:
 He practices ungodliness
 and spreads error concerning the LORD;
 the hungry he leaves empty
 and from the thirsty he withholds water.
[7] The scoundrel's methods are wicked,
 he makes up evil schemes
 to destroy the poor with lies,
 even when the plea of the needy is just.
[8] But the noble man makes noble plans,
 and by noble deeds he stands.

Original Meaning

CHAPTERS 28–29 SPOKE of the false leaders, and chapters 30–31 spoke of their false counsel. Now chapters 32–33[1] speak of the true leader and the characteristics of his reign. The section is divided into four parts. The first is a general introduction (32:1–8), describing the nature of true leadership; the second (32:9–20) describes the Spirit as being necessary for such leadership; in 33:1–16 the necessity of divine intervention on Judah's behalf is explained; finally, 33:17–24 contains a graphic illustration of the rule of the King.

---

1. From a literary perspective, chs. 31 and 32 may go together as a single "woe" unit. From a thematic perspective, chs. 32 and 33 go together as discussing the true leader.

In contrast to the drunkenness, blindness, and confusion of the leaders described in chapters 28–29, the "king" whom God promises here will bring in a completely different atmosphere. His reign will be characterized by "righteousness" and "justice." Who is this king? Scholars have debated whether this is a prediction of the messianic king. While the language is more prosaic than that used in such undoubtedly messianic passages as 9:1–6 and 11:1–16, it is still true that what is described here is more than the best of human kingdoms. Thus, there seems good reason to see this material as God's promise of his Messiah in view of the failure of all the human messiahs.[2]

"Each man" (32:2) probably refers to the "rulers" (32:1) in the messianic kingdom. Instead of devouring their people for their own sakes (as the false leaders described in chs. 28–29 did), these leaders will be a blessing to their people. Their blessing is described in four vivid similes: a "shelter," a "refuge," "streams of water," and shade in the desert. In this new kingdom the conditions that resulted from Isaiah's ministry (6:9–10) will be drastically reversed (see also 30:20–21). Instead of deafness and blindness, "eyes" will see and "ears" will hear (32:3). Instead of dullness and insensitivity, hearts (NIV "mind") will have knowledge and understanding.

Both Jeremiah and Ezekiel make similar promises about the human heart in the new messianic age (Jer. 31:33; Ezek. 36:26). The Messiah will not only rule for his subjects rather than himself, but his subjects will want to know his will and obey it. Furthermore, as intimated in 2:1–5 and directly stated in 66:19, the Israelites will be able to declare God's Word to the nations with "fluent" and "clear" speech.

In 32:5–8 is a lengthy contrast between the "fool" (*nbl*) and the "noble" (*ndb*). As in the Hebrew language, so in life it is easy to confuse the *nbl* and the *ndb*. In Hebrew thinking, the "fool," like the "scoffer" (see comments on 28:14), is a strongly negative term.[3] It describes someone who has consciously rejected God and his ways (32:6; see also Ps. 14:1; 53:1); it is not merely, as in English, someone who is stupid and ridiculous. In fact, the "fool" in the Bible may be someone who is brilliant and attractive. He has simply built his life on a lie (I am accountable to no one but myself) and has dedicated his life to propagating that lie. As a result, the kind of ethics that permeate the Bible are foreign to him. The only language he understands is power. Thus, when it serves his ends, he may do good things for the poor

---

2. See Oswalt, *Isaiah 1–39*, 579–80, for an extended discussion; see also Childs, *Isaiah*, 239–40. Seitz, *Isaiah 1–39*, 230–33, argues at some length that the reference is to Hezekiah, but there is no biblical evidence to show that the years after the deliverance in 701 B.C. brought about the kind of situation predicted here.

3. See Chou-Wee Pan, "נבל," *NIDOTTE*, 3:11–13.

and needy. But if they get in the way of his "schemes," he has no concern for them at all (32:7).

Many times in life a "fool" is treated as someone honorable—a "noble"—simply because he has gained power and wealth. That is not the pattern in the Messiah's kingdom. Those are called "noble" whose actions are "noble," that is, generous and giving.[4] The "plans" and "deeds" of noble persons are for others, not for themselves (32:8). They have learned that the gracious God can be trusted to supply their needs, and thus they no longer need to be grasping but can become giving.

 THIS PATTERN WHERE the "fool" is called "noble" has been repeated in Europe for centuries. Someone who was really nothing more than a glorified pirate was given the rank of nobility by the king, and with it vast lands and holdings on which he could treat "common" people as he wished. Much of the surge of immigration into America in the 1800s was an attempt to escape the oppression that this system fostered. The tragedy is that this system was not only blessed by the church, but it was perpetuated by it, as wealthy benefactors who were simply trying to buy forgiveness while continuing in their sins were loaded down with ecclesiastical honors.

It was this pattern that drove Francis of Assisi out of the establishment and back to a ministry to the poor. The film *Brother Sun, Sister Moon* powerfully portrays Francis's conflict with a calcified, self-serving church hierarchy. In the end that hierarchy could not deny that the basis of St. Francis's "revolt" was biblical. Likewise, it was the resistance of the rich and the powerful in England to John Wesley's message of changed living that drove him out of the doors of the established church to preach to the poor, who embraced the message with joy.

 WE IN THE CHURCH today run the same danger just described. We need money to run our institutions, so how easy it is to commit the sin described by James in James 2:2–4:

Suppose a man comes into your meeting wearing a gold ring and fine clothes, and a poor man in shabby clothes also comes in. If you show

---

4. See E. Carpenter and M. A. Grisanti, "נדב," *NIDOTTE*, 3:31–32.

special attention to the man wearing fine clothes and say, "Here's a good seat for you," but say to the poor man, "You stand there" or "Sit on the floor by my feet," have you not discriminated among yourselves and become judges with evil thoughts?

We give honors to people who do not deserve them, to people whose money has been made in sharp but questionable practices—all the time telling ourselves that money has no morality. No, money has no morality, but the people who make it and give it do. It is sometimes urged that by giving our wealthy, and worldly, benefactors an opportunity to give to a good cause, we may be helping them to find a "ministry" and may be able to bring them to a new relationship with the Lord. I do not question the truth of this in principle, but my experience in Christian higher education tells me that the practice often falls far short of the principle. In fact, the "fool" believes that he or she owns you now and has the right to tell you how to conduct your business in a more "up-to-date" (read "less Christian") way. And because we feel "beholden" to our benefactor, we are cautious about offending him or her.

James did not seem to have had this problem. His words to the rich sound as if they come straight from the mouth of an Old Testament prophet (James 5:1—6):

> Now listen, you rich people, weep and wail because of the misery that is coming upon you. Your wealth has rotted, and moths have eaten your clothes. Your gold and silver are corroded. Their corrosion will testify against you and eat your flesh like fire. You have hoarded wealth in the last days. Look! The wages you failed to pay the workmen who mowed your fields are crying out against you. The cries of the harvesters have reached the ears of the Lord Almighty. You have lived on earth in luxury and self-indulgence. You have fattened yourselves in the day of slaughter. You have condemned and murdered innocent men, who were not opposing you.

By all means let us have a ministry to rich "fools." But let our "ministry" not be one of confirming them in their folly by conferring undeserved "nobility" on them. Let our ministry be one of confronting them with the direction and consequences of their lives, thus helping them to find their way to the feet of the Messiah, in whose kingdom they will change their behavior into a truly "noble" kind.

Isaiah 32:9–20

⟨⟩

⁹ YOU WOMEN WHO are so complacent,
    rise up and listen to me;
  you daughters who feel secure,
    hear what I have to say!
¹⁰ In little more than a year
    you who feel secure will tremble;
  the grape harvest will fail,
    and the harvest of fruit will not come.
¹¹ Tremble, you complacent women;
    shudder, you daughters who feel secure!
  Strip off your clothes,
    put sackcloth around your waists.
¹² Beat your breasts for the pleasant fields,
    for the fruitful vines
¹³ and for the land of my people,
    a land overgrown with thorns and briers—
  yes, mourn for all houses of merriment
    and for this city of revelry.
¹⁴ The fortress will be abandoned,
    the noisy city deserted;
  citadel and watchtower will become a wasteland forever,
    the delight of donkeys, a pasture for flocks,
¹⁵ till the Spirit is poured upon us from on high,
    and the desert becomes a fertile field,
    and the fertile field seems like a forest.
¹⁶ Justice will dwell in the desert
    and righteousness live in the fertile field.
¹⁷ The fruit of righteousness will be peace;
    the effect of righteousness will be quietness and
        confidence forever.
¹⁸ My people will live in peaceful dwelling places,
    in secure homes,
    in undisturbed places of rest.
¹⁹ Though hail flattens the forest
    and the city is leveled completely,
²⁰ how blessed you will be,
    sowing your seed by every stream,
    and letting your cattle and donkeys range free.

IT HAS BEEN COMMON for critical scholars, imbued with the principles of source and literary criticism, to treat 32:9–14 and 32:15–20 as two originally unrelated pieces brought together more or less accidentally in the editorial process. More recently, commentators such as Childs and Seitz have felt the unsatisfactory nature of this explanation as they seek to understand the text in its present unity.[1] If these texts were originally unrelated, what did later editors see in them to put them together in this way, and if suitable connections can be found to explain their now being together, why could not an original author have put them together?[2]

The unit as it stands now shows a consistent train of thought as it continues to address the issue that everything in chapters 7–39 ultimately goes back to: trust and security. Verses 9–14 condemn "women" who are "complacent" and "secure,"[3] apparently because of a good harvest. The prophet tells them that their complacency is terribly misplaced, for in only one year, all that will be changed. They should start mourning now (32:11–12) because of the agricultural disaster about to come on them.

Verse 13, with its use of "thorns and briers," suggests that the prophet has more in mind than a mere physical disaster. This pair has been used in a symbolic way in both chapters 5 and 27 to speak of the spiritual condition of the nation (5:6; 27:4).[4] Not only will the land itself become barren and deserted, but this is the condition of the nation as well. "Merriment" and "revelry" will cease (32:13), and all the places where strength and rule could be expected will be abandoned (32:14). All the false trusts will have failed.

But that will not mean God has failed. As so many times previously, the prediction of tragedy and defeat is immediately followed with God's promise of hope (32:15–20). If the nation has trusted in all the wrong things and

---

1. Childs, *Isaiah*, 237–42; Seitz, *Isaiah 1–39*, 229. Childs addresses the issues more directly, but I cannot help but feel he sidesteps the central issue to a certain extent. He seems to accept the scholarly explanation of the growth of the material but then dismisses that supposed growth as irrelevant to the message of the present unit. I do not believe authorial intent can be so easily avoided.

2. This is not to insist that they have to have been first written or spoken together. They may have been originally separate. But if they were, they both come from the same mind, as the use of *ša' ănannot*, a rare word outside of Isaiah, in both parts indicates. Thus, as the larger composition began to emerge in the prophet's mind and heart, it was easy for him to combine pieces like these in order to make his larger point. This is different from supposing multiple editorial levels in which pieces from many different origins and settings are combined on almost mechanical principles.

3. "Secure" here is a fem. participle of *btḥ*, "trust" (so also in vv. 10, 11).

4. See also 7:23–25; 9:18; 10:17.

become barren and unproductive, God has something in mind that will make possible true productivity and security, namely, his own "Spirit" (32:15).

The leaders and the counselors have exhibited a spirit of confusion, self-service, and rebellion. The result has been, and will be, disaster and profound insecurity. But in the context of the messianic kingdom, God has a prescription for that condition. He will pour out his Spirit from "on high." Just as the rain falls and the formerly barren earth springs to life, so the Spirit will fall on barren hearts, and the things that the covenant required but could not produce—"justice" and "righteousness"—will spring up. In place of the frantic busyness that self-dependence requires, those on whom the Spirit falls will be able to live in continual "quietness" and trust (NIV "confidence," 32:17), because they will have truly relinquished their lives into the hands of their covenant Lord. Their "homes" will be places of "peace," trust (NIV "secure"), and "rest" (32:18).[5]

Unlike those whose trust is placed in mere physical circumstances, this rest cannot be disturbed by physical disaster (32:19). Resting in the Spirit of God, they have inner resources of blessing that transcend the changing physical and material world. They have "streams" by which to plant the "seed" of their lives and from which to nourish those who depend on them.

Bridging Contexts

IT IS HARD for those of us who live in an urbanized culture to realize how tenuous was the life of those who lived in the agricultural world of the ancient Near East. This was especially the case in Canaan, where there were no large rivers that could be used for irrigation. Everything depended on the coming of the fall and spring rains. If these rains did not come at the proper time, famine and starvation would result in short order. Furthermore, since there were no means for long-term storage of food, a good harvest in one year offered no insurance against a bad one the following year. This explains in part the fixation of Canaanite religion— and to some extent, all the ancient Near Eastern religions—on matters of fertility and reproduction. It was truly a matter of life and death from one year to the next.

Perhaps the closest parallel in modern culture to this deep insecurity is that found in the most crime-ridden areas of our inner cities. A recent newspaper article tells of a man whose home has been broken into more than twenty times in the last ten years, despite bars and locks. He says, "I don't know why

---

5. The word translated "rest" here is *šaʾ ᵃnannot*, the same word rendered "complacent" in verses 9 and 11. In those places the women were resting on the wrong things.

they keep doing it. I ain't got nothing left to steal!" That is insecurity. When will it happen again? What will they take this time? And where is security to be found? In a new alarm system? Not likely. This is the kind of context in which Isaiah offers an inner security that will produce a godly character even in the least likely circumstances.

WE HAVE ALREADY seen in 11:1–16 the close association of the Holy Spirit with the messianic promise. It is because the Spirit of the Lord rests on the Messiah that he is able to rule as he does— with justice, knowledge, and the fear of the Lord. Here that connection is broadened. Not only is the Messiah himself to be characterized by the life of the Spirit, so are the members of his kingdom (cf. 32:1–8). John the Baptist underscored this when he differentiated himself from the Messiah by saying that he only baptized with water, whereas the Messiah would baptize with the Holy Spirit and fire.[6] Jesus reiterated this prior to his ascension when he said much the same thing as John had (see Acts 1:5).

But Jesus did not wait until his ascension to connect his ministry with that of the Holy Spirit. We are told in John 7:37–39 that he promised the Spirit to all who would believe in him.

> On the last and greatest day of the Feast, Jesus stood and said in a loud voice, "If anyone is thirsty, let him come to me and drink. Whoever believes in me, as the Scripture has said, streams of living water will flow from within him." By this he meant the Spirit, whom those who believed in him were later to receive. Up to that time the Spirit had not been given, since Jesus had not yet been glorified.

Thus, Jesus says that those who believe in him will not only experience the flowing in of the Holy Spirit, but they will give positive evidence of his presence by the kind of life that flows out from them.

The apostle Paul echoes this same principle in Romans 8. He had said in chapter 7 that the law was unable to produce the kind of defeat of sin in one's life that being identified with Christ necessitated (cf. 6:11). Unless God made some provision for us, the Christian would be as frustrated as the Jew had been in trying to live a godly life. But God has indeed made that provision. The Spirit has come to do in us what the law could not do (8:3–4). The

---

6. Matt. 34:11; Mark 1:8; Luke 3:16; John 1:33. Note that only in John is the Baptist quoted as referring to the sacrificial death of the Messiah. Clearly John saw beyond the means (cleansing and forgiveness) to the ultimate goal, namely, Spirit-filling.

law could provide forgiveness, but it could not enable a person to live a righteous life. So now, just as Isaiah had promised, the Messiah, through the Holy Spirit he has given, makes it possible for Christians to live a life of true nobility—one of generosity and self-giving, one of justice and righteousness, one that the uncertainties of existence cannot ultimately disrupt. There are inner resources with which to meet everything that comes to us and to triumph over them.

Isaiah 33:1-16

❦

¹ WOE TO YOU, O destroyer,
  you who have not been destroyed!
Woe to you, O traitor,
  you who have not been betrayed!
When you stop destroying,
  you will be destroyed;
when you stop betraying,
  you will be betrayed.

² O LORD, be gracious to us;
  we long for you.
Be our strength every morning,
  our salvation in time of distress.
³ At the thunder of your voice, the peoples flee;
  when you rise up, the nations scatter.
⁴ Your plunder, O nations, is harvested as by young locusts;
  like a swarm of locusts men pounce on it.

⁵ The LORD is exalted, for he dwells on high;
  he will fill Zion with justice and righteousness.
⁶ He will be the sure foundation for your times,
  a rich store of salvation and wisdom and knowledge;
  the fear of the LORD is the key to this treasure.

⁷ Look, their brave men cry aloud in the streets;
  the envoys of peace weep bitterly.
⁸ The highways are deserted,
  no travelers are on the roads.
The treaty is broken,
  its witnesses are despised,
  no one is respected.
⁹ The land mourns and wastes away,
  Lebanon is ashamed and withers;
Sharon is like the Arabah,
  and Bashan and Carmel drop their leaves.

¹⁰ "Now will I arise," says the LORD.
  "Now will I be exalted;
  now will I be lifted up.

¹¹ You conceive chaff,

you give birth to straw;

your breath is a fire that consumes you.

¹² The peoples will be burned as if to lime;

like cut thornbushes they will be set ablaze."

¹³ You who are far away, hear what I have done;

you who are near, acknowledge my power!

¹⁴ The sinners in Zion are terrified;

trembling grips the godless:

"Who of us can dwell with the consuming fire?

Who of us can dwell with everlasting burning?"

¹⁵ He who walks righteously

and speaks what is right,

who rejects gain from extortion

and keeps his hand from accepting bribes,

who stops his ears against plots of murder

and shuts his eyes against contemplating evil—

¹⁶ this is the man who will dwell on the heights,

whose refuge will be the mountain fortress.

His bread will be supplied,

and water will not fail him.

THIS SECTION CONTINUES the description of the kingdom of the true Messiah.[1] It is introduced by the sixth and final woe in the series begun in chapter 28, but this one is not addressed to the people of Israel or its leaders. It is addressed to the enemy of Jerusalem, almost certainly Assyria. The true king is the one who can bring about the deliverance that the drunken leaders cannot. The unit is divided into two

---

1. Many scholars today separate ch. 33 from chs. 28–32 because of its supposed liturgical and apocalyptic flavor. See H. Williamson, *The Book Called Isaiah* (Oxford: Clarendon, 1994), 221–39, for a review of recent positions and a lengthy argument that the chapter was originally designed by "Deutero-Isaiah" as a bridge from his collection of earlier prophetic writings to his own. This view is highly theoretical and, in my mind, does not adequately account for the present location of chs. 34–39. Childs, *Isaiah*, 245–46, 249, speaks favorably of W. Beuken's attempt to show that ch. 33 is an example of intertextuality, in which an editor has reused earlier references in order to pull those earlier materials together ("Jesaja 33 als Spiegeltext im Jesajabuch," *ETL* 67 [1991]: 5–35). But Childs says this has not broken the essential narrative structure within which the material functions. In that case it seems difficult to me to distinguish author from editor.

parts. The first (33:1–6) includes the "woe" itself (v. 1) and an appeal to God (v. 2) based on his character and power (vv. 3–6). The second part (33:7–16) begins with a statement of the hopelessness of the situation (vv. 7–9) and moves to a promise by God to take action (vv. 10–16). Surely such a God should be trusted.

The Woe and an Appeal to God (33:1–6)

THE EMPHASIS ON betrayal in 33:1 has suggested to many that the specific occasion for this woe was when Sennacherib accepted Hezekiah's payment to break off his attack on Judah and then did not break off the attack.[2] However, if that were the case, the material has been placed here in a much larger theological context. The fact that Assyria is not named is indicative of this. All the destructive and deceptive character of earth's nations is used as a foil to depict the radically different character of the biblical God and of the kingdom he will build.

In 33:2 we see the outcome that has been desired throughout this section. Speaking for the people, the prophet says that they will wait (NIV "long") for the Lord (cf. 30:18). Perhaps the Israelites have been forced to because the promised Egyptian help has proven useless. Nevertheless, they are now no longer trusting the nations to deliver them from the nations. They have nowhere else to turn but to God, and Isaiah has no question about God's ability to deliver. When God speaks, "nations" and "peoples" will "scatter." All the "plunder" they have stolen from other nations will be stripped away from them as though by "locusts."

This is so because the Lord is the only One who is truly "exalted" (33:5). All the attempts by humans to exalt themselves by force and deception will ultimately fail, because God alone sits "on high" (cf. 14:4–21). He does not, however, use his position as a justification for oppression. Instead, his character will provide a "foundation" on which people can live with confidence (cf. 28:16–17). That foundation is "justice" and "righteousness" (33:5), and on it can be erected "salvation," "wisdom and knowledge." All of this is available to the person who acknowledges that God is the Lord and gives him reverent obedience: "the fear of the LORD" (33:6).

Deliverance to Come from God (33:7–16)

THIS SECTION, AS noted above, first describes the desperate need for deliverance. Verses 7–9 paint a picture of hopelessness. Again, what is described

---

2. See 2 Kings 18:13–16; cf. Smith, *Isaiah 1–39*, 2 vols., rev. ed. (Expositor's Bible; London: Hodder & Stoughton, 1927), 331–32.

is consistent with the situation after Sennacherib took Hezekiah's tribute and then refused to leave. There is no place left to turn. The soldiers are crying, and the peace "envoys" are weeping. Neither military strength nor diplomacy can do any good now. Since the "treaty is broken," there is no possibility of further negotiation. That is the last hope; only raw aggression is left. As a result, the roads are empty; everything breathlessly awaits the attack.

Verse 9 depicts the situation in terms of a drought. There is no relief in sight, nor is there cooling breeze or restorative rain. The result is that even in the most fertile areas, those most typically blessed with rainfall— "Lebanon," "Sharon," "Bashan," and "Carmel"—have none; the dead "leaves" are falling from the trees.

But there *is* hope. There is no Assyria that is greater than God, and God will make that fact plain. He alone will be "exalted." All the great plans of the destroyer will one day be visited back on itself. In that hour of destruction, it will become plain that all that the destroyer has achieved in plundering the nations is to fill his storehouses with dry "chaff" and "straw," a tinderbox his own "breath" will light (33:11). Assyria started a fire sweeping across the ancient world with its imperial aggression and oppression, and Isaiah says that one day God will bring that fire back on the one who started it. Assyria's own "peoples" (33:12) will be consumed in the blaze. The destruction of Sennacherib's army in Judah is only a foretaste of the destruction of the entire empire less than a hundred years later (621–609 B.C.).

The Assyrians and all the other mighty nations of earth are not the main actors in this scene; the Lord is. It is his "power" (33:13) that rules the earth and brings the empires down to ashes. If the nations produce the tinder and provide the spark, the "consuming fire" is the Lord himself. He is the "everlasting burning" with whom people must somehow come to terms. But how can such a thing possibly be done? If he is the fire that lights the sun and consumes the nations, what incredible mystical operations will be needed for mere humans to "dwell" with him (33:14)!

In fact, there are no arcane mystical rites necessary. For in the end, as Isaiah realized in his vision recorded in chapter 6, it is not God's mystical essence that separates us from himself; rather, it is his character. Thus, it is the "sinners" and the "godless" who tremble before him, not the finite or the mortal. So what is required of us to live in the presence of "the consuming fire"? On the surface remarkably little. All that is required is a change of character on our part.

The opening words of 33:15 give a general description of this character: Do and say "what is right," that is, what is in keeping with some standard. In the Bible that standard is obviously determined by God. In 33:15c–

16, the specifics of "right" behavior are spelled out. As is usually the case in such lists, the behaviors are primarily relational. Persons who will survive the fire do not extort money from those weaker than they; they do not accept "bribes" to pervert justice; they will not listen to "plots of murder," nor will they pay attention to anything "evil." That is, they value others just as God values others. Such a person can "dwell" with God on the "heights." In that setting they will be secure ("refuge") and will have all their needs supplied. God can do what human leaders cannot and what Egypt cannot. Should he not be trusted?

GOD PROMISED THAT the plunder accumulated by the destroying nations would be stripped from them. One of the fulfillments of this promise had to do with the sacred vessels of the temple in Jerusalem. Nebuchadnezzar carried these vessels off to Babylon (2 Kings 24:13), and Belshazzar went so far as to drink toasts to his gods from them (Dan. 5:2–3). Undoubtedly he did this to demonstrate his and his gods' conquest of the Lord. But one of the first things Cyrus the Persian did after taking Babylon was to offer to rebuild the temple in Jerusalem (2 Chron. 36:33; Ezra 1:2–4; cf. also *ANET*, 316). Where did the money for that enterprise come from? Much of it came from the coffers of conquered Babylon, which in turn had come from places like the Jerusalem temple, stripped of its gold. Cyrus also directed that the vessels of the temple be given to those who were returning so that they could be restored to their rightful place (Ezra 1:8–11).

Today, it is interesting that one of the continuing stories in Europe concerns the restoring of Nazi plunder to its rightful owners. Whence comes this instinct that the plunder ought to be restored? The fact is that the right to the possession of one's property is written on the hearts of God's creation. There is a real sense that ownership of property is a sign of personal identity. Those who have suffered robbery often speak of the sense of personal violation they feel as a result of the theft. This is one more sign of God's lordship in the world. Because God in the Trinity is personal, he values personhood. Therefore, he has given us this sense of individual property rights, which undergirds civil laws around the world. Power may think it can break that creation law, and it may do so for awhile. But since God is God, it cannot do so forever. Right and justice will prevail. It does so now in a proximate way and will do so absolutely in the heavenly kingdom.

One of the characteristics of statecraft, both ancient and modern, is the weighing of alternatives. How much can one get away with? Sennacherib had to decide if there would be enough international displeasure with his breaking his agreement with Hezekiah to make that breach too costly. Evidently he decided that since he was the only power of any consequence left standing, he could do what he wanted.

Japan made a similar judgment when it decided to break modern rules of warfare in its surprise attack on Pearl Harbor in December of 1941. The Japanese were gambling that if they could cripple the U.S. Pacific fleet for a few years, they could cement such a hold on the Far East that it would be too expensive for the United States to dislodge them. And who knows how history would have been different if they had been able to destroy the fleet's aircraft carriers and not just its largely obsolescent battleships. But they were not able to do so, and in the end all their plunder was wrested from their grip. God is still God, and the betrayer is still betrayed, and the destroyer is still destroyed.

IN THE WEST TODAY, ethics, not only national but personal, have become largely utilitarian. Like Imperial Japan in 1941, we decide what is right on the basis of what we think we can get away with. If it seems good for me at this moment, then I don't care what it does to you. But Isaiah tells us that this kind of personal or national self-exaltation is dangerous. There is only One who is truly exalted, only One who can truly see the end from the beginning, only One who has established what is right out of his own character. There are standards that we violate to our own hurt.

In particular, Christians need to reconsider how the utilitarianism of the day is creeping into our behavior. One of these areas has to do with obedience to the laws of the community in which we live. It is easy to say that something like traffic laws are simply a human creation and have no divine sanction, so that I can obey them or not as I please. What we do not see is that this inevitably erodes all our ethical considerations because those human laws have their authority as an extension of divine legal authority. This is what Paul argues in Romans 13. It is impossible to separate our attitudes toward God's authority from our attitude toward the authority of the human government under which we live.

It is true, of course, that no human authority is absolute; only God's is. If the state ever intrudes itself into the realm of God, there is no question which has priority. But the place where our attitude toward obedience to God is formed and reformed is in our everyday behavior. If we place ourselves above the law in these mundane areas, inevitably we will find ways to do so in the more critical areas of our behavior in respect to God himself. It is no accident that 33:6 tells us that "the fear of the LORD is the key to this treasure" of "salvation and wisdom and knowledge." If we will not honor the Lord as Almighty God in careful obedience, we can have no meaningful relationship with him.

Like 30:19–20, Isaiah 33:16 addresses the fundamental issues of the book and of the human race: What is the best way to get my most basic needs supplied? As I have already said several times, the basic needs of humans are the same around the world: security, basic physical needs, and comfort and pleasure. All three are closely interrelated. For example, having our basic physical needs supplied in an atmosphere of insecurity and stress will result in sickness. The question in the Garden of Eden is the same question today. Who supplies my needs? The obvious answer is, "Myself; who else?" And the method of supplying the needs seems equally obvious, "By my effort in manipulating the environment in which I find myself."

But Isaiah and the rest of the Bible say something very different. No one says it more dramatically than Jesus Christ: "But seek first his kingdom and his righteousness, and all these things will be given to you as well" (Matt. 6:33). Most of us are so familiar with these words that they have lost their radical nature for us. Jesus is saying that God supplies our needs and does so as a gift. Moreover, they come to us as a by-product, not as a direct result. Do one thing, and this other thing will happen "as well." We don't supply our needs or get them supplied through our efforts. Rather, they get supplied for free to those who demonstrate their allegiance to God's rule.

This is precisely what Isaiah is talking about: Stop trying to save your own necks by making deals with your Egypts or Assyrias and start trying to please God. Leave those other concerns in his hands and focus your attention on becoming what he wants you to be. Then you will discover your needs being supplied in gracious ways you could never have imagined.

This does not necessarily mean you will be uninvolved in the process. For instance, God gave the land of Canaan to his people. They did not take it; that point is made again and again (Josh. 1:2–3; 2:9; etc.). Note how in Joshua 1–5 the people had to spiritually prepare for the Conquest. At the same time, the people were involved in the process of taking the land. Everything is centered on priorities. Is the maintenance of your relationship to your King primary, or is the King simply another means for you to try to manipulate as you scramble to take care of yourself? If the former is the case, you will discover that in the presence of the Lord a table is spread for you that no one can drive you away from. If the latter is the case, you will discover that no matter how much you accumulate, it is never enough.

> The LORD is my Shepherd,
>> I shall not be in want....
> You prepare a table before me
>> in the presence of my enemies....
> and I will dwell in the house of the Lord
>> forever. (Ps. 23:1, 5, 6)

Isaiah makes it plain here in Isaiah 33:14–16 and elsewhere that the mark of being a member of God's kingdom is to behave as the King does. This is the same principle as in the Sinai covenant. Do you want to be my people? Then you must live like me. You must be holy in the same ways that I am holy. This holiness is not first of all a matter of divine essence.[3] Rather, it is a matter of character and lifestyle. As in Psalm 15, ritual cleanliness has nothing to do with access to the Holy Place, where sacrifices were given and prayers offered. Rather, it is a matter of behavior. Those who act like God may live in his presence; others "need not apply."

But it is important for us to put this truth into the whole biblical context if we are to understand its significance for us today. This is an important corrective for modern "sinning religion." I was involved in an editorial conference for a modern-language translation of the Bible and heard an older "saint" object to a translation of Romans 6:17–18 that said we are no longer "slaves to sin," because, he said, "we are always enslaved to sin." Thank God that is not so. God expects us to share his character, and we can.

The New Testament will never, however, let us believe that we can *earn* a place in God's house because we live like him. No one can earn a place with God by righteous behavior. Rather, we are *given* that place, just as the Israelites were given freedom from Egypt. God gives us that place because Jesus Christ has died in our place. But once there, how shall we live? The Israelites thought they could obey the commandments in their own strength, and they failed miserably. But God has not only given us eternal life, he has also given us his Spirit so that we can do what the Israelites could not.

> For if you live according to the sinful nature, you will die; but if by the Spirit you put to death the misdeeds of the body, you will live, because those who are led by the Spirit of God are sons of God. (Rom. 8:13–14)

---

3. In this respect Rudolph Otto, in his *The Idea of the Holy*, 2d ed. (London: Oxford Univ. Press, 1950), has done us a grave disservice. He has excluded the biblical idea from his primary research and has used pagan religions where the concept is marginal at best to form the foundation for thinking about the biblical idea. For a better understanding, see J. Wells, *God's Holy People: A Theme in Biblical Theology* (JSOTSup 305; Sheffield: Sheffield Academic Press, 2000). See also J. Oswalt, *Called to Be Holy* (Nappanee, Ind.: Evangel, 1999).

Isaiah 33:17–24

¹⁷ YOUR EYES WILL see the king in his beauty
    and view a land that stretches afar.
¹⁸ In your thoughts you will ponder the former terror:
    "Where is that chief officer?
    Where is the one who took the revenue?
    Where is the officer in charge of the towers?"
¹⁹ You will see those arrogant people no more,
    those people of an obscure speech,
    with their strange, incomprehensible tongue.

²⁰ Look upon Zion, the city of our festivals;
    your eyes will see Jerusalem,
    a peaceful abode, a tent that will not be moved;
  its stakes will never be pulled up,
    nor any of its ropes broken.
²¹ There the LORD will be our Mighty One.
    It will be like a place of broad rivers and streams.
  No galley with oars will ride them,
    no mighty ship will sail them.
²² For the LORD is our judge,
    the LORD is our lawgiver,
  the LORD is our king;
    it is he who will save us.

²³ Your rigging hangs loose:
    The mast is not held secure,
    the sail is not spread.
  Then an abundance of spoils will be divided
    and even the lame will carry off plunder.
²⁴ No one living in Zion will say, "I am ill";
    and the sins of those who dwell there will be forgiven.

THIS SEGMENT CONCLUDES chapters 32–33, which stress that the divinely provided leader will be for Israel what the drunken, confused leaders have never been. He is the gracious promise for which they wait (33:2). This promise was fulfilled in multiple ways throughout Israel's history. It was immediately fulfilled when Hezekiah, the anointed king, trusted God for deliverance and experienced that deliverance in dramatic ways. It was fulfilled later when God delivered his people from Babylonian captivity and restored them to their own land. It was fulfilled in the more distant future when God revealed his Messiah in Jesus Christ. And it will be finally fulfilled in the last days, when the Messiah rules the earth by the rod of his mouth.

In the context of chapter 33, there can be little question that the "king" referred to here is the Lord. Not only is it clear in verses 1–16 that he is the monarch of the earth, but verse 22 specifically identifies "the LORD" as "our king." It is hard to imagine that Isaiah might have Hezekiah, the only likely human claimant in the late 700s, in mind in verse 17 when verse 22 is so specific. Moreover, the realm of Hezekiah was anything but stretching "afar." It was closely constricted.

Instead, the "king" here is the One to whom Hezekiah goes in humble subjection (37:16–20) and who thereby removes the Assyrian siege "towers" and tribute (NIV "revenue") officials from Jerusalem (33:18). This divine king makes it so that the alien Assyrian speech is not heard in Judah for a long time (33:19; cf. 28:11). Now there is "peaceful [secure]"[1] "Zion," a place whose "festivals" will no longer be disgusting to God (cf. 29:1–2). The prophet uses a bit of an oxymoron to describe the city as a permanent "tent." Perhaps the thought is that all our human habitations are as fragile as tents—and always will be. But if those tents are given over to God, he can make them more secure than the mightiest fortress that is only dependent on human power for its survival (see also 54:2).

From the metaphor of the tent, the author moves to water imagery. The city will have peaceful "rivers and streams" flowing through it. As in Psalm 46, a river is a symbol of peace and abundance. The waves of the sea crash and roar destructively, but a river flows quietly along, providing water for all sorts of constructive uses. Isaiah underscores the peaceful nature of God's supply when he says no vessel of war ("galley") will sail on the rivers of Zion. Why? Because of the righteous character of the Lord, who is Israel's "king"

---

1. This is the unusual word *šaʾǎnan*, which appeared three times in ch. 32, one other time in Isaiah, and only five other times in the rest of the Old Testament.

(33:22). He will bring in order ("judge"); he will bring in obedience to the Torah ("lawgiver"). He is Moses, Samuel, and David all rolled together. With One like that in charge, peace and prosperity are assured—even better, salvation. Such a One can deliver us from any situation of life, whether it be aggression from enemies, or a broken law, or a world of disorder.

It is not clear who is being addressed in the first half of 33:23. However, in the overall context, it is most likely the destroying, betraying nation with which the chapter began. This warship tried to sail against Zion, but it came up against a greater enemy in the Lord than it had planned for. Like a mighty windstorm he has whirled down on them, leaving the "sail" collapsed and the "rigging" sagging. Thus, all the "plunder" they had collected will be carried off by their intended victims (cf. 33:4).[2]

The final promise for the "Zion" ruled by the Messiah is that it will be a place of health, both physical and spiritual. All the effects of "sin" will be done away with, and creation will be seen again in the manner in which it was first intended.

IT IS HARD for those of us who live in democratic countries to relate to this emphasis on a king, since we have had a long tradition of government by the people. However, it does not take much disorder in our lives before we begin to clamor for a strong leader. This is what happened in Germany in the 1930s. To be sure, their experience of representative democracy was limited, but they were a strong, capable people. Nevertheless, when the Weimar Republic began to come apart with raging inflation and widespread unemployment, Hitler had no difficulty in convincing the German populace to give him all the powers of a king and then some.

The same thing had happened earlier in Russia. When the inept Czar Nicholas was finally deposed, the situation in Russia was chaotic. In that setting, Lenin was able to impose his will on the nation and become in effect the new czar. Tragically, he proved much more despotic than Nicholas had been. In the United States in the 1930s, many Americans were more than willing to make Franklin Roosevelt president-for-life. To be sure, his powers were sharply circumscribed by the Constitution and by Congress. Nevertheless, the similarity is clear: When society and government begin to break down, we want a strong leader to take charge. That is what Isaiah is promising

---

2. An alternative is that the reference is to the present condition of Israel that can only be rectified by the Messiah (see Oswalt, *Isaiah 1–39*, 605).

his people. God will give them a leader who is both strong and righteous, visionary and compassionate.

AS NOTED ABOVE, we can apply this message to at least four different historic settings. The first is in Isaiah's own day, as godly Hezekiah led his people to trust God and in so doing led them into a wonderful experience of God's power and trustworthiness. The second is the deliverance from Babylon that was completed during the time of Nehemiah, Ezra, and Malachi. The people of Judah once again experienced a secure Zion where God's bounty was provided. The fourth is in the consummation of all things, when there will be no rival to God's kingdom. The third is the one in which we live today, the one in which God's Messiah has been fully revealed and in which we see that God's promises are spiritual before they are physical.

One of the ways in which the revelation of Christ solves a potential problem in this passage as well as other messianic promises in the Old Testament is in his divinity. On the one hand, we see a king who is human. Isaiah 32:1–8 depicts a realm in which humans are active. To be sure, they are active in remarkable ways, but it is still a human realm that is being described.[3] On the other hand, the king described here in chapter 33 can be none other than the Lord—but he is the Lord who somehow fulfills the role previously filled by humans: judge, lawgiver, king.

When we think of what is called the first Christian creed ("Jesus is Lord," cf. Rom. 10:9) and recognize Jesus as the God-Man, this apparent contradiction is resolved. God rules both on earth and in heaven. He does not rule from heaven as an absentee ruler, nor does he rule on earth as a limited and finite human.[4] We can imagine the prophet puzzling over what he has said, and wondering like Mary did many centuries later, "How can these things be?" They can be if the human Messiah is also the divine King.

What does Christ offer us today? Several things emerge from this passage. He offers beauty and wide opportunities (33:17). He offers security (33:18–20). He offers us deliverance (33:22). He offers us health in its most comprehensive form (33:24). We may think of *beauty* as a nonessential, but that is obviously not how God sees it. When we look at creation, we see an abundance of things beautiful. Why is beauty a characteristic of this heavenly-

---

3. Thus Seitz, *Isaiah 1–39*, 229, argues that the intended reference must be to Hezekiah.

4. Note the same problem in Mal. 3:1. The "messenger of the covenant" will come, but then it is said that the Lord himself is the Coming One. Which is it, the messenger of the Lord or the Lord himself? The answer, of course, is that it is both.

earthly King? Among the factors that make for beauty are harmony, symmetry, rhythm, and balance. When Christ becomes the King of our lives, these are some of the things he brings to us. He is in perfect harmony with the Father as he lives out a life of rhythmic giving and receiving. He is never off-balance, attempting to secure his own will. In the quiet confidence of the Father's provision, there is a serenity and a wholeness that shines out of him. He offers this same beauty to us.

In Christ there are *endless opportunities*. He does not press us into a mold in order to produce robots who will serve him. Rather, he calls us friends, allowing each of us to achieve the maximum of what we were designed for. He allows each of us to develop in our own way because he, our King, delights to serve us. In such a relationship and with all the power of heaven at our disposal, even the most restrictive of earth's situations offers endless openings.

In Christ there is complete *security*. When we know that even in our darkest hour we were loved by him, we know that there is nothing we can do to make him stop loving us. Nothing can wrench us out of his hand. Could a day come when we demand that he let us go? Yes, that possibility exists. But until such a time, we are held in an unfailing grip. Inside that shelter we dare anything, knowing that in even the most tragic failure, we are his and he is ours.

In Christ there is *health*. Like beauty, there is both outer health and inner health, and the two are closely connected. When our sins are forgiven and our future is assured, and when we have the confidence of full provision for our needs, we can rest in him. In a rest like that, there is a soul health that will have an impact on our physical health. And even if the "earthly temple" is falling into that inevitable decay that is the fate of all until Christ returns, our inner life may radiate health and wholeness through Christ.

Isaiah 34:1–17

¹ COME NEAR, YOU nations, and listen;
    pay attention, you peoples!
Let the earth hear, and all that is in it,
    the world, and all that comes out of it!
² The LORD is angry with all nations;
    his wrath is upon all their armies.
He will totally destroy them,
    he will give them over to slaughter.
³ Their slain will be thrown out,
    their dead bodies will send up a stench;
    the mountains will be soaked with their blood.
⁴ All the stars of the heavens will be dissolved
    and the sky rolled up like a scroll;
all the starry host will fall
    like withered leaves from the vine,
    like shriveled figs from the fig tree.

⁵ My sword has drunk its fill in the heavens;
    see, it descends in judgment on Edom,
    the people I have totally destroyed.
⁶ The sword of the LORD is bathed in blood,
    it is covered with fat—
the blood of lambs and goats,
    fat from the kidneys of rams.
For the LORD has a sacrifice in Bozrah
    and a great slaughter in Edom.
⁷ And the wild oxen will fall with them,
    the bull calves and the great bulls.
Their land will be drenched with blood,
    and the dust will be soaked with fat.

⁸ For the LORD has a day of vengeance,
    a year of retribution, to uphold Zion's cause.
⁹ Edom's streams will be turned into pitch,
    her dust into burning sulfur;
    her land will become blazing pitch!
¹⁰ It will not be quenched night and day;
    its smoke will rise forever.

From generation to generation it will lie desolate;
  no one will ever pass through it again.
¹¹ The desert owl and screech owl will possess it;
  the great owl and the raven will nest there.
God will stretch out over Edom
  the measuring line of chaos
  and the plumb line of desolation.
¹² Her nobles will have nothing there to be called a kingdom,
  all her princes will vanish away.
¹³ Thorns will overrun her citadels,
  nettles and brambles her strongholds.
She will become a haunt for jackals,
  a home for owls.
¹⁴ Desert creatures will meet with hyenas,
  and wild goats will bleat to each other;
there the night creatures will also repose
  and find for themselves places of rest.
¹⁵ The owl will nest there and lay eggs,
  she will hatch them, and care for her young under the
    shadow of her wings;
there also the falcons will gather,
  each with its mate.

¹⁶Look in the scroll of the LORD and read:

None of these will be missing,
  not one will lack her mate.
For it is his mouth that has given the order,
  and his Spirit will gather them together.
¹⁷ He allots their portions;
  his hand distributes them by measure.
They will possess it forever
  and dwell there from generation to generation.

CHAPTERS 34–35 OFFER a conclusion not only to chapters 28–33, but more largely to all of chapters 13–33.[1] Throughout chapter 7–39, which I have entitled "Lessons in Trust" (see outline), God through the prophet has been showing the people of Israel why they should trust him and not the nations. Now in chapters 34–35 the alternatives are depicted in glaring contrast. To trust the nations is to become a desert (ch. 34), but God can be trusted so that even if we have chosen the nations, he can make the desert burst forth with flowers (ch. 35). The point should be clear: Trust God!

Chapter 34 is composed of two parts. The first (vv. 1–4) is a general announcement of judgment on the nations of the earth. Then this announcement is particularized by applying it to the nation of Edom (vv. 5–17). In this case, the graphic illustration is three times as long as the general statement it illustrates.

General Announcement of Judgment (34:1–4)

THE GENERAL ANNOUNCEMENT of judgment sounds a good deal like the opening stanzas of chapters 13 and 24. The language is that of the court. God calls the defendants, the "nations" and the "peoples," to hear the decree pronounced against them. But the judgment does not merely involve the "earth"; it affects the entire cosmos, with the "stars" being "dissolved" and the "sky rolled up" (34:4).[2]

God's anger is particularly directed against the "armies," which aptly symbolize the arrogance and pride of "nations." He will devote them to complete destruction (34:2). The verb used here (and the corresponding noun in v. 5) is *ḥrm*, which speaks of ritual destruction for offenses against God. It is the same term used of the Canaanites in Joshua 6:17 and of the Amalekites in 1 Samuel 15:3. This is not merely a contest to see who is stronger; it is a conflict between the Creator and those who have rebelled against him, a conflict with cosmic consequences.

Edom As an Example (34:5–17)

WHEN IT IS ASKED why Edom should be singled out to represent the nations of the earth in their hostility to God and their eventual destruction, the

---

1. It is becoming popular among scholars to see chs. 34–35 as a bridge between chs. 1–33 and chs. 40–66. See Childs, *Isaiah*, 252–56 for a handy summary of the arguments. I believe that creates some insuperable problems for the placement of chs. 36–39.

2. Throughout the book "the host of heaven" refers not only to the physical stars but also to the pantheon of pagan gods. Thus, the statement here that "the starry host will fall" has theological significance as well as cosmic.

answer seems clear. As early as the entry of Israel into the land of Canaan, Edom opposed God's plan (Num. 20:14–21). This hostility continued through the kingdom period, with one king after another having to face warfare with the Edomites.[3] In Psalm 60:9 Edom is used in a representative way. Ultimately the antagonism issued in the Edomites assisting Babylon in sacking Jerusalem (Ps. 137:7; Obad. 10–14).

The section on Edom can be divided in two parts. The first (34:5–8) begins and ends with the causal *ki*, "for" (the first is not translated in the NIV). These verses speak of the bloody destruction that is going to fall on Edom for Zion's sake. The second part (34:9–17) speaks of the desert that Edom will become. It will be a home for unclean birds and animals.

As already noted, *hrm* is repeated in verse 5, which emphasizes the representative role of Edom among the nations. The repetition of "blood" and "fat" (vv. 6–7), terms commonly used in instructions for sacrifices, makes the sacrificial setting that much clearer. The nations of earth, refusing God's grace, have become the sacrifice for their own sin. "Wild oxen" and "bulls" are the symbols of great strength and the rampaging assertion of the will. But the Lord will hold his creatures accountable for their behavior. There will be a payback, not merely as a negative judgment on sin but also on behalf of the faithful, who are integral to God's plan to redeem the earth. The destruction of the nations is intended "to uphold Zion's cause."

The description in 34:9–17 goes into considerable detail to make its point. The language of verses 9–10 is reminiscent of the destruction of Sodom and Gomorrah in Genesis 19. It is also appropriate to the region at the south end of the Dead Sea, where Edom is located. It is a barren land, where "pitch" and "sulfur" deposits can be found. This may be another reason why Edom is chosen to represent the destruction of the nations: Its territory is largely desert, which is nearly uninhabitable. Thus it fits what Isaiah wants to say about the results of trusting human glory.

To underline his point about the uninhabitability of this desert, the prophet stresses that it will become the home of all the unclean birds and animals (34:11–15). There is considerable discussion about the precise identity of many of the birds and animals listed here, and different translations show some variation. But the general point is clear: No human can live there, and if they could, they would not want to. The Creator has reassigned it to inhabitants other than human. In verse 11 "measuring line" and "plumb line" are used in an ironic way. These tools were normally used in construction with positive results. But since God is the Maker, he has the capacity to use tools in different ways. Edom has not lived up to the Creator's

3. See Motyer, *Prophecy of Isaiah*, 268–69 for a helpful review of this evidence.

standards. Therefore, those standards will be used as the measurements for destruction.[4]

Verses 16–17 assert that this prediction about the birds and animals nesting in Edom is a certainty. To establish this certainty, the prophet appeals to "the scroll of the LORD," where the hearer can supposedly read that each of the animals mentioned will be there.[5] In the book of nature as established by the "mouth" of God, there are certain fixed realities, like the mating of animals. Just as God has assigned the places and conditions of the animals, so he has also assigned the places and conditions of humans. He is like a landowner who can divide up the plots of land as he wishes. Thus, there is a fixed rule in the moral universe that is no more changeable than the laws of nature. The nations of the earth have chosen to flaunt their rebellion and must pay the price for doing so.

ONE MAJOR AREA of this chapter poses a problem for us today. Most of us are far removed from the world of bloodshed. If we encounter it at all, we see it through the distancing eye of the television camera or the movie camera. It is not a part of our lives. We eat meat, but we never give a thought to the butchering process. Moreover, apart from the horrifying slaughter that took place on the Civil War battlefields, those of us who are Americans have been by and large insulated from warfare and bloodshed in our own land.

Neither of these were true for Isaiah's first hearers. Blood and gore were a part of their everyday life. They took it as a matter of course. The whole family was involved in the butchering process, and sadly, they knew at firsthand the realities of brutal warfare. Thus, one of the things they fervently hoped for was that the people who had brutally slaughtered their family members would someday have "a taste of their own medicine." Thus, language that we

---

4. The Heb. of v. 12 is difficult. Lit. it reads: "Its nobles and there is nothing there, a kingdom it will be called. And all its princes will come to an end." The proposal of *BHS* to take "nobles" from the beginning of this verse and add it to the end of the previous on the basis of LXX is not warranted by the LXX. The NIV makes as good a sense as any. For some other proposals, see Oswalt, *Isaiah 1–39*, 616, n. 14.

5. It is not clear what this "scroll" is. Some scholars suggest it is a previous prophecy of Isaiah, but there is no such prophecy extant. Others suggest that a postexilic editor is referring to the previous passage and noting that the prophecy has been fulfilled in the destruction of Edom and its large-scale abandonment afterward. But the text cannot be used to authenticate the text. Most likely this is a rhetorical reference to the hypothetical Book of the Lord (see Mal. 3:16), where everything is written. Thus, the writer is simply saying, "You can believe this; it is as certain as the laws of nature."

find horrifying and offensive was probably actually comforting to many of those first hearers. There was going to be justice in the world after all. Though the "poor" and the "needy" of Judah may be too weak and helpless to redress the balance of the scales of justice, a day would come when God would do it for them, and the Edoms of the world would pay for what they had done.

Almost certainly this is why Jonah did not want to go to Nineveh. He wanted the Assyrians to suffer for all the suffering they had brought to Israel. But he knew how compassionate God really is and that if even an Assyrian would repent, God would not impose the judgment on them. He wanted the Assyrians to pay.

How can we relate this to our own times? We may think of the bombing of the Federal Building in Oklahoma City. It was interesting to hear persons who lost family members in the bombing speak of the impending execution of the convicted bomber. There was not a lot of passion in their voices, nor was there any of the feel of a mob demanding blood. But there was a sense that they could not feel "closure" in their own experience until the one who made the bomb had paid the full price for his crime. So even though we may not feel comfortable with the language of blood and slaughter that Isaiah uses, when the experience does come home to us, we want the scales of justice balanced. And if we will not let God place his Son in the balance for us, then justice says that we ourselves must take that place and go to destruction with Edom.

TRUSTING THE CREATURE. How do we in the contemporary world relate to such a savage text? First, we must relate to it in its literary context. As I have tried to demonstrate above, it functions to draw together all that has been said in the previous chapters about the folly of trusting the nations. Thus, as we read it today, we must ask ourselves where our trust really resides. Does it reside in the Edoms of the world? If so, we are headed into the desert with those Edoms. To put our ultimate trust in creatures instead of the Creator is truly stupid. It is to fly in the face of reality and ultimately to crash into that reality with devastating effect.

But how do we know whether we are trusting the creature or not? Most of us are not in a position to affect national policy about alliances, so what do all these admonitions have to do with us? They touch our lives at two points: the church and our own personal walk.

(1) To trust the nations is to trust the glory of humanity. What are our churches trusting in? Large budgets, impressive plant, powerful preaching? If so, we have put our trust in the creature. The place given to prayer in a local congregation is a good measure of where a church's trust really is. If its only focused praying is the Sunday morning pastoral prayer, that congregation is

headed into the desert. Whatever they may say, they as a church are trusting the creature. By contrast, when a congregation like the Brooklyn Tabernacle makes real, earnest prayer a top priority, it is actually making a practice of trusting God and is headed into a garden. The pastor who teaches the congregation to pray and the congregation who teaches their pastor to pray has gone far toward a change of allegiance from the world to God.

(2) This chapter touches us personally as well. Does my life have too many of the features of a desert? Is it possible that I have been trusting humanity, myself included, for what only God can give? What does it mean to trust God radically? Sometimes it means deliberately not doing what I could for myself and letting God do it instead. Sometimes it means taking a radical step of faith without the absolute assurance that the ground is there to step on. We may think of the main character in the film *Indiana Jones and the Last Crusade*, when he is faced with a chasm he cannot cross. Remembering words he had been told previously, he steps off into the chasm, and suddenly a walkway appears under his feet.

Have we ever given God a chance to do that kind of thing in our lives? Or has everything been so carefully planned and organized that God has no room to work? If so, a day will come when we are unable to solve the problem with our plans, organization, and effort. Then we will cry, "God, why have you abandoned me?" And the answer will be, "I have not, but because you never learned to trust me in the easy times, you don't know how to trust me now."

Vengeance. How do the passionate promises of vengeance apply to the life of the contemporary Christian? Do not Jesus' words about turning the other cheek and loving our enemies radically contradict these words of Isaiah? In fact, may we not say that this is a "pre-Christian" text that has been invalidated by the New Testament? The answer to both questions is "No." These words and those of the New Testament are closely interrelated.

The key idea here is that of Paul found in Romans 12:19: "Do not take revenge, my friends, but leave room for God's wrath, for it is written: 'It is mine to avenge; I will repay,' says the Lord." How can we find the grace not to seek revenge? It is precisely in the knowledge that there is a just Judge of all the universe who will see that justice is done in the end. We do not need to destroy the Edom that may have crushed us under its heavy boot because we can trust God to do the right thing in the end, both for Edom and us.

How freeing this is. It takes the justice of the world off our shoulders and frees us from carrying around a heavy load of anger and resentment. Surely one of the things that brought down President Nixon in the end was his "list of enemies." If he and his staff had been less concerned about their enemies and more concerned simply to do what is right in the confidence that God would redress the balances, the Watergate scandal might never have happened.

Isaiah 35:1–10

¹ THE DESERT AND the parched land will be glad;
   the wilderness will rejoice and blossom.
Like the crocus, ²it will burst into bloom;
   it will rejoice greatly and shout for joy.
The glory of Lebanon will be given to it,
   the splendor of Carmel and Sharon;
they will see the glory of the LORD,
   the splendor of our God.

³ Strengthen the feeble hands,
   steady the knees that give way;
⁴ say to those with fearful hearts,
   "Be strong, do not fear;
your God will come,
   he will come with vengeance;
with divine retribution
   he will come to save you."

⁵ Then will the eyes of the blind be opened
   and the ears of the deaf unstopped.
⁶ Then will the lame leap like a deer,
   and the mute tongue shout for joy.
Water will gush forth in the wilderness
   and streams in the desert.
⁷ The burning sand will become a pool,
   the thirsty ground bubbling springs.
In the haunts where jackals once lay,
   grass and reeds and papyrus will grow.

⁸ And a highway will be there;
   it will be called the Way of Holiness.
The unclean will not journey on it;
   it will be for those who walk in that Way;
   wicked fools will not go about on it.
⁹ No lion will be there,
   nor will any ferocious beast get up on it;
   they will not be found there.
But only the redeemed will walk there,
¹⁰   and the ransomed of the LORD will return.

> They will enter Zion with singing;
>   everlasting joy will crown their heads.
> Gladness and joy will overtake them,
>   and sorrow and sighing will flee away.

THIS CHAPTER IS the mirror image of Isaiah 34. That passage spoke of the fate of the arrogant nations and all who trusted in them. This one speaks of the destiny of those who turn from that path to a resolute trust in God. It may be argued that there is no mention of trust in this chapter (or in ch. 34, for that matter). That is certainly correct. However, the larger context on both sides of these chapters makes the point clear enough. Throughout chapters 28–33, the central issue was the stupid advice of the leaders that the Judeans should trust Egypt. In chapter 36, the Assyrian officer will mock the idea of trusting God. Thus, even though the words are not used here, the question of trust is the underlying concept. What happens if we trust in God instead of the nations? The answer to that question is beautifully presented here.

First of all, in a powerful contrast, God will turn the "desert" into a garden (35:1).[1] The "burning sand will become a pool," and the places "where jackals once lay" will become grassy meadows (35:7). These latter statements certainly make it appear that they are intended as a direct reference to the preceding chapter. Even the desolation that endured from generation to generation (34:10, 17) can be changed by God if we will let him. God will display his "glory" to his people by restoring them, making them as rich and abundant as the forests on "Lebanon" and "Carmel" or the grasslands of the plain of "Sharon" (35:2; cf. 33:9). When the rains of God fall, what appeared to be a barren waste springs into riotous color almost overnight.

Verses 3–6a and 8 make it plain that this restoration is a spiritual one. Those who are discouraged and fearful will be given courage and strength. They have remained faithful while the nation has gone down and down. They have seen evil triumph again and again, and they have wondered if

---

1. Since this is poetry, it is unwise to try to find a precise literal referent for the images used here. In other words, we should not ask what literal desert is being referred to, nor should we attempt to narrow down to one option the place from which the people are returning. It seems to me that the author intends to talk about several things simultaneously: the return from exile in 539 B.C. and later, the ultimate ingathering of all believers at the end of time, and the journey of the unbeliever to faith, restoration, and healing. On the correct reading of biblical poetry, see R. Alter, *The Art of Biblical Poetry* (New York: Basic Books, 1985), 186.

God's day would ever come. But, as I commented on chapter 34, the Lord will balance the scales of justice, and they will see the day when both wickedness and righteousness receive their true reward from God. Furthermore, in an apparent allusion to Isaiah 6, the promise is made that those who did not remain faithful—the "blind" and the "deaf," the spiritually "lame" and "mute"— will be delivered from their afflictions and become full participants in the community of faith.

This idea is furthered with an additional image in 35:8–10, namely, that of a "highway."[2] In the rugged highlands of Judah and Ephraim as well as in the desert east and south of Judah's central ridge, a straight and level highway would be a wonderful thing. That is what God promises to those who will turn to him in trust. He will make a way through the most difficult circumstances. Note that this is another contrast with chapter 34. In 34:10, the prophet said the conditions of the desert would obstruct all passage. But that is not the case in God's country. There is ready access to him and to all the blessings of his creation.

This highway is the way to God, as seen in its title, "the Way of Holiness." The meaning of the phrase is further spelled out in 35:8–9. Negatively, there will be no one "unclean" on it, there will be no "fools" there,[3] nor will there be any devouring animals. Positively, God's way is a way of purity, obedience, and safety. It is the way of holiness on which the "redeemed" walk. Verse 10 describes the end result of this journey through the desert. It is to come to the city of God, Zion, where "gladness" and "joy" will forever displace "sorrow and sighing" (cf. 25:7–8).

Bridging Contexts

FOR THOSE OF US who have lived through the creation of the modern superhighway system, the picture of the highway here is vivid. We can remember when a journey of two hundred miles would take five or six hours as we crawled through small towns with their many traffic lights or crept up long hills behind heavy trucks. What a great day it was when the new interstate highway opened up and that same journey could be covered in about three hours. That is the kind of thought expressed here. God does not want to place any barriers in the way of people coming to him. If there are barriers, they are of our making, not his. He does not want us

---

2. For other occurrences of "highway" in Isaiah, see 11:16; 19:23; 40:3; 43:19; 49:11; 62:10. In each case it is either to provide a way for people to come to God or for God to come to his people.

3. *'wil*, a morally perverse person, cf. 19:11 (not the same word used in 32:5–6).

winding our way through a mountainous desert on a pothole-filled, two-lane highway, where drug lords rule. He wants us to come to him with pleasant companions on a four-lane highway through a garden spot, where each new vista is more charming than the last. This is what God promises to those who will abandon their trust in humanity and hurl themselves on him.

TWO COMINGS ARE described in this chapter: the coming of God to his people, and the coming of the people to God's house. Both are necessary, and this is the proper order. We humans have made our world into a desert and are helpless in it. We can intuit that there is a God to whom we are accountable, but we don't know who or what he is. All our attempts to reach him or even describe him founder on the depravity of our nature and the inadequacy of our ability to communicate (e.g., the Tower of Babel, Gen. 11:1–9). God is other than we, and we are unable to even imagine him except as being a duplicate of ourselves.

But that way lies a barren desert. If God is only humanity written large, then he is just as much subject to fate as we are; he is just as much in the dark about the future as we are and just as unable to change his moral behavior. For him too, survival at all costs is all that matters—a survival that depends on rightly assessing where the power is and determining how to seize and hold it. I say again: That way lies a desert.

But God is radically other than we, and that means we can never know him unless he first comes to us. He must take the initiative both to disclose himself to us and then to deliver us from the desert into which we have condemned ourselves. We are helpless, both in our ignorance and in our sin. This is some of the meaning of the deceptively simple statements with which the Gospel of John opens:

> In the beginning was the Word, and the Word was with God, and the Word was God. He was with God in the beginning.
> Through him all things were made; without him nothing was made that has been made. In him was life, and that life was the light of men. The light shines in the darkness, but the darkness has not understood it. . . .
> The Word became flesh and made his dwelling among us. We have seen his glory, the glory of the One and Only, who came from the Father, full of grace and truth. (John 1:1–5, 14)

At the heart of God is communication. It is not an afterthought or an "add-on." Where God is, there is communication. The creation itself is an expression of that communication. And since creation has fallen and an additional barrier other than finiteness, the one of sin, has been placed between us, God has come to this earth to be one of us. He did that because there was no other way in which we could see what his true glory consists of (cf. Isa. 35:2).

But his self-revelation is not merely to impart true information, because the imparting of information is only the thinnest edge of communication. Real communication involves the sharing of personality. That is not possible for those sunk in despair and discouragement (35:3–4). Neither is it possible for those who have been spiritually crippled by their own sin (35:5–6). If God is to communicate his person to us, those barriers will have to be broken down. That is exactly what he did in the Word, Jesus Christ. "God was reconciling the world to himself in Christ," says Paul in 2 Corinthians 5:19. He reconciled the world *to himself* by coming all the way to us.

Why has he come? *In order that we might come to him.* Throughout the Scriptures life with God is described as a walk. Abraham was told to "walk before me and be blameless" (Gen. 17:1). Moses told the Hebrews that the fulfillment of God's commands involved walking "in all his ways," which involved serving and loving him with one's whole "heart" (Deut. 10:12). Hezekiah asked God for a longer life because he had "walked before you faithfully and with wholehearted devotion" (2 Kings 20:3). Jesus told his disciples to "walk while you have the light" (John 12:35). First John 2:6 says that those who claim "to live in him must walk as Jesus did." Paul prefers the more abstract "manner of life" (cf. Phil. 1:27), but he has the same concept in mind (cf. Eph. 5:2, "walk in love"). Life with God is not static.

In other words, God has not delivered us from our sins so that we can simply sit and contemplate our saved condition until the day we die. Rather, he has delivered us from our sin so that we can participate in his life and character in a progressive, ongoing way. This is what Paul has in mind when he says that believers are to "work out your salvation with fear and trembling, for it is God who works in you to will and to act according to his good purpose" (Phil. 2:12–13). God has come to us and day by day makes it possible for us to walk with him in greater and greater likeness to him, until that last day when we arrive in the heavenly city where gladness will displace sorrow forever.

Isaiah 36:1–37:7

‌🔥

IN THE FOURTEENTH year of King Hezekiah's reign, Sennacherib king of Assyria attacked all the fortified cities of Judah and captured them. ²Then the king of Assyria sent his field commander with a large army from Lachish to King Hezekiah at Jerusalem. When the commander stopped at the aqueduct of the Upper Pool, on the road to the Washerman's Field, ³Eliakim son of Hilkiah the palace administrator, Shebna the secretary, and Joah son of Asaph the recorder went out to him.

⁴The field commander said to them, "Tell Hezekiah,

"'This is what the great king, the king of Assyria, says: On what are you basing this confidence of yours? ⁵You say you have strategy and military strength—but you speak only empty words. On whom are you depending, that you rebel against me? ⁶Look now, you are depending on Egypt, that splintered reed of a staff, which pierces a man's hand and wounds him if he leans on it! Such is Pharaoh king of Egypt to all who depend on him. ⁷And if you say to me, "We are depending on the LORD our God"—isn't he the one whose high places and altars Hezekiah removed, saying to Judah and Jerusalem, "You must worship before this altar"?

⁸"'Come now, make a bargain with my master, the king of Assyria: I will give you two thousand horses—if you can put riders on them! ⁹How then can you repulse one officer of the least of my master's officials, even though you are depending on Egypt for chariots and horsemen? ¹⁰Furthermore, have I come to attack and destroy this land without the LORD? The LORD himself told me to march against this country and destroy it.'"

¹¹Then Eliakim, Shebna and Joah said to the field commander, "Please speak to your servants in Aramaic, since we understand it. Don't speak to us in Hebrew in the hearing of the people on the wall."

¹²But the commander replied, "Was it only to your master and you that my master sent me to say these things, and not

to the men sitting on the wall—who, like you, will have to eat their own filth and drink their own urine?"

[13]Then the commander stood and called out in Hebrew, "Hear the words of the great king, the king of Assyria! [14]This is what the king says: Do not let Hezekiah deceive you. He cannot deliver you! [15]Do not let Hezekiah persuade you to trust in the LORD when he says, 'The LORD will surely deliver us; this city will not be given into the hand of the king of Assyria.'

[16]"Do not listen to Hezekiah. This is what the king of Assyria says: Make peace with me and come out to me. Then every one of you will eat from his own vine and fig tree and drink water from his own cistern, [17]until I come and take you to a land like your own—a land of grain and new wine, a land of bread and vineyards.

[18]"Do not let Hezekiah mislead you when he says, 'The LORD will deliver us.' Has the god of any nation ever delivered his land from the hand of the king of Assyria? [19]Where are the gods of Hamath and Arpad? Where are the gods of Sepharvaim? Have they rescued Samaria from my hand? [20]Who of all the gods of these countries has been able to save his land from me? How then can the LORD deliver Jerusalem from my hand?"

[21]But the people remained silent and said nothing in reply, because the king had commanded, "Do not answer him."

[22]Then Eliakim son of Hilkiah the palace administrator, Shebna the secretary, and Joah son of Asaph the recorder went to Hezekiah, with their clothes torn, and told him what the field commander had said.

[37:1]When King Hezekiah heard this, he tore his clothes and put on sackcloth and went into the temple of the LORD. [2]He sent Eliakim the palace administrator, Shebna the secretary, and the leading priests, all wearing sackcloth, to the prophet Isaiah son of Amoz. [3]They told him, "This is what Hezekiah says: This day is a day of distress and rebuke and disgrace, as when children come to the point of birth and there is no strength to deliver them. [4]It may be that the LORD your God will hear the words of the field commander, whom his master, the king of Assyria, has sent to ridicule the living God, and that he will rebuke him for the words the LORD your God has heard. Therefore pray for the remnant that still survives."

⁵When King Hezekiah's officials came to Isaiah, ⁶Isaiah said to them, "Tell your master, 'This is what the LORD says: Do not be afraid of what you have heard—those words with which the underlings of the king of Assyria have blasphemed me. ⁷Listen! I am going to put a spirit in him so that when he hears a certain report, he will return to his own country, and there I will have him cut down with the sword.'"

ISAIAH 36–39 FORMS the last section in the second major subdivision in the book (chs. 7–39, see outline). Its three subsections are all focused on the question: Shall we put our trust in God or in the nations?[1] (1) In chapters 7–12, Ahaz gave the wrong answer to Isaiah, and the implications of that response are explored both for the near term and the long term, especially as it provides the basis for the coming messianic kingdom.

(2) Chapters 13–35 then explain why trust in the nations is so foolish. All human beings are under the judgment of Israel's Holy One (chs. 13–23), who will bring history to a close with the redemption of the faithful of all nations as well as his own people (chs. 24–27). These general truths are applied to the specific circumstances leading up to the attack by the Assyrian Sennacherib in 701 B.C. (chs. 28–35). Isaiah speaks forcefully against the folly of trusting Egypt instead of God in that situation.

(3) After these lessons in trust, the test as to whether to trust God or the nations is administered once again, this time to the son of Ahaz, Hezekiah. Thus, Isaiah 36–39 is anything but a historical appendix. These chapters are the climax of the whole argument of the book to this point. The prophet has

---

1. Many commentators speak of chs. 36–39 as a historical appendix. In part this is true because the material closely parallels parts of the Hezekiah section in 2 Kings. Thus, Bernard Duhm has posited that the material was simply lifted more or less as is from Kings by a postexilic editor. Supposedly the editor did this because he needed a bridge between the two blocks of material he wanted to put together: chs. 1–35 (First Isaiah) and chs. 40–55 (Second Isaiah). Modern redaction criticism takes a much less mechanical view than this, and many scholars today who accept multiple authorship for the book would still argue that the material has been edited to serve a particular function in the present form of the book. There are basically three views on the relationship of the material here and in Kings: priority of Kings (cf. Childs, *Isaiah*, 260–66), priority of Isaiah (cf. Seitz, *Isaiah 1–39*, 243–44), and both dependent on a common source (cf. Motyer, *Prophecy of Isaiah*, 285–86). In my view, the present order of the incident narrated in chs. 36–39 of Isaiah only makes sense in the context of Isaiah and demonstrates that the Kings account has been at least influenced by Isaiah (as Motyer recognizes).

asserted over and over again that God can be trusted. But is that all just rhetoric? Are they just words that have no historical significance? No, everything the prophet has said is true. The only question is whether anyone is listening or not. In the upshot, the answer is a short-term "yes" but a long-term "no."

It is the combination of these two answers that sets the stage for this section. Because Hezekiah says "yes," the sovereign power and unique trustworthiness of God are demonstrated and do not need any further explanation. The point of God's absolute rule over the world and his ability to care for those who trust him has been made, and now it is possible to move on to further points in God's and the prophet's theological program.

Yet Hezekiah's failure to witness these same truths to the Babylonian envoys is also important to what follows. Up to this point, it may have been thought this devout and trusting Hezekiah is the promised Immanuel (7:14). Perhaps he is the one who will be the savior of his people, and perhaps his kingdom is the one promised in chapters 9, 11, and 32–33. By placing this failure at the end of the section (ch. 39), the author-editor is not merely pointing ahead to the coming defeat by Babylon. Much more importantly, he is saying that Hezekiah is *not* Immanuel and that we must look to someone else yet to come for the fulfillment of the messianic promises. In my view, this is the only satisfactory explanation for reversing the chronological order of Isaiah 36–37 and 38–39.[2]

The date of the event described in chapters 36–37 seems to be unquestionably 701 B.C., based both on Assyrian records and on those found in the Bible. But it does create one serious problem. First Kings 18:1 is explicit that Hezekiah began to reign in the third year of Hoshea of Israel, that is, about 727 B.C. But that would place his "fourteenth year" in 715, which is impossible. The solution seems to be that he was coregent with his father, Ahaz, until Ahaz's death in 716, and that the years of his reign, unlike those of other coregents, were only counted from his full accession to the throne. Thiele does not accept this suggestion and argues that there is a twelve-year discrepancy in the accounts that has not been fully harmonized.[3]

---

2. Aside from the fact that there is a question as to whether Merodach-Baladan was still active in 701 B.C., the promise in 38:6 that God will deliver the city from the Assyrian king means that Hezekiah's illness and the visit of the Babylonian envoys occurred at least somewhat prior to the destruction of the Assyrian army described in 37:36–38. See Oswalt, *Isaiah 1–39*, 629–30, for further discussion.

3. For a full discussion, see E. R. Thiele, *The Mysterious Numbers of the Hebrew Kings*, 3d ed., 118–54. Young (*The Book of Isaiah*, 2:540–42) argues cogently that "fourteen" is an error for "twenty-four."

The Speech of the Field Commander (36:1–22)

"THE FIELD COMMANDER" (36:2) is the third highest-ranking officer in the Assyrian army, so this move against Jerusalem is a serious one. The main army is engaged in the siege of Lachish, about thirty miles southwest of Jerusalem on the edge of the coastal plain. This is the last remaining Judean walled city except Jerusalem; all the rest have fallen to the Assyrians (36:1). As long as Lachish stands firm, there is danger to the rear of any army attacking Jerusalem, for Lachish is large and can hold numerous troops. At the same time, as long as Jerusalem holds out, it poses a danger to the troops surrounding Lachish. So it is greatly to Sennacherib's advantage to persuade the leadership in Jerusalem that their situation is hopeless and that their only option is to surrender. This would save the expense and aggravation of yet another siege and would probably help to bring Lachish down.

It is significant that the field commander stands in exactly the same spot where Isaiah stood some thirty-four or thirty-five years earlier when he had confronted Ahaz (36:2; cf. 7:3). The warnings Isaiah gave over the folly of trusting Assyria instead of God are all coming true with a vengeance. He said that the Assyrians would flood the land right up to its neck (8:7–8), and that very flood tide was now swirling around them. Ahaz had only been faced with his two northern neighbors: Israel and Syria. Hezekiah now faces a much larger and more deadly enemy. Have the lessons of Isaiah's preaching during the last thirty-five years made any difference? Will Hezekiah trust God in much more risky circumstances than those where his father did not trust?[4]

The field commander's speech is not logically developed. At one point he says that the Lord has sent them to attack Jerusalem (36:10), but in another that the Lord cannot protect Jerusalem from the hand of Sennacherib (36:18–20). It appears that he is simply hammering the fearful Judeans with every possible argument that might undermine their trust—and trust is clearly what this conflict is about. His opening words make that clear: "On what are you basing this confidence of yours?" (36:4). Then he proceeds to demolish, from his point of view, each possible basis. He starts with military power and says they are trusting a "splintered reed," Egypt, for their strength. That reed will break if they put any weight at all on it (36:5–6). That proved true as the Assyrian army was able to defeat the one Egyptian foray under Tirhakah handily.[5]

---

4. Note that although Shebna is still in the king's "cabinet" as secretary, he has been deposed as Isaiah prophesied and Eliakim has been put in his place as "palace administrator" or prime minister (cf. 22:20–21).

5. See *ANET*, 287–88.

The commander then turns to another possible source of help, the Lord (36:7). Here he betrays a deficiency in his background briefing, believing that God is unhappy at the destruction of the high places outside of Jerusalem where local people were worshiping him. The pagan Assyrian cannot understand that the unity of God is undermined by worship of him in places other than Jerusalem. Furthermore, many high places were formerly pagan worship centers, so the worship of the Lord there was often diluted with paganism. It was for these kinds of reasons that God, through Moses, had commanded that he was to be worshiped only in the place he himself chose (Deut. 12:2–5). But the Assyrian cannot understand that and assumes that God is angry at this destruction and will not likely help someone like Hezekiah, who engineered the destruction.

Then the field commander turns back to military might and mocks the weakness of Judah. So powerful is Assyria that they could afford to give two thousand horses to Judah and still be confident of defeating them. But he is not worried because he knows that little Judah cannot muster two thousand trained horsemen to ride the horses even if they were given. In that light, the help from Egypt is useless (36:9), because Judah cannot make good use of whatever military assistance they might receive.

Then the Assyrian field commander switches gears again, asserting that "the LORD," the God of Israel, has directed him to "destroy" the "land." It would be interesting to know where this idea came from. It is certainly not what we think of as typical Assyrian thought. It may well be that the Assyrian foreign office has done its homework and discovered that these were the kinds of things the prophets of Israel were saying. Yet the field commander's brutal assertion that his master, the king, can defeat Judah's God just as he has every other god (36:18–20) makes it clear that all he really believes in is power.

It is clear from the interchange in 36:11–12 that a part of the purpose of the field commander's expedition is to erode the morale of the city. When the ambassadors of King Hezekiah ask him to continue his presentation in Aramaic, the common language of the Assyrian Empire and one that the Judean officials understand but not the common people, he flatly refuses. He feels all the Israelites should know what horrors they are going to face if their leaders are so foolish as not to surrender. Presumably the people might become so panic-stricken that the leaders will be forced to surrender even if it is against their own best judgment.

It is interesting that the Assyrian refers to his master as "the king" on several occasions (36:8, 13, 14, 16, 18) but never once accords that honor to Hezekiah. Whenever he refers to the king of Judah, it is only by his name. Here is one more part of the power play: The ruler of this petty nation does not even have the right to be called a king in any comparison with the true king of the universe, Sennacherib. How does he dare to oppose his will to that of the only true king?

The real issue comes out in 36:14–20. It is a contest between the Lord and the king of Assyria. Note that it is not a contest between the Lord and the gods of Assyria, but between the mightiest and most glorious man of the age and the Lord God. Here is the height of the human arrogance that has been attacked throughout the book thus far, and here all the teaching of the book thus far comes to its climax. Will we trust human glory, a humanity that dares to call itself "king"? Or will we trust the One who *is* Glory, the One who *is* King, and be given a message of hope for the nations?

The Assyrian officer says in the bluntest of terms that Hezekiah "cannot deliver you" (36:14), because "the LORD will [not] deliver" them (36:18–20). But before he comes to that reason, he dares to ask the Judeans to trust his master, Sennacherib. If they will entrust themselves to this master tyrant instead of to the Lord, he will lift the restraints of the siege from them and they will be able to go back out to their farms (36:16) until they are transported to just as good a place as this. One has to admire the Assyrian's capacity to put a good face on the deportation, which everyone knows will follow any surrender at this stage in Judean-Assyrian relations.

Then, in the kind of sudden reversal that is typical of hard-line inquisition, the tone changes from conciliatory to brutal. What will happen to them if they are so foolish as to believe Hezekiah's promise that "the LORD will deliver us" (36:18)? All the terrible things that they have heard have happened to every other city of consequence up and down the eastern coast of the Mediterranean Sea. The gods of all those cities were helpless before the king of Assyria, so how can they imagine that their God is any different? Interestingly, he never comes right out to say God cannot deliver, but he says that no other god has, so how can this one?

Perhaps the field commander would arouse some competitive zeal if he were so bold as to say God cannot deliver, but if he can just let the facts speak for themselves, the people will surely be forced to the conclusion he wants them to draw. But the Assyrian's argument has a fatal flaw in it. He assumes that the Lord is just one more of the gods. But that is not true. As Isaiah has been saying all along, the Lord is not one of the gods; he is a different sort of being altogether.

The representatives of King Hezekiah make no attempt to answer this collection of arguments.[6] That is certainly just as well, because they are not meant to answer. This is psychological warfare, an attempt to break the enemy's will to resist. And it seems to have been effective because the rep-

---

6. The NIV has "the people remained silent," but the Heb. does not specify the subject of the verb. It seems more likely that it is the embassy, since it is hard to believe that everyone listening on the wall would have done something the king commanded just because he commanded it.

resentatives go back to the king in a state of shock and grief, as attested by their having "torn" their clothing.

Hezekiah's Response (37:1–7)

HEZEKIAH'S RESPONSE TO his advisors' report is instructive. He also tears his clothes (37:1), puts on sackcloth or burlap (the traditional sign of mourning), and goes into the temple. He does not closet himself with his advisors and consider what "spin" to put on the events. To be sure, if the sequence of the materials in 2 Kings also corresponds to the sequence of events, Hezekiah has already tried to buy himself out of the situation by giving Sennacherib a large sum of money, so in one sense this is a last resort. We need not make Hezekiah look better than he is. But it is hard to imagine either Jehoiakim or Zedekiah in the Babylonian crisis a hundred years later turning to God this openly or directly at any point in the process.

Not only does Hezekiah himself turn to God, he also sends an impressive delegation to consult with Isaiah (37:2). Hezekiah's message to Isaiah carries much the same tone as that found in his prayer later in chapter 37. He is particularly concerned about the disgrace that this situation brings on God. Hezekiah and at least some of his people have publicly declared their belief that God will not let them fall to the Assyrians. But now they *are* going to fall unless God intervenes in some miraculous way. The Judeans have no strength with which to bring about their own deliverance. This is the point of 37:3. Like the mother who has labored and labored to the point of exhaustion, they have no strength left (see also 26:16–18; 54:1; 66:9). But the Assyrian has not only ridiculed the Judeans for the apparent failure of their trust, he has ridiculed "the living God" himself. Rather hesitantly, Hezekiah wonders if God will let that go by (37:4).

The response God gives to Isaiah makes it clear he does not intend to let the challenge pass unaddressed. The difference from the hesitancy of Hezekiah's tone is marked. The king may be terrified, but the God who speaks through Isaiah is not. God's words are brisk and matter-of-fact. He returns a bit of his own ridicule when he refers to the high Assyrian officers as "underlings" (37:6).[7] But he says that he has not merely been ridiculed by the Assyrian, he has been blasphemed. As a result, he will not allow the Assyrian to succeed in his plans but will send him home by means of nothing more than a "spirit."[8] There, supposedly secure in his own fortress, Sennacherib will die by the "sword." God is not mocked.

---

7. Heb. *na'ar*, "lad."

8. It is interesting that Isaiah does not foretell the destruction of the Assyrian army, nor does he give any hint as to what the "certain report" (37:7) will contain. This leads some

Bridging Contexts

WE MAY THINK of an incident similar to this in our own times. In December 1944, Hitler threw his carefully hoarded reserves into the weakest part of the Allied line in the Ardennes forest of Belgium. He hoped that by a lightning thrust northwestward to the coast at Antwerp he could divide the British and American sections of the Allied army and gain the time necessary for his secret weapons, the V–2 rockets, to soften up the British and perhaps bring the Allies to the bargaining table. The result was the so-called "Battle of the Bulge."

Initially, the Germans were successful as they punched a large hole through the Allied front lines. The terrible winter weather favored the Germans as it kept the Allied air forces grounded. However, although the front line had been broken, the second and third lines only bent backward. And in the middle of the "Bulge," surrounded by German forces, was the important crossroads town of Bastogne. As long as Bastogne was held by the Allies, it constituted a serious threat to the German supply lines. So major German forces were committed to capturing it, forces that were sorely needed in the westward push if it was to succeed.

After more than a week of hammering, during which the American forces holding the city were more and more constricted, a German representative appeared under a white flag, demanding the surrender of the city. Brigadier General Anthony McAuliffe responded to the demand with one of the tersest replies to a surrender demand in all history, "Nuts!" The German representative withdrew somewhat mystified but understanding that no surrender was forthcoming, and a few days later the city was relieved by American troops driving northward through the shoulder of the "Bulge." Hezekiah, unlike General McAuliffe, had no promises of a Patton-led Third Army coming to his rescue. He only had the Lord. But that was enough to make him give a response to the Assyrians that must have sounded a good deal like McAuliffe's.

There are some striking similarities between the field commander's attempts to break the Judeans' will to resist and that which is practiced today. One of these is the bombardment with arguments, even if some of the arguments actually contradict each other. So it did not matter that "God sent us" (36:10) and "God is no match for us" (36:18–20) could not both be true.

---

scholars to maintain that the account of the destruction of the army is a later legend (see below on 37:36–38). Motyer, *Prophecy of Isaiah*, 279, maintains that the army's destruction was already predicted in 14:24–27 and that here the focus is on what will happen to Sennacherib for his blasphemy. The latter point is certainly correct whether or not we agree with that interpretation of 14:24–27.

Truth is beside the point in this kind of situation. The point is to get prisoners reeling, hitting them with another argument before they can formulate a response to the previous one. The desired result is a feeling of helplessness and hopelessness under the sheer weight of the arguments.

A second similarity is the sudden alternation between apparent kindness and brutality. The "subject" has been expending tremendous energy resisting when suddenly the pressure is relaxed, and perhaps even some kindness is shown. One experiences great relief, believing that "the worst is over." But in that moment the interrogator returns to the attack with much greater brutality than before. In many cases, the "subject," having dismantled his or her defenses, is simply unable to erect them again. The Romanian pastor Joseph Tson experienced something like this when after months of interrogation, the interrogator suddenly backed him up against a wall and, holding him by the lapels, began banging Tson's head against the wall. Pastor Tson said that he shouted at the top of his voice, wanting everyone in the building to know what was happening. But, like Hezekiah, he did not break under the pressure. He had inner resources that were superior to those of the interrogator.

The field commander's reference to the "two thousand horses" and horsemen to ride them (36:8) may well be a boast about the latest military technology. At this time the use of mounted cavalry was first being promoted alongside the use of chariotry. The cavalry were even more flexible and mobile than chariot forces, which had dominated warfare for the previous five hundred years. If it is indeed a reference to cavalry, it is probably a mocking reference to Judah's being out of touch with the latest developments. If they were going to depend on military technology to protect them from Assyria, then they had to have the latest technology, and that they clearly did not have. They had no one trained to ride the horses even if they did have them.

In today's world, dependence on technology has the same drawbacks. Is technology a tool, or is it the source of our strength? If it is the latter, then we have no choice but to commit ourselves to the latest technology even if it means abandoning a perfectly serviceable older approach. If our identity is tied to technology, then we can never afford to be one moment behind. As the Assyrians learned to their dismay, the God on whom Hezekiah trusted was not dependent on military technology, so it really did not matter whether the Judeans were up to date or not. This is not an argument that we should cultivate technological backwardness. But it is to say that if our true identity is somewhere else than in technology, then we will not need to be ruled by the latest developments in the field. In days of rapid change, this can be a real blessing, as the latest development may well be a dead-end.

WHOLEHEARTED DEVOTION. Where is the source of strength when all the forces of the world seem ranged against us, intent on hammering us into the ground and breaking all our resistance? Perhaps for Hezekiah, this was the culmination of a whole series of choices. We do not know how carefully he had listened to Isaiah across the years, but the biblical record depicts a man who had, from the outset, tried to do what he believed God had wanted. So when he came to this crisis moment, there was a sense in which he was already fully committed. He had torn down the idol altars; he had reinstituted the kind of worship God had directed; he had gone so far as to try to reintegrate people from north Israel into worship at the Jerusalem temple. He had tried to clean up the priesthood (cf. 2 Kings 18:2–8; 2 Chron. 29:1–31:21). As he testifies in Isaiah 38:3, he had lived for God with "wholehearted devotion."[9]

What does this mean for us? Perhaps it may be illustrated by the sequel to the story of Joseph Tson told above. Tson says that that night as he was filled with righteous indignation over what had been done to him, he felt Jesus speaking to him. Jesus said something like this, "Joseph, I thought you wanted to know me."

Tson responded, "Yes, Lord, I do!"

"Well," Jesus replied, "as my servant Paul said, that means you want to share the fellowship of my suffering. But the way you are going on, it appears to me you don't really want to know me that deeply."

The next morning, before the interrogator could open his mouth, Pastor Tson said to him, "I want to apologize to you."

The interrogator blurted, "For what?"

"For harboring resentment and hatred in my heart toward you. Last night my Jesus showed me that you are his instrument to help me to know him better through sharing the fellowship of his suffering. So please forgive me."

The interrogator mumbled something, and Tson says, "He never laid a hand on me again." I suppose the man did not want to give Jesus any help.

The point is that Tson was personally and spiritually prepared for what was going to happen to him. He had long ago decided who was going to be the King in his life, and he had long ago decided that nothing would keep him from knowing Jesus in his fullness. Thus, when a spurious "king" presented himself, this was not a new issue to be faced. It had already been faced. Furthermore, because of a living relationship

---

9. Lit., "a perfect [unblemished] heart."

with Jesus, Tson was in a place to hear the voice of Jesus in a way that could make the incident actually creative from a spiritual standpoint. So the question for each of us must be: Is Christ the King of my life today? If he is, then adversity and persecution will not catch us off-guard and shake us.

The New Testament writers constantly counsel us in this regard. Peter says, "Do not be surprised at the painful trial you are suffering, as though something strange were happening to you. But rejoice that you participate in the sufferings of Christ" (1 Peter 4:12). He also says, "But in your hearts set apart Christ as Lord. Always be prepared to give an answer to everyone who asks you to give the reason for the hope that you have" (3:15). John says to each of the seven churches that they can and must "overcome," and that if they do, eternal rewards await them.[10] Paul advised the elders of the church at Ephesus to keep watch over themselves and the "flock," because enemies from both without and within would seek to destroy them (Acts 20:28–31). In other words, we need to expect adversity and be spiritually prepared for it when it comes.

Trusting God. There is a second important factor if we are to stand firm when we are challenged to trust other things than God. This is the truth of Psalm 46:10, which has been translated traditionally as "Be still, and know that I am God." A more colloquial translation might be, "Relax and find out that I am God." We need to be entrusting God with the small things of our lives so that when the crisis comes, it is easy for us to continue trusting him. We need to allow God to demonstrate his love and care to us on a daily basis by taking our hands off some things that we could supply for ourselves and letting God supply them in his way and in his time.

As a seminary professor I have seen my students living this way again and again. They pull into town with everything they own in a rented trailer, with no job, no place to live, nothing but the conviction that this is where God wants them. We faculty sometimes shake our heads and say, "Here is another crazy couple"; yet again and again I have seen God provide for people like that in unusual ways. When they finish their seminary career, they know that God can be trusted; they have seen him in action. The rest of us who plan so carefully and provide for ourselves so fully have never put God to the test; he has never had to demonstrate his special trustworthiness to us. So when the day comes that we are faced with a taunting Assyrian, we may have a much greater leap of faith to trust God than the person who put himself or herself at risk for God long before. Oswald Chambers says it this way:

---

10. Rev. 2:7, 11, 17, 26–29; 3:5, 12, 21.

Trust entirely in God, and when He brings you to the venture, see that you take it. We act like pagans in a crisis, only one out of a crowd is daring enough to bank his faith in the character of God.[11]

Another aspect of this narrative as it relates to trust has to do with the validity of the Assyrian's charge that the Judeans were trusting Egypt. Sometimes we give our opponents ammunition to use against us because we have betrayed our trust in God by trusting the world instead. In the case of Judah and Egypt, the trust was one God had prohibited, and now the Assyrian was able to mock them for doing such a foolish thing.

By all means, then, let us look at the things we are trusting and see if they are in fact a denial of our supposed faith in God. If there are any practices or relationships in our lives that will give others a chance to say that we talk a good show but are really no different from the world in the way we live, we must get rid of them now. There may also be some things that are legitimate and permissible but which will still give the impression that we do not actually trust God for our needs, and we should dispense with those too so that it will become as clear as possible where our trust really is. These kinds of decisions are personal, between us and the Lord, but the real issue for all of us is: Do I really trust the Lord for the supply of my needs, or does my behavior say that I lie?

---

11. O. Chambers, *My Utmost for His Highest* (New York: Dodd, Mead, 1935), 151.

Isaiah 37:8–38

W HEN THE FIELD commander heard that the king of
Assyria had left Lachish, he withdrew and found
the king fighting against Libnah.
⁹Now Sennacherib received a report that Tirhakah, the
Cushite king of Egypt, was marching out to fight against him.
When he heard it, he sent messengers to Hezekiah with this
word: ¹⁰"Say to Hezekiah king of Judah: Do not let the god
you depend on deceive you when he says, 'Jerusalem will not
be handed over to the king of Assyria.' ¹¹Surely you have
heard what the kings of Assyria have done to all the countries,
destroying them completely. And will you be delivered? ¹²Did
the gods of the nations that were destroyed by my forefathers
deliver them—the gods of Gozan, Haran, Rezeph and the
people of Eden who were in Tel Assar? ¹³Where is the king of
Hamath, the king of Arpad, the king of the city of Sepharvaim, or of Hena or Ivvah?"

¹⁴Hezekiah received the letter from the messengers and
read it. Then he went up to the temple of the LORD and
spread it out before the LORD. ¹⁵And Hezekiah prayed to the
LORD: ¹⁶"O LORD Almighty, God of Israel, enthroned
between the cherubim, you alone are God over all the kingdoms of the earth. You have made heaven and earth. ¹⁷Give
ear, O LORD, and hear; open your eyes, O LORD, and see;
listen to all the words Sennacherib has sent to insult the
living God.

¹⁸"It is true, O LORD, that the Assyrian kings have laid
waste all these peoples and their lands. ¹⁹They have thrown
their gods into the fire and destroyed them, for they were not
gods but only wood and stone, fashioned by human hands.
²⁰Now, O LORD our God, deliver us from his hand, so that all
kingdoms on earth may know that you alone, O LORD, are
God."

²¹Then Isaiah son of Amoz sent a message to Hezekiah:
"This is what the LORD, the God of Israel, says: Because you
have prayed to me concerning Sennacherib king of Assyria,
²²this is the word the LORD has spoken against him:

"The Virgin Daughter of Zion
      despises and mocks you.
The Daughter of Jerusalem
      tosses her head as you flee.
23 Who is it you have insulted and blasphemed?
      Against whom have you raised your voice
and lifted your eyes in pride?
      Against the Holy One of Israel!
24 By your messengers
      you have heaped insults on the Lord.
And you have said,
      'With my many chariots
I have ascended the heights of the mountains,
      the utmost heights of Lebanon.
I have cut down its tallest cedars,
      the choicest of its pines.
I have reached its remotest heights,
      the finest of its forests.
25 I have dug wells in foreign lands
      and drunk the water there.
With the soles of my feet
      I have dried up all the streams of Egypt.'

26 "Have you not heard?
      Long ago I ordained it.
In days of old I planned it;
      now I have brought it to pass,
that you have turned fortified cities
      into piles of stone.
27 Their people, drained of power,
      are dismayed and put to shame.
They are like plants in the field,
      like tender green shoots,
like grass sprouting on the roof,
      scorched before it grows up.

28 "But I know where you stay
      and when you come and go
      and how you rage against me.
29 Because you rage against me
      and because your insolence has reached my ears,

I will put my hook in your nose
    and my bit in your mouth,
and I will make you return
    by the way you came.

30"This will be the sign for you, O Hezekiah:

"This year you will eat what grows by itself,
    and the second year what springs from that.
But in the third year sow and reap,
    plant vineyards and eat their fruit.
31 Once more a remnant of the house of Judah
    will take root below and bear fruit above.
32 For out of Jerusalem will come a remnant,
    and out of Mount Zion a band of survivors.
The zeal of the LORD Almighty
    will accomplish this.

33"Therefore this is what the LORD says concerning the king of Assyria:

"He will not enter this city
    or shoot an arrow here.
He will not come before it with shield
    or build a siege ramp against it.
34 By the way that he came he will return;
    he will not enter this city,"

                              declares the LORD.
35 "I will defend this city and save it,
    for my sake and for the sake of David my servant!"

36Then the angel of the LORD went out and put to death a hundred and eighty-five thousand men in the Assyrian camp. When the people got up the next morning—there were all the dead bodies! 37So Sennacherib king of Assyria broke camp and withdrew. He returned to Nineveh and stayed there.

38One day, while he was worshiping in the temple of his god Nisroch, his sons Adrammelech and Sharezer cut him down with the sword, and they escaped to the land of Ararat. And Esarhaddon his son succeeded him as king.

ALTHOUGH SOME SCHOLARS believe the material in 37:9–38 to be a second account of the same event narrated in 36:1–37:8,[1] there are enough differences between the two to make that unlikely. In particular, we may note that the challenge has moved to focus exclusively on God's ability to deliver, that Hezekiah's own commitment seems much more forthright and direct, and that the oracle from God is much more forceful and direct. Motyer has proposed that Hezekiah, encouraged by Isaiah's words recorded in 37:6–7, has moved beyond a hesitant faith and responded to the field commander's challenge with the assertion that the Lord will deliver Jerusalem (cf. 37:10). Thus Sennacherib's letter is a response to Hezekiah, and Hezekiah's prayer is indicative of his now-total reliance on God.[2] This seems a plausible explanation of the facts.

Hezekiah's Prayer (37:8–20)

WE DO NOT KNOW precisely where "Libnah" (37:8) was located. Two different sites have been suggested, one about six miles north of Lachish and another about ten miles north. Presumably Lachish has already fallen,[3] and the Assyrian army is "mopping up" the last pockets of resistance. But it is also possible that the "rumor" (cf. 37:7) of an Egyptian attack plus continuing unrest in Babylon has made the Assyrian king cautious, and he is pulling back north to keep from having Jerusalem directly in his rear.[4]

In any case, Sennacherib does not want to relax any of the pressure on Hezekiah. Unable to spare the highest officers this time, he sends messengers with a letter directly from himself. No longer is it a question of Hezekiah's deceiving the people about God's deliverance (36:14). Now the challenge is directly to God: "Do not let the god you depend on deceive you" (37:10). The "gloves are off," and the Assyrian king flatly says that he has "destroyed" the nations of every other god, and he will destroy the nation of Judah's god as well. Once again, the contest is not between the gods of

---

1. See the discussions in Childs, *Isaiah*, 272–76; and Seitz, *Isaiah 1–39*, 250.

2. Motyer, *Prophecy of Isaiah*, 280–81.

3. It has been suggested that the huge reliefs of the fall of Lachish in Sennacherib's palace in Nineveh represent something of a consolation prize. Surely the Assyrian would have rather had depictions of the fall of Jerusalem.

4. It is often pointed out that Tirhakah was not actually "king" of Egypt in 701 B.C. He did not assume this position until several years later. However, since the final edition of the chapter was not written until after Sennacherib's death in 681, it is probable that Tirhakah is given the title here that the writer knew he eventually held. This was a common practice in ancient literature. Cf. Young, *The Book of Isaiah*, 2:478–79.

Assyria and the God of Judah. It is a contest between a man and the God of Judah. Sennacherib's fatal mistake is that he does not realize that Judah's God is not man-made, like all the rest.

Here Sennacherib deigns to call Hezekiah "king" (37:10), but it is only to associate him with the "kings" of all the previously captured cities (37:13). There is something of a personal threat here, because the Assyrians treated rebellious kings with special brutality. If Hezekiah insists on trusting his God, then he should remember what will happen to him when this God fails. He can expect something like being skinned alive, so he had better think twice before defying the mightiest man alive.

This time Hezekiah does not ask Isaiah to pray for the "remnant" (37:4); rather, he goes directly to God himself. His ascription of praise in 37:16 is a marvelous compendium of the attributes and character of God. He is the "Lord Almighty," that is, "Yahweh of heaven's armies." All the hosts of heaven are at his beck and call; he can do whatever he wishes. He is the "God of Israel," the One who has stepped into time and space to graciously create a people through whom he can save the world. He is "enthroned between the cherubim" with all that phrase connotes of both unapproachable holiness and of covenant faithfulness. He is the sole "God over all the kingdoms of the earth," a stunning statement of faith, surrounded as Judah is with polytheistic cultures. But there is a reason for such a statement, and that is Hezekiah's final ascription: God "made heaven and earth." Because he alone is the Creator, then he alone is God of the entire cosmos.

Hezekiah's petition (37:17) particularly stresses the fact that God is not an idol but is the "living God."[5] Idols have ears, but they cannot hear; they have eyes, but they cannot see (cf. Ps. 115:4–8; 135:15–18). God has no eyes, but his "eyes" are always on his creatures; he has no ears, but his "ears" are always open to his people's cries. Hezekiah prays as Elijah did on Mount Carmel (1 Kings 18:36–37), with the confidence that his God not only can hear but wants to hear.

Perhaps the most striking thing about this prayer is its focus on God's vindication rather than on the deliverance of the people. Hezekiah calls on God to see the way in which Sennacherib has insulted God. The most crucial issue here is not whether the city of Jerusalem is taken. Rather, it is whether the claim will stand that Yahweh is just one more of the gods created by humans, which other humans can destroy at will. Later on the city

---

5. This phrase, which appears some thirty times in the Bible, usually appears in contexts that at least imply a contrast with idols. Cf. Deut. 5:26; 1 Sam. 17:26; Jer. 10:10; Dan. 6:20, 26; Acts 14:15.

did fall, but God's identity and character were not on the line there. Jeremiah had foretold the event, claiming God was in fact doing it (cf. Jer. 37:6–10).

But here God has said it will not happen while Sennacherib has said it will. Who is right? Hezekiah admits that what the Assyrian has said about the other kingdoms and cities and their gods is right (37:18–19), but he insists that they are not gods at all. They are human creations, products of human skill and ingenuity. Of course, this is primarily addressing the fact of idolatry. But it is profoundly true of pagan thought itself. The entire system is a product of human speculation on the nature of existence and, as such, is a human creation. Compared to the God of the Bible, who has broken in on us and revealed himself to be dramatically different from our speculations, those things are not even worthy to be called "gods."

Isaiah 37:20 brings the prayer to a fitting climax. Why does Hezekiah pray for the deliverance of his city? Significantly, it is not as he prayed for himself in chapter 38. He does not claim that the city deserves deliverance because of its righteousness or even because of its special place in the plan for God. One reason alone is given: "so that all kingdoms on earth may know that you alone, O LORD, are God."

In many ways this is the climax of all the teaching found in chapters 7–35. Unlike Ahaz, whose fear led him to trust the nations more than God, Hezekiah has learned the lessons taught in the intervening chapters and is willing to stake everything, including his own life, on the uniqueness of the living God. Here is trust on the highest level. Here is trust befitting a descendant of that David who was not willing for a giant to stand unmolested and "defy the armies of the living God" (1 Sam. 17:26). If Israel is to be the vehicle through which all the nations will come to know the true God (Isa. 2:1–5), then trust like this is an imperative. Israel must allow itself to be put in a place where the uniqueness and sole saviorhood of God can be seen. In the crisis Hezekiah comes through with flying colors.

God's Response to Hezekiah's Prayer (37:21–38)

GOD'S RESPONSE TO this prayer comes through Isaiah and is recorded in 37:21–35.[6] It appears in three parts, the first of which is addressed directly to Sennacherib (37:22–29). The second is addressed to Hezekiah (37:30–32), and the third is spoken of Sennacherib (37:33–35). If the message of the field commander betrayed a certain familiarity with Judean life and thought, this oracle shows remarkable familiarity with the Assyrian royal annals. Especially verses 24–25, which quote the boasts of Sennacherib, sound much

---

6. For a discussion of the authenticity of the statement as coming from "Isaiah son of Amoz," see Oswalt, *Isaiah 1–39*, 658–59.

like what appears in those annals. Possibly there were publicists with the Assyrian armies who circulated these kinds of poetic celebrations of Assyrian might. If so, Isaiah has picked up on them and uses them to show how foolish they are in the light of the reality of the living God.

The opening phrase "the Virgin Daughter of Zion" (37:22) suggests that the Assyrian attack on Jerusalem is comparable to a dominant male seeking to rape a beautiful young girl. On the surface, there is nothing to keep him from carrying out his will. But Assyria, the would-be rapist, has not taken into account "the Holy One of Israel" (37:23). Or rather, he has dismissed the "LORD" as being of no account. He has put himself on the level of God, lifting his "eyes in pride" and in the process blaspheming God by bringing him down to Sennacherib's own level. Once more we encounter the theme of the folly of self-exaltation on the part of the creature (cf. 2:6–22; 14:4–22; etc.). There is only One who is "high and lifted up." For anyone else to presume to that position is to invite destruction. As a result, the "Daughter of Jerusalem" will be able to toss "her head" in mockery at the mighty man as he runs away in ignominy.

Verses 24–25 seem to extol Sennacherib by reference to extremes. Verse 24 speaks of the "heights" he has scaled in the north ("Lebanon"), while verse 25 speaks of the deep "wells" he has "dug" in the south ("Egypt"). Surely this man is the master of the world, from north to south and from heights to depths. He can fell the tallest trees and stop up the mightiest rivers. Nothing can stop him.

But what he does not know is that all of this has been "long ago . . . planned" by the God of one of the little countries the Assyrian has so contemptuously trampled on (37:26). This theme of the plan of God in relation to Assyria has been encountered at least twice before (10:6, 15; 14:24–27). Not only is this not a contest between what the God of Israel wants and what Assyria wants, but the Assyrian is not even on the stage by his own volition. He is a puppet being moved by Israel's God! God has "brought it to pass" that Assyria has conquered the "fortified cities" and reduced their inhabitants to wilted, "scorched" "plants" (37:27). As a result, Sennacherib cannot hide from God. Just as God has brought him on the stage, he can take him off again (37:28–29). To God, the mighty Assyrian monarch is no more than a bull with a ring in his nose[7] or a horse with a "bit" in his mouth.

Verses 30–32 constitute a sign to Hezekiah that this is indeed a word from God. Like several of the other signs in the book (7:14; 8:3; 16:14), it is forward-looking. It does not create faith, but it promotes it in that God has

7. In Ezek. 29:4 "hook" seems to denote a fishhook. But in Ezek. 19:4 and 38:4 the idea seems to be more of a ring in the nose, as is suggested here by the parallelism with "bit."

gone on record that he will do what he says and has given a means for checking the veracity of what he has said. Probably the "three years" is not three
full years from the date of the prophecy but parts of three different calendar
years. One possibility is that the Assyrians will retreat in the fall of "this
year" when it is too late for planting to take place. Thus, though the Assyrians will be gone in the next, or "second" year, the only food plants growing
will be those that come up on their own. Finally, planting can take place in
the fall of that "second" year, so that there will be plenty of food to be harvested in the "third" year.[8]

But in God's mind, the more important point is that he will preserve a harvest for himself from among his people (37:32). The Assyrian thought to devastate God's "field" and take all the crop for himself. But although God has
permitted a large measure of devastation to take place, he will not allow total
destruction to occur. He has too great a passion ("zeal") for his people to allow
that to happen. He will preserve a "remnant" for himself.

All God's promises are summed up in 37:33—35, where Isaiah makes two
assertions about what will happen—one negative (v. 33) and one positive
(v. 34)—and then gives a supporting reason for these assertions (v. 35). The
negative assertion is that the Assyrian will not mount any kind of an attack
against the city. Not only will they not conquer God's city, they will not
even "shoot an arrow" there. On the surface of it, this is amazing. Hezekiah
is the leader of the revolt; to leave him unpunished would send a bad message, from an Assyrian point of view, to all the other potential rebels in the
area. But not only will the Assyrians not mount a siege against the city, they
will leave the area completely (37:34). The reason given for this amazing turn
of events is that God "will defend" the city "and save it." Sennacherib has said
he will destroy the city, whereas God has said he will save it. Now we will
see who is right.

Verses 36—38 are stunning in their terse, matter-of-fact reporting. They
are so plain and unadorned as to be almost anticlimactic. Perhaps the point
is to show that there is simply no contest here.[9] This is not some earth-
shaking conflict between evenly matched contestants. This is definitely a "no
contest" match. God simply sends the angel of death. Nor is the angel finished on the Philistine plains. Just because Sennacherib is at home in what
should have been the safest place on earth for him ("the temple of his god"),
God's word is still true (37:7), and his rule is still effective. His own sons "cut
him down" (37:38) and flee.[10] Despite all his boasts, Sennacherib cannot

---

8. See Delitzsch, *Commentary on Isaiah*, 2:30.

9. See Dan. 5:30 for a similar kind of statement. After the lengthy pronouncement of
judgment on Belshazzar in vv. 1—29, the actual event is reported in one verse.

10. Cf. 14:21. See also 10:15—19, 28—34.

stand against the living God.[11] Hezekiah has proved that it is foolish to trust the nations in place of the living God, "the Holy One of Israel" (37:23).[12]

THE PAGAN VIEW OF REALITY. At the heart of this material is the conflict between the biblical view of reality and the pagan view. Yehezkel Kaufmann has shown that the pagan view of reality was rooted in the idea that the gods emerged from matter, were identical with its various forms, and were conditioned by it. Thus, they "correspond" with the natural realm and are indeed continuous with it.[13] The thought that the gods might have come into existence before matter is simply unthinkable. Matter, existing in chaotic form, has always existed and always will, and the gods are the result of tensions in this stuff. Whether you call it "Yin" and "Yang," or "Good" and "Evil," or "Positive" and "Negative," the point is the same.

Thus, the gods have no real freedom. They play the role assigned to them by their "fate." The sun god cannot shine in the night; the moon goddess cannot shine in the day. Furthermore, the gods have no purpose when they "create"—or perhaps more precisely, when they "procreate." They are to be understood by analogy with the world of nature, and just as nature is without purpose as it produces life, so are the gods without purpose. Since there is no purpose, there is no goal toward which they are moving. Life came from nowhere and goes nowhere.

This continuity with nature necessarily issues in idolatry. If the gods have emerged from matter and are conditioned by it, what could be more sensible

---

11. In his annals, Sennacherib boasts that he forced Hezekiah to give back the loyal king of the Philistines whom Hezekiah had been holding captive in Jerusalem, and he says he exacted heavy tribute from him and "shut him up like a bird in a cage." But that is the end of the report of that campaign. In the next nineteen years he does not report campaigning in the west again. The Bible explains why he did not capture and execute the rebel Hezekiah and why he did not pursue the capture of Egypt any further (cf. *ANET*, 288).

12. It is common today to assert that verses 36–37 are a legendary explanation of what was just an accident of history (cf. R. Clements, *Isaiah 1–39*, 288–89). Childs, *Isaiah*, 276–78, is to be commended for attempting to save the theological value of the text, insisting that although the event did not occur, this account is still a "true" witness to God's activity in history. However, we must ask how the assertion of a historical fiction supports theological "truth." Paul's statement in 1 Cor. 15:17, "If Christ has not been raised, your faith is futile," expresses the connection between historical fact and faith that the Bible makes from beginning to end. Note that a "legendary" explanation of Sennacherib's death is not supplied. If the destruction of the army is legendary, one might expect the king's death to have been given the same treatment.

13. Y. Kaufmann, *The Religion of Israel*, trans. M. Greenberg (Chicago: Univ. of Chicago Press, 1960), 21, 29.

than to represent them in material forms? Furthermore, the understanding of the correspondence between the gods and matter means that by manipulating the idol, I can manipulate the god and in so doing manipulate the natural force behind the god.

Kaufmann notes that the biblical writers never seem to pay attention to the deity behind the idol and argues forcefully how this shows a complete ignorance of the thought world of myth in the Bible.[14] However, it seems to me that he has made too much of this evidence. To think that the Israelites were so isolated from the surrounding cultures that they did not even understand how those cultures thought is to ask far too much. To think that Elijah and Elisha did not understand how the Baal religion functioned presupposes an almost unbelievable obtuseness. Furthermore, when the Israelites fell into the worship of idols, it is unimaginable that they did not do so for the same reasons their pagan neighbors did: the attempt to manipulate the forces of nature with which the idols corresponded.

No, the reason the biblical prophets concentrate on the folly of making idols (see comments on 40:18–20; 42:17; 44:9–20) is that this is the Achilles heel of paganism. Rather than go into a complex (and abstract) argument on the nature of transcendence and continuity, they simply ask how a piece of stone or a block of wood can save us. Even though this argument seems simple, it has profound implications, for behind it is the much larger question: How can the natural system save us from the natural system? How can what manifestly has no purpose infuse our life with purpose? How can what is obviously without meaning give us meaning? Such things do not merit the title of "gods." Thus, idolatry is the symptom, but by addressing the symptom, the biblical writers are necessarily getting us to focus on the disease.

Today, the disease is all around us, and the symptoms are beginning to reemerge. Many of the most intelligent among us insist on the eternity of matter. "Spirit" is only a by-product of electrochemical forces inherent in that matter, forces they might describe as "positive" and "negative." They insist that all life is evolving but admit that they do not know why nor to what end. But there is also emerging a sense that there is more to reality than merely electrochemical forces, that we need to somehow "personalize" these forces. No longer is cold, impersonal reason a satisfactory basis for life. So we face the reemergence of the same conflict with which Hezekiah was faced. We must again ask whether the living God is any different from, or superior to, what this world calls "gods."

---

14. Ibid., 146, etc.

Human boasting. The Assyrian kings did not suffer from false humility. In a report to his god Ashur, Sargon II (724–705 B.C.) said the following words that sound a good deal like those Isaiah quoted:

> I put the armies of Shamash and Marduk across the Lower Zab, whose passage is difficult like a canal. I entered through the passes of Kullar, the high mountain of the land of Lulumi which they call Zamua. . . . I passed through the midst of Nikipa and Upa, high mountains, which are covered with all kinds of trees, whose midst is chaos, whose passes are fearful, whose shade spreads over that region like a cedar forest so that one who goes through them does not see the ray of Shamash. I crossed over the Buya, a river between them, 26 times. My army in its mass did not fear the high waters.[15]

But when we think of the posturing in the ring by members of the World Wrestling Entertainment, these words sound almost modest. We may smirk and comment that the wrestlers, like their performances, are just so much air, a make-believe world for consumption by the gullible. But before we dismiss the spectacle too easily, we must remember that people pay large ticket prices to see these performances. This suggests that people in some way enjoy such posturing. It may suggest there is something we actually admire in it, and perhaps we secretly wish we could get away with such blatant self-promotion.

HUMILITY. The Bible again and again speaks of God's preference for the lowly. Isaiah says in 57:15:

> For this is what the high and lofty One says—
> he who lives forever, whose name is holy:
> "I live in a high and holy place,
> but also with him who is contrite and lowly in Spirit."

Jesus says, quoting the Old Testament, "Blessed are the meek, for they will inherit the earth" (Matt. 5:5). He says of himself, "I am gentle and humble in heart" (11:29). Peter follows up on this with the words: "Humble yourselves, therefore, under God's mighty hand, that he may lift you up in due time" (1 Peter 5:6). Yet, we see that the "winners" in this world, like

---

15. D. Luckenbill, ed., *Ancient Records of Assyria and Babylonia* (Chicago: Univ. of Chicago Press, 1927), 2:42–43.

Sennacherib, are often masters at self-promotion and intimidation. A best-selling book of a few years ago was entitled *Winning Through Intimidation*, and many people learned to practice its techniques.[16] Is the Bible hopelessly out of touch? Or is it the kind of thing we are expected to give a nod of approval to while admitting that it is not practical in "the real world"?

Everything depends on whether we have really met God or not. For Sennacherib and the World Wrestling Entertainment performers, their lives and their futures are in their own hands. Their success depends completely on themselves. So the adage runs, "If you don't blow your own horn, nobody else will." The same will be true for all of us. We may try to find ways that are a little more socially acceptable than the braggadocio of the WWE, yet in the end we must carefully cultivate our own reputation and put ourselves forward. It is a matter of "self-respect," we are told. It is a person with "no backbone" who lets oneself be walked on by others.

To be sure, there are persons who feel themselves to be worthless, who feel that they do not get any "breaks" because they don't deserve any. There are also those who try to win our sympathy with a "false modesty." They are constantly putting themselves down in such a way that we are forced to focus our attention on them as we try to assure them they are much more deserving and capable than they say. Neither of these are what the Bible has in mind with its teachings on humility. Hezekiah's responses are instructive. He does not bandy words with the oppressor. His first instructions to his representatives is that they are to keep silent (37:21). He is not going to get into a shouting match. He is not going to try to say that he is better or that what they say about themselves is untrue. He refuses to play the game of one-upmanship.

Then he takes his concerns to the Lord. He has put his reputation in the hands of God. This is the key. A person who responds to the love of God knows a number of things, according to 1 John 5. We know how much we are worth: the life of the Son of God (5:11–12). We know that pulsating in us is eternal life (5:13). We know that we have instant access to the throne room of our Father (5:14–15). We know that we can live lives like God (5:18). We know that we are in a life-and-death battle with the powers presently ruling this world (5:19). We know that Jesus has given us the power to understand the issues in the battle and to remain true (5:20).

The person who knows all these things does not have to brag and pose. But neither does he or she have to go through life with a "hang-dog" expression. We are infinitely valuable to God, and our future, both near-term and long-term, is secure in God's hands. If he is who he says he

---

16. Robert J. Ringer, *Winning Through Intimidation* (New York: Random House, 1976).

is, then we do not have to worry about our "image." Instead, we can concentrate on reality: "attaining to the whole measure of the fullness of Christ" (Eph. 4:13).

Paul defines this kind of attitude as "maturity." And surely this is maturity—having a correct estimate of your abilities and your liabilities, one that is not dependent on the opinions of others, and being secure in who you are and who you are becoming. But this is not really possible without the perspective of heaven. When we get ourselves "off our hands" and into God's hands, we no longer need to worry about how we are looking. Now it is God's reputation that matters to us, and we are freed from that debilitating self-concern that will otherwise eat us up. That is the picture we see in Hezekiah's prayer. Here is a man whose personal success and survival are no longer paramount. This is a free man.

Prayer versus ritual manipulation. Pagan ways of thinking have an insidious way of slipping into our practices without our being aware of it. Perhaps this is so because even in our highest spiritual achievements, we remain the fallen children of Adam and Eve. I do not want to suggest that economic theory is inherently evil, but there is something slightly perverse about our constant wish to get the greatest return for the smallest outlay. We do not easily or naturally ask, "Where can I make the greatest contribution?" Instead it is, "Where can I get the biggest return with the least input from me?"

This is what drives the gambling instinct, and this is what drives pagan thought. Pagan thought says, "I know what my needs are, and I must find the means to supply those needs at the least cost to myself." Biblical thought says, "Your transcendent Creator-Father knows what your needs are and wants to supply them out of his bounty. In order to receive that supply, give yourself away to him without reservation." Our answer is the same as Adam and Eve's, and as the man who was given one talent said (Matt. 25:25): "We're afraid of you." The price God asks seems too high. Maybe he will take our all and give nothing back. So the pagan option looks good. We will find ways to manipulate God and make him give us what we want/need while keeping ourselves for ourselves.

When we begin to do this, much of our religious life begins to change its complexion. We go to church, we read the Bible, we tithe, we pray, we reject sin—all as a means of manipulating God. Slowly but surely these behaviors begin to take on the shape of idolatry. The physical acts become the spiritual reality. Current bestsellers on prayer have this real potential. We are encouraged to repeat a specific biblical prayer over and over, using the precise words of the biblical text, with the promise that in so doing we will receive the blessings of God. It may not be the intention of the authors of these books, but quickly humans see such a prayer as a mechanical device whose purpose is to get the maximum out of God with the minimum of an investment of themselves.

The Hebrew prophets destroy such an idea. Again and again they weigh in against it. Isaiah has already done so in the first chapter and will do so again in chapter 58. Unlike pagan religious activity, biblical rites have no efficacy in and of themselves. They are symbols of interpersonal relationships between God and the worshiper. Jesus makes this point when he says we are not to pray like pagans who believe that they will be heard because they repeat a rote formula (Matt. 6:7).

Another illustration can be found in the parable of the Pharisee and the tax collector. One man's prayer was heard and the other's was not, and the hearing and not hearing were dependent on the attitude of the person's heart (Luke 18:14–19). One of the reasons the prophets so often call for activity on behalf of the poor as the sign of true religion is because it is hard to turn this into a manipulative activity. It requires too much investment with too little evident return.

Hezekiah's prayer is a wonderful antidote to pagan prayer. He is far from trying to manipulate God. He does not suggest that God owes him or his people anything. He focuses on God's character and nature. Neither does he promise to do anything for God if God delivers them. He is concerned that God be known properly in the world and wants for that to happen in the context of the oppressor's boast, for that is the level on which this conflict has been pitched. Hezekiah places himself and his people in the position of simple trust. He cannot make God bless them and does not try. Rather, he commits himself to God without any qualifications or caveats.

We, too, can pray and live in this way. We can give ourselves to God absolutely and without limit. As we continue in the Christian life, we will discover ever deeper levels where that earlier surrender will have to be actualized, but that does not diminish the reality or the completeness of that first moment of total, unreserved trust. In such a relationship, we can surrender our needs to God. To be sure, he invites us to tell him what we think our needs are because our trust is deepened as we see God providing the very things we asked for. But that does not mean that we demand he work for us. It means we lay our supposed needs at his feet for him to supply as he sees best. This kind of prayer is no longer an exercise in manipulation. Now it is a conversation between a trusting child and a loving Father.

The God of history. The Bible makes human historical experience the arena in which God is revealed. This is startlingly different from the pagan understanding. While pagans believed their gods acted in history on behalf of their favorites, they had no concept of an overarching plan or purpose, nor did they believe anything of the gods' natures could be learned from such experience. It was in the recurring cycles of nature that the gods were truly seen. Thus, the idea of keeping a record of God's activities in human history and his inspired interpretations of the meaning of those activities is something unique to the Bible.

In a real sense, then, God was revealing himself by incarnation long before Jesus Christ was born. Jesus was the culmination of what God had been doing from the outset. The Hebrews are able to say to us, "We know God and commend him to you because we have seen him at work in the context of our experience." Some writers would say that God was no more at work in Israelite history than he was in Canaanite history but that the Israelites just chose the vehicle of human history to express their faith.[17] This is not the place for a lengthy discussion on the subject; suffice it to say here that unless the Hebrews had continuing and convincing evidence that God was doing this, there is no satisfactory explanation as to why they chose this mode of expression. None of their more sophisticated and thoughtful neighbors did such a thing.

Thus, it continues to be of critical significance whether the historical claims the biblical writers make are correct. If they are not, then there is every reason to abandon the strange faith of the Bible. It flies directly in the face of the way in which reality has been otherwise viewed around the world, and if it is only the bizarre creation of the Israelites, we ought to, as Paul says, give it up. However, if the biblical writers' testimony is not their own creation but an honest report of what actually happened, then regardless of the popular view or even the majority view, their religious conclusions are inescapable, and we must, like the Christians in the Colosseum, stand on them.

---

17. Cf., e.g., W. T. Stevenson, *History As Myth* (New York: Harper, 1969).

Isaiah 38:1–22

I N THOSE DAYS Hezekiah became ill and was at the point of death. The prophet Isaiah son of Amoz went to him and said, "This is what the LORD says: Put your house in order, because you are going to die; you will not recover."

²Hezekiah turned his face to the wall and prayed to the LORD, ³"Remember, O LORD, how I have walked before you faithfully and with wholehearted devotion and have done what is good in your eyes." And Hezekiah wept bitterly.

⁴Then the word of the LORD came to Isaiah: ⁵"Go and tell Hezekiah, 'This is what the LORD, the God of your father David, says: I have heard your prayer and seen your tears; I will add fifteen years to your life. ⁶And I will deliver you and this city from the hand of the king of Assyria. I will defend this city.

⁷"'This is the LORD's sign to you that the LORD will do what he has promised: ⁸I will make the shadow cast by the sun go back the ten steps it has gone down on the stairway of Ahaz.'" So the sunlight went back the ten steps it had gone down.

⁹A writing of Hezekiah king of Judah after his illness and recovery:

> ¹⁰I said, "In the prime of my life
>   must I go through the gates of death
>   and be robbed of the rest of my years?"
> ¹¹I said, "I will not again see the LORD,
>   the LORD, in the land of the living;
>   no longer will I look on mankind,
>   or be with those who now dwell in this world.
> ¹²Like a shepherd's tent my house
>   has been pulled down and taken from me.
> Like a weaver I have rolled up my life,
>   and he has cut me off from the loom;
>   day and night you made an end of me.
> ¹³I waited patiently till dawn,
>   but like a lion he broke all my bones;
>   day and night you made an end of me.
> ¹⁴I cried like a swift or thrush,
>   I moaned like a mourning dove.

My eyes grew weak as I looked to the heavens.
I am troubled; O Lord, come to my aid!"

¹⁵But what can I say?
He has spoken to me, and he himself has done this.
I will walk humbly all my years
because of this anguish of my soul.
¹⁶Lord, by such things men live;
and my spirit finds life in them too.
You restored me to health
and let me live.
¹⁷Surely it was for my benefit
that I suffered such anguish.
In your love you kept me
from the pit of destruction;
you have put all my sins
behind your back.
¹⁸For the grave cannot praise you,
death cannot sing your praise;
those who go down to the pit
cannot hope for your faithfulness.
¹⁹The living, the living—they praise you,
as I am doing today;
fathers tell their children
about your faithfulness.

²⁰The LORD will save me,
and we will sing with stringed instruments
all the days of our lives
in the temple of the LORD.

²¹Isaiah had said, "Prepare a poultice of figs and apply it to the boil, and he will recover."
²²Hezekiah had asked, "What will be the sign that I will go up to the temple of the LORD?"

Original Meaning

I HAVE ARGUED that chapters 36–39 stand in relation to chapters 7–12 as a kind of a mirror image. Chapters 7–12 show the consequences of Ahaz's refusal to trust God and his trusting the nations (in particular, Assyria) instead. The result was near destruction at the hands of the very nation he trusted. But the chapters conclude on a hopeful note, because God will not break his promise either to his people or to the house of David. He will send a Davidic Messiah to restore his people and rule them in peace and justice. Chapters 36–37 reverse the picture. Isaiah's prophecy has come true, and Judah has been devastated by Assyria. But Hezekiah, Ahaz's son, does put his trust in God and does not surrender to Assyria. As a result God proves his trustworthiness by keeping his word and delivering Judah from Sennacherib.

But the mirror image effect continues. Whereas chapters 7–12 began badly and ended well, chapters 36–39 begin well and end badly. Chapters 38–39, which are closely connected, depict a Hezekiah who is both mortal and fallible. This segment ends with the prediction of the Exile under Babylon, with Hezekiah's descendants in the Davidic dynasty serving the Babylonian king as eunuchs. What is going on? This question is intensified when we realize that the events in at least chapter 38 took place before the deliverance in 701 B.C. In other words, they have been pulled out of chronological order for some reason. What could the reason be?

Since the Scripture does not answer the question explicitly, any answer we give must be tentative. Many commentators have suggested that the materials have been pulled out of chronological order in order to put the prediction of the Babylonian exile at the end of the segment and thus to provide a transition from the Assyrian section of the book to the Babylonian one. That is probably correct, but I suggest a more complex reason for changing the order. Not only does it provide a chronological transition, but it also provides a theological one. Who is this promised Davidic Messiah? Is it not Hezekiah? He is the one whose faithfulness has secured continued life for the nation. He is the one who has manifested the kind of spirit that makes true leadership possible. We also know from Kings and Chronicles that he restored both justice and religious faithfulness in the land during his reign. Surely this is the child of chapter 9, the root from the stump of Jesse in chapter 11, the man on the throne in chapter 16, and the righteous, beautiful king in chapters 32–33.[1]

Chapters 38–39 tell us this is not the case. However good a man Hezekiah may have been, he is just that, a man. Even if he receives extended life (ch. 38), death is still his fate, as the focus of the psalm in 38:9–20 emphasizes. He is not the one who can usher in an eternal kingdom. Nor is he the almighty God (9:6). His behavior, however commendable, is not infallible (39:1–8). Instead of using the opportunity to glorify the God who had delivered him from death, Hezekiah tries to impress the Babylonian envoys with his wealth and armaments. Trust is a way of life, not an affair

---

1. This is the position of Seitz, *Isaiah 1–39*, 255, etc.

of the moment. So these chapters not only prepare us for the coming Babylonian exile, they also prepare us for a further revelation of the nature and character of the promised Messiah. If it is not Hezekiah, then who is it? Chapters 40–66 address this question, and chapters 38–39 prepare the reader for it.

Hezekiah's Prayer (38:1–8)

SEITZ POINTS OUT that chapter 38 reverses the flow of chapters 36–37. There the story of the one who mocked God goes from life to death. Here the story of the one who trusts God goes from death to life. The reason for this is prayer. Although Hezekiah's prayer in 38:3 is not as lofty and unselfish as that in chapter 37, it is still a model of the direction the trusting heart takes in the time of crisis. God's word from Isaiah is unequivocal: Hezekiah is "going to die." This is not a word of judgment; it is simply a fact. But the king does not accept the announcement passively. He knows something of the heart of God, that he does hear and listen (cf. 38:5) to the cries of his people even if all the signs point to a fixed outcome. Thus, he turns to God. As far as the evidence indicates, this kind of personal dependence expressed through communication with God is foreign to Ahaz, but it seems entirely natural for Hezekiah.

It is interesting that Hezekiah does not actually ask for lengthened life. What he does is simply remind God that he has conducted his life ("walked before you") with faithfulness (lit., "truth") and "wholehearted devotion" (lit., "a perfect heart"). This is reminiscent of God's command to Abraham in Genesis 17:1: "Walk before me and be blameless [lit., perfect]." In short, Hezekiah, who was only thirty-nine years old at the time, is saying to God that he has met God's requirements for long life (cf. Ps. 34:11–14) and is asking by implication if it is fair to cut his life short as though he were a wicked man (cf. Ps. 37:35–36).

God responds to this argument and sends Isaiah back with a different word, one of fifteen additional years.[2] He also promises to "deliver you and this city" from the Assyrians. This may indicate that the event occurred during Sennacherib's attack on the land. Of course, that threat had been inescapable from the time that Samaria fell in 721 B.C., so the historical setting of the words may have been as early as 710, the first time Merodach-Baladan (cf. 39:1) was

---

2. Manasseh, Hezekiah's son, is apparently only twelve years old when Hezekiah dies (2 Kings 21:1). That suggests that Hezekiah had no heir at the time of this illness. If that is correct, it offers further explanation for the particular bitterness of Hezekiah's weeping. The thought of the end of the Davidic dynasty is too awful to contemplate. This may also explain the appellation for God, "the God of your father David," in the response in 38:5.

active. At any rate, the point is made again: Trust God and not the nations; he can deliver.[3]

Like his father before him, Hezekiah is offered a sign to confirm God's gracious promise of deliverance. Ahaz refused the sign because he had already made arrangements to take care of himself. Hezekiah has no such encumbrance, so he is happy to receive whatever evidence God cares to give. Perhaps this particular sign, with the sun's shadow moving back up the steps, is chosen to signify that just as God can move time backward, so he could add days to our lives.[4]

Hezekiah's Lament (38:9−20)

THESE VERSES ARE often referred to as Hezekiah's psalm of thanksgiving for his deliverance from death. However, the meter of the Hebrew lines is that of a lament, and several of the other features of a lament, though not all, are present. Only 38:16, 17, and 19 sound notes of thanks and praise.

In fact, the psalm seems to be largely a meditation on mortality. In 38:10−14 Hezekiah speaks of the untimeliness of the announced death. In "the prime of my life" (v. 10) relates well to his situation, as does "robbed of the rest of my years." It is particularly fellowship with God and with other humans "in the land of the living" that he hates to lose (v. 11). But at its best, life is transient, and Hezekiah uses two different figures of speech to express this transience: a "shepherd's tent" and cloth on the "loom" (v. 12). The tent is never very long in one place as the shepherd keeps moving to follow the flock. And although a cloth seems permanently attached to the loom, there must inevitably come a day when it is "cut" loose. Life is just as impermanent.

In both verses 12 and 13, Hezekiah repeats the phrase "day and night you made an end of me." This emphasizes that our lives are always in God's hands, but it also emphasizes the inevitability of death at God's hands. There was no place to get away from God, either in light or dark. Hezekiah thought he would feel better when day came (38:13), but there was no release. But

---

3. There may be a parallelism between the lengthening of the life of Hezekiah and the lengthening of the life of the nation. From a merely human standpoint, Judah's life as an independent kingdom was over. If the wealthier and more powerful Israel had fallen, there was no question that Judah too would soon fall. But that leaves God out of account. If he decides that Judah's life should be extended, it will be extended, in spite of Assyria. Cf. P. Ackroyd, "An Interpretation of the Babylonian Exile: A Study of II Kings 20 and Isaiah 38−39," *SJT* 27 (1974): 329−52.

4. The version of the account in 2 Kings 20:9−11 has Hezekiah being given a choice whether the shadow should move forward or back. He chooses back as being the harder thing to do.

just as death is from the Lord, so is life. If there is to be any hope, it is from "the heavens"; if any "aid," it is from the Lord (38:14).

It is unclear whether 38:15 is to be taken negatively or positively.[5] If it does begin with an expression of thanks, it has a muted tone. The point seems to be that all of "this," both the disease and its subsequent removal, is the work of God and not of Hezekiah. What lesson should Hezekiah draw? He should certainly not stride through life in arrogance as though his life were his own. He has come through great "anguish of ... soul" and has been delivered, so he should live with that awareness, both in gratitude and with a sense of responsibility.

Verse 16 continues to be somewhat ambiguous because the referent of "such things" (Heb. "them") is unclear. Probably it denotes both the devastating illness and the gracious deliverance. Hezekiah determines to rest his "life" in the awareness that each new day is a gift from God. He believes that the "anguish" he went through has been beneficial (38:17). Perhaps one benefit is a new realization of God's "love" and mercy. Despite his profession in 38:3 that he has been completely loyal to God, the king is aware that if God were to treat him in complete justice, his "sins" would merit nothing but death (cf. Ps. 130:3).

Verses 18–19 express the idea that it is to God's benefit to keep the faithful alive since those in the "grave" (Heb. $\check{s}^{\ni}ol$, the underworld) "cannot praise" God for his "faithfulness." Rather, it is "the living" who praise God and who pass along their testimony of his faithfulness to their children (38:19). These ideas seem to be in line with those found in the Psalms.[6] The idea of a blissful afterlife with God is not yet developed in Old Testament thought. This made death especially fearful in that time.

Verse 20 moves to an unambiguous note of praise. It fits the "vow of praise" with which the lament form typically closes. The speaker is confident of God's deliverance even before it has taken place or before it has been completed. Here Hezekiah, in ways that fit in with what we know of his work with the Levitical singers (2 Chron. 29:25–26), promises that as long as he is alive, there will be joyful music to the saving God in his "temple."

Additional Notes (38:21–22)

IN MY JUDGMENT these last two verses were not part of the original in Isaiah. They do not fit with each other, and they appear to be out of context. This

---

5. Calvin took it negatively; most modern commentators take it positively.

6. See Ps. 6:5; 30:9; 88:10–12; 115:17–18. Motyer, *Prophecy of Isaiah*, 295, argues that all these references refer to dying with unforgiven sin, and thus being out of favor with God. However, as here, to have one's sins forgiven is, in fact, to be delivered from death. There are no references to dying with sins forgiven.

is especially clear when we look at the parallel account in 2 Kings 20, where they are integrated into the flow of the narrative. I propose that the Isaiah account and the Kings account were both dependent on a common source and that the original Isaiah did not include these details, perhaps in order to highlight the psalm. But a later editor, comparing the two accounts, thought that the details had been unintentionally left out and added them on at the end, not wanting to disturb the flow of the original.[7]

Verse 20 shows us that healing is from the Lord even if some intervening means is used to promote the healing. Verse 21 may explain why the sign involved the "stairway of Ahaz" in 38:8. As the sun moved up and down that stairway, so Hezekiah would once again move up and down the stairs of the "temple."

ILLNESS AND SIN. Hezekiah's reference to God's having put all Hezekiah's sins behind his back (38:17) brings us to a common issue when we deal with illness. Frequently when we are ill, we wonder what we have done to deserve this. This question is intensified when we discover people in the Bible who became ill as a result of sin. Note, for example, Gehazi, the servant of Elisha. When Elisha refused the lavish gifts of the Syrian general Naaman, Gehazi thought that he would get them for himself. So he followed the Syrian entourage and told them that his master had changed his mind. As a result Gehazi contracted leprosy (2 Kings 5:16–27). A similar thing happened to King Uzziah when he insisted on burning incense in the temple (2 Chron. 26:16–20).

At the same time, the classic story of suffering in the Bible is that of Job, where it is clear that his suffering had nothing to do with sin. Jesus made the same point when he was questioned about whose sin made a certain man blind. He replied that there was no sin involved, but that the man was blind so that God could be glorified (John 9:2). These accounts tell us that while sin may be involved in certain illnesses, that is not always the case. The causes of illness are much more complex than we can ever discover.

The more significant issue is the one of deserving. Neither Job nor the blind man "deserved" their illness. Neither did Hezekiah, as God's response to his prayer seems to indicate. So illness should be a stimulus to self-examination, and if we can find no disobedience to God, it should be an

---

7. For further discussion on this point see Oswalt, *Isaiah 1–39*, 690–91. Seitz, *Isaiah 1–39*, 260–61, argues that they are original and show an intentional theological shaping of the material, but his arguments seem strained.

opportunity for deepening our trust in him and our dependence on him for resources to triumph through the illness.

Afterlife. It is troubling to some to discover that the Old Testament has no clear picture of the afterlife. The Hebrews apparently thought of the realm of death (Sheol) as a shadowy place where disembodied spirits lived a rather joyless life (cf. Isa. 14:9–11). This is troublesome because it would seem that if the doctrine of heaven is true, it ought to appear in all parts of the Scripture. But such an idea fails to take into account the nature of Scripture. The Bible is not a heavenly product dropped onto the earth. The Muslims look at the Quran in much that way, but that is not how we got the Bible. The Bible is the result of God's interactions with specific people in specific times and places. This means that he accommodated himself to the understanding and development of those people.

It also means there is a progressive quality to God's revelation. An example is the deity of the Messiah. Before God could reveal that truth, he had first of all to demolish the idea of many gods. That task required virtually the entire Old Testament era. Only after the oneness of God had been fixed in the people's minds was it possible to begin to reveal the plurality that exists in the one God.

The same thing was true with regard to the afterlife. In the pagan view the physical world is not the real world. It is a dim reflection of the invisible world, where reality exists and where everything that happens here is determined. It took great effort on the part of God to demonstrate to people steeped in those ideas that they were wrong. This *is* a real world, and we have the freedom here to make real choices that have ultimate significance. We can participate here in the life of God in such a way that our behavior here is forever changed. Until this concept was firmly placed in the people's minds, any talk of a blissful afterlife would be dangerous. But once the reality of this world was implanted, then the truth that there are further dimensions to reality could be revealed.

GOD'S SOVEREIGN WILL. One issue guaranteed to provoke vigorous discussion among believers is the idea that God can change his mind. It is usually asserted that such a thing is impossible. After all, it will be said, God knows everything and he is perfect, so it is impossible for him to change his mind. Often a verse like 1 Samuel 15:29 is quoted: "He who is the Glory of Israel does not lie or change his mind; for he is not a man, that he should change his mind."

But we must make an important distinction here. God does not change his mind concerning the basic nature of things. He does not condemn adultery one day and commend it the next. Just because his favorite David committed adultery did not mean that it was acceptable behavior. Furthermore, God's basic purposes with humanity are not changeable. He intends to share his presence with us, and to do that he intends to remake us into his own character and likeness. So he would not change his mind concerning the judgment he pronounced on Saul. Through the series of events related in 1 Samuel 13–15, we see a Saul more and more fixated on himself and his success until there no longer remained the possibility of God's using him.

But this unchanging commitment to do good to people means that God will gladly change what he has said about us if it can become a greater means to our blessing. Jonah knew that when he was sent to Nineveh (Jonah 4:1–3). This is the situation here as well. In the normal course of events Hezekiah contracts a disease that will mean the end of his life. But Hezekiah calls out to God, and God sees that his intervention will be a means of greater blessing for both Hezekiah and his people. Did God know that before? Of course he did. But the issue is whether Hezekiah will turn to God in faith at such a moment. If he will not, then there is little God can do for him and through him.

The "openness of God" debate at the present time seems to me to try to solve this problem with an excessive use of human logic. One kind of logic says that if God knows everything in advance, then human freedom is an illusion. All our choices are conditioned, and while we may think we are free to choose, we are not. The problem with this is that the Bible depicts people who have real choices to make and who experience the just consequences of those choices. Thus, another kind of logic is brought into play. If humans are really to be free, then God's foreknowledge must be limited.

If the first kind of logic makes God a puppet master, then this second kind of logic makes him helpless. Furthermore, it flies in the face of what Scripture, especially Isaiah, teaches us about God. The special proof that God is God alone is that he alone can tell the future (cf. 43:8–13; 48:5–8). The simple fact is that the Bible teaches both that God is sovereign and that humans have the capacity to make real choices. Any attempt on our part to reduce these teachings to simple logic will inevitably do harm to one or the other element. We must simply assert the truth of each and live in faithfulness to what the Scripture teaches. Like Hezekiah, we need to bring our petitions to God with intensity and conviction, confident that he will be consistent with his own nature and that he will always work for our best.

A perfect heart. Hezekiah's claim that he lived a life of "truth" (NIV "faithfully") with a "perfect heart" (NIV "wholehearted devotion") is rather off-putting to modern ears. We have become suspicious of extravagant claims to righteousness—and that is as it should be. All of Jesus' teachings are critical of those who are proud of the righteousness they have achieved.

But there is a sense in which we have swung too far in the opposite direction. As we listen to popular Christian music, we rarely hear someone singing of the joys of living in unbroken fellowship with God. Instead, we hear constant confessions of recurring sin and brokenness and of God's continuing forgiveness. It is as though we have absolutized Romans 7, forgetting that it is encased in Romans 6 and 8.

We have also forgotten that Jesus told his disciples that their righteousness must exceed that of the Pharisees (Matt. 5:20). The fact is that the Pharisees were not too righteous; rather, they were not righteous enough. They believed that the righteousness they had achieved, an external righteousness, was enough. God, however, wants an internal obedience that expresses itself in external behavior (cf. Jer. 31:33), something that in the end is only possible through his grace. This is what Moses called for when he said that we should love the Lord "with all your heart and with all your soul and with all your strength" (Deut. 6:4).

So what is Hezekiah saying, and how does that translate for today? First, he is not claiming infallibility, nor is he claiming perfect performance. His mention of God's putting his sins away (38:17) is evidence enough of that. But he is saying that on the conscious, intentional level, he has kept his promises to God. This is the meaning of "walking in truth." Hezekiah has not willingly deceived God or others. He has been careful about what he promised and has found the grace in God to keep his promises. How has this been possible? The answer is that his "heart" belongs wholly to God. The Hebrew concept of the "heart" is of the "control panel" of the life, where thought, affection, and will come together. The Hebrews do not separate these three aspects of human personality, as if they each function independently of each other. Hezekiah is saying that as far as it is up to him, his "heart" has been focused on one thing only: serving, pleasing, and obeying God.[8]

If such a life was possible for an Old Testament believer, it is certainly possible for us, who now have the Holy Spirit within us (Rom. 8:12–14; Gal. 5:16–18). This does not mean we will always do everything right or that we will never have to ask forgiveness. It is instructive to note that Asa had such a heart (NIV his "heart was fully committed to the LORD"), but he did not remove the shrines ("high places") outside Jerusalem where Yahweh was worshiped (1 Kings 15:14). Evidently, his failure to do this was out of ignorance and not out of defiance. So his performance was flawed, but his heart was wholly God's. The tragedy of Solomon's life is that in the end his heart became divided and was no longer given over completely to God (1 Kings 11:4).

---

8. The word translated "perfect" in KJV is the Heb. *šalem*, which has the idea of being whole or undivided.

Every believer today should aspire to have the same testimony on our deathbed that Hezekiah had. To be sure, we live in an increasingly fractured and corrupt society, where it is not as easy to be faithful and to have undivided hearts as it may have been for some of our ancestors. But if ever there was a fractured and corrupt society, it was the one in which Hezekiah lived. Shall we today, the children of Christ, live below the standard of Hezekiah?

Isaiah 39:1–8

A T THAT TIME Merodach-Baladan son of Baladan king of Babylon sent Hezekiah letters and a gift, because he had heard of his illness and recovery. ²Hezekiah received the envoys gladly and showed them what was in his storehouses—the silver, the gold, the spices, the fine oil, his entire armory and everything found among his treasures. There was nothing in his palace or in all his kingdom that Hezekiah did not show them.

³Then Isaiah the prophet went to King Hezekiah and asked, "What did those men say, and where did they come from?"

"From a distant land," Hezekiah replied. "They came to me from Babylon."

⁴The prophet asked, "What did they see in your palace?"

"They saw everything in my palace," Hezekiah said. "There is nothing among my treasures that I did not show them."

⁵Then Isaiah said to Hezekiah, "Hear the word of the LORD Almighty: ⁶The time will surely come when everything in your palace, and all that your fathers have stored up until this day, will be carried off to Babylon. Nothing will be left, says the LORD. ⁷And some of your descendants, your own flesh and blood who will be born to you, will be taken away, and they will become eunuchs in the palace of the king of Babylon."

⁸"The word of the LORD you have spoken is good," Hezekiah replied. For he thought, "There will be peace and security in my lifetime."

Original
Meaning

"MERODACH-BALADAN" was a Babylonian leader who was twice able to make himself king of Babylon in defiance of the Assyrians: from 721–710 B.C. and from 705–703. Even after he was ousted by Sennacherib in 703, he escaped to Elam (modern Iran), where he continued to plot against the Assyrians until his death. Obviously he was interested in encouraging any others in the Assyrian Empire who were potential allies or who would draw Assyrian attention away from him and onto themselves. The fact that he heard about Hezekiah's illness and recovery tells us both that he had a good intelligence system and that communication between the various parts of the ancient world was better than we in our modern parochialism might imagine.[1]

It is easy to understand why Hezekiah would be glad to receive the "envoys" (39:2). After all, here is a great world leader paying attention to little Judah. There is something immensely flattering when someone whom we consider more important than we pays attention to us. But there is also something dangerous as well, namely, that we will succumb to the temptation to convince the important person that the attention being given is justified.

Sadly, that is the temptation into which Hezekiah falls. Here is a wonderful opportunity to declare the glory of God to the nations. The illness and recovery may have been only a pretext for Merodach-Baladan to do some political fence-building, but it still is the ostensible basis of the visit. So Hezekiah could have used the visit to tell the story of what the sole God of the universe did for him. But instead of making God look good, Hezekiah, like Moses long before (Num. 20:9–12), takes the opportunity to make himself look good. The detailed list of what he shows the Babylonians and the summary statement "there was nothing . . . Hezekiah did not show them" is Isaiah's way of emphasizing how completely Hezekiah falls into the trap.[2]

While it is impossible to say for certain, the dialogue between Hezekiah and Isaiah in 39:3–4 seems to emphasize Hezekiah's difficulties. Isaiah appears unbidden with a direct and blunt question about what the men said and where they came from. Interestingly, Hezekiah does not tell what was said. Was there talk of political alliances? He only says they were from faraway Babylon. Perhaps he is suggesting this is different from an alliance with nearby Egypt. Isaiah does not respond to this but moves on to ask what they saw "in your palace." This suggests that he knows perfectly well that Hezekiah has been showing off.[3] To Hezekiah's credit, he does not lie. Instead, he brazens his way through, saying that they have seen "everything."[4]

Again, Isaiah does not respond directly to Hezekiah but simply announces on the authority of "the LORD Almighty" (39:5) that what the men have seen—that is, "everything in your palace"—will one day belong to the Baby-

---

1. A modern equivalent for Merodach-Baladan might be Yasser Arafat. Arafat seems as indefatigable and resilient as the Babylonian was. No matter how many battles he loses, he keeps bouncing back.
2. In 2 Chron. 32:31 we read that God was testing Hezekiah in this instance.
3. Note that Elisha asked similar questions of Gehazi after Gehazi had gone to try to get something for himself from Naaman. When Gehazi tried to lie his way out, Elisha told him he had supernaturally seen the whole thing (2 Kings 5:25–27).
4. "Everything" (lit., "all") and "there is nothing" are emphasized in the Heb.

lonians (39:6). Not only that, but some of Hezekiah's "descendants" will be eunuchs in the palace of the king of Babylon. This idea receives special emphasis when the prophet says that these will be the king's "own flesh and blood who will be born to you" (39:7). It is not just his possessions that will be carried off but his family too. Nothing Hezekiah has will be left.

If we had only Hezekiah's reply, "the word of the LORD ... is good" (39:8), it might be possible to put it in a good light. We might think that this is humble submission to God's judgment. But when we are given the reason why he said that, there is no way to clear him.[5] He says the Lord's word is good because the judgment is not going to fall on him. How sad, and how short-sighted. This is not how we would like to remember such a good man. Yet this is how Isaiah has chosen for us to remember him. And when we recall that this event probably occurred before those of chapters 36–37, we are forced to ask why the material has been ordered in this way. In actual fact, Hezekiah rose above this point in his trust in God when faced with Sennacherib. So why are we not allowed to remember him in that way instead of this?

I believe the answer is that Isaiah wants to show us why his book cannot end here and why it was necessary to project it out into the future in the coming chapters. Yes, God has shown that he was completely trustworthy in regard to the Assyrians. But what about these lessons in trust when the enemy is no longer Assyria but is Babylon? What will those lessons be worth when Jerusalem is *not* delivered from Babylon? If the book had ended with chapter 37, future readers could well say that in Babylon God's people met a force superior to Sennacherib. Furthermore, those readers could say that the Messiah whom Isaiah predicted had come in the person of Hezekiah and that the promises had nothing more to offer them.

However, by showing that Hezekiah is both mortal and fallible, Isaiah does two things. (1) He shows that trust is intended to be a way of life, not a one-time experience. This is not only true for Hezekiah but for the nation as well. The possibility of trust had been demonstrated, but something more was necessary to enable the nation to practice such trust in an unreserved way. What that something was must yet be revealed, but it would be in the chapters to come. (2) Isaiah is showing that there is no final salvation in a human being, no matter how good he might be. Our hope is not in the perfectibility of humanity. The Messiah we look for is better than that.

---

5. Seitz, *Isaiah 1–39*, 264–66, attempts to do so because of his view that the ending of "I Isaiah" demands a positive conclusion. However, he can only do so by pointing out that there is no direct judgment on Hezekiah and that 2 Chron. makes his wealth a sign of divine blessing. This is not enough to counteract the text itself.

Bridging Contexts

THE BABYLONIAN EXILE did not occur because of Hezekiah's failure to seize an opportunity to glorify God before the Babylonians. To be sure, it is intriguing to think of how history may have been different if he had, but that is not the point Isaiah is making. Hezekiah's behavior is illustrative, not causal. Why did the Babylonian exile occur? Because the nation, like Hezekiah, saw trust as a one-time affair rather than a way of life. So Hezekiah's reign, perhaps the best overall in Judah's history, was followed by Manasseh's, unquestionably the worst (cf. 2 Kings 21:10–15).[6] That this was so is in part a testimony to the character of the people. If the revival under Hezekiah had produced a different people, their king would have behaved differently.

The same thing is true with Josiah, Manasseh's grandson. For reasons that the text does not specify, he had a heart for God and led his nation in a remarkable revival (cf. 2 Kings 23:1–3). Yet after his untimely death, the revival seems to have disappeared overnight, and his son Jehoiakim led as cynical a regime as one could imagine.[7] Again, it is the people who failed in their trust. They saw trust as a means of getting out of a crisis rather than as the lifelong expression of a covenant relationship.

Perhaps more to the point, they saw trust only as a means of getting their needs met. But that reduces trust into a device for manipulation. When it is used in that way, it is bound to fail, for God cannot be manipulated. The result is the same today as it was in Judah and Israel: We turn to other means of manipulation to supply our needs—in their case, the worship of other gods.

As I have said frequently before, idolatry is an attempt to manipulate our environment in such a way as to meet our needs. The idolatrous instinct is ever-present with us, and as soon as we abandon trust in God, idolatry in one form or another is waiting in the wings. This is even more likely if we evaluate our success in life, as Hezekiah seems to have done, by our possessions. We keep confusing ends and means. The intended end of our lives is abundant life, the life in which God's fullness is poured into ours. A by-product of that fullness is physical and material blessing. But that is *only* a by-product. When we make it an end and put it forward as the evidence of our success in life, manipulation of God in order to secure that end is almost inescapable. Manipulation and trust are incompatible.

---

6. It is tempting to wonder if Hezekiah's attitude, "There will be peace and security in my lifetime," offers any kind of an explanation for Manasseh. Did Hezekiah's lack of concern for the future beyond himself mean that he did not give the kind of attention to his son and the formation of his spiritual life that he should have?

7. Note his destruction of the scroll containing the prophecies of Jeremiah (Jer. 36:22–23).

THE QUESTION THIS chapter raises for us is, Who gets the glory? If both Moses and Hezekiah failed at this critical point, we are certainly not immune. In both cases they were faced with seemingly impossible situations. For Moses there was nothing around but rocks and gravel, yet his people were dying of thirst. Hezekiah was faced with the apparent inevitability of his death. Both men did the right thing in turning to God in their distress. Neither prayer is an attempt to tell God what to do or to manipulate him with some super-faith. Both are simply appeals from the heart. In both cases God took immediate action. But here is where the tragedy emerges. Moses says, "Must *we* produce water for you, you rebels?" And he struck the rock with his rod, making it appear as if he were producing the water. We know what Hezekiah did.

When we pray the Lord's Prayer and say the words "Hallowed be your name," what are we saying? We are asking that God will be seen in the world as he truly is: high and lifted up, both in power and in character. Yet how often do we take the credit for what goes right in our lives and blame God for what goes wrong? When we have ended up in an impossible situation and then have somehow gotten out of it, who gets the credit in the eyes of the world? Us or God?

Even beyond that, what are we showing to the world? Are we showing them our accomplishments, or even our spirituality? Who gets the glory? There are, of course, ways of drawing attention to ourselves by constantly dragging God into all our conversations. I am not talking about that. But the person who has cultivated a life of trust, who knows that everything he or she has is a gift from God, will be constantly deflecting the praise and honor from himself or herself to God. If that kind of deflection is not occurring, then perhaps I need to ask myself if I truly believe that what I am and have is a gift, or do I believe I produced it, either through my physical effort or, worse, through my spiritual effort. Hezekiah and his achievements cannot save the world; only Christ can. Neither can your achievements or mine. Who is getting the glory?

Isaiah 40:1–31

¹ COMFORT, COMFORT MY people,
    says your God.
² Speak tenderly to Jerusalem,
    and proclaim to her
that her hard service has been completed,
    that her sin has been paid for,
that she has received from the LORD's hand
    double for all her sins.

³ A voice of one calling:
"In the desert prepare
    the way for the LORD,
make straight in the wilderness
    a highway for our God.
⁴ Every valley shall be raised up,
    every mountain and hill made low;
the rough ground shall become level,
    the rugged places a plain.
⁵ And the glory of the LORD will be revealed,
    and all mankind together will see it.
                    For the mouth of the LORD has spoken."

⁶ A voice says, "Cry out."
    And I said, "What shall I cry?"

"All men are like grass,
    and all their glory is like the flowers of the field.
⁷ The grass withers and the flowers fall,
    because the breath of the LORD blows on them.
    Surely the people are grass.
⁸ The grass withers and the flowers fall,
    but the word of our God stands forever."

⁹ You who bring good tidings to Zion,
    go up on a high mountain.
You who bring good tidings to Jerusalem,
    lift up your voice with a shout,
lift it up, do not be afraid;
    say to the towns of Judah,
    "Here is your God!"

¹⁰ See, the Sovereign LORD comes with power,
    and his arm rules for him.
  See, his reward is with him,
    and his recompense accompanies him.
¹¹ He tends his flock like a shepherd:
    He gathers the lambs in his arms
  and carries them close to his heart;
    he gently leads those that have young.

¹² Who has measured the waters in the hollow of his hand,
    or with the breadth of his hand marked off the heavens?
  Who has held the dust of the earth in a basket,
    or weighed the mountains on the scales
    and the hills in a balance?
¹³ Who has understood the mind of the LORD,
    or instructed him as his counselor?
¹⁴ Whom did the LORD consult to enlighten him,
    and who taught him the right way?
  Who was it that taught him knowledge
    or showed him the path of understanding?

¹⁵ Surely the nations are like a drop in a bucket;
    they are regarded as dust on the scales;
    he weighs the islands as though they were fine dust.
¹⁶ Lebanon is not sufficient for altar fires,
    nor its animals enough for burnt offerings.
¹⁷ Before him all the nations are as nothing;
    they are regarded by him as worthless
    and less than nothing.

¹⁸ To whom, then, will you compare God?
    What image will you compare him to?
¹⁹ As for an idol, a craftsman casts it,
    and a goldsmith overlays it with gold
    and fashions silver chains for it.
²⁰ A man too poor to present such an offering
    selects wood that will not rot.
  He looks for a skilled craftsman
    to set up an idol that will not topple.

²¹ Do you not know?
    Have you not heard?
  Has it not been told you from the beginning?
    Have you not understood since the earth was founded?

²²He sits enthroned above the circle of the earth,
    and its people are like grasshoppers.
He stretches out the heavens like a canopy,
    and spreads them out like a tent to live in.
²³He brings princes to naught
    and reduces the rulers of this world to nothing.
²⁴No sooner are they planted,
    no sooner are they sown,
    no sooner do they take root in the ground,
than he blows on them and they wither,
    and a whirlwind sweeps them away like chaff.

²⁵"To whom will you compare me?
    Or who is my equal?" says the Holy One.
²⁶Lift your eyes and look to the heavens:
    Who created all these?
He who brings out the starry host one by one,
    and calls them each by name.
Because of his great power and mighty strength,
    not one of them is missing.

²⁷Why do you say, O Jacob,
    and complain, O Israel,
"My way is hidden from the LORD;
    my cause is disregarded by my God"?
²⁸Do you not know?
    Have you not heard?
The LORD is the everlasting God,
    the Creator of the ends of the earth.
He will not grow tired or weary,
    and his understanding no one can fathom.
²⁹He gives strength to the weary
    and increases the power of the weak.
³⁰Even youths grow tired and weary,
    and young men stumble and fall;
³¹but those who hope in the LORD
    will renew their strength.
They will soar on wings like eagles;
    they will run and not grow weary,
    they will walk and not be faint.

CHAPTER 40 INTRODUCES the third major division of Isaiah: chapters 40—55. The question of the Lord's trustworthiness has been thoroughly answered. But the question remains: What will motivate the people of God to actually trust him and become the servants that they are called to be? Furthermore, how will it be possible for sinful Israel to become God's servants at all? What is to be done about the sin that has alienated them from God?

To answer these questions the prophet projects himself out into the future where these questions will be seen in their full poignancy. In the context of the coming Babylonian exile, he addresses the questions he knows the exiles will be prompted to ask by that crisis. Chapters 40—55 answer the questions in two subdivisions. (1) Chapters 41—48 address Israel's captivity in Babylon. If they are to be the redeemed servants of the Lord, they need to be free in order to worship God in the land of the promises. These chapters speak of God's capacity to deliver and his desire to do so. (2) Chapters 49—55 address the prior issue of what needs to be done about the sin that got the people in their dilemma in the first place.

Isaiah recognizes that the Exile will bring up questions about these issues. Although the questions are never specifically stated, answers are given again and again to implied questions. The first answer is: "I am God, and there is no other; I am God, and there is none like me" (46:9, etc.). The second is: "So do not fear, for I am with you; do not be dismayed, for I am your God" (41:10, etc.). What, then, are the questions? They are: "Has not God been defeated by the gods of Babylon?" and "Has not our sin separated us from God forever?" To both of these, Isaiah answers with a resounding "no." God has not been defeated either by the Babylonian gods or by his people's sin. In fact, God will use the evidence of their lives to demonstrate his sole Godhood. Far from being cast off, they will be his witnesses in his case against the idols.

These two themes emerge at once in chapter 40. The chapter has two main divisions: verses 1—11 and verses 12—26, with verses 27—31 acting as a kind of summary conclusion. In the first section, the question of whether God has cast his people away is addressed. Echoing the words of Isaiah 12, where this event is anticipated, God speaks not judgment but comfort. He will deliver them, and they will be in a position to tell the world of the deliverance. Then in 40:12—26, he speaks of his ability to deliver them. He is the incomparable God, like whom there is no other. The nations of earth are nothing to him, so they need not fear that they have been abandoned. They need only to wait in hope for the time to come (40:27—31).

The dominant idea here is that of the undeserved grace of God. This is what will motivate the people to trust God, just as was intimated in chapter 12. When God delivers his people without any deserving on their part, they will at last be willing to cast themselves on him without reservation. So if chapters 7–39 were about trust as the basis for servanthood, chapters 40–55 are about grace as the motive and the means of servanthood.

God's Promised Deliverance (40:1–11)

THESE VERSES ARE often referred to as the "prologue" to the book of "Second Isaiah." Some have even seen them as the call of the anonymous prophet who is supposedly responsible for the book.[1] More recent thinking has suggested that the real significance of the material is not as a new call but as an extension and expansion of chapter 6.[2] No longer is the prophetic message to be primarily one of judgment. That point has been made and will be confirmed in the fires of the Exile. Now, however, the message is to be one of hope. Special prominence is given to speech in the passage. Although the people have withered and fallen like dried grass, God's word as spoken by his prophet will not fail. Just as he had said that judgment would come, and it had, so he now says restoration will come, and it will!

Verses 1 and 2 provide an introduction and set the tone for the following three three-verse stanzas. The idea of the word translated "comfort" (v. 1) is to "encourage," as is "speak tenderly" (v. 2).[3] Isaiah sees a day when God's servants will be crushed to the ground under the burden of their sins. They will feel sure that all is lost and that all the promises have been nullified by their rebellion. But the message to be proclaimed to them is that this is not so.[4] The

1. Cf. Westermann, *Isaiah* 40–66: *A Commentary*, trans. D. Stalker (OTL; Philadelphia: Westminster, 1969), 32; N. Habel, "Form and Significance of the Call Narrative," *ZAW* 77 (1965): 314–16.

2. Cf. C. Seitz, "The Divine Council: Temporal Transition and New Prophecy in the Book of Isaiah," *JBL* 109 (1990): 229–47. Hanson, *Isaiah* 40–66 (Louisville: John Knox, 1995), 15–24, goes to great lengths to exegete the significance of the use of the divine assembly in these verses. But as a matter of fact, there is no reference to the divine assembly, and it is highly conjectural that there is even any implication of it (see Oswalt, *Isaiah* 40–66 [NICOT; Grand Rapids: Eerdmans, 1998], 48, 50).

3. Lit., "speak to the heart"; cf. Gen. 34:3; 50:21; Ruth 2:13; 2 Sam. 19:8; 2 Chron. 30:22.

4. It is interesting to note that the person to whom these commands are addressed is not specifically identified, nor are the "voices" in vv. 3 and 6. Childs (*Isaiah*, 302–3) says that the intent is to present these words as a continuation of those of Isaiah of Jerusalem and cites Delitzsch approvingly when he says that Isaiah is treated "like a spirit without visible form." If that is the intent but not the fact, I cannot help wondering why later writers felt it necessary to engage in this deception. An alternative view is that since Isaiah is speaking to

Exile is not to destroy them but only to punish them. Now that punishment is complete ("double"), and God has a word of hope for them.

In the first stanza (40:3–5), some of the language of chapter 35 is resumed. There is a "highway" in the "desert/wilderness." But in this case, the highway is for "our God." As in 52:7 and 63:1, it is God who comes to helpless Zion to set her free. Nothing can prevent his swift coming to his people's aid, neither mountains nor valleys. The highway will be level and straight, so that God can come quickly. Once again, the identity of the one speaking is not important. Rather, it is the word to be spoken. If there is to be deliverance for God's people, it must come from God's direct intervention. There is no other hope.

That fact is underlined in the second stanza (40:6–8), where perhaps another voice (though possibly the same voice as in vv. 3–5) cries out that "all men [Heb. flesh] are like grass." This has a twofold implication. On the one hand, Judean flesh is like grass. They have been consumed by their sins, and there is no permanence in them at all, nor is there anything they can do to help themselves. But it is also true that Babylonian flesh is as grass. If the Judeans are to be delivered, God will have to do it. But if he *does* decide to do it, there is nothing the Babylonians can do to prevent it. There is no permanence in anything human, but if God speaks a promise, that "word" will stand, and nothing earthly can alter it.

Because that is so, "Zion" has a word to declare to the surrounding villages. There is some controversy about the speaker in this final stanza (40:9–11). One possibility is that represented in the NIV text, namely, that there is yet a third unidentified speaker, who is commanded to bring the "good tidings to Zion."[5] There is a certain attractiveness to this proposal since the content of the previous stanzas has been addressed to Zion.

However, the most natural way to read the Hebrew is that Zion is this messenger of good tidings. There is a consistency in that point of view also, in that Zion's place is not merely as a recipient of God's grace but also as a messenger of that grace to the surrounding world. The good news, as it is stated later in 52:7, is about the intervention of God in the world: He "comes." The Creator breaks into his world, both to break the power of evil with his strong "arm" (40:10) and, "like a shepherd," to gather up the broken in his gentle "arms."

---

persons far in the future, in another historic context than his own, the details of his own setting are no longer significant. In fact, if that were the case, this lack of specificity might be exactly what we would expect.

5. Motyer, *Prophecy of Isaiah*, 301, argues that since the first two voices are indefinite, we should expect the third to be also, but then he is required to hypothesize an unknown woman since mᵉbaśśeret, "you who bring good tidings," is feminine.

God's Ability to Deliver His People (40:12—26)

THE FIRST SECTION (40:1—11) has verified God's desire and intention to deliver his people, but can he do it? After all, from one perspective, he seemed unable to prevent the Babylonians from capturing the land and city in the first place, so why should we think he can deliver the people from them?[6] This question becomes even more pointed when we recall that there is no evidence any people have ever gone home from captivity before. In all the long history of exile up until the fall of Babylon, there is no report of that ever happening. Thus, for God to say that it is going to happen for the Israelites is to make a large claim.

Isaiah's approach to answering the question as to whether God can deliver from Babylon is to assert that God is unique. He is able to deliver not because he is greater than the Babylonian gods; he is able to deliver because *he is the only God!* As Hezekiah said of his neighbors' gods (37:19), what the Babylonians were worshiping are not gods at all.

Isaiah 40:12—26 can be divided into two sections that parallel each other in general ways (vv. 12—20 and vv. 21—26). Each unit begins with an assertion, in the form of rhetorical questions, that the Lord is the sole Creator (40:12—14, 21). This is followed by an affirmation that the Lord is the Ruler of all nations and rulers (40:15—17, 22—24). Next is a rhetorical invitation to compare God with anything else (40:18a, 25). Finally, there is the claim of absolute superiority over the gods, whether conceived of as idols (40:18b—20) or as the heavenly host (40:26).[7]

In 40:12—14 the prophet employs a series of rhetorical questions intended to bring the reader to the point of saying that Yahweh is the sole Creator. The doctrine of creation is important to the argument of this part of the book.[8] The concept is not developed in logical proofs as much as it is assumed and built upon.[9] The prophet has received it and accepts it gladly as a part of his arsenal. Here he develops the point by insisting that God is other than creation. He is *not* the mountains or the oceans or the heavens, but he is *other*

---

6. We tend to focus on Jeremiah's message that it was God's will for Judah and Jerusalem to fall to Babylon, but for one Jeremiah there seem to have been dozens of others prophesying in the name of the Lord that God would not let the city fall into the hands of the Babylonians. Thus, it would have been easy for many to believe that God had failed.

7. See Motyer, *Prophecy of Isaiah,* 302—303, for a somewhat similar analysis. Other commentators vary widely. For instance John. D. W. Watts, *Isaiah 34—66* (Waco, Tex.: Word, 1987), 84—90, extends the unit from v. 10 to v. 31 and sees an intricate five-part chiasm.

8. The Heb. *br³*, "to create," occurs fifty-four times in the Old Testament in the Qal and Niphal. Of these, twenty-one are in Isaiah, and thirteen of those occurrences are between 40:26 and 45:18.

9. Cf. C. Stuhlmueller, "'First and Last' and 'Yahweh-Creator' in Deutero-Isaiah," *CBQ* 29 (1967): 495—511.

than all of these. He is not them but holds them in his hand. He originated the world, but he is not the world.

Verses 13–14 seem particularly aimed at the polytheistic religions, where a counselor/magician among the gods assists the other gods in realizing their purposes. Isaiah insists that there are no such beings, that "understanding" originated with the Originator of all things. To think otherwise is to give up transcendence, and to give that up is to be dropped into the morass where life is only the outworking of a deterministic cycle coming from nowhere and going nowhere.

Compared to the One who holds the oceans in his hand, the nations of the earth are "nothing" (40:17). Unlike the other gods, the God of Israel is not a personalization of his nation. He brought all the nations into existence, but he is not an extension of any one of them. To him the most important of the nations does not weigh enough to even move a balance scale. Babylon and Assyria and Egypt may be great in their own eyes and in the eyes of their neighbors, but in the eyes of the One who spoke light into existence, they mean little. Verse 16 illustrates this point by saying that no earthly sacrifice is sufficient to manipulate him in favor of earthly concerns. If all the forests of Lebanon were set on fire and all its animals burned on the fire, it would not affect him at all.

Thus, if the Lord is the sole Creator and the Lord of the nations, will we say that an idol is comparable to him? Certainly not! The diatribe against the idols in 40:18b–20 is the first of several in this part of the book (41:6–7; 42:17; 44:9–20; 46:5–7; 48:5). It is the complement to the prophet's insistence on the transcendence of God. If God is not the world, then any attempt to represent him in the forms of this world has deadly consequences. It immediately links him to the world and begins the process of ultimately making him identical with the world. The emphasis on the making of the idol is surely intentional. How can something made by humans possibly be the maker of the humans who made it?

The cycle begins again with 40:21, where the prophet asserts that God is not only other than the world but also other than the heavens, having stretched them out "like a tent" (40:22). As a result, he is not overawed by the "rulers" (40:23) of this earth. In fact, their destiny (like Sennacherib's) is in his hands (cf. Dan. 4:34–35). Verse 24 with its comparison of the kings of earth to plants seems to reflect 40:6–8. Like plants, the kings grow up quickly and wither away. The reflection may extend to the breath of God ("blows") being associated with the word of God (40:8). The tender plants of humanity are no match for the eternal judgments of God.

Thus, once again we, the readers, are asked—this time by God himself—if we know of anything to compare with him. If it is not the gorgeous idols of the craftsmen, perhaps it is the stars of heaven, the "starry host" that the pagans believed were representations of the gods (cf. 2 Kings 17:16; 21:3). To that suggestion Isaiah retorts that God "created" them and brings them out night after night "by name," like a shepherd calling his flock. Is the product on the same plane as the maker or the sheep on the same plane as the shepherd? No, the stars only exist because of the "mighty strength" of Judah's God.

Waiting in Hope (40:27–31)

BOTH OF THE questions the exiles will be asking have now been fully answered. What is an appropriate response? That question is answered in these closing verses. In 40:27 the prophet anticipates the attitude of the exiles, who will be saying that they are either now outside of God's vision for them ("my way is hidden") or else God has given up on them ("my cause is disregarded"). To this Isaiah responds that to think in this way is to have much too low a view of God. He reminds them of who God is in 40:28–29, dealing with the Creator's endless power and wisdom in the first verse and his wonderful desire and ability to share that power with the "weak" and the "weary" in the second. So he speaks of both the being and the person of God.

Thus, his question in 40:28 is rather incredulous. How could you say such things about God when you know perfectly well who he is and what he is like? He knows your situation perfectly, and he can and will do something about it. The fact is that the most vigorous things in creation ("young men") cannot keep themselves going. They are not self-generating but are dependent on outside sources for their strength. God is not like that; he *is* self-generating, and that means he has abundant strength to give away to those who will wait for (NIV "hope in") him.

Here we come back to the theme of trust. This concept of trust as waiting has appeared three times previously in the book (8:17; 25:9; 33:2) and will appear twice more (49:23; 64:4).[10] To "wait" on God is not simply to mark time; rather, it is to live in confident expectation of his action on our behalf. It is to refuse to run ahead of him in trying to solve our problems for ourselves. Thus, just as Isaiah called on the people of his own day to trust God to solve their problems, he calls on the exiles in the age to come to do the same thing. If they are worn out and weary, hardly daring to believe that there is any future for them, the God of all strength can give them exactly what they need at the right time, whether to "soar," "run," or "walk."

---

10. The Heb. root is *qwh*. The parallel term is *hkh*, which occurs in 8:17; 30:18; 64:4.

Bridging Contexts

TRANSCENDENCE AND IMMANENCE. The idea of God's coming is a central one for the biblical message. Since God is conceived of as being "outside" of creation, it is critical whether he can enter into his creation. This has been a chief criticism of the doctrine of transcendence from the outset. After all, if God is truly other than the world, can he possibly be present in it or participate in its life? This is what led Plotinus to his idea of the "Good Mover." If there really is a first cause, he reasoned, then that force must be incapable of being acted upon by any other cause. Similarly, the Gnostics of the early Christian era argued that this dark and sinful world cannot be entered into, or even have been created by, the one who is altogether good. So they reasoned that there must be an infinite number of mediators between us and that One.

More recently the school of thought known as *process theology*, as first expounded by A. N. Whitehead, has sought to address the same problem. These theologians believe that unless God is somehow identified with the unfolding process, we have no choice but to abandon the concept of God altogether as irrelevant to our concerns. Thus, they identify him as the love that drives the process and to which the process tends as its goal.

But this is another example of the danger of forcing the biblical data into our logical boxes. As with sovereignty and human freedom, both the absolute otherness of God *and* his ability to be present with his creation are taught by the Bible, and if we diminish either in an attempt to make them conform to our logical limitations, we have done damage to the full revelation. For instance, if God is not transcendent, then he lacks the power to change our circumstances. But more importantly, we also have lost any reason to change those circumstances because they are simply part of the ineluctable consequences of being caught on the wheel of existence that has neither beginning nor end. But if God is only transcendent, then he neither knows nor cares what is happening in our lives. He is simply other than we, bringing us into existence and providing the energy that powers the cosmos, but he remains untouched by the changing, fluctuating movements of the world.

The Bible insists that *both* propositions are equally true. On one account, God "sits above the circle of the earth" (40:22). He is not the sun, moon, or stars, nor is he to be identified with any process of earth, whether physical, political, or psychological. He is above and beyond all of that. But at the same time, he *is* love. Immediately, we must say that this is not to reduce God to all that we call love. It seems to me that this is one of the dangers of process theology. Paganism identifies the gods with the natural systems of time and space, while process theology identifies God with the psychological and historical systems of time and space. Furthermore, it was a good deal easier to say that the historical process was leading us toward the goal of love in 1901 than it is in 2001. No, to say that God is love is to move the connection in the opposite direction. It is to say that everything we know and think of as love is partial and derivative of the totality that love is in God. What this means is that God is intimately involved with the life of his creation but is not at the same time just an expression of that life.

This truth is summed up in Isaiah 40: God is outside of the systems of time and space, which means he is not conditioned by any of those systems. He can intervene in them at will and change any of them to suit his grand design. Furthermore, it means he can *have* a grand design. He can have a plan that is not merely an expression of what is but something to which the "is" can be made to conform. Yet even though he is outside of time and space, he is not limited by them. He is aware of our distress and our captivity, our joy and our accomplishments, and he is able to come to us, sharing the joy and delivering us from our distress. He is great enough to be able to help, and he is near enough to want to help.

All of this is summed up in Jesus Christ. Thus, it is entirely appropriate that the New Testament sees John the Baptist as the second voice here, who prepares the way for God's coming in the desert (Mark 1:2–3). It is also significant that like the anonymous voice here, emphasizing the central importance of the message, John says, "He must become greater; I must become less" (John 3:30). The identity of the herald is not that important, but the One who is coming, the eternal Word, is all-important.

Without worrying about logical contradiction, all four Gospels insist that Jesus is God and man at the same time. His humanity is assumed, but his deity is also both implied and asserted. Matthew says in the mouth of Peter, "You are the Christ, the Son of the living God" (Matt. 16:16). In Mark, in response to the question as to whether he is "the Son of the Blessed One," Jesus responds, "I am. And you will see the Son of Man sitting at the right hand of the Mighty One and coming on the clouds of heaven" (Mark 14:62). Luke expands both the question and the answer. The rulers ask, "Are you then the Son of God?" And Jesus replies, "You are right in saying I am" (Luke 22:70). But it is in John that the equation is made most explicit. References can be multiplied, but two must suffice. In John 10:30 Jesus says, "I and the Father are one," and in 14:9 he says, "Anyone who has seen me has seen the Father." Paul too states the principle in unequivocal terms in Philippians 2:6–11:

Who, being in very nature God,
    did not consider equality with God something to be grasped,
but made himself nothing,
    taking the very nature of a servant,
    being made in human likeness.
And being found in appearance as a man,
    he humbled himself
and became obedient to death—
    even death on a cross!
Therefore God exalted him to the highest place
    and gave him the name that is above every name,
that at the name of Jesus every knee should bow,
    in heaven and on earth and under the earth,
and every tongue confess that Jesus Christ is Lord,
    to the glory of God the Father.

In Jesus Christ the linking of the transcendent God with the immanent God has come to its climax. In him the transcendent God has come to us in both humility and power. He not only knows our condition and is moved by it, he has even entered into that condition. He has come!

The doctrine of creation. Closely related to the doctrine of transcendence is the doctrine of creation. In some ways all the rest of biblical faith stands or falls with this truth. It is important to say at once that this is not to espouse a particular theory of creation. There are those today who insist that unless you accept that the cosmos was created in seven twenty-four-hour days about six thousand years ago, you do not really believe in creation. This is to confuse expression and truth. The truth of creation is that God, who is a spirit, existed before matter, that the cosmos came into existence at his command and was not the result of a conflict between eternal forces of good and evil, that creation conformed precisely to a preexisting plan, that creation was both orderly and progressive, that God directed every phase, and that humanity is the apex of creation.

Precisely how these principles were worked out in scientific terms leaves open any number of possibilities, so that to spend a great deal of time trying to defend the literal nature of the Genesis accounts misses the point. The key point is that these ideas are diametrically opposed to the stories of the origin of the cosmos both in the ancient Near East and elsewhere in the world. They are unparalleled, and the whole structure of biblical faith rests on them.

Let me develop some of the implications of the biblical doctrine of creation briefly, especially as they relate to this chapter. (1) If matter were to precede spirit, human personality is only of an accidental nature and is finally insignificant. (2) If the cosmos happened by chance, life is without both meaning and purpose. (3) If the cosmos originated out of eternal conflict, whether called "good" and "evil," or "positive" and "negative," the human quest for peace and personal integration is useless, grasping for the wind. (4) If the present condition of the cosmos is the result of an evolution governed by the interrelationship of mindless, irresistible forces, there is no possibility of personal transformation. "Salvation" can never be more than self-actualization.

In fact, if the Bible's doctrine of creation is wrong, then everything the Bible holds out to us is not only wrong, but also positively perverse. It prompts us to reach for beautiful hopes that are nothing more than soap bubbles in the air. But in fact, what the Bible teaches us is so odd that we cannot account for it in any other way than the one the biblical writers give us: They got it from God. Their disembodied voices that come to us across the centuries are the very Word of God, which does not pass away.

CONTRADICTIONS IN THE WESTERN WORLD. We live today in a self-contradictory world. It is a world that has resulted from taking some of the premises of the Bible while rejecting others. We passionately believe, for example, in the worth of the individual and are willing to fight to the death for the absolute right of human choice. Where has that idea come from? It comes straight out of the Bible, where humans are called to voluntarily enter into a relationship with the eternal God, one who knows them by name. The Bible is not about a "people movement" or "national development." It is about real, distinctive individuals, from Adam to the apostle Paul. To be sure, they were a part of a people, a nation. But the story is not first about the nation. It is about people in the nation.

The greatest story in the ancient Near Eastern world was the Gilgamesh Epic. It is found everywhere in one form or another. In it Gilgamesh seeks the meaning of life, and the story is engaging. But Gilgamesh is not a historical individual; he represents humanity. That is not the case in the Bible; it records the acts of real people. Where the Bible has not penetrated, individual human worth does not exist.

We also believe in progress. We believe that we are not locked in, that we can go someplace else and do something else; in words that now sound a little quaint, we can "better ourselves." Where did that notion come from? It comes from the Bible. God had a plan for an Abraham, a Moses, a David, and we can trace how that plan unfolds not only in progress but sometimes in regress. God had a plan for a people in bondage to the greatest powers of their day. We see those plans unfolding as people leave the husks of the past behind them and are transformed. Where has the idea of progress existed in the world? Wherever the Bible has gone.

But now the Bible is increasingly lost in Western society, and with it we have lost its central idea, the idea of transformation. So we fight for individual rights, and yet we increasingly deny any responsibility for our choices, arguing that we really do not have any choices since we are conditioned by society, our family, some tragedy, or even our genes. What has happened? We have kept the Bible's conclusion but denied its premises. We have accepted human worth while buying into deterministic evolution.

But it does not work that way. If we are simply the end product of mindless forces, without real choices of our own, then we have no freedom and no worth. On the one hand, if we really believe that a killer has no choice but to do what he does, then we should let him go, for it is unjust to punish him for what he cannot help doing, and there are no "corrective influences" on earth that are going to change a lifetime of genetic and social conditioning. On the other hand, if in society's collective wisdom his behavior is not conducive to the progress of evolution, then we simply ought to rub him out on the spot without a lot of moralizing about justice and right and wrong. Those principles do not exist in a world without creation.

The same thing has happened to our view of progress. The biblical view is profoundly linear. Believers are not trying to get back to the place they started. Once Eden was lost, there is no recovering it. But it is possible to have something even better! The new heavens and the new earth are better than Eden, and the blessings of the redeemed as described in the eschatological parts of the Bible are something better than the blessings of Eden.[11] That is the kind of God we serve. But without a Creator able to do new things, there may be change, but there is no progress.

That is what has happened to us. We no longer really believe we can transcend our past. We no longer believe that we can escape its dead hand on us. In a frenzy of activity we keep changing, but always with the sick knowledge that we are simply doomed to do it all over again in a different way. So we cry for "progress," having thrown away the only basis on which real progress can rest, namely, the possibility that the transcendent God can break in from outside and change us.

---

11. To be sure, there is a harmony between the past and the future. Thus, the "tree of life" that stood in the Garden of Eden (Gen. 2:9) reappears in the new Jerusalem (Rev. 22:2, 14, 19). What this says is that the new things God does are always consistent with what he has done already. But it is not merely a circling back to re-create the past. See comments on 43:16–19.

But what about the world where creation does exist? What about a world where humans have been created in the image of God? What about a world that originally conformed to a master plan and, though terribly marred, still has its outlines? What about a world whose omnipotent Maker is determined to give abundant life to every person who will let him? The Judeans in captivity were much like us. They did not believe there was any way God could transform them or their circumstances. They insisted on their "freedom" to personally do as they wished while all the time believing that their situation could never really be changed.

Hope. It is into a setting just like ours that Isaiah speaks by inspiration. He speaks to people who have lost hope. The impossible has happened. They were sure their nation could not fall, that their temple could not be destroyed, and that their God would not let them down. Yet all that happened. Whatever the future might hold, it would always be one of regret. Yes, God may have acted in the past, for other people, but this situation is beyond him. It is beyond his compassion ("he has forgotten me"), and it is beyond his power ("my way is hidden from him").

Isaiah says to us as he said to them, "No! There is nothing beyond his compassion or his power. Have you not known? Have you not heard?" There is nothing that a caring Creator cannot change. We are persons of worth to him, and that means that we really can choose to be and act differently than we have. Are there chains of conditioning on us as real as any captivity the Judeans endured? Of course there are. But the Creator can break those chains. To be sure, the way he chooses to do that is his business. One of the recurring themes in the following chapters is the discomfort the people have with the ways God chooses to act on their behalf. We cannot dictate the terms or the means, but we can hold on to him with confident hope.

In the same way, we can believe that God can change our circumstances. There can be real change for the better. That is, there can be if we believe in a God who is both outside of and inside of history. Precisely because process theology is wrong and God is not a historical process, he can intervene in that process and change it. But so much depends on our faith. I am not talking here about getting some idea and then doing a mental number on ourselves until we really believe it is going to happen. I am talking about a life of faith in God, a life where we truly release ourselves into his hands without any reservation, a life where we are constantly giving ourselves and our concerns into the caring Creator's hands.

This is clearly what the Judeans were going to have difficulty doing in the crisis of the Exile, and Isaiah knew it. In a real sense the problem he addresses in his own day and the problem he addresses in that future day are the same. In his own day, the people did not think they could trust God to deliver them from the nations, so they trusted other nations instead. In the exilic age, the people do not believe that God can deliver them either! That is why "cry" and "shout" and "speak" are so prominent.

These people needed to hear the Word of God in ways that changed how they thought. That is what we need too. We need lives of faith that are shaped by the Word of God, its view of reality, and the principles that emerge from it. If I cannot "believe" God and "hope" in him in the sense of surrendering my life to him in a kind of life that I know pleases him, then his power cannot transform me. But if I will actively believe his Word, there really are no limits to what he can do for me, for my family, and for my society.

Isaiah 41:1–20

1 "BE SILENT BEFORE me, you islands!
   Let the nations renew their strength!
Let them come forward and speak;
   let us meet together at the place of judgment.

2 "Who has stirred up one from the east,
   calling him in righteousness to his service?
He hands nations over to him
   and subdues kings before him.
He turns them to dust with his sword,
   to windblown chaff with his bow.
3 He pursues them and moves on unscathed,
   by a path his feet have not traveled before.
4 Who has done this and carried it through,
   calling forth the generations from the beginning?
I, the LORD—with the first of them
   and with the last—I am he."

5 The islands have seen it and fear;
   the ends of the earth tremble.
They approach and come forward;
6   each helps the other
   and says to his brother, "Be strong!"
7 The craftsman encourages the goldsmith,
   and he who smoothes with the hammer
   spurs on him who strikes the anvil.
He says of the welding, "It is good."
   He nails down the idol so it will not topple.

8 "But you, O Israel, my servant,
   Jacob, whom I have chosen,
   you descendants of Abraham my friend,
9 I took you from the ends of the earth,
   from its farthest corners I called you.
I said, 'You are my servant';
   I have chosen you and have not rejected you.
10 So do not fear, for I am with you;
   do not be dismayed, for I am your God.
I will strengthen you and help you;
   I will uphold you with my righteous right hand.

¹¹"All who rage against you
    will surely be ashamed and disgraced;
  those who oppose you
    will be as nothing and perish.
¹²Though you search for your enemies,
    you will not find them.
  Those who wage war against you
    will be as nothing at all.
¹³For I am the LORD, your God,
    who takes hold of your right hand
  and says to you, Do not fear;
    I will help you.
¹⁴Do not be afraid, O worm Jacob,
    O little Israel,
  for I myself will help you," declares the LORD,
    your Redeemer, the Holy One of Israel.
¹⁵"See, I will make you into a threshing sledge,
    new and sharp, with many teeth.
  You will thresh the mountains and crush them,
    and reduce the hills to chaff.
¹⁶You will winnow them, the wind will pick them up,
    and a gale will blow them away.
  But you will rejoice in the LORD
    and glory in the Holy One of Israel.

¹⁷"The poor and needy search for water,
    but there is none;
    their tongues are parched with thirst.
  But I the LORD will answer them;
    I, the God of Israel, will not forsake them.
¹⁸I will make rivers flow on barren heights,
    and springs within the valleys.
  I will turn the desert into pools of water,
    and the parched ground into springs.
¹⁹I will put in the desert
    the cedar and the acacia, the myrtle and the olive.
  I will set pines in the wasteland,
    the fir and the cypress together,
²⁰so that people may see and know,
    may consider and understand,
  that the hand of the LORD has done this,
    that the Holy One of Israel has created it.

THERE IS NO agreement among scholars about the structure of chapters 41 through 46. Many different proposals have been put forward, ranging from the argument that there is no structure at all to complex parallelisms.[1] What this tells us is that the material is complex and that any proposal must be presented with diffidence. The prophet's method of presentation in these chapters seems to be the repetition of key themes in varying ways with a certain degree of increasing specificity. Then chapter 47 draws the conclusions of what has been said as regards Babylon, and chapter 48 is a call to trust and belief.

One feature that many commentators have noted and have taken as structural indicators are the hymnic portions in 42:10–13 and 44:23. They understand these segments to bring a previous unit to a close and to introduce a new one. But those who see the material in this way do not agree as to whether these segments should be treated as the closing of the previous unit or the opening of the succeeding one.[2] This subtlety of transition as a feature of the book has been noted several times above. I consider them to be the opening of the succeeding unit and so see the structure as 41:1–42:9; 42:10–44:22; and 44:23–47:15.

Within 41:1–42:9, we can identify two subsections, each beginning with a challenge to the idol worshipers to present their best case that their gods are truly divine. (1) Isaiah 41:1–20 speaks of the terror that God's activities are inducing among the idol worshipers (vv. 2–7) but goes on to assure his servant Israel that they need not be afraid (vv. 8–20). (2) Isaiah 41:21–42:9 begins with a strong argument for God's superiority over the idols because he alone has foretold the future (41:21–29) and concludes by introducing the ideal Servant, through whom God will bring justice on the earth (42:1–9).

God's Challenge to the Nations (41:1)

THIS FIRST VERSE introduces a key feature of this section: an imaginary court case between God and the idols in order to determine who is really God. Each

---

1. A. Schoors, *I Am God Your Saviour: A Form-Critical Study of the Main Genres in Is. XL–LV* (VTSup 24; Leiden: Brill, 1973); R. Melugin, *The Formation of Isaiah 40–55* (BZAW 141; Berlin: de Gruyter, 1976); R. Merendino, *Der Erste und Letz: Eine Untersuchung von Je. 40–48* (VTSup 31; Leiden: Brill, 1981); J. Goldingay, "The Arrangement of Isaiah 41–45," *VT* 29 (1979): 289–99.

2. Some commentators who take it as the end of the preceding section are: Childs, Motyer, and Watts. Some who take it as the beginning of the next section are C. North, J. Mckenzie, and P. Bonnard, *Le Second Isaïe: Son disciple et leurs éditeurs (Isaïe 40–66)* (Paris: Gabalda, 1972). C. Westermann and P. Hanson take the hymns as independent units.

side is to bring forward evidence to prove their point. Here God calls the "nations" from the farthest ends of the earth (the "islands") to "be silent" in the presence of the Judge of the universe and to hear his evidence. Then they must make whatever response they can. By this means God will demonstrate to his fearful people that their captivity in Babylon in no way calls his power or lordship into question.

God's Activities As Evidence (41:2–7)

As HIS FIRST evidence (41:2–4), God begins with a rhetorical question in verse 2 and then repeats and answers it in verse 4. The question has to do with who called the "one from the east." God insists that he alone has done this. Almost certainly the person being referred to is the Persian Cyrus (45:1), who was to bring down the Babylonian Empire. So God is appealing to his unique activity in history as evidence that he alone is God. He is not appealing to some activity in the cycles of nature or to some conquest over monsters in the realm of myth. This argument will be repeated and intensified several times in the next few chapters as this court case continues.

Not only does Isaiah say that God has called Cyrus forth, he also says that it is God who has given the "nations" into his hand (41:2). Cyrus is able to subdue every nation he encounters with ease, treating them like grain to be threshed because this is in the God of Israel's plan. This is expressed in 41:4 with the first occurrence of another idea that will be prominent in the next several chapters: that God knows the beginning from the end. He called forth the "first" generation, and he will be "with the last" generation when it quits the earth (cf. 43:10; 44:6; 46:10; 48:12.) He is not just a part of the process, as the pagan gods are. Rather, he stands outside of time, calling it into existence, directing its path, and bringing it to an end. "I am he" is a statement both of self-existence and self-identity. Reflecting Exodus 6:3, God says he is the One who "is." Every other life form on the planet is derivative. But he is the One who has neither beginning nor end. He simply "is."

When the "nations" of earth hear of Cyrus's earth-shaking conquests, they will be terrified (41:5–7). But what can they do? They know of no gods who rule history on the basis of a righteous plan. So they do the only thing they can do: make better idols. This idea, already encountered in 40:25–26, will also be repeated in the coming chapters (41:22–24; 44:9–20; 46:6–7). Because there is no encouragement to be had from their gods, idol worshipers must encourage one another (41:6–7).

The author describes the complexity of the process by referring to four different classes of workers needed to make the god. It is hard work to make your maker. The comment "it is good" (41:7c) reminds us of Genesis 1, where

God the Creator repeatedly says this of his creation. Most likely Isaiah is asking, "Now who is the Creator and who is the created in this picture?" If we do not have the God who has revealed himself to us, then we will have to have gods we have made for ourselves.

No Need for God's People to Fear (41:8–20)

IN THIS SECTION God asserts that unlike the powerful nations around them, the Judean captives have nothing to fear. Their God is no idol whom they have made. Of course, it is not enough merely to insist that he is powerful enough to do something about their situation. The other issue is whether he *wants* to do anything for them. These verses insist that God has not cast them off because of their sin. In fact, they are his "servant," his "chosen" (41:8, 9). God has not forgotten his promise to "Abraham."

Just as the Lord God took Abraham from Mesopotamia and the descendents of Jacob out of Egypt, he can take this generation out as well. God is "with" them, to "strengthen," "help," and "uphold" them (41:10). God is not at some far-off point, shouting instructions. He is personally present with his people, so they have nothing to "fear." Since the phrase "do not be afraid" is repeated so often in this section of the book, we know it is a central issue for the people in captivity. They are afraid God has abandoned them, so Isaiah reminds them again and again that this will not happen.

Of course, they are not only afraid that God has left them, they are also afraid that their many enemies will overpower them. That is the issue addressed in 41:11–16. God will protect them, and their enemies will simply evaporate before the Lord (41:11–12). Why? Because "I am the LORD," language that is reminiscent of the Exodus. God will demonstrate his lordship by helping his people (41:13–14). He will take an active hand in their defense. Encouragement comes from knowing that God is personally present with them in their distress and from knowing that he will be directly involved in the outcome.

The word "Redeemer" appears here in 41:14 for the first time in Isaiah, but it will appear thirteen more times between now and the end of the book (ten of them before 54:9).[3] Here it is given a special association with "the Holy One of Israel." In chapters 1–39 this latter expression for God most frequently conveyed his transcendent power and glory. In this part of the book it is especially associated with his power to bring his own back to him.

---

3. This is the term *goʾel*, used of Boaz in relation to Ruth and Naomi (Ruth 2:20). Boaz will marry Ruth and raise up a son to carry on the family line of Naomi's husband, Elimelech. Thus, a redeemer protects from harassment and possible slavery, preserves a posterity for the future, and provides a structure of belonging.

In 41:15–16 God continues to offer his people protection from their enemies, but now the focus moves from defense to offense. Just as Cyrus will use his sword to thresh his enemies (41:2), so God is going to use Israel. A "threshing sledge" was constructed from pieces of wood with sharp stones ("teeth") driven into them. This device was pulled around over a pile of cut grain so that the kernels of grain were separated from the husks both by the weight and by the cutting effect of the stones. God will use Israel in his plan of world history. They will not be passive by-standers, a helpless "worm" (41:14), but will be active participants with God in his work. We might think of Daniel in this respect, with his influence in both Babylon and Persia (Dan. 6:25–28), and also of Esther and Mordecai (Est. 10:1–3).

Verses 17–20 are a graphic summary of what has been said to this point. Isaiah uses the language of nature to depict a God who can do the impossible. His people are spiritually dry and desolate. Their hopes are gone and their dreams broken. Yet this God, who is not a part of the cosmic system and thus is not captive to it, can do what is new and unheard of. He can make "rivers" flow on mountaintops and cause "pools" to spring up in the "desert."

The language here reminds the attentive reader of chapter 34, where God said that he could turn the desert into a garden, indeed into a veritable forest. God reiterates that promise here, but he goes a step further in verse 20 by giving the reason for doing this for his people: so that the world may see the evidence in what God has done for Israel that he is indeed God, the Holy One. Ezekiel makes a similar point when he says that God will show himself holy among his people so that the world may know who he is (Ezek. 36:23).

GOD AND HISTORY. The argument that is fundamental to this passage and, indeed, to this entire part of the book is that God is not part of the historical process. The conflict with the idols is made to rest on this issue. Paganism understands its gods to be continuous with this world. Thus, they cannot know how the cosmic process began or how it will end. In fact, for all practical purposes there is no beginning and end to the process. Existence is an endless cycle of birth, life, and death that, so far as we know, goes on forever. Those beings who are within the process cannot tell if there is any meaning to the process. They do not know why things happen, how long they will endure, or what they will accomplish.

If we start with the cosmic system and try to reason out to ultimate reality from it, that is where we are going to end up. All things are contingent on all other things, there is no meaning or purpose to existence, the forces of the cosmos are fundamentally impersonal, and their behavior is completely determined by their relationship to each other. This is a system made up by humans to try to explain life as we encounter it. The pagans attempt to personalize theses forces the better to understand and control them, but in the end the gods remain simply the forces of existence, whether in nature, in human society, or in the human spirit, only wearing human-like masks.

But Isaiah's response is that those forces are not gods. They have no right to be called "holy." By definition, the holy is the "other," but these beings are not other. They are part of the system. The diatribes against idols are aimed squarely at this point. Rather than go into a somewhat abstract presentation like the one just given, Isaiah is much more concrete. He says, "You have made your own gods from your own environment. So, if you made them, what can they do for you?" They cannot tell the future because they do not know the future. Neither can they tell you where you came from and what the meaning of your life is. You made them!

Only a Being who is outside of the system can bring the system into existence and give it direction. Such a Being can tell you what will happen before it happens. That Being can never be found out by starting with the system. To be sure, with his guidance, the system can give you a good deal of collateral information about him, but since he is not the system, it cannot take you to what it is not. In the end, God will have to reveal himself from beyond.[4] That is precisely what he has done. And proof that he is beyond the system is that he can tell what will happen in advance. He is the One who has called the man from the east.

Fear. Isaiah is speaking to a people debilitated with fear. They are in a situation that is completely foreign to them. They grew up secure in their own land, confident that because they served the living God and had his temple in their midst, nothing bad could happen to them. Undoubtedly, the deliverance under Hezekiah helped foster that kind of complacency. Furthermore, since no one ever came back from captivity and since God had promised this land to them, the captivity could not occur. So when it did occur, the result was complete devastation.

We get a glimpse of this in the prophet Ezekiel. Chapters 1—24 were written before the Exile, and in them we see Ezekiel working hard to convince his hearers that Jerusalem is going to fall. Chapters 33—48 were written after the fall of Jerusalem. Here we get the sense that Ezekiel is having just as hard a time convincing his hearers that Jerusalem is going to be rebuilt.[5]

---

4. In vv. 22, 23, and 26 the Hiphil form of the verb *ngd* ("to reveal, declare") occurs five times, as God dares the gods to give some revelation. He is the only One who can do that.
5. See I. Duguid, *Ezekiel* (NIVAC; Grand Rapids: Zondervan, 1999), 20.

In a situation where all the old, familiar landmarks are gone and insecurity is rampant, fear is the dominant and debilitating emotion.

In his trilogy *The Lord of the Rings*, J. R. R. Tolkien tells of the old king Theoden who has become convinced by his counselor Wormtongue, who is really an enemy agent, that the situation is hopeless. So he sits dejected in his darkened palace, waiting for the enemy to come and bring his kingdom and his life to an end. But one of the members of the Fellowship of the Ring, Gandalf, comes and tells Theoden that he may indeed die, but that for himself he would rather die confronting the enemy on his charger than sitting in gloom on a meaningless throne. Theoden's mind is not changed at once, but eventually under Gandalf's prodding he sees Wormtongue for who he really is. When that happens, the atmosphere changes. Theoden rises to his full height and calls for his warriors, who come with relief, and they ride to battle. In the darkest hour, a miracle occurs and the battle is won. But if fear had prevailed, there would have been no battle and no miracle.[6]

NEW AGE RELIGION. One of the great features of the so-called Enlightenment era was the dominance of reason. Everything had to bow at the bar of reason, and if something was not amenable to human reason, it was discarded. For this reason Thomas Jefferson felt it necessary to write an abridged version of the New Testament, explicitly leaving out all references to miracles. On this basis, Rudolf Bultmann, a German New Testament scholar of the first half of the twentieth century, argued that the New Testament had to be "demythologized" for humanity "come of age" by stripping out all mention of the supernatural.

But if the emphasis on reason had significant dangers, it at least had the benefit of preventing the rise of ideas that are merely based on fancy. Now, however, the situation is changed. There is widespread disillusionment with reason in anything but the technical arena. In the realm of ultimate meaning, reason is now looked at skeptically. Two world wars have something to do with that, but also there is the sense that reason has failed to make life any more meaningful or worthwhile and that it has stifled emotions and hampered free expression.

The result is that ideas and formulations no longer need to conform to logic. If they seem good and useful to someone, then they are true. This means that paganism, which was long held at bay by reason, is back among us with new vigor. Someone can now use a computer, which is the product

---

6. J. R. R. Tolkien, *The Two Towers* (New York: Ballantine, 1965), 147–53.

of pure logic and will only respond when used according to logical principles, to discourse on how he was once a knight in King Arthur's court in a previous life!

This new situation means that Isaiah's arguments have a new relevance for our day. The central issue is the one of how we know truth. Does truth come to us from inside the cosmic system or outside of it? Reason argued strongly that it came from inside the system and that the human intellect could discover all essential truth. Now that reason has been dethroned, we still believe that truth comes from inside the system, but now believe that "truth" need no longer be self-consistent or coherent. Now truth comes by intuition, and if it "works" for me, it is "true."

That is exactly the basis of paganism. Working from within the system, we imagine the various parts of it in whatever ways will make the system most amenable to control by me. These imaginings do not need to be consistent with each other, nor do they need to be logically defensible. In fact, the more effectively we can turn off the reasoning faculty, the more likely we are to encounter the divine.

Isaiah's answer to this is not a retreat to philosophical reasoning. Rather, it is an appeal to experience. Isaiah insists that truth does come from outside the system but that God has broken into the system and has shown himself to faithful witnesses. Moreover, he has shown himself to us in ways that are fully consistent and coherent. In the end, it is the Bible that shows the importance of reason. It does so through the use of reason, constantly demonstrating the link between cause and effect in the activity of God. The problem occurred when Enlightenment thinkers tried to make human reason superior to God. Isaiah's Holy One never acts in irrational ways, but at the same time, he is never capable of being fully explained by human rational capacities. Why would we ever think he could be if he is the Holy One?

So what we need today is a rediscovery of the Word of God, both in its written and in its experiential form. We need to see the evidence in the Scriptures that there is a God who is outside the system and who can both predict in advance what the system will do and can redirect that system as necessary to achieve his goals. Then we need the evidence of changed lives that will demonstrate to the world around that there is a faithful, consistent, true God, who has broken in upon us and "has done this" (41:20). Far from disengaging us from the world in contemplation of ourselves, God wants to reengage us with the world by delivering us from ourselves.

Fear. Franklin D. Roosevelt, President of the United States during World War II, said, "We have nothing to fear but fear itself." That statement, of course, is rhetorical hyperbole, but there is a great measure of truth in it. Fear and discouragement have a way of defeating us before we even attempt anything. Nothing can be accomplished through us because we are afraid to start. In many cases, if we can overcome our fear enough to begin a task, positive results occur. But how do we overcome our fear? It is because we are afraid that we cannot overcome our fear!

God's answer to fear today is the same as it was in Isaiah's day. He reminds us that we are not alone. He is with us (41:10). Nor is the One who is with us merely a projection of ourselves, as in paganism. No, the One who made us, who stands outside of all things, and who orders all things has broken into the system to be with us. Nor is this mere rhetoric. In Jesus Christ, the promise of Immanuel (Isa. 7:14) has been fulfilled (Matt. 1:23). God has stepped into our time and space, into our flesh, and is with us in every aspect of our lives.

This is the significance of Jesus' "I am" statements in the Gospel of John. He is not a dim reflection of God or a distant intermediary; he is God himself. Just as God says here, "I am he" (41:4), so Jesus said, "I am he" (John 8:58; 18:5). God has lost none of his power or holiness in coming to us. Rather, by coming to us he is able to elevate us to his level. His presence does not guarantee success in our endeavors, but we need not fear to try because we know his presence is not contingent on success; he has promised never to leave us or to forsake us (Heb. 13:5). The seal of that promise is the presence of the Holy Spirit. Jesus told his disciples that he would leave them but then would come to them (John 14:17–20). He has done that in his Spirit. He is with us.

Not only does he promise to be with us, he promises to help us (41:14). With the help of the entire universe at our backs, why should we be afraid? Again, this is not merely ourselves trying to magically harness the forces of the universe to do our will. It is the almighty, independent Creator, who freely comes to stand at our sides and do through us what we cannot.

There is an incredible condescension here. Why should God "help" us? What need has he for us? Why does he not just tell us to stay out of the way and watch him do his work? But no. He has given us the dignity of sharing his own image, and he will not demean us by making us merely robots to speed his cause. Why should we fear when God has bequeathed a dignity like that on us? So Christ gave his disciples the impossible task of making other disciples across the world (Matt. 28:18–20). What an unimaginable task, and yet what an incredible honor! He intends to use us in the achievement of his work. And why not, if he is with us and will help us?

Isaiah 41:21–42:9

²¹"PRESENT YOUR CASE," says the LORD.
   "Set forth your arguments," says Jacob's King.
²²"Bring in ⌐your¬ idols to tell us
      what is going to happen.
   Tell us what the former things were,
      so that we may consider them
      and know their final outcome.
   Or declare to us the things to come,
²³   tell us what the future holds,
      so we may know that you are gods.
   Do something, whether good or bad,
      so that we will be dismayed and filled with fear.
²⁴But you are less than nothing
      and your works are utterly worthless;
      he who chooses you is detestable.

²⁵"I have stirred up one from the north, and he comes—
      one from the rising sun who calls on my name.
   He treads on rulers as if they were mortar,
      as if he were a potter treading the clay.
²⁶Who told of this from the beginning, so we could know,
      or beforehand, so we could say, 'He was right'?
   No one told of this,
      no one foretold it,
      no one heard any words from you.
²⁷I was the first to tell Zion, 'Look, here they are!'
      I gave to Jerusalem a messenger of good tidings.
²⁸I look but there is no one—
      no one among them to give counsel,
      no one to give answer when I ask them.
²⁹See, they are all false!
      Their deeds amount to nothing;
      their images are but wind and confusion.

^{42:1}"Here is my servant, whom I uphold,
      my chosen one in whom I delight;
   I will put my Spirit on him
      and he will bring justice to the nations.

² He will not shout or cry out,
    or raise his voice in the streets.
³ A bruised reed he will not break,
    and a smoldering wick he will not snuff out.
In faithfulness he will bring forth justice;
⁴   he will not falter or be discouraged
till he establishes justice on earth.
    In his law the islands will put their hope."

⁵ This is what God the LORD says—
he who created the heavens and stretched them out,
    who spread out the earth and all that comes
        out of it,
who gives breath to its people,
    and life to those who walk on it:
⁶ "I, the LORD, have called you in righteousness;
    I will take hold of your hand.
I will keep you and will make you
    to be a covenant for the people
    and a light for the Gentiles,
⁷ to open eyes that are blind,
    to free captives from prison
    and to release from the dungeon those who sit
        in darkness.

⁸ "I am the LORD; that is my name!
    I will not give my glory to another
    or my praise to idols.
⁹ See, the former things have taken place,
    and new things I declare;
before they spring into being
    I announce them to you."

WE NOW COME to Isaiah's second statement of his case against the idols (41:21–29) and his second address to the servant of the Lord (42:1–9). The case against the idols is similar to the first except that it is considerably more pointed. The address to the servant is very different from the first, so much so that we must conclude a different servant is being addressed.

The Case Against the Idols (41:21–29)

ONCE MORE GOD calls on the idol worshipers to present their case that the things they worship are really gods. In 41:22 it is not specified what they are to "bring." The NIV supplies "idols," and that is a reasonable hypothesis. Another alternative is that they are being challenged to bring forth arguments, as in verse 21.

Here Isaiah strikes directly at the heart of the pagan worldview. The prophet calls on the idolaters to give evidence that their idols have ever specifically predicted the future. The reference to "the former things" (41:22) may be understood in one of two ways. It may be speaking of the time in the past when a prediction was made. But another possibility is that Isaiah is asking for an explanation of the past and why things have happened as they have. I believe the latter explanation is more likely. The prophet is asserting that because there is neither a sense of purpose or of overarching meaning in the worldview of continuity, there is no possibility of understanding why anything happens. And if the past cannot be explained, then what about the "future"? Have any of the gods ever given a specific prediction of something that had never happened before but that then subsequently did occur?

The answer to this question is, "Of course not." Just as the thunderstorm cannot predict where it will go or what it will do, neither can an idol. In fact, the gods are incapable of doing anything of a free or unconditioned nature (41:23). They are a part of the cyclic functioning of the cosmic system and must do what the cycle requires. They cannot vary from that pattern. So God mocks them, daring them to do anything at all. If they cannot do anything good for their worshipers, then perhaps they can do something frightening against their enemies.

But there is no answer. So God pronounces judgment (41:24). These gods are "nothing"; their works are "worthless," and those who worship them are an offense against creation (NIV "detestable"; KJV "abomination"). In attempting to deify creation, the pagans have actually committed an offense against it.

In 41:25–27 God responds to the challenge. He does have a plan for history, and what will be unfolding before the exiles' eyes will be the evidence of it. God has brought the conqueror who is coming down on Babylon like a brick-maker or a "potter," who jumps into the vat where the clay is and treads it into liquid form.[1]

---

1. The reference both to the "north" and "from the rising sun" as this conqueror's point of origin is somewhat confusing. One possibility is that the prophet is speaking from the perspective of the land of Israel. Attackers from eastern lands always had to come from the north because of the desert to the east (cf. Jer. 1:13–14). Thus, Isaiah is simply using

It is one thing to assert that Cyrus's coming is at the direction of "Jacob's King" (41:21), but it is quite another to prove that the assertion is so. Anyone can make the claim to have done so after the fact. But Isaiah is ready for that approach, and he has both negative and positive evidence. First of all, none of the idols predicted Cyrus's coming at all (41:26). No one can come forward and say, "That's right! That's just what my god said was going to happen." By contrast, says Isaiah, the God of Israel did make such a prediction in advance (41:27). In fact, that is exactly what he is doing through Isaiah, his "messenger of good tidings" in this very writing. The prediction is being made in what Isaiah is writing during his own lifetime. Then when that writing is read with opened eyes (when it is "unsealed," 8:16; 29:11–12) amidst its fulfillment during the Exile (150 years later), it will become its own confirmation.[2]

Isaiah 41:28–29 is the pronouncement of judgment on the idol worshipers. They have been unable to give any "answer" to the questions God has asked. There is "no one" among them who can give evidence that their gods are even in the same category as Yahweh. He alone is truly Other, and thus he alone is truly Holy. All who worship something other than the true God are doomed to become like their gods: nothing, worthless, wind, and chaos.[3] Their lives are doomed to become as meaningless as their gods are.

An Address to the Servant (42:1–9)

As in 41:1–21, the court case against the gods is followed by an address to the Lord's servant. Like the prior instance, the content of the address

---

a convention of speech. Another possibility is that although Cyrus hailed from Persia to the east of Babylon, his actual approach to attack Babylon was from the north.

2. These statements have been an embarrassment to those commentators who deny the possibility of predictive prophecy. They have had to say that "Second Isaiah" must have predicted Cyrus's ultimate victory prior to this writing at the time when he first began to make his moves against the Babylonian Empire, but that that prophecy has since become lost. Childs (*Isaiah*, 322) says that "Second Isaiah" is referring to statements located in "First Isaiah," in such passages as ch. 13. However, if those words in ch. 13 are actually "Second Isaiah's," as Childs seems to maintain, then the argument is fictitious, and "Second Isaiah" knows it. See Oswalt, *Isaiah 40–66*, 99–103.

3. As Motyer, *Prophecy of Isaiah*, 318, notes, not only the structure but also much of the vocabulary in vv. 24 and 29 are parallel. Also, with the exception of "wind," the same sequence of terms occurs in the description of the nations in 40:17. The Heb. word *tohu* ("chaos"; NIV "confusion") is a favorite of Isaiah, occurring four times between chs. 41 and 45 and seven times elsewhere in the book. In this section it appears that the ancient Near Eastern creation myth of the gods bringing order out of chaos may have been in the prophet's mind. He asserts that far from doing such a thing, they themselves are chaos and plunge their worshipers into chaos. That is not, however, what the Lord God does (see 45:18–19).

seems to follow the content of the case presented. There the fearful servant needed to be reassured that although Cyrus's coming meant terror for the idol worshipers, it need not cause the servant any fear. Here, while the connection is not as clear, the address seems to be a further reflection on Yahweh's control of history. Just as he was able to bring down the Babylonian Empire through Cyrus, so he will bring "justice" (42:1, 3, 4) to the earth through his "servant." Verse 9 makes the connection clear by stating explicitly that the prediction concerning the servant is one of the "new things" that the gods could not declare in advance, but that the Lord can do so with impunity.

The identity of this "servant" has been the source of endless controversy.[4] The differences between him and the servant Israel[5] are striking. The servant Israel is fearful and blind, yet God loves him and will deliver him so that he can be God's evidence to the nations that he is indeed God. But this Servant, who only appears here in chapters 40–48 and but three times in chapters 49–50, is of a different sort. He is always obedient and responsive to God, his mission is to bring justice to the nations for God, and he is to be a "light" to the nations and a "covenant" to the people (of Israel, see 49:6). In contrast to the promises of divine blessing constantly being given to the servant Israel, this servant receives no benefits through his ministry but only increasing difficulty.[6] In sum, whoever this is, it is not the nation of Israel; it is another figure altogether.

The reiterated statement that this person is going to bring justice on the earth, that God's Spirit will be on him (42:1), and that his accomplishment of this end will not be through oppression (42:3) reminds us of the prophecies of the Messiah in Isaiah 9, 11, and 32. Thus, we have a complementary picture to the one there. There we had the servant as King. Here we have the king as Servant. The idea that the ends of the earth ("the islands"), which could not defend the deity of their gods (41:1), will "put their hope [lit., wait for, trust] in his law" is further indication that this figure is a messianic one (cf. 2:1–5 and comments).

The further description of the ministry of this Servant in 42:6–7 confirms that this is not the nation but someone who will function for the nation and indeed for the world. Where Israel was blind and deaf, captive to the powers of this world, this Servant will give sight and freedom. This ministry will be the ultimate revelation of the "glory" of God, which fills the earth (6:3) and belongs to no idol (42:8).

---

4. For further discussion, see Oswalt, *Isaiah 1–39, 49–52; Isaiah 40–66*, 107–8, 113–15.

5. See 43:18–19; 44:1–2, 21; 45:4; 48:20 and related descriptions in each case.

6. See the descriptions in 49:1–7; 50:4–9; 52:13–53:12.

PREDICTIVE PROPHECY. Isaiah hangs his claim that Yahweh is the only being worthy of the title "God" squarely on the possibility of predictive prophecy. Commentators who do not believe in that possibility find themselves in something of a quandary.[7] Brevard Childs, for example, dismisses the idea as a belief in "clairvoyance."[8] Yet at the same time he correctly admits that the second part of Isaiah wants its readers to believe that the Exile really had been predicted by Isaiah. Everything, then, hangs on whether we admit that such a thing is possible. If we conclude it is not possible, then I would claim that all of the lofty theology of Isaiah 40–55 is suspect. If the unknown writer of the book has to falsify evidence to support his claims that God is who he says he is, then there is no reason to believe that God is any of the things this person says he is.

However, if there is such a God as Isaiah says has revealed himself to him, why is it so difficult to believe that God can tell the future? If he did create the world for a purpose, if he is leading all of history to the fulfillment of that purpose, and if he is outside of time and space but has the full capacity to intersect those realms at any point, why should we think it impossible for him to tell us what will happen in advance?

It may be urged that this is a magical and superstitious view, but that is the furthest case from the fact. The biblical prophets did not practice magical rituals in order to find out the future. Magic ritual is based on the idea of continuity. The ancients believed the position of the stars or the shape of a sheep's liver was directly related to human events, so whenever certain conditions were observed, certain events would occur. That is far from what the biblical prophets did. They were called by God into a relationship with him in which he revealed his word to them unbidden. That word addressed current conditions among his people especially in relation to their obedience to the covenant, and it pointed out the future implications of that obedience or lack thereof. This was no attempt to find out the future for the benefit of one's client.

---

7. Some commentators are irate that the writer claims the gods cannot predict the future. B. Duhm, *Das Buch Jesaja* (HKAT; Göttingen: Vandenhoeck & Ruprecht, 1892) in particular charged that "Deutero-Isaiah" knew perfectly well that the gods regularly predicted the future but simply chose to deny the facts. But Isaiah is not denying that the gods, or their representatives, have sought to tell the future. What he is denying is that they ever made *specific* predictions (such as naming Cyrus) that subsequently were proven correct. Westermann, *Isaiah 40–66*, 91, eloquently supports this general argument, although he certainly does not attribute the naming of Cyrus to "First Isaiah."

8. *Isaiah*, 3–4.

Prediction had three main functions in the Bible. (1) It was a means of calling people to obedience, because such obedience would have positive future consequences. (2) It was a means of encouraging faith; the God whom we serve cannot be surprised by events beyond his control. (3) It served to confirm God's trustworthiness when the predicted events occurred.

Justice as right order. The Hebrew word translated "justice" in 42:1, 3, and 4 is *mišpaṭ*. In many ways it is the antonym of *tohu*, "chaos" (see n. 3, above). It is much more than merely legality, as "justice" has come to connote in English. Rather, it has the idea of "right order." This explains why it is often paralleled to *ṣᵉdaqah*, which is usually translated "righteousness" but simply has the idea of "doing the right thing." This means that *mišpaṭ* has a much larger pool of connotations than does our word "justice." To be sure, a world where the innocent are punished and the oppressors go free is a world where *mišpaṭ* is lacking. The word contains everything we think of as "justice," but it contains more than that as well.

This can be further seen in the usage of the related word "judge." Many a child, hearing Samson called a "judge," has suffered from some disorientation. How could this mighty man be called a judge? That is not the way judges act today! Of course, the point of the book of Judges is that when the people have disobeyed and are being beaten down by oppressors, they are not experiencing the kind of right order that God intended in his world. So when in response to repentance and faith God sends a champion who will restore them to the kind of life God intended for them, *mišpaṭ* is restored in the land.[9] So Isaiah is saying that the coming Messiah will do all that is necessary to restore God's right order on the earth.

PREDICTIVE PROPHECY. It seems to me that the believer has to walk a middle road on the subject of prophecy in the Bible. This was brought home to me some years ago when I was teaching an adult Sunday School class. As we came to the end of one study, I asked the members of the class what part of the Bible they would like to go into next. The consensus was that they would like to study "prophecy." I was delighted with the idea and began the next week with an overview of Amos, proceeding on through Hosea and Micah. But I began to see a questioning look in the members' eyes. Although they were too polite to say so, something was wrong.

Finally, I stopped and asked them what the trouble was. After much hemming and hawing, one of them finally blurted out, "Well, we were kind of

---

9. Cf. Richard Schultz, "שפט," *NIDOTTE*, 4:213–20.

wondering when we were going to get to prophecy." Suddenly it dawned on me. When they said "prophecy," they meant predictions associated with the end of time, or "eschatological prophecy," material limited to the final chapters of Ezekiel, Daniel, and Zechariah in the Old Testament. What they really wanted was a study of the book of Revelation, supplemented by the Old Testament material.

This is a view we need to be careful of. Any attempt to use eschatological prophecy to create a timetable or roadmap of future events is filled with difficulties. If nothing else, a study of all the wrong conclusions drawn from the eschatological prophecies in the last two hundred years should lead us to a healthy caution. Furthermore, as I tried to indicate above, simple knowledge of the future is not the purpose of prediction in the Bible. The point of the predictions of Jesus' return, for example, is not so that we can figure out exactly when it will happen.[10] Rather, it has the three purposes outlined above: We should be obedient to all of his commands, knowing that he could return at any time; we can live confidently in difficult times, knowing that evil cannot triumph in the end; and we can look forward excitedly to the hour when he returns, knowing that our faith will be climactically confirmed.

But if overfascination with eschatological prediction is to be avoided, there is another extreme that, if anything, should be even more assiduously avoided. That is a certain tendency to deny that the Bible really contains predictions. This is one of the illogical ways in which Enlightenment rationalism continues to hang on. We see those today who on the one hand insist that we can each create our own truth, while at the same time insisting that it is rationally impossible for the Old Testament writers to have predicted the coming of Christ. What the New Testament writers called prediction, they say, is simply the result of those writers having gone through the Old Testament text with a fine-toothed comb and using whatever they could find to bolster their belief that Jesus had been predicted in advance.

The first question to be posed to such a view is why the New Testament writers even thought of doing such a thing. Why did they think that his coming would have been predicted? The answer to the question is that in passages such as Isaiah 41–42, God's use of prediction is made the central evidence of his Godhood. The New Testament writers expected there would be predictions of the Messiah because that is what the Old Testament statements led them to.

---

10. Remember the booklet entitled 88 *Reasons Why Jesus Will Return in 1988* that was distributed to many pastors in the United States in the spring of 1988. When Jesus did not return in September of 1988 as the author predicted, he published a supplement explaining how he had made a one-year mistake and that Jesus would come in 1989. There have been no subsequent supplements.

The second question to those who question whether the Old Testament really predicted Christ is regarding the standard used to determine what is a valid prophecy. For instance, if we believe that the material was revealed to the writer by God, then it is not necessary that every writer understood the full implications of what he was saying about Christ for his statement to be a valid prediction. Did Micah understand all the historical implications of his statement that the "ruler over Israel" would come from Bethlehem (Mic. 5:2)? I very much doubt it. But that does not mean that those who concluded that the place to look for the Messiah was in Bethlehem were misusing an Old Testament text (Matt. 2:4–6).

It is also important to distinguish those places where there is direct prediction from those places where the New Testament writers use the Old Testament allusively or illustratively. When all is said and done, we must come back to this text and say that if the possibility of genuine prediction is denied, then one of the Bible's chief arguments for the unique deity of its God has been undercut and with it much of what else the Bible says about him and his Son.

The ministry of the Servant. If we conclude that Isaiah 42:1–9 is a prediction of the ministry of Christ, which I believe is a correct conclusion, we can see in these verses a number of indications about the dimensions of his ministry and its nature. (1) As we said above, that ministry is above all to restore God's right order in the world. This point is made three times in short order. This should remind us that to suggest that the cross of Christ is only about forgiveness of sins is unwarranted. To be sure it is about that, but it is about much more. It is about dealing with all the effects of sin in the world and about restoring God's work on all levels of society.

This message has been true of the church from the outset. It is possible to trace the progress of the church across the world by the schools and hospitals it has left in its wake. To be sure, the church has contributed its share of suffering and bloodshed. But these other benefits cannot be gainsaid. The Servant's ministry is for the restoration of God's order in the world.

(2) Moreover, it is a worldwide ministry. The Spirit who was on Christ (42:1; cf. John 1:32–34) impels his disciples to take his "law" (Heb. *torah*, "teaching, instruction") to the ends of the earth, because people everywhere are waiting for it. His light is meant to shine through his disciples to all the nations (Isa. 2:2; 66:23; Matt. 28:19–20). If a new understanding of multiculturalism means that we must constantly be on guard against merely cultural overtones in our presentation of the gospel, it must not dampen our enthusiasm for taking the gospel of Christ to the whole world. A postmodern perspective insists that all people have light, but they just have a different take on what the light consists of. Isaiah knows better. People who have

made God in their own image are in the darkness, and they desperately need the light that streams from the Cross and the empty tomb.

(3) A third aspect of the ministry of the Servant that is especially relevant for our time is its manner. The ancient kings boasted about the ferocious ways in which they brought "justice" to their kingdoms and about the heavy yokes they imposed on any whom they conquered. This Servant brings God's right order into the world not from a position of strength but of weakness. He does not break an already-bent reed, nor does he quench a candle flame that is already flickering. Christ disarmed his enemies with love and grace and gentleness.

We must minister in the same way. In many ways this is the most difficult part of the ministry of Christ for many of us. We find it difficult to give up the assertiveness that has manifested itself in us since we were born. We want what we want when we want it, and there are many different justifications offered for an assertive, dominating Christianity. But the word of God still stands:

> He made himself nothing; he took the humble position of a slave and appeared in human form. And in human form he obediently humbled himself even further by dying a criminal's death on a cross. (Phil. 2:7–8 NLT)

> A disciple is not above the teacher, nor a slave above the master. (Matt. 10:24 NRSV)

Isaiah 42:10–43:7

[10] SING TO THE LORD a new song,
  his praise from the ends of the earth,
  you who go down to the sea, and all that is in it,
  you islands, and all who live in them.
[11] Let the desert and its towns raise their voices;
  let the settlements where Kedar lives rejoice.
  Let the people of Sela sing for joy;
  let them shout from the mountaintops.
[12] Let them give glory to the LORD
  and proclaim his praise in the islands.
[13] The LORD will march out like a mighty man,
  like a warrior he will stir up his zeal;
  with a shout he will raise the battle cry
  and will triumph over his enemies.

[14] "For a long time I have kept silent,
  I have been quiet and held myself back.
  But now, like a woman in childbirth,
  I cry out, I gasp and pant.
[15] I will lay waste the mountains and hills
  and dry up all their vegetation;
  I will turn rivers into islands
  and dry up the pools.
[16] I will lead the blind by ways they have not known,
  along unfamiliar paths I will guide them;
  I will turn the darkness into light before them
  and make the rough places smooth.
  These are the things I will do;
  I will not forsake them.
[17] But those who trust in idols,
  who say to images, 'You are our gods,'
  will be turned back in utter shame.

[18] "Hear, you deaf;
  look, you blind, and see!
[19] Who is blind but my servant,
  and deaf like the messenger I send?
  Who is blind like the one committed to me,
  blind like the servant of the LORD?

²⁰You have seen many things, but have paid no attention;
　　your ears are open, but you hear nothing."
²¹It pleased the LORD
　　for the sake of his righteousness
　　to make his law great and glorious.
²²But this is a people plundered and looted,
　　all of them trapped in pits
　　or hidden away in prisons.
They have become plunder,
　　with no one to rescue them;
they have been made loot,
　　with no one to say, "Send them back."

²³Which of you will listen to this
　　or pay close attention in time to come?
²⁴Who handed Jacob over to become loot,
　　and Israel to the plunderers?
Was it not the LORD,
　　against whom we have sinned?
For they would not follow his ways;
　　they did not obey his law.
²⁵So he poured out on them his burning anger,
　　the violence of war.
It enveloped them in flames, yet they did not understand;
　　it consumed them, but they did not take it to heart.

^{43:1}But now, this is what the LORD says—
　　he who created you, O Jacob,
　　he who formed you, O Israel:
"Fear not, for I have redeemed you;
　　I have summoned you by name; you are mine.
²When you pass through the waters,
　　I will be with you;
and when you pass through the rivers,
　　they will not sweep over you.
When you walk through the fire,
　　you will not be burned;
　　the flames will not set you ablaze.
³For I am the LORD, your God,
　　the Holy One of Israel, your Savior;
I give Egypt for your ransom,
　　Cush and Seba in your stead.

⁴Since you are precious and honored in my sight,
  and because I love you,
I will give men in exchange for you,
  and people in exchange for your life.
⁵Do not be afraid, for I am with you;
  I will bring your children from the east
  and gather you from the west.
⁶I will say to the north, 'Give them up!'
  and to the south, 'Do not hold them back.'
Bring my sons from afar
  and my daughters from the ends of the earth—
⁷everyone who is called by my name,
  whom I created for my glory,
  whom I formed and made."

IN ONE SENSE what has preceded this section in chapters 40–42 has been introductory. Chapter 40 gave a general introduction to the two great themes, God's love and his unique power. Then 41:1–42:9 gave a more specific introduction to God's case against the idols and to the two servants: the one fearful and the other ministering God's justice to the world. Now in 42:10–44:22 there is even greater specificity as God declares his intention to deliver his people from their distress and to use them as his witnesses against the idols. The section has two parts, generally following these two themes: 42:10–43:7 addresses the certainty of God's deliverance, and 43:8–44:22 deals with how that deliverance will witness for God and against the idols.

A Hymn of Praise (42:10–17)

AS NOTED ABOVE (see comments on 41:1–20), there is considerable disagreement as to whether 42:10–13 goes with the previous section, belongs to the following one, or stands alone. I do not believe these verses are intended to stand alone, but there are good arguments for reading it with either the previous section or the following one. I believe it fits best with what follows.[1]

---

1. On the side of reading it with the preceding is that it can be seen as an expression of praise for what God has promised to do both through Cyrus and through his Servant. In this sense it is somewhat analogous to ch. 12, which concludes chs. 7–12. The majority of commentators take it this way. However, 42:10–12 looks much like the opening call to praise that characterizes the hymn form in the Psalms, followed by the reason for that call.

Isaiah calls on the whole world to give praise to God (42:10–12). Normally such a call is followed by a general statement of the reason for giving praise to God (cf. 42:13) and then an expanded discussion of that reason (cf. 42:14–17). The extremities of earth (e g , the "ends of the earth" and the "islands") are particularly emphasized, probably as a way of expressing totality (cf. 41:5; 42:4). Likewise, the "sea," the "desert," and "the mountaintops" all convey the idea of the extremes of earth. Isaiah is emphasizing that the Lord is not simply the God of Judah. He is the God of the whole world, and what he is going to do for Judah has joyous implications for the whole world. If he can deliver Judah from all its captivities, then there is no one whose distress and difficulty is beyond his care and his delivering power.

Verses 14–17 expand on the promise of verse 13, where God is depicted as "warrior" coming to the defense of people.[2] If it seems to them that he has "kept silent" (v. 14) for a long time as they have endured the Exile, that time is coming to a rapid close. Just as the nine months of gestation come to a sudden climax in birth, so God is going to birth a new thing on behalf of his people. Whatever obstacles may stand in the way, whether forested mountains or rapid rivers, will present no obstacle to God (v. 15). He will make a "smooth" way for his people to travel on (cf. 35:8–10), and even though they are "blind," he will lead them, giving them "light" for their darkness (42:16). This means that their worst fears—that God has either abandoned them or is helpless to come to their aid—are groundless.

By contrast, the Babylonian gods will be helpless to assist their people (42:17). The Judeans should not make the mistake of thinking that since they are in Babylon, the Babylonian gods have won so that they should now put their trust in those gods. Anyone who trusts in them will be put to "shame"; that is, it will be shown that they trusted the wrong things. Those gods are helpless to do anything for their people. They must inevitably fail them. So the contest with the gods is moved to a new level. Not only are they unable to explain the meaning of life and to tell the future, they are also unable to care for and deliver their worshipers.

The Issue of God's Deliverance (42:18–43:7)

THIS NEXT SECTION expands on the promise of God's deliverance that was introduced in the preceding call to praise (42:10–17). It begins in 42:18–25 by calling on the people to recognize that what befalls them in the Exile will not be the result of God's failure to deliver them but precisely because he sent them there. The underlying logic is that if the Babylonians had

---

2. Childs, *Isaiah*, 332, says "the theme of the unit [14–17] is not fully clear." I think that is so because he has separated it from vv. 10–13.

indeed taken the people from God's hand against his will, there is no way he could now be strong enough to take them back. But that is not the case. Because God is the One who sent them into exile, he is fully able to take them back whenever he chooses.

Verses 18–20 remind us that servant Israel is not in a position to do anything for itself or for the world. As 6:9–10 predicted, they became "blind" and "deaf" under the ministry of Isaiah and all the prophets. The more they heard of God's admonition and instruction, the more "blind" and "deaf" they became. Because God does what is right ("for the sake of his righteousness"), he made his truth (*torah;* NIV "law") as "great and glorious" as possible (42:21). He gave it in the wonder and the terror of Sinai and adorned it with the lives and the witness of saints and prophets through the years. Yet everything he did seems to have been of no avail. The people plunged deeper and deeper into their sin until all that they worked so hard for, and even they themselves, became "loot" and "plunder" (42:22).

But now the prophet commands the "deaf" to "listen." Perhaps the tragedy of the Exile will unstop their ears a little. He calls on them to ask why they are in exile (42:22–24). It is not by accident or because of Babylon's great might. Rather, they are in exile because of sin against God. They did not obey his "law," his instruction, which formed the terms of their covenant with him, and as a result he gave them over to be looted and plundered. Yet, even as this was unfolding, as prophets like Jeremiah and Ezekiel were speaking and as these words of Isaiah were there to be read, no one seemed able to learn the obvious lessons (42:25). God brought them down to destruction in punishment for their sin, but no one seemed to get the point.

So what is God to do after the looting and plundering have become fact? The shift in tone from 42:25 to 43:1 is breathtaking. What God will now do is grace. Interestingly, there is nothing the Judeans have to do in advance for this grace to become available to them. They do not have to repent or promise to change their ways. God simply declares, as in 40:1–2, that he has "redeemed" them. It is a completed fact. The association with creation in 43:1 is important. It is because God created them that he can redeem them. God, as Creator, is free from any constraint by the system he created. Therefore, he can do a new thing and can redeem his people both from their captivity and from their sin. So he insists that the judgment that befell them was not intended to destroy them and will have no power to do so (43:2). The only way of hope for these people is through the fires of judgment (see comments on ch. 5). But it *is* the way of hope and not the way of destruction, as they feared.

The key to all of this is the personal relationship of God to his people. The recurrence of the pronouns "I" and "you" throughout 43:1–7 is striking.

Twice God says, "I am/will be with you" (vv. 2, 5). He identifies himself by relation to them, calling himself "the LORD, *your* God, the Holy One of Israel, *your* Savior" (v. 3). The Creator of the universe deigns to give himself to them as their personal possession because he loves them, they are "precious" to him. Again, this is cause for wonder. Why would the One who is beyond the stars even pay any attention to rebel beings on this small planet? But he does, and although these particular people have broken their covenant with him time and again, he will keep his side of the bargain.

The reference to exchanging Egypt and Cush for them (43:3) has been taken by some to refer to the Persian conquest of Egypt. Thus, God will permit Cyrus and his descendants to conquer that land in return for letting his people go home. But most commentators agree that the picture is larger, and more poetic, than that.[3] God is simply asserting that he is willing to pay any price to ransom his own.

In 43:5–7 the promise first made in 11:11 is reiterated: God will recover his people from all the lands where they have been taken. The special emphasis here is on "your children," a theme of special prominence in this part of the book.[4] Would the heritage of Israel finally be cut off, as succeeding generations became increasingly mixed into the Babylonian population? Had the ancient promises to Abraham finally failed? God insists that is not the case. Even if the exiles themselves do not go home, their children, who are God's own "sons" and "daughters" (43:6), will. God's promises will not fail. He "created" Israel for his "glory," and that purpose will be realized.

Bridging Contexts

INTERPRETING PROPHECY. This passage illustrates some of the difficulties of interpreting prophecy, especially when that prophecy is couched in poetic language, as much biblical prophecy is. Some interpreters claim to interpret prophecy "literally" and insist that anyone who does not do so does not really believe the Bible. But how literally is prophecy meant to be taken? In many cases, we must confess that we do not know until after the fact. Such diffidence does not sell many books, since the public wants certainty, not more questions. Nevertheless, it is still a fact, and it is incumbent on interpreters to recognize it.

A case in point is located here in 42:15–16. How is God going to deliver his people from Babylon? These verses make it clear, do they not? He is going to blast the mountains, dry up the Euphrates, make the sun shine in

---

3. Cf., e.g. Young, *The Book of Isaiah*, 3:143.
4. See, e.g., 45:11; 47:8–9; 49:20, 25; 51:18, 20; 54:1, 13; 60:9; 65:23; 66:8.

the daytime, and create a smooth highway for the blind Judeans to walk on. We can easily imagine "prophecy teachers" saying such things to the exiles. After all, that is what the Bible says.

In fact, none of those things occurred, according to Ezra and Nehemiah. Neither of the returns from Babylon was accompanied by miracles of the sort just described. So did the prophecy fail? Not at all! The Judeans *did* return home, and they did so because of Cyrus's specific act. God did act in history, as Isaiah and other prophets foretold, and did something that in the prophets' own time was called impossible. God intervened. But he did not intervene in the precise ways described in this poetic passage.

If that is so, why does the prophet use such excessive language? I believe it is because he knows he needs to move the emotions and will of a people crushed into apathy. Believe God and prepare to leave a captivity that has absorbed my whole life adjusting to it? No, that old life is over, and I might just as well give up that antique faith of mine and let it go. In such a situation, a low-key, reasoned presentation will not get the job done. Rather, the truth must be presented with a kind of emotional impact that will break past the apathetic barriers and capture the will.

Similarly, as we read prophecy not yet fulfilled today, we must be careful not to fall into this kind of trap. Will God's promises be fulfilled? Yes, by all means! And will they be fulfilled in ways that fully conform to the central affirmations being made? Yes! But will they be literally fulfilled according to all the images and figures used to express the point being made? That is another question altogether, which calls for much more modesty on the part of interpreters. Certainly literal fulfillment can be considered as a possibility. But other possibilities ought to be presented as well, all the time recognizing that one of the most important keys to interpretation is the kind of literature being dealt with. Along with this more nuanced interpretation, we must stop anathematizing those who read the significance of the imagery in different ways from our way.

The work of God in history. Throughout this part of the book Isaiah insists that God rules history and that this is one of the evidences of his Godhood. The difficulty for us today is that we do not have inspired prophets who can make those assessments for us. Is this the work of God, or is that? While some can claim to know and make large pronouncements on the basis of their supposed knowledge, the evidence is not there to support their claims. So is history still under the rule of God or not?

Yes, it is. The evidence of the Old and New Testaments is given to us to convince us of the fact so that we can live in faith in these days. The coming of Christ and the growth of the church is surely an evidence of that control. Likewise, the survival of the Jewish people in spite of all odds against such a survival is strong evidence. In recent times the defeat of the German Nazis and the Japanese militarists demonstrates his control, as does the sudden and shocking collapse of Russian communism. If the revelation of God is now complete and we lack inspired prophets to point out the specifics of God's activities, the Word of God gives us enough guidance to recognize the main outlines of his hand at work in today's history.

TRIUMPH OVER ADVERSITY. One of the things this passage of Scripture helps us to see is the way to overcome adversity. Too often we succumb to a dualistic worldview that sees good things coming from God's hand and bad things coming from the hand of the devil. When we do that, we are slipping back into a pagan way of thinking. We see existence as a playing field where eternal good and eternal evil are using us as pawns to advance their respective causes. That is basically how the Babylonians viewed things, and it is how the Judeans were tempted to believe. That is, if more bad things happen to us than good things, it is because the bad gods are winning. So we need to do more religious things to strengthen the good gods and weaken the bad ones. That is *not* the biblical perspective.

The biblical perspective begins with God as sole Creator and Lord (43:1, 7). Nothing exists outside of him. Evil is not an eternal principle existing on its own. It is nothing other than the failure to surrender to and obey the good God. This means that nothing happens to us apart from God's will. Logically, this should lead to determinism, wherein God causes everything to happen and we simply do what we must, for good or ill. But the Bible offers a different perspective by also presenting humans as being fully responsible for real choices.[5]

There is no fully effective middle way between these two poles. If there were, the debate over this issue would have ceased long ago. But let it simply be said here that the Old Testament is willing to live with the problem because of the complete unacceptability of the alternative: that other divine or semidivine beings can cause things to happen contrary to God's purposes.

What this means is that if there is adversity in my life, it is not there in defiance of God's control. It is helpful to think here of the concept of God's permissive will or of the idea of secondary and tertiary causation. God has

---

5. Note how this paradox is developed in Rom. 9–11. If Rom. 9 is read alone, one can only conclude that the Jews rejected Christ because that is what they were predestined to do. But if one read ch. 11 alone, one will conclude that the Jews rejected Christ solely because they chose to do so. The truth encompasses both teachings.

made a world of cause and effect. In other words, God does not directly cause everything that happens. If I slip and put my finger in front of a moving saw blade, God does not cause me to slip, and he certainly does not independently cause the saw to cut my finger. But he certainly permits the saw to cut my finger in keeping with the ways in which he made the world.

But if God did not directly cause this event, neither did he intervene to prevent it from happening, as he could have (and perhaps does far more often than we know). Instead, he chose not to do so and permitted normal cause-and-effect principles to function. So we need not think that God specifically wills such an event to take place. However, God does permit such things to happen, and that means it is still within his control. That in turn means he can enable me to deal with it and to use it for positive purposes.

But the situation described here is more than the permissive will of God. The Hebrew people of Isaiah's prophecy have chosen to live in defiance of God's instructions for life, his *torah* or "law." Just as in the physical world, there are certain consequences of such acts. The Creator of the universe has made the universe that way. So if I find myself in adverse circumstances, I need to ask myself if I have been living in sin.

That is not a popular question today. But then it was not popular in Isaiah's or Jeremiah's day either. We do not like to believe that the way we have chosen is wrong. After all, I am doing what I want, and what I want cannot be bad, can it? But Isaiah's words come through to us: "Which of you will listen to this or pay close attention in time to come?" (42:23). Will we be like those who, being consumed by the fire, "did not take it to heart" (42:25)? If we will admit our sin, we can admit that the trouble we are experiencing has been caused by God. And if it is caused by him, then we can turn to him to deliver us from it, or through it. If, however, the devil is the ultimate source of our trouble, there is a real question whether God can do anything about it. But if no trouble comes to us except through the hand of God and if we know that his hand is always moved by love, then we know that nothing can separate us from his love (Rom. 8:35−39).

Priority of grace. One of the fundamental principles of the kingdom of God is that his grace precedes everything else. That emphasis in 43:1−7 reminds us of this truth. This is what the serpent called into question in the Garden of Eden. He suggested that God does nothing for free. If he tells his children not to eat from the tree of the knowledge of good and evil, it is not because he freely cares for them but because he is trying to protect himself. Note how the Abraham narrative begins with free, unconditional promises (12:3). If there is to be hope for the human race, it will have to come from God's side and not from ours. Once the relationship was severed by the sin of Adam and Eve, there was no way they or we could reestablish it. God's holy nature had been offended, and only he could remedy that situation. He began to do so by reaching out to Abraham and Sarah with gracious promises.

That situation continued in Egypt. Note that Sinai does not precede the Exodus. Rather, the giving of the law on Mount Sinai follows the Exodus. This fact indicates that the descendants of Jacob were not saved from Egypt by their obedience. They were delivered from that bondage by grace alone. Then, *and only then,* came the call for obedience. Obedience never produces deliverance, but gracious deliverance should issue in obedience.

That is the paradigm presented here in Isaiah. To be sure, God calls his people to listen to and believe the promises he makes to deliver them. But his grace is declared to them even before they are necessarily prepared to listen and believe. Nor is the grace presented in any way that makes it conditional on obedience. God simply announces through the prophet that he *will* deliver them. It is stated as a fact.

The most concise statement of this truth in the New Testament is found in Romans 5:8: "But God demonstrates his own love for us in this: While we were still sinners, Christ died for us." That is, God did everything necessary to deliver us from the consequences of our sin before there was any indication that we would respond to that free act. If ever there was a refutation of Satan's slander, it is there. The characteristic of the Triune God is free, self-giving love, without the slightest taint of "what's in it for me." The ultimate proof of that fact is the cross of Jesus. God comes to us in Christ offering himself to us (see comments on Isa. 53:10). There is nothing we have done or can ever do to merit such an offer. It is free.

Personal relationship with God. As I have stated elsewhere, the Bible is not unique in its concept of God as the transcendent One, nor is it unique in its claim that God is personal with the human-like qualities of caring, passion, and compassion. But what is unique is its combining of these two. Nowhere else in religious or philosophical thought do we find this combination. Like sovereignty and free will, it is logically contradictory, yet the Bible maintains it everywhere throughout its pages. The Creator is your Redeemer, but more than that, he is your Lover. His transcendence is not diminished by his passion, nor his passion by his transcendence.

That is wonderful news. If the absolute principle of this universe were unfeeling, implacable, mindless force, then our condition would be bleak indeed. It is no wonder that one of the concerns of many cosmologists is to find intelligent life elsewhere in the universe. Not only are they seeking to validate chance evolution, but they are also reacting out of the terrible loneliness that a "force" theory of origins must result in.

But the Bible tells us that there is a Person who inhabits the universe, a Person who has a deep concern for his creatures and, as amazing as it seems, wants to be known by those creatures. On the surface of it, this is astounding. What possible benefit could the Triune One possibly gain from such a relationship? God is not lonely. In himself there is perfect fellowship. But perhaps that itself is the answer to the question. He does not seek to be known by us for himself but for ourselves. Anything made in the image of God is made for fellowship, and it is made for fellowship with the ultimate Fellowship. Thus, we will be ever incomplete until we are included in that eternal Fellowship.

God acts out of concern for our well-being. He does what he does for us because he values us. He finds us "precious," we are his special heritage. In the end, of course, it was not the kingdoms of Egypt, Sheba, and Cush he gave in exchange for us, but his own self in the person of his Son, Jesus Christ.

What this means is that biblical faith is not first of all adherence to a set of intellectual principles, nor is it the acceptance of certain behavioral dicta or the adoption of a set of moral norms. To be sure, it is all of these, but they are not what the faith is *first of all* about. Rather, it is first of all about a personal relationship with one's Creator. To some, the words "personal relationship" strikes too much of an evangelical, Protestant ring. But I would argue that a passage such as this one shows us that these words or, more to the point, this concept is not a special possession of one wing of the Christian church. Rather it is biblical, even Old Testament, in its basis.

Can it be doubted that the God who walks in the garden with Adam and Eve, who admonishes Cain, who eats supper with Abraham, who wrestles with Jacob, who speaks "mouth to mouth" with Moses, who calls Samuel by name, who offers a house to David, who shouts and weeps and sings through the prophets wants a personal relationship with people? To be sure, all of that is immensely heightened when God comes in flesh and says to ordinary people, "Come and be with me." But it is not some strange new idea. It is the culmination of what has been so throughout the Old Testament.

What is the significance of all this for today? It is to express the concern that for all too many contemporary Christians, the personal relationship side of their faith is much more theory than fact. For too many of us the passion of God for us is more of an idea than a reality. Our faith is a system of beliefs, more or less coherent, or it is a set of habits more or less followed. But to personally relate to God on a day-to-day basis is foreign to many of us. We do not read the Bible; we do not pray; we do not consciously pay attention to his voice throughout the day. That is not the way God wants it to be. We are his special treasure, and if we are to become all we can be, we need to be living in that reality.

Isaiah 43:8–44:5

⁸ LEAD OUT THOSE who have eyes but are blind,
   who have ears but are deaf.
⁹ All the nations gather together
   and the peoples assemble.
Which of them foretold this
   and proclaimed to us the former things?
Let them bring in their witnesses to prove they were right,
   so that others may hear and say, "It is true."
¹⁰ "You are my witnesses," declares the LORD,
   "and my servant whom I have chosen,
so that you may know and believe me
   and understand that I am he.
Before me no god was formed,
   nor will there be one after me.
¹¹ I, even I, am the LORD,
   and apart from me there is no savior.
¹² I have revealed and saved and proclaimed—
   I, and not some foreign god among you.
You are my witnesses," declares the LORD, "that I am God.
¹³   Yes, and from ancient days I am he.
No one can deliver out of my hand.
   When I act, who can reverse it?"

¹⁴ This is what the LORD says—
   your Redeemer, the Holy One of Israel:
 "For your sake I will send to Babylon
   and bring down as fugitives all the Babylonians,
   in the ships in which they took pride.
¹⁵ I am the LORD, your Holy One,
   Israel's Creator, your King."

¹⁶ This is what the LORD says—
   he who made a way through the sea,
   a path through the mighty waters,
¹⁷ who drew out the chariots and horses,
   the army and reinforcements together,
and they lay there, never to rise again,
   extinguished, snuffed out like a wick:

¹⁸"Forget the former things;
do not dwell on the past.
¹⁹See, I am doing a new thing!
Now it springs up; do you not perceive it?
I am making a way in the desert
and streams in the wasteland.
²⁰The wild animals honor me,
the jackals and the owls,
because I provide water in the desert
and streams in the wasteland,
to give drink to my people, my chosen,
²¹   the people I formed for myself
that they may proclaim my praise.

²²"Yet you have not called upon me, O Jacob,
you have not wearied yourselves for me, O Israel.
²³You have not brought me sheep for burnt offerings,
nor honored me with your sacrifices.
I have not burdened you with grain offerings
nor wearied you with demands for incense.
²⁴You have not bought any fragrant calamus for me,
or lavished on me the fat of your sacrifices.
But you have burdened me with your sins
and wearied me with your offenses.

²⁵"I, even I, am he who blots out
your transgressions, for my own sake,
and remembers your sins no more.
²⁶Review the past for me,
let us argue the matter together;
state the case for your innocence.
²⁷Your first father sinned;
your spokesmen rebelled against me.
²⁸So I will disgrace the dignitaries of your temple,
and I will consign Jacob to destruction
and Israel to scorn.

^{44:1}"But now listen, O Jacob, my servant,
Israel, whom I have chosen.
²This is what the LORD says—
he who made you, who formed you in the womb,
and who will help you:

Do not be afraid, O Jacob, my servant,
   Jeshurun, whom I have chosen.
³For I will pour water on the thirsty land,
   and streams on the dry ground;
I will pour out my Spirit on your offspring,
   and my blessing on your descendants.
⁴They will spring up like grass in a meadow,
   like poplar trees by flowing streams.
⁵One will say, 'I belong to the LORD';
   another will call himself by the name of Jacob;
still another will write on his hand, 'The LORD's,'
   and will take the name Israel."

THIS PASSAGE IS part of a larger unit, which I have identified as 42:10–44:22. The first part of this unit (42:10–43:7) dealt with the certainty of Israel's deliverance from the Babylonian captivity. This second part shows how God will use that deliverance as the evidence that he alone is God. This material can be further subdivided into 43:8–44:5, which discusses Israel's role as a witness for God, and 44:6–20, the ultimate diatribe against the helplessness of the gods.

God's Courtroom Scene (43:8–13)

ISAIAH 43:8, WHICH almost certainly refers to the servant Israel, leaves no doubt that their hope is not in themselves. They are "blind" and "deaf" (cf. also 42:18–19). They are not in a position to give ministry (as in 42:1–9) but only to receive it. They are once more called into the courtroom along with the "nations" and the "peoples" (43:9). Once more the question is put to them: What idol has "foretold this"? It is not clear what "this" refers to. It may denote the coming of Cyrus and the fall of Babylon, though commentators offer a variety of opinions.[1] The indefiniteness of "this" may encompass the whole of God's redemptive work in the world.

Now the nations are called on to produce "witnesses" who can give evidence that any of their gods have made a prediction in the past ("the former

---

1. Motyer, *Prophecy of Isaiah*, 334, who takes 43:1–7 as referring to the Exodus, believes "this" is referring to that event. Young, *The Book of Isaiah*, 3:148, takes it to refer to the conversion of the nations. Childs, *Isaiah*, 335, says the parallel with "former things" shows that the gods are being called on to explain the past.

things") that has then come true. Their silence proves that they have no such evidence. But now the One who is both judge and defendant turns to his blind and deaf servant and says, "You are my witnesses." What incredible courage on God's part to rest his case on evidence like that. It means that God is going to have to do an amazing work on their behalf so that they can be the evidence he deserves.

Verses 10–13 relate in general terms what Israel's relationship is to God and what they know to be true if only they will open their eyes and ears. They have been called into a relationship with God whereby they will "know" (affective) and "believe" (volitional) and "understand" (cognitive) that "I am he." We have already encountered this latter phrase in 41:4, and we will see it twice more in this chapter (43:13, 25; see also 46:4; 48:12; 51:12). This is God's ultimate statement of identity. A more colloquial translation might say, "I'm the one." He is the One all society is looking for, the One who made all things, the One to whom all things will return, and therefore the only One who can save (43:11). There is no one else in his category, and the Israelite people have been called in order to experience that truth and demonstrate it to the nations of the world.

This probably explains the interesting combination of verbs in 43:12. God has not merely "revealed" truth about himself to them, nor has he merely "saved" them, nor has he merely "proclaimed" the meaning of what he has done. He has done all three together and simultaneously so that his revelation is a wholistic one, touching the whole of human personality. No one else but the Lord has done this, and the Hebrews know it. They have experienced all of this: They are "witnesses . . . that I am God." The term translated "God" here is ʾel, the more inclusive word whose cognates in the Semitic languages almost mean "deity." God is saying that he is the totality of deity, as revealed by what he has done on the earth for and through the Israelites. The conclusion in 43:13 is inescapable: There is no one who can successfully contest his will. He is "it"; there is no one else.

Promises of Deliverance (43:14–21)

IN THESE VERSES God tells his people once again that he is going to deliver them from Babylon. They are witnesses to how he has delivered them in the past, and this is what they will be witnesses of in the future. Once again, relational terminology is prominent. He is "your Redeemer," "your Holy One," "your King." They are "my people, my chosen," "formed for myself." It is because of them that the almighty God will "bring down" Babylon. He is not going to deliver them merely to prove some abstract theological point. Rather, he will deliver them, as 43:4 says, because he loves them.

But how is he going to deliver them?[2] Verses 16–17 invite the people to remember what he did in the Exodus. There God demonstrated his lordship over both nature and human nations. He also showed both his desire and his ability to save. But after reminding them of those facts, he suddenly says in 43:18 that they are to "forget" all that. What is going on? We can imagine people beginning to get excited over the prospect of deliverance, and they know just how God is going to do it. He will raise up a deliverer from among them, who will divide the Euphrates River so that they can cross dry-shod, and then he will bring the river back over the Babylonian army and drown them all. As humans we like everything to be predictable.

But God is not predictable like the gods. He is the Creator, who loves doing things in "new" ways (43:19). So whereas formerly he made a "way through the sea" (43:16), this time he will make a "way in the desert" (43:19). In language reminiscent of several places in the earlier part of the book (e.g., chs. 13; 32; 34; 35), God promises to transform the desert created by arrogance and false trust, the place where unclean animals live, into a place of "water" and "streams" where his "chosen" may have all their needs supplied (43:20).[3] As a result, his people will bear witness to his deity; they will "proclaim my praise" (43:21).

The Present Reality (43:22–28)

THEN, IN WAYS reminiscent of what we saw several times in chapters 1–39, the prophet steps back from that glorious future for a moment to talk about present reality. That reality seems to have two foci here. Not only does Isaiah point to the unbelief that will characterize so many people during the Exile, but people are also reverting to the unbelief rampant in Isaiah's own day, for which judgment is still to come (43:28).[4] There is an implied charge against God to which these verses are the answer, namely, that it is beside the point to talk glowingly of God's deliverance from the Exile, for it seems so unfair of God to have sent his people into exile in the first place. After all, they were assiduous about performing all the rituals God commanded, so if in fact God sent them into captivity, he is the one in the wrong.[5]

---

2. Note the slowly increasing specificity. In ch. 41 it is only a man from the east whose coming will terrify the nations. In ch. 42 deliverance is promised; Babylon will fall, and God will deliver in a different way from what they might expect. This type of specificity will increase through ch. 47.

3. R. P. Carroll, "Second Isaiah and the Failure of Prophecy," *ST* 32 (1978): 119–31, cites passages like this to show that "Second Isaiah" predicted a miraculous deliverance from Babylon and was proven wrong. See comments on 42:15–16.

4. The NIV choice of the future tense for the imperfect verbs in this verse is a viable one, although other possibilities must be allowed. See Motyer, *Prophecy of Isaiah*, 341, n. 1.

5. See Westermann, *Isaiah 40–66*, 130.

God's answer to this charge reflects the kind of hyperbolic, ironic language that the prophets often resort to when discussing ritual and cultic activity.[6] Amos, for example, implied that none of Israel's sacrifices in the desert were actually to God (Amos 5:25); Jeremiah said God had no interest in the temple (Jer. 7:1–9), and Isaiah has already said that the whole thing made God sick (Isa. 1:11–15). Almost certainly the reason for this strong language is that the trap of believing cultic behavior has an automatic effect on God is such an easy one to fall into. So God says that, in fact, they have not been calling on him at all; rather, they have wearied themselves with their sacrifice (43:22; cf. Mal. 1:13). They have not really brought sacrifices to God when they did these things, and in fact God never said that he wanted such things (43:23). What have they done? They have just piled up more and more sin until God could not bear it any more.

What are we to make of such statements? Surely God had commanded the Israelites to bring sacrifices to his altar (Lev. 1–6), and there were some severe penalties for those who did not do so or who did it in wrong ways (cf. Lev. 10:1–3). So what is Isaiah's point? He is trying to drive home the truth that in a world of transcendence, we cannot manipulate God by manipulating the physical world. The Hebrews were continually falling back into the worldview of their neighbors, in which, since the gods are a part of the cosmic system, doing something to the system does something to the gods. But God is not part of the system, and instead of the ritual having automatic effects, it was intended to symbolize a change in personal relations.

God does not have to be manipulated into forgiving us. In fact, he cannot be so manipulated. He has already done that (43:25), and he has done it for his own sake. We have only to receive what he has done. The sacrifices were to be symbols of changed hearts and changed lives. So God truly did not want their *sacrifices*; he wanted *them*, as symbolized by the sacrifices. But many of the Israelites had succumbed to the temptation to try to keep themselves for themselves and to try to placate God, to "get him off their backs" as it were, with their sacrifices and rituals. So, in fact, all the offerings they kept bringing and all the rituals they engaged in, which they blamed God for burdening them with, were just adding to the mountain of their unconfessed sins that they kept piling on God's back.

Thus, God suggests in 43:26 that his people might want to review the "case" they are making against him. Far from being unfair because of their

---

6. This was one of the elements that caused J. Wellhausen and other scholars in the heyday of higher criticism to conclude that prophets and priests were sworn enemies, a position that is much modified now. See J. Sawyer, *Prophecy and the Prophets of the Old Testament* (Oxford: Oxford Univ. Press, 1987), 19–22.

careful ritual, the Exile became the more necessary because of them. From their "father" Jacob (cf. Deut. 26:5; Hos. 12:2–4) right up to the present they have continued in sin. The inevitable result is the one that occurred in 586 B.C., when God consigned "Jacob to destruction."

God's New Work (44:1–5)

BUT, AS ALWAYS in this book, destruction is not the last word God intends to speak. Once again, he implores his people to "listen."[7] Do not rely on mechanical rituals but enter into a relationship by listening to the One who speaks, who has been speaking since the dawn of time.

Again, the appeal is to creation. If the exiled Israelites are tempted to think that God has given up on them, that their sin has become too much for him to do anything about, they should remember that God has a special interest in them. He "made" them, forming them "in the womb." If a mother cannot forget her child (cf. 49:15), God cannot forget those he created.

Just as God is strong enough to do something about their physical captivity, so he is great enough to do something about their persistent sinning. Not only has he found a way to forgive their sin without destroying the justice on which the world rests; he has also found a way to transform a proud, self-centered people, who seem incapable of giving themselves away, into those who will gladly find their central identity in their surrender to their Father. The means of that transformation is his Spirit (44:3).

Just as in the earlier occurrence in 32:15, the work of the Spirit is to enable God's people to do what they cannot. In 32:15 they could not live lives of justice and righteousness, and God promised that his Spirit would enable them to live such lives. Here the people are unable to surrender their proud self-ownership and enter into a completely committed relationship with God. But God says that when his Spirit is poured out on the "dry ground" of their "offspring," they will be glad to identify themselves as belonging to the Lord (44:5). No longer will they try to retain ownership to themselves while trying to manipulate God with sacrifices.

WITNESSES. Jesus quoted Isaiah 43:10 when he said to his disciples "You will be my witnesses" (Acts 1:8), and he was using the term in the same sense that Isaiah used it. He was calling on his disciples to give evidence out of their own personal experience that Jesus Christ was who he said he was. They were not first of all to preach sermons

---

7. See 40:28; 42:18, 23; 43:1, 14.

but to tell what they knew to be so in life. This is also what John does in the beginning of his first letter, as he tells his readers that he has touched and seen and heard Life (1 John 1:1–3). This means that unless there is a vital, first-hand experience of Christ that has transformed the way the witness lives, there is nothing to witness to. This is demonstrated by the sons of Sceva, who were evidently trying to minister out of a secondhand knowledge of Christ in Acts 19:14–16:

> Seven sons of Sceva, a Jewish chief priest, were doing this. One day the evil spirit answered them, "Jesus I know, and I know about Paul, but who are you?" Then the man who had the evil spirit jumped on them and overpowered them all. He gave them such a beating that they ran out of the house naked and bleeding.

The only Savior. The point in 43:11 about God's being the only Savior seems to be a sweeping claim. But it is rooted squarely in the worldview issues that are at the center of this section and, indeed, at the center of the book, namely, that there is no salvation in paganism. The system cannot save us from the system. While one part of the system might pretend that it can save from another part, it is not true in the long run, for no part of the system is independent of any other. The result is that unless there is a Being from beyond the cosmic system who can intervene in the system at will, there is no real deliverance. We cannot be delivered from ourselves, from our past, or from the effects of our sin. All of these factors are inescapable, and we must simply make the best of them, realizing that we are all victims and victimizers.

The only "salvation" paganism, either ancient or modern, can offer is either Stoicism, which seeks to look realistically at a situation and make the best of it, or Epicureanism, which champions "eat, drink, and be merry, for tomorrow we die." A modern combination of these two is "self-actualization," in which I simply discover who I am and capitalize on that. But what the disciples of self-actualization do not realize is that one of the most self-actualized persons we can meet is the serial killer. If we are really only the product of all of our conditionings and if we really have no option but to obey them, then to be "self-actualized" is to embrace all that conditioning in an iron grasp and to leap into the abyss.

The nature of biblical revelation. Isaiah 43:12 gives us a good snapshot of the process of revelation. Sometimes both the friends and the enemies of revelation agree in that they make it far too simplistic: God dictated his word to human secretaries, putting in stylistic variations just to give it some "local color." If we do not accept that picture, so we are told, then we must believe that humans originated the Bible as a fallible "witness" to a faith that is only a little different from the Canaanite religions from which it emerged.

One version of this view posits that God really has acted in human experience (revelation) but that the reports of that action are only human. The great defect of this idea is that we cannot know *whether* God acted, but only that fallible people thought he did. There is little there on which to stake one's eternal destiny. But in fact, as the Bible describes it, revelation is a more nuanced and relational process than either of these oversimplifications. The terms Isaiah uses here ("revealed," "saved," "proclaimed") lend themselves to understanding this process. The biblical material sees the following four phases in revelation, all of which are directed by God:

God intervenes in human experience.
He inspires a person or persons with the interpretation of that experience.
He superintends the recording and transmission of that interpreted report.
He applies the meaning of that interpreted report to the hearts of
    hearers and readers.

All of this process is revelation, and no one part of it can be cut off from the others. So God says here that both his actions ("saved") and his interpretations ("proclaimed") are part of the process by which he has "revealed" himself.

A new thing. We humans do not very much like surprises. We like to have everything neatly packaged and predictable. That is the way the gods are. They do what they have always done; they have no choice. As representations of the cosmic system, they are fated to do the same things over and over again. The sun does not have the option of rising in the west.

But Yahweh is the Creator; he loves to do things differently. Because he is faithful, he will always be consistent with himself, so he will never be arbitrary and heartless. Yet that does not mean he must therefore always repeat himself. He will do things in new ways. The reason for calling the people's attention to the Exodus (43:16–17) and then telling them to "forget the former things" (43:18) is that God wants us to learn things about his character and nature from the past but not to enshrine the methods of the past. Tragically, we are prone to do the opposite: enshrine the methods while forgetting the theological truths they were first devised to teach.

Ritual. There are three common views of ritual in the world. (1) The pagan view is the one I call "continuity." In this view the symbol and the reality are identical. What one does to the symbol, one does to the reality. This is the principle that lies behind voodoo and all other forms of sympathetic magic. In this view I can do things here that will automatically affect the divine realm. It does not matter whether I am repentant or whether I am trusting the god. If I do the ritual right, the god must do what that ritual requires.

(2) The second view posits a radical break between the symbol and the reality. If the first view is more Platonic, this one is more Aristotelian. The

symbol is only a mental representation of the reality, so you can do whatever you want to the symbol and it will have no effect on the reality at all. This view has dominated Western thought since the eighteenth century.

(3) But the Bible seems to take a middle way between these two. On the one hand, it is clear, as this passage testifies, that manipulating a symbol, such as a sacrifice, has no automatic effect on God. On the other hand, certain symbols have a more than casual relation with the reality they symbolize.

Some years ago a translation of the Bible got in trouble with this point. The translators reasoned that "the blood of Christ" was simply a metaphor for the death of Christ, there being nothing magic about Christ's blood. But when their translation came out with the "death of Christ" where the "blood of Christ" had been, there was a great deal of uproar—and not merely from traditionalists, who did not like to have treasured images tampered with. Whether the critics of the translation could have expressed it or not, they were recognizing that certain symbols have greater communicative power than equal abstractions because reality is multidimensional. There is something about "blood" that speaks of sacrificial, atoning death in ways that mere "death" does not. What this means is that while we cannot treat the symbols of our faith as if they have power in and of themselves, neither can we interchange the symbols with impunity. Coke and donuts will not take the place of wine and bread in the Lord's Supper.

WITNESSES. Many people today are terrorized by the prospect of being witnesses for Christ. They think that they must go door to door, passing out religious literature, or that they have to collar people in the bus terminal with "The Four Spiritual Laws." In part this is the result of preaching that has used guilt as a device for gaining acquiescence in the message. One expression of this terror is to attempt to justify oneself by saying, "Well, I just live my witness." But all too often this means no witness at all.

I believe the present passage can help us through some of the impasse. (1) Notice that there is no command to be witnesses here. Rather, God simply declares a fact: "You *are* my witnesses." Jesus says the same thing. The people of Israel and the disciples experienced some things that forever changed them. It was a fact. The same is true for us if we have genuinely encountered Christ in our lives. Like it or not, we have been changed. We *are* evidence of his divine, delivering, transforming power. It is not something we must do; it is something we are.

(2) Note too the incredible condescension of God in this process. To think that he would rest his claim to Godhood on the likes of the Israelites, or the

disciples, or us is all but unbelievable. Yet he does it in the full knowledge of our fallibility. His witnesses then were "blind" and "deaf," and not much more could be said for the disciples or for us, and he knows all that. Still, when idols are called to bring out their witnesses, we are the ones God points to in order to support his case. What love, what dignity, what worth this act bestows on us. It told the exiles they were not cast away, and it should say the same to us. Witness is not an onerous demand but an incredible privilege.

(3) One's witness is the expression of one's experience. The exiles were not expected to make speeches but to report what they knew to be so out of their own lives. They could report that God had indeed predicted the Exile long before the fact, going all the way back to Moses in his final address to them (cf. Deut. 4:25–31). They could report how they had persisted in sin and how God had tried again and again to woo them back to him, until there was no more hope and the Exile became inevitable. But they could also report that God had promised a deliverer and that they even knew his name: Cyrus. The day would shortly come when their final witness would be given as they walked out of the gates of Babylon. It is the same for us. The Scriptures tell us to be ready with a reason for the eternal hope we have (1 Peter 3:15). It does not have to be dramatic or attention-grabbing. It is simply our story and what that story says about the reality of Christ and his ability to save.

(4) Finally, the concept of witness *does* require that God in Christ has done something in our lives. In Ezekiel 36, God says that the people have "profaned my name" by going into exile and making it appear that he was helpless to deliver them. If they were going to be the evidence of his unique holiness, he would have to deliver them not only from the consequences of their sin but also from the causes of it: their penchant for idolatry and the stubbornness of their hearts. That theme is at least alluded to in Isaiah 44:1–5. God in wonderful condescension deigns to rest his claim to be the sole God on the evidence of our lives. We must ask what the content of our daily walk to the witness stand really is. Are we allowing God to deliver us or not?

Remember the lessons of the past, but forget the methods of the past. Most of us have a hard time learning this lesson. It requires a flexibility, an openness, a daring that most of us do not possess. Life is a complex business. From the moment we make our entrance into the world, one painful experience after another impresses this complexity upon us. It is made clear to us that if we are to have our needs met, we must quickly find ways of managing this apparently chaotic complexity. So whenever we find something that works for us, we hang on to it with all the tenacity of a leech. There seem to be so few things that work most of the time that we treasure the ones that do. In some ways maturation is the process of accumulating things that work and discarding those that do not. In fact, when you look at wisdom literature, that is what you see: The wise person knows what works in life and the fool does not.

Now along comes someone who says, "Let go of all those things that have worked in the past." What? Why? Because you and I are not God. The great danger of maturation is calcification. We have finally figured things out. We know what we want, and we know how to get it. The result is that we don't need faith any more. We know the questions, and we know the answers, so God, who seems to enjoy disturbing the comfortable, needs to keep his distance. Here is where God comes to us and dares us to believe him for a new thing in our lives, something that will force us to let go of some of the hard-won strings of control, daring to let God stretch our vision. This is the vision of a Caleb, who says at age eighty, "Give me this hill country [to conquer]" (Josh. 14:12).

However, this is no call for novelty for its own sake. If maturity is too often devoted to methods that have worked in the past, young people are too likely to say the opposite: "If it's new, it's right." But not everything new is right. For instance, not every contemporary praise chorus can outshine every Wesley or Watts hymn. So God introduces the new thing he is about to do by reminding the people of what the past events have taught them about him. If the new that we are proposing results in some sort of spiritual amnesia, something is wrong. It is true that the seven last words of the church are, "We've never done it that way before." But it is also true that when new methods obliterate the old truths, that is not good news, either for the church or for the lost world.

The nature of true religion. Throughout the Bible, the great danger to "true religion" is what we may loosely call *sacramentalism*, which is a substitution of religious forms for a vital, personal relationship with God. This relationship is the hallmark of biblical experience of God. From the reference to Adam and Eve's walking with God in the cool of the evening (Gen. 3:8), to Enoch's walk with God (5:22–23), to Abraham (17:1), to the Psalms (cf. Ps. 27:8), to Jesus and the disciples (Mark 3:14), to Paul's impassioned cry to know him (Phil. 3:10), to the saints around the throne in the book of Revelation (Rev. 7:9–11), biblical religion is about a personal relationship with God.

It is not surprising, then, for Micah to say that all God's requirements can be summed up in three verbs: "To act justly and to love mercy and to walk humbly with your God" (Mic. 6:8). In the same way, Jesus sums up the scriptural requirements with one verb: "'Love the Lord your God with all your heart and all your soul and all your mind.' This is the first and greatest commandment. And the second is like it: 'Love your neighbor as yourself'" (Matt. 22:37–39).

But personal relationships are never easy to manage or to quantify. Do I love God more today than yesterday? Am I more like Christ today than the day before? It is much easier to quantify religious performance. It is much easier to say that I have rigorously confessed my sins and taken communion, or have been baptized, or have had an unbroken record of attendance at church and Sunday School, or have not missed a day of devotions in months, or have spent hours in the service of the poor. So we, like the Jews, would prefer to measure our religious attainments on the basis of religious performance than upon a daily love relationship with our Creator and Redeemer. Having performed at a fairly high standard, we then think that we have a claim on him for blessings in our lives while keeping control of our lives for ourselves.

At the same time, we cannot say that these activities have no relation to the reality that underlies them. If I say I love my wife passionately but am never home at night for weeks on end, if I never talk to her, never give her a gift, and never do what she asks me to do, you would be justified in saying that I am deluding myself. I do not love her, and there is really no relationship between us. So if I say we cannot congratulate ourselves on our great relationship with God simply because we go to church, neither dare I say that since our relationship is not performance-based, it doesn't matter whether we go to church. It does matter, but it is not the end; it is, instead, the means, and we must not confuse the two.

Life in the Spirit. There is a much more than casual relationship between 43:22–28 and 44:1–5. The problem identified in the first passage is the one we have just noted: the tendency to substitute formalism for genuine personal surrender. This was a problem throughout the Old Testament. There was a solution, but it was not in greater human effort. Many Old Testament saints had tried that road and found nothing but increased frustration. That is what Paul is testifying to in Romans 7. The solution was as it is here: God promised to pour out his Spirit on his children. That promise is for us today.

Romans 8 makes this clear. The covenant (or the law) could not solve the problem of our persistent rebellion. That self-willed, self-centered attitude that Paul calls "the flesh" (NIV, usually "the sinful nature") was too strong for the covenant. So God has made his Spirit available to everyone through God's Son, the Messiah. What will the Spirit do for us when we allow him to fill us? Isaiah spells it out in 44:4–5. He will enable us to identify with our Lord and with his people without reservation. To be "double-minded," as James describes it (James 1:8; 4:8), is to try to live partly for God and partly for myself, to be partly identified with God and partly identified with the world, to expect God's blessing while retaining the key to my heart for myself. It is not possible to resolve that conflict in our own strength. But the Spirit has come, and he will make it possible for us to say without any reservation, "I belong to the LORD" (Isa. 44:5).

Isaiah 44:6–22

❦

⁶"THIS IS WHAT the LORD says—
    Israel's King and Redeemer, the LORD Almighty:
  I am the first and I am the last;
    apart from me there is no God.
⁷Who then is like me? Let him proclaim it.
    Let him declare and lay out before me
  what has happened since I established my ancient people,
    and what is yet to come—
    yes, let him foretell what will come.
⁸Do not tremble, do not be afraid.
    Did I not proclaim this and foretell it long ago?
  You are my witnesses. Is there any God besides me?
    No, there is no other Rock; I know not one."

⁹All who make idols are nothing,
    and the things they treasure are worthless.
  Those who would speak up for them are blind;
    they are ignorant, to their own shame.
¹⁰Who shapes a god and casts an idol,
    which can profit him nothing?
¹¹He and his kind will be put to shame;
    craftsmen are nothing but men.
  Let them all come together and take their stand;
    they will be brought down to terror and infamy.

¹²The blacksmith takes a tool
    and works with it in the coals;
  he shapes an idol with hammers,
    he forges it with the might of his arm.
  He gets hungry and loses his strength;
    he drinks no water and grows faint.
¹³The carpenter measures with a line
    and makes an outline with a marker;
  he roughs it out with chisels
    and marks it with compasses.
  He shapes it in the form of man,
    of man in all his glory,
    that it may dwell in a shrine.

¹⁴ He cut down cedars,
>> or perhaps took a cypress or oak.
> He let it grow among the trees of the forest,
>> or planted a pine, and the rain made it grow.
¹⁵ It is man's fuel for burning;
>> some of it he takes and warms himself,
>> he kindles a fire and bakes bread.
> But he also fashions a god and worships it;
>> he makes an idol and bows down to it.
¹⁶ Half of the wood he burns in the fire;
>> over it he prepares his meal,
>> he roasts his meat and eats his fill.
> He also warms himself and says,
>> "Ah! I am warm; I see the fire."
¹⁷ From the rest he makes a god, his idol;
>> he bows down to it and worships.
> He prays to it and says,
>> "Save me; you are my god."
¹⁸ They know nothing, they understand nothing;
>> their eyes are plastered over so they cannot see,
>> and their minds closed so they cannot understand.
¹⁹ No one stops to think,
>> no one has the knowledge or understanding to say,
> "Half of it I used for fuel;
>> I even baked bread over its coals,
>> I roasted meat and I ate.
> Shall I make a detestable thing from what is left?
>> Shall I bow down to a block of wood?"
²⁰ He feeds on ashes, a deluded heart misleads him;
>> he cannot save himself, or say,
>> "Is not this thing in my right hand a lie?"

²¹ "Remember these things, O Jacob,
>> for you are my servant, O Israel.
> I have made you, you are my servant;
>> O Israel, I will not forget you.
²² I have swept away your offenses like a cloud,
>> your sins like the morning mist.
> Return to me,
>> for I have redeemed you."

THIS PASSAGE, THE ultimate accusation against the idols, concludes the unit of 42:10–44:22. While one further passage will address idols (46:1–7), it lacks the intensity and the air of judicial challenge that comes to its climax here. The diatribe here reflects the trajectory that has developed in the earlier ones. Initially, the case against the idol gods was focused on their inability to explain the meaning of the past and tell the future (41:21–29). In the second presentation of the case (43:8–13), another element was added: their inability to save their people or prevent Yahweh from saving his people from them. Now in this third presentation, although their inability to predict the future takes first place (44:7–8), it is quickly succeeded by their inability to save, and that issue takes up the rest of the case.

The statement of the case begins in 44:6–8 with another claim to absolute uniqueness by God. The body of the charges is presented in 44:9–20. Finally, 44:21–22 forms the conclusion by issuing a call for Israel to take to heart all that this means for what their God can, and will, do for them. Like the other presentations of the case against the idols, this one has an "evangelical" function. It is not a cool philosophical discourse but attempts to convince apathetic, discouraged people not to put their hopes in things that will ultimately fail them; they must wait confidently and expectantly for what the one God, the Creator, their Holy One, will do for them.[1]

God's Absolute Uniqueness (44:6–8)

IN WORDS AND phrases that are now familiar to anyone working straight through the book, Yahweh declares his absolute uniqueness. But he first identifies himself inextricably with Israel. Although he is the only God, "the first and . . . the last," he is also the One who has made himself known in the context of a relationship with a small, insignificant people. The gods cannot explain why he has done this nor where the relationship is going to go in the future. But God has, and the people of Israel are "witnesses" to that fact (44:8). In an always changing, unstable world, there is One who does not change, a "Rock" to which beaten, battered people may cling.

Charges Against the Idols (44:9–20)

IN CONTRAST TO this Rock, what do the other peoples of earth have to cling to? Nothing. They "treasure" worthless things, trash, and as a result have

---

1. As I have observed elsewhere (Oswalt, *Isaiah 40–66*, 170–71), this is another example of the use of a "graphic summary" to drive a point home. This contrasts with the widespread scholarly argument that vv. 9–20 are not original. See also Motyer, *Prophecy of Isaiah*, 343, n. 1; and Oswalt, *Isaiah 40–66*, 174, n. 36.

become "nothing" themselves (44:9).[2] This thought is developed further in a general way in 44:10—11. The gods are nothing because they are made by human "craftsmen." Such gods must fail their worshipers, putting them to "shame" and thereby making the worshipers as valueless as the things worshiped. Once again (see comments on 40:18—20 and 43:8—13) the question is: How can something made by humans ever save humans?

In 44:12—17 the prophet describes the process of making idols in great detail, showing how difficult it is to make one's own gods when the true God can be so easily found. Isaiah takes us backward through the complex process, beginning with the last step of plating the wooden form with precious metal (v. 12). Then he describes how the carpenter made the wooden form (v. 13). Next he describes the process of choosing the wood for the form (v. 14). In all of this he describes the difficulty and the complexity of the process.

In 44:15—17 Isaiah comes to the heart of his argument. When the idol maker cuts down a tree for the form of his god, he also uses some of that same tree for firewood! How in the world, the prophet asks, can a piece of wood, another part of which has been used to cook food and supply warmth, ever be expected to save a person, especially when so much human effort has had to be lavished on it to make it what it is?[3] The answer is, of course, that it cannot do so, and anyone who thinks it can has been mentally and spiritually blinded (44:18).

The ultimate seriousness of paganism and its consequences is seen in 44:19—20. God hates the thing that has reduced humans to "nothing," that has destroyed their power to think logically. So it is not mere hyperbole when he calls the idols an "abomination" (NIV "detestable thing," v. 19). In the Old Testament an "abomination" (*to'ebah*) is a violation of God's creation order.[4] It is to use a created thing in a way that violates its character. That is surely the case with idolatry. God has given all of nature to humans to care

---

2. Motyer's observation (*Prophecy of Isaiah*, 343) that the idols have no power to change the human heart is apropos.

3. Many modern commentators are embarrassed for the prophet because they think he is ignorant of the complexity of pagan thought, or worse, knows it but can only attack it on the superficial point of idolatry. See, e.g., Hanson, *Isaiah 40—66*, 90—93, who suggests that "Second Isaiah" as a whole is actually teaching tolerance toward other cultures' expressions of deity. In fact, that is the opposite thing to what this book is teaching. It looks forward to the day when the other cultures will abandon their false conceptions and come to the Holy One of Israel. As I have argued both here and elsewhere, there is no reason why Isaiah would not have understood the worldview of paganism as thoroughly as he understood how idols were made. He is simply attacking paganism where the fundamental flaw in its conception of reality is most obvious—and most vulnerable.

4. See, e.g., Lev. 7:18; 11:10; 18:22; Deut. 7:25—26; 12:31; 18:9—13.

for in a way that will produce blessing (Gen. 1:28–30). For us to elevate nature to the place of God and bow down to that which was made for us is just such a violation. Spiritually speaking, it is to feed "on ashes" (Isa. 44:20).

A Call to Take Heart (44:21–22)

THESE TWO VERSES give us God's appeal to his people on the basis of what he has just said. They have not made their God; rather he has "made" them. Therefore, he is no prisoner of creation, and they need not be either. If they will "remember" all that he has been, is, and will be, they need not fear that he will "forget" them. Nor do they need to fear that their sins have become irremovable aspects of their fate. God is not bound by fate; if he determines to forgive their "offenses" and to redeem them from their captivity, he will find a way to do those things. There is nothing that can stop him (cf. 43:13).

ACCESS TO TRUTH. The forcefulness of the language used here and elsewhere in Isaiah in reference to idol worship strikes our modern ears harshly. This is because we have come to the place where harsh language is tolerated only when it is directed against intolerance. In the modern West, intolerance and politically incorrect speech are the only sins left. And intolerance is defined in the widest terms possible: believing that someone else is wrong. We have lost all confidence that anything is true in the realm of ultimate meaning. What you believe is just as likely to be true as what I believe; therefore, how dare either of us criticize the other? I may adhere to any strange creed I wish as long as I do not insist you should believe it.

What has happened is this: For the first fifteen hundred years of Christendom the church maintained the authority to determine what was right and wrong. Then for the next three hundred years the Bible was the authority. Then the Enlightenment replaced the Bible with reason. Now we have lost faith in reason's ability to show us the truth. This means that each person now determines truth for himself or herself, but with one major caveat. Anything that society determines demeans the absolute worth and freedom of any individual will be attacked with draconian energy.

So, to use modern parlance, where is Isaiah "coming from"? How can he speak so forcefully about someone else's cherished beliefs? He can do so because he believes that he has access to "the truth." That is the critical question. Does he have access to such truth, or is his "truth" of no more value than that of the Canaanites or the Babylonians? If the latter is true, then we must hang our heads for him and tell him to "pipe down." If, however, he does know the truth, then he must not keep silent. Should a person who knows that a highway bridge has collapsed a few miles ahead keep silent? That would be criminal neglect. Such a person has an obligation to warn everyone he can of the danger they are facing.

So the overriding issue in all of this is whether the "truth" about life, its meaning, and its purpose can be known. And if so, by what means is that knowing possible? If, however, life is without meaning, then that is the end of the discussion. "Right" and "wrong" are meaningless terms that should be expelled from our vocabulary. Yet the most avid secularist is not willing to give up such terms, especially when he or she feels "rights" have been violated. We *do* think some things are so, so the question is: How do we know them? The answer given everywhere today is: experience. Our experience, individual and collective, teaches us that certain things are so. However, beyond some broad generalities, everyone's experience is different. So it is impossible to say that there are particular principles that are true for everyone.

But before we go very far down that road, we should look at the five thousand years of human history that have preceded us. When unaided human experience has been made the means for discovering "truth," the results have been markedly similar around the world. I have already talked about them at various places in this commentary, but let me recap them briefly: The world is divine; all physical-psycho-social forces are gods; conflict is eternal; sexuality is the life force; sympathetic magic is the means of manipulating and identifying with the gods; all ethics are relative (though since no society can exist for long without certain ethical norms, the ethics a given society deems effective will have to be enforced with coercion); all time is cyclical; progress is an illusion; individuals are only of value as they are a part of the larger whole of humanity, but humanity itself is of no particular value. The history of the human race tells us that this is where the theory of knowledge the Western world now espouses will lead us. Is that really where we want to go?

The only viable alternative to that theory of knowledge is the one offered in the Bible. Again we have talked about it elsewhere: It is the principle of revelation. Truth is mediated to us from beyond ourselves. It is mediated by both language and action as God, who transcends us in every particular, intersects us in our own context.

This mode of knowledge has led to some startlingly different conclusions about reality. There is one transcendent Creator of the universe, who is a personal Spirit. He created the universe freely and joyously as an expression of his own creative love. Humans, and indeed, individual humans, are an expression of his character and nature and are thus of the highest value to him. Since he is transcendent, he cannot be manipulated by sympathetic magic. He can only be identified with through the means of personal relationship he makes available to us. Since he is the one Creator and is utterly consistent, the world has a purpose and a goal. That in turn means it is possible to determine what is effective in reaching that goal and what is not effective. This also means that it is possible to keep track of progress toward that goal. There is thus an absolute ethic that is rooted in the very nature of things, which, when followed, brings blessing to the human race and which, when denied, brings disaster.

This is where Isaiah is coming from. And it is the same place that Jesus Christ was coming from when he said to Nicodemus, "I have spoken to you of earthly things and you do not believe; how then will you believe if I speak of heavenly things? No one has ever gone into heaven except the one who came from heaven—the Son of Man" (John 3:12−13). Jesus was claiming to have direct access to the truth. More than that, he was claiming to be the means of that truth's being revealed to the world. This is where the passion of an Isaiah and a Jesus come from: the conviction that the truth about nature and life has been revealed to us and that we can then speak with assurance about the right ways to live and the wrong ways. That is what is at issue in a passage like this.

CONFRONTING AND SHAPING OUR AGE. The challenge that a passage like this places before contemporary Christians, especially young Christians, is whether we will confront our age as directly as Isaiah and the rest of the prophets of Israel did. Young people are under terrific pressure to conform to the dominant culture of the day. Part of that pressure comes from within. How do I differentiate myself from my parents (a necessary step if maturity is to occur)? The immediate tendency is simply to reject everything about my parents—the way they think, the way they dress, the preferences they have—and to adopt whatever is new and current.

But this internal pressure has been dramatically reinforced from outside by the collapse of American culture that has occurred with increasing speed since the 1960s. Young people have been encouraged to look at the past, and particularly at their parents, with contempt. They have been encouraged to flaunt their defiance of all authority as though authority in itself is an evil. The ethics without which no society can exist (as best epitomized in the Ten Commandments) are consciously attacked in popular music, and music critics rush to laud the "provocative honesty" of the "artists," while all the time the "artists" are laughing. All they intended was to be outrageous and shocking in as rude a fashion as possible.

In this atmosphere, it is imperative that Christian young people be willing to be marked men and women. On the one hand, they need to temper the internal pressure to negate everything of their parents. They need to look critically and yet appreciatively at these persons who gave them life. This is surely why the fifth commandment was given in the first place. If it was the easy, natural thing to honor one's parents, no commandment would have to be given. It is because it is so easy to dishonor one's parent that a commandment was necessary. So if the Christendom of one's parents is full of inconsistencies, that does not mean the whole thing should be dispensed with. Do it better by the grace of God. Bring it back to the Bible and to the authority of God. The children of the exiles in Babylon had the opportunity to trust God in ways that would put their parents' little faith to shame, and by the grace of God they did it. Let the children of Christian parents today do the same thing and go beyond their parents' faith.

On the other hand, let Christian young people today refuse to bow to the false gods of this world just as believers did in Babylon 2,700 years ago. The meaninglessness and pointlessness of life in a world where the transcendent God has been shut out is vividly portrayed in all the media today. We are already reaping the bitter fruits of the view that this world is all there is. Can things made with human hands save us from ourselves today any more than they could then? Not in the least. So the god and goddess of unlimited sex, the god of power through wealth, the god of alcoholic gaiety, and the goddess of beauty must all be rejected by Christians today as we seek the face of the one God more than anything else. He alone can redeem us from the dungeons in which those other gods will abandon us at the end of the day.

This will require increasing courage and the willingness to be rejected and ultimately disenfranchised. Unless our society undergoes a major revival, Christians will soon be seen as the enemy of the state. But God is writing our history and no one else, so we can dare to be different, and in so doing continue to be lights for the truth so that others lost in the dark can find their way home to the Father.

Isaiah 44:23–45:13

²³ SING FOR JOY, O heavens, for the LORD has done this;
   shout aloud, O earth beneath.
Burst into song, you mountains,
   you forests and all your trees,
for the LORD has redeemed Jacob,
   he displays his glory in Israel.

²⁴ "This is what the LORD says—
   your Redeemer, who formed you in the womb:

I am the LORD,
who has made all things,
who alone stretched out the heavens,
who spread out the earth by myself,

²⁵ who foils the signs of false prophets
   and makes fools of diviners,
who overthrows the learning of the wise
   and turns it into nonsense,
²⁶ who carries out the words of his servants
   and fulfills the predictions of his messengers,

who says of Jerusalem, 'It shall be inhabited,'
   of the towns of Judah, 'They shall be built,'
   and of their ruins, 'I will restore them,'
²⁷ who says to the watery deep, 'Be dry,
   and I will dry up your streams,'
²⁸ who says of Cyrus, 'He is my shepherd
   and will accomplish all that I please;
he will say of Jerusalem, "Let it be rebuilt,"
   and of the temple, "Let its foundations be laid." '

⁴⁵:¹ "This is what the LORD says to his anointed,
   to Cyrus, whose right hand I take hold of
to subdue nations before him
   and to strip kings of their armor,
to open doors before him
   so that gates will not be shut:
² I will go before you
   and will level the mountains;

508

I will break down gates of bronze
    and cut through bars of iron.
³ I will give you the treasures of darkness,
    riches stored in secret places,
so that you may know that I am the LORD,
    the God of Israel, who summons you
            by name.
⁴ For the sake of Jacob my servant,
    of Israel my chosen,
I summon you by name
    and bestow on you a title of honor,
    though you do not acknowledge me.
⁵ I am the LORD, and there is no other;
    apart from me there is no God.
I will strengthen you,
    though you have not acknowledged me,
⁶ so that from the rising of the sun
    to the place of its setting
men may know there is none besides me.
    I am the LORD, and there is no other.
⁷ I form the light and create darkness,
    I bring prosperity and create disaster;
    I, the LORD, do all these things.

⁸ "You heavens above, rain down righteousness;
    let the clouds shower it down.
Let the earth open wide,
    let salvation spring up,
let righteousness grow with it;
    I, the LORD, have created it.

⁹ "Woe to him who quarrels with his Maker,
    to him who is but a potsherd among the potsherds
            on the ground.
Does the clay say to the potter,
    'What are you making?'
Does your work say,
    'He has no hands'?
¹⁰ Woe to him who says to his father,
    'What have you begotten?'
or to his mother,
    'What have you brought to birth?'

> [11] "This is what the LORD says—
>   the Holy One of Israel, and its Maker:
> Concerning things to come,
>   do you question me about my children,
>   or give me orders about the work of my hands?
> [12] It is I who made the earth
>   and created mankind upon it.
> My own hands stretched out the heavens;
>   I marshaled their starry hosts.
> [13] I will raise up Cyrus in my righteousness:
>   I will make all his ways straight.
> He will rebuild my city
>   and set my exiles free,
> but not for a price or reward,
>   says the LORD Almighty."

AS WITH 42:10—44:22, the next section (44:23—46:13) appears to me to be a two-part unit introduced by a call to praise, in which the plan of God involving his servants (44:23—45:13) is followed by a declaration of God's absolute superiority over the idols (45:14—46:13).[1] I will discuss the two parts separately, but I believe the basic line of thought continues throughout.

In 44:23—45:13, God reveals the name of the person who will be his "anointed" to deliver his people from the Babylonian exile. After the opening call to praise (44:23), the prophet celebrates God's power to do as he wishes, concluding with the announcement of Cyrus's name (44:24—28). Then follows God's commission to Cyrus (45:1—8). Finally, in response to an apparent challenge to the appropriateness of using a pagan in this way, God asserts that he has a perfect right to do this if he chooses (45:9—13). Han-

---

1. As noted in the comments on 42:10—43:7, the structure of this part of the book is a source of endless controversy among scholars. It is difficult to find two commentators who agree as to the precise divisions of the material. The ideas are developed in a kind of helical motion, where earlier themes reappear often with some of the same phrasings, and yet there is an advance in the thought, primarily in greater specificity. This has led some, like Schoors, *I Am God Your Saviour*, and R. Kratz, *Kyros im Deuterojesaja Buch* (FAT 1; Tübingen: Mohr Siebeck, 1991), to deny that there was any original structure but that a variety of originally independent forms have been woven together by various editorial devices and insertions. Childs, *Isaiah*, 349–50, utters an appropriate word of caution about the tendency of such an approach to make the final form of the text irrelevant.

son points out the prominence of first-person pronouns and verbs referring to God in the section.[2] Although the naming of Cyrus is the dramatic center, the passage is about God, not Cyrus.

A Call to Praise (44:23)

THIS VERSE FUNCTIONS as a transition between the former unit and the following one, just as 42:10–17 did. It is a call to praise, in which the "heavens" and the "earth," which at the beginning of the book were called to witness Israel's rebellion (1:2), are now called to rejoice over the salvation promised in 44:21–22 and revealed with more clarity in 44:24–45:7. The rest of nature ("mountains," "forests," and "trees") is then commanded to join in the song of redemption. In this visual (and auditory) way, Isaiah emphasizes again that the Creator of the world is the only One who can redeem the world. Also, nature, in whom God's creative "glory" is seen, is called upon to praise God for his greater redemptive "glory" that will be displayed "in Israel." Truly his glory fills the earth (cf. 6:3).

God's Redemptive Plans (44:24–28)

THE "REDEEMER" NOW SPELLS out in the greatest detail yet what his redemptive plans are. Here he names the "one from the east" (41:2) who will be Israel's savior. Furthermore, he specifies why Jerusalem will have good tidings to share with the surrounding towns (cf. 40:9). The man's name is "Cyrus," the Persian king who will conquer Babylon and who will see to it that Jerusalem's temple is rebuilt (44:28).

But the naming of Cyrus is only the final act in a long list. As the punctuation in the NIV shows, 44:24–28 comprises a single sentence consisting of a succession of participles that define "I am the LORD" in 44:24.[3] Here God identifies himself and demonstrates his lordship by what he does. He is the Creator, who "made" everything, stretching out "the heavens" and spreading out "the earth." He is the Lord of history (44:25–26a), revealing what he is doing to "his servants" the prophets and making "fools" of those who try to predict the future by means of magical continuities. He is the Redeemer (44:26b–28), who is able to rebuild the ruined "Jerusalem" and its surrounding

---

2. Hanson, *Isaiah 40–66*, 96. There are more than forty such occurrences here.

3. Whereas Heb. infinitives express pure undefined action ("running"), participles focus on the one performing the action, the actor ("one who is running"). Cf. B. Waltke and M. O'Connor, *An Introduction to Biblical Hebrew Syntax* (Winona Lake, Ind.: Eisenbrauns, 1990), 614–15.

towns.[4] Because he is the Creator and the Lord of history and the Redeemer, he is even able to use a pagan emperor to accomplish his purposes.

The Commission of Cyrus (45:1−8)

CYRUS NOW RECEIVES his commission from God. He is specifically said to be God's "anointed" or Messiah (45:1). The victories that will come to him will be gifts from God's hand (45:1−3). They will not be his own accomplishments but will come from God for two purposes: that Cyrus himself might know that Yahweh, "the God of Israel," is "the LORD," and that his work in history might be done "for the sake of Jacob my servant."

Twice is it said that God has called Cyrus "by name." This underlines the importance of the naming of Cyrus as an act of predictive prophecy. Isaiah has repeatedly insisted that God alone can tell the future[5] and that the attempts to do so by the devotees of the gods only make them look like "fools" (44:25). His ability to name the deliverer far in advance is the climactic demonstration of this fact. If we deny the obvious predictive claim that Isaiah of Jerusalem is making and instead posit some unknown person simply declaring after the fact that Cyrus was God's man, we have made this unknown prophet deny the very thing he claims. God has, then, *not* named the deliverer in advance and the prophet knows it. That is not great theology; it is misrepresentation of the facts.[6]

One of the evidences of God's lordship is that he knows the name of one who does not know God's name (45:4−5). Even if Cyrus has never heard of Yahweh of Israel, Yahweh knows about Cyrus even before he is born. It is neither the Persian Ahura-mazda nor the Babylonian Marduk who rules the world of time and space, but Yahweh. The statement that Cyrus will recognize this eventually is an interesting one, and depending on how the identity of Darius in the book of Daniel is resolved,[7] that book may give evidence of the realization of the promise (cf. Dan. 6:26−27). At the same time, Cyrus's

---

4. It is not clear why the drying up of the "deep" is referred to in the context of redemption. Many contemporary commentators see this as an allusion to the triumph of the "creator" god over chaos (cf. Hanson, *Isaiah 40−66*, 99−101), and that is certainly a possibility in view of the clear allusions in 27:1 and 51:9. However, there is also the possibility that the Exodus is being alluded to, and that would make more sense in the context of redemption (cf. Ex. 15:5; Ps. 106:9). So Motyer, *Prophecy of Isaiah*, 375.

5. See 41:21−24, 26−27; 43:12; 44:7, 26; see also 45:20−21; 46:10; and 48:3.

6. See Oswalt, *Isaiah 40−66*, 192, 196−97, for further discussion. See also Motyer, *Prophecy of Isaiah*, 355−56; Young, *The Book of Isaiah*, 3:192. Hanson, *Isaiah 40−66*, 98−99, offers an imaginative reconstruction of "Second Isaiah's" choice of Cyrus that ignores this issue entirely.

7. See T. Longman III, *Daniel* (NIVAC; Grand Rapids: Zondervan, 1999), 157−58.

acknowledgment that he was called by the Lord to release his people (cf. Ezra 1:2) may be as much as this statement intends for him to do.

This segment ends much as the previous one (44:23–28) began: with a declaration of the absolute uniqueness of God (45:5–8). There is none like him, and his goal is that people all over the world will recognize his uniqueness. Three different times the Lord makes the statement that there is no other god than he (45:5–6).

This is all summed up in 45:7 with its dramatic statement that nothing on earth occurs apart from him. In this assertion Isaiah is denying the pagan understanding that good and evil (or light and dark) are two eternally coexistent principles battling in the universe. There is only one first principle, and he is light and good. If darkness and evil exist, they do so because the one God permits them to exist. In that sense, he is responsible for their existence.[8]

But if the thought ended here, we might conclude that God has a kind of neutral position on the direction of the world. Verse 8 shows that is not the case. God does care passionately about the direction his creation takes. He expects that "right" (understood as an expression of his own character) will prevail and that "salvation" (in the sense of deliverance from all the effects of evil) will rule. That is what he "created" the earth for.

God As Sole Creator and Redeemer (45:9–13)

BUT DOES GOD have a right to do such a thing as he has just promised? Does he have the right to use someone who does not even know him to save his believing people? This section answers such questions. God asserts that as the sole Creator and Redeemer he does have the right to do this. Here we recall the admonition of 43:18 to forget the former things. That would not have been easy for that faithful remnant, whose very life had come to center on the study of the Scriptures (as seems to be the case during the Babylonian exile). Surely if God were going to raise up a deliverer for them, it would be someone like Moses, a man who knew and loved the Lord and through whom God could reveal himself to his people.[9]

---

8. For a good rebuttal to the idea that Persian dualism is specifically in mind here, see Motyer, *Prophecy of Isaiah*, 359. The Heb. word *ra'* is an inclusive term like the Eng. "bad"; it can range all the way from "misfortune" to "moral wickedness." The NIV "disaster" is a good attempt to catch the more general connotation here; "calamity" is another alternative. For a more detailed discussion, see Oswalt, *Isaiah 40–66*, 203–5.

9. Childs, *Isaiah*, 354, says that "a close reading does not support such a quasi-psychological interpretation" and argues that vv. 9–13 are addressed to the nations. I do not know what is meant by "quasi-psychological" in this context, but I cannot imagine any reason why

But God responds to this idea with strong words. He pronounces doom ("woe," 45:9–10) on those who challenge the rightness of his activity. He compares it to a pot criticizing the way the potter makes it, or a baby saying to its parents that it does not approve of being born in this way. We may ask why the response is so strong.

In fact, just as the predictions of the future become more specific throughout chapters 40–48, so do the challenges to the hearers. The strongest of all can be found in chapter 48. If the exiles will not let God deliver them in his own way, they have not learned the lesson of his lordship. He is still their "God in a box," to do with as they choose. So in 45:11–12 God once more asserts that he is not only Israel's "Holy One" and "Maker," but also the Maker of the whole cosmos and the Creator of all "mankind." If he does not have a right, as an expression of his own "righteousness," to set his "exiles free" (45:13) as he chooses, who does?

"I AM THE LORD." This phrase is repeated four times in the first two stanzas of this unit (44:24; 45:3, 5, 6). In one sense, the whole Bible is about humans coming to know who "the LORD" is. From the Exodus, where knowing who the Lord is was a central purpose of the plagues and Israel's deliverance, to Leviticus, where his identity is the basis of his commandments, to Kings, where Elijah demonstrates who the Lord is on Mount Carmel, to Ezekiel, where the phrase occurs more than sixty-five times, the true identity of God is central.

This phrase is complicated for us in English because it is not immediately clear to us that "the LORD" is actually an English substitution for God's personal name in Hebrew, which was probably, though not certainly, pronounced "Yahweh." So the statement is, "I am Yahweh." "I am Yahweh" suggests rulership, absolute sovereignty, and the like. But what does "you will know that I am Yahweh" mean? If we have reconstructed the name correctly, the name is a verbal sentence meaning "he causes [everything] to be." That is, he is the origin, the foundation, the basis, and the end of all things. To know that God is all these and to know that he is these things for me personally changes everything. He is not merely my Lord; he is my everything, including the next breath that I take.

---

the nations would object to the call of Cyrus to deliver people from Babylonian oppression. This is the issue, as is shown by v. 13. I would also argue that a close reading shows a more personal and direct tone than is to be found in God's addresses to the nations in this part of the book.

This is why the New Testament statement of faith is so shocking. Who is Jesus Christ? He is the "Lord" (Rom. 10:9–10)! The Old Testament said that the Hebrew people would know their God is Yahweh on the basis of his delivering them from Egypt and Babylonia (Exodus and Ezekiel) and on the basis of his moral character being worked out in their lives (Leviticus). The New Testament says the same things for every person who has ever lived when it says that we will know Jesus is Yahweh when he delivers us from our sin and plants the character of the Father in us by making the Holy Spirit available to us.

Challenge to unbelief. When we think of the sharp challenge here to those who question God's ways, we also think of Jesus' challenges to the Pharisees. Unquestionably some of the harshest words in the Bible come out of Jesus' mouth in talking to this group of people. When we think about this phenomenon, it seems a bit strange. After all, the Pharisees were some of the most devout Jews in the country. If we imagine that some of them were cold and priggishly self-righteous, we must think that there were many others who were sincerely trying to serve God with their whole hearts, such as Nicodemus and Joseph of Arimathea. The Pharisees were not like the Sadducees, who were mostly devoted to furthering their own power and positions. Oddly, as far as the Gospels are concerned, Jesus has almost nothing to say to the Sadducees.

What should we make of this phenomenon in Isaiah and Jesus? While we cannot be dogmatic, perhaps the reason is that it is precisely those who are most faithful who are in the greatest danger of "putting God in a box" and thus limiting what he can do in and through them. The flagrant sinner either ignores God altogether or in despair invites God to do "whatever" to address the crisis of his or her soul. Superficial believers have only an academic interest in God. They have been inoculated with just enough religion to ensure that they are far from contracting the real thing. But it is those who are passionate about their faith who stand in the greatest danger. They have such great possibilities, yet if they cannot break beyond the limitations that their own study and involvement have placed on them, all those possibilities will be lost.

A football coach once said to a group of us players, "If I stop yelling at any of you, start worrying, because that will mean I have given up on you." Maybe that is what is going on here and in the ministry of Jesus. Perhaps it is precisely because there are such great possibilities for either truth or error that God addresses these people so harshly and directly. They need to be shaken out of their dangerous confidence that they know the almighty Creator so well that they can tell him what he is going to do next.

MODERN PHARISEES. We as evangelical Christians need to be careful that we do not fall into the trap the Pharisees did. We also need to be careful that we do not automatically, and wrongly, exclude ourselves from that group. The law and grace debate might lead us in that direction. If we say that a Pharisee is someone who believes that he or she can make himself or herself acceptable to God by right behavior, then most of us evangelicals can immediately assume that we are not of that group. After all, we are those who follow the Reformation creed of *sola gratia*—grace alone. We know that none of us brings anything in our hands when we kneel at the cross. So that means we could not possibly be grouped with the Pharisees.

But suppose we expand the definition of "Pharisee" to those who are passionate students of Scripture, who are zealously concerned to know and please God? What then? Would not many of us fall into that category? I believe that is a more appropriate definition, at least for our purposes here. It was people who zealously studied the Scriptures who could not believe that Jesus could be the promised Messiah. It was people who wanted to please God who could not accept his friendship with notorious sinners. It was people who had almost made a life's work of studying God's ways who could not allow Jesus to deliver people in ways that seemed to violate how God was supposed to act. We may say that they had not studied the Scriptures well enough or that they were more concerned about justifying God's ways to themselves than they were about applying them to human hearts. But the question here is whether that behavior is descriptive of me and whether the strong words of Isaiah and Jesus might be directed at me.

Inclusivism. I commented in the previous unit on the pressure for tolerance in the modern world. This unit lends itself to further discussion of that point. If we were to apply today's postmodern thinking to the Judean experience in captivity, what would we have expected them to say the experience had taught them? Surely it would go like this:

1. Let us repent of our sinful idolatry in insisting that our god is the only god.
2. Let us welcome the evidence of the pervasiveness of the Divine as seen in the Babylonian religion and in the other religions we have encountered.
3. Let us admit that other expressions of faith are as good as, and in some cases better than, our narrow conceptions.
4. Let us admit that our god is nothing other than one more flawed attempt (and more flawed than most) to encapsulate the All.

But, as a matter of fact, what we get from Isaiah precisely counters that. It is:

1. Our sin is in not insisting firmly enough on God's absolute uniqueness.
2. What the Babylonians call "gods" are not gods at all; they are the product of human ingenuity applied to this world.
3. These "gods" do not know where we came from or where we are going, but ours does and he has told us!
4. Our God is *not* the All—he is distinctly Other than us and our experience.

Isaiah is concerned that the experience of the Exile will *not* make the Judeans more "inclusive." He would share that same concern for us today. This is not the time to dilute our faith and admit that other faiths "contain a lot of the truth too." Would Isaiah say that about the religion of Canaan or Babylon? No! This is not to say that every concept in the non-Christian religions is wrong or perverse. As C. S. Lewis says, if the resurrection is true, then we ought not to be surprised to find the dying and rising god motif in the pagan religions.[10] But that does not mean the fertility religions are true; it means Christianity is true! It may well mean that the proponent of the fertility religion will be better prepared to accept the truth of Christ's resurrection. But what we should never say to that person is, "See, you have a faith in resurrection, too. You are already a believer." Christians do not believe in resurrection; we believe in the resurrection *of Christ*, and there is a vast difference between the two.

This is not to say that we may therefore be rude or vicious in our contacts with persons of other faiths or of no faith. We must value them as creations of the Father and as persons for whom Christ died. The grace in which we stand gives us no grounds for feelings of superiority or for patronizing those who have not yet responded to the grace that has been extended to them. Christ's command to love our neighbors does not only apply to believing neighbors. But that command to love them does not mean that we must confirm them in the error that is destroying them. It is interesting that some of those who argue most strongly for inclusivism would be the first to argue forcefully with a cigarette smoker that what he or she is doing is deadly and should be stopped at once. So exclusivism in the realm of the physical is perfectly acceptable. It is only in the realm of the spiritual that it is seen as an expression of intolerance.

---

10. C. S. Lewis, "Myth Became Fact," in *God in the Dock: Essays on Theology and Ethics*, ed. W. Hooper (Grand Rapids: Eerdmans, 1970), 63–67.

Isaiah 45:14–46:13

〽

THIS IS WHAT the LORD says:

"The products of Egypt and the merchandise of Cush,
　and those tall Sabeans—
they will come over to you
　and will be yours;
they will trudge behind you,
　coming over to you in chains.
They will bow down before you
　and plead with you, saying,
'Surely God is with you, and there is no other;
　there is no other god.'"

[15] Truly you are a God who hides himself,
　O God and Savior of Israel.
[16] All the makers of idols will be put to shame and disgraced;
　they will go off into disgrace together.
[17] But Israel will be saved by the LORD
　with an everlasting salvation;
you will never be put to shame or disgraced,
　to ages everlasting.

[18] For this is what the LORD says—
he who created the heavens,
　he is God;
he who fashioned and made the earth,
　he founded it;
he did not create it to be empty,
　but formed it to be inhabited—
he says:
"I am the LORD,
　and there is no other.
[19] I have not spoken in secret,
　from somewhere in a land of darkness;
I have not said to Jacob's descendants,
　'Seek me in vain.'
I, the LORD, speak the truth;
　I declare what is right.

²⁰"Gather together and come;
  assemble, you fugitives from the nations.
 Ignorant are those who carry about idols of wood,
  who pray to gods that cannot save.
²¹ Declare what is to be, present it—
  let them take counsel together.
 Who foretold this long ago,
  who declared it from the distant past?
 Was it not I, the LORD?
  And there is no God apart from me,
 a righteous God and a Savior;
  there is none but me.

²² "Turn to me and be saved,
  all you ends of the earth;
  for I am God, and there is no other.
²³ By myself I have sworn,
  my mouth has uttered in all integrity
  a word that will not be revoked:
 Before me every knee will bow;
  by me every tongue will swear.
²⁴ They will say of me, 'In the LORD alone
  are righteousness and strength.'"
 All who have raged against him
  will come to him and be put to shame.
²⁵ But in the LORD all the descendants of Israel
  will be found righteous and will exult.

^{46:1} Bel bows down, Nebo stoops low;
  their idols are borne by beasts of burden.
 The images that are carried about are burdensome,
  a burden for the weary.
² They stoop and bow down together;
  unable to rescue the burden,
  they themselves go off into captivity.

³ "Listen to me, O house of Jacob,
  all you who remain of the house of Israel,
 you whom I have upheld since you were conceived,
  and have carried since your birth.
⁴ Even to your old age and gray hairs
  I am he, I am he who will sustain you.

I have made you and I will carry you;
    I will sustain you and I will rescue you.

⁵"To whom will you compare me or count me equal?
    To whom will you liken me that we may be compared?
⁶Some pour out gold from their bags
    and weigh out silver on the scales;
they hire a goldsmith to make it into a god,
    and they bow down and worship it.
⁷They lift it to their shoulders and carry it;
    they set it up in its place, and there it stands.
    From that spot it cannot move.
Though one cries out to it, it does not answer;
    it cannot save him from his troubles.

⁸"Remember this, fix it in mind,
    take it to heart, you rebels.
⁹Remember the former things, those of long ago;
    I am God, and there is no other;
    I am God, and there is none like me.
¹⁰I make known the end from the beginning,
    from ancient times, what is still to come.
I say: My purpose will stand,
    and I will do all that I please.
¹¹From the east I summon a bird of prey;
    from a far-off land, a man to fulfill my purpose.
What I have said, that will I bring about;
    what I have planned, that will I do.
¹²Listen to me, you stubborn-hearted,
    you who are far from righteousness.
¹³I am bringing my righteousness near,
    it is not far away;
    and my salvation will not be delayed.
I will grant salvation to Zion,
    my splendor to Israel.

THESE VERSES (the second part of 44:23–46:13) sum up the case for God's superiority over the idols. The first segment (45:14–25) contrasts God's ability to save with that of the idols in a general way. The second (46:1–7) continues this contrast in much more concrete imagery. In both of these the theme of "carrying" is prominent. In the final section (46:8–13), Isaiah calls on his hearers to take all this to heart and not to give up hope that God will deliver them.

God's Ability to Save (44:14–25)

THIS SEGMENT OPENS with a picture of people from the ends of the earth[1] coming humbly to Israel, admitting that Israel's God is the only God (45:14). The next three verses offer some reflection on this picture. The gods of the idol makers will fail them and leave them in "disgrace" as they "go off" into captivity (45:16). But God's people will not be "disgraced," for the opposite thing will happen to them: They will be "saved" from captivity (45:17).

Verses 18–19 give the reason why this affirmation can be made: God is the sole Creator of the universe, and he created it for a purpose. That purpose, as revealed in his promises to "Jacob's descendants," is a saving one. Though he may be hidden in his transcendent essence (cf. 45:15), he is anything but hidden in his desire for relationship with his human creatures. He has revealed this desire as he has "spoken" to them again and again, inviting them to "seek" him (45:19).[2]

After this introduction, the idol makers are once more called to present themselves before God (45:20). But their description here is unusual. They are the "fugitives from the nations" (as in 45:14). In other words, the discussion has proceeded to the point where the idols are now seen as having failed, and their worshipers know this. So they come into the assembly carrying their useless images. In 45:21 the Lord once again asks who predicted this situation, and the answer is that he alone has done so. Thus, he is the only God.

What follows next is surprising. We might expect words of judgment, as in 44:9–20, but instead we have an invitation to these people from the "ends of the earth" to "turn" to the Lord "and be saved." This expresses God's

---

1. In this case "Cush" (Ethiopia), considered at the time to be the southern end of the earth, represents all the most distant places of earth.

2. It seems likely that Isaiah is consciously contrasting the Hebrew understanding of creation with that of the pagans. The pagans believed that "chaos" (45:18; NIV "empty," Heb. *tohu*) was the first principle from which the gods emerged and that humans were created as an afterthought to serve the gods.

ultimate purpose in the conflict with the idols. He does not want to destroy the idol makers but to save them. As with Israel, his ultimate purpose in judgment is not destruction but redemption. If he is the only God, then he is also the only Savior. And if he created the world and humanity in it for good, then he is the One to whom all persons must eventually turn if they are to realize the purpose of their lives. But, as Childs remarks,[3] this is not a blanket offer of universal salvation. There are those who accept God's offer and come, and there are those who refuse to come. "Shame" and defeat will be the lot of the latter.

Illustration of God As the Only Savior (46:1–7)

THE THEME OF God as the only Savior is now graphically illustrated. Those who have depended on the Babylonian gods "Bel" and "Nebo" load their idol gods onto oxcarts, to be "carried" off "into captivity" (46:1–2). The worshipers, instead of being saved by their gods, have to save the gods! In an especially poignant rejoinder, God reminds his people that he is the One who has "carried" (46:3) them ever since their conception in the womb, and he promises to continue to carry them through their "old age" (46:4). He is their Maker and will carry them.

The alternative is spelled out in 46:5–7. If people choose to make their own gods, they will have to carry what they have made. When they put the god down, it will not move an inch from where it is put. Would we compare the Maker and only Savior of the world to that? Surely not!

Final Appeal to Idol Worshipers (46:8–13)

THESE VERSES CONSTITUTE the final summation and appeal in the disputation with the idols. The case has been presented several times, moving from the inability of the idols to explain the past or tell the future to their inability to save those who worship them.[4] Now God calls on his people to make their decision. Will they give up their ancient biblical faith and be sucked down into the "black hole" of paganism, or will they refuse to succumb to their sense of discouragement and despair and instead reaffirm their confident hope in God and in his promises to deliver them?

They are to remember that in "former" times God predicted what is taking place at this moment and that he has kept his promises in the past. Cyrus, "the bird of prey" coming "from the east," will arrive in direct fulfillment of the prediction and purpose of God. These things show that Yahweh is God

---

3. Childs, *Isaiah*, 356.
4. See 40:25–26; 41:6–7, 21–29; 43:8–13; 44:9–20; 45:20–21; 46:1–7.

alone and that "there is none like" him. The issue now is whether the exiles will believe it and keep their faith through forty-five dark, uncertain years so that when Cyrus is revealed, there will still be a remnant who can reach out and take hold of God's hand. God's "righteousness" in keeping his promises is about to be revealed. At that time will there be any left who have been righteous (done the right thing) by believing God (cf. Gen. 15:6)?

Bridging Contexts

THE ONLY SAVIOR OF THE WORLD. Isaiah 45:22–25 reminds us of the New Testament appropriation of the Saviorhood of God. Paul says of Jesus the very things that are said of Yahweh here, that every knee will bow and every tongue will swear allegiance to him (Phil. 2:10–11). How can Paul say such a thing? It is because he has become convinced that Jesus is the way in which God will manifest his world-saving power. It is in and through Jesus Christ that persons will be able to say that "in the LORD alone are righteousness and strength" (Isa. 45:24).

The identity of Yahweh and Jesus was the core of Paul's preaching immediately after his conversion (Acts 9:20) and continued to be at the heart of his thought for the rest of his life (cf., e.g., Titus 2:13; 2 Tim. 4:1). That he applies this passage, with its strong affirmation, "I am God, and there is no other" (Isa. 45:22), to Christ is a clear indication of how deeply the truth of Jesus' deity grasped him.

It is sometimes argued that the missionary thrust of Christianity has been imposed on the more ethnically based Old Testament faith. To be sure, that faith is ethnically based. That was the only way to ensure that it was passed on effectively from one generation to another. This is why Moses was so insistent that the Torah of God be taught to one's children and lived out and reflected upon in their presence on a daily basis (Deut. 6:6–9). But from the outset, it was not exclusively ethnic. The place of the foreigner or alien was a special one in the Israelite community. Any "strangers" who wished to join the community could do so if they took on themselves the obligations of Torah. For males this meant circumcision, but females were welcome too, as the book of Ruth demonstrates.

Solomon's dedicatory prayer for the temple shows this same truth. That building was to be a house of prayer for all nations. The statements of Isaiah and Micah about all the nations coming to Jerusalem to learn Torah carry this idea forward (2:1–4; Mic. 4:1–3). And while it is possible that Jesus' remark about the Pharisees going around the world to make one proselyte may denote their attempt to recruit other Jews to the outlook of the Pharisees, it may also refer to an attempt to bring Gentiles into the Jewish faith.

Thus, although the Old Testament faith was ethnically based, it was by no means exclusively so.

The arguments we have seen in the last several chapters of Isaiah help us to see why this worldwide outreach of biblical religion would come to pass. If indeed Yahweh is the only God of the whole world and its sole Creator, if Yahweh created the world in order to engage humans in a relationship of blessing with himself, and if the entire human race has been corrupted by sin, it follows that there is only one Being who can restore humans to that original purpose: Yahweh. Thus, not only is he Israel's only Savior, he is the world's only Savior. In other words, God's purposes are not for Israel alone; they are for the whole world, and Israel has been chosen to be the means whereby those purposes are realized.

The new thought that Christianity introduced was that it was no longer necessary to be incorporated into the ethnic community in order to have a relationship with God. Rather, it is possible to meet him directly in Jesus Christ. While the principles taught in the Torah remain in force for the believer in Christ, its specific practices have been shown to be external forms not essential to the truth being taught. But at its heart, the motivation that impels Christians to go to the ends of the earth is an Old Testament one: There is only one God, and that means there is only one Savior. It is for him that all the ends of the earth wait. In these last days the Savior has been manifested as the Son of God; in him we see the image of the invisible God.

THE BURDEN OF THE GODS. Few in the Western world have idols that they carry with them from place to place (although one wonders what Isaiah's response might be to processions of saints and icons). If we may regret the artistic loss when Protestant Reformers smashed statues and stained glass, we may still recognize a similar impulse in the Old Testament prophets. But does this passage speak to us at all? It certainly does, because many contemporary persons are carrying a whole host of gods, and the burden is killing them.

I am referring to all the things that have come to replace God in our lives—perhaps a job, a house, a car, a love relationship, or even one's self-image. The pagans personalized all these, but they were seeking in the gods what we seek in these. These are the things that give us our sense of identity and meaning in life. Yet many of us are suffering from burnout or breakdown because we have all these things to carry and they have become too much for us. We need them for what they do for us, but the burdens they impose are devastatingly heavy. Instead of our using them, they use us, and the results are all around us. To escape them, we must have increasingly stimulating and exciting diversions, but then the diversions themselves become a burden.

Isaiah's answer to such contemporary problems is the same as it was 2,700 years ago. We must stop carrying those things and let the One who is in fact carrying us anyway do it for us. The issue is whether we are willing to entrust all those aspects of our lives that we feel are so necessary to us into God's hands. If we are not willing, we effectively make them idols and try to use them to provide things they cannot.

Meaning, purpose, identity, and fulfillment are ultimately only things God can provide. We truly begin to experience God's carrying of us when we take our hands off these things and relinquish them into God's hands. And why should we not? The reason is that we are afraid—afraid that God will do a worse job of directing our lives than we are able to do. On the surface of it, that is a ridiculous thought, but it is the fact. Until we are willing to do what the remnant did during the Exile and release our survival into God's hands, we are allowing our fears to keep us from knowing God's care and deliverance.

The righteousness of faith. The word "righteousness" is prominent in this section, occurring twice in 45:24–25 and twice in 46:12–13. In each case the Lord's righteousness and human righteousness are paralleled. In the first passage, we are told that righteousness is in the Lord and that in the Lord the descendants of Israel will be found righteous. In the second passage, God says his people are far from righteousness, but his righteousness is about to be revealed.

What is at stake here? First of all, it must be said that it is not incorrect to equate deliverance here with God's righteousness.[5] He is "right" to deliver his people even though they have sinned, because such an act is an expression of his gracious nature. But to say that the righteousness of the people is their deliverance seems more questionable. Rather, Isaiah is saying that just as God can act righteously in delivering his people, we can also act righteously. But what is that act in this context and in ours? I believe it is analogous to what Abraham did in Canaan when he believed the incredible promises of God and was accounted as righteous (Gen. 15:6). That is, Abraham did the one right thing a human can do: He believed God. That is what the exiles will be called upon to do—to believe God's promises and thus not cast away their faith. According to 46:12 they are in danger of doing that very thing. They "are far from righteousness." But in God they can "be found righteous" if they will believe what he says (45:25).

---

5. Note that in the NRSV, only the first of these four occurrences is translated with "righteousness"; the others are translated "triumph" (45:25) and "deliverance" (46:12, 13).

The application for us today is first of all in relationship to Christ. Paul tells us that we too can be accounted "right" if we believe God's promise that eternal life is to be found in Christ. If we seek to be right with God by doing right things, we only condemn ourselves to separation from him, because we are then saying that he is wrong in calling us hopelessly sinful in everything we do. We are not believing in his promises, we are believing in ourselves, and that is not "right." But when we agree with God when he says we are hopelessly lost, and when we believe his statement that in Christ all our sins have been forgiven, then we are "right" with God.

But this "righteousness" is also an ongoing life of faith. When we are faced with an impossible obstacle and we turn to God, believing that he will carry us through it or around it or over it, we are doing the "right" thing. To try to surmount it in our own strength or to allow it to defeat us is definitely not "right," because God's intention is that we should be "more than conquerors." So the life of faith is the life of righteousness. And as we live in constant surrender to God and trust in his promises, we will discover his plan of transformation for us, so that our behavior is more and more like his—righteous.

Isaiah 47:1–15

1 "GO DOWN, SIT In the dust,
     Virgin Daughter of Babylon;
 sit on the ground without a throne,
     Daughter of the Babylonians.
 No more will you be called
     tender or delicate.
2 Take millstones and grind flour;
     take off your veil.
 Lift up your skirts, bare your legs,
     and wade through the streams.
3 Your nakedness will be exposed
     and your shame uncovered.
 I will take vengeance;
     I will spare no one."

4 Our Redeemer—the LORD Almighty is his name—
     is the Holy One of Israel.

5 "Sit in silence, go into darkness,
     Daughter of the Babylonians;
 no more will you be called
     queen of kingdoms.
6 I was angry with my people
     and desecrated my inheritance;
 I gave them into your hand,
     and you showed them no mercy.
 Even on the aged
     you laid a very heavy yoke.
7 You said, 'I will continue forever—
     the eternal queen!'
 But you did not consider these things
     or reflect on what might happen.

8 "Now then, listen, you wanton creature,
     lounging in your security
 and saying to yourself,
     'I am, and there is none besides me.
 I will never be a widow
     or suffer the loss of children.'

⁹Both of these will overtake you
   in a moment, on a single day:
   loss of children and widowhood.
They will come upon you in full measure,
   in spite of your many sorceries
   and all your potent spells.
¹⁰You have trusted in your wickedness
   and have said, 'No one sees me.'
Your wisdom and knowledge mislead you
   when you say to yourself,
   'I am, and there is none besides me.'
¹¹Disaster will come upon you,
   and you will not know how to conjure it away.
A calamity will fall upon you
   that you cannot ward off with a ransom;
a catastrophe you cannot foresee
   will suddenly come upon you.

¹²"Keep on, then, with your magic spells
   and with your many sorceries,
   which you have labored at since childhood.
Perhaps you will succeed,
   perhaps you will cause terror.
¹³All the counsel you have received has only worn you out!
   Let your astrologers come forward,
those stargazers who make predictions month by month,
   let them save you from what is coming upon you.
¹⁴Surely they are like stubble;
   the fire will burn them up.
They cannot even save themselves
   from the power of the flame.
Here are no coals to warm anyone;
   here is no fire to sit by.
¹⁵That is all they can do for you—
   these you have labored with
   and trafficked with since childhood.
Each of them goes on in his error;
   there is not one that can save you.

ISAIAH 47–48 SHOULD be considered together as two sides of the final conclusion of chapters 40–48.[1] If God is to keep his promises, two things must happen: Babylon must fall (ch. 47), and the exiled people must listen to God and believe him so that when Babylon does fall and they have the opportunity to return home, they will dare to act on the opportunity (ch. 48).

Most commentators consider chapter 47 to be a self-contained poem constructed on the model of the oracles against the nations.[2] With relentless vigor it declares the fall of proud Babylon. It makes its point in three stanzas: Babylon's humiliation (vv. 1–4), Babylon's false pride (vv. 5–11), and Babylon's helplessness (vv. 12–17).[3] The central issue in the poem is the humiliation of Babylon and her inability to do anything about it. Ultimately, then, the issue is pride, the same issue dealt with in regard to the nations in the earlier part of the book.[4] Can any of the nations of earth compare to Israel's Holy One? Once again, the answer is a resounding no.

Babylon's Humiliation (47:1–4)

BABYLON WAS THE queen of the world, the mightiest of the mighty, but she will soon meet one mightier than she, who says that she must leave her "throne" and "sit on the ground" (47:1). Although she is beautiful and "delicate," like a "virgin daughter" of kings, she will be forced to do menial labor (47:2). More than that, she will be sexually humiliated. This language is used elsewhere in the Old Testament to describe being taken into exile (cf. 20:4) and to refer to nations who have allied themselves with other nations being failed or mistreated by those allies.[5]

Babylon had been on the mistreating end of that relationship for a long time, but the time is coming when she will experience what she has meted

---

1. In agreement with Motyer, *Prophecy of Isaiah*, 371, and differing from my earlier proposal in *Isaiah 40–66*, 17, 190, where I saw ch. 47 as the conclusion of the unit beginning at 44:23.

2. See, e.g., Westermann, *Isaiah 40–66*, 188–89.

3. The NIV essentially agrees with this structure, although it has divided vv. 5–11 into vv. 5–7 and vv. 8–11. Motyer, *Prophecy of Isaiah*, 371, argues for vv. 1–7, 8–11, 12–15. Childs, *Isaiah*, 365–66, noting considerable variation among scholars, cautiously decides for the structure advocated here.

4. For a study of the similarities and dissimilarities between chs. 14 and 47, see Chris Franke, "The Function of the Oracles against Babylon in Isaiah 14 and 47" (SBLSP 32; Atlanta: Scholars Press, 1993), 250–59.

5. Isa. 57:8; Lam. 1:8; Ezek. 16:37; Mic. 1:11; Nah. 3:5.

out to others. This introductory stanza is brought to a conclusion with an ejaculation of praise to the One who is bringing all this to pass, "the Holy One of Israel." He may not have seemed much to great Babylon, but he is "Yahweh of Heaven's Armies" (NIV "LORD Almighty"), and in any contest for greatness with him, Babylon does not have a chance.

Babylon's False Pride (47:5–11)

THE BABYLONIANS THOUGHT that they could do whatever they wanted to captive nations (47:6), because there was no one greater than they. They made the fatal error of thinking that they were self-existent and self-perpetuating: "I am, and there is none besides me" (47:8, 10). It never occurred to them that they might be the agents of One infinitely greater than they who will hold them to account for their actions (47:7). But there is such a Person (cf. 43:10; 44:6; 45:5, 21; 46:8), and for Babylon to have tried to usurp his prerogatives was a deadly mistake.

Part of the deadliness of that mistake is complacency. Queen Babylon is so convinced of her ascendancy that she cannot imagine herself as a widow bereft of children (47:8–9). Her complacency robs her of that beneficial self-criticism that asks whether what we are doing may reap bad consequences. Babylon has none of that, so that "wickedness" runs rampant (47:10). Part of that wickedness is the attempt to control the spirit world through magic "spells" and "sorceries" (47:9–11). The Babylonians were intelligent and devoted that intelligence to mastering magical arts, so they are sure that they can ward off any "calamity" that threatens them. They do not reckon with a God who is beyond all magical manipulation, who is complete in himself, and who knows nothing of fate or destiny (cf. 65:11).

Babylon's Helplessness (47:12–15)

THIS FINAL STANZA expands on the last thought of the previous one. On a sarcastic note, the prophet tells Babylon to go ahead with her magic. Maybe it will work out after all (47:12)! But of course, it is futile. All the energy expended to divine the future and control its events has been wasted (47:13). What the sorcerers have set in motion is like a fire that does no one any good; it will only burn up those who started it (47:14). Babylon has done business with these sorcerers and magicians for years. But in the final crisis, they will abandon the city to go their own way.[6]

---

6. Lit., "stray off to his own region"—probably the equivalent of the modern "every man for himself."

THE BUSINESS OF MAGIC and divination was big business in Babylon. There were classes of priests whose business was to read the significance for the future of the shape of a sacrificial animal's entrails. These omens were carefully cataloged and recorded; their official listing ran to more than seventy tablets. When we think of the tremendous effort that went into compiling and categorizing these, we get some idea of what Isaiah is talking about. But along with that work we can only imagine what effort was required to get proficient in the interpretation of the omens and in remembering where in the tablets a given phenomenon was discussed. By comparison, it makes the acquisition of a Ph.D. degree today look a little less daunting. At the same time, one would have to gain great skill in obfuscation and nuancing in order to cover the 51 percent of the time when one's prognostications would be wrong.

The same kind of incredible effort went into the study of the horoscope. How much time must have been spent staring into the night sky in order to find some coordination between the placement of the stars and current events. Along with that went the effort of cataloging and categorizing all those observations so that they would have some utility for those who would try to make use of them to tell the kings and rulers whether to undertake certain activities. In some ways, they would have been better off if they had not had so much intelligence. They would not have been able to find all the spurious connections that gave them the illusion of being able to control the fates that ruled their lives.

The amazing fact is that the horoscope still is functional today. People who deny that Jesus ever did a miracle will open the newspaper to the horoscope every day. This is nothing other than a continuation of that failed Babylonian wisdom. The organization of the sky is according to the Babylonian system, and the names of the signs of the zodiac are Greek versions of the Babylonian names. How much effort goes into saying something each day that gives the illusion of meaning while being so vague and general that it can cover anything that happens!

What is its attraction? The same attraction that it has had for five thousand years. I can get control of my life by getting a glimpse of what is fated to occur today. God asks me to surrender my life and my future into his hands for his direction, multiplication, and blessing, but we humans would rather not surrender. We would rather apply our formidable intelligence to getting control of the world for ourselves.

THE STATEMENT THAT Babylon's wisdom and knowledge misled them has haunting applications to the present. We can think of Germany and Japan, two of the most brilliant and energetic peoples on the earth. Where had their wisdom and knowledge led them in 1945? Into ruin. Think of how much of the world's resources were consumed in destruction between 1914 and 1945. Think of how many brilliant minds were consumed in finding more efficient ways to kill people. And think of how many brilliant and creative minds were destroyed by the engines of war.

But even in peace, intelligence not surrendered to God can be a terrible curse for the human race. Harry Emerson Fosdick's maxim "rich in things and poor in soul" continues to define us all too well. Our tremendous intelligence is, as it was for the Babylonians, aimed at making ourselves self-existent and self-perpetuating. What will cloning mean in a world where researchers have long ago denied any overarching ethical accountability that is incumbent on all people?

In an interview on National Public Radio persons advocating fetal-tissue research admitted that there are ethical issues but focused completely on the political tactics that would be necessary to get federal funding for the research. Not once did they discuss the ethics of killing the weak in order to indefinitely preserve the life of the strong.[7] Their argument was simply that since we now have the technology do this sort of thing, we must. Our wisdom and knowledge have misled us. How long will it be before the Redeemer, whose name is Yahweh of Heaven's Armies, the Holy One of Israel, tells us to get off our throne and to take our place in the dust?

---

7. The interview occurred on *Morning Edition*, June 22, 2001.

Isaiah 48:1–22

¹ "LISTEN TO THIS, O house of Jacob,
  you who are called by the name of Israel
  and come from the line of Judah,
you who take oaths in the name of the LORD
  and invoke the God of Israel—
  but not in truth or righteousness—
² you who call yourselves citizens of the holy city
  and rely on the God of Israel—
  the LORD Almighty is his name:
³ I foretold the former things long ago,
  my mouth announced them and I made them known;
  then suddenly I acted, and they came to pass.
⁴ For I knew how stubborn you were;
  the sinews of your neck were iron,
  your forehead was bronze.
⁵ Therefore I told you these things long ago;
  before they happened I announced them to you
so that you could not say,
  'My idols did them;
  my wooden image and metal god ordained them.'
⁶ You have heard these things; look at them all.
  Will you not admit them?

 "From now on I will tell you of new things,
  of hidden things unknown to you.
⁷ They are created now, and not long ago;
  you have not heard of them before today.
So you cannot say,
  'Yes, I knew of them.'
⁸ You have neither heard nor understood;
  from of old your ear has not been open.
Well do I know how treacherous you are;
  you were called a rebel from birth.
⁹ For my own name's sake I delay my wrath;
  for the sake of my praise I hold it back from you,
  so as not to cut you off.
¹⁰ See, I have refined you, though not as silver;
  I have tested you in the furnace of affliction.

¹¹ For my own sake, for my own sake, I do this.
How can I let myself be defamed?
I will not yield my glory to another.

¹² "Listen to me, O Jacob,
Israel, whom I have called:
I am he;
I am the first and I am the last.
¹³ My own hand laid the foundations of the earth,
and my right hand spread out the heavens;
when I summon them,
they all stand up together.

¹⁴ "Come together, all of you, and listen:
Which of the idols has foretold these things?
The LORD's chosen ally
will carry out his purpose against Babylon;
his arm will be against the Babylonians.
¹⁵ I, even I, have spoken;
yes, I have called him.
I will bring him,
and he will succeed in his mission.

¹⁶ "Come near me and listen to this:

"From the first announcement I have not spoken in secret;
at the time it happens, I am there."

And now the Sovereign LORD has sent me,
with his Spirit.

¹⁷ This is what the LORD says—
your Redeemer, the Holy One of Israel:
"I am the LORD your God,
who teaches you what is best for you,
who directs you in the way you should go.
¹⁸ If only you had paid attention to my commands,
your peace would have been like a river,
your righteousness like the waves of the sea.
¹⁹ Your descendants would have been like the sand,
your children like its numberless grains;
their name would never be cut off
nor destroyed from before me."

²⁰ Leave Babylon,
flee from the Babylonians!

Announce this with shouts of joy
   and proclaim it.
Send it out to the ends of the earth;
   say, "The LORD has redeemed his servant Jacob."
²¹ They did not thirst when he led them through the deserts;
   he made water flow for them from the rock;
he split the rock
   and water gushed out.

²²"There is no peace," says the LORD, "for the wicked."

AS WE HAVE noted earlier, chapters 40–55 deal primarily with two questions that the exiles would be asking, which were two phases of a single larger question: Does not the fact of the Exile prove that God has been defeated? Either he has been defeated by the Babylonian gods, or he has been defeated by our sin. While both issues are addressed in chapters 41–47, the primary focus is on demonstrating that the gods have not defeated God in the slightest degree. With the announcement of judgment on Babylon, that argument has come to its climax. But will the exiles believe the promises that have been given to them, or will they give up their faith along the way so that when the prophecies of deliverance are fulfilled, there will be none left to act on them?

Clearly, Isaiah, looking at his own experience (cf. 48:8), sees that as a real possibility. So this chapter is a stirring call to faith. Words for hearing occur ten times in this chapter as the prophet reminds the people that it is because they have not listened in the past that they are in their present condition; he then admonishes them to listen to the promises now that they are in exile.

Opening Words (48:1–2)

THESE TWO VERSES are strongly negative. The people identify themselves as the descendants of "Jacob" and as being "from the line of Judah." They consider themselves to be God's people. But Isaiah says that is not so. While he does not explain why he says this here, 48:4 and 8 do. They have not been obedient people; rather, they have been stubborn and rebellious. They have a name, but their behavior has shown that they do not have a relationship.[1]

---

1. B. Duhm advocated removing part or all of this chapter from the work of "Second Isaiah," because he felt it was inconsistent with the note of grace that he believed was characteristic of this author. However, careful reading shows that admonition is inherent in the material now comprising chs. 40–48 and that this chapter is simply the climax of that admonition.

The Nature of Israel's God (48:3–11)

AFTER THE ATTENTION-GRABBING opening words, God sums up his claim to be an entirely different order of being than the gods. He begins by referring to the past. The people have heard all the predictions God has made, and they know all his predictions have come true (48:3). He made the predictions precisely so that when the events occurred, it would be impossible to say that some idol god performed the actions (48:4–5). In 48:6a, Isaiah calls the people to "admit" the truth of their experience and to draw the appropriate conclusions from that experience.

Then in 48:6b, the prophet turns to the future. He will predict new things that have not been heard before. What these things are, are not specified, and indeed that is not the point of the statement.[2] The point is that God can do new things, something the idols cannot do. He is the Creator and can therefore say and do things that have never happened before. He is doing this precisely so that no one can "defame" him by comparing him to an idol and so that no idol may share his "glory" (48:11).[3]

God's Appeal to His People (48:12–22)

THESE VERSES SHARPEN God's appeal to his people. Three times they are commanded to listen (48:12, 14, 16). As with a number of Hebrew words, the word *šamaʿ* ("listen") does not permit a separation between perception and action. Thus, if you truly "hear" an admonition, you will obey it. If you do not obey it, then you evidently did not "hear" it. Here, then, if God's people "listen" to what God says, they will believe his words and act accordingly. They will retain their faith in him in spite of adverse circumstances, will be ready to leave the known in Babylon, and will take the risk of the unknown in returning to Judah when the time comes.

Verses 12–16 recap the reasons why the people should listen to (and put their faith in) God. He is the sole Creator (vv. 12–13), before everything and after everything. He is the Lord of history (vv. 14–15). Just as he summons the stars of the heavens and they obey (v. 13), so he can also summon a Persian emperor, who will do what God has purposed all along (v. 14). No idol can predict such a thing in advance as God has because they are captive to the cycles of time and fate. They can only do what they have always done.

---

2. Motyer, *Prophecy of Isaiah*, 377, and Young, *The Book of Isaiah*, 3:251, both take these "new things" to be the way in which God will deal with human sin through his Servant. Since that is the theme of chs. 49–55, this is a plausible suggestion.

3. For a discussion of the implications of this chapter for the authorship of the book, see Oswalt, *Isaiah 40–66*, 270–72.

Neither do they have any overarching purpose for human experience. So they cannot possibly do what God has done in foretelling a hitherto unheard of thing and in bringing it to pass.

The challenge to hear is summed up in 48:16 with a reiteration of the claim that God is the speaking God. From the beginning of time God has spoken in terms that are intelligible to humans. He has not hidden himself in the babble of diviners and mediums (8:19–20; 29:4) but has used ordinary, straightforward language (45:19). He has done this by inspiring persons with his "Spirit" so that their own words became the very words of God.[4] If God has spoken, surely humans should listen.

Verses 17–22 sum up everything that has been said in the chapter and, in some ways, in the entire subdivision (chs. 40–48). In keeping with this idea of summation, verse 17 identifies God by a group of his names and titles: "the LORD ... your Redeemer, the Holy One of Israel," and "your God." The last three of these denote the special relationship of God to Israel. Not only is he the speaking God, but he is also the God of grace and love. He cares deeply about the choices we make and the directions our lives take. So he has made his will known to Israel and called them to follow it. If they had "paid attention" (cf. 28:23; 32:3) in the past, none of the tragedies that are to befall them in the Exile would have occurred. Instead, all the promises that God had made to them would have been fulfilled (48:18–19).

But even though they did not listen in the past, that does not mean God has been defeated by their sin and has given up on them. If they will believe God now, they can be delivered from Babylon, into which their deaf ears and hardened hearts have delivered them. For the One who created the earth is capable of redeeming those whom he has created. In the world of the gods, the world of continuity, where all things are as they have always been, ruled by inexorable fate, there is no possibility of redemption. The gods cannot change anything. But God's creation is not a world of continuity. Just because no one had ever gone home from exile before does not mean it cannot happen. The Creator can break in and make "water flow" from rocks if he chooses.

---

4. The final sentence of v. 16 has been a puzzle to commentators because the antecedent of the pronoun "me" is not clear. In the first two sentences, the speaker is clearly God, but it is equally clear that cannot be the case in the last sentence. The reference to the Spirit has led several commentators (including Delitzsch, Young, and Motyer) to conclude that the Messiah is being referred to, since the Spirit is associated with the Messiah in several places in the book (cf. 11:2; 42:1; 61:1). However, apart from that point, there is nothing else to indicate the Messiah is the referent here. I believe (with Calvin) that "me" refers to the prophet. He is saying that God has spoken in the past and is continuing to do so right up to the present through the prophet himself.

The allusion to the Exodus is clear here. What he has done in the past shows that he can be equally creative to redeem his people again. "Announce this with shouts of joy!" But joy is not the final note here. As always in this book (cf. ch. 5; 25:10–12; etc.), the prophet is careful not to let the wonderful promises of the future delude his hearers into believing that they can leave their present condition unaddressed (48:22). If they persist in wickedness, none of these promises are for them. They must change their way of responding if they are to have a part in the coming joy.

THE NATURE OF REBELLION. From beginning (1:2) to end (66:24) the book of Isaiah is addressing rebellion. That is entirely appropriate, for the Bible as a whole does the same thing. Rebellion is the refusal to "stay within the lines," which is just what Adam and Eve did in Eden (Gen. 2–3). That kind of behavior is what is being talked about in Revelation 21:8 and 22:18–19. God has created us to live in certain ways, and refusal to do so results in disaster.

The word "refusal" is important in all this. Rebellion is not an ignorant missing of God's ways. It is an intentional and deliberate refusal to do what we know we should, and beneath that is the rejection of a relationship of dependence that acknowledges God has the right to declare what is right and wrong for us. This is a part of the significance of the Sinai covenant. As humans we are in a de facto relation of dependence on our Creator (cf. Rom. 1:18–23). But God clearly desires our relationship with him to be personal and not merely de facto. The theme of "dwelling in your midst" (cf. Num. 5:3) that ultimately issues in "remain in me" (John 15:7) shows this. In other words, the covenant puts the whole element of obedience and dependence squarely in the relational arena.

Thus, what the Hebrews did when they rebelled against God was not just disobedience, but, as it is defined here (48:8), "treachery," a breaking of faith. God never intends for our lives to be shaped by conformity to a list of abstract rules. Rather, he intends for them to be shaped by a joyous pursuit of greater and greater likeness to the character of our covenant Lord, our Father.

So in the end "rebellion," "stubbornness," and "treachery" are what sin is all about. It is entirely appropriate that Christ should have been betrayed by one of his own disciples, because that is what God's family have been doing to him since the dawn of time. We have not just accidentally fallen into a ditch. Instead, like the two-year-old who has been told not to go down a steep stairway alone and who looks to make sure that he is being watched and then starts down the stairs, we have consciously and willfully chosen to walk in the ditch.

The importance of revelation. Central to this chapter is the idea that God has revealed himself, the nature of reality, and his will for human behavior. He has spoken. If this premise is wrong, then it is not merely this chapter that must be discarded; the Bible and the whole structure of Christian faith will go with it. After all, the idea of revelation, namely, that God has spoken to us, is at the center of the biblical claims.

This is as it should be, given the doctrine of transcendence. If God is truly other than creation, then it is impossible for us who are a part of creation to know him in any ultimate way through creation. Certainly, as Psalm 19 tells us, creation can tell us some things about the Creator (Ps. 19:1–6). But if we are to know his true character, nature, and will, he will have to communicate those things to us in ways that are intelligible to us, and that means language (19:7–14). Thus, if the Bible is not an inspired record of the speech of God and the implications of that speech but only one more attempt to express human groping for the ultimate, it is both deceptive and wrong.

One evidence that the Bible does indeed stem ultimately from God is the worldview of transcendence and the concepts that flow from it. If the transcendent God did not himself explain reality in this way, it would be impossible to explain where these ideas, such as monotheism and the prohibition of idolatry, have come from. In recent years the Bible's uniqueness and the uniqueness of its view of God have come under concerted attack. In part this attack was deserved, since advocates for uniqueness have sometimes made claims that were excessive. However, the attackers have gone too far in the opposite direction.

One example is the work of Mark Smith, who argues that the religion of Yahweh is an evolutionary development from Canaanite theology.[5] He bases his conclusions on certain similarities, both in language and practice, between Yahwism and the Canaanite theology. But he does not pay adequate attention to the radical differences between the end results of the two faiths. This is a bit like showing that dogs and humans share many features and then asserting that there is no essential difference between humans and dogs.

This claim to revelation means that in the end the Christian faith cannot coexist with other religions as one more way of thinking about God. If God is the only Creator, who has revealed himself uniquely to Israel and whose revelation culminated in Jesus Christ, then Jesus is the only means of access to God. This is, of course, what the Bible claims. If those claims are not correct, then Christian faith is simply wrong from top to bottom.

---

5. M. Smith, *The Early History of God: Yahweh and the Other Deities in Ancient Israel* (San Francisco: Harper & Row, 1990).

C. S. Lewis made the point in a well-known statement: "A man who was merely a man and said the sort of things that Jesus said would not be a great moral teacher. He would either be a lunatic—on a level with a man who says he is poached egg—or else he would be the Devil of Hell."[6] We cannot have his teachings without his deity. Either he is who he is claimed to be by the Scripture, speaking to us as the Creator of the world, first and last, covenant Lord and Holy One, the only Redeemer, or we are living a delusion. There is no middle ground. If the Bible is not finally the speech of God, then the faith it proclaims must be discarded, for it will not live alongside the other view. Either the world is an effusion of the divine, or the Holy One of Israel is the world's Creator. Both ideas cannot be so, and if the former is so, then deity only "speaks" from within us. There is no god to speak to us from beyond ourselves because in the end there is nothing beyond ourselves.

The exercise of faith. Paul says that faith comes by the hearing of the Word (Rom. 10:17). In a real sense that is what Isaiah is saying as well. Faith is an obedient response to revelation. It is to "hear" God's Word in the active sense described above. It is not merely to hear and do nothing. In the end, that is rebellion. Rather, it is to hear and to take action on what is said. Thus, it is wrong to describe faith as merely a set of beliefs. That is not one's faith. The devils, we are told, "believe" in God (James 2:19). They know intellectually that God exists. They even know what is said in his Word, because the demons recognized that Jesus was the promised Messiah (Luke 4:34). They have an orthodox set of beliefs, but they have no faith.

On the other hand, faith is not what is today referred to as "spirituality," that is, a loosely defined set of mystical emotions and experiences. To disconnect one's intellect and will from one's perceptions in an attempt to participate in the divine is not faith. In fact, it may be the furthest thing from faith, for it involves no obedience to an imperative Word from beyond ourselves. Rather, it seeks to avoid the reality of the distinction between creature and Creator and to find a way into the divine that demands no obedience at all. That way lies disaster, for what we will be absorbed into is not God, but that whole set of his creatures who have also tried to find an access to his power and being without obedience.

No, to have faith is to truly hear a word of invitation, of hope, and of command from the One who is unutterably far beyond ourselves. But it is also to hear a word of condemnation and destruction from One who is light to our darkness, purity to our filth, strength to our weakness. These words leave us no option but to move. Bartimaeus, imprisoned in his blindness, heard the words, "Cheer up! On your feet! He's calling you!" and he threw off his cloak

---

6. C. S. Lewis, *Mere Christianity* (New York: Macmillan, 1952), 56.

and came to Jesus (Mark 10:46–52). To do otherwise would be to condemn himself to darkness for the rest of his days. That is faith. It is to construct your life in active response to the revelation of God. It is to live in accordance with what he has said and is saying in his Word.

THE BIBLE AND WORLDVIEWS. There can be little doubt that the Western world is steadily losing its hold on the Bible. One indication of this is found in a children's book titled *The Green Book*.[7] This book is about a group of people who are forced to leave a dying earth to colonize a distant planet. Because of weight limitations, each person can take only one book. The plot then revolves around what books are brought and the incredibly important place these books come to have in the life of the community. The author's premise is that "story" is profoundly important in shaping one's perception of oneself and the world.

This is certainly a correct insight. But the interesting thing is that in the context of such works as *The Odyssey* and *Grimms' Fairy Tales*, the author neglects to have anyone bring a Bible. The enormity of this omission is incredible. It says a good deal about the author, but it also says a good deal about our society. There is no doubt that the single story that has shaped the West is the Bible. It is the best-selling book of all time. Yet at the end of the twentieth century a book can be written about the perpetuation of human civilization that ignores the Bible.

Another evidence of this phenomenon is the mounting influence of a nonbiblical worldview on us. The worldview of continuity, which knows nothing of transcendence, sees no real possibility of change. Human beings are caught in the continuous cycles of time, where everything is changing but nothing is really different. As the aphorism has it, the more we change, the more we are the same. Deterministic naturalism is only an abstract and scholarly way of saying what the ancient myths said: Choice is an illusion. We each do what we must do as a result of all the conditioning that has occurred in our lives.

In the ancient world this was known as fate. You could not change your fate; you could only react to it. This is the central idea in Greek tragic dramas. The hero is caught in a web of fate, and the plot revolves around how he meets that fate in a noble way. So Oedipus is fated to have sexual relations with his mother. He leaves his country and changes his identity in order to avoid this terrible thing. But years later and in another place, he falls in love

---

7. J. Walsh, *The Green Book* (New York: Farrar, Straus & Giroux, 1982).

with a beautiful older woman. When their love is culminated, it is revealed to them that they are mother and son.

This idea is a contemporary one. Displayed in a jet airliner in 2001 are the words, "If you can't change your fate, change your attitude." In other words, there is really no hope of transcending your past. You cannot change the ways you react and behave. You cannot conquer ingrained habits and tendencies. All you can do is accept them without whining and complaining and go to your doom with your head held high. If you deny the biblical worldview, there is only one other option, the same one held by the ancient Babylonians and Greeks, by Hindus and Buddhists—and it is no different in the supposedly irreligious West today. If we will not listen to the biblical story, then we *will* listen to the other one. It is the only other option.

But if the biblical understanding of reality is no longer a part of the furniture of many of our minds, it continues to be a wonderful option for us. The cycles of time and existence are not all there is, nor is psychological conditioning. There is One who "sits above the circle of the earth" (40:22), who is not a prisoner of its cycles or its conditioning. He is able to break into it and do something never done before. Just because Israel has had a long history of rebellion and treachery does not mean it is doomed to continue in that way or that every single Israelite is doomed to continue in that way. By the power of the transcendent Redeemer, they can change. They can be responsive and obedient, walking in his ways and following his instruction, his Torah. He has done everything necessary for that change if they will just listen.

The same is true for us today. We can leave the "Babylons" that have enslaved us. We can be delivered from the guilt and shame of all our past sins. In Jesus Christ, God has made a way for us. If ever there was a new thing, the coming of Christ was it. Can the immortal God become mortal? Can the eternal Spirit take up a body of flesh? Can the One who is everywhere present be localized and contained in a womb? If we do not believe in transcendence, the answer is no. These things have never happened before, and they are not a part of the recurring story of life as we know it.

But if we believe that the Creator of the universe is not limited by his creation, the answer is yes. God can do the impossible and bring about genuine change. He can do for us what we cannot do for ourselves. So he has reconciled us to himself (2 Cor. 5:19), nailing our death certificate to Christ's cross (Col. 2:14). This means that "I can do everything through him who gives me strength" (Phil. 4:13). And if God can do what he has done in Christ, he can do anything, including delivering us from all that has "fated" us. We are not doomed to simply trying to accept our fate with some sort of heroic, noble demeanor. Our fate can be changed. God can make new creatures.

But the issue is the same for us as it was for the ancient Israelites: Will we believe it? Will we "listen" to what God says in his revealed Word? Unless we do so, all his revelation is in vain. This is a startling thought. The power of the transcendent Creator/Redeemer is limited by our response to it, just as was undoubtedly the case when many of the exiled Judeans did not believe the words of the prophet and thus were unprepared to go home when the opportunity came. We must "hear" God's revelation in the active sense of responding to it and obeying it. Christian salvation offers the possibility of real change in our lives as God does new things for us. But that change is only available to those who "listen."

Isaiah 49:1–13

¹ LISTEN TO ME, you islands;
    hear this, you distant nations:
 Before I was born the LORD called me;
    from my birth he has made mention of my name.
² He made my mouth like a sharpened sword,
    in the shadow of his hand he hid me;
 he made me into a polished arrow
    and concealed me in his quiver.
³ He said to me, "You are my servant,
    Israel, in whom I will display my splendor."
⁴ But I said, "I have labored to no purpose;
    I have spent my strength in vain and for nothing.
 Yet what is due me is in the LORD's hand,
    and my reward is with my God."

⁵ And now the LORD says—
    he who formed me in the womb to be his servant
 to bring Jacob back to him
    and gather Israel to himself,
 for I am honored in the eyes of the LORD
    and my God has been my strength—

⁶he says:

  "It is too small a thing for you to be my servant
    to restore the tribes of Jacob
  and bring back those of Israel I have kept.
  I will also make you a light for the Gentiles,
    that you may bring my salvation to the ends
      of the earth."

⁷ This is what the LORD says—
    the Redeemer and Holy One of Israel—
 to him who was despised and abhorred by the nation,
    to the servant of rulers:
 "Kings will see you and rise up,
    princes will see and bow down,
 because of the LORD, who is faithful,
    the Holy One of Israel, who has chosen you."

⁸This is what the LORD says:

"In the time of my favor I will answer you,
   and in the day of salvation I will help you;
I will keep you and will make you
   to be a covenant for the people,
to restore the land
   and to reassign its desolate inheritances,
⁹ to say to the captives, 'Come out,'
   and to those in darkness, 'Be free!'

"They will feed beside the roads
   and find pasture on every barren hill.
¹⁰ They will neither hunger nor thirst,
   nor will the desert heat or the sun beat upon them.
He who has compassion on them will guide them
   and lead them beside springs of water.
¹¹ I will turn all my mountains into roads,
   and my highways will be raised up.
¹² See, they will come from afar—
   some from the north, some from the west,
   some from the region of Aswan."

¹³ Shout for joy, O heavens;
   rejoice, O earth;
   burst into song, O mountains!
For the LORD comforts his people
   and will have compassion on his afflicted ones.

CHAPTERS 49–55 ADDRESS the second problem that will confront the exiled people. The first is their captivity in Babylon. If they are to be the redeemed servants of the Lord, they need to be set free and to live and minister in the land of God's promises. That issue was dealt with in chapters 41–48: God has a plan of deliverance for his people, even before the tragedy has occurred, and there is nothing the Babylonian gods or the Babylonian power can do to stop that plan from being accomplished.

But there is a second problem confronting both God and his people. What is to be done about the sin that got the people into this dilemma in the first place? God has declared repeatedly that they are his chosen servants. But how can this be? How can these sinful people ever serve a just and holy God? He cannot simply ignore their sin, so what is to be done? In its own way, this alienation from God is a much more serious problem than their captivity in Babylon. So what can God's grace do to address this problem?

The answer to that question is given in chapters 49–55. Although the language and imagery of captivity continues, specific reference to Babylon and its idols is conspicuously absent, as is any further reference to Cyrus. In other words, a different kind of captivity is being addressed here, and the deliverer from this captivity is the Servant of the Lord, who was first introduced in 42:1–9. He will be for Israel what Israel could not be in itself. His servanthood will make possible theirs—and ours. As he becomes the means of Israel's restoration to God, he makes them the prototype for the restoration of all the world.

This subdivision has three sections. In 49:1–52:12 God repeatedly insists that he has not cast his people off. In other words, the hope of the world begins in the heart of the Creator, who is unwilling to let his people go. But the section is also marked by an increasing intensity of anticipation. Somehow God is going to deliver his people from their captivity to sin. This intensity reaches its climax in chapter 52, with its ringing call to leave the captivity that has held them. The third section (54:1–55:13) is marked by an invitation to participate in a deliverance that is seen as accomplished.

What accounts for the change from anticipation to participation? It is the second section (52:13–53:12), the fourth and last of the so-called "Suffering Servant" passages, which provides the answer to our question, as the preceding "Servant Songs" (49:1–13; 50:4–9) have led us to expect. The Servant of the Lord will give his life so that God's people may be restored from their alienation into his fellowship and his service.

The Salvation Task of the Servant (49:1–6)

IN CHAPTERS 41–48, with only one exception, the emphasis was on the servanthood of the nation of Israel. For the most part, all of those references were encouraging a blind and rebellious Israel to believe that God had not cast them off and that God would use them as evidence in his case against the idols. The one exception was the second reference to "servant" (42:1–9). Here the Servant was announced as the obedient One who would bring God's justice to the nations and who would be a covenant to "the people." I argued there that this Servant was not the nation of Israel but Israel's ultimate Deliverer, introduced there before focusing again on the more immediate problem of the captivity in Babylon.

Now with that problem of the Exile having been thoroughly dealt with, however, we can return to address the second problem, the one that the

Servant will solve.[1] We can imagine Isaiah's readers saying, as they come to the end of what is now chapter 48, "Alright, we're listening and we can believe that God can and will restore us from Babylon by means of Cyrus. But who can restore us to God? That's the real problem." Isaiah's answer is given in these verses. It begins with a continuation of the call to "listen." The prophet is continuing to unfold God's plan, which calls for yet a further obedient, believing response. But now it is the Servant himself who calls for the entire world to listen to what he is going to reveal.

The first revelation is one of call and confidence. The Servant has no doubt of his call (49:1), his divine enablement (49:2—3), or his ultimate vindication (49:4). He has been called from the womb, so his vocation is no secondary thing. Furthermore, he is perfectly suited for whatever task God may have for him. Like a "sharpened sword" or a "polished arrow" he will accomplish exactly what God wants at the appointed time. There is no hint of blindness or rebellion in this Servant. Even though his servanthood seems futile (the first emergence of a theme that will grow in 50:4—9 and 52:13—53:12), he knows that God will not fail him.

The contrast with the nation is obvious here. But if that is so, why is the Servant specifically named "Israel" in 49:3? This question has raised a great deal of controversy, which I cannot discuss in detail here. In general, there are three options: The passage is referring to the nation, to the prophet, or to some ideal Israel.[2] As I have said, the descriptions here do not match what is said of Israel, and if there is any further question, 49:5—6 seals the issue: Israel cannot be the agent to restore Israel to God. As far as this person being the prophet himself, the language is far too sweeping to be applied to any ordinary human. This leaves only the third option, which I have already advocated above. The Messiah will be "Israel" as Israel was meant to be. He will display the Lord's "splendor" (49:3) as an obedient Israel might have done, and in so doing, he will be the One "who restores the tribes of Jacob" to the Lord.

How that will be done is left unanswered here, but it will be answered a few chapters later. Whatever it is will be so far-reaching that it will reach to the ends of the earth, including even "Gentiles" in its scope (49:6).[3] "Salvation"

---

1. On the connections between 42:1—9 and 49:1—13, see Childs, *Isaiah*, 383.

2. Childs, *Isaiah*, 383—85, presents a strong argument for ideal Israel, although he carefully avoids identifying this figure with any specific person. Hanson, *Isaiah 40—66*, 128 says that it is both individual and collective, which makes it difficult to extract any meaning from the passage.

3. Motyer, *Prophecy of Isaiah*, 388, is correct in saying that the Heb. of v. 6 does not have the Servant "bring" salvation to the ends of the earth. Rather, it says he will "be" God's salvation. He also makes the interesting observation that while words having to do with salvation are common throughout the book of Isaiah, they are relatively rare elsewhere in the Old Testament.

here corresponds to "justice" in 42:1 and helps to amplify the meaning of "justice" to divine order, as discussed there. For God to "save" the world means to bring it into the order he intended, and for God to bring about that order it is necessary for him to save it from the bondage sin holds over it.

The Servant's Task As Representative of God's Covenant (49:7–12)

IN THESE VERSES God addresses the Servant in ways that are reminiscent of the dialogue in Psalm 2. God declares that although the Servant is "despised" and reduced to the level of a slave, a day will come when kings and princes will honor him because of God's faithfulness in his life (49:7; cf. Phil. 2:5–11).[4] In particular, the Servant's task is to be a representative of God's "covenant" to his people. Like a new Joshua he will settle the people in a land of freedom and abundance, where the God of "compassion" will tend them as a shepherd tends his flock (Isa. 49:8–11). While 49:12 may be intended to speak of the remnant returning from all directions, it may also be another indication of the worldwide scope of the Servant's ministry. People of all sorts from all kinds of places will find restoration to God through him.[5]

Outburst of Praise (49:13)

AS IN 42:10–17, the announcement of the work of the Servant results in an outburst of praise. As there, nature is called on to sing the praise of its Creator and Redeemer. As nature has involuntarily experienced the effects of human sin (Gen. 3:17), so also it will experience the effects of our redemption (see also 44:23; 55:12–13; note the promise in 65:17). The terms "comfort" along with "his/my people" are reintroduced here for the first time since chapter 40; they will recur several more times in the immediately following passages.[6] Having dealt with the questions about God that the captivity would raise, the prophet can now return to the opening themes of the division (chs. 40–55) and show how the ideal Servant will make them possible.

---

4. Once again (as in 48:17), the Lord is identified as "the Redeemer, the Holy One of Israel." In chs. 1–39 "the Holy One of Israel" is used primarily to express the sovereign power of the Lord as ruler of the nations. Now the ultimate purpose of that power is revealed: redemption.

5. The word translated "Aswan" in 49:12 is *sinim*. The DSS reads *synym*, which gives some support to an earlier suggestion that Syene (Aswan) was intended. There is no other reference to "Sinim" in the Old Testament.

6. See "comfort" in 51:3, 12, 19; 52:9; 54:11; "his/my people" in 51:4, 16, 22; 52:4, 5, 6, 9.

THE CONCEPT OF SERVANT. "Servant" is not an easy concept for us to deal with today for several reasons. One is its unfortunate association with American slavery. As a result of that association, the term is surrounded with connotations of brutality, deprivation, and injustice. A second difficulty is the association of this term with house servants in Europe. Although coercion is not a factor there, it still involves the idea of lower-class, menial work. For these reasons it is difficult for us to envision all that is going on in the term.

Unquestionably, the word connotes taking a lower place. Also, "servant" connotes the idea of ownership. But slavery in the ancient world was not at all like the plantation slavery of the American South. For instance, in Greece and Rome, the teachers of children in noble families were often slaves. Thus, educated and even upper-class people might be in slavery for a time. In the Old Testament, a person might voluntarily enslave himself or herself for a time to someone else if the burden of debt became too great to bear (Lev. 25:39–41). Not only did this provide a way of getting on one's feet again, it also provided protection from creditors. In both America and Europe, this practice continued in the form of "indentured servitude."

But beyond these matters, the concept of "servant" is a larger one than we normally think of. It partakes of the same idea that caused people two hundred years ago to close their letters with the phrase "Your obedient servant." To be sure, that was primarily flowery, formal language. But it also expressed the idea that each of us, no matter what our position in life, may be of service to others. Thus, high officials in the government were called "servants" (a word that developed into "ministers") of the king. Thus, for God to call someone his "servant" is not to say, "You are my boot-black," or "You are the one who does the difficult, demeaning work I don't want to do." It is to say that the servant will perform an essential service for someone whom they gladly recognize not only as master but also as savior. That servant finds both protection and hope in a relationship with someone who is stronger and more resourceful than he is. That servant is the key agent for the accomplishment of the master's work in the world.

Ultimately, the task of servanthood can be a position of high honor, as when the king says to someone, "I would like you to be my Prime Minister (First Servant)." Although in the government of heaven the position of "Prime Minister" is already filled by the Son of God, what an honor it is to be invited to take any position in that government. So, yes, accepting the place of servant of the Lord involves a limitation of our autonomy, but that autonomy was a delusion anyway. In return for that voluntary limitation, we gain deliverance, protection, and a position from which we can perform valuable service for the King.

EXPERIENCING THE MINISTRY OF JESUS. What does it mean for us to have experienced the ministry of Jesus Christ, God's Servant, in the light of this passage? It means both benefits and character, according to the New Testament. These are made available to us through a mystical union with Christ. Jesus says that we are the branches of his vine and that his life flows through us (John 15:5–8). Paul speaks of our dying with Christ to the old life of sin and being raised to a new life characterized by his "mind" or attitude toward life (Rom. 6:1–4; Gal. 2:20; Phil. 2:1–5).

In the comments on chapter 48 I spoke about the danger of mere "spirituality" divorced from a genuine "listening" to the revealed Word of God. I want to underline what I also said there that this does not reduce the Christian life to adherence to a set of mental constructs or of moral ideals. Rather, we have the privilege of participating in the life of God as we follow the guidance he gives in his Word. We can become the servants of God as we share the life of the Servant.

The benefits we experience in this participation include a sense of calling, enablement, and confidence. Just as Christ was called from the womb (49:1, 5), so Christian servants can know that they too have a calling that is suited particularly to them. That does not mean we will necessarily be performing the same tasks throughout our lives as may have been more common in another generation. But it does mean that God has put us together in a certain kind of way and that we can find that way of living out our lives in fulfillment of his will and calling.

It is apparently the sociologist Max Weber who coined the phrase "the Protestant work ethic" as he studied the impact of this truth of divine calling as emphasized by Martin Luther. Luther recognized the fact that God does not merely call people to religious professions, as was the implication of Roman Catholic tradition. He calls all persons, and each one of us can fulfill our daily tasks with that joyous sense of carrying out the very call of God.

Furthermore, as those who participate in the life of the Servant, we too can have that sense of enablement by God. We too can become aware of being a "sharpened sword" or a "polished arrow" in his hand (49:2). This does not mean we are necessarily doing something earth-shaking as the Servant, Jesus Christ, did. However, as we perform what may seem to be simple tasks, they may have more significance than we will ever know on this side of the grave. But in the daily round we can have that sense of having been divinely fitted for just what it is we are doing.

This does not mean we will never feel that our lives are pointless and futile. The clear implication of 49:4 and 7 is that Christ felt that way. At the end of a long day of verbal jousting with the religious leaders who ought to have been the most responsive and were yet the most recalcitrant, he must have felt that way. Similarly, when the disciples failed to grasp a simple spiritual truth for the fourteenth time, he must have felt that way. And when the great crowds of his early ministry began to drift away, there is something almost plaintive in his question to the disciples, "You do not want to leave too, do you?" (John 6:67). In other words, do not think that to have a sense of calling and of divine enablement means you will always feel "on top of things." He did not, so why should we?

But in the midst of that frustration and sense of futility, Jesus never lost the confidence of who he was and what that meant. He knew that he was God's and God was his (cf. "my God" in 49:4). He knew that if he would only be faithful, he could trust the outcome of his service into God's hands. He might be despised and abhorred by people (49:7), or he might be honored by them, but they were not the ultimate dispensers of the rewards. He knew, as we can know, that "my reward is with my God" (49:4). In the words of Psalm 56:4:

> In God, whose word I praise,
> in God I trust; I will not be afraid.
> What can mortal man do to me?

Isaiah 49:14–50:3

[14] BUT ZION SAID, "The LORD has forsaken me,
the Lord has forgotten me."

[15] "Can a mother forget the baby at her breast
and have no compassion on the child she has borne?
Though she may forget,
I will not forget you!
[16] See, I have engraved you on the palms of my hands;
your walls are ever before me.
[17] Your sons hasten back,
and those who laid you waste depart from you.
[18] Lift up your eyes and look around;
all your sons gather and come to you.
As surely as I live," declares the LORD,
"you will wear them all as ornaments;
you will put them on, like a bride.

[19] "Though you were ruined and made desolate
and your land laid waste,
now you will be too small for your people,
and those who devoured you will be far away.
[20] The children born during your bereavement
will yet say in your hearing,
'This place is too small for us;
give us more space to live in.'
[21] Then you will say in your heart,
'Who bore me these?
I was bereaved and barren;
I was exiled and rejected.
Who brought these up?
I was left all alone,
but these—where have they come from?'"

[22] This is what the Sovereign LORD says:

"See, I will beckon to the Gentiles,
I will lift up my banner to the peoples;
they will bring your sons in their arms
and carry your daughters on their shoulders.

²³ Kings will be your foster fathers,
 and their queens your nursing mothers.
They will bow down before you with their faces to the
   ground;
 they will lick the dust at your feet.
Then you will know that I am the LORD;
 those who hope in me will not be disappointed."

²⁴ Can plunder be taken from warriors,
 or captives rescued from the fierce?

²⁵ But this is what the LORD says:

"Yes, captives will be taken from warriors,
 and plunder retrieved from the fierce;
I will contend with those who contend with you,
 and your children I will save.
²⁶ I will make your oppressors eat their own flesh;
 they will be drunk on their own blood, as with wine.
Then all mankind will know
 that I, the LORD, am your Savior,
 your Redeemer, the Mighty One of Jacob."

⁵⁰:¹ This is what the LORD says:

"Where is your mother's certificate of divorce
 with which I sent her away?
Or to which of my creditors
 did I sell you?
Because of your sins you were sold;
 because of your transgressions your mother was
   sent away.
² When I came, why was there no one?
 When I called, why was there no one to answer?
Was my arm too short to ransom you?
 Do I lack the strength to rescue you?
By a mere rebuke I dry up the sea,
 I turn rivers into a desert;
their fish rot for lack of water
 and die of thirst.
³ I clothe the sky with darkness
 and make sackcloth its covering."

THIS PASSAGE CONSISTS of the people's negative response to the proclamation of the Servant's redemptive work (49:14) and God's extended rejoinder (49:15—50:3). In words reminiscent of 40:27, the people declare that the great promises about the Servant's ministry are in vain because it is plain that "the Lord has forgotten" them. To this God replies that he can no more forget them than a nursing mother can forget her baby (49:15—16). He goes on to declare that the proof of his love for them will be seen in the abundance of "descendants" that will be born to Zion when she thought herself forever barren (49:17—21). God will cause the nations to bring the lost children home (49:22—23).

But these promises elicit another pessimistic answer: Who can break the grip of the captors (49:24)? Again God responds that he can do that very thing (49:25—26). The third response is only implicit, but on the basis of God's response in 50:1—3, it seems to be something like: "But you are the one who (arbitrarily) sold us to those captors in the first place." To that God responds again that he has not cast them off and has the power to restore them at will.[1]

The language of return here is clearly out of proportion to the actual returns that occurred in 538 and 445 B.C. Those were relatively small affairs. There certainly was not, as Motyer phrases it, "a population explosion" in the Exile so that more returned than those who went into exile in the first place.[2] So if these statements were intended to be a prediction of literal events, the prophet is sadly mistaken.[3]

But there is good reason to understand that these statements were never intended to be taken literally. As I said above, the focus is now on the return *to God*, and Isaiah is speaking figuratively about a worldwide response to God's reconciliation through the work of the Servant. God has not forgotten his ancient promises to Abraham. The patriarch will indeed have more children than the stars of the heavens or the sand of the seashore. Even if Zion's sin and exile make it appear as if Abraham's line has come to an end, that is not the case. Another evidence that the physical returns from Babylon are not in view is the appearance of these same figures of speech in chapters 56—66, which have their historical setting in the postexilic period. There the return has already occurred, yet the promises of Zion's abundant motherhood continue to be made (cf. 60:9; 66:7—11, 20).

---

1. One evidence that 50:1—3 should be taken together with 49:14—26 is the recurrence of "This is what the LORD says" (49:22, 25; 51:1).

2. Motyer, *Prophecy of Isaiah*, 394.

3. See R. N. Whybray, *Isaiah 40—66* (NCBC; Grand Rapids: Eerdmans, 1975), 144, 146.

Once again, the issue of possibility and impossibility is at the heart of what is taking place here. From this world's perspective, it is impossible for Israel to be restored into a relationship with God. She has been divorced by him (50:1), and her children are either dead or sold into captivity (49:21). A barren, bereaved woman without a man in her life cannot have children. This is a fact of nature. But God insists that not only will the exiled children return (49:17–18) but that more children will be born to the mother (49:19–21). No wonder the incredulous remark, "Where have they come from" (49:21)?

The transcendent Creator, who could do a new thing in making Babylon give up the captives, can also do a new thing and get the very nations who threatened the life of Israel to be the ones to assist her in fulfilling her calling to be a blessing to the world. As he promised before (11:10, 12), the Servant/Messiah will be the banner God raises to call the nations to himself (49:22). They will come gladly, owning their debt to Israel as God's people (49:23).[4] All of this will confirm two things for the Israelites: Yahweh is indeed the Lord, the one who causes all things to be, and those who "wait for" (NIV "hope in"; cf. 30:18) him "will not be disappointed" (49:23). The God who can defeat the power of all the Assyrias and the Babylons of the world can also defeat the power of sin.

But the astonishing thing is that he cannot do these things for his people if they will not give him an opportunity, by putting their trust in him. As we have said earlier, chapters 40–55 focus on the motivation to trust God. Chapters 7–39 have amply demonstrated that God can and should be trusted. But ultimately it is only the grace of God that can actually motivate persons to believe what he says and to exercise that trust (cf. 12:1–2). This passage is an expression of that grace, reaching its climax in the passionate words of 50:1–3, where God insists that he has both the will and the power to redeem his people.

To be sure, it is no accident of history that the Judeans experienced the Exile; it was because of their sin (50:1). But just as no nation on earth can stand up to God, neither can sin. Do they think he has divorced them? Where is the certificate? There is none. Do they think he was somehow forced to "sell" them against his will? Of course not. But just as he alone could

---

4. In regard to 49:26, it is important to recognize again that the language throughout this passage is highly figurative. God is saying that those who arrogantly oppress his people will actually be bringing their own destruction on themselves. More than that, those who persist in sin of any sort are doing that thing. A verse like this is not a warrant for the modern state of Israel to brutalize its enemies, nor for Christians to do such a thing. Rather, it is simply a statement of fact, which can be seen again and again in history. One example is that of Robespierre, who instituted the "reign of terror" during the French Revolution only to fall prey to that violence himself.

deliver them from the power of the nations, he alone has the power to deliver from sin. His "arm" is not "short" and weak; rather, it is full-sized and powerful. He can "dry up the sea" and turn off the sun; what is so difficult about defeating sin?

Bridging Contexts

WAITING ON THE LORD. The recurring theme throughout this passage is God's attempt to overcome an unwillingness to believe what he says. This is particularly evident in the contrast between 49:13 and 14. God has promised "comfort" and "compassion," but the people say that it is not true because God has forgotten them. This attitude is reminiscent of what Isaiah encountered in his own day. God had promised deliverance to the people of Judah from the Assyrian threat if they would only "wait" for him. But they had refused to do so, preferring to trust an Assyria to deliver them from the threat of Israel and Syria or an Egypt from the threat of Assyria. Evidently the same tendency was to persist into the Exile, where people gave up on God and turned to accommodating themselves to the Babylonian culture.

The book of Daniel shows that not all of the Judeans succumbed to this pressure, but the book also shows how persistent and pervasive the pressure was. Nebuchadnezzar was king of the universe, and he was not about to permit a "fifth column" close to the center of his empire to suggest that there was a king greater than he. So it was no easy thing to "wait" for the Lord to fulfill his promises.

This was especially true in regard to the promises of the Servant/Messiah, who would defeat the power of sin and bring in the kingdom of right. It only took a little less than seventy years from the time the first captives were taken in 605 B.C. until the first return in 538 B.C., but it took hundreds of years for the Servant to take his throne. Why did God make his people wait so long for the fulfillment of the promise?

While we can talk about further revelation that was necessary before the Messiah could come and the unique possibilities for dissemination of the message that the Roman Empire would make possible, the ultimate answer to that question rested in the mind of God. The only point is that those to whom these promises were made never saw their fulfillment. Nevertheless, some of them waited with faith undimmed for God's time to be fulfilled. Thus, when Christ came, there were people like Anna and Simeon, who were ready to recognize him (Luke 2:25–38). They were the end of a long line of people who had waited confidently, and in the end, their faith was not disappointed (49:23).

WAITING. We too are called to live with that confident expectation that is the expression of faith and trust. Waiting believingly is our way of relinquishing control of our lives (see comments on ch. 32). When we rush ahead to solve our problems in our own way without waiting on God to show us how he wants to deal with those problems, we have effectively said to him that we know better than he does and we are better able to solve the problem than he is. This is why Jesus required his disciples to wait in Jerusalem for him to fill them with his Holy Spirit. They and their devices were not the way to carry out Jesus' command to make disciples of all nations. God was going to use them in dramatic ways to fulfill that purpose, but it was going to be in his way and through his power, not theirs.

But not only are we called upon to wait on God in the daily round of our lives. There is another waiting that is incumbent on us, and it is even more in line with what God was asking of the exiles in this passage. We are called upon to wait as they did for the ultimate fulfillment of the promises made here. In many ways we have seen them fulfilled. All the nations have flowed to Jerusalem and have poured out their wealth and devotion on the city of Zion, the church of the living God. The number of Abraham's descendants has swelled into the billions. Those who have set out to destroy God's people have ended up by destroying themselves.

But we still wait for the final establishment of God's kingdom on earth. That is the confident expectation to which Christ calls his followers. The question of Luke 18:8 is still addressed to us today: "When the Son of Man comes, will he find faith on the earth?" In other places, he spoke of the need not to lose focus in our waiting for his return. He spoke of the "foolish virgins," who were not prepared for the bridegroom's coming (Matt. 25:1–13). He spoke of those who got busy doing other things and were not ready (Matt. 24:36–44).

Already in the years immediately after Jesus' return to heaven, some lost hope and said he was not coming back. The question for us is whether we will remain in that sort of line that culminated in Anna and Simeon, or whether we will lose hope and effectively finish the line for our family and our descendants. God promises not to disappoint those who wait for him. But that means continuing to wait for as long as he decrees and not losing hope in the meantime.

Accepting God's love. Part of the reason that some of the exiles lost hope was that they could not really believe in God's love for them. Undoubtedly there were a number of different types of thinking in that group. (1) Some frankly thought that God had treated them unfairly. After all, the people of

Judah were not that bad, and there were other people around them who were at least as bad, maybe worse (cf. Hab. 1). Moreover, if their parents had been so bad, as bad as the prophets insisted they had been, then God should have punished them and not their "innocent" children (Ezek. 18). So this group would say, "If God loves us so much, we shouldn't be in this mess at all" (cf. Isa. 40:27).

(2) Others admitted that God had treated them fairly. This generation was just as unfaithful as the preceding ones had been, and God had given them exactly what was coming to them. Being as bad as they were and having failed God so miserably, they could not imagine that God could ever love a people such as them.

(3) Finally, there were those who said, in effect, "So what?" These people looked at their circumstances and concluded that the situation was hopeless. Whether they had gotten into this fairly or unfairly was beside the point. The point was that there was no way out. So God could say he loved them all he wanted, but it simply would do no good.

Those same groups of people exist today. In every way possible God is saying that he loves us and wants us in fellowship with himself. He promises to give us spiritual abundance and fruitfulness. But we cannot truly "hear" his words in the sense of receiving them. (1) Some of us say, "If God really loved me, he would not have allowed me to be born into this abusive family." Or, "If God really loved me, he would not have made me poor." Or, "If God really loved me, he wouldn't have let me get pregnant when we were not married." (2) Others say, "God can't love me, not after what I've done." Or, "God can't love me when I just keep on sinning after I said I wouldn't do it again." Or, "God can't love me; I am just so worthless. Nothing I say or do is worth anything." (3) Finally, others say, "It doesn't make any difference whether God loves me or not; my situation is hopeless. He can't do anything about this."

To all of these God says the same things as he said 2,700 years ago: He can no more forget us than a mother can forget her nursing baby. And we have even more evidence of that truth than Isaiah did, for when he speaks of our names as being "engraved . . . on the palms of my hands" (49:16), we think of the nail scars in the hands of God's Son. When he has done that for us, how could he forget us?

(1) To those among us who believe they have been treated unfairly, he calls them to face their own liability in their situation. Undoubtedly there were individual Judeans who truly did not deserve the Exile. They were people of faith who had been living in obedience to God, yet this terrible thing happened to them (e.g., Daniel and his three friends, and Ezekiel). But the question in that circumstance is not "Why?" and holding God hostage for an

answer. Rather, it is, "What now?" and looking to God for resources to go on. For such persons, God's affirmation of love will be their lifeblood as they seek to cope with the "unfairness" of life. The fact is that we are part of a much larger web of cause and effect than simply our own actions, and if circumstances do not turn out as we might wish, that is no indication that God does not love us or care for us.

(2) The second group longs for God's love and forgiveness but simply cannot believe that God can forgive them for what they have done. This is often a reverse form of pride: "What *I* have done is too much for God." It is often also the expression of an inability to forgive oneself. If I am this disappointed in myself, think how infinitely more disappointed God is. What is called for is a radical surrender of oneself into God's hands. Of course he is disappointed, but that does not change the fact of his love. In the humiliation of admitting that ours is not the worst sin in the world and that our disappointment in ourselves is not the issue, there is a possibility of realizing that God *wants* to forgive us if we will only let him. In receiving that forgiveness, there is finally the possibility of forgiving ourselves.

(3) The situation of the third group is much the same as that of the second: If God's love is to be experienced, it must be surrendered to. The pride that says "My situation is hopeless" is one that refuses to believe God is greater than anything this world can present to him. What God asks for is the opportunity to try. He asks us to test him in faith, not in doubt, and to allow him to show us the love he has for us and to demonstrate that love can conquer any obstacle it meets. His arm is not too short to ransom us, nor does he lack the strength to rescue us (50:2).

Isaiah 50:4–51:8

[4]THE SOVEREIGN LORD has given me an instructed tongue,
    to know the word that sustains the weary.
He wakens me morning by morning,
    wakens my ear to listen like one being taught.
[5]The Sovereign LORD has opened my ears,
    and I have not been rebellious;
    I have not drawn back.
[6]I offered my back to those who beat me,
    my cheeks to those who pulled out my beard;
I did not hide my face
    from mocking and spitting.
[7]Because the Sovereign LORD helps me,
    I will not be disgraced.
Therefore have I set my face like flint,
    and I know I will not be put to shame.
[8]He who vindicates me is near.
    Who then will bring charges against me?
Let us face each other!
    Who is my accuser?
    Let him confront me!
[9]It is the Sovereign LORD who helps me.
    Who is he that will condemn me?
They will all wear out like a garment;
    the moths will eat them up.

[10]Who among you fears the LORD
    and obeys the word of his servant?
Let him who walks in the dark,
    who has no light,
trust in the name of the LORD
    and rely on his God.
[11]But now, all you who light fires
    and provide yourselves with flaming torches,
go, walk in the light of your fires
    and of the torches you have set ablaze.
This is what you shall receive from my hand:
    You will lie down in torment.

^{51:1}"Listen to me, you who pursue righteousness
    and who seek the LORD:
Look to the rock from which you were cut
    and to the quarry from which you were hewn;
²look to Abraham, your father,
    and to Sarah, who gave you birth.
When I called him he was but one,
    and I blessed him and made him many.
³The LORD will surely comfort Zion
    and will look with compassion on all her ruins;
he will make her deserts like Eden,
    her wastelands like the garden of the LORD.
Joy and gladness will be found in her,
    thanksgiving and the sound of singing.

⁴"Listen to me, my people;
    hear me, my nation:
The law will go out from me;
    my justice will become a light to the nations.
⁵My righteousness draws near speedily,
    my salvation is on the way,
    and my arm will bring justice to the nations.
The islands will look to me
    and wait in hope for my arm.
⁶Lift up your eyes to the heavens,
    look at the earth beneath;
the heavens will vanish like smoke,
    the earth will wear out like a garment
    and its inhabitants die like flies.
But my salvation will last forever,
    my righteousness will never fail.

⁷"Hear me, you who know what is right,
    you people who have my law in your hearts:
Do not fear the reproach of men
    or be terrified by their insults.
⁸For the moth will eat them up like a garment;
    the worm will devour them like wool.
But my righteousness will last forever,
    my salvation through all generations."

Original Meaning

ONCE AGAIN THE SERVANT is introduced, and as in 49:1–6, he speaks in the first person (50:4–9). This is followed, as in chapters 42 and 49, with a commentary (50:10–51:8).[1] There are two connections with the preceding section: the contrast between the transgressions of Israel (50:1) and the obedience of the Servant (50:5), and the fourfold repetition of "the Sovereign LORD."

As far as the structure of the present section is concerned, 49:14–50:3 had insisted that the Sovereign Lord (cf. 49:22) has both the power and the will to deliver his people from their sin. But how will he do so? According to 50:4–9, he will do it through the obedience of his Servant, even if it means the Servant must suffer to accomplish the Sovereign Lord's purpose. Then 50:10–11, with its comment on the Servant's words, provides the transition into the body of the commentary (51:1–8). Those who "obey the word of his servant" (lit., "listen to the voice of his servant"; note the recurrence of "listen" in 51:1, 4, 7) will have light, while those who manufacture their own light will find destruction. The Servant will speak a message to which those who are seeking God's "righteousness" will listen (51:1). His "justice" (not theirs) will be a light to the nations (51:4; cf. 42:1; 49:6), and in him they will find "salvation" (51:8).

The Obedience of the Servant (50:4–9)

THIS THIRD OF the so-called "Servant Songs" reveals yet more clearly that the servant's obedience to the Lord will result in suffering for him. This "servant" is clearly not the nation of Israel, since they did not suffer because of their obedience but because of their rebellion.[2]

There is also a further indication (cf. 49:2) that the Servant will reveal God through speech. His "ears" have been "opened" to hear God's message (50:5), and his "tongue" has been "instructed" (50:4) how to declare it. But if the message is declared, there is going to be abuse (50:6), and the Servant is willing to bear that abuse because he knows that God will vindicate him in the end (50:7–9). No one will be able to successfully accuse him of either disobeying God or of falsifying the message. Nor will those who "beat" him

---

1. Many commentators see 51:1–52:12 as a unit; for example, Motyer, *Prophecy of Isaiah*, 402ff. does, but he also notes an "easy progress" from ch. 50 into ch. 51. For a similar understanding of the structure of this section to that proposed here, see Watts, *Isaiah 34–66*, 193ff.; Hanson, *Isaiah 40–66*, 144–45. Westermann, *Isaiah 40–66*, 233–34, argues that 50:10–51:8 is a composite of miscellaneous materials and that the genuine words of "Second Isaiah" begin again at 51:9.

2. For further discussion on this point, see Oswalt, *Isaiah 40–66*, 322–23.

and pull out his "beard" be able to make him stop obeying his Lord. In fact, his accusers will be unable to stand at the end.

The certainty that the Lord will "vindicate" him in the end means that the Servant has the courage to be obedient, setting his "face like flint" to do his Master's will. The emphasis on the servant's speech reminds us of what is said about the Messiah elsewhere. He will "strike the earth with the rod of his mouth" (11:4), and "the LORD has anointed me to preach good news to the poor" (61:1).

Words of Transition (50:10–11)

THIS BRIEF INTRODUCTION to the commentary on the Servant's words high-lights the emphasis on obedience to his message that will be prominent in the commentary proper (51:1–9). It also contains a significant synonymous parallel between the Lord and the Servant. To "fear the LORD" is synony-mous with obeying "the word of his servant," and vice versa (50:10). Once again, this "servant" cannot be the nation but someone else, One who brings God's word to the nation. Nor is it the prophet, for to obey the prophet's word is not synonymous with fearing the Lord. More and more clearly, this Servant is in a unique position.

Clearly, one's response to the Servant is in the nature of a watershed. Those who have "no light" can walk safely if they will entrust themselves to God in the way that he has revealed. But those who reject God's revealed way and try to manufacture their own light will find that the way they have cho-sen leads to "torment" (50:11).[3] Furthermore, to listen to the Servant is to "trust" God, while refusing to listen to what he says is tantamount to refus-ing to trust God.

A Commentary on the Servant's Words (51:1–8)

THESE VERSES EXPAND on the theme of "listening to/obeying" the words of the Servant. The ones being addressed are those among the Judeans who are inclined to put their trust in God. The others have been dismissed in 50:10. But these are addressed as those who "pursue righteousness" and "seek the LORD" (51:1) and those "who know what is right" and "have my law in your hearts" (51:7). The message that the Servant will reveal is for them—and it is a message of deliverance. But as noted in the introductory comments on

---

3. The NIV rendering "provide yourselves with flaming torches" is not strong enough for Heb. "gird yourselves," which at the least has a more intensive connotation and may even imply fastening the torch to one's waist (in order to have the hands free). See Motyer, *Prophecy of Isaiah*, 401; Oswalt, *Isaiah 40–66*, 328, n. 44.

chapters 49–55, the deliverance here is not primarily from Babylon. Instead, it has both a universal (51:4–6) and a timeless (51:6, 8) quality.

This fact emphasizes again that Israel's primary problem is not captivity in foreign lands. Rather, their ultimate problem is the same as that of the whole human race: alienation from God. Deliverance from Babylon without this other deliverance will accomplish little. Unless God can find a way to deliver from the bondage to sin that produces injustice and oppression, there is no final hope for humanity. Furthermore, it is plain that God's deliverance goes beyond sincere obedience and well-motivated living. If those qualities of life could take away divine-human alienation, there would be no need for further deliverance. But in fact, it is particularly persons with those characteristics who will be able to receive that further deliverance. Their heartfelt commitment to the law of God does not deliver them from their alienation, but it means they are in a position to receive that deliverance if they will.

The commentary may be divided into three stanzas: 51:1–3, 4–6, and 7–8.[4] (1) In verses 1–3 God and the Servant call on the righteous ("Listen to me") to look back. They are invited to remember God's dealings with Abraham in election love (v. 2) and behind that to recognize the creative power that brought the world into existence in the first place. If the Israelites are tempted to despair over God's willingness to restore them, God points them to their origins as a people. He took a single couple and from them brought a whole nation. Surely he will not abandon them now. Nor is there any question about his power to do so. The God who brought the world into existence will have no problem in restoring the "ruins" of "Zion."

The particular imagery for creation used in 51:3 is significant. Here it is not the founding of the earth and the stretching out of the heavens that is so frequently used in this part of the book. Instead, the creative activity that resulted in a garden is emphasized. Isaiah's point is that the Creator originally created a world of beauty, harmony, and blessing. Yahweh is not merely the Creator; he created the world with the specific plan in mind of blessing. So if God is characterized by election love and creative power for blessing, his people need not fear that they will be left in the ruins and despair that their sins have created. The lessons of the past are clear: The Lord is a God of "comfort," "compassion," and power, and he will not rest until the world is once more a place of "joy and gladness," "thanksgiving," and "singing."

---

4. Westermann, *Isaiah 40–66*, 233, observes correctly that the first two of the so-called "Servant Songs" (42:1–9 and 49:1–7) are followed by commentaries, like this one, but in the previous cases, the commentary ends with a song, whereas this one does not. He therefore pulls 51:3 out and puts it after 51:8, calling it "a fragment of a song." This seems unnecessary to me. There is a lyrical quality about the entire segment that seems to belie the need for a formal expression of song (see also comments on 54:1–17).

(2) The next stanza begins as the first did, with a call to "listen." The emphasis here is the universal and eternal work of the Servant. This deliverance that will be accomplished is not merely for the children of Abraham but for the children of Adam, as 49:6 made plain. Not only will the people of Israel wait for the mighty arm of God's deliverance to be revealed (51:5; cf. 50:2; 51:9; 52:10; 53:1), but indeed the whole earth waits. The "law" of God and the "justice" that is a consequence of it will go out to all the nations and become the light that the Servant brings to the "Gentiles" (42:6; 49:6). What God will do for his people truly has universal impact.

Furthermore, the "salvation" God is offering is beyond the limits of time and space. It will have relevance even when "the heavens" and "the earth" cease to exist and when all the inhabitants of earth have died. It could be argued that this is merely hyperbolic language, but even if that were granted, the point cannot be denied that something beyond mere deliverance from Babylon and the restoration of earthly Zion is being talked about.[5]

(3) The third stanza of the commentary on the third Servant Song also begins with a call to listen (51:7). There are words both by and about the Servant that especially those who are seeking God need to hear. They need to be encouraged (comforted) by the assurance that God has not abandoned them and that their commitments to know God and to do his will have not been in vain. They need this encouragement because of the persistent fact that a fallen world has nothing but "reproach" and "insults" for those trying to live the life of the holy God.

What God wants them to hear is that the reproaches and the insults are being spoken by those who are passing away like garments eaten by moths (51:8). In other words, all of that will pass, and pass more quickly than they might think. But the righteous salvation of God will endure forever (cf. 40:8). Note that this same figure was also used by the Servant (50:9). The servants may share the same confidence as their Servant, and sharing it, they need not lose hope, even in the midst of the uncertainties of hope deferred and mockery from a lost world.

Bridging Contexts

TO LIVE, AND more than that, to speak, for God is to invite abuse. This passage begins and ends on that note. The Servant does nothing but obediently speak the words he has been instructed to speak (50:4–5), and the next thing that happens is that he is offering his back to those who beat him (50:6). There is no explicit connection between the

---

5. Cf. Childs, *Isaiah*, 402; Delitzsch, *Isaiah*, 2:250.

two, but the fact is there. To speak for God is to be abused. At the end of this passage (51:7–8), those who love God's law experience the same thing. In both cases, the anchor that is offered to hold both the Servant and the servants is the righteousness of God, which will in the end vindicate his own.

Believers are persecuted throughout the Bible and up to the present. While it should not be surprising if the unbelieving world does so, it is extremely disheartening when the abuse comes from those who consider themselves to be believers as well. But it is a fact of life. In the first incident reported after the fall of humanity in the garden, Abel is killed by Cain because Abel's faith was vindicated and Cain's was not (Gen. 4). It continues with Joseph, who was attacked and sold into slavery by brothers jealous of God's promises for his life (Gen. 37:19–20). Unless God had intervened to save their lives, Joshua and Caleb would have been stoned because they challenged the people to believe that the land could be taken with God's help (Num. 14:10).

This pattern continued on through Israel's history, with the prophets in particular coming in for abuse and murder. Thus, Jesus could say that the Jews had shed the blood of the prophets from the beginning of the world until the present generation (Luke 11:51). It is in that light that he said to his disciples, "Blessed are you when people insult you, persecute you and falsely say all kinds of evil against you because of me" (Matt. 5:11). To Jesus, the ultimate evidence that disciples were being faithful to him was their being persecuted (cf. John 15:18–16:4).

This was certainly the case with the apostle Paul. He could testify that he had been beaten, stoned, and imprisoned because of his faith (2 Cor. 11:23–26). It has also been true of Christians through the ages. We think of those who died in the Colosseum as the quintessential martyrs, but they are only the beginning of an endless line up to and including Sudanese Christians, who are being slaughtered and enslaved even as these words are being written.

In the context of Isaiah 50:4–9, it is important to notice that Jesus was not so much abused for what he did as for what he said. If he had not claimed to be the Son of God, if he had not pronounced judgment on the religious leadership, and if he had not said he alone was the Way, he might not have been put to death. Words and language are at the heart of God's revelation. He spoke blessing on his creatures (Gen. 1:28) and laid down the terms of life in the Garden of Eden in explicit language. The experience of the prophets with God was profoundly linguistic in nature: God had a message for his people and was determined to communicate it to them. Jesus Christ, the Servant, is the ultimate communication of God to humans.

Thus, John's inspired labeling of Christ as "the Word" could not have been more apropos, though this is not to say that in Jesus communication was only his being and that verbal communication was no longer necessary.

Hardly! No one can read the Gospels and believe that. Jesus spoke, and it was in part precisely because he spoke that he died. But he could die in confidence because he knew that the Word of God is one of eternal salvation and that that Word will never pass away (cf. Isa. 40:8; 55:11).

WE TODAY HARDLY THINK of persecution as a sign of blessedness. We think we are blessed when all people speak well of us. But in the Sermon on the Mount Jesus says that such a thing is not a good sign, for it means we are no longer "salt" and "light." We no longer stand out from the unbelieving crowd, and what we say and do no longer brings what the crowd does and says under obvious condemnation.

We believers in North America have been largely free of persecution for three hundred years, and it has dulled us to the reality of life. Surely some Western believers have suffered for their faith, but they are isolated instances. The majority of us have even experienced favored status as the government was for years peopled with at least nominal believers. That is changing today, and most of us are unprepared for it. Some preachers are still calling people to become Christians so that they may become rich, prominent, and comfortable. Books that seem to offer a biblical "mantra" that can produce abundance merely by repeating it daily sell in the millions.

That is not the message of Isaiah 50:4–51:8, nor is it, I am convinced, the message of Christ. It is certainly not the experience of millions of Christians around the world. We are called to submissive obedience, knowing perfectly well that in the short term this will probably mean we will not be as comfortable, wealthy, powerful, or prominent as we might be otherwise. But we must "set our faces like flint" (cf. 50:7) to obey God at all costs, following in the footsteps of our Master. We do so, not with long faces and self-inflicted mortification but with joy. That joy is both because we know we are living in the way our Creator intended and because we know that in the end, faith will be vindicated and unfaith unmasked for the tragedy it is.

For us Christians this faith is a good deal easier than it was for the people in Isaiah's day. We have seen the promises of the Servant/Messiah fulfilled. Isaiah had the Servant say that he knew his obedience would be vindicated; we have seen that to be the case. Not only has the promised Servant come, living as Isaiah and the other prophets foresaw, but he has also been vindicated by the Father in incredible ways. When he left the earth, he left behind at most 120 followers. By all the laws of reason that group should have dwindled to nothing in a matter of months. Far from it! Today his followers number more than one billion and can be found on every continent. His faith and obedience have been vindicated, so we can walk in the same way with confidence.

But this passage says even more to us. It is not merely the example of the Servant that we follow. The worldwide, eternal salvation that the Servant proclaimed is ours. To be sure, we continue to walk in faith as we look to the final consummation of creation when the blessing of Eden returns to creation without the curse of sin. But we have seen the birth of the promised seed of Abraham and have received the Holy Spirit, who is the down payment on the final payment of that blessing. Therefore, those who seek God today and attempt to live in the light of his covenant commands can draw even further strength from the lessons taught here. We too can look back on the goodness of the Creator's intent and on the election love of Abraham's friend. But we can also look back on the coming of the promised Servant, the Son of the Father. With those things to look back on, we can look ahead with confidence.

Our looking ahead should be with even greater confidence than those exiles in Babylon were able to muster. We have seen the down payment on that universal, timeless salvation. Sin has been defeated through the death and resurrection of Christ, and all that is necessary to reconcile humans to the Father has been accomplished. In that light, it ought to be many times easier for us to believe in that final day when every knee will bow and proclaim that Christ is Lord. It ought to be much easier to look forward confidently to the new heaven and the new earth that Isaiah promises us (65:17–25). With that kind of confidence—not the arrogant confidence of conquerors but the humble confidence of the redeemed—we in the West ought to be able to face any persecution and hatred that will come with the same kind of quiet endurance that our brothers and sisters in the rest of the world have manifested and continue to do.

Isaiah 51:9–16

⟨⟩

⁹ AWAKE, AWAKE! CLOTHE yourself with strength,
   O arm of the LORD;
awake, as in days gone by,
   as in generations of old.
Was it not you who cut Rahab to pieces,
   who pierced that monster through?
¹⁰ Was it not you who dried up the sea,
   the waters of the great deep,
who made a road in the depths of the sea
   so that the redeemed might cross over?
¹¹ The ransomed of the LORD will return.
   They will enter Zion with singing;
   everlasting joy will crown their heads.
Gladness and joy will overtake them,
   and sorrow and sighing will flee away.

¹² "I, even I, am he who comforts you.
   Who are you that you fear mortal men,
   the sons of men, who are but grass,
¹³ that you forget the LORD your Maker,
   who stretched out the heavens
   and laid the foundations of the earth,
that you live in constant terror every day
   because of the wrath of the oppressor,
   who is bent on destruction?
For where is the wrath of the oppressor?
¹⁴   The cowering prisoners will soon be set free;
they will not die in their dungeon,
   nor will they lack bread.
¹⁵ For I am the LORD your God,
   who churns up the sea so that its waves roar—
the LORD Almighty is his name.
¹⁶ I have put my words in your mouth
   and covered you with the shadow of my hand—
I who set the heavens in place,
   who laid the foundations of the earth,
   and who say to Zion, 'You are my people.'"

ASSUMING I AM CORRECT that 50:10–51:8 is a commentary on 50:4–9,[1] Isaiah 51:9–16 opens the unit that stands between the third and the fourth so-called "Servant Songs." This unit (51:9–52:12) progresses through three stages from question to affirmation: 51:9–16 deals with the uncertainty over why God has not yet acted; 51:17–23 affirms that it is now Zion's oppressors who will suffer; 52:1–12 announces the imminent deliverance from captivity. Each of these sections begins with the repeated call "Awake, awake," and the motif of the "arm of the LORD" both opens and closes the unit (51:9; 52:10).

Isaiah 51:9–11 presents the question and 51:12–16 gives the Lord's answer. The opening verses have some of the characteristics of a community lament in that they express both doubt and hope. There is the hope now and even the confidence (v. 11) that the Lord will intervene and redeem his people from their sin and its effects. The despair and the hopelessness seen in 40:27 and 49:14 have been somewhat mitigated. Yet there remains the nagging question, "Why hasn't the Lord acted on our behalf long before now?" After all, he was the One who redeemed Israel from Egypt, so there is no question of his ability. None of the powers of evil in the world can stop him, so it is time for that mighty arm (cf. 51:5) to swing into action.[2]

At the same time, as in the lament form, there is the confidence that God will indeed act. In language reminiscent of 35:10, Isaiah 51:11 looks forward to the day when "the ransomed" will return to "Zion with singing." So the captives to sin no longer doubt that God *will* act, but they wonder why he is waiting so long.

God does not directly answer the question, but he does respond by calling on the captives to be sure that their focus is on him and not on their oppressors.[3] The double "I" in 51:12 highlights this emphasis. He is the Creator of all things. Why should they pay more attention to mortals, who are

---

1. See comments on 50:4–51:10 for discussion of this position.

2. As in 27:1 and 30:7, Isaiah uses the mythological imagery of the sea monster. Esp. in Babylonian and Canaanite mythology, the chief god was supposed to have defeated the monster of watery chaos prior to bringing this world into existence. While that imagery is alluded to here and in the other places, no use is made of the myth itself. Rather, Egypt is seen as the monster and the Red Sea is what was overcome. Evil is not defeated in some other-worldly realm on a continual basis but rather in the context of human experience, where God intervenes in nonrepeatable acts of grace and redemption. For further discussion see Motyer, *Prophecy of Isaiah*, 408; Oswalt, *Isaiah 40–66*, 341–42.

3. The change in gender and number of the subjects and objects in 51:12–16 has prompted scholars to posit a number of different hands behind the verses. The change is from masculine plural in verse 12a to feminine singular in v. 12b to masculine singular in verses 13–16. But if it is understood that the movement is from the captives to Zion to Israel to the Servant, the sequence is intelligible.

little more than "grass" (51:12; cf. 40:6–8; Ps. 56:4, 11), than to the eternal Creator, who is also the One who seeks to "comfort" them?

There is no point in focusing on the "oppressor" (51:13), because he will soon be gone. He may be "bent on destruction," but he is not the ruler of the world, and the One who does rule asserts that the "prisoners . . . will not die in their dungeon" (51:14). Far better to focus on the Comforter, to whom both the seen and the unseen worlds bow in obedience (51:15). The way in which God's creative power and election love will come together to redeem Zion from her sin can be seen in the Servant. As elsewhere in the book, the Servant's ministry is to reveal God. He will declare God's words, and nothing will be able to thwart those plans for him.

THE CRIES OF the oppressed for justice and deliverance have hardly ever been heard so loudly as in the twentieth century. The brutality of oppressors was not new, but science and industry gave them an ability to extend and multiply their oppressive force in previously unheard-of ways. As a result, we have had the terrors of Auschwitz and the "killing fields" of Cambodia. In situations such as these, the cry comes again, "Awake, awake, O arm of the LORD." And again, there comes the question, "How long, O LORD?" Why does God not act on behalf of his people, or if they are not his people in particular, at least on behalf of the helpless and downtrodden, whom the Bible declares have a special place in the heart of God?

If there were an easy answer to this question, it would have been given long ago, and there would be no more books on the problem of evil. But, as in the book of Job, the Bible does not answer the question. What it does is to offer us an alternative. We can serve a good, all-powerful Creator, who does do justly in the long term and who will ultimately balance all the books; the only other option is to have a world in which we and our abilities are supreme. A wise person will certainly choose the former, as Job did, for to choose the latter is not to answer the question but to render it, and indeed all questions, mere gibberish. If there is a good and just God, then we have hope that indeed oppression can be, and will be, overcome. But if we are ultimate, then an honest view of history must tell us there is no hope at all.

THE BIBLICAL LAMENT is a wonderful piece of literature insofar as it bridges two attitudes in life that are often treated as excluding each other: doubt and hope. The result of this exclusion is that people are often deprived of the encouragement and assurance that can be theirs. We are often told that if you entertain doubts, you do not have faith and hope is impossible for you. As a result, there are people who never face their doubts and are forced to live lives of denial and superficiality. By contrast, there are those whose doubts are undeniable and who therefore conclude that faith is impossible for them. Both kinds of persons need to look carefully at passages such as this and at the longer laments in the Psalms (e.g., Ps. 6; 22).

What the laments show us is that doubt and faith are *not* mutually exclusive. But it may be helpful at the outset to draw a distinction. There is a kind of doubt that demands proof before it will be surrendered. Perhaps this is what the writer of James has in mind when he says that we "must believe and not doubt" (James 1:6). But there is also a kind of doubt that bespeaks uncertainty and sincerely seeks reasons to believe. So the man said to Jesus, "I do believe; help me overcome my unbelief" (Mark 9:24). It is in this latter case that the laments come to bear.

Too often we think that to have any questions about God or his actions is to have no faith. Conversely, if we really had faith, we would have no anxieties. Laments like this one in Isaiah show us that this is not the case. We may be certain that God will in the end answer all our prayers and bring us to Zion with singing. But at the same time we may be in deep anguish over God's prolonged failure to act. That anguish does not mean that our hope is not genuine, but neither does genuine hope mean that we will feel no anguish. We can be honest about our feelings without denying the hope that is truly ours.

But how can we be sure that our questions and uncertainties do not overwhelm our hope? Isaiah gives us the key. It lies in our focus. We need not deny the world and all the questions it raises. We need not pretend that all is well when all is far from well. But those things must not become our central focus. If they do, they will overwhelm us. "The oppressor" and his evil purposes will put us under. Rather, our focus must be on our Creator/Redeemer and all that has been revealed about his character, nature, and will. Undoubtedly we will still have questions, and many of them will still be unanswerable, but we will be able to live with them knowing that we know the One in whom all the questions of life have their "Yes" (cf. 2 Cor. 1:20).

Without question, this insight has come out of the furnace of Isaiah's own experience. Why did his preaching actually turn his own generation from God? There is no easy answer for that. But God has given him the key. "Focus on me and my holiness," he said, "and I will be your sanctuary. If you focus on the world, as your compatriots are doing, I will only be a stumbling block to you as I am to them" (cf. 8:12–14).

Isaiah 51:17–52:12

¹⁷ Awake, awake!
  Rise up, O Jerusalem,
you who have drunk from the hand of the Lord
    the cup of his wrath,
you who have drained to its dregs
    the goblet that makes men stagger.
¹⁸ Of all the sons she bore
    there was none to guide her;
of all the sons she reared
    there was none to take her by the hand.
¹⁹ These double calamities have come upon you—
    who can comfort you?—
ruin and destruction, famine and sword—
    who can console you?
²⁰ Your sons have fainted;
    they lie at the head of every street,
    like antelope caught in a net.
They are filled with the wrath of the Lord
    and the rebuke of your God.

²¹ Therefore hear this, you afflicted one,
    made drunk, but not with wine.
²² This is what your Sovereign Lord says,
    your God, who defends his people:
  "See, I have taken out of your hand
    the cup that made you stagger;
  from that cup, the goblet of my wrath,
    you will never drink again.
²³ I will put it into the hands of your tormentors,
    who said to you,
    'Fall prostrate that we may walk over you.'
  And you made your back like the ground,
    like a street to be walked over."

^{52:1} Awake, awake, O Zion,
    clothe yourself with strength.
Put on your garments of splendor,
    O Jerusalem, the holy city.

The uncircumcised and defiled
will not enter you again.
² Shake off your dust;
rise up, sit enthroned, O Jerusalem.
Free yourself from the chains on your neck,
O captive Daughter of Zion.

³For this is what the LORD says:

"You were sold for nothing,
and without money you will be redeemed."

⁴For this is what the Sovereign LORD says:

"At first my people went down to Egypt to live;
lately, Assyria has oppressed them.

⁵"And now what do I have here?" declares the LORD.

"For my people have been taken away for nothing,
and those who rule them mock,"
declares the LORD.
"And all day long
my name is constantly blasphemed.
⁶Therefore my people will know my name;
therefore in that day they will know
that it is I who foretold it.
Yes, it is I."

⁷How beautiful on the mountains
are the feet of those who bring good news,
who proclaim peace,
who bring good tidings,
who proclaim salvation,
who say to Zion,
"Your God reigns!"
⁸Listen! Your watchmen lift up their voices;
together they shout for joy.
When the LORD returns to Zion,
they will see it with their own eyes.
⁹Burst into songs of joy together,
you ruins of Jerusalem,
for the LORD has comforted his people,
he has redeemed Jerusalem.

¹⁰ The LORD will lay bare his holy arm
    in the sight of all the nations,
and all the ends of the earth will see
    the salvation of our God.

¹¹ Depart, depart, go out from there!
    Touch no unclean thing!
Come out from it and be pure,
    you who carry the vessels of the LORD.
¹² But you will not leave in haste
    or go in flight;
for the LORD will go before you,
    the God of Israel will be your rear guard.

NOW GOD TURNS the tables on his people. In 51:9, they had called on him to step up and bring to reality the promises he had been making. If their sins were really to be defeated and they were to be restored to God's favor, then let it happen! Awake, awake! But now God says it is not for him to awake but for them. Twice (51:17; 52:1) he says it is they who must rise up and take by faith what is offered to them. It is not a question of needing to persuade God to do what he is reluctant to do. Rather, it is a question of the people's developing and maintaining such a faith that when God acts, they will be ready to receive what he has done.

As noted in the comments on 51:9–16, these two sections (51:17–23 and 52:1–12) are a development of the promise made in response to the call for action in 51:9–10. In 51:17–23 God declares that Zion's punishment is now ended and that the things the nations visited on her will now be visited on them. In 52:1–12 the tone of anticipation becomes more intense as God calls on Jerusalem to do the very opposite of what Babylon was required to do in chapter 47. There Babylon was called to go down from the throne and sit in the dust in rags. Here Jerusalem is to "put on your garments of splendor," "shake off your dust," and "sit enthroned" (52:1–2). This section goes on to say that God's honor is at stake because the nations claim he cannot deliver his people (52:5–6). Therefore, he will "bare his holy arm" (52:10) and deliver them in the sight of "all the ends of the earth." In a climactic conclusion God calls on his people to "depart" with all deliberate speed, knowing that God goes both before and behind them (52:11–12).

One of the recurring images of Scripture is the "cup of wrath," found from Psalms through Revelation.[1] Its origins may have been in the idea of one person's intentionally getting another person drunk in order to reduce sexual inhibitions (cf. Hab. 2:15). But the cup also symbolized the sum total of a person's allotted experience (Ps. 16:5). So those who have sinned against God must drink the cup that their sins have filled up. In Israel's case, that cup was the apparent destruction of her heritage. With the destruction of the northern kingdom and then the southern kingdom, it looked as if the mother would die alone, her children dead and destroyed (51:18–20). But now, God says, the day of destruction is past, and the cup of God's wrath is placed in the hands of the "tormentors" for them to drink (51:23). As elsewhere in the book, although the enemy nations were used by God to punish his people, they too are accountable for their proud and cruel behavior.[2]

Isaiah 52:1–12 represents the climax of God's promises not to allow his people to remain alienated from himself. Although the imagery of captivity and release is central to the promises, it is significant that Babylon itself is not mentioned. This suggests again that it is not merely physical captivity that is the problem God must solve.

This segment falls naturally into two parts. In 52:1–6, just as God demonstrated his unique deity in delivering his people from Egypt, so he will do again in delivering them from this new bondage (52:4–6). Once again, an important piece of evidence for that uniqueness is his ability to predict the whole thing in advance (52:6). Jerusalem will be transformed from slave to queen (52:1–2), and the transformation will not be the result of some deal between God and the captors (52:3). He was not forced to sell them into slavery in the first place, and there is no one who can stand up to him and demand payment for their return.

The second part of this climactic unit (52:7–12) brings to a conclusion all that has been said about redemption, not only since 49:1 but indeed since 40:1.[3] Both the ability and the desire of God to restore his people to himself have been amply demonstrated; all that remains is for the paeans of song (52:9) to begin. As is so typical of this book, Isaiah utilizes a graphic illustration to conclude the point. He pictures a besieged city waiting for news from a delivering army. Will the army be able to break through the besiegers? If so, there is hope; if not, all is lost.

---

1. See Ps. 75:8; Jer. 25:15, 17, 28; 51:7; Lam. 4:21; Ezek. 23:32–33; Hab. 2:16; Zech. 12:2; Matt. 26:42 (w. parallels in Mark and Luke); Rev. 14:10; 16:19; 17:4; 18:6.

2. See Isa. 10:12–19; 14:24–27; 34:1–8; 47:4–7.

3. Note the recurrence of such terms as "comfort," "arm of the LORD," and messenger of "good tidings" on the "mountain."

Suddenly, the watchmen on the walls of the city begin to "shout for joy" (52:8). They have seen a messenger far away on the mountain, and he is signaling the "good news" (52:7) of victory. God has bared "his holy arm," defeated the enemy, and "redeemed Jerusalem." Nothing remains but for Israel to lay hold of this promise in faith and to leave behind the old way with its sin and uncleanness. Nor is this to be some furtive sneaking off, lest the enemy discover what is happening and prevent it. No, the enemy is completely defeated and can do nothing to retain its hold on the former captives. They are free, free indeed, through the power of God.

MODERN PARALLELS. It is hard to imagine a clearer example of God's causing Israel's enemies to drink the cup they had once forced on Israel than that of modern Germany. From the *Krystallnacht* in the early 1930s, when the windows of Jewish-owned stores were smashed and the goods looted, through the terrible destruction of the Warsaw ghetto, through the degradation and terror of the death camps, Germany made the Jewish people drink a cup of almost unimaginable horror.

Whether God permitted this because of the Jewish people's refusal to recognize Jesus as Messiah is highly debatable, but the parallels with the Assyrian and Babylonian exiles are noteworthy. It is clear that God held the German people accountable for what they had done. The great German cities, the flower of European culture, were razed to the ground, from Hamburg to Dresden. The cup had been taken from the hands of the helpless Jews and put into the hands of the all-conquering Germans. The end came when the Red Army raped its way into Berlin. That was the final straw of degradation and humiliation. If Germany was permitted to do what it did by God, it was not able to escape his justice in the end.

A further parallel between the events of 1930–1950 and those described by Isaiah is the recognition of the Jewish state. It is possible that the Jewish state may never have been recognized if it were not for the shame of the Western powers over their silence concerning the Holocaust and if it were not for the influx of Jewish survivors into Palestine after World War II. Thus, the Nazi attempt to exterminate the Jews actually resulted in their becoming established in their own land again after nearly two thousand years of wandering. What the enemy intended for destruction was actually turned into hope, and the destruction that the enemy intended was visited back on himself.

A parallel event to what Isaiah pictures in 52:7–9 also occurred during World War II. During the so-called Battle of the Bulge in December 1944, the American forces in the Belgian city of Bastogne were surrounded by the

German troops. The American situation seemed hopeless, but they refused to surrender. Everything depended on whether the American Third Army, some hundred miles south of Bastogne, could force its way northward over snow-clogged roads and in the face of desperate German defenses. The Third Army commander, General George Patton, is said to have told his tank commanders, "Do whatever you have to, just keep going." That is just what they did, in one case outflanking the Germans by taking a road the Germans considered impassable and had not fortified. When American defenders met the American attackers on the outskirts of Bastogne, there were shouts of excitement. The siege was broken, and the faith of those who refused to surrender was justified.

GOD TO THE DEFENSE. This passage speaks of those who are powerless to defend themselves. The picture is of a widow who hopes to depend on her children to help her as the contents of the cup she is forced to drink leaves her staggering, but she has no children to take her hand, to help her. Her children too have fallen under the blows, and she is left alone, helpless. But, as a matter of fact, that is not the case. The "therefore" at the opening of 51:21 is significant. Precisely because there is no other help, "your God, who defends his people," will take action.

This enunciates an important spiritual principle. Contrary to that favorite aphorism "God helps those who help themselves," the Bible tells us that God helps those who cannot help themselves. This is the one aspect of the repeated admonition in Isaiah and elsewhere: "Wait on the LORD." It is often only when we have come to the end of all of our resources that we are able to turn to the Lord in faith and receive what he wants to do for us. This is surely a part of the reason why God placed Abraham and Sarah in a position of being utterly dependent on him, even to the extent of not knowing where they were going.

But why? Why does God wait until we are helpless, or at least aware of our helplessness before he acts? One of the main reasons is that we are usually unwilling to give up our control of the situation until we come to that extremity. That is what happened to Jacob. It was not until he had done everything he could and was finally in a place where he had no other resources that he was able to become utterly serious with God (Gen. 32:22–32). In a real sense this was the same situation with Hezekiah. Only after Sennacherib had taken Hezekiah's tribute and still refused to lift the siege on Jerusalem was Hezekiah ready to receive the help God had to offer. Gideon offers us a similar example. With 30,000 men against 100,000, the battle was a difficult proposition, but not an utterly hopeless one. With only 300, it *was* hopeless. In each of these cases, God's power was available before the final extremity, but it was not until that hour that the central figure was able to lay hold of it.

The same thing is true today. As long as we think the solution to our problems is somehow in ourselves, we are liable to think of God as an assistant or as a fall-back device. But to think of the almighty Creator in such a way is to deprive ourselves of his aid. He is not our servant. This is especially true in regard to our relation to him. As long as we think that we can do something to earn his favor, we are unlikely to cast ourselves on the Savior whom God has provided. We think we don't need a Savior—perhaps a teacher, or an example, or a friend, but not a Savior. This is why Paul takes the first three chapters of the book of Romans to demolish the idea that there is any righteousness in us at all. It is only when we admit that there is nothing we can do for ourselves to remove our sins and our sinning that we will turn to the Savior and receive the forgiveness, cleansing, and empowerment he has been wanting to give us all the time.

Why God acts. Someone has said that if it were not for the people in it, the church would be a wonderful institution. C. S. Lewis addresses this thought when he has Screwtape, a senior devil, instruct his young protégé, Wormwood, whose "subject" has started attending church, to get him to focus on the human foibles of the people worshiping next to him. The fact is that God is as frequently blasphemed (52:5) because of the behavior of those who claim to know him as for any other reason. Thus here in Isaiah, God says he must deliver his people from their captivity because their captors are using it as an occasion to blaspheme him. Ezekiel says much the same thing (Ezek. 36:19–20). Thus, God says here that he must raise Jerusalem out of the dust and dress her in splendid garments so that the world will know him for who he really is. A similar thought appears in the New Testament in Ephesians 5:25–27:

> Christ loved the church and gave himself up for her to make her holy, cleansing her by the washing with water through the word, and to present her to himself as a radiant church, without stain or wrinkle or any other blemish, but holy and blameless.

When we live as captives to sin, we make it appear to the watching world that God is unable to deliver us. When our lives are not marked by his holiness, we make it appear as if he is just one more of the gods, not the unique Creator and Redeemer of the world, whose moral character is unlike that of any of the so-called gods. For us to "know his name" (52:6) is not merely to know facts about God and his nature. Rather, it is so to participate in his life that his nature and character become ours. This is what Jesus meant when he prayed, "Holy Father, protect them by the power of your name—the name you gave to me—so that they may be one as we are one" (John 17:11).

The joy of redemption. Isaiah 52:7–12 is about the wonder and the joy of the "good news" of redemption. The early Christians understood that their message about Jesus Christ was the ultimate "good news," and they realized that the "good news" referred to in such Old Testament passages as this one found their ultimate meaning in Christ. But why was this message of God's coming "good news"? It was only so because the people in the besieged city realized the terrible danger in which they stood. If they had been stoutly denying that they were in any danger, the news of God's breaking through the enemy lines would have been treated not as good news but as useless news, or even worse, as bad news. What right does God have to come barging into our city? We are getting along very well, thank you.

In other words, a prerequisite for hearing good news may be first of all that we receive the true bad news. So John Wesley said to his young preachers, "Preach the Law until they are convicted, then preach Grace until they are converted." It is great good news to a person who knows he has just fallen out of an airplane to be told he has a parachute. By contrast, if that person is not aware of what is happening to him and does not realize that he is plunging toward the earth at an alarming rate of speed, the news about the parachute will seem irrelevant at best.

A good churchwoman wondered why she had so little a sense of God's grace in her life. She mentioned this to a wise counselor, and the counselor asked her, "When did you first know you were lost?" The woman responded indignantly, "I have never been lost! I have always known God from my earliest childhood." The counselor did not press her, and they went on to other things. But the woman kept thinking about that question. One night a few weeks later, she suddenly woke up in terror. She saw herself hurtling down a dark abyss, unable to stop. She was sure it was a dream and yet she was fully awake. She threw herself down at the side of her bed and cried, "Jesus, save me." Suddenly the vision of the abyss stopped, and she had an incredible sense of being held in strong arms. As she later recounted the story, her face lighted up with a smile: "I didn't know God's grace before because I didn't think I needed it. You can't be found until you know you are lost!"

Isaiah 52:13–53:12

❦

¹³ SEE, MY SERVANT will act wisely;
    he will be raised and lifted up and highly exalted.
¹⁴ Just as there were many who were appalled at him —
    his appearance was so disfigured beyond that of any man
    and his form marred beyond human likeness—
¹⁵ so will he sprinkle many nations,
    and kings will shut their mouths because of him.
For what they were not told, they will see,
    and what they have not heard, they will understand.

^{53:1} Who has believed our message
    and to whom has the arm of the LORD been revealed?
² He grew up before him like a tender shoot,
    and like a root out of dry ground.
He had no beauty or majesty to attract us to him,
    nothing in his appearance that we should desire him.
³ He was despised and rejected by men,
    a man of sorrows, and familiar with suffering.
Like one from whom men hide their faces
    he was despised, and we esteemed him not.

⁴ Surely he took up our infirmities
    and carried our sorrows,
yet we considered him stricken by God,
    smitten by him, and afflicted.
⁵ But he was pierced for our transgressions,
    he was crushed for our iniquities;
the punishment that brought us peace was upon him,
    and by his wounds we are healed.
⁶ We all, like sheep, have gone astray,
    each of us has turned to his own way;
and the LORD has laid on him
    the iniquity of us all.

⁷ He was oppressed and afflicted,
    yet he did not open his mouth;
he was led like a lamb to the slaughter,
    and as a sheep before her shearers is silent,
    so he did not open his mouth.

⁸ By oppression and judgment he was taken away.
 And who can speak of his descendants?
For he was cut off from the land of the living;
 for the transgression of my people he was stricken.
⁹ He was assigned a grave with the wicked,
 and with the rich in his death,
though he had done no violence,
 nor was any deceit in his mouth.

¹⁰ Yet it was the LORD's will to crush him and cause him
  to suffer,
 and though the LORD makes his life a guilt offering,
he will see his offspring and prolong his days,
 and the will of the LORD will prosper in his hand.
¹¹ After the suffering of his soul,
 he will see the light of life and be satisfied;
by his knowledge my righteous servant will justify many,
 and he will bear their iniquities.
¹² Therefore I will give him a portion among the great,
 and he will divide the spoils with the strong,
because he poured out his life unto death,
 and was numbered with the transgressors.
For he bore the sin of many,
 and made intercession for the transgressors.

ISAIAH 52:1–12 BROUGHT to the climax God's "comfort" (49:13; 51:3, 12, 19; 52:9) of his people in his insistence that their sin has not finally alienated them from him but that he has found a way to bring them back to him. Particularly in Isaiah 50–52 this ability to restore his people, and indeed all people, to himself is referred to as "the arm" of the Lord, an image of his incomparable power (50:2; 51:5, 9; 52:10). So we, the readers, are brought to a fever pitch of anticipation, particularly by the final call in 52:11–12 to leave the unclean and go out from bondage, both led by and followed by the Lord. Clearly, the "arm of the LORD" is about to be revealed.

We have had some hints about this arm in 42:1–6; 49:1–6; and 50:4–9, where God in each case promises to deliver not only his own people but the entire world by means of his obedient Servant. However, there have been increasingly disturbing overtones in these passages. They have not sounded like paeans of victory. To be sure, ultimate victory is promised, but it does not seem to be through smashing conquest. Rather, it is through an obedient revelation of God[1] in the midst of rejection and abuse.

Those overtones are now amply confirmed in 52:13–53:12. The arm of the Lord looks nothing like our stereotypical conquering hero. Especially after the exultant tone of 52:7–12, the somber notes of the present passage come as a shock. But that means that this section is in this place on purpose. To suggest it is here by accident or because of some obscure word association with the preceding or the following strains credulity beyond the breaking point. Someone, whether author or editor, was trying to make a point by placing this poem between the material of chapter 52 and that of chapter 54. That point is clearly to demonstrate an instrumental relationship between 52:13–53:12 and what both precedes it and follows it. Who is the mighty arm of the Lord (49:1–52:12) who makes possible the glorious invitations found in chapters 54 and 55? By what means is the alienation of sin overcome? The arm of the Lord is the ideal Servant—Israel as he was meant to be.

This poem is divided into five stanzas of three verses each. It moves from an introduction (52:13–15) to the Servant's rejection (53:1–3) to his carrying of "our" sins and transgressions (53:4–6) to the results of that carrying (53:7–9) to a revelation of the atoning nature of the carrying (53:10–12). This careful structuring demonstrates both the care with which the prophet approaches this particular statement and the importance he attaches to it.

Introduction (52:13–15)

THE POEM BEGINS with a note of triumph. The idea behind "act wisely" is to act in such a way as to succeed (thus the NASB's "will prosper"). There is no question about the outcome of the Servant's work. A day will come when the very same words will be used of him ("raised and lifted up") as are used only of God elsewhere in the book (6:1; 57:15). It is important to note that the poem closes on the same note of triumph ("a portion among the great ... divide the spoils with the strong," 53:12). The spoils belong to the victor. There is a reason why that point is made both at the beginning and the end of the poem. It is because nothing in between looks in the least like victory, certainly not any victory that proud, dominating humans can conceive of.

This anomalous view is presented immediately after the opening words. The disfigurement of the Servant is utterly shocking.[2] He hardly appears to

---

1. Note the references to speaking in the second and third of the so-called "Suffering Servant" passages (49:2; 50:4).
2. The pronoun translated "him" by the NIV at the end of the first clause in 52:14 is actually "you." Two possible interpretations exist, represented by the NIV and NASB. The first

be human. He is not the attractive figure that so many of the world's conquerors have been or pretended to be. Whether this thought continues into 52:15 depends on what is done with the first main verb in that verse. The meaning of the verb *nzh* in Hebrew is to sprinkle something on something else. But in each of its occurrences, what follows is what is sprinkled, and the indirect object—what is sprinkled upon—is marked by a preposition. Thus, normal syntax would require that here the nations are being sprinkled upon something else.

The absurdity of that picture has prompted the observation that in Arabic there is another root having these consonants, meaning "to startle." This would provide a good parallel to "shut their mouths" (in astonishment), which "sprinkle" does not provide. If we retain the meaning "sprinkle" (NIV and NASB) and assume that the object being sprinkled is not stated, then the sense of 52:15 is that the kings are struck dumb by the thought that the supposed conqueror has actually come to purify the nations by sprinkling something (blood? sacred water?) on them.[3] If "startle" is correct (NRSV, REB, JB, CB), the thought carries through from verse 14 to 15. Those to whom the Servant will bring justice are appalled that he will do so by means of his own injury and abuse. They have never "heard" of such a thing, yet now they "see" it.

Rejection of the Servant (53:1–3)

THIS SECOND STANZA continues the discussion of the response to the revelation of the Savior. But now we move beyond the initial astonishment to outright rejection. Isaiah makes it explicit that this Servant is "the arm of the LORD" that had been promised (53:1). But that report is clearly disbelieved. Why? Three reasons are given. (1) He comes onto the scene in a quiet and unassuming way (53:2). (2) He has no extraordinary beauty or attractiveness to draw people to him; his "appearance" was quite ordinary. (3) Finally, he is rejected because he takes on himself the pain and "suffering" of the world (53:3).

This suffering should not be restricted to physical suffering in the light of what else is said in the poem, but neither should it be construed to exclude such suffering, which is often as much the result of sin as murder or warfare

---

(cf. NIV) is that there is a mixing of second and third pronouns in referring to the Servant. This kind of mixing of pronouns is not infrequent in the prophets; see *Gesenius' Hebrew Grammar*, ed. E. Kautzsch, tr. A. Cowley (Oxford: Clarendon, 1910), 462. The other possibility is that "you" refers to the captive people, so the NASB inserts "my people" after "you." I believe the first interpretation is correct. See also Motyer, *Prophecy of Isaiah*, 425.

3. See Motyer, *Prophecy of Isaiah*, 425–26, for a defense of this view. See Oswalt, *Isaiah 40–66*, 374, n. 56, for the counterargument.

is. But we find pain and suffering disturbing, both because we do not know what to say in sympathy and because it reminds us of our own vulnerability. So we try to ignore it ("hide [our] faces") and not to think about it ("esteemed him not"). The Servant has come to take away the sins of the world, but no one pays any attention to him.

The Servant's Carrying of Sin (53:4–6)

IF THERE WERE any question about why the Servant suffers, these verses answer the question once and for all. Despite what "we" thought, he is not suffering because God has inflicted deserved punishment on him (53:4). It is our suffering that he bore, and it is for "our transgressions" and "our iniquities" that he suffered (53:5). The repetition of first-person plural pronouns hammers home that the Servant has suffered in "our" place.

There has been endless debate about who the first readers understood the "we" to refer to.[4] It seems plain to me that the obvious referents are the prophet and the people he is addressing. This makes it utterly clear that the people, while remaining the servants of God to bear witness to his saving power, are not the Servant of the Lord who will bring justice and deliverance to the earth (as some claim). Verse 6 drives this point home with imagery. "We," the blind, rebellious people of God (cf. 42:18–25), are the sheep who have gone astray, but he is the one who gets beaten for our willfulness!

The Results of Carrying Our Sin (53:7–9)

THIS STANZA DETAILS the Servant's innocence and submission and the injustice of the treatment he receives. The Servant is now compared to a sheep, and with very different results. In him it is the mild, defenseless nature of the sheep that is the basis of comparison. Although his suffering is manifestly unjust, he accepts it without protest (53:7). It is significant that the only extended metaphor in the poem deals with sheep, the animals of sacrifice.

The injustice of what the Servant suffered is further underlined in 53:8–9. He is deprived of justice, but he is also deprived of "descendants," evidently "cut off" in the prime of life.[5] As a final insult, he is buried with the rich.

---

4. See D. Clines, *I, He, We and They: A Literary Approach to Isaiah 53* (JSOTSup 1; Sheffield: JSOT Press, 1976). See also E. J. Young, *Isaiah Fifty-three: A Devotional and Expository Study* (Grand Rapids: Eerdmans, 1952).

5. An alternate interpretation of the Heb. is to be found in the NASB: "as for His generation, who considered / That He was cut off. . . ?" If this understanding is correct, then it is the idea, as in v. 3, that no one even cared enough about him to consider the injustice of his fate.

But is this an insult? Surely the Old Testament frequently treats riches as a blessing from God.[6] But it also has a more ambiguous view of riches, especially in the Prophets. Isaiah's statement in 5:8, "Woe to you who add house to house and field to field till no space is left and you live alone in the land," more accurately reflects the view of such prophets as Hosea and Amos (and Jesus). In their view, riches have all too often been amassed through violence and deceit.[7] The contrastive "though" seems to make clear that that is the sense here. The Servant is buried with the rich even "though" he did not do what they did.[8] As he had not opened his mouth in self-defense (53:7), neither had he opened it in "deceit" (53:9).

The Atoning Nature of the Carrying (53:10–12)

WHY HAVE THESE things happened to the Servant? The answer is given in this final stanza. They were not accidental; they were intended. Moreover, it was God's intention. The opening lines of 53:10 are terrible. What good father could *wish* for his son to be crushed? It is only possible if there was some unquestionably greater good to be obtained. And what greater good could possibly justify the crushing of the Servant? The answer is given in the second half of the verse. It is when the "life"[9] of the Servant is offered as a sin offering that God's purpose in bringing him to this place is realized ("prosper"). Then will the injustice of being deprived of children and a long life be rectified. The Servant did not come to tell people what God wants; rather, he came to *be* what God wants *for* us.[10] But how can someone who has been cut off from the land of the living without descendants

---

6. That point is clearly made in such passages as Deut. 6:10–12; Prov. 10:22; 14:24; and 19:4. However, there is the underlying theme that riches are a gift from God and should be held and used as such.

7. See Ps. 37:16; Prov. 11:4, 28; 13:7–8; 16:8; Hos. 12:7–8; Amos 3:14–4:1; Matt. 6:19–21.

8. The NASB tries to solve this problem by making the contrast between the "wicked" of v. 9a and the "rich" of v. 9b. But the Heb. does not support this.

9. The Heb. word *nepeš* ("life, soul, being, self") is associated with the Servant in all three verses of this stanza (NIV, "life," v. 10; "soul," v. 11; "life," v. 12). In all three cases the underlying idea is that the Servant has given his life for the sins and transgressions of others.

10. Unfortunately the NIV has obscured some of the power of the statement. The particle *ʾim* is better translated "if" or "when" than "though." It is *when* the Servant is offered up that God's purpose is achieved. The form of the verb is somewhat ambiguous, which accounts for three different translations. As it stands, it is either third fem. sing. or second masc. sing. If it is the first, then evidently "soul" (fem.) is the subject: "When she offers his soul [i.e. herself]. . . ." This has prompted some to correct to "When he [the Servant] offers his soul. . ." (cf. NRSV). If the second option is correct, then "you" is either the hearer or God. The NIV has opted for the latter; I opt for the former. See Oswalt, *Isaiah 40–66*, 401–2.

ever have these things? It certainly looks as though resurrection is the only answer.[11]

Verse 11 gives a more theological statement of what was accomplished in the Servant's death. It begins by recapping the previous statement, but this time from the Servant's point of view, saying that when his life has been offered up for others, he will "see" it and be "satisfied."[12] The hard struggle will have been worth it.

But what does that struggle accomplish for people who accept it on their own behalf? The second half of verse 11 answers that question in a tightly connected statement. Because the Servant knows God ("by his knowledge") in intimate relationship (see 42:1—6; 49:1—6; 50:4—9) and indeed shares God's own righteousness (lit., "the righteous one, my servant"), he will in turn be able to make many people righteous. How? By bearing "their iniquities," which is clearly what the "suffering of his soul" was about at the beginning of the verse.

Everything is summed up in 53:12, as the opening "therefore" indicates. But it is as though the author does not want anyone to miss the reason for God's ("I") giving the Servant the spoils of victory, because even though the cause has been fully stated in 53:4—11, he restates it again in the closing bicola of the verse. Why does God give his servant the victor's wreath? "Because" he was treated like one of the rebels when he was not and thus could bear their punishment and make "intercession" for them. If there are any remaining question about how the Servant brings God's justice to the world, this verse should clear it up.

SACRIFICE FOR OTHERS. As early as Philip's encounter with the Ethiopian eunuch (Acts 8:26—40), it has been normal for Christians to understand that Jesus Christ is the Servant about whom Isaiah is speaking in this chapter.[13] Despite myriad attempts to find a figure

---

11. R. N. Whybray, admitting that resurrection would be a logical conclusion if the Servant had indeed died, instead tries to demonstrate that he is not represented as having actually died (*Thanksgiving for a Liberated Prophet: An Interpretation of Isaiah 53* [JSOTSup 4; Sheffield: JSOT Press, 1978], 79—105). This seems to be a conclusion searching for evidence.

12. The MT simply says "he will see and be satisfied." The LXX adds "light" after "see"; this is supported by all the Qumran editions of Isaiah. This is a strong argument in favor of its originality, especially since the consonants of "light" (*ʾor*) could be confused with those for "see" (*rʾh*). The NIV addition "of life" has no textual support.

13. Childs's comment that Phillip did not identify Jesus as the Servant but only used the passage to preach to the eunuch the good news of Jesus Christ (*Isaiah*, 423) seems to me to be so fine a distinction that it can only have meaning for a late twentieth-century biblical critic.

in the sixth century B.C. who might be the referent in this passage, none has been successful.[14] By contrast, the congruence with Jesus' life is remarkable—so remarkable that those who deny the possibility of predictive prophecy have had to say that that Jesus consciously modeled himself on Isaiah's Servant to make it appear that he was the fulfillment of that prophecy. This from a man on whose lips was no deceit!

Jesus did indeed appear on the earth without any kind of fanfare or dominating presence (apart from the celebration of the angels). He was horribly disfigured, as all descriptions of the facts of crucifixion make plain. He did go to his death without any protest about its manifest injustice and without any attempt to defend himself, going so far as to ask Peter if he would have him disobey his Father's will (John 18:11). The prayer in the Garden of Gethsemane makes it clear that his death was indeed the Father's will. And his own words, uttered at the Last Supper, demonstrate that he understood his death to be a substitutionary one: "This is my blood of the covenant, which is poured out for many for the forgiveness of sins" (Matt. 26:28).

Those around him understood it that way as well. John the Baptist's identification of him as "the Lamb of God, who takes away the sin of the world" (John 1:29) cannot be understood in any other way. Likewise, Peter's sermon that inaugurated the Christian church stresses that baptism in the name of Jesus is "for the forgiveness of . . . sins" (Acts 2:38). Paul makes the point even more explicit when he says in Colossians 1:19–20:

> For God was pleased to have all his fullness dwell in him, and through him to reconcile to himself all things, whether things on earth or things in heaven, by making peace through his blood, shed on the cross.

And it seems clear that the inspiration for the famous "self-emptying" hymn in Philippians 2:5–11 is Isaiah 53, beginning and ending as it does with the Servant's transcendent glory and between those end points the downward staircase that ends at a cross.

But the Philippian passage also reminds us that there is a bridge not merely to the New Testament but to the present as well, for Paul calls his hearers to emulate the attitude that Christ had. Clearly, that attitude was one of self-denial for the sake of others. Just as the Servant did not hold on to the "rights" that were his but cheerfully gave them up so that others might live, so we are called to walk the same road. We too are called upon to consider others better than ourselves so that they can live.

---

14. The most concerted recent attempt to do so was by R. N. Whybray in his *Thanksgiving for a Liberated Prophet*. But the fact that he has to go to great lengths to show that the apparent meaning of the text is not correct suggests that the undertaking is a futile one.

On a secular level, we can think of the man who, having survived a plane crash into the icy waters of the Potomac River, kept refusing offers to pull him out while he assisted others. In the end, it is believed that he himself died. On another level we think of the five young men who wanted so desperately to bring the gospel to the Auca tribe in Ecuador. Misunderstanding their intentions, the Aucas murdered them all. Although the young men had pistols, they refused to use them on their murderers. But the selfless lives of those young men have inspired countless others to live as they lived, and today there are countless thousands who know Christ who would not know him otherwise. So Paul's question to the alleged followers of Christ is whether we are choosing to give up our lives for the sake of others.

ACCEPTING THE OFFERING. There are two levels at which this fourth revelation of the Servant has significance today. Both levels involve our response to what Jesus Christ, the Servant, the mighty arm of the Lord, has done. The first is our response to his self-offering. Verses 4–6 make it perfectly plain that the reason he suffered the abuse and injustice described in verses 7–9 was because of "our" sin. There is a certain anonymity in that plurality. Yes, "we" have sinned and "we" need to repent and do better. But in practice that often means that each of us accepts little responsibility for the sin and its consequences

Yet if I read verse 10 correctly (see comments above), the prophet focuses us down from the comfortable anonymity of the plural into a very direct second singular "you." He says that it is when each of us makes a sin offering of Jesus' life that he will see his children, live a long life, and see the success of his Father's plan for him. It is as though Christ comes to us with his own broken body in his arms and says, "Here, offer me up to the Father as an offering in your place." What will we say?

Another image is suggested by verse 11. We are told that after the suffering of his entire being (*nepeš*), "he will see ... and be satisfied." Although the word translated "suffering" is not that used of birth pangs but connotes more the idea of misery or unremitting effort, there is still a parallel to the act of giving birth. I was present in the delivery room when our third child was born. It did not take great reasoning powers to recognize that "natural" childbirth is not the same as "painless" childbirth. Karen, my wife, was fully conscious and was doing all the right things, but pain and struggle were written eloquently on her face and body. Finally, there came the great moment when Peter was born. I confess that I did not think he was very attractive; he was red and wrinkled and yowling. But when the obstetrician laid him on

Karen's breast, I watched in wonder as all the pain and struggle washed out of her face and she beamed with love at that little boy. Go through it again? No. Worth it? Yes. That is how it is with Jesus. He "sees" the newborn Christian and is "satisfied." He considers all that it cost him to redeem us as not too much.

But suppose when he offers himself to us, we respond that we don't need a sin offering. Suppose we have rejected the "old-fashioned" idea of sin and consider ourselves to be as worthy as the next person of the blessings of God. What then? It would be as though, after all the labor and struggle, the baby is stillborn. Then indeed it was all for nothing. Then indeed the Savior finds no satisfaction in the offering he made.

Can humans thwart the will of God? Not in any ultimate sense. There *will* be a new heaven and a new earth, and all the redeemed *will* inhabit them. There *will* be a great crowd of the redeemed. But those who are invited first may choose not to come in (Luke 14:16–24). From God's side he has done everything necessary, and "whosoever will may come." But we must accept the offering made on our behalf. Without that "wedding garment" the door of the banquet hall remains closed, and the Savior's sufferings are in vain for us (Matt. 22:11–12).

Living the life. If we have accepted the offering of Christ in our place, there is a further response incumbent on us—the one Paul presents in Philippians 2:5–11. We too are called on to live the Servant's life. That life begins and ends in a sense of triumph. It was precisely because Jesus knew who he was, where he had come from, and where he was going that he was able to move from heaven to a barn, from knowing everything to knowing nothing, from supplying all the world's needs to becoming dependent on the breast of a little refugee girl for his very life. He could lay aside the robes of glory because he knew who he was.

We need that same kind of absolute assurance. A man rushed into church one evening and shouted to those gathered there for the service, "I've read the end of the book! We win!" Those who have the witness of the Holy Spirit that they are the children of God (Rom. 8:16) and who know that their sins are forgiven are those who can overcome the world with love (1 John 5:1–5). They do not need to worry about their "image" or "position." They are free to take the lowest place and to "prosper" there. Their highest concern is to be in tune with their Father's will for their lives. They can confidently give themselves without reservation, facing success with humility and failure with stability, knowing all along that in the end all things are theirs.

That kind of assurance will be necessary for servants because their lot is one of astonishment and rejection. We all want the balm of servanthood, but who can bear its twisted face? The person who gives unstintingly will always be looked at with distrust. "What's her angle? What's he trying to prove?" Who wants to be known as a "goody-goody"? And if you really seek to implement the teachings of Christ, such as love your enemies, it will not be long before people look on you as not merely strange and unnatural but somewhat subversive.

Perhaps the worst aspect of the cross we are called to bear for Christ's sake is simply being taken for granted. You are pouring out your life for others, and they simply take the cup of water you spent so much time drawing, swig it down, throw the cup on the ground, and go on, without even a look in your direction, let alone a "thank you." They "esteemed him not." If that's what they did to the Master, why should we servants expect to be treated better (John 15:20–21)? So if we are to endure this and not become either cynical and embittered or pious and prudish, there will have to be in us, and singing through us, the song of final triumph.

What is the burden of our servanthood? If we look at the picture of the Servant here, it is clear. We are called upon to bear the griefs and sorrows, the burdens, of those around us. This is hard. It is easier to tell them what the cure for their troubles is. That way we do not have to become involved with them. But that was not the way of the Servant. He did not tell us where to take our burdens. No, he took them.

In a practical way, this means we must help put our shoulders under the grief and sorrow of the AIDS patient, the struggle of the single parent, the confusion of the pregnant teenager. He *bore* our griefs and sorrows. To be sure we cannot bear these in the way the Savior could and can, but we can help those around us carry them to the place where they can be unloaded onto him. In our worst nightmares, we need to see ourselves lifting spotless, pharisaic hems lest the sins and transgressions of the world should besmirch them.

A fact of the Servant's ministry was its apparent failure in the short term. According to 53:7–9, he died childless in the midst of life, deprived of justice and treated as though he had been violent and deceitful. But he was content if he was simply doing his Father's will. The same must be true for servants today. If we make success as the world counts success our goal, we run the serious danger of losing everything. If we are to walk in the footsteps of Isaiah and of the Son of God, we need to be prepared to leave the outcome of our servanthood in God's hands, bending everything in us to one end, being faithful.

There is nothing wrong with seeking to be a success for God—much better that than trying to be a failure for God! The only issue here is the subtlety of "success." If success is obedience, that is one thing. But if success defined in this world's terms is the evidence of obedience, that is another thing. Someone has said that if you hope to be a successful megachurch pastor, you cannot talk about sin or money. Yet those are two of the things the Bible talks about most. Suppose Isaiah or the other prophets had never talked about sin. Neither Israel nor the church would exist today. As the Servant was determined to be faithful and to leave the outcome of his service to God, so must we.

Ultimately, of course, our servanthood cannot be redemptive in the way Christ's was. He alone is the Redeemer. That reminds us of the ultimate impossibility of separating the "personal" and the "social" gospel. A "personal" gospel that does not impel us into society is deficient, just as a "social" gospel that does not spring from a transformed person is deficient. On the one hand, when we bear the burdens of a hurting world, our goal is to bear them to Christ. To clothe, to feed, to assist, and yet not to bring persons to a personal knowledge of God through the cross of Christ is to have missed what the good news is about in the first place. On the other hand, simply to help people deal with their guilt while failing to show how sin has effects in all corners of life and failing to help people deal with those effects is not to serve in the way of the Servant.

Isaiah 54:1–17

¹"Sing, O barren woman,
  you who never bore a child;
burst into song, shout for joy,
  you who were never in labor;
because more are the children of the desolate woman
  than of her who has a husband,"
                          says the LORD.

²"Enlarge the place of your tent,
  stretch your tent curtains wide,
  do not hold back;
lengthen your cords,
  strengthen your stakes.
³For you will spread out to the right and to the left;
  your descendants will dispossess nations
  and settle in their desolate cities.

⁴"Do not be afraid; you will not suffer shame.
  Do not fear disgrace; you will not be humiliated.
You will forget the shame of your youth
  and remember no more the reproach of your
    widowhood.
⁵For your Maker is your husband—
  the LORD Almighty is his name—
the Holy One of Israel is your Redeemer;
  he is called the God of all the earth.
⁶The LORD will call you back
  as if you were a wife deserted and distressed in spirit—
a wife who married young,
  only to be rejected," says your God.
⁷"For a brief moment I abandoned you,
  but with deep compassion I will bring you back.
⁸In a surge of anger
  I hid my face from you for a moment,
but with everlasting kindness
  I will have compassion on you,"
  says the LORD your Redeemer.

⁹"To me this is like the days of Noah,
when I swore that the waters of Noah would never
again cover the earth.
So now I have sworn not to be angry with you,
never to rebuke you again.
¹⁰Though the mountains be shaken
and the hills be removed,
yet my unfailing love for you will not be shaken
nor my covenant of peace be removed,"
says the LORD, who has compassion on you.

¹¹"O afflicted city, lashed by storms and not comforted,
I will build you with stones of turquoise,
your foundations with sapphires.
¹²I will make your battlements of rubies,
your gates of sparkling jewels,
and all your walls of precious stones.
¹³All your sons will be taught by the LORD,
and great will be your children's peace.
¹⁴In righteousness you will be established:
Tyranny will be far from you;
you will have nothing to fear.
Terror will be far removed;
it will not come near you.
¹⁵If anyone does attack you, it will not be my doing;
whoever attacks you will surrender to you.

¹⁶"See, it is I who created the blacksmith
who fans the coals into flame
and forges a weapon fit for its work.
And it is I who have created the destroyer to work havoc;
¹⁷   no weapon forged against you will prevail,
and you will refute every tongue that accuses you.
This is the heritage of the servants of the LORD,
and this is their vindication from me,"
declares the LORD.

AS WITH THE THREE other Servant Songs, there is a commentary following the fourth one. But unlike the others, where a song of praise forms the conclusion of the commentary (cf. 42:10–13; 49:13; perhaps 51:7–8), here the entire commentary (chs. 54–55) has a lyrical quality. As I observed at the beginning of the subdivision of Isaiah 49–55 (see comments on ch. 49), the tone of chapters 54–55 reflects the assurance that God's promises to restore his people to himself in chapters 49–52 have come to their fulfillment. Now anticipation changes to invitation and celebration. To be sure, the revelation in God's Son to make this reconciliation possible will not take place for nearly seven hundred years. Nevertheless, the revelation is now complete, and those who accept the promise can enjoy that reconciliation in advance.

In reality Isaiah 54–55 forms two parts of a single whole. Chapter 54 is a love song by God to Zion, his estranged bride, telling her all the things he is going to do in restoring her. Chapter 55 is the invitation proper, calling on the bride not to miss through unbelief what is hers. Together they constitute one of the most beautiful pieces of literature in the entire Bible.

Restoration and Hope for a Disgraced Woman (54:1–10)

IN THESE TEN VERSES God speaks to Israel in the image of a disgraced woman. She is the barren one (vv. 1–3), the widow (vv. 4–5), the divorced one (vv. 6–8). To each of these, God promises restoration and hope, and the promises are brought to a climax in verses 9–10. In these climactic verses God makes it clear again that the problem being addressed in this section is not captivity in Babylon but alienation from his presence. Here he says that his "unfailing love" and "his covenant of peace" are forever.

This does not mean that Israel will no longer be subject to condemnation and punishment, as later history shows. It means rather that somehow God is now reconciled in himself to his people. Whatever was necessary to satisfy the righteous anger of God at human sin has been done, and God can proclaim that there is no longer any barrier to persons experiencing that reconciliation. Humans need never be separated from him again. Clearly, what was described in 52:13–53:12 is the means to this end.

In the ancient Near East almost the worst fate that could befall a woman was to have no children. This idea runs through the Bible from Genesis to Galatians, where it is the symbol of the inability of human resources to solve either human or human-divine problems.[1] Here (54:1–3) God says that those who have experienced his grace will no longer be fruitless but will live lives of unexpected abundance, with more "descendants" than they can account for.

Widowhood was also considered a disgrace in many parts of the ancient world (54:4). A woman made her contributions to society through her husband, and now she was left alone, no longer a contributor but just a liability. Yet God says that Israel should no longer consider herself to be a widow. Her "Maker" is her "husband."

Who is this one who has "married" her, delivering her from the disgrace? Verse 5 rings with his titles. Not only is he the Creator, he is also the One who has all the host of heaven at his command ("Yahweh of heaven's armies; NIV, "LORD Almighty"). He is Israel's "Holy One," whose holy nature is not turned to judgment (as in much of chs. 1–39) but to redemption ("Redeemer"). Nor is his creative, redemptive power limited to some locale or to some group. He is the "God of all the earth." *This* is the One who has taken you as his own! Who could be sad?

But there was an even worse disgrace than childlessness or widowhood: divorce. At least in widowhood your husband had left you alone involuntarily. The divorced woman was one who had been found wanting in some way and was willfully "rejected" (54:6). This was Israel: She had failed God and was cast out of her home. But God has found a way and brought her back to himself. His "anger" was for a "moment," but his "compassion" is "everlasting" (54:7–8). In the work of the Servant the righteous anger (the justice) of God is satisfied so that his "unfailing love" (54:10) can find expression for those who will receive it.

Restoration and Hope for a Ruined City (54:11–17)

THE IMAGE NOW changes from disgraced woman to a ruined city. The people are like a city that has been "lashed by storms" (54:11), subjected to "tyranny" and "terror" (54:14), and has experienced "havoc" (54:16) within it. But since God is the One who brought all that to pass (54:16), he is the One who can change it all (54:15, 17).[2]

Again, the promises are lyrical in tone. In place of weathered, broken walls stained with smoke, there are "battlements of rubies" glittering in the sun. In

---

1. Barrenness and inability to give birth are also key themes in Isaiah (see 26:16–18; 29:22–23; 37:3; 66:9).

2. All the prophets make this important point in one way or another: Since it was God who caused disaster in the first place, he had the power to deliver those who met the conditions for such redemption (see, e.g., Isa. 10:5–6, 17–19). If the disaster had occurred in spite of him, then he could hardly have the ability to deliver them.

place of tyranny and terror, there is true learning, "peace" (*šalom*), "righteousness," and security. These blessings are for those who gladly accept the role of "servants of the LORD." How can sinful, rebellious Israel enter into such a role? Through the ministry of the Servant of the Lord. Through his self-giving, all the promises made to his servants in chapters 40–48 can be realized.[3]

AN OLD MAN lies in a hospital bed. The story of his life is written in the deep furrows on his face, his heavily veined nose, and his bloodshot eyes. But deeper than those more superficial evidences lies the flat, bleak look in those eyes. He has tasted life to the full, and the taste has been bitter. Now he waits for the end, wondering if what lies beyond will be even more bitter. To the side of his bed comes a woman. Life has not been very kind to her either. Her dress is not in the latest fashion, nor is her hair dressed in a becoming way. Her complexion is sallow, and attempts to improve it with make-up have not been entirely successful. But here the similarity between the two figures ends, for out of her eyes shine eagerness, humor, hope, and love. "Hello, Dad," she says with a smile.

He turns his head slightly to look at her and then turns away. "I know what you want to say to me, and you might as well save your breath. It's too late." Too late for forgiveness from God, too late for a new start, too late to change the past.

"But Dad, it's never too late! Look what Christ has done for me! I was in the gutter, drinking myself to death, just as you said I would. But he saw something in me to love! Everybody else said I was no good, and he told them to 'shut up.'"

"Daughter, you don't know what I've done. I was a preacher! Now I've done things I can't even talk about. If your God is so good and loving, he wouldn't have anything to do with me. I'm too far gone."

"Daddy, you look at me! Nobody is too far gone for Jesus Christ! He took every sin that was ever committed or ever will be committed on this earth. If you think you're the worst sinner there ever was, you've got another think coming. He died for Hitler! Do you think you're worse than Hitler? No, you're just like Hitler, too proud to get down on your face and ask God to forgive you. He will forgive you, Daddy! He will! Just tell him you're sorry and ask him!"

---

3. Note that while all but one of the references to the "servant" in chs. 40–48 are clearly to the nation as a whole, the proportions are exactly reversed in chs. 49–55, where only one of the references (this one in 54:17) is to the nation.

The old man turned his head to look at his grown daughter. Touched by her intensity, he looked at her as he had not in a long time. And looking at her, he saw what was undeniably true—she was being transformed from the inside out. Suddenly, he was overcome with an almost unbearable longing. He was a wreck and his life was a wreck, and it was soon coming to an end. Was it possible that even at this late date some of that light on his daughter's face could be his? So, hesitantly, he reached his hand out from under the sheet and took hers. In the next moments as he brokenly confessed his sins and his need and confessed a very tiny faith bolstered by his daughter's kiss, barrenness became fruitfulness, solitary disgrace became the welcoming embrace of the world's Maker, and rejection became joyous acceptance. When he opened his eyes, the broken walls of his life had become battlements of rubies.

THIS PASSAGE SHOWS us the heart of the gospel of Christ. God has reconciled his lost world to himself. He has not waited for us to find a way to bridge the gap between him and us, as he certainly could have in his own righteousness. After all, we are the ones who created the breach between him and ourselves, so let us find a way across it. But of course, there is no way from our side. For God to wait in the lonely isolation of his moral perfection for us to come to him would be to wait for all eternity. Our sinfulness makes it impossible to get ourselves to a place where we can stand before his blazing purity and survive. "The soul who sins ... will die" (Ezek. 18:4).

Yet the amazing thing about God is that he gets no satisfaction from the richly deserved death of the sinner (Ezek. 18:32; 33:11). Some of the family members of the victims of Oklahoma City bomber Timothy McVeigh were disappointed when they were prevented from seeing him die. They wanted that satisfaction. Not so with God. Not even the death of the most heinous criminal brings a grim smile of satisfaction to the face of God. Rather, there is grief in his heart like the grief of a David who cried, "O Absalom, my son, my son," over the death of his rebel son, who would have killed his father without a qualm.

So what did God do as an expression of his "unfailing love," his "everlasting kindness," his "covenant of peace"? What did he do so that the "barren woman" could be surrounded with laughing children, the "widow" could be married to the most wonderful husband in the world, and the "rejected" divorcée could know that the rejection was only for a moment while the acceptance was forever? What he did was to take all that proud emptiness, all that solitary self-sufficiency, all that demand for our own way, into himself.

This is the true face of God—not the stern, implacable Judge dispassionately rehearsing the endless list of our crimes and in the end grimly meting out exactly what we have deserved. No, this "Maker," this "God of all the earth," is our Father, who will go to any lengths to see that we do *not* get what we deserve. The judgment has been taken by the Judge, who can now proclaim that there is no more judgment outstanding against the accused.

Thus, from God's perspective, he will never pronounce judgment again (54:9). From his perspective, "no weapon forged against" his people will ever succeed again (54:17). That is, no further punishment or discipline is necessary because it has all been taken by God himself.

But that is from God's side. Suppose we do not continually avail ourselves of his provision of grace and mercy. Suppose we decide to use that grace so that we can persist in a life of sin. This would be like God's saying to us as he finishes cleaning out the garbage dump where we have been living and turning it into a lush vegetable garden, "You will never be sick and hungry again." That is true from God's perspective. But it assumes that we will continue to live in the middle of that garden. If we decide to move over to the next garbage dump and still try to claim those promises, we will discover that while the effects of that move are also covered in what God did for us in his self-giving, they will continue if we choose to live outside his grace.

There is nothing more God needs to do for his "covenant of peace" to be ours forever. "The punishment that brought us peace was upon him, and by his wounds we are healed" (53:5). We are "accepted in the beloved." But there is something we must do to experience that covenant forever: We must continually choose to live under its terms.

Isaiah 55:1–13

¹ "COME, ALL YOU who are thirsty,
    come to the waters;
and you who have no money,
    come, buy and eat!
Come, buy wine and milk
    without money and without cost.
² Why spend money on what is not bread,
    and your labor on what does not satisfy?
Listen, listen to me, and eat what is good,
    and your soul will delight in the richest of fare.
³ Give ear and come to me;
    hear me, that your soul may live.
I will make an everlasting covenant with you,
    my faithful love promised to David.
⁴ See, I have made him a witness to the peoples,
    a leader and commander of the peoples.
⁵ Surely you will summon nations you know not,
    and nations that do not know you will hasten to you,
because of the LORD your God,
    the Holy One of Israel,
    for he has endowed you with splendor."

⁶ Seek the LORD while he may be found;
    call on him while he is near.
⁷ Let the wicked forsake his way
    and the evil man his thoughts.
Let him turn to the LORD, and he will have mercy on him,
    and to our God, for he will freely pardon.

⁸ "For my thoughts are not your thoughts,
    neither are your ways my ways,"
                                    declares the LORD.
⁹ "As the heavens are higher than the earth,
    so are my ways higher than your ways
    and my thoughts than your thoughts.
¹⁰ As the rain and the snow
    come down from heaven,
and do not return to it
    without watering the earth

and making it bud and flourish,
>so that it yields seed for the sower and bread for
>>the eater,
[11] so is my word that goes out from my mouth:
>It will not return to me empty,
but will accomplish what I desire
>and achieve the purpose for which I sent it.
[12] You will go out in joy
>and be led forth in peace;
the mountains and hills
>will burst into song before you,
and all the trees of the field
>will clap their hands.
[13] Instead of the thornbush will grow the pine tree,
>and instead of briers the myrtle will grow.
This will be for the LORD's renown,
>for an everlasting sign,
>which will not be destroyed."

WE TURN NOW from the announcement in chapter 54 that all is forgiven to the invitation to experience that forgiveness. The tone is one of earnest appeal with no less than twelve imperative or jussive verbs occurring in the first seven verses. Everything has been done, the tables are set, all is in readiness. How tragic it would be if those who are invited fail to come. Once again, we sense the great significance of what was prophesied in chapter 53. Something is revealed there that has changed the tone of all that follows. The bride *is* restored, the city *is* rebuilt. What a tragedy if those for whom all this has been done fail to enter into it. They *must* come.

In 55:1–5 the invitation is expressed in the strongest terms to those who have no resources in themselves. It begins in physical imagery ("come to the waters," "come, buy and eat," vv. 1–2) and moves onto a more spiritual plane ("that your soul may live," v. 3). God's invitation is not merely to find a supply of bodily needs but to satisfy a person's whole being (*nepeš;* NIV "soul") with true life. Once again, as in 54:10, the language of "everlasting covenant" is used. The old covenant was broken and thus legally annulled after the allotted punishment had been meted out. But God promises another covenant, this one on the pattern of the unconditional one given to "David" (55:3).

But more is going on than simply a similarity between the covenants. It is plain that in some sense this "everlasting covenant" *is* the covenant with

David. For what David was in part, "a witness to the peoples" (55:4), the nation now will be able to bring to fulfillment (see also 43:8–13).[1] The nations of the world will flock to restored Israel because of their God (55:5).

This is, of course, exactly what was predicted in Isaiah 2. This everlasting covenant, evidently made possible by what was described in chapter 53, will mean that God's people really will be enabled to fulfill the servanthood promised to them at the beginning of the book. But they must accept what God has done for them. A banquet table is worse than useless to the person who is either too proud or too ashamed to come and eat from it.

Verses 6–11 address the universal problem of people who hear the invitation of God with clarity. They cannot deny the reality of the choice before them: to stay where they are in unbelief or to go forward in immense uncertainty. Surely for people in Isaiah's own day, but no less so for those who read these words in the Exile, the message of what is now 52:13–53:12 was largely a mystery. What in the world was God talking about? Who is this person, and how in the world can what he did make it possible for God to be *eternally* reconciled to his people?

God's challenge to these people is to exercise faith first and let understanding come afterward. God promises that what he says (his "word," 55:11) is indeed reliable and that forgiveness and abundance are theirs now and in the future, if they will only seek him sincerely and unreservedly. Once again, the issue is not deliverance from physical captivity but deliverance from alienation from God—the real problem. If the "wicked" will turn from their "way" and "thoughts" (55:7) to God's "ways" and "thoughts" (55:8–9), even if those "ways" and "thoughts" are not perfectly intelligible to them, they will be pardoned and restored.

All of this is brought to a close in 55:12–13. While much more than deliverance from physical captivity is being talked about, that imagery would communicate most immediately in the circumstances of the Exile. All nature will rejoice in the redemption of humanity (cf. 42:10; 44:23; 49:13), and in place of sorrow and sighing there will be "joy" and "peace" (cf. 35:10; 51:11) as the captives return to their God.

Bridging Contexts

JESUS USES THIS same intensity of invitation in his parable of the king's banquet (Luke 14:23). When those who were first invited to the banquet refused to come, the king told his servants to go out "to the roads and country lanes and make them come in, so that my house will

---

1. Westermann, *Isaiah 40–66*, 283.

be full." God has made all the preparations, and he *will* find people to respond to his invitation. As Paul says, not many of these will be mighty or wise or noble, as the world defines those (1 Cor. 1:26–29). The mighty, the wise, and the noble demand that God's ways and thoughts be made intelligible to them first. But the lowly, the helpless, and the broken don't have to have things explained to them; they simply see the open door and the loaded tables.

An illustration of both the gravity and the intensity of this invitation can be illustrated by a time of tragedy, such as a flood. A mother, a son, and a daughter are clinging to the upper branches of a large tree surrounded by raging flood waters. The rescue team in a boat cannot get right up to the tree because of debris, but the distance between the boat and the tree can be jumped with effort. The team in the boat shout with urgency, "Jump, jump," but the family members are afraid. Finally, summoning up courage, the son jumps and lands safely in the boat. Then the daughter jumps. She falls into the water, but the rescuers are ready and quickly pull her into the boat. Now the rescuers along with the son and daughter plead with the mother, "Jump, jump, you can do it! We'll catch you if you fall short." There is a compelling urgency in the invitation. But she is afraid, and as she debates whether to jump or remain in the apparent safety of the tree, there is a terrible crack, the tree falls, and she is swept away with it. "Seek the LORD while he may be found."

TRUST AND SURRENDER. From Abraham to the present the nature of faith has remained the same. We ask ourselves why God called Abraham to start journeying without knowing his precise destination (Gen. 12:1). It is because of the human problem. We want to decide what is right and wrong for ourselves. Nothing has changed since the Garden of Eden. We do not wish to be told by our Creator that something is wrong for us when everything appears so delightful. Neither do we wish to be told that something is good for us when it looks as though it is going to take a lot of effort and may actually bring us some pain. We want to hold the place of God in our lives and have God serve us, supplying our needs as we dictate. So faith always involves letting go of secure footholds and (apparent) certainties to do things God's way.

This is what Zerubbabel was assured of in Zechariah 4:6: "'Not by might nor by power, but by my Spirit,' says the LORD Almighty." And this was what Peter grasped for a moment as he stepped over the side of the boat onto the surface of the heaving waves (Matt. 14:29). As long as we first insist that everything about God's ways and plans be made completely intelligible to us before we decide to act on his invitation, we will never act.

If, however, we will surrender our right to decide what is best for us and allow God to determine that, we are on our way home. We have turned that most critical corner—the corner of surrender. Now we are allowing God to be the Creator and to dictate to us the terms under which we were made to operate. So God's invitation comes to all of us, not merely those who have never entered a relationship with him.

To be sure, it comes to us as he desperately pleads with us to jump from that apparently secure tree of pride and self-sufficiency into his arms. It is a plea to jump from appearance to reality. The life outside of God is only apparently secure and abundant. It really has none of that to offer in the end. To remain in its hold is to choose loss and poverty. It is to live in defiance of the Holy One who made us. That way cannot possibly lead in any other direction but final loss. So God calls us to jump out of what is only an appearance into what is a reality. Come from hunger to food, from thirst to water, from sadness to joy, from death to life. The person debating whether to jump says, "But I already have food, and water, and joy, and life." The fruits of faith are only apparent after you have jumped. Then, looking back, you can say, "Oh my, what I thought I had was only an illusion."

But the invitation is also for those who have been living the life of faith for many years. One of the problems of living on earth is that the longer we live here, the more its ways become our ways. A child has no difficulty in believing in the unseen world; it is only adults who tend to "pooh-pooh" it. In the same way, a child has no difficulty in believing that God can do the impossible. It is only adults who feel they have to temper "childish enthusiasm."

I am not speaking here about our increasingly pagan "mind over matter" philosophy with its suggestions that we can find ways to manipulate the spirit world to make it serve our purposes. That is the door to death. Rather, I am saying that it is at God's urgent invitation that we are to leave our comfortable worldly ways and launch out in paths of service and living that do not depend on our strength but on his. When he speaks, his word will bear the fruit he intends in wonderful ways in our lives.

Isaiah 56:1–8

T HIS IS WHAT the LORD says:

"Maintain justice
and do what is right,
for my salvation is close at hand
and my righteousness will soon be revealed.
² Blessed is the man who does this,
the man who holds it fast,
who keeps the Sabbath without desecrating it,
and keeps his hand from doing any evil."

³ Let no foreigner who has bound himself to the LORD say,
"The LORD will surely exclude me from his people."
And let not any eunuch complain,
"I am only a dry tree."

⁴For this is what the LORD says:

"To the eunuchs who keep my Sabbaths,
who choose what pleases me
and hold fast to my covenant—
⁵ to them I will give within my temple and its walls
a memorial and a name
better than sons and daughters;
I will give them an everlasting name
that will not be cut off.
⁶ And foreigners who bind themselves to the LORD
to serve him,
to love the name of the LORD,
and to worship him,
all who keep the Sabbath without desecrating it
and who hold fast to my covenant—
⁷ these I will bring to my holy mountain
and give them joy in my house of prayer.
Their burnt offerings and sacrifices
will be accepted on my altar;
for my house will be called
a house of prayer for all nations."

⁸ The Sovereign LORD declares—
    he who gathers the exiles of Israel:
"I will gather still others to them
    besides those already gathered."

ON THE SURFACE, it might seem as if the book should have ended with chapter 55. What more could remain after those stirring promises that God's grace is freely available to all who accept the urgent invitation? Isaiah 55:12–13 with its benedictory tone sounds like the climax of all that can be said about the divine-human relationship.

Yet the book is far from over. In our chapter arrangement no less than eleven chapters remain. Bernard Duhm, the late nineteenth-century commentator, felt the division between chapters 40–55 and 56–66 so strongly that he proposed that there was yet a third editor/author of the book, whom he designated "Trito-Isaiah."[1]

However, it is not necessary to go to such lengths to understand what is taking place in this segment and in the book as a whole. A careful reader will note an apparent contradiction between the teachings of chapters 1–39 and those of chapters 40–55. This seeming contradiction may be illustrated by the differing uses of the word "righteousness." In chapters 1–39 it is used exclusively for behavior that is in keeping with the statutes of God. But in chapters 40–55, except for two places, the term refers to God's "righteousness" in faithfully delivering his people in spite of their previous sin. In other words, if the book ended at chapter 55, the reader might well assume that since righteousness is basically impossible for humans, we are delivered into a "position" of righteousness by God's grace through his Servant and that the stress on righteous living in the first part of the book is not incumbent on those living in grace.

In a remarkable way, chapters 56–66 synthesize the teaching of the two earlier sections, showing that actual righteous living is a requirement for the servants of God (i.e., chs. 1–39) but that such righteousness is only possible through the grace of God (i.e., chs. 40–55). Thus, far from being an unfortunate and miscellaneous appendix to "the real book," these chapters form the

---

1. Duhm, *Das Buch Jesaja*. While Duhm thought that most of the material in chs. 56–66 was the work of one person, subsequent thinking has largely moved to seeing the material as a rather disparate collection of writings from many members of the exilic community. For a select bibliography on the topic, see Childs, *Isaiah*, 439. As in earlier segments, Childs attempts to pay tribute to this point of view while still reading the material as a theological unity, something I do not believe is possible.

necessary conclusion and climax to the book's teaching. As such, they show us the expected characteristics of the life of servants of the Lord.[2]

I must touch on a second matter concerning the structure of this segment of the book. A number of recent commentators have proposed a chiastic or concentric structure, in which chapters 60–62 form the centerpiece.[3] I believe this is correct. The function of a chiasm is to give the midpoint special prominence. Thus, we find the culmination of the servants' and the Servant's ministry in focus in chapters 60–62 as restored Jerusalem fulfills the promised ministry of being a light to the nations.

But why not put this material at the end of the book (note the promise of the new heaven and the new earth in ch. 65)? I believe that this is directly in line with a common feature in the book. Isaiah is unwilling to end any segment in the book with the kind of promise that will leave readers with the feeling that their present behavior is unimportant because of the certainty of future promises of blessing. So, although "Jerusalem, the light of the world," is highlighted in the center of the literary structure, the final words of the book have to do with the necessity of obeying God if we are to be among that worshiping crowd from every tribe, tongue, and nation.

The chiastic structure looks like this:

A. Obedient foreigners (56:1–8)
   B. Necessity of ethical righteousness (56:9–59:15a)
      C. Divine warrior (59:15b–21)
         D. Jerusalem, light of the world (60:1–62:12)
      C' Divine warrior (63:1–6)
   B' Necessity of ethical righteousness (63:7–66:17)
A' Obedient foreigners (66:18–24)

It is important to observe that B' is not merely a mirror image of B. There are important advances in the thought there even though the general topic is the same (see the book outline at the conclusion of the introduction).

Verse 1 provides an immediate illustration of the synthesizing function mentioned above. It calls on the reader to "maintain justice and do what is right" in language similar to that found repeatedly in chapters 1–39. But in the same breath it says we should do this because God's "righteousness"—

---

2. For a fuller discussion of this point, see my "Righteousness in Isaiah," 177–91. I do not disagree with Motyer's identification of these chapters as "The Book of the Anointed Conqueror" (*Prophecy of Isaiah*, 461), although the ultimate vision of the Messiah is certainly central to the material. I only wonder if that title does enough justice to the large blocks devoted to the righteousness, or lack thereof, of the Lord's servants.

3. These persons extend from Westermann, *Isaiah 40–66*, to Motyer, *Prophecy of Isaiah*. For a fuller discussion see Oswalt, *Isaiah 40–66*, 461–65.

that is, his "salvation"—is at hand. We can only do righteousness because of God's righteousness made available to us.

A superficial reading of chapters 40–55 may have led us to believe that since we are unable to do right and since God has delivered us from the effects of that failure by a righteous act of grace, right living is not really incumbent on us except as a kind of unrealistic ideal. No, says Isaiah, righteous living, as expressed in Sabbath-keeping and the rejection of "evil" (56:2), is the absolutely necessary expression of God's righteous salvation.

That thought is reinforced in dramatic, even shocking, ways by the following verses. It may have been easy for persons reading chapters 40–55 to conclude that it was really one's birthright that secured salvation. Why had the Israelites been delivered from captivity? Certainly it was not because they deserved it, nor is there any demand in those chapters for changed living. The people were delivered from captivity for one reason alone: God had made some promises to their ancestor Abraham. "Thus," someone might say, "it really doesn't matter how I live; I simply need to accept the privileges of my birthright and not give up hope in God."

But verses 3–8 radically refute such an idea. The person who is pleasing to God is not the purebred Israelite who is doing his part to continue the physical line of Abraham. If the "foreigner," who is not part of that line, and the "eunuch," who cannot pass that line on, choose to live in obedience to God's "covenant" (vv. 4, 6), they are more pleasing to God than the Israelite who lives in rebellion against that covenant. God will give the eunuch a better heritage than children, "an everlasting name" (v. 5).

But this righteousness is more than legalistic law-keeping. Verse 6 speaks in relational terms of binding oneself to God as an act of love, service, and worship. Those who do this will be brought into God's "house of prayer," there to participate in the worship of that place, because God's purpose is to gather "all nations" to himself (vv. 7–8).

By beginning the final section of the book on this rather shocking note, the prophet is both tying us back to the beginning of the book, reminding us that the redeemed servants of the Lord have a mission, to draw all the world to the "holy mountain" (56:7; cf. 2:2–3), but also telling us that being a member of the covenant community is not a matter of inheritance but of obedience.

Bridging Contexts

THE STRUGGLES OF the early Christian church illustrate the problem addressed here. In the intertestamental period, the Jewish community had veered directly from one ditch into the other. In the century after the return from exile, there was a tendency to maintain no distinction between themselves and the surrounding pagan nations (see Ezra, Nehemiah, and Malachi). Instead of being a light to the nations, drawing them to the God of Israel, the Israelites were being sucked into the generalized, syncretistic paganism of the nations. Under the ministry of the priest (Ezra), the governor (Nehemiah), and the prophet (Malachi), the community finally recognized its peril and began to restrict the influence of the surrounding peoples. But having escaped the ditch of syncretism, they plunged straight across the road into the ditch of isolationism. Judaism cut itself off from the surrounding world, making a fetish of its purity before God.

As a result, it took severe upheavals within the church before the early Christians could accept the truth that Isaiah is teaching here. Peter had to have a vision from heaven to convince him that it was even appropriate to share the gospel with non-Jews (Acts 10:9–16). Even then, when conflict arose over association with Gentiles, Paul had to confront Peter publicly to keep him from reverting to the old ways (Gal. 2:11–14). The fact that the Gentiles accepted the work of the Jewish Messiah, Jesus, and bound themselves in obedient love to the God of the covenant did not really enter into the picture. They did not have the birthright. Fortunately, the ancient truth prevailed, and it became clear, especially through the ministry of Paul (Eph. 3:4–13), that it was a part of God's eternal plan to "gather still others" (Isa. 56:8).

Little has changed today. A Christian worship service is beginning, and two young men come in who are clearly out of place. Their clothes are outlandish and not very clean. Their hair is lank and long. Their arms are covered with tattoos. They are clearly not of the evangelical subculture. Are they earnestly seeking salvation? Are they believers who have left all to follow Christ? Who knows? Who cares? They don't belong because they are different from us. So an usher, perhaps tactfully or perhaps rudely, goes up to them and tells them that they are not welcome here. They don't have the right family credentials, so they don't belong. And God may well say to us the same thing he said to the returned Israelites, "Don't you dare exclude them from my house. They love me more than you do, as you could tell from their lives if you took the time to look. That loving obedience is the only family credentials that matter to me."

THERE IS A CLEAR message to the evangelical wing of Christendom in this passage—and indeed, in this entire section of Isaiah. There is a real danger of our falling into this same error. We ask ourselves who are the elect of God. Obviously, it is those who have "believed on the Lord Jesus Christ." They are the children of God, his servants; they have been adopted into his family; they have the birthright. There is a positive side to this, for in the nonevangelical church one often senses a lack of assurance about a relationship to God. If a person is asked, "Are you going to heaven," he or she responds, "Well, I hope so. I am doing my best." And of course, "doing my best" is not what Christianity is all about. As the elder John says, it is about having Jesus Christ (1 John 5:12). So the assurance that comes from knowing that you personally have exercised faith in God through Christ and that God keeps his word to deliver such a person from the condemnation of his or her sins is a good thing.

But there is a "down side" to this understanding of the faith, namely, the conviction of many people that since they have *once* exercised faith in Christ and have not actively repudiated that confession, therefore they *are* saved regardless of how they live from day to day.

This conviction is fostered by a reading of Romans 7 in isolation from Romans 6 and 8, which results in a direct contradiction of the point Paul is attempting to make. Paul is saying that we as Christians *must not* continue to live lives of sin (6:15—18) and that we need not so continue because we have the Spirit of Christ in us. Through the Holy Spirit we can "put to death" the deeds of our sinful nature (8:13). Yet influential Christian preachers and teachers tell us that Romans 7, which speaks of the bondage to sin experienced by those who, like the Jews, attempt to defeat sin in their own strength, depicts the normal Christian life. This implies that being Christian is really only a matter of birthright, of adoption, and has no real impact on how we live. It may change our ideals, but it does not change the realities. Thus, we see the spectacle in North America of persons claiming to be "born-again" Christians whose ethical lives are no different from those of a lost world.

That is the very opposite of the truth. Unless our adoption into a new family changes our behavior into the likeness of the Head of that family, there is reason to doubt the reality of the adoption. The German pastor and professor Dietrich Bonhoeffer, killed by the Nazis because of his involvement in a plan to assassinate Hitler, spoke to this issue in his book *The Cost of Discipleship*. He spoke of a "cheap grace" that promises an eternity of bliss with no cost to us now and no expectations of a changed life.[4] God says to us as he says to the returned Israelites, "It is not the proof of your pedigree that counts; it is your life of glad obedience to me that demonstrates your real pedigree."

Christians today must recover the understanding that while it is indeed by grace through faith, not our works, that we are saved (Eph. 2:8—9), it is *for* good works that we have been saved (Eph. 2:10). Our righteousness earns us no favor at all with God, but that righteousness is the proof positive that we have been transferred from the kingdom of darkness into the kingdom of light (Col. 1:12—13). There really is no other evidence.

---

4. D. Bonhoeffer, *The Cost of Discipleship* (New York: Macmillan, 1963), 45—46.

Isaiah 56:9–57:13

⁹ COME, ALL YOU beasts of the field,
   come and devour, all you beasts of the forest!
¹⁰ Israel's watchmen are blind,
   they all lack knowledge;
 they are all mute dogs,
   they cannot bark;
 they lie around and dream,
   they love to sleep.
¹¹ They are dogs with mighty appetites;
   they never have enough.
 They are shepherds who lack understanding;
   they all turn to their own way,
   each seeks his own gain.
¹² "Come," each one cries, "let me get wine!
   Let us drink our fill of beer!
 And tomorrow will be like today,
   or even far better."

⁵⁷:¹ The righteous perish,
   and no one ponders it in his heart;
 devout men are taken away,
   and no one understands
 that the righteous are taken away
   to be spared from evil.
² Those who walk uprightly
   enter into peace;
   they find rest as they lie in death.

³ "But you—come here, you sons of a sorceress,
   you offspring of adulterers and prostitutes!
⁴ Whom are you mocking?
   At whom do you sneer
   and stick out your tongue?
 Are you not a brood of rebels,
   the offspring of liars?
⁵ You burn with lust among the oaks
   and under every spreading tree;
 you sacrifice your children in the ravines
   and under the overhanging crags.

⁶The idols among the smooth stones of the ravines are
    your portion;
    they, they are your lot.
Yes, to them you have poured out drink offerings
    and offered grain offerings.
    In the light of these things, should I relent?
⁷You have made your bed on a high and lofty hill;
    there you went up to offer your sacrifices.
⁸Behind your doors and your doorposts
    you have put your pagan symbols.
Forsaking me, you uncovered your bed,
    you climbed into it and opened it wide;
you made a pact with those whose beds you love,
    and you looked on their nakedness.
⁹You went to Molech with olive oil
    and increased your perfumes.
You sent your ambassadors far away;
    you descended to the grave itself!
¹⁰You were wearied by all your ways,
    but you would not say, 'It is hopeless.'
You found renewal of your strength,
    and so you did not faint.

¹¹"Whom have you so dreaded and feared
    that you have been false to me,
and have neither remembered me
    nor pondered this in your hearts?
Is it not because I have long been silent
    that you do not fear me?
¹²I will expose your righteousness and your works,
    and they will not benefit you.
¹³When you cry out for help,
    let your collection of idols save you!
The wind will carry all of them off,
    a mere breath will blow them away.
But the man who makes me his refuge
    will inherit the land
    and possess my holy mountain."

 AFTER THE OPENING commendation of obedient, covenant-keeping foreigners and eunuchs in the previous section, this section resounds with a kind of judgmental language that has not been found in Isaiah since chapter 34. What is going on here?

Words of Judgment to the Leaders (56:9–57:2)

THIS SECTION BEGINS with an attack on "Israel's watchmen" (56:10), who are compared to "dogs" who do not bark because they are asleep with full stomachs (56:10–11). They are stupid "shepherds," who are only interested in taking care of themselves and have no concern for the flock. Clearly this is the leadership of the nation, and with what follows, they are evidently the religious leaders. The nation is in a desperate spiritual condition, and the leaders do not care. This is similar to what Amos said when he accused the elite of northern Israel of indulging their appetites with no awareness of the tragic condition of the house of Joseph (Amos 6:6).[1]

Isaiah is implying that simply a return from captivity will not guarantee a new set of behaviors for the people unless there is a radical change in the attitude and behavior of the leaders from that which he has experienced in his own day (cf. chs. 26–28). If the leaders continue to be self-centered and power hungry, the flock entrusted to them will continue to be overtaken by their spiritual enemies (56:9). Moreover, there will be so little spiritual perception that the disappearance of the "righteous" from among them will go unnoticed (57:1–2). The passing away of an older, more faithful generation will cause no alarm. The fact that they have been graciously delivered from the increasing chaos of a degenerate society will never occur to either the leaders or the followers in that degenerate society.

---

1. The clear connection of what is said here (and indeed throughout this entire division) with the preexilic religious environment has constituted a problem for those who believe in multiple authorship. Westermann hypothesized the reuse of certain preexilic prophecies (*Isaiah 40–66*, 325). Childs (*Isaiah*, 463) seeks to solve the problem with an appeal to "intertextuality." He suggests that the editor responsible for this part of the book has consciously used some of the language of "First Isaiah" in order to make a point that the same spiritual attitude (although not actually the same practices?) persists in this new eschatological age. A much simpler explanation is that Isaiah is speaking about the spiritual condition in his own day *and* in the future in language that is familiar to him. He only sees those details of the distant future that are directly relevant to the revelation he is giving. That is why it has been so difficult for modern commentators to decide what the actual historical setting of "Third Isaiah" is. Isaiah is speaking to the general setting he foresees. There *is* no detailed historical setting for this material.

Words of Judgment to the People (57:3–13)

NOW ISAIAH TURNS directly to the people, addressing them as "you." In strong language he speaks to those who believe that they are "the elect" and that cultic righteousness is all that is required of them. He accuses them of really being idolaters at heart. Like those who worship rocks and trees (57:5–7), who engage in ritual prostitution (57:8), and who sacrifice their children (57:5, 9), their only real desire is to manipulate divine power to their own advantage. They mock those who are passionate about obeying God's austere covenant (57:3–4) and prefer their own lush, amorphous syncretisms.[2] After all, they are the elect; they are free.

Of course, the attempt to manipulate divine power to one's own advantage is hard work (57:10). One has to learn a lot of arcane religiosity and put up with a good deal that is boring and repetitious. But in the end, the worshipers tell themselves, it will be worth it, and so they gather up what energies they can find from within themselves and soldier on.

Following the description of the people's behavior, God pronounces his judgment. He begins with a question: "Whom have you so dreaded and feared that you have been false to me?" (57:11). This is the God who graciously delivered them from captivity in Egypt, who kept them through all the years of apostasy, and who now in the end has delivered them once again, this time from Babylon. How could they not have "remembered" (57:11) all this and have so easily turned aside to the religions of their own making?

In an ironic aside, he asks whether it is because he has not spoken to them that they do not fear him. Of course, he has spoken to them again and again. No, the answer to these two questions lies in the depravity of the human heart. God has revealed all they need to know, and there is no other god who has terrified them into abandoning what they know. It is simply that God asks too much. He asks them to give up control of their lives and to abandon themselves into his hands in glad obedience (57:13b). That is too much. So they would rather construct a religion that seems to give them control over

---

2. While it is not clear how much of the actual pagan practices the returned Jews engaged in, it seems probable that the integration into the pagan world that both Nehemiah and Ezra fought so vigorously would have included such practices. The argument of syncretism would have been strong: Since Yahweh is Baal and Baal is Yahweh, since Molech is Yahweh and Yahweh is Molech, therefore Molech and Baal's practices are Yahweh's as well. Instead of being a light to the world and bringing foreigners to the good news of the only Creator and Savior, the returnees were being sucked into the religion of the foreigners. It is also possible that Isaiah was describing a future apostasy in terms of the behavior of his own times. See J. Payne, "The Eighth Century Background of Isaiah 40–66," *WTJ* 29 (1967): 179–90; 30 (1968): 50–58, 185–203.

their destinies, that seems to let them decide what is right and wrong for them and to provide a means of avoiding that wrong and producing that right. But such a religion is worthless in the end.[3] It cannot stand up when the winds of adversity blow upon a life. It will collapse and blow away (57:13a).

BEING AN IDOLATER IN SPIRIT. Too often we restrict our understanding of idolatry to worship involving imagery. Since we do not use images in our worship, either public or private, we think none of this talk about pagan religion has any relevance to us. It is obvious, of course, that "idols" are a part of "idolatry." But there is an attitude that leads to the worship of images that is separable from the images themselves. We get a clue to what this is when Paul refers to "greed" as "idolatry" in Colossians 3:5 and Ephesians 5:5.

What does the apostle mean here? He means that there is an attitude behind covetousness that says if I can just have all the things I want and I see, I will be happy. If some is good, more is better. There is also an attitude about reality evident here. What I really need is connected to material, physical things. The worship of images then springs from this attitude. If I can just figure out how to manipulate the physical world so as to guarantee physical abundance for myself, I will have solved the riddle of life.

With such an attitude, it is possible to be an orthodox Christian and yet to be an idolater in spirit. I can believe all the right things mentally and still be trying to use my religion to achieve my goals, to serve my ends, to supply my needs. The pronoun in the last three phrases of the previous sentence is significant: "my." Thus, prayer and devotion, worship and service, all become devices to serve my ends, and my Christianity is actually only another form of paganism: the attempt to manipulate the divine for my ends. The result is that the religion will become more and more formal and more and more lifeless—as Paul says, "having a form of godliness but denying its power" (2 Tim. 3:5).

This condition is especially deadly in leadership (cf. Isa. 56:9–12). When the leaders are motivated by what they can get out of their positions, whether it be remuneration or adulation, they will have no real concern for the spiritual life of the flock. In fact, the flock will begin to emulate the leaders,

---

3. It is interesting that the Heb. of 57:13 only has "let your collection save you" (not "collection of idols"). This suggests that the prophet may not be restricting his thinking merely to idol worship but to all kinds of worship that are simply a collection of human attempts to manipulate the divine.

often unconsciously. They will absorb the attitudes and approaches of the leaders and come at life in the same ways. As a result, they are decimated by the world, and the leaders are not even aware of what is happening.

PASTORAL LEADERSHIP. There are at least three areas in which this passage relates to contemporary life. The first is the area of pastoral leadership. Some say that pastors are no more prone to moral failure today than they have ever been. It is only that in this day of instant communication, more of us are aware of it than people were in the past. The knowledge of a moral tragedy could be hidden from all but a few then; it cannot now. Wherever we come out in that discussion, Nathaniel Hawthorne's *The Scarlet Letter* and other works like it certainly show us that moral failure among pastors is not something that has only emerged in the late twentieth century. But the question is what to do about it, and this passage offers some helpful guidelines.

These leaders are characterized by an obsessive interest in themselves and their own gratification. They love to sleep; they love to eat; they love to drink; above all, they want their own way. These are people who, like King Saul, have never gotten themselves off their own hands. Unlike King David, they have never learned to forget themselves in the love of God and of others.[4]

If I as a pastor can be honest about my own inclinations to sin and, at the same time, will put my reputation, my achievements, my status, my success, and my rights on the altar of God both for all time and anew each day, then the possibility of that kind of self-forgetfulness in glad service will be a real one. Then I as a pastor can know that neither I nor my people will be the ones to satisfy my needs. I must surrender my needs to God and can trust God to meet those needs. When the freedom of that self-forgetfulness is coupled with a sense of divinely given responsibility for the flock, there is a real possibility of the pastor's becoming a sterling example of loving faithfulness, even if that faithfulness leads to a cross.

The fine line between gluttony and asceticism. Not only have the leaders in Isaiah's day made the satisfaction of their desires primary, but so have the people. As I said above, to do so is to reduce one's religion to a form of paganism. I practice it to satisfy my desires. There is frightening evidence that

---

4. The great failure for which David is remembered, the adultery with Bathsheba, is so glaring because it is a blatant denial of this very characteristic in his life. David descends down to the level of serving and protecting himself.

this is so among us today. In so many ways the satisfaction of supposed needs is all-important to us: We drink to excess, we eat to excess, we cannot get enough sex of all sorts, we lie and cheat to get more money to buy more things to put into more storage facilities, and we sacrifice our children, both the unborn and the living, to the satisfaction of these needs.

What is the answer? For centuries the church has said that the answer is "the mortification of the flesh"—in other words, asceticism. That is, true saints are those who, in an impressive show of dedicated self-denial, refuse to satisfy their needs except to maintain the bare necessities of life. This is the all-or-nothing approach. The only way to secure victory for the spirit over the desires is to completely deny the desires.

But Paul tells us that in fact that kind of rigorous asceticism has no power to control the passions (Col. 2:23). So where is victory? It begins in the recognition that God made our desires and they are good. He takes joy in seeing that they are satisfied. The key is in self-surrender. Paul calls it "dying to oneself" (Rom. 6:11; Gal. 2:20; Col. 3:3–5). We surrender our needs to him, determined to be faithful to him and his ways above all else, leaving the fulfillment of our needs in his hand. Here there is freedom without excess, satisfaction without satiation, because we know that in the end it is God we want and that another half-gallon of ice cream will never satisfy that longing.

Syncretistic religion. In the Persian Empire at the time of the return from the Exile (ca. 538 B.C.), people had a heightened awareness of the rest of the world. Undoubtedly the careful organization of the empire and the increased communication involved had something to do with it. As a result, there came an increased sense that all forms of religious expression and all religious conceptions were essentially the same. Unquestionably this was true for the pagan religions in the ancient Near East. The similarity of the basic worldview and the expressions of the worldview are startlingly similar from Sumer in the East in 2000 B.C. to Rome in the West in 2 B.C. So to represent Greek Zeus as Syrian Baal or Babylonian Marduk as Roman Jupiter or Phoenician Anat as Greek Athene was nothing more than might be expected.

But the problem arises with the religion of Yahweh, for that religion is startlingly different from all the rest at all the major points. Yahweh is *not* the same as Baal, and his worship is not the same as Marduk's. This is the truth for which the Judeans Hananiah, Mishael, and Azariah (Shadrach, Meshach, and Abednego to the Babylonians) were willing to die. And it was this truth that the restored Judeans were apparently all too willing to surrender to the prevailing views in the Persian Empire and in the later Greek ones.

We are under similar pressure. Many today argue that all ways of thinking lead to God (assuming, incorrectly, that all religions are only human gropings after God) and that all expressions of God are at the same time partial and partially true. Thus, for the adherents of any one religion to insist that they know the only way to God is not only arrogant but positively sinful.

But suppose that what is true in the physical world is also true in the spiritual world, that is, that there are things that are absolutely so and things that are absolutely not so. Black is not white, and no amount of intellectual obfuscation will make it so. Neither will any amount of wishing make it so. Paganism refuses to believe this because if it were so, we would have to admit that we are not God and that we can neither find our way to him nor manipulate him to take care of us. Paganism must insist that we can find God on our own and that therefore my way is as good as yours because nothing spiritual is absolutely so.

Today, as in the days of the Persian Empire, we must stand on the uncomfortable facts. There is a God who is other than the created universe. Because this is so, human intellect cannot comprehend him. It can see the evidence for his existence, but that does not make him either intelligible or capable of manipulation by us. Thus, the only way we can know God is if he reveals himself to us in ways that we can comprehend. He has done so in the life of the descendents of Abraham, originally physical and ultimately spiritual. That revelation has culminated in the life, death, and resurrection of Jesus Christ.

As there is only one Creator, so there is only one Savior. There is the truth, and there we must stand. Because the Judeans ultimately were willing to stand on what they knew at that time and because the first Christians were willing to stand on the further revelation that came in Christ, the Christian faith exists today. If either group had succumbed to the intense syncretistic pressures that existed in their day, there would be no Christian faith today. It is not one more of the world's great religions. It is either the only religion, or it is an incredible figment of fevered imaginations that does not deserve to exist.[5]

---

5. For a sensitive yet unflinching declaration of this truth, see A. Fernando, *Sharing the Truth in Love: How to Relate to People of Other Faiths* (Grand Rapids: Discovery House, 2001).

Isaiah 57:14–21

❧

A ND IT WILL be said:

"Build up, build up, prepare the road!
Remove the obstacles out of the way of my people."
¹⁵For this is what the high and lofty One says—
he who lives forever, whose name is holy:
"I live in a high and holy place,
but also with him who is contrite and lowly in spirit,
to revive the spirit of the lowly
and to revive the heart of the contrite.
¹⁶I will not accuse forever,
nor will I always be angry,
for then the spirit of man would grow faint before me—
the breath of man that I have created.
¹⁷I was enraged by his sinful greed;
I punished him, and hid my face in anger,
yet he kept on in his willful ways.
¹⁸I have seen his ways, but I will heal him;
I will guide him and restore comfort to him,
¹⁹   creating praise on the lips of the mourners in Israel.
Peace, peace, to those far and near,"
says the LORD. "And I will heal them."
²⁰But the wicked are like the tossing sea,
which cannot rest,
whose waves cast up mire and mud.
²¹"There is no peace," says my God, "for the wicked."

Original Meaning

THESE VERSES STAND in sharp contrast to 56:9–57:13. There the stress was on the inability of humans to live the righteous lives that their redemption called them to live; here the focus is on the activity of God to "revive" (57:15) and "heal" (57:18–19) them. There the focus was on the failings of "you" (more than twenty-five occurrences of "you," "your," and "yours" in 57:3–13); here the focus is on what "I" will do (twelve occurrences of "I" and "my"). God will do for his people what they cannot do for themselves.

619

The stage was already set for this statement at the end of 57:13, where the prophet says that the one who takes "refuge" in God (instead of in idols) will inherit the land.[1] While righteousness is expected of God's people, any attempt to produce it on their own will result in the most corrupt spiritual pride. The only hope is for God to deliver his people from sinning just as he delivered them from the consequences of sin when he restored them from captivity.

Once more the highway imagery comes to the fore. But this is not a highway for God (cf. 40:3–5), nor is it a highway for the people to return from captivity (cf. 11:16). Rather, this is a highway on which the "contrite" (57:15) can return to God, admitting their own inability to do what is right (cf. "the Way of Holiness," 35:8).

The third occurrence of the "high and lofty" pair is found in 57:15 (cf. 6:1; 52:13). In one of the most beautiful statements in Scripture, the One who is utterly separated from the inhabitants of earth in his "holy" place says that his dwelling is also with the lowly and the contrite. This is not to say that God will become less than transcendently holy; rather, he will bring humans to share that character. He has "created" humans, and he cannot bear to be in a position where he can do nothing but "accuse" them (57:16; cf. Hos. 11:10–13). Rather, his intention is not merely to punish (Isa. 57:17) but to go beyond that to giving his people a changed nature, where rebellion and pride will be replaced by "praise" and "peace."

Once again we see that the problem here is no longer captivity but the inability to live righteous lives. God does not merely promise forgiveness for sin but a healing for those who "mourn" (57:19) over the state of Israel. Not only do they mourn for the absence of righteousness in the community, they mourn for its absence in their own lives (see 59:1–15a). In this way, they are in sharp contrast with the "wicked" (57:20–21). Because the wicked refuse to recognize their sinfulness and turn from it, they cannot experience the "peace" (*šalom*) that God promises. These final verses emphasize once again

---

1. The difficulty of determining the precise historical setting for chs. 56–66 supports the contention of this commentary that although the chapters are broadly addressing the concerns of those who returned from the Exile, their real context is the literary and theological one within the present book (see comments on chs. 40 and 56). Hanson, *Isaiah 40–66*, 202–3, illustrates the problem. He concludes that this segment was written by disciples of "Second Isaiah" shortly after the Return and was originally a word of encouragement to the disheartened returnees. However, he opines that later editors, immersed in a fierce conflict between the establishment and the visionaries, reused the words here to encourage the visionaries. This reconstructed setting is entirely imaginary. Childs, *Isaiah*, 473, agreeing that the theological purpose provides the main setting, responds sharply to Hanson and others that "attempts to replace Third Isaiah's own theological rendering with a sociological theory of competing groups in strife runs flatly in the face of the canonical shaping of the entire Isaianic corpus."

that God's promises are not for the nation as a whole merely because they are the descendants of Jacob, but specifically for those inside the nation—and outside—who recognize their need and turn to God in contrition.

THIS PASSAGE SPEAKS of the sovereignty of God in human behavior. This is not to say there is some sort of deterministic element in it. But the question is, "How can human beings keep covenant with God?" Isaiah 56:1–8 established the priority of that requirement, praising the least expected who did that. But 56:9–57:13 made it plain that those who set out to produce their own righteousness would inevitably produce something spurious (57:12), whatever form that so-called righteousness may have taken.

Jesus' parable of the Pharisee and the tax collector (Luke 18:10–14) is an illustration of this fact. The Pharisee was proud of his own achievements, while the tax collector came to God acknowledging his failure and his need. What was the issue? It was one of pride and self-reliance versus reliance on God and seeking a dependent relation with him. If humans are to be healed of their sinful behavior, it must be God who does this, and he will do it for those who live in humble reliance on him. The language of "dwelling" in 57:15 is significant in this respect, reminding us of the language in John 15:5, "I am the vine; you are the branches. If a man remains in me and I in him, he will bear much fruit; apart from me you can do nothing."

Righteousness is not an end in itself. Whenever it becomes so, it merely becomes another idol, a device to earn the favor and blessing of the divine world. God does want righteousness, but only as a by-product of our relationship with him. He, "the high and lofty One," wants to live with and in us. In that way alone will we be able to live lives that reflect his character. So again, Isaiah 56–66 represents a resolution of the themes of chapters 1–39 and 40–55. The first block of material tells us that righteousness is a necessity and that its absence brings judgment. The second block tells us that deliverance is a work of God's grace alone, requiring nothing but persistent trust that God will deliver. This section, then, reiterates the demand for righteousness but shows us that that righteousness is only possible by means of God's persistent grace.

TODAY AMERICA IS suffering from a failure of evangelical theology. The 1970s and 1980s were widely recognized as the age of the evangelical. The movement was large enough and influential enough to gain the attention of the national media; leading figures in the movement became forces to be reckoned with. Yet, concurrent with that popular recognition was the hastening moral decay of the nation. The connection between these two is not coincidental. To a generation that wanted to "feel good" at all costs, we declared a feel-good religion. All one has to do to gain a heaven of bliss and an earthly life of abundance is to say "yes" to Jesus' wonderful plan for life. This decision has no necessary bearing on a person's behavior.

While it is desirable to live like Jesus, it is also understood that this is not really possible. The transaction between God and believer is almost entirely legal. The "yes" to Jesus is all that is necessary to transfer a person from one jurisdiction to another, from one birthright to another. We expect to continue in sin—and not surprisingly, we do, with national polls showing that today the lives of evangelical Christians are indistinguishable from the world around us.[2] Our "righteousness" is just like the world's "righteousness."

This is much like the situation described in Isaiah 56–57. "Birthright" in itself means nothing. Just as God did not really care whether a person was a physical descendant of Jacob, neither does he really care whether we have made a profession of faith. What he wants to see is evidence of his behavior, his attitudes, and his passions being replicated in the lives of those who say they know him. This is true faith, as the book of James makes clear.

So we evangelicals need to come to God in contrition—contrition for spiritual pride, contrition for our arrogant dependence on accepting Christ as a magical act, contrition for bringing reproach on the name of God, contrition for not allowing God to heal us, individually and collectively, of our persistent sinning, contrition for not believing that God can indeed impart his righteousness to us, contrition for our unwillingness to fully surrender to God, contrition that our "standing" before God has been more important to us than our relationship with him.

But the good news is that God is merciful. He wants to live with us and in us. He wants to heal us. The worst thing we can do is to return to the kind of legalistic righteousness of earlier generations. No, the message of these verses, and indeed of this entire last part of the book, is that while God expects real righteousness and justice in our lives, he also expects to do that in us and for us as a by-product of our loving relation with him. When it is he whom we want, then righteousness will be as natural to us as the grapes are on the branch. That righteousness, instead of having the stink of pride, will be a gentle fragrance because it will be all unconscious.

2. G. Barna, *Boiling Point: It Only Takes One Degree* (Ventura, Calif.: Regal, 2001), 79.

Isaiah 58:1–14

¹"SHOUT IT ALOUD, do not hold back.
   Raise your voice like a trumpet.
Declare to my people their rebellion
   and to the house of Jacob their sins.
²For day after day they seek me out;
   they seem eager to know my ways,
as if they were a nation that does what is right
   and has not forsaken the commands of its God.
They ask me for just decisions
   and seem eager for God to come near them.
³'Why have we fasted,' they say,
   'and you have not seen it?
Why have we humbled ourselves,
   and you have not noticed?'

"Yet on the day of your fasting, you do as you please
   and exploit all your workers.
⁴Your fasting ends in quarreling and strife,
   and in striking each other with wicked fists.
You cannot fast as you do today
   and expect your voice to be heard on high.
⁵Is this the kind of fast I have chosen,
   only a day for a man to humble himself?
Is it only for bowing one's head like a reed
   and for lying on sackcloth and ashes?
Is that what you call a fast,
   a day acceptable to the LORD?

⁶"Is not this the kind of fasting I have chosen:
to loose the chains of injustice
   and untie the cords of the yoke,
to set the oppressed free
   and break every yoke?
⁷Is it not to share your food with the hungry
   and to provide the poor wanderer with shelter—
when you see the naked, to clothe him,
   and not to turn away from your own flesh
      and blood?

⁸ Then your light will break forth like the dawn,
and your healing will quickly appear;
then your righteousness will go before you,
and the glory of the LORD will be your rear guard.
⁹ Then you will call, and the LORD will answer;
you will cry for help, and he will say: Here am I.

"If you do away with the yoke of oppression,
with the pointing finger and malicious talk,
¹⁰ and if you spend yourselves in behalf of the hungry
and satisfy the needs of the oppressed,
then your light will rise in the darkness,
and your night will become like the noonday.
¹¹ The LORD will guide you always;
he will satisfy your needs in a sun-scorched land
and will strengthen your frame.
You will be like a well-watered garden,
like a spring whose waters never fail.
¹² Your people will rebuild the ancient ruins
and will raise up the age-old foundations;
you will be called Repairer of Broken Walls,
Restorer of Streets with Dwellings.

¹³ "If you keep your feet from breaking the Sabbath
and from doing as you please on my holy day,
if you call the Sabbath a delight
and the LORD's holy day honorable,
and if you honor it by not going your own way
and not doing as you please or speaking idle words,
¹⁴ then you will find your joy in the LORD,
and I will cause you to ride on the heights of the land
and to feast on the inheritance of your father Jacob."
The mouth of the LORD has spoken.

Original Meaning

WE RETURN AGAIN to the inability of the people to do righteousness, as they were commanded in 56:1. Whereas in 56:9–57:13 their own attempts at righteousness were depicted as idolatrous, here those attempts are seen as being selfish and oppressive. Instead of their religion making them a blessing to those around them, as God intended, it made them a curse. Interestingly, the people were being caught up in what God had not particularly commanded—fasts[1]—and were neglecting what he had specifically commanded—the Sabbath feast.

Verses 1–3 introduce the subject. The people give every appearance of piety and genuine concern to know God's will. But in fact, says Isaiah, they have "forsaken the commands" of God and are in a state of "rebellion." The evidence of this fact is in their approach to their cultic behavior. Why are they engaging in this behavior? Is it to express gratitude and submission to God? No, for as their quotation in verse 3 indicates, they are engaging in the behavior for the very same reasons the pagans do, to manipulate God to act in their favor.

Verses 4–12 expand on this theme. God *does* want to bless his people (58:8–9, 10b–12), but that blessing cannot be obtained by cultic manipulation. It is given freely to those who are in unbroken covenant relations with him. What evidence can the Israelites give that they are in such a relationship? Ethical behavior. Only twice in the Old Testament does God command persons to fast. But in hundreds of places he commands his people to treat other people, especially those weaker than they, with respect, justice, and kindness. So here God tells the people that if they want to stop doing something, they can stop oppressing the poor (58:6–7).

In fact, they fast for the very opposite reason of what God intends for his people. Instead of abandoning themselves and their needs into the hands of God and instead of giving themselves away to others, their religious activities have become self-serving. Verse 5 suggests this self-serving aspect with the phrase "a man to humble himself" (lit., "to afflict oneself"). The worshiper is merely doing something to himself to show how devoted he is. Verse 3 makes it even more explicit: "You do as you please." It is not surprising, then, that such religious behavior issues in oppression, violence, and hatred. Whenever human needs are exalted above everything else, the supply of those needs justifies any behavior at all.

God calls for behavior that is self-forgetful and outward-looking. Let acts of self-denial be for the sake of others and not for one's own sake. Work "to set the oppressed free" (58:6). Eat less in order to have food to give to the "hungry." Wear less-expensive clothes in order to clothe the

---

1. The only fast specifically commanded in the law is that associated with the Day of Atonement (Lev. 16:29). The only other place where fasting is commanded by God is in Joel (1:14; 2:12, 15). All the other references are to fasts imposed by leaders, or voluntarily assumed, in moments of crisis (2 Sam. 12:23; 1 Kings 21:9; 2 Chron. 20:3; Ezra 8:21; Neh. 9:1; Est. 4:3; 9:31; Ps. 35:13; 69:10; 109:24; Jer. 14:12; 36:6, 9; Dan. 9:3; Zech. 7:3; 8:19). While Westermann, *Isaiah 40–66*, 335, is correct in asserting that Zech. 7 and 8 express a concern over fasting, it is not correct to say that an interest in fasting is especially characteristic of the postexilic period. See Robert J. Way, "צום," *NIDOTTE*, 3:780–83.

"naked" (58:7, 10). This is the kind of cessation and self-affliction God has "chosen."

The reference to "light" in verses 8 and 10 looks both backward and forward. It looks back to the promises to the Servant in 42:6 and 49:6. By means of the Servant, God's light of justice will shine through his people to be a light for the nations. That theme is found as early in the book as 2:5 and continues through 30:26 and 51:4. The theme reaches its climax in 60:1−3, the passage to which this one looks forward. Through God's people the blessings of his covenant will be extended to the whole earth. Then the people who have walked in darkness will indeed see a "great light" (9:2).

Verses 13 and 14, speaking about the Sabbath, are connected to the preceding as a way of further saying what kind of cessation God *would* like. He would like his people to stop doing as they "please" on the Sabbath day (cf. 58:3). Again, the issue of going one's "own way" is central. Cult, even costly and self-denying cult, is attractive because it seems to offer a way to get God to do what we want. But ceasing work (for ourselves) and ceasing self-enhancing activities is not at all attractive. Nevertheless, the Sabbath is enjoined as one of the feast days and is to be considered as a time of delighting in the Lord and in all his blessings to us. It does not manipulate God but is a means of developing the all-important relationship with him.

IN COLOSSIANS 2:20−23, Paul says that one of the failings of rigorous self-discipline and careful attention to the forms of worship is that they cannot restrain the passions. No place is that more evident today than around the Church of the Holy Sepulcher during Passion Week. People have fasted all week, preparing themselves for the Easter celebrations. What happens? Processions from each of the branches of Christendom, all led by priests garbed in every kind of glittering and costly vestment, jostle with one another seeking pride of place. And quickly jostling and harsh comments descend into full-scale riots, with golden crucifers and shepherds' crooks being used as battleaxes. Is this the religion of Christ, who laid down his life for his enemies? Hardly! We can envision him standing again on the Mount of Olives, looking at the spectacle with tears streaming down his face.

But just as painful is another picture, one of a wealthy evangelical employer who gives liberally to missions but refuses to pay his employees anything above the minimum wage and refuses to contribute to retirement and health-care plans for them. Certainly the Lord does not want him to stop giving to missions, but doing that is no justification for mistreating people.

THE ILLUSTRATIONS ABOVE demonstrate that the issue is the same for us today as it was 2,700 years ago. We are still just as tempted to use religious behavior as a way of manipulating God for our selfish ends as our Israelite forbears were. It is interesting that Isaiah uses fasting, because that continues to be a practice of Christians today who seek a more disciplined life. Other activities, however, have replaced Israelite cultic activities, such as church attendance, daily devotions, prayer, tithing, and so on, and these are all liable to the same dangers.

The danger is that we engage in them in order to wring blessings from a God who, we feel, is disinclined to give blessings unless we manipulate him in some way. Insofar as these attitudes, either consciously or unconsciously, govern our behavior, to that extent our religion is nothing more than idolatry. By contrast, to the extent that our religious life is characterized by self-forgetful service, freely given with no return expected, to that extent it is mirroring the life of God. And to those who are in the flow of God's life, blessing is a natural and abundant by-product. In this kind of behavior we show that we know God and are not in a relationship with him for what we can get, but for love.

However, it is important to remember the larger context of Isaiah here, for the point being made is the same as that found in the New Testament. We cannot live this kind of covenant life in our own strength. It is only as God empowers us with his grace that we are able to lay aside our self-serving attitudes and give ourselves away in love to God and others.

In this regard, there is cause for concern over the phenomenal popularity at present of the so-called "Prayer of Jabez" (1 Chron. 4:9–10). While there is no indication this is the intent of those who have popularized it, the idolatrous use of this prayer is a real danger. To repeat a set of words as though its mere repetition guarantees divine favor is the furthest thing from biblical faith. Yet one hears this use of the prayer touted in many quarters. People say things like, "I've said that prayer every day for a month, and my business has never been so good." Surely the idea is not to repeat Jabez's words but to emulate his attitude of committing himself to God. We do not find strength to deny ourselves and cultivate the life of the Holy Spirit by repeating words. We find such strength in abandoning ourselves to the sanctifying grace of God.

Isaiah 59:1–15a

¹ SURELY THE ARM of the LORD is not too short to save,
nor his ear too dull to hear.
² But your iniquities have separated
you from your God;
your sins have hidden his face from you,
so that he will not hear.
³ For your hands are stained with blood,
your fingers with guilt.
Your lips have spoken lies,
and your tongue mutters wicked things.
⁴ No one calls for justice;
no one pleads his case with integrity.
They rely on empty arguments and speak lies;
they conceive trouble and give birth to evil.
⁵ They hatch the eggs of vipers
and spin a spider's web.
Whoever eats their eggs will die,
and when one is broken, an adder is hatched.
⁶ Their cobwebs are useless for clothing;
they cannot cover themselves with what they make.
Their deeds are evil deeds,
and acts of violence are in their hands.
⁷ Their feet rush into sin;
they are swift to shed innocent blood.
Their thoughts are evil thoughts;
ruin and destruction mark their ways.
⁸ The way of peace they do not know;
there is no justice in their paths.
They have turned them into crooked roads;
no one who walks in them will know peace.

⁹ So justice is far from us,
and righteousness does not reach us.
We look for light, but all is darkness;
for brightness, but we walk in deep shadows.
¹⁰ Like the blind we grope along the wall,
feeling our way like men without eyes.

At midday we stumble as if it were twilight;
  among the strong, we are like the dead.
¹¹ We all growl like bears;
  we moan mournfully like doves.
We look for justice, but find none;
  for deliverance, but it is far away.

¹² For our offenses are many in your sight,
  and our sins testify against us.
Our offenses are ever with us,
  and we acknowledge our iniquities:
¹³ rebellion and treachery against the LORD,
  turning our backs on our God,
fomenting oppression and revolt,
  uttering lies our hearts have conceived.
¹⁴ So justice is driven back,
  and righteousness stands at a distance;
truth has stumbled in the streets,
  honesty cannot enter.
¹⁵ Truth is nowhere to be found,
  and whoever shuns evil becomes a prey.

THIS PASSAGE IS one of the more poignant statements of human sinfulness and fallibility in the entire Bible. Interestingly, it begins with condemnation of others in the second-person plural (59:2–3), then moves to the third-person plural (59:4–8), but closes with confession in the first-person plural (59:9–15a). The prophet seems to understand that as true as the condemnation of others may be, in the end he cannot exclude himself from that condemnation. Like everyone else, he is not able to produce in his own strength the righteousness God requires.

Verses 1 and 2 seem to hark back to the opening of Isaiah 58. From their point of view, the people have done everything necessary to procure God's blessings for themselves. Yet it does not seem to be happening. What is the matter with God? Is he weak (his "arm ... too short")? Or is he inattentive ("his ear too dull")? Of course not! Their lack of blessing is not God's fault but theirs. Their "iniquities" and "sins" have come between them and God (59:2).[1] And as chapters 57–58 have shown, some of those sins are their very religiosity.

---

1. The fact that vv. 1–2 seem to respond directly to the question of 58:3 may explain the use of the second-person pronouns. The appearance of the third person in vv. 4–8 may signal a wider reflection on the sin problem.

Coupled with that are the twofold evidences of a broken social system: violence and injustice (59:3–4).[2] As has been said repeatedly above, one of the purposes of the covenant was to promote a society in which the ethics of the Creator were lived out in human relations. But Isaiah envisions a day, all too much like his own, when the religious forms of the covenant are adhered to with some rigor while its relational content is dismissed with hardly a glance.

The closing of 59:4 seems to provide the basis for yet one more of Isaiah's graphic illustrations. That verse ends with the suggestion that the evil in the restored community will not be a superficial matter but something that is endemic to them, something conceived and given birth to. And the things they give birth to, or produce, are like the "eggs of vipers" and the webs of spiders (59:5–6a). They are not only "useless" but worse, deadly.

This thought is further expanded upon in 59:6b–7. All the faculties of these persons are given over to evil: their "hands" to "acts of violence," "their feet" to the shedding of "innocent blood," and "their thoughts" to "evil." Thus, it is no surprise that the characteristic behavior of their lives, "their ways," is ruinous and destructive. This thought is expanded on in 59:8. Taken with 59:7d, verse 8 gives us the catalog of the major words for "highway," "path," and "road" used so frequently throughout this book.[3] In contrast to the highway of holiness that God will prepare for his people (35:8) or to the level highway on which he will come to deliver his people (40:3–4), these "roads" are "crooked," and those who embark on them will find destruction and disintegration, not the wholeness, the "peace" (*šalom*), that God offers (52:7; 57:19).

As noted above, in 59:9–15a the prophet moves from condemnation to shared confession, using first-person plurals. Here he is speaking for all the faithful of the land, people who by their very nearness to God realize their own propensities and their own need. Unquestionably the calling of a prophet was a spiritually dangerous one. It would have been easy, becoming so intimately allied with the holy God and being aware of just how terrible the sin of the people was, to consider oneself above such things. But if the

---

2. Hanson, *Isaiah 40–66*, 210, aptly observes that in such a society, "rewards go not to the honest person seeking to contribute to society but to those seeking to rob it for their own gain."

3. Heb. *mᵉsillah* (59:7d, "way") occurs elsewhere at 7:3; 11:16; 19:23; 33:8; 36:2; 40:3; 49:11; 62:10, and only fifteen times elsewhere in the Old Testament; *derek* (59:8a, "way") occurs forty-eight times in the book (total of 706 in the Old Testament); *maʿgal* (59:8b, "path") appears here and in 26:7 (total of sixteen in Old Testament, with seven in Prov.); *nᵉtibah* (59:8c, "road") occurs elsewhere in Isa. at 42:16; 43:16; 58:12 (total, twenty-one).

prophet was closely allied with God, he was also still inextricably part of his human community. Tragically, any member of that community, if left to himself or herself, is capable of the worst sins imaginable. The mark of the truly great prophets was that they did not forget the latter in their absorption in the former.

This confession is one of a person who has reflected deeply on the human condition. This is not a little regret over a few "unfortunate slip-ups." Rather, it is a recognition of the profound incapacity of humans to produce the very conditions on which "justice" and "righteousness," the things God called for in 56:1, depend. Not only is no "justice" to be found (59:9, 11, 14), neither are "truth" (59:14–15) and "honesty" (59:14). The condition is one of complete "darkness" (59:9), into which "light" cannot penetrate. The reason for this is that the prophet confesses that "we" do not have the moral "eyes" (59:10) to see the light.[4]

In 59:12, in words reminiscent of Psalm 51:4, the prophet makes it plain that the reason injustice and unrighteousness are such serious sins is not that they are first of all crimes against humanity but sins against the Creator who made us. They are acts of "rebellion" against the Lord of the universe. *That* is why they are terrible sins. If there were no Creator to whom we are responsible, no one can logically say that the strong snatching resources for survival from the weak is a bad thing. In fact, evolutionary theory would suggest that this is a necessity if "higher forms of life" are to emerge. But Isaiah will not have it, for what we do to one another are heinous crimes against God. Having revolted against God and thereby denying the "truth" of our existence, there is no truth in any of our relationships to the extent that those who take a stand against "evil" become the target to be attacked.

Thus, the prophet paints a picture that seems truly hopeless. If this is the condition of the people of God even after they have returned from exile, what hope is there? God continues to call for righteousness and justice as fruit of their restoration, but they are utterly incapable of doing those things. We may say that it is a realistic picture, born of the most searching reflection on the human condition. But that offers no comfort. Are humans doomed to continue in sin, recognizing that they ought to do differently but are constitutionally unable to do so? Isaiah is definitely not saying that. Rather, he is showing the need for something other than merely stern discipline and good intentions if God's commands are to be fulfilled. What that something is will be uncovered in the next segment.

---

4. As Motyer, *Prophecy of Isaiah*, 487, observes, on the physical plane there is some hope of curing blindness, but if a person has no eyes, the situation is hopeless.

REVIVALS. One of the facts of history is that when revival comes to a people, it never starts among those furthest from God. Typically, it starts among those closest to him. Thus, the well-known revival text, 2 Chronicles 7:14, begins with the words, "If *my* people, who are called by *my* name, will humble themselves and pray...." The revival does not come from among those who are not God's people but those who are and who gladly name themselves as such.

The revival that broke out at Asbury College in Wilmore, Kentucky, in February 1970, which some credit as being formative in the emergence of the so-called "Jesus Movement" of the 1970s, began with a group of students meeting for prayer for more than a year, asking God to visit the campus. There had been a difficult presidential transition, and there was a good deal of bitterness and animosity in the college and in the small town where the college was located. But God began to answer those prayers when one of those praying students, certainly one of the "best" in the student body, had an opportunity to speak in chapel and began to confess his own need for God.

That confession was the match that lit the fire, a fire that continued on the campus for several weeks and touched tens of thousands as "witness teams" of students scattered across the country to share what God was doing. And while their message did call for "you" to change and for "them" to stop sinful ways, it did not focus there. Rather, the focus was on "our" need and the faithfulness of God to meet that need.

WHENCE OUR INHUMANITY TO OTHERS? This passage is one of the most candid expressions of the human condition to be found in a brief compass anywhere in human literature. It lays bare one of the realities of human existence that philosophers struggle to explain: Why do we do things that are so obviously destructive of even our own best interests in the long run? Why do we choose to do things to one another that are not merely self-serving but egregiously vicious and cruel? Whence comes our fascination with the violent and horrible?

Many who do not wish to admit that the problem could be systemic have put forward environmental explanations. Two recent ones are Karl Marx's suggestions that the problem is one of economics and John Dewey's claim that the problem is one of ignorance. Both of these have been proven to be false during the twentieth century. The promise of communism that when the means of production are put into the hands of the workers and when the petty bourgeoisie are forcibly removed from the scene, all evil and all coercion disappear has turned out to be one of the cruelest jokes ever perpetrated on humanity. One of the facts that has been lost on us in the blizzard of horrors in World War II is that communism was responsible for the deaths of upwards of thirty million people in the 1930s. No, the problem is not economics.

Nor is the problem ignorance. Was there ever a more educated populace than that of Germany in the 1930s? Yet it was the Germans who embraced Hitler enthusiastically, and it was the Germans who swallowed Goebbels's propaganda, blinding themselves to the evident evils of the system these men were foisting on them. Nor did the wonderful educational system of the United States save us from the terrible tragedy of Vietnam. In fact, it may be argued that one of the main things the burgeoning education of the twentieth century made possible was the construction of more terrible tools to be employed in the service of evil.

In fact, as the Bible insists, the problem of evil is systemic, although not in the way that many world thinkers have maintained. These thinkers have believed that "Good" and "Evil" are eternal entities in the universe. They are a given in existence, and it is out of their constant conflict that the visible world has emerged. Humans cannot be relieved of this conflict except perhaps, as in Buddhism and Hinduism, by gaining release from the very wheel of existence.

Over against this, the Bible offers another picture. Creation preceded evil. God is light, and in him is no darkness at all (1 John 1:5). He created the universe as an expression of his own goodness (Gen. 1:4; etc.). But he has permitted his creatures the possibility of choosing not to live within his purposes, and that choice on the part of our first parents was like introducing a virus into the body. It has infected the entire system, most especially the human system, and it manifests itself in the corruption of one of the central features of humanity, our capacity to image. Genesis 6:5 says that the very way we form the images in our hearts (the place where intellect, feelings, and will combine for the Hebrews) has become intensively and extensively corrupted. Thus, just as cancer cells are able to capture the cells around them and turn them to their own destructive purposes, the Bible insists that there is a moral cancer let loose in the human system. This is the picture Isaiah is painting for his readers.

Honesty compels us to admit the correctness of that picture in our own societies and in our own lives. None of us can pretend that in ourselves we are above the common human experience. If we pretend that we can somehow achieve the righteousness of God in our own strength, we are both deluded and deceitful—deluded because we have blinded ourselves to the facts and deceitful because in the deepest recesses of our souls we know the facts but won't face them. We are like the Pharisee who "prayed to himself" (NIV margin) and said, "I thank you that I am not like other men" (Luke 18:11).

If there is a cure for the disease, it does not lie in ourselves any more than the cure for cancer lies within the cancer victim. Our hope is the same as that of the tax collector in the parable just mentioned. It lies outside of us in the "mercy" (Luke 18:13) of our Maker, in the possibility that he can somehow solve the problem we cannot. He must make it possible for us to pay the high price of justice, for justice is costly. To give the other person his or her due without taking advantage of them presupposes a kind of inner security in which the one giving justice does not need to worry about being taken advantage of in turn.[5] This is freedom. But is that kind of freedom truly possible in view of the depth of the human problem? That is the question Isaiah's realism poses for us today.

---

5. It is interesting to watch secular humanism, in championing justice for the poor, enthusiastically embracing an evolutionary theory that denies any basis in a creation order. Instead, they base their theory on "unalienable rights." But whence come these rights? The American Declaration of Independence says that we have been endowed with them by our Creator. If there is no Creator, there are no rights; it is "survival of the fittest."

Isaiah 59:15b–21

^{15b}THE LORD LOOKED and was displeased
    that there was no justice.
¹⁶He saw that there was no one,
    he was appalled that there was no one to intervene;
so his own arm worked salvation for him,
    and his own righteousness sustained him.
¹⁷He put on righteousness as his breastplate,
    and the helmet of salvation on his head;
he put on the garments of vengeance
    and wrapped himself in zeal as in a cloak.
^{18,9}According to what they have done,
    so will he repay
wrath to his enemies
    and retribution to his foes;
    he will repay the islands their due.
¹⁹From the west, men will fear the name of the LORD,
    and from the rising of the sun, they will revere his glory.
For he will come like a pent-up flood
    that the breath of the LORD drives along.

²⁰"The Redeemer will come to Zion,
    to those in Jacob who repent of their sins,"
                        declares the LORD.

²¹"As for me, this is my covenant with them," says the
LORD. "My Spirit, who is on you, and my words that I have
put in your mouth will not depart from your mouth, or from
the mouths of your children, or from the mouths of their
descendants from this time on and forever," says the LORD.

THIS PASSAGE CONCLUDES not only 59:1–15a but
also the block of material beginning at 56:1. The
people were commanded to do righteousness and
keep justice (56:1), and the fact that the eunuch
or the foreigner who did these things would be considered a full member of
the community (56:3–8) emphasized the importance of the command. But
apart from 57:14–21, where God promised to heal the contrite, the material

from 56:9 to 59:15a narrates a sad account that climaxes in the tragic statement of 59:9–15a. The burden of that account is that God's people seem unable to keep his commandments. In some cases they try to keep them in false ways. But in the end they admit that even with the best will, they cannot do either what God has commanded or what they agreed to when they accepted the covenant with him.[1]

So what is to be done? The answer is found in 59:15b–21. God will come and do for his people what neither they nor anyone else can do for them. That is, the same "arm" (59:16) that made it possible for them to be restored to fellowship with God (53:1), the Servant, will now defeat the sin that reigns in them and will make it possible for them to be, in truth, the servants of the Lord (as promised in 2:1–5 and elsewhere throughout the book). Whereas in 52:13–53:12 the Servant was submissive, undergoing the punishment the erring sheep had brought on themselves, now the arm of the Lord is revealed as a conquering warrior (59:17).[2]

The "enemies" he will defeat are not outside oppressors, as both the literary and the historical context make clear. Rather, it is the sinners in Israel who will be conquered. But we notice that he is not doing this on behalf of the righteous in Israel. Instead, he is doing it for those "who repent of their sins" (59:20). Thus, what he is really defeating is sin itself as it reigns in his people. He is not coming here to vindicate the righteous (59:1–15a made it abundantly clear there are no such persons). No, he has come to do what the people, sinners and righteous alike, cannot do, namely, defeat the power of evil in their lives. Moreover, this victory has a worldwide impact. People all over the world ("from the west ... and from the rising of the sun") will be affected by the witness of a righteous Israel (cf. Ezek. 36:21–27). They will give God "glory" and turn to him in obedience ("fear the name of the LORD," 59:19).[3]

---

1. Many commentators do not see this kind of integral connection of 59:15b–21 with what precedes it. For fuller discussion, see Oswalt, *Isaiah 40–66*, 525–32. Childs (*Isaiah*, 484–91) has now taken a similar position.

2. Hanson, *Isaiah 40–66*, 212–17, goes to some lengths to identify and interpret this passage as a retreat to an apocalyptic vision by a marginalized and discouraged minority who see no possibility of deliverance in the historical era. In fact, this description of the Lord's arm is no more obviously apocalyptic in tone than are the four passages revealing the ideal Servant in chs. 40–55. All five passages speak of the central figure in metaphorical and sweeping terms and point to future action by the figure. It is only that in the former ones evil is conquered by submission, whereas here (and in 63:1–6) it is conquered by victory. That does not make the material apocalyptic. For a discussion of apocalyptic, see J. Oswalt, "Recent Studies in Old Testament Apocalyptic," in *The Face of Old Testament Studies*, ed. D. Baker and B. Arnold (Grand Rapids: Baker, 1999), 369–90.

3. The second sentence in 59:19 constitutes a problem. The NIV and other modern translations take ṣar ("oppress, constrict") to be an attributive adjective modifying "river,"

Verse 21 concludes all that has been said in chapters 56–59. God's goal for his people is for them to be witnesses to the world of his nature and character, that he, the only God, is indeed the only Savior. But that witness has been silenced by the unclean lips of the nation, just as the unclean lips of the prophet had rendered him speechless (6:5). The goal of the divine warrior is not merely so that the people can enjoy the holy life of God. The goal is that the "Spirit" of God can fill the lives and mouths of his people, making the witness promised in 2:1–5 not just a possibility but a reality. This is the fulfillment of the "covenant of peace" (54:10; 55:3–5).

THE REV. PAUL BLACKHAM of All Souls Church in London delivered an address on "Mission in a Post-Modern World" at Amsterdam 2000. One of the significant points he made in that address is that logic and argument are greatly devalued in the postmodern mind-set. They are approached with an almost infinite skepticism. Human experience, however, is treated with near reverence. Thus, the quality of the life of a witness is given much more credibility than the quality of his or her argument. Blackham went on to say that this is good news for the Christian evangelist, because the entire biblical approach to witness and mission revolves around the testimony of the witness's life. Thus, the cry of Isaiah for transformed lives that demonstrate the redeeming power of God continues to be echoed and underscored in the twenty-first century. Words about transformation are useless if they are contradicted by lives that are not transformed.

THE CONTEMPORARY CHURCH desperately needs to recapture not merely the truth but the experience pointed to in these verses. We have come to believe that Romans 7 (and Isaiah 59:1–15a) is all we can expect. God has forgiven us of our sins (delivered us from our Babylon), but he is helpless to deliver us from our sinning. "God forbid" (to quote the KJV of Rom. 6:2)!

To be sure, if we merely rely on discipline and will to enable us to conform to God's expectations, we will be left in Romans 7, which is precisely

---

as the word order suggests (thus, "like a pent-up flood"). The KJV, because of an agreement problem, elected to read *ṣar* as "an oppressor." In the second colon, the question revolves around the meaning of the rare verb *nosˤsah*. "Drive along" makes better sense in the context of a pent-up river than does the alternative "raise a banner."

Paul's point. He says in Romans 6 that we must defeat sin, and in Romans 7 he shows us why the Jews, he being one of them, had been unable to do so. The law simply could not provide the dynamic necessary to overcome entrenched self-centeredness. But that is all lead-in to Romans 8. Sin, as a way of behaving and relating, *can* be defeated in our lives because of what God has done for us in the divine warrior, Christ. He has done what the law could not do, deliver us from sinning.[4]

He does this through the power of the Holy Spirit. It is widely recognized that the Spirit is the dominant figure in Romans 8, occurring seventeen times in Romans 8:1–16. Here the promise of Isaiah 59:21 is explained in detail. Christ will live his life within us through the Holy Spirit, and we will be enabled to live a quality of life like that described in Colossians 3:12–16:

> Therefore, as God's chosen people, holy and dearly loved, clothe yourselves with compassion, kindness, humility, gentleness and patience. Bear with each other and forgive whatever grievances you may have against one another. Forgive as the Lord forgave you. And over all these virtues put on love, which binds them all together in perfect unity.
>
> Let the peace of Christ rule in your hearts, since as members of one body you were called to peace. And be thankful. Let the word of Christ dwell in you richly as you teach and admonish one another with all wisdom, and as you sing psalms, hymns and spiritual songs with gratitude in your hearts to God.

Such a life is not possible for those who are only forgiven. But unless it *can* be made possible, it is merely one more hopeless burden believers are required to carry. We are commanded to do something we cannot. What Isaiah and Paul are saying is that Christ came to make it a possibility through the gift of the Holy Spirit. We can keep covenant with God, with no credit for the feat accruing to us at all but all glory to the conquering Christ. He enables us to live "blameless" lives (1 Thess. 5:23), to walk in a "blameless" manner (Gen. 17:1), and to keep us in that walk until the coming of Christ.[5]

---

4. The law was capable of enabling people to remain in relationship with God. What it could not do, because of the power of entrenched self-centeredness, which Paul calls "the flesh," was to stop them from sinning. But the Spirit of Christ can. Thus, the life described in Rom. 8:4–8 is in complete contradiction to that described in 7:14–25.

5. For more on these ideas, see J. Oswalt, *Called to Be Holy* (Nappanee, Ind.: Evangel, 1999).

Isaiah 60:1–22

᷉

¹ "Arise, shine, for your light has come,
   and the glory of the LORD rises upon you.
² See, darkness covers the earth
   and thick darkness is over the peoples,
   but the LORD rises upon you
   and his glory appears over you.
³ Nations will come to your light,
   and kings to the brightness of your dawn.

⁴ "Lift up your eyes and look about you:
   All assemble and come to you;
   your sons come from afar,
   and your daughters are carried on the arm.
⁵ Then you will look and be radiant,
   your heart will throb and swell with joy;
   the wealth on the seas will be brought to you,
   to you the riches of the nations will come.
⁶ Herds of camels will cover your land,
   young camels of Midian and Ephah.
   And all from Sheba will come,
   bearing gold and incense
   and proclaiming the praise of the LORD.
⁷ All Kedar's flocks will be gathered to you,
   the rams of Nebaioth will serve you;
   they will be accepted as offerings on my altar,
   and I will adorn my glorious temple.

⁸ "Who are these that fly along like clouds,
   like doves to their nests?
⁹ Surely the islands look to me;
   in the lead are the ships of Tarshish,
   bringing your sons from afar,
   with their silver and gold,
   to the honor of the LORD your God,
   the Holy One of Israel,
   for he has endowed you with splendor.

¹⁰ "Foreigners will rebuild your walls,
   and their kings will serve you.

> Though in anger I struck you,
>> in favor I will show you compassion.
> ¹¹ Your gates will always stand open,
>> they will never be shut, day or night,
> so that men may bring you the wealth of the nations—
>> their kings led in triumphal procession.
> ¹² For the nation or kingdom that will not serve you
>> will perish;
>> it will be utterly ruined.
>
> ¹³ "The glory of Lebanon will come to you,
>> the pine, the fir and the cypress together,
> to adorn the place of my sanctuary;
>> and I will glorify the place of my feet.
> ¹⁴ The sons of your oppressors will come bowing
>> before you;
> all who despise you will bow down at your feet
> and will call you the City of the LORD,
>> Zion of the Holy One of Israel.
>
> ¹⁵ "Although you have been forsaken and hated,
>> with no one traveling through,
> I will make you the everlasting pride
>> and the joy of all generations.
> ¹⁶ You will drink the milk of nations
>> and be nursed at royal breasts.
> Then you will know that I, the LORD, am your Savior,
>> your Redeemer, the Mighty One of Jacob.
> ¹⁷ Instead of bronze I will bring you gold,
>> and silver in place of iron.
> Instead of wood I will bring you bronze,
>> and iron in place of stones.
> I will make peace your governor
>> and righteousness your ruler.
> ¹⁸ No longer will violence be heard in your land,
>> nor ruin or destruction within your borders,
> but you will call your walls Salvation
>> and your gates Praise.
> ¹⁹ The sun will no more be your light by day,
>> nor will the brightness of the moon shine on you,
> for the LORD will be your everlasting light,
>> and your God will be your glory.

20 Your sun will never set again,
  and your moon will wane no more;
 the LORD will be your everlasting light,
  and your days of sorrow will end.
21 Then will all your people be righteous
  and they will possess the land forever.
 They are the shoot I have planted,
  the work of my hands,
  for the display of my splendor.
22 The least of you will become a thousand,
  the smallest a mighty nation.
 I am the LORD;
  in its time I will do this swiftly."

Original Meaning

ISAIAH 60–62 FORM the center section of the chiastic structure in which chapters 56–66 are arranged (see the comments at 56:1–8). These three chapters display the glorious future of a Jerusalem in which God's glory shines through his anointed Servant (61:1–3). That glory is an expression of the reality that will exist when the divine warrior's conquest of sin is complete. But even prior to that final consummation, many aspects of it have already been realized. God's light has dawned in Zion in the person of Jesus Christ; as a result, many of the world's great nations have come to Jerusalem. In the process many of the dispersed peoples of Israel have been restored to the land. From Jerusalem a witness has gone out to all the world, and that witness continues to this day.

Chapter 60 may be divided into four stanzas. (1) Verses 1–3 form a vividly poetic introduction. (2) Verses 4–9 focus on the return of Zion's dispersed sons and daughters, accompanied by the wealth of the world. (3) In verses 10–14 the kings of the oppressor nations submit to Zion. (4) Verses 15–22 demonstrate how God will not cast off Israel forever but will fully restore it to himself.

Poetic Introduction (60:1–3)

THE EMPHASIS ON "light" in this section is all the more striking because of the contrast with 59:9. Where there was complete "darkness," there will now be "light" like that of the rising sun. There is no question as to the source of this light. It is not something that originates from within Zion; rather, it is a reflection of the "glory of the LORD."[1] Something has occurred that makes it possible for the glory of the Lord to be seen in his people. That something is the conquest of sin by the divine warrior. As 42:6 and 49:6 said, the Servant will be a "light for the Gentiles [nations]," and Zion will be the lamp out of which that light shines on the nations (60:3).

The purpose of God's sharing his glory with his people becomes explicit in 60:2—3. Israel has a mission: The "nations" are in "darkness" because they do not know the one Creator, who is thereby the one Savior. When the light of God dawns in Israel, the nations will recognize it for what it is and "come" flowing to it. Zion's light is not for itself but for others.

Return of Zion's Dispersed Sons and Daughters (60:4–9)

THE FINAL THEME of the introduction is expanded in two ways: Isaiah 60:4– 9 stresses that the nations will bring wealth with them to Jerusalem; in 60:10– 16 the emphasis is on the submission that these nations, who once oppressed Israel, will offer. Both stanzas contain references to the fact that the nations will restore Zion's scattered children.

In 60:4–9 Isaiah emphasizes the worldwide nature of the pilgrimage of the nations, coming from the far southeast ("Sheba") and from the distant west ("Tarshish").[2] They will come with every kind of conveyance, from camels to ships. The wealth will be of every sort as well: incense, flocks, rams, silver, and gold. But there is no question what this wealth is intended to honor, for it is "proclaiming the praise of the LORD" (60:6), it is "to the honor of the LORD your God" (60:9). It is neither to praise nor to honor Zion, for Zion is only the lamp from which the light shines. To be sure, if it were not for the lamp, there would be no vehicle out of which the light could shine, because God has chosen to reveal himself in the context of human life. So the "splendor" with which he endows his people is an expression of his own generous abundance, but even more it is so that the world may know him.

---

1. "Glory" and "the glory of the LORD" are important themes in Isaiah. All attempts by humans to glorify themselves, whether in accomplishments (3:8) or in making the gods in the image of humanity (44:13), are doomed to failure because the earth is "full of [the LORD's] glory" (6:3) and none other (cf. also 24:15; 26:15; 35:2; 40:5; 41:16; 42:8, 12; 58:8; 59:19; 60:19; 66:18, 19). But the wonder is that he intends to share that glory with his people, as is seen here (cf. also 4:2, 5; 44:23; 60:19).

2. It is not clear why special emphasis is given to peoples of Arabia and other areas southeast of Judah: Midian, Ephah, Kedar, and Nebaioth (vv. 6–7). Since Midian, Ephah, and Nebaioth are all named in Genesis as descendants of Abraham (Gen. 25:2, 4, 13), there may be some intention of specifying that all of Abraham's children will be reunited. There may also be an allusion to the incidents of Judg. 6–8.

Along with their wealth, the nations will also bring back Zion's "sons" and "daughters" (60:4, 9). This figure of speech pictures Zion as a bereaved wife and mother.[3] What she thought was gone forever God will restore. He is able to make his people productive and fruitful again in every area of their lives. Note also the restoration to Israel of her scattered people. If the promises to Abraham are to have any meaning, the forced dispersion of Abraham's descendants cannot be permitted. In a coming day, all those who wished to return will be able to do so; moreover, the nations that carried them off will be the ones to bring them home (60:4, 9).

Submission to Zion (60:10–14)

THE NATIONS WILL not only bring their wealth to Zion, but they will also come to serve her. The "kings will serve you" (60:10), and if not, their "kingdom ... will be utterly ruined" (60:12). This seems to stand in contradiction to such statements as 2:1–5; 56:1–8; and 66:20–23 (not to mention 60:6, 9), which have the nations as equal participants in the worship of the Lord. Probably two points are being made. (1) As Isaiah has said throughout the book (e.g., 10:5–32), those who oppress God's people, even as an instrument in his hand, are accountable for their behavior. Thus, the day will come when there will be a complete reversal, in that the oppressors will become servants of a redeemed people. Sin will be punished.

(2) A choice is implied in the two kinds of passages. If one does not choose to become a participant in worship with God's redeemed people, the only other option is to become their servants. The option of continuing to be their oppressors will no longer exist. But notice again that the service is not finally given for the aggrandizement of Zion. Instead, it is given "to adorn the place of my sanctuary" (60:13; cf. 60:7). The service is given to Zion for the Lord, because she is "Zion of the Holy One of Israel." It is when God's people have truly laid aside their own self-seeking through the work of the divine warrior (59:15a–21; 63:1–6) and exist for God's glory alone that all these by-products come flowing to them.

Restoration of Israel to God (60:15–22)

A PROMINENT FEATURE of this final stanza is the recurrence of first-person pronouns referring to the Lord (60:15, 16, 17, 21, 22). Isaiah closes by asserting that all of the benefits that will accrue to God's people result from one thing alone: the gracious power of the Lord. Twice he asserts that "the LORD will be your everlasting light" (60:19, 20). It is he who will transform Zion

---

3. Cf. 49:21; 51:18–20; 54:1–8; 66:7–9.

from being "forsaken" and abandoned (60:15) to being suckled at the "breasts" of royalty (60:16).[4] It is he who will replace silver, iron, and stones with gold, silver, and bronze (60:17). It is he who will take away violence, ruin, and destruction (60:18) and give peace and righteousness (60:17), salvation and praise (60:18) in their place.

Isaiah does not foresee a day when Israel will finally "get it all together" and bring in the kingdom of God. Rather, he sees a day when Israel will finally allow God to do his work in them and through them. This is, of course, similar to the point that was made in Isaiah 9−11, where God demonstrated his trustworthiness in gracious deliverance. The recognition of 60:16 is identical in theme if not in words with that of Isaiah 12. When God is allowed to do his gracious transforming work in persons, then they "will know that I the LORD, am your Savior, your Redeemer, the Mighty One of Jacob."

But the ultimate transformation that the Savior produces is not changing bronze into gold or iron into silver. Rather, it is changing people who are helpless in sin, incapable of acting in righteous ways, into "righteous" people (60:21), people who are truly seen as the kind of "shoots" that the Lord has set out. These are the people who have in them a "brightness" (60:19) that outshines the sun or the moon. The Creator himself, the Holy One of Israel, shines out of their lives.[5] What higher place in the order of reality can there be than to be "the work of my hands, for the display of my splendor" (60:21)? Thus, Israel will truly be a servant of the Lord.

Bridging Contexts

A THEOLOGICAL SETTING. Determining the historical setting the prophet has in mind for Isaiah 60−62 is not easy. If we are correct in thinking that chapters 56−66 are primarily addressed to people in the postexilic era, then he is not talking about the return from Babylon. That conclusion is confirmed when we compare chapters 56−66

---

4. The figure of speech is reminiscent of the Egyptian representations of the pharaoh sitting in the lap of the goddess Isis nursing at her breast. It is a way of saying that the pharaoh is divine. So here Isaiah is saying that Zion goes from being an orphan to a child of royalty.

5. Westermann, *Isaiah 40−66*, 363−64, and Whybray, *Isaiah 40−66*, 237, consider 60:19−20 to be intrusive because they speak of a time when there is no sun or moon, and this is supposedly a feature of later apocalyptic. However, note that 60:1−2 already mention that "the glory of the LORD *rises* upon you." Already, then, the poetic language of the passage is treating God as the sun. It is a small step from there to saying that the sun and moon are not needed.

with chapters 40–48. The problem addressed in this section is clearly not physical bondage. That fact also suggests that the prophet is not envisioning some other major return relatively soon after the first return. Once again, deliverance from a foreign country is not the major problem facing the people.

But did Isaiah have a specific event further in the future in mind? If so, we are hard-pressed to identify it. We must say that in contrast to his earlier predictions of exile in Babylon, release by Cyrus, and restoration to the Promised Land—all of which were specifically fulfilled—the predictions in Isaiah 60 have not been fulfilled. We can certainly say that the Messiah of 61:1–3 has come, proclaiming deliverance to the captives of sin, and that since his coming the wealth of the nations has certainly flowed to physical Jerusalem in praise of the glory of God in Christ. We can even say that within the last 125 years what was previously unimaginable, the establishment of a Jewish state in Palestine, has occurred. But this is talking about events scattered over a period of two thousand years.

Even yet we cannot say that all of these predictions have been fulfilled in a final way. Nevertheless, if everything is focused on the final triumph of Christ at the end of time, it is surprising that some of these things have already occurred, at least in part. Perhaps the answer to all the questions is "yes." Perhaps no one historical setting is intended but rather a compilation of all the kinds of things that will take place to give final vindication to the faith of Israel.

In other words, the primary setting for these thoughts is not historical but theological. That is, the primary point is to say that it is only when God's grace is released in the lives of his servants that they can manifest his righteous character in such a way as to allow the nations of the world to see him and come to him as he desires. Precisely when and how these events are to occur is of secondary importance to this theological point.[6] I am not suggesting that it is of no importance whether the events described here occur. But predicting what they are is not as important to the prophet as is getting God's point across.

Thus, the modern reader must ask if his or her spiritual context is like that which has been described in the chapters prior to chapter 60 or if it is like that described in chapter 60. The need for servants of God to be lamps through whom his life can shine undimmed has never been greater than it is at present.

---

6. Whybray, *Isaiah 40–66*, 229, says that the words "have lost the sharp outlines of a concrete expectation" and that "a future *state* [author's emphasis] of Jerusalem" is depicted "rather than a concrete *act* [author's emphasis] of salvation."

THE GLORY OF GOD IN US. Perhaps the primary place where the message of Isaiah 60 is made applicable to contemporary life is in the prayer of Jesus recorded in John 17. Here, in his so-called "high priestly prayer," the theme of "glory" appears repeatedly. At the heart of this repetition is the mutuality of the glory. Christ asks God to "glorify" him so that he in turn can "glorify" God (17:1, 5). This "glory" is something that has been freely shared among members of the Godhead since before time began (17:5), and Christ's work on earth has the function of bringing "glory" to God (17:4). But Jesus has also received "glory" through the lives of the disciples (17:10), with whom he has shared the "glory" God had given to him (17:22, 24). In the end he wants his disciples to see the "glory" he shares with the Father.[7]

It becomes more than a little mind-boggling to try to sort all of this into some kind of logical order. But I do not think that is the point. The point is simply to say in a variety of ways that "glory" is never for oneself. It is always to be shared, given away, reflected. In Hebrew, the word "glory" (*kabod*) does not have the ephemeral connotations that "glory" has in English. In fact, it is just the opposite. *Kabod* connotes what is weighty, significant, even real. This is what Christ has come to give us—the very reality of God. But just as he has given it to us from God, we are to give it back to him. As the light of his reality shines in us, it is not to draw people to us but to God. No accolades should come to us but to the God who shines through us.

What is the reality, the significance of God, that Christ came to share with us? It is his character. When the seraphim cried, "the whole earth is full of his glory" (Isa. 6:3), they were not talking about an "aura" or a "halo." The meaning of the word "glory" is defined by the preceding sentence, in which God is described as the only truly holy being. Leviticus 18–25 leaves no doubt that "holy" for this divine being does not first of all designate separation but is ethical. So the "glory" of God that rises on his people and draws the nations to him is the solid reality of God's holy character. That character shines out of lamps that may not always have the most attractive appearance but which, if they are clean and spotless, will do nothing to obscure the shining of their light.

If we take away the lamp imagery, what is left for us today? Just this: There can be no question concerning the Lord Jesus' commission to us, namely, that we draw all nations to him, making them his disciples. How? Isaiah says that the nations will come to him, as he is seen "shining" in us. How

---

7. For a discussion of this prayer see G. Burge, *John* (NIVAC; Grand Rapids: Zondervan, 2000), 458–80.

does he shine in us? Isaiah 56–59 have made it clear: God "shines" through us when his ethical life is reproduced in us by his grace. When we lay down our pride in submission to him (57:15), when we put the good of others ahead of our own religious accomplishments (58:1–14), and when we live lives that embody his truth and justice (59:1–15a), then where there had been darkness, there will be light—a light that is not our own but reflects the glory that the Trinity shared before the beginning of time.

This latter point should be underlined. Just as the Christian enters into a relationship with God by his grace alone, so the Christian reflects God's glory to the world only by means of divine grace. Only as the life of God is graciously reproduced in us is it reproduced at all.

The heresy of Galatia is still with us—that is, the idea that while we enter this life by grace, we maintain it by effort, all the while knowing we are doomed to failure. That is not the case, as Paul so vigorously asserts (Gal. 3:1–5). It is the Holy Spirit who initiated us into the life, and it is the same Holy Spirit who enables us to live the life of God, not as a burdensome requirement but as a glad expression of his own nature set free within us (Gal. 5:16–26). This process will draw the nations not to us but to God. It is hard to improve on Motyer's way of saying this: "It is when the Lord in his holiness is present among his people, and manifestly so, that the world is magnetized."[8]

---

8. Motyer, *Prophecy of Isaiah*, 497.

Isaiah 61:1–11

¹ THE SPIRIT OF the Sovereign LORD is on me,
  because the LORD has anointed me
  to preach good news to the poor.
He has sent me to bind up the brokenhearted,
  to proclaim freedom for the captives
  and release from darkness for the prisoners,
² to proclaim the year of the LORD's favor
  and the day of vengeance of our God,
to comfort all who mourn,
³   and provide for those who grieve in Zion—
to bestow on them a crown of beauty
  instead of ashes,
the oil of gladness
  instead of mourning,
and a garment of praise
  instead of a spirit of despair.
They will be called oaks of righteousness,
  a planting of the LORD
  for the display of his splendor.

⁴ They will rebuild the ancient ruins
  and restore the places long devastated;
they will renew the ruined cities
  that have been devastated for generations.
⁵ Aliens will shepherd your flocks;
  foreigners will work your fields and vineyards.
⁶ And you will be called priests of the LORD,
  you will be named ministers of our God.
You will feed on the wealth of nations,
  and in their riches you will boast.

⁷ Instead of their shame
  my people will receive a double portion,
and instead of disgrace
  they will rejoice in their inheritance;
and so they will inherit a double portion in their land,
  and everlasting joy will be theirs.

⁸"For I, the LORD, love justice;
  I hate robbery and iniquity.
In my faithfulness I will reward them
  and make an everlasting covenant with them.
⁹Their descendants will be known among the nations
  and their offspring among the peoples.
All who see them will acknowledge
  that they are a people the LORD has blessed."

¹⁰I delight greatly in the LORD;
  my soul rejoices in my God.
For he has clothed me with garments of salvation
  and arrayed me in a robe of righteousness,
as a bridegroom adorns his head like a priest,
  and as a bride adorns herself with her jewels.
¹¹For as the soil makes the sprout come up
  and a garden causes seeds to grow,
so the Sovereign LORD will make righteousness and praise
  spring up before all nations.

IN THIS CHAPTER we are introduced once again to the means whereby God's people will be enabled to live righteous lives, which will in turn draw the nations to God. That means is the Anointed One, the Messiah (61:1–3a). Then follows a list of the benefits that the Messiah's people will receive (61:3b–7). In 61:8–9 God speaks, making it explicit that covenant righteousness is what he desires and that he is the One who makes that righteousness possible. Finally, the servant people break forth into a psalm of praise to God, who makes them a righteous people in the sight of the nations (61:10–11).

Scholars have long debated the identity of the person in 61:1–3. He has been identified with the Servant of chapters 40–55, with Trito-Isaiah, with some unknown disciple of Deutero-Isaiah who is leading the faithful during postexilic times, and with someone like Ezra.[1]

Whybray argues against the first position because he says that there is no mention of the Servant's mission to the nations here. However, that is not strictly correct. To be sure, the Servant does not deal with the nations directly here, but he does have a mission to them. As God intervenes through the

---

1. Delitzsch, *Commentary on Isaiah*, 2:396–99; Whybray, *Isaiah 40–66*, 240; Hanson, *Isaiah 40–66*, 223–24; Watts, *Isaiah 34–66*, 301–2.

Servant in the lives of his people, they are freed from the bondage of sin and enabled to live in righteousness *before* the nations. When that happens, the Servant's mission to the nations will become possible (see 61:9, 11).

Of more significance than identifying the speaker is the calling given to him. He has been anointed by the Spirit of God, both to "preach good news" (61:1) and to provide "beauty" instead of "ashes," "gladness" instead of "mourning," "praise" instead of "despair" (61:3), so that God's people will be "oaks of righteousness." This is not the work of a human prophet; rather, it is the work of the Messiah, the Anointed (see the reference to the Spirit in 11:2), who is prophesied throughout the book.[2] He will make of his people what they cannot make of themselves.

The results of the Messiah's work are detailed in 61:3b–7, beginning with God's people becoming "oaks of righteousness." This is the opposite of what was said of them in 1:27–31, where they were an "oak with fading leaves" because of the unrighteousness and injustice practiced among them (1:21). But even there God promised that Jerusalem would one day "be called the City of Righteousness, the Faithful City" (1:26). Now he reveals the means whereby that will become a reality. The Servant/Messiah's work will not only deliver but also transform.

That deliverance and transformation is expressed in the language of rebuilding in 61:4 and in the language of freedom in 61:5. The nations will make it possible (61:5–6) for the people of Israel to fulfill their ancient calling, to be a royal priesthood (Ex. 19:6), serving God in the beauty of holiness. They will move from "disgrace" to the "inheritance" of a firstborn son— the "double portion" (Isa. 61:7).

The words of God in 61:8–9 underline again the central point in this final section of the book. Why will the people of God enjoy the inheritance of the firstborn son? Because (NIV "for") "I, the LORD, loves justice." What is the logic there? Is it merely that oppression of the Israelites by the nations is unjust and God is not going to permit it to continue indefinitely? "Robbery and iniquity" suggests that is not the case. Rather, it is that God loves justice and hates robbery and iniquity in his people, and one of the effects of the

---

2. See 9:1–7; 11:1–16; 16:5; 32:1–7; 33:13–19. Childs, *Isaiah*, 505, gives a guarded endorsement to this position, saying that when early Christians linked Servant and Messiah, that was a "legitimate reader response," but that we must not "read back a servant/Messiah figure into Isa. 61." With respect, I do not believe those two statements are compatible with each other. A reader-response that is not consistent with the author's intent is not legitimate. If Childs means to say that Isaiah did not have a fully developed picture of the way in which Jesus Christ would flesh out the things that are said of him here, I fully agree. But that is not to say that he was speaking of someone other than the Messiah when he said these words. See Motyer, *Prophecy of Isaiah*, 499, for a clear insistence that the Messiah is intended.

"everlasting covenant" (61:8) he will make with them is that they will be able to live the life of God's true children. "All who see them" (61:9) will recognize this fact.

As has happened before when the work of the Servant/Messiah is presented, the response is a paean of praise.[3] Israel sees herself as a bride whom the Groom has dressed in beautiful wedding garments. What are the garments? They are "salvation" and "righteousness" (61:10). The figure changes in 61:11. Now Israel sees herself as a fruitful field in which God has planted the seeds of flowers, namely, "righteousness" and "praise." In the overall context of Isaiah 56–66, there can be no doubt of the import of these words. God will give his people the righteous behavior they have been unable to produce in themselves. He will do this for his own praise and glory before the nations as a witness to his almighty power.

THE WEDDING SYMBOLISM. The New Testament uses the same language as Isaiah does, the language of the wedding dress, to talk about the same issues. In his famous comparison of the church as the bride of Christ, Paul says that the church will appear before Christ "without stain or wrinkle or any other blemish, but holy and blameless" (Eph. 5:27). In Revelation 19:7–8 the same point is made: "For the wedding of the Lamb has come, and his bride has made herself ready. Fine linen, bright and clean, was given her to wear. (Fine linen stands for the righteous acts of the saints.)"

In two other places Paul uses the same language, although without specific allusion to the wedding dress. In 1 Thessalonians 3:13 he writes, "May he strengthen your hearts so that you will be blameless and holy in the presence of our God and Father when our Lord Jesus comes with all his holy ones." And he makes the point again at the end of the book: "May God himself, the God of peace, sanctify you through and through. May your whole spirit, soul and body be kept blameless at [or 'until'] the coming of our Lord Jesus Christ" (5:23).

With these images and statements the New Testament is saying what Isaiah says: that God wants us to share an intimate relation with himself in which he will do for us what we cannot do for ourselves, that is, to make us like himself, to make us behave as he does. In ancient times the week leading up to the consummation of the marriage was a time of celebration, with the men celebrating in one area and the women in another. On the day of

---

3. See 12:1–6; 42:10–13; 49:13–21; 54:1–17.

the wedding, the bride was led to her groom's home dressed in a gown he had provided for her.[4] There another round of feasting occurred before the bride and groom went to the wedding chamber.

The church is now in that week of celebration. God through his Son, Jesus, has sent to us a "garment of praise," a dress that will have all the onlookers uttering "oohs" and "ahs" as we walk through the streets to go to his house. Shall we go to the Groom clothed in the rags of our own failures to live a life where sin is defeated? Surely not! We can go to him clothed in a gown of the righteous behavior that he has enabled us to experience.

RIGHT LIVING. The challenge for the contemporary church is to believe in Christ. On the surface that seems like a simplistic statement. Surely that is what it is to be the church—to believe in Christ. Even the most liberal expressions of Christianity today admit that "belief" in Christ is basic. But that is just the question. What does it mean to "believe in Christ"? Does it merely mean to take him as our model (with varying descriptions of what that might be)? Many would say, "No, no, it means far more than that," namely, to have faith in Christ not only as our personal Savior from sin but also as the Savior of the world.

But what does it mean to be "saved from sin"? In too many circles today, it only means that the believer is delivered from the guilt and condemnation of his or her sin. The idea that Christ's life, death, and resurrection have as their ultimate goal the breaking of the power of continued sinning has become almost strange to modern Christian ears. Yet this passage makes it perfectly clear that that is the goal. The Messiah proclaims "the year of the LORD's favor" (61:2) so that God's people may become "a planting of the LORD for the display of his splendor" (61:3). What is his splendor but his character?

Can anyone seriously believe that a proud, boastful, self-serving, "born-again Christian" is a display of God's splendor? If they do, they are denying the plain statements of the New Testament, where we read such things as these:

> Jesus Christ, who gave himself for us to redeem us from all wickedness and to purify for himself a people that are his very own, eager to do what is good. (Titus 2:13–14)

> What good is it, my brothers, if a man claims to have faith but has no deeds? Can such faith save him? (James 2:14)

---

4. J. Thompson, *Handbook of Life in Bible Times* (Downers Grove, Ill.: InterVarsity Press, 1986), 89.

For everyone born of God overcomes the world. This is the victory that has overcome the world, even our faith. (1 John 5:4)

Many modern Christians miss the significance of these latter two passages because they separate faith and works, or better, faith and Christian living. In other words, they believe we are brought into a relationship with God through Christ by faith. In this faith relationship we experience forgiveness of sins. Then, *as an expression of our faith,* we try to do "good works," believing that we are expected to but also knowing that, by and large, we will fail. This is a faulty understanding. In many different ways the New Testament tells us that faith in Christ is for the purpose of changing us into Christ's (and thus God's) likeness.[5] Forgiveness of sin is not the end; it is only the means. The end is that we should live out the righteousness of God *by faith.* Failing to believe Christ to make our character like his, and attempting to do this merely as an expression of our faith and in our own strength, we cannot help but fail.

But some will say, "I have asked Christ to make me like him, and there have been some changes in my life, but I still fail to be all that I know he wants me to be." This brings me back to the opening statement in this section. We have asked, but have we believed? "Faith" is an act of complete trust in which we renounce all other supports. Have we truly surrendered our own way, our own desires, our own will into the hands of the Savior?

Most of us want God's power for holy living while retaining a firm grip on the steering wheel of our lives. We would like to be "better" Christians but are unwilling to become bond-slaves. God's awesome power to be loving when we are not loved, to be kind in the midst of cruelty, to be clean in the midst of filth, to be self-forgetful when everything around us says to "take care of yourself at all costs" is not available to those who would use it for their own ends.

A second factor is that too often we allow the accuser to defeat us. We do not see instant, painless change in our behavior and so we allow doubt to replace faith. But the point of failure is the point at which we must ask God to show us what in us is preventing his power from being released in us. As we give God the freedom to probe around in our persons and to excise what is killing us, we may enter into a painful process. But it is also a process that leads to wonderful freedom and joyous growth.

In the end, the only question is one of belief. Do we believe that Christ wants to deliver us from habitual sinning? Do we believe he can do that? Will *we,* personally and intentionally, believe him to do that in our lives? Will we keep on believing him to remake us into his image, despite setbacks and difficulties, right to the end of the road?

---

5. Cf. Rom. 12:1–2; Gal. 5:22–25; Eph. 2:10; 4:17–24; Col. 2:20–3:11; Heb. 9:14.

Isaiah 62:1–12

¹ FOR ZION'S SAKE I will not keep silent,
    for Jerusalem's sake I will not remain quiet,
  till her righteousness shines out like the dawn,
    her salvation like a blazing torch.
² The nations will see your righteousness,
    and all kings your glory;
  you will be called by a new name
    that the mouth of the LORD will bestow.
³ You will be a crown of splendor in the LORD's hand,
    a royal diadem in the hand of your God.
⁴ No longer will they call you Deserted,
    or name your land Desolate.
  But you will be called Hephzibah,
    and your land Beulah;
  for the LORD will take delight in you,
    and your land will be married.
⁵ As a young man marries a maiden,
    so will your sons marry you;
  as a bridegroom rejoices over his bride,
    so will your God rejoice over you.

⁶ I have posted watchmen on your walls, O Jerusalem;
    they will never be silent day or night.
  You who call on the LORD,
    give yourselves no rest,
⁷ and give him no rest till he establishes Jerusalem
    and makes her the praise of the earth.

⁸ The LORD has sworn by his right hand
    and by his mighty arm:
  "Never again will I give your grain
    as food for your enemies,
  and never again will foreigners drink the new wine
    for which you have toiled;
⁹ but those who harvest it will eat it
    and praise the LORD,
  and those who gather the grapes will drink it
    in the courts of my sanctuary."

¹⁰ Pass through, pass through the gates!
   Prepare the way for the people.
Build up, build up the highway!
   Remove the stones.
Raise a banner for the nations.

¹¹ The LORD has made proclamation
   to the ends of the earth:
"Say to the Daughter of Zion,
   'See, your Savior comes!
See, his reward is with him,
   and his recompense accompanies him.'"
¹² They will be called the Holy People,
   the Redeemed of the LORD;
and you will be called Sought After,
   the City No Longer Deserted.

THE THEME INTRODUCED in 61:4–11 (and parallel-ing that of 60:1–22) continues here. It is introduced in 62:1 with a declaration of God's intent for Zion. The paralleling of "righteousness" and "salvation" is significant in two ways. (1) It reminds the reader that Israel's righteousness is only possible because of the saving activity of God; it is not something Israel can produce on her own. (2) At the same time, the combination makes it plain that the only goal of God's saving activity is unmistakably righteous living.

This statement is followed by eight verses (62:2–9) of direct address to Israel. There has been much scholarly debate over who the speakers are. If God is the speaker in verses 1 and 6, then perhaps verses 2–5 and 7–9 are to be seen as prophetic amplifications on these themes. This blurring of the distinction between God and the prophet is a well-known characteristic of biblical prophecy. The theme of these verses, recalling the promises of chapters 49–52,[1] is an insistence that God has not cast off Zion (62:4) but

---

1. There are a number of other reminiscences of chapters 40–55 here, such as "watch-men" (62:6; cf. 52:8); "highway" (62:10; cf. 40:3); "reward . . . recompense" (62:11; cf. 40:10). Whereas this feature might be taken as evidence for single authorship of the book, most modern scholars, having a prior commitment to multiple authorship, see this as a striking example of "intertextuality," the idea that later biblical writers allude to earlier ones. Cf. B. Sommers, *A Prophet Reads Scripture: Allusion in Isaiah 40–66* (Stanford, Calif.: Stanford Univ. Press, 1998). He argues for the unitary authorship of Isa. 35 and 40–66 on the basis of what he sees as a common pattern of allusion. He does not grant that the allusions to the earlier chapters of the book can support unitary authorship of the whole.

that he "rejoices" (62:5) over her as a groom does a bride (continuing the imagery of 61:10).[2]

In this statement of God's joy in his people, the idea of the display of his handiwork before the nations is never far from the surface. "The nations will see" the "glory" that is their "righteousness" (62:2). The nation will be a beautiful "crown" in God's "hand" (62:3). Zion will be "the praise of the earth." One aspect of this is the idea of "recompense" (62:11): Just as Israel has been a butt of Gentile jokes, so they will become the object of Gentile praise and wonder. Some of that same idea is found in 62:8–9, where God assures his bride that the produce of the fields that once was taken by the "enemies" (cf. Deut. 28:33, 39) will no longer so be taken but will be eaten by those who planted it[3] and so become a source of "praise" in the "sanctuary."

The concluding segment (62:10–12) actually concludes the unit that began at 60:1. As already mentioned, these verses show some interesting parallels with chapter 40, with its call to "build up the highway" and "raise a banner for the nations." This is the same language used in the discussion of the messianic kingdom in chapter 11. Here Isaiah is drawing together strands from throughout his book in an effort to call the people to take action to receive the promises God is making to them. They *can* be the righteous people of God, his "Holy People" (62:12), who will draw all nations to him.

Now, as compared to 40:10, it is not the "Sovereign" who is coming but the "Savior" (62:11). The "ends of the earth" are to hear the Lord's "proclamation" that a Savior has come to Zion and to make their adjustment accordingly. They can come to the city that is now "Sought After," there to share in its salvation, or they can continue to range themselves against it and be reduced to become its servants.

Bridging Contexts

IF ANY OF US has ever been in a situation where we felt completely abandoned and rejected and then, unaccountably, found ourselves welcomed and taken in, we can understand what this chapter is about. I had an experience like that in college. There was a girl in my class whom I admired from a long way off. She was pretty, she was witty, she was popular, she had it all. Whenever anything was going on, she was always in the middle of whatever it was. I was the opposite, or so I felt. I was not good-

---

2. The textual evidence is in favor of retaining "sons" in v. 5. This creates a problem for the imagery since laws of incest prohibit a son from marrying his mother. Perhaps there is a mixing of metaphor and literal here, with the joy of the return of the descendants to the land being compared to the joy of a wedding (cf. 62:4, "your land will be married").

3. Isa. 37:30; 65:20–21; Jer. 31:5; Amos 9:14.

looking, my attempts to be funny usually fell flat, I tended to be loud-mouthed, and I was always on the fringes.

This girl and I happened to be in a speech course together. One of the assignments was for each of us to assess the personality of another class member, understanding that one of our assets (or liabilities) as a speaker was the personality we projected. On the day the assignments were due, we had to share them (privately) with the person we were assessing. When I saw that this girl was the one who had been assigned to assess me, I can hardly describe the terror I felt. I knew that she was going to fillet me like a fish. I knew that when she finished with me, I would be able to slither out under the door of the room without opening it. To my surprise yet today, she singled out trait after trait of mine that she found attractive and compelling. She handled areas that needed improvement with tact and insight. In fact, when I left the room, I could have floated out the window. She had found some things in me that were valuable. I have never forgotten that gift.

That is what God is doing here. Not for the first time in this book he is saying to all people that he sees worth and value in us. He wants to be with us, he likes us, we are important to him. To a great extent, this is so because of him and not because of us. Because God is the kind of person he is, he is able to see things in us that lie buried beneath layers of sin and shame. He is able to see possibilities where nothing but failure would be perceived by anyone else. But even more than that, he is able to uncover those hidden things, to let loose those possibilities, because he has taken all the failure, the sin, and the shame into himself. So he is able not only to show us what is there but to set it free. He is able to give each of us on a cosmic and eternal level the kind of gift that girl gave me so many years ago in speech class.

WE LIVE IN a time of strange paradoxes. One of those is that we have never had such emphasis on self-esteem coupled with such a high suicide rate. What explains this? I am not suggesting that our emphasis on self-esteem is causing the suicides, of course. But I would suggest that increasing our (artificial) attempts to induce self-esteem does not address the problem. What causes feelings of self-worth? What enables people to go on living when problems seem to mount above eye level? On the other hand, what diminishes our sense of worth? And beyond that, what does that have to do with Isaiah 62?

Paul Tournier, the Swiss psychologist, writes:

If we tried to cast off all our social apparel, we should tend to become individuals and not persons. The notion of the person is bound up

with the human community, a spiritual solidarity, a common patri-
mony, and therefore to a certain conventional form of expression
which partakes of the nature of the personage.[4]

What he was putting his finger on more than forty years ago is the fact that
one's sense of oneself is in some sense a by-product of a whole web of relationships. We have not learned that lesson yet. Western society, especially
North American society, continues to fragment. Families are now such complicated things, with step-step-mothers and siblings with whom we have no
blood ties at all, that it becomes increasingly difficult to say I belong anywhere. I am an individual and not a person.

Oddly enough, self-esteem outside of a positive complex of relationships
is not a good thing but a bad one. The serial killer often feels good about himself and has nothing but contempt for his victims. In other words, we are
focusing on the wrong thing. We should be helping people to find complex,
stable webs of relationship in which they play a vital and necessary part. In
such a setting they will know themselves to be of worth, but that worth will
not be the most important thing to them. What will matter is that we find
our "self" by giving it away to others.

This is, of course, what is at the heart of Trinitarian theology, which gave
rise to the very concept of "person." The persons of the Trinity exist in mutually dependent relations with each other, and the identity of each is dependent on the others. There is no "Father" unless there is a "Son," and there is
no "Son" without the "Father." And the "Spirit" is the "Spirit *of* the Father and
the Son." That is why God is the kind of God he is. God reaches out to us
with open arms, seeking to draw us in. We are his "crown," his "bride," his
"My-delight-is-in-her," his "Holy People," his "No Longer Deserted." The
Trinity want to take us into their society, where we find ourselves by surrendering ourselves into their love. John beautifully expresses this truth when
he writes that his reason for telling what he knows about Jesus is so that his
readers can have fellowship with each other—a fellowship that is shared
with the Father and the Son (1 John 1:3). We give up our lonely individuality to find our true personality.

This is what the church, though broken and fallible, is all about. As we
become a part of the people of God, we discover how valuable and important we are. When the church is the church, each of us playing our own part
in the complex dance, we find ourselves. We do not have to be told that we
have worth. We know it. Like the people of Israel contributing to the building of the tabernacle, we each, moved by the Spirit, have something to con-

---

4. P. Tournier, *The Meaning of Persons*, trans. E. Hudson (New York: Harper & Row,
1957), 75.

tribute (Ex. 35:20–29). Those who cannot sing can do the accounts, and those who cannot teach can organize fellowship meals. Each one has a vital part to fill (cf. 1 Cor. 12:4–11; Eph. 4:11–16). Those on the outside of such relationships look in with wonder and longing, just as God says the nations will look in upon his redeemed people.

Isaiah 63:1–6

¹WHO IS THIS coming from Edom,
    from Bozrah, with his garments stained crimson?
Who is this, robed in splendor,
    striding forward in the greatness of his strength?

"It is I, speaking in righteousness,
    mighty to save."

²Why are your garments red,
    like those of one treading the winepress?

³"I have trodden the winepress alone;
    from the nations no one was with me.
I trampled them in my anger
    and trod them down in my wrath;
their blood spattered my garments,
    and I stained all my clothing.
⁴For the day of vengeance was in my heart,
    and the year of my redemption has come.
⁵I looked, but there was no one to help,
    I was appalled that no one gave support;
so my own arm worked salvation for me,
    and my own wrath sustained me.
⁶I trampled the nations in my anger;
    in my wrath I made them drunk
    and poured their blood on the ground."

Original Meaning

WE RETURN FROM talking about the future when the light will have dawned on a redeemed Israel, and through them on the whole world, to the less rosy present and what it will take if that light is to dawn. As I said in my opening comments on Isaiah 56–66, the material is arranged chiastically (see comments on 56:1–8). Chapters 56–59 speak of the inability of the people to do righteousness, but this is interspersed with, and finally concludes with, the promise that God will enable the righteousness he requires (59:15b–21). Chapters 63–66 return to this theme, but this time the promise of his intervention begins the segment, signaling that these two elements (human inability to do righteousness, divine ability to produce that righteousness) are reversed.[1] Here the primary emphasis is on God's power to enable his servants to live righteous lives.

How can an unrighteous people manifest the light of God that will bring the nations to his feet? The answer is the divine warrior. God will defeat every enemy of his people, including the most dangerous of all, sin. Because of the physical and military imagery used in these verses, it might be easy to think that what is intended here is an announcement that God will defeat all the nations who oppress Israel in the future. That is certainly true, but it goes beyond that.

This is made clear by the succeeding context. Israel's problem is that they are weak because they are sinful. In response, God does not say in 63:1–66:24 that he will destroy their physical enemies in spite of their sinfulness. Rather, he will destroy the sinners *among his people* and will vindicate those among his people who allow him to make them righteous, using these latter people to call the nations to worship the righteous God. They are his true servants (65:13–16; cf. 54:17).

Thus, the blood that stains the garments of the Victor (63:1, 3) is the blood of sinners from all nations, including his own nation, who have defied him. This defiant character of humanity is symbolized by the nation of Edom (63:1; cf. 34:5–15; also Obad.). Why could no one else do this (Isa. 63:3, 5)? Because he alone did not have to die for his own sins (53:4–10). He alone is the righteous Judge, who is without sin. But this is not destruction for its own sake. Rather, it is for the purpose of making "redemption" and "salvation" (63:4–5) available. Until sin and those who propagate it are defeated, there is no genuine salvation available. The idea that redemption and continued sin can coexist is not biblical; it is certainly not Isaianic.

Bridging Contexts

FOR MOST OF US, this picture of a blood-spattered warrior striding exultantly off a field of battle strewn with corpses is a distasteful one. This is especially true for us in North America, who have known so little bloodshed in comparison to the rest of the world. However, we need to put this in another perspective. Think about the prisoners in a Nazi concentration camp. Striding up to the barbed-wire gates comes a blood-spattered, smoke-begrimed GI, who with one burst of his

---

1. The divine ability appears in 63:1–6; 65:6–25; 66:7–16, 18–24; human inability in 63:7–65:5; 66:1–6.

submachine gun blasts the locks off the gates. Does he look distasteful to those prisoners? Not in the least! He is the most beautiful thing they have seen in years. He means freedom; he means deliverance; he means life from the dead. Can you imagine any of them saying, "Now Yank, those Nazis are really nice people, and if you had just talked to them gently and rationally, I am sure all of this unpleasant violence would have been unnecessary"? Hardly! On that field, there was only one approach, a fight to the death and winner take all.

The same is true in the spiritual world. There can be no negotiation with sin, for it is the sworn enemy of all that God is. It is sin that killed the Son of God, and it is sin that will kill all God's creatures if it can. The idea that we can have a negotiated peace where God holds one part of the creation while sin holds another is ludicrous. In the end, either the righteous God will rule the world or sin will. The same thing is true of the human heart. The thought that we can have forgiveness of sin by the blood of Jesus while continuing to practice that which killed him is ludicrous. Christ the warrior comes to destroy sin and set us free.

As Christians, we look to the day when sin will be defeated on the earth. The Bible promises that Day in both Testaments. We do not know when the divine warrior will be manifested to complete that defeat, but we know that it will happen.

But that faith has implications for the present. It means that no quarter can be given to sin. Someone has said, "Republicans are death on sexual sins and any limitation of personal freedom but really don't care about inequity, while Democrats will fight to the death against inequity while jumping from bed to bed. But both of them are in favor of greed." To whatever extent that is true, it is a sad commentary. How can we make a place in our lives for what we are confident must be destroyed in the end if Christ is to reign? How can we act as if personal sin is laughable while structural sin is a terrible evil? How can we excoriate promiscuity while winking an eye at those who are gouging the poor? How can I excuse my sins while condemning yours? How can we act as if sin is anything but the sworn, deadly enemy of all we hold precious?

Harry Emerson Fosdick said it well, "Save us from weak resignation to the evils we deplore." If Christ is the divine warrior, who will eventually triumph over sin in the world at large, the time is now to let him defeat sin in our own lives and to give us a thoroughgoing hatred of it in all its forms. This is the underlying theme in each of Paul's letters: You have come to Christ, who has extended his grace to you; that means you cannot continue to live in sin. Stop stealing, stop lying, stop raging against each other, stop committing adultery, stop oppressing the poor, stop boasting. You can't keep that up and have the One who destroyed sin on the throne of your life.[2]

Isaiah 63:7–14

⟨leaf ornament⟩

⁷I WILL TELL of the kindnesses of the LORD,
    the deeds for which he is to be praised,
    according to all the LORD has done for us—
  yes, the many good things he has done
    for the house of Israel,
    according to his compassion and many kindnesses.
⁸He said, "Surely they are my people,
    sons who will not be false to me";
    and so he became their Savior.
⁹In all their distress he too was distressed,
    and the angel of his presence saved them.
  In his love and mercy he redeemed them;
    he lifted them up and carried them
    all the days of old.
¹⁰Yet they rebelled
    and grieved his Holy Spirit.
  So he turned and became their enemy
    and he himself fought against them.

¹¹Then his people recalled the days of old,
    the days of Moses and his people—
  where is he who brought them through the sea,
    with the shepherd of his flock?
  Where is he who set
    his Holy Spirit among them,
¹²who sent his glorious arm of power
    to be at Moses' right hand,
  who divided the waters before them,
    to gain for himself everlasting renown,
¹³who led them through the depths?
  Like a horse in open country,
    they did not stumble;
¹⁴like cattle that go down to the plain,
    they were given rest by the Spirit of the LORD.
  This is how you guided your people
    to make for yourself a glorious name.

Original Meaning AFTER INTRODUCING GOD'S ability to defeat sin in all of its forms, Isaiah returns to a discussion of the human inability to do what is right (from 63:7 to 65:16). But this iteration of the theme (in contrast to the way it is presented in chs. 57–59) has more of an emphasis on the recognition that human failure will always be the case unless God intervenes. So there is not only a lament over the failure but also the question why God allows this condition to persist.

The groundwork for this question is laid in 63:7–14, and then the question itself is brought out in 63:15–64:12.[1] The forceful answer from God appears in 65:1–5. In 63:7–14 the prophet begins the discussion by rehearsing the theological significance of the Exodus. He lays the emphasis on the elements of God's character that were revealed in the Exodus events. His "kindnesses"[2] and "compassion" (63:7) were revealed, as were his "love and mercy" (63:9). He is One who does "good things" (63:7) in saving and redeeming (63:9) his people.

But the Exodus events also reveal the rebellious character of God's people. After all God had done for them, the Israelites turned against him. Interestingly, Isaiah does not put this rebellion into either a legal or a royal context. That is, he does not say that they broke their covenant or they disobeyed their King. Rather, they "grieved [God's] Holy Spirit" (63:10). That is the language of personal relationship, for the "Holy Spirit" is God's personal presence among his people. Note too 63:14, where "the Spirit of the LORD" gave "rest" to the people (the language is reminiscent of Ps. 23). Clearly the "Spirit" here is a way of speaking about God's personal involvement with humans.[3]

This atmosphere is reinforced by such language as "lifted them up and carried them" (63:9; cf. 46:3–4). All this makes the rebellion more unthinkable. It is not a king or a judge who has been disobeyed or whose authority has been denied. Rather, it is a Father's love, care, and concern that has been treated as worthless. The result is that their Lover became their "enemy" (63:10). Love and personal relationship do not invalidate the law of cause and effect.

---

1. Whybray, *Isaiah 40–66*, 255, notes that 63:7–64:12 fits the pattern of a communal lament (see, e.g., Ps. 80), with a recounting of God's saving work in the past (Isa. 63:7–14), an appeal for help (63:15–64:5), a confession of sin (64:6–7), and a renewed appeal for help (64:8–12).

2. In both occurrences of "kindness" in v. 7, the Heb. *ḥesed* is used. There is no single English word that captures all the nuances of the Heb. term. At its heart is the idea of "passionate commitment of one who has to one who has not, especially when the commitment cannot be compelled" (see D. A. Baer and R. P. Gordon, "חסד," *NIDOTTE*, 2:211–18).

3. Delitzsch, *Commentary on Isaiah*, 2:431, argues that a developed understanding of the Trinity is presented here with the "angel of his presence" (63:9) representing the second person of the Trinity.

But if the Exodus events illustrate both the undeserved grace of God and the shocking rebellion of the people, they also illustrate what older theologians called the "biddability" of God. For in spite of the rebellion of the first generation in the desert, God did not abandon his people. Although he would have been justified in wiping them off the face of the earth in response to their repeated breaking of the covenant, he did not do so. This is implicit in 63:11–14. Given God's initial grace and his continuing patience, what of the future? Can God provide a new Moses who will be the "arm of the LORD" (63:12; cf. 52:10; 53:1) for a fallen people? Can he not deliver them from their persistent rebellion and grieving of the Holy Spirit?

THE THREE THEOLOGICAL themes of this segment of Isaiah are the perennial ones of church history. There is first of all the incredible, undeserved grace of God. Where better can this be seen than in the birth of the church? How could a group of people who were neither the intelligentsia nor the elite of their day have the kind of impact on the world that those first Christians did? It was only the result of the grace of God. Over and over again Paul marvels at that grace in permitting him to be the one to reveal the mystery of the ages to the Gentiles. And because the Holy Spirit was at work in those early believers, they did not merely revel in that grace but were able to become channels of it to a world that God had prepared to hear.

But the other theme is there as well. In many ways, just as the story of the Old Testament is a story of apostasy, so is the story of the church. We look at the medieval papacy with horror. How could the things that were done there be done in the name of Christ? Every one of the seven deadly sins was practiced right in the hierarchy of Christ's church. There is no grace that will make it so the evil in the human heart cannot be expressed.

But the third theme is there as well. Across the centuries, time after time, when a merely human interpretation would have said that the church had finally gone beyond the point of restoration, that very thing occurs. A Francis of Assisi appears, or a Bernard of Clairvaux, or a Martin Luther, or a Count von Zinzendorf, or a John Wesley. Alongside these, there have been millions of nameless people who have turned to God in failure, despair, and shame and found not merely restoration to favor but more than that, genuine cleansing and revitalization. In our rebellion, we have experienced God's incredible willingness to hear the prayer of desolation and come back home to our hearts once again.

Contemporary Significance

THE CHURCH IN the West today is in precipitous decline, and we need the message of these verses. While Christendom is still the established religion in most of the western European countries, it clearly has no hold on the hearts of the vast majority of the populace, who see Christianity as irrelevant to their lives. In North America the so-called "mainline churches" are in a state of near free fall, with millions departing their rolls annually, while their leaders speak piously of the "purging of the church." A recent book title speaks about life "after Christianity."[4]

Isaiah calls us to return to our first love. It is not the stern Judge or the distant King who calls us but the One who has carried us through all the years (cf. 46:3–4). He is the One who gave us birth in the first place, who held our arms when we took our first steps, and who faithfully guided us out of the desert into green pastures. The whispers of the Holy Spirit are those of a brokenhearted Lover who tells us that it is not too late to return to his arms.

But this Lover is no weak-chinned stripling, who can be treated like a doormat, thankfully allowing us to use him over again whenever we are between other enchantments. He is Almighty God, whose ways are truth and whose law is eternal. To grieve his heart is to fall off a cliff. If he becomes our enemy, all of life will turn against us. Christians who have a sentimental idea of a God who exists for them are in for a rude shock, and it is time that we woke up to that reality.

But if we do wake up to it, there is no end to what God will do for us. He has breathed new life into his church before, and he will do it again. Contemporary writers, like the author of the Dune series of science-fiction novels, envision a future where a sort of hybrid religion exists because they have only known a church in decline. But that is not historically accurate, because history shows that God will not let his church go. The only question is when, and the answer to that question depends on us.

---

4. Gianni Vattimo, *After Christianity* (Italian Academy Lectures; New York: Columbia Univ. Press, 2002).

Isaiah 63:15–64:12

¹⁵ LOOK DOWN FROM heaven and see
from your lofty throne, holy and glorious.
Where are your zeal and your might?
Your tenderness and compassion are withheld
from us.
¹⁶ But you are our Father,
though Abraham does not know us
or Israel acknowledge us;
you, O LORD, are our Father,
our Redeemer from of old is your name.
¹⁷ Why, O LORD, do you make us wander from
your ways
and harden our hearts so we do not revere you?
Return for the sake of your servants,
the tribes that are your inheritance.
¹⁸ For a little while your people possessed your holy place,
but now our enemies have trampled down your
sanctuary.
¹⁹ We are yours from of old;
but you have not ruled over them,
they have not been called by your name

⁶⁴:¹ Oh, that you would rend the heavens and come down,
that the mountains would tremble before you!
² As when fire sets twigs ablaze
and causes water to boil,
come down to make your name known to your enemies
and cause the nations to quake before you!
³ For when you did awesome things that we did not expect,
you came down, and the mountains trembled
before you.
⁴ Since ancient times no one has heard,
no ear has perceived,
no eye has seen any God besides you,
who acts on behalf of those who wait for him.
⁵ You come to the help of those who gladly do right,
who remember your ways.

But when we continued to sin against them,
    you were angry.
How then can we be saved?
⁶ All of us have become like one who is unclean,
    and all our righteous acts are like filthy rags;
we all shrivel up like a leaf,
    and like the wind our sins sweep us away.
⁷ No one calls on your name
    or strives to lay hold of you;
for you have hidden your face from us
    and made us waste away because of our sins.

⁸ Yet, O LORD, you are our Father.
    We are the clay, you are the potter;
    we are all the work of your hand.
⁹ Do not be angry beyond measure, O LORD;
    do not remember our sins forever.
Oh, look upon us, we pray,
    for we are all your people.
¹⁰ Your sacred cities have become a desert;
    even Zion is a desert, Jerusalem a desolation.
¹¹ Our holy and glorious temple, where our fathers
        praised you,
    has been burned with fire,
    and all that we treasured lies in ruins.
¹² After all this, O LORD, will you hold yourself back?
    Will you keep silent and punish us beyond measure?

IN THE PREVIOUS SECTION, we noted that 63:7–65:12 have, as an underlying theme, both a lament over human failure to do what is right and the question why God allows this condition to persist. The present section gives us the lament proper, which is addressed directly to God.[1] We may divide these verses into four sections: 63:15–19; 64:1–5; 64:6–7; and 64:8–12.[2]

---

1. There are an unusual number of complex textual problems found in this unit. For discussions of them, see Oswalt, *Isaiah 40–66*, 609–11, 617–20, 627–28.

2. Motyer, *Prophecy of Isaiah*, 516, divides the lament into seven stanzas, chiastically arranged, but as with many of his suggested chiasms in the book, I remain unconvinced that this literary design is really present here.

The Complaint (63:15–19)

THESE VERSES, SPOKEN by the prophet as a representative of the people, express the complaint element of the lament. In brief, it is that God is far away from his people, exalted in lonely isolation in his unapproachable holiness and glory. He has "withheld" his "might" and "compassion" from them (63:15). This is not right because God is the true "Father" (63:16) of Israel, much more so than the mere physical ancestors, "Abraham" and Jacob ("Israel"). This is a profound insight. Isaiah understands that Israel is not merely an ethnic, linguistic, or national group. They are first and foremost a spiritual group. They are who they are because of the covenant love of God, who is not merely the "Father" of the nation but also its "Redeemer." If that love should ever be withdrawn, their reason for existence would be called into question.

Yet that seems to be precisely what has happened. The people "wander from" God's "ways" with hardened hearts that do not know how to fear him (NIV, "do not revere you"). It is not clear to what extent the prophet is merely representing what the people are saying or is speaking for himself. Most likely he is speaking for the people, who are trying to disclaim some of the responsibility for their own condition. To say that they are sinning because God will not let them do otherwise is a gross slander of God, which God summarily rejects in 65:1.

To be sure, unless God softens the depraved and hardened human heart, there is no way we can ever turn to him (cf. 1:9). But the fact is, he has already done all that is necessary for that softening to occur. What is missing is the human will to appropriate what God has done. God does not have to be implored to "return" (63:17) to his people. As Malachi says (Mal. 3:6), God has not changed. If his people will return to him, he will return to them.

Isaiah 63:18–19 continues the complaint, saying that although Israel, "your people," once "possessed your holy place" and were "yours from of old," it is now as if they had never "been called by your name."[3] "Enemies have trampled down your sanctuary," with all that implies of either God's helplessness or his lack of concern. As those in despair often do, the speaker has magnified the tragic and minimized the positive. God's people carried his name and possessed his sanctuary for a long time. But looking back, it seems like such a short time.

---

3. A lit. trans. of v. 19 is "Behold us, from of old you have not ruled over them; your name was not called over them." The comparative prefixed to the relative (ka'ašer) is implied. Thus: "We are like those over whom you never ruled, those who were never called by your name." Cf. NASB, NRSV, NLT, etc.

The Petition (64:1–5)

ISAIAH MOVES FROM complaint to petition, calling on God in the name of the people to leave his isolation in the "heavens" and to come to their aid (64:1). The reason for his doing so has been noted throughout this part of the book: that the nations may know the "name" (64:2) of God, that is, that they might know exactly who God is, the sole Sovereign of the universe. Only when those nations see God blessing and defending a transformed people will they recognize him appropriately.

God's actions in the past demonstrate that this petition is not based in fantasy (64:3–4). Whenever God had manifested himself in the past, dramatic things occurred, from the parting of the Red Sea (Ex. 14:21–22) to the stopping of the rain for three years (1 Kings 17:1). Nor were these merely divine fireworks. Unlike any of the other so-called gods, the Lord performed his miracles on the behalf of his people. In sum, God can act and he has acted, so it is not foolish to ask him to act again.

But if Isaiah knows that God can act, he also knows that there are conditions for that to occur (64:4–5). God acts in behalf of those who "wait for him," that is, those who put their trust in him and not in their own devices (cf. 30:18; 40:31). One evidence of such a trust is a life of godliness. To "remember [his] ways" is not merely an intellectual awareness of God's character and expectations, nor is it only to give intellectual assent to those matters. Rather, as Deuteronomy shows, it is to live in accord with those "ways" (cf. Deut. 8:10–20).

That is confirmed by the parallel phrase "gladly do right" (Isa. 64:5). Relationship with a holy God while doing what is contrary to his character is a contradiction of terms. Yet the prophet admits that is exactly what has happened. Far from remembering God's ways by following them, the people of God have sinned against those ways. Thus, instead of God's presence being a blessing to the people, it has become a curse.[4] So while it is theoretically possible to petition God to break through the barriers of time and space and make them a righteous people, their very unrighteousness prevents the petition from being heard. How indeed can they "be saved"?

The Contradiction (64:6–7)

THE RECOGNITION OF the contradiction at the end of 64:5 is now expanded. If the people tended to blame God for their hard-heartedness, at least they did not minimize the reality of their condition. They could not have a

---

4. That's why God had said to Moses that he could not go with the rebellious people, lest his very presence should kill them (Ex. 33:3).

relationship with God and fulfill their mandate of being a light to the nations as long as they continued to live lives that were a reproach to his holy character. They are "unclean"; even the "righteous" things they do are defiled and contaminated (64:6).[5] This underlines the Old Testament understanding that sin is not first of all behavioral dysfunction but rather an offense against the very nature of life, which finally must end in death and decay.

This thought is continued with the image of a dead leaf swept away on a wind of sin. Further reflection occurs in 64:7. What is it to be among the people of God? How is one's life to be lived out in a believer? Is it a matter of discipline and commitment? No, first of all it is a matter of laying "hold" of God, of calling on his "name." It is to be in a vital relationship of dependence and self-renunciation. When that is so, right behavior will follow. But if right behavior becomes the focus, that behavior quickly becomes self-serving and is reduced to nothing more than "filthy rags." God's "face" cannot help but be "hidden" from such people, and they are left to "waste away" in their "sins" (64:7). Here we are at the conundrum again: We are wasting away in our sins because we won't turn to you, and we won't turn to you because you have hidden your face from us. What is to be done?

The Petition Repeated (64:8–12)

ISAIAH CRIES OUT again for God to take unilateral action.[6] Surely God can break the cycle, stop the punishment, and restore his people to himself. These final verses of the lament, then, reiterate the petition. Once again Isaiah asserts that the nation only exists because of God, the "Father," who brought them into existence, the "potter" who formed their "clay" on his wheel (64:8). He should not allow the people's "sins" to make him forget that they are his creation (64:9), nor should he overlook the fact that all the "sacred" spaces that he presumably treasures are in "ruins" (64:10–11). The closing verse picks up the original plea of 63:15. The Lord must not "hold [himself] back"; he must not be "silent" while he goes on punishing them relentlessly.

---

5. "Filthy rags" is lit. "menstrual cloths."

6. It is to be wondered if perhaps the prophet designed this lament on purpose, not only to expose once again the sinful condition of the people but also to expose a false approach to the problem, in which the onus for its solution is taken off the sinner and placed on God. The response of God in ch. 65 suggests this may be the case.

Bridging Contexts

A STRAW MAN? As I remarked in footnote 6, we may wonder if this block of material (63:15–64:12) is not a "setup"—the presentation of a "straw man" that can be demolished in the next segment. And, indeed, that demolition is precisely what happens. In 65:1–16 God replies to this lament with devastating directness, demonstrating that the responsibility for the people's condition lies precisely with them and not on his shoulders. If this "setup" scenario is correct, then Isaiah is consciously presenting the false argument as clearly and as convincingly as he can so that when the returnees from the Exile are tempted to say these things, they will discover that the prophet has already said it even better than they could!

At the same time, the very passion and poignancy of the material suggests that while the "setup" scenario may be correct, it is more than a "straw man." There is more than a degree of truth in what is said here, and we cannot simply dismiss it. The relationship between the human will and the divine will is a complex one that modern theological parties tend to reduce to "sound bites." Arminians sometimes suggest that God is looking on, anxiously wringing his hands while wondering what we humans are going to do next. But Calvinists can make it appear that God merely needs to consult his vast blueprint to determine what each one of us will be compelled to do next.

A careful student of the Bible recognizes that both of those oversimplifications misrepresent the biblical positions. In fact, I would go so far as to say that *any* attempt to reduce the biblical data to a neatly complete system fully comprehensible to the human mind results in a defective system. The most recent example of this is process theology and its evangelical twin, the so-called "openness of God." These two positions have determined that the only way to preserve the reality of human free will is to posit a God who does not know the future and who is as much a part of the unfolding of existence as we are. Despite the best intentions of the open theists,[7] any attempt to make a place for free will by limiting the degree to which God knows and can predict the future ends up with a God who is less than the One described in the Bible.

The problem with both oversimplifications is just that: They are oversimplifications. They attempt to make the ways of the infinite God conform to the limitations of human reason. From the outset such an enterprise is doomed to failure. If God's ways can be made perfectly intelligible to my finite brain, then he is no longer God. The challenge is to hold simultaneously two

---

7. A recent expression of this position is that of G. Boyd, *God of the Possible* (Grand Rapids: Baker, 2000).

positions that *from within our limitations* seem mutually contradictory. From within those limitations, God must either be sovereign or we must be free. But the Bible maintains both, and that means, as difficult as it may be, we must make room for both in our thinking.

Paradox in practice. What does that mean in practice? It means that I cannot evade responsibility for my actions. I cannot say, "It's not my fault; God made me do it." At the same time, it means that God is not merely an interested bystander, watching the drama of unfolding human choices. God's holy, redemptive will is going to be accomplished in life, either through me or in spite of me. It also means that there will be an ongoing interaction between God's will and my choices.

This is nowhere better seen than in the account of the "hardening" of Pharaoh's heart (Ex. 4:21; etc.). Did God do something to Pharaoh that was contrary to something this man or any other Egyptian pharaoh would have done under normal circumstances? Not in the least! This was not a kindly, gentle man, concerned to do the best he could for a "minority" in his kingdom. Rather, this man was prepared to do anything in order to secure his power base, including genocide. But he became that sort of person as a result of choices he had made over his lifetime.

God has designed this world so that our choices successively form us into persons we have no other choice but to be. Thus, the Bible says that God knew Pharaoh would harden his heart (Ex. 3:19), that Pharaoh did harden his heart (8:15), that Pharaoh's heart became hard (7:13), and that God hardened Pharaoh's heart (7:3). All are true. The point is that Pharaoh felt he was God with an absolute range of choices he could make if he wanted. In fact, that was not the case. Pharaoh was a creature in a world he had not designed and where his choices and his ability to choose had become strictly limited.[8]

Thus, in this passage it is not true that God *made* the people sin. He did not do it to them, and he does not do it to us. They chose to sin—and chose to do so against God's clearly expressed will. On the other hand, having chosen to sin, it became easier and easier for them to sin and harder and harder for them to stop. This is the way God has made his world.

Thus, it *is true* that unless God intervenes and breaks this pattern, there is no way it is going to be broken. It is true that if God does not choose to intervene, people are going to continue in their sin and the consequent alienation from God, from God's creation and from their truest selves. But (and here is the rub) this is not merely a matter of God's deciding whether to intervene. The question is, will they meet the necessary conditions for that intervention

---

8. See Motyer, *Prophecy of Isaiah*, 517, on this point.

to occur? Will they cry, as the Galilean man did hundreds of years later, "I do believe; help me overcome my unbelief!" (Mark 9:24)? That is, were God's people willing to have certain patterns of behavior broken in their lives? Were they willing to have certain precious ties broken? Or did they want God's blessings *while they continued to do what they had always done?* The fact is, we humans want to have our way *and* God's blessings. That can never be.

 POSSIBILITIES. We live in a world that has increasingly come to accept the mind-set of the old world. One of the reasons immigrants came to the new world was because of the limited options of the old world. The lines of class and place were firmly fixed when a person was born. What you would be and where you would do it were determined from your first cry.

Not so in America. "The sky's the limit" is more than just a cliché. While it is not totally true, there is more than a grain of truth in the conviction that the only limitations on a person here are those that person places on himself or herself. The only limits are those of vision and diligence. We really believe that all have been created equal in terms of opportunity. Of course, there have been tragic departures from this dream. The slaves from Africa were excluded from it, as were many women. But even though the opportunities for American women were markedly less than those for American men, they were still vastly improved over many European women.

That consciousness of unlimited possibilities certainly resonates with the biblical message. That message flatly contradicts the view of paganism that saw all of life as directed by the fates, where the position of the stars on the day of your birth determined the possibilities for the rest of your life. In a stunning contrast, the Bible declares that every person has real choices to make regarding the meaning and purpose of life and that every person will be held accountable for those choices.[9] If those choices are good ones, unlimited possibilities open up. If they are bad ones, no position or status can change the results. It does not matter if the person is a David; sin will have its effects. But neither does it matter if the person is an eighty-year-old runaway like Moses; obedience will reap a harvest that will bear fruit to the end of time.

---

9. This is one reason why God often chose the rejects of society, such as second-born sons or barren women, as the objects of his special favor. If they would respond to his offers with faith and obedience, he would show the world through them that there are limitless possibilities in him.

So the new world has been a place where the biblical message can bear fruit in spectacular ways. The idea that *anybody* can be converted regardless of their past life and can become a new person in Christ makes perfect sense. It does not matter what people have done or what kind of a terrible background they come from; God can remake them and bring something bright and clean and new out of it. Does that message pay inadequate attention to some of the conditionings of life? Yes. Does it sometimes bring despair because it seems to offer more than it can deliver? Undoubtedly. Nevertheless, expectations can mean everything when it comes to possibilities. Those who expect little are often able to receive no more than they expect. On the other hand, there are no such limitations on those who expect much.

Overcoming the backward slide. Today in America we are sliding back into a belief in fate. There are a number of reasons for this. One is that it is a frankly easier view of life, and increasingly we are looking for the easy way out of everything. We don't want to work for what we receive; instead, we want to get it handed to us. The rise of state-run lotteries and state-sponsored gambling institutions is both a symptom of this situation and a contributing factor to it. Thus, it is easy to believe that since my situation is all determined for me, I cannot be expected to rise above it.

A second factor is, of course, the rise of the naturalistic behavioral sciences, which, having no other model from which to explain life than a mechanistic one, see us as nothing other than the sum total of our biological and sociological conditionings. The idea that any of us can possibly transcend these and take control of our conditioning is not only bizarre, it is hateful, because it introduces into the equation a factor that cannot be quantified.

A third factor is the fact that our lives have become much more complex. Success or failure no longer seems to depend as much on our own efforts and will. There seem to be so many more outside contributing factors now.[10]

This attitude has come to infect our religious thinking as well. Much like the ancient Judeans, we see ourselves as helpless victims. We don't like our sinful condition and admit that it is far from what God would like us to be— and even what we would like to be. But we feel helpless to change. It is "just the way I am," and no one can do anything about it. Perhaps if God would break in and make me a different kind of person, things might be different. And God knows, I have asked him to do that often enough, but he just doesn't seem to do it. Thank God for the grace of Jesus that tells me I am accepted anyway. This is the line of those who feel they are religiously fated.

---

10. At the same time, when we read of all the setbacks and disappointments that pioneer families suffered while still retaining their faith in themselves and God and in the possibility of eventual success, we have to say that life was terribly complex then too.

They cannot live out the life of Christ in the world unless they become other than what their psychological conditioning has made them to be, and since that does not happen, they cannot become Christlike.

Years ago a wise pastor under whose ministry I had the good fortune to sit helped me to see that such an attitude is a "cop-out." God is not going to make us into different persons from what we are. If we think that redemption is to have our personality destroyed, we have misunderstood what it means for God to be the Creator. He loves the unique features that make each of us different from every other person on this planet. Why would he destroy what he has expressly made?

To be sure, what he has made has become corrupted, deeply and desperately so. But that does not mean his creation must be destroyed. It must be cleansed and purified but not destroyed. It is one thing to be impulsive and passionate; it is another to be ruled by an uncontrollable temper. That temper is like a cancer in the personality, and it must be done away with. But when it is, that person can still expect to be impulsive and passionate, though now with constructive results. God does not want to make you and me into persons other than who we are. What he wants to do is to free us from the blights on our personalities that in fact blur our uniqueness and make us just like millions of other sinful people.

But how is that cleansing and purifying to take place? Here is the difficulty. We want God to "zap" us, to do something to us so that there will be no more struggle in our relationship with him. That is not the way it takes place. We hear the apostle Paul saying "Everyone who competes in the games goes into strict training. . . . I do not fight like a man beating the air. No, I beat my body . . . so that . . . I myself will not be disqualified for the prize" (1 Cor. 9:25–27). We hear him telling us that those who belong to Christ have "crucified the 'flesh'" (self-willed living; NIV "the sinful nature," Gal. 5:24). In other words, it is up to us to appropriate the spiritual power that is ours in the Cross and in the Holy Spirit.

God has already placed his Spirit in every believer (Rom. 8:9). So we do not need to "get" the Holy Spirit. What we need to do is to turn him loose, as we believe God will make us like himself, as we identify those specific behaviors that are an offense to him, and as we isolate the causes of those behaviors, learn what triggers them in us, avoid the places where we are likely to fall into them, celebrate our successes, stop beating ourselves for our failures, and walk on. God's power is unleashed in us when we step toward him in faith, take the hammer in hand, and do what we need to do in order to crucify the self-will that is God's enemy.

Isaiah 65:1–16

¹"I REVEALED MYSELF to those who did not ask for me;
    I was found by those who did not seek me.
To a nation that did not call on my name,
    I said, 'Here am I, here am I.'
²All day long I have held out my hands
    to an obstinate people,
who walk in ways not good,
    pursuing their own imaginations—
³a people who continually provoke me
    to my very face,
offering sacrifices in gardens
    and burning incense on altars of brick;
⁴who sit among the graves
    and spend their nights keeping secret vigil;
who eat the flesh of pigs,
    and whose pots hold broth of unclean meat;
⁵who say, 'Keep away; don't come near me,
    for I am too sacred for you!'
Such people are smoke in my nostrils,
    a fire that keeps burning all day.

⁶"See, it stands written before me:
    I will not keep silent but will pay back in full;
    I will pay it back into their laps—
⁷both your sins and the sins of your fathers,"
    says the LORD.
"Because they burned sacrifices on the mountains
    and defied me on the hills,
I will measure into their laps
    the full payment for their former deeds."

⁸This is what the LORD says:

"As when juice is still found in a cluster of grapes
    and men say, 'Don't destroy it,
    there is yet some good in it,'
so will I do in behalf of my servants;
    I will not destroy them all.

⁹I will bring forth descendants from Jacob,
 and from Judah those who will possess my mountains;
my chosen people will inherit them,
 and there will my servants live.
¹⁰Sharon will become a pasture for flocks,
 and the Valley of Achor a resting place for herds,
 for my people who seek me.

¹¹"But as for you who forsake the LORD
 and forget my holy mountain,
who spread a table for Fortune
 and fill bowls of mixed wine for Destiny,
¹²I will destine you for the sword,
 and you will all bend down for the slaughter;
for I called but you did not answer,
 I spoke but you did not listen.
You did evil in my sight
 and chose what displeases me."

¹³Therefore this is what the Sovereign LORD says:

"My servants will eat,
 but you will go hungry;
my servants will drink,
 but you will go thirsty;
my servants will rejoice,
 but you will be put to shame.
¹⁴My servants will sing
 out of the joy of their hearts,
but you will cry out
 from anguish of heart
 and wail in brokenness of spirit.
¹⁵You will leave your name
 to my chosen ones as a curse;
the Sovereign LORD will put you to death,
 but to his servants he will give another name.
¹⁶Whoever invokes a blessing in the land
 will do so by the God of truth;
he who takes an oath in the land
 will swear by the God of truth.
For the past troubles will be forgotten
 and hidden from my eyes.

THESE SIXTEEN VERSES constitute God's answer to the preceding lament. While some scholars dispute this, saying that there is really no answer to the charge that God has been silent,[1] the fact is God answers the real issue: the continuing rebellion of the people. They have sought to placate God with a reliance on cult and liturgy that is as offensive to him as any of the pagan worship. They have relied on their status as the elect of God while continuing to live lives of self-willed, self-serving sin. They call themselves the "servants of God," but they are not.

God's Continuing Revelation (65:1)

THE OPENING VERSE addresses this issue in ways that cannot be mistaken.[2] In the previous section, 64:7 stated that "no one calls on [God's] name," because "you have hidden your face from us." Isaiah 65:1 directly refutes that statement by saying that in fact God had "revealed" himself to people who did not call on his name. In other words, the reason they did not call on him was *not* because he had not revealed himself to them. He has been continually revealing himself. The problem lay in the people, not in God.

Israel's Problem (65:2–7)

SO WHAT WAS their problem? They have been "obstinate" (*sorer*, see also 1:23; 30:1), walking in "not good" ways that they have devised for themselves. These three ideas—obstinacy, devising one's own ways, and ways that are not good—describe in a brief compass precisely what the human problem is. Rather than obediently submitting to the ways of living that the Creator has designed for us, we have rebelled and tried to devise other ways of living for ourselves. By definition, "good" is that which corresponds to the Creator's plan (cf. Gen. 1:3; etc.). Therefore, anything we try to replace those ways with is, by definition, "not good."[3]

So what is it we humans have devised? We have devised worship practices that we believe will make it possible to manipulate God to act in our favor

---

1. Whybray, *Isaiah 40–66*, 266–67.

2. Motyer, *Prophecy of Isaiah*, 523–24, argues that v. 1 is actually the introduction to the final two chapters and that the reference is to God's calling of the Gentiles. I think this flies in the face of the nearer context. See the comments above.

3. Note that the initial description of human moral corruption in Gen. 6:5 speaks of the complete corruption of the way we form the devisings of the heart. The ways we devise for ourselves are necessarily corrupt.

while we retain the option to live our lives for ourselves. This was the function of heathen ritual. By doing certain things here on earth, the pagans believed that the attitudes and behaviors of the gods were automatically altered. The attitude of the worshiper was unimportant; what mattered was whether the ritual was done correctly. If so, then the desired results could be expected.

That is the very attitude that Isaiah sees in his pious readers. Why is God not more evident in their public and private lives? Why does he not make them act in just and righteous ways? The reason, he says, is that, to use the imagery of Joel, they are tearing their garments in rituals of repentance while their hearts are left whole to serve themselves (cf. Joel 2:12–13). They are depending on their position as God's people and on ritualistic religion to manipulate God in their favor while they continue to disobey the terms of their covenant with him.

The worship practices described in 65:3–5, 7 look markedly like the preexilic Canaanite practices that were so attractive to the Israelites. What are they doing here in this section of Isaiah? There are three possible explanations for this. (1) The returnees from exile are continuing to engage in these practices. But even those who take this point of view admit that there is no convincing evidence outside of Isaiah 56–66 in support of it. (2) Other scholars see this as evidence the book was written by a preexilic prophet and was addressed to preexilic people. But what is being said in these chapters is much more intelligible if we understand the general context to be the postexilic period. (3) The preexilic prophet is using images with which he is familiar to talk about the response of God to postexilic ritualism. This last one seems to me to be the most likely explanation.

The prophet does not intend these verses to be taken literally. Rather, he is throwing together a collection of the most horrendous images he can think of to try to convey how disgusting God finds ritualism *of any sort* when it is not expressing the important thing, a changed heart. Thus, I doubt that the returnees were actually engaging in these behaviors. But if they gave a whole burnt offering just as prescribed in Leviticus in an attempt to force God to forgive their sins and to bless them while they kept on sinning, the prophet says they might as well be sitting in a tomb and drinking mouse broth (see 66:3, where this very point is made).

In these circumstances, the people's pretensions to holiness procured by ritual magic are ludicrous (65:5). That being the case, they might rather prefer for God to remain silent instead of responding to their lament and rending the heavens to speak to them! But the prophet says God "will not keep silent" (65:6). They want God to act? Well, act he will—and he will fully repay them for all they have done (65:7).

A Remnant of the Faithful (65:8–11)

BUT IF GOD CASTIGATES the spurious holiness of those who think that they can manipulate him through their rituals, it does not mean that there is no remnant of the faithful among the people. Just as in Elijah's day (1 Kings 19:18), if many in the nation abandon the truth in the postexilic period, there will also be many who do not. God's promises to create himself a people will not return to him void (55:11). These are the ones God calls his "servants." While the behavior that marks these as God's servants is not specified here, its content can be safely inferred. These are the people who "seek" the Lord (65:10).

What does seeking the Lord mean? This is the language of Deuteronomy. "But if from there you seek the LORD your God, you will find him if you look for him with all your heart and with all your soul" (Deut. 4:29). To seek the Lord is to seek his ways, to seek to please him, to seek his presence. These are the primary goals of a believer, not his blessings. Moreover, seeking involves one's whole being. Ultimately, it is expressed in the language of Deuteronomy 6:5: "Love the LORD your God with all your heart and with all your soul and with all your strength." The servants of God stand in stark contrast with those who try to bypass a submissive relationship with God and seek to gain control of their "destiny" through religious behavior (Isa. 65:11).

God's Promises Remain (65:12–16)

GOD HAS NOT abrogated his promises. "Jacob" will have "descendants," and "Judah" will possess the "land" of promise (cf. 65:9). But that does not mean everyone called by the names of Jacob or Judah will share in the promise. As 56:1 stated and as 66:18–24 will reiterate, it is not birthright but behavior that marks the servants of God. Thus, 65:13–16 details the differences between "you" (i.e., those who have been trying to manipulate God for blessings) and "my servants" (i.e., those who seek God for himself with changed lives). In fact, the very blessings that the manipulators sought and were denied will fall on the servants who seek God first and his blessings only secondarily.[4]

THE ESSENCE OF RELIGION. In every age the human problem seems to be the same. We want benefits without personal cost. The greatest good is seen to be personal freedom expressed ultimately in the right to determine what is right ("good") and wrong ("evil") for

---

4. Much the same argument can be found in the book of Malachi, where the prophet insists that the blessings of God have eluded the people because they are seeking blessing and not God. See J. Oswalt, *Where Are You, God* (Nappanee, Ind.: Evangel, 1999).

ourselves. That is, we are determined to deny the fact of creation. We refuse to admit that there is a Creator who has defined the norms of human existence and that these norms are nonnegotiable. As a result, God calls and calls to us (65:1, 12), but we do not hear. At the same time we accuse him of being unresponsive to our calls. We are deaf to him because we want him to speak to us on our terms. We want him to approve our sinful self-reliance and wonder why he is silent.

In fact, he is not silent at all. It is as though we refuse to purchase cable television service and then accuse the television broadcasters of not broadcasting anything because we cannot get programs on channel 73. The signals are all there; it is just that we have not met the conditions for receiving them.

The problem is compounded when we bring religion into the picture. As the tragedies of September 11, 2001, have made clear, the idea that a purely secular culture is a possibility is a fiction. In crises, the native human religiosity manifests itself again, much to the disgust of the committed secularists. What is religion? Paul Tillich said it was to have a concern for ultimate issues.[5] Frankly, I think it is much more mundane than that. I believe religion is the attempt to get on the good side of whatever forces I conceive to have control of my destiny by the easiest and simplest means possible.

That being so, and given our deep need to keep control of the core of our being, externals come to play the central part in our religious lives. If I think God likes praising, I will praise. If I think God wants praying, I will pray. If I think God wants offerings, I will offer. If I think God wants abstinence, I will abstain. If I think God wants obedience, I will obey. But none of these behaviors is for its own sake. They are all means to obtain blessing. Therefore, I will calculate to the finest point possible the minimum of these I can give and still get the blessing.

The problem is that God doesn't want these things. By themselves he finds them disgusting. They are so because they are one more expression of human pride. It is as though we say, "Alright, God, you have a commodity I want, and I have some things you want. So let's engage in a little trade. I give you what you want and you give me what I want. But you need to recognize, God, if you don't give me what I want, you're not going to get what you want."

Such activity is not the behavior of a servant of God. A servant of God recognizes that God needs nothing, that he has already freely given everything I need or want, and that in fact, there is nothing I could ever do to earn

---

5. D. M. Brown, *Ultimate Concern: Tillich in Dialogue* (New York: Harper & Row, 1965), 49–51.

these things. The two of us are not now, and never will be, on anything like a par. Rather, what I need is God's presence in my life, and that presence is only possible when I renounce my right to myself and in a paroxysm of love and gratitude hurl myself into his arms, committed with all my being to be like him, simply because I want to.

ATTITUDES SPEAK LOUDER THAN ACTIONS. What does it mean to be a Christian? In all too many ways we find ourselves in a similar position to those Isaiah is addressing in this passage. We gauge our faith on the basis of certain externals.

- So one person says, "I am a Christian because I am a formal member of that body of people known as the Christian church. I am a Christian in just the same way that the Judeans were members of the people of God. We may say that we are adopted, but the relationship is the same: We are members of an elect group."
- Someone else says, "That is not true. Church membership means nothing. You must have received Christ as your personal Savior. Then you are a member of the church universal. You are part of the family forever."
- A third person says, "That is really not any necessary indication of your heart condition. A Christian attends worship with the body on a regular basis. Christians worship God with sacraments and music and prayer and the hearing of the Word of God."
- Another says, "There is more dead form at 11:00 A.M. on Sunday than any other hour of the week. Christians feel the presence of God in their hearts when they worship him spontaneously and energetically."
- Finally, someone else says, "What you're 'worshiping' is the exciting feel of worshiping. A Christian is someone who gives a cup of cold water to the thirsty, a coat to the freezing, a word of encouragement to the despairing, all for Christ's sake."

Well, what *is* it to be a Christian, for heaven's sake? I believe it is all of the above and none of the above. What do I mean? That with the right attitude every one of the above is characteristic of the Christian, and that with the wrong attitude every criticism of the above is correct. That is, if we gauge our Christian faith by external behaviors alone—any external behaviors— it is all dust and ashes. So a Malachi can say for God, "I am sick of your worship. I just wish you would shut the doors and go away" (cf. Mal. 1:10). Unless we have come to the place where our service to God is growing out of a glad servant heart, it is all in vain. Can you imagine a bridegroom asking a minister how many hours a month he has to spend with his bride to keep the marriage in force? If he does ask this question, we know something is severely lacking in his devotion to his bride, and we also know the relationship is doomed.

By contrast, if we really have a loving bond-slave relationship with the Lord, we will want to express that love in every possible way, from meeting together with Christian brothers and sisters to worshiping him in the most profound ways possible, to telling others about him, to reaching out to the downtrodden for him, to working for justice in his world. So Malachi can say to the people that if they truly love God, it will not be a problem to give their best, and Haggai can say that if they are truly God's servants, they will show it by building God's house. The point, then, is this: If external behaviors are in place of a loving servant heart, they are worthless, but if a loving servant heart does not express itself in external behaviors, we are deceiving ourselves.

17 "BEHOLD, I WILL create
    new heavens and a new earth.
  The former things will not be remembered,
    nor will they come to mind.
18 But be glad and rejoice forever
    in what I will create,
  for I will create Jerusalem to be a delight
    and its people a joy.
19 I will rejoice over Jerusalem
    and take delight in my people;
  the sound of weeping and of crying
    will be heard in it no more.

20 "Never again will there be in it
    an infant who lives but a few days,
    or an old man who does not live out his years;
  he who dies at a hundred
    will be thought a mere youth;
  he who fails to reach a hundred
    will be considered accursed.
21 They will build houses and dwell in them;
    they will plant vineyards and eat their fruit.
22 No longer will they build houses and others live
      in them,
    or plant and others eat.
  For as the days of a tree,
    so will be the days of my people;
  my chosen ones will long enjoy
    the works of their hands.
23 They will not toil in vain
    or bear children doomed to misfortune;
  for they will be a people blessed by the LORD,
    they and their descendants with them.
24 Before they call I will answer;
    while they are still speaking I will hear.
25 The wolf and the lamb will feed together,
    and the lion will eat straw like the ox,
    but dust will be the serpent's food.

> They will neither harm nor destroy
> on all my holy mountain,"

says the LORD.

THESE VERSES OPEN up one of the critical aspects of biblical revelation. God had a basic problem to confront as he began to reveal himself to the Hebrew people. They were surrounded by peoples who believed this visible world was actually only a dim reflection of the invisible world of the gods. What was really important took place in that world, preconditioning everything that took place here. Thus, human beings had no real choices to make but simply reduplicated the actions of the gods.

That is, of course, wholly untrue. This is a real world, and humans do have real choices to make, choices that have cosmic consequences. So, to make that point, for much of the Old Testament, God makes no reference to any reality beyond this world at all. Our choices are made here, and the effects are experienced here. This is a real world.

But this world is not all there is to reality. If we have gotten the point that this world is real and is not merely a reflection of invisible realities, we are perhaps ready to have the curtain pulled back in order to get a glimpse of the rest of reality. That is what is happening here. The fact is that all the effects of human choice are not experienced in this life. Justice is not entirely served here, as any of us can relate. All the good that is done here is not rewarded here, and all the evil that is done here is not punished here. So if God says that his servants will be blessed, as he did in 65:13–16, either he is a liar, or this world is not all there is to reality. These verses tell us that the latter is the case.

But this is not an accommodation to a pagan view, as some students of apocalyptic maintain.[1] It is not the *real* heaven and earth that is now revealed, nor the *real* Jerusalem that is let down from heaven. Rather, they are *new* (65:17). What that means is that God will "create" something that, while being in continuity with what had been, will yet be a completely new expression of that reality (see comments on 43:14–21). The earthly realities give shape to the new realities instead of the earthly expression being merely a duplication of what already exists in heaven. But because they are new, the tragic realities of this world need not be repeated there. Thus, we may experience the reality of joy without the reality of weeping (65:18–19). Likewise,

---

1. See J. Oswalt, "Recent Studies in Old Testament Apocalyptic," 369–90.

we may experience the delight of birth without the despair of death (65:20). The satisfaction of building will not be accompanied by the fear of destruction and conquest (65:21–23).

So God says that what he has said is true: Those who believe his word, who obey him, and who live his life *will* be "blessed" (65:23). There are consequences to our choices; they begin now and will come to their ultimate fruition when the Creator concludes his creative activity in the coming days. The language of 65:25 is closely related to the vision of the messianic kingdom in chapter 11, with the final line of the verse being an exact duplicate of the first colon of 11:9. This makes it plain that what we have here is not merely a poetic expression of the certainty of justice in some general sense but a prediction of real events in the age to come.

THE DUALISM AND FATALISM of paganism are never far from us. Nowhere is that more clear than in our thinking about the existence of good and evil in the world. It is easy for us to think that sin is in the world because of Satan. God is the good god and Satan the bad god; these two are at war, and we humans are the chess pieces on their board or, to put it another way, the game pieces in a cosmic session of some giant computer war game. Thus good and evil are the cosmic realities, and we are fated to play the part chosen for us. One expression of this can be seen in the tattoos of many prison inmates with some version of "Born to be bad" or "Born for Hell."

But that is not true. The Bible tells us that sin is in the world for one reason only: human choice. Satan did not make Eve sin, nor is there anything in Genesis about the tempter's being sinful. It is only said that he is more "subtle" than any other creature. Whatever Satan may have done before earthly time began had no conditioning effect on the choices of Eve and then Adam. Creation was in a pristine condition even though Satan was in it. And if our first two parents had not sinned, the clear implication is that creation would still be in that pristine condition today.

My point is that it is human choice that determines the shape of reality, not cosmic reality that shapes human choice. There will be a slain Lamb on the throne of heaven because we humans have sinned. We were not doomed to sin because there had to be a slain Lamb on the throne of heaven.

Thus, as we look to the new heaven and the new earth, we must not think that because they are coming, it doesn't matter what we do. The truth is the other way around. Because they are coming, we can choose to be faithful today, secure that if we live out our lives in poverty, justice *will* be served. We do not have to worry about the consequences of our actions being seen today, because we know that the reality that is to come will reflect our right choices. By the same token, we must remember that just because we "get away" with something now, that does not mean that wrong act is not being imprinted on the reality that is to come. *We* shape our future.

 EVANGELICALS SPEND a good deal of time arguing about "the Millennium." I remember an older gentleman who said to me when I was in college, "I grew up in a liberal church, so I was a postmillennialist. But then I saw the error of that, got converted, and became a premillennialist." This gives us a sense of how critical some considered this issue in the midst of the "modernist-fundamentalist" debates of the 1920s and 1930s.

Even today in some denominations, premillennialism is an article of faith. The specific issue, of course, is whether Christ returns before the establishment of the reign of God's righteousness on the earth or after. But the deeper issue is that of biblical interpretation: How literally is one to take poetic imagery? People whose general orthodoxy no one can doubt differ significantly on this subject. All orthodox persons agree that Christ will return in physical form; what they disagree on is whether there will be a physical reign of Christ on earth prior to the final judgment and prior to the revelation of the new heaven and earth. If the language of Revelation 19–21 is given any literal credence at all, this seems to be the case, and it is where I stand personally.[2]

But as interesting as those arguments might be to some of us, the most important issue for us is to think about the implications of this theology for our daily lives. If it is true that the reality we experience in the days to come will be shaped by our choices now, then those choices are of critical importance. Far from saying with the television comic, "the devil made me do it," we need to be thinking about the cosmic effects of our choices on the world to come. Our actions are not predetermined. Instead, our actions will bear fruit from now on and forever. This ought to make us think a good deal more soberly about what we do. Far from being merely a duplicate of something

---

2. If I am right that these verses include reference to a literal reign of Christ on a redeemed earth, how are we to understand the mention of death in v. 20? There are at least two possibilities. (1) There will continue to be cessation of earthly life in the Millennium, but it will no longer be an occasion of fear (see C. S. Lewis, *Out of the Silent Planet* [New York: Macmillan, 1972]). (2) The language is still figurative to speak of a kind of life that is full and fulfilling.

that has always existed, we have the possibility of shaping the reality that is to come. This is what Paul meant when he said to Titus in Titus 2:11–13:

> For the grace of God that brings salvation has appeared to all men. It teaches us to say "No" to ungodliness and worldly passions, and to live self-controlled, upright and godly lives in this present age, while we wait for the blessed hope—the glorious appearing of our great God and Savior, Jesus Christ.

By the grace of God we have a coming world to look to. That being so, how should we live now to be assured that the reality we are shaping will be a joyous one? If it is true according to the old adage that "some people are so heavenly minded, they are no earthly good," it is also true, and perhaps more so today than previously, that there are many people who have effectively forgotten that the story we are telling has its end only on the other side of the grave.

Isaiah 66:1–24

THIS IS WHAT the LORD says:

"Heaven is my throne,
    and the earth is my footstool.
Where is the house you will build for me?
    Where will my resting place be?
² Has not my hand made all these things,
    and so they came into being?"

declares the LORD.

"This is the one I esteem:
    he who is humble and contrite in spirit,
    and trembles at my word.
³ But whoever sacrifices a bull
    is like one who kills a man,
and whoever offers a lamb,
    like one who breaks a dog's neck;
whoever makes a grain offering
    is like one who presents pig's blood,
and whoever burns memorial incense,
    like one who worships an idol.
They have chosen their own ways,
    and their souls delight in their abominations;
⁴ so I also will choose harsh treatment for them
    and will bring upon them what they dread.
For when I called, no one answered,
    when I spoke, no one listened.
They did evil in my sight
    and chose what displeases me."

⁵ Hear the word of the LORD,
    you who tremble at his word:
"Your brothers who hate you,
    and exclude you because of my name, have said,
'Let the LORD be glorified,
    that we may see your joy!'
    Yet they will be put to shame.
⁶ Hear that uproar from the city,
    hear that noise from the temple!

It is the sound of the LORD
    repaying his enemies all they deserve.

⁷"Before she goes into labor,
    she gives birth;
before the pains come upon her,
    she delivers a son.
⁸Who has ever heard of such a thing?
    Who has ever seen such things?
Can a country be born in a day
    or a nation be brought forth in a moment?
Yet no sooner is Zion in labor
    than she gives birth to her children.
⁹Do I bring to the moment of birth
    and not give delivery?" says the LORD.
"Do I close up the womb
    when I bring to delivery?" says your God.
¹⁰"Rejoice with Jerusalem and be glad for her,
    all you who love her;
rejoice greatly with her,
    all you who mourn over her.
¹¹For you will nurse and be satisfied
    at her comforting breasts;
you will drink deeply
    and delight in her overflowing abundance."

¹²For this is what the LORD says:

"I will extend peace to her like a river,
    and the wealth of nations like a flooding stream;
you will nurse and be carried on her arm
    and dandled on her knees.
¹³As a mother comforts her child,
    so will I comfort you;
    and you will be comforted over Jerusalem."

¹⁴When you see this, your heart will rejoice
    and you will flourish like grass;
the hand of the LORD will be made known to
        his servants,
    but his fury will be shown to his foes.
¹⁵See, the LORD is coming with fire,
    and his chariots are like a whirlwind;

he will bring down his anger with fury,
    and his rebuke with flames of fire.
¹⁶ For with fire and with his sword
    the LORD will execute judgment upon all men,
    and many will be those slain by the LORD.

¹⁷"Those who consecrate and purify themselves to go into the gardens, following the one in the midst of those who eat the flesh of pigs and rats and other abominable things—they will meet their end together," declares the LORD.

¹⁸"And I, because of their actions and their imaginations, am about to come and gather all nations and tongues, and they will come and see my glory.

¹⁹"I will set a sign among them, and I will send some of those who survive to the nations—to Tarshish, to the Libyans and Lydians (famous as archers), to Tubal and Greece, and to the distant islands that have not heard of my fame or seen my glory. They will proclaim my glory among the nations. ²⁰And they will bring all your brothers, from all the nations, to my holy mountain in Jerusalem as an offering to the LORD—on horses, in chariots and wagons, and on mules and camels," says the LORD. "They will bring them, as the Israelites bring their grain offerings, to the temple of the LORD in ceremonially clean vessels. ²¹And I will select some of them also to be priests and Levites," says the LORD.

²²"As the new heavens and the new earth that I make will endure before me," declares the LORD, "so will your name and descendants endure. ²³From one New Moon to another and from one Sabbath to another, all mankind will come and bow down before me," says the LORD. ²⁴"And they will go out and look upon the dead bodies of those who rebelled against me; their worm will not die, nor will their fire be quenched, and they will be loathsome to all mankind."

THERE HAS BEEN considerable disagreement among commentators concerning the structure of this final chapter of Isaiah. In large measure this disagreement has resulted from uncertainty about the place and function of 66:5–6 and 15–16. Some scholars have taken them with the units preceding them, while others have taken them with what follows, while still others have treated them independently.[1] Recently, however, a minor consensus has emerged (though not always as a result of the same reasoning) that the units should be seen as verses 1–6, 7–14, and 15–24.[2]

A Final Diatribe Against Ritualism (66:1–6)

ALTHOUGH SOME HAVE taken 66:1 as an indication that some in the return from exile opposed rebuilding the temple, there is nothing in the biblical record to support such a claim.[3] Rather, this verse should be put into the larger context of 66:1–6, which presents the prophet's final diatribe against ritualism. It is not that God has anything against the temple per se. In fact, he inspired the prophets Haggai and Zechariah to move the apathetic people to get on with the task of rebuilding. By the same token, he has nothing against sacrifices per se. He inspired Malachi to condemn those who refused to give their best animals. No, the point here is the same as that of 57:3–13 and 65:1–5: Empty ritualism that does not symbolize a genuinely repentant and obedient heart is worse than useless.

From the outset of the book and up to its very end, the central problem it has identified in the human race is that of self-exaltation. We try to solve the basic problem of our extreme fragility, both physically and psychologically, by lifting ourselves up in order to gain power. For it is by means of power that we can protect ourselves and ensure the satisfaction of whatever we consider our needs to be. When all is said and done, that is what ritualistic religion is about. The religious elite discover how to manipulate divine power.

But, in fact, that approach is all wrong. In this universe God alone is exalted, and any attempt by humans to exalt themselves and usurp God's power for themselves is doomed to fail. So God says here that it is the "humble and contrite in spirit," who tremble at his word, whom he esteems (66:2). To try to use ritual to enhance one's own power or to satisfy one's own needs is to do nothing other than to choose one's "own ways" (66:3), even if the rituals are those promulgated by God himself. Once again, God insists that it is not he who has been silent when they called, as they had charged in 64:12. Instead, the very opposite is true. He has "called," and they have been silent (66:4). They have devised their own ways of relating to God, and when he calls them to a different kind of response, they are deaf.

---

1. For some of the alternatives proposed, see J. Oswalt, *Isaiah 40–66*, 665, n. 13.

2. See W. Beuken, "Isaiah Chapters LXV–LXVI: Trito-Isaiah and the Closure of the Book of Isaiah," *Congress Volume, Leuven 1989* (VTSup 34; Leiden: Brill, 1991), 204–21; Childs, *Isaiah*, 539; Oswalt, *Isaiah 40–66*, 664–65; E. Webster, "A Rhetorical Study of Isaiah 66," *JSOT* 34 (1986): 93–108.

3. Cf. Hanson, *Isaiah 40–66*, 250.

In 66:5–6, God turns to speak once again to the remnant, those whom he designated as his "servants" in chapter 65. These are the people of whom he spoke in 66:2, those "who tremble at his word" (66:5). Because they have chosen lowliness and powerlessness, they are easily victimized by the powerful, who mock them for their simplistic piety. But God says that the lowly have one powerful thing going for them—God! He will vindicate those who care more about what God says than whether their needs have been met. In the very temple where the ritualists think they have God at their command, that God, who calls them his "enemies" (cf. 1:24), will pay them back for their rebellion.

Hope and Abundance (66:7–14)

AS THROUGHOUT THE book, judgment and destruction quickly give way to hope and abundance. This next unit describes Lady Zion. Here the promise made in chapter 1 comes to its fruition. The dross has been purged away, and instead of being a harlot, Zion has become the faithful city, the mother of nations (cf. 1:25–27). The image of the fruitful mother reminds the attentive reader of all the places in the book where barrenness and childlessness were alluded to.[4] The pagan fertility rituals were focused on the critical need to maintain the fertility of field and womb if life was to defeat death in the world. But Isaiah says that the only real life is that which is given as a free gift by God in response to surrender and obedience.

Nor does God give in a "tit for tat" fashion. His gifts are out of all proportion to whatever we have done. When humans meet their own needs, it is arduous and painful work, like giving birth. But God's gifts are childbirth without labor (66:7–9). Our needs are not met by our work but by our being in a position to receive the results of God's work. This is the significance of nursing at the "breasts" of Zion (66:11). A baby does nothing to satisfy its own needs; it must simply own its absolute dependence and receive what has been provided.

In such a position there is rest, rejoicing, and wholeness, or "peace" (66:12). As in 12:1 and elsewhere,[5] the idea behind the word "comfort" (66:13) is to encourage. Those who have felt the weight of their sin, have known their own powerlessness to deal with that sin, but have still come to God in penitent faith, believing that he can do something about it, will find themselves encouraged just as a child does on its mother's lap. The case is not hopeless, all is not lost, this thing can be recovered from. That is comfort.

But if judgment is never God's intended last word, neither is hope without conditions. Isaiah never wants his readers to be left in a position where they

---

4. See 26:16–18; 29:23; 37:3; 49:19–21; 51:17–20; 54:1–3.
5. See 40:1; 49:13; 51:3, 12, 19; 52:9; 54:11; 57:18; 61:2.

are so secure in God's election love that they forget the real possibility of judgment. The Lord's "hand" (66:14) of deliverance, redemption, and power will be revealed to "his servants," but it is "his fury" that "will be shown to his foes." Once again the question emerges: Am I among his servants or his foes?

Judgment and Hope (66:15–24)

THIS SECTION CONCLUDES the book in a characteristic fashion, with an interplay of the twin themes of judgment and hope. Just as the two have been intertwined throughout the book, they are intertwined here. The beginning (66:15–17) and the end (66:24) speak of the judgment that lies ahead for those who rebel against God and attempt to gain control of his power for themselves. For the present God has taken the fire of his judgment into himself in the person of his Servant. But that will not always be so. A day will come when that "fire" (66:15–16, 24) will be unleashed against an unrepentant world.

Judgment is a reality that humans must reckon with. Just as in the natural world, where there are inescapable consequences of our choices, so also in the spiritual world. Thus, instead of ending with 65:17–25 and its vision of the new heaven and the new earth, or even with chapters 60–62, with a picture of the light streaming from Zion, the book brings this grim note of judgment directly to the fore in its closing words.

But judgment is not what the Creator God wants, and that is equally clear in this final section. Isaiah 66:18–23 speak of the universal redemption that is God's desired way of bringing this sinful world to its close. Verse 18 is especially interesting in this regard. Although the text is difficult,[6] the sense seems to be that God will use the very sins and schemes of the rebellious to reveal the glory of his salvation. The people of Zion ("them" in v. 19) who "survive" (see 4:2) all the attempts of an evil world to destroy them will be sent to all the "nations" with a "sign" of God's "glory." In one sense their very survival will be the sign, but in view of the importance of "signs" in the ministry of Christ, it is hard to avoid the conclusion that Christ is the sign they take—the preeminent evidence of God's glory in triumphing over evil.[7] This, of course, accords closely with the thought of Isaiah 2 that Israel has a mission to declare God's glory to the nations in such a way that they will be drawn to him.

---

6. A lit. rendering of the first part is: "But I—their works and their plans—it (fem.) is coming to gather. . . ." Perhaps the sense is: "But I [know] their works and their plans and [the time] is coming to gather. . . ." There is no consensus among the versions. See the discussion in Oswalt, *Isaiah 40–66*, 681, n. 60.

7. See esp. Matt. 24:30; Luke 11:30; John 1:14; 12:18.

The response of the nations to Israel's mission will be to restore the last remnants of the Israelites ("your brothers," 66:20) to Israel in a last great ingathering. The breadth and the scope of this return is underlined by the variety of means used to make that possible. Its importance is emphasized by the comparison of that return to the bringing of the best and purest of "offerings."

Then comes the most stunning statement of all: "I will select some of them also to be priests and Levites" (66:21). While we cannot be absolutely certain of the antecedent of "them" in this statement, the most obvious one is "the nations." If that is correct, and most commentators agree that it is,[8] this is the strongest statement in the book that the election of Israel is not for Israel but for the world. That understanding is furthered by 66:22–23, which speaks of the entire human race coming to worship God. This is the goal of all that God has done on earth—that we, his creatures, may have fellowship with him.

But what about 66:24? Why end the book on this grisly note? The answer goes as far back as chapter 1. There Isaiah could speak of the day when the unfaithful city, whose sins he has carefully delineated, will be transformed by righteousness and justice into "the Faithful City" (1:21–27). But just as he would not leave his hearers there in chapter 1, ending that chapter instead with an announcement of the destruction awaiting those who did not repent, neither will he leave them with unmitigated hope here. For the wonderful promises of God have nothing to do with any who persist in rebellion. If the rebels are lulled into complacency by these good promises, they will be lost.

On the one hand, the promises of God are yea and amen (2 Cor. 1:20): There *will* be a new heaven and a new earth (Isa. 66:22), and those who rejoice to worship the one true God *will* participate in it. On the other hand, whether any of us participate in those promises is strictly up to us, and Isaiah never wants that to be forgotten.

 **Bridging Contexts**

A NUMBER OF the key themes of the book and of this final part of the book appear in this chapter: humility and contrition as opposed to ritualism and rebellion; God's gift of abundance to Lady Zion (as opposed to the fundamental barrenness of the earth mother of the nations); fire as a symbol of God's holiness, making it either destructive or

---

8. Cf. Childs, *Isaiah*, 542; Motyer, *Prophecy of Isaiah*, 542–43; Westermann, *Isaiah 40–66*, 426; Whybray, *Isaiah 40–66*, 291–92.

cleansing; the place of the nations in the worship and service of God; and the ultimate goal of creation as worship and fellowship with the Creator. Most of these have been dealt with at some length even in recent chapters. Here I want to focus on three: humility and rebellion, the source of abundance, and the goal of life.

Humility and rebellion. In some ways the United States was born out of rebellion. Before that there was the Peasants' Revolt in Germany. In both of these cases, orthodox Christian leaders spoke out forcefully on the side of authority. Luther, for example, argued vehemently that the peasants were sinning against God in turning on their masters. In the case of the American Revolution, John Wesley wrote a tract employing his considerable force of logic and eloquence in calling on the American colonists to cease their revolt against their God-appointed king. This tract created such hostility against Wesley's followers in America, the Methodists, that some Methodist preachers had to return home to England and others, like Francis Asbury, had to go into hiding during most of the Revolution. This means that we Americans have a soft spot in our hearts for rebels, for people who refuse to be limited by the self-serving mandates of those in authority.

How does that bear on Isaiah's continually inveighing against rebels? It seems to me that there are two kinds of rebels. (1) There are the "good" rebels. These are people like most of the founders of America, who were reacting against injustice and wrong. They are also like inventors, people who are reacting against doing things the old way just because that is the way it has always been done. These are not people who merely have to have their own way and who refuse to be bound by any strictures except their own. They are simply looking for a better way. (2) The "bad" rebels are not looking for a better way. They do not care about the condition of others. They merely want their own way, no matter what it may cost or what it may destroy.

The difference between the two types of rebels is the difference between humility and arrogance. I think this is why Isaiah continually stresses that rebels try to create "their own ways."[9] For these kinds of persons, it is not that the other ways—in this case, God's ways—are necessarily so bad; it is just that they want their own ways. Here is the deadliness of arrogance. Arrogance says, "Even if it kills me, I will do what I want." The fact is, God has made the world so that arrogance does, in fact, kill. It kills on a variety of levels. It kills relationships, it kills families, it kills churches, it kills companies. Some years ago, a student of business reached the shocking conclusion that one of the traits America's most excellent companies shared was "love." That

---

9. See 59:7; 65:2; 66:3.

is, they loved their product, they loved their employees, and they loved their consumers.[10] However we may define love, it is at the least a focus beyond oneself.

That is what Isaiah is calling his hearers to: the kind of humility that is willing to project the focus of one's life not primarily on what is good for me but on what is good for those around me (Rom. 12:5–6). This is humility, focusing on others before oneself. This person may well become a "good" rebel, refusing to sit by while others are demeaned and oppressed by arrogant authorities. But the "rebellion," the refusal to submit, has nothing to do with some need to project myself, to have my way, to show "them" that "they can't boss me around." Humility, the self-forgetfulness that arises from a deep sense of worth and security, is the key to it all. Others may get the praise and the "perks" for awhile, but the truly humble know that in the end those are not the things that matter.

The source of abundance. Throughout Isaiah, as throughout the Bible, this question is stressed: Who supplies my needs? The answer is found in another of the divine paradoxes that fill the Bible: to grab is to lose, to let go is to get. That is, if I make my abundance the goal of my existence, I invariably discover that the abundance I have gained is an abundance of nothing.

A roustabout managed to rise through the ranks of his company until the day came when he owned the company. Later he said, "I gave everything I had to climb to the top of the heap. Then I discovered that the heap I was climbing was a manure heap." That story can be multiplied thousands of times. So in Isaiah 47 Lady Babylon looks out on a world she reduced to ruins and says, "I am, and there is none besides me" (47:8, 10). What she realizes too late is that in gaining everything, she has only gained ruins—nothing. This picture is picked up and further developed in Revelation 18: Babylon is fallen.

The reason why this is so is that the world is not self-sustaining. When I was in high school, I spent a good deal of time trying to construct a perpetual motion machine. I was arrogant enough to think that even though no one else had ever done this, I could. Eventually I gave up and went on to other, often equally futile, enterprises. I had to admit that there must always be a supply of energy from outside a given system if that system is to continue to function.

At the time I did not realize the profound significance of the discovery I had made. There *are* no perpetual motion machines. That includes the physical universe. On every level, energy must come from somewhere beyond that

---

10. Thomas J. Peters and Robert H. Waterman Jr., *In Search of Excellence* (New York: Harper & Row, 1982), 76ff.

level to keep it functioning. Yet we arrogant humans believe that somehow we are complete in ourselves and can, from within our own resources, supply our own needs. It is only when we, like trusting infants, relax in the embrace of Mother Zion that our needs are met from beyond ourselves. Who supplies Mother Zion's need? Zion's Creator and Lord, the source of all things. Surrendering all things to him, we gain all things.

The goal of life. The book of Isaiah ends with the world worshiping God. Interestingly, worship is where the book of Exodus, the Old Testament book that arguably defines the nature of salvation, ends as well. And most interestingly of all, that is where the Bible itself ends in the book of the Revelation.

What's the point? Let's begin with Exodus. Why does God bring his people out of Egypt? An unthinking answer might be so that he can take them into the land of Canaan. But then what is the purpose of Exodus 19–40? If the ultimate goal of the Exodus is the Conquest, then everything relating to the covenant and the tabernacle is just so much "filler." In fact, it is the other way around, as a study of the word "inheritance" shows. Canaan is the "inheritance" (or perhaps better, "special possession") of Israel, but *Israel* is the "inheritance" of the Lord.[11] God brought the people of Israel out of Egypt in order to bring them, and through them the world, to himself (cf. Ex. 19:4). That is why Exodus ends as it does, with the people encamped around the tabernacle and the glory of the Lord filling the tabernacle. "Canaan," our blessing and bliss, is not the end; it is only a means to the end, and that end is already announced in Exodus 40: worshipful fellowship with God.

That, then, is why the Bible ends on the same kind of note. Revelation 4–22 ultimately describes one continuing service of worship. What is going on? Is the God of the universe some megalomaniac who constantly needs to be told how great he is? Hardly! The point is that our life is not about us, just as the life of each member of the Trinity is not about himself. All too easily we think of the next life as a place where *we* are rewarded, where *we* finally get the "goodies," where *we* get blessed.[12] Not true. Just as here, where the greatest blessings of life are when we become part of something greater than ourselves, so it will be in the next life. When we are taken up into the glory and wonder of the Creator, when we lose ourselves in the joy and love that radiates from him, when we know what it is to be united with, but not absorbed into, the One whose greatest delight is in us whom he has made, we will have truly found ourselves forever.

---

11. Ps. 78:71; Isa. 19:25; Jer. 10:16; Joel 3:2.

12. To a great extent that *is* the vision of heaven presented in the Qur'an. It is all about rewards. Even in heaven the idea of intimate fellowship with Allah is faintly blasphemous.

THE INEVITABLE CHOICE. This Sunday school chorus captures the heart of this chapter:

One door and only one, and yet its sides
are two.
I'm on the inside; on which side are you?

This chapter is about the fundamental choice facing humanity. Those who confess that Israel's God is Creator of the universe and accept his created ways in humility will enjoy fellowship with him in a new heaven and a new earth. Those who deny that reality, arrogantly seeking to define the terms of their existence for themselves, will perish eternally.

This fact has some important implications for us today. (1) We must be careful not to minimize the reality of this choice in our presentation of the biblical message. It is often said that people today respond better to positive messages than to negative ones. I suspect that is not more true than it has ever been. But the danger we run is in failing to warn people about the risk of refusing the positive message. We may fail to communicate to people that this is a life-or-death issue. We tell people that God loves them and has a wonderful plan for their lives. Do we ever tell them what happens if they reject God's wonderful plan? A person is in the backseat of a car hurtling out of control down a hill toward a sharp turn and a sheer cliff. Do we only tell them that if they jump out life will be less anxious? Do we consider the reality of these options in our own decisions?

(2) One of the tragedies of modern child-rearing theory is that we have forgotten that always allowing a child to "have it your way" is ultimately deadly, because it fails to teach the child that our choices have inescapable consequences. But this is difficult. Only those who have attempted to rear children know how rock-hard a child's determination is to have his or her own way. Somehow we who are parents must steel ourselves to the inevitable conflict of the will that *must* occur as we try to bring our children to surrender their own way or face the consequences. This is the only way to strength of character and, much more seriously, the only way to heaven.

Adults who have always had their own way and have been shielded from the consequences of those choices by indulgent parents are almost impervious to the good news of Christ. They refuse to take responsibility for their actions and thus have nothing to repent of. The idea that Jesus asks them to give their lives away in worshipful service to him is more than offensive to such persons. Let us remember that it is not merely our children's future as contributors to society that is at stake, it is their eternal destiny.

The source of abundance. The fact that we cannot supply our own needs is another idea that seems radically countercultural today in a world of radical individuality and determined self-sufficiency. But it is a theme that runs through the Bible. It was self-sufficiency that tempted Adam and Eve, and it was self-sufficiency that Abraham surrendered and in so doing brought hope to the world. It was their inability to rely on God's sufficiency that doomed a whole generation to die in the desert. It was the need to supply their own needs that made so many Israelites susceptible to the blandishments of Baal and Asherah. In the end, it was the need to supply their own needs that drove the Pharisees to devise a means of earning a right standing with God.

We are no different. The idea of truly surrendering our needs to God and resting on his lap as serenely as a nursing baby is *very* difficult. How can we get there? (1) We must recognize our own grasping, self-sufficient tendencies. (2) We must ask God to sensitize us to all the ways we try to satisfy our needs without depending on him, including the manipulation of him through rituals of one sort and another. (3) We must allow him to show us what our *real* needs are. (4) Finally, we must wait patiently for him to show us how he wants to meet the needs. Usually it will be through the ordinary means he has already placed in our hands. But when we engage in those, it will be entirely different from what it was before. Now we will realize that God is at work within us. No longer will we be tempted to praise ourselves for what we have accomplished (and in so doing thank ourselves for the gifts that God had actually given to us in the first place!). And sometimes he will satisfy our needs in ways that are completely beyond ourselves. Those are moments to be treasured for a lifetime, moments when we know beyond a doubt that God cares for us and that there is nothing he cannot or will not do for us.

The goal of life. This thought relates closely to the previous one. When we have learned to live in the constant relinquishment of our needs into God's hands, we learn that in the end our only real need is for him. With him, we have everything; without him, everything is nothing.

So many people make God a means to the end of blessing. They serve him to get something else. That leads to the perverted view of heaven as a place where I get riches. God? Jesus? The Holy Spirit? Oh yes, they'll be around someplace. But they will be talking with the big shots: Abraham and Moses and David and Elijah and Peter and Paul. But I won't need him; I'll have his blessings. Horrible! Heaven will be about being what we were made to be in him. How can every redeemed person on earth be in intimate worshipful fellowship with him at the same time? I have not the faintest idea, but I am also sure that for him it will not be a problem.

What does that mean for life today? It changes our whole view of what the Christian life is about. Too easily we have come to believe that the Christian life is about a position that guarantees the believer with certain benefits. Not so! In fact, that is exactly what Isaiah has been attacking throughout his book, especially in chapters 56–66. The survivors from the Exile clearly believed that they had survived because of their special status as the elect of God. Therefore, the promises were guaranteed for them no matter what they did. As long as they did all the religious things that manifested their elect status, they were in.

The Lord responds differently. The person who knows me is the person who humbly and joyously manifests my life in his or her behavior. That will never be possible as a result of human effort or performance but only as a result of complete reliance on me. God calls us today to manifest his righteous life in our relationships. We can only do that as we live in that submissive relationship to God in which our will is utterly surrendered to the Holy Spirit so that his life can be lived through us. That is what heaven will be, and that begins now.

God has delivered us from each of our Egypts by the blood of Jesus Christ. He has done this in order to write his covenant on our hearts through the power of the Holy Spirit and thus to take up residence in the tabernacle he desires most of all—the tabernacle of our hearts. He longs to fill that tabernacle with the glory that fills the earth. He wants to move each of us from that place where we cry out in horror, "Woe to me . . . for I am a man of unclean lips . . . and my eyes have seen the King, the LORD Almighty" (6:5), to the place where we can "come and see [his] glory" (66:18)—and not merely to survive the experience but actually to have that glory reside in us. That is the goal of life.

Scripture Index

Subject Index

Subject Index

Asbury, Francis, 86, 698
asceticism, 276, 617
Ashdod, 244, 261
asherah poles, 231, 311
Ashur, 25, 419
Ashurbanipal, 24, 241
assurance, 590, 610
Assyria, 19, 20–26, 28–30, 44, 46–47, 61, 116, 119, 126, 136–37, 14–42, 150–51, 160, 164–66, 174–81, 187, 189, 193, 198–201, 209, 211–12, 219, 225, 235–36, 241–44, 246, 261–62, 264, 274, 317, 319–20, 330–31, 344–45, 348–50, 358–60, 372–74, 377, 380, 389, 401, 414–15, 435, 556, 577
Assyrian language, 322
astrology, 531
atheism, 302
atonement, 263, 311
Auschwitz, 215, 571
authority, 83, 376, 504, 506; of the Bible, 120, 143, 287; of God, 255
authorship of Isaiah, 398, 681
Azekah, 262

Baal, 31, 89–90, 241, 614, 617; worship of, 418
Baal-Shamayim, 31
Babylon, 18–19, 23–32, 43, 46–47, 49, 51–52, 116, 119, 176, 181, 189, 198–212, 253–56, 261–62, 274, 352, 387, 403, 435–36, 459, 468, 480, 490, 497, 507, 511, 529–30, 532, 542, 545, 564, 575, 577, 595, 614, 699; lost location of, 201
Babylonian envoys, 49, 399, 426
Baghdad, 248
banners, 42, 189
barrenness, 595
Bartimaeus, 540
Bastogne, 578
Bathsheba, 616
bats, 49
Battle of the Bulge, 404, 577
bearing, 269
beatitudes, 355
beauty, 382–383, 507
Beckett, Samuel, 157
beer, 323
Beer Elim, 224

behavior, 250, 282, 378, 433, 526, 622, 627, 684
behavioral science, 676
Bel, 31, 522
belief, 525, 572; in God, 307
Belshazzar, 29, 254, 255
Bernard of Clairvaux, 666
Bethlehem, 187, 248
Bezalel, 187
Bible, 191, 332–33, 431, 507, 539, 541, 566; as revelation of God, 55; historicity of, 423; reading, 80, 421
biblical, 333; claims, 143; literacy, 453; revelation, 431, 494–495, 687; worldview, 453
bier, 209
binge drinking, 323
birds, 388
Bismarck, Otto von, 220
bitter grapes, 113
Blackham, Paul, 637
blamelessness, 638, 651
blasphemy, 403, 579
blessing, 355–56, 363, 504, 567, 586, 590, 625, 627, 629, 671, 682, 688; of God, 44; to the world, 555
blindness, 149, 331, 335, 363
blood, 305–6, 387, 496, 661–62, 703
bloodshed, 388
Boaz, 223, 460
bodies, 217
bondage, 351; to sin, 610
Bonhoeffer, Dietrich, 610
Book of Immanuel, 164; of Yahweh, 388
boomers, 131
born again, 63
bourgeoisie, 633
bragging, 420
branch, 72, 108, 128, 187; of Yahweh, 106
bride, 658; of Christ, 182
Britain, 154–55, 202; commonwealth of, 275
broken promises, 258
Brooklyn Tabernacle, 390
brotherly love, 166
brothers Grimm, 34
bruised body, 73–74
Buddhism, 542, 633
Bultmann, Rudolf, 463

Subject Index

contentment, 157

continuity, 31, 56, 60, 78, 244–45, 284, 332, 414, 417–18, 468, 471, 495, 537

contrition, 621–22, 697

control, 28, 79, 101, 280, 312, 333, 614, 683

Corinth, 313, 325

cornerstone, 326

corporate, 589

corruption, 125, 263, 633

council, 127

counter-culture, 304

court, 49, 386, 469, 489–90, 492, 502

covenant, 49, 54, 61, 73, 78–80, 113, 136, 263, 282, 313, 327, 336, 339, 438, 499, 538, 568, 601, 614, 621, 625, 627, 630, 638, 649, 651; breaking of, 267; maker, 75; of peace, 595, 598–99, 637

covetousness, 615

creation, 394, 451–54, 493, 504, 513, 521, 564, 633; in God, 56

Creator, 73, 75, 89–90, 95, 97, 100, 117, 120, 174, 202, 216, 231–32, 245, 282, 292, 321, 326, 338, 359, 386–87, 413, 446–48, 454, 460, 481, 483, 491, 495, 502, 506, 511, 513, 521, 536–37, 548, 570, 572, 596, 599, 603–4, 634, 644, 683, 688, 696, 701

crime, 368

criticism, 34

cross, 59, 62, 131, 325, 326, 474, 485, 516, 677

cruelty, 215, 632

crusades, 361

Cullmann, Oscar, 192

cult, 308, 626; of Yahweh, 330

cultic activity, 81, 329

cultic behavior, 625

cup of wrath, 576

curds and honey, 141

cure, 634

curse, 282, 671

Cush, 189, 198, 230, 481, 521

cycles, 28, 31, 121, 249, 284–85, 423, 447, 453, 461, 468, 536, 541–42

cynicism, 113–14, 257, 319

Cyprus, 273

Cyrus, 28–30, 40, 208, 375, 461, 469–70, 478, 481, 489, 497, 510–12, 514, 522–23, 546–47, 645

Czech Republic, 302

Czechoslovakia, 256

daily devotions, 145

Damascus, 21, 137, 149, 174–75, 198, 224, 230

Daniel, 25, 28, 461

Darbyism, 361

Darius, 30, 512

darkness, 642

dating, 199; of Isaiah, 310, 399; of Sennacharib, 218

David, 116, 136, 144, 161, 179, 186–87, 190, 268, 381, 452, 486, 598, 602, 616, 675; covenant, 17; kingdom, 137

day, of atonement, 625; of Yahweh, 176, 242

Dead Sea, 224–25

deafness, 683

death, 74, 103, 132, 146, 157, 208–10, 213–15, 227, 290, 293–94, 300, 308, 319, 356, 429, 597, 688; of sinful nature, 610; of the servant, 587; to self, 287; to sin, 279, 550

deceit, 586

deception, 152, 256

Declaration of Independence, 634

decline of church, 667

defeat, 254, 367; of death, 294; of enemies, 346; of God, 535; of sin, 555–56, 568, 575, 636, 638, 662, 665

defender in court, 337

defense of Jerusalem by God, 22, 374, 403

defenses, 261, 263

deliverance, 53, 243, 280, 294, 299, 336, 382, 485, 490, 491, 497, 515, 535, 546, 564, 602, 614, 621, 645, 650, 696; from sin, 395; of God, 380, 479; need for, 373

democracy, 381

demythologization, 463

dependability, 265

dependence, 114; on God, 23, 275, 354, 427, 431

depravity, 579, 629, 633

dereliction, 125

descendents, 128; of Abraham, 53

desert, 42, 47, 143, 344, 387, 390, 394

desolation, 106

720

humbling by God, 274; of the proud, 273
humiliation, 95–96, 99, 211, 226, 264
humility, 103, 263, 289, 419–20, 697–99, 701
hymns, 458, 478
hypostatic union, 450

I am statements, 465
ICBM's, 202
icons, 524
identity, 700
idolatry, 97, 100–101, 104, 108, 225, 245, 311–12, 355, 406, 414, 417, 421, 438, 614–15, 624, 627
idols, 40, 48–49, 61, 84, 96, 118, 175, 231, 241, 254, 272, 312, 330, 347, 359, 413, 418, 447–48, 460–62, 467–68, 475, 497, 502–3, 510, 521–22, 524–25, 536, 620; manufacturing of, 503, 521; worship of, 458, 468–69
ignorance, 633
illness, 430; of Hezekiah, 435
illustration, 263–64, 291, 301, 320, 386, 438, 576, 603, 630
image, 268; of God, 56, 58, 454, 486, 633, 653
images, 615
imagination, 304
immanence, 449–51
Immanuel, 136, 140, 142, 144–46, 148–50, 160–61, 399, 465
immorality, 308
impassibility of God, 431
imputed, 54
inadequacy, 245
inattention, 585, 591
incarnation, 146, 162, 423, 450
inclusivism, 58, 517, 609
incontinence, 151
indescribability of God, 129
India, 195
Indiana Jones, 390
individualism, 62
inhumanity, 632
iniquity, 131
injustice, 549, 585–86, 589
insecurity, 369
inspiration, of Israel, 199; of Scripture, 38
instrument of God, 116
integrity, 145

intelligence, 530, 532
intentional sin, 538
intercession, 587
interpreting prophecy, 481
interrogation, 405
interstate, 393
intertestamental period, 608, 307
intolerance, 504
invitation, 521, 540, 583, 595, 601–4
Iran, 201
irony, 209
Isaac, 144
Isaiah ben Amoz, 36, 41, 72, 89, 199, 250, 512
Isaianic school, 34–35
Islam, 302, 361, 431
isolationism, 609
Israel, 136–37, 141, 150–51, 160, 165–67, 174, 180, 186, 230–31, 400, 428, 556; as blessing, 300; restored to God, 644
Issus, 30

Jacob, 130, 231, 243, 337, 354, 486, 578, 670
Japan, 236, 376, 483, 532
jealousy, 566
Jefferson, Thomas, 463
Jehoiachin, 25–26, 30
Jehoiakim, 25–26, 403, 438
Jeremiah, 26, 349
Jericho, 262
Jeroboam, 20
Jerome, 224
Jerusalem, 84, 89, 177, 198, 248, 261, 292, 311, 319, 329–31, 607, 641, 650
Jesse, 186–87
Jesus, 29, 35, 37, 80, 108, 113, 116, 121–22, 127, 129, 133, 142–43, 153, 156, 162, 168, 183, 247, 267–68, 276, 286, 306, 353–55, 369, 377–78, 380, 390, 395, 419–20, 422, 430, 432–33, 450, 465, 486, 493, 496, 506, 516, 523, 539–42, 557, 566–67, 572, 586, 588–89, 602, 652, 658, 662, 703; as Lord, 515, 523
Jesus movement, 632
Jewishness, 609
Jews, 336, 577
Jezreel, 160

Subject Index

uncertainty, 572
unclean, 127
understanding, 602; of the prophets, 474
underworld, 209
unfailing love, 595–96, 598
unharvested field, 73
uniform, 264
uniformity, 246–47
unity of Isaiah, 18, 329, 372, 446
unity of Scripture, 168
universal, judgment, 310; redemption, 696; salvation, 310–11
universality, of Christianity, 91; of Yahwist religion, 90
unmoved mover, 59, 60
upraised hand, 166
utilitarianism, 120, 333, 376
Uzziah, 20, 33, 72, 126, 430

valley, 261
vassals, 22
victim, 676
victory, 583; of God, 302–3, 308, 350
Vietnam, 226, 633
view, 119; of God, 17
vine, 550, 621
vineyard, 99, 112, 115, 297, 301, 310–12
violence, 89, 91, 625, 630, 632
virgin, 140, 162; daughter, 415, 529
virtue, 215
vocation, 127, 550
voice, of God, 348; of Jesus, 407
vow of praise, 429

wadi of Egypt, 311
waiting, 152, 290, 304, 335, 346, 373, 448, 556–57, 578, 598, 671
walking, 79, 89, 91, 96, 122, 145, 304, 393, 395, 427, 433, 498, 563, 568, 638
wall, 345
wandering, 670
war, 254–55, 308, 388
warning, 505
warrior, 46, 54, 98, 161
Warsaw, 577
watchmen, 254–55, 577, 613, 655
water, 137, 380
Watergate, 390
way, 630; of holiness, 393, 620
weakness, 268, 351
weapons, 360

Weaver, Dennis, 213
Weber, Max, 550
wedding, 651–52, 656, 685; supper of Lamb, 294
weeping, 224, 263
Weimer Republic, 381
Wesley, John, 157, 276, 364, 580, 666, 698
Whitehead, Alfred North, 449
whoredom, 263
Whybray, R. N., 649
wicked, 620; tenants, 116
wickedness, 538
widower, 141
widowhood, 596
wife of Isaiah, 140, 149
willfulness, 212
wine, 323
Winning Through Intimidation, 420
wisdom, 48, 96, 241–42, 245, 331, 498, 583
wise men, 241
witness, 194–95, 496, 602, 636–37, 641–42, 645–46, 659
witnesses, 493, 496, 502
woe, 113, 174, 317, 329, 335, 343, 358, 362, 372–73, 514, 703
women, 99, 141; of Zion, 99
wood, 503
word, 566; of God, 464; pictures, 177; play, 113, 138
Wordsworth, William, 287
work of Christ, 195
works, 610, 653
works righteousness, 62
world, 119
world war, 102, 191, 215, 236, 256, 265–66, 275, 360, 404, 419–20, 463–64, 577, 633, 662
worldview, 58, 248, 356, 483, 539, 541
worldwide pilgrimage, 642
worship, 32, 77–78, 145, 181, 231–32, 242–43, 249, 293, 311–12, 330–33, 347, 401, 521, 615, 626, 661, 681, 684–85, 698, 700; of the dead, 330; of God, 643
wrath, 299, 301; of God, 348, 390
wreath, 317–18, 321

Yahweh, 227, 240, 241
Yam, 273

Subject Index

A PARTICULAR OBEDIENCE

a novel by

DAVID WARD-NANNEY

MUD SEASON PUBLISHING

Published By
Mud Season Publishing
PO Box 2150, SS6 0AJ, United Kingdom
www.mudseasonpublishing.com

ISBN 978-0-9562639-0-2

Thank you, Agnes Stevens,
for all that you do.

CONTENTS

Our Granddaughter

1

STOCKARD woke up one August morning in 1963 in a sweat. It wasn't just that her grandmother had no air conditioning at Sefer Farm, where she spent her summers. It had been the dream, like The Nightmare. Not a nightmare, but *The Nightmare*, the painting by Henry Fuseli. She had seen it just last week in one of her mother's art books.

The dream itself was nothing like the painting, in which Fuseli depicted a woman asleep on a couch, a gargoyle sitting on her chest. It was not a restful sleep. A horse peeked through a curtain in the background.

Her dream had been set in Sefer Farm's barn. She had wandered into the barn on a pitch black night and found herself unable to leave. There was someone else in the barn. Or something else in the barn. She could feel the presence. It was dark. What little light there was could have been made by candles, although she could not see what exactly made the light. She could not see what was there.

She was terrified. Whatever was in the barn approached her from one side. It enveloped her like a dark forceful blanket, and it covered her from all sides. She felt it pressure her chest and her breathing came in gasps. It had a hold of her. It was going to kill her. Just when she reached out, to try and grab something for leverage, just when she felt her lungs begin to labor painfully and her heart beating hard, she awoke.

Her heart racing, she looked down to see her t-shirt and boxer shorts soaked with sweat. Her summer brown legs lay out before her. She had thrown the sheet aside.

It was her room at Sefer Farm. She was safe.

She lay back down, her heart easing off its pace. The dream had not been at all like Fuseli's *The Nightmare*. Except maybe the horses. But there had been no horses in her dream. She had been in the barn. That was the only similarity, which was not similar at all. But she had felt a tremendous pressure on her chest as if someone had been sitting on her chest. There had been no gargoyle in her dream, either.

Despite the dissimilarity, Stockard could only think of *The Nightmare*. She got out of bed. It was a single four-poster bed, dark stained wood like everything else at Sefer Farm. It appeared to be an extension of the floor, the staining of the two so similar that Stockard wondered if the man who had stained the floor had not also stained her bed, although it had not always been her bed. She had some framed Monet prints on the walls and some pictures on a chest of drawers. There was one of her mother, her grandmother, Rose and herself, the only people in the house on this morning.

She remembered *The Nightmare* and decided to pay the house library an early visit and look at the print in the art book. She could not get it out of her head. Why had her dream led her to the picture?

When she opened her bedroom door and peered down the hall-way, there was an unusual stillness in the house. Early mornings in the summer of the South. Nothing moved. The heat of the night had so completely drained the landscape of energy that it slept peace-fully only in the early morning. She would take a left into the main living room, a massive cavern of a room with a fireplace so big that you could park a car in it. The irony, she thought as she passed it, was that the stones in the fireplace were probably the coolest things in the house right now. Come the first autumnal chill, Rose's husband, Ebern, would be stacking wood next to it, and there would be a fire in it from early morning until almost midnight.

That was months away. Stockard passed through the living room, where sofas and armchairs and wingchairs were grouped into sitting areas. She had seen the room full of people for Thanksgiving parties, for Christmas parties, for birthday parties. When it was only her family they congregated around the two sofas that faced each other, the fireplace on one side. She then entered the old part of the house, the part that her great-grandfather had built as a hunting lodge, when her grandmother came out of the kitchen. She looked gaunt.

"Good morning, Stockard," she said. "Did you sleep well?" She looked Stockard over, from head to foot.

Stockard was aware that she had not brushed her hair. She had not brushed her teeth. She was a mess, her long brown hair breaking off at various points like tributary rivers. Her face was still sticky and shiny from her nightmare. She was just about to say no, she had not slept very well but caught something from her grandmother. Her grandmother was not really focused on her. She had taken only a cursory look at Stockard and then stood in the doorway of the kitchen, distractedly fingering her black reading glasses. Stockard nodded and was about to say she had slept fine when her grandmother, skinny and already dressed in khaki trousers and a white shirt, said, "Your Uncle Abe is dead."

Dead? What do you mean dead? Stockard nodded her head, feeling it go sideways, a horse asking a question. Dead? "Yes, ma'am," she said.

They looked at each other for a long moment. "An accident. On their farm."

Stockard had been on her aunt and uncle's farm. It was nothing like Sefer Farm, which was part monument to carpentry, part monument to her great-grandfather, Seth Griffin, who had made the family money with a sawmill and then a full-blown regional lumber operation. It was also her family's full-time retreat from the world, just thirty minutes from Nashville, the only place where her grandmother wore trousers and allowed herself a cigarette on the porch. "Ladies do not smoke in public," she had said.

Uncle Abe and Aunt Evelyn's farm was an hour-and-a-half drive from their Upper East Side brownstone, set in rolling Connecticut hills. It was a big-city person's version of what a farm should be. No actual work happened on their farm, just horse riding and weekend guests being entertained.

What kind of accident could happen on that no work farm? What kind of accident could kill Uncle Abe?

"You'll want to pack a bag after your bath," her grandmother said. "A black dress. Do you have a black dress?"

Stockard stood there, blinking, slowly understanding what her grandmother was saying. She would need a black dress for the funeral. "Yes, ma'am." She did have a black dress, a sleeveless light wool one. She could wear a cotton cardigan over it. "And you'll need some other dresses. It's the city. Remember."

Her grandmother always said this when Stockard was packing to go see her cousins in New York. "What about Eve and Emily?"

"In shock. Evelyn said they were in shock. They don't know…"

They don't know their father is dead? But they are in shock over it? What was her grandmother talking about?

"They don't know," said her grandmother again, "about it. They know their father is dead, but they don't know the circumstances."

It came to Stockard like a lightning flash. It was her grandmother's use of the word "circumstances." It was the way she hesitated. "Grandmother, what is it? How did Uncle Abe die?"

The deal between grandmother and granddaughter was a simple one. They were honest with each other. Stockard's grandmother had never candy-coated anything for her, not like her grandmother had done for Stockard's mother. There was an understanding between the two, as if early on Stockard and her grandmother had known they could tell each the truth, no matter how harsh or silly. It did not mean they told each other everything, but what they did tell each other was unfiltered. Stockard had been on the verge of telling her grandmother why she was on her way to the library to look at Fuseli's *The Nightmare* when her grandmother had blurted out that Uncle Abe was dead.

Now her grandmother took a step forward as if to say something secret, to say something softly. "Your Uncle Abe committed suicide last night. He used a shotgun on the sofa."

It would be months before everyone realized that Abe had used one of Seth Griffin's shotguns for his final act. Seth Griffin, the man who had built Sefer Farm, who had made their money. It was a Browning single-barrel twelve-gauge, a heavy old thing, ironic because Abe had been a Wall Street investment banker, Jewish, educated to within an inch of his life, and was uncomfortable with guns. Stockard's grandfather had never made it past sixth grade, was only vaguely aware of the Old Testament God, and had spent most of his life with either a gun or a fishing rod in his hands. Two different men used one gun for such different results.

Stockard had seen paintings of suicides. She imagined Uncle Abe taking his shoe off, probably one of those handmade oxfords that he wore to work. It was Wednesday. He took off one of his black wool socks, shoved the barrel in his mouth and then pulled the trigger with a toe. That's how you committed suicide with a shotgun. With a toe.

"Why?"

"I'm not sure, dear child."

They stood in the hallway for an eternity, looking at each other, Stockard finally saying, "I'll go get ready."

She would not open her mother's art book that morning and stare at *The Nightmare*, wondering why the dream had been so terribly frightful and why there had been a pressure on her chest when she awoke and why all she could think of was Fuseli's painting.

2

RETURNING to New York City was a shock to Stockard's senses. It always had been.

She had been going to New York all her life, ostensibly to see her aunt and uncle and cousins. Her grandmother also had business there and twice a year she had loaded her daughter and her grand-daughter onto a train to make the nearly two-day trip from Nashville. They had flown once, only once, but Stockard's mother, nervous by nature, was terrified of planes. The one time they flew, her mother had lapsed into silence as the plane lifted from the Nashville runway and then had kept silent for three days afterwards, huddled in a bed, taking only milk.

Stockard's mother was like that. She was fragile. The world had a severe impact on her and the slightest thing could set her off. The bed was her retreat.

Stockard was not at all like her. There was the physical difference. Stockard was medium height for a woman and had a thick frame, wide hips and large boobs. Her mother was the same height but appeared taller because she was skinny and flat-chested with a pale face and sandy blond hair. Stockard had a dark complexion and brown hair that was as rich and deep as mink.

And things did not bother Stockard the way that they did her mother.

By the time that they arrived in New York, Uncle Abe was already buried.

"It is the Jewish way," explained her Aunt Evelyn. "They want the funeral to take place within twenty-four hours of death."

Stockard had forgotten that Uncle Abe was Jewish. Their last name was Goldfarber. She always thought of them as Griffins, which was her last name and her mother's last name and her grandmother's last name. This despite her mother and grandmother having both been married. Her grandmother's husband had wrecked his plane in a field not far from Sefer Farm. Her mother's husband, Stockard's father, had long been banished, their marriage being annulled a few months after their civil service across the border in Kentucky, in a town where marriage was done quickly.

Now, Stockard wondered, would her Aunt Evelyn and her cousins, Eve and Emily, become Griffins by name?

They had taken a cab from Grand Central to her aunt's house and as soon as they were standing on the sidewalk, a porter loading their bags into the back of the cab, Stockard remembered what it was like to be in the city. On Sefer Farm, the air itself was lonely. In New York City, there was movement all around her, the dirty smells of garbage and exhaust fumes, people streaming down sidewalks, the homeless perched against the station and the ever-present smell of urine. It was summer in the city, when everything that was bad about it overwhelmingly smelled bad.

There had been quiet conversation, Stockard's grandmother asking her aunt how she was.

"Shocked," was her aunt's answer. "Oh, I'm bearing up fine." She had cut her eyes to Eve, her eldest daughter, who was six months younger than Stockard. Stockard had seen how Eve was withdrawn into herself as everyone looked at her. It drove Stockard to the window, wanting to pull herself away from the scene. She hated seeing people in the spotlight, people who did not want to be in the spotlight. Eve was pale like her mother.

The window was on the second floor, where the living room was. Her aunt had a penchant for French fabrics, this room done in bright golds and deep reds, the furniture darkly polished and ornate. The floor-to-ceiling windows allowed Stockard a view of the street below as her family congregated behind her.

New York, she was reminded, was easily forgotten when not here. She could be in Nashville right now and looking out a window from their house and see maybe two or three cars pass in thirty minutes. Her grandmother's house was located in a good neighborhood, well removed from any busy streets. Below her aunt's brownstone, yellow taxis sped and jostled for position, slowing abruptly at the stoplight just ahead. It was supposed to be a quiet New York street, more exclusive than her grandmother's neighborhood, but it was much busier. Through the glass, Stockard could hear the busy sounds of the big city.

Compared to the mad dash through traffic and clogged intersections on their ride from Grand Central, her aunt's street and house was tucked away. Stockard could place her face close to the window and look down the street to see Central Park. The Metropolitan Museum of Art was just around the corner.

Finally Emily came down the stairs, the last member of the Griffin women to enter the living room. Emily was the youngest. She had changed the atmosphere. She had been noisy coming down the stairs and was dressed in her trademark corduroy skirt, a brown one, and a white t-shirt. Emily had thrown herself into her grandmother's arms, the two hugging a long moment, her grandmother saying, "Oh, darling, I'm so sorry."

"I know," Emily had whispered.

Emily had then hugged Stockard's mother.

As the two stood in silence, Stockard watched, having turned around from her window perch and wanting to say hello to Emily. Emily was her favorite.

Stockard watched her mother and her cousin hug for what felt like a long time. Her mother's arms gripped her cousin once, twice, three times and then the sobs came, first the sniffling of the nose, then the gasping of the air, the hug intensified, and then Stockard's mother burst into a full sobbing fit, and it was Emily who was stroking her mother, saying it was all right. Everything would be all right.

The two had to sit down, awkwardly changing how they held on to each other. Stockard stood to the side, still waiting to say hello to her cousin, her mother's reaction dwarfing such pleasantries as a warm greeting. Stockard took in the others. Her grandmother was standing with her left hand on her hip and her right hand holding her reading glasses. Her aunt hovered between the living room and the kitchen, as if she was about to offer drinks or food. Her cousin Eve sat on a sofa corner furthest from everyone else, watching the scene with a look of disgust.

"Evelyn, I'd like a refreshment if that's possible," said Stockard's grandmother.

"Yes, mother," said Aunt Evelyn and went through a swinging door into the kitchen. She appeared a minute later with a gin and tonic for her mother.

Stockard, when she looked back on that trip, the trip to go to Uncle Abe's funeral, which they missed, the trip to console her aunt and cousins, could only see this single incident which would explain why they moved from Nashville to New York City to live with her aunt and cousins. Something had happened in that room that day. It was not just her mother having a breakdown and Emily being the one to console her. It was something else, as if Uncle Abe's death had created an opportunity, a reason for all the Griffin women to live under one roof.

Stockard's mother had said they moved to New York City to help out. Her grandmother said that Evelyn could not continue to manage the day-to-day duties of the family business and that she would have to take over, temporarily. The businesses in Nashville, she said, could take care of themselves for a couple of years without her.

Why her cousins and aunt could not move to Nashville was never explained. Her aunt had grown up in the same house in which Stockard had grown up, so that was not the issue. There was plenty of room.

Why would her grandmother sell the Nashville house and move them all to New York?

She did not sell Sefer Farm and she had declared that when she returned to the South for good that she would live her remaining days on it.

Her aunt had sold the Connecticut farmhouse.

That was how Stockard found herself living in New York City after having spent the previous sixteen years of her life in Tennessee. Her aunt made special arrangements so that she could attend the same all-girls school, Morary's, that Eve and Emily attended. It was four blocks away and the three girls walked there together, Stockard unaccustomed to the grey and red uniform. While Eve was a somber companion, Emily was always ready with a wry comment or was pointing out something which made her laugh. The first few months of all the Griffin women living in the brownstone were awkward, each woman figuring out what the new order meant for her. Only Stockard's grandmother was unshakeable in her confidence, spending a half day at her office at Forest & Griffin, the venture capital firm which she had started with her partner, Andrew Forest.

3

Eve asked Emily and Stockard to go with her to the main branch of the New York Public Library, where she would do research for a paper on New York's religious history. She hated leaving their neighborhood alone.

Emily and Stockard both agreed to go. While Eve sat at a desk stacked with New York state history books, they sat in the periodicals room, reading whatever took their fancy. Stockard got her first glimpse of the *Village Voice*. She was immediately engrossed.

By the time that Emily had flipped through various art magazines, she had noticed that Stockard could not put the *Voice* down and looked over her shoulder.

"Looking for a date?" she asked.

Stockard jumped and went red, the two laughing a stifled library laugh as Emily put her hands on Stockard's shoulders to calm her.

"Have you seen this?" Stockard held up the paper with the personal ads.

"Uh huh."

"It took me a minute to figure out 'Fet.' Fetish, right?"

"And why would you think I'd know that?"

Stockard looked up at Emily to see if she was serious. "What does 'WE' mean?"

"I'm not sure about that one."

They were whispering, the creaking of the leather sofa masking their conversation.

"Okay, check this out." Stockard flipped the page and there were two pages dedicated to fortune tellers and alternative medicines. "I don't know that we have such things in Nashville, honey." She liked to roll the final syllable of "honey" out for a mile. "Ho-neeeee."

"Oh, yeah," said Emily. "We've got everything here." She read some of the highlights out loud. "Tea leaves, astrology, pendulum,

crystals, crystal balls, tarot, ruins, palm readers. Of course, palm readers. How handy to carry around your fortune in your hand."

Stockard sniggered a little. "Have you been to any of these?"

"Not once. Quackery."

"I wonder what they do."

"Well… let's find out." Emily reached down, flexed the wooden
rod at an odd angle and removed the two pages from the *Village
Voice*, having to take four pages total to avoid making a ripping sound,
that noise which echoes off the canyons of a library, signalling to the
world that a library thief is at work.

Abe had left most of his money in trust for his daughters.

The girls had cash and a mission, to see what their fortunes held.
And that's what they did. They visited all they could, every card reader, every palm reader, every aromatherapists, every herbalist, every ad
they could.

It was almost a year and a half later when Stockard and Emily
visited an acupuncturist. It was Stockard's senior year at Morary's
and she had less than four months before graduation. Eve begged
out of at least half of their explorations, citing homework or a particular dislike as excuses. She complained that the crystal ball was simply too much of a stretch for her so had skipped that visit. Ditto for
ruins and numerology, although her natal chart was stuck above her
bedroom desk. She had skipped the acupuncturist, saying, "Needles,
no way!"

The acupuncturist's son had taken a liking to Stockard while she
waited for Emily to have her patterns of disharmony reharmonized
with about forty needles, stuck mainly in her back. The reception
room was heavily oriental in decoration, red silk tassels hanging in an
archway, a black table serving as the reception desk. The acupuncturist's son had pointed to the book in Stockard's hand and said, "You
read go?"

Stockard was not reading *Go*, the portrayal of Beatnik life in
1940s Manhattan by John Clellon Holmes. The book was in her hand,

but she was holding it for Emily while under the needles. Stockard thought for a moment what would be the correct answer and found herself nodding with a smile. It was a radiant smile. It's hard to resist a beautiful woman with such a smile. Stockard and the acupuncturist's son, who served as a kind of receptionist behind the black desk where he could study after school, talked of Beat culture and the body of literature for thirty minutes before her cousin emerged, her patterns apparently reharmonized. It occurred to Stockard that now the son would speak with Emily and figure out that it was her cousin who was the real Beatnik fan. Emily was the one in a corduroy skirt, a black turtleneck and a jean jacket, not Stockard. Her blue wool skirt with its wide pleats looked more like Mayfair than Greenwich Village.

Besides a slightly electric feeling in her back and a need to go to sleep afterwards, Stockard was unphased by acupuncture. It was simply another notch on the mystical belt of exploration.

On the way out of the acupuncturist's office, the son had handed Stockard, not her cousin, a worn soft brown paper bag, saying: "Something for you. When you get home." He had smiled and bowed his head ever so slightly.

Stockard had opened the bag once on the sidewalk. There was a pipe about a foot long. It was lacquered red and had a gold dragon snaking up the side. It took a moment for both girls to realize what it was. There was also a parcel of tin foil. It contained a nice neat square of hash.

"Me thinky you chasey dragon," said Emily in her best Charlie Chan voice.

"Huh?"

"I think he's just given you a ticket to opiumville," said Emily.

"What for?"

"To get you high, my dear." Emily reflected on how men always did things for her cousin. Stockard had that Southern accent, that long brown hair, and that smile. Her accent was honestly earned, where "yes" became "yeeeess," often imitated in film and literature, but as real as butter and grits for Stockard. When the two went out together, men always paid attention to Stockard and ignored Emily. "What did you say to him?"

"We just talked about your book. *Go.* Did you talk to him?"

"Not a word," said Emily. "He just sat behind the desk and read."

4

THERE were three rooms on the fourth floor of the brownstone. The TV room, Stockard's bedroom, and the bathroom. The ceilings sloped at odd angles with the rooms, interrupted by a few dormers front and back. No one but the girls and Ismelda made it up to the fourth floor.

Ismelda was the Guatemalan maid who lived in the basement apartment. She would go out early for fresh bagels, the warmness of a just-baked bagel a New York memory that had always been with Stockard. Her aunt had a giant Gaggia espresso machine for coffee. Stockard and her grandmother preferred café au lait, which was much gentler than the espressos that her aunt drank. Ismelda only came up to the fourth floor in the mornings, starting her cleaning chores at the top and then working her way down. As Stockard, Emily and Eve left for school, they could hear the distant sound of the vacuum cleaner on the fourth floor.

Stockard loved being the sole inhabitant of the fourth floor. Hearing Ismelda making everything tidy gave her a rush. She knew she would return to a space that was her own and clean and neat. It was her retreat, and when she settled on her bed for a nap or to read, she was in a cozy tower, somewhere far away and untouchable by the rest of the world.

The TV room had an old sofa at one end. In front of the sofa was a large blanket chest, which the girls used as an ottoman.

At the other end of the room sat the television, with an almost circular glass front which projected the black and white images that floated in from the air. The Andy Griffith Show. Hated for its simplistic view of life. The Beverly Hillbillies. Hated for its simplistic view of Tennessee. Jeopardy. Loved it. Bewitched. Hated the sneaky way the women had to get things done, but loved the idea that women controlled things, even if they were witches.

That night after visiting the acupuncturist, Emily, Eve and Stockard had gotten stoned for the first time in the TV room. It was well after dinner. Emily had brought a book of matches. They fumbled with the pipe, the hash falling out of the bowl a couple of times. Emily burnt her finger holding a match too long. But in just a few minutes, all three girls were stoned.

They sat silently in front of the television, eyes blinking, not paying attention to My Three Sons. Hated. Why couldn't they do My Three Daughters?

Stockard imagined this was what it felt like to float in space, only with oxygen and warm air. To float on a warm pillow. Her mouth had gone dry and the air itself was thick with the blue-black rays from the television, little dust particles picking up the light, causing Stockard to follow them around and see great waves of dust moving in the room. She looked over at Emily and Eve. They were far away.

"Do you think Mom can smell it downstairs?" asked Eve in a monotone, still facing the television.

"No," said Emily. "She's two, probably three floors down."

Emily, Eve and Stockard's mother had bedrooms on the third floor.

Stockard looked at Emily again. This time Emily was looking back and she grinned a most mischievous grin, glassy-eyed and delighted all at once.

Nothing mattered anymore, thought Stockard. She wasn't worried about corralling her hair tomorrow morning for school. It was a giant mess of wet when she came out of the shower and she never felt like her efforts with her hair matched the neatness of her school uniform.

She didn't care about other things that had bothered her. Early after they had moved to New York, Stockard had watched Emily get berated for bringing a B back on her mid-term report card. In Chemistry.

It was at dinner one evening. "You've always done so well in science," said Aunt Evelyn. "Why a B?"

Stockard was thinking that her aunt might cut her cousin a little slack. Her father had just committed suicide, after all. Emily was making As in all the rest of her classes. Four As and one B. That was pretty good, especially under the circumstances.

The conversation would have happened when no one else was at the house, no one but Evelyn, Eve and Emily. There had been the first few weeks after Stockard and her mother and grandmother had arrived, when Stockard felt more like a visitor, like when she would visit her cousins in the summer in the Hamptons. She had been an outsider to those things that make family life so peculiar and private, the daily details, Emily getting chewed out for making a B in Chemistry.

Stockard could not get the moment out of her head and had revisited it over the months. At first she felt sorry for Emily. Having her shortcomings made public. Stockard would have blushed and mumbled apologies and wanted to die on the spot. Emily looked her mother straight in the eye and said it would not happen again. Emily could do that. She could close down a topic in five words or less.

It made Stockard feel like she was sitting on the porch at Sefer Farm, listening to the katydids playing their sorrowful song in the heat of the summer. Her mother had once described the sound as the most lonely sound she had ever heard.

She could be sitting in class, especially Calculus, where Dr. Noud was working through a problem on the blackboard. Stockard could see how the problem could be worked but she resisted it. It was simply too much work to make her mind follow Dr. Noud's snail pace. She knew he had to do it that way. He had to make sure that everyone in the class followed him, but oh the boredom made Stockard want to scream. Her mind would turn to other things. She would take a look at his attire. A yellow shirt and red tie today. He had no fashion sense. All of her math teachers had been the same. They had no idea how to dress. Then her mind would drift and inevitably she would return to Emily's mid-term B in Chemistry. The bone chill emptiness came with it. How dare her Aunt Evelyn be so mean? And poor Emily.

Poor Emily.

Stockard's grandmother had looked at her report cards, all of them, signing the copy that went back to school. She would say, "Excellent as usual," and read a few of the comments out loud. That was it. At most it was a five-minute exchange, usually in her grandmother's office at home. Stockard would tuck the return report card into one of her books or put it on her dresser, and still someone at the school would have to chase it down. Stockard was always the last person to turn in her report card, often crinkled and sometimes stained by spilt Coke or smeared with a bit of chocolate.

Over time, the moment had grown. Aunt Evelyn had positively yelled at Emily. Emily had broken down in tears, sobbed and run upstairs to quietly sob on her bed. Or in a corner of her closet.

Stockard knew this was not so. She knew her imagination was playing some kind of trick on her. But why? Why was this seemingly innocuous family moment starting to loom and haunt and make her feel so terrible and lonely?

After the dragon pipe, she didn't care. Less than an hour later Stockard drifted into a deep sleep on the sofa and when she awoke, the TV was still on although no more programs were being broadcast, just the black and white fuzz of no reception, the Ant Races as they called them. Emily and Eve had gone, presumably to their beds. It was an almighty effort to take the ten steps to her bed and take her clothes off. Reaching around to unsnap her bra had taken her remaining energy and she had collapsed to sleep the deepest sleep.

The next night they did it again and the next night again and what Stockard found was that those thoughts of Emily's chastisement and why Fuseli had visited her, they had disappeared. They chased the dragon and left their cares far behind, the chase exhilarating and fun.

Emily had swiped a Bunsen burner from her physics lab—she had indeed made an A in Chemistry the previous year and had moved on to Physics in her junior year—and the girls had become proficient with the pipe. Stockard and Emily had returned to the acupuncturist one more time, this time so that Stockard could ask his son for more hash.

She had been nervous. "What if he asks me out for a date?"

"Tell him you've got a boyfriend," said Emily.

"But he won't give it to me."

"Oh, he will."

"What if he won't?"

"Surely there are other places to buy hash."

"Oh, I hate it. Buying drugs."

Emily snorted. "Buying drugs! Oh, no, my dear, we're not buying drugs. We're buying fun. A lot of fun."

"I don't want to. What do I say?"

They spent a disproportionate amount of time talking in this way, wondering how Stockard would ask for drugs and finally their small supply got impossibly small and they made the appointment and Stockard, hoping that acupuncture would calm her nerves, went into the doctor's room first and afterwards, when she was sitting in the reception, working herself up to ask the son, who was still sitting behind the desk, reading a textbook, and she was trying small talk, trying to get him to talk about the Beats, about acupuncture, he cut her off and said, "Your cousin said you liked the present."

"Why, yes! I did. We did. My cousin and me." Stockard actually found herself blushing and smiling and devoid of what to say next. "We did." Her voice trailed off.

"Here then." He came around from behind the desk and handed Stockard another tin foil parcel, this one four or five times the size of the last one.

"Oh! That is so kind." She knew her Southern accent was so thick that it was getting caught in the air between her mouth and his ears, a distance of several feet. How does one say thank you for the gift of drugs? "Thank you. I, um, really appreciate it."

"When you need some more, just call me. My name's Jerry. Call me here."

"Oh, um, thank you." Stockard looked at the foil packet and then thrust it into her coat pocket, thinking that was the place for it, not out in the open, although it could be anything wrapped in tin foil. Brownies. Cake. Something from the acupuncturist. Something medicinal. "Oh, how much do I owe you?"

Stockard was a nervous wreck. She had no idea how these things were supposed to be handled.

"Don't worry about it," said Jerry.

"Don't worry about it!" said Emily when they were on the sidewalk, walking home. "Don't worry about it. Yes, Stockard, don't worry about it. It's all taken care of."

"Did you pay?"

"No. Not money. Jerry and I are meeting at the Guggenheim Saturday for a browse and lunch. I think he's too scared to ask you out for a date, but he asked me."

Too scared. She contemplated the irony of her being nervous about asking for drugs and him being nervous about her beauty. She had missed it, missed it again, but for the next seven months, the girls always had plenty of hash and then Eve and Stockard were off to school. She loved smoking hash, yes, she did.

5

Eve and Stockard had both applied to Berkeley and Stanford. It had come as a surprise when Stockard was accepted to Stanford and not Berkeley and vice versa for her cousin Eve. They would go to school clear across the country from their New York brownstone, but still fifty miles apart.

Their grandmother had arranged for them to share a car.

"Someone on Andrew's staff has it all set up for you," she had explained. "You'll go to the Volvo dealership in Oakland, choose a color and they'll give you a car."

"We're driving a Volvo?" Eve had never shown an interest in cars.

"It's a very safe car," said their grandmother.

Someone from Andrew Forest's staff had also arranged for both girls to have telephones installed in their dorm rooms. This was not typical in 1967, but the staff member had harangued at least two university officials and actually pulled some strings with a Ma Bell board member to make it happen.

The first time Stockard's phone rang and she picked it up to hear her mother's voice, she was stoned.

"It's your mother. I was calling to see how you are."

"Oh, well, um, I'm very well, thank you." Stockard knew she was being unusually formal with her mother.

"Have I called at a bad time?"

"Um, a little bit."

"Well, call me back when you have a moment."

"I will."

"Stockard, I miss you."

"I miss you, too, Mother." Stockard could see them all sitting around the dinner table that night, that omnipresent clan of women. "I miss all of you. Tell grandmother and Aunt Evelyn and Emily I said hello!"

"We love you."

"I love you, too." Stockard replaced the phone on the cradle. She sat there for a moment, the sounds of her residence, Branner Hall, layered around her. A door closed just down the hall, two people talked in a stairwell, people walked in and out of the lobby, passing through arched hallways. She did not know any of those people who were making sounds, a fact that intensified her loneliness, her feeling that all the people in the world who loved her were not there. They were all so very far away. She missed her grandmother and her mother and Aunt Evelyn and Emily, although they already knew that Emily would be coming to Stanford next year. She wanted to be with her family and she felt her heart for the first time. It sank in her chest. This is homesickness, she thought and began to cry.

The next morning Stockard called her mother first thing.

"Sorry 'bout yesterday."

"It's not a problem. I know you're busy. There's so much to do. Are you settling in?"

"Yes, ma'am."

"Do you need anything?"

"No. Uncle Andrew has everything taken care of."

"Is he sending you money?"

"I think so. He said there would be money in an account and gave me a checkbook. The checks don't bounce, so it must be for real."

"He did the same thing for me. Be careful with those checks. One of his bookkeepers used to send me letters warning me not to spend another dime until the first of the month and even then your grandmother said I always spent too much."

"Well, how much can I spend?"

"Oh, I don't know. Why don't you call Uncle Andrew and ask? What courses are you taking this semester?"

Her mother wanted to know everything Stockard was doing. They quickly catalogued Stockard's first semester courses and the books she was reading for classes. Philosophy 101, she said, was a lot of activity for not many answers. Plato, Mill, Descartes. "My professor has a thing for Rousseau's Social Contract. He keeps working in references. I think Rousseau will loom large on the final exam."

"Philosophy treads a fine line between mental masturbation and societal guidepost," her mother said. She had the trick of remembering her own freshman year classes, taken some twenty-five years ago. She remembered what she had read and studied at Sewanee and even what she had thought at the time. It gave Stockard a sense of continuity, as if she was going through the same process of going to college that generations before her had gone through and that she was both a continuation of those generations and also separate, doing it in her own way. Stockard knew she was seeing different things than her mother, especially on the West Coast. Her mother had never been west of the Mississippi.

Stockard tried to describe the rotation of friends she made, her mother reassuring her that this was how the freshman year was. You tried on new friends like clothes at the store and cast them off as easily. The analogy was so true and so familiar that Stockard wondered if her mother was again testing her literary recall. There was getting used to Stanford, the constantly perfect weather, the mission architecture and odd new traditions, like fountain hopping. Stockard tried to describe the parties but carefully avoided the drugs. Everyone smoked pot. A lot of people did other drugs. LSD was very popular.

6

"I HAD this dream," said Stockard down the telephone line, "that Grandmother was with me. We were in the desert. There was this man, a big muscle man, sort of a cross between the Hulk and Jack Lalane, and stranger than that. There was that cartoon quality to him, that reality where the laws of physics do not apply and he was both unreal in how he looked but ferocious, vicious in what he could do. But the funny thing was that Grandmother looked at him and said that if he didn't behave, she would pay to have him neutered and if that didn't elicit good behavior, she would simply have him put down. 'Put down,' that's what she said, like you do a dog. Only it wasn't exactly Grandmother."

"That sounds like your grandmother to me," said her mother. "She just beats up on men…" Her mother often trailed off the last word of a sentence, leaving it to hang out there without the formality of a full stop, sometimes unexpectedly continuing it, "basically threatens castration."

"Uh huh?"

"You know what I'm talking about. You've heard the stories. Workers at one of the mills threatened to unionize. Your grandmother brought in lawyers and people who break up unions and it looked like they would unionize anyway, so she took the sawmill where most of the organizers worked, shut it down, sold the equipment, tore the building down and then sold the land to K-Mart."

"Good Lord," said Stockard. "She actually sold the equipment and tore the building down?"

"And had it all published in the newspaper, right down to how much she sold the land for. We were all surprised that land could sell for that much. It was her way of telling her employees that she could make money with or without them."

"Did it work?"

"Yes, honey, it certainly did. I told her she just as well have burnt the sawmill down and erected a monument to the passing of unions."

This is what dreams did for Stockard. They led her to Fuseli. They led her to her mother, who had taken a new interest in Stockard since she had gone to Stanford. Once she had awoken with the funny image of her grandmother chewing out a hulk man, she did not even bother to get out of bed. She dialed her mother straight away, saying good morning or was it afternoon to Ismelda, and burrowing back into her quilt while the line went humming silent and Ismelda fetched her mother. Her roommate had a boyfriend and was never there. She had even taken her pillow with her. Stockard had the full run of their room and it was a mess she surveyed before her mother came on the line. Clothes were strewn over her roommate's bed, left on the floor, and draped over her desk chair. There was a collection of empty Coke and Miller Lite bottles on flat surfaces.

She had other dreams that she told her mother. There was the one where she was riding with her great-grandfather, Seth Griffin, whom she had never known. He had died thirteen years before she was born. But there he was driving a car in her dream and Stockard was riding in the passenger seat and Seth dropped something on the floorboard. He leaned over to pick it up, completely ignoring the road and Stockard, amused at his absent-mindedness, had taken the wheel while he rooted around on the floor for whatever it was he had dropped.

"That does not sound like your grandfather," her mother had said.

"My great-grandfather?"

"Right. That does not sound like your great-grandfather. Old Seth never let loose of anything, much less steering apparatus."

"What was he like?"

"Tough as shoe leather. I only knew him when he was much older. By then he just walked around Sefer Farm, shooting things and catching fish. I was a little scared of him. He had that air about him, like he could tear you apart. Evelyn used to hunt and fish with him, but we didn't do much together. I hated guns and couldn't stand to touch the fish."

The dreams meant something, Stockard knew that. When she awoke, they were so vivid and the moods they created stayed with her for hours. She could still summon the cold sweat panic of her Nightmare dream and her amusement at Seth ignoring the steering wheel. But understanding them, try as she might, was elusive. Someone was sending a Morse code message from very far away, an important but not urgent message, and she did not understand Morse. Tap tap tap went each dream, entertaining her like an art house movie, illogical and fantastic, and all she could do was watch it and not decipher it.

She had even tried to read some Freud. He was a clear writer and his pieces on dreams and dream interpretation all came down to sex, which she could not stomach. Freud's ideas were like her philosophy class, cold ideas that could be batted about like a beach ball, but really not sticking with her.

Stockard's freshman year was notable, she had decided, for two events. The first was that her hair changed. She woke up one morning, showered and was combing her hair out when she realized that her hair no longer wanted to be parted on the right, but preferred the left. A rolling curve had sprung up, seemingly overnight, that made her hair over her forehead curl luxuriously, like one of the waves off the North Shore of Hawaii. She preferred to towel dry her hair, always had. Blow dryers left her hair dry and looking as if she had just arrived from a windstorm. She would comb it out and let it finish drying naturally. Her hair looked the same slightly damp as dry.

That curl, which now exposed her long forehead, had not been there yesterday. She combed it some more, wondering if it was a fluke. For weeks afterwards, she would look in the mirror at her hair, now parted on the left and with a curl the French would be proud of, and she shook her head. Her body had forced a new coif on her.

The other major event of her freshman year had been the abandonment of her virginity. She could not force herself to use the term "loss." She was not going to lose her virginity. She would not misplace it. Once gone, she would not be able to find it at the Lost and Found. But her virginity was this thing, a being of its own, and it had become oppressive. She had decided that it had become such a nuisance, that it must be abandoned. It must be dumped.

The genesis of this thought, Stockard had decided, could be blamed on the hippies. Stockard liked to think of herself as above such trivial concerns, but sex was everywhere. She was a freshman during 1967 and 1968 and California was aflame with people her own age throwing themselves into hallucinogenics, wispy clothes, nakedness, and a maddening lack of logic. Worst of all and most nagging was Free Love. The hippies pushed sex into her daily almost hourly awareness.

"It's a goddamned nuisance," she would say to herself as she sat in the medical library that spring, studying. Medical students were practically non-existent in the medical library. It was a quiet place to read and a change of surroundings from her room, which could be oppressively monotonous after a couple of hours. But in the silence of the library with spring arriving her mind often wandered. Not that spring arrived in Stanford. The weather was always spring-like. But she thought she felt the laziness of spring in her bones.

Stockard's vision of having a lover was ridiculous, she knew. She tapped a pencil on the books she read, leaving little rainstorms of lead marks on the pages.

"Ridiculous" was a word her grandmother used to dismiss the rising cost of eggs and the ostentation of new money.

Ridiculous as they were, the sweet visions of gentleness, silk sheets and cozy embraces afterwards persisted. It was like a goddamned Jane Austen novel if Jane Austen had written a lovemaking scene, which she certainly had not. Stockard knew her ideas about sex were absurdly wrong. Why would anyone in a Stanford residence have silk sheets? Did they even make silk sheets for single dorm beds? She thought silk sheets were tacky anyway. Yet she could not get the vision out of her head as she first contemplated sex.

The next step was to figure out who would take her nuisance virginity.

Sometimes she thought anyone would do. Just get it over with. Then she would look at available prospects.

"One of the maintenance men leers at me," said Stockard to Emily.

"I am sure all of the maintenance men leer at you," her cousin replied. "Still, that doesn't mean you want them to be your first. Don't you want someone who is… like you? I mean, someone who is, you know, scrubbed and groomed and educated like you? You don't want some smelly old maintenance guy breathing on you. I'll bet they smell like the homeless."

She could talk to Emily about these things. Emily was still in New York, finishing her senior year at Morary's and safeguarding the dragon pipe. Stockard had no problem finding marijuana at Stanford. Emily would come back to Stanford with Stockard next year, but until then, they phoned each other at odd times, often in the dead of the New York night, when Emily, always, was awake. It helped to talk to Emily.

"Well, I don't want to be slutty with someone I know, I don't think," said Stockard to Emily.

"Slutty. That's a word my mother would use."

"Yeah, I guess. Used the way she does, it means that nearly every girl at Stanford is slutty."

"The times, they are a changing," said Emily. She was going through a Bob Dylan period, her coffee house manners somehow being set to folk music.

They covered all of the topics. Would it be painful as reported? Would she get pregnant even with a condom? Would he have a condom? She could not bring herself to buy condoms. Emily enjoyed the speculation about her virginity abandonment more than she did.

Stockard did not share one worry with Emily. Would people be able to tell she was no longer a virgin?

An especially stupid question. She knew that her rationality was coming off the rails. If people could tell she was no longer a virgin then they could tell she was a virgin now. She couldn't look at other people and know if they were or were not virgins. Was it something that only ex-virgins knew? It was a ridiculous notion and she kept putting it out of her mind.

Stockard found an extra joint a day helped to take the edge off her thoughts.

One Thursday night, about a week into her hailstorm of distracting thoughts, when really it felt like not a week but a goddamned eternity, pages of textbooks littered with lead marks and the ends of pencils chewed into irregular golf ball patterns, Stockard was drawn to a room party down the hall, where some of the partygoers had gathered outside, cups in hand, joint in the open. She recognized Melody and Nancy, roommates two doors down. Melody's great-grandfather had worked on the railroads and Melody herself had one foot in San Francisco's Chinatown and one foot in Golden Gate Park. Stanford, Stockard knew, was the next step on her family's socio-economic climb. Melody was one of the more regular drifters into Stockard's social life.

Nancy was a San Diego beach girl. Stockard had still not figured how or why she was at Stanford. The three stood in the doorway criticizing their Survey of Western Literature teacher's choice of ties. Stanford teachers generally did not wear ties. A hopeful boy, skinny with hands shoved into jean pockets, stood mutely to the side.

"Well, I'll just excuse myself to the bar, Ladies," said Stockard as she walked into the room, automatically taking the can of Schlitz proffered to her. She was saying things to people and smiling and nodding, but she found that she had no idea what she was saying, because one of the room's residents, her presumed host, Jake something or another, was on the periphery of her vision.

Jake was a fellow freshman. He was careful and nice. He was good looking, too. He was very much of the same mold as herself. He had been raised conservatively in Boston, his one act of rebellion was in not going to Harvard as the men in his family had for three generations. He, too, still dressed as he would have at home, wearing plaid Bermudas, a Lacoste shirt and boat shoes. Neither Jake nor Stockard had given in to the wispy clothes of the time.

There were a lot of smiling guys and girls. Everywhere. She knew them all and had that sensation of being in the middle of people she knew, but each from a different place, from different classes or Branner or the medical library, where serious students studied.

Jake was more a drinker than a stoner. Stockard had needled her way into a small circle of familiar faces who were passing a joint. She was eager for a few more tokes as she felt the tension begin to increase between herself and Jake. She could feel him in the room, even when she couldn't see him. And then Jake was sitting next to her, at first hardly able to make eye contact and then drunk enough to have flowing conversation with her. Stockard was not a bit surprised. It had all gone to plan.

Had she planned this, she asked herself. Had she decided to let Jake relieve her of her virginity? The questions ran along a parallel track in her mind, in the background, as he smiled. He had such nice teeth.

Hardly without bidding, Jake followed Stockard back to her room. She had used the pretense of getting more dope, although her head swam as they walked down the hallway. Once back in her room, she fished her stash out of her desk and rolled one last joint—she told herself it was for good measure—and then offered Jake a beer and a toke. He took both and somewhere in the sipping and toking they found their way to each other, locked in a rolling kiss.

Jake broke away. "You are so beautiful, Stockard."

"Thank you." She leaned back in to kiss him, now too nervous, despite her advanced stage of being stoned, to know what a better response would be. She thought, sometimes you run out of things to say. The thought tickled her and she giggled a little, her eyelids opening to see Jake, up close, as if she were peering at him through a microscope, the pores of his high-bred skin looking like a plastic sponge, the muscles of his face working slowly with the kiss.

Jake broke away again. "I need to run off for a second." He stood up and looked towards the door. "That dope's really good." He took a step. "I don't normally smoke that stuff." He took another step. "Goes to your head."

Stockard was now a million miles away. She had smoked way too much dope and found that mixing it with booze had resulted in a kind of paralysis, she hovering ever so slightly above the scene, like the newly dead, unable to do or say anything. She saw Jake put one foot in front of the other, he did a sort of lumbering walk and took maybe three or four steps before he fell to his knees in front of the trashcan and began throwing up, without restraint.

Despite the violence of his throwing up, Jake managed to do it with some style, one knee on the floor, one hand on the floor, as if he was bowing to a queen. The other hand was on the trashcan. Stockard wondered what was in the trashcan. A corrected draft of a history paper, "A Survey of European Kings," for her Western Civ class. A couple of empty beer cans. Maybe an old tampon box. When had she last emptied it?

It would now need to be emptied and washed out, she thought, and it would probably smell anyway.

Jake finished throwing up, stood up while wiping his mouth with his left hand, turned to Stockard and said, "Sorry."

She smiled at him. It was a benevolent, distant smile. She still did not know what to say nor could she have gotten her mouth to create the sounds if she had.

"I think I'll…" Jake threw himself on her roommate's bed and then unceremoniously passed out, head thrown to the side, mouth open, his eyes clinched shut.

Stockard, laid out on her own bed like an immobile patient on a gurney, drifted into sleep shortly afterwards.

7

AFTER the Griffin women had made their way to FDR to watch fireworks and then tried futilely to hail a cab, Stockard's grandmother had said, "I'm ready to go home."

She was not complaining about the lack of cabs on the 4th of July. She did not want to return to their brownstone. She was done with New York City and wanted to return to Sefer Farm. That was home.

They were back at the farm three days later. Stockard, her mother and her grandmother had taken a train. The farm was distant from everywhere.

Stockard had found in her grandfather's hangar—an old barnlike structure built forty years ago to house a couple of barnstormers—an invitation to Seth Griffin's annual turkey shoot, an event that figured often in her grandmother's recollections of Sefer Farm. Her grandmother would still hold the occasional turkey shoot, always complaining about the bother. "It is a men's event," she had said, "and I only do it when I need to reach out to certain men in business. They are still shocked to see that I can shoot."

On the invitation were the directions to Sefer Farm. "Twenty-five minutes outside of Nashville on the Murfreesboro Road you'll pass Kimbro and in less than five minutes look for a navy blue gate in the middle of a thick forest on the left. Go through the gate and shut it behind you, please. The house is at the end of the road."

That blue gate. Now it was motorized. Stockard had been very young when brick walls had been built on either side of the gate and the long road to the farmhouse had been paved, the black asphalt growing paler every year. Rose, who was the third generation of women in her family to keep house for the Griffins, and her husband Ebern had cleaned and livened up the house. They had been caretaking Sefer Farm for the past two years. Before Rose, there had been Rose's mother, Cissy, who had been her grandmother's age. Lilly had been Rose's grandmother, who had actually helped midwife

Stockard's grandmother into this world. They had all at one point or another taken care of Sefer Farm and they and their husbands had been buried in Sefer Farm's cemetery. It had been Ebern who had picked them up from the train station. Once Ebern had parked the farm Suburban at the front, Stockard had carried her formless duffle bag against Ebern's pleas to her room.

Her mother had disappeared "for a bath and a nap." Her grandmother had marched into her office "to catch up on work." They had just spent two days on a train together in close quarters and given the first chance, they dispersed.

Stockard threw her duffle onto her bed, dug around for a pair of shorts and a sleeveless shirt and then changed. She retraced her steps back through the house, the same path that she had taken on the morning that she had learned of Abe's suicide.

She walked down the hallway that connected the family's bedrooms, through the doorway into the living room, the massive fireplace anchoring the sofas and chairs, still holding their positions three years later. Here in passing was her first feeling that Sefer Farm was something special. She had the sense of coming home as the scenery from the train had changed from industrial rolling hills to wooded land. When the train had arrived at the Nashville train station, she knew she was getting closer and closer to something so familiar. Those blue gates that announced Sefer Farm, those too had stirred a powerful sense of returning to a place she knew as well as any. But as she made her way towards the library, her spine tingled with Sefer Farm. She had grown up in this house, had crawled on these floors. So had her mother. So had her grandmother. And that towering figure of Griffin mythology, Seth Griffin, he had built this house. It was hers. It was theirs. It was a part of her and she kept the house alive and would continue to keep the house living and breathing and in this realization, the two woke up together at that moment and embraced each other, Stockard slowing her pace, uncertain

whether to stop and focus on the moment or continue to where she
knew she had to go and collect the feeling in a net, to look at later.

She walked into the hallway that connected the kitchen and the
library and into the library, which had recently been dusted and polished, the mounted heads of deer, elk, moose and a single grizzly
bear, all staring down on her. They were trophies from her great-
grandfather's midlife hunting trips, frozen in time, hardly the gnash-
ing massive vicious beasts that Seth Griffin had set out to track and
kill. On a low shelf were the art books, and her mother's book was
there. She grabbed the dictionary of artistic symbols next to it and
a Merriam-Webster dictionary from another shelf. All three were
reference books, large and heavy, and before she was out on the back
porch, Stockard could feel the weight in her arms. She kept walking.

The farmhouse was built on the highest spine where three rolling
hills came together. From the top of the farmhouse, Stockard could
see into the three coves that the hills made. One cove held the entrance road to the farm. Another cove held her grandfather's hangar,
the barn-like structure. The field had been graded for an airplane to
take off and land, although none had done so in Stockard's lifetime.
Ebern trimmed the field every two weeks with a tractor and a Bush
Hog when it grew. The third cove held the actual barn on the farm,
where horses and hay and tack were kept. Ebern kept a few chickens nearby for the eggs. Her grandmother had said that they used
to keep pigs, chickens and occasionally sheep as food and that the
field next to the barn had been plowed once, all part of keeping the
farm inhabitants fed. Now food came from the Kimbro grocery store.
Even the horses had been sold when they moved to New York. It was
an unused barn.

There was an oak tree that looked down onto the barn cove, and
that is where Stockard headed with her cache of books, her arms
hurting a little more with each step. Stockard had always loved sitting under the oak tree. The sun would set over the hills across from
the tree. It was the prettiest of the three coves. The house could not

be seen from the oak tree, but Stockard could see anyone who approached it, giving her the same sense of privacy and security as a soldier in a foxhole. She sat down, looking around. Her great-grandfather had planted rows of such trees, strong ones, walnuts, oaks, all along the spines of these hills, and they were now mature big trees, looking all the more massive at the tops of the hills. She looked around and felt again the peace of returning home, the moment of comfort, of being where everything was known, had been known for years and years and years.

She picked up her mother's art book. It was the 1948 version of *Gardner's Art Through The Ages*. She found Fuseli in the index. Swiss born. Lived in England. She turned the page to the plate of *The Nightmare*. An incubus squatting on a sleeping woman, a horse poking its head through a curtain. The horse's eyes were bulging and crazy. She looked at the picture for a long time.

There was nothing in the symbols dictionary about the incubus, but horses as symbols had a lengthy entry. Carriers of life and death. Possession. Initiation. Horse sacrifice. Water-god. Driving force of the libido. Horse of the sun. Horse majestic. Steed of the gods. She read the entry, nothing standing out.

Then she went back to the Gardner's plate of *The Nightmare*. There it was. She had not even bothered to read the accompanying text. Fuseli specializes in night moods of horror and gothic fantasies, in the demonic, the macabre, the sadistic.

The text ended with, "Fuseli's art is near the start of an enterprise that will lead to the uncovering of the dark terrain of the human subconscious."

"Point noted," said Stockard to herself. She knew of Freud's definition of the subconscious from her dream interpretation reading, but it was vague at this moment. The dictionary was of no help. "Beyond consciousness." She would have to revisit her Freud volumes or root around at a bookstore for a better definition.

She tried "incubus" in the dictionary.

"1. An evil spirit believed to descend upon and have sexual intercourse with sleeping women."

Stockard looked up. It was late on a summer afternoon, the sun having done the most damage it could have. It was always humid in Tennessee in the summer. Sweat had formed on her forehead and beaded just above her lip. Her back was damp. She looked back at the barn and realized it was the barn of her nightmare. There had been no horses nor incubi in her dreams. There had been a presence in the barn, and whatever it was, it reminded her of this painting, of Fuseli's nightmare.

She looked at the barn. She should go down there, she decided. Go to the barn and see if she could conjure up the presence that had been her dream. Would it scare her? She tried to imagine entering the barn, the heat, the crawling creatures that were part of a barn in the South, the smell of the hay and the dirt.

It dawned on her, slowly. Her dream had been about sex. Was that it?

For three years she had remembered the dream. She had similar dreams where a dark presence weighed on her, but nothing as explicit as her Nightmare. It had continued and stayed with her and she had known all along that she would return to Sefer Farm and spend this moment trying to understand what it was that had woken her in such a panic and now it was all perfectly obvious. It had been about sex, sex as demon creature, the horse as the appetite, preying upon her, and it had bubbled up from some deep dark place to haunt her, just as Fuseli's image must have haunted him and only now, three years later, could she put it together. How strange and wonderful the human mind is, she thought to herself as she pulled a slightly bent and wrinkled joint out of her pocket and lit it. It was her moment alone, while everyone else was settling back home and tomorrow the routines would begin again. For a moment her world stopped and she watched as the sun continued its descent towards the hill, disappearing behind the row of hardwoods which her great-grandfather had planted.

She was jelly under the oak tree and dozed off, waking up to dread the walk back up to the house, hating that she had brought three enormous books to lug, all the heavier in the wake of being high.

Rose was in the kitchen, scraping and banging. Stockard could smell buttermilk biscuits in the oven and chicken being pan fried. She was stuck between this world, where she was home again and the familiar would be her daily life until the end of August and that world, the world of her nightmare, something that she understood as a fact, a dream about sex, but whose very presence, despite being understood, continued to haunt her.

The smell of the food made her stomach jump.

8

THE back porch on the farmhouse was where people gathered at night unless the weather was too cold. In the summers it was a cool, covered place that was tucked between the kitchen and her grandmother's bedroom, and its deck spilled past the house, allowing nooks and crannies where naps could be had or a book could be read. There were rocking chairs, a few wooden arm chairs with tied cushions, a porch swing and a porch bed. Stockard and her mother spent their evenings out there, drinking beer and one evening talking about Abe's suicide.

It had been a taboo subject in the brownstone and even when Stockard called her mother from Stanford, she knew that to have her mother talk about it while still in the brownstone was a foolish move on her part. So she had let it be.

Despite her implicit agreement with her grandmother to be honest with each other, when Stockard had asked why Abe killed himself, her grandmother had said, "Some things do not need to be talked about." Stockard knew that when her grandmother left prepositions hanging, she was uncomfortable. All her grandmother would say was that Abe "made a mess of things and took the cowardly way out." And she would only say that when it was just the two of them.

Her mother was more forthcoming that night in August, before Stockard would return to Stanford for her sophomore year. It was the kind of conversation she would not be able to have because Emily would be her roommate.

Uncle Abe had kept a mistress in Greenwich Village. It wasn't just he. Another man, someone he knew through business, had helped keep the woman, too, paying for her apartment.

"It was a bit lewd," said her mother. "She was a rough woman, into strange things, weird sex. I gather the two men shared the woman. There's probably more to it. A great deal more."

42

Stockard had to weigh whether or not to ask what constituted weird sex and finally decided against it. "How did they know her?"

"Your Uncle Abe was involved with several arts things. Foundations. Councils. From what we can tell, he met her through one of those. She wasn't an artist, but apparently could always be found with artists. Whatever that means."

"So Uncle Abe was having an affair and that's why he killed himself?" She looked at her mother, who would stare out into the night when she wasn't talking.

"They were into other things, drugs mainly. He had started to do drugs. Hallucinogenics. Peyote. Mescaline. LSD. And not in his spare time. He started going to work on them."

"No!" Stockard was trying to imagine Uncle Abe in one of his suits, tripping at work amongst other suited bankers.

"Yes. No one could tell. Some people later said he was distracted and looked tired, but no one suspected heavy drug use. When your Aunt Evelyn finally found out..."

"How did she find out?"

"Oh, the other man, the one who helped keep the woman, he finally had a nervous breakdown. He had a heart attack, ended up first in the hospital and then in the nut house. He was under pressure. His wife found out and then came and told Evelyn. Somehow Abe found out that she knew and he went out to their farmhouse. He couldn't even face Evelyn. He just killed himself when he knew the game was up."

"It seems like an excessive reaction."

"Sometimes the world is too much. If he was suffering for a long time, if whatever it was that sent his friend off the edge had been eating at Abe and then he found out that his wife had found out. And you know what a tough cookie Evelyn can be. Then maybe it was the only way he could see. In many of the Asian cultures, in Ancient Greece, it was the honorable thing to do, to knock yourself off rather than face the world with such shame."

Now that was power, thought Stockard. If someone would rather kill himself than face Aunt Evelyn, then Aunt Evelyn had real power.

"People don't know what they do to people. I think suicide is essentially a selfish act," said her mother. "He left behind two daughters. If nothing else, he should have thought of his daughters. Eve has become so bitter and withdrawn. She's sold out to the hippies."

Stockard knew her mother's information about Eve was second hand, mainly from herself. She had seen Eve every two or three weeks during their freshman year. Eve hadn't even wanted the car so Stockard would drive to Berkeley, usually on a Saturday and spend the night with Eve in her dorm room.

Emily had become even more Emily. "Emily on the other hand is clever. If anything, she has taken her grief out in her art. She spends so much time painting and drawing, especially late at night, even when she talks to you." Her mother took a sip of beer and crossed her legs the other way. "I always liked Abe. You could tell that circumstances had wound him tighter than he liked. I think given the chance and in the right…"

While Stockard's mother was searching for the right word, Stockard looked into the darkness of the night. Off the porch she could hear the slow tweets and twitters of a warm Southern night. These people who she knew all her life, they still surprised her.

"Given the right environment, Abe could have enjoyed life more. His family was terribly old fashioned. Strict Jews. Those people he worked with, bankers, they were not the most free of people. Some of them were downright mean. He used to call them Barracudas. And then there's Evelyn. She can be so tough, and I think if Abe had someone a bit softer at home, the rest of it wouldn't have been so bad. It must have been terrible."

Stockard continued to look into the darkness as a silence settled over them. She thought her mother must be talking about herself, too. There was no one soft around her, either. Only Stockard and Emily, and only now that they were all grown up. Stockard felt sad for her because the two people she felt most comfortable with would soon be far away from her. Her mother was being left behind, left on Sefer Farm with her own mother, who even now at that late hour was in her study, working. As soon as Stockard thought of her grandmother, she materialized on the porch with a bourbon on ice in a silver cup. Those silver cups and a giant silver water pitcher were fixtures of the farm.

She looked at Stockard and her mother, taking in the beer bottles, and said, "I still think of beer as something you have with lunch. If you are a man. I can remember in England, they all drank beer at lunch. In France, it is wine."

"I dare not drink at lunch," said Stockard's mother.

Stockard knew what she meant. It was too easy being drunk all the time. Stockard had the same problem with dope. It would be too easy being stoned all the time. She had to set her own boundaries and lunch was out for imbibing.

Her grandmother dug around in a pocket and produced a pack of Salems and a lighter, offering a cigarette to Stockard and her mother. They all three puffed their cigarettes red, Stockard and her mother leaning back into their chairs.

It was a routine. The evenings always ended up like this, Stockard's mother talking about what she was reading, usually salacious history. Her reports on Nero and Caligula had sent them into peels of laughter when horror should have been the correct response. Sometimes her grandmother would retell a bit of family history, the story of how Seth Griffin won the silver pitcher or how Evelyn had sold her birthday horse for a profit when they found out his father was a racing winner.

Afterwards, often while Stockard sat in bed and read, and before she went to sleep, she would think about how the three of them lived together. Despite how close Stockard had become with her mother in the last year, it was her grandmother who still dominated the conversation, a fact that made Stockard wonder where her mother had been until she was eighteen years old. She had been physically present, but it was not until Stockard had gone off to school, had escaped, that her mother had shown any real interest in Stockard. It was difficult for her to reconcile the two feelings. On the one hand she was so glad to have discovered her mother, a witty and warm friend. On the other hand, this same person, her very own mother, had not taken much interest in raising her.

9

STOCKARD returned to Stanford for her sophomore year with Emily, now a freshman and her roommate. They heard from her mother every other day. Sometimes her mother would catch Emily while Stockard was at class and the two would talk, confirming Stockard's suspicion that while Emily and her mother lived at the brownstone, they had grown close.

But the voice that was so persistent in Stockard's head was her grandmother's, even though they did not talk nearly as often as Stockard did with her mother. It was a trick of her imagination, she figured. By not having as much contact with her grandmother, she had recreated her. And at the oddest times. In the oddest ways.

Her grandmother's voice came to her on a Saturday afternoon in the spring of her sophomore year. Emily and she had driven across the Bay Bridge to visit Eve, part of their weekend routine to sit on Eve's sofa in her off-campus apartment. There they drank beer and smoked dope and made occasional forays into Eve's Berkeley social circle.

Emily emerged from Eve's kitchen and said, "Who drank the last beer?"

Emily and Eve looked at Stockard, whose beer still had the condensation on the can. "Okay. I guess I did."

"You're the pack mule," said Emily. It was a rule that whoever had the last beer had to go out and get more.

Ten minutes later Stockard found herself at the 7-Eleven, alone, staring at the beer fridge. A man next to her had been eyeing the beer cooler, too. He was big and dirty and looked as if he had just worked a day at construction. It was his body odor that stood out to her. It smelled like honest work, like something she would smell around Griffin Lumber, the family lumber business that her great-grandfather had started. For a moment, she could smell woodchips and sap and grease. All of those machines, the rip saws, the forklifts, the trucks, they had all needed grease.

He caught Stockard looking at him. He did a double take and realized that this college co-ed, young and beautiful and somehow more carefully put together than any woman he had ever seen, who he knew was wholly out of his reach, was looking at him, taking him in.

"You want to play, little girl?"

It took a moment for the euphemism to register with Stockard.

"You look like you're interested," he said.

Stockard was having problems pulling away from the smell of her childhood, a very particular slice of her world. "Oh… no, thank you."

"You look like you're not so sure."

Was that a Boston accent? "No, no, sorry," she said, finally coming out of her little trip down memory lane. "I was just… you look like someone I know."

"That's a sexy accent you got."

"Thank you," said Stockard, grabbing a six pack of Budweiser from the refrigerator. Her grandmother's voice, clear as a bell, said, "There's nothing wrong with him." She hesitated, feeling the heat in her cheeks. Confused, she made her way a bit too hastily past the rack of potato chips and a tub of Slim Jims to pay at the counter. She could feel his eyes on her all the way out of the store and she did not look back, jumping into the Volvo and driving away. Too quickly she would later believe.

It would remain with her for the rest of her life. He was not her type, and yet she had been powerfully drawn to him. There was a moment when she had actually considered going with him and letting him do with her whatever he wanted. The loss of control, the being ravaged, the whole scenario had stoked her imagination. She wondered if he drove a truck and would he have taken her on the truck seat. She could see his dirty fingers against her white flesh.

48

And what the hell did her grandmother say to her? Her grandmother wouldn't even consider a man like that. Would she?

In her constant analysis of the scene, she had fled because she was simply fearful of not knowing what to do, more so than doing it with him. She told no one about the incident. What could she have said?

10

A T the time, Stockard's sophomore, junior and senior years looked very different. In retrospect, they looked all the same, except the last two months of her senior year. Emily and Stockard had the same Branner Hall room all three years and the same telephone, a worn black rotary dialer with a grey metal dialing ring.

In her junior year, Stockard returned feeling that Stanford was so familiar, a lesser version of how she felt about Sefer Farm. Hoover Tower, Palm Drive, and the Claw were all part of the scenery now, expected and invoking a sense of comfort. The foothills behind the campus buildings were unlike Tennessee foothills. Tennessee was plush and wooded. Stanford was bare and scrubby. It was the kind of detail that would remind her that she was not at home at Stanford, not like at Sefer Farm.

Even their friends had been whittled down and honed to no more than half a dozen Fine Arts students, diehards from her sophomore year, mostly girls. Boys came and went and never penetrated the circle of Griffin women.

It was a Saturday morning in March of her senior year and Stockard woke up in her Branner bed smelling Rose's soup, being cooked some 2,000 miles away. A sit-down Saturday lunch had been her grandmother's tradition for a very long time. They would cook steaks and baked potatoes tomorrow night. She wondered what kind of soup Rose had cooked. Rose had so many soups. Vegetable, cream of broccoli, onion and split-pea. Stockard thought a big breakfast might be in order.

Emily was already at the studio, having left art books open around their room. She often liked to be in the studio when it opened at 7:00 AM. She said it was the best time to work, early in the morning. Saturdays and Sundays were especially good because so few students were in the studios on the weekends.

Stockard believed Emily awoke full of hormones, making it the best time to work. Emily would return just before noon, looking like someone who had labored, spent and ready for lunch. Then they would make their way to Berkeley to see Eve.

Stockard was much slower in the mornings.

She showered and settled in front of the mirror in her green bathrobe to brush out her hair. She was just running a last brush through when the door to her room opened and in walked a man with his head down.

He was saying, "Are you ready," as he picked his head up.

At first all Stockard saw were his pink trousers. They had tiny green frogs embroidered on them. His green golf shirt matched the green of the frogs. She then looked at his face. He had cheek bones that would cut leather and a head of carefully coiffed blond hair that spelled California Beach.

He was doing his own observation, taking Stockard in from head to toe and then back up again.

"Well, hello," said Stockard. Moved by she knew not what, Stockard found herself taking two steps towards the intruder, dressed for golf. "Snappy trousers."

Like a trashy romance novel, Stockard thought to herself, the man took three steps towards her and the two came together in one swift motion, dancers coming together on the dance floor. That was how Stockard, one March Saturday of her senior year, lost her virginity, finally. She did not so much lose it as throw it to Mills Andrew. "Shouldn't it be Andrew Mills instead of Mills Andrew?" Stockard would ask afterwards.

"Logically, it should be," said Mills, whose Southern accent was now apparent. "But my mamma's maiden name was Mills and it's a family tradition. The second born son takes his mother's maiden name."

"Bit of a bummer if your mother's maiden name is Petunia."

The two giggled for a moment. Stockard was well familiar with customs of the South and in the familiarity she found herself, the silence after the laugh giving her a moment to think and want, pulling Mills back on top of her. The first time had hurt but it was a hurt that came with a pleasure subtle, explosive, warm, hot, varied in a thousand delicious ways in an instant.

"Are you okay," he asked.

"I think it's stopped." Stockard had spent sometime in the bathroom cleaning up the mess of her deflowering.

"Is that normal?"

"I don't know," said Stockard.

Mills sat up in bed. "You mean this is your first time? Was your first time?"

"Well," said Stockard, "if you have to know, yes, it was."

"We don't even know each other, do we?" He drew out the "do" to "dooo."

"No, I don't think we do. Do you know Emily?"

"Who is Emily?"

"My roommate. She's also my cousin."

"No. I was looking for Chad."

"Chad lives next door."

"Does he?" Mills was smiling now, maneuvering himself back into Stockard. "Well… what a mistake."

11

WITH two months until graduation, Stockard should have been busy saying goodbye to her undergraduate years. She should have been drifting to a stop in her studies, enjoying the last moments of college friendships and looking at her surroundings wistfully. It was not the time for her to be forming new attachments.

At nine o'clock, Mills poked his head into Stockard's room, took one look around and said, "Oh, sorry, wrong room." Then he pulled his head out of the room and closed the door.

"What a handsome stranger," said Emily.

"He certainly is," said Stockard.

"Did you get a load of those trousers?" Emily was flipping through an issue of *Art News*.

Mills had been wearing green trousers with yellow bumble bees.

"Reminds me of home," said Stockard.

It was the second Saturday after Stockard and Mills had their first encounter. The previous Saturday Mills had again walked in "mistakenly," this time at nine o'clock.

"Our tee time is at 10:30. I'm supposed to get Chad at 10:00. I thought I might come visit you an hour earlier," he had explained.

"Oh, you did, did you Mr. Andrew? Don't you think that's a bit presumptuous?" Stockard was in her familiar green bathrobe.

"Maybe I just wanted to talk, you know, to get to know you better."

"That," said Stockard sliding off her robe, "would be a shame." She dove into her bed.

Stockard was not ready to come clean with Emily and Eve about no longer being a virgin nor how it had happened. Stockard and Mills sought each other for an hour on Saturday mornings, fleeting pleasures as casually taken as a walking ice cream and nothing else. It had come out that Mills was in a marriage-bound relationship with a hometown sweetheart in Winston-Salem. He was surprisingly non-committal about his upcoming marriage and did not express any clear signs of emotion about the girl. Stockard thought he might just be playing it cool for her sake. He was supposed to go to the University of North Carolina law school and then join his father's firm to carry on the family practice.

Stockard planned on spending the summer with her mother and grandmother on Sefer Farm. Beyond that, she had no idea what the future held.

The Saturday after Mills aborted his visit, he came through the door again at nine o'clock sharp.

"Oh, sorry, wrong room again," he said.

"Hah hah, she's gone to the studio," said Stockard. "Please, get in here."

Stockard had read that the breath was the one earthly sign of the soul. To kiss was to have two souls mingle. She believed it now. Mills' breath was minty fresh on Saturday mornings. At ten he would part as he had come, with a kiss.

With three weeks until graduation, Stockard watched her alarm clock tick past 10:15 and then 10:30 before saying to Mills, "You'll miss your tee time."

"No golf today."

They were lounging in Stockard's single bed, which was more than roomy enough for them. Stockard had started to dread Mills' ten o'clock departures on Saturday mornings. He would leave her bed, pulling on his brightly colored trousers, run his fingers through his hair, it apparently springing back to perfection without so much as a glance in the mirror. Then he would be gone. As their Saturday assignations had continued, Mills departures began to leave a void behind, a lonely fast cooling impression on her bed.

"Oh," she said.

Mills had turned on his side to look into Stockard's eyes. "I thought we could spend some more time together."

"Oh."

"Is that okay? Do you have other plans?"

Stockard tried her most serious look and said in a deadpan voice, "I would like nothing better."

"We don't have to." Mills had expected a smile, at least.

Stockard had never seen Mills hesitant nor apprehensive.

She wanted to dismiss him, send him back to his room and explain that it would be bad for them to spend any more time together. Graduation was just around the corner. After that, they would not see each other again. It was a thought that began to worry her. She knew that she would miss Mills very badly. She would miss not just the sex, but more so the banter, the strange relaxed conversation which Stockard would believe, starting from this moment, to be the cornerstone of any good relationship with a man.

It was the thought of graduation and the ending of all that she had enjoyed that forced a smile to her face. "I'm just teasing."

They decided to drive to Carmel for lunch to avoid Emily's return.

From that moment until the Thursday before graduation, they spent every possible moment together.

"I wish," said Stockard after a long lovemaking session, "well, you know."

"That we'd done this more than just on Saturday mornings?" They were already in a routine, spending the afternoons at Mills' room. He had a single in Roble Hall. They would risk Stockard's room only when Emily was out, which was often with the final frenzy leading up to exams.

"Yes. That's it." They were in bed, Stockard lying on top of Mills, her head buried in the pillow to the side of his head. "I thought it might be too… ensnaring? Confining?" She had a way of timing the words, feeling his heart beat under her, she would allow two beats, and then say the word. "Conventional. Committed. Undesirable."

Mills was running his left hand through her hair. "I thought you didn't want me around. That I was convenient. On Saturday mornings. Only."

"If you had walked into the wrong room when I was a freshman, it would have been inconvenient. Your timing was perfect."

Stockard stopped studying and abandoned herself to Mills. Somewhere in the anticipation of seeing him the next time, in her utter contentment at being with him and at the pain of leaving him when she would tear herself away for a moment at her room, Stockard realized she was in love.

Her first great love eclipsed everything else, making the beauty of Stanford in the hot spring an accessory to her brilliant mood. Food was irrelevant. A terrible pressure was being exerted on her heart.

It was unbearable as graduation came closer and closer.

Stockard and Mills had set aside the Thursday before graduation to spend the afternoon and evening together. At one o'clock that afternoon, Mills called her.

"Hey," Mills whispered.

"Hey," Stockard whispered back, thinking it was a game.

"My parents showed up," said Mills.

"I thought they were supposed to," said Stockard.

"I wasn't supposed to see them until tomorrow morning."

"Oh… Well, what do you want to do?"

"I want to come see you."

"Maybe we could squeeze a quickie in," said Stockard. "Why are you whispering?"

"We're at Kip's." It was a restaurant just off campus. "They're a couple of tables away."

There was an awkward moment of silence. Stockard knew something was wrong.

"Mills, don't worry about it. If we can see each other, that's great, but there's no reason to put anybody off. Your parents are probably so proud. My mother and grandmother will be here tomorrow anyway. Hopefully we can catch up sometime later."

"Got a pen handy," Mills asked.

"Yes, sir."

"Take this down." Mills gave Stockard his parents' address in Winston-Salem. "If worse comes to worse… I'll try to sneak out and see you."

"Like Romeo and Juliet!"

"Hah hah. I gotta go. They'll be wondering where I am."

"Bye."

"Bye."

What Stockard wanted to say was, "I love you." Her every instinct was to tell him that she loved him and that she wanted to meet his parents and she wanted to break up his relationship with his girl-friend and be with him and the world be damned.

Stockard smoked a joint, the first one in more than three weeks, and was asleep within an hour, a long deep dead sleep. She awoke feeling disoriented. She wished that she had woken with Mills at her side. She loved falling asleep with his warm long body next to her. She loved waking up, hearing him breathe. Once he had woken her up by making love to her.

She decided she'd just wander by his residence to see if she could catch a glimpse of him. If she could not be with him, she might at least see him. That, she thought, might provide some relief.

There he was, standing right next to his parents, talking just out-side the front door of Roble Hall.

Next to him was a girl, a little younger than he. Stockard knew that Mills did not have a sister. Stockard also knew the type well. In her silk headband and sleeveless oxford shirt, the girl was Chapel Hill sorority to a tee. She kept rubbing her hand on Mills' shoulder. Mills was intent on talking with his parents. He knew the girl's touch.

Stockard was walking parallel to Roble when she stopped to look at the scene.

That bastard didn't even have the balls to tell her that his girl-friend had shown up. She knew something like this would happen. She would get hurt. It was stupid because Stockard knew all along that Mills had a serious girlfriend. He had been honest up front. She had liked the moment and had never thought that someone else's claim on Mills would disturb her in the least. But it did! Now the pressure she felt around her chest changed to a searing burn and the first tear welled up.

She was in plain sight. If Mills turned his head to the left and raised his eyes, he would surely see her. Then what? Would he come rushing over to her and explain the situation? Would he apologize and explain to his fiancée, right there in front of his parents, that he did not love her, that he loved Stockard.

Stockard was wondering what his fiancée would do. Would she get on the next plane back to Chapel Hill? Would she stay in spite of the betrayal? How awkward would that be?

Mills would not be so callous. Despite the exposure, despite being seen any second, Stockard kept running the possibilities through her head, cursing the haze of a nap and a joint. It occurred to her that nothing good could come out of this confrontation. Mills simply might ignore her, or worse, introduce her as a "friend." Stockard would have to sit there and make nice to his fiancée. It was this thought that made her do a quick about-face and walk back to Branner Hall.

As soon as she walked through the door, the phone rang.

She hoped it was Mills. He had seen her and was calling to explain that his girlfriend had shown up unexpectedly with his parents and that he had to play the good boyfriend for now. But he would sneak out to see Stockard later. She willed a tear back into her eye and cleared her sinuses before picking up the phone, saying, "Hello?"

Sefer Farm

1

"I HATE to sound like an ingrate, especially after you bought the horses, but could we have air conditioning?"

Margaret looked at her granddaughter Stockard, who had just asked the question. They were in the tack room of the barn. Stockard was taking off the thick dried pink emollient from the saddles and reins that was used for long-term storage and rubbing in saddle soap. She loved the smell of the tack room. Musty barn, nice leather.

This must have been what it was like when Margaret, 21 years old, had asked her own father if she could look at the Griffin Lumber books. When Margaret asked Seth for anything, no matter what it was, he gave it to her. It had been her own mother who had cautioned her against being spoiled. Margaret looked at Stockard buffing a saddle. There wasn't much chance that her granddaughter was going to be spoiled. She was all grown up now, freshly graduated from Stanford and moping around the farm. That was why she had bought horses, to give Stockard and Eve and Emily something else to do. To cheer them up. Eve and Emily would spend all of July at Sefer Farm. It would be a full house.

Margaret did not really want air conditioning. She knew what it would mean for the house. Duct work would have to be retrofitted. Some of the carefully fitted woodwork would be damaged or have to go. The air conditioning unit was a big, noisy, expensive thing.

"Well, certainly we can," said Margaret. "I don't know why I haven't put air conditioning in yet. While I'm at it, I'll put central heating in, too." It had taken her five years after her father's death to get the farmhouse to look and function how she wanted. Now she was about to mess it up for her granddaughter. So be it, she thought to herself.

When Seth Griffin had bought the land for the farm and built the house, he had one intention. He wanted a place to hunt and fish. The two lakes on the farm had been known as the South Pond and the North Pond since before he had paid for the land. Between the two lakes were the kind of forested rolling hills that led up to the Cumberland Plateau. A higher spine connected three of the hills and it was on the highest point of the spine that the farmhouse was built. Originally it was a practical dwelling. It was meant to be a barebones hunting lodge, a simple two-story house with a couple of big rooms on the bottom floor and a series of bedrooms and bunkrooms on the top floor. After the farmhouse was completed, there was often a group of men at the farm on the weekends for hunting or fishing. Seth hosted a couple of big shoots in the fall, the Thanksgiving Turkey Shoot being the longest standing and the most famous.

Over the years, the farmhouse had changed. First a good-sized kitchen was attached to the house. It made the simple house into an L shape. The next year a large covered porch was built onto the back of the house and a barbeque fire pit was laid just off it.

When Margaret had returned from Vassar, she had convinced Seth to build a large section on the other side from the kitchen. There, she had said, comfortable bedrooms and modern plumbing could have their rightful place. While she was at it, she had beefed up the original kitchen addition to balance out the structure, which became a large U.

After her father had died, Margaret had looked at the house and pronounced the whole thing a hodgepodge of styles and additions and redone the entire farmhouse, filling in the bottom half of the U with a large living room, using the original fire pit as the foundation for a fireplace and building an extensive back porch in the upper half of the U. She had brought in the best trim carpenters to completely refit the house and there were rooms where the wood was more expensive than the cost of the original farmhouse. By 1940, the house was complete. It was in the form in which it would remain for decades to come.

The physical form of the farmhouse in its many manifestations was nearly irrelevant. From the time that Seth had wandered the farm with a shotgun or a fishing rod until Stockard had spent her summer after graduation riding horses around it, Sefer Farm had been the retreat for the Griffin family, a place where they could rest their minds and enjoy themselves. It had become the geographic center of the family, a place where they could always return together or individually.

After Margaret had made a mental checklist of things that needed to be done for the air conditioning installation and knew which phone calls she would make first, she looked at Stockard and said, "If you'd prefer, Ebern could do that."

"Oh, I don't mind," said Stockard. "It's the least I can do. Thank you so very much for the horses. It'll be nice to ride again."

"You are most welcome," said Margaret, who sat down next to Stockard on the bench. "I hope the horses will brighten you up. You are not your usual smiley self."

"I know," said Stockard, who continued polishing. "It's a man. I miss a man." She tried to say it with the frankness with which her grandmother could discuss business.

"I am sorry," said Margaret as she watched Stockard. "Why don't you invite him to the farm?"

There was a guest room that was reserved for Uncle Andrew, who made regular trips to the farm to talk business with Margaret. Over the years, he had left a whole wardrobe in there. He favored the attire of a British sportsman while on the farm. The closet was full of tattersall and gunchecked shirts, corduroy and moleskin trousers and a great big tweed hunting coat. Stockard had peeked in there several times as a child and could not reconcile so many clothes with a man who was not there every day.

Other than Andrew, Ebern, and the occasional workmen, Stockard had never seen another man on the farm. Abe would make holiday visits when he was alive, but even then he had favored the library, where he would read in an armchair. She tried to imagine

Mills on the farm. She could not get the image of him with his girl-friend out of her mind. "It didn't end so well."

"I am very sorry. It makes it all the worse, doesn't it? These things need closure or to be patched up. Have you considered writing him?"

"No, ma'am."

"Well, it's not my place to tell you what to do, but you might consider it. Men are a strange breed. They will play to the basest instincts naturally, so it's up to women to keep the game up to a proper standard. Good manners are a start."

"Yes, ma'am."

"I am very glad you are here for the summer. You can stay as long as you want, you know?"

Stockard thanked her grandmother, who departed saying she was on her way to her study to get the air conditioning installed lickety-split.

The barn in isolation reminded her of *The Nightmare*, that damned dream that had plagued her for so long. Now she had finally had sex and she could not connect the dark haunting presence of *The Nightmare* with that strangely physical and spiritual act with Mills. It had not been just physical. There was something about having him so close, smelling his breath, running her fingers through his hair, the beams of light that were his blue eyes, something that the physical carried to her soul, something deeply fulfilling.

It had not ended well.

The thought of him nearly brought tears as she used a wet yellow cloth to remove the emollient from a pair of reins. The bit could have used some buffing but she wondered if the chemicals would upset the horses. Ebern would know. She could feel her eyes watering.

When Stockard had returned to her Branner Hall room after spotting Mills with his girlfriend and the phone had rung, she had picked the receiver up, and said a ponderous hello.

"Stockard?"

"Hello, Eve."

"You all right?"

"Why, yes, I am. You?"

"You don't sound so good."

"Oh, I just woke up from a nap. Bad dream. What are you up to?"

"Nothing. I've been calling for the last week. Where have you and Emily been?"

"Exams and all that."

"Graduating seniors don't study for final exams, especially with your grades." There was a peculiar excitement to Eve's voice, more like she remembered Eve when she was a child, excited before Christmas.

Stockard did not know what to say.

"Anyway," Eve broke the silence, "since everyone arrives tomorrow, I thought you might want to come to Berkeley tonight. We could eat out, smoke, watch some TV and then go to the station tomorrow. You have the car."

"That would be great," Stockard droned, aware of her unenthusiastic voice. She did not want to be alone and have nothing to do. She tried to pep her voice up. "I'll wait for Emily to come back and see if she wants to come, too."

"See you when I see you."

Emily walked through the door five minutes later, her arms full of painting supplies and some sculpting tools. Her exams were over and she had cleaned out her studio locker. She was ready for a night with her sister and her cousin before the maternal steel curtain arrived for the ceremonies.

In her need to be distracted, she did not realize that she had also removed herself from her room and her phone, the only ways for Mills to find her.

It was only after Stockard had left Stanford for good, only when she had returned to Sefer Farm, that she realized that Mills did not have her address. He had no way of knowing how to get a hold of her. If he wanted to.

The question of whether Stockard wanted to hear from Mills was a big one. She spent days saying yes and no and yes and no to herself and it was not until her grandmother, who had shown her typical common sense, had said it needed either closure or putting straight that Stockard began to imagine the letter she would write to Mills.

She finally sat down and wrote it, a piteous thing, confused with outrage, sorrow, cold logic about how it worked out the best, remorse for letting him go, anger at his girlfriend. It was a scrawling rambling six-page letter and when Stockard was done with it, she needed a nap.

The next day she laughed as she read it. "You're nuts," she said to herself. "You can't send that."

She could not bring herself to rip it up and instead folded and stowed it in the dictionary, in the m's. It was the dictionary she kept on her bedside table.

A couple of days later, there were four workmen in the house, pulling trim off the walls and floors, cutting holes, banging and sawing and talking over lunches that Rose made for them to eat on the porch. The air conditioning was on its way. She wrote a second letter. "Dear Mills, I am so sorry we didn't get to see each other before we both left Stanford but I wanted to let you know how much I enjoyed your company..."

It was more formal, less emotional, and ended with her wishing him the best. It was the kind of letter she imagined her grandmother writing, although she couldn't imagine her grandmother being in such a situation. She folded the letter, put it into an envelope and addressed it.

She lay the letter on her dresser and looked at it. Her room at Sefer Farm was exactly the same as it had been when she had awoken from *The Nightmare*. The darkly stained furniture appeared to sprout from the darkly stained floor. There were boxes stacked in a corner, still unpacked from Stanford, mostly full of books. There was a red rug. It had been the first thing her grandmother had bought for

Sefer Farm. It was an intricate oriental with golds and navies and a few spots of green. It was at least double Stockard's age. More, she thought, trying to refocus on the letter, but it sat there, wanting to be ignored. It was the right thing to do.

The next day she looked at the envelope after she had first woken up and thought, if this is your way of saying good bye, it will work. There is not one thing in that letter that will bring Mills back to you.

The question started all over again. Did she or did she not want Mills in her life?

She knew this was not the letter she would send either and placed it next to the first letter in her dictionary.

Well, she did want Mills back, she decided and now she focused on the likelihood of him coming back to her. In a couple of months he would be in law school. For all she knew, he was already engaged, or even worse, married to that girl.

That girl. How much did Mills love her? How much did he love me?

Was he the kind of guy who would give it all up to be with Stockard? In her best moments, she would send a confessional letter to Mills, saying that she loved him and missed him. After reading it, Mills would move to Nashville, go to Vanderbilt law school and they would settle in a nice house in Nashville, not too far from Sefer Farm.

In her worst moments, she imagined writing the confessional letter and never hearing back from him.

Stockard spent the entire two weeks of the air conditioning installation worrying about the question. She had already decided that the third letter would have to be the confessional and she had played in her head with the wording. It must come as a surprise to you—or maybe not—that I am in love with you. I miss our laying in bed together. She could see herself writing the letter, sweeping handwriting, slow violins playing in the background, the moment full of emotion.

Her routine had been to sleep late and have coffee on the porch after a shower. They would eat lunch out there, too, often times with the workers. Her grandmother was a case study in manners. She could talk to the men in a way that was both friendly and formal, exacting the best behavior from them. They even used their napkins.

Stockard's mother, on the other hand, reminded her of Robert Browning's poem, *My Last Duchess*. "She had a heart too soon made glad, too easily impressed."

It was the first time that Stockard had ever noticed how her mother reacted to men and them to her. She knew that it was her grandmother's position and manners that kept them from openly flirting or worse with her mother. That was the way it had always been, she saw. Her grandmother had kept her mother out of trouble. As much as possible. After all, Stockard herself was the product of such a relationship. Her mother had fallen in love with a local soap maker, Sammy, Stockard's father.

Stockard would spend the rest of her afternoons reading or napping, sometimes in her room, sometimes on the porch, although she hated being out there with workmen all over the house. Sometimes she would read or nap under her oak tree. Around five, when the hottest part of the day was gone and the first softening of the heat began to hit the shadows, she would put on jeans or jodhpurs and go for a ride. Ideally she should ride first thing in the morning, but she could not get up early enough. After her ride, she would change back into shorts and have dinner with her mother and grandmother. Later in the evening they would meet again on the porch, where Stockard and her grandmother would smoke cigarettes. Her grandmother would have a bourbon on ice, poured with that silver water pitcher and into one of the silver cups. Stockard and her mother still drank beers.

Stockard never wrote that third letter. She worried it into a thousand shapes and finally realized that she hadn't thought about it for a day or two. By the end of June, the air conditioning was installed and blowing cool air throughout the house and Stockard was looking forward to her cousins coming to the farm for July. What was left of her love of Mills had been exhausted by emotion and she wanted to forget the whole thing, for a little while.

2

O N July 1st, Eve and Evelyn came off the plane at the Nashville airport not speaking to each other. They had gotten into an argument that morning over what Eve was wearing, a flowing white robe-like thing with clunky brown leather sandals. Eve had been absorbed into the hippie culture of Berkeley, even once being arrested at the People's Park demonstration, thereby making her a lifelong enemy of Ronald Reagan. Reagan had campaigned successfully for the California governorship. One of his campaign promises was to clean up Berkeley. Eve had become difficult about certain things, clothes being one of them. Aunt Evelyn, Stockard knew, had the exact same conservative views on clothes as her grandmother.

Stockard looked at Eve and had to admit that her clothes did not appear to fit. She had watched the Summer of Love disappear and demonstrations against the war pick up, and just as she had found the hippie's Free Love a painful thorn in her side, so she found the demonstrations alienating. It wasn't that she had approved of the Vietnam War. The bloody images that came over television and in newspapers made her sick. She simply found the screaming activists unappealing. Her grandmother's voice, again unsolicited and clear in her head, would say, "They do not know better."

Rose cooked a ham, corn in cream, butter beans, mashed potatoes and corn bread. Afterwards the Griffin women sat on the porch and ate hot apple pie with ice cream, watching the remnants of a thunderstorm disappear. It had been raining all day. Aunt Evelyn was the first to bed, citing a long travel day. Soon Emily, Eve and Stockard were left alone. The rainy day had left behind a drippingly humid night, still warm despite the darkness. Emily fetched the dragon pipe from her room, saying in her well worn Charlie Chan voice, "Me thinky we chasey dragon." Stockard came back from the mud room with trip supplies: an orange plastic poncho, a flashlight, a candle and a box of matches.

She led the way in the darkness of the night to her oak tree, where they spread the poncho on the wet ground. They used the candle to light the hash, cupping their hands over the bowl to keep the smoke from escaping after the nugget was lit.

In the long silence after the hash was burnt, they sat with their backs to the oak tree, their butts on the ground between the pipe-like roots. Emily reclined, looking at the stars as they made their patchy appearance. "All those stars," she said. "So many places to see."

Eve and Stockard were looking down into the cove, where the barn sat, obscured by the heavy darkness of the night. Eve asked what the horses were like.

"Slow," said Stockard, feeling the words come out of her mouth, awkward at first. "Quarter horses. Not young ones either. They're solid, though."

"Like the Volvo. Grandmother always wants us going places in safe slow things." Emily kept looking at the stars. It was a new moon, non-existent.

"I think I'll get up early and ride," said Eve. "I'm beat." She got up, still in her flowing white robe, and went to bed, eschewing the offer of the flashlight, instead making the journey alone and in the dark.

After they could no longer hear Eve's footsteps disappearing towards the house, Emily said, "She hates this place. She railed about being stuck on some hillbilly farm and how it was all tainted money…"

"Tainted money?"

"Eve's become anti-money lately. She thinks there's no way to honestly make money. Not a lot of money. Not honestly. She especially likes the word 'honestly.' I think she means something else, like legally or morally."

"We didn't make it. Our great-grandfather made it. It's not really ours, anyway. And I don't think it's a lot."

"That's not what Eve thinks. She thinks grandmother was the one who really made it and not honestly. See. Now I can't even say the word without laughing. And she believes we have an obligation to rid ourselves of the money."

"Well, thank God we don't have the money. I'd hate to see her just throw it away. What about your father's money? Is that honestly gotten?"

"Tainted for other reasons, but not so much. I think it is because Eve knows how much it is and how Father earned it. That's what makes the difference. Still, she hardly touches it."

"I don't understand her," said Stockard, wondering how you question a thing like money. It was an inanimate object, she thought, and then found herself rethinking the thought. "It doesn't matter to me. Where it comes from. I think. Just the presence doesn't matter nor where it came from. But it makes things easier in a way." She heard herself talking about money and began to realize that she had no formed opinions about it. The thought disturbed her. "I don't think I'll ever see any money, anyway. Grandmother hasn't said a word about it."

Now money became an issue. Heartbreak had filled her June, but every once in awhile a thought would break through, a thought that she might one day get over the suffering and the searing pain and then what? Would she remain on Sefer Farm forever, like her mother? Doing nothing? What was she going to do? Work? She had no idea what she was fit to do nor what she wanted to do.

Each time the thought occurred, Stockard set it aside, but a funny thing had started to happen. The thought began to linger longer and longer. She was damned glad when Emily had produced the dragon pipe. Such thoughts could be banished into a cloud of smoke. At least that was her hope even though Emily had unintentionally brought the subject up again despite their being stoned. It worried her. Damn Eve, she thought to herself.

They sat with the candle burning between them, the warm Southern night enveloping them. The candle was starting to attract insects so Stockard reached over with licked fingers and put it out.

"Speaking of obligations," said Emily as their eyes tried to adjust to the darkness, "your mother said you were still suffering from heartbreak. Still suffering, she said."

"Oh… well."

"Stockard, what is she talking about? Were you in love at Stanford?"

Stockard had put it away. She had carefully filed the heartbreak into a steel cabinet, somewhere deep and cold and away from her heart. She had quietly forgotten it, mostly. Now it was back and she could see for an instant Mills' beaming blue eyes and could feel the warmth of his body and could hear his laugh, his delighted and delightful laugh. She sniffed a few wet sniffs, choked a sob, and then really let loose. She felt Emily's hand grab her by the neck and pull her face to Emily's chest. It felt good to finally cry, to have someone she loved and trusted to cry on and she savored the feeling. The hash had heightened her perceptions. She could feel the pique of Emily's shirt, smell her skin, a mixture of jet travel and humid night. She went on like that for ten minutes, maybe more, before Emily asked, "Who on earth was it?"

Stockard told her the whole story. It was the first time she had ever told anyone the whole story. She described Mills walking into her room and how the attraction was instant. Their Saturday "appointments." The last two weeks.

"Who would have ever guessed? And you didn't tell me!"

"I wasn't ready. I didn't… it all sounded so silly, so improbable. I couldn't tell you. It was trivial. At first."

"Not Stockard Griffin abandoning her virginity! My God, it was," Emily trotted out her faux Tennessee accent, "a historical moment."

Somewhere in Stockard's sophomore year Emily had admitted her own deflowering while a senior at Morary's in New York. She would not say with whom, but afterwards sex subsided into the background for them.

"Then I knew that it was just something we did on Saturdays. You saw him once."

"No! The guy who came in by accident. That deadly good looking one in the ridiculous trousers?"

"That was Mills."

"Oh, my God."

"He aborted when he saw you." By now Stockard was sitting upright again.

They talked on until the blackest part of the night came and even the buzzing insects buzzed no more. Even the nocturnals began to sleep. They knew that if they did not make the walk back to the house then they were in danger of passing out under the tree. They walked side by side, Stockard shining the flashlight in front of them, Emily carrying the pipe and the folded orange poncho. Emily asked, "Do you think Grandmother would take us out shooting?"

"Oh, yes, I'm sure she would. Why?"

"I've never handled a gun and thought it might be nice to learn."

"Oh, I've got one in my room…"

"Stockard!"

"Grandmother taught me when I was, oh, ten or so. She said I needed to know. She bought me a thirty-eight. It's still a little heavy for me, but she said it was lady-like. We can go shoot tomorrow. I'll see if I can find some more bullets."

"You didn't have that thing at Stanford, did you?"

"Certainly not. It's always been just for the farm."

"I always wondered if grandmother took her gun with her. So she didn't?"

"She does. She had a revolver in New York, tucked in her nightstand. She let me know. Said just in case. Funny, because she never tells my mother where the gun is."

In the early hours of the morning when it was still dark, Stockard finally fell into bed and slept, having a dream that the farm hangar caught on fire. Her grandfather used to fly planes and had built it. It looked like a very large version of the barn, which was in the next cove. Now it was used for storage. It was full of crates and boxes and furniture and even a Ford Model T. Stockard knew her old clothes were in there.

She could not summon her grandfather's face in her dream. There was only one picture of him in the house, hung in the library near one of her great-grandfather's stuffed buck heads.

In her dream, she watched from across the cove as the hangar began to smoke and then the flames became visible. She could not tear herself from watching. It only vaguely occurred to her that she needed to get help, that the fire needed to be put out, but she was more interested in watching it. Quickly the flames enveloped the whole structure, and the grass around it caught too, a line working its way towards the trees. It was only then that she saw the danger. All of those beautiful old trees that her grandfather had planted would catch fire and then the farmhouse would burn, too, leaving nothing. It would be the burning of Atlanta from *Gone With The Wind*. Just as she realized the significance of the fire and that it might be too late, she woke up. She lay in bed, her limbs leaden with beer and hash residue. She did not understand it and eventually drifted back to sleep, but not before hearing her grandmother leave her bedroom and walk softly towards the kitchen.

The early footsteps that Stockard did not hear were Eve's.

3

T HE next morning, Emily and Stockard slept late. They slept late every morning, getting up somewhere between ten and eleven. Stockard's mother had usually not been up for long, either. They would nibble leftover toasted buttermilk biscuits and drink coffee in the kitchen while Rose prepared lunch, which was a sit-down affair. Since the air conditioning had been installed, they had opted to eat first in the dining room, which was too formal. Eventually they ate on a table in the living room that looked out onto the porch with its view. They were all grateful to escape the heat of high noon.

Afterwards, they would disperse. Margaret went to her office to continue the constant caretaking of her businesses. Eve and Evelyn, who were early risers, often took naps. Eve liked to ride first thing in the morning, while it was still cool.

On the porch, Stockard's mother, April, would read, alternating her love of the salacious but literary novel with her constant analysis of the petty details of history. That summer she read *Go Ask Alice* and a hefty tome on sex in the Italian Renaissance.

Emily would haul a clunky wooden box of paints and an easel to a vantage point on the farm and paint while Stockard would sit nearby with a book.

"All I can do on this farm," said Emily one day, as she concentrated with brush in hand and her eyes occasionally scanned the juncture of the barn and hangar coves, "is landscapes, and they're all starting to look the same."

"You said that yesterday," Stockard replied. She was lying on her back, holding a book just above her face, reading. She could only read in this position for five minutes before her arms gave out. She was liable to fall asleep with the book on her face.

"It hasn't changed." Emily gave a big sigh. "This is not inspirational. I've done the coves from every angle imaginable. I could try an outer space perspective, I suppose."

"There are other things, you know. The lakes."

"The ponds. It's just not doing it for me. Even my drawings are flat." Emily had been using pencil to do quick drawings at the lunch table, at the dinner table, in the kitchen, when they were sitting on the porch at night. "I think it is the place. Sefer Farm doesn't inspire me. Do you really think you can spend the rest of your life here?"

"Who said anything about the rest of my life?"

"You haven't said you're leaving."

"It doesn't mean I'm not."

"Do you have any plans?"

Stockard had been rereading Flannery O'Connor short stories. She set the book pages down, cover splayed up, and rolled over on her side, looking at Emily, her cheek now in touch with the old quilt on the ground. "No."

Emily dabbed and painted a few strokes. "Look, we told grandmother we'd be here for all of July, but good Lord, that seems like an awfully long time now. I love being with you and everyone else, even cranky Eve, but there's just so much you can do here. We're tapped out. Eve wants to go somewhere in August. She keeps saying she wants to go see the west."

"We just spent four years out west."

"She means the rest of the west. Arizona, New Mexico, Colorado, Wyoming, places like that. She wants to go drive around. She wants to road trip."

"Are you going to do it?"

"Probably. What else am I going to do? Go back to New York? I'm tired of the city. I'm tired of Sefer Farm. I need to do something. Are you coming?"

"I haven't been invited." Stockard picked her book up and made like she was reading again.

"Suit yourself," said Emily, dabbing paint on her canvas again. "You'll die a miserable, old-fashioned, lonely death in this place. It's great to visit, but…"

"I wouldn't want to live here."

But Stockard did live here. It was not a place to visit. It was her home. Emily, whom Stockard loved, had hit on a most hateful point. Sefer Farm was in the middle of nowhere. It was not a place where young people went to fully engage in life. Yet she was terribly attached to home. The financial issue, how she could leave Sefer Farm, compounded the problem. Her grandmother had given her $100— five crisp $20 bills—when Stockard had first arrived on the farm, saying, "You probably need pocket money." She had not mentioned money since. Stockard did not know where she stood. Could she ask for more? Her grandmother had always anticipated her needs, taking her shopping for clothes and make-up, giving her money for bookstore runs, and then Andrew had picked up where her grandmother had left off when Stockard went off to school. But since graduation, neither Andrew nor her grandmother had said anything about Stockard's long-term money prospects.

Now that Stockard was about to lose the two people her age on the farm, money was something she thought about all the time, try as she may to kill the thoughts with the dragon pipe.

4

ON the morning of the 18th, a voice seeped into Stockard's dense black sleep. At first she thought she was dreaming. Her limbs were heavy. She could not move her mouth, but she knew it tasted like morning breath, which she had labeled "mourning breath," mourning the beer and hash and whatever they had eaten the night before and mourning that she had been too stoned to brush her teeth before collapsing in bed. It had been part of their routine. Eve, like the first night after they arrived, would stay up with Emily and Stockard for one round of the pipe and then she would go to bed. Emily and Stockard were night owls and late sleepers. Stockard kept meaning to go to sleep with a glass of water because she always awoke with cotton mouth. Or mourning mouth.

Which she could taste and feel as she listened, trying to hear the voice. It was ever so faint. A woman's voice. She made out the words.

"Help. Help. Someone, help."

Stockard's eyes clicked open and she sat up in bed at once, stopping to listen again. The voice was coming from outside her window, down the hill, somewhere in the cove where the hangar was. She was sick from moving so quickly, a fullness suddenly weighing her stomach down. It was a feeling, she knew, before she threw up. Then she heard a horse clomping by her window.

In a flash Stockard reached into her bedside table and pulled out the .38 that her grandmother had bought her. A couple of times a year, Rose would take it to Ebern, who would clean it, test fire it and then reload it. It had been, to this point, the only use the gun had seen. It was a black Smith & Wesson with a long barrel. For a second, Stockard saw how the darkly stained grip was like the furniture and the floor, deep and rich. For some reason, it annoyed her. She could not escape darkly stained wood.

She was wearing a pair of men's boxers and a t-shirt, her standard sleeping attire. The fastest way to the side of the house was through the living room and out the double doors onto the porch, where she came through the door so fast that she startled Aunt Evelyn, who was reading a three-day old *New York Times*. She received them in the mail and read them religiously.

Evelyn screamed and then said, "Stockard, you scared…" She took in Stockard's gun and her eyes widened again. "What…"

Stockard covered the distance from the doors to the porch steps at a trot, taking in for an amused split second Aunt Evelyn's reaction, saying breathlessly, "Someone is yelling help!" She was off the porch, her bare feet feeling the pine needles and cold dark dirt as she went running.

Just as Stockard hit the tree line, she glimpsed a saddled riderless horse next to the house, right outside her bedroom window, and she would have stopped but heard again the pitiful cries. "Help! Help! Help me, someone! Help!"

"Eve!" cried Stockard, and she set off down the hill towards the hangar, her reactions so instinctive now that she would later look back and wonder what had happened. "Eve, I'm coming." She had not consciously identified the voice as Eve's, but the words were coming out of her mouth. She went down the hill in a glade of old-growth pine trees. It needed clearing. Some of the recent storms had taken off branches and there was the odd fallen tree. Even as Stockard moved towards Eve's voice, which was saying, "Help! I'm over here!", Stockard was noticing the fallen trees and wondering how that had happened. These trees stay together, they don't fall individually. Towards the bottom of the hill, just as Stockard could feel the sour spit of hard exercise in her mouth and her lungs were laboring, she found Eve.

At first all she recognized were the polished brown leather riding boots against the white jodhpurs. Very Connecticut, Stockard had said the first time that Eve appeared in her riding outfit. Overdone for Tennessee, she had thought but dared not say, but who besides

the family was going to see her? This was the very same Eve, ironically, who had flown into the Nashville airport in a white flowing robe.

Eve was lying on the ground, a brown smear of pine bark across
one white jodhpurred leg. "Oh, Stockard, thank God!"

"Eve? What on earth?" Stockard came running up to her cousin,
noticing the rest of her outfit. A pink Lacoste shirt, riding gloves that
matched her boots and a brown suede riding helmet. She was on her
right side and Stockard noticed her left arm had the same brown
smear as her trousers, only there was a splotch of red.

"My arm," said Eve, who was now speaking in a groan. "My arm.
That stupid horse. He wiped me off. He used a tree. My arm's broken."

By now Stockard was leaning over Eve, trying to see what was
wrong with her, trying to understand what she was saying. Stockard
now tried to focus on Eve's left arm. Stockard was breathing hard.
She could feel the sweat running down her forehead.

"Is that a gun?" Eve had for a painful moment raised her head to
look at Stockard.

"All I heard was 'help'," said Stockard. "I didn't know what for."
She lay the gun down.

"Go shoot that goddamned horse," said Eve.

"Hold on, missy, we've got to get you out of here." Stockard looked
more closely at Eve's arm. There was brown and red and some pink
flesh and then Stockard saw the white. "Oh, no."

"What?"

"This is… it doesn't look so good."

"Well it hurts like a motherfucker!"

"I've got to get someone. We've got to get you out of here."

"Don't leave me. Everything's going white."

"You're just going into shock." Stockard heard a faint noise on
the pine floor just up the hill. Her senses were on high alert still and
she could feel the presence of someone else before she heard the
footsteps.

She looked up to see Aunt Evelyn, who was stalking her way down the hill with a shotgun, tucked Churchill, butt into her right armpit, left arm leading the barrels. "Aunt Evelyn," yelled Stockard, "it's okay. Eve just got thrown from a horse!"

Evelyn nodded her head and then looked to her right.

"Mamma," said Evelyn in a voice that Stockard had never heard, a country voice born in Tennessee, "did you hear that?"

Stockard looked to where Evelyn was speaking and there was her grandmother, standing about two hundred feet from Evelyn, a shotgun pointed straight up, finger on the trigger guard. Stockard looked back at Eve and said, "I think the cavalry has arrived."

Eve had laid her head down, her complexion had gone white and her eyes were half closed. "Good," she said and let out a groan of pain.

Her grandmother said, "I'll bring the car around. Y'all take Eve down to the tree line." Stockard watched as she turned, shotgun still pointed straight up, and hurried up the hill. It wasn't a walk nor was it a run. For a moment she wondered if her grandmother had ever run. Running was not a lady-like thing to do.

Evelyn was quickly with them. She hesitated for a moment, looking at her daughter and then saying, "Oh, baby, it's going to be okay. It's a nasty break. We'll get you to the hospital." Her peculiar Vassar-New York-Tennessee accent had returned.

Stockard was alarmed at how much new blood there was since she had been standing there.

"We need to get you down into the cove, out of the trees," said Evelyn. "Can you stand up?"

"I think so," said Eve. She made to turn her body over and let out a howl. Tears followed and she said between chattering teeth, "It hurts so bad, Mamma."

"Mamma." Stockard knew her mind was registering strange details, the blue blue color of the sky through the canopy, the smell of pine needles, the darkness of the bark, but she had never heard Eve call her mother "Mamma" before.

"I know it does, honey. Stockard and I can carry you. Hold on a minute." Before Stockard could move, Evelyn was at the top of Eve, putting one hand in Eve's right armpit and grabbing Eve by the belt. "Stockard, grab her by the knees."

Stockard leaned to Eve, encircling her knees.

"Honey, this is gonna hurt but the sooner we get you out of here, the sooner we can get you to a doctor." Evelyn looked at Stockard and said, "Keep going no matter what. Let's go." She picked Eve up and Stockard lifted, too.

Instantly Eve screamed, startling Stockard for a minute.

"Keep going, Stockard," said Evelyn.

By now Eve was sobbing and squirming and screaming. It did not take them more than two minutes to get Eve down the hill and to the edge of the trees, but to Stockard it felt like ten or fifteen minutes, the longest ten or fifteen minutes in her life. She and her aunt were physically hurting Eve. Neither of them was strong, but Evelyn kept a tight grip on her daughter and Stockard managed to control her thrashing legs, and soon they were on the edge of the field.

When they finally lay Eve down, she was crying and whimpering. Evelyn leaned over to her daughter and said, "I'm so sorry, dear, but we had to get you out of there."

There was no direct road from the farmhouse, where the Suburban was parked, to the hangar cove. Margaret would have to drive half way out the entrance road of the farm and then cut down a double track around the base of the foothill and finally into the hangar cove. It could take fifteen minutes to make the trip.

Stockard was starting to wonder if Eve was going to make it. Her arm was bleeding. She had never seen a compound fracture. She had never seen so much blood. Some of the blood was on Stockard. Some on Evelyn. A lot was on Eve. Stockard didn't know how much blood a person could lose before they died but Eve had lost a lot.

Evelyn said, "If Mother isn't here soon, we're going to need to tourniquet that arm."

"Amputation" was the word that flashed through Stockard's mind. She could see Eve without an arm.

Evelyn took off her belt, a thick leather one, and said to Eve, "I'm going to use my belt to slow the blood flow. You're losing blood, honey and we need to slow it."

Eve by now had stopped speaking and merely groaned.

Stockard watched as Evelyn carefully threaded the belt under Eve's armpit and then used the buckle to ratchet the pressure. Eve gave another scream.

When the Suburban hit the cove, Stockard looked up. She had never seen the old car going so fast, a tail of dust following it, the wheels bobbing up and down willy nilly across the field. For a split second, she wondered if her grandmother would be able to stop it in time.

Margaret eased the Suburban so that one side was two feet from where they stood. She left the motor running and came around, where Stockard and Evelyn were already loading Eve into the back seat. They were not nearly as gentle this time. Time was of the essence, now, and they worked as a wordless efficient team.

Evelyn slid into the back seat while Margaret headed for the driver's seat.

"Stockard," said her grandmother, "take those guns back to the house. Get your cousin and your mother and borrow Ebern's truck. We're going to the Vanderbilt Hospital."

"Yes, ma'am," said Stockard as she watched the driver's door shut, and the Suburban was off, still picking up speed as it disappeared down the double track out of the cove and into the woods. She stood there for a moment, watching the dust settle and then she looked down at her bare feet. She had blood on her shirt and her boxers and smeared on her legs. She had a few cuts and abrasions from hauling Eve with bare feet, but she could not feel anything, just an exhaustion. It was a struggle carrying the shotgun and her revolver up the hill and she was surprised to see the horse up top, still standing right under her bedroom window. She waved at it and said, "Buck, you shameful thing. Ebern will come to take care of you in a minute."

She walked into the kitchen where Rose stood next to the stove with a frying pan in one hand. Her mother, having just showered, was sitting in a chair with her first cup of coffee.

"Stockard," her mother said, "what on earth are you doing with a... Is that blood?"

Rose said, "Child, what on earth has happened?"

Emily as it turned out had slept through the entire thing. Stockard ducked into Emily's room and said, "Wake up. Your sister's been thrown from a horse. Broke her arm. We've got to go to the hospital."

"What?" Emily's eye had popped up from the covers.

"Get up!" Stockard disappeared from the door frame. She went to the bathroom and stripped, washing the blood off quickly and then hurried down the hallway, clad in a towel, to her room, where she got dressed. Rose had run to find Ebern, who was stacking hay next to the barn. Fifteen minutes later, Stockard, who was already exhausted from the morning, was driving Ebern's pickup truck with her cousin and her mother sitting next to her. They found Margaret in the Emergency waiting room. Eve was already being scheduled into surgery.

It would be two days before Eve was finally brought back home with a cast from the first knuckle to her shoulder and a special harness for her arm. At dinner that night, they pieced together what had happened.

Eve rode the same route every morning. From the barn she would ride to the North Pond and then southeast to the South Pond, coming back through the hangar cove and then she would ride rough through the trees up the hill and back into the barn cove. Eve had tried all four horses that her grandmother had bought and decided that Buck was the most surefooted of them. She had grown attached to him and would bring him an apple every morning before they went out together. Buck knew the route as well or even better than

Eve and he had taken to avoiding particular holes in the dirt roads and particular ditches in the trees. He didn't want too much hassle.

On the morning of the 18th, Eve went to the barn to find Buck skittish already. He wouldn't stay still as she saddled him and Eve had finally had to tie his head directly to the post to keep him from moving around. Once Eve was on Buck, he took off, which he had never done before, staying to their trail, just taking it faster than usual. Eve thought Buck just needed a little exercise so she trotted and then cantered him. He really picked up speed on the canter and it was Eve's first realization that something was wrong with him. He had never run that fast. Midway between the North Pond and the South Pond, she had decided to abort the ride because Buck was becoming more and more uncontrollable. She had to kick him hard to get him into the hangar cove and once there, he had taken off for the farmhouse, going around the hangar, staying close to the tree line. Eve couldn't control him. When she tried to rein him in, yanking on his head as hard as she had ever pulled reins, Buck had tried to buck. Eve was an accomplished rider and knew how to ride a bucking horse. No quarter horse was going to get rid of her, she had said. Then Buck headed straight for a tree and managed to rub Eve off him. He used the tree. Eve, who had never seen a horse do that, was completely surprised and didn't realize the state of her injuries until she tried to get up, angry as hell and ready to teach Buck some discipline. That's when she had rolled over and started yelling for help, waking Stockard out of her heavy morning sleep.

"Well, what was it? What spooked Buck?" Margaret asked her granddaughter over dinner.

"I don't know, but he wouldn't come near the hangar when we entered that cove. He kept looking at the hangar and going away from it, sliding around it. That's when he finally flipped. He's never done that before. We used to ride by the hangar twice every day."

"Crazy horse," said Emily. She had taken to Ole Stew, who really was old and fat and slow, like riding a sofa.

"There are some strange things in that hangar," said April.

5

THE first night after Eve had returned from the hospital, she had still been on painkillers and had slipped from a hazy fluffy world into a sleep on a sofa in the living room. Stockard and Emily made their ritual visit to the oak tree without her.

"So how does Eve's accident affect your plans?" Stockard startled Emily. They had been staring silently into the night for a long time.

"You mean in August?"

"Yeah. The trip out west."

"I don't know. I haven't brought it up, yet. I don't think Eve is going anywhere with that giant cast on her arm. She can't even lie down properly. Did you see how she went to sleep in the living room. Half of her body on an ottoman, arm propped under mounds of pillows, her head flung into the corner of the sofa? It looked terribly uncomfortable. Can you see her driving all over the country with that cast?"

Stockard tried to imagine Eve in the Volvo, the arm propped on a stack of pillows or maybe a wooden box. In the back seat, looking out the window as the dry dramatic western scenery went by. She wouldn't be able to drive. The Volvo was a manual transmission. There wasn't room in the driver's seat for a big cast and a body, even if she could drive and shift gears with one hand. "Actually I can." It was her only way off the farm, she had decided, her one shot at leaving.

Stockard's sleep was no longer deep and restful. The one thought that she had gone to sleep and woken up thinking was, "I'm going to be stuck here just like my mother, for the rest of my life."

"I'll ask her in a couple of days when she's more collected. Who knows? If we go, are you coming?"

"I don't know." Stockard wanted to say hell, yes, cousin, wouldn't miss it for the world.

"What's there not to know?"

"It's the money. Grandmother hasn't said anything about money and I don't know if I have any, if I can afford to go on the trip."

Emily laughed a stoner's low and rhythmical laugh. "Money! You're thinking about not going because of money? What about that checking account?"

"I thought that was for Stanford. Nothing else."

"I don't know about that. You might want to check with Uncle Andrew. If you've got no money, don't worry about it! I've still got money from Dad and my checkbook from Uncle Andrew still works fine. I'll spring for you, how's that?"

It was splendid. It was her last resort, Stockard had figured, and she was loathe to ask Emily for money directly. Maybe she would try another check from her checkbook and even if it didn't work, Emily would pick up the tab. Whatever reservations she had about using her cousin's money to gain freedom from Sefer Farm disappeared into the alternative, her dread of being stuck there. After living with Emily for five years, she had gotten used to Emily having her own money, the money that her father had left for her. Emily as a result paid for a lot of things along the way. Sometimes Stockard would watch Emily picking up the tab at a restaurant or paying for another round of beers and have the slightest pang of guilt, but by now it had become a habit.

If Stockard was relieved on the walk back to the farmhouse, she realized that her money problems were not really fixed, just delayed a month or two. Emily would return to Stanford and take her money with her. She would have to deal with it, eventually. But at least she could get off the farm.

The question remained, what would Stockard do? How would she earn money and her independence? As soon as the outlines of the farmhouse came out of the darkness, Stockard could only think of tomatoes.

Their routine was to come in by way of the kitchen door off the back porch, making a quick raid on the fridge, eating up leftovers and anything else that looked fair game. Stockard liked to eat to-matoes when she was stoned, slicing them with one of Rose's old big knives. Ebern kept all of the knives sharp. She would shake a little salt on them and then devour. Emily went for sliding pieces of leftover meat between cold buttermilk biscuits. It was the last effort of the evening and they would eat in silence before disbanding to their rooms.

That night they had replaced the poncho, the candle and the flashlight in the mud room and then entered the kitchen from the porch. "I love leftover lamb," said Emily, thinking of dinner leftovers. She would spread some mint jelly on sliced bread and make a lamb sandwich.

Stockard was headed for the tomatoes on the window sill, her salivary glands already working, like Pavlov's dog she thought to herself, when they heard a yell. Not a scream. It was a yell.

In the silence that followed, Emily and Stockard stood dead still, looking at each other, the kitchen large and empty, they waiting for another sound.

"What was that?" whispered Stockard.

"Who was it?" Emily led the way from the kitchen down the old part of the house and into the living room, where Eve had long since left the sofa to try and sleep in her bed. They stood in the living room for a moment, not making a noise. They heard a door open and automatically crept towards it. From where the five downstairs bedrooms were connected by a hallway they saw their grandmother standing in her bedroom doorway, wearing a robe. Stockard, who was still stoned, couldn't remember ever seeing her grandmother in her robe. She was torn between this strange vision and the yell that they had heard.

Her grandmother whispered, "Did you hear that?"

"What was it?"

"Someone called out."

"It sounded like someone yelled."

"That's what we heard."

Then another door opened and Stockard's mother joined them, whispering, "I think it came from Evelyn's room."

The party of four walked quietly to the end of the hallway, which turned left where Evelyn's bedroom was the only door before the hallway spilled into the entrance hallway. There was light coming from underneath the shut door. Emily, Stockard and her mother linked arms behind Stockard's grandmother. They stopped in front of Evelyn's room, Stockard's grandmother knocking twice on the door and saying, "Evelyn, are you all right? Evelyn, we heard a yell." She knocked again.

"Is that you Mamma?" Again, Stockard noticed how her aunt's accent had reverted to a Tennessee drawl.

"It's me, honey, are you okay?" Her grandmother opened the door and there was Evelyn with her covers gripped to her chin, her bedside light turned on. "What is it Evelyn?" They all four peeked into her room.

"It's going to sound crazy, but someone has snatched the covers off my bed," said Evelyn. "Twice."

"Who," asked Margaret.

"I don't know." Evelyn peered at the group of women, hovering behind the threshold. Neither she nor they moved towards each other.

"You mean you didn't see who it was?"

"No," said Evelyn drawing out her words, "I didn't see anything. There was no one in the room. The door didn't open. It didn't close. My covers just… were pulled off the bed. Twice. I had the light on the second time and had just drifted off to sleep when it happened again. There was nobody there."

The four women, framed by the doorway, stood staring at Evelyn, Emily finally saying what was on their minds, "Spooky."

Stockard felt a chill run up her spine, like someone had opened a window or a door in the house, creating a draft. Something was wrong on the farm. She could not formulate her thoughts better than that. Something was terribly wrong.

It was the first time in a long time that women slept together in that house. April slept with Stockard. Evelyn slept with Emily. Margaret locked her door and Stockard knew that her grandmother probably had searched her closet, her bathroom, behind the drapes and very likely had her revolver in one hand as she slept.

Eve had the cold comfort of painkillers and beer and slept through the whole incident.

It was the first time that Stockard had ever thought it would be nice to have a man in the house.

6

STOCKARD'S sleep continued to be restless. Two days later she woke just in time for lunch. Afterwards, Emily wanted to paint in the hangar because she had a dream in it.

Stockard and Emily walked silently down the trail into the hangar cove. Stockard was starting to feel entrapped on the farm. Even if she did make an escape in August, she was convinced it would only be temporary. She had graduated from Stanford having studied nothing practical, nothing like accounting. She had made fun of the business majors, especially those that studied accounting. While they had to pour over boring numbers, she was learning the lessons of the world and history, the secrets of the human soul that only the arts could teach. Now, stranded on the farm, in the middle of nowhere with no money and no alternatives, she occasionally thought that accounting was not such a bad thing. Accountants at least knew what they could do and could get a job.

The trail came out a hundred or so yards from where, just four days previously, Stockard and Evelyn had carried an injured Eve and her grandmother had driven like a bat out of hell through the cove. It felt like a month had passed. It was a hot dull day.

The cove was a giant V with the hangar positioned at the closed end. The hangar was two maybe three times as large as the barn and much simpler in its design, four large and long walls, a simple tin roof. The hangar had been painted the same green of the barn and Ebern had put a fresh coat on just a couple of years ago. The cove itself was a broad expanse of level grass, now a patchy mixture of burnt brown and pale green. August was traditionally the hottest month and all of the grass would be brown soon. Even in the heat it was the most serene and picturesque of all the coves, preserved in time, still and unused, its peace only occasionally broken by Ebern pulling a mower behind a tractor.

Stockard was carrying the easel, her sunbathing quilt and a collection of Wodehouse stories. She needed to read something funny. Her mood and the mood of the house had been somber since Aunt Evelyn's nocturnal visit. Even last night her mother had climbed into Stockard's bed long before Stockard had gone to sleep. Emily and Stockard and Eve had opted to forego the dragon pipe. The atmosphere was too nervy to go traipsing out to the oak tree in the dark and come back crowded with new paranoia.

There was a pair of hangar doors across two-thirds of one wall facing into the cove. They were bolted from inside. The girls first had to go through a small door on the side of the hangar, leaving the art supplies and quilt outside. Emily had retrieved the key from a peg in the mud room. The lock had been oiled and maintained over the years so that the door came open like it was used every day. "Ebern sure takes good care of this farm," said Emily.

"Three hundred and sixty-five days a year," said Stockard. "I've seen him splitting wood on Christmas day."

Inside the hangar was a vast empty space, boxes and furniture stacked in one corner, barely taking up a quarter of the space. The Model T stood in another corner, up on lifts and looking positively prehistoric. Despite Ebern's fastidiousness, the hangar was dusty and bits of dirt had blown underneath the sliding doors. The only windows were high up under the eaves, the light fading as it came towards the ground. Emily and Stockard stood looking at it for a moment.

"Not like my dream," said Emily.

"How so?"

"The light was red, like it was lit by a fire, like a really big fire, a bonfire. There was a plane, an old one, and the propeller was going. It was loud and was blowing like a wind storm in here. And…" Emily stood still looking off into nothingness.

"What?"

"A man was in here, like one of the locals, a mean dirty man with wild eyes. It was our grandfather. He came over to me, the wind blowing and the red light behind him and he squatted down in front of me. It was odd because when he squatted, we were eye-to-eye, like I was a child and he needed to squat to look into my eyes and he said, 'Leave.'"

"Just 'leave'?"

"Yep."

Stockard felt the chill run down her spine, again. "And you wanted to come down to the hangar to paint?"

"I wanted to paint the dream. Maybe it'll help me understand. Here, let's open the doors so there's more light."

Stockard and Emily looked at the bolt a little before finally figuring out how to release the lock. It slid cleanly, but the doors were harder to open, making a tremendous amount of rusty metal on metal noise. Stockard was glad to get them open. The hangar was starting to creep her out. They went around to get the supplies and Stockard lay her quilt just inside the hangar, in the shade. She bunched up one corner to use as a pillow. Once Emily was all set up, she started to paint. She had brought two canvases, which was unusual. She normally only worked a single canvas each day, sometimes going back three or four times to the same spot to work on the same canvas. Thirty minutes into the second canvas, Emily finally spoke. "What do you think it meant?"

"Your dream?"

"Uh huh."

"Our grandfather wants you to leave? Could it be that simple?"

"Why not?"

"Couldn't it be more metaphorical? One of our unknown ancestors, representing a forgotten side of our family—no one talks about Lee Wilson—is telling us to stay out of the hangar, a forgotten part of the farm?"

"Don't nose around in the past?"

"Why not?"

"It doesn't feel right. I think he was telling me to leave the farm. That's all."

"I had a dream about this hangar. The day ya'll arrived, I dreamt that it burnt down and then the field caught fire and the fire started to go towards the house."

Emily did not respond but kept working while Stockard lay on the quilt, looking at the tall ceiling, wondering what Emily was thinking. Wodehouse's prose was quick and pleasant to read. Jeeves was taking her out of herself, cheering her up. She was about to start reading again when Emily said, "Why are we dreaming about fire and this hangar?"

"Fire. Symbol of civilization. Symbol of the spirit unbounded." Stockard's nightmare did not recur but had been persistently on her mind over the years. She had started to take more interest in symbols and the strange language of dreams and would occasionally find herself buried in another one of Freud's essays or a dictionary of symbols. She was sporadic in her interest, an especially vivid dream driving her to the books, and she still did not feel as if she had a good grip on what those dreams meant.

"Look," said Emily.

Stockard swung her head around to see Emily holding up a flattened tube of paint.

"No more red paint. How can I paint a dream of fire without red?"

"Are we done?"

"I think so. Done with no answers and one and a half paintings."

Stockard shook the quilt several times to get the dirt out, stirring up more dust. She began to sneeze. Emily packed up, putting her paints away and folding up the easel. It was normally awkward the two of them carrying a wet canvas and a wet palette along with the other things, but two wet canvases was too much. They decided to leave them inside the hangar, next to the small door. They would pick them up later.

Stockard stopped to look at the painted canvases. The first one looked the most complete. The air itself was red, blowing around in gusts. Emily had borrowed some textured swirls from Van Gogh's *Starry Night*. It was difficult to show hot swirling air in a painting. But there was no Lee Wilson.

In the second painting, Emily had painted Lee's face first, again borrowing some facial features from Van Gogh's *The Potato Eaters*. Lee's eyes were wild, yellow on the outside, reflected red in the middle. Emily was just starting to paint the walls when she had run out of red paint.

"Having a Van Gogh kind of day," asked Stockard.

"I can see what he meant. It is so difficult to portray lunatic moods with smooth paint."

"What about Bosch?"

"Yeah yeah."

"Or Munch?"

"Okay, I got the point. It's difficult for me to paint this mood. How's that?"

"Sorry, sorry, I just thought you wanted examples."

"I'm having problems putting down on canvas whatever it is..." They stood looking at the paintings a moment before Emily continued. "It's making me grumpy. It comes from painting too many goddamned boring landscapes."

They broke away from the drying paintings to stack everything else outside of the large sliding doors and then shut them. The doors took a great deal more effort to close than to open. Both girls grunted a few times and worked up a sweat.

Once the sliding doors were closed, Emily and Stockard stood inside. They had been unusually quiet that afternoon and now their silence was encapsulated in the empty structure. Stockard felt the loneliness of it and was at a loss for thoughts or words or even movement. Emily, she could tell, was in the same state of mind. They stood looking at the hangar for a minute, then two, time drawing into the dull light, the dust swirling and then settling, the smell of closure, of being sealed off for a long time, all around them.

Stockard looked at the boxes and furniture stacked in the corner. There were some wooden crates. The boxes were a hodgepodge of cardboard and sizes, some looking new, some ancient. She recognized a lot of the furniture from the Nashville house, which grandmother had sold when they all moved to New York. There were two sofas, one upside down and stacked on the other, making a piece of furniture that had legs on the floor and sticking up in the air. It had been wrapped in polyethylene, taped at the corners with one big piece of tape going around the middle. There was a large china cabinet, unwrapped, sitting aloof from the rest of the furniture. She could remember the Nashville house, now, and was struck by how a house could be reduced to a shell, its contents taking up so little space in a far-away building. She turned to Emily, meaning to say something along these lines and at the same time aware that their conversations were becoming ponderous and philosophical, not as much fun as they used to be, but she found Emily standing next to her, tears running down her cheeks.

"What on earth, Emily?"

Emily began to cry harder. Stockard felt for a moment that she understood why. It was the weight of the situation. Being trapped on Sefer Farm. Eve's bizarre horse accident. Aunt Evelyn being haunted. Their dreams being haunted. It had become too much. Stockard was on the verge of tears herself, but Emily suddenly and completely stopped crying, as if she had just turned a switch off. She wiped her eyes and her nose on Stockard's t-shirt, laughing afterwards. "I'm so sorry," she said, "but I've realized that I can't stay here anymore. I've got to go."

"I know. I've got to go, too."

"Can we go tomorrow? I don't think I could stay here any longer."

"We told grandmother we'd stay until the end of July." Stockard was thinking of how grandmother always came to the lunch and dinner tables with a smile on her face. She was happy to have her family around her. She liked those nights on the porch, the Griffin women smoking and drinking and talking. Talking. Talking. "A week more. That's all."

Stockard heard the certainty in her voice. It had not been there before. She did have to go. She had to leave Sefer Farm. She wanted to go back out into the world, unencumbered by a university dorm and classes, on her own, to find out what the world had in store for her, because she knew that by staying here, she would never find out and this awful trapped feeling would persist and begin to rob her of oxygen, and soon she would just be suffocating and suffocated, not even a caged animal, which is how she was starting to feel. It didn't matter what happened when Emily went back to school. If she had to work at the 7-Eleven or McDonald's, she would do exactly that and the world be damned if that was the price that Stockard had to pay to be out on her own. Now she was determined to get the hell out of there.

It was the first time in her life that she knew she had to do something. She was literally being compelled to leave Sefer Farm. She knew not only that she had to go, but it didn't matter where or for what reason. She simply had to move. Her trust in the compulsion, a driving force unlike anything she had ever felt before, was complete. She did not question it. She did not try to explain it. She submitted to it, obediently. All of this hit Stockard in an instant, like a lightning bolt and after the dull period of the thoughts being absorbed and mulled over, Stockard began to wake up from a long sleep, just like she had been kissed by a prince and the world looked very different.

They joked on the way up the hill, arriving at the farmhouse in a much better mood than when they had left it. Stockard had chosen to be there for a week more. She didn't have to be there.

7

THE mail slot had been cut into the stone wall that hinged the blue gated entrance to Sefer Farm. The slot had a brass flap over it, spring loaded so that it would snap closed. It emptied into a metal box on the other side of the wall. It was painted matt black and had a brass padlock on it. The slot had been cut large enough to handle a ream of paper flat packed. Much of Margaret's business correspondence was delivered through this slot.

The mail man usually made it to Sefer Farm just before lunch, bringing that summer the usual mixture of bills, Margaret's business correspondence, Evelyn's *New York Times,* and the occasional personal letter. Ebern would usually bring the mail to the house before dinner. Everything at Sefer Farm moved deliberately. The routines were like machines that moved at just the right speed, not too fast, not too slow, and never ever missing a beat.

By the time that Stockard and Emily had returned from the hangar, Ebern had delivered the day's mail. Stockard walked into her room to change for a ride before dinner. Emily had agreed to carry on as normally as possible until the end of July and then they were gone.

An unopened letter was sitting on her dresser. It was rare for Stockard to receive a letter, a fact that had intensified her sense of being trapped on the farm.

She flipped it over, looking for a return address and there was the name she knew would be there. "Mills Andrew."

"You have got to be kidding," she said. She held the letter for a moment wondering what would be in there. Did she want him in her life or not? The old dialogue played in her head like a scratchy record. She did not want to open it. She didn't want to know. She had just gained independence for the first time. She now knew what her compulsion was. It was an urge to do as she pleased. It was like a freight train, she thought, just taking off from the station, she enjoying all of the high hopes of a journey just beginning. Like a freight train, she knew it could not be stopped easily. What was in the letter?

Would it stop her?

She opened it with a finger, leaving a jagged tear across the middle of the envelope. Mills used bright white stationery, his name and address printed across the top. Very Emily Post, thought Stockard. He had typed the letter.

"Dear Stockard, I had to lie to the Stanford Alumni Association to get your address, which explains why I am so late in writing to you."

Formal, thought Stockard.

"I hated not saying goodbye," continued the letter, "but I did try to call you a couple of times. I looked everywhere for you at graduation and only saw you on the stage when it was your turn. I lost you in the crowd afterwards."

I saw you, too, on the stage and had to look away. I practically ran out of graduation when it was over.

"I just wanted to say how much I enjoyed our time together..." Stockard let out a peal of laughter.

It was a formal letter, non-committal, but he had made the effort to write her. He said he was working for his father that summer, as planned, and was still starting law school at Chapel Hill in the fall. He wanted to see her if she ever came his way. He would be in Asheville in August and wondered if there was any way they could see each other, either half way or he might be able to come her way for a couple of days.

This was what life did, Stockard realized. It messed you about. When you had determined to do one thing, something else tried to keep you from it. There were diversions and dead ends. Pit stops. Rest stops. Wrecks. She was starting to understand how life could be difficult.

She read the letter a second time, more slowly, afterwards lying down on her bed for a moment, feeling slightly paralyzed.

Like a spring, she sat up and put the letter and the mauled envelope into her nightstand drawer. She was through her doorway and into the living room without thinking and right in front of her grandmother's study door, which was closed. She knocked.

Her grandmother's voice came from behind the door. "Yes?"

Stockard stepped in. Her grandmother was at her desk, reading glasses perched on her nose, a page full of type in her left hand. She looked around at Stockard and said, "Hello, my dear."

"Hello." Stockard took two steps in, hesitated and then closed the door behind her. "I, um… I think Emily is going to go west in August." No preliminaries, Stockard thought, just get it out as best you can. "She wants to drive around and see some of… Colorado and Wyoming and New Mexico."

"That sounds nice," her grandmother said, looking once at the sheet of paper in her left hand and then putting it down. She swiveled in her chair to face Stockard. "Is Eve going with her?"

"She doesn't know, with the cast."

"What about you? I'd hate to think of Emily going alone."

"Well, that's what I came to talk with you about. Would you mind if I went?"

"Dear child, I wouldn't mind at all. I think it'll be good for you to get out and see the world, or at least some of it. As much as you'd like to see."

Stockard stood looking at her grandmother, slightly disoriented now with no expectations, just a need to get through what needed to be said, "Well, I hate to ask, but I might need some money, you know… for food and things." It occurred to Stockard that she didn't really know what she needed money for and she tried to think of traveling. Gas. Hotel rooms. Would they stay in hotel rooms?

"Of course you'll need money!" Her grandmother looked at Stockard and then pulled her reading glasses off and set them on her desk. "Why don't you sit down? I've been meaning to talk to you about your money, but I could never find the right time."

"Your money," Stockard heard. She was hyper sensitive to her grandmother's language.

"You have money. Well, what you have is income. It's been all set up. Your Uncle Andrew. Before you went off to Stanford. You can keep using that checkbook and I've got something..." She opened one of her desk drawers and flipped through file folders, finally pulling one out. "I've got something for you." She pulled out two things and handed them to her. "Gas cards. A Shell one and an Exxon one. So you can buy gas on the road. I thought you'd do more driving around this summer. You've stayed awfully close to home."

"I didn't want to hog the Suburban."

"Hog the Suburban? Why don't you just go buy yourself a car?"

"Can I do that?" New rules, Stockard thought, these are not the rules I lived by when I walked into this room.

"Of course you can. You'll have to. Unless you and Emily want to fly back to Stanford to get that Volvo."

"Oh." It was a stifled joy that Stockard found. She tried not to look too overjoyed and she was torn between controlling her face, her heart rate and asking herself why she didn't just let loose and run and jump and scream. But it was simply not done with her grandmother. The way that her grandmother was saying all of this was as if nothing could be more natural than for Stockard to realize that money was not a problem. At least not the kind of problem she had been making of it.

"Just call Uncle Andrew and someone on his staff will set it up for you. Do you know what kind of car you'd want?"

No, she did not. "I liked the Volvo."

"Well, get another one if you want. It's a safe car. Do you think you'll be gone for long?"

"I don't know," said Stockard, thinking she wouldn't be gone for too long, maybe a couple of months. Sefer Farm was not as entrapping as it had been. "August for sure."

"Well, I'll miss you," said her grandmother and then she got up and came to Stockard, throwing her arms around her. "I knew this day would come. College is just… college, but leaving home afterwards, well, I won't know when I'll see you next, will I?"

Stockard was lost in the moment and slow to get her arms around her grandmother. She was a skinny woman. "Grandmother, I will always be coming back here to see you."

"I hope so." She pulled back from Stockard and gave her a look. "Will you do me a favor?"

"Anything."

"Will you take that revolver?"

"Uh, the one in my room?"

"Yes. Ebern could get you a new one if you'd prefer something smaller, but I hate to think of you girls on the road without protection."

"I'll take it, but I dare not say a word to Emily. We went out to shoot one day and she did not like it one little bit."

"They're city, my dear. That mess with Abe probably did not help. You know better." Her grandmother sat back in her desk chair. "We'll talk about money some more, later, but I want to warn you about it. Andrew—or someone on his staff—will tell you how it works. You should be fine. Here's my warning. Don't make too much of it. And don't make too little of it. You've never been foolish with money, not like your mother. Now that you are on your own, you'll have to find out what money means to you. In some ways, it is another relationship. To some people money means everything. To others, it means nothing. You can't do very much without it. I wouldn't equate money with freedom, but for a moment imagine taking a trip out west without it. You'd have to take a bus or hitchhike. You'd sleep… well, you can let your excellent imagination roll over the possibilities. Think about that on your travels. I hope you'll be back for Christmas. We can talk some more then."

Stockard didn't know whether to stay or leave and finally after the two sat looking at each other in silence, she got up, saying, "Emily's probably looking for me to go riding."

"See you at dinner, my dear." Her grandmother turned back to her sheet of paper, small black type requiring her reading glasses.

Stockard hesitated at the door, looking back at her once. Her grandmother was already reading, again. As she went through the door, she wondered what money meant to her grandmother.

Stockard felt an electric charge as she walked through the hallway into the living room and back to her room, where she hesitated for a moment, remembering the letter that had just come. "I'll deal with you later," she said to the nightstand, and found a pair of white jodhpurs in a drawer, smelling freshly laundered.

Whatever tension had been in the air was gone. The horses had run well for Emily and Stockard. Emily complained that Pudd'n Head was too goddamned slow, slower than even Ole Stew. The Griffin women sat down for dinner and were all smiles. Even when Emily, Eve and Stockard went out to the oak tree, they were excited about what lay ahead. Eve said she was going out west, cast be damned. She sure as shit, adding a Tennessee accent of her own making, wasn't staying at the farm and wasn't going back to New York.

8

THE excitement they had felt after passing through Memphis and over the Mississippi had given way to road fatigue in Amarillo. "I have never seen a more boring landscape," Emily said as she looked at the flat land, the big sky and I-40, which had been ruler straight forever.

Eve was grumpy from the start, always near an open car window to stop her cast from sweating. Her arm could take as long as 18 months to heal, she was told, and 18 months was too long to stay any one place, especially in her mood. She jibed Emily about her sketch book. "Why don't you just buy a camera?"

"Not the same," quipped Emily, the pages flapping as she tried to capture the banality of the Great Plains, rubber bands holding her sketch book page in place.

The atlas was their guiding symbol, brand new when they left Nashville. Stockard had selected a middle of the range Volvo, a blue 144, a boxy sedan. It was the strangest feeling to have something so big, so expensive, in her name, something that was hers. Legally. Sometimes she felt it was a loan, it was not really hers. Just holding the key in her hand felt good. This was freedom, she knew, an extension of whatever it was that she had found in July on Sefer Farm.

Emily had bought the atlas, a big AAA folio with a soft cover, at a 7-Eleven. "For people who want to go from point A to point B," she had said as she flipped through it. It was so easy to drive from circle to circle on the map, from city to city. From Amarillo to Albuquerque. Through the dry as a bone landscape. From Albuquerque to Flagstaff.

The Grand Canyon was due north from there. It was their first planned destination and they stood in the August heat, looking down into the great chasm cut into the earth.

"It's a hole," said Eve.

"It's a big hole," said Stockard, agreeably. There were families at their viewing spot atop a promontory. The kids would look and then dash off, chasing each other or heading for the ice cream truck. The parents would stand a few extra moments, torn between a natural wonder that they had traveled hundreds of miles to see and the feeling that they had seen it before, that it was all not as incredible as it should be. Stockard could read their expressions like a book.

"A gash an angry God sliced into the earth," said Emily. "All those poor mugs, hiking down to the bottom of a hole to see a river running through the bottom of a hole."

They saw Las Vegas. Hoover Dam. Death Valley. The Canyonlands. Pike's Peak. Long's Peak. Old Faithful.

They had seen Washington, Jefferson, Roosevelt and Lincoln jack hammered and blown into the side of a mountain. They had seen Thoreau-like colors in the Badlands and bought a Wall Drug Store bumper sticker for the car. They drove and they drove and when they turned towards Denver after three weeks, they suffered from an unshakeable road fatigue.

They were due in Denver on the 23rd of August, where Eve's doctor had arranged for a substitute doctor to x-ray her arm and change the cast. Despite the rattling car and hauling her broken arm everywhere, Eve got a clean bill of health and a new, less-cumbersome cast. The doctor told her to use a sling more.

They had run out of hash and were tired of the highways. Through a perverse need to drive back roads and find an isolated place to spend their last week together before Emily flew back to school, they ended up in Steamboat Springs. They stayed in the Rabbit Ears Motel and hiked around Rabbit Ears Pass during the day. At night they foraged around the bars. The town was nearly deserted.

One night Emily and Stockard were dancing at The Tin Roof, the only busy bar in town. Local pickup bands played nearly every night. Emily had easily scored a supply of pot there and they found the atmosphere congenial and better than sitting in the Rabbit Ears Motel getting stoned. Eve was stuck at a table with her casted arm resting on top of a chair back. She had begun to take her misery out on beer, although she was no dancer, she told herself, so it didn't matter too much. Stockard and Emily said they were no dancers either, but they couldn't just sit around much longer, and they had started saying yes to anyone who wanted to dance. It was there that Luke first approached Eve, asking how she had broken her arm. Eve had the story well rehearsed and she was delighted when Luke said, "That's a real bummer. We could have used a riding instructor."

"We?"

"I work at the C Lazy U. It's a dude ranch about ten miles up the road. We never have enough riding instructors."

"My cousin," Eve pointed to Stockard, who was self-consciously swaying to a metallic and huffy harmonica song, "she rides. She's been riding longer than I have."

That was how Stockard began working at the C Lazy U and Eve found a boyfriend.

When Emily flew out the next Monday, she said she was glad that Eve and Stockard had finally found a place to stay still. She would be graduating one semester early and would be back in December.

They would remain in Steamboat Springs until May of next year, 1972.

The Blue House

1

WHEN Emily returned to Steamboat Springs on December 19th, she was toting a new camera bag. Her graduation and Christmas gift to herself was a Nikon F2 Photomic.

She had put the camera body in Stockard's hand and said, "See how heavy it is?"

It felt like a brick to Stockard.

Emily had given up painting, sculpting, drawing and printing. She had decided that photography was her medium. "I'm never going to be any good as an artist and I like taking pictures the most." Eve said she had told her so.

The next six months of Emily's pictures told the story. There were the pictures of Stockard and Emily on the ski slopes of Steamboat Springs. Stockard always looked beaten up on a pair of skis. She had only skied a couple of times before living in Steamboat and she had a lot of learning to do. Emily had grown up going to Vermont for winter ski breaks and was more comfortable and less frazzled on skis. After ski season, they had driven all over the Rockies in Colorado, leaving Eve in a deadly dull routine with Luke. Emily had taken pictures of them driving around Colorado, revisiting Pike's and Long's Peaks, wandering amongst summer tourists in Vail and Aspen, and in front of a raft on the Arkansas River.

When they finally stopped in Boulder to see what all the fuss was about, they decided not to leave.

In 1972, Boulder was a hippie town, a retreat for mainstream hippies who wanted out of the limelight, unlike Haight Ashbury. It was a drug town. It did not take much effort to stumble into an excessive lifestyle. Stockard and Emily found a house under Mount Sanitas, on the opposite side from The Hill. It was an important distinction in their minds. The Hill represented the University of Colorado. It was full of college students. They did not want to be part of the daily college experience and felt themselves to be well beyond it even if only a year or less from school themselves. They did not really want to be a part of the full on hippie culture around downtown Boulder either. The community around Mount Sanitas was neither hippie nor college, but not remote from either. It bordered normal neighborhoods, where men went off to work and women stayed home, where children played in the backyard and there was a dog or three at every house. They wanted to be in between the various Boulder contingents and they moved into a three-bedroom house on Mapleton Drive.

The third bedroom was ostensibly for Eve, but Emily quickly had it fitted with a sink and converted into a darkroom beneath the notice of their landlord. Their house always smelled of photographic chemicals and there was film and photographic paper stacked in the refrigerator. Stockard was getting used to hearing the click of the shutter or seeing Emily leave the house, camera bag on one shoulder, a heavy tripod in the other hand. She was getting deeply and daily absorbed in taking and developing pictures.

The plumber was stoned when installing the sink and he did not do a very good job of soldering the cold-water line. They had been in Boulder just six months when the landlord, Jeff something or another, showed up on their doorstep one morning.

Stockard answered the persistent knocks on the door. It was ten o'clock in the morning and she was not fully awake, blinking in the sunlight that came through the open front door. "May I help you?" She had never shed her Southern accent and she could hear the "you" draw out unnaturally long. "May I hep yoooouuuuuuuu?" She needed coffee.

"I think you've got a leak somewhere," said Jeff.

"Huh?" Stockard kept blinking, slowly recognizing their landlord.

"I think you've got a leak somewhere. Your water bills come to me and the consumption has gone through the roof. I cannot imagine that you girls are using that much water and I think you've got a leak."

"Oh." More information, thought Stockard. So much to take in, so little consciousness.

"Have you noticed any water under the sinks or pooling on the floor of the kitchen or the bathroom?"

"No." Stockard kept on blinking, thinking this simple physical act would help wake her.

"Do you mind if I look around?"

"It's a little messy. Can you come back after we've cleaned up? We don't normally let it go…"

"If there's a leak, it could be damaging the house so I better look now. I am, after all, the owner of the house. My asking you is me being nice."

Stockard let the front door swing open, her familiar green bathrobe now on full display. It had become worn over the years. It was the most comfortable piece of clothing that she owned. "Help yourself." She knew what she looked like and did not want to think what Jeff thought of her. It was her grandmother's voice that was saying a lady never answered the door in her bathrobe, this despite their generally ragged appearance in Boulder.

Jeff crawled around underneath the kitchen sink and made some noises in the bathroom before he came into the living room, where Stockard was sitting on the sofa, wondering what he was going to say next.

"I need to go underneath the house. Everything looks fine. It does look… neglected."

"Okay."

Jeff returned after ten minutes, knocking on the door. "It's the damndest thing, but there is a leak, but it's coming from a place where I don't remember there being any sink or bathtub or anything. One of the bedrooms. Is anyone in there?"

"Which one?" Stockard already knew the answer to her question.

"The one in the middle."

"No one's in there."

"Well, I better take a look." Jeff made a beeline for the bedroom door.

Stockard sat back down on the sofa, trying to imagine the scene.

Emily had made several attempts to keep her darkroom orderly, but it simply was not in her makeup. Jeff opened the door to a room whose appearance had been radically altered. In addition to a utility sink being installed, the walls had been painted matt black to dampen stray light. Black wooden shutters had been mounted over the window. A rubber mat had been laid across the floor. Steel tables had been installed along three of the walls. It reeked of film processing chemicals. There were strings of negatives hanging from lines that had been nailed into the walls. It was a mess.

Stockard heard the door open and the click of the light switching on. There was silence. She knew that Jeff was standing there, either in shock or taking the scene in. She wished she had a cigarette. She wanted to light one up. It would give her a chance to think. She was now of that class of smokers who never bought cigarettes, but often bummed one in a crowd. Jeff's heavy footsteps came back down the hallway.

"What have you done?" Jeff stood in front of the sofa, looking down at Stockard.

It was the first time that Stockard had ever had a man stand above her and demand to know something. His voice was stern and angry.

"My cousin is a photographer. Amateur photographer." Stockard looked at Jeff from head to toe. Maybe "amateur" was the wrong word. He was ridiculous in his anger. She wanted to flick her make-believe cigarette ash on the floor and blow smoke at him. "She takes it very seriously." She had used a very cool and very measured tone of voice.

"Well, you fucked up that room. You put a sink in there and it's going to cost me money to get it right. The floor will never be right. The plumber cut into the floor. He did a sloppy job. It's a hardwood floor! It will never be right. I cannot believe it." Jeff glared at Stockard for a minute. "And the whole rest of the house looks terrible. You and your cousin are just going to have to move out."

They would have to box everything up. They would have to find another place in Boulder. They would have to right Emily's darkroom and find another house where she could do the same. They were definitely staying in Boulder. Emily and Stockard loved living in Boulder.

"Look, there's no reason to be unreasonable," said Stockard. As she heard the words come out of her mouth, she had heard them before, maybe in a movie. "So we're messy. I'll give you that. I hadn't really thought about it before, but you're right, the place is a real pig sty. I need to get a maid. Neither one of us cleans worth a damn. You're right about the darkroom. We made some changes and we didn't ask you about it. The room's a disaster from a landlord's point of view, but why do you own this place?" She was surprised that she had shut him up. She continued, "To make money, right?"

Jeff nodded and looked at Stockard in a way that made her uncomfortable. He was finding her attractive. She stood up and instinctively walked to the other side of the blanket chest that acted as their coffee table.

"How much were you going to make on this place? Do you have a mortgage? Let's say you do." The words came out of her mouth without any effort. Her brain had no interaction with her mouth, her mouth simply spouted the words and they sounded surprisingly accurate. "You've got a fifteen-year mortgage and you were looking to make fifty dollars a month on rental." She knew the figure was high, but it would flatter Jeff. She was essentially saying that he was a better businessman than he actually was. "You're looking to make six hundred dollars a year plus your equity build up." She did not remember ever having used the word "equity" before. The words and the math continued to come from nowhere. "The house is worth, what, twenty thousand dollars." She knew, again, that she was overestimating.

Jeff nodded. He had crossed his arms.

"Okay, so let's say I buy the house from you. You get your equity stake up front and then I'll pay a premium on the house so that you get your investment back."

"What did you have in mind?"

"Thirty-five thousand dollars." Stockard knew it was too much money.

"You're crazy. You can't come up with that kind of money."

"What if I can?"

"It's a deal."

Stockard loved to see the change in Jeff. First he had been curious, poking around in his rental property. Then he was indignant. Then he saw her as a piece of ass. Finally he was putty in her hands. All it took was money.

"But if you can't come up with the money by the end of the week, I'm evicting you and your cousin and slapping you with a lien to recoup damages."

"Deal." A week was a long time, she figured.

After Jeff left, Stockard had a shower and brewed a pot of coffee. She called Uncle Andrew. She tried to make the story as brief as possible, explaining that she wanted to buy a house. He said that was great and he would contact an attorney in Boulder to help find a real estate agent and make sure that the deal was handled correctly. Stockard then had to tell the whole story, taking more of Andrew's time than she wanted. Andrew was never rude and never impatient with Stockard, but she had been raised by her grandmother saying that Andrew was an important man. His time was valuable. When she was done with her story, he said he understood perfectly. He took down the landlord's name and telephone number and then said, "Sometimes it is easier to pay to make a nuisance go away. If you can afford it."

"It's true. Thanks for understanding, Uncle Andrew."

Andrew asked, "So Emily has not given up photography?"

"She cannot leave it alone. I've never seen someone tinker so persistently. Even at parties! That camera goes everywhere!" Stockard was wondering if Uncle Andrew could see Emily taking her camera into the bathroom.

"It is a sign of the real thing. I like her pictures."

It was an innocuous comment, but it sounded so odd for some reason. It would stick out in Stockard's mind. At that moment, she was still absorbed with the events of the morning. She let it pass.

She had just said goodbye to Andrew when Emily came through her bedroom door, rubbing her eyes, her hair mashed into one side of her head. She wore flannel pajamas, red ones with pastries, to bed.

"Good morning, Sunshine," said Stockard.

"Morn'n. Why are you up so early?"

"Things to do."

"Like what?"

Stockard eyed Emily for a beat. "Like buy this house."

"Why would you do a thing like that?"

"I think I'm ready to settle down here, for awhile."

"Oh. Mind if I stay?"

"Do you want to buy it with me?"

Emily sat down in a chair, facing Stockard. She ran her fingers through her hair. "I'd like to. I like living with you and I like my darkroom. I finally have a place to work, although I wonder if I'll want a studio one day. But I have a confession."

Stockard waited in the silence. Emily rarely paused. "Well, what is it?"

"I'm broke."

"Huh?"

"I'm broke, at least for this year. I gave most of this year's income away. Don't look so shocked. I just didn't want all that money. When Uncle Andrew explained it, the money, I started to have these crazy thoughts. One minute I wanted a big diamond, the next I wanted a flat in Paris. Paris! What the hell do I care about Paris? Stupid thoughts, although not as stupid as Eve, but they were not good. So I put aside enough to live on. The rest I gave away. I gave it to a charity. Believe it or not, it made me feel better."

"Uh."

"I'd love to help out with the house. I think it's a great idea, I just cannot until next year. I'm more than happy to make it up next year."

"Uh."

"Well," said Emily, "since we're on the topic, I've also volunteered to go away for six months."

"Huh?"

"Something like the Peace Corps. It's fruity as hell, but I thought I'd go to Peru. They've got tons of things that need to be done, and I was talking to one of the recruiters. It sounds like something I can do to be useful. So I've signed up for a six-month tour in Peru. Some project building a bridge or a well or something. I leave in a week."

"Ah."

"Is it okay if I leave my stuff here? I've got enough money for rent."

"Of course. Don't worry about the rent. I've pretty much bought the house."

Stockard found that she was ready for a nap just after lunch.

Eve and Luke had lasted until July and then she had packed her things and moved to Boulder. Her cast was long since gone, although she still walked as if her left arm was in a sling. By then, Stockard and Emily's house was full of furniture, darkroom equipment and various other odds and ends, especially books. There was no room for Eve. Much to Stockard's chagrin, Stockard and Emily had offered to find a bigger house, but Eve had insisted on getting an apartment of her own, down on Spruce in a converted house. She had taken a job in a small bakery that sold whole grain breads and pastries. She worked the early shift and was turning the ovens on at three in the morning. Her schedule was at odds with Stockard and Emily's, who were lucky to be out of bed by noon. They sometimes had a late lunch together, but Eve was noticeably absent from their lives. She had given up telling Emily and Stockard her suspicions about the family money, but she was continuing her trend of working at places that she could have bought.

Stockard thought Eve had finally gone off the deep end. After Emily's revelation, she decided she was the only sane one of the three.

2

For ten years, Boulder would be the home for the three girls. They would follow the basic trends that they set up when they first arrived. Eve appeared frozen in 1971, maybe even 1968. Her clothes did not change. Tie-dye and bell bottoms. Her hair did not change. Long and straight and in a bandana for work. She continued to work at the bakery. It was a big event when she started to work the morning shift rather than the early-morning shift. She had a series of boyfriends similar to Luke, men who existed with her, suspended in a routine. They were never very far from her and never too close.

Emily's trip to Peru was her first of many such trips. She became disenchanted with the Peace Corps-like mission after the first trip. "Those people are naïve," she said. "They show up young, starry-eyed idealists thinking that a simple-minded pity will help people out. They are culturally out of it. The irony is that just when they realize their mistake, they either give up in defeat or they create an even more fanatic illusion to help them get through their mess. I hate the lack of comprehension. They think a cheer and sincere charity will solve world hunger."

"What are you going to do?" Stockard was aware that Emily could not stay still. She had been back from Peru less than a week when this conversation took place.

"I'm going to immunize people, or at least help."

"Huh?"

"The CDC people put me into contact with several groups that run immunization programs in third-world countries."

"I never understood what that meant, third world."

"It means poor and unimmunized. So next week I'm due in Cairo to meet with some people who are setting up programs in Africa."

"You're leaving already?"

"Well, next week."

"We better celebrate or something. That's not much time. What do you want to do?"

"Go buy a camera. Want to come?"

Emily had been in a Lenten frame of mind when she had prepared to leave for Peru, her first charitable trip. As she had tried to explain to Stockard why she was leaving her precious Nikon behind, Stockard had interjected, "You must give up what you are to be selfless." She wasn't sure if she was quoting soterology or Zen Buddhism. It was part of the language that people spoke in Boulder. It didn't matter. She understood what Emily was saying better than Emily, who was saying it.

Within a week of arriving in that overgrown Peruvian village, Emily knew she had made a mistake. By the end of the trip, she swore she would never be caught without a camera again. And she wanted to start shooting medium format.

That afternoon, Emily and Stockard went to a camera shop in Denver and bought her first Mamiya, a boxy black thing even heavier than the Nikon. For the next week, Emily spent hours fiddling with the camera. She made a special stop in New York on her way to Cairo, ostensibly to visit her mother, but also to buy lenses and various other accessories to go with her new camera. She also bought a hard shiny silver case for the camera and enough film to shoot a movie. She still had her Nikon, the smaller camera, over her shoulder, but going forward Emily's obsession with seeing the world through a lens and placing the image on film one frame at a time only grew.

Stockard was as different from her cousins as could be. She had become interested in the process of buying her house. There had been the heat of the initial argument with Jeff. Stockard enjoyed having to think quickly. She enjoyed having an opponent. She pulled things from her depths that she did not know she knew. She thought that she had never paid attention to her grandmother and her aunt when they talked business. They rarely talked about the family businesses in front of the other Griffin women, but they chewed over other financial matters in front of them. That was Stockard's only explanation for knowing that a mortgage was normally a 30-year loan and equity was what you actually owned.

As a Denver attorney had guided the transaction to a smooth closure, Stockard found that she could not leave it alone. When she found out that the actual documents were being sent to New York for review by one of Andrew's staff, she ordered the Denver attorney to send her duplicates.

Packets of documents began to arrive. Some were stapled. Some were spiral bound. The vast majority of the documents were margin to margin full of tiny text. She read it all, calling the Denver attorney so often that he finally suggested that she take a real estate course to satisfy her curiosity. He wasn't angry. He lived by the billable hour and even if he was busy, he knew a billable client when he met one.

Aunt Evelyn had once said, "Business majors are the most ignorant people coming out of college."

Stockard knew what she meant. All they knew were numbers and strange axioms for gaining shareholder value and profitable margins. They knew nothing about the world, about what had inspired men and women for centuries, about the frailties of the human heart, about what a mind and a culture under pressure could produce, about art and the consolation of the human spirit through the lens of history.

Stockard had waded into the various steps of buying her house. The offer. The inspection. The title search. The closing. As she read the documents she began to ask herself how her aunt and her grandmother knew about these things if they had not learned them in college. She knew they had both taken accounting courses. "A necessary evil," her grandmother had said, "because in business you've got to know how much a thing cost and how much you can sell it for. And of course there's the mess of running the business. Overhead. Otherwise I would have avoided accounting." Her grandmother knew she would be going into business even as a Vassar undergraduate.

Did they take other business courses?

Stockard had arrived for the closing in jeans and a sweater and felt immediately that she was underdressed. There was her Denver lawyer in a grey suit. Jeff's attorney was in a suit. Even Jeff was wearing a sport coat, looking like the grinning Cheshire cat. Despite her clothes, they treated her with deference and respect. When she saw the certified check go from her attorney to Jeff's, she understood why. It was the power of money. It commanded respect, and she by association had commanded respect because she could marshal the funds to follow through on her promise.

Afterwards her attorney had taken the deed, saying, "Your people in New York requested that I send the deed to them, for safekeeping. Is that okay?"

"Could you send me a copy?"

Of course he could. With a shake of the hand and a request to call him if she needed anything else, he was gone.

Now she had a car and a house in her name. The car had represented freedom. The house represented permanency. She spent days thinking how different they were.

Eventually Stockard enrolled in a Continuing Education course at CU. Real Estate 101. It was taught in an auditorium that seated 500. She started looking at houses for sale. She started going to the foreclosure auctions. She took the Real Estate Law course. And then the Real Estate Finance and Investment Analysis course. It was her little secret. She bought her first investment house two years after buying her house. This time she did not overpay. She slightly underpaid, but spent too much fixing it up. After she had rented it out and was carefully laying out the numbers on a piece of graph paper and using an HP calculator, she saw by how much she had overspent on the fixing up. She knew where to cut corners on the next one. She was starting to understand how money worked.

3

STOCKARD had a few misgivings about the Rabchaus when she first met them. Primarily she wondered about Etta, the wife, who had left the following note to herself on the refrigerator door.

I take a stand for:
Experiencing things as they are, in total clarity and ease
Operating at 100% all the time
Having love be at the center of my life
Letting the mystery pass thru me & to pass the mystery on
Being willing at any moment to step into the creative unknown

Stockard's first instinct was to laugh. The grammar was bad enough and the temptation was strong for her to take a pen to the note and correct a few things. But Stockard knew that as soon as she bent down with a pen, she would start writing questions.

"What does this mean?" In particular the bit about the mystery was mysterious. "Letting the mystery pass thru me & to pass the mystery on." Was "thru" even a word? What was The Mystery? Why would anyone place something like this on the refrigerator? Stockard was trying not to let her mind run away with the possibilities.

"Having love be at the center of my life" was easy for Stockard to figure out.

Etta was married to Bill, who made good money doing something or other for a large beer distributor. They were in their early thirties and when their marriage of seven years started to wane, they had agreed that they loved each other very much, but they needed to spice it up. Bill thought sleeping with other women would spice it up nicely. After several weeks, Etta came around to believing that taking a lover might help, too.

Bill knew exactly whom he wanted as a lover. Her name was Cadence and she worked at the bakery where Bill picked up a muffin and a cup of coffee every morning on his way to the beer distributor. She was younger than Bill and Etta. Bill had gotten used to seeing

Cadence's long, dark hair pulled back in a ponytail. She always wore jeans, faded with holes. She looked delicious in jeans. She normally wore a t-shirt. Bill could see puffs of flour against the blue t-shirts, a perfectly natural thing for bakery staff. There was something about the way that Cadence wore her work that drove Bill mad.

Stockard never found out exactly how Bill had taken Cadence as his lover and how Etta made it clear that it was okay for Bill and Cadence to be together. Very likely Bill explained to Cadence that Etta had her own lover, Christopher Shishin, whom Etta had met at a Tiep Hien fundraiser. When Stockard had asked Cadence what Tiep Hien was, Cadence's reply was, "some Buddhist school or something."

Etta tried to explain it more precisely. "It's from the Zen School of Lin Chi."

A Tiep Hien magnet held her personal manifesto on the fridge.

"Oh." Stockard wondered did everyone in Boulder know these things?

"There are fourteen precepts to Tiep Hien," Etta said as she tossed a salad. "It's all based on Engaged Buddhism. Would you like to come to a meeting and learn more?"

"Maybe." Boulder did this to you, thought Stockard. You found yourself doing things that you normally would never have done elsewhere. You took things seriously which elsewhere would have made you laugh. Not that Buddhism made Stockard laugh. It was more the unquestioning reverence afforded anything alternative that made Stockard laugh.

"Shishin can explain it better than me. Did you know he was my lover?"

Really! Stockard was still surprised at the frankness of these people. Her grandmother's voice had continued speaking in her head over the years. She was now eighty-one and living on Sefer Farm full-time. She never left, not even to get her hair cut. A hairdresser from Kimbro made a trip to the farm every month. Her grandmother's voice was saying, "This is something that people should keep to themselves."

Her mother was living with her grandmother on Sefer Farm, too. She had just sent James Fox's *White Mischief* with a note that read: "Thoroughly entertaining. Rich people behaving very badly in colonial Kenya. Not what we see in Tennessee. How about in Boulder?"

Stockard knew Cadence through Eve. They worked at the same bakery. Cadence and Eve were only casual friends, but one time Cadence and Stockard saw each other at a party and the two had become fast friends. Stockard was now thirty-three years old. Cadence was almost ten years her junior, but there was an immediate rapport. Cadence would call to have a beer or a cup of coffee. Stockard, who had troubles developing a social life without a job or being part of one of the cliques in Boulder, never let a social opportunity pass.

In the ten years that Stockard had been in Boulder, she had tried running, but her boobs were too big to make that enjoyable. She had done some hiking and liked that until she started dragging a large backpack around for longer, multiple-day hikes. She still loved tromping around Mt. Sanitas and Flagstaff for a couple of hours at a time. She occasionally skied, but the drive to the resorts was rarely worth a simple day trip. She had met some people through these sports. Along the way, Stockard always felt as if she was being invited to a different Buddhist meeting. There were so many! She had heard of Tiep Hien, but sorting out all the details of what they stood for and what it meant was too much for her. They never drank booze at those meetings and she found they had a limited interest for her. If she contributed money to the upkeep of a temple, then it was a monumental effort to keep the fundraisers away. They always wanted more money. There was a time when Stockard had known several teachers from Naropa University, itself a local college based on Buddhist teachings. The University of Colorado and Naropa University staff never mixed.

When Cadence had invited Stockard to Bill and Etta's house for dinner, Stockard did not know what to expect. She had written off her initial embarrassment at their openness as her problem. They did talk about their "lovers" and their "spirituality" with an inappropriate frankness. Stockard thought it was her East Coast and Southern upbringing that made her embarrassed.

Stockard was doubly surprised to find out that she was the fifth wheel at the dinner party. The two pairs of known lovers were the only others in attendance. Bill and Cadence. Etta and Christopher Shishin. Despite their frankness about their relationships, they were surprisingly well behaved at dinner. Stockard had not known what to expect, but there they all sat at the Rabchau's dinner table, the room lit by a lot of candles, and they ate their curry and rice and talked like normal people about Ronald Reagan's chance for re-election and how Boulder was the only city in the United States to dislike him. They talked about the good old days before Pearl Street Mall had been created and how the commercialization of Boulder would bring the worst kinds of people, tourists or businessmen. Bill cast out a comment about the CU Buffs' dismal football record but no one took the bait.

Stockard was very relaxed by the time they moved into the Rabchau's living room for dessert and herbal tea. They had drunk a lot of wine, and the living room had two overstuffed sofas and large pillows in the remaining floor space. Stockard had to look twice to realize that Bill was sitting on one sofa rubbing Etta's shoulders. Etta sat on the floor between his legs. Cadence was lying across the other sofa with her head in Christopher Shishin's lap. He was stroking her hair. Stockard was leaning against a couple of pillows on the floor and it took a moment to realize that this was more normal than what she had expected. The husband and wife were being affectionate and the two single people were taking care of each other. It was uncharacteristically confusing. They kept on talking about the most pedestrian topics.

Stockard had a thought that made her sit up. Maybe she was supposed to be watching this scene. Maybe she was being asked by merely her presence to join this group. She began to mull the thought over as Christopher Shishin was expounding his views on the sell-out culture of Boulder versus the blue-collar mentality of Denver. Christopher was not her type. He was skinny and moved carefully. Stockard had seen many sensitive men like Christopher at the Buddhist gatherings and she found they lacked substance. Bill was a stocky man but not very deep. She was more attracted to Bill but she knew he was intellectually thin, a strike against him.

As Stockard caught herself appraising the two men around her and wondering what on earth she was thinking, a loud snore stopped everything.

Etta had fallen asleep.

Bill, with a smile, leaned over to look into his wife's face. She let out another snore, even louder.

"Gee, I think she's asleep," said Cadence.

Etta let a deeper, louder snore go.

"Whoa, that's pretty much how I feel," said Christopher. "I think it's time for me to go."

Stockard's dark suspicions, whatever they were, went out the door with Christopher, who kissed the sleeping Etta on the cheek on his way out. The dinner party was over. Cadence and Stockard left shortly afterwards, both walking in the same direction home.

At Pine and 6th Street, where Stockard would continue north and Cadence would go east, they stopped for a moment. Cadence said, "You are one of us. You fit so well into our little group."

"Oh, thanks. I like everyone."

"I think everyone loves you. Well," Cadence leaned over and hugged Stockard, giving her a kiss on the cheek, "time to sleep."

4

A<small>T</small> four o'clock the next afternoon, Stockard answered a knock on the front door and was not surprised to find Bill Rabchau. He had been on Stockard's mind and she wondered if her thoughts had summoned him to her doorstep.

He looked like a lion, lazy by nature, who had just woken from a long nap to find that there was something new and interesting in the jungle.

"Hello, Bill."

"Hello, Stockard," said Bill. "I was…"

Stockard was mentally finishing the sentence while he hesitated. I was just in the neighborhood and wanted to know if you'd like to fuck. Me. Fuck me.

In his hesitation, Bill took a deeper look into Stockard's eyes and began again. "I was just thinking of you." He was silent.

"How nice," said Stockard. She did not expect the hesitation. She was prepared for him to barge in. It changed what she expected of him. He might not be so cocksure after all. She was about to invite him in when he spoke again.

"I've been thinking about you since you left last night."

"Oh," said Stockard. She heard a note of cinematic longing in his voice. She leaned into the edge of the door, hiding a part of herself behind it. "Bill, I don't know if it's a good idea, you coming in."

"That's okay," he said. "I just wanted to drop by and say what I've said."

They stood for a moment, looking at each other, Bill fully self-possessed. He was very comfortable staring at Stockard, waiting for her to say something. It was Stockard's turn to hesitate.

"Well, thanks." She couldn't ask about his wife. Etta apparently would not care if Bill was looking for another lover. Besides, Stockard did not necessarily want to shoot him down. She was simply at a loss for what she wanted to say. After a moment that stretched on and on for Stockard, Bill spoke again. "Look at it as an open invitation. We could have fun together. Ask Cadence. I hope we'll see each other soon."

Bill turned and walked very casually down the porch steps and strolled to his car. He waved as he opened the car door and then was gone before Stockard even noticed what kind of car he was driving.

When she looked back at the moment, Bill had managed the whole thing so well. It was grown up. There was no sense of embarrassment or jitteriness, at least not on his part. This, Stockard thought, was how adults approached each other. There was no false pretense, no sex as an ulterior motive. What Bill wanted he asked for and he did it with genuine good manners. Sex was the motive.

Stockard leaned on the door she had closed on Bill and took a look at her house. Just after she had overpaid for the house, she'd had the wood floors stripped, restained and then polished. Then she had all of the walls painted white. Over the years, Emily's photographs had eaten up all available wall space.

Then they took up the floor space.

Now when Emily returned from one of her trips, there were two or three weeks when she would constantly be in her darkroom, developing film and making prints. As the best of the pictures were printed, Emily would mount them and have them framed. Older pictures would come off the walls and the new ones would go in their place. Old pictures leaned against the walls and furniture. Stockard knew she was a terrible housekeeper and now she could see the dust buildup on the pictures. She had tried a succession of maids over the years, but they had done a lousy job cleaning, missed cleaning days for pitiful excuses or displayed a bad attitude. She would have to get someone in before Emily returned from Malawi, the latest third-world country she was visiting to help set up schools or immunization programs or irrigation plans. Stockard could no longer remember where Emily was nor what she was doing. There were the pictures to remind Stockard, but they were so crystal clear and dramatic that she forgot that they were a depiction of Emily's life during certain periods.

Stockard also had shelves built along a section of wall in the living room and on three walls of her bedroom. She was still a reader and the books had piled up over the years.

"That's what we are," Stockard said to herself, "two girls, a lot of photographs and a lot of books." Now something else was offering itself to her.

One day while she had been hiking up Sanitas, she had overheard a woman commiserating with a man. They looked as if they were two or three years out of college. The man had just found out that his girlfriend had cheated on him with two guys. The woman was incredulous. "Is that even possible? How do they do that?"

It had been a bright, blue-sky day in the spring. Their conversation kept breaking into Stockard's own happy thoughts. They had been hiking just behind her. The Sanitas trail is steep and their voices floated up to Stockard. At first she thought she was listening to a radio program. As the story unfolded, Stockard heard the terrible suffering in the man's voice. It was a mixture of desperation and numbness. He kept saying, "I can't believe it. I thought she was the one."

All Stockard could wonder was why the woman couldn't figure out how a ménage à trois worked. Was she really that innocent? She was genuinely stumped by the mechanics of two guys and a girl.

With Bill safely away, Stockard found herself on the other side of that conversation. She was now wondering what had led the man's girlfriend into having sex with two guys. Was it spontaneous? Was she drunk? Was she promiscuous? A slut? Each option was so different. Was she adventurous and then torn with guilt so she 'fessed it up to her steady, creating one of those nuclear moments, dropping a bomb that would forever decimate the landscape of a relationship?

Or had the girl stumbled into her own version of the Rabchau open marriage?

Despite Bill's sleaziness—again a word that her grandmother would use—Stockard found herself wondering what it would be like to sleep with him. Would he be one of those callous men? She searched for her copy of Florence King's hilarious book on Southerners, simply titled, *Southern Ladies and Gentlemen*. It was on a bedroom bookshelf. She looked up the description of The Bad Good Ole Boy: "He makes his grand exit seven seconds after the grand entrance and murmurs: 'I sure pleasured you, Velma Lee, dint I?'" Was that how Bill would be? Not likely, not if Cadence was still seeing him. She was the kind of woman that a man wanted to love slowly and carefully. She had beauty that wanted to be worshipped.

Stockard had four lovers in her ten years in Boulder. Each had a slightly different approach to making love, but the limits were quickly reached and she found that within six months, she felt thoroughly conventional. And bored. The very idea of sex degenerating into a routine had kept her away from men's approaches for more than a year. There had been no one interesting, either.

"Bill visited," said Stockard. She had gone to the bakery where Eve and Cadence worked, purposely showing up just after ten in the morning. It was a slow time and she knew that Cadence would be manning an empty counter. Eve had long since gone home. There might be someone in the back cleaning up from the night's baking. There were no customers. "Yesterday. He made a proposition, if that's the right word."

Stockard was looking carefully at Cadence to see her reaction. Strands from Cadence's ponytail were starting to escape. She was in her typically faded jeans and flour dusted t-shirt. She looked so good. Stockard could see how any man who stumbled on her at this moment could not help but see an understated, painfully simple beauty.

"I figured," said Cadence. She had a slightly ambiguous smile. "He's got a thing for you."

"What do you think?"

"I can't blame him. I'd have a thing for you, too." Cadence's smile was full now. "But that's not what you're asking, huh? Well, you ought to give Bill a try. He knows the ropes."

The mistress of a married man was recommending to a possible second mistress that the man was a good time.

It was the language of her grandmother. Mistress. Married Man. The labels carried connotations. A church wedding. Proper society. She knew how proper people behaved. A mistress was something that Parisian men had. It was not something a Southern man had. Uncle Abe had a mistress. He blew his head off because of it. The church vows that she had heard so many times did not apply to Etta and Bill. There was the image of Bill stroking Etta's hair that night. He was so loving with his wife, but across the room sat the woman he was sleeping with. The possibilities were liberating for Stockard.

The second time that Bill knocked on Stockard's door, she was ready.

"Hey." He was dressed for work, having no doubt just finished his daily duties for the beer distributor.

He wanted another crack, Stockard thought. "Hello, Bill. Come on in."

Stockard turned and made for the sofa. She heard the door close behind her. She felt her ponytail tugged. She stopped and began to turn around when Bill steadied her shoulder, not allowing her to move, not to see him. His other hand stayed on her ponytail, grasping it, his thumb working the elastic band off. Stockard could feel his body moving slowly towards her. He ran one hand down the length of her released ponytail, spreading her hair out, slowly. With both hands, he began to claw, even more slowly, cat-like, at the end of her hair, working his way up until he reached her head. Stockard felt herself stepping back into Bill.

In the coming weeks, Stockard would begin to understand how different making love with Bill was compared to her previous boyfriends. For one thing, Bill was not her boyfriend. She supposed he was her lover, but she hated the word. It sounded like something cheap, an endearment between habitually married people, "Lover Come Back." It reminded her of the relentless virginity of Doris Day. Or it meant a person you were fucking but needed a better way of saying it.

Whatever Bill and Stockard were doing, she knew there was not much love in it. Bill was a technician. He knew all the right buttons to push. He could be slow, like the first time they made love on Stockard's floor, right in front of the front door. He touched every part of her skin, carefully removing each piece of clothing, pulling a cushion down from the sofa at one point, a lap robe a little later. Actual rapprochement did not come for more than an hour and then they lay on the floor, surrounded by their clothes, Bill saying the strangely obligatory, "That was nice."

"Yes, it was very nice," said Stockard, who did not necessarily want to nuzzle into him. "Like an expertly guided tour."

Mills Andrew was now long in her past. There had been a playfulness to their sex that she had missed ever since. It was the newness of the act, at once pleasurable, intuitive but intense, that had led Stockard into more and more sex with Mills. Afterwards, they had been witty careless friends, the world a joke from their cushion of bliss. Stockard had never found the same whimsicality with a man again.

She had dated Dorn Bury, who was dumb, but had a great runner's body. There was no playfulness in the man. Joe Kinwald was a new music teacher at the university who was as madly devoted to Stockard as he was to his music. He was too dramatic and within a week of their dating was convinced that they were soul mates. Smug Charlie was a knee surgeon, a distant sun in his own solar system. Stockard could not remember ever actually having sex with Charlie. Finally Stockard had met dirty Evan, who was doing card tricks on the Pearl Street Mall for donations. He was raising money for a commune in Sunshine Canyon, where he was living. Evan appeared deep from the outside but exhibited a nebulous core. Sex with Evan was surprisingly routine and tedious. He preferred the missionary position by the third time and his idea of foreplay was a fifteen-second kiss. He loved the inner light of Stockard, he said. Once she was over the shock of such brightly colored, smelly plumage that was so boring, she ended her Evan dalliance to renounce men and sex. Why, she would always wonder, did people from communes smell so bad? Did they not have showers? Then Bill came along.

Stockard had never been a devotee of food, but for the range of sex in her life so far, it was the only comparison she could make. Most people ate at McDonald's. Each burger looked like the last. There were steel counters to keep the people from getting too comfortable at the register. It was all part of the business plan. Serve as many people as quickly and uniformly as possible. The food factory. The industrial revolution had arrived for food.

Look what had happened to the experience. The food had become so predictable, so bland, that eating had moved from a basic gratification of taste and smell, a joyful ode to the primal need to eat, to feeding your face. Fast food took a page from Southern cuisine and used fat and sugar to keep the largest number of people happy.

Stockard realized that Mills Andrew was not this. The other four had been various flavors of fast food, the physical routine supplanted only by the primal wired nervous system that enjoyed the physical attention of another and a single climactic moment.

Mills Andrew had been love. Stockard had spent the last ten years regretting her loss of Mills. She had written that last letter before leaving Sefer Farm. She was formal, just as he had been. She had just gained freedom and painful as it was, she knew that she had to keep moving west, not go back east. Stockard had written Mills that she was traveling for awhile and would miss him, but she would be in touch after she settled. She had left it there. A few years ago she had retrieved the letters from her dictionary at Sefer Farm, the two that she had written and never sent.

To continue the lovemaking metaphor, Bill knew every wine on the wine list. He knew what vintages were good. He knew when a piece of beef was overdone, when a sauce had reached a perfect balance. He knew al dente. His breath was always minty and his fingernails were always carefully manicured. Beyond the technical perfection of his technique and the sheer explosiveness of their making love, Stockard noticed that they kissed very little. Sometimes he liked to start off kissing her, but mostly he would initiate a moment by caressing her hair. Once underway, he would kiss her skin, especially around her throat, he would kiss her back, he would kiss her inner thigh on his way to somewhere else, but he rarely kissed her on the mouth. She also noticed his breathing, which was steady and controlled until he was on the verge of his own climax. Then he huffed and groaned and was as near physical violence as other men had been. Bill took his time for his own release, saving it for the very end. They would lay loosely together for five or ten minutes and then he would leave with a final brief kiss.

Stockard had felt clumsy early on and had at one point tried to take Bill in her mouth.

"No, not yet," he had whispered. It was his standard reply whenever Stockard tried to become the fellatrice.

5

BETWEEN Stockard's house and Cadence's apartment were two blocks of old houses. They had large lots and tall, mature trees, the kind of trees that made you think of Fairy Tales, the woods of Hansel and Gretel, the walk of Little Red Riding Hood, the tangled archetypal tales of humanity. The houses and lawns were in various states of repair or disrepair. An eighty-four year old man, who had lived in one of the houses for fifty-nine years, did not wake up one September morning in 1982 and a For Sale sign was on the still green front lawn within a week.

Stockard was the first person to view the house.

A week before, Stockard had received a postcard. On one side was a sunset picture of the Taj Mahal, the great white building with its onion-shaped dome and flanking towers pointing up, set against a sky of purples and pinks. On the other side was Emily's handwriting: "Hey Roomie, Will be home in time for Thanksgiving and will not leave until the New Year, I think. Miss you and Eve. Lots of love, Emily."

The postcard was the impetus for Stockard to buy the newly available house around the corner. With the imminent arrival of Emily, she needed to separate her life into two houses. Her current house would be where Emily and she continued to live, Stockard's books everywhere that Emily's photographs were not.

The other house would be where she and the Rabchaus and Cadence and even Christopher would meet. It took three weeks to have the walls plastered and painted and the floors sanded and refinished. Andrew had another bright young assistant, a recent Yale graduate, who arranged for the speedy delivery of funds and for a different Denver lawyer to hop to the transaction. Andrew was very good natured about Stockard's real estate investing. He would send her kind notes in March each year to say that he had noticed her house rental business was showing a steady profit. She was delighted.

Stockard bought a few Persian rugs and cushions for the downstairs and a queen sized bed for the largest bedroom upstairs. In the kitchen she stocked six antebellum sterling Jefferson cups. By early October the house was finished, largely unfurnished, and Stockard could breathe a sigh of relief knowing that when Emily finally returned from her latest goodwill trip, she would be none the wiser to the strange world in which Stockard now dwelled.

It would be known as The Blue House.

It had all started with Christopher, who had called Stockard to see if she wanted to go out for a beer.

In the sexually charged atmosphere, an invitation for a beer was not simply an invitation for a beer. At least Stockard did not take it as such. She had ho and hawed to Christopher and finally agreed to meet him in a couple of days at a bar on Pearl Street. In the meantime, she would bring up the matter with Cadence, who knew just what to do in awkward situations.

Stockard loved Cadence's youth. She was dancing to INXS, her laughter cackling as she threw her hands up and twirled and bounced around the sofa where Stockard sat. Cadence at times was so very young. It was the way she smiled, carefree. Stockard wanted to be like Cadence and knowing that such ringing laughter was not in her makeup, she had decided to keep Cadence close.

"What about Christopher?" Stockard asked as the song ended.

Cadence ran her fingers through her hair, which she had let down. "What about him?"

"Have you ever?" Stockard made a forward movement with her head. She hoped the nod delivered the rest of the message. "Have you ever slept with him?"

"Nah, although he… hovers, I guess. He's interested. I think of him as Etta's domain." Cadence slipped in behind Stockard on the sofa and put her arms around her.

"I thought you might have," said Stockard, leaning back into Cadence, "the way he was stroking your hair that first dinner. It is just that kind of, uh, scene."

"Strange, huh? We're so open, but they are, like, exclusive. I think Christopher wants to, but Etta won't let him."

"Ah." Stockard could feel Cadence's breathing and they sat very still for a moment.

"Why, are you interested in Christopher?" Cadence started brushing the side of Stockard's head.

"No. You?"

"Not so much. Maybe I'm a little curious, but I'm more interested in you."

Stockard leaned her head to the side and waited for Cadence to kiss her. As Cadence's face came slowly closer to her own, Stockard saw, with the new magnification that we see a lover, her eyelashes and her perfect nose and her lips. It was the first time that she had ever kissed a woman.

The next week, it was Etta who was asking Stockard, "And you don't think your grandmother had other men? No one else pursued her?"

"I never knew of anyone."

"How odd. It's one of two things that everyone needs. Romantic affection. It usually comes in the flavor of sex."

"What's the other?"

"Food." They were standing in the Rabchau's kitchen. Etta swept a hand from the stove to the refrigerator, where Etta's list was still posted.

The list caught Stockard's eye, again.

"That first night I came to dinner, you had that list," Stockard's hand automatically pointed towards the refrigerator, "and I thought you were, you know, sort of out there." It was the counterpoint to what she was thinking, that Etta had her head screwed on unusually straight for a Boulderite.

Etta looked where Stockard was pointing and then walked to the list. "I take a stand for," read Etta, "experiencing things as they are, in total clarity and ease. Very hokey. I actually wrote that in a workshop. It sounds like I'm stoned, but that's what happens around here. You get in with particular people and for a moment, you become part of their madness. Beats discussing the price of milk in Cleveland. I put it up because it made me laugh so hard. Bill thought there was some truth in it, but I hate the way it was written. I can't bear to say things like that out loud or even write them. I'll burn it one day."

Stockard's impromptu visit to Etta had started as a low level buzz. Cadence had called it "Sexual Congress." It was a term that made Stockard laugh every time, partly because Stockard had no good way of describing what exactly the five of them were doing. First was Bill's visit, the two of them ending up on her living room floor, clothes in neat little piles around them. Then there was making love to Cadence on her sofa. Christopher had been so kind in his approaches, so genuinely affectionate towards Stockard, that she had woken up one day and realized that she had three valentines.

"Three members of your sexual congress," Cadence would say.

It was an idea that Stockard had to avoid. It was a foursome, although Bill and Christopher were not inclined towards each other as far as Stockard and Cadence knew. If Stockard could keep focused on specifics, on how Cadence felt at the door of her apartment when she hugged Stockard, on how Bill could look at her, on how Christopher could be like a friendly puppy dog, then she could enjoy the moment. It was only when she tried to summarize the situation that she felt icky. The image of all four of them, naked, eagerly at each other, turned Stockard's stomach. They had avoided group sex.

No one minded. Everyone enjoyed the moment.

Etta was the lone voice of opposition, Stockard had decided. It somehow marred Stockard's enjoyment to have Etta holding out, to be so close to the group, but not fully involved.

So one September Thursday Stockard had found herself unable to eat lunch and next on the Rabchau's doorstep, ringing the doorbell. Bill, she knew, was at work. Etta had practically leapt across the doorstep to hug Stockard.

They had come to the subject of Stockard's grandmother after Stockard had stumbled through various versions of why she was visiting. "How are you? I haven't seen you in a couple of weeks and, you know, it's not the same hearing about you. I was wondering, you know…" Stockard finally found Etta's eyes. At first Etta's expression was uncomprehending, but as the silence stretched out, she understood that Stockard was trying to ask her a question and she knew it was about the group hanky-panky. It was a problem for Stockard to even define exactly what was going on. She had no clear vocabulary to describe the state of affairs and therefore it was impossible for her to politely ask Etta why she was not taking part in the sex. She could not bring herself to use Cadence's hilarious term with Etta. Sexual Congress.

Stockard finally asked Etta, "Do you disapprove?"

"No, not at all." Etta visibly relaxed when Stockard got the question out.

"But you're not really a part of it?"

"No, not really." Etta caught Stockard's roaming eyes again. "It is going to sound strange, but I am old fashioned. Don't look so surprised."

"Oh, God, I thought I was the only one."

"Not at all."

Stockard was leaning against the kitchen counter now, somewhat relieved. "I can hear my grandmother's voice commenting on the whole thing. She would not approve at all."

"Approve of what? What in particular?"

"Pre-marital sex. Adultery." Stockard winced at the term. "Those two things would make me a loose woman. She would never use the word 'slut' but it wouldn't be far from her mind. She wouldn't understand sleeping with two men and the very idea that I would be sleeping with another woman, well, the weight of the moral disapproval. I can hear her voice on occasion. So that's really why you do not... participate?"

"Bill had this bee in his bonnet about other women. He loves me dearly but he's not sexually interested in me. I think it's normal for men. At least in Boulder. They get so tired of the same old same old. I figured I had a choice between him doing it behind my back or with my full knowledge and approval. Strangely, it doesn't really matter who he sleeps with. We have been more like friends for the last three or four years anyway. So I find Christopher fun, occasionally, but in terms of your question, in terms of why I'm not 'participating', it boils down to why I'm not sleeping with you and Cadence."

"Oh," said Stockard, who felt herself blush outrageously.

"Stockard, don't be flustered. It's not that I'm not interested. I've just never been with a woman. I wouldn't know where to begin."

That's how Etta, the final holdout, became part of the group.

If Stockard found the situation unusual, she could not imagine what Emily would have thought. It was Emily's postcard and impending return to Boulder that had driven the group to The Blue House. Emily had barely mentioned men in all the years of what they called her Good Works. She had not talked about the work itself very much either. She did talk about the pictures. She talked about the cameras and the equipment. She had never strayed too far from Nikon for 35mm and she was a diehard lover of Mamiya for medium format. Emily could talk zoom lenses versus fixed focal and grainy versus smooth film. Her monologue on filters nearly put Stockard to sleep one day. Stockard loved her cousin and often found herself sitting with Emily in front of opened camera cases as Emily showed her a new lens or a new motor.

"So you really have never found a man in your Good Works," Stockard asked one time.

"Find a man? Sure, finding them's the easy part," said Emily. "Getting rid of them is much more difficult. I've got other things to do."

Pictures are what Emily meant. There were now stacks of acid-free boxes in the attic, representing years of negatives and prints. Emily's darkroom was still curtained in negatives.

Stockard took Emily's pronouncements on men with skepticism. It had come out years later that she would have sex at the Stanford art studio often. When Stockard had asked why Emily had not confessed this while at Stanford, she had replied, "I didn't want to get in your way."

Eve on the other hand always had a man around. Despite the change in names, Stockard could see no difference in Eve's men. They were all throwbacks to the 60s, aging ex-hippies with long hair, dirty jeans and thinly bearded faces. They all wore round gold-rimmed glasses. Stockard could not remember their names. Not once had Eve talked of marriage. She carried on with her routine, working at the bakery and living in a tiny apartment, accompanied by the bearded escorts who disappeared into the background wherever they were. She did not drink and did not smoke pot.

"Your cousin," Stockard's mother had said on her last visit to Boulder, "has become lodged in the firmament of the 60s. Berkeley did something to her and not something of which Ken Kesey would approve."

6

STOCKARD gave the first key to Cadence. She had called Cadence, given the address and they had met five minutes later. The house still had the chemical smell of fresh paint and refinished floors. It was quiet and huge and empty as Stockard showed Cadence around. They were standing in the living room, the sense of a vast empty space intensified by the sparse furnishings, a single large rug of deep reds and dull golds with navy and green highlights. Tasseled pillows were laid in the center. The house was so overwhelming that it drove Stockard and Cadence closer together.

"So this house is for us?" Cadence was looking at Stockard in a way that she had never looked before.

Stockard was trying to decipher the look. "Yes." Cadence looked dumbfounded, a term Stockard had never used for her. "You, Etta, Bill, Christopher."

"And you." Cadence was now looking at the ceiling, where Stockard had left the original light fixture, a crystal chandelier. "One bed. That's all you thought it would take?"

Stockard was looking at the chandelier, too, and thinking that her grandmother had never bought anything so gaudy. Her aunt had. "Why, I thought we could fill out the furnishings as…" Stockard was thinking of the chairs and other beds the house might need. She caught the half smile on Cadence's face. "Do you think we'll need more?"

Cadence had by now leaned into Stockard, pushing her breasts into her arm, a grin on her face. "Why don't we go upstairs?"

There was a knock at the front door.

"Who is that?" Cadence was very still.

The knock had startled Stockard. "I don't know. No one else knows, not yet. Maybe they'll go away."

There was another knock at the front door. And then a third, very loud this time. Stockard found that the urgency of the knocks pulled her towards the front door without a word. Cadence stayed behind.

The entrance hallway was as cavernous as the rest of the house, the large wooden double door appearing more like the entryway into a castle. Stockard opened one of the doors to find a lady just under five feet in height and no younger than eighty years old. What was left of her grey hair sat on the top of her head like a giant fluffed grey cotton ball. Stockard took the woman in and said, "Hello?"

"Hello, dear," said the little old lady in a voice that was more like a bark. "Are you my new neighbor?"

It took Stockard a beat to understand what she was asking. "Why, yes, I am." Stockard leaned out to shake her hand and now saw that the lady held a cake in her hands.

"Here you go, dear," said the old lady, offering the cake to Stockard. "I baked this a couple of days ago, but I was a bit premature, I'm afraid. You haven't been around. I just wanted to say, Welcome to the neighborhood."

The icing was white. It was the kind of cake, Stockard knew, that contained copious amounts of sugar and butter. It would be very good. It was set in a glass cover on a marble circle, like at a lunch counter. The weight of it surprised Stockard as she took it out of the little old lady's hands.

"That is so very nice," said Stockard. "I would ask you in, but I have no chairs…"

"Don't worry about it, dear." The old lady hovered for a moment.

"Oh, I am so sorry," said Stockard, "my name is Stockard Griffin." She had not said her name in so long that it surprised her. Stockard Griffin. I was certainly not born Stockard Griffin, she thought, and what I've become is not what I expected, the thought disappearing as she balanced the cake in her left hand and extended her right hand.

Taking Stockard's hand, the old lady said, "Florence. Florence Melos." She pointed to her right. "I live in that house."

Stockard swung her head outside of the door frame just enough to take the house in, a huge Tudor with a carefully kept lawn.

"If you need anything," said Florence, "please knock on the door. It is nice to make your acquaintance."

Stockard smiled as Florence turned and carefully set off down the porch stairs. She watched as Florence cut across a flower bed into her own yard, turning for a final wave at Stockard and finally disappearing into the Tudor. She looked at her own lawn and made a mental note to have the same landscaping company that maintained her other houses come around to take care of The Blue House lawn.

Stockard and Cadence used a comb to cut the cake.

"I'll have to get some things for the kitchen," said Stockard as they ate their slices with their hands.

The second key went to Etta, who shared reheated quiche and a bottle of wine with Stockard for lunch at The Blue House. Stockard had bought flatware and glasses and a kitchen knife by then. Bill got the third key later that night over gin and tonics. He hated drinking beer and would only drink wine or liquor. Stockard assumed it had something to do with his working in the beer business. Christopher took the fourth key in the basement the next day as they lay on their clothes, post coitus, the cold cement floor touching parts of Stockard's skin.

They had descended to the basement after passing the door and Christopher had asked, "What's down there?"

Where Bill was a technician, Christopher was animal. He had the kind of lust that could be sparked by odd things, in this case a naked light bulb in a damp basement, the skeleton beams and studs of aged wood and the dark brick walls. Cadence had wanted to make love on the living room rug. Etta and Bill had stuck to the bed.

Stockard couldn't make it up the basement stairs without Christopher wanting to do it again, right there on the staircase, and then a third time in the kitchen as they opened a bottle of wine. The house brought something out of Christopher, something that

Stockard had not seen before. His horniness took on a ravenous nearly violent aspect. It was unpredictable.

"Has Christopher made a rear entry, yet?" Cadence was staring at the living room chandelier again. They had turned the heat up. As autumn turned colder, the house became disproportionately colder, the old windows letting in the chill. There were drafts that started on the first floor and worked their way up to the third floor.

"Huh?" Stockard had been staring at the chandelier, too, and been thinking she should get rid of it.

Cadence and Stockard liked to lounge and make love in the living room, under the chandelier, with only the oriental carpet and pillows for comfort. Stockard had added a wool blanket to the mix.

"Has he given it to you up the ass?" Cadence laughed at the way she had said it. It was a masculine matter of fact tone.

"No. You?"

"It's all he knows with me. He doesn't even kiss."

"Yeah, he doesn't kiss me either, not anymore. He just gets down to the essential act. It's almost desperate the way he wants to do it, like a meal he's starving for. It borders on violent."

"He's definitely violent with me."

"Does he hit you?" Stockard sat up.

"No, but it's more the way he takes me. Like he wants to damage me." Cadence kept looking at the chandelier.

"He's not that way with me, just horny as hell. Not at all like Bill."

"Bill doesn't even participate with me anymore," said Cadence. "He simply drives me, if you know what I mean."

"No," said Stockard, "I'm not sure I do."

"He doesn't even want to have intercourse with me. It's more like he wants to worship me. He simply gratifies me, not even himself. He won't let me do anything. I'm treated like a princess."

"Again," said Stockard, "I'm one step removed from how he treats you. I can see his reverence towards the act and his… technical perfection…"

"Technical perfection," purred Cadence. "A skilled craftsman."

Stockard was ostensibly trying to work out the difference between Bill and Christopher and more importantly how they treated Cadence and herself. It was not a typical conversation, but she found that Cadence could talk about anything with a disarming frankness. As Stockard continued to think about Cadence and Bill and then Cadence and Christopher, she was startled to find herself jealous.

She was not jealous of Cadence. She was jealous that anybody else possessed Cadence. It had been the images that had done it to her. Stockard could imagine Cadence on a pedestal, Bill doing what he did so well. She could imagine Cadence being manhandled by Christopher. It burnt Stockard. It was a terrible surge of emotion that started in her heart and went to her legs.

Cadence asked, "Are you all right?"

"Uh huh, why?"

"You are wriggling around a lot."

"Oh, sorry. I was just thinking about Christopher. Do you like him?"

"He's fine, harmless in his own way."

Stockard was trying to lie still and focus on the chandelier. "Do you like what he does?"

"I don't dislike it. It's just different from…"

"The missionary position," Stockard finished the sentence for her. She had been hoping that Cadence would say she didn't like Christopher, didn't like what he did to her, didn't like Bill. Stockard wanted her to say she wanted Bill and Etta and Christopher to go away and only wanted to be with Stockard, because Stockard had realized in her jealousy something that had been growing and becoming steadily more apparent over the past few months, mainly that she was in love with Cadence and did not want to share her with anyone.

That fragile barrier between two people had been broken so many times between the five of them that they had early on set out to foster a sense that each was equally special to the others. It was the only way that it would work. They had been raised to respect another person's physical barrier, that space ever so slight that stood between oneself and another. Half of the excitement was first breaking that barrier, gently and carefully, reaching out for another person and then as the other person accepted touch, the two people came together slowly but surely, drinking each other up. To treat people otherwise, to not respect the space of another person was not merely rude, it was morally wrong. It was a realization that Stockard had been playing with ever since she had kissed Cadence for the first time. To not respect what was happening between other people as they entered the same sacred relationship was morally wrong, too. And how they pulled it off, how they lived in such close physical violation of each other's space was by setting up a very small community, a very large relationship and the assumption was that as Stockard loved Cadence or at least respected and adored her, so Stockard should feel about Etta and Bill and Christopher. And Etta should feel the same sacred respect for Cadence, Christopher and Stockard. Etta was already in holy vows to respect Bill. It was what made the whole situation odd and improbable, but it had worked well until Stockard realized that she loved Cadence and she did not necessarily love Bill nor Christopher nor Etta.

Etta loved only Stockard. Stockard could see it in the way that Etta would look at her. Etta called Stockard to meet her at The Blue House more than anyone else by Stockard's reckoning, especially in the mornings during the week, when Etta knew that the others were working and unavailable. Etta lingered closer and longer to Stockard than the others did. Etta looked very deeply into Stockard's eyes.

Stockard knew and noted all of this because she did exactly the same things to Cadence, right down to calling Cadence to meet her at The Blue House when no one else was likely to show up.

With this realization that Stockard had fallen in love with one member of the group, Cadence, and that Etta had fallen in love with Stockard, Stockard knew that The Blue House was falling apart. She had even started to sneak over to Cadence's apartment to see her without going to The Blue House, where everyone had a key.

The only funny thing about The Blue House was Florence, their neighbor. Stockard figured that Florence must watch The Blue House like a hawk, because Florence often knocked on the door when Stockard was in. No one else reported being disturbed by the little old lady from the Tudor next door.

Florence had dropped off some carrot cupcakes for Halloween. They had ivory icing and an orange pumpkin candy on top. They were gone in two days. Food follows sex, Stockard thought to herself when she saw the empty cake holder, the one that Florence had used to deliver both the Halloween cupcakes and the Welcome Wagon cake. Stockard washed it in the sink and dried it with a cotton napkin. She had considered putting a washer and dryer in the house. All she had to wash were the kitchen linens and the sheets. It was not enough to justify a washer and dryer. Maybe she could have bought one of the small ones, the kind that were stacked dryer on washer. It would help with her deception. She smuggled the sheets and napkins into her real house. Emily had finally returned from India and points east. She spent most of her time sleeping so Stockard found the deception easy, but necessary. Soon Emily would catch up on her sleep and begin to spend more and more time in the darkroom, developing the cases of film she had brought back. Then she would sit in the living room with the prints spread out on every flat surface, various pieces of camera gear spread about for cleaning. It was at that point that Emily would ask questions about Stockard's comings and goings and hauling bed linen into the house for washing. It would be nice to have a washer and dryer in The Blue House then.

Eve would never be a problem. There was no reason that she would notice Stockard's habits.

Stockard had finished wiping Florence's cake platter dry. She had looked out the kitchen window onto the backyard, noticing how large it was. The landscapers had raked the leaves and the yard stood still, cold and unused. For a moment she could imagine children out there, playing in the fallen leaves. She lifted the cake platter, made her way through the house, from the kitchen down a hallway, through the living room and out the front door. She cut across the same flower bed through which Florence had cut and was in front of the great brown timbered door of the Tudor, ringing the doorbell.

So quickly did the door open it was as if Florence had been on the other side of the door, waiting for Stockard to knock.

"Hello, dear," said Florence.

Stockard looked down, remembering how short she was. "The cupcakes were divine." She handed the cake platter to Florence, watching as the little old lady took it with a grunt.

"Well, I'm glad you enjoyed them." Florence had a way of pausing, the awkwardness of the silence and moment forcing Stockard to respond. Her mother's pauses bridged two thoughts, the completion of a sentence. Florence simply stopped talking.

"I must have you over for lunch, sometime, Mrs. Melos, but I must get proper furniture first," said Stockard, who could imagine Florence watching the parade of regulars go in and out of the front door of The Blue House. She must have been thinking, well, dear, you have enough furniture to entertain an awful lot of guests now, but not enough to entertain me. Or did Stockard see in that wry right eye a knowing look. Did Florence know that something funny was going on at the house next door? How could she not if she really kept a close watch. Would her old mind ever entertain the notion that five people were fucking each other next door? Stockard found herself stopping on her choice of word. "Fucking." It was the first time that she had mentally used the word in describing what they did. She was only vaguely aware of the uncomfortable silence that Florence had started. Stockard was now extending it on and on and then she was thinking to herself, well, is the old bat even aware that we are two humans standing in her doorway saying nothing to each other. Stockard was thinking of what exactly she could say to break the silence, her social skills abruptly bankrupt. Maybe she would take Florence out to lunch. She probably never got out of the Tudor anymore. It would be nice…

"Stockard?"

The voice came from behind Stockard and jolted her.

"Stockard?" It was Eve's voice.

Stockard turned around to see Eve, standing at the gate of the Tudor, about thirty feet away.

"Eve?" Stockard noticed for the first time the stone wall that enclosed the Tudor's front. It was knee height and as old as the house, weathered and beautiful in the autumnal light. She had a pang of homesickness. She wanted to be back at Sefer Farm.

"Who's that, dear?" Florence had bobbed onto the porch of her own house, the marble cake dish still in her hands.

"That's my cousin, Eve," said Stockard. She watched in disbelief as Florence waved Eve to the front porch, and Eve was drawn, like at the end of a string, right to Florence, opening the black iron gate and walking up the stone path.

Stockard's homesickness turned to dread bordering on panic. Three of her worlds, each carefully kept from the other, threatened to collide in one moment.

Eve was wearing faded jeans and a baggy sweater, a brown cable knit sweater that she had bought while at Berkeley. Berkeley clung to her, and the world worked even more desperately against her. Her old nemesis, Ronald Reagan, the man who had made Berkeley his target, the man who had sent the National Guard to the People's Park protest, was now president of the country. She was thoroughly put down and had withdrawn further into herself. She looked terrible as she walked up the path, having no resemblance to the girl that Stockard had grown up with. Stockard could remember Eve dressing in red velvet for Christmas when she was eight and nine and ten years old. Eve had a wonderful smile growing up, Stockard remembered now. Where had that smile gone?

"Mrs. Melos," said Stockard when Eve had joined them on the porch, "this is my cousin, Eve Griffin." They had all changed their last names somewhere along the way, Stockard now remembered. The Griffin women had become Griffins, all of them, even Eve and Emily. "Eve, this is Mrs. Melos."

"Please call me Florence. How do you do?"

Eve had gone to shake Florence's hand when she spotted the cake platter, still in her hands.

Stockard saw Eve's extended hand and Florence still holding the platter. She must have a steel worker's arms, thought Stockard, as long as she's been holding that heavy thing. "Here, let me take that," she offered.

Florence and Eve shook hands and then a whole new kind of silence opened up between the three of them. Stockard's mind had been racing with the possibilities of what she should have said to Florence and now that Eve had joined them, she found her mind was completely blank. She had no idea what to say to either of them, either individually nor as a collective.

Eve turned to Stockard and said, "I was just out for a walk, on my way to Mount Sanitas."

"Yes, dear," said Florence, "it is such a lovely park."

"And I saw you," continued Eve, "here." She looked around the porch.

It was a question, Stockard thought, by the very tone. I saw you here. What are you doing here on this old lady's porch, talking to her as if you have known her all your life? Holding her cake platter? She was aware that both Eve and Florence were looking at her, waiting for her to speak. Stockard had a fleeting thought that Florence would invite them into her house for a full-blown tea and then it was sure to all come out. Florence was sure to say that she had never seen Eve visit Stockard, not of all the people that Florence had seen visit Stockard. There were really only four who were there frequently. Then Eve would be asking how Florence saw two blocks away to

Stockard's house and no, dear, Florence would be saying, didn't you know? Your cousin lives right next door.

No, Eve did not know that. She did not know that her cousin had bought a gigantic Victorian house in Boulder. She would lie and sprout the secret that she was one of Boulder's landlords, which was true, and Eve still didn't know about her extracurricular property acquisitions. It had been Stockard and Andrew's secret. She could fold The Blue House into that secret and expose it, avoiding the fucking. That word again.

Stockard could feel her face falling as she contemplated the outcome of her stupid good intention to deliver the cake platter, cleaned and timely, to her dear old neighbor. She tried to fix a smile on her face. It would be her poker face, but she felt her eyes and forehead falling in resignation.

"I would invite you in," said Florence, sending Stockard into a collapse of relief, "but I was just about to step out to get my hair done. I daren't be late."

"Of course," said Eve. "It was so very nice to meet you."

"I'll walk with you," said Stockard to Eve.

Just like that Eve and Stockard were on their way towards Stockard's other house and Florence was pulling out of her driveway. Stockard noticed that she was driving a very new Mercedes. Florence reversed out of her driveway recklessly fast. Stockard wondered if she bothered with the mirrors.

On the walk, Stockard found herself maintaining an irrelevant light conversation with Eve while she wondered if she had left the door to the other house unlocked. Of course she had. It compounded her feeling that everything was a mess.

Bill and Christopher knew something was up. They did all of the calling. None of the women called them to meet at The Blue House. Their group of five was starting to unravel. Now she was willfully deceiving her two cousins. Eve was easy to deceive. Stockard wanted to avoid Eve's constant disapproval at all costs. Emily was different.

Why did she want to keep The Blue House away from Emily, who was her oldest and best friend? Now her deception from Florence was nagging at her. What did she care about the old bat next door?

In front of Stockard's house, the one that she and Emily shared, Stockard asked if Eve might like a cup of tea before continuing on to Sanitas?

"Sure," said Eve and the two walked up the little driveway and into the house.

Emily was sitting on the sofa with prints spread around her, drinking coffee.

"Look who I ran into," said Stockard as they came through the door.

"Hello," they said to each other, Emily making a slow motion attempt at a hug before sitting back onto the sofa.

"More sand and poor people," said Eve, taking in the pictures around Emily.

Stockard caught the look on Emily's face. It was stern.

"Emily's been using some new wide-angled lenses," said Stockard. "There's some really interesting views of the Taj Mahal, some strange looks at Kashmir." She went to the kitchen to make tea.

She had boxes of the local herbal tea, Celestial Seasonings. It was a Boulder thing that had evidently become very big business. Just the other week there had been an article in the Boulder Daily Camera about how big Celestial Seasonings had become. They sold their tea all over the world. There must have been twenty different boxes stacked in the cabinet. Red Zinger. Morning Thunder. Sleepy Time. Some locals had made the business from the local vegetation, picking herbs and other weedy things in the surrounding hills, drying them and selling them. Now they sold Sleepy Time everywhere.

Meanwhile her cousin was helping the poor everywhere.

What was the difference? What made the local hippie capitalists different from Emily?

Eve's comment about sand and poor people was rude. Stockard had found herself covering up for Eve's rudeness, moving conversations along or apologizing after Eve had offended yet someone else, but in a way, Eve was right on this count. Emily took pictures of sand and poor people.

She watched steam come out of the kettle until it was coming out fast enough and making enough noise to convince her that it was boiling. The water hissed as it hit the mugs and made the little white tea bags bulge and float to the top.

Emily had avoided life all these years. She had been jumping on planes, toiling for the distant poor and lost in the world of still pictures for as long as Stockard could remember. In a way, the camera was the perfect metaphor for Emily. She witnessed the world. She did not engage it.

Stockard caught another glimpse of Eve's brown sweater and had the exact same thought about her. Eve was not living a life, either. She was stuck in some kind of dead routine, too.

Ten years of nothingness, thought Stockard. That's what I've done in ten years. Nothing. Now that she was fully engaged in the present, the past looked indifferent.

As Stockard brought the smelly mugs of tea into the living room, she asked, "What the hell's wrong with us?"

Eve replied, "I beg your pardon."

Emily slowly and quietly said, "It is a question that I have been asking for years."

The phone rang.

"I need to see you," Christopher said once Stockard had the phone to her ear.

Stockard was trying to think of an excuse, trying to think of how she could say no without eliciting Eve and Emily's suspicion. They could hear everything that she was saying.

"I need to see all of you," he said. "I've called everyone else and we're meeting at The Blue House. At seven tonight. Okay?"

"I'll be there." Stockard was left with the dead receiver in her hand, wondering why Christopher sounded so ominously flat.

In her search to explain her absences to Emily, Stockard had created a different Etta. The new Etta was sensitive and easily traumatized. The new Etta called Stockard often to unload her burdens and she was too shy to come over to Stockard's. It was Etta the Excuse that allowed Stockard to come and go without too much explaining.

In a couple of weeks, Emily, Stockard and Eve would make their annual trip to Nashville. Christmas at Sefer Farm was a tradition. Thoughts of the farm, of growing up there, smelling the hardwood trees in the autumn, kept breaking into the moment at hand. By the time that Stockard had returned to the living room, her faux paux of calling the Griffin women crazy, had been forgotten, apparently.

7

THAT night was very cold and Stockard wore a bulky goose down jacket to The Blue House. Cadence, Etta and Bill were already there.

"What's up with Christopher," asked Bill as soon as Stockard walked through the door.

"I don't know. You, either, huh?"

"No one has a clue."

"I'll bet he's getting married," said Cadence, "and he's dropping out of The Blue House. I knew it would come to something like this."

"Christopher getting married?" Etta was sitting in a bay window. "It would be all of the sudden. I suppose he wouldn't tell us if he's been seeing someone else, but we were trying to keep everything above board."

Christopher made his entrance, quietly. "Hello."

He was wearing a large blue overcoat. Stockard noticed he didn't bother to take it off, but walked right into the middle of the room, under the chandelier, standing away from where they were sitting. "I'm afraid I have some bad news and I'm not going to beat around the bush. Have any of you heard of AIDS?"

There was a long silence as Christopher looked at them. "It is a disease that attacks the immune system."

"Uh huh." Only Cadence made a sound.

"It is relatively new. It is incurable and it is fatal. I found out last week that I have it. It is also sexually transmitted."

"What?"

"That's about it. I have a sexually transmitted disease and there's a chance that you do, too."

The thing about Christopher, Stockard was thinking, is that he's not normally like this. He's not firmly spoken and sure of himself. Except whatever The Blue House unleashed in him.

He had no expression on his face. "You all need to be tested."

"Christopher," said Etta, "you say this disease is fatal?"

"They do not have a cure for it right now and it is my understanding that the medical community has not really started to take this disease seriously."

"Oh, God," said Cadence.

"How is it transmitted," asked Stockard.

"Sexually."

"How specifically?"

"The fluids. There has to be broken skin or some way for an infected person's fluids to enter the blood stream. That's actually difficult to do except under certain circumstances."

"Intercourse?"

"If it's rough. Anal intercourse more easily." Christopher looked at Bill.

"Oh, God," said Cadence.

"Hetero intercourse is safer than male homosexual. Female homosexual intercourse is surprisingly safe."

"But we need to be tested," said Etta.

"Yes."

"Where did you get it," asked Bill.

"That is the question."

"Well," said Etta.

"There's someone I see when I'm in San Francisco."

"Someone you see?" said Etta. "I thought we were keeping it within this group?"

"I can't remember who said that, but no one asked if it was okay. We didn't all agree to it."

"How the fuck can you say that," asked Stockard.

"It's not really going to help to get angry about this. There's a chance you don't even have it."

Cadence abruptly rose from her sitting position on the floor and walked out of the house. She did not say a word. Stockard got up to follow her.

Seth's Daughter

1

No one expected Margaret to crumble under the weight of grief. She had already been running Griffin Lumber for eighteen years and had recently formed Forest & Griffin with her business partner, Andrew Forest, when her husband buried his plane into the Tennessee turf after an afternoon of bourbon. Forest & Griffin was a venture capital firm before the label was used. Margaret was 37 when her husband died. She did not mourn or celebrate. She carried on building a tidy fortune in the midst of the Great Depression. It was an unlikely time and she was an unlikely woman.

It was said that Margaret Griffin had once threatened the governor of Tennessee over proposed commercial forest taxes, that she had personally vowed to burn down every single Griffin Lumber mill before allowing unions in, that she had gone with her father on snowy January mornings to shoot bucks and that she had once shown up at a logging site in trousers and driving a muddy Model T to find out why the cutters could not keep pace with production numbers.

She was tough as nails, as the people of Nashville said. And that's what you expected of Seth Griffin's daughter, despite her Vassar education and her ability to ride sidesaddle. It was the kind of toughness that put men off. And she meant it to do just that. In a time when a woman's property was customarily subsumed by her husband, she never again intended to become chattel. She took back the Griffin name a year after the crash and never gave control over to any man again.

2

TRIP was back, carrying a Gladstone bag in his left hand and a full bottle of whiskey in his right hand. The contents of the Gladstone were a mystery until he sat down at the table and pulled out a handful of sterling silver spoons.

"Anybody mind if I say each one of these," waving a spoon in the air, "is worth a dollar?"

There was silence as the other five men looked at Trip, taking in the grandson of the great Civil War general, Augustus Rosecrans Bedford, known more simply as The General. It occurred to a few of them that The General himself might have eaten off one or all of those silver spoons. The General was the last person in the Bedford family who could afford such finery. All of the family's silver had been buried during the Civil War. It was probably one of the few things that the Bedfords had emerged from the defeat of the war still owning. They also had a big plantation house a couple of miles out of town and about one percent of the land that went with it before the war.

There most of the Bedfords still lived, including Trip and Trip's father, Augustus Rosecrans Bedford, Jr. No one had ever called him The General Junior. He was widely seen as not half the man that his father was. Junior carried the defeat of his father, indeed the defeat of the entire South, heavily on his shoulders. He could be seen walking around town, his head down and those burdened shoulders down and pushed inwards, as much a physical cower as one man could manage and still be walking. The General himself had died a slow, painful death at the end of the Civil War. Gangrene had eaten away first at a knee injury suffered on his horse in battle and then it had taken his entire body. Junior simply did not have the vim and vigor of his father, and the family had lapsed into the background of the town, becoming one of Nashville's families that got along in the shadows. Junior worked at one of the local banks and was rarely seen even there.

His son, Augustus Rosecrans Bedford III—known as Trip because he was the triple of the stock—came into the world full of the very same fire as The General. At Amsted's that night, he wasn't just down on his poker luck and out a few dollars. He had already made a first visit to the room over Amsted's Saloon and had lost several hundred dollars, what was considered a small fortune in 1899. He had lost it all to Seth Griffin, the father of Margaret Griffin and the great-grandfather of Stockard Griffin. It would be Seth's shotgun with which Margaret's son-in-law would blow his brains out. By the time of this poker game, Seth did not yet own that shotgun. He was twenty-four years old and could not afford such a nice shotgun. Not yet.

Trip Bedford didn't just return with the burden of the earlier evening's loss. He was carrying an awful three-generation weight that had started when his grandfather had won Civil War battles but his army had lost the war. Trip believed, in his lucid moments, that his grandfather had died of a broken heart, a terrible sense of shame at what he and his fellow generals had handed succeeding generations. Outwardly it might have been gangrene that had taken his grandfather, but if The General's army had won the war, Trip believed he could have whipped gangrene and anything else that mother nature could have thrown at him. It was this sense of frustration that made Trip desperately pissed off and mostly drunk, the two things playing havoc with the atmosphere over Amsted's. Trip could never complete things like his grandfather. He never made successes and losing all of his money to one no-name over Amsted's was another in a long line of examples.

All of this, the generational frustration, the hot temper, sat in the room with Trip over Amsted's that night. The other five men were well aware of it. They also knew that sitting in that Gladstone was bound to be a gun, some kind of pistol, maybe a Colt .45, loaded and at Trip's frustrated fingertips.

"It's a dollar?" Trip was still waving a spoon.

"Let's call it three. Each piece's worth three dollars, all right?"

Now everyone was looking at Seth, who had made the offer. The silence hung over the table, heavier than the cigar smoke, overwhelming the ever louder voices of the bar underneath their feet. No one had ever heard Seth speak in that tone before, a strict mean tone, as if to say, "You're a fool to bring your family's silver in here and if I'm going to take it, I'll take it for an honest price, not what some goddamned desperate drunk wants to lose it for."

It was not like Seth Griffin at all. He was the quiet one whose sleepy eyes signaled a lack of motivation, a non-threatening complacency. Seth was laid back. He was certainly not ambitious. He was not outspoken. But he held Trip's cash money in a stack in front of him and he aimed to take as many of those silver spoons as he could.

When Margaret looked at Stockard's sleepy deep brown eyes, she saw her father's eyes. It was one of the physical traits that Seth and his great-granddaughter shared, although the two would never meet. Seth would die while napping on his farm porch thirteen years before Stockard would be born. It was only Margaret who could remember Seth's eyes, how gentle they could be, how he too had always looked like he was either on his way to a sleep or just waking up.

Margaret had only said it once. "Dear, you have my father's eyes." Stockard was eight years old.

The spoons came out of the Gladstone and made their way one or two at a time to Seth. Then the forks and knives. A number of jokes presented themselves, Seth sitting at a table, silverware and money stacked around him as if he was a miser counting the family fortunes or as if he was a mad host, doing an inventory for an elaborate dinner party, the money for a fine big turkey and a roast beef. Seth's soft eyes never changed as he continued to win. Then there was a little gasp from the table as the first serving piece came out of the bag, after

Seth had made a nice stack of soup spoons. He could serve a table of twenty at that moment.

Judge Baker, one of the five original players at the table, had said what was on everyone else's mind. After they had watched so many five and ten dollar bills go from Trip to Seth on Trip's first losing visit to the table, Judge simply laid it out. "Trip, you can't fight it. Seth's on a roll."

Trip had been in denial and now the real depth of that denial was evident. He pulled out, and lost, a dozen sterling cups. Next came the big serving pieces, weighing as much as four or five spoons but Trip was playing them as if they were three dollars each. All of the sudden everyone was bluffing and playing for the big pieces and Seth was still taking each hand. It was an incredible run of luck and would have been noted at each hand if Trip's frustrated misery had not hung over the whole game. Everyone knew it was the end of the game when Trip reached down and pulled out a silver pitcher, a great monstrous thing, hand engraved.

The pitcher itself was one of two, a matched pair commissioned by The General. He had taken two large canvas bags of silver dollars to a silversmith in 1834 and had the silver melted, molded and then hammered into the shape of two large water pitchers, each standing nearly a foot and a half high. He was celebrating the completion of the Tuscumbia, Cortland & Decatur railway. He had been one of the investors. It was the first non-farming non-plantation investment that Augustus had made. He was delighted to be making money on industry and not farming.

The pitchers were weighty, impractical things, the kind of service item that a man with strong servants could afford. An engraver had spent three months decorating the pitchers. They were the centerpiece of the family's silver collection and had been the very first items wrapped in felt, then placed in paraffin coated sacks, crated and buried in the field during the Civil War.

The silence was deafening. It overwhelmed the room. The whole town had heard about the matched pair of silver pitchers when they were first made. The silversmith had a big mouth and it was the single biggest commission he had ever received. He had never had someone show up with two bags of silver coins before.

The room had come to a halt, Amsted's underneath had frozen, the town was in repose, and the silence from Nashville in that moment radiated across Tennessee, north to Kentucky. For a brief moment the world stopped. On the table sat something of deep significance to everyone. It was a symbol of some past glory, some communal pride, and it was being gambled away, the cheapest and tawdriest and most desperate way to lose a thing.

"You gents won't mind if I say this is fifty dollars," Trip said.

"Fifty's okay by me," said Seth.

It was a bluff and Seth made short work of it. He took that pitcher with three of a kind, nines in fact. Trip had a pair of jacks.

Seth pulled the pot towards himself, setting the pitcher on the table to his right.

"I think that's all for me," said Seth. He started putting the forks and the knives and the spoons and the serving pieces into the pitcher. It was that big. They all fit. During the clink clink of the loading, everyone sat silently, the breath having been knocked out of the room. They were in shock. No one could look at Seth. No one could look at Trip.

Seth started shoving all of the bills into his pockets when Trip leaned into the table to break the silence. "You can't take that," said Trip. His long right index finger was pointed at the pitcher.

Seth's response was instantaneous, as if he had been waiting for Trip to say exactly that. "I won it, fair and square."

"You can't take that pitcher," said Trip again. His face was fierce.

Seth stood up, ready to leave.

Trip stood up and was about to say something, to reach into that bag and pull the gun they all knew was there. He was not going to let the pitcher leave the room. In one fluid motion, Seth reached across the table with his left hand and grabbed Trip by the collar. Those arms were suddenly so long! No one had ever noticed Seth's size before. It took an unusually long arm to reach across the table like that. Trip, who was drunk, fell into the table, reaching out to catch himself with both hands. Before his hands had really hit the table, Seth's right arm came around, the pitcher, full of shifting silver, in his hand. The sound was a mixture of silver clanging on itself and a thud, like a sack of potatoes hitting the ground. The second thud was Trip hitting the floor, out cold.

It did not matter whether the second pitcher was in the Gladstone or whether there really was a gun in there. The night was over. Two men carried Trip to one of the bedrooms over Amsted's, which was where he woke up the next day, just before noon. By then, Seth had already visited Citizens National Bank, the very same bank where Trip's father worked. He had placed his cash winnings into a bank account, the very first account he ever had. He showed the silver to the bank manager and said he wanted to place it in the bank's vault for safekeeping, unless the manager had other ideas about what to do with it. The word had already reached even the bank manager. There had been a helluva poker game over Amsted's the night before, and Seth Griffin, a name that everyone knew now, had cleaned the Bedford family out of their silver.

Within two weeks Seth had bought his first run of mature forest land. Within a month, a sawmill was sitting on the edge of the land, the sounds of axes ringing and horses dragging downed trees.

One day that sawmill would be renamed Griffin Sawmill No. 1. There would be a number two and three and four, all the way into the twenties. There would be Griffin Forest No. 1, Griffin Lumber Supply No. 1 and Griffin Fleet Maintenance No. 1. There would be number two and three and four of those, too.

Seth married Ruth, a school teacher, and they had one child, Margaret.

3

THE antebellum elements of Nashville society regarded Seth Griffin as an intruder. He might have won that poker game over Amsted's fair and square, but he had no right to the silver that he had won. He had taken it from the Bedford family just as a marauder would smash a door open and claim the spoils of war. A foot soldier with a silver service. Trip Bedford was a drunk fool, they knew, but with the curious sympathy of Southern society, people said that Seth Griffin should have returned every piece of silver to the Bedford family. Or at least negotiated a swap for something the Bedfords had that was equally valuable. Seth had no right to such finery.

The silver pitcher had pushed the story into the sensational. No one could imagine one of those pitchers leaving the plantation house of the Bedford's. But to think of it sitting in a bank vault and money being borrowed against it to finance a lumber company. Well, a lot of heads shook at how such a thing could happen.

Seth for his part paid no attention. He ran his lumber company and grew it relentlessly. His biggest asset, he believed, was land, the very land that antebellum society was selling off to finance their lifestyles. He bought their land, especially the remote patches, still covered with forests.

Ruth and Seth bought a house in a new neighborhood, where driveways curved up to recently built Queen Annes with eight, nine, even twelve chimneys. They had chosen the neighborhood for their daughter, just after she was born. Ruth wanted a good safe neighborhood for Margaret. She wanted her close to a model school, too. The best schools, her experience as a teacher had taught her, were closest to the affluent neighborhoods.

Seth wanted Margaret to have "a leg up."

Ruth knew what he meant. Literally he wanted Margaret to have one leg higher than the other children, like a rider getting on a horse, or for Seth like cutters in the forest climbing trees. Seth, she thought, was not getting his metaphors right. He should have said, "I want Margaret to cut with a sharp axe." But she never corrected him. Seth was not one of her students. Not that she taught anymore.

One of Margaret's neighborhood friends was Harriet Mayfield, who lived two streets north. They were the same age and had grown up going to the same schools. The Mayfield's house was slightly larger than the Griffin's, but the furnishings were far more palatial.

The Mayfields had moved into their fashionable neighborhood several years after the Griffins and had made a commotion by dedicating a large room upstairs for a bathroom, complete with oversized bathtub and a water closet in a side room.

The Griffins had a small bathroom upstairs with a tub and a sink. The wc was in the basement.

The Mayfields also had Tiffany mirrors at the top of the stairs and Baccarat chandeliers in the dining room and the entrance hall. It was grand in a way that fascinated a young Margaret.

When she went over for dinner, she was aware—and she had no idea where this awareness came from—that they dined on silverware that had been in the Mayfield family for four generations. The plates and cups were from France and the crystal was from England. Harriet had shown Margaret the wine cellar in the basement.

In the Mayfield's wine cellar, the two girls unsettled a small cloud of dust. Margaret wondered out loud at how dirty the bottles were. Harriet said that it helped the wine age. Wine apparently wanted to grow older before it was drunk. Margaret was not even sure what wine was. Harriet picked up a particularly old, and what she knew to be precious to her father, bottle of wine and made to hand it to Margaret, and somewhere in the exchange of the dusty bottle and the dark strange surroundings, the bottle was dropped. And broke. Loudly.

Mr. Mayfield came down the stairs in a hurry, his fat footfalls sounding like troops moving over wooden planks, and he was there, taking in the scene at once. He hissed, "Get out of here." The girls had scampered out through the door, Margaret only residually aware of the broken glass on the floor and the wine which had splattered on her legs and dress. It was traumatic because Margaret had never seen a man angry before and all the worse because she had caused him to be angry. Worst of all was what she heard once at the top of the stairs through the door into the kitchen. She heard Mr. Mayfield say, "Baseborn."

It would take several years for Margaret to realize that Mr. Mayfield was calling her baseborn. It was the only logical conclusion. Margaret knew what it meant. It meant low born. Margaret had no generals in her ancestry. She had no exceptional history in her family. Her father made his way from sawmill worker to lumber company owner and everyone knew how he had done it. It was luck. He had a lucky poker game. Her mother had been a schoolteacher, respectable in itself, but only a step off dirt floors. Despite their fine house in the same neighborhood, Margaret knew that the Old South still saw her as "baseborn." There was nothing she could do about it, and once she realized it, she found in herself something more independent and fierce, something that allowed her to make her own rules. She had other things to learn about the Old South.

Seth had told his daughter that you could always tell when an old landed family was in financial trouble. They sold the land the furthest from Nashville. They sold it for next to nothing. They had no more expensive land to sell.

The few lucky or smart ones sold their land close to Nashville. It fetched a high price. If a family's timing was right and they could wait long enough, their remote land would eventually be required for growing Nashville and then the price would go up. Otherwise, fortunes based on land tended to dwindle.

Seth had bought land from Chester Mayfield, who was not clever with his timing. He had bought the Mayfield land not more than three months before the Mayfields bought and furnished their house, just north of the Griffin house.

When Margaret heard that, she wondered who was baseborn. Chester Mayfield had sold nearly his last tract of land and spent the proceeds on a ridiculously ornate house and stocked it full of wines. It was the last party before the reckoning. Meanwhile her daddy had turned the Mayfield land, now Griffin Forest No. 15, into another lumber producing patch. He had turned the Mayfield folly into a long-term, steady, revenue-generating property.

If Margaret knew that Chester Mayfield called her baseborn out of a silly overvaluation of fermented grape juice and anger at having to sell his family's land to support their dwindling lifestyle, and she knew that her father was much more clever than Harriet's father, she also knew that her place in society was between groups. She was most definitely not part of the Old South society.

But even society below was closed to her. Even Bill Haywood, the son of one of Seth's cutters, the very same child who was one year younger than Margaret and who Margaret had taught how to shoot a slingshot at the annual Griffin Lumber picnic when he was eight years old, that Bill Haywood had become more and more shy over the years, talking less and less to Margaret and barely able to look her in the eyes.

By the time that Margaret was halfway through high school, Bill Haywood was working full-time at Griffin Lumber as a cutter, following in his father's footsteps.

Margaret's mother one day showed her a letter.

1 May 1915

Dear Margaret,

I was so very happy to receive your letter of 21 April. Seth must be doing extremely well if your daughter is considering a college education. It is a joy to have friends find success.

How I dealt with the problem you describe is by going to a good Yankee school, Wellesley, as you know. What I have never told you is how that came about. My father had the great foresight to see that he had the money but not the pedigree to join Bowling Green society. Moonshiners do not drink with their well-to-do customers. But he did have a few customers who were sympathetic to his position and he saved all of their goodwill until he needed a favor for me. He went to one of the town's grand old matrons—Mamma says that he wore a suit and even made an appointment by post, getting her to write the letter—and he asked what a loving father should do in his circumstances.

I believe the matron had a soft spot for his approach because she went on vacation to New York that spring and invited me to go along with her. We visited a number of schools in the northeast and she took me to the finer shops and I learned how big city people dress and walk and talk. When I returned to Bowling Green after Wellesley all the old boys were practically beating the door down to have tea with my family.

There is something to this method, hateful as it is to enter the enemy cities. By making an escape to a place far away and bringing back a whiff of the respectability of other people, it will smooth the way for your daughter when she returns. It will also add a polish, what the Yankees call "finish," to that delightful daughter that I know you have raised.

Another route that others have taken is to send their daughter to Paris, where there are various schools and matrons who perform the same service, just in a Continental style. With the war on, this option is not possible.

What I would suggest is that you and your daughter join me in a tour of New York City and parts of New England. Along the way, we shall endeavor to find a school that would serve your daughter well.

I miss our childhood days and the time we spent together before responsibilities took us apart. It would be a lovely way for us to catch up if you should accept my offer.

With cherished love,

Jessica Truett

That was how Vassar and Margaret found each other.

4

O NE morning Margaret was back at the Nashville house, Vassar Bachelor of Arts framed on the wall. She was a habitual early riser with nothing to do. Her father came into the kitchen dressed in a suit.

"There's no need to get all dressed up for me," said Margaret.

Seth looked up in time to see his daughter wink at him.

"Be seeing some bankers later," he said. "I never feel right meet'n 'em in work clothes." He straightened his tie, a blue and green stripe silk tie that Margaret had bought him in New York. "Never feel right in a suit either, to tell the truth."

"What are you seeing the bankers about, if I may be so bold as to ask?"

"A loan, one for a run of forest down south."

"Is a loan a good idea?"

"If I had the cash, I'd not do it. Besides, the land'll pay the loan in two years. Nothing to it, except putting on a suit."

Margaret almost said, "Too much effort," but was stopped by the impulse to go and change into one of the dresses she had bought in New York City and go with him. She did not know where the impulse came from, only that something was not right. While she was trying to clarify what exactly was not right, she tried to keep up a patter of conversation to keep her father occupied, but he was distracted and was soon walking out the door, leaving Margaret alone with her thoughts.

"Daddy," Margaret said a few nights later, "suppose I wanted to take a look at Griffin Lumber."

"Supposing you did," Seth had replied. "Ain't nothing to it that you've not seen before. Men cutting trees down. Men cutting trees up. Men selling lumber. More men driving trees and lumber all over. What more is there to see?"

"I want to look at the books," she said. She looked at her father while the statement sank in. He was handsome in a most unconventional way. His face was as plain as it could be and twenty years ago no one noticed him, she imagined. Experience had done something to that face. His skin was tanned from having spent every day outside. At first he was out looking over his lumber operations. As things began to run better and he began to relax, as money piled up in the bank, Seth spent more time either hunting or fishing. He was always carrying a gun or a fishing pole somewhere. Seth had bought Sefer Farm on the outskirts of Nashville because it had two big lakes and miles of woods. He rarely hunted or fished anywhere else.

"I mean the accounts," said Margaret. "I want to look at the accounts." She had waited long enough for his response.

Seth sighed and said, "I know you do, darling." He had looked away, nowhere in particular, for a moment.

He had crows feet around his eyes. What Margaret saw was comfort. That's what had changed him into handsome. He was a man who was comfortable with the world. He had fought for and earned what he had. You could tell he'd do it all over again, if he had to. His comfort came from the fact that he could.

Seth knew that he had spoiled his daughter. He couldn't help himself. He had watched Ruth waddle around pregnant for almost six months with their only child. Ruth had gotten large fast and Seth watched as his little wife became big and her walk changed into the sideways walk, the shifting of hips down on one side, up on the other, then seesawed the other way as her shoulders and head bobbed left to right, right to left. He loved Ruth more every day as she carried the baby. He had not given a single thought to the actual baby as a human being until Dr. Kinney had called him into their bedroom, some sixteen hours after Ruth had gone into labor.

Lilly, who had been hired at Seth's insistence as soon as Ruth started to show her pregnancy, was standing just inside the bedroom, a baby swaddled in white sheet in her dark arms. She was crying, those great big white eyes in that black face had gone red and there were wet patches on her cheeks.

"What on earth, Lilly?" Seth was genuinely concerned.

"Mister Seth, your wife has done give birth to the most beautiful baby girl." She cried harder, trying to look down at the baby in her arms and at the same time to get the baby closer to Seth.

Seth had never seen Lilly cry, had never seen a woman cry. He had been raised around men, his mother dying in childbirth when he was four years old. Ruth certainly never cried.

Seth came and caught a glimpse of Ruth out of the corner of his eye. He looked at his wife in their bed. Her hair was soaking wet and perspiration stained the pillows. She was sleeping ever so quietly.

"Ruth's fine," said Dr. Kinney. "She's just worn out." Dr. Kinney had slapped his hand on Seth's back, pushing him closer to Lilly. "You got a baby girl there, Seth. Made of the same stock as your wife. She came out determined to be here."

Then he saw the little face peeping out of the swaddling, the eyes closed, the skin rubbed red and newborn patchy brown. Lilly pushed the swaddling into his arms, and Seth Griffin stood looking into that face. He stood and he stood, looking at that little face and he was a lost man, his heart had been stolen and he knew that someone else had entered his life and that his life, his heart, would never be the same.

"Seth, you all right over there?"

Seth could not help standing there, the baby in his arms, looking at her little face.

"Sure thing, Doc."

"You never seen a baby before?"

"Don't suppose I have."

Seth figured he started a second life the day that Margaret was born. He had never felt pain before. He had never feared death. He had never worried about someone the way he worried about Margaret. Now he was a wreck. Now he discovered in his daughter a helpless being who needed him. And she grew, learned to crawl and walk, began to speak and it wasn't that long before he knew that Margaret loved him nearly as fiercely as he loved her. He figured you had to have a child to love the way he did.

He tried to keep this new Seth Griffin hidden from the rest of the world.

When Margaret, twenty-one years of age, had asked Seth if she could stick her nose into his company's accounts, he knew he'd say yes. He knew he didn't have a prayer of saying no. He could not say no to his beloved daughter.

So in that fall of 1921, when he had turned back to look at her, his lovely child, he said, "Darling, I don't mind if you take a look at the books, but will you do your father a favor?" He looked at her nodding a slow yes. "Can you be quiet about it?"

"Yes, sir."

"I don't know what you are looking for, but I don't think you're looking because it's good reading. And I don't want people spooked or feeling bad. That okay?"

"Yes, sir." She would start visiting the main office of Griffin Lumber on the weekends, when no one was around. She would take daddy's key ring, the one which was too heavy to keep in his pockets. In the mornings he would carry it from his dresser to his office desk and the evening he would bring it back to his dresser. At Sefer Farm, he'd leave it in the bottom of the gun cabinet. For years to come, Margaret Griffin would look at a key ring and see exciting things to come, the unlocking of things, not the locking.

5

THE bright red Studebaker, ornate and shiny, stood in sharp contrast to her black Model T, plain as plain could be. She had seen the Studebaker around town before, but now she was stuck behind it on the Murfreesboro Road. "Who would need such a thing in Tennessee? Who would want such a thing?" she asked of her reflection in the windshield.

In the cab of the Studebaker sat Lee Wilson, driving and trying to read the directions on the printed invitation. "Twenty-five minutes outside of Nashville on the Murfreesboro Road, you'll pass Kimbro and in less than five minutes look for a wooden gate painted a dark blue in the middle of a thick forest on the left. Go through the gate and shut it behind you, please. The house is at the end of the road."

He hated the Murfreesboro Road. In 1921 it was heavily rutted from use, the dirt tracks carved wet by automobile tires and wagon wheels and then left to dry hellishly bumpy. The ruts made his car jump left and right. He had to drive slower. He would be even later than he already was. He was like a kid late for Christmas. Seth Griffin's Thanksgiving Turkey Shoot was an event, a chance to shoot on a well-kept farm with men who ran Tennessee. It had been held the weekend before Thanksgiving for as long as anyone in Nashville could remember. Lee was a new face in town, although certainly not new to the town, and he understood that the invitation to shoot turkeys was an invitation to access to the center of power in the state. Just thinking about it made him press the gas pedal a little harder.

Margaret was trying to keep her mind on Doyle Carter and the mess awaiting her at the farm. How was she going to handle herself around Doyle? Her father and she would split the hunters into two groups, taking their groups to separate blinds. There could be as many as twenty in the hunting party, which was too many for a single group. Ten, if she thought about it, was too many for a blind, but half of them would be hungover and not even have put cartridges in their shotguns when turkeys appeared, if the turkeys bothered to appear to be shot at all. The thing about the farm was that Daddy had hunted so often over so much acreage that Margaret sometimes wondered if the animal kingdom wasn't getting wise. If the deer and the boar and the turkeys didn't know when Seth had walked out the front door with a gun, then Darwin was wrong and beings did not evolve. Usually he carried a Winchester sixteen-gauge pump as the perfect all around shotgun. Even when he went fishing, Seth carried a pistol and had more than once brought back both largemouth bass and rabbit.

What would she do if Doyle Carter ended up in her shooting party? She'd be nice to him Saturday and Sunday and then look two-faced on Monday. Maybe Daddy wouldn't deal with the problems of his accounting department until Tuesday. She hated the idea that she would have to be nice to a man who was stealing outright from her father. It had taken two months of digging in the Griffin Lumber books for Margaret to see that it had to be Doyle. The more she thought about it, the more angry she got.

She was yanked out of her anger, momentarily, when the Studebaker came to a screeching halt in front of her. Margaret had to slam on the brakes and swerve to the right of The Ridiculous Thing to miss it.

"Moron," Margaret said to the rear of the Studebaker.

She realized that they were stopped right in front of the gate to Sefer Farm.

"It's gonna be a humdinger of a weekend," said Margaret, picking up her father's accent. "We got your drunk morons with shotguns let loose on Sefer Farm."

The Studebaker pulled into the farm entrance and before the driver had a chance to get out to open the gate, Margaret decided to keep driving down the Murfreesboro Road for a little. She could not face the unknown moron, not just yet. She thought another ten minutes of driving would give her a chance to clear her mind of Doyle Carter and her anger.

As she drove she kept thinking about the moron in the Studebaker and she wondered if the usual group was going to be there or if something had changed. By the time she returned to the blue gate, she had no heart to be sociable. She knew the back porch would be crowded with men full of whiskey. Lucius was the big black caretaker of the farm and he would be with the men, the only one not drinking. He would be hovering over a fire pit, turning steaks for Seth's guests. That would leave her to mingle with father's friends. The thought took all of the stuffing out of her.

She opened the blue gate, pulled the Ford through, hopped out on the other side and closed the gate. The Griffin Lumber cutters had carved the road that led from the gate to the farmhouse through a heavy wood of pine trees. They were tall, mature trees and the November night became that much darker as she entered into the tunnel of pine. Just when she saw the lights of the house, she cut the car lights. She had decided to sneak in.

It was a sharply cold night, the earthy smells of fall just barely floating above the freeze. The air was full of trees having died their yearly death. Sloughed hardwood leaves and pine needles had long since fallen and started their slow return to the soil. Margaret could picture the fields close by, with crops harvested and the dirt plowed for the winter freeze.

Once out of the Model T, she could smell the fire off the back porch.

In through the front door, Margaret removed her shoes and padded in socked feet towards the kitchen, where Cissy came into view. She was Lucius' wife and kept the farmhouse clean and its occupants fed. Cissy and Lucius lived in a cabin just off the main farm road.

In a whisper through the kitchen door, Margaret asked Cissy to sneak a plate of food up to her room and not tell anyone that she was there.

"Yo daddy been wondering where you is."

"Well, tell him I've got a headache and have gone to bed. I'll see them at breakfast."

"Yes, ma'am."

"Don't tell Daddy too loud. And ask him to make me a whiskey." She smiled and pointed to her head. "Medicinal. For the headache."

"For the head," said Cissy—it sounded like "Fo d' dead"—and turned to go out on the porch, where Margaret could hear the ever rising tone of men talking. She padded up the stairs. Margaret's bedroom was on the second floor, directly over the kitchen. Both rooms were on the foot of the L shape of the farmhouse.

She walked across the creaky floorboards, her socks running smoothly across them until she was inside the door of her bedroom, where she had put a red Persian rug. It made the floor less shocking in the cold mornings. She pulled the desk chair up to the window that overlooked the backyard and sat looking down on her father's stag party.

The fire pit was between the kitchen and back porch that ran off the other side of the house and Lucius was stacking wood next to it. The fire was a smooth bed of dark orange coals and Margaret could smell meat cooking over an open flame, her stomach knotting. Three men stood on the other side of the fire pit from Lucius, one with his foot up on the stones of the pit. Margaret knew there were ten or twelve men in rocking chairs on the covered porch; she could not see under the porch from her bedroom. Five others sat in pine chairs around a pine table just off the porch. Her father's face appeared from underneath the porch, looking straight into her window. He held up a metallic flash in his right hand, jingled it at her and then blew a kiss with his left hand. She knew he couldn't see her, but she blew a kiss back, saying, "Ah, Daddy."

Then he disappeared back under the porch. A minute later, Margaret heard Cissy's footsteps, first mounting the stairs and then coming around the corner, and then the knock on the door.

She brought everything on a tray, had gotten out specially a china plate, a sterling fork and knife, and a folded linen napkin. The silver cup that Seth had waved at her completed the tray. It was her father's one concession to luxury. He always drank his whiskey from a silver cup and so did everybody else at the farm.

Cissy slipped the tray onto a table next to the window.

"Thank you, Cissy," said Margaret, who was transfixed out the window.

"Yes ma'am." Cissy looked out the window from behind Margaret. "They sure do love coming to his farm."

"I suppose they do. They like Daddy's whiskey, that's for sure. You'd think they'd never heard of prohibition."

"Your daddy sure was smart, buying all that whiskey."

"I don't think Daddy was thinking of prohibition, Cissy. He was thinking of other things. Anyone new down there?"

"Same every year. There's a young one. Got here just before you did. He's sitting on the porch."

Margaret raised the window a little and immediately the men's voices followed the cold air into the room.

"… flying between the rigs and refineries."

"That's him," said Cissy. "Lee Wilson. That's his name. He's awful young."

"The flying was funner than the work," said Lee, out of sight. "I used to fly a Jenny. It's like nothing I've ever done before, float-ing above the ground like a bird. You could actually fly above the birds and see them going south or north in their great big groups. Everything looks different up there. You can see how the fields are divided up and the neat lines that trees make…"

"You want me to light the lamp?"

"No, thank you, Cissy."

"I'll just be leaving you alone, then."

"Thank you, Cissy. I'll see you in the morning."

"Yes, ma'am."

By the firelight, Margaret could just make out the steak and baked potato on her plate. Her father had given her a straight bourbon and the first sip burnt her throat, a nice warmth flowing down into her stomach.

"The St. Clair brothers bought our refinery and kept me on. I think I must have worked for three, maybe four years, before I woke up one day and said, 'Enough.' The brothers couldn't afford to pay in cash at first so I was paid mostly in stock. You don't need much cash in Oklahoma to begin with and even less when all you are doing is working. So by the time I quit, St. Clair Oil was worth something and so was my steak."

"Stock, you moron," whispered Margaret, realizing that he had probably been chewing on steak while telling this story.

Looking out on the little world of men underneath her, Margaret was so tired. She hated closing the window before going to sleep. She thought it was unhealthy to sleep in an unventilated room, but they would be up until late, talking and drinking and eating. She hated locking her bedroom door, too, but drunken men looking for the wc could wander anywhere. She kept a twelve gauge loaded with slugs next to her bedside and wanted to avoid an accident. With a locked door, there would be no accidents.

6

THE next morning Lee Wilson was the last man to enter the dining room. He was resplendent in tweed jacket and crisp moleskin trousers, his hair pomaded into place, and a purple cashmere scarf tucked into the collar of his jacket. By far he was the most expensively dressed in the room.

Most of the men were wearing a combination of worn canvas and beaten sweaters. Margaret had Dutch braided her hair and wore thick blue wool trousers and a grey sweater with a large leather patch on the right shoulder. Her father was accustomed to seeing her in men's clothes, but she had raised other eyebrows.

This was the difference between being a girl and a woman, she had been thinking. Girls get away with wearing trousers around men. Women do not. Most of the men had seen her in trousers as a girl on the farm. They took no notice of her attire before now. She was starting to understand how age changed what other people expected of her.

"Lee, I'd like you to meet my daughter," said Seth.

Lee already had a biscuit in one hand and was reaching for a plate of ham with the other when he looked up, first at Seth and then to Margaret.

His mouth dropped open. "Why, I'm so sorry. I didn't see you…"

He put the plate of ham down and stood up, his chair wobbling backwards and rocking forward on its front legs with a crack as Lee walked to the other side of Seth, to where Margaret was sitting. He moved the biscuit from his right hand to his left, leaving a few crumbs on the hand he extended awkwardly to Margaret over her right shoulder, barely clearing her breast.

Men, transfixed by the scene unfolding directly across the table, saw Margaret's mouth drop open at exactly the same moment that Lee's had dropped open.

Lee was the best looking man she had ever seen and it had taken a minute for her eyes to move beyond his ridiculous costume. She had expected no less from a man who drove a bright red Studebaker. Then she looked at his face. She twisted in her seat to shake Lee's hand, finally asking, "How do you do?"

One of the first to the breakfast table, Margaret had become steadily more irritated by how long it took some of the men to wake up, get dressed and have breakfast. She had greeted each as they had come through the door, her voice becoming a little chillier as time passed. By the time Lee came through the doorway, that purple scarf leading like a flag squad at a parade, she was smirking and silent. She could feel the heat rise into her cheeks when she realized that the entire table had been watching the exchange between Lee and herself. She was doubly embarrassed because Lee was blushing, too, and she could feel her father's eyes.

"I thought," said Seth with a sideways glance, "that you could take Mr. Wilson with you this morning. He likely needs some younger company after being around us old fogeys last night."

Margaret looked from Lee to her father, catching his curious eyes. Then she looked back to Lee, who had not moved and was gazing deeply into her eyes.

She realized that they were still holding each other's hand, the shaking long since ceased. She pulled her hand back with a jerk, startling Lee.

"I would welcome the opportunity," said Margaret in her most formal hostess voice, "to show Mr. Wilson where we hunt on our little farm." She looked around the table. "Mr. Wilson and nine or ten of you dreadfully hungover Old Fogeys. Assuming you gentlemen are done with breakfast."

Margaret's group would include two bankers, the state secretary, three businessmen, a newspaper editor, and a municipal utilities director. She wasn't sure what Lee was. Doyle Carter, Margaret's real problem for the weekend, had thankfully gone with her father's group to the northernmost lake. She would take her group to what had been christened the South Pond, the two lakes and the farmhouse making up a triangle on the farm. The two bankers were both named Sumner. Sumner Bumpus and Sumner Craig. They even dressed alike, thought Margaret, coolly taking in their grey hunting coats.

It was still dark when Margaret's group had set out for the South Pond, where Seth had built one of numerous blinds on the farm. Frank Stainbeck, the local furniture baron, brought up the rear with one of the lanterns. Success had gone to Frank's stomach, which barreled forward and made him walk more slowly than the rest of the group. George Paulett, the state secretary, carried a second lantern in the middle. He was as nondescript as the bankers. Margaret led the way, carrying the third lantern. Lee walked right next to Margaret, trying out small talk about the farm, about how long she had lived in Nashville, about hunting and finally asking her, "Did you go to Vanderbilt?"

"I graduated from Vassar, Mr. Wilson, last May." She could feel the eyes of the men walking behind her, looking for any sign of flirtation. Many of the men in her group had watched Margaret grow up and they were oddly subdued around her.

Lee was openly flirtatious. There was something about his smile and the way he walked, looking at her and not where he was going. Margaret quickened her step and tried to keep her answers short without being defensive and cold.

"I never heard of it. Where is it?"

"North of New York City, a little place called Poughkeepsie." She had begun to whisper.

"What kind of school is it? Did you like it?" Lee was trying to whisper and walk quietly.

"Liked it a lot. I'm thinking about going back to school, but I'm not sure what I'd study. Daddy thinks I need to settle down, get married and have children, but I'd like to do something with my life beyond just that. We should be quiet until we get to the blind."

Lee gave a nod and crooned forward, trying to walk quietly.

The South Pond was a series of three small circular lakes that had run together, forming a kidney shape. They made their way to the southern most part of it, where wild turkeys had been seen for more than ten years. In the darkness, the lamps caught some of the dark shimmer of the lake, but there was an extra chill in the air, a better indication that a body of water was close by.

The blind was a wooden box, framed in four-by-fours and sided with broad planks. There were various trap doors on the sides and the top. The outside had been painted with random swirls of brown and green. Branches had been attached to the edges, giving it the appearance of a house for elven Robin Hoods. Benches had been built on the inside, allowing the party to face out the opened trap doors. By the time everyone was settled in the blind, the blackness of the night had given way to a pale blue sky, but the night still clung close to the ground, in the trees and all around the hunters.

The quiet gave Margaret a moment to think about what she had said to Lee Wilson. What would she do next? Despite her father's wishes, there was no man she would consider marrying.

During high school in Nashville, she had been friendly with the boys but elusive as a love interest. She had been very comfortable with the kind of boys in high school who liked her, but not attracted to them. They were not interesting.

Vassar had provided a pool of young men that was completely different. The campus was littered with Yale undergraduates. "Yalies" they called themselves and were called by others. Margaret had never before encountered men so self-confident and so ready to display their self-confidence. The nice ones were harmless and uninteresting. The arrogant ones were distasteful to Margaret.

Century McCormick was a Yalie name that made her wince while she sat in the blind, her shotgun propped in front of her. Margaret first thought his friends called him "Cen" as a shortened version of his name. Later she believed it was "Sin." He had not been derogatory about Tennessee or her accent as so many had been. Not that others had been openly dismissive of Tennessee, but there were facial expressions, comments and the occasional mocking accent, all so barely perceptible or just out of range that Margaret second guessed herself. The thought that came back to Margaret again and again during her freshman year at Vassar was that she knew she was an outsider from the society of Nashville and the workers of Griffin Lumber. She felt as if she belonged to Nashville but not necessarily the people of Nashville. She had to work very hard to feel comfortable around her social peers and she worked hard to make Griffin Lumber workers comfortable around her. At Vassar, she was so much the outsider that she felt no restrictions. She was cowed by nothing and determined to graduate from Vassar with a good education. She was open to what came along with that education.

Century was a gentlemen and beyond such trivial considerations as geography, and he was interested in Margaret.

The sun slowly dawned and thirty minutes, maybe an hour had passed in silence, except the quiet snores of Frank, the rotund manufacturer of furniture. Margaret heard the distinct pop of a cork leaving a bottle. It stopped her from dwelling on Century McCormick, for whom she had fallen. Who had burned her. Margaret was trying to put the exact events out of her mind when the bottle of whiskey was opened. They had all been so quiet, waiting for a turkey to appear. Margaret was thinking of how heartbreak had given her a new self-possession in college. She had become even more herself, a Tennessean, the daughter of Seth and Ruth. One of the Sumners, sitting to her right, had just taken a swig of the bottle and turned to Margaret. She whispered "Thank You" and took a big swig.

It was skinny John Hallum, who owned a lot of flour and grist mills in Nashville and Memphis, and who was sitting with his back roughly to Margaret's back, who spoke first.

"It always makes me feel funny sitting with a bunch of men… no offense Margaret."

"None taken."

"It always makes me feel funny," John began again, "sitting with a bunch of men in such close quarters and saying nothing."

They had dispensed with whispering and were talking normally now.

The other Sumner, sitting next to John, said, "I like you better, John, when you say nothing, no matter how close you are."

Margaret had already anticipated the guffaws and Sumner slapping John on the back.

The group could hear gunfire in the distance.

"They've found something to shoot," said Francis, who had come out of his slumber.

"Where Daddy is concerned," said Margaret, "that's a very broad statement."

To her left she saw George pull a small wooden box from the game pocket of his coat. He caught Margaret's eye. "Cigars," he said.

That was it, she figured. The morning's hunt was over. Margaret leaned over and unloaded her gun. Several others followed her example.

"Well," said Margaret, "let's walk up to where Daddy is and see what he's shooting. We'll go up to the northwest of Daddy's blind and come from behind so they don't end up shooting us."

7

MARGARET was surprised to see Lee Wilson bringing up the rear of the group. Had she known it, Lee had had a fitful night of sleep, had been hungover and now the bourbon and cigar were working powerfully on Lee's stomach. He simply did not feel well and did not have the energy to continue the small talk with Margaret.

Good, she thought to herself, if I keep Mr. Wilson at bay, I can corner Daddy when we get back to the farmhouse and explain what I found in the Griffin Lumber books. She was going over how she would say it to her father in her mind. "Daddy, let me put it to you straight. Doyle Carter is stealing from you." Too damning and direct, she thought, even if it was true.

She looked back at the group of men. They were a drag ass weary lot.

That's when she saw a buck emerge from a clearing to the rear of the group and she stopped cold, her mouth dropping wide open, because it was headed right for Lee Wilson. The deer had a big rack, at least twelve points, and it was trotting like she'd never seen a deer trot before. John Hallum, with his head down and not realizing that Margaret had stopped, ran into her, bringing them both down to the ground. Margaret was able to look up to see the collision.

It all happened in slow motion.

The buck did not see the group and ran right into Lee Wilson. There was an unusually loud thud like a twenty-five pound sack of potatoes being thrown off a roof. For an instant, Lee and the buck lay on the ground, motionless. The buck was up at once, shook off the fall and ran into the woods, continuing on his way.

There was gunfire. Margaret looked back to see both Sumners with shotguns shouldered, firing at the buck. The buck was gone before the turkey shot hit the trees.

Frank the Furniture Baron said, "Boys, you gonna need something bigger than ten gauge to bring that big sucker down."

There was a groan. It was Lee. He had not moved. He lay on the ground, a crumpled heap of clothes, that purple scarf, dirty now, partially laid out beside him. Margaret was the first to get to him.

"Mr. Wilson," she said while grabbing a hold of one of his shoulders, "Mr. Wilson, are you all right?"

"Ooohhh, shit," he said.

From the ground, Lee could smell the loveliest smell, something feminine. He had smelled it before when he was walking next to Margaret, but now the world was upside down, and he tried to roll over. There was a sharp crack of pain in his left arm and he felt remote, only smelling Margaret, the only thing he could think of.

"Are you okay," she asked again.

"No," he said.

"Where does it hurt?"

"My arm. Left arm."

By now the entire group had encircled Lee. Margaret and John Hallum had rolled him onto his back. Even though it was gently managed, Lee gave a restrained yelp.

Frank offered Lee the whiskey bottle.

Margaret's state of mind was a mess. She still thought that Lee was foolish with his purple scarf and his red Studebaker. He had brought along a brand new L. C. Smith shotgun for the hunt. It too stood out amongst the shotguns as expensive and flashy. No amount of extra finery could disguise that accent of his. It was not an educated twang. She hated such peacockery, such pretension.

But he was handsome and his incessant questions, so clearly good intentioned and genuinely curious, were starting to work on her. Now he had been injured while she was his guide. She felt awful and confused while leading the way back to the house. Two of the party had gone to the North Pond to fetch Daddy and his hunting party. The rest were behind her, encircling Lee, asking him if he was okay and pouring more bourbon into him.

"He was chasing a doe in heat," said Seth when he returned to the farmhouse. "I saw the doe a minute before the buck came through our camp. If I'd had a slug, it'd be venison and turkey for Thanksgiving."

The second shooting party had done much better, having shot nine turkeys, a mix of gobblers and hens in a fruitful confused moment of lead, powder and the silence afterwards of the kill. They had been sitting outside the blind, the turkeys in canvas bags, passing a bottle of bourbon and smoking cigars, about to set out and meet Margaret's group when Francis and George had finally found them. The group was in a splendid mood. They had a good hunt, enough turkey that everyone could have some for the coming Thanksgiving holiday, and they had a helluva good hunting story. The weekend wasn't even halfway done.

Lee, on the other hand, was humiliated. He was immersed in a chemical and biological cocktail. He was smitten with Margaret. By the time they finally left the blind, Lee was exhausted and ashamed of how he felt about her. He had been bringing up the rear because he thought he'd made a fool of himself on the walk from the house. He was working hard to get a grip on himself, but he still found himself looking at the back of Margaret as she led the group to the farmhouse. He knew he was pining and he didn't realize how ridiculous the look on his face was until Margaret turned around and looked right at him. He was just about to smile at her when the buck drove him to the ground.

He didn't know what had hit him. The buck had driven a shoulder into Lee and his antlers had been pointed to the left, to where he was running, narrowly missing him. He was still in shock when he heard the others gather around him.

When Margaret had bent over him and asked if he was okay, she had emerged from a dream. Her smell, a mixture of soap, shampoo and something indescribably feminine, had brought him back through the smell of wet dirt. It was afterwards that he realized how ridiculously beaten he looked. On the long, painful walk back to the farmhouse, his arm had started to hurt more and more and was positively throbbing with pain by the time they reached the farmhouse. Margaret had used his purple scarf as a sling for his arm. He could scarcely look at Margaret as she had tied it. He hated the idea that she had seen him beaten up. He knew at one point a few heroically restrained tears had rolled down his cheeks. It felt like the worst moment of his life to have the woman that you love see you cry.

Once back at the farmhouse, he said to Margaret, "If you don't mind, I think I might go lie down for a minute."

"Nonsense," said Margaret, "you've broken your arm. I'm driving you back into Nashville and we're going to get your arm set and put into a cast."

Lee tried to protest but Margaret was adamant. "You've been injured and you need someone to intercede on your behalf. You don't know how bad it really looks. Wait here and I'll go get your things."

She left Lee on the front steps of the farmhouse, several of his hunting party standing around him, making small talk. Frank had produced another bottle of whiskey and was feeding it to Lee, sometimes taking a swig himself.

She had driven him back to Nashville and directly to Dr. Kinney's house, where the good doctor had a small home-examining room. Mrs. Kinney dipped the plaster bandages in water and handed them to Dr. Kinney while Margaret told the story. Lee's mood began to brighten as Margaret put the story in such a kind light. She made it sound less humiliating. Then Dr. Kinney had given Lee a morphine injection, saying, "This will take the edge off the pain better than whatever you've been drinking." As soon as Margaret saw Lee fall into the slow dream state of morphine and he could not answer the basic question "Where do you live," she had decided to put him into their guest bedroom at the Nashville house, where Lilly could take care of him. Torn between her duty to be at the Turkey Shoot, her need to tell her father about Doyle Carter and having an injured man for whom she felt responsible, she opted to stay in Nashville.

8

Lee Wilson was well enough on Monday to be packed off to his boarding house with a hamper of food that Lilly had made.

Margaret knew that the men of the turkey shoot would all have left by Tuesday.

At five-thirty on Wednesday morning, Margaret and Seth were sitting in the blind at the North Pond, sipping coffee they had brought in a thermos. Seth had carefully laid a line of shotgun shells on the empty window sill in front of him. He always did that, thought Margaret, like a kid lining up dominos, the brass caps down, the tan paper up. Two slugs on the right. Turkey shot on the left. The bird shot was in his right coat pocket.

Margaret looked at their boots, which she could hardly make out in the bluing darkness, just shapes that disappeared at the end of their legs. She knew what they looked like all too well and could conjure the image in her mind's eye. They both wore lumberjack boots with a kiltie at the bottom of the laces. They were worn and oiled. That's the difference, she thought, between the purple scarf, the silver pitcher and our boots. The purple scarf was new money, the kind that drove a bright red Studebaker and lived in a boarding house. The silver pitcher was old money, no self-discipline, no clamp on craving, just an expectation of luxury to come. And here we sit, new money and the second generation, only we're not like either the purple scarf nor the silver pitcher. It was a simplistic view, she knew, but the thought persisted, we're stronger than…

"Doyle Carter asked if things were going all right," said Seth. He never whispered in a blind, but he could talk with a low soft voice that sounded like the root of a tree growing towards you.

"What'd you say?"

"I told him everything's fine. No need to disturb anything until…" Seth drew a breath through his nostrils as if he had smelt prey approaching, "until you need to."

"He's doing it through a company called Needle Top. It's not smart, the way he's doing it."

"Doyle's not smart."

"He's got Needle Top, nothing to it, just a business with a bank account…"

"Which bank?"

"Planters."

"Figures. I don't know anyone there. Just a country bank, long ways away."

"He drops a bill into the payables about once a month, already approved." Margaret knew she didn't have to explain anything more. Doyle paid the payables so the theft was a closed loop. No one else saw the invoice. "Been doing it for nearly three years."

"How much?"

"The amount varies month by month. The total is… a lot. Enough to buy a nice run of land. Without a loan."

Seth went back to breathing through his mouth and he was still for awhile, waiting for something to move outside the blind. They'd already made enough noise to scare off anything worth shooting.

"It's always the same, the bill," said Margaret, after she had waited long enough. "A single line that says Cutter Maintenance and Repairs."

"You sure about this?"

"Doyle left the Needle Top papers in his desk. His name is all over them."

"Greedy and stupid. Well, if you were in my boots, what would you do?"

"I'll go back into town before lunch," the other thought branched out as she spoke, the thought that her father was asking her for advice, "to see John Sutter…"

"A lawyer? Is that necessary?"

"Doyle'll be out until Monday so we need to meet with him first thing Monday morning. Now he thinks you might know something is up. Did anyone in the office tip Doyle off to my visit last Friday? Either way, there's a chance he's ready for us. Not much of a chance. I've got his Needle Top papers. They were sitting in our desk, the desk we gave him to work on." There was a trace of outrage in Margaret's voice. "Monday morning we meet with him first thing and we need someone there. A lawyer will send the message to Doyle how serious this is. And if there's any trouble, we'll be ready."

"So you think John will be in his office today?"

"If not, he'll be at home. John'll understand."

"Okay, Monday it is."

John Sutter arrived at Griffin Lumber at 8:30 the following Monday morning. John, Margaret and Seth made small talk in Seth's office until Doyle finally arrived at his office at 9:15, where one of his girls relayed that he was needed first thing in Seth's office.

Doyle looked chubby in a suit. Margaret thought everyone looked better in hunting clothes. He had the wan appearance of one who had enjoyed a long hard holiday week, and he was cheerful when introduced to John Sutter, who was thin and sober in one of Seth's chairs, his briefcase on the floor, sitting next to him. Margaret was wearing a black flannel skirt and jacket, one of the somber outfits she had bought in New York City at a store that brought clothes from London.

Only Seth did not wear a suit. He wore a pair of newish wool hunting trousers and a thick flannel shirt. He looked like he was ready to grab a saw and go to work on a tree after the meeting, this despite not having worked on the production line for twenty years. Once everyone was seated and the air had thickened up as Doyle's inner ear picked up a serious tone, Seth said, "Doyle, there seems to be a few problems in the books. Ah, um, it appears we are paying a company… a company that I've never heard of, a monthly sum, that, well, stands out."

Margaret could barely contain herself. She wanted to leap out of the chair and wave the Needle Top papers at him. She couldn't believe how soft her father was, coming out like Doyle had just spilled some coffee on a rug rather than stolen money from him.

Doyle eased back into his chair and said, "Well, Seth, if you tell me which company, I'll go back and look into it. If there's a mistake, I'll get it fixed. You can count on me." He was all smiles.

It wasn't a genuine smile, Margaret knew. She had seen how he had tensed up, sat forward in the chair, his belly sticking out over the edge, nearly over his knees. He knew he'd been caught. Was he trying to cover his tracks by getting back to the books this morning? Did he already know how to get himself out of this? Or was he buying time, time to think of how to save his skin? Or was he trying to flee? Once through the door, he'd be gone.

Seth's office hadn't changed as long as Margaret could remember. It was in the back of their main lumber yard, a simple matter, four walls with windows on three walls. Two windows looked out onto the land behind the lumber company. The other window looked out onto the people, mostly women, who took care of the paperwork that kept the business going. They sat in desks lined up in four columns.

Margaret looked at the closed door. She wouldn't let Doyle through that door until this matter was taken care of. She got up from her chair, the silence irritating her, tucked the papers under her left arm and walked over to the door, turning and standing in front of it. Doyle and John had to turn awkwardly in their chairs to see her. She looked at her father. She could tell he wanted to put his feet up on his desk. She finally broke the silence. "Doyle, it's Needle Top."

"That the name of the company?"

"Yes, Doyle," said Seth in the middle of a sigh, "that's the name of the company."

"Well, let me go see what I can find," Doyle made to get up.

Margaret stepped towards Doyle and put a hand on his shoulder, gently sitting him back down. "That won't be necessary, Doyle." She saw her daddy smile, a small one, fleeting, across just a corner of his lips. She walked to the side of Seth's desk and lay the papers down.

"We know all about it." She flipped a sheet of paper. "You are the sole officer of Needle Top. Doyle," she flapped a sheet of paper in her right hand, "you used your home address as the business address."

Doyle looked at Seth and said, "Seth, what is this? You think I…"

Seth said, "Margaret's telling you, Doyle."

"Doyle," said Margaret, putting a sheet of paper in front of him, "here's a list of all the money you've taken out since June 1918." She waited for him to look at the paper. He wouldn't raise his eyes from it. "I've got the books here," she said, pulling a box from behind Seth's desk, "with all the details. And the invoices, too. Doyle, you didn't even bother to get rid of the evidence." She looked at Doyle Carter, the cause of so much of her own anger. He was hunched over the sheet of paper, his eyes glued to it, his breathing pronounced. He was very still. John Sutter was practically invisible. Margaret wondered how he had done it. Was it something he had learned in law school? "Doyle, we're gonna give you two options. John here has a piece of paper. It says that you are willing to acknowledge what you've done and you are handing over what money's left. It also says that you haven't done anything else. So I'm going to ask you once, is that true?"

Doyle looked up. "What's the other option?"

"We're calling the police. We'll have you arrested and make an example of you. Whatever you've got, we'll take it to repay us. House. Car. Land. Shotgun. Whatever you got. Someone from John's firm is waiting at the police station, ready to file charges. All we have to do is make the call. There's someone else at the courthouse ready to file a civil case against you." Margaret's voice was stern. She could feel a part of her melting, looking at Doyle, a man who had been whipped. He was ashamed, she knew by the way his eyes wandered away from her, away from her daddy, towards the floor corners.

"Doyle," this time it was Seth who spoke, "I just as soon bury you in the trash ditch at Sefer Farm. But Margaret keeps telling me it is illegal to kill a man, no matter how he has betrayed your trust, no matter what he's done to you. Look at me when I'm talking to you. I'll come over there and pop you upside…"

Margaret held her hand out to John Sutter and said, "Give me that affidavit."

The briefcase was off the floor in an instant, clicked open, and paper handed to Margaret, briefcase snapped close and on the floor.

"Go ahead, Doyle, read it. There's nothing else, is there?" Margaret was shaken by her father's anger, a magnified reflection of her own. Physical violence was beyond her, but she understood what her daddy wanted to do. It didn't mean it was the best thing to do, letting anger take over like that.

"No, ma'am. That's it." Doyle read the document with a complete focus, and then said, "You have a pen, Margaret?"

After Doyle signed the paper, Margaret took it and handed it back to John, who returned it to his briefcase as efficiently as it had come out. "Now, Doyle," she said, "you and John and I are going to take a little trip to Planter's…"

"Now? I don't have the…"

"I've got the passbook," said Margaret. "We're taking a trip out to Planter's and you are going to close that account."

Later that afternoon, when the Doyle Carter matter was about as closed as it would ever be, Margaret sat in Seth's office, the two alone, finally, after the day's events. She said, "Doyle's not your only problem, Daddy."

"Is that so?" Seth was tired and he had raised his eyebrows not so much out of surprise as out of weariness.

"No one else is stealing, not like Doyle. But there are things not working the way they are supposed to."

"Is that so?" Margaret could hear the frustration in her daddy's voice.

"I've got a friend," she said, "a smart man who knows things about business. He's third or fourth generation… his grandfather lent money in Philadelphia and his father works on Wall Street. He's been working for his daddy since last June. I could write and ask him to come down and take a look at what we got. He might be able to give us advice."

"What's his name?"

"Andrew Forest."

9

ANDREW's reply came a week later in small precise handwriting. "I can be in Nashville on the 5th of January."

Andrew also wrote that he was engaged to Joan Brannon, one of Margaret's Vassar classmates. Margaret wondered how a Boston debutante would fare with a Wall Street banker. Joan liked Cape Cod in the summer and thought New England was the heart and soul of the nation. Andrew only liked to vacation for a few days at a time and preferred Long Island. He thought of New York as the only city in the U.S. and all other places as the backwoods. But Andrew's reserved manner and Joan's proper ways worked well, when Margaret thought about it. She could not imagine either Joan or Andrew marrying someone else. That was usually the test against which she weighed a match.

When she finished reading Andrew's letter, she looked at it for a moment. Stiff white stationary with a discreet letterhead. What would he think of Nashville? Would this be too trivial for him? Would he sneer at the whole state? Margaret knew that she needed help, so she set aside her reservations and tried to focus on what she would need to prepare for Andrew. Seth had already gone to Sefer Farm for the holidays, so she encamped herself in Seth's office at Griffin Lumber. Word had spread about what she had done to Doyle Carter. The staff was quiet and responsive around her. Seth had left word that Margaret was to have whatever she wanted. They had agreed that Margaret's preparations for Andrew should be open knowledge.

The preparations were laborious. Seth's books were old fashioned written ledgers. She could total two or three ledgers and always come up with different numbers. Even some of the column totals in ledgers did not add up correctly. The actual listings of assets were not organized into clear categories.

They had one Remington typewriter and one girl, Sally Anne Jones, who was trained on it. Margaret co-opted Sally Anne, at first trying to put ledgers and inventories in front of her. Sally Anne, who was born and bred in Nashville and had the perky demeanor of someone who wanted to learn typewriting in 1921, was not a natural collator of information, so Margaret did it herself, quickly laying out how she wanted each piece of paper to look and what numbers and information went where. The office was used to not having Seth around in December and they were noticeably irritable at Margaret's presence as Christmas approached.

That didn't bother Margaret. She liked that they worked harder with her around.

Out in the field, Margaret could see that the cutters and haulers and sawmill staff were not letting up. She visited all of the sawmills with the inventories in hand. She also visited the biggest forests in production. Finally she met with the managers of the three biggest stores, hating that she did not have time to look at each and every piece of the operation. But come December 23rd, most of the Griffin Lumber operation would shut down until January 2nd. By then Margaret felt like she had as good a grip on the operation as she was likely to have.

During this time, Margaret found that her mood got better and better. She could only ascribe the feeling to fixing something that had nagged at her for a very long time, like finally oiling a squeaky door. She had known somewhere in the back of her mind that her father was not as involved in the business as he should have been, but it wasn't until he had gone off for a loan that she sprang into action. Now the picture was becoming very clear and her knowledge and control of the situation made her mysteriously and surprisingly happy. The main beneficiary of her good mood was Lee Wilson, who had been persistently present.

First came flowers, not just for Margaret, but for Ruth and Lilly as well. There was a nice note. Lee wrote simply and came to his point easily. He appreciated them taking care of him and he was on the mend. He did not put on the airs that you'd expect from a man who would wear a purple scarf at six in the morning on a turkey shoot.

Then Lee had visited them at the Nashville house, bringing chocolates and more flowers. Once Ruth had gone to Sefer Farm for the rest of the month, Margaret was left alone in Nashville. Lilly was only needed for breakfast and the washing. Margaret, surrounded by papers, ate lunch at a diner near the lumber company. By night, Lee Wilson entertained her with restaurants, the moving pictures, and the speakeasies in Printer's Alley. It was a vibrant time in the country, the post war prosperity lifting everyone's spirits and working against prohibition.

Where very few people at Griffin Lumber spoke to Margaret casually, it was a relief to have Lee do most of the talking. He had gone to Oklahoma, just as she had heard that night of the Turkey Shoot. He had gone to make money and had come back having made it, at least by Nashville standards. Lee was clever in that way. He was obviously satisfied with himself, but he made it clear to Margaret that he knew where he fitted in the world. In terms of fortunes, he was small potatoes. In Nashville, he did okay. What was left of his family was spread all over Appalachia. In some sense, he had no family.

Margaret had both a family that she adored and Vassar, a sort of stepping stone. When she looked at Lee by the candlelight of a dinner or the dark lighting of a speakeasy, she felt a maternal care. He had no family and no education. How was he going to find his place in the world, she wondered. He had practically stumbled into her father's turkey shoot. Seth had been shaking his head over Lee's Studebaker in downtown Nashville when Lee found him. Lee couldn't help but agree with Seth that a horse could go where a motor car could not, but a car could do all right, he had said. To prove it, Lee had driven Seth at that very moment in a drizzling rain out to Clyde's Pond to go fishing. The trip would have taken forty minutes by horse, but Lee made it in less than half that. Seth, to show his appreciation, had sent him the turkey shoot invitation.

To hear Lee tell how he had made money in Oklahoma, he had stumbled into that, too. It was only because the St. Clair brothers had no cash when they hired Lee that he had been paid in stock. That stock, which was issued in 1919 and 1920, was zooming in value by 1921, when Lee finally had had enough of being their whipping boy. Now Lee was making even more money on the stock market and that too was luck, thought Margaret.

What she thought she liked about him was that he had come from next to nothing and carried no baggage and he assumed the same of everyone else. He did not want to know about the Griffin family history, did not seem to think there was anything to it. As far as Lee was concerned, Seth was born running Griffin Lumber. Curiously, he knew when Seth was leaning over his Studebaker who he was and which company was his. There was nothing calculating in the way Lee said this.

Lee did not have a care in the world and he picked Margaret up each night as enthusiastically as if it were their first date. He would ask about her day, but Margaret knew better than to give more than a passing mention of her work at Griffin Lumber, what she dismissed as "helping Daddy." Then they would be off, talking to everyone. Lee was a talker, especially when he drank, and when there was a quiet moment, he looked as contented as a just-fed dog.

10

MARGARET found Lee at the barn, where he had parked the Jenny, the airplane he had bought after they got married and he realized that she intended to keep working at Griffin Lumber. He was drinking whiskey and sitting on a bench, looking at the airplane. "Hey there, stranger," she called from a distance. It was a hot, humid, sunny September day, not a hint of fall in the air. The grass around the barn was still brown from the summer heat. The barn after a hot summer was ready for a new coat of paint. Lee looked over to her and gave her a smile and a wave.

As Margaret approached Lee, his features came into focus and she was still struck by how good looking he was. "Thought we might walk up to the North Pond and see if we can bag duck or teal." She carried a twenty-gauge side-by-side in her left arm. It was a strange sensation to have the cold weight of a gun in her left arm after having the warm lightness of Evelyn in the same arm for the last four months. She realized she had not handled a gun since Evelyn's birth.

Almost as soon as Evelyn was born, Lee had complained that between Griffin Lumber and the new baby, he was practically a widower. Then he had begun to spend all of his time at Sefer Farm, flying his plane.

Lee was looking at her, expressionless, as she walked up to him. She sat next to him, leaned over and kissed his cheek.

"I was getting ready to go up." He motioned towards the Jenny. "Wanna come for a ride?"

Margaret looked at the half-empty whiskey bottle. She wondered if it had started the day full. "Maybe so," she said. She had never seen Sefer Farm from the air. For a moment she tried to imagine what the birds saw as they flew over the farmhouse. She looked back at the whiskey bottle and immediately thought of Evelyn, her baby who was waiting for her in Nashville. She had seen plenty of men drink bottle after bottle of whiskey and still be able to aim a gun. Why couldn't he fly a plane, she wondered. She would have felt better if she knew how to fly it, just in case.

Lee caught her glances at the whiskey bottle. "Nothing to it. Plane practically flies itself. If you were wondering."

She knew if she said no it would be an insult to Lee. He was proud of the plane, she could tell. "I know it's been a busy time," she said, thinking conversation would take his mind off flying. "I'm sorry about that. We haven't had much time together. I know you understand that, especially with Evelyn. We've got it good with Lilly and Mamma always taking care of her, but a baby needs her parents." She looked over at Lee, who was still staring at the Jenny. It was a great big thing next to the barn. From where they sat, they could see underneath the top wing, which was longer than the bottom wing. The body was painted silver. Margaret could see the wood supports of the wing pressing through the cloth. Lee had cleaned it up. "The business is a different matter," she said, finally filling in the silence.

"I thought your daddy was running it."

"No," said Margaret. "Daddy's only back in Nashville because of Evelyn. He'll be back here soon. He thought he could help out when I was pregnant, but he's more like a figurehead, now. He's the company historian and anything that's not written down, he knows. He told us, about a year ago, that we're in charge now."

"You mean you and Andrew."

"That's right."

"I thought Andrew was going back to New York."

"He was, but he thinks we've got something. He says he'll have to return next year, but he's talking about the land we have, how that'll appreciate and how we're really just one step away from setting up a construction company. He wants to go buy a brick kiln and a cement plant next. It's exciting."

"I'll bet it is," said Lee, who kept staring at the Jenny, "for you. But you don't need any help."

Margaret took a deep breath. "Lee, we've talked about this. We're in a good position. I wouldn't want you there unless you were a partner with us, but we've got all the management we need right now. Maybe that'll change in the future. As we grow."

"Maybe so."

That was better, thought Margaret. Lee had once shouted that she didn't take him seriously, not in business. He had money, too, he'd said.

This time, he was quiet and just kept staring at the Jenny. He finally took a drink from the bottle. "Well," he said, "that's that. Mind helping me start the plane?"

Margaret was half open to a plane ride now. She felt sorry for him. She was trying to be nice, but she knew what she was doing. She had long thought that a man should be able to take care of himself. Once she thought it meant that a man should be able to make money and take care of his family. Now she looked at Lee, who had made money, and she decided it meant that just because a man had been pushed to the outside because his wife ran a business and had a baby, he should be able to find his own way, whatever that would be. It'd make him feel better if he could show her his plane. "What do I do?"

"Well, you can either climb into the cockpit and I'll show you what to do or turn the propeller. The propeller's easier but it takes a bit of muscle. I usually get Lucius to do that."

"I'll turn the propeller," she said.

Lee walked up to the plane, setting the whiskey bottle on the ground before showing her. She grabbed the propeller, which swung with some resistance. It felt heavier than it looked. Lee moved awkwardly around her to pick up the bottle, like he didn't want to touch her, and then he climbed into the cockpit, the rear one. After he looked intently into the cockpit, Margaret saw him look around at her and say, "All right, give it a try."

She grabbed the propeller and pulled down. This time the propeller left her hands at the bottom of the rotation, and before she knew it, the propeller came back around, surprising her with the air, rushing, being pulled around her head. She could feel the hairs on her arm blow as the engine made a few sputtering sounds, and then the engine started, the propeller steady in front of her. She was so close to it that she stumbled backwards a step. As she regained her footing, she looked up to see Lee, still looking out the cockpit, his head bent at a funny angle to see her.

She was still in shock at the noise and proximity of the propeller and her mind was trying to make sense of it, when she noticed the movement in the wing. The left wing was coming towards her. Goddamn, that plane made a lot of noise. Lee had pulled it forward and turned it, and now the edge of the propeller was inches from her face. Just in time she stepped back two more steps and then two more, this time her heart racing. She looked back up at Lee. She knew her expression was blank, her mouth open. He was looking down into the cockpit and she could see his lips moving. He jerked his head back up and their eyes met.

You son of a bitch, Margaret thought when their eyes locked, you meant to do that. You meant to kill me. She thought she might have said it. He couldn't hear it. The plane was too noisy. But he could see her lips moving and the way she had said it left little room for Lee to interpret it as anything but anger. He looked at her for a moment, the propeller spinning regular and loud, the wind blowing her hair every which way. Once he saw the anger in her eyes, he gave a big sigh, his shoulders going up and then down with the breath, and then he revved the engine and taxied away from Margaret, who had gone back to the bench to get her gun. It was an instinctive reaction for her. As the plane revved and began to roll down the field, she heard him laugh a long cackling laugh.

11

I N May of 1927, Charles Lindbergh crossed the Atlantic in an airplane without stopping. It was the icing on the cake, the cake being the Roaring Twenties. Everything was possible. People danced to Jazz and drank illegal booze in speakeasies. The markets, witnessed first-hand by the Dow Jones Industrial Average, had bottomed out at 63 in 1921 when Margaret and Andrew were really beginning to do their work on Griffin Lumber. As Lindbergh made his flight, the DJIA was a short step from 170. It was financial abundance that everyone could see, and many had money in the markets. For Lindbergh, there was a tickertape parade in New York City.

Lindbergh's plane, *The Spirit of St. Louis,* was propelled by a Wright J-5 Whirlwind engine, the very same engine that propelled the Stearman that Lee bought the next year. For a period, Lee was sober and he flew his new Stearman every day. It was an expensive plane, built to fly three people fast and far. It was then that he built the hangar in the empty cove to house both his Jenny and the Stearman.

The two planes could not have been more different. The Jenny was unreliable and had to be repaired often. Lee had bought several surplus Jenny engines for parts. He could break the engine down and rebuild it with ease. It was the very unreliable nature of the Jenny that made it so easy to maintain. Repairs were a habit.

The Stearman was big and complicated and the first time that Lee attempted a simple tune-up of the massive engine, he had to bring a mechanic from Nashville to finish it. It was a reliable plane and did not need a lot of work, but when it needed work, it needed expensive parts and an expensive mechanic.

Margaret always believed it was the Stearman that finally broke Lee and severed whatever bonds remained between the two of them.

She realized this one cold Sunday morning in February of 1929. The entire family was at Sefer Farm. That morning Seth, Margaret and seven-year-old Evelyn had made a trip to the North Pond blind and come back in time for breakfast. Seth, Margaret noticed, was getting slower. Afterwards, Margaret had been sitting in her study, looking over Griffin Lumber papers, wondering how on earth the firm was making so much money. The decade had been especially good to them. While Margaret had wanted to expand, Andrew in the last year had been very cautious, and they had begun to build up an even larger cash cushion. She had been second-guessing Andrew. He had never left Griffin Lumber. The two had tentacles in a lot of different businesses now. They were preparing to launch their own holding company to roll it all up under one umbrella.

She heard the tap on the door, a single large knuckle rapping on wood and she half expected to look up and see her father. It was Lee. "Hello," she said.

"Margaret," he said. They were long past diminutives. "Mind if we have a word?"

"Come on in," Margaret said, watching as he closed the door behind him, she wondering, wondering, wondering.

"See you're still working on that," he nodded in the direction of the stack of papers on her desk. "How are things?"

"Good. Real good." She was taking him in. He had bathed that morning. His eyes were still blood shot and he was a little pale. The veins on his cheeks were starting to break red. She decided to wait and see what he was going to say. As harmless as he had been, she was still wary. The children were forbidden to go near the hangar when Lee was there.

Lee looked away and said, "I've uh got a favor to ask."

Margaret nodded. A show of silence was her caution. She talked when she wanted to put people at ease. It was a simple formula and it always worked.

"I'm a bit short of money." He sighed, looking briefly at his wife, whose face had not changed. "I don't need that much, just some for the fuel. That Stearman goes through it."

"Not a problem, Lee. How much do you need?"

"I need to find out from the field. I was putting everything on account but haven't paid and they said…"

"Just get a bill from them and I'll write you a check. We can do that every month if you need. Is there anything else?"

"Well, sometimes the Stearman needs things, and it can be expensive."

Margaret was watching Lee carefully now. She took in his drooped shoulders, the way he could not look her in the eye but for a split second and she realized it: he was defeated.

"Lee, if you need money, it is not a problem. Just give me the bills and I'll pay them. You probably need pocket money, too." She noticed that Lee winced when she said "pocket money." Good, she thought, he should be ashamed and cowed. "We've had a good year at Griffin Lumber. We've had a good run of years."

"That's good. I guess you're right. What's yours is mine. In a way. As we're married and all."

Margaret did not hear what he said afterwards, something about being broke being temporary. He had found a hole in her defenses. What was hers was his and vice versa, although she did not want anything he had.

When their marriage had begun to come off the rails and Lee had begun to drink so much, she worried that he would want other things from her. She worried that he would come to her bed at night. He never dared, much to her relief. Then she had worried about the safety of her children. She had taken precautions, making sure that gun cartridges and shotgun shells were locked up. Lee had long since started sleeping in one of the upstairs rooms, far away from the family rooms that had been built across from the kitchen wing. She had even instructed Cissy to keep an eye on April, who had been born three years after Evelyn, and to make sure that when she wandered, she did not wander to the hangar cove. She was still just four years old and did not wander very far.

Now Margaret saw where the real danger was. She had left herself open to financial danger. He was right. They were married and he might sober up enough to make money demands, and if he was really smart, he'd find someone to put the law behind his demands.

12

By the time Lee sold the Stearman in 1931, he was swearing to anyone who would listen that the market was at its bottom. It was poised to make a triumphant comeback and he would ride it back up. But first he needed money and he had long since stopped asking Margaret for money to play the market. Instead he found a buyer for the Stearman, a Chicago meat packer who had supplemented his business with Canadian booze smuggled across Lake Michigan.

The Stearman had not been flown for a year and the new owner had to send a mechanic from Chicago with spare parts. The pilot, who had arrived on a Thursday, stayed in one of the upstairs bedrooms at Sefer Farm. Evelyn, who had always been a curious child, peppered the pilot and the mechanic with questions. On Sunday, they finally started the Stearman.

Margaret heard the low rumble of the engine as it started and idled. She left her study and walked through the house, out the back porch and along the ridgeline that looked down into the cove. She could see the hangar and the full expanse of the field that acted as the runway. The pilot was in the rear seat and the mechanic was on a ladder, peering into the engine. He was close to the propeller, reminding Margaret of the feeling. They were yelling at each other, indistinct short sentences, plane speak she figured. Finally the pilot climbed down the ladder and walked around the plane, looking at it and occasionally pulling or pushing at something, all the time yelling in his short sentences at the pilot.

Lee, she noticed, was absent from the scene.

Margaret had thought that Lee's simplicity was like her father's. It had taken years before Margaret understood that her father was not simple at all. Seth's outward calm concealed a stoicism and cleverness that was like a magic trick, it was so well hidden.

216

Lee, on the other hand, was like a kid at a birthday party, and when the party was over, he was twisted against himself. There was nothing stoic nor clever about him.

After some more yelling, the mechanic returned the ladder to the hangar and then climbed into the front seat. She heard the pilot now: "Ready?"

The engine revved to a new loudness and then it lurched forward, gaining speed on its trajectory out of the cove. The pilot had spent his waiting days cleaning the plane. The butter yellow body and the chocolate brown wings gleamed in the sunlight. It lifted carefully into the air, passing out of the cove, becoming quiet and smaller as it left. Margaret watched it with one hand visoring her eyes. It made a slow arc, the wings splayed up and down as it banked into a turn. It came back towards the farmhouse. He's going north now, thought Margaret, to Chicago. It was just after breakfast. They'd make Chicago that evening if everything went well. The plane came back over the farm.

It was still a head turner. Even the engine winked a metallic glint at her. It was the end of Lee, Margaret knew, for that plane to fly away from him.

The money that Lee had earned from the sale chased the panic-stricken losses of his other financial misadventures. The market had not bottomed out. It wouldn't bottom for quite a while.

Lee was left with only the Jenny and the clothes in his closet. Margaret had made sure he had the parts and fuel to keep the Jenny in the air. It was the one thing, she believed, that got him out of bed, whenever he bothered.

13

MARGARET and Andrew unveiled Forest & Griffin, Inc. at the end of 1934. It was in essence a holding company, although they used it to do much more than hold their various companies into a single controllable entity. They invested their capital from Forest & Griffin and quickly began to invest other people's money into new ventures.

Seth had been perplexed when they had added their fifth Remington typewriter and had six trained typists in 1926. By 1927, his daughter and Andrew Forest had shown such steady returns and had so far outstripped his own ambitions that he had made Margaret his proxy and had withdrawn from Griffin Lumber completely. Margaret had expected her father to be guarded and irritable with his company, just as he had been when they had discovered Doyle Carter. As Andrew sat down with Seth at the end of each quarter, Seth had been gradually more happy, his only concern coming as the markets plunged in 1929. When Andrew was able to explain how they had anticipated the crash and what they had done to prepare for it, Seth told Margaret they were on their own. He was officially quit from the company.

Only now would Seth disappear for three and four weeks at a time, going to Colorado to hunt elk, to hunt grizzlies and moose in Montana and to fish for trout in Wyoming. Often he took one of his friends, old men that Margaret knew from shoots at the farm.

It was a bittersweet moment for Margaret. She hated to see her father give up on what he had fought for and created and grown. Yet she was proud that she could carry on the family business, not just maintaining it, but making it something more than her father had foreseen. As the veil of the Great Depression lifted, she knew that they had played their cards very carefully. No luck was needed. Now they were ready for anything to come. That's when she and

Andrew had decided to form Forest & Griffin. Now they were really ambitious.

Seth's sole ownership of Griffin Lumber had been swapped into a large chunk of Forest & Griffin stock. And there the money began to grow.

When Seth died in 1936, his stock rolled into a trust.

Seth had been napping on the back porch of Sefer Farm one warm spring day. He had not bothered to remove his boots and instead had propped them on the arm of a swinging bed, specifically designed for day naps on the porch. He had removed his coat but had used it like a blanket. It was an old tin hunting coat, rigid with age and dotted with paraffin patches. Cissy had come out to wake Seth and found his eyes wide open and his skin ice cold to the touch.

"Mr. Seth," said Cissy, "I know you's in good hands now."

The final prolonged note of the organ ceased its nose-wriggling vibrations and left a silence in the First Baptist Church. Margaret heard the shuffles in seats, the thumping of wooden pews with shoes and one baby snoring lightly just behind her. She sat on the end of the first pew. Next to her was Evelyn, April, Ruth and Lee. She knew that Lilly, Lucius, Cissy and Cissy's young daughter, Rose, were in the gallery. The church was packed, Seth's coffin sitting at the front and center, unmistakably the reason they were all there.

Reverend Madge shuffled to the pulpit and adjusted the small gold glasses on his nose. His black gown accented his shortness and his fatness. He looked at Ruth and gave her a look of knowing sympathy. His eyes swept across the row, finally settling on Margaret. "We will all miss Seth Griffin," he began, "for when a great man, a man whose presence…"

Margaret snapped out of her haze when Reverend Madge had looked her in the eye. She had seen his expression go from sympathy to a sort of query, as if he was wondering, in one facial sigh, where have you been my child?

On second thought it was not a rebuke, Margaret decided. It was a simple reacquaintance. Margaret and Reverend Madge had not seen each other in a very long time. She could see in his expression that she had changed. She had become something he did not recognize. As the Reverend continued on, "I think we'll all remember Seth as…", Margaret thought of her father in that box. She had held his cold dead hand for a second and realized that it was not her father. It was just a body, a dead cold body, the life gone out of it.

Where was he? There was no way that such a person merely disappeared from the world. She knew his spirit must be somewhere. Was it true that his soul could find another body, maybe a baby or a horse or a dog? She didn't believe in reincarnation and her dipping into the thought made her grimace.

She could remember sitting on her daddy's lap in front of the fire while her mother read bedtime stories. He would hold her hand but otherwise sit still. He smelled like the lumber yard, freshly cut pine, sawdust, maybe a whiff of generator exhaust. He was always nursing a bourbon in a silver cup at night.

As soon as he saw her, it didn't matter where they were, his face lit up with a smile, and now Margaret thought of how he had smiled at her when she had returned after her first semester at Vassar. They had spoken on the phone a couple of times and she had written a lot of letters, but he was hesitant when first seeing her at the train station, as if he wasn't certain who was getting off the train. She had thrown herself into her daddy's arms and was instantly comfortable, his chin on her head, his arms around her. He had loved her so much. There were a million signs, little signals, the way he lingered when they would run into each other in the hallway at Sefer Farm, or how he'd ask if she wanted to stroll up to the North Pond, his shy eyes expecting her to outgrow him one day, and you could see he was dreading that moment, had been dreading it since she was born, and Margaret knew this and was determined to not let him down. She would always need him, she told herself, and she sent the message to him, never saying it, but in other ways, how they would stand close to each other. She did not want to think of her marriage nor of the later years when Seth had resigned himself to being supplanted at Griffin Lumber. His stepping aside had been an act of love. After all, Griffin Lumber had been his creation and he had ruled it with the same persistence he had shown that night over Amsted's, when he had clobbered the grandson of The General.

Reverend Madge, if he was looking, would have seen expressions flickering across her face. Smile, frown, sad lips, smile, sad eyes. A couple of times tears had welled up.

She became aware of April crying and her mother sniffling. She looked for a hanky in her bag, thinking that one day Ruth would no longer be there either. Margaret could not have foreseen Ruth's quiet death on December 8th, 1941, the day after the attack on Pearl Harbor and the United States' entry into World War II, the political furor eclipsing her mother's funeral. Ruth had always been content in the background.

The Reverend called for a hymn, stirring her out of her thoughts. As she fumbled in her bag and the congregation stood up, she saw the hanky being offered to her from behind. It was Andrew.

The burial was on Sefer Farm later that morning. Seth had never said anything about what he wanted when he was dead, but Margaret and her mother had agreed that it would be unnatural to bury him anywhere but Sefer Farm. They had set aside a spot off the road between the front gate and the farmhouse. Five cutters had made a clearing deep in the trees with a little path. Later Margaret would put an iron fence around it. It was the beginning of their family graveyard, a place you had to know existed it was so well hidden by the trees. When Seth's coffin was lowered into the hole, the woods were full of people, all facing towards the black-gowned Reverend Madge, who finished with a reading from Ecclesiastes.

A wide circle of spring blue sky crowned the clearing. People looked strange in black dresses and suits, standing in the trees on

Sefer Farm, the very forest in repose as Lucius put the first shovel of dirt onto the coffin. No one, Margaret had said, will put dirt on Daddy's coffin but one of us. And Lucius had certainly been one of them. She thought of Lucius and his family and all the people at Griffin Lumber, so many who were packed into the woods at that moment, and the people who relied on Forest & Griffin, and most importantly of her two daughters, Evelyn ashen, April still sniffling by Ruth's side. Now, thought Margaret, it is time for me to take control of the family. I am the only person all these people can rely on. It was at once a crushing and liberating thought, and she found mixed in her grief a tiny seed of relief that now she could act without Seth's moral weight always pressing on her. It was a thought she could barely admit to herself.

It was several hours later that visitors began to clear out of the farmhouse, where they had been offered a fried chicken lunch. Margaret had never seen so many people eating off plates everywhere, on the porch, on the picnic tables, in the dining room, even in the library, perched on the sides of sofas and sitting on steps.

Afterwards Margaret had gone to her study. She needed to be alone. She had been on the edge of tears all morning. Already the house was missing something. She knew it was Seth. There would never be life in the halls again.

When a knuckle rapped on her door, she knew this time it was Lee.

Margaret had confirmed and reconfirmed that St. Clair Oil had never employed a Lee Wilson. No one in Tulsa could remember a Lee Wilson. The only Jenny that Lee had ever flown, the detectives said, was one he owned in Omaha, Nebraska, where he lived for several years, apparently doing crop dusting and giving rides in his plane for a fee, neither of which Lee pursued full-time nor for very much money. He just liked flying the Jenny.

Lee did have money at one time. He had paid cash for the Studebaker, the Jenny, the Pierce-Arrow and the Stearman. But where he had gotten it from, the detectives could never find.

All that Margaret knew about Lee was that he had a lot of family, poor and spread out from the other side of the Cumberland Plateau clear to the western edge of the Appalachians. Whatever Lee had become, he had made himself. Because Margaret didn't know how and paid detectives couldn't find out how, she wondered who it was who sat in one of her armchairs.

"I'm real sorry, Margaret," began Lee. She could tell he was already drunk. He held his liquor well, but there was a heaviness to his movements and speech, a deliberateness which a drunk knows well. "I'm gonna miss Seth."

"Thank you, Lee." She was in no mood for talking.

"I sometimes think Seth was the only one who didn't mind me being on this farm."

Margaret's eyes had drifted out the window and she had to refocus them on Lee. "Lee, you are welcome here, you know that."

"Well, I don't think I'd be missed if I left."

Margaret took him in. He was unusually focused, sitting on the edge of his seat. His hair was gone. He was fat. His shoulders hunched forward. His manner, like an alert animal, worked against his dilapidated form.

"I figure it might be time for me to leave," said Lee, his speech hurried now. "That maybe things have run their course."

Margaret wondered where he would go but dared not ask the question. "If that's what you want to do," she said. She thought about losing another man, how it would be a shame. Despite his slackass presence, Lee and his buzzing Jenny had become a part of that farm. It was another thought she dare not voice.

"Well, Margaret, I'll lay it out for you. I ain't got no money and I can't go anywhere without some."

"Of course. How much do you need?"

"I figure twenty thousand should set me up."

At least, she thought, he didn't have the audacity to look her in the eyes when he asked for it.

"Lee, I'll give you a thousand. That should get you a fresh start."

"A thousand? What kind of fresh start are you talking about? I'm thirty-eight years old." Margaret forgot he was that young. He looked so much older. "I'm not exactly a spring chicken and raring to go. Besides, I figure you owe me. We're married. What's yours is mine."

"Lee, I own nothing."

Lee's mouth dropped open. "What you say?"

"Lee, I own nothing. I get paid a dollar a year by Forest & Griffin. Everything else," she indicated the house with a sweep of her arm, "is held by a trust."

"A trust?"

"It's a vehicle…"

"I know what a trust is." He sat back in the chair.

It took thirty more minutes of Margaret trying to explain how the trust was structured and finally, when she had enough, she stood up and left Lee in her study. She didn't care if he looked through the drawers. It was all numbers and operations and not very exciting material. The documents that mattered were sitting in a safe at Forest & Griffin.

What Margaret didn't tell Lee was that the trust had a dissolving mechanism, a way for the Griffin family's assets to roll to Margaret in their entirety and the trust would break itself up. The mechanism's trigger was Lee's death.

14

ONE day April was walking back from the stables, taking the long way, when she saw her father sitting in his chair at the side of the hangar. She saw the camp cup, ever present in his left hand.

"Hello, sugar," said Lee. "Have you been out riding?"

"No, sir. I was just visiting the horses. I don't think Evelyn spends enough time with them and they get lonely."

"That's probably true."

"Why don't you ride, Daddy?"

"I do, I just don't ride horses. I like my Jenny just fine. Say, do you want to go for a ride in her?"

Her mother had warned her about the old plane. She had explicitly said she was not to go up in it and certainly not with her father. April was aware that the camp cup meant Lee was not himself sometimes. But he was so happy, smiley, and cheerful. He was glad to see April. Maybe he would not go too far with the plane. It was probably no different from riding in a car, only further off the ground.

She changed her mind when sitting in the front seat of the plane, the propeller whirling with so much noise that the vibration set her jaw to grinding. Lee was gunning the engine at the far end of the cove, ready to take off. April was about to turn around and say to her daddy that she didn't want to go, that she was scared, but the seatbelt held her firmly. Lee had buckled it tightly. She was not tall enough to turn her head and be seen by Lee in the cockpit behind her.

At the other end of the cove, Margaret appeared, waving her hands, her mouth open, shouting something. April thought she would stop the whole thing.

Suddenly the plane lurched forward, bouncing all over the field as the landscape passed by more and more quickly and April grabbed a handle in the little cockpit, her teeth now clenched. The bump bump of the wheels got more intense and then the plane lifted itself off the ground and everything was smooth if not loud. For a moment all the terror of take off disappeared and April lost herself in how different things looked from above. It looked as it should. It was so obvious now. She could see how the roads went on and on and how the forests ended and the little houses were plopped right in the middle of clearings and it all was so obvious, a sort of truth that was being revealed for the first time to April. She was delighted.

Then their farm came back into sight and her daddy was heading back into the cove. That was short, she thought. He was going to land and it would all be painless and safe. She thought she had been silly to be so scared.

Lee cut a diagonal line across the cove, gradually lowering the plane just off the ground, heading straight for Margaret, who stood still where she had tried to stop Lee from taking off. He edged the plane ever lower, aiming it right at her.

April heard her father laughing, loud and rhythmically, and she saw her mother through the propeller blades, at first a tiny spec at the end of the cove, and gradually she got bigger and bigger and then April could see that she was wearing a pair of khaki trousers and a white shirt, typical of what her mother wore around the farm, one hand on her hip and the other shielding her eyes. It was a sunny day, a warm October day.

Just when April thought the plane would hit her mother and then the ground and the trees behind her, it pulled up, making a deeper noise, and she saw the tree line go from above her to just barely below her. She thought she could have reached out and touched the trees, which quickly disappeared and there was nothing but blue sky.

"That son of a bitch," said Margaret. She watched as Lee pulled the plane straight up and then rolled it, slowly, the plane upside down, hanging in midair for a moment. She heard one scream, April's, for a moment, and then Lee let the plane fall into a dive back towards the cove. April did not scream again.

Lee flew the Jenny for ten more minutes, rolling and diving around the cove and Margaret stood watching, shaking her head, occasionally saying, "That son of a bitch!"

Finally Lee made the approach from the other side of the cove, easing the wheels onto the field. Margaret was surprised to see Ruth and Evelyn make for the stopping plane first. They had come running from behind her. She caught up with them as the engine cut off and the propeller spun to a slow halt.

"Goddamn it, Lee, don't you ever take her up again."

"I think she liked it." Lee had a big grin on his face.

"She's scared stiff. Look, she can't even move."

Evelyn had climbed to the cockpit and unbuckled April.

"Oh, April," said Evelyn and then looked at her mother. "She's messed herself."

Evelyn and Ruth helped April out of the cockpit. It was Ruth who took her up to the farmhouse, holding her by the shoulder.

Margaret and Evelyn stayed behind.

"You can't do that to a twelve year old girl, you son of a bitch," said Margaret.

"I thought it would be fun. How was I supposed to know that she wouldn't like it?"

"You know April is fragile. She can't take things like that. She can't even ride the horses because she's so scared of them."

"I didn't know that." Lee had stayed in the cockpit.

"Of course you wouldn't know that. You're so goddamned drunk all the time, I'm surprised you even remember her name. If you ever take her up in a plane again, I'll kill you." Margaret walked away.

She could hear Evelyn's footsteps behind and just before they got to the farmhouse, Evelyn said, "Mother, I found something in the seat, something wedged behind April."

"What's that?"

Evelyn handed her a lipstick.

Margaret looked at it for a second and then took it out of Evelyn's hand, uncapped it and screwed it up. It was a bright red color.

They looked at it for another moment and then Margaret said, "Throw it away, honey. That's nothing a lady would wear."

Evelyn knew what she meant. It was not a color that she nor her mother would ever wear.

15

A TWENTY-THREE year old April was wandering through the house, trying to work herself into finally telling her mother Some of Grandfather's most prized kills hung above the library shelves. There was an eighteen-point buck and a moose with as big a rack. They stared at each other from opposite walls. It was this sense of heaviness and being watched, as if the dead, stuffed animals looked down on her, that made it such an uncomfortable room for April. There was her mother's office, a small room off the kitchen. It had two armchairs and a writing desk and was full of floral patterns.

Her mother's office was the heartbeat of the house. Even Andrew Forest had been in that room every week to talk with her mother about Forest & Griffin. In that room, April had found her sister and her mother after her father's funeral. She had awoken from a bad dream. She had been twelve years old. It was one of the many inexplicable images from her childhood. She had always thought it had been a dream, their smiles, the air of celebration, her mother still in her black dress.

"Go back to sleep, dear," her mother had said, and that's what April had done.

April was standing in the same doorway now, full of secret, when her mother came from the kitchen door down the little hallway to her study.

"Looking for me?"

"Just wandering," said April. "Mother, would you like to eat lunch out?"

"Cissy can cook us something," said Margaret.

"But mother, I thought it might be nice if we ate out."

"It's cheaper to stay in and what will Cissy do with her spare time?"

"Cissy could use a rest now and then. Besides, she's always got something to do around this house." April tried to wave her hand around, making an uncertain motion that perplexed them both.

Margaret stopped abruptly, looking like a dog about to point. "I just thought we could take lunch on the porch. It's a lovely day."

"Why don't' we go over to Thelma's diner?" April tried to beam a smile, but she could feel her lip quiver. "And have grilled cheeses?"

Margaret caught the quiver. "If that's what you want, child. It is a long way to travel for what Cissy can whip up in five minutes with an iron, but if you want to get out of the house, then we shall get out of the house."

"I'll even drive," said April, "so that this is as effortless for you as possible." She fluttered her eyelids and looked skyward the way she did when a conversation had become unbearable.

"Only if you promise to pay attention. I sometimes wonder how you got your driver's license, the way you go flying through intersections."

"I'll be careful."

Margaret had bought a new Cadillac convertible the year before. Momentarily distracted, she thought it would be good for April to drive since she was at home, freshly graduated from Sewanee. The Cadillac was a hellious big thing, painted a shiny black with a tan rag top. It was safe and yet feminine. The fenders were massive and reminded Margaret of the motorcycle sidecars so often seen in World War II newsreels. She had reasoned that April, who was a spotty driver, could plow headlong into a truck or a train, and she would be fine in such a massive thing. It moved down the road with weight.

Margaret was distracted by April's insistence that they go out for lunch and then April wanted to pull the rag top back, which they did together. Margaret looked to the back of the car to help her daughter back the giant car out of the driveway and as soon as April had it aimed down the street and was rolling forward, Margaret was scanning the horizon for stop signs, stoplights, yield signs, large trees, oncoming traffic, anything that April could hit with the car. She was pleased as punch when April negotiated two intersections. Maybe she had overstated the case of how bad a driver April really was. Margaret began to relax a little. She looked at April.

"What is that on your finger," asked Margaret.

April looked down at her hands, both gripping the top of the driving wheel. She had forgotten to take off the ring that morning.

April's mind froze. She felt as if the moment was suspended in a hazy glue. "Oh, that," she said. She accelerated from a stop through the intersection. "That's a wedding band."

"I know that, child, but what is it doing on your finger?" A horn sounded on their left. Sounds and sights and the air moving into the car overwhelmed them. "Maybe you should pull over," said Margaret.

"I'm sorry, Mother, I meant to tell you before now."

"April," Margaret watched a stop sign go by, "pull this car…"

It was more of a thump than a crash. They T-Boned a car which had pulled into the intersection. Margaret knew the expression well but still found it odd. A T-Bone was a steak, so named because it had a bone that ran down the middle of the cut and ended on one side like a T. To create such a figure with two cars was to T-Bone.

"Such creativity," said Margaret, thinking of the T-Bone steak and how many of those she had seen Lucius grill at Sefer Farm, how someone had transferred the phrase to car accidents. There was the eerie silence just after the crash, as if the sound that the two cars made coming together was loud enough to make the world pause, as if they had interrupted the world for a moment. Then the sound returned.

Margaret looked over at April and said, "Dear, are you all right?"

"Mamma, I'm fine. Are you all right? You've got a cut. Here, I've got a handkerchief in my bag."

Margaret could feel the stinging of the cut where she had smacked her head against the upper windshield frame. She felt the warm moistness of the blood. A finger touched to the forehead brought back a bright red fingertip. April scooted across the seat, put her right arm around her mother and her left hand came up with the white handkerchief.

"Mamma, I love him and I just didn't know how to tell you."

"Are you two okay?" It was the man from the other car. He had gotten out on the other side—the driver's door was crushed in—and had come around to April's side of the car. He held his left arm close to his chest, like a dog with a bum leg.

"Oh, I think we're fine," said Margaret. "Are you okay?"

"My arm's not too hot." He raised it slightly and immediately winced.

"I do apologize," said April. "I just wasn't paying attention."

The man looked into the convertible and saw a pretty young lady who was holding her mother in one arm and a bloody handkerchief in the other. The mother looked a little shocked but otherwise just fine. There were tears streaming down the young lady's face and her lower lip was starting to wobble. He had been late for his appointment and had at first thought he had run the intersection, but then he remembered hating every stop sign in this neighborhood and not seeing any car at the intersection as he stopped. Normally he would have been upset. He could be quick with harsh words, but the occupants in the nice big shiny car looked like they had been more affected than himself. They looked like they had been run over. There was something about them that looked more traumatized than he felt. Women were delicate like that.

"As long as we're all right, there's no real harm done. Let me go up the road and call for the police and a couple of tow trucks." He tried to turn to go and found himself looking at the scene in front of him.

It was at this moment that Margaret realized that taking care of April would be a lifelong responsibility and there would be car wrecks, train wrecks and calamity that threatened them, always. It would be three more weeks before Margaret heard April throwing up in the bathroom and she wondered if the child she knew was on the way would be like April, too. Stockard had been the fourth person in the car accident, although no one knew that would be her name.

Obedience

1

ONCE she was at the sidewalk, Stockard found herself turning left, towards her house, not to the right towards Cadence's.

As she walked along the sidewalk, she felt the cold air of Boulder, first against her face. Her ears always went cold. She had tried wearing hats, but forgot them. Her hair was just below her shoulders, but the cold got her ears anyway.

Was this the price, she wondered, of a dissolute life, for fucking people indiscriminately? That was what she was doing. Somewhere in the sexual chaos of having four constant partners, she had decided that she was better off, morally, than a sheik with his harem or those goddamn Mormons with their multiple wives. The women of their little group had become the gatekeepers. The men were kept happy by their whim. This, she had decided, was not a violation of her moral self. The very idea of a moral self was foreign until The Blue House. Now there was a chance that her immorality would kill her.

Even at this moment, she was making a distinction in her thoughts between her personal morality and the Southern views of morality with which she had grown up. The Bible Belt had surrounded her with people who had rigid views of what was right and wrong. Boulder had been the opposite. Everyone in Boulder had seen the world from their own extremely flexible viewpoints. Morality was a bad word. Morality implied the Missionary Position. It ruled out too many things in life and imposed a puritanical code on each person, thereby not allowing a person to be a person. Stockard, as she faced Christopher's message of doom, was neither feeling the vengeance of a Bible Belt God nor adrift in the relativity of hippie morals. She simply wondered if there was not something deeper in herself that had revolted against her enjoyment of The Blue House.

For some reason she kept going back to her freshman philosophy class. There was something about morality. Her teacher had been a

Rousseau nut. What could Rousseau say about group sex? She'd go find the Rousseau book they had used when back home.

As she passed through her front door, all thoughts of The Blue House, of Christopher's unknown disease, and of her attachment to Cadence disappeared. There was Emily sitting on the sofa with her familiar photographs all around her. Poor people and sand. Over the next week, she would emerge from the darkroom with freshly print-ed photos, large ones. She would cut the mounts herself and then prop a series against a wall. The better prints she would have framed.

The Blue House was the polar opposite. The walls were bare. The furnishings were still sparse. She liked to think it was very Zen, a place where she could concentrate on the task at hand. Pleasure.

Emily said, "Hello." She could draw out the l's and the o. "Hellllll-o." She had started saying "hello" in that way as a way of poking fun at Stockard's slow Southern accent, but it had become Emily's standard greeting to everyone. "You are looking well."

A pinpoint of light opened to a flood on the moment and Stockard saw not just her cousin sitting on the sofa, littering their living room with photographs. She saw how much it meant to her and how routine had dulled it, how she had never reached out to fully engage this world.

"Hell, yeah, partner, doing better than a cowboy at the end of his drive." She let out a whoop and leapt across the sofa, watching Emily's eyes widen in surprise. She was not used to seeing her cousin plummet towards her. Stockard landed next to Emily, sending some of the contact sheets flying. "And you?"

"Coming around. Tired. I think it's the cold. It was so deliciously warm on the subcontinent."

"I'll turn the heat up."

"Don't bother. I need to get used to it, again."

"Let's look at the pictures."

"They're… I like them. I cannot imagine not taking them, but I'm starting to wonder how good they are. You know how many I've taken, literally thousands of pictures. This house is full of them. I'm starting to wonder why I do it."

Stockard picked up one of the contact sheets. It had pictures of the desert, the sun sending shadows over the sand, the bright blue sky overhead, a quarter moon visible in some.

"When did you start shooting color?"

"A year ago? Maybe more. This is the third or fourth batch."

"I wonder why I didn't notice."

"I'm thinking of giving it up. Black and white is better, I think."

Stockard looked at the desert shots again. She used the loupe this time.

"These are extraordinary. Look at how there's a richness to the brown of the sand. I can almost make out the granules."

"That's the medium format. I'm half fiddling with trying large format."

"And the deep blue of the sky. That's the blue sky of the Rockies. Only more so. Then you've captured these magnificent shadows."

"The light was similar to Joshua Tree, I thought."

"But my God, these are extraordinary. They are so good."

"Well, thanks."

She could not believe how vivid the images were. Emily went back to leafing through contact sheets. Stockard got off the sofa and looked at the walls, taking in the photos that were framed and hung. There were several stacks of mounted photos on the floor.

"You've got to do something with these," said Stockard.

"What? My photos?"

"Yes."

"Do you want me to clean them up? Are you sick of having them everywhere?"

"No. I don't mean that. You've got to show them." Stockard was on the floor. She was flipping through a stack of pictures. "Other people need to see these. I think other people would really enjoy them."

"Well, I didn't really take them for other people. Sometimes for you. I just like the process."

"You are mad. You do all of this work and you want to keep these photos, these amazing pictures, to yourself. You've got to show them to other people. A show. In a gallery."

"There's no place in Boulder to show them."

"I don't mean in Boulder. I mean in New York. Or Los Angeles. New York would be the place."

"You're joking."

"No, I'm not. These are serious pictures."

"I know a little about photography and I don't think my stuff is good enough for a gallery." Emily watched Stockard flipping through another stack of photographs for a moment. "Just my opinion."

"Will you do me a favor?"

"Sure."

"Let me choose six pictures and you blow them up to a nice size and let me take them to New York, to shop around?" Stockard had moved to a stack behind the sofa.

"I think you're the one who is crazy now," said Emily.

"Maybe. Will you do it?" Stockard stopped and stood up to look Emily right in the eye.

"Yes."

The next day Stockard went through Emily's boxes, crammed full of contact sheets, negatives and prints, making sure that she had not missed anything. It occurred to her that she had never seen Emily's pictures before. She had seen them as Emily's folly, but for more than ten years she had only seen her cousin's efforts. Emily had been relentless with a camera, always preferring to spend the day and night in her darkroom rather than go out for a beer. Only now did Stockard see how unique Emily's eye was. Her perspective was museum-quality. It was a revelation. Not every photograph was a revelation, but she could tell that Emily had kept on working towards something, and every once in a while, she captured it perfectly These particular pictures were Emily and no one else. It was always something different. Emily captured the harmony of light and landscape in the desert. You could actually feel the endless, barren but beautiful quality of the desert. Her pictures of Malawi were lush and stark. There was a tension to everything that Emily saw and then she manipulated the camera, the film, and the lens to capture that tension.

Stockard was close to Emily's message. She could see something in Emily's pictures that she could almost articulate. It was at once a thought and a feeling, comprehensive but not clearly described. She chased the words around in her head.

The phone rang. It had been in the background all day, like the low hum of electricity. Then it came forward and she remembered where she was. She answered the phone. "Hello?"

"Stockard? It's me. Etta." Edda. Stockard could hear the traces of the Midwest accent.

Stockard had put the events of the previous evening away, out of her mind. She had taken Christopher's terrible revelation and the heavy emotion that hung over it and she had placed them very neatly aside, like a parcel, wrapped in brown paper on a hall table. Even as Etta's voice came across the phone line, Stockard could only vaguely remember what had happened. It was like waking out of a dream.

"Hello, Etta."

"Is everything all right?"

"Yes."

"You sound so… distant… and formal."

"Sorry. I was working on something and had lost myself."

"How are you doing?"

"Fine. You?"

"Shocked, of course. Scared silly, too. Bill's no better than Christopher. That son of a bitch has slept with more than our little group. All women. Tons of them. Especially lately…"

Stockard heard Etta's voice trail off as a stack of pictures next to the phone took her interest.

"Stockard? Stockard? Are you there?"

"Oh, sorry. Can I call you back?"

Before she heard Etta's "Why, yes," Stockard was already putting the phone down.

The phone began ringing, again. It rang four times, five times six times, the rattling sound coming from the base impossibly loud Finally it went silent. Stockard took the arm off the cradle, made sure no one was on the other end of the line, and then placed it all into a drawer, where she would not hear it. She put several dish towels over it to make sure. She went back to looking at the pictures.

She found a picture of her and Andrew in the snow at Sefer Farm. Emily had snapped it after one of those rare Christmas snow storms in Tennessee. Stockard had tromped after Andrew in the snow to help him gather wood. Against his protests. Emily had yelled at the two while they were gathering wood. When they had turned around, she had taken ten pictures with the press of a button and the whirl of the motor. They had then posed for a couple more shots.

The picture that Emily had printed was of Andrew, leaning over for a piece of wood. Stockard was standing in front of him with wood in her arms. They had both turned their heads to look at Emily, both smiling.

Stockard leaned it against the lamp on her nightstand. Just below the picture in the drawer was her gun. For a moment she thought of it. Uncle Andrew had never slept with a gun in his nightstand. She knew that because she knew Uncle Andrew's room at Sefer Farm. She would have to ask him one day why not.

Soon Emily walked through the front door, returning from a trip to Denver for printing paper and picture mounting supplies.

Stockard skipped a greeting. "I was thinking you've got two shows here, maybe three. You've got the Humanitarian. You've got hundreds of pictures of lines of people getting shots, getting food.

Most of those have really nice follow up shots. Or maybe they are shots before. Where you show the people going about their daily lives. There's some great stuff here. The second show is Travel. You've taken literally thousands of pictures of your journey and how you get from one place to another and everything you see in between. You must have a hundred photos of the door of this house, coming and going. I wanted to do a whole series of this house just for our amusement. I had no idea it had changed so much and so little over ten years. The trees have grown, the door needs to be painted. So here's what I wanted to do. We do twelve large photos, say sixteen by twenty…"

"I only brought back eleven by fourteen."

"Oh. Let me see." Emily pulled a white Ilford box from a stack in her arms and set it in front of Stockard. "That looks small."

Emily was looking exasperated. "Look, I think this is a total waste of time. No one is going to like my stuff that much."

"Maybe." Stockard was looking at Emily, as she put the rest of the boxes on the kitchen table. There were the Kodak and Ilford logos on some of them, the Kodak boxes bright yellow, the Ilford ones white. "But let me try."

"This is going to take so much work."

"What I was going to suggest is that we then take two series of pictures for each show and put them together in five by sevens. I could list out twenty, maybe thirty sequences for each show. Prepare the descriptions and work on the titles. I'll hop down to a printer and see if we can get some mockups done."

"This is so overboard."

"What else are you going to do?"

Emily looked at Stockard, who already had a notepad next to her, writing scribbled across the top page. "Okay."

Four days later, after every flat surface in the house had been covered in photos, and every vertical surface had been used to prop photos, and Emily was complaining that she was getting high from the darkroom chemicals and Stockard was tired of eating delivered pizzas, there was a knock on the door. Stockard opened it to find Eve standing on the doorstep. "Hello, missy," said Stockard.

"I've been trying to call for two hours."

"Oh, yeah, I took the phone off the hook. Come on in."

Eve stepped into the house. It was a sea of photographs. "What is Emily up to?"

"Oh, yeah, be careful. We're working on something."

"We?"

"I thought Emily's work should be shown. So we're working on pitching it."

"Grandmother's sick."

"Huh?"

"She had a stroke six days ago."

"Oh, no."

"She wouldn't let anyone know about it. Then she had another one last night. Your mother called. She's been trying to get a hold of you, too. My mom is on the way to Nashville right now. They're asking that we come to Nashville early."

For Christmas, thought Stockard. She meant early for Christmas. We were all due to fly out in two weeks for the holidays. Stockard imagined Sefer Farm in the winter landscape, the trees barren of leaves. She could see her grandmother, lying in bed, sick. Grandmother would refuse to go to a hospital.

"Of course we'll go. I'll get us booked on the first flight in the morning."

"Already done. My mother took the liberty."

"I can't believe it. Let me get Emily. She's in the darkroom."

2

EVELYN was waiting for the girls in the Nashville air terminal to meet the flight from Denver. The girls knew the routine. They would pile into the Suburban, a blue one bought just a couple of years ago. The parking lot would smell of burnt jet fuel. There would be the sounds of planes taking off and arriving. People would be coming and going all around them. It always occurred to Stockard when she was in an airport that no one would go to an airport unless they had to. Her ideas of pleasure did not include holidays and vacations, four-color spreads of swimming pools and beaches, perpetually smiling families.

From the airport they would drive out to Sefer Farm, first on the highway, each road becoming smaller and older, until a two-lane road split a rolling countryside, the blue gate a timeless entry into that world, that persistent constant steadfast world of her grandmother's farm.

As the plane arrived under a cold grey winter sky, Stockard knew that a Tennessee Christmas was rarely a postcard event. Normally the girls would be in a good mood, but they had worried each other on the flight. They did not know that much about their grandmother's condition. Stockard had a shivering moment when she feared that her grandmother was about to die, but the world could not do without her. Fate did not work that way. They did not exactly understand a stroke or from what their grandmother was suffering. Emily had seen a stroke victim in India who could not move his entire right side of his body, his arm permanently bent. His left side would drag his right side down the street.

Evelyn was all smiles at the gate. She hugged each, Stockard last. As they parted, Stockard asked, "How is grandmother?"

Evelyn's smile was unusual, the darkness that followed the question not. "Girls, your grandmother died last night."

"Oh, no," said Emily.

"It was a very peaceful death," said Evelyn. "Andrew said that she breathed very hard for a minute and then passed away, her eyes closed the whole time."

The last breath, normally a strong one, a last gasp, a struggle before giving in, thought Stockard.

Eve asked, "Andrew?"

"He's been with your grandmother the whole time. He had come down early for business. We still run the lumber business out of Nashville. Some other operations. He likes to keep an eye on things, although he's not as involved. But he was down when mother had her first stroke. He's taken care of her the entire time. He... he even followed the hearse back to the funeral home. At two o'clock this morning. Finally they had to banish him. I don't suppose they wanted... a witness watching the actual embalming."

Evelyn and April had been on the phone all that morning, notifying relatives, friends, and the great number of people who knew and loved their mother through business. "The undertakers promised to have your grandmother back to us tonight..."

"Back at the farm?" Eve had interrupted.

"Yes. They said it wasn't possible but I gather Andrew had a word. So we'll have our time alone with her before people start coming. It's more like a wake. The newspaper will run the notice tomorrow and then the funeral will be Monday."

It was Thursday. Stockard had never heard of a body being in a house for five days before burial and she was balancing her slight repulsion at the thought versus the flatline shock that her grandmother was dead. The ride was silence punctuated by the occasional question. There would be no autopsy. Margaret had been under a doctor's care and the cause of death was known. The funeral home would issue the death certificate. An embalmed body lasted a very long time. The coffin had been made by Griffin Lumber employees. The very existence of the coffin had been a surprise to Aunt Evelyn but Andrew knew about it. As they drove down the final stretch of two lane road and Stockard realized what it meant, that now she was about to enter Sefer Farm for the first time without her grandmother being alive, a commanding presence on the farm, the stark reality of her grandmother's death came upon her and she could feel the tears first well up in her eyes, her nose prickly and then she lost all restraint. Emily was in the back seat with her and they moved together to hold each other as the car turned left, Evelyn reaching up to click the remote button that opened the front gate electrically. The wooden gates were still a shiny blue. The paved driveway looked as old and weathered as the trees that still hung over it, creating the tunneled entry. Here, thought Stockard, is a void. The master of Sefer Farm is dead, even the trees themselves felt the loss and leaned sadly against the sky, a tinny taste in her mouth. This is the taste of death. By the time Evelyn parked the car in front of the house, all four women were wiping their faces and sniffling.

April and Andrew sat in the living room with its giant fireplace lit. Both were already in black, Andrew a suit, Stockard's mother a black skirt and cardigan, a white blouse peeking out. It was a somber reunion, Andrew quietly withdrawing into himself, refusing anything to drink or eat and staring off into a point to the side of the fireplace. They all stayed in the room until Margaret was returned to her home, the shiny dark coffin standing against one wall. Evelyn had directed where it should be placed, thinking out loud about where people would sit, and how they would walk by the coffin. They could take food in the dining room and library and they would serve drinks in the hallway. Evelyn was already orchestrating the visitation days. Tomorrow she would select the plot in the farm graveyard. She was the most self-possessed. Andrew opened the coffin and they stood looking at Margaret's body. It was late in the afternoon and it had already turned dark outside. After awhile Stockard heard Evelyn quietly walk away and return with a jingling tin. She looked up to see her aunt with one of the silver cups. Her aunt offered it to her and she took it, her aunt returning to the kitchen for another one.

That night, after they had huddled over soup and sandwiches in the kitchen and had drunk bourbon and smoked cigarettes and Andrew had stayed by Margaret's coffin, sipping a scotch, and the girls had turned in early, shock giving away to weariness, Stockard fell asleep in her room, the very same one she had slept in for thirty four years. It had once had a crib in it and now Stockard realized that it was her room because it was closest to her grandmother's. It had always been her grandmother who had taken care of her. Who had taken care of grandmother?

There were always men in her family, but they were invisible somehow allowing the women to come into their own. Her great-grandfather, Seth, was titanic in the family mythology. He was the one to break out on his own, to see an opportunity in a silver pitcher and a poker game and walk with his own independence.

There was Lee Wilson, whom no one talked about now, and even Uncle Abe, who had disappeared into the shadows of disgrace. Her own father had been forgotten.

But Uncle Andrew was a constant. He had always been there, ever so discreet, and working with Grandmother to take care of the Griffin women's money. The more Stockard thought about it, the more her grandmother looked like the titanic figure of the family. Now she was gone. Stockard finally drifted into a restless sleep and for the first time in as long as she could remember, she dreamed.

The old farmhouse creaked in the winter night as the fires went out and the timbers cooled. The central heating system was programmed to come on at four o'clock in the morning, slowly warming the house, waking it. This was how Margaret insisted on it being set up. Until her first stroke, she had always slept with her window open.

An hour after the heat came on, Stockard woke with a start. She could feel the change in the temperature in her room. The cold of the night, which drove her deeper into her comforter, had finally relented and she got up to go to the bathroom. All that bourbon. As she left the bathroom, there was a moment when she was walking down the hall and it was so unusual to see her grandmother's door open that she walked past her own door and peered in.

Margaret had preferred heavy fabrics, gold brocade drapes and a white tapestry bed cover. It was a Queen's bedroom, thought Stockard, complete with heavy stately furniture. Despite the furniture and fabrics, Margaret's room was surprisingly bright. It was a corner room and the windows on two sides were undraped, the light inexplicable at that time of the morning at that time of the year. She had a massive four poster bed and she now lay in it, propped up with several pillows, her arms on her chest as before in the coffin, the covers tucked up under her elbows. Andrew was in bed with Margaret. There they sat, propped by the same pillows. Andrew was in a different suit, a grey chalk stripe. He wore a black tie. One of Andrew's arms was under her grandmother's head, like a couple asleep, like a final embrace.

Stockard could see in Andrew's empty skin tone that he was as dead as her grandmother, their faces so close to each other, pallor matching pallor. On the nightstand was an envelope, "April" written across the front.

It was a dream. It was not.

3

MARGARET's italic hand had written, Dearest April, we discussed the writing of this letter for what felt like a lifetime. Indeed it was for your lifetime. By now we are beyond such cares.

This letter is to explain to you that Andrew Forest is your father. It is simply written.

Lee Wilson, who was supposed to be your father, became troublesome and unpleasant early in our marriage. I know you will recall his late dilapidated state, but the same torn man when he was young was much more difficult. I had Evelyn to raise and worry about. I did not have much time to take care of a grown man. It all went wrong.

There had always been a friendship between Andrew and me, ever since our college years. We forged a stronger friendship in business. We both spoke the language of money and somewhere in our day-to-day dealings with each other, we more than got along. When Lee Wilson's descent had become apparently irreversible, Andrew consoled me. He meant it as a friend but nine months later, dear April, you came along.

We opted for secrecy for many reasons. First was Andrew's own family. Second, we never wanted dear Evelyn to have any doubts about her place in our family. Then, there is the public implication of a married man and a married woman—not married to each other—having a child with each other. It sounds so squalid. But the reality was that the great friendship that led to your birth could never be publicly portrayed with any sympathy.

We thought of you girls as precious gifts—and of your daughters as even sweeter ones. Not a day passed without talking about each of you, sometimes in an office, often late at night over a phone.

I hope you understand our desire for secrecy, which brings us to this letter. There is a certified copy of this letter with our attorney, J. Brown, in New York. It will remain locked away under seal unless needed. You may do with this letter and the information contained within it what you will. It is now time for you to do as you please and make your own decisions, but we ask that you act with careful thought. You have more than enough money to last you the rest of your life.

If there are any parting words that might help explain our relationship, then it must be these. We found each other by accident and held on to each other no matter what our individual responsibilities were, and we each had many. I always wanted to lecture both you and Evelyn about the importance of having someone else, but how could I when the appearance contradicted me? You need someone to hold in bed, someone to reach for during the horrors of the night. Someone you can go to bed with and wake up with.

No matter how much time we spent with you, we always wanted more. I hope this brings some peace and clarity to your mind.

The letter was signed by both Margaret and Andrew, "Mother" and "Father." "Love."

At just after five in the morning, Stockard had climbed into her mother's bed, turned on the bedside lamp, and handed the envelope to her. They had both read it several times before turning the lamp off, holding each other as a glow seeped around the edges of the curtain.

"I always wondered," said April after awhile, "about that night." And she told her daughter a story.

4

It started with a dream. She could see her grandfather, Seth, looking at her. Only it wasn't exactly her grandfather, but it was. She couldn't make her mind up. Seth and she had been walking along a beach and had discovered a cave, more like something she had seen on the side of the Cumberland Plateau. They stood at the entrance, a tiny little hole where the sand met the rocks. She thought only she could squeeze in and her grandfather would not be able to go into the cave with her. She didn't want to go into the cave but found that Seth was telling her she had to. Seth leaned over and kissed her. She could feel the scrape of his beard and the smell that she associated with old people. His beard was rough and Seth never had the smoothness of skin that her father had after he had shaved. Her grandfather's kiss lingered a little too long and April pulled away and ran towards the cave, crawling into the hole and down a little shaft as the light grew dimmer and dimmer. She was scared and woke up.

Her room was dark, black like the clothes they had worn that day at Daddy's funeral. She was the only one to cry and the tears ran down her face, she trying to not make a noise. She was sitting next to her grandmother, who had leaned over with a handkerchief, a practical white cotton one that she had pulled out of her black bag. Ruth had wiped April's face and then cupped her nose as April had blown. She remembered walking down the aisle of the church after the ceremony was over, her mother and sister in front of her, holding hands. Ruth held her hand. They had followed the casket out. Unlike Seth's funeral, Lee Wilson's brought few people to the First Baptist Church.

April got out of bed in the darkness of her room, not bothering with the light. She walked out into the hallway, where light reflected up the staircase, casting shadows upwards. Down the stairs, several lamps in the hallway were on and she knew it was late. She could hear voices in Mother's study, a nice little room off the butler's pantry, where her mother had a couple of armchairs and a small writing desk and a telephone on its own line. She heard a cackle of laughter and was at her mother's study door after softly padding down a hallway, through the kitchen and the butler's pantry, and passing a small wc. The Nashville house was not like Sefer Farm, which sprawled on and on. Everything here was close together.

She cracked the door and saw Evelyn and her mother, both with champagne glasses in their hands, Evelyn stuffing a large piece of chocolate cake into her mouth. They were both smiling. April looked for a moment and saw a bottle of champagne upside down in a silver wine bucket. It would be years before April realized that they were drinking champagne and that it was a champagne bottle. It had taken decades for her to put the pieces together.

Margaret suddenly looked at the door. "April, dear, what are you doing awake?"

"I had a bad dream."

"It's over, honey, now go back to bed, okay?" It had been Evelyn's voice, strange and light.

"Do you want to go crawl into your grandmother's bed?"

"Can I come in with you?" April stood in the doorway, feeling the bright lights hit her.

"It's time to go back to bed." Margaret set her glass down and came to the door. "I'll take you up and get you settled."

"Good night," said Evelyn, who then had another fork of cake.

April could never get those smiles out of her mind, her mother and her older sister, on the night of her father's funeral, up late and the atmosphere of a birthday party gone joyous and fun in that little room. Her mother smelled like booze but different from how her father had smelled like booze. Even Seth smelled like booze before he died, but mother smelled like booze and perfume. There was a liveliness to her smell. Father had worn his booze like bitterness. She never saw her mother and her sister drunk again. She went back to sleep, perplexed, the events of the past week, tragic and awful, not making sense with their champagne mood.

5

"They were celebrating Lee Wilson's death?"

"It doesn't make much sense, does it?" April said. "Unless…"

"Unless they wanted him to die?"

They lay in bed for a long silent moment, almost hearing each other's brain click through thought after thought.

"You don't think they… helped Lee Wilson… into the grave?" Stockard tried to make it sound like an improbable scenario, but she knew it with a certainty that startled her.

They lay there for another long moment, the sound of a door opening down the hallway breaking their silence.

"It's Evelyn," said April, out of bed at once and at the door, beckoning her sister.

Evelyn appeared, fully bathed and made up, in a black wool dress. She said, "I was just going to see Mamma."

"Evelyn, she's not there," said April. "She's been moved."

"What?"

"Here, read this first," said April, shoving the letter into her sister's hands.

They had to move fast. It took all three women to move Margaret back to her coffin. How on earth had Andrew done it on his own, they had wondered. Stockard was shocked by the effects of rigor mortis. Her grandmother's body was as stiff and straight as a board. And then Andrew had to be moved to his room, notable now for its proximity to Margaret's room. "Well, that makes sense," said Stockard, her comment coming out at the odd moment when they had just struggled to get his body through the door. While Evelyn called the funeral home—she had wondered out loud how am I to explain two deaths in the same house in three days—April tidied up her mother's coffin and Stockard jumped in the shower. By the time the two men arrived from the funeral home, all three women were dressed in black. The men were nonplussed. "Happens all the time," one said, "one dies of natural causes, the other dies of a broken heart."

It was Evelyn who had called Andrew's wife, capping a surreal morning for all three. "Joan was surprisingly level headed," said Evelyn. "She said it was just like Andrew to follow his business partner into a new venture."

Emily walked around the house saying, "I can't believe it," recovering in time to photograph Andrew on his deathbed and the removal of his body. Eve looked knowing when she was told of Andrew's death, but she did not know what had happened. It was a secret between Evelyn, April and Stockard. Evelyn was a steel trap, a cold operator who kept secrets with ease.

By that afternoon Joan had called back to say that arrangements had been made to move Andrew's body from Nashville to New York. Evelyn had waivered on the phone, expecting for there to be a surprise in Andrew's will. There might be another letter or a request to be buried at Sefer Farm. "Joan," she probed, "did he keep his papers at Forest & Griffin, in the safe? Do you know? I can have someone bring them to you right away."

"Oh, the only things he kept in our safe were his will and some cash. Pocket money, he called it. I've just read his will. It's all very straightforward. There's a family plot at Woodlawn. I don't think Andrew's grandfather had anticipated the current state of the Bronx when he bought it."

Joan and her daughters and her grandchildren had spent their summers on Cape Cod for as long as Evelyn could remember and she was about to ask her if she would be buried at Woodlawn. She suspected not. She knew the Brannons had a family plot in Boston. But she caught herself, wondering how the day's events had loosened her tongue. She promised to see Joan as soon as she was back in New York. Joan apologized for not being able to make Margaret's funeral. Their goodbyes were hesitant and uncertain. Evelyn was relieved to finally be off the phone.

Stockard was ready for the day to be over by the time that Emily came through the back door with a camera case slung over her shoulder and carrying two canvases. "Look at this," she said, leaning the pictures against a sofa.

"We forgot them," said Stockard. "That was a long time ago."

"Twelve years," said Emily.

The two canvases were Emily's dream, the one she had painted in the hangar. Now they made sense.

6

Iт took Stockard several weeks to digest the facts and arrange them into a neat package for herself. She found herself using blunt language.

Her grandmother and quite possibly her aunt had killed a man. Not just any man. Her grandmother had killed her husband. Her aunt had killed her father. It was like something out of Greek tragedy. Or mythology.

If a murdered Lee Wilson had haunted the farm the July that all the Griffin women spent on Sefer Farm, why had it been only then? Why had he not haunted the farm persistently since his death?

It had been a decisive moment for Stockard, she knew. If she had not struck out on her own at that time, she wondered if she would have ever escaped Sefer Farm. Lee Wilson was a warning sign. Stay here and you will become just like your grandmother.

Her grandmother had betrayed her husband. Stockard's mother, and therefore Stockard herself, were products of that betrayal.

Her grandmother had carried on a sixty-year affair with a married man.

What other unsavory deeds, she wondered, had her grandmother done?

How did The Blue House stack up against that?

The next year proved to be very busy, and in her few idle moments Stockard found time to think long and hard about what kind of person her grandmother had been.

First had come the conversation with her aunt. It was just after the New Year and everyone except Eve was still at Sefer Farm. Eve had gone back after Christmas, her excuse was that the bakery needed her. Even Eve could see it wasn't much of an excuse but no one bothered to confront her.

Stockard's aunt had been sorting through papers in her mother's office. It was just after six and her aunt had been in that office all day, so Stockard brought her a drink, the farm standard bourbon in a silver cup.

"Thank you," Evelyn said, taking a sip.

Stockard looked around her grandmother's office. It had been cleaned every week since her death but the papers had remained in the same stacks. Now Evelyn was going through each stack, putting things in folders, labeling some, throwing others in the trash can. Stockard found herself taking a seat as if the sight of that office without her grandmother had taken the strength out of her legs. "Is it very difficult? Sorting through all of this?"

"No. Not really." Evelyn swiveled in the chair and pointed to a stack. "Your grandmother was a demon on detail. She looked at everything. You have to remember that she lived through the Great Depression. That generation, they're suspicious. She kept cash and gold everywhere. We found a gold brick in her closet. She had painted it black and used it as a door stop. That's how she was with her businesses. She suspected everyone and would double-check everything. Andrew used to say we could have cut our accounting staff by a third if your grandmother had trusted people more. Most of this," she waved her arm across the papers of the desk, "is such detail. I never look at this much detail. Never found the need. Time reveals all mistakes, all crimes."

Stockard looked up to see her aunt registering what she had just said. "Is there anything I can do?"

Her aunt uncharacteristically paused. Stockard had expected an automatic answer, "No, but thank you for offering." Instead she said, "What did you have in mind?"

"I know I can't help with what's on the desk." Stockard pointed that way. "I don't really know anything about the businesses. But I wondered if you needed someone else to help out. I meant someone from the family."

"Would you like to enter the business? Forest & Griffin?" Evelyn had asked the question very slowly, very carefully.

"Well, yes, actually, I would." Stockard looked at her aunt and decided it was time. "It's something… I've realized something very important. You know Emily and I have been working on her pictures. I'm nearly ready to go to New York and pitch them and already I know how it will work. They are going to sell. And I think I know who they will sell to. I don't know how I know, I just do."

"When I was corralling Emily into the idea that her pictures would sell, while I was getting her organized, I realized that this is what I do well. I manage. I know how to manage. Did Andrew ever tell you about what I've done in Boulder, about the houses?"

"Fourteen houses in eight years. Collectively they've appreciated just over two hundred percent. And they are always rented."

"So you know. Well, that was how I had fun."

"So let me be very clear," said Evelyn. "You would like a long-term job with Forest & Griffin?"

Her aunt had become formal. It made Stockard pause for a moment. Was she about to say no or was she otherwise uncomfortable about having Stockard in the family business?

"Yes, that is correct."

Her aunt got up and closed the study door, this time sitting in the chair next to Stockard's. "Your grandmother had learned that it was better to give people some distance. That's why she never bullied you. Well, about what you were going to do with your life. She knew she had made mistakes with your mother, but with you, she did much better. She was far more clever with you. Your money, as you know, had been taken care of. But there was a clause, a trigger as your grandmother used to call it, that would hand your money back to you. That trigger was if you decided of your own volition that you wanted to enter the business."

Stockard had pulled the trigger. She thought it was not the right word. Her grandmother would have meant it as a good thing. You aim and hit with the pull of a trigger, but Stockard in the moment could only think that the trigger did not mean control and safety, not like a gun in the nightstand did for her grandmother. She had never needed a gun. But her decision to go into the family business what had been an idea that had bubbled up, hot and smelly, from somewhere deep in herself, had represented control, not necessarily safety. It was what she had to do.

Her aunt carried on. "Your grandmother had mixed emotions about it. She wanted you to do as you pleased, but she also wanted someone to pick up where I'll leave off. Eve, well, she's not so hot on money. Emily, as you can see, is an artist. You were the only one who found any fun in making money. Your real estate investments and the rental business have done very well. But no one, according to your grandmother's rules, could tell you the option was there. It was a choice only you could make."

It was what Stockard wanted to do. But first she had to get Emily's work shown and sold, and she was going to have to confront The Blue House, and what aftermath was left.

For a little in the New Year, Stockard had been nagged by the fear that she had AIDS. All that rough sex with Christopher, but the test had come back clear and the follow up six months later had come back clear, too. Cadence had not been so lucky. Christopher had moved to San Francisco where his true love would nurse him to the end. Cadence had moved to her parents' house in Malibu, where her father was a professor at Pepperdine. All this Stockard had gotten from Etta, a departing phone call before she and Bill moved back to Minneapolis. They had had enough of Boulder. She wanted kids and a normal life now. Whatever it was that had tied the group together was gone.

7

B Y May Stockard was in New York, going to the office every morning with her aunt. She was living at her aunt's brownstone and working day and night to catch up on all the things she needed to know. Some of it was horribly boring and when she had resigned herself to some remedial accounting classes at Columbia in the fall, she knew that some boredom was in order.

But there was a side to her that called out persistently and clearly and dreams appeared to be the vehicle. They had always been. Her dreams had terrorized her, like her nightmare. They had led her to ask questions about her family, to ask questions about herself, like breadcrumbs left on the trail; and as she came home each day and fell into an exhausted sleep each night, what refreshed her were her dreams and she knew she had to do something about them. It was part of her new self, the person who had given up being perpetually stoned and at loose ends, the person who had drifted through so many years. If she was going to do the work during the day, her payoff would be to follow her dreamscapes and find out what they all meant.

She contacted both the Jung Institute and the Freudian Society in New York and met with their referral directors. Lists of appropriate therapists and analysts came back and in all she visited six over a period of three weeks. In each one of her interviewing sessions—for surely she was interviewing each one of these men and women—Stockard laid out the dream that she had the night that her grandmother died.

"I'm at a house, a big one, some elements from our farm, some from my house, others from classical buildings, the Parthenon for example, and the furnishings are a mishmash, but everything is there in abundance. I am in a big room and I have to push my way through a crowd to get to the front, where everyone is looking. There is a sofa up front and on it sits my grandmother with her father and my

Uncle Andrew. When my grandmother sees me at the front, she beckons me forward and I go up to her. She hands me a box, a wooden thing about the size of a writing box, only it is natural wood, not dark stained like everything else at our farm. The hinges and handles and lock are made of stone. I look at my grandmother and say thank you and she says, when you've opened it, you will not thank me. In this box I give you death. I'm confused and my heart is racing and I look around. Behind the sofa are people I know, my cousins, my aunt, my mother and even my grandfather, Lee Wilson. The people in the crowd, the people I had to push through, I don't know them. Some of them are happy to see me. Some are glad I've been given a cursed gift. Some are indifferent, but I know I have to push my way through them to leave, but I don't know what to do. And then I wake up."

It had been Fran Raim, a Jungian, who had asked, "And then what happened?"

"And then I found my grandmother and my real grandfather in their last embrace."

The others had simply asked what Stockard thought it meant. So Stockard had settled on Dr. Fran Raim, who wore dark suits and starched cotton blouses and had an office near Wall Street, near where Forest & Griffin had their Manhattan office.

On Thursdays just after lunch, Stockard would see Dr. Raim for a fifty-five minute hour and the two were simpatico.

It was no time before Stockard was asking the question, "What is in store for the second half of my life?"

8

THERE were other reasons, stories untold, for having a blood test and Stockard had dashed into the overpriced silver store Marley's, which conveniently had a near Wall Street store. She was going to be clever with her announcement. She went straight to the cups and was ho humming about the quality of the various little things on display when a pitcher caught her eye and stopped her dead in her tracks.

"Excuse me," she said to the man behind the counter. Her Southern accent had not gone away. "Excoooooose me." The man was grey and old and finally heard Stockard. "This pitcher," she said poking her finger frantically at it, "may I see it."

"Of course," he said with a born and bred New York accent. He carried a ring of keys and fumbled with the cabinet, finally swinging the door open, and pulling the pitcher down. "It's heavy," he said, giving it to her and not letting go until he was sure that she could handle the weight.

She looked deep into the silver reflection, seeing herself warped by the curve of the pitcher and in a flash of light against the silver she knew.

It wasn't just luck that brought Seth his money, it was knowing when you were lucky and riding it until it was done. And then stepping away. Seth Griffin had been a smart player, diving into the stream of life at just the right moment.

She knew that Rousseau was right. She had found the quote that had nagged at her for more than six months after Christopher had made his dreadful announcement.

Jean-Jacques Rousseau, the favorite of her Philosophy 101 teacher, had written: "To be driven by appetite alone is slavery, and obedience to the law one has prescribed for oneself is liberty." It was a quotation that worked for her, on its own. Here. Now.

She knew that whatever it was that had passed, whatever her life had been up to this point, it was only just beginning and that what lay ahead, no matter how boring or how difficult, it would be necessary and—she could hardly summon the word in her mind —satisfying.

After the flash, Stockard became aware of her breathing and then the pitcher and the store and the man standing next to her. He said, "I can find nothing about it, not the mark, not the design, nothing. It is, apparently, one of a kind."

"I own its brother," said Stockard. She looked at the old man and pulled the pitcher closer to her. "No one will be separating them again."

Lightning Source UK Ltd.
Milton Keynes UK
02 September 2009

143275UK00001B/116/P